HUMAN RIGHTS IN SCOTLAND:
TEXT, CASES AND MATERIALS

Tony,

with best wishes

Keith

AUSTRALIA
Law Book Co.
Sydney

CANADA and USA
Carswell
Toronto

HONG KONG
Sweet & Maxwell Asia

NEW ZEALAND
Brookers
Wellington

SINGAPORE and MALAYSIA
Sweet & Maxwell Asia
Singapore and Kuala Lumpur

HUMAN RIGHTS IN SCOTLAND: TEXT, CASES AND MATERIALS

By

Keith D Ewing
King's College, University of London

and

Kenneth Dale-Risk
Lecturer in Law, Napier University, Edinburgh

THOMSON

™

W. GREEN

Published in 2004 by
W. Green & Son Ltd
21 Alva Street
Edinburgh EH2 4PS

Typeset by YHT Ltd, London
Printed in Great Britain by The Bath Press, Bath

No natural forests were destroyed to make this product;
only farmed timber was used and replanted

A CIP catalogue record for this book is available from the British Library.

ISBN 0 414 014499

PREFACE

This book is the successor to a slim volume which first appeared in 1982 under the title *Civil Liberties in Scotland: Cases and Materials* by K D Ewing and W Finnie. Believed to be the first book on the subject in Scotland, that book went into a second edition in 1988. Although expanded in size, the second edition was still much shorter than the present volume. There are no doubt several reasons why this book is significantly longer than its predecessors. But not the least of these is the new human rights culture which has washed over the Scottish legal system since 1998.

The new human rights culture creates a new contradiction for the Scots lawyer. In his influential pamphlet on *The Scottish Legal Tradition*, Lord Cooper wrote that "law is the reflection of the spirit of a people, and so long as the Scots are conscious that they are a people, they must preserve their law". That opportunity has been seized and reinforced by devolution, though quite what Lord Cooper would have made of this is unknown. We do know, however, that he was critical of modern legislation, seeking to re-assure the "layman" that:

> "despite this enormous accretion of the indispensable apparatus of the
> complicated modern state, it is still the common law of Scotland that regulates
> and defines all the main rights and duties of the Scottish citizen".

Not any more. It is the Westminster Parliament through the Scotland Act and the Human Rights Act that has defined some of the "main rights and duties of the Scottish citizen", and other legislation which has defined what remains. But what these former measures have done—by incorporating Convention rights—is to reinforce many of the rights and duties acknowledged by the common law, though also to authorise the continued operation of many of the restraints on the exercise of these rights. There are, however, areas (notably in relation to contempt of court) where the balance has swung from State to citizen, or more accurately in this case from State to multinational media corporations.

The incorporation of human rights legislation has also equipped the courts with powers—should they choose to use them (and there is not much evidence of this so far)—to take on the regulatory state. This is particularly true in Scotland where primary legislation as well as executive action must comply with convention rights. But the contradiction of all this—which was noted in the preface to the second edition of *Civil Liberties in Scotland: Cases and Materials*—relates to Lord Cooper's second concern. If the first was with regulatory legislation eating into the common law, the other was with the distinctive identity of Scots law. Although devolution will help with this latter objective, the human rights component of the devolution settlement is bound to encourage a greater "convergence" of laws.

In preparing this new volume it has been possible to some extent to follow much of the structure of the predecessor volumes, and even to retain some of the text and materials. The book has, however, been substantially rewritten to take account of the legal changes introduced by the Scotland Act 1998 and the Human Rights Act 1998. But notwithstanding the nature and scale of these changes, it is important not to lose a sense of historical perspective, or to lose sight of the fact that these instruments have been grafted onto an existing legal system with established recognition of and restraints on the rights and liberties of the people of Scotland.

It has been necessary to revise and to rewrite every chapter: such is the nature and scale of change. It has also been necessary to include some new chapters, notably Chapter 2 on the Human Rights and the Scottish Parliament, Chapter 5 on The Right to a Fair Trial, and

Chapter 10 on Emergency Powers and the 'War on Terror'. The inclusion of Chapter 2 is not only a reflection of the importance of devolution, but is also a recognition that the protection of human rights is not just a judicial function: it is a responsibility of all branches of government. It should be made clear, however, that this book does not attempt to provide an exhaustive account of all Convention rights.

Although this is a much larger volume than its predecessors, the aim remains the same. That is to say, it is designed principally for law students coming to the subject for the first time. This has also informed some of the decisions made about the selection of material. We hope that we have produced the core material that will be needed by all first time students of human rights and that the volume may be of value to those proceeding to more advanced work. We also acknowledge, however, that in making our selections, we will inevitably have outraged someone by excluding his or her favourite case or cases.

In preparing this volume we have inevitably acquired many debts. Our first debt is to Wilson Finnie of the University of Edinburgh who provided much of the intellectual stimulus, energy and insight which this volume inherits. We are also indebted to Chris Himsworth, for reading and commenting on two of the chapters, though he is not responsible for the errors of law or judgment that remain. Finally we record our debt to Jill Barrington and Rachel Cryer at W Green & Son for their remarkable patience in what has been a long gestation. The second named author is primarily responsible for Chapter 4 and part of Chapter 6; the first named author for the rest.

K D Ewing

K Dale Risk

September 30, 2004

CONTENTS

TABLE OF CASES

TABLE OF STATUTES

Chapter 1

THE CONSTITUTIONAL BACKGROUND

I. INTRODUCTION

Human rights law has been transformed by the constitutional changes which have been introduced since 1997. This chapter is designed to explain the background to these changes by examining their historical, constitutional and political context. We begin with an account of Scotland's position in the United Kingdom before devolution, and the factors leading to dissatisfaction with what has been described as the democratic deficit in Scotland. We then consider the possible legal limitations on the power of the Westminster Parliament as contained in the Treaty of Union to assess the extent to which they could be deployed to protect the human rights of the people of Scotland. The failure of the Treaty of Union to provide any safeguard whatsoever (despite the bold claims made about it undermining the "English" principle of parliamentary sovereignty) leads to a consideration of the status of the European Convention on Human Rights in Scots Law before its formal incorporation in 1998. As we will see, by 1997 the ECHR could be relied on by the courts though it could not be directly enforced in legal proceedings. In Chs 2 and 3 we examine how that has now dramatically changed.

II. SCOTLAND IN THE UNITED KINGDOM

Until 1707 Scotland was a sovereign nation, albeit one that shared its monarch and head of state with another since 1603. Since 1707, however, Scotland has been a part of the United Kingdom and as such has been dwarfed politically by England. For all practical purposes the destiny of the nation was determined in London. There developed, however, a complex system of executive or administrative devolution to the Scottish Office based in Edinburgh, the political head of which was the Secretary of State for Scotland who was a member of the Cabinet. The responsibilities of the devolved administration could impinge on human rights in one of a number of different ways. These responsibilities included local government, schools and colleges (though not universities), as well as the police, prisons and the civil and criminal law. Matters not within the administrative jurisdiction of the Scottish Office were the responsibility of the specialist British government departments. So the Ministry of Defence, the Department of Trade and Industry and the Home Office might all sponsor legislation or engage in activity which has an important bearing on the human rights of the people of Scotland. In the case of the Home Office, the Home Secretary had and still has national responsibility for matters such as broadcasting, immigration and counter terrorism.

Agee v Lord Advocate
1977 S.L.T. (Notes) 54

On February 16, 1977 the Home Secretary made a deportation order under s.5 (1) of the Immigration Act 1971. The order required the petitioner (Agee) to leave the United Kingdom on the ground that the Home Secretary had deemed it to be conducive to the public good to deport the petitioner. The order was served in Edinburgh where Agee was residing. Thereupon he sought suspension of the order and a declarator that it was *ultra vires*. The petitioner also sought interdict and interim interdict against the Chief Constable of the Lothian and Borders Police from arresting him and enforcing his removal from the jurisdiction of the court. The motion for interim interdict was refused:

LORD KINCRAIG: "The sole ground advanced by counsel for the petitioner as justification for the motion was that there was a real question to try between the parties, namely, whether the deportation order, not having been made by the Secretary of State for Scotland, could effectively be enforced in Scotland, having regard to the provisions of s.2 of the Secretary for Scotland Act 1887. Section 2 (1) of the 1887 Act is in the following terms: 'All powers and duties vested in and imposed on one of Her Majesty's Principal Secretaries of State by any Act of Parliament, law, or custom, so far as such powers and duties relate to Scotland, and so far as they have not already been transferred to, vested in, and imposed on the Secretary for Scotland, shall, subject to the exceptions hereinafter mentioned, be transferred to, vested in, and imposed on the Secretary for Scotland.'

The office of Secretary for Scotland was initiated by the Secretary for Scotland Act 1885, to which Secretary certain powers and duties of Her Majesty's Principal Secretaries of State under certain enactments were transferred (see s.5 of the 1885 Act). Counsel for the petitioner submitted that by virtue of s. 2(1) the exercise of any powers and the performance of any duties given by Acts of Parliament to a Principal Secretary of State, so far as they relate to Scotland, must be exercised and performed by the Secretary of State for Scotland, the successor to the Secretary for Scotland. He argued that as the Immigration Act 1971 applied to Scotland, and the power to enforce a deportation order was to be exercised in Scotland, that power could not be exercised by Mr Rees [the Home Secretary] but by the Secretary of State for Scotland only, and the order not having been made by the Secretary of State for Scotland was not a valid warrant for requiring the petitioner to leave Scotland, or for any proceeding to enforce the order.

This is a question of law which is capable of being answered without further procedure. Unless counsel for the petitioner can show that his submission is correct in law interim interdict must be refused.

In my judgment the submission which was made to me is fallacious. The office of Secretary for Scotland remained in existence until 1926 when, by the Secretaries of State Act 1926, it was abolished. Section 1 (1) of that Act provided that after the appointment of an additional principal Secretary of State: 'all the powers and duties of the Secretary for Scotland shall ... become powers and duties of a Principal Secretary of State, and the office of Secretary for Scotland and the office of Parliamentary Under Secretary for Health for Scotland shall be abolished.' The particular Secretary of State to whom the powers of the Secretary for Scotland were to pass is not stated in the section, and accordingly the section means that the powers and duties of the Secretary for Scotland shall become the powers and duties of any Principal Secretary of State. This is clear from the terms of s.1(2), which provided that on the appointment of the additional Secretary of State, all property which at the time of the appointment was vested in the Secretary for Scotland as such, was to he transferred to and become vested in that additional Secretary of State. Further, s.12 of the Interpretation Act 1889 provides in subs.(3) that in every Act whether passed before or after the commencement of the 1889 Act the expression 'Secretary of State' shall mean one of Her Majesty's Principal Secretaries of State for the time being. Thus the powers and duties of the Secretary for Scotland became vested in any one of Her Majesty's Principal Secretaries of State, including the Home Secretary.

The Immigration Act 1971 provides that powers of deporting persons under that Act shall be exercised by the Secretary of State, which means one of Her Majesty's Principal Secretaries of State. The Home Secretary is one of these. By virtue of s.1(1) of the 1926 Act he is empowered to exercise the powers of the former Secretary for Scotland in so far as they relate to Scotland. For these reasons I hold that the attack on the validity of the deportation order, in so far as the enforcement of it in Scotland is concerned, fails, and that on that ground the petitioner's motion for interim interdict must be refused."

The writ of the Home Secretary still runs in Scotland: see *Saini v Home Secretary*, 1999 S.L.T. 1249 and *Hider v Home Secretary*, 2004 S.L.T. 145.

Although there was thus a measure of administrative devolution, it remained the case that since 1707 Scotland's Parliament was at Westminster. There were, however, modifications of the Westminster system of government to accommodate Scotland. Scotland was over-represented in the House of Commons in terms of the ratio of seats to population. Following the creation of the Scottish Parliament, the number of Westminster constituencies in Scotland is to be reduced. Another modification of the Westminster system was the creation in 1894 of the Scottish Grand Committee consisting of all Scottish members of the House of Commons. The second reading debate on Bills could be referred to the committee provided that the Speaker certified that the matter related exclusively to Scotland, and provided the Minister moved a motion to refer. But although the debate might take place in the Scottish Grand Committee, the vote would take place on the floor of the House, thereby ensuring that the outcome would be determined by British members of the House. So although the Westminster system was modified in these and other ways in response to the Scottish dimension, these modifications served only to reinforce the uncertain legitimacy of the system under which Scotland was governed. Regardless of how the people of the country voted, Scotland was governed through Parliament by an executive drawn from a party that may not have commanded the confidence of the Scottish people. These uncertainties were bitterly exposed during the Thatcher years.

T.M. Devine
The Scottish Nation 1700–2000

"Scottish opposition to Thatcherism went much deeper than simple hostility to an unpopular government. While the Scots remained loyal to the idea of state and community, the Conservatives made a virtue out of promoting nationalism, competition and privatization. The government's values had been rejected in the humiliating defeat of several Conservative candidates in 1987 but were nevertheless still to be imposed because of its electoral ascendancy elsewhere in the UK. Scottish protests against the poll tax, introduced to popular fury on April Fool's Day 1988, or against the privatization of public utilities were ignored. Mrs Thatcher disregarded the tradition of the union as a partnership in which Scottish interests had been taken into account and instead seemed to consider there to be no limit to the absolute sovereignty of the Westminster parliament. When Michael Forsyth became Scottish Minister for Education and Health in 1987, he vigorously pursued a strategy of appointing ideological supporters of the government to the committees and quangos of the Scottish Office which advised on a range of important matters and which had hitherto jealously guarded their professional autonomy. Forsyth saw this as essential to the success of the free market revolution and the destruction of the corporatist consensus. But his opponents saw the strategy as an intolerable undermining of independent bodies for reasons of party political advantage and a sinister confirmation of the inexorable centralization of power taking place under the Tories. Increasingly, the problem of governance in Scotland was seen not simply as being rooted in Thatcherism but instead derived from the very nature of the British constitutional system itself."

Alongside administrative (or executive) devolution and parliamentary (or legislative) accommodation, there was also a measure of judicial autonomy in the period between the Union in 1707 and the introduction of legislative devolution in 1999. A measure of judicial autonomy had been guaranteed by the Treaty of Union itself, with Art.XIX providing:

> "XIX. That the Court of Session or Colledge of Justice do after the Union and notwith-standing thereof remain in all time coming within Scotland as it is now constituted by the Laws of that Kingdom and with the same Authority and Priviledges as before the Union subject nevertheless to such Regulations for the better Administration of Justice as shall be made by the Parliament of Great Britain. ... And that the Court of Justiciary do also after the Union and notwithstanding thereof remain in all time coming within Scotland as it is now constituted by the Laws of that Kingdom and with the same Authority and Priviledges as before the Union subject nevertheless to such Regulations as shall be made by the Parliament of Great Britain and without prejudice of other Rights of Justiciary And that all Admiralty Jurisdictions be under the Lord High Admiral or Commissioners for the Admiralty of Great Britain for the time being And that the Court of Admiralty now Established in Scotland be continued ... And that all other Courts now in being within the Kingdom of Scotland do remain but subject to Alterations by the Parliament of Great Britain And that all Inferior Courts within the said Limits do remain subordinate as they are now to the Supream Courts of Justice within the same in all time coming And that no Causes in Scotland be cognoscible by the Court of Chancery Queens-Bench Common-Pleas or any other Court in Westminster-hall And that the said Courts or any other of the like nature after the Union shall have no power to Cognosce Review or Alter the Acts or Sentences of the Judicatures within Scotland or stop the Execution of the same And that there be a Court of Exchequer in Scotland after the Union for deciding Questions concerning the Revenues of Customs and Excises there..."

It is to be noted, however, that the Scottish legal system did not and does not enjoy complete autonomy. There was—and still is—a right of appeal in civil cases from the Court of Session to the House of Lords which is Scotland's supreme court in non-criminal matters. Although by convention two Scottish Law Lords sit in Scottish appeals, Scots lawyers were and are unlikely to be in the majority. The criminal law was, however, administered only from Scotland. Although a right of appeal in criminal cases was introduced by the Criminal Appeal (Scotland) Act 1926, no provision was made for an appeal from the High Court of Justiciary to the House of Lords. The Scottish judges thus had an important role to play in developing the common law so far as it affects human rights and in interpreting statutes that impose criminal penalties. However, it is one of the curious paradoxes of devolution that it threatens the limited autonomy of the Scottish courts. This is because of the jurisdiction of the Privy Council over devolution matters which has been shown to include a significant area of Scottish criminal procedure. Fresh concerns about the autonomy of the Scottish legal system have been aroused by the Government's proposals for a new Supreme Court for the United Kingdom to replace the appellate committee of the House of Lords: see G.L. Gretton, "Scotland and the Supreme Court", 2003 S.L.T. 265; and H.L. MacQueen, "Scotland and a Supreme Court for the UK?", 2003 S.L.T. 279. Compare C. Himsworth, "A Supreme Court for the United Kingdom?" (2003) SCOLAG Bulletin.

III. PARLIAMENTARY SOVEREIGNTY AND THE TREATY OF UNION

An important feature of the Westminster system is the principle of parliamentary sovereignty. Indeed this may be said to be the fundamental rule of the British Constitution. It means that there are no legal limits on the power of Parliament. "For us an Act of Parliament duly passed by Commons and Lords and assented to by the King, is supreme, and we are bound to give effect to its terms" (*Mortensen v Peters*, 1906 8 F. (J.) 93 at 100–101, *per* Lord Justice General

Dunedin). The principle can be defended in the democratic age on the ground that it enables the wishes of the people to be translated into law. In this sense it is a legal or constitutional principle which gives effect to the political principle of popular sovereignty. In practice, however, the legal or constitutional principle gives the Executive (not the legislature) enormous political power. In our system of government the Executive controls the legislature in the sense that the leading members of the Executive (the Prime Minister and the Cabinet) are also members of the legislature, by the fact that almost all legislative proposals are initiated by the Executive, and by the fact that for political reasons M.P.s are bound to vote for their party in the House. In a very real sense, and to a very large extent, the legislature simply gives legal authority to the wishes of the Executive. As a result it is doubtful whether there is adequate parliamentary scrutiny or control over legislation in the Westminster Parliament. Nevertheless it remains the duty of the courts to give effect to legislation passed by Parliament, as the following case shows.

Sillars v Smith
1982 S.L.T. 539

Four accused persons were charged with vandalism, contrary to the Criminal Justice (Scotland) Act 1980, s.78(1). Each of them argued before the sheriff that the 1980 Act had no legal validity. The argument was rejected by the sheriff who convicted each of the accused. They then appealed by stated case to the High Court.

SHERIFF MACVICAR: "The pleas and arguments stated by all four appellants were identical, as are the matters which it is desired by them to bring under review. I have therefore taken the liberty of stating a single case in respect of all the appellants.

The only matter which is sought to bring under review is my decision to repel the plea to the competence of the proceedings. The first-named appellant presented the argument, on behalf of himself and the other appellants, in the form of a prepared statement which he read to the court, and which is annexed to the complaint. The attack on the competence of the proceedings was founded on the proposition that the Criminal Justice (Scotland) Act 1980 (s.78 of which created the offence of vandalism with which the appellants were charged) has no constitutional validity and therefore no legal force. The argument in support of that proposition may be summarised as follows: 1. The Scotland Act 1978(now repealed) provides for the creation of a Scottish Assembly (s.1(1)). That Assembly was empowered to make laws, to be called Scottish Assembly Acts, but such an Act should be law only to the extent that it was within the legislative competence of the Assembly (ss.17 and 18). A provision was to be within the legislative competence of the Assembly if, and only if, the matter to which it related was a devolved matter (Sched. 2, art.1). A devolved matter was one of those included in the groups in Pt.I of Sched.10 to the Act (s. 63(2)). Group 25 (crime) of Pt. I of Sched. 10 was to cover all criminal matters, including offences against property. Therefore if the Scotland Act 1978 had become law, the passing of the Criminal Justice (Scotland) Act 1980 (or any equivalent statute) would have been within the legislative competence of the Scottish Assembly, and not of the Parliament of the United Kingdom at Westminster. 2. Section 83 (1) of the 1978 Act provided:

'The preceding provisions of this Act (and the Schedules relating to them) shall not come into operation until such day as the Secretary of State may by order appoint.'

Section 83 (4) provided: 'The first order under this section shall not be made unless a draft of it has been laid before Parliament and approved by a resolution of each House of Parliament.' Section 85 provided: (1) Before a draft of the first order to be made under section 83 of this Act is laid before Parliament a referendum shall be held in accordance with Schedule 17 to this Act on the question whether effect is to be given to the provisions of this Act. (2) If it appears to the Secretary of State that less than 40 per cent of the persons entitled to vote in the referendum have voted 'Yes' in reply to the question posed in the Appendix to Schedule 17 to this Act or that a majority of the answers given in the referendum have been 'No' he shall lay before Parliament the draft of an Order in Council for the repeal of this Act. (3) If a draft laid before Parliament under this section is approved by a resolution of each House Her Majesty in Council may make an Order in the terms of the draft.' The question to be asked in the referendum referred to in s.85, in terms of Sched.17 was: 'Do you want the provisions of the Scotland Act 1978 to be put into effect?'. 3. A referendum was duly held, in accordance with the provisions of s.85, on 1 March 1979. Thereafter, the Secretary of State laid before Parliament the draft of an Order in Council for the repeal of the 1978 Act, proceeding upon the narrative that it appeared to him, on consideration of the result of the referendum, that he was required by s. 85(2) of the said Act, to lay before Parliament such an order. The said draft was approved by resolution of each House, and on 26 July 1979 the Scotland Act (Repeal) Order 1979 (S.I. 1979 No. 1978) was made and came into operation. The 1978 Act was thereby repealed. 4. The repeal of the 1978 Act was not in accordance with the wishes of the Scottish people, as may be deduced from the following considerations: (a) although the published figures of the voting in the referendum disclosed that less than 40 per cent of the persons entitled to vote had voted 'Yes' in reply to the question posed, a clear majority of about 77,000, of those who actually voted, voted 'Yes'; (b) at the general election in May 1979, a clear majority of electors voted against the Conservative (or Unionist) party, which was committed to the repeal of the 1978 Act. Conservative (or Unionist) Members of Parliament were returned in only 22 out of the 71 Scottish seats; (c) about two-thirds of the Scottish Members of Parliament voted against the resolution of the House of Commons which approved the said draft Order in Council. 5. In any event, the Secretary of State acted unlawfully in laying the draft order before Parliament. He stated publicly that he was not satisfied with the accuracy of the electoral register, and was not justified in stating in the order that it appeared to him that he was required by s. 85 (2) to lay the draft order before Parliament. 6. The supremacy of Parliament is not unchallengeable in Scotland. There is good authority for the view that this has always been so (*MacCormick v Lord Advocate*, 1953 S.L.T. 255, per Lord President Cooper, Lord Carmont concurring). Further, Parliament itself has recognised that its will must on occasion yield to the authority of bodies other than itself, both by the introduction of referenda into the process of legislation, and by its acceptance of the principle that its sovereignty can by subjected to orders of the European Economic Community. 7. In these circumstances, Parliament acted unlawfully in resolving that the Scotland Act 1978 should be repealed. Accordingly, the passing of the Criminal Justice (Scotland) Act proceeded upon a pre-existing illegality, and was therefore itself tainted with illegality, which rendered the Act invalid. Quod erat demonstrandum. I found it unnecessary to consider the argument in detail. I rejected the plea to the competence of the proceedings, upon the view that it is not competent for a court of summary criminal jurisdiction to question the validity of an Act of Parliament."

At the hearing of the appeal, the appellants repeated many of the arguments which had been raised before the sheriff. The High Court (Lord Justice-Clerk Wheatley, Lords Hunter and Dunpark) dismissed the appeal, and the following opinion was delivered:

"We go straight to the fundamental question whether the vires of an Act of Parliament which has gone through the whole parliamentary process, has received the Royal Assent and been brought into operation can be competently challenged in a Scottish court. That question has been definitively answered by two Scottish cases which span over a century in time. In *The Edinburgh and Dalkeith Railway Company v Wauchope* (1842) 1 Bell's App. Cas. 252 in the House of Lords Lord Campbell said at p. 279: 'All that a court of justice can look to is the parliamentary roll; they see that an act has passed both Houses of Parliament, and that it has received the royal assent, and no court of justice can enquire into the manner in which it was introduced into parliament, what was done previously to its being introduced, or what passed in parliament during the various stages of its progress through both Houses of Parliament. I therefore trust that no such enquiry will hereafter be entered into in Scotland, and that due effect will be given to every act of Parliament, both private as well as public, upon the just construction which appears to arise upon it". In *MacCormick v Lord Advocate*, 1953 S.L.T. 255 Lord President Cooper said: 'This at least is plain that there is neither precedent nor authority of any kind for the view that the domestic Courts of either Scotland or England have jurisdiction to determine whether a governmental act of the type here in controversy is or is not conform to the provisions of a Treaty'. While that was said in the context of the issue in that case it is a clear illustration of the principle enunciated by Lord Campbell (supra).

We are satisfied that there is sufficient in these passages alone to warrant the rebuttal of the appellants' plea to the competency, based as it is on a submission that the Act of 1980 which had gone through all the parliamentary processes and received the Royal Assent is invalid. In that situation we find it unnecessary to deal with the ancillary arguments which were adduced in purported support of that basic argument, since they fall within Lord Campbell's veto.

The question of law stated by the sheriff is: 'Did I err in law in repelling the plea to the competency of the proceedings?'. We answer that question in the negative and refuse the appeal."

The principle of parliamentary sovereignty distinguishes the United Kingdom from many other countries, and has huge implications for the judicial protection of human rights. Unlike in the United States, the British courts could not invalidate or refuse to apply an Act of Parliament no matter how far it might restrict human rights. The unique constitutional position of Scotland within the United Kingdom did, however, provide the courts with some opportunity to develop a doctrine that would give them an enhanced role. The principle of parliamentary sovereignty expressed by Lord Dunedin above is not a view necessarily shared by all Scots lawyers. In the view of Lord Cooper in *MacCormick v Lord Advocate*, 1953 S.L.T. 255, "the principle of the unlimited sovereignty of Parliament is a distinctively English principle which has no counterpart in Scottish constitutional law" (at 262). Lord Cooper continued in a passage of some importance:

"Considering that the Union legislation extinguished the Parliaments of Scotland and England and replaced them by a new Parliament, I have difficulty in seeing why it should have been supposed that the new Parliament of Great Britain must inherit all the peculiar characteristics of the English Parliament but none of the Scottish Parliament, as if all that happened in 1707 was that Scottish representatives were admitted to the Parliament of England. That is not what was done. Further, the Treaty and the associated legislation, by which the Parliament of Great Britain was brought into being as the successor of the separate Parliaments of Scotland and England, contain some clauses which expressly reserve to the Parliament of Great Britain powers of subsequent modification, and other clauses which either contain no such power or emphatically exclude subsequent alteration by declarations that the provision shall be fundamental and unalterable in all time coming, or declarations of a like effect. I have never been able to understand how it is possible to reconcile with elementary canons of construction the adoption by the English constitutional theorists of the same attitude to these markedly different types of provisions."

It is not clear how convincing an analysis this is. It appears to be based on a model of a static constitution: it is as if the Scottish constitution of 1707 had been preserved in formaldehyde. But constitutions are living and dynamic organs which change as the reasons for them change. Who is to say that like the English constitution, the Scottish constitution would not also have adapted a principle of parliamentary sovereignty as the best way in the democratic age to give effect to the wishes of the people? Who is to say that the principle of parliamentary sovereignty would not also have emerged in Scotland as a means of giving effect to the popular sovereignty of the people? And who is to say that the Scottish people would have been content about the prospect of unelected judges (usually educated privately and at English universities) second-guessing the wishes of their representatives? It is one thing to say that certain Treaty guarantees were fundamental law, but it would be something else to go beyond that. It appears, however, that Lord Cooper's views on parliamentary sovereignty did not amount to much in practice, for even if the legal powers of Parliament were constrained by the Treaty of Union, they were, even on Lord Cooper's analysis, legal restraints which could not be legally enforced by the domestic courts. For as Lord Cooper also said:

"Accepting it that there are provisions in the Treaty of Union and associated legislation which are 'fundamental law', and assuming for the moment that something is alleged to have been done—it matters not whether with legislative authority or not—in breach of that fundamental law, the question remains whether such a question is determinable as a justiciable issue in the Courts of either Scotland or England, in the same fashion as an issue of constitutional *vires* would be cognisable by the Supreme Courts of the United States, or of South Africa or Australia. I reserve my opinion with regard to the provisions relating expressly to this Court and to the laws 'which concern private right' which are administered here. This is not such a question, but a matter of 'public right' (Articles XVIII and XIX). To put the matter in another way, it is of little avail to ask whether the Parliament of Great Britain 'can' do this thing or that, without going on to inquire who can stop them if they do. Any person 'can' repudiate his solemn engagement but he cannot normally do so with impunity. Only two answers have been suggested to this corollary to the main question. The first is the exceedingly cynical answer implied by Dicey (*Law of the Constitution*, 9th ed., p. 82) in the statement that 'it would be rash of the Imperial Parliament to abolish the Scotch Courts and assimilate the law of Scotland to that of England. But no one can feel sure at what point Scottish resistance to such a change would become serious.' The other answer was that nowadays there may be room for the invocation of an 'advisory opinion' from the International Court of Justice. On these matters I express no view. This at least is plain that there is neither precedent nor authority of any kind for the view that the domestic Courts of either Scotland or England have jurisdiction to determine whether a governmental act of the type here in controversy is or is not conform to the provisions of a Treaty, least of all when that Treaty is one under which both Scotland and England ceased to be independent states and merged their identity in an incorporating union. From the standpoint both of constitutional law and of international law the position appears to me to be unique, and I am constrained to hold that the action as laid is incompetent in respect that it has not been shown that the Court of Session has authority to entertain the issue sought to be raised."

In this way Lord Cooper both raised and dashed the hopes of those who believed in the limited sovereignty (if such a status is possible) of the Westminster Parliament. A number of attempts have been made nevertheless to challenge legislation of the Westminster Parliament on the ground that it breaches the Treaty of Union. These challenges have not been made to legislation affecting fundamental questions such as the Church of Scotland or the Scottish courts, both of which are expressly protected by the Treaty. Rather the challenges have been based on other grounds, including Art.XVIII to which Lord Cooper refers in the immediately preceding passage. Article XVIII provides as follows:

"That the laws concerning regulation of trade customs and such excises to which Scotland is by virtue of this treaty to be liable be the same in Scotland from and after the union as in England and that all other laws in use within the Kingdom of Scotland do after the union and notwithstanding thereof remain the same as before (except such as are contrary to or inconsistent with this treaty) but alterable by the Parliament of Great Britain with this difference betwixt the laws concerning public right policy and civil government and those which concern private right that the laws which concern public right policy and civil government may be made the same throughout the whole United Kingdom but that no alteration be made in laws which concern private right except for evident utility of the subjects within Scotland."

This is a provision of great importance which in the hands of creative and confident judges could have been a means of imposing significant practical limits on the power of Parliament. Indeed, it could be argued that Art.XVIII offered the possibility that a Bill of Rights could have been introduced into Scots law indirectly. However in the following case—a challenge to Britain's membership of the EEC as it then was—the courts demonstrated an understandable reluctance to be drawn into battle with Parliament.

Gibson v Lord Advocate
1975 S.L.T. 134

Gibson was a fisherman from Banff. Before the accession of the United Kingdom to the European Communities he was one of a small number of United Kingdom fisherman having exclusive rights to fish in United Kingdom territorial waters. Article 2 of EEC Regulation 2141/70 would give him only the same rights as all other EEC fishermen in United Kingdom waters. He contended that these provisions affected a matter of private right, were not for the evident utility of the subjects of Scotland, and that therefore s.2(1) of the European Communities Act 1972, which gave them domestic effect, was contrary to Art.XVIII of the Treaty of Union and null and void. Gibson sought declarator to that effect, but was unsuccessful. On the question of the applicability of Art.XVIII:

> LORD KEITH: "In addition to the argument on relevancy there were addressed to me interesting arguments upon the question of jurisdiction and the competency of the action. These arguments raised constitutional issues of great potential importance, in particular whether the Court of Session has power to declare an Act of the United Kingdom Parliament to be void, whether an alleged discrepancy between an Act of that Parliament and the Treaty or Act of Union is a justiciable issue in this court, and whether, with particular reference to Article XVIII of the Act of Union, this court has power to decide whether an alteration of private law bearing to be effected by an Act of the United Kingdom Parliament is 'for the evident utility' of the subjects in Scotland. Having regard to my decision on relevancy, these are not live issues in the present case. The position was similar in *MacCormick v Lord Advocate* . . . Like Lord President Cooper, I prefer to reserve my opinion on what the question would be if the United Kingdom Parliament passed an Act purporting to abolish the Court of Session or the Church of Scotland or to substitute English law for the whole body of Scots private law. I am, however, of opinion that the question whether a particular Act of the United Kingdom Parliament altering a particular aspect of Scots private law is or is not 'for the evident utility' of the subjects within Scotland is not a justiciable issue in this court. The making of decisions upon what must essentially be a political matter is no part of the function of the court, and it is highly undesirable that it should be. The function of the court is to adjudicate upon the particular rights and obligations of individual persons, natural or corporate, in relation to other persons or, in certain instances, to the state. A general inquiry into the utility of certain legislative measures as regards the population generally is quite outside its competence."

The foregoing cases suggest that—so far as Scots law is concerned—the Westminster Parliament may not be sovereign, but that the courts will not readily intervene to uphold the Treaty. The cases also suggest that while the courts may do so to protect the Church or the courts, they would not do so to protect the human rights of the people of Scotland—the latter is a political question for Parliament to determine. This is perhaps the first example of the courts recognising that it is the responsibility of Parliament to determine and protect human rights. In this way Scotland's judges passed the opportunity to use Art.18 creatively to impose restraints by Parliament on the human rights of the people of Scotland. The unwillingness to engage was

confirmed by a trilogy of cases in which a number of individuals tried unsuccessfully to challenge the much despised poll tax or community charge which had been introduced under the
Conservative government of Mrs Thatcher by the Abolition of Domestic Rates etc (Scotland)
Act 1987. In these cases the courts demonstrated a reluctance to engage with the Treaty of
Union, Art.XVIII, and were reluctant to find a breach even where they directly addressed the
question: *Murray v Rogers*, 1992 S.L.T. 221 and *Fraser v MacCorquodale*, 1992 S.L.T. 229. The
same is true of attempts to use Art.18 to challenge the Skye bridge toll: *Robbie the Pict v
Hingston (No 2)*, 1998 S.L.T. 1201. The most recent consideration of the Treaty of Union was
in the context of the House of Lords Act 1999 which reduced to 92 the number of hereditary
peers who could sit in the House of Lords. It was argued in *Lord Gray's Motion*, 2000 S.C.
(H.L.) 46 that this violated the Treaty of Union on the ground that it violated Art.22 which
guaranteed that 16 Scottish peers would have a place in the House of Lords after the Union.
However, the House of Lords Committee on Privileges rejected the claim on a number of
grounds. For his part Lord Slynn of Hadley doubted whether a provision "even if regarded as
fundamental and as part of the constitution, cannot be altered by Parliament" (at 49). Lord
Hope of Craighead was reluctant to "question the extent and application of the doctrine of
sovereignty" (at 62). But he did not dismiss as "entirely fanciful" the argument that "the
legislative powers of the new Parliament of Great Britain were subject to the restrictions
expressed in the Union agreement" (at 59).

IV. THE EUROPEAN CONVENTION ON HUMAN RIGHTS

In the absence of any entrenched human rights, it was necessary to look to international law for
protection. There are in fact a large number of international treaties dealing with human rights,
but of these the European Convention on Human Rights has assumed a greater degree of
prominence than most. The ECHR is a treaty under international law signed in Rome in 1950,
ratified by the United Kingdom in 1951, coming into force in 1953. The Convention is confined
to civil and political rights, and generally excludes matters of a social and economic nature.
There is, *e.g.* no protection of the right to work, the right to social security, or the right to just
conditions of work. But these matters are dealt with in the Council of Europe's social charters,
these are not enforced with the same degree of rigour as the ECHR. There have been many cases
taken against the British government since under the ECHR, the very first in the 1970s, though
it is not the case as sometimes suggested that Britain has a worse record than any other Council
of Europe Member State for breaching the Convention. These complaints against the United
Kingdom cover a wide range of issues, though only a small proportion have been made in
relation to developments in Scotland.

European Convention on Human Rights
"The governments signatory hereto, being members of the Council of Europe,
    Considering the Universal Declaration of Human Rights proclaimed by the General
Assembly of the United Nations on 10th December 1948;
    Considering that this Declaration aims at securing the universal and effective recognition
and observance of the Rights therein declared;
    Considering that the aim of the Council of Europe is the achievement of greater unity
between its members and that one of the methods by which that aim is to be pursued is the
maintenance and further realisation of human rights and fundamental freedoms;
    Reaffirming their profound belief in those fundamental freedoms which are the foun-
dation of justice and peace in the world and are best maintained on the one hand by an
effective political democracy and on the other by a common understanding and observance
of the human rights upon which they depend;
    Being resolved, as the governments of European countries which are like-minded and
have a common heritage of political traditions, ideals, freedom and the rule of law, to take

the first steps for the collective enforcement of certain of the rights stated in the Universal Declaration,

Have agreed as follows:

Article 1—Obligation to respect human rights

The High Contracting Parties shall secure to everyone within their jurisdiction the rights and freedoms defined in Section I of this Convention.

Section I—Rights and freedoms

Article 2—Right to life

1. Everyone's right to life shall be protected by law. No one shall be deprived of his life intentionally save in the execution of a sentence of a court following his conviction of a crime for which this penalty is provided by law.

2. Deprivation of life shall not be regarded as inflicted in contravention of this article when it results from the use of force which is no more than absolutely necessary:
   a. in defence of any person from unlawful violence;
   b. in order to effect a lawful arrest or to prevent the escape of a person lawfully detained;
   c. in action lawfully taken for the purpose of quelling a riot or insurrection.

Article 3—Prohibition of torture

No one shall be subjected to torture or to inhuman or degrading treatment or punishment.

Article 4—Prohibition of slavery and forced labour

1. No one shall be held in slavery or servitude.
2. No one shall be required to perform forced or compulsory labour.
3. For the purpose of this article the term "forced or compulsory labour" shall not include:
   a. any work required to be done in the ordinary course of detention imposed according to the provisions of Article 5 of this Convention or during conditional release from such detention;
   b. any service of a military character or, in case of conscientious objectors in countries where they are recognised, service exacted instead of compulsory military service;
   c. any service exacted in case of an emergency or calamity threatening the life or well-being of the community;
   d. any work or service which forms part of normal civic obligations.

Article 5—Right to liberty and security

1. Everyone has the right to liberty and security of person. No one shall be deprived of his liberty save in the following cases and in accordance with a procedure prescribed by law:
   a. the lawful detention of a person after conviction by a competent court;
   b. the lawful arrest or detention of a person for non-compliance with the lawful order of a court or in order to secure the fulfilment of any obligation prescribed by law;
   c. the lawful arrest or detention of a person effected for the purpose of bringing him before the competent legal authority on reasonable suspicion of having committed an offence or when it is reasonably considered necessary to prevent his committing an offence or fleeing after having done so;
   d. the detention of a minor by lawful order for the purpose of educational supervision or his lawful detention for the purpose of bringing him before the competent legal authority;
   e. the lawful detention of persons for the prevention of the spreading of infec-

tious diseases, of persons of unsound mind, alcoholics or drug addicts or vagrants;

    f. the lawful arrest or detention of a person to prevent his effecting an unauthorised entry into the country or of a person against whom action is being taken with a view to deportation or extradition.

2. Everyone who is arrested shall be informed promptly, in a language which he understands, of the reasons for his arrest and of any charge against him.

3. Everyone arrested or detained in accordance with the provisions of paragraph 1.c of this article shall be brought promptly before a judge or other officer authorised by law to exercise judicial power and shall be entitled to trial within a reasonable time or to release pending trial. Release may be conditioned by guarantees to appear for trial.

4. Everyone who is deprived of his liberty by arrest or detention shall be entitled to take proceedings by which the lawfulness of his detention shall be decided speedily by a court and his release ordered if the detention is not lawful.

5. Everyone who has been the victim of arrest or detention in contravention of the provisions of this article shall have an enforceable right to compensation.

Article 6—Right to a fair trial

1. In the determination of his civil rights and obligations or of any criminal charge against him, everyone is entitled to a fair and public hearing within a reasonable time by an independent and impartial tribunal established by law. Judgment shall be pronounced publicly but the press and public may be excluded from all or part of the trial in the interests of morals, public order or national security in a democratic society, where the interests of juveniles or the protection of the private life of the parties so require, or to the extent strictly necessary in the opinion of the court in special circumstances where publicity would prejudice the interests of justice.

2. Everyone charged with a criminal offence shall be presumed innocent until proved guilty according to law.

3. Everyone charged with a criminal offence has the following minimum rights:

    a. to be informed promptly, in a language which he understands and in detail, of the nature and cause of the accusation against him;

    b. to have adequate time and facilities for the preparation of his defence;

    c. to defend himself in person or through legal assistance of his own choosing or, if he has not sufficient means to pay for legal assistance, to be given it free when the interests of justice so require;

    d. to examine or have examined witnesses against him and to obtain the attendance and examination of witnesses on his behalf under the same conditions as witnesses against him;

    e. to have the free assistance of an interpreter if he cannot understand or speak the language used in court.

Article 7—No punishment without law

1. No one shall be held guilty of any criminal offence on account of any act or omission which did not constitute a criminal offence under national or international law at the time when it was committed. Nor shall a heavier penalty be imposed than the one that was applicable at the time the criminal offence was committed.

2. This article shall not prejudice the trial and punishment of any person for any act or omission which, at the time when it was committed, was criminal according to the general principles of law recognised by civilised nations.

Article 8—Right to respect for private and family life

1. Everyone has the right to respect for his private and family life, his home and his correspondence.
2. There shall be no interference by a public authority with the exercise of this right except such as is in accordance with the law and is necessary in a democratic society in the interests of national security, public safety or the economic well-being of the country, for the prevention of disorder or crime, for the protection of health or morals, or for the protection of the rights and freedoms of others.

Article 9—Freedom of thought, conscience and religion

1. Everyone has the right to freedom of thought, conscience and religion; this right includes freedom to change his religion or belief and freedom, either alone or in community with others and in public or private, to manifest his religion or belief, in worship, teaching, practice and observance.
2. Freedom to manifest one's religion or beliefs shall be subject only to such limitations as are prescribed by law and are necessary in a democratic society in the interests of public safety, for the protection of public order, health or morals, or for the protection of the rights and freedoms of others.

Article 10—Freedom of expression

1. Everyone has the right to freedom of expression. This right shall include freedom to hold opinions and to receive and impart information and ideas without interference by public authority and regardless of frontiers. This article shall not prevent States from requiring the licensing of broadcasting, television or cinema enterprises.
2. The exercise of these freedoms, since it carries with it duties and responsibilities, may be subject to such formalities, conditions, restrictions or penalties as are prescribed by law and are necessary in a democratic society, in the interests of national security, territorial integrity or public safety, for the prevention of disorder or crime, for the protection of health or morals, for the protection of the reputation or rights of others, for preventing the disclosure of information received in confidence, or for maintaining the authority and impartiality of the judiciary.

Article 11—Freedom of assembly and association

1. Everyone has the right to freedom of peaceful assembly and to freedom of association with others, including the right to form and to join trade unions for the protection of his interests.
2. No restrictions shall be placed on the exercise of these rights other than such as are prescribed by law and are necessary in a democratic society in the interests of national security or public safety, for the prevention of disorder or crime, for the protection of health or morals or for the protection of the rights and freedoms of others. This article shall not prevent the imposition of lawful restrictions on the exercise of these rights by members of the armed forces, of the police or of the administration of the State.

Article 12—Right to marry

Men and women of marriageable age have the right to marry and to found a family, according to the national laws governing the exercise of this right.

Article 13—Right to an effective remedy

Everyone whose rights and freedoms as set forth in this Convention are violated shall have an effective remedy before a national authority notwithstanding that the violation has been committed by persons acting in an official capacity.

Article 14—Prohibition of discrimination

The enjoyment of the rights and freedoms set forth in this Convention shall be secured without discrimination on any ground such as sex, race, colour, language, religion, political or other opinion, national or social origin, association with a national minority, property, birth or other status.

Article 15—Derogation in time of emergency

1. In time of war or other public emergency threatening the life of the nation any High Contracting Party may take measures derogating from its obligations under this Convention to the extent strictly required by the exigencies of the situation, provided that such measures are not inconsistent with its other obligations under international law.
2. No derogation from Article 2, except in respect of deaths resulting from lawful acts of war, or from Articles 3, 4 (paragraph 1) and 7 shall be made under this provision.
3. Any High Contracting Party availing itself of this right of derogation shall keep the Secretary General of the Council of Europe fully informed of the measures which it has taken and the reasons therefor. It shall also inform the Secretary General of the Council of Europe when such measures have ceased to operate and the provisions of the Convention are again being fully executed.

Article 16—Restrictions on political activity of aliens

Nothing in Articles 10, 11 and 14 shall be regarded as preventing the High Contracting Parties from imposing restrictions on the political activity of aliens.

Article 17—Prohibition of abuse of rights

Nothing in this Convention may be interpreted as implying for any State, group or person any right to engage in any activity or perform any act aimed at the destruction of any of the rights and freedoms set forth herein or at their limitation to a greater extent than is provided for in the Convention.

Article 18—Limitation on use of restrictions on rights

The restrictions permitted under this Convention to the said rights and freedoms shall not be applied for any purpose other than those for which they have been prescribed."

To the original text have been annexed 12 protocols, not all of which have been ratified by the United Kingdom. The additional protocols deal with a range of substantive and procedural issues, in the sense that they expand the list of rights covered by the treaty, and revise the procedures for enforcing treaty obligations. So far as substantive matters are concerned, the most significant is the First Protocol, which was ratified by the United Kingdom. This provides that:

"Article 1—Protection of property

Every natural or legal person is entitled to the peaceful enjoyment of his possessions. No one shall be deprived of his possessions except in the public interest and subject to the conditions provided for by law and by the general principles of international law.

The preceding provisions shall not, however, in any way impair the right of a State to enforce such laws as it deems necessary to control the use of property in accordance with the general interest or to secure the payment of taxes or other contributions or penalties.

Article 2—Right to education

No person shall be denied the right to education. In the exercise of any functions which it assumes in relation to education and to teaching, the State shall respect the right of parents to ensure such education and teaching in conformity with their own religious and philosophical convictions.

Article 3—Right to free elections
The High Contracting Parties undertake to hold free elections at reasonable intervals by secret ballot, under conditions which will ensure the free expression of the opinion of the people in the choice of the legislature.

Also important is the Sixth Protocol which deals with the elimination of the death penalty, ratified by the United Kingdom. Article 1 of the Sixth Protocol provides that "the death penalty shall be abolished", and that "no one shall be condemned to such penalty or executed", the only exception being made "in respect of acts committed in time of war or of imminent threat of war" (art.2). Protocol 12 deals with protection against discrimination and has not been ratified by the United Kingdom.

So far as the procedures for enforcing the Convention are concerned, two types of complaint are permitted. The first are inter state complaints where one country makes a complaint against another (as in *Cyprus v Turkey* (2002) 35 E.H.R.R. 731), and the second are individual applications. The latter are by far the most common in practice as well as being a novel feature of the procedure. It means that an individual or a non-governmental organisation may bring a complaint against a state, revealing a remarkable willingness of states to expose themselves to scrutiny by judges in an international forum. For it is another remarkable feature of the procedure that the complaints are dealt with by a judicial body in the form of the European Court of Human Rights. The procedures were revised by the Eleventh Protocol which was a response to the growing sclerosis of the enforcement machinery. The treaty has always included provisions designed to control the flow of cases. Thus it has always been necessary for individual complainants to exhaust domestic remedies and to bring their complaints in good time. The original procedure was nevertheless cumbersome, with complaints screened first by the European Commission of Human Rights before proceeding for disposal to either the Committee of Ministers or the European Court of Human Rights. With the increase in the number of countries ratifying the ECHR as the boundaries of the Council of Europe extended to encompass the former allies of the USSR (and the Russian Federation itself), these arrangements were simply untenable. Indeed, even in the so-called streamlined proceedings, delay caused by an excessive workload is a serious problem. The procedures introduced by the Eleventh Protocol have been incorporated as amendments to the treaty. The procedural provisions which are to be found in the rest of the treaty are not reproduced here.

V. PARLIAMENTARY SOVEREIGNTY AND HUMAN RIGHTS

Although an extremely important treaty, the status of the ECHR in domestic law was greatly affected by the dominant principle of parliamentary sovereignty. It's time that the principle of parliamentary sovereignty was (depending on one's point of view) undermined or modified as a result of British membership of the EEC (as it then was) on January 1, 1973. Under the European Communities Act 1972, s.2, Community law directly effective Community law may be enforced in the British courts. Under the 1972 Act, Community law is to be enforced even though there may be domestic law (including an Act of Parliament) to the contrary. In the *Factortame* case, the House of Lords held that this meant that Community law was to take priority over the Merchant Shipping Act 1988: *R. v Secretary of State for Transport, ex p. Factortame (No.2)* [1991] 1 A.C. 603. This was the first time that a British court had refused to apply an Act of the Westminster Parliament since the English Bill of Rights of 1688 which asserted politically and established legally the sovereignty of Parliament. Nevertheless the principle of parliamentary sovereignty remains a powerful one and has been deployed, in the context of the Government's programme of constitutional reform since 1997, to justify limiting the extent of incorporation of the European Convention on Human Rights as well as the powers of the Scottish Parliament. As the fundamental principle of the British constitution it has two effects. The first is that the courts cannot challenge the validity of or refuse to apply an Act of Parliament regardless of what it says or does (subject to the qualification already alluded to). Secondly, the courts cannot give effect to international treaties which have been ratified by the United Kingdom, unless these treaties have been formally incorporated into British law by an Act of Parliament. It was for these reasons that attempts to protect human rights in the Scottish courts before 1998 foundered. These attempts were based on trying to enforce the European Convention on Human Rights, an international treaty of the Council of Europe. It is not an EC Treaty and hence not incorporated by the 1972 Act.

Kaur v Lord Advocate
1981 S.L.T. 322

This was a case brought by a mother who was to be deported from the United Kingdom. Her three children were born in the United Kingdom and were legally entitled to remain. The mother sought a declarator that her deportation was a violation of Arts 3 and 8 of the ECHR: the former seeks to prohibit inhuman or degrading treatment or punishment, while the latter creates a right to respect for "private and family life". The action was unsuccessful.

Lord Ross: . . . "In my opinion the Convention cannot be regarded in any way as part of the municipal law of Scotland. I accept that the Convention sets forth a number of very important principles relating to human rights, but the provisions of the Convention have never entered into the law of Scotland. As I understand it, the law of Scotland is to be found partly in enactments by a body with legislative power and partly in the common law. A treaty or a convention is not part of the law of Scotland unless and until Parliament has passed legislation giving effect to the treaty provisions . . .

I was also referred to various English cases. This is a field of law where it would be proper to seek assistance from reported decisions in the English courts although these decisions are not binding in Scotland . . .

I now summarise the conclusions which I draw from these cases. (1) In England, it is accepted that conventions such as the European Convention on Human Rights are not part of the municipal law of England. [Here Lord Ross excerpted a number of comments.] (2) The second conclusion which may be drawn from the English authorities is that if there is any ambiguity in a United Kingdom statute, the court in England may look at and have regard to the Convention as an aid to construction. Lord Denning M.R. said as much . . . in *R. v Secretary of State for Home Affairs, ex p. Bhajan Singh* [1976] Q.B. 198 at p. 207:

> 'What is the position of the Convention in our English law? I would not depart in the least from what I said in the recent case of *Birdi v Secretary of State for Home Affairs* (1975) 119 S.J. 322. The courts can and should take the Convention into account. They should take it into account whenever interpreting a statute which affects the rights and liberties of the individual. It is to be assumed that the Crown, in taking its part in legislation, would do nothing which is in conflict with treaties. So the court should now construe the Immigration Act 1971 so as to be in conformity with a Convention and not against it.'

[Lord Ross then cited a number of other dicta to similar effect.]

With all respect to the distinguished judges in England who have said that the courts should look to an international convention such as the European Convention on Human Rights for the purpose of interpreting a United Kingdom statute, I find such a concept extremely difficult to comprehend. If the Convention does not form part of the municipal law, I do not see why the court should have regard to it at all. It was His Majesty's government in 1950 which was a High Contracting Party to the Convention. The Convention has been ratified by the United Kingdom, but, although this probably means as counsel pointed out, that the Convention had been laid before both Houses of Parliament before it was ratified (the Ponsonby Rule) ... , its provisions cannot be regarded as having the force of law ... Under our constitution, it is the Queen in Parliament who legislates and not Her Majesty's government, and the court does not require to have regard to acts of Her Majesty's government when interpreting the law. It is significant that in art. 6 of the condescendence the pursuers aver 'the Government of the United Kingdom is bound by the terms of the said Convention'. The government may be so bound, but I do not see how or why the courts should be bound by the Convention...

So far as Scotland is concerned, I am of opinion that the court is not entitled to have regard to the Convention either as an aid to construction or otherwise...

Counsel for the pursuers, however, contend further and in any event that the Convention was enforceable as part of Community law. Counsel referred to the European Communities Act 1972 and drew attention to the wide terms of s.2 (1) of the Act which deals *inter alia* with the enforceability of all rights 'created or arising by or under the Treaties' ... Counsel also submitted that the Court of Justice of the European Communities ... had already expressed the view that the Convention was part of the law which has to be enforced under the treaties and that this court was obliged to follow that ruling and to enforce the Convention as part of Community law. Alternatively, if the matter was in doubt counsel for the pursuers submitted that I should refer the matter to the European Court.

Counsel for the pursuers relied in particular upon the judgment of the European Court in *Firma J Nold v EC Commission* [1974] 2 C.M.L.R. 338 ... Counsel contended that the present case fell directly under the decision in the case of *Nold* and that the law of Scotland must be regarded as including those principles referred to in *Nold* because they were part of European law. Alternatively, if the matter were in doubt counsel contended that a reference should be made to the European Court ... It seems clear that for some purposes at least the European Court does enforce the principles contained in the Convention. There are a number of cases where the European Court has emphasised that it must ensure that the fundamental rights of individuals contained in the general principles of the law of the Community are enforced ... [In *Nold* it is stated at p. 354:]

> 'As this Court has already held, fundamental rights form an integral part of the general principles of law which it enforces. In assuring the protection of such rights, this Court is required to base itself on the constitutional traditions common to the member-States and therefore could not allow measures which are incompatible with the fundamental rights recognised and guaranteed by the constitutions of such States. The international treaties on the protection of human rights in which the member-States have co-operated or to which they have adhered can also supply indications which may be taken into account within the framework of Community Law...'

I agree with counsel for the defender that the European Court does not deal with fundamental rights as such in the abstract; it only deals with them if they arise under treaties and have a bearing on Community law questions ... In *State v Watson and Belmann* [1976] 2 C.M.L.R 552 in the opinion of the Advocate General ... at p. 563 ... the Advocate General said:

> 'On the basis of this analogy between rules of Community law and rules of international law accepted by all the member-States, some learned writers have felt justified in concluding that the provisions of the said Convention must be treated as forming an integral part of the Community legal order, whereas it seems clear to me that the spirit of the judgment did not involve any substantive reference to the provisions themselves but merely a reference to the general principles of which, like the Community rules with which the judgment drew an analogy, they are a specific expression. ... The extra-Community instruments under which those States have undertaken international obligations in order to ensure better protection for those rights can, without any

question of their being incorporated as such in the Community order, be used to establish principles which are common to the States themselves ...'

In *Allgemeine Gold v Commissioners of Customs and Excise* [1978] 2 C.M.L.R 292, Donaldson J. (as he then was), observed that although fundamental rights enshrined in the Convention are relevant to a consideration of the rights and duties of the Community institution and may be a background against which the express provisions of the EEC Treaty have to be interpreted, they do not form an implied, unexpressed part of the Treaty itself ...

In concluding that the pursuers' argument is not well-founded, I am also influenced by the fact that the issue raised in the present case has no Community law content at all. The pursuers here are not seeking to protect some economic right, but merely to assert a right alleged to be conferred on them by the Convention ...

For all these reasons, I am of opinion that the pursuers have not averred that they have any right under Community law. It follows that the pursuers' case is irrelevant and incompetent since they are seeking declarator of a right which they do not have either under the municipal law of Scotland nor under Community law. The action therefore falls to be dismissed."

The decision in *Kaur* was the subject of a valuable article in which it was argued that it was a decision of "great importance to Scots law, emphasising the need to enact the ECHR if the full benefit of its protection is to be assured in domestic law": W. Finnie, "The European Convention on Human Rights" (1980) J.L.S.S. 434. Although deploring the "practical effect" of the decision, it was nevertheless contended by Finnie that it was "correct and desirable" given the important constitutional principle underlying it. The case was, however, the start of a short journey which was to culminate in the enactment of the Scotland Act 1998 and the Human Rights Act 1998, both of which provide an opportunity to enforce Convention rights in the domestic courts. Mrs Kaur would now be able to pursue her claim against the appropriate minister under the Human Rights Act. Yet despite these changes, it is by no means clear that Mrs Kaur would be any more successful in legal proceedings today than she was in 1981. As we shall see, it may simply be that the reasons for her failure would be different. Nevertheless, in the course of the journey towards that incorporation, the judges began to depart from the unequivocal and constitutionally sound position adopted by Lord Ross, attempting to carve some role for the Convention in domestic legal proceedings. The following case reveals how far the courts had come on the eve of enactment of the Scotland Act and the Human Rights Act.

T, Petitioner
1997 S.L.T. 724

This is a case in which a homosexual man living in a stable relationship with another man applied to adopt a four-year old boy who had a number of disabilities. The adoption was thought by a number of parties to be in the best interests of the child. However, the issue which arose was whether the courts should sanction an adoption where it was proposed that the child would be brought up by an adoptive parent living in a homosexual relationship. The First Division took the view that there was no objection and the adoption order was made. In the course of its decision, the court reconsidered the status of the ECHR in Scots Law.

LORD PRESIDENT (HOPE)

"(b) European Convention on Human Rights

The amicus curiae suggested that, if we were unclear as to whether the provisions of the 1978 Act were intended to allow applications such as that made by the petitioner, we should consider whether regard should be had to the European Convention on Human Rights as an aid to the construction of the Act. As he pointed out, Lord Ross in *Kaur v Lord Advocate*, 1981 SLT at p 330 said that, as the Convention was not part of the municipal law of the United Kingdom, the court was not, so far as Scotland was concerned, entitled to have regard to the Convention either as an aid to construction or otherwise. That opinion was expressed after a careful review of the English authorities. These consisted largely of various dicta in the Court of Appeal, where the judges stated that, if there was any ambiguity in the United Kingdom statute, the court may look at and have regard to the Convention as an aid to construction. But Lord Ross said that he shared the view of Diplock LJ, as he then was, that the Convention was irrelevant in legal proceedings unless and until its provisions had been incorporated or given effect to in legislation. For my part, I think that, read as a whole and in context, Diplock LJ's remarks in *Salomon v Commissioners of Customs and Excise* [1967] 2 QB at p 143, were not intended to indicate that the Convention could not be looked at in order to resolve an ambiguity. What he was saying was that the terms of the statute could not be departed from if they were clear and unambiguous. However that may be, Lord Ross's opinion, although widely quoted in the textbooks as still representing the law of Scotland on this matter, has been looking increasingly outdated in the light of subsequent developments, and in my opinion, with respect, it is time that it was expressly departed from.

It is now clearly established as part of the law of England and Wales, as a result of decisions in the House of Lords, that in construing any provision in domestic legislation which is ambiguous in the sense that it is capable of a meaning which either conforms to or conflicts with the Convention, the courts will presume that Parliament intended to legislate in conformity with the Convention, not in conflict with it: see *R v Home Secretary, ex p Brind* per Lord Bridge of Harwich at [1991] 1 AC, pp 747H–748A. Similar views with regard to the relevance of the Convention were expressed by Lord Reid in *R v Miah* [1974] 1 WLR at p 694B-E, and by Lord Keith of Kinkel in *Derbyshire County Council v Times Newspapers Ltd* [1993] AC at pp 550D–551G. In *Anderson v HM Advocate* the opportunity was taken at 1996 SLT, p 158, to refer to the Convention and to Lord Bridge's observations. But an opinion was reserved as to whether these observations were part of the law of Scotland also, as the court was not concerned with a matter of statutory interpretation in that case. It is however now an integral part of the general principles of European Community law that fundamental human rights must be protected, and that one of the sources to which regard may be made for an expression of these rights is international treaties for the protection of human rights on which member states have collaborated or of which they are signatories: see *Stair Memorial Encyclopaedia*, Vol 10, "European Community Law", para 95. I consider that the drawing of a distinction between the law of Scotland and that of the rest of the United Kingdom on this matter can no longer be justified. In my opinion the courts in Scotland should apply the same presumption as that described by Lord Bridge, namely that, when legislation is found to be ambiguous in the sense that it is capable of a meaning which either conforms to or conflicts with the Convention, Parliament is to be presumed to have legislated in conformity with the Convention, not in conflict with it.

The question then is whether, if the petitioner's application for adoption were to be held not to be within the intendment of the 1978 Act because he is living with a third party in a homosexual relationship, this would conflict with the Convention. If such a conflict were to be demonstrated, it would point in favour of a construction of the 1978 Act which would remove it. There are three possible grounds for complaint. The first is that such a decision would constitute an unjustified interference with the petitioner's right to respect for his private and family life, contrary to art 8(1) of the Convention. The second is that it would constitute a violation of his right to found a family, contrary to art 12. The third is that it would constitute discrimination on the ground of sex, contrary to art 14. But, in regard to the first ground, the European Commission on Human Rights has held that the relationship of a homosexual couple does not fall within the scope of the right to respect for family life: eg *S v United Kingdom*, Application no 11716/85, decision of 14 May 1986; *Kerkhoven,*

Hinke and Hinke v The Netherlands, Application no 15666/89, decision of 19 May 1992. A complaint under art 8 of unjustified interference with the right to respect for his private life would also be likely to be held inadmissible, as in *Dudgeon v The United Kingdom*, where the European Court accepted that it was legitimate to take special measures to protect those who are specially vulnerable because they are young and to have regard to strong public feelings in determining what measures states consider necessary for the protection of morals by way of restraint on homosexual relationships: see also *Kerkhoven, Hinke and Hinke v The Netherlands*. A complaint under art 12 would be likely to be held inadmissible, as in *X and Y v United Kingdom*, Application no 7229/76, decision of 15 December 1977, the Commission held that art 12 did not guarantee a right to adopt a child who was not the natural child of the couple concerned. The cases of *S v United Kingdom* and *Kerkhoven, Hinke* and *Hinke v The Netherlands* also demonstrate that a complaint under art 14 would be likely to be held inadmissible.

In these circumstances I agree with the amicus curiae that the relevant cases point to the conclusion that, if the court were to hold that the petitioner's application was not within the intendment of the 1978 Act, there would be no conflict with the Convention. But there is nothing in these authorities to suggest that there is anything in the Convention which would require the court to hold that it was the intention of Parliament that an adoption order should not be made in these circumstances."

VI. CONCLUSION

Under the British constitutional arrangements in force before the general election in 1997, the position regarding human rights in Scotland were scarcely different from the position elsewhere in the United Kingdom. This would not have justified comment but for:

- the legal claims that Scottish constitutional law was different from English constitutional law, a claim that was to prove to be hollow; and
- the political claim that the people of Scotland were being governed from London by an administration which enjoyed little popular support in Scotland.

An interesting feature of these times is that the courts were unwilling to flex their muscles by using the former (constitutional law) in response to the latter (the democratic deficit). To the extent that Convention rights were becoming to have a potentially greater influence in Scots Law (as in *T, Petitioner*, above), this was as a result of the vicarious influence of developments in the English courts on Scottish judges. It was not a result of the emergence of a distinctive Scottish view reflecting a distinctive Scottish constitutional law. Indeed in *Kaur*, above, Lord Ross had demonstrated an impeccable commitment to Imperial doctrine for reasons which were wholly convincing. Those wishing directly to enforce Convention rights from Scotland thus had no option but to use the right of individual petition in the ECHR. There were in fact very few decisions of the European Court of Human Rights dealing with Scottish complaints.

Chapter 2

HUMAN RIGHTS AND THE SCOTTISH PARLIAMENT

I. INTRODUCTION

The transformation of human rights law in Scotland has taken place in two ways and by means of two legal instruments. First by the Scotland Act 1998 and secondly by the Human Rights Act 1998. In this chapter we are concerned with some of the key features of the devolution settlement of 1998. Our main concern is to examine how human rights considerations are woven into the fabric of that settlement. We begin by examining the nature and powers of the Scottish Parliament. We then proceed to examine the ways in which the Parliament must have regard to Convention rights and to the measures taken to ensure that it does not legislate in violation of these rights. In the final substantive section of this chapter we examine the role of the courts in ensuring that Convention rights are not breached by either the Scottish Parliament or the Scottish Executive. We defer until Ch.3 a consideration of some of the major cases which address the respective powers of the Parliament and the Executive. In the context of British constitutional law, however, we are thus dealing with a constitutional novelty of the greatest importance. Here we have a body with power to make primary legislation which can be struck down in the courts not only because it has legislated on reserved matters, but also because it has violated the human rights of natural or legal persons in an area of devolved authority.

II. THE SCOTTISH PARLIAMENT

Legislative devolution is an idea of some antiquity, with the House of Commons resolving as long ago as 1894 that "it is desirable, while maintaining the powers and supremacy of the Imperial Parliament, to establish a legislature in Scotland for purely Scottish affairs". A similar resolution was passed in 1895 and in 1908 a Bill was introduced to give self-government to Scotland, and was passed on a third reading by a large majority. Scottish devolution bills were also passed in 1911, 1913 and 1920, while in 1912 the House of Commons resolved again that "the measure providing for the delegation of parliamentary powers to Ireland should be followed by the granting of similar powers of self-government to Scotland as part of a general scheme of devolution". The issue of Scottish devolution (which enjoyed the support of both Keir Hardie and Ramsay MacDonald) was kept alive by the Government of Scotland Bill 1924 introduced by a number of government backbenchers during the short tenure of the first Labour government. The Bill—modelled on the earlier measure of 1920—was quite properly described as proposing "fairly large powers" for a proposed Scottish Parliament (consisting of the King and a House of Representatives). The Parliament would have the power to make laws "for the peace, order and good government of Scotland", and would also have tax-raising powers, which might include taxes based on property or income. Apart from the obvious geographical exception, the Parliament would have no power in relation to the Crown, the making of peace and war, the defence of the realm, treaties, external trade and the Post Office. Scottish appeals to the House of Lords would be discontinued, with appeals to be heard by the Judicial Committee of the Privy Council which would also be empowered to rule on the validity of any acts of the Scottish Parliament.

Although the Labour Party manifesto in 1929 included a commitment to a Scottish Parliament, it was another 40 years before the matter was to resurface as an active public policy issue. However, this time the dynamic driving the process proved to be unstoppable despite a false start in 1979.

N. Burrows
"Unfinished Business: The Scotland Act 1998"
(1999) 62 M.L.R. 241

"The Royal Commission on the Constitution (1969–1973) had recommended that legislative competence be devolved to Scotland. The Labour Government enacted the Scotland Act 1978. That Act was to devolve certain specified areas to a Scottish Parliament, which was to be elected following the result of a referendum, provided that the referendum achieved a positive vote of 40 per cent of the electorate in favour of devolution. The referendum target was not achieved with only 32.5 per cent of the electorate voting in favour of devolution. The 1978 Scotland Act was, therefore, repealed. In May 1979 the election of a Conservative government opposed to devolution meant that devolution was no longer on the official political agenda.

Within Scotland, however, devolution remained a live issue particularly in the light of dwindling political support for the Conservatives culminating in the May 1997 election when no Conservatives were returned from Scottish seats. The Campaign for a Scottish Parliament continued its work and established a Committee, which, in July 1988, recommended the formation of a Scottish Constitutional Convention 'to make plans for the future governance of Scotland'. In early 1989, a cross party group was established to discuss ways of moving the project forward. The Conservatives refused to participate and the Scottish Nationalist Party (SNP) withdrew support preferring to continue its fight for independence. At its inaugural meeting in March 1989 the Scottish Constitutional Convention adopted a *Claim of Right for Scotland* echoing earlier Claims of Right. The modern version acknowledges 'the sovereign right of the Scottish people to determine the form of government best suited to their needs'. It states that the purpose of the Scottish Constitutional Convention is 'to agree a scheme for an Assembly or Parliament for Scotland', to encourage popular support for it and to 'assert the right of the Scottish people to secure the implementation of the scheme'.

Membership of the Scottish Constitutional Convention was drawn from the political parties (Conservatives and SNP excepted although individuals within these parties did support the movement), representatives of local authorities, the churches, civic organisations including women's groups, trade unions and business organisations. It claimed to be 'the most broadly representative organisation in Scotland'. The Scottish Constitutional Convention met in plenary sessions and in working groups until November 1990 when it presented its report *Towards Scotland's Parliament*. At that stage, there was not agreement on the method of election or on certain other matters and an independent commission was established under the convenership of Joyce McMillan to report on these matters. The findings of the McMillan report were incorporated into the conclusions of the 1990 report and a final document, *Scotland's Parliament; Scotland's Right* was presented to the Scottish people on St Andrew's Day 1995.

The involvement of the Labour Party throughout this process means that the 1995 report has a particular significance in relation to the Labour Party's proposals for devolution. The Labour Party was elected on the basis of a pledge to introduce a devolved parliament for Scotland and has made frequent references to the work of the Scottish Constitutional Convention and the principles underlying its work. An understanding of *Scotland's*

Parliament: Scotland's Right is therefore crucial to an understanding of the Scotland Act despite the fact that there are some significant differences between them. In July 1997, the new government issued its White Paper, *Scotland's Parliament*, which set out to translate the Labour Party's commitment 'into a sound and durable constitutional settlement'. Whilst acknowledging a debt to the Scottish Constitutional Convention, the white paper reorients the debate on devolution. Whereas the Scottish Constitutional Convention and the Claim of Right had sought to anchor a new political settlement in a concept of sovereignty based on the will of the people, the White Paper states unequivocally that:

'the UK Parliament is and will remain sovereign in all matters: but as part of the government's resolve to modernise the British constitution Westminster will be choosing to exercise that sovereignty by devolving legislative responsibilities to a Scottish Parliament without in any way diminishing its own powers.'

The consequences of this approach are discussed below in considering the provisions of the Scotland Act. At this stage, it is perhaps sufficient to note that, in Scotland the 'doctrinal incubus of parliamentary sovereignty' has not gone uncontested.

Before introducing the Scotland Bill, the government decided to ascertain the wishes of the Scottish electorate on devolution. The reasons for holding a referendum were outlined by the Secretary of State, Donald Dewar, in the debates on the Referendums (Scotland and Wales) Bill 1997. He argued that:

'There is advantage in popular consent. In our unwritten constitution, popular consent gives a certain legitimacy. In a sense it is a way to build the devolution scheme into the system and to give it roots ... If we get the right result, we have moral authority to speed the passage of devolution.'

Donald Dewar had, of course, been a signatory to the Claim of Right and therefore had some attachment to the notion of the 'settled will of the people'. His claim that popular consent assists in providing legitimacy reflects the Scottish debate and perhaps suggests a slight ambivalence towards any theory of the sovereignty of the UK Parliament in political if not legal terms.

The Referendums (Scotland and Wales) Act 1997 provided that a referendum was to be held on 11 September 1997. In Scotland, two questions were put to the electorate; the first asked whether there should be a Scottish parliament and the second whether that parliament should have tax varying powers. The Labour government rejected SNP demands for a third question on independence. It also rejected Conservative demands that the timing of the referendum should be delayed until after the debate on the contents of the Scotland Bill had taken place. In 1978, the referendum had taken place after the Scotland Act had received Royal Assent. The government's response was to state that if there were not significant support for devolution then it would be pointless to waste valuable parliamentary time. The results of the referendum reflected widespread popular support for the creation of a parliament and for that parliament to have tax varying powers. On a turnout of 60.4 per cent, 74.3 per cent voted in favour of the creation of a Scottish parliament with 25.7 per cent against and 65.6 per cent voted in favour of tax varying powers with 36.5 per cent against. From this time on, the Labour government was able to quote the settled will of the people in support of its devolution proposals. Accordingly the Scotland Bill was published in December 1997."

The Scotland Act 1998 creates the Scottish Parliament with limited powers, as an act of the sovereign Westminster Parliament. The Act has been dubbed a "constitutional statute", meaning for this purpose that its provisions cannot be impliedly repealed: *Thoburn v Sunderland City Council* [2003] Q.B. 151 at 186 (Laws L.J.). The Scottish Parliament is a unicameral Parliament of 129 members elected every four years on the additional member electoral system.

There are thus 73 members representing individual constituencies, and 56 members representing the regions. This has contrived to ensure that no one party has a majority of seats in the Parliament and also a greater representation of small parties than is possible under the Westminster electoral system. Acts of the Scottish Parliament must be passed by the Parliament and receive the Royal Assent. It is expressly provided that the validity of an Act of the Scottish Parliament is not affected by "any invalidity in the proceedings of the Parliament leading to its enactment" (Scotland Act 1998, s.28(5)). The Parliament has only a limited authority in the sense that it may legislate on matters other than the long list of reserved matters which remain within the jurisdiction of the Westminster Parliament, and it has only limited tax-varying powers. The validity of Acts of the Scottish Parliament can be challenged in the courts, to ensure that the Parliament does not stray from the authority conferred upon it by the sovereign Westminster Parliament. It is arguable, however, that whatever sovereignty Westminster retains over Edinburgh, it is purely formal, disconnected from political reality. There can be no question of the Scottish Parliament being stripped of its existing powers or of Westminster exercising a power to override Edinburgh. As in the Westminster Parliament, the Scottish Parliament supplies the government. The First Minister and the other Ministers must be recruited from among the members of the Scottish Parliament, and together the members of the Scottish Executive are referred to collectively as the Scottish Ministers.

Whaley v Lord Watson of Invergowrie
2000 S.L.T. 475

The petitioners were active members of the hunting community who were trying to stop the enactment of legislation designed to ban hunting with wild dogs. Lord Watson proposed to introduce a private members' bill and was supported by an anti-hunting organisation. The petitioners sought by interim interdict to prevent him from introducing the bill on the ground that he was disqualified from doing so because he was in breach of the rules relating to members' interests. These were contained in reg.6 of transitional regulations. The conduct and standards committee of the Parliament had found that Lord Watson was not in breach, and the Lord Ordinary dismissed the petition. His decision was upheld on appeal, though in the course of its decision the Inner House had occasion to comment on the nature of the Scottish Parliament and its relationship with the courts. It will be seen that the Court of Session has taken a very assertive view of its role in the new constitutional order. It will also be seen that the members of the court refer to s.40(3) and (4) of the Scotland Act. The former provides that in any proceedings against the Parliament, "the court shall not make an order for suspension, interdict, reduction or specific performance", but may only make a declarator. The latter provides that in any proceedings against a member of the Parliament, the court is not to make any order "if the effect of doing so would be to give any relief against the Parliament which could not have been given in proceedings against the Parliament".

LORD PRESIDENT (RODGER): "I have emphasised the origin and nature of the transitional order on members' interests because, at times during the course of the argument for the first respondent before us, it seemed as though counsel wished us to regard art 6 of the order as in some way a mere matter of the regulation of the internal affairs of the Parliament upon which, preferably, the court should not intrude at all and on which, if the court did intrude, it should do so only with some particular degree of circumspection. In particular counsel stressed that the standards committee of the Parliament had considered the question of whether the first respondent had breached art 6 of the order and had come to the conclusion that he had not. The committee, rather than the court, were the appropriate body to rule on this matter and the court should respect their decision by exercising a discretion not to grant interdict against the first respondent.

This line of argument found some favour with the Lord Ordinary in a passage which I quote fully, including the opening sentences which have a more direct bearing, however, on another argument for the first respondent about the scope of s 40 (3) and (4) of the 1998 Act:

'It is obvious in my opinion that what the legislature at Westminster intended in subs (3) by reference to the question of declarator and restriction on the remedy of interdict was freedom of action as far as the Scottish Parliament was concerned and that that was to be protected by subs (4) by not allowing interference with its affairs which would not be permitted by way of interdict against it directly, to be achieved indirectly through the back door.

In my opinion what is being proposed here by the petitioners is precisely that. They are seeking, through an allegation of a breach of the Parliament rules, the advocacy position which, for present purposes I take as read, to stop the introduction of a Bill, the competence of which would not be affected by the fact that its promoter had breached the advocacy rules. It would still have been a competent Bill provided the Presiding Officer had provided the necessary certificate. Thus, by the back door, it is my opinion that what is being sought to achieve here is exactly what subs (4) was designed to prevent. It goes further because quite apart from the general power of the Parliament to regulate its own affairs, which was not disputed by counsel for the petitioners, the result of granting this interdict would be effectively to suspend or overturn the decision of the standards committee as to whether or not the rules had been breached by the first respondent in relation to the question of paid advocacy, a matter which must be for that committee to determine. I expressly reserve my opinion as to whether or not there might be circumstances in which an interdict against an individual member of the Parliament could be competency [sic] achieved in this court if the proviso to subs (4) did not apply. What I consider is being attempted by the petitioners in this case is to achieve, by a roundabout method, the obstruction of the legitimate presentation of a Bill to the Parliament which must be allowed to regulate its own affairs and determine whether or not in its opinion the member is competent to present it. That has already been decided and that this [sic] in my opinion is a matter for Parliament and the standards committee.

The matter seems to me to be compounded by the fact that if persons such as the petitioners had a legitimate concern, and maybe they have, that the lobbying rules had been breached, it seems to me that their remedy is by way of complaint, petition or even public address. This court, in my opinion, is not in the position of interfering with legitimate decisions of the Parliament as to its own affairs and certainly not to rehear a decision that the standards committee has already taken. This seems to me to be inherent in what was intended by the proviso to subs (4) of s 40.'

A little later his Lordship observed:

'In my opinion the actionable wrong, assuming it to have been committed, is against the rules of the Parliament and its committee. In my opinion it is for the Parliament to decide whether or not in those circumstances the member in question is entitled or not to present the Bill. It seems to me to be a recipe for disaster to allow members of the public who are aggrieved by the potential consequences of a particular piece of legis-lation to have the right to enter into the procedure of the Scottish Parliament and require this court to declare that it has misdirected itself. There has been a vast development in the last 20 years of the concept of judicial review, but it has always been very carefully orchestrated against the background of Lord Diplock's celebrated dicta which are now too well known even to be recorded. The Scottish Parliament is entitled to make its own determination, in my opinion, upon its own rules and this court should not even look at it on grounds of irrationality. It may be in due course that if there is a fundamental irrationality in its approach to the legislation it passes such could be challengeable by a number of reasons based on its legislative competence upon the view that an organisation that is acting beyond its powers is acting irrationally and therefore not within its competence. In the case of the Parliament that is legislative competence. I offer no further view on that subject. What I am entirely satisfied about is that it is quite inappropriate for pressure groups, individuals, however their interests may be affected, to have the right to tell, by way of legal action, a committee of this Parliament that its own view of its own rules is inappropriate or even wrong. That, in my opinion, is far beyond what the legislation contemplated the extent of intervention by the Court of Session would be in the activities of the Scottish Parliament.'

These remarks of the Lord Ordinary contain some general observations about the relationship between the courts and the Scottish Parliament which had a bearing on his reasoning and which I am unable to endorse.

The Lord Ordinary gives insufficient weight to the fundamental character of the Parliament as a body which—however important its role—has been created by statute and derives its powers from statute. As such, it is a body which, like any other statutory body, must work within the scope of those powers. If it does not do so, then in an appropriate case the court may be asked to intervene and will require to do so, in a manner permitted by the legislation. In principle, therefore, the Parliament like any other body set up by law is subject to the law and to the courts which exist to uphold that law. In the 1998 Act Parliament did, however, put one important limitation on the powers of the court in proceedings involving the Scottish Parliament. In s 40 (3) and (4), which I examine more fully below, it provided that in such proceedings the court should not grant an order for suspension, interdict, reduction or specific performance but might instead grant a declarator; nor should it grant any order against an individual which would have equivalent effect. It is unnecessary for present purposes to consider the position where Community law rights are involved. ... Subject to s 40 (3) and (4), however, the court has the same powers over the Parliament as it would have over any other statutory body and might, for instance, in an appropriate case grant a decree against it for the payment of damages.

Some of the arguments of counsel for the first respondent appeared to suggest that it was somehow inconsistent with the very idea of a Parliament that it should be subject in this way to the law of the land and to the jurisdiction of the courts which uphold the law. I do not share that view. On the contrary, if anything, it is the Westminster Parliament which is unusual in being respected as sovereign by the courts. And, now, of course, certain inroads have been made into even that sovereignty by the European Communities Act 1972. By contrast, in many democracies throughout the Commonwealth, for example, even where the parliaments have been modelled in some respects on Westminster, they owe their existence and powers to statute and are in various ways subject to the law and to the courts which act to uphold the law. The Scottish Parliament has simply joined that wider family of parliaments. Indeed I find it almost paradoxical that counsel for a member of a body which exists to create laws and to impose them on others should contend that a legally enforceable framework is somehow less than appropriate for that body itself.

Members of the Scottish Parliament hold office by virtue of the 1998 Act and, again, their rights and duties derive ultimately from the Act. Qua members of the Parliament, just as in all the other aspects of their lives, they are in general subject to the law and to the decisions of the courts. Of course, in ss 41 and 42 the Act makes certain specific provisions to ensure freedom of speech for members of the Parliament and to permit proper reporting of its proceedings. In addition s 40 (4) recognises one particular respect in which the position of members vis a vis the courts is different from the position of other people: in certain situations the courts cannot grant an order for suspension, interdict, reduction or specific performance (or other like order) against them. But the immunity thus granted to the members of the Parliament is not granted in order to afford protection to the members themselves but simply to buttress the immunity of the Parliament from orders of that kind. In other respects the law applies to members in the usual way. In particular—to come to the specific issue in this case—the first respondent is legally bound by the terms of art 6 of the transitional order on members' interests. If he breaches that article, then he contravenes the law of the land and indeed commits an offence. The breach may have other consequences which make it proper for the civil courts to notice it. Since subss (3) and (4) of s 40 have been specifically enacted to exclude certain powers of the court in relation to proceedings against the Parliament, the inference must be that in other respects the law applies in the usual way to both the Parliament and to members of the Parliament. Under reference to the opinion of Lord Woolf MR in *R v Parliamentary Commissioner for Standards, ex p Al Fayed* at [1998] 1 WLR, p 670G-H, counsel for the first respondent submitted, however, that this court should exercise 'a self denying ordinance in relation to interfering with the proceedings' of the Scottish Parliament. Lord Woolf used that expression to describe the attitude which the courts have long adopted towards the Parliament of the United Kingdom because the relationship between the courts and Parliament is, in the words of Sedley LJ, 'a mutuality of respect between two constitutional sovereignties'. The basis for that particular stance, including art 9 of the Bill of Rights 1689, is lacking in the case of the Scottish Parliament. While all United Kingdom courts which may have occasion to deal with proceedings involving the Scottish Parliament can, of course, be expected to accord all due respect to the Parliament as to any other litigant, they must equally be aware that they are not dealing with a parliament which is sovereign: on the contrary, it is subject to the laws and hence to the courts. For that reason, I see no basis upon which this court can properly adopt a 'self denying ordinance' which would consist in exercising some kind of discretion to refuse to enforce the law against the Parliament or its members. To do so would be to fail to uphold the rights of other parties under the law. The correct attitude in such cases must be to apply the law in an even handed way and, subject to the residual discretion described by Lord Watson in *Magistrates of Kirkcaldy v Grahame* at 1882, 9 R (HL), pp 91–93, to grant to parties the remedy which they seek and to which they are entitled. In particular, where a competent interim remedy is sought against a member, the correct approach will be to apply the law in the usual way and to have regard to all the relevant factors in deciding where the balance of convenience lies.

These general observations provide a background to the more specific arguments which counsel for the first respondent directed against the petitioners' case. The argument which the Lord Ordinary accepted and which really lies at the heart of his decision relates to the construction of subss (3) and (4) of s 40 of the 1998 Act and their application to the facts of this case. In short, the Lord Ordinary held that it would be incompetent to grant the proposed interdict against the first respondent because the petitioners were seeking by a back door to achieve exactly what subs (4) was designed to prevent. For that reason the Lord Ordinary appears to have felt able not merely to refuse the motion for interim interdict but actually to dismiss the petition at this early stage.

In my view the Lord Ordinary construed subs (4) too widely. As I have pointed out above and as indeed the Lord Ordinary accepts, subs (4) exists to prevent parties from circumventing the terms of subs (3). Subsection (3) provides that the court is not to grant various forms of relief, including interdict, in proceedings against the Parliament. So, for example, the court could not grant an interdict against the Parliament considering a Bill, even if it would not be within the legislative competence of the Parliament. That protection for the Parliament could easily be rendered worthless if, for instance, it were possible for interdict to be pronounced, on the same basis, against the Presiding Officer granting the necessary certificate of legislative competence—which would have the effect that the Bill could not be introduced and hence could not be considered by the Parliament. Subsection (4) outlaws such stratagems. The terms of both subss (3) and (4) are plainly modelled on the familiar terms of s 21 of the Crown Proceedings Act 1947—even down to the use of the term 'relief' in a manner which is not altogether usual in Scots law....

Despite these powerful factors which can be advanced on behalf of the petitioners, I have come to the conclusion that the balance of convenience does not favour the grant of interim interdict since the issue turns on the construction of the Members' Interests Order and not on any matters of fact which remain to be clarified. We have heard full legal submissions on the point and I have considered the matter on the most favourable version of the facts from the petitioners' point of view. On that basis I have concluded that the petitioners' case is unsound. That being so, it appears to me that an interim interdict would serve no legitimate purpose. On the other hand, it would prevent the first respondent from introducing a Bill which has the necessary support from other members and which the Presiding Officer has certified to be within the legislative competence of the Parliament. While the first respondent could point to no particular reason why this Bill should be considered by the Parliament in the near future, other things being equal, it would seem to be in the public interest that a member who has a Bill which is drafted and ready to be considered by the Parliament should be able to introduce it as soon as he is ready to do so.

For these reasons I would recall the Lord Ordinary's interlocutor dismissing the petition and sustaining the first respondent's first plea in law. *Quoad ultra* I would adhere to the Lord Ordinary's interlocutor insofar as he refused the petitioners' motion for interim interdict."

III. HUMAN RIGHTS AND LEGISLATIVE SCRUTINY

So far as the Scotland Act and human rights are concerned, it is important at this stage to establish just how human rights are formally protected under the new regime. Section 29 of the Scotland Act provides that an Act of the Scottish Parliament is not law so far as any provision of the Act is outside the legislative competence of the Parliament. By virtue of s.29(2) there are a number of reasons why a provision might be outside the competence of the Parliament. Apart from the long list of reserved matters, these include a provision that is "incompatible with any of the Convention rights or with Community law". Convention rights for this purpose have the same meaning as in the Human Rights Act 1998, which is dealt with in Ch.3 below, and with which the Scotland Act tends to overlap. It is ultimately for the courts to determine whether a matter is outside the competence of the Parliament. In order to help avoid legislating outside the competence of the Parliament, an extensive network of scrutiny devices has been introduced. These involve Executive scrutiny by the responsible Minister; legislative scrutiny by the presiding officer; and judicial scrutiny by the Judicial Committee of the Privy Council:

Scotland Act 1998

"Scrutiny of Bills before introduction
31.—(1) A member of the Scottish Executive in charge of a Bill shall, on or before introduction of the Bill in the Parliament, state that in his view the provisions of the Bill would be within the legislative competence of the Parliament.

(2) The Presiding Officer shall, on or before the introduction of a Bill in the Parliament, decide whether or not in his view the provisions of the Bill would be within the legislative competence of the Parliament and state his decision.

(3) The form of any statement, and the manner in which it is to be made, shall be determined under standing orders, and standing orders may provide for any statement to be published.

Submission of Bills for Royal Assent
32.—(1) It is for the Presiding Officer to submit Bills for Royal Assent.

(2) The Presiding Officer shall not submit a Bill for Royal Assent at any time when—
    (a) the Advocate General, the Lord Advocate or the Attorney General is entitled to make a reference in relation to the Bill under section 33,
    (b) any such reference has been made but has not been decided or otherwise disposed of by the Judicial Committee, or
    (c) an order may be made in relation to the Bill under section 35.

(3) The Presiding Officer shall not submit a Bill in its unamended form for Royal Assent

if—

    (a) the Judicial Committee have decided that the Bill or any provision of it would not be within the legislative competence of the Parliament, or

    (b) a reference made in relation to the Bill under section 33 has been withdrawn following a request for withdrawal of the reference under section 34(2)(b).

  (4) In this Act—

"Advocate General" means the Advocate General for Scotland,

"Judicial Committee" means the Judicial Committee of the Privy Council.

Scrutiny of Bills by the Judicial Committee

33.—(1) The Advocate General, the Lord Advocate or the Attorney General may refer the question of whether a Bill or any provision of a Bill would be within the legislative competence of the Parliament to the Judicial Committee for decision.

  (2) Subject to subsection (3), he may make a reference in relation to a Bill at any time during—

    (a) the period of four weeks beginning with the passing of the Bill, and

    (b) any period of four weeks beginning with any subsequent approval of the Bill in accordance with standing orders made by virtue of section 36(5).

  (3) He shall not make a reference in relation to a Bill if he has notified the Presiding Officer that he does not intend to make a reference in relation to the Bill, unless the Bill has been approved as mentioned in subsection (2)(b) since the notification."

Unlike in the Westminster Parliament, there is no Human Rights Committee of the Scottish Parliament. The Joint Committee on Human Rights is a joint committee of the House of Commons and the House of Lords which—among other things—scrutinises bills to determine whether they are compatible with Convention rights. The Committee then reports on its findings to both Houses. There are occasions when the Committee does point out that Bills fall short of Convention obligations. The role of the Presiding Officer under s.31(2) of the Scotland Act is perhaps the closest procedure to parallel the Westminster procedure. However the two are by no means identical, though if anything the power of the presiding officer to block a bill is much greater than the power of the JCHR to scrutinise one. Nevertheless, there is considerable support for greater scrutiny by members of the Scottish Parliament. In the meantime it would be a step forward if the presiding officer were to publish the reasons for his views that legislation is compatible with the ECHR and otherwise within the powers of the Parliament. This could be done by an amendment to the Standing Orders which provide as follows:

Scottish Parliament
Standing Orders 2004

"Rule 9.3 Accompanying documents

  1. A Bill shall on introduction be accompanied by a written statement signed by the Presiding Officer which shall—

    (a) indicate whether or not in his or her view the provisions of the Bill would be within the legislative competence of the Parliament; and

    (b) if in his or her view any of the provisions would not be within legislative competence, indicate which those provisions are and the reasons for that view.

  2. A Bill shall on introduction be accompanied by a Financial Memorandum which shall set out the best estimates of the administrative, compliance and other costs to which the provisions of the Bill would give rise, best estimates of the timescales over which such costs would be expected to arise, and an indication of the margins of uncertainty in such estimates. The Financial Memorandum must distinguish separately such costs as would fall upon—

    (a) the Scottish Administration;

(b) local authorities; and

(c) other bodies, individuals and businesses.

3. An Executive Bill shall also be accompanied by—

(a) a written statement signed by the member of the Scottish Executive in charge of the Bill which states that in his or her view the provisions of the Bill would be within the legislative competence of the Parliament;

(b) Explanatory Notes which summarise objectively what each of the provisions of the Bill does (to the extent that it requires explanation or comment) and give other information necessary or expedient to explain the effect of the Bill; and

(c) a Policy Memorandum which sets out—

(i) the policy objectives of the Bill;

(ii) whether alternative ways of meeting those objectives were considered and, if so, why the approach taken in the Bill was adopted;

(iii) the consultation, if any, which was undertaken on those objectives and the ways of meeting them or on the detail of the Bill and a summary of the outcome of that consultation; and

(iv) an assessment of the effects, if any, of the Bill on equal opportunities, human rights, island communities, local government, sustainable development and any other matter which the Scottish Ministers consider relevant.

3A. Any Bill other than an Executive Bill may also be accompanied by—

(a) Explanatory Notes, as defined in paragraph 3(b);

(b) a Policy Memorandum, as defined in paragraph 3(c) (but with the reference in paragraph 3(c)(iv) to the Scottish Ministers read as a reference to the member introducing the Bill)."

Although there is no separate human rights scrutiny committee of the Scottish Parliament, the "lead committee" (which considers and reports on the Bill's general principles at the first main stage of scrutiny (Stage 1), would normally consider ECHR-issues that arise in a particular Bill at this point of the process. The legislative committees are "general purpose" committees in relation to legislation—combining the separate functions of "select" and "standing" committees at Westminster. The Justice Committees and before them the Justice and Home Affairs Committee are particularly concerned to address Convention issues which tend to arise in a number of ways. The first is in relation to those bills which have been introduced to give effect to Convention obligations. As might be expected, the Committee considers whether the Bill meets these obligations. A good example of this is the intense scrutiny by the Justice and Home Affairs Committee of the Bail, Judicial Appointments etc. (Scotland) Bill 2000. This important bill was said to be the first piece of legislation dealt with by the Executive and the Parliament that specifically addressed ECHR concerns. The Committee was extremely critical of the Bill, with the reasons for these criticisms being outlined in the following extract which also reveals the extent to which individuals and interest groups can raise their concerns before the Scottish Parliament in advance of legislation, thereby minimising the need for judicial review afterwards.

Justice and Home Affairs Committee
6th Report, 2000
Stage 1 Report on the Bail, Judicial Appointments etc. (Scotland) Bill
S.P. Paper 147: Session 1 (2000)

"Introduction and background

1. On 6 April 2000, the Minister for Justice (Jim Wallace) announced to the Parliament (during a debate on the Regulation of Investigatory Powers Bill) that the Executive was to introduce a bill 'to deal with a number of ECHR issues'. In particular, the bill would 'amend certain provisions of the Criminal Procedure (Scotland) Act 1995 in relation to bail ... amend the District Courts (Scotland) Act 1975 in relation to justices of the peace and certain prosecutions in the district court ... [and] create a new judicial office of part-time sheriff'. The Minister said he hoped to introduce the bill 'as soon as possible after Easter' (col 1465).

2. In the event, the Bail, Judicial Appointments etc. (Scotland) Bill (SP Bill 17) was not introduced in the Parliament until 25 May 2000. On the same day, the Parliament formally designated the Justice and Home Affairs Committee as the lead committee on the Bill. The Bureau also referred the provisions of the Bill that confer powers to make subordinate legislation to the Subordinate Legislation Committee ... Because of the time pressures imposed on the Stage 1 process, this Committee has not had an opportunity to consider that Committee's report before finalising this one.

3. From the outset, the Executive has made clear its anxiety to have the Bill enacted and in force by 2 October this year. That is the date on which the Human Rights Act 1998 is to be brought into force, making it unlawful for any public authority to act in any way incompatible with the Convention rights. Additional urgency has been created by the decision of the High Court in *Starrs v Ruxton*, 2000 S.L.T. 42 that a court presided over by a temporary sheriff is not an independent and impartial tribunal within the meaning of article 8 of the Convention. The use of temporary sheriffs has been suspended since 11 November 1999, following that decision, creating considerable practical difficulties for the processing of cases in the Scottish courts.

Time constraints and evidence taken by the Committee

4. In order to allow the Committee to complete Stage 1 consideration of the Bill in time to allow the 2 October deadline for commencement to be met, the Executive provided draft versions of the Bill and its accompanying documents some three weeks before the Bill was introduced. These drafts were largely identical to the published Bill and accompanying documents.

5. The Committee took evidence on the draft Bill on 15 May from Professor Christopher Gane of Aberdeen University and on 22 May from the Deputy Minister for Justice (Angus MacKay), Victim Support Scotland and the District Courts Association. Finally, on 30 May, the Committee took evidence on the Bill itself from Jamie Gilmour, a solicitor and former temporary sheriff, the Sheriffs' Association, the Law Society of Scotland and the Scottish Rape Crisis Network. Written evidence was received from various District Courts. We are grateful to all our witnesses, many of whom have agreed to give evidence at extremely short notice.

6. Even allowing for the availability of the draft Bill, the Committee has faced some difficulty dealing with the complex issues raised by the Bill within what has been an extremely tight timescale. While we fully appreciate the need to complete the Bill's passage in time to meet the 2 October deadline and the added necessity of resolving the crisis situation in courts due to the removal of temporary sheriffs, we do not fully understand why the Executive was unable to introduce the Bill earlier. It is now some considerable time since that deadline was announced and since the need to make some of the necessary

legislative changes proposed—particularly in relation to temporary sheriffs—was first recognised.

7. We mention the short timescale within which we have had to consider this Bill not because of the difficulties it has caused the Committee in terms of additional workload or disruption to other work—although it has had those effects—but from a genuine concern that there may not be time to ensure both that the new provisions are in place in time and that they are right.

...

Part 1—Bail

Extension of circumstances in which bail may be granted

9. Part 1 of the Bill makes various changes to the Criminal Procedure (Scotland) Act 1995 in relation to bail. Section 1 of the Bill requires courts to decide whether to grant bail to an accused person on first appearance, regardless of whether an application has been made. Section 2 provides that an accused may be admitted to bail for an offence even if he or she is serving a prison sentence or has been refused bail in respect of another offence. Section 3 removes the current restrictions on granting bail in cases of murder or treason, while section 4 extends the right to appeal against a refusal of an application for bail to include cases where the application was made before full committal.

10. The Sheriffs' Association explained that currently the High Court, but not the Sheriff Court, had discretion to grant bail in cases of murder or treason (col 1337). Professor Gane believed the necessity of the changes was beyond doubt. 'The European Court of Human Rights has clearly said that an individual arrested on suspicion of having committed an offence has the right to have his or her deprivation of liberty considered automatically without application ... If we did not remove the distinction between bailable and non-bailable offences, come 2 October—if not at the moment—any instance in which [consideration of] bail was denied to a person who was, for example, charged with murder, would be incompatible with that person's Convention rights. Simply on that ground, his detention would be an unlawful act.' (col 1253–4).

11. According to the Minister, these changes would not necessarily result in more serious offenders being granted bail. Courts would continue to apply established common law criteria in deciding whether to grant bail, including considerations of public safety and the likelihood of the accused re-offending, absconding or intimidating witnesses (col 1274). The Law Society of Scotland agreed that the Bill was unlikely to make a significant difference to the number of people granted bail in practice (col 1345). The Scottish Rape Crisis Network, however, was concerned that women's safety would be put at risk (col 1348).

Criteria for bail decisions

12. An important difference that arose in evidence was on the question of whether the Bill should include criteria to guide the courts in making decisions on bail. In the Policy Memorandum, the Executive argues that including such criteria would 'add nothing and might simply confuse the position'. Statutory criteria would 'make it more difficult for the courts to reflect future developments in domestic or Strasbourg case law' and it was better to let judges 'take a reflective and reactive approach as Convention jurisprudence and social conditions and attitudes develop' (paragraph 17).

13. Professor Gane, however, was unconvinced. He regarded the lack of bail criteria as a 'significant weakness in the Bill', and he was also concerned that it did not specify clearly where the burden lies in establishing whether bail should be granted or the standard to be applied in making that decision (cols 1253–4). In agreeing with Professor Gane, Scottish Rape Crisis Network asked that statutory guidelines be included in the Bill (col 1348–9).

14. Far from creating confusion, Professor Gane believed that statutory criteria would help to resolve current difficulties with the common law position. In his view, the courts were being put in the unfair position of having to 'work out as they go along' whether

existing common law criteria were compatible with Convention case law. Many of the existing common law criteria appeared to be compatible, but the European Court had decided that neither the gravity of the offence nor the strength of the case against the accused was in itself a sufficient ground for refusing bail. He did not think it 'beyond the ingenuity of legislative draftspersons to construct a set of statutory guidelines that indicated which of the present criteria should continue to be used and the relative weight that should be given to them'. Statutory criteria would also help to ensure that bail decisions were taken on a more consistent basis across Scotland, and while some of the benefits of consistency could be achieved by guidance issued through judicial channels, it was 'not ... necessarily appropriate, in a democracy, to concede to the judiciary what might be more appropriately regarded as legislative matters' (cols 1254–5, 1257).

15. The Minister, however, said that including statutory criteria for bail would 'go far beyond the intended purpose of the Bill'. Because of the difficulties involved in getting the criteria right, there was a danger of such provisions being found to be incompatible (col 1279). On the one hand, there was a danger that statutory criteria would be 'overtaken by future decisions'; on the other, they would have to be interpreted in the light of developing case law and so it was 'not clear what would be gained by seeking to codify the position in statute' (col 1279).

16. The Minister also did not accept Professor Gane's point about consistency, saying that guidance was already made available to procurators fiscal by the Crown Office. Although this guidance was not directly available to the defence, it informed decisions of the courts which were then reported and available to all parties (cols 1280–1). The Sheriffs' Association, like the Executive, was also not persuaded that there was any danger of inconsistency in relying on the common law. According to Sheriff Wilkinson, 'a degree of inconsistency is inevitable, because one is dealing with uncertain subject matter and with imponderables ... it is inevitable that different sheriffs will attach different weight to one consideration compared with another' (col 1338). The Law Society of Scotland took a similar view (col 1346).

17. The Committee does not consider that, in view of the conflicting evidence received, it is in a position to reach a conclusion on whether a case for statutory bail criteria has been established. In any case, this is not an issue that we regard as central to what Part 1 of the Bill is aiming to achieve ... All the same, we are not convinced the Executive has fully addressed the legitimate points raised on this matter in evidence. It may be that more could usefully be done to clarify the non-statutory guidance available to the courts, and make that widely available, as a means of improving consistency in relation to bail decisions. There may also be a case for providing better training to assist sheriffs in this area.

...

Part 2, Chapter 1—Temporary and part-time sheriffs

Replacement of temporary sheriffs with part-time sheriffs

21. Section 5 of the Bill repeals section 11(2) of the Sheriff Courts (Scotland) Act 1971, which provides for the appointment of temporary sheriffs. It also allows such sheriffs to continue to act in relation to cases already in progress. Section 6 then inserts into the 1971 Act four new sections, 11A to 11D, providing for the appointment of part-time sheriffs, their removal from office and associated matters.

22. Questions were raised in evidence about the length of time taken to address this issue. According to Jamie Gilmour, a solicitor and former temporary sheriff, the Executive had been warned over a year before the *Starrs and Chalmers* case that temporary sheriffs were open to challenge on ECHR grounds (col 1319). The Sheriffs' Association, similarly, said that they had made repeated representations to the Executive about the position of temporary sheriffs. It would be useful to know, in this connection, what action the Executive has taken to establish whether other aspects of the judicial system will also need to be reformed (for example, the children's hearing system and local council planning committees).

23. It is clear from the evidence the severe disruption that has been caused by the suspension of all temporary sheriffs following the *Starrs* judgment. The Sheriffs' Association said that sheriffs had been put under extreme stress and cases were adjourned for weeks as a matter of course, resulting in increasing backlogs. There was a 'state of near crisis every day', particularly in Tayside, Central and Fife. The Association was therefore extremely keen to see a legislative solution to the problem effected as soon as possible (col 1322).

24. For that reason, the Association offered a general welcome to the creation of part-time sheriffs (col 1322). However, both it and Jamie Gilmour had grave doubts about aspects of the relevant provisions in the Bill.

Removal of part-time sheriffs

25. Their greatest concern was with the new section 11C, which provides a mechanism for removal of a part-time sheriff. Subsection (1) provides that a part-time sheriff can be removed from office only by order of a tribunal, appointed by Ministers in accordance with subsection (3). The tribunal may order the removal of a part-time sheriff from office, under subsection (2), only if, after investigation at the request of Ministers, it finds evidence of 'inability, neglect of duty or misbehaviour'. Subsection (3) of the new section is different in the Bill as introduced from the equivalent subsection in the draft Bill, which read as follows:

(3) The tribunal, which shall consist of not fewer than three persons, shall be constituted by the Scottish Ministers in accordance with regulations made by them.

26. In the opinion of the Sheriffs' Association, the draft version was 'fatally flawed'. Although the newer version was an improvement, the tribunal 'remains a body nominated by the Executive; its members may not themselves be independent of the Executive ... The proposals leave serious questions about compatibility with the European Convention on Human Rights' (cols 1323–4). The Association recognised that there was a body of opinion according to which such an arrangement was compatible: 'We are not saying that the case is open and shut; we are saying that this is not an occasion for experiment or for those kinds of risks to be run. We are therefore opposed to the new section 11C' (col 1324).

27. Jamie Gilmour agreed, saying that the fact that a 'quasi-judicial body' would be able to remove someone from a judicial position raised a question about the security of tenure of part-time sheriffs and whether they had a sufficient guarantee against outside pressures. He was struck by the fact that the new removal mechanism was not the same as the existing mechanism for removal of a sheriff (under section 12 of the 1971 Act), despite the fact that part-time sheriffs were to have the same obligations and responsibilities as their full-time counterparts. He wanted the procedures for removal to be the same in the two cases (col 1315).

28. Although the Sheriffs' Association reached the same conclusion, it recognised that the Lord President and the Lord Justice-Clerk might not welcome the additional burden, and that the procedures involved could be awkward. The Association could accept an alternative mechanism, so long as it 'left the removal of part-time sheriffs essentially in judicial hands'. This was the case in England and Wales and was also what was proposed later in the Bill for removing justices from district courts—a discrepancy that was 'not only odd, but open to challenge' under ECHR (col 1324). Its preference was for removal 'with the concurrence' of the Lord President or Lord Justice General after an investigation carried out by a judge (cols 1332–3).

29. The Law Society of Scotland endorsed the Sheriffs' Association view, although with the caveat that a great deal would depend on the content of regulations to be made under section 11C(2). The 'devil [was] in the detail'—if the regulations provided for a standing tribunal whose members could not be removed, that might allay some of the Society's concerns (col 1342). The Society also pointed out the lack of a right of appeal for the part-time sheriffs themselves against a decision to remove them from office. Although an appeal

mechanism might be included in regulations, the Bill itself left open the question of whether the human rights of the new part-time sheriffs had been adequately provided for (col 1342).

30. Having heard this evidence, the Committee is convinced that some change to the removal procedures in the Bill is essential to address the points raised. If the Executive is not disposed simply to make part-time sheriffs subject to the same removal procedures as their full-time counterparts, we would urge it to consider whether the suggestion made by the Sheriffs' Association offers a suitable alternative.

Duration of appointment

31. Under subsection (1) of the new section 11B, part-time sheriffs are appointed for five-year terms, renewable under subsection (5). The Law Society of Scotland was 'against this instinctively' as it had the potential 'to undermine the independence of the appointees' given that the decision in *Starrs* was that temporary sheriffs might be 'seen to be compromised because his or her appointment was coming to an end'. Although the Court of Session in *Clancy v Caird* had found 'no objection in principle to time limiting the appointment of judges', the Society was not convinced this would prevent challenges to part-time sheriffs on fixed-term appointments (col 1341).

32. Jamie Gilmour took a similar view. The Executive seemed to be relying on the decision in *Clancy v Caird*, 2000 SL.T. 546 that temporary judges were independent and impartial in terms of the Convention. But for him the 'fundamental distinction between the temporary judge and the temporary sheriff is that the work of a temporary judge is under the control of the Lord President, whereas the work of the temporary sheriff is under the control of the Scottish Executive justice department' (col 1321).

33. What was more, in his view, there was no provision for re-appointment of temporary judges and it was for the Lord President to determine when they sat. The Lord President had also issued guidelines to prevent temporary judges sitting in cases involving the Secretary of State, Scottish Ministers or the Lord Advocate. Because part-time sheriffs, by contrast, could be regarded as on probation for re-appointment or for a full-time position it was 'arguable that the impartial observer would take the view that a part-time sheriff might be influenced, even unconsciously, when considering cases involving the Executive or a public interest' (col 1315).

34. Concurring with the opinion of the Lord Justice Clerk in *Starrs*, Mr Gilmour argued that it was essential to give permanent contracts to part-time sheriffs. 'If the Bill is passed as it is currently drafted, as sure as sparks fly upwards, within three or four weeks that would be tested in the courts'. The only reason he could envisage why the Executive had not opted for permanent appointments was to reduce the risk of having to pay them pensions (col 1317).

35. We recognise that the Executive is likely to have given this point careful thought in drafting the Bill, and no doubt has reasons for believing that the short-term appointments envisaged are compatible with the Convention. Nevertheless, it is not the Executive's lawyers but the sheriffs who will decide any cases involving challenges on ECHR grounds to the provisions in the Bill—and the fact that at least some of those sheriffs believe that such a challenge could succeed is, in our view, a sufficient reason for thought to be given to amending the Bill to give part-time sheriffs permanent appointments.

Role to be played by part-time sheriffs

36. Witnesses were also doubtful about the role envisaged for part-time sheriffs. Under the new section 11A(6), they would be 'subject to such instructions, arrangements and other provisions' as the relevant sheriff principal makes. The Sheriffs' Association was uncertain how this would work and thought that some improvements could be made to these parts of the Bill. However, it acknowledged the difficulty of finding a scheme that would work satisfactorily across the country.

37. The Association also recognised a dilemma with part-time appointments. It was of the opinion that unless there was some prospect of permanent appointment, it would be

difficult to attract people of sufficient calibre. It was concerned, however, that the 'liberty of the public and other considerations affecting their material interest should not be in the hands of people who are being tried out' (col 1335).

38. Jamie Gilmour wanted the Bill to specify the reasons for appointing part-time sheriffs. To him, it was 'constitutionally fundamental that authority for part-time appointments should be given to cover only for illness, absence and sudden pressure of business' (col 1314). Instead, the Bill gave Ministers a general power of appointment, which could allow them to use part-time sheriffs as a way of 'running the whole Scottish justice system on the cheap' (col 1319).

39. The Sheriffs' Association had in the past objected to the over-use of temporary sheriffs, who had effectively become essential to the routine operation of the courts, something the Association had regarded as unacceptable (col 1325). The additional full-time sheriffs who had recently been appointed had the capacity to deal with only two-thirds of the workload that had been borne by the temporary sheriffs before their suspension (col 1329). The Law Society of Scotland also felt that temporary sheriffs had been used more than they should, but it had not yet formed a view on whether a similar danger arose in relation to the new part-time sheriffs (col 1343).

40. We agree with witnesses that the new part-time sheriffs ought to be employed only where, for temporary or exceptional reasons, the complement of full-time and permanent sheriffs is unable to cope with the workload. The flexibility that this allows is vital to the efficient operation of the justice system, but should not be abused in the interests of economy. Whether there needs to be provision in the Bill to ensure that part-time sheriffs are appropriately deployed is a matter on which we have not yet taken a view—but it may be something we will wish to consider further at Stage 2.

Number of working days each year

41. The proposed new section 11A(7) requires sheriff principals to 'have regard to the desirability of securing that every part-time sheriff is given the opportunity of sitting on not fewer than 20 nor more than 100 days' each year. In Jamie Gilmour's view, this was a 'nebulous' provision that put a 'doubtful duty' on sheriffs principal to follow a guideline that was not under their control: 'it is not sheriffs principal who will assign part-time sheriffs to courts, but the booking unit of the Scottish Executive justice department' (col 1316). He believed the provision had been included in response to criticism of perceived 'sidelining' of some temporary sheriffs, a practice in which those regarded as less competent by the Executive were employed less often. However, in his view, it did not succeed in sufficiently distancing the Executive from the process, and so remained vulnerable to ECHR challenge.

42. For the Law Society of Scotland, the concern was that there was no fixed maximum number of days that part-time sheriffs would be able to sit. Even 100 days represented 20 weeks in the year, which was a sufficiently large proportion to create the risk that the part-time sheriff would be seen to be dependent on that work. 'That might undermine the perception of his or her independence in seeking reappointment'—again raising potential problems in relation to the European Convention (col 1341). The Sheriffs' Association was uncertain whether a maximum should be specified in the Bill. On the one hand, no maximum would provide for flexibility but, on the other, a set maximum might preserve independence and guard against part-time sheriffs becoming substitute full-time sheriffs (col 1331).

Limitation on appointment of solicitors

43. Subsection (6) of the new section 11B prohibits part-time sheriffs who are also practising solicitors from sitting in a court in the same district in which his or her court is located. Although Jamie Gilmour recognised that that would formalise a longstanding convention, he thought it was anomalous that part-time sheriffs were not to be subject to the same outright ban on practising law as applied to full-time sheriffs (col 1316).

44. Although this is not a point on which the Committee is in a position to take a definite

view, it raises once again the possibility that the provisions in the Bill do not go far enough to minimise the risk of successful legal challenge on the ground of independence and impartiality of part-time sheriffs.

Part 2, Chapter 1—Conclusion

45. As the Sheriffs' Association said, 'there is no advantage in having this bill on the statute book if the office of part-time sheriff is open to challenge on similar grounds to those advanced successfully against temporary sheriffs' (col 1323). On the basis of this and other convincing evidence, the Committee believes there is a real danger that the provisions of the Bill as currently drafted for the appointment and removal of part-time sheriffs will be open to successful legal challenge on ECHR grounds. To avoid this possibility, we believe this Chapter of the Bill requires to be amended to put its compatibility with the Convention beyond doubt.

...

Recommendations

68. The Committee would be extremely reluctant for this Bill to be passed by the Parliament without a number of significant amendments being made, particularly in relation to part-time sheriffs. While we fully acknowledge that the Bill is necessary in order to address existing problems of incompatibility with the Convention, there seem to be good reasons to think that some of the changes it makes are insufficient to ensure compatibility, while others may not be necessary for that purpose. Whatever the urgency of getting this Bill into force, there is no point in doing so if it does not succeed in addressing the problem it is intended to solve. Indeed, it would be little short of disastrous if the resulting Act were immediately to be successfully challenged in the courts.

69. The Committee therefore urges the Minister for Justice to give a commitment at the Stage 1 debate that he will bring forward amendments at Stage 2 in order to put beyond doubt the ECHR-compatibility of Part 2 of the Bill. In order to allow the Bill to be so amended, and on condition that it is, the Committee recommends to the Parliament that its general principles be agreed to at Stage 1."

The Justice and Home Affairs Committee was instrumental in securing a number of changes to the Bill. In the Stage 3 debate the Deputy First Minister and Minister for Justice (Mr Jim Wallace) said:

"I hope that the Executive has co-operated and collaborated during the passage of the bill. We have listened carefully to the views that have been expressed by distinguished lawyers and experts on human rights, such as Professor Chris Gane, and by the Law Society of Scotland, Victim Support Scotland, the Sheriffs Association and the District Courts Association. When it has made sense to do so, we have willingly lodged amendments, and the bill is the better for all the work of the Justice and Home Affairs Committee and the representations that it received, distilled and put forward in its reports.

We have removed the power to appoint the members of the tribunal to remove part-time sheriffs from ministers' hands and put it into judicial hands. Greater security of tenure has been conferred on part-time sheriffs by stipulating that their reappointment will be automatic unless one of the grounds that are specified in the bill applies. We have brought the procedure for removing a justice of the peace into line with that for the removal of a part-time sheriff. We have also lodged an amendment that allows councillor justices to remain eligible for appointment to the justices committee."

Mr Wallace also confessed to having been 'impressed by the readiness of members to accept the key importance of the convention and the need for Scotland to ensure that our laws and procedures are constructed in accordance with the rights that are guaranteed by it' (Scottish Parliament, Official Report, July 5, 2000, col 1056). Further consideration of the Bail, Judicial

Appointments etc. (Scotland) Act 2000 is deferred until Ch.5 where there is also an account of one of the cases—*Starrs v Ruxton*, 2000 S.L.T. 42 —that created the need for its enactment.

In the meantime it is to be noted that another bill designed to implement Convention obligations (though not directly as a result of a decision of the Scottish courts) is the Regulation of Investigatory Powers (Scotland) Bill 2000. Although the Justice and Home Affairs Committee had some concerns about aspects of the Bill, it recognised the Executive's case for bringing it forward and concluded that 'the regulatory framework it will establish to govern the use of covert investigatory techniques strikes an appropriate balance between effective crime prevention and the safeguarding of the rights of the individual': 5th Report, 2000. Turning to Bills not intended specifically to implement Convention obligations, these have typically been subject to much less scrutiny on Convention grounds.

However, Convention issues may arise and the Committee may wish to be satisfied that there is no question of incompatibility. The issue arose in relation to the Land Reform (Scotland) Bill 2001 where the Committee appeared to be reassured by the Minister that there was no breach of art.8 of the Convention: S.P. Paper 541 Session 1 (2001). The matter also arose in relation to the Sexual Offences (Procedure and Evidence) (Scotland) Bill where the Committee was concerned about compatibility with art.6, and appeared to be assured by witnesses that there would be no breach: S.P. Paper 446 Session 1 (2001).

Yet despite these developments, there is a concern that Convention issues are not being adequately dealt with during the legislative process. This concern was addressed by the Justice 1 Committee in its report on the Convention Rights (Compliance) (Scotland) Bill (S.P. Paper 290 Session 1 (2000)):

> "116. John Scott [of the Scottish Human Rights Centre] expressed concern about the way in which the Executive carried out the ECHR audit. He said, 'if, effectively, the same people who draft legislation later certify a Bill as ECHR-compliant, that does not seem to offer the degree of independence that one would want'. Similarly, in its report, the Equal Opportunities Committee recommends that the audit process be clarified. It seeks an undertaking from the Executive that future Bills of this kind should provide such detail. John Scott was also concerned that it is difficult for an ordinary MSP to find out whether there are ECHR issues which have not been addressed by the Executive. He believes that this may highlight the need for an independent human rights commission fulfilling a pre-legislative scrutiny role."

These concerns are addressed in the following extract, which is from the Scottish Executive's proposals for a Scottish Human Rights Commission. This will add yet another dimension to the protection of human rights in Scotland, the proposed functions of the Commission to include giving advice to the Scottish Parliament on legislation after the introduction of Bills in the Scottish Parliament.

Scottish Executive
The Scottish Human Rights Commission
Consultation Paper (2003)

"The Commission, as an expert body, will be able to provide advice to the Scottish Parliament which should add to the effectiveness of human rights scrutiny during the passage of a bill

What does this function mean?

The Scottish Executive views providing advice to the Scottish Parliament on legislation after introduction as a key function of the Commission. Many international human rights commissions can advise their Parliaments on legislation.

There are effective and comprehensive mechanisms currently in place in Scotland to ensure that legislation complies with the human rights obligations enshrined in the Scotland

Act. It is the formal responsibility of Scottish Ministers to certify that a Bill is within the competence of the Scottish Parliament (this includes compliance with the ECHR) at or before its introduction in the Scottish Parliament. The Presiding Officer of the Scottish Parliament is also required to give his view on whether a Bill is within competence. In addition, human rights points must be covered in the policy memorandum that accompanies all Executive Bills introduced to the Scottish Parliament. Moreover, the Advocate General, the Lord Advocate or the Attorney General may refer a bill to the Judicial Committee of the Privy Council for a decision on competence: so consideration of legislative competence does not end on introduction.

In accordance with the views already expressed by Ministers, this function is to be limited to advice on 'legislation after introduction' to preserve the existing arrangements for consideration of competence. We intend that this function should be clearly defined in legislation and should be sufficient to cover the following:

- All 'Public Bills'—that is Executive, Member's and Committee Bills;
- Scottish Statutory Instruments.

How this function might work
We need to consider the mechanisms by which the Commission might offer advice to the Scottish Parliament. We present the Executive's views here to contribute to the discussion: however, the way forward would, of course, be a decision entirely for the Scottish Parliament to take once a Commission has been established. There are two main possibilities:

- Establishing a specialist Human Rights Committee in the Scottish Parliament;
- Lead Committee scrutiny at Stages 1 and 2.

One option would be to establish a separate Human Rights Committee in the Scottish Parliament to conduct human rights scrutiny and to have the primary relationship with the Commission. This committee might be similar in form to the Joint Committee on Human Rights (JCHR) at Westminster.

One potential advantage of a separate Human Rights Committee would be that there would be one point of contact for a Commission. The committee itself could also develop specialist skills. It might therefore be able to bring a strong focus to human rights work in the Scottish Parliament. However, setting up a Human Rights Committee would also have resource and staffing implications for the Scottish Parliament. Creating another committee could place undue pressure on staff and MSP resources. There is also the question of whether establishing such a committee might lead to duplication with the work of the Commission.

The majority of Bill scrutiny in the Scottish Parliament takes place in committees, with the general principles being considered at Stage 1 and detailed amendments considered at Stage 2. Lead committees currently consider human rights issues to some extent at Stage 1. This seems to be a logical point at which the Commission should provide advice. Advice given at Stage 1 would feed easily into the evidence the committee gathers for the Stage 1 report to the Scottish Parliament and would allow human rights consideration to take place early in the legislative process.

Although this is expected to be an important function for the Commission, the Scottish Executive does not envisage the Scottish Parliament adopting a practice of waiting for the Commission's comments before proceeding to the next stage of a Bill—the Commission would be expected to provide its advice on the general principles of the Bill at Stage 1. Whilst it will be open to the Commission, as it is to any other body, to comment on Stage 2 and 3 amendments, that should not in any way delay the progress of the Bill.

How legislation is brought to the Commission's attention
We have also considered how legislation should be brought to the Commission's attention. There are two options:

- The Scottish Parliament could be asked to consider amending standing orders to include a new duty to send all legislation introduced to the Commission;
- The Commission could monitor legislation introduced as part of its own administrative procedures.

The Northern Ireland Act conferred a statutory duty on the devolved Assembly to refer all devolved legislation to the Northern Ireland Human Rights Commission for comment—the Commission then decides what to comment on. Something similar could be proposed for the Scottish Commission. This would require amendment to the standing orders of the Scottish Parliament and would be for the Parliament to decide. Creating a binding requirement is likely to mean that a greater proportion of the Commission's resources would be taken up in considering and then prioritising every piece of proposed legislation introduced to the Parliament. We feel that prioritising from the outset would be more effective and that the Commission should be able to decide on its own priorities. On balance we propose that the Commission should develop its own procedures to ensure that it monitors legislation as it is introduced.

Relationship with the Scottish Parliament

In keeping with the independence of the Commission, it should not be established as a Parliamentary 'advisory' body in the sense that this would imply some sort of different or exclusive relationship with the Scottish Parliament above that of any other body. The Commission should not be under the direction of the Parliament. In addition, Parliamentary committees should not be under any obligation to ask for or take into account advice given by the Commission.

Committees should certainly be encouraged to call for advice and evidence from the Commission when it is relevant. When a human rights issue arises, it is extremely likely that they will call on the Commission. In addition, we feel that it should be open to the Commission to provide evidence on legislation after introduction without any specific request from the Scottish Parliament. This is in keeping with the current arrangements in relation to proposed legislation. In practice, therefore, the Commission would be able to submit written evidence; could ask to submit oral evidence (but it would be for the Scottish Parliament to take the decision); and could be specifically invited to give evidence.

As part of the Bill process, it seems likely that most contact would be with committees. However, individual MSPs should also be able to ask the Commission for advice as part of the Bill process e.g. in relation to an amendment they wish to put down at Stage 2 or Stage 3.

In addition to the Commission's relationship with the Scottish Parliament in respect of this function, we anticipate that the Commission should be able to engage at all levels with the Parliament. The Commission should be able to answer any query it receives from MSPs and the Scottish Parliament Information Centre (SPICe) researchers. This means that all levels of the Scottish Parliament should be able to treat the Commission as an expert body and request its advice, observations and evidence on human rights issues outwith the specific function of providing advice on legislation after introduction.

Preferred Approach

* **We are not in favour of asking the Scottish Parliament to consider establishing a separate Human Rights Committee;**

* **The Commission should put its own procedures in place to ensure that it is in a position to monitor legislation as it is introduced;**

* **The Commission should not act on the direction of the Parliament and there should be no duty on Scottish Parliament committees to ask for or to take the Commission's advice into account;**

* **MSPs should be able to treat the Commission as an expert body and request its advice, observations and evidence on human rights issues going beyond the specific function of providing advice on legislation after introduction."**

IV. HUMAN RIGHTS, JUDICIAL REVIEW AND REMEDIAL ORDERS

Pre-legislative scrutiny is not on its own a guarantee that legislation will be within the competence of the Scottish Parliament or that it complies with human rights principles. One reason for this is that human rights principles are evolutionary and progressive: what may have been acceptable for one generation may not be acceptable for another. A good example might be the changing attitudes to homosexuality which has seen the need to change discriminatory practices by both public and private sector employers to reflect the changing nature of our understanding about human rights. Acts of the Scottish Parliament can be challenged in the courts at any time on the ground that they violate Convention rights, and at the time of writing challenges have been made to at least three statutes: *A v Scottish Ministers*, 2002 P.C. 63 (Mental Health (Public Safety and Appeals) (Scotland) Act 1999); *Adams v The Scottish Ministers*, 2003 S.L.T. 366 and *Whaley v Scottish Ministers*, 2004 S.C. 78 (Protection of Wild Mammals (Scotland) Act 2002); and *Flynn v H M Advocate*, [2004] UKPC D1 (Prisoners and Criminal Proceedings (Scotland) Act 1993, as amended by Convention Rights (Compliance) (Scotland) Act 2001). However, given the amount of executive and parliamentary scrutiny of bills on human rights grounds, it could only be in the most exceptional circumstances that a court would be justified in striking down an Act of the Scottish Parliament. The ready use of this power would be controversial: human rights are a matter of judgment not science. The need to use such power to declare legislation outside the competence of the Parliament ought to be diminished still further by the Scotland Act 1998, s. 101 which requires the courts—where possible—to read legislation in a manner which is compatible with the power of the Parliament:

Scotland Act 1998

"Interpretation of Acts of the Scottish Parliament etc

101.—(1) This section applies to—
   (a) any provision of an Act of the Scottish Parliament, or of a Bill for such an Act, and
   (b) any provision of subordinate legislation made, confirmed or approved, or purporting to be made, confirmed or approved, by a member of the Scottish Executive,
which could be read in such a way as to be outside competence.

(2) Such a provision is to be read as narrowly as is required for it to be within competence, if such a reading is possible, and is to have effect accordingly.

(3) In this section 'competence'—
   (a) in relation to an Act of the Scottish Parliament, or a Bill for such an Act, means the legislative competence of the Parliament, and
   (b) in relation to subordinate legislation, means the powers conferred by virtue of this Act."

Section 101 was used in *Flynn v H M Advocate*, [2004] UKPC D1, where the Prisoners and Criminal Proceedings (Scotland) Act 1993 (as amended) was read in such a way as to avoid any conflict with Convention rights and so prevent the Privy Council having to declare that it had no effect. In addition to the restrictions on the Scottish Parliament, there are similar restrictions on the powers of the Scottish Ministers on whom powers have been conferred and to whom powers have been transferred. Here it is provided that a member of the Scottish Executive has no power to make any subordinate legislation or do any other act so far as the legislation or act is incompatible with Convention rights (s.57(2)). This does not apply "to an act of the Lord Advocate (a) in prosecuting any offence, or (b) in his capacity as head of the systems of criminal prosecution and investigation of deaths in Scotland, which, because of subsection (2) of section 6 of the Human Rights Act 1998, is not unlawful under subsection (1) of that section" (s.57(3)).

Section 6(2) of the Human Rights Act provides that the acts of public authorities are not unlawful if what they have done was required by primary legislation. Apart from the creation of the Scottish Parliament and the Scottish Executive, the Scotland Act has a number of important implications for the Scottish legal system. The Lord Advocate and Solicitor General for Scotland are now Scottish Ministers serving the Scottish Executive, with the new position of Advocate General for Scotland advising the United Kingdom government on Scottish matters. However, in addition to the movement and creation of institutions, the other main development is the procedure for challenging Acts of the Scottish Parliament or decisions of the Scottish Executive in legal proceedings. This is done by means of raising a devolution issue, in accordance with Sch.6 of the Scotland Act 1998. This provides that:

Scotland Act 1998
Schedule 6

"DEVOLUTION ISSUES

PART I

PRELIMINARY

    1. In this Schedule "devolution issue" means—

    (a) a question whether an Act of the Scottish Parliament or any provision of an Act of the Scottish Parliament is within the legislative competence of the Parliament,

    (b) a question whether any function (being a function which any person has purported, or is proposing, to exercise) is a function of the Scottish Ministers, the First Minister or the Lord Advocate,

    (c) a question whether the purported or proposed exercise of a function by a member of the Scottish Executive is, or would be, within devolved competence,

    (d) a question whether a purported or proposed exercise of a function by a member of the Scottish Executive is, or would be, incompatible with any of the Convention rights or with Community law,

    (e) a question whether a failure to act by a member of the Scottish Executive is incompatible with any of the Convention rights or with Community law,

    (f) any other question about whether a function is exercisable within devolved competence or in or as regards Scotland and any other question arising by virtue of this Act about reserved matters.

    2. A devolution issue shall not be taken to arise in any proceedings merely because of any contention of a party to the proceedings which appears to the court or tribunal before which the proceedings take place to be frivolous or vexatious.

PART II

PROCEEDINGS IN SCOTLAND

Application of Part II
    3. This Part of this Schedule applies in relation to devolution issues in proceedings in Scotland.

Institution of proceedings
    4.—(1) Proceedings for the determination of a devolution issue may be instituted by the Advocate General or the Lord Advocate.

    (2) The Lord Advocate may defend any such proceedings instituted by the Advocate General.

    (3) This paragraph is without prejudice to any power to institute or defend proceedings exercisable apart from this paragraph by any person.

Intimation of devolution issue

5. Intimation of any devolution issue which arises in any proceedings before a court or tribunal shall be given to the Advocate General and the Lord Advocate (unless the person to whom the intimation would be given is a party to the proceedings).

6. A person to whom intimation is given in pursuance of paragraph 5 may take part as a party in the proceedings, so far as they relate to a devolution issue.

Reference of devolution issue to higher court

7. A court, other than the House of Lords or any court consisting of three or more judges of the Court of Session, may refer any devolution issue which arises in proceedings (other than criminal proceedings) before it to the Inner House of the Court of Session.

8. A tribunal from which there is no appeal shall refer any devolution issue which arises in proceedings before it to the Inner House of the Court of Session; and any other tribunal may make such a reference.

9. A court, other than any court consisting of two or more judges of the High Court of Justiciary, may refer any devolution issue which arises in criminal proceedings before it to the High Court of Justiciary.

References from superior courts to Judicial Committee

10. Any court consisting of three or more judges of the Court of Session may refer any devolution issue which arises in proceedings before it (otherwise than on a reference under paragraph 7 or 8) to the Judicial Committee.

11. Any court consisting of two or more judges of the High Court of Justiciary may refer any devolution issue which arises in proceedings before it (otherwise than on a reference under paragraph 9) to the Judicial Committee.

Appeals from superior courts to Judicial Committee

12. An appeal against a determination of a devolution issue by the Inner House of the Court of Session on a reference under paragraph 7 or 8 shall lie to the Judicial Committee.

13. An appeal against a determination of a devolution issue by—
   (a) a court of two or more judges of the High Court of Justiciary (whether in the ordinary course of proceedings or on a reference under paragraph 9), or
   (b) a court of three or more judges of the Court of Session from which there is no appeal to the House of Lords,
shall lie to the Judicial Committee, but only with leave of the court concerned or, failing such leave, with special leave of the Judicial Committee."

It will be noted that the final court for dealing with devolution issues is the Judicial Committee of the Privy Council rather than the House of Lords. Some of the difficulties surrounding the meaning of a devolution issue have already been addressed by the Judicial Committee in some detail, and these are dealt with in Ch.3, below. The cases in question have generally related to the powers of the Lord Advocate in the field of criminal justice where there has been concern about the failure to comply with the Convention rights of accused persons. Most of these cases arose under Sch.6, para.12 above. There is, however, also a procedure under Sch.6, para.33 (not reproduced) whereby the Lord Advocate, the Advocate General and the Attorney General "may require a court or tribunal to refer to the Judicial Committee any devolution issue which has arisen in proceedings before it to which he is a party". *Kelly v H M Advocate*, 2003 S.C. (P.C.) 77 is one such case. The Privy Council only has jurisdiction to hear appeals: it has no original jurisdiction to consider devolution issues (*Follen v H M Advocate*, 2001 S.C. (P.C) 105). By an Act of Sederunt (SI 1999/1345), a devolution issue should be raised in the pleadings before the evidence is led, unless "on cause shown" the court otherwise directs. Should the courts hold that the Scottish Parliament or Scottish Ministers have acted in breach of Convention rights, an expedited parliamentary procedure enables legislation to be introduced in appropriate cases to give effect to such a decision. (It is to be emphasised that these powers can be used not only in direct response to a judicial decision).

Convention Rights (Compliance) (Scotland) Act 2001

"Remedial orders

12.—(1) In the circumstances set out in subsection (2) below, the Scottish Ministers may, by order (in this Part of this Act, a 'remedial order'), make such provision as they consider necessary or expedient in consequence of—

(a) an Act of Parliament or an Act of the Scottish Parliament;

(b) any subordinate legislation made under any such Act;

(c) any provision of any such Act or subordinate legislation; or

(d) any exercise or purported exercise of functions by a member of the Scottish Executive,

which is or may be incompatible with any of the Convention rights.

(2) Those circumstances are that the Scottish Ministers are of the opinion that there are compelling reasons for making a remedial order as distinct from taking any other action.

(3) A remedial order may—

(a) make different provision for different purposes;

(b) relate to—

(i) all cases to which the power to make it extends;

(ii) those cases subject to specified exceptions; or

(iii) any particular case or class of case;

(c) make—

(i) any supplementary, incidental or consequential provision; or

(ii) any transitory, transitional or saving provision,

which the Scottish Ministers consider necessary or expedient;

(d) modify any enactment or prerogative instrument or any other instrument or document relating to the exercise or purported exercise of functions by the Scottish Ministers;

(e) make provision (other than provision creating criminal offences or increasing the punishment for criminal offences) which has retrospective effect;

(f) provide for the delegation of functions.

(4) A remedial order shall not, however, create any criminal offence punishable—

(a) on summary conviction, with imprisonment for a period exceeding three months or with a fine exceeding the amount specified as level 5 on the standard scale;

(b) on conviction on indictment, with a period of imprisonment exceeding two years.

(5) The conferring by subsection (1) above of the power to make remedial orders does not prejudice the extent of any other power.

Procedure for remedial orders: general

13.—(1) A remedial order shall be made by statutory instrument.

(2) No remedial order shall be made unless laid in draft before and approved by resolution of the Scottish Parliament.

(3) Before laying a draft remedial order for the purposes of subsection (2) above, the Scottish Ministers shall—

(a) lay a copy of the proposed draft order, together with a statement of their reasons for proposing to make the order, before the Scottish Parliament;

(b) give such public notice of the contents of the proposed draft order as they consider appropriate and invite persons wishing to make observations on the draft order to do so, in writing, within the period of 60 days beginning with the day on which that public notice was given or the day on which the draft order was laid under this subsection, whichever is earlier, or, if both those actions occurred on the same day, that day;

(c) have regard to any written observations submitted within that period.

(4) When laying a draft remedial order for the purposes of subsection (2) above, the Scottish Ministers shall lay before the Scottish Parliament a statement—

   (a) summarising all the observations to which they had to have regard under sub-
      section (3)(c) above; and

   (b) specifying the changes (if any) which they have made in the draft order and the
      reasons for them.

   (5) In reckoning, for the purposes of subsection (3)(b) above, any period of 60 days no
account shall be taken of any time during which the Scottish Parliament is dissolved or is in
recess for more than four days.

Procedure for remedial orders: urgent cases

   14.—(1) Where it appears to the Scottish Ministers that, for reasons of urgency, it is
necessary to make a remedial order without following the procedure under section 13(2) to
(4) above, they may do so.

   (2) After so making a remedial order, the Scottish Ministers shall forthwith—

   (a) give such public notice of the contents of the order as they consider appropriate
      and invite persons wishing to make observations on the order to do so, in writing,
      within the period of 60 days beginning with the day on which it was made;

   (b) lay the order, together with a statement of their reasons for having made it, before
      the Scottish Parliament.

   (3) The Scottish Ministers shall have regard to any written observations submitted within
the period mentioned in subsection (2)(a) above.

   (4) As soon as practicable after the end of that period, the Scottish Ministers shall lay
before the Scottish Parliament a statement—

   (a) summarising all the observations to which they had to have regard under sub-
      section (3) above; and

   (b) specifying the modifications (if any) which they consider it appropriate to make to
      the remedial order.

   (5) If modifications have been specified under subsection (4)(b) above, the Scottish
Ministers shall—

   (a) make a remedial order by virtue of this subsection giving effect to those mod-
      ifications and replacing the remedial order made under subsection (1) above; and

   (b) lay the remedial order made by virtue of this subsection before the Scottish Par-
      liament,

or (where the modification specified consists only of the proposed revocation of the
remedial order), by order, simply revoke the remedial order made under subsection (1)
above.

   (6) If, at the end of the period of 120 days beginning with the day on which a remedial
order was made under subsection (1) above, the Scottish Parliament has not, by resolution,
approved the order or any remedial order made by virtue of subsection (5) above replacing
it, then the remedial order or, as the case may be the replacement remedial order ceases to
have effect (but without that affecting anything done under that order or the power to make
a fresh remedial order, whether under the procedure set out in section 13 above or this
section).

   (7) Subsection (6) above has no effect where the Scottish Ministers have, before the end
of the period referred to in that subsection, simply revoked the remedial order made under
subsection (1) above.

   (8) An order made under subsection (5) above simply revoking a remedial order made
under subsection (1) above shall be made by statutory instrument which shall be subject to
annulment in pursuance of a resolution of the Scottish Parliament.

   (9) In reckoning, for the purposes of subsections (2)(a), (6) and (7) above, any period of
60 or 120 days, no account shall be taken of any time during which the Scottish Parliament
is dissolved or is in recess for more than four days."

A similar provision exists in the Human Rights Act 1998, enabling remedial orders to be
introduced to modify legislation of the Westminster Parliament. However, s.10 of this Act is

more narrowly drawn than the corresponding provisions of the Convention Rights (Compliance) (Scotland) Act 2001, which was strongly criticised by the Justice Committee (on which see below). The power to introduce remedial orders in the Human Rights Act applies only after a court has declared legislation to be incompatible with Convention rights, or only after a decision of the European Court of Human Rights has called into question the compatibility of a piece of domestic legislation with the Convention. As in the case of the Convention Rights (Compliance) (Scotland) Act 2001, the power in the Human Rights Act 1998 to by-pass normal parliamentary proceedings applies only when a Minister of the Crown considers that there are "compelling reasons" to do so in order to remove the incompatibility. Any remedial orders introduced in the Westminster Parliament are scrutinised by the Joint Committee on Human Rights. By March 2004, the power to introduce remedial orders under the Convention Rights (Compliance) (Scotland) Act 2001 had yet to be used, though a number of such orders had been introduced at Westminster.

Justice 1 Committee
2nd Report, 2001
Stage 1 Report on the Convention Rights (Compliance) (Scotland) Bill
S.P. Paper 290: Session 1 (2000)

"Part 6—Powers to make Remedial Orders

Principal provisions of Part 6

98. Section 10 of the Human Rights Act 1998 ('the 1998 Act') confers upon UK Ministers powers to make remedial orders to remedy certain legislative provisions which are or may be incompatible with ECHR. In addition, section 107 of the Scotland Act 1998 confers upon UK Ministers the power by remedial order to make provision in consequence of any Act of the Scottish Parliament; subordinate legislation made under an Act of the Scottish Parliament or any act of the Scottish Ministers which is or may be incompatible with ECHR.

99. The powers under section 10 of the 1998 Act are available to the Scottish Ministers to a limited extent. They could exercise those powers where a Scottish court finds a provision of a Westminster Act relating to devolved matters incompatible with ECHR or where they consider that a provision in a Westminster Act or Act of the Scottish Parliament may be incompatible as a consequence of a Strasbourg decision taken after 2 October 2000.

100. The Executive proposes to confer a new power on the Scottish Ministers, which will extend the range of circumstances under which they are able to make remedial orders to remedy actual or perceived incompatibilities with ECHR. Provision has been made in the Bill for a general remedial power, similar in scope to that already available to UK Ministers under section 107 of the Scotland Act. The Bill also makes provision for a remedial order to have retrospective effect other than a provision creating criminal offences or increasing the punishment for criminal offences.

101. The Scottish Ministers will therefore be able to make a remedial order in a wider range of circumstances than they can under section 10 of the 1998 Act and can amend provisions in an Act of the Scottish Parliament which have been found by a Scottish Court to be incompatible with ECHR; provisions in a Westminster Act extending to Scotland which correspond to provisions in a Westminster Act extending to England and Wales which an English court in England and Wales has declared to be incompatible and which UK Ministers have remedied by remedial order under the 1998 Act; any exercise of functions by the Scottish Ministers found by a court to be incompatible with ECHR, and any provision in legislation or any function of the Scottish Ministers which is thought to be incompatible.

102. Sections 13 and 14 of the Bill set out the procedure for making a remedial order which would oblige the Scottish Ministers to publicise the contents of the proposed draft

order and take into account any comments made within a period of 60 days and for the draft order then to be laid before the Scottish Parliament for approval by resolution, together with a statement on any comments made, specifying any changes made and why. There is also a truncated procedure which will be followed in 'exceptional cases', which the Executive explains in the Policy Memorandum will only be used in 'the most urgent circumstances' (SP Bill 25-PM para 146).

Legislative competence
103. The Committee notes that the Bill's accompanying documents include a statement from the member in charge of the Bill (Jim Wallace, Minister for Justice) stating that, in his view, its provisions are within the legislative competence of the Scottish Parliament. Similarly, there is a statement from the Presiding Officer indicating that he is of the same view (SP Bill 25-EN, paras 162–163). In providing oral evidence to the Committee, Michael Clancy of the Law Society of Scotland stated that 'I think that the *vires* of the Scottish Parliament and the Scottish ministers, as contained in the Scotland Act 1998, sections 28 and 29, and schedules 4 and 5 ... would constrain the Scottish Ministers from exceeding their authority' (col 2117). However, in a written submission to the Committee the Faculty of Advocates questions the legislative competence of the provisions contained within Part 6 and whether an Act of the Scottish Parliament is the proper way to transfer functions, create shared functions or curtail UK functions in this area (Annexe E). The Committee notes the concern of the Faculty of Advocates and considers that the Executive should explain the basis of its view on legislative competence to the Parliament in the Stage 1 debate. It is worth noting that there is an opportunity for the law officers to make reference to the matter of legislative competence under the Act after it is passed and before it receives Royal Assent. The Committee is aware that ultimately the Courts will decide on this matter.

The need for these powers
104. Under the 1998 Act, Scottish Courts can strike down incompatible provisions in Acts of the Scottish Parliament with immediate effect. The Executive explained to the Committee that 'the power would help us to avoid an impossible situation arising or the striking down of a piece of legislation' (col 2069). The Law Society of Scotland echoed this concern, 'when the courts have declared that a piece of Scottish legislation is incompatible with the European Convention on Human Rights, it is important that there is swift and effective remedy' (col 2116). Similarly, in its report, the Subordinate Legislation Committee observes 'that there are persuasive arguments that legislation to implement obligations under the Convention ought not to be liable to amendment particularly of a wrecking or delaying nature' (Annexe A).
105. The Committee questioned whether the procedure proposed in the Bill would be faster than emergency primary legislation. The Executive answered that the normal procedure would probably take less time than taking primary legislation through quickly, but not necessarily (col 2067). Some members were concerned that these measures take away the right to democratic scrutiny of all legislation. John Scott of the Scottish Human Rights Centre was not comfortable that the Executive will be able to decide on the appropriate way to proceed with either remedial powers or primary legislation (col 2073). The Executive claimed that 'if there is a strong view that something in the draft of the draft (remedial order) is unacceptable, that would be taken on board' (col 2067).
106. We are concerned that there is no real opportunity to amend these orders. It is either a case of accepting an order in its entirety or rejecting it. The Law Society of Scotland agrees 'that would be an issue if the Scottish Ministers found it was necessary or expedient to lodge a remedial order under section 12, because it would be a take-it-or-leave-it situation' (col 2116). Similarly, Professor Gane said, 'I am not sure that it is constitutionally a good idea to bypass Parliament when (the Executive) believes that something might be wrong' (col 2154). He continued, 'we might all agree that there is a problem and

that we need to do something about it, but just because something needs to be done quickly does not mean that the Executive will necessarily get it right with its proposed solution' (col 2154).

107. The Committee is concerned that the Executive could not easily suggest an example of where this provision would have been used in the past (col 2069). In fact, the Minister for Justice admitted that when addressing the ECHR problem with regard to temporary sheriffs, 'as events transpired, it took us some time to get it right' (col 2177). This proves that democratic scrutiny is very important and should not be bypassed unless absolutely necessary. On reflection, the Minister suggested that Part 4 of this Bill could have been achieved through such a remedial order. Professor Gane agreed, 'I am not wholly convinced by the argument that such a power should be used when it is thought that something might be wrong. I am more inclined to say that such powers should be assumed only when it is known that there is something wrong—when the Executive has been told authoritatively and the matter is not merely a matter of Executive judgment' (col 2158). The Committee agrees that where a court decision has been made, where there is no question that a provision is incompatible, and where there is a very simple solution, it may be appropriate to use a remedial order.

108. The Minister for Justice assured the Committee that there is no intention that the general remedial power should become a replacement for primary legislation (col 2161). **The Committee considers that, except for in exceptional and urgent cases, it would be more appropriate to use primary legislation than the proposed remedial orders to remedy actual or perceived incompatibilities with ECHR and recommends that this power be used sparingly.**

Test to be applied
109. The Subordinate Legislation Committee believes that the scope of the power is too wide. It reported that the Committee's concern with the provision would be met if it is amended to include wording to the effect that the Minister should have urgent and compelling reason to use the procedure (Annexe A). Professor Gane agrees, 'using special procedures to remedy *demonstrated* conflicts between legislation and Convention rights is one thing (although this was severely criticised during the debates on the Human Rights Bill), but to use such powers in respect of *possible* conflict is quite another' (Annexe D).

110. Similarly, the Faculty of Advocates questions the appropriateness of the power proposed. It points out that under existing Westminster legislation, for the exercise of an equivalent power, there are two tests. Under the higher test it is only competent for Ministers to use remedial orders to remove incompatibilities where there are 'compelling reasons' for using that route, where primary legislation has finally been declared incompatible or disapproved by a competent court, or where subordinate legislation has been quashed by a competent court. The lower test applies under section 107 of the Scotland Act where a Minister of the Crown can 'remedy' proceedings of the Scottish Parliament or the Executive by remedial order where the Minister considers it 'necessary and expedient'. Part 6 of the Bill proposes that the lower test be applied (Annexe E). Professor Gane claimed that 'the Human Rights Act 1998 probably achieves the right compromise between Executive authority and democratic scrutiny' (col 2155).

111. The Executive has now proposed that it will bring forward amendments at Stage 2 of the Bill to introduce such a higher test—requiring Ministers to prove that they have urgent and compelling reasons for using a remedial order (col 2161). The Committee welcomes this commitment. **However, the Committee notes that although there might be compelling reasons to act, the actions that are taken might go beyond what is necessary to address the problem, and there would be no control over that.**
...

Recommendation
130. **The Committee ... has grave concerns about the breadth of the powers given to Scottish Ministers in Part 6, and notes the Executive's intention to bring forward an**

amendment at Stage 2 to apply a higher test to the use of these powers. Given that commitment, all but one member of the Committee recommends to the Parliament that the general principles of the Bill be agreed to."

V. CONCLUSION

We have thus come a long way in a short time since the decision of Lord Ross in the *Kaur* case. At that time Scotland operated within the Westminster system with a sovereign Parliament. There was little or no scope for the courts in protecting human rights based on international treaties and there was no dedicated human rights scrutiny of legislation. Indeed the Select Committees of the House of Commons were still in their infancy. How the scene has changed, at least at the institutional level. The aim of this chapter has been to demonstrate the great transformation that has taken place since 1997. This transformation has seen a quite extraordinary level of protection of human rights within the context of the devolved settlement. An important feature of that settlement as it has developed, however, is that human rights protection is the formal responsibility of all three branches of government, with the result that the judges ought to perform a role only as sweeper. This indeed is one of the most interesting and important features of the constitutional reforms, though it is understandably overshadowed by the power of the courts to declare invalid the primary legislation of the Scottish Parliament. It is clear, however, that the institutional structures for the protection of human rights are not yet complete, and that a Scottish Human Rights Commission with a wide range of functions will add another dimension to the position in Scotland. While such a body is no doubt desirable, it is nevertheless important that the current obsession with human rights is not seen to suffocate parliamentary government itself. The formal protection of human rights will be a poor substitute for a vital and vibrant democracy.

Human Rights Scrutiny of Scottish Legislation

Scottish legislation is subject to the most fascinating range of pre and post legislative scrutiny to ensure compatibility with the powers of the Scottish Parliament. Among other things, the Parliament may not legislate in breach of Convention rights. Human rights scrutiny thus takes the following forms:

- Executive scrutiny of bills before they are introduced (Scotland Act 1998, s.31(1));
- Parliamentary scrutiny by the presiding officer on or before introduction (Scotland Act 1998, s.31(2));
- Parliamentary scrutiny of bills for convention related matters by the lead committee, but typically the Justice Committee;
- Judicial scrutiny of bills by the Privy Council following a law officer's reference where there are doubts about its validity (Scotland Act 1998, s.33);
- Judicial interpretation of legislation where possible to ensure that it is within the powers of the Parliament and compliant with convention rights (Scotland Act 1998, s.101);
- Judicial scrutiny of legislation by the courts after it has been introduced on the ground that it is outside the competence of the Parliament.

Chapter 3

HUMAN RIGHTS AND JUDICIAL REVIEW

I. INTRODUCTION

A remarkable feature of human rights law since the end of the Second World War has been the cascade of human rights from international law to constitutional law. This means that these human rights obligations on states are supervised in the national arena but in some cases enforced in national courts. This gives rise to a number of questions, the first of which is to determine what rights should be protected in this way. Many countries distinguish between civil and political rights (such as those covered by the ECHR) and social and economic rights (such as those covered by the Council of Europe's Social Charter), but by no means all do. A second question is whether entrenchment can be said to be compatible with democratic principle, to the extent that it empowers the courts to challenge decisions made in the political process. The answer to that question will depend in part on the form that entrenchment takes. The democratic concern is more urgent if the courts have the power to strike down legislation than if they have the power only to ensure that executive action is consistent with the Bill of Rights. These are questions which have assumed considerable importance in Scotland following the Scotland Act 1998 and the Human Rights Act 1998 which in different ways enable Convention rights to be enforced in the Scottish courts, with the ECHR forming the backbone of a Scottish Bill of Rights.

Diversity in the Constitutional Protection of Human Rights

Bills of Rights take many different forms. In a valuable article in 1980 Wilson Finnie developed the idea of a ladder in terms of the way in which the ECHR might operate in a domestic legal system: W. Finnie, "The European Convention on Human Rights" (1980) J.L.S.S. 434. On the top rung of the ladder was entrenchment giving the courts the power to strike down legislation inconsistent with the Bill of Rights being the highest form of incorporation or effect. On the lowest rung of the ladder in contrast was the duty to interpret legislation consistently with the Bill of Rights being the weakest form of incorporation or effect. There are a number of intermediate positions between these extremes. Adapting the idea of a ladder and applying it to the experience of Bills of Rights in different countries, it is possible to trace their effects as follows, moving from the strongest to the weakest forms of Bills of Rights in the common law world.

- *A power to strike down legislation that is incompatible with the Bill of Rights (the US model).*
- *A power to strike down legislation, subject to a statutory override allowing legislation to apply notwithstanding that it violates the Bill of Rights (the Canadian model).*
- *A power to declare legislation incompatible with the Bill of Rights in circumstances where the legislation continues in force until amended or repealed (the United Kingdom model).*

- *A power to interpret legislation consistently with the Bill of Rights, but not otherwise to challenge the validity of the legislation (the New Zealand model).*

Although the United Kingdom model comes towards the bottom of the ladder, the position is different with regard to Scotland specifically. The Privy Council enjoys a power with regard to legislation of the Scottish Parliament which is similar to that of the US Supreme Court, though not quite the same for two reasons. The first is that (as we shall see), the Privy Council is constrained by what is in effect a statutory presumption in favour of validity (Scotland Act 1998, s.101), and the second is that the decisions of the Privy Council can always be overruled by the Westminster Parliament. Only a constitutional amendment can reverse a decision of the US Supreme Court.

II. HUMAN RIGHTS AND DEMOCRACY

There is a great debate between those who argue that individual rights constrain the collective will and those who argue that the individual needs to be protected from the arbitrary exercise of power by the majority. The democratic argument against entrenched rights is fuelled by two concerns. The first is the very idea that judges should act as a veto on the democratic process. It seems the simplest thing to say that governments and parliaments should be stopped by the courts from violating the human rights of the people. However, the difficulty is that these rights are not self evident. Thus, what does it mean when we say that everyone has the right to freedom of expression or the right to freedom of association? Does the former mean that the government may not introduce legislation prohibiting tobacco companies from advertising cigarettes? Does the latter mean that the government may not introduce legislation authorising trade unions to exclude racists and fascists from membership? There is also the question of the circumstances in which restrictions may lawfully be imposed on Convention rights. Thus several articles of the Convention (arts 8 to 12) permit restrictions to be imposed if these are "in accordance with the law" and "necessary in a democratic society" for one of a number of reasons. The question here is simply this: who is best able to determine what is necessary in a democratic society? Those who are elected, representative and accountable, or those who are appointed, socially and economically elitist, with tenure for life?

These are highly contested questions, which give rise to other questions about why the judges should be given a veto over the way in which the community chooses to be governed. Legislation is made by inclusive, representative and accountable institutions. The legal process fulfils none of these essential preconditions of democracy. Under the Scotland Act 1998 the final say on what the Scottish Parliament can do (unless Westminster says otherwise) is not the Scottish people but the Privy Council sitting in panels of five judges at a time, only two of whom may be Scottish judges. One answer is to say that judges who operate this veto on the democratic process must themselves meet some basic democratic principles in terms of the manner of their appointment and the method of their operation. Although the principle of judicial independence is of the greatest importance and is not to be diminished, it is no excuse for a judiciary that is neither representative nor accountable. The requirement that the judiciary should be representative means that it should fairly represent the community it serves in terms of gender, race and social origin. This will not be achieved by an independent judicial appointments commission if the pool of people eligible for appointment to the Bench are mainly white men educated in the leading public schools. The requirement that the judiciary should be accountable means that it should be prepared to engage more fully with the people through their parliamentary representatives. This suggests in turn a need for parliamentary approval of judicial appointments and a role for parliamentary committees in questioning judges in order to enhance understanding about the development of the law.

J. Waldron
"A Right-Based Critique of Constitutional Rights"
(1993) 13 *Oxford Journal of Legal Studies* 18

"It is odd that people expect theorists of rights to support the institutionalization of a Bill of Rights and the introduction of American-style practices of judicial review. All modern theories of rights claim to respect the capacity of ordinary men and women to govern their own lives on terms that respect the equal capacities of others. It is on this basis that we argue for things like freedom of worship, the right to life and liberty, free speech, freedom of contract, the right to property, freedom of emigration, privacy and reproductive freedoms. It would be curious if nothing followed from these underlying ideas so far as the governance of the community was concerned. Most theories of rights commit themselves also to democratic rights: the right to participate in the political process through voting, speech, activism, party association, and candidacy. I have argued that these rights are in danger of being abrogated by the sort of proposals [for a Bill of Rights] in the United Kingdom.

The matter is one of great importance. People fought long and hard for the vote and for democratic representation. They wanted the right to govern themselves, not just on mundane issues of policy, but also on high matters of principle. They rejected the Platonic view that the people are incapable of thinking through issues of justice. Consider the struggles there have been, in Britain, Europe and America—first for the abolition of property qualifications, secondly for the extension of the franchise to women, and thirdly, for bringing the legacy of civil rights denials to an end in the context of American racism. In all those struggles, people have paid tribute to the democratic aspiration to self-governance, without any sense at all that it should confine itself to the interstitial quibbles of policy that remain to be settled after some lawyerly elite have decided the main issues of principle.

These thoughts, I have argued, are reinforced when we consider how much room there is for honest and good faith disagreement among citizens on the topic of rights. Things might be different if principles of right were self-evident or if there were a philosophical elite who could be trusted to work out once and for all what rights we have and how they are to be balanced against other considerations. But the consensus of the philosophers is that these matters are not settled, that they are complex and controversial, and that certainly in the seminar room the existence of good faith disagreement is undeniable. Since that is so, it seems to me obvious that we should view the disagreements about rights that exist among citizens in exactly the same light, unless there is compelling evidence to the contrary. It is no doubt possible that a citizen or an elected politician who disagrees with my view of rights is motivated purely by self-interest. But it is somewhat uncomfortable to recognize that she probably entertains exactly the same thought about me. Since the issue of rights before us remains controversial, there seems no better reason to adopt my view of rights as definitive and dismiss her opposition as self-interested, than to regard me as the selfish opponent and her as the defender of principle.

Of course such issues have got to be settled. If I say P has a right to X and my opponent disagrees, some process has got to be implemented to determine whether P is to get X or not. P and people like her cannot be left waiting for our disagreements to resolve themselves. One of us at least will be dissatisfied by the answer that the process comes up with, and it is possible that the answer may be wrong. But the existence of that possibility—which is, as we have seen, an important truth about all human authority—should not be used, as it is so often, exclusively to discredit the democratic process. There is always something bad about the denial of one's rights. But there is nothing specially bad about the denial of rights at the hands of a majority of one's fellow citizens.

In the end, I think, the matter comes down to this. If a process is democratic and comes up with the correct result, it does no injustice to anyone. But if the process is non-democratic, it inherently and necessarily does an injustice, in its operation, to the participatory aspirations of the ordinary citizen. And it does *this* injustice, tyrannizes in *this* way, whether it comes up with the correct result or not.

One of my aims in all this has been to 'dis-aggregate' our concepts of democracy and majority rule. Instead of talking in grey and abstract terms about democracy, we should focus our attention on the individuals—the millions of men and women—who claim a right to a say, on equal terms, in the processes by which they are governed. Instead of talking impersonally about 'the counter-majoritarian difficulty', we should distinguish between a court's deciding things by a majority, and lots and lots of ordinary men and women deciding things by a majority. If we do this, we will see that the question 'Who gets to participate?' always has priority over the question 'How do they decide, when they disagree?'

Above all, when we think about taking certain issues away from the people and entrusting them to the courts, we should adopt the same individualist focus that we use for thinking about any other issue of rights. Someone concerned about rights does not see social issues in impersonal terms: she does not talk about 'the problem of torture' or 'the problem of censorship' but about the predicament of each and every individual who may be tortured or silenced by the State. Similarly, we should think not about 'the-people' or 'the majority', as some sort of blurred quantitative mass, but of the individual citizens, considered one by one, who make up the polity in question.

If we are going to defend the idea of an entrenched Bill of Rights put effectively beyond revision by anyone other than the judges, we should try and think what we might say to some public-spirited citizen who wishes to launch a campaign or lobby her MP on some issue of rights about which she feels strongly and on which she has done her best to arrive at a considered and impartial view. She is not asking to be a dictator; she perfectly accepts that her voice should have no more power than that of anyone else who is prepared to participate in politics. But—like her suffragette forebears—she wants a vote; she wants her voice and her activity to count on matters of high political importance.

In defending a Bill of Rights, we have to imagine ourselves saying to her: 'You may write to the newspaper and get up a petition and organize a pressure group to lobby Parliament. But even if you succeed, beyond your wildest dreams, and orchestrate the support of a large number of like-minded men and women, and manage to prevail in the legislature, your measure may be challenged and struck down because your view of what rights we have does not accord with the judges' view. When their votes differ from yours, theirs are the votes that will prevail.' It is my submission that saying this does not comport with the respect and honour normally accorded to ordinary men and women in the context of a theory of rights."

Apart from questions of democratic legitimacy, the other concern with entrenched rights is the effect that they have on progressive legislation or on progressive institutions. Judges historically have a poor record when it comes to respect for representative institutions or progressive governments, whether national or local. In England (and Scotland), the courts have presented difficulties for trade unions, which are still regarded as being in restraint of trade (*Boddington v Lawton* [1994] I.C.R. 478), and which have been subjected to judicial restrictions on their liberty from which they have had to be rescued by Parliament. This latter legislation (which was consistent with the requirements of international human rights law) was said by one judge in 1980 to "stick in judicial gorges": *Express Newspapers Ltd v McShane* [1980] I.C.R. 42 at 57 (Lord Diplock). The courts have also undermined the powers of local authorities to develop fair wages and equal pay (*Roberts v Hopwood* [1925] A.C. 578), subsidise transport for the elderly (*Prescott v Birmingham Corporation* [1955] Ch.210), and encourage the use of public transport by reducing fares in a manner inconsistent with business-like principles (*Bromley L.B.C. v Greater London Council* [1983] 1 A.C. 768). At the level of national government, in the 1970s the courts undermined the attempts by the then Labour Government to extend the principle of comprehensive education, eliminate racial discrimination and extend the right of workers to be represented by a trade union in the workplace. The last was said by one judge who was to become one of the most "liberal" Law Lords as being the equivalent to the compulsory acquisition of the employer's property (*Powley v ACAS* [1978] I.C.R. 123). All of this mischief could be created without a Bill of Rights. The fear was that with a Bill of Rights the courts could go a whole lot further, these fears being reinforced by developments in Canada where corporations were emboldened to use the Canadian Charter of Rights and Freedoms successfully to challenge a number of irritating restrictions. These included a ban on Sunday trading, restrictions on tobacco advertising and limits on election spending: *R. v Big M Drug Mart* (1985) 18 D.L.R. (4th) 321; *RJR-MacDonald Ltd v Canada* (1995) 127 D.L.R. (4th) 1; and *National Citizens' Coalition Inc v Attorney-General for Canada* (1985) 11 D.L.R. (4th) 481.

These concerns do not apply so forcefully where the Bill of Rights does not apply to legislation, but only to administrative action. However, even here scholars warn of judicial "upgrade" whereby the courts given limited powers by Parliament seek inevitably to extend them. This has been said to be the experience of New Zealand where the Parliament enacted an "interpretive" Bill of Rights. The courts, however, have moved to convert or "upgrade" the document into one whereby they feel empowered to declare that an Act of the New Zealand Parliament is inconsistent with its terms, thereby increasing the pressure on the government to bring forward amending legislation: J. Allan, "Turning Clark Kent into Superman: The New Zealand Bill of Rights Act 1990" (2000) 9 *Otago Law Review* 613. One possible response would be to encourage a greater degree of executive and legislative scrutiny of legislation to ensure compliance with human rights principles, so that the responsibility for ensuring compliance with human rights obligations rests principally with the Government and Parliament. Executive scrutiny of bills to ensure compliance with human rights or constitutional obligations is to be found in the USA, Canada and New Zealand. It usually takes the form of scrutiny by the attorney general's department. Parliamentary scrutiny was pioneered in Sweden where the powerful Constitutional Committee of the Riksdag has the power to block the enactment of legislation that is said to violate the Constitution which includes a chapter on fundamental rights. This procedure has since been complemented by the incorporation of the ECHR which can now be enforced in the courts. Indeed it is arguable that parliamentary scrutiny can only be effective where the government knows that it will face trouble in the courts if it ignores the concerns of Parliament. This is particularly true of parliamentary systems of government where the legislature is dominated by the Executive. We have considered in Ch.2 the extensive arrangements for executive and legislative scrutiny in Scotland.

Lord McCluskey
Law, Justice and Democracy

"A Bill of Rights embodies semi-permanent choices between the conflicting interests of citizens. And to present such choices as if they are the gratuitous enlargement of the human rights of all is to misuse language. Rights are not to be regarded as if they were roses without thorns. Any Bill of Rights which guarantees some rights and denies or conspicuously omits others—for example, economic or cultural rights—is entrenching one set of values at the expense of alternative sets of values. If those whose task it was to select the rights to be protected were to be situated behind a veil of ignorance, so that they did not know how the various alternatives would serve or hinder different interests; if, therefore, they had to choose on the basis of timeless principles acceptable to all right-thinking men; if they were clever enough to choose golden words to express those rights, words so pure and unambiguous that no man, no judge, who had to apply them to real life could possibly fail to ensure that the principles they encapsulated would be applied fairly and equally to all men in all circumstances, then no doubt they could fashion an honest charter of enduring freedoms that would do more than just buttress the interests and values of one class and one generation against the interests and values of their successors.

But how realistic is that hope? A Bill of Rights could serve certain interests and prejudice others. Thus a provision about a right to life would, depending upon how it was phrased by the draftsman and interpreted by the judges, favour one side or the other in the abortion argument. It could hardly avoid doing so. A right of freedom of association is bound to determine or to enable judges to determine, in some degree, and possibly totally, the arguments about the closed shop and collective bargaining. If rights are conferred upon but confined to human persons the results will be entirely different from those which would flow from the conferring of rights upon corporate or legal persons, such as limited companies or trade unions. The essential nature of rights is that they restrict the freedom of those who must respect them. A child's right not to be caned is a restriction upon a teacher's freedom to impose disciplinary sanctions. A worker's right not to join a trade union is a restriction upon the power of his fellow workers to present collectively a monolithic united front to the employer. A right to freedom of speech may be so large, so widely interpreted, that it interferes with the right of accused persons to a fair trial, because it permits the press to publish information which directly or more subtly prejudices the minds of potential jurors or judges. A right to choose freely how one's children are to be educated or one's illnesses are to be treated may confer advantages upon those who can afford to exercise their choice, but leave those who cannot afford to do so with meaningless paper rights. Indeed, the conferring of such rights in relation to education or health care might gravely prejudice the capacity of the community as a whole to allocate and distribute limited educational and health care resources in such a way as to benefit those in need or those who can benefit, rather than those who can pay. The point of offering such examples is not to indicate a preference for or against abortion, the closed shop, private medicine or public schools. The point is that these matters, and countless others, involve political choices. And their character does not alter because they are cast in the noble language of fundamental human rights.

Bear in mind that one of the principal arguments for conferring certain rights in an entrenched charter is that they should not be able to be disturbed by a temporary political majority which in a parliamentary democracy commands the legislature and executive for five or ten years.

Of course that argument has some force; particularly for those who cannot win such a majority, because it opens up for them a route for obtaining and preserving rights which the majority want to modify or remove. But it also means that if a particular coalition of interest groups can at the moment of enactment of the charter win a sufficient majority to ensure that their interest is secured and entrenched in the form of a charter right, then later parliamentary majorities cannot adjust that and related rights in accordance with the wishes of the majority. Charters of entrenched rights provide a favourable environment for the single-issue fanatics, such as the American Prohibitionists of the 1920s. The 18th Amendment introducing Prohibition has been described as the crowning achievement of a movement which had become the 'rallying-point of those who wished to save the Republic from the corrupting effects of alcohol, the saloon, machine politics, jazz and the movies, from all the sins which robbed the nation of its purity'.

Even if, when the charter is enacted, there is no consensus to frame a particular interest as an explicit right, it may well be possible to smuggle it in, in a vague and delphic form of words, leaving alive the hope that by interpretation judges will ultimately make explicit that which the charter left obscure. So the power lies with the judges. The real alternatives are not, on the one hand, some timeless noble document which eloquently distils and expresses the best essence of civilised experience and, on the other, an elective dictatorship abusing its temporary stewardship by trampling on the rights of minorities.

What are the alternatives? On the one hand, we can make political choices and buttress them against change—whether they are spelled out explicitly or left to be teased out of the wording by the judges. On the other, we can leave such choices to be made and re-made, by elected representatives who must answer to the electorate for their decisions. As time passes, the alternatives can surely become rule by the words of yesterday's charter majority as filtered through the minds of today's judges versus rule by today's elected representatives.

To leave profound policy issues to judges in this way is to avoid a principled and fully informed consideration by society itself of the problem of where in a civilised and free society the lines fall to be drawn and the balances struck. If the judges are required to put flesh on the bare bones of vaguely worded rights, where are they to draw their inspiration from? They may choose to look at the United States, which has had to address such questions; but they will find some funny answers. The Supreme Court has had to consider, for example, what limits, if any, fall to be placed on the freedom of speech guaranteed in the First Amendment and how that freedom can be squared with the Sixth Amendment guarantee of a fair trial by an impartial jury or the Fourteenth Amendment guarantee of due process. In the result, the media can carry almost unrestricted information about the life and circumstances of a person who is to face trial on criminal charges even though potential jurors may read that information and be prejudiced by it. So it may take weeks to select a jury and it may have to consist of people who read no newspapers and watch no television. We in Britain would treat such publication as being in contempt of court, because we think that the need to ensure a fair trial overrides the need to sell newspapers. Why should the judgment of Parliament on such a matter be abdicated to judges, even if, as our history suggests, the judges would, in that particular case, probably make a good job of it?

In the United States, the judges have hardly been uniformly and conspicuously successful, by comparison with the United Kingdom, in securing and extending fundamental human rights and freedoms. What are held by some as the glittering achievements of the United States Supreme Court in asserting civil liberties or fundamental rights fail to be seen in their context. The advances in human rights achieved in the Supreme Court can be assessed only against the background. Occasionally, that background is so oppressive, so prejudiced and so cruel that one is left wondering how a society conceived with such nobility of rhetoric and purpose could have created such oppression, inequality and prejudice. That is an historical matter. But a lawyer who tried to form a picture of American society by reading nothing but the reports of cases in the Supreme Court would end up with a depressing view of that society.

In studying even recent liberal decisions of the Supreme Court one tends to break off from applauding the answers in sheer dismay that it was still necessary to ask the questions. Sometimes even the answers cause equal dismay. The Supreme Court has, for the past three decades or so, advanced the cause of human rights against the opposition not just of those opposed to such rights but also of those who believed that the unelected judges have no warrant in the constitution for such judicial activism. But even on the human rights front if we go back beyond the 1950s we find a history of the court's reluctance to use the same Bill of Rights for the same purpose. As Justice Thurgood Marshall, the first black to sit on the bench of the Supreme Court, said in a case in 1978: 'During most of the past 200 years, the constitution as interpreted by this court did not prohibit the most ingenious and pervasive forms of discrimination against the Negro.'

I do not seek to deny that recently much has been achieved both in civil rights and elsewhere. But even the broad, unqualified statements of rights which the Supreme Court Justices have had to apply did not prevent them, until recently, from taking a narrow, legalistic, laissez-faire perspective on freedom so as to strike down as unconstitutional legislation designed to stop the exploitation of workers, women, children or immigrants. They legalised slavery, and when it was abolished, they legalised racial segregation. They repeatedly held that women were not entitled to equality with men. They approved the unconstitutional removal by the Executive of the constitutional rights of Americans of Japanese origin after the bombing of Pearl Harbour.

In truth, statements of fundamental rights can seldom be enacted with precision. They are full of notions like 'due process' or 'respect for family life' or 'freedom to manifest one's religion'. And the rights are then qualified by equally elastic concepts, like 'reasonable', or 'necessary in a free society' or 'national security'. When rights are created in vague and imprecise terms, their content to be discovered by judges whose choices are not determined by familiar and well understood rules of law, no one really knows, till the courts have decided, what his rights are.

So, unless it can be shown that it is, on balance, necessary to enact a Bill of Rights to enable our citizens to achieve rights not available through the processes of democracy, unless it can be shown that we can agree on the content, and the precise expression, of particular rights, we should be slow to confer upon our judges an unreviewable power to evolve a miscellany of actual rights and restraints whose real content we cannot sensibly predict.

However inconvenient and untidy it is for our judges to have to stand aside and observe European judges, whether in Luxembourg or in Strasbourg, decide human rights and discrimination questions on the basis of materials not available to the domestic courts, that is not an argument for creating the great cloud of uncertainty that a domestic Bill of Rights would bring.

I cannot do better than to end with the words of the American judge, Learned Hand: 'I often wonder whether we do not rest our hopes too much upon constitutions, upon laws and upon courts. These are false hopes; believe me, these are false hopes. Liberty lies in the hearts of men and women; when it dies there no constitution, no law, no court can save it; no constitution, no law, no court can even do much to help it. While it lies there it needs no constitution, no law, no court to save it.'"

III. HUMAN RIGHTS AND DEMOCRACY: A RESPONSE

There are a number of responses to these concerns, though these focus more on attempts to legitimise the process of judicial decision-making, rather than its malign effect on social policy. The most impressive and persuasive of these responses is the argument developed by John Hart Ely (*Democracy and Distrust* (1980)) who argues that the US Bill of Rights—with its powerful scope for judicial review of legislation—can be justified as being necessary to deal with the situation where democracy "malfunctions". Writing in these terms, Ely was seeking to justify the liberal approach adopted by the US Supreme Court under the leadership of Chief Justice Warren. The court is famous for its decisions reversing State legislation that was socially very conservative, and particularly famous for its decision in *Brown v Board of Education*, 347 U.S. 483 (1954) in which it struck down laws providing for racial segregation in education: America's apartheid laws which were authorised by the Constitution until this momentous decision overturned an earlier decision permitting the "separate but equal" treatment of the races (*Plessy v Ferguson*, 163 U.S. 537 (1896)). In *Brown* the Supreme Court woke up from a long sleep and demonstrated a remarkable progressive streak which saw it strike down State laws restricting certain forms of consensual heterosexual conduct and most notably a Texas law restricting a woman's right to choose whether to terminate a pregnancy (*Roe v Wade*, 410 U.S. 113 (1973)). In this period the court also delivered a number of important decisions on free speech, in one case restricting the right of public figures to sue for libel (*New York Times v Sullivan*, 376 U.S. 254 (1964)).

According to Ely democracy "malfunctions" in two situations. The first is where the channels of political change are blocked, perhaps by incumbents who seek to gerrymander the political process to their advantage. However, it is not clear which laws have this effect. It is clear that the gerrymandering of electoral boundaries to the benefit of a particular party or group would fall within this definition. But what about a law that imposes a limit on election expenses, such as the one that was struck down in *Buckley v Valeo*, 424 U.S. 1 (1976)? Is this one that protects incumbents because they already enjoy the benefits of public recognition? Or does it promote electoral fairness by ensuring that wealthy incumbents are unable to buy electoral success? The second way in which democracy "malfunctions" is when the political majority use their power to discriminate against "discrete and insular minorities" who are never likely to constitute a political majority. Such groups might include ethnic minorities, political minorities, asylum seekers, gays and lesbians, transsexuals and prisoners. In relation to these and other groups, however, the courts traditionally have not responded well, and indeed much of the discrimination that takes place does so in the shadow of the law and because it is permitted by the common law in particular. It is true that *Brown v Board of Education*, above, was a great trophy for this perspective on judicial review. However as Lord McCluskey pointed out in the above extract, there are many cases in which the US Supreme Court turned its back on minorities in need of its protection, whether they be Japanese Americans interned without trial during the Second World War (*Korematsu v United States*, 323 U.S. 214 (1944)), or Communists persecuted during the cold war (*Dennis v United States*, 341 U.S. 494 (1951)). These latter cases are a reminder that elegant theory does not always translate well in practice.

J H Ely
Democracy and Distrust

"Thus the two arguments that follow, each overtly normative, are if anything more important than the one I have just reviewed. The first is entirely obvious by now, that unlike an approach geared to the judicial imposition of 'fundamental values,' the representation-reinforcing orientation whose contours I have sketched and will develop further is not inconsistent with, but on the contrary is entirely supportive of, the American system of representative democracy. It recognizes the unacceptability of the claim that appointed and life-tenured judges are better reflectors of conventional values than elected representatives, devoting itself instead to policing the mechanisms by which the system seeks to ensure that our elected representatives will actually represent. There may be an illusion of circularity here: my approach is more consistent with representative democracy because that's the way it was planned. But of course it isn't any more circular than setting out to build an airplane and ending up with something that flies.

The final point worth serious mention is that (again unlike a fundamental-values approach) a representation-reinforcing approach assigns judges a role they are conspicuously well situated to fill. My reference here is not principally to expertise. Lawyers *are* experts on process writ small, the processes by which facts are found and contending parties are allowed to present their claims. And to a degree they are experts on process writ larger, the processes by which issues of public policy are fairly determined: lawyers do seem genuinely to have a feel, indeed it is hard to see what other special value they have, for ways of insuring that everyone gets his or her fair say. But too much shouldn't be made of this. Others, particularly the full-time participants, can also claim expertise on how the political process allocates voice and power. And of course many legislators are lawyers themselves. So the point isn't so much one of expertise as it is one of perspective.

The approach to constitutional adjudication recommended here is akin to what might be called an 'antitrust' as opposed to a 'regulatory' orientation to economic affairs—rather than dictate substantive results it intervenes only when the 'market,' in our case the political market, is systemically malfunctioning. (A referee analogy is also not far off: the referee is to intervene only when one team is gaining unfair advantage, not because the 'wrong' team has scored.) Our government cannot fairly be said to be 'malfunctioning' simply because it sometimes generates outcomes with which we disagree, however strongly (and claims that it is reaching results with which 'the people' really disagree—or would 'if they understood'— are likely to be little more than self-deluding projections). In a representative democracy value determinations are to be made by our elected representatives, and if in fact most of us disapprove we can vote them out of office. Malfunction occurs when the *process* is undeserving of trust, when (1) the ins are choking off the channels of political change to ensure that they will stay in and the outs will stay out, or (2) though no one is actually denied a voice or a vote, representatives beholden to an effective majority are systematically disadvantaging some minority out of simple hostility or a prejudiced refusal to recognize commonalities of interest, and thereby denying that minority the protection afforded other groups by a representative system.

Obviously our elected representatives are the last persons we should trust with identification of either of these situations. Appointed judges, however, are comparative outsiders in our governmental system, and need worry about continuance in office only very obliquely. This does not give them some special pipeline to the genuine values of the American people: in fact it goes far to ensure that they won't have one. It does, however, put them in a position objectively to assess claims—though no one could suppose the evaluation won't be full of judgment calls—that either by clogging the channels of change or by acting as accessories to majority tyranny, our elected representatives in fact are not representing the interests of those whom the system presupposes they are."

Another approach comes from Canada where Hogg and Bushell, ("The Charter Dialogue between Courts and Legislators" (1997) 35 *Osgoode Hall Law Journal* 75) suggest that the virtue of a Bill of Rights (or in this case the Canadian Charter of Rights) is that the judges are involved in a dialogue with legislatures. The authors acknowledge that "dialogue" may not "seem particularly apt to describe the relationship between the Supreme Court of Canada and the legislative bodies". This is because "when the Court says what the Constitution requires, legislative bodies have to obey". The question is how is it possible "to have a dialogue between two institutions when one is so clearly subordinate to the other"? Hogg and Bushell reply by contending that where a judicial decision is open to legislative reversal, modification or avoidance, "then it is meaningful to regard the relationship between the Court and the competent legislative body as a dialogue". For in that case, "the judicial decision causes a public debate in which Charter values play a more prominent part than they would if there had been no judicial decision". The legislature in turn, "is in a position to devise a response that is properly respectful of the Charter values that have been identified by the Court, but which accomplishes the social and economic objectives that the judicial decision has impeded". This is also an attractive theory which has been seized upon by a beleaguered Supreme Court of Canada anxious to justify and explain its role in the wake of some public criticism. A good example of the court endorsing its suggested role as a partner in a dialogue is provided by the following dictum in the leading case *Vriend v Alberta* [1998] 1 S.C.R. 493. According to Iacobucci J. at 565–566:

"As I view the matter, the Charter has given rise to a more dynamic interaction among the branches of governance. This interaction has been aptly described as a 'dialogue' by some (see eg Hogg and Bushell, supra). In reviewing legislative enactments and executive decisions to ensure constitutional validity, the courts speak to the legislative and executive branches. As has been pointed out, most of the legislation held not to pass constitutional muster has been followed by new legislation designed to accomplish similar objectives (see Hogg and Bushell, supra, at p 82). By doing this, the legislature responds to the courts; hence the dialogue among the branches.

To my mind, a great value of judicial review and this dialogue among the branches is that each of the branches is made somewhat accountable to the other. The work of the legislature is reviewed by the courts and the work of the court in its decisions can be reacted to by the legislature. ... This dialogue between and accountability of each of the branches have the effect of enhancing the democratic process, not denying it."

The idea of dialogue has also found supporters from British commentators: F. Klug, "Judicial Deference under the Human Rights Act 1998" (2003) E.H.R.L.R. 125. Indeed it might be argued that it is an idea that is peculiarly well suited to the British system given that the Human Rights Act 1998 enables the courts only to declare legislation incompatible with Convention rights. In contrast to the position in Canada there is no power to strike down legislation under the Human Rights Act (though the position is different under the Scotland Act). The United Kingdom courts can suggest, the Government can consider, and Parliament can respond, or not. It has been suggested that the Human Rights Act has thus produced:

"a creative tension between the judiciary on the one hand and Parliament and the executive on the other. It binds the principal constitutional actors into a dialogue with each other in which all agree on the objective of securing Convention rights, and disagreements about their interpretation or the resolution of conflicts between them are mediated by a new relationship between courts and Parliament, both of which have an explicit role in pronouncing on human rights issues." (M. Hunt, "The Human Rights Act and Legal Culture: The Judiciary and the Legal Profession" (1999) 26 *Journal of Law and Society* 86.)

It has also been suggested that "the only factor missing" from Hunt's description is "the people". However, never fear, we "still have the opportunity, under the British Bill of Rights model, to engage in this 'dialogue' through participating in the political process directly or through various modern means of communication". "In this way", it is claimed, "no one need be barred from the national debate over where the appropriate balance between rights lies. While ministers can be lobbied, judges can not" (F. Klug, *Values for a Godless Age* (2000), pp.181–182). But have the British people not always had this "opportunity", with the difference being that it was an opportunity undiluted by the need to defer to the voices of those who were beyond their direct influence? This in fact is the real problem with the dialogue idea. While it feigns to dilute the role of the courts in the political process, it carefully elides the questions of legitimacy which are left unanswered. Indeed dialogue simply invites traditional questions to be asked in a different form. Thus on what basis can we justify giving a privileged status as interlocutors to an unelected, unrepresentative and unaccountable body? Why should judges—rather than say the BBC, the STUC or the Church of Scotland—be given a privileged station in a conversation? A better metaphor than dialogue would be censorship. Judges are not so much interlocutors in a dialogue with the Government but censors whose disapproval the law-maker is constantly devising means defensively to avoid.

P. W. Hogg and A. A. Bushell
"The Charter Dialogue between Courts and Legislators"
(1997) 35 *Osgoode Hall Law Journal* 75

"Where a judicial decision striking down a law on *Charter* grounds can be reversed, modified, or avoided by a new law, any concern about the legitimacy of judicial review is greatly diminished. To be sure, the Court may have forced a topic onto the legislative agenda that the legislative body would have preferred not to have to deal with. And, of course, the precise terms of any new law would have been powerfully influenced by the Court's decision. The legislative body would have been forced to give greater weight to the *Charter* values identified by the Court in devising the means of carrying out the objectives, or the legislative body might have been forced to modify its objectives to some extent to accommodate the Court's concerns. These are constraints on the democratic process, no doubt, but the final decision is the democratic one.

The dialogue that culminates in a democratic decision can only take place if the judicial decision to strike down a law can be reversed, modified, or avoided by the ordinary legislative process. Later in this article we will show that this is the normal situation. There is usually an alternative law that is available to the legislative body and that enables the legislative purpose to be substantially carried out, albeit by somewhat different means. Moreover, when the Court strikes down a law, it frequently offers a suggestion as to how the law could be modified to solve the constitutional problems. The legislative body often follows that suggestion, or devises a different law that also skirts the constitutional barriers. Indeed, our research, which surveyed sixty-five cases where legislation was invalidated for a breach of the *Charter*, found that in forty-four cases (two-thirds), the competent legislative body amended the impugned law. In most cases, relatively minor amendments were all that was required in order to respect the *Charter*, without compromising the objective of the original legislation.

Sometimes an invalid law is more restrictive of individual liberty than it needs to be to accomplish its purpose, and what is required is a narrower law. Sometimes a broader law is needed, because an invalid law confers a benefit, but excludes people who have a constitutional equality right to be included. Sometimes what is needed is a fairer procedure. But it is rare indeed that the constitutional defect cannot be remedied. Hence, as the subtitle of this article suggests, 'perhaps the *Charter of Rights* isn't such a bad thing after all.' The *Charter* can act as a catalyst for a two-way exchange between the judiciary and legislature on the topic of human rights and freedoms, but it rarely raises an absolute barrier to the wishes of the democratic institutions.

Our conclusion is that the critique of the *Charter* based on democratic legitimacy cannot be sustained. To be sure, the Supreme Court of Canada is a non-elected, unaccountable body of middle-aged lawyers. To be sure, it does from time to time strike down statutes enacted by the elected, accountable, representative legislative bodies. But, the decisions of the Court almost always leave room for a legislative response, and they usually get a legislative response. In the end, if the democratic will is there, the legislative objective will still be able to be accomplished, albeit with some new safeguards to protect individual rights and liberty. Judicial review is not 'a veto over the politics of the nation,' but rather the beginning of a dialogue as to how best to reconcile the individualistic values of the *Charter* with the accomplishment of social and economic policies for the benefit of the community as a whole."

IV. HUMAN RIGHTS AND THE SCOTLAND ACT 1998

Acts of the Scottish Parliament may be challenged in the courts if they fail to comply with Convention rights, the Government having decided that the Scottish Parliament should have no power to legislate in a way that is incompatible with the Convention (Cm. 3782, 1997, para.2.21). For the first time in the democratic era the courts in this country have the clear and unequivocal power (and duty) to strike down legislation passed by a democratically elected Parliament. The paradox of this arrangement is that the Scottish Parliament has in place a number of pre-legislative scrutiny devices designed to ensure that legislation is consistent with Convention rights. As we have also seen there is the possibility that these could be extended with the introduction of a Scottish Human Rights Commission. We thus have the possibility of "rights conflict", with the courts empowered to challenge decisions and conclusions taken by and within the Parliament that a particular piece of legislation is consistent with human rights. In view of the fact that human rights are so imprecise and open textured, such arrangements ought to indicate a need for deference on the part of Her Majesty's judges in Scotland. There is a need to defer generally to the decisions of an elected body, as well as specifically to judgments made in good faith about human rights obligations. Human rights are matters of judgment, and there is no reason why, as a general rule, the judgment of lawyers and judges should be seen to be superior to the judgment of civil servants and politicians.

A v The Scottish Ministers
2002 P.C. 63

This was a challenge to the very first Act of the Scottish Parliament: the Mental Health (Public Safety and Appeals) (Scotland) Act 1999 which amended the Mental Health (Scotland) Act 1984. The Act was an emergency measure—passed after a judicial ruling—designed to prevent the release of people who had been ordered to be detained under a hospital order. However, the condition for which they were detained was not treatable which meant in the case of two applicants—A and D—that they could apply to the courts for their immediate release, even though they were still thought to be a danger to the public. The position of a third applicant was different, in the sense that he was detained under conditions that if he could not be treated under a hospital order he would be returned to prison. The 1999 Act allowed for the continued detention of all three applicants on the ground that it was necessary to protect the public from serious harm. This was stronger in the case of A and R who would be released into the community if they succeeded than in the case of D who would be "released" back to prison, rather than amongst the public at large. It was argued by the appellants that the detentions under the 1999 Act violated their rights under art.5(1)(e) and (4) of the Convention. The Judicial Committee upheld the decision of the Inner House that there had been no breach.

Lord Hope of Craighead:

"The legislation

[4] I should like to say a word first about the structure of the legislation which provides the context for the determination of a devolution issue as to the legislative competence of the Scottish Parliament. The issue has been defined by the appellants in these terms: 'Is section 1 of the Mental Health (Public Safety and Appeals) (Scotland) Act 1999 a provision (in whole or in part) outwith the legislative competence of the Scottish Parliament by virtue of section 29(2)(d) of the Scotland Act 1998 and accordingly not law, in terms of section 29(1) thereof.'

[5] Section 29(1) of the 1998 Act provides that an Act of the Scottish Parliament is not law so far as any provision of the Act is outside the legislative competence of the Parliament. Section 29(2) defines the limits on that legislative competence. Paragraph (d) of that subsection provides that a provision is outside that competence if it is incompatible with any of the Convention rights. Section 126(1) provides that the expression 'the Convention rights' has the same meaning as in the Human Rights Act 1998. Those are the rights set out in the European Convention for the Protection of Human Rights and Fundamental Freedoms to which effect is given by sec 1 of the Human Rights Act 1998 for the purposes of that Act. Among these rights are those in art 5 of the Convention which are concerned with the right to liberty.

[6] The Advocate General drew attention to various safeguards which have been built into the Scotland Act 1998 to ensure so far as possible that there is no breach of the limits of the Parliament's legislative competence. These are to be found in secs 31 and 33 of the Act. Section 31(1) provides that a member of the Scottish Executive who is in charge of a Bill shall, before its introduction, state that in his view it is within the legislative competence of the Parliament. This corresponds to sec 19 of the Human Rights Act 1998, which requires a Minister of the Crown before second reading of a Bill in either House of the Parliament at Westminster to make a statement of compatibility. Section 31(2) requires the Presiding Officer, on or before the introduction of the Bill, to decide whether the Bill would be within the Parliament's legislative competence and to state his decision. This enables him to issue a warning to the Parliament if he is of the opinion the Bill would be outside its competence.

[7] Important though these two safeguards may be in practice to the work of the Scottish Parliament, they are no more than statements of opinion which do not bind the judiciary. With that in view sec 33 enables the Advocate General, the Lord Advocate or the Attorney General to refer the question of whether a Bill or any provision of a Bill would be within the Parliament's legislative competence to the Judicial Committee for its decision. This procedure is available to the Law Officers after the passing of the Bill but before it receives Royal Assent: see sec 32(2). In the present case the Law Officers notified the Presiding Officer that they did not intend to make a reference. This enabled the Presiding Officer to submit the Bill for Royal Assent without delay. But the fact that the Law Officers decided not to test the matter in this way is of no consequence at this stage. The court has power to deal with it as a devolution issue under sched 6 to the Act after the Bill has been enacted if a member of the public claims that the provision was outside the Parliament's legislative competence.

[8] Before the court reaches the stage of making a determination that an Act of the

Scottish Parliament or any provision in such an Act is outside the legislative competence of the Parliament there are a series of questions that it may have to address. These are to be found in secs 100 to 102 of the Scotland Act 1998. (a) A person cannot bring proceedings on the ground that an 'Act', which includes making any legislation, is incompatible with the Convention rights unless he would be a victim for the purposes of art 34 of the Convention if proceedings in respect of the Act were brought in the European Court of Human Rights: see sec 100(1). So the first question is whether the person by whom the challenge is made is or would be a victim of the provision which he says is outside the legislative competence of the Parliament. (b) Any provision of an Act of the Scottish Parliament which could be read in such a way as to be outside competence is to be read as narrowly as is required for it to be within the legislative competence of the Parliament, if such a reading is possible, and is to have effect accordingly: see sec 101. The aim of this provision is to enable the court to give effect to legislation which the Scottish Parliament has enacted wherever possible rather than strike it down. So the second question is whether the provision which is in issue can be read and given effect in such a way as to avoid the incompatibility. (c) The court has power, if it decides that an Act of the Scottish Parliament, or any provision in such an Act, which cannot be read compatibly is outside its legislative competence, to make an order removing or limiting the retrospective effect of the decision or suspending its effect for any period and on any conditions to allow the defect to be corrected: see sec 102(2). The power to suspend enables the court to give the Scottish Parliament time to reconsider the legislation and to amend it in such a way as to remove the incompatibility. So the third question is whether the case is one where one or other of the orders contemplated by sec 102(2) should be made as part of the determination of the devolution issue.

[9] Each of these three questions is, to a greater or lesser degree, in play in the present case. They are, of course, bound up with the underlying question as to whether sec 1 of the Mental Health (Public Safety and Appeals) (Scotland) Act 1999 ('the 1999 Act'), or any part of it, is incompatible with the patients' Convention rights. But I think that it is important not to lose sight of them, especially in the case of D which presents certain difficulties which do not apply in the other two cases of A and R.

The issues

[17] A and R are both being detained under a hospital order in the state hospital as restricted patients, because they are patients who are subject to a restriction order: see sec 63 of the Mental Health (Scotland) Act 1984. They cannot be returned to prison in the event of their obtaining a discharge under sec 64 of that Act as, under the law in force at the time when the hospital orders were made, they were not sentenced to any term of imprisonment. In the event of their discharge from hospital they would have to be released into the community.

[18] D is in a different position. He is a restricted patient because he is subject to a restriction direction. He was sentenced in Northern Ireland to a period of imprisonment which he was still serving when he was diagnosed as suffering from a mental disorder which was considered to be treatable. He was admitted to hospital by reason of a transfer direction together with a restriction direction made by the Secretary of State for Northern Ireland under arts 53 and 55 of the Mental Health (Northern Ireland) Order 1986 (SI 1986/595). There were no suitable facilities for his detention in Northern Ireland, so he was transferred under sec 81 of the 1984 Act to the state hospital. The effect of the restriction direction which was made in his case is that the Scottish Ministers must return him to prison to complete his sentence in the event of his being granted a discharge: sec 74 of the 1984 Act, read with sec 81(2).

[19] The cases of A and D differ from that of R in respect that on 8 July and 22 July 1999 respectively they lodged summary applications at Lanark sheriff court seeking a discharge from their detention as restricted patients on the grounds set out under sec 64 of the 1984 Act. So their applications were already pending when the 1999 Act was brought into force on 13 September 1999. R did not lodge his application for a discharge until 8 March 2000.

But the Scottish Ministers accept that all three appellants satisfy the victim test laid down in sec 100(1) of the Scotland Act 1998, on the assumption—which they dispute—that the mental disorder from which they are suffering is not treatable.

[20] Section 1 of the 1999 Act is said to be incompatible, in whole or in part, with art 5(1)(e) and art 5(4) of the Convention. The issues which the case raises are the following: (a) Is sec 1, in whole or in part, incompatible with art 5(1)(e)? Article 5(1) provides that no one shall be deprived of his liberty save in the cases which it describes, which in para (e) include the lawful detention of persons of unsound mind, and in accordance with a procedure prescribed by law. This issue is raised by all three appellants. (b) Is the case of D under art 5(1)(e) to be distinguished from those of A and R? D wishes to obtain a discharge so that he can be returned to prison to serve the remainder of his sentence of imprisonment. He is not seeking to be released into the community. (c) Is sec 1, in whole or in part, incompatible with art 5(4)? Article 5(4) provides that everyone who is deprived of his liberty by arrest or detention shall be entitled to take proceedings by which the lawfulness of his detention shall be decided speedily by a court and his release ordered. This issue also is raised by all three appellants. (d) Is the retrospective application of sec 1 to pending proceedings incompatible with art 5(4)? This issue, which relates to the right known as the right to equality of arms, is raised only by A and D.

Compatibility with article 5(1)(e) generally

[21] The jurisprudence of the European Court of Human Rights indicates that there are various aspects to art 5(1) which must be satisfied in order to show that a person's detention is lawful for the purposes of that article: see *R v Governor of Brockhill Prison, ex p. Evans* [2001] 2 A.C. 19, p 38B–E, where I set out my understanding of what is involved.

[22] There are three distinct questions that need to be addressed. The first question is whether the detention is lawful under domestic law. Any detention which is unlawful in domestic law will automatically be unlawful under art 5(1). As the court said in *Winterwerp v The Netherlands* (1979) 2 E.H.R.R. 387, para 39, the lawfulness of the detention for the purposes of art 5(1)(e) presupposes conformity with the domestic law in the first place and this covers procedural as well as substantive rules. The second question is whether, assuming that the detention is lawful under domestic law, the domestic law also complies with the general requirements of the Convention. These are based upon the principle that any restriction on human rights and fundamental freedoms must be prescribed by the law: see arts 8 to 11 of the Convention. They include the requirements that the domestic law must be sufficiently accessible to the individual and sufficiently precise to enable the individual to foresee the consequences for himself. The third question is whether, again assuming that the detention is lawful under domestic law, it is nevertheless open to criticism on the Convention ground that it is arbitrary because, for example, it was resorted to in bad faith or was not proportionate: *Engel v The Netherlands (No 1)* (1976) 1 E.H.R.R. 647, para 58.

[23] As the court said in *Winterwerp v The Netherlands*, para 45, the domestic law must itself be in conformity with the Convention, including the general principles expressed or implied therein. That is the background to sec 29(2)(d) of the Scotland Act 1998, which defines the limits of the legislative competence of the Scottish Parliament in regard to the Convention rights. Nevertheless the wording of art 5, as interpreted by the court, shows that it is in the first instance a matter for the domestic law to lay down the substantive and procedural rules which regulate the detention of persons of unsound mind.

[24] In the present case the answer to the first question as to the position in domestic law is that the appellants are being detained under Part VI of the Mental Health (Scotland) Act 1984 as amended by the 1999 Act. The legislation as it now stands permits the continued detention of restricted patients who no longer satisfy the condition which sec 17 of the 1984 Act lays down for detention in a hospital that their mental disorder is treatable if the sheriff or the Scottish Ministers, as the case may be, are satisfied that the patient is suffering from a mental disorder the effect of which is such that it is necessary, in order to protect the public

from serious harm, that the patient continue to be detained in hospital, whether for medical treatment or not: secs 64(A1), 68(2A) and 74(1B) of the 1984 Act as amended. The effect of the amendment 'was to reverse the decision in *R. v Secretary of State for Scotland*, 1999 S.C. (H.L.) 17. Assuming for the moment that the relevant provisions of the 1999 Act are compatible with the appellants' Convention rights—as the first question refers only to domestic law—the continued detention of the appellants is authorised by the amendments which it made to the 1984 Act. It is lawful under the domestic law which no longer requires, in the case of restricted patients whose continued detention in a hospital is necessary on grounds of public safety, that their mental disorder is treatable.

[25] As for the second question, it has not been suggested that the relevant provisions of the 1984 Act, as amended by sec 1 of the 1999 Act, are inaccessible or insufficiently precise. The procedure which the law prescribes for the appellants' continued detention satisfies the requirements mentioned in para 45 of the *Winterwerp* case. It is stated in that paragraph that the notion underlying the words 'in accordance with a procedure prescribed by law' in art 5(1) is one of fair and proper procedure, namely that any measure depriving a person of his liberty should issue from and be executed by an appropriate authority, and the procedure under which this is done should not be arbitrary. Although the appellants' counsel did not contend otherwise, the fact that they are being detained under a procedure prescribed by domestic law which complies with the general principles of the Convention is an important factor on the issue of compatibility. The 1999 Act satisfies these tests.

[26] The third question is the one to which the appellants' counsel directed their argument. In *X. v United Kingdom* (1981) 4 E.H.R.R. 188, para 43 the court said that the object and purpose of art 5(1) is precisely to ensure that no one should be deprived of his liberty in an arbitrary fashion. In other words, what the Convention requires is that there must be no element of arbitrariness. That is the context in which, in para 39 of its judgment in the *Winterwerp* case, the court laid down the three minimum conditions which have to be satisfied for there to be lawful detention of persons of unsound mind within the meaning of art 5(1)(e). These conditions were restated in *X v United Kingdom*, para 40, in *Luberti v Italy* (1984) 6 E.H.R.R. 440, para 27 and in *Johnson v United Kingdom* (1997) 27 E.H.R.R. 296, para 60. In the *X* case they were said to be that: 'the individual concerned must be reliably shown to be of unsound mind, that is to say, a true mental disorder must be established before a competent authority on the basis of objective medical expertise; the mental disorder must be of a kind or degree warranting compulsory confinement; and the validity of continued confinement depends upon the persistence of such a disorder.'

[27] As the Lord President said, [in the present case], the system which the 1999 Act lays down satisfies these criteria. The sheriff or the Scottish Ministers must be satisfied that the patient is suffering from a mental disorder (the first *Winterwerp* criterion) and that it is such as to make it necessary for the protection of the public that he continue to be detained in hospital (the second and third *Winterwerp* criteria). As all three criteria are satisfied, the system does not appear to be open to the criticism that, in Convention terms, it is arbitrary.

[28] The appellants' counsel nevertheless contended that the system was incompatible with art 5(1)(e) on the ground that the article, read purposively with art 18 which limits restrictions on rights permitted under the Convention to the purpose for which they have been prescribed, did not permit the detention of persons of unsound mind in circumstances where there is neither a genuine intention to provide medical treatment to that person nor the possibility of benefit from such treatment. In my opinion the jurisprudence of the Strasbourg court does not support this proposition. In *Winterwerp v The Netherlands*, para 51 the court said that a mental patient's right to treatment appropriate to his condition cannot as such be derived from art 5(1)(e). In *Ashingdane v United Kingdom* (1985) 7 E.H.R.R. 528, para 44 the court looked again at the question whether the expression 'lawful detention of a person of unsound mind' could be construed as including a reference to matters such as the conditions of detention. It held that, although there must be some relationship between the ground of permitted deprivation of liberty relied on and the place and conditions of detention, the article was not in principle concerned with suitable

treatment or conditions.

[29] The conclusion which I would draw from these cases is that the question whether a person who is deprived of his liberty on the ground that he is a person of unsound mind in circumstances which meet the *Winterwerp* criteria should also receive treatment for his mental disorder as a condition of his detention is a matter for domestic law. So too is the place of his detention, so long as it is a place which is suitable for the detention of persons of unsound mind. It follows that the fact that his mental disorder is not susceptible to treatment does not mean that, in Convention terms, his continued detention in a hospital is arbitrary or disproportionate.

[30] In *Guzzardi v Italy* (1980) 3 E.H.R.R. 333, para 98 and *Litwa v Poland* (2001) 33 E.H.R.R. 53, para 60 the court recognised that a predominant reason why the Convention allows the persons mentioned in art 5(1)(e) to be deprived of their liberty is not only that they are dangerous for public safety but also that their own interests may necessitate their detention. So the need to protect the public from serious harm is in itself a legitimate reason for the detention of persons of unsound mind, provided always that the *Winterwerp* conditions are satisfied. In this context the fair balance which is inherent in the whole of the Convention between the demands of the general interests of the community and the requirements of the protection of the individual's fundamental rights favours the general interests of the community.

[31] For these reasons I agree with the judges in the Inner House that sec 1 of the 1999 Act is not incompatible with the appellants' rights under art 5(1)(e) of the Convention. I would hold that it was not incompatible with the appellants' rights under art 5(1)(e) for the Scottish Parliament to require the continued detention of restricted patients in a hospital where this is necessary on grounds of public safety, whether or not their mental disorder is treatable.

D's case under article 5(1)(e): restriction direction patients

[32] Senior counsel for D said that he was a criminal who simply wished to go back to prison. As he had been sentenced to imprisonment for life, there was no prospect of his being released from hospital into the community. Section 65 of the 1984 Act requires the sheriff, in the event of his being of the opinion that a patient who is subject to a restriction would, if subject to a restriction order, be entitled to be discharged under sec 64 of the Act, to notify the Scottish Ministers with a view to his being remitted to any prison where he might have been detained if he had not been removed to hospital. His complaint was that, due to inadequate drafting, he had been sucked by sec 1 of the 1999 Act into a system which was designed to protect the public from restricted patients subject to restriction orders who would have to be released into the community in the event of their obtaining a discharge from hospital.

[33] Senior counsel said that D would be content to be told that he did not satisfy the victim test because sec 1 of the 1999 Act did not apply to him. But his arguments were presented on the assumption that his case was caught by sec 1 and that but for its provisions he would be entitled, on proof that his mental condition was not treatable, to be remitted to prison under sec 65 of the 1984 Act. As I understood the argument, it was that, whatever might be the position in regard to patients who were subject to restriction orders, the system laid down by sec 1 of the 1999 Act did not meet the second test in *Winterwerp* in D's case as he was subject to a restriction direction, not a restriction order, and that for this reason the section was incompatible with art 5(1)(e).

[34] At first sight it might seem odd to hold that a provision was outside the legislative competence of the Scottish Parliament because the class of persons to whom it applied included a single individual with whose Convention rights, in contrast to all other members of that class, it was incompatible. But I think that this is the inevitable consequence of the restriction which sec 29(2)(d) has imposed on its legislative competence. If the class of persons to whom the provision is to apply is defined too widely, so that it includes any one or more persons who ought not to be there because to include them would be incompatible

with their Convention rights, the provision as a whole must be held to be outside the legislative competence of the Parliament. It is, of course, an overriding requirement that those who seek to challenge a provision on the ground of an incompatibility with the Convention rights must satisfy the victim test in sec 100(1) of the Scotland Act 1998. But, provided this test is satisfied, it is open to any individual who claims that the provision is incompatible with his Convention rights to challenge its legislative competence on this ground irrespective of whether anyone else is affected by the provision in this way. It is fundamental to a proper understanding of this new system to appreciate that the Convention exists to protect the fundamental rights and freedoms of each and every individual. This is not a situation in which a solution that is good for most people must be accepted as good for everybody.

[35] Appreciating that it would not be in the public interest for sec 1 of the 1999 Act to be struck down simply because it was incompatible with D's Convention rights, senior counsel suggested that an order should be made under sec 102(2)(b) of the Scotland Act 1998 suspending the effect of the decision for a period of three months to enable the Scottish Parliament to correct the defect which he had identified. If the only solution to the problem he has raised was to hold that sec 1 was invalid on the ground that it was outside the Parliament's legislative competence, I would have thought it appropriate to make such an order in this case.

[36] But it is only if the legislation cannot be read and given effect by reading it as narrowly as is required for it to be within competence that the question can arise as to whether it should be held to be outside competence. So the first point to be addressed under the system which the Scotland Act 1998 lays down is how the legislation ought to be interpreted. I think that the solution to the problem which has been raised by D's case is to be found by making use of the interpretative obligation which is laid down by sec 101(2) of the Act, bearing in mind the observations which I made in *R. v Lambert* [2001] 3 W.L.R. 206, paras 78–81 as to how the corresponding obligation in sec 3(1) of the Human Rights Act 1998 ought to be used.

[37] The word 'public' in the phrase 'in order to protect the public from serious harm' in each of the various amendments included in sec 1 of the 1999 Act is capable of meaning either the public in general or a section of the public, as the context requires. In D's case, there is no question of his coming into contact with the public in general as he would be remitted to prison in the event of his discharge from hospital. But the persons with whom he would be liable to come in contact in a prison may be regarded as a section of the public. They include prison officers, other inmates and a variety of people who visit prisons for religious, educational, social work or other purposes. Read in this way, the effect of the amendments introduced by sec 1 of the 1999 Act is to require the sheriff or the Scottish Ministers, as the case may be, to be satisfied in D's case that it is necessary for him to be detained in a hospital to protect that section of the public from serious harm.

[38] In my opinion, on this narrow interpretation of the word 'public', the amendments introduced by sec 1 of the 1999 Act are consistent with the second *Winterwerp* test in D's case, as there would be no element of arbitrariness in a decision that the risk of serious harm to that section of the public warranted his compulsory confinement in a hospital. It could not be said that his continued detention in the state hospital was disproportionate to the legitimate aim of protecting that section of the public from serious harm. But it must also follow that, if the sheriff or the Scottish Ministers are not satisfied that it is necessary for D to continue to be detained in a hospital to protect that section of the public from serious harm, he will be entitled to be transferred back to prison if the psychiatric evidence shows that his mental condition is not treatable.

Compatibility with article 5(4) generally

[39] The function of art 5(4) was explained by the court in *Winterwerp v The Netherlands*, para 55, where it was said that the very nature of the deprivation of liberty under consideration in art 5 would appear to require a review of lawfulness at reasonable intervals. In

para 58 the court said, in the case of the special category of the detention of persons of unsound mind, the absolute minimum for a judicial procedure was the right of the individual to present his own case and to challenge the medical and social evidence adduced in support of his detention. Thus, the domestic remedy available under art 5(4) should enable judicial review at reasonable intervals of the conditions which are essential for the lawful detention of a person on the ground of unsoundness of mind: *X. v United Kingdom*, paras 52, 53; *Ashingdane v United Kingdom*, para 52. The review must encompass the lawfulness of the detention under art 5(1)(e) as well as its lawfulness under domestic law.

[40] The appellants maintained that the review provisions now contained in secs 64(A1) and 64(B1) of the 1984 Act as amended by sec 1 of the 1999 Act were incompatible with art 5(4) as they did not require a review of whether the grounds which made their detention lawful under art 5(1)(e) existed or continued to exist. Senior counsel for A said it was necessary for the review to include a consideration of the therapeutic element. That argument loses its validity if, as I would hold, it is not a necessary condition of the lawfulness of their detention on Convention grounds that the mental disorder from which they are suffering should be treatable. But there remain senior counsel's broader arguments, which were (1) that the introduction of the overriding test of public safety enables the appellants to continue to be detained without there being any review of the lawfulness of their continued detention on the basis on which they were originally admitted and detained, and (2) that when he is applying the public safety test the sheriff is not conducting a review but exercising the function of a primary decision maker.

[41] In my opinion the answer to the first argument lies in the fact that the domestic law has been changed since the appellants were originally admitted and detained. As senior counsel for the Scottish Ministers said, the lawfulness of the detention must be assessed at the time of the assessment. The original basis on which the appellants were admitted was that, as required by sec 17 of the 1984 Act, they were suffering from a mental disorder which was treatable. Treatability remained a condition of their detention in hospital until the law was changed by sec 1 of the 1999 Act. The effect of that change is that they are now subject to a further and overriding condition which prevents their release, irrespective of whether their mental condition remains treatable, if the Scottish Ministers can show that it is necessary to protect the public from serious harm that they be detained in a hospital. For reasons already given, I consider that this condition is compatible with the three tests which were identified in *Winterwerp*. So their continued detention on this ground is lawful in terms of both domestic law and the requirements of the Convention.

[42] As for the second argument, art 5(4) does of course require judicial review at reasonable intervals of the question whether the appellants' continued detention in a hospital is still necessary on public safety grounds. On one view a decision by the sheriff that a patient must continue to be detained in a hospital on public safety grounds is that of a primary decision maker. But the context in which that decision is made is one where the patient in question is already the subject of a restriction order or a restriction direction made on grounds of public safety. It is also one in which the Scottish Ministers are continuing to detain the patient in the light of the reports on his condition prepared under sec 62(2) of the 1984 Act by the responsible medical officer at regular intervals. In this context the exercise which the sheriff is required to conduct by secs 64(A1) and 64(B1) at reasonable intervals is one which can properly be described as a review. It is a review of the patient's continued detention in the light of the new rules which have been introduced on public safety grounds by the Scottish Parliament. I would hold that it is not incompatible with art 5(4).

Conclusion

[47] For these reasons ... I would hold that sec 1 of the 1999 Act is neither in whole nor in part outwith the legislative competence of the Scottish Parliament in terms of sec 29(1) and 29(2)(d) of the Scotland Act 1998. I would dismiss all three appeals."

Two points of significance emerge from the foregoing case. First, it reveals the extent to which the domestic courts are constrained by the jurisprudence of the Strasbourg Court. It is particularly important that the latter is followed closely, in view of the likelihood that government departments will be guided by the jurisprudence when framing legislation. However, it is to be noted that there is no measure in the Scotland Act equivalent to the Human Rights Act, s.2. This provides that the courts are to have regard to but are not bound by the Strasbourg jurisprudence. Nevertheless, "the Scottish courts have been fully prepared to apply ECHR case law in delimiting what constitutes competent behaviour by the Executive in terms of s.57(2) of the [Scotland Act]": S. Tierney, "Devolution Issues and s. 2(1) of the Human Rights Act 1998" [2000] E.H.R.L.R. 380. The second point relates to Lord Hope's bold declaration that both ministerial statements *and* presiding officer statements are merely "statements of opinion which do not bind the judiciary". These are statements—particularly that of the presiding officer—which it might be thought deserve some respect. It is of course much too early to be able to identify a coherent theory on the part of the courts to attempts to challenge the primary legislation of the Scottish Parliament. However, the cases which are beginning to emerge nevertheless reveal more than a hint "at a general reluctance on the part of the courts to interfere with legislation passed by the Scottish Parliament" (S. Tierney, "Constitutionalising the Role of the Judge" (2001) 5 Edin. L.R. 49 at 71). The following decision of Lord Nimmo Smith is a particularly sensitive and persuasive attempt to determine the proper role of the courts when presented with a challenge to primary legislation.

<h2 style="text-align:center">Adams v The Scottish Ministers
2003 S.L.T. 366</h2>

The Protection of Wild Mammals (Scotland) Act 2002 makes it a criminal offence to engage in mounted fox hunting with dogs, or to permit land or dogs to be used for this activity. The first petitioner (Adams) was a self-employed manager of foxhounds for the Duke of Buccleuch, while the others were landowners, farmers and unincorporated bodies (such as the Fife Hunt, the Buccleuch Hunt Supporters Club, the Jedforest Hunt, the Countryside Alliance and the Master of Foxhounds Association). They challenged the validity of the Act on the ground that it was incompatible with arts 8 and/or 14 of, and/or art.1 of the First Protocol to the ECHR. The petitioners failed.

LORD NIMMO SMITH:

"Introduction
[1] This application for judicial review raises important issues about the legislative competence of the Scottish Parliament and the relationship between this court, the Parliament and the executive in respect of legislation enacted by the Parliament. It was described to me by counsel for the Lord Advocate as the first challenge in the courts to an Act of the Scottish Parliament in which petitioners who (either in person or through representative organisations) actively campaigned against and made representations about the policy of the legislation during its progress through the Parliament seek to continue the debate about that policy through the courts after Royal Assent has been given...

The discretionary area of judgment of the Scottish Parliament
...[92] Having considered the authorities to which reference was made, I find that what appears to me to be the most correct and helpful expression in considering the extent to which this court will defer to the Scottish Parliament, whose act is said to be incompatible with the Convention, is the 'discretionary area of judgment' recognised by Lord Hope in *Kebilene* [2000] 2 A.C. 326 and Lord Bingham in *Brown v Stott*, 2001 S.L.T. 59...
Counsel for the petitioners recognised that in principle the prevention of cruelty to animals is capable of amounting to a legitimate aim of legislation. This may be regarded as having traditionally fallen within the constitutional responsibility of the legislature. There

has for many years been legislation having as its aim, or one of its aims, the prevention of cruelty to animals, and such legislation makes provision *inter alia* for the species of animals that may be killed, the methods by which they may be hunted and otherwise treated, and so on. The enacting of such legislation necessarily involves the making of moral judgments. There is no doubt that there is considerable public controversy about questions such as whether mounted foxhunting with dogs should be prohibited; this is reflected in the whole history of the attempts, ultimately successful in Scotland, to introduce legislation having this effect. Issues of this kind are, in general, recognised as being more appropriate for decision by a democratically elected representative legislature than by a court. I have already discussed the position of the Scottish Parliament as a legislature having power to pass Acts having the character of public general statutes. This, moreover, is an area in which the Parliament required to strike a balance between the aim of the legislation and the interests of those affected by it; the Convention rights relied upon by the petitioners require to be weighed against the public interest. To regulate the way in which animals may be hunted and killed appears to me to be far more within the constitutional responsibility of the Parliament as the elected legislature than within the constitutional responsibility of the courts. All of these considerations appear to me to point to its being appropriate for this court to defer to a greater rather than to a lesser extent to the Scottish Parliament in respect of legislation such as the Protection of Wild Mammals Act. Moreover, this is not an area where the subject matter lies more readily within the actual or potential expertise of the courts: the making of a moral judgment is more suitable for a legislature than for a court, and the Scottish Parliament has procedures which enabled it to obtain such evidence as it thought appropriate in order to make the judgment. In that the Parliament took it upon itself to form judgments as to whether mounted foxhunting with dogs is a sport, whether it can be described as cruel, whether it can be distinguished from other methods of controlling fox numbers in terms of the efficiency, the relative suffering of the fox and so on, these all appear to me to fall within the discretionary area of judgment to which the court should defer. It follows that if and insofar as a balancing exercise requires to be carried out, the prohibition of mounted foxhunting with dogs is capable of being regarded as necessary in a democratic society for the protection of morals (art 8(2)) and necessary in accordance with the general interest (the second paragraph of art 1 of the First Protocol). I shall examine questions of proportionality in my discussion of each of these provisions...

Article 8 of the Convention

...[102] In my opinion, on the facts of the present case as averred by the petitioners and as discussed in Dr Marvin's report, art 8 is not engaged, because mounted foxhunting with dogs is not an activity which falls within the concept of private life as explained in the European jurisprudence. While Mr Adams's tied house is clearly his home, the prohibition on mounted foxhunting with dogs will have, at most, a consequential rather than a direct effect on it, if his employers decide to terminate his employment, and the tied house that goes with it. I do not regard this as interference with his house within the meaning of art 8. I do not regard the land owned by Mr Murray, Mr Holman-Baird and Mr Scott Plummer as being the 'home' of any of them within the meaning of the article. To deal with the second point first, it is clear from the averments which I quote in para 106 about the extent of the land owned by each of them that each owns a large estate with ample space for a variety of open air activities to be carried on, well away from their houses. No doubt the concept of 'home' is a flexible one, depending on the circumstances of the case, but the principal connotation is of a person's dwellinghouse or habitation and its immediate surroundings. It is only in an extended sense, which I do not believe is the sense used in the European jurisprudence, that it can apply to a large estate.

[103] Foxhunting appears to me to have no characteristic that would bring it within the concept of private life. It is carried on in the open air. It involves a fairly large number of participants. It is open to all comers and is thus inclusive rather than exclusive. It may be carried on, principally at least, on private land rather than on public roads, but it is private

land to which all who wish to participate are admitted for the occasion. It constitutes a spectacle for them as well as for those who use the public roads to follow the hunt. It is, I believe, because of these features that counsel for the petitioners thought it necessary to place so much emphasis on Dr Marvin's discussion of the social aspects of foxhunting. These very aspects appear to me to emphasise the public rather than the private nature of the activity, because its social consequences are so diffuse. As it was put in *Botta v Italy* (1998) 26 E.H.R.R. 241, foxhunting gives rise to interpersonal relations of such broad and indeterminate scope that it cannot be described as the private life of its participants. It goes well beyond the 'certain degree' contemplated in *Niemietz v Germany* (1992) 16 E.H.R.R. 97, and cannot be regarded as falling with the 'personal sphere' recognised by the European Court of Human Rights.

[104] If I had had to go on to consider the application of art 8(2), I would have taken account of the considerations which I have already mentioned in my discussion of the area of discretionary judgment of the Scottish Parliament: see para 92. I would also have taken account, in considering the question of proportionality, of the fact that the legislation goes no further than to prohibit the method of hunting and killing foxes which the Parliament has decided to characterise as cruel and less efficient than other methods, while providing exceptions for those other methods.

Article 1 of the First Protocol
... [129] To deal with the position of Mr Adams first, it is in my opinion sufficiently clearly averred that his livelihood as a self employed manager of foxhounds, and the tied house that goes with it, are possessions within the meaning of art 1 of the First Protocol. The clearest authority which leads me to this conclusion is *Tre Traktörer Aktiebolag v Sweden* (1989) 13 E.H.R.R. 309, with which *Karni v Sweden* (1988) 55 D.R. 157 appears to me to be consistent. The issue does not appear to me to be so much one of loss of future profits, or loss of goodwill, as the loss simply of an opportunity to make a living by pursuing a particular activity. Mr Adams's economic interest in acting as a self employed manager of foxhounds appears to me to be as much a 'possession' as similar interests in operating a licensed restaurant or in carrying on medical practice. In my opinion, therefore, to the extent that the legislation may have the direct, and not merely consequential, effect of preventing Mr Adams from engaging in an activity in which he has hitherto engaged and from earning a living from day to day by practising the appropriate skills, it is sufficiently relevantly averred that the legislation has the effect of controlling the use of this possession. In so far as the tied house forms part of his emoluments, it may be regarded as a tangible demonstration that this possession is a current asset. Accordingly, I regard the Wild Mammals Act as having the effect of controlling the use of this possession. The same, in my opinion, applies to the hounds. On the basis of the authorities referred to above, I regard the prohibition on their being used for a particular purpose as a control of use, rather than *de facto* expropriation: no rights in relation to the hounds are transferred or otherwise extinguished.

[130] It is next necessary to consider the balancing exercise provided by the second paragraph of the article. As previously discussed in para 92, it was in my opinion within the discretionary area of judgment of the Scottish Parliament to decide to prohibit mounted foxhunting with dogs. Legislation having this effect has been in prospect for some time. It prohibits certain acts. It does not transfer any right to the state or to anyone else. Mr Adams may currently earn his livelihood from this particular method of hunting and killing foxes, but it is by no means certain that he will cease to be employed, or in any event will be unable to continue to earn his living by using skills which he uses at present. The control on the use of land does not affect any activity which is said to be central to its economic exploitation. There is no averment that there will be a loss in the value of the land, or the income derived therefrom, that will be directly rather than consequentially attributable to the prohibition of mounted foxhunting with dogs. There is no certainty that the hounds will be put down, and if they are it will be as a result of a decision made by their owners. Leaving sentiment aside, the hounds are no different from specialised tools. There is no

averment, in any event, of the economic value of the hounds. In short, there is no identifiable financial loss in respect of the matters founded upon by the petitioners for which
compensation might be expected."

Notwithstanding the decision of Lord Nimmo Smith, a second challenge to the Protection of
Wild Mammals (Scotland) Act 2002 was made in *Whaley v Lord Advocate*, 2004 S.L.T. 424. On
this occasion, the challenge was broadened to include claims that the Act violated a number of
international treaties by which the United Kingdom was bound, as well as a breach of Arts 9, 10
and 11 of the ECHR. The treaties in question were: the Rio Declaration on Environment and
Development of 1992, the Rio Convention on Bio Diversity of 1992, the Final Act of the
Helsinki Conference on Security and Cooperation in Europe of 1975, the United Nations
International Covenant on Economic Social and Cultural Rights of 1966, the United Nations
International Covenant on Civil and Political Rights with the Optional Protocol of 1966, and
the Universal Declaration of Human Rights of 1948. However, in an impressive judgment of
some considerable length and learning, this challenge also failed. According to Lord Brodie, the
court could not grant a declaration of incompatibility as between the Protection of Wild
Mammals Act and the international obligations of the United Kingdom. This does not mean
that these treaties are not relevant in the construction of Convention rights, and indeed Lord
Brodie strongly resisted an argument for the Lord Advocate that the courts were not equipped
to deal with such treaties; but it does mean that they cannot be enforced in the Scottish courts as
free standing obligations. It was also acknowledged, however, that "the Scottish Parliament,
unlike the Westminster Parliament, is not sovereign. Unlike the Westminster Parliament (except
where the matter is subject to Community law), the Scottish Parliament is therefore under legal
control". However, like Lord Nimmo Smith before him, Lord Brodie made clear that "where
what is under consideration is a conscious decision by the democratically elected Parliament in a
matter which came to turn on moral judgments, it is appropriate that the court, in exercise of its
purely supervisory jurisdiction, should accord considerable deference to such judgments as the
Parliament has made". In taking this view he rejected the audacious arguments of the huntsmen:

> "I must make it clear that I reject, as entirely irrelevant, the considerations urged on me by
> Mr Friend in support of his motion that I allow a second hearing, that there was no upper
> chamber in the Scottish Parliament, and that the Rural Affairs Committee of the Parlia-
> ment had recommended that the Bill which was enacted as the Protection of Wild
> Mammals Act be not passed ... The Scottish Parliament is constituted as it is constituted.
> Neither are its powers reduced nor are the powers of the court increased by the fact that the
> Parliament is a unicameral rather than a bicameral body. The court does not, as Mr Friend
> submitted it did, 'serve the function of an upper chamber'. That is not a power conferred
> upon the court but, in any event, 'serve the function of an upper chamber' is an entirely
> meaningless expression when used of a unicameral institution. No criticism is made in this
> petition of the procedures by which the Protection of Wild Mammals Act was enacted. The
> Parliament was entitled to reject the recommendations of the Rural Affairs Committee. In
> any event, in terms of section 28 (5) of the Scotland Act, the validity of an Act of the
> Scottish Parliament is not affected by any invalidity in the proceedings of the Parliament
> leading to its enactment."

V. HUMAN RIGHTS AND THE SCOTTISH EXECUTIVE

In addition to the restraints on the Scottish Parliament, there are also constraints on the Scottish
Executive. As already pointed out in Ch.2, s.57(2) of the Scotland Act 1998 provides that:

> "A member of the Scottish Executive has no power to make any subordinate legislation, or
> to do any other act, so far as the legislation or act is incompatible with any of the Con-
> vention rights or with Community law."

An exception is made in s.57(3) for acts of the Lord Advocate in prosecuting any offence, or in his or her capacity as head of the systems of criminal prosecution and investigation of deaths in Scotland. However, the exception applies only in relation to acts which are covered by the Human Rights Act 1998, s.6 which applies only to circumstances where a public authority is required to act in a particular way being directed to do so by primary legislation. Before examining two of the key cases on s.57(2), it is to be noted that s.58 of the Scotland Act provides that the Secretary of State for Scotland may give directions to a member of the Scottish Executive, requiring him or her to comply with Britain's international obligations.

Brown v Stott
2001 S.L.T. 59

The respondent was prosecuted for two offences: theft; and driving a car after consuming excessive alcohol, contrary to s.5(1)(a) of the Road Traffic Act 1988. She indicated her intention to plead not guilty to both charges. On July 1, 1999 the respondent gave written notice of her intention to raise a devolution issue under s.98 of and Sch.6 to the Scotland Act 1998. The issue was whether, compatibly with the respondent's rights under Art.6 of the European Convention on Human Rights, the Procurator Fiscal at Dunfermline, as prosecutor, could rely at trial on the respondent's admission compulsorily obtained under s.172(2)(a) of the 1988 Act. This requires the person keeping a vehicle to give information about the driver on request by the police. It is an offence under s.172(3) to fail to provide the information. The point was dismissed by the sheriff, but accepted on appeal by the High Court of Justiciary which declared that the Procurator Fiscal had no power to lead and rely on evidence of the admission which she had been compelled to make under s.172(2)(a) of the 1988 Act. The High Court took the view that the admission made under s.172 violated the right against self-incrimination which the High Court thought to be part and parcel of the right to silence. The Privy Council reversed the decision of the High Court. Here we are concerned only with whether the matter raised a devolution issue, and we return to the substantive points in the case in Ch.5.

LORD HOPE OF CRAIGHEAD: "This is an appeal under para 13(a) of sched 6 to the Scotland Act 1998, with leave of the High Court of Justiciary, against a determination of a devolution issue by that Court. Its determination took the form of a declarator that, in the circumstances of this case, the procurator fiscal had no power when he was prosecuting the respondent on a charge of driving after consuming an excess of alcohol under sec 5(1) of the Road Traffic Act 1988 to lead and rely on evidence of an admission which the respondent was compelled to make under sec 172(2)(a) of that Act that she had been the driver of a motor vehicle at or about 2.30 am on 3 June 1999 which was parked in the car park of the Asda Superstore at the Halbeath Retail Park in Dunfermline.

Is the issue raised a 'Devolution Issue'?
It is necessary to consider first whether the issue in this case raises a devolution issue within the meaning of para 1 of sched 6 to the 1998 Act. This is because the jurisdiction which has been conferred upon the Judicial Committee under sched 6 of the Act is limited to the determination of devolution issues as defined in that paragraph: see paras 10, 11, 12 and 13 of the schedule. There was a difference of view in the courts below on this point. The sheriff refused to hold that the minute lodged by the respondent's agent had raised a devolution issue. But in the High Court the Solicitor General did not seek to support the sheriff's reasoning. The Lord Justice General (Rodger) described that reasoning as manifestly untenable. He expressed his own conclusion on the point in these words (p 331C): 'I need therefore say no more about it except to confirm that the minute discloses a sharp devolution issue in terms of para 1(d) of sched 6 to the Scotland Act 1998'.
Doubts as to the soundness of that view and of observations to the like effect in other cases in the High Court of Justiciary were raised by their Lordships in the course of the

hearing by the Judicial Committee of the appeals in *Montgomery v HM Advocate*, 2001 S.L.T. 37, the reasons for decision in which were delivered on 19 October 2000. In the event, the Board were able to dispose of those appeals without coming to a concluded view on the point. As Lord Slynn of Hadley observed at p 39, all parties were prepared to argue the case on the assumption that it was a devolution issue and, indeed, all parties argued that it was. But it is unsatisfactory that this important issue should be left unresolved. In the present case their Lordships have had the advantage of detailed submissions from, on the one hand, the Solicitor General who has contended that no devolution issue has been raised and, on the other, the Advocate General who has contended the contrary. Counsel for the respondent adopted the submissions that were advanced by the Advocate General. So I believe that it is now possible for the Board, having heard argument on both sides, to reach a decision on the matter. It is important, in the interests of certainty, that it should now do so.

The two competing arguments may be summarised as follows. On the one hand there is the argument which the Solicitor General advanced with reference to the wording of art 6(1) of the Convention and the observations in *Montgomery v HM Advocate* of Lord Hoffmann. On the other there is the argument advanced by the Advocate General with reference to the wording of the Scotland Act 1998 and my own observations in that case. The essential point of difference between these two arguments is whether the solution to the problem lies simply in the opening words of art 6(1) of the European Convention for the Protection of Human Rights and Fundamental Freedoms ('the Convention') which describe the Convention right to a fair trial, or whether it lies in the provisions of the Scotland Act 1998 which describe the functions of the Lord Advocate as a member of the Scottish Executive and provide a system for the determination of questions which arise in proceedings before a court or tribunal whether he has purported to act or proposes to act outside his powers under that Act.

The position which was contended for by the Solicitor General was that the act of leading and relying upon the evidence of the admission could not of itself cause any unfair determination of the charge within the meaning of art 6(1). The prosecutor's act was not incompatible with the respondent's right to a fair hearing. It was for the court to determine whether or not the evidence should be admitted, so it was only at the stage of the determination of the matter by the court that the question of fairness would arise. If the evidence was admitted the respondent would be entitled then to argue that the court, as a public authority within the meaning of sec 6(1) of the Human Rights Act 1998, had acted in a way that was incompatible with her Convention right. She would be entitled to seek a remedy under that Act by appealing against her conviction on the basis of that evidence. But that would not raise a devolution issue within the meaning of para 1(d) of sched 6, for the obvious reason that the court is not a member of the Scottish Executive.

The position which was contended for by the Advocate General was that the act of the prosecutor in maintaining the prosecution and inviting the court to rely upon the evidence was outwith the powers of the Lord Advocate as a member of the Scottish Executive because it was incompatible, within the meaning of sec 57(2) of the Scotland Act 1998, with the respondent's Convention rights. While the court had the primary responsibility to ensure that the respondent had a fair trial, the effect of the Scotland Act 1998 was that this was also a responsibility of the prosecutor. The importance of this division of responsibility was underlined by the fact that, prior to the coming into force of the Human Rights Act 1998 on 2 October 2000, the only way of safeguarding a person's Convention right to a fair trial under the devolution settlement was by challenging the acts of the prosecutor. Parliament had chosen to give effect to the international obligations of the State under the Convention when it enacted the Scotland Act 1998 by imposing corresponding limits on the competence of the Scottish Parliament and the powers of the Scottish Executive. The system for the determination of devolution issues which was laid down in that Act was designed to ensure that a remedy was available in domestic law for any infringement of a person's Convention rights as soon as the relevant provisions of the Scotland Act 1998 were brought into force on 6 May 1999.

For the reasons which I expressed more fully in my judgment in *Montgomery v HM Advocate* I consider that the solution to the problem is to be found in the provisions of the Scotland Act 1998. The approach which that Act has taken to the question as to how best to ensure that effect is given under the devolved system to the Convention rights is that the right of the accused to receive a fair trial is a responsibility of the Lord Advocate in the prosecution of offences as well as of the court. I base this view on an analysis of the provisions of that Act. It is of cardinal importance to a proper understanding of the point to appreciate the overall context in which the relevant provisions were enacted. At the heart of the whole question lies the scheme which Parliament has constructed for the devolution of legislative and executive competence to Scotland from Westminster.

Article 13 of the Convention provides that everyone whose rights and freedoms as set forth in the Convention are violated shall have an effective remedy before a national authority. This article is not one of the Convention rights to which effect is given by the Human Rights Act 1998, but it has not been overlooked. The reason which was given for its omission from the articles set out in sched 1 to that Act was that secs 7 to 9 of the Act were intended to lay down an appropriate remedial structure for giving effect to the Convention rights as defined by sec 1(1) of the Act. The State's obligation to provide an effective remedy before a national tribunal in the event of a violation of the Convention rights also forms an important part of the background to the devolution legislation. The structure of the devolved system of government which is set out in the Scotland Act 1998 takes account of the State's obligations under the Convention in the same way as it takes account of its obligations in Community law. In both respects Parliament has chosen to legislate in a way which ensures that those obligations are respected both by the Scottish Parliament and the Scottish Executive by limiting their competence. It has also chosen to ensure that questions which arise as to whether the Parliament or the Executive have acted or are proposing to act in a way that is incompatible with any of the Convention rights or with Community law may be resolved, as devolution issues, under the system laid down in sched 6. The same system has been adopted for the determination of devolution issues under the Government of Wales Act 1998 and the Northern Ireland Act 1998. These systems seek to achieve uniformity in the determination of these issues throughout all parts of the United Kingdom by reserving to the Judicial Committee of the Privy Council the power of final decision in all these matters.

One of the matters which was devolved to the Scottish Parliament and to the Scottish Executive was the system of criminal prosecution for which the Lord Advocate is responsible. The Scotland Act 1998 provides that the Lord Advocate is a member of the Scottish Executive: sec 44(1)(c). It contains provisions which are designed to ensure his independence as public prosecutor. Section 29(2)(e) restricts the legislative competence of the Parliament in regard to any provision in any Act which would remove him from his position as head of that system. Section 48(5) provides that any decision by him in that capacity is to be taken by him independently of any other person. Section 52(6) ensures that the functions which were exercised by him immediately before he ceased to be a Minister of the Crown on the coming into force of the Scotland Act 1998 are exercisable only by the Lord Advocate. It is in the light of these provisions that sec 57(3) falls to be read. It qualifies the position of the Lord Advocate in regard to the general restraint on his competence in sec 57(2), which provides that a member of the Scottish Executive has no power to do any act which is incompatible with any of the Convention rights or with Community law. Section 57(3)(a) provides that that subsection does not apply to an act of the Lord Advocate 'in prosecuting any offence' which, because of sec 6(2) of the Human Rights Act 1998, is not unlawful under subsec (1) of that section.

Alongside these provisions are the powers which are given to the Advocate General for Scotland, for whose appointment provision was made by sec 87 of the Scotland Act 1998. The Advocate General for Scotland is a Minister of the Crown. As such she is a member of the United Kingdom government. Her functions include that of safeguarding the interests of the United Kingdom in the operation of the devolution settlement. Those interests include that of seeing to the fulfilment of the State's international obligations, in particular those which it owes as a Contracting State under art 13 of the Convention. That is the purpose of the powers that she has been given by paras 4 and 33 of sched 6 to institute proceedings for the determination of a devolution issue and to require a court or tribunal to refer a devolution issue to the Judicial Committee. In the exercise of these powers she is entitled to exercise her own judgment independently of, and even contrary to, the views of the Lord Advocate.

It seems to me to be clear from these provisions that it was the intention of Parliament that acts of the Lord Advocate in prosecuting offences should be subject to judicial control under the devolved system. In his case, as in the case of any other member of the Scottish Executive, the question whether or not an act or proposed act of his or of any prosecutor for whose acts he is responsible is within his competence depends upon the application to that act of the concept of compatibility. If the act or proposed act is 'incompatible' with any of the Convention rights it is outside his competence.

The opening words of art 6(1) provide: 'In the determination ... of any criminal charge against him, everyone is entitled to a fair and public hearing'. But the relevant question, for the purposes of the system of devolution which has been constructed under United Kingdom domestic law, is not whether these words impose a correlative obligation on the Lord Advocate in his capacity as public prosecutor. If that were the sole question, there would be much force in the argument advanced by the Solicitor General that, as the determination during a criminal trial of the criminal charge in all its aspects is a matter for the court and not the prosecutor, the acts of the Lord Advocate in that capacity lie outside the scope of the article. But the test which sec 57(2) applies to his acts is not expressed in the language of obligation. It takes a broader and more inclusive form, as it requires that his acts must be compatible with any of the Convention rights. It is sufficient for this restraint on his powers to operate that his purported or proposed act is inconsistent with the obligations which the State has assumed under the Convention. The acts which he performs in the course of the trial when he is leading and founding upon evidence are brought by this means within the scope of the article.

It is sufficient to satisfy the test laid down in sched 6 that a devolution issue has 'arisen' for there to be a question as to whether or not a purported or proposed exercise of a function by a member of the Scottish Executive is incompatible with a Convention right. There is no need at this stage to inquire as to whether some other person or some other public authority, such as the court, also has responsibility for giving effect to the same Convention right. The fact that that other person or other public authority has the last word or has the power to intervene in such a way as to preserve or give effect to the Convention rights may enable the question as to incompatibility to be answered in the negative. It may be possible to reach that answer as a matter of relevancy or, without further inquiry, on agreed facts. But that is not to say that a devolution issue has not arisen. On the contrary, it is to answer the question that has been raised.

It is, of course, important to appreciate that the mere raising of a question will not be enough to satisfy the definition in para 1 of sched 6. Paragraph 2 of the schedule provides that a devolution issue shall not be taken to have arisen merely because of any contention of a party that appears to the court or tribunal to be frivolous or vexatious. Moreover, as the High Court of Justiciary has already held, it is not enough merely to assert that a devolution issue has arisen: *British Broadcasting Corporation, Petitioners (No 2)*, 2000 S.L.T. 260, per Lord Kirkwood. Sufficient detail must be given in support of that proposition to show that there is a point of substance that needs to be addressed. It may be clear from the detail that has been provided that the raising of the issue is premature, or it may be clear that the question which has been raised is not a devolution issue at all within the meaning of the paragraph. In the latter case it will be proper for the court or tribunal to say that, in the circumstances described, a devolution issue has not arisen without having to go so far as to describe the contention as frivolous or vexatious in terms of para 2 of the schedule. That was what the Board did in *Hoekstra v HM Advocate*, 2001 S.L.T. 28 when it refused the petitioners' application for special leave to appeal.

But that is not the situation in this case. The Lord Justice General dealt with this point when he said that, as the Solicitor General had indicated in deliberately unequivocal terms that it was the procurator fiscal's intention to lead the evidence of the respondent's reply under sec 172 and to rely on it in seeking a conviction, the evidence of her admission would constitute a significant element of the evidence showing that she had driven the car on the occasion in question. He said that for this reason it was convenient, in this particular case, to decide the devolution issue relating to this evidence before the trial. In my opinion this approach, with which I agree, serves to reinforce the point that a devolution issue has indeed been raised in this case which the Judicial Committee has power to determine under the jurisdiction that has been given to it by para 13(a) of the schedule.

I would hold therefore that the respondent's minute discloses a devolution issue which the Judicial Committee has power to determine."

This broad view of a devolution issue has meant that a wide range of issues are treated as devolution issues. They include:

- Indicting and continuing proceedings against the accused: *Montgomery v H M Advocate*, 2001 S.L.T 37.
- Continuing to prosecute the accused in a manner allegedly in breach of Convention rights: *Buchanan v McLean*, 2001 S.L.T. 780.
- Conducting and prosecuting proceedings before a temporary sheriff: *Millar v Dickson*, 2001 S.L.T. 988.
- Bringing a case against the accused to trial after an unreasonable delay: *Dyer v Wilson*, 2002 S.C. (P.C.) 113.
- Whether proceedings against the accused in the district court would infringe Convention rights: *Clark v Kelly*, 2003 S.L.T. 308.

Questions arise however about the overlap between the Scotland Act and the Human Rights Act. The right to challenge the prosecutor under the former was particularly important before the Human Rights Act 1998 came into force on October 2, 2000. This is because under that Act courts and tribunals are defined as public bodies which must comply with the Act (s.7). So in the conduct of its proceedings, a court must ensure that the parties appearing before it have a fair trial in accordance with art.6 of the Convention. However, as Lord Hope pointed out in *Brown*, until the Human Rights Act came into force "the only way of safeguarding a person's Convention right to a fair trial under the devolution settlement was by challenging the acts of the prosecutor". Following the introduction of the Human Rights Act the question then arose as to whether the accused could choose to enforce Convention rights under either the Scotland Act or the Human Rights Act. It has been pointed out that:

"Most practitioners appear to consider that parties have a choice of taking human rights points against Scottish Ministers or the Lord Advocate either under the Human Rights Act or under the Scotland Act. Furthermore, they consider that, when they raise proceedings under the Human Rights Act, this does not give rise to a devolution issue and therefore the special procedural provisions in Sch 6 to the Scotland Act and the relevant rules of court do not apply. This has considerable attractions, particularly in criminal proceedings, because it means that human rights issues can be raised and dealt with during the trial whereas, if they are treated as devolution issues, they would require to be raised and dealt with as preliminary issues and notification would have to be given to the Advocate General for Scotland .... As a result, the number of human rights issues which have been notified as devolution issues in criminal proceedings has dropped dramatically since 2 October [2000]." (I. Jamieson, "Relationship Between the Scotland Act and the Human Rights Act", 2001 S.L.T. 43.)

The following case gives further guidance on s.57(2), and also explores the relationship between the Scotland Act and the Human Rights Act in relation to the protection of Convention rights. It gives primacy to the former.

H M Advocate v R
2003 S.L.T. 4

The appellant had been charged with a number of offences of indecent conduct towards a number of girls. The girls had complained to the police in 1995, and the accused was cautioned and charged, but the Crown decided not to proceed because of a concern about the sufficiency of the evidence. After further allegations were made by other girls against the accused several years later, fresh charges were made in respect of these further allegations. The indictment also resurrected the 1995 allegations and included charges which were similar in terms to those which had been made then, with the prosecution due to commence on October 2, 2001. The accused claimed that the Lord Advocate had no authority to proceed with these charges because to do so would violate the accused's rights under Art.6 of the ECHR to be tried within a reasonable time. Lord Reed disagreed, as did the Criminal Appeal Court which gave leave to appeal to the Privy Council. By this time the minute had been amended to include an alternative submission that the Lord Advocate had no power to proceed under s.57(2) of the Scotland Act. In the Privy Council, a majority of 3:2 held that there was a breach of Art.6 and the charges against the accused were dismissed. An interesting (though for present purposes incidental) feature of the case is the fact that a majority of the Board in this case were Scottish judges (Lords Hope of Craighead, Clyde, and Rodger of Earlsferry). The two English judges dissented from a decision which provided a very robust defence of the rule in Scots law that requires trials to be started within a reasonable time.

LORD HOPE OF CRAIGHEAD:

"The issues
    33. The joint statement of facts and issues states that the following issues (which I have re-worded slightly) arise in this appeal:
    1. Whether the continuation of this prosecution by the Lord Advocate on charges 1 and 3 after a reasonable time has elapsed constitutes a violation of article 6(1).
    2. Whether, in view of section 57(2) of the Scotland Act 1998, the Lord Advocate still has power to prosecute the appellant on charges 1 and 3 after a reasonable time has elapsed.
    3. Assuming that the Lord Advocate does still have power to prosecute notwithstanding the elapse of a reasonable time, whether the remedy should nevertheless have been for the prosecution on charges 1 and 3 to be discontinued.
    4. Whether in any event the act of the Lord Advocate in continuing to prosecute the appellant after a reasonable time has elapsed constitutes an 'act' within the meaning of section 57(2) of the Scotland Act 1998.

An 'act' of the Lord Advocate?
    38. I propose to consider this issue first, as it is directed to what is in effect a preliminary issue. Its purpose is to challenge the proposition that the complaint which the appellant has made raises a devolution issue within the meaning of paragraph 1(d) of Schedule 6. If the Lord Advocate is right on this point, the appeal would have to be dismissed on the ground that the Judicial Committee does not have jurisdiction. The appellant's complaint that his Convention right has been violated would not be one that could be dealt with under Schedule 6 to the Scotland Act 1998.
    39. As the written case for the Lord Advocate explains, he seeks to restrict the ambit of the word 'act' in section 57(2) so that it excludes, in all but the rarest of cases, any act in prosecuting an offence which is carried out by him or on his authority. He contends that the word does not embrace any of the acts which are inherent in the proceedings themselves, such as serving an indictment, calling witnesses, lodging productions or inviting the court to take this or that procedural step. He bases this argument on two considerations. The first is that a broad construction of the word could lead to numerous points being taken as

devolution issues and to the Judicial Committee becoming the final court of appeal in a wide variety of Scottish criminal matters. The second is that it would duplicate the protection which is now afforded in Scots law in criminal cases by section 6(1) of the Human Rights Act 1998, in a manner which would be peculiar to Scotland. It is not to be found anywhere else in the United Kingdom, as the devolution arrangements for Wales and Northern Ireland in the Government of Wales Act 1998 and the Northern Ireland Act 1998 do not provide for the transfer of prosecution functions to the Welsh Assembly or to a Northern Ireland Minister. ...

44. Mr Davidson's argument [for the Lord Advocate] was that, on its proper construction, the word 'act' in section 57(2) was confined to the issuing of departmental circulars, guidelines, statements of practice and other documents. He pointed out that the first part of section 57(2) was concerned with the making of subordinate legislation. He said that in that context the words 'doing any other act' should be read as referring to acts of a legislative or administrative character in the promulgation of what might be conveniently described as soft law. He accepted that there would have to be strong indications from the context to justify giving such a restricted meaning to these words. But he said that it was clear from the context that the purpose of the subsection was to control the acts of the Scottish Executive, not to give rights to those who might claim to be the victim of a violation of their Convention rights. He also drew attention to the definition of 'devolution issue' in paragraph 1 of Schedule 6 to the Scotland Act. He said that it indicated that the primary concern of the Scotland Act was with functions and with devolved competence, and that an expansive meaning of the word 'act' was difficult to fit in with the mechanism which the Act had provided for the control of powers which were being exercised by the Scottish Executive. He maintained that protection against a violation of a person's Convention rights, and the remedies which were to be afforded to persons who claimed that their Convention rights had been, or were at risk of being, violated, were to be found not in that Act but in the Human Rights Act 1998.

45. I would reject these arguments. They fall into two parts, and I regard each of them as unsound. On the one hand there are indications within section 57 itself and elsewhere in the Scotland Act 1998 that the word 'act' does not have the restricted meaning which was contended for by Mr Davidson but is capable of extending to all acts performed by the Lord Advocate in the exercise of his functions as prosecutor. On the other there are the wider considerations as to the aims and function of the Scotland Act and its relationship with the Human Rights Act 1998 which are wholly inconsistent with Mr Davidson's argument that the Scotland Act is not concerned with the provision of remedies against violations of a person's Convention rights.

46. The fact that section 57(3)(a) provides that subsection (2) of that section does not apply to an act of the Lord Advocate 'in prosecuting any offence' which is not unlawful under section 6(1) of the Human Rights Act 1998 because of section 6(2) is in itself a powerful indication that the word 'act' in subsection (2) is not confined to acts which relate to the making of soft law. Mr Davidson was unable to explain what acts in the course of prosecuting an offence would fall within the restricted meaning of the word for which he contended. Nor did he explain why the word 'act' in section 57(2) should be given a narrower meaning than that which it has, according to his own argument, in section 6(1) of the Human Rights Act. That subsection makes it unlawful for a public authority to act in a way which is incompatible with a Convention right.

47. A further indication that the word 'act' is used in an unrestricted way in the Scotland Act 1998 is to be found in section 52(5), which provides that subsection (4) of that section which provides for acts or omissions of members of the Scottish Executive to be treated as acts of the Executive collectively does not apply in relation to the exercise of retained functions of the Lord Advocate. Among the retained functions of the Lord Advocate are the functions which he exercised as head of the system of criminal prosecution in Scotland prior to the coming into force of the relevant provisions of the Scotland Act. Section 52(5) indicates that things which the Lord Advocate does in the exercise of that function may

properly be described in this context as 'acts'. I do not see why the same word should be given a different meaning in section 57(2). I should add that I agree with my noble and learned friend Lord Rodger of Earlsferry, for the reasons he has given, that the term 'act' in section 57(2) does not include a failure to act. Section 57(2) does not mention an omission or a failure to act: contrast sections 52(4) and 100(4)(b) and paragraph 1(e) of Schedule 6, but compare the use of the word 'act' in section 50 and the word 'action' in section 58. It deals only with positive acts of the Lord Advocate. ...

50. As for the wider considerations as to the aims and functions of the Scotland Act, I would refer to what I said on this subject in *Montgomery v H M Advocate*, 2001 S.L.T. 37, 17G–19H and again, with the approval of all the other members of the Board, in *Brown v Stott*, 2001 S.L.T. 59. I do not think that it is possible to reconcile Mr Davidson's contention that the system for the protection of an accused person's Convention rights is to be found only in the Human Rights Act 1998 and not in the Scotland Act 1998 with the ordinary meaning of the words used in sections 57(2) and (3) and 100(1)(b) of the Scotland Act. Moreover the scheme of the Act seems to me to be clear. Although the Act was careful to provide in sections 52(5) and 53(2) that the retained functions of the Lord Advocate are to be exercisable only by him and not by the other Scottish Ministers, the restraint on his powers in section 57(2) extends to his retained functions as well as all the other functions which he may perform as a member of the Scottish Executive. This means, as Lord Rodger has explained, it is not open to an accused person who seeks to rely on his Convention rights against the Lord Advocate to pick and choose between the Scotland Act and the Human Rights Act. His challenge must be brought under the Scotland Act.

51. As I have just indicated, the prohibition from doing anything which is incompatible with the Convention rights and with Community law in section 57(2) has to be read with section 100, which seeks to ensure that Convention rights are protected by the Scotland Act in a manner which is consistent with the Human Rights Act. It provides that a person cannot bring proceedings in a court or tribunal on the ground that an act is incompatible with the Convention rights, or rely on any of the Convention rights in any such proceedings, unless he would be a victim for the purposes of article 34 of the Convention within the meaning of the Human Rights Act if proceedings in respect of the act were brought in the European Court of Human Rights. Among the proceedings which section 100(1)(b) contemplates are those in which an accused person complains that his Convention rights are being, or at risk of being, violated. There would have been no point in enacting this provision if, as Mr Davidson contended, the only way in which an accused person could make such a complaint was by invoking the provisions of the Human Rights Act. It points to the opposite conclusion, which is that it is under the provisions of the Scotland Act that he must seek his remedy.

52. For all these reasons I would hold that the proceedings about which the appellant complains in his devolution minute fall within the scope of section 57(2), as for the Lord Advocate to proceed to trial on charges 1 and 3 of the indictment in the exercise of his prosecution powers would amount to the doing by him of an act within the meaning of that subsection. I would also hold that the question whether the doing of that act in the exercise of his functions would be incompatible with the appellant's right to a hearing within a reasonable time under article 6(1) of the Convention is a devolution issue within the meaning of paragraph 1(d) of Schedule 6 to the Scotland Act."

Lord Hope then turned to the main issues in this case. He held that there had been a breach of Art.6. The remaining part of his judgment is reproduced in Ch.5, below.

These decisions on these two issues—what is an act of the Lord Advocate on the one hand and the appropriate manner for raising Convention concerns on the other—are significant in that they both serve to increase the powers of the Privy Council on Convention rights. Is there good cause for this power grab by the senior judges? As is suggested in the cases themselves, if these matters had been decided differently, it would have been necessary on the former point and possible on the latter point to raise Convention issues relating to Scottish criminal procedure under the Human Rights Act. Given that these issues would be raised in the context of criminal law matters, there would have been no appeal to the House of Lords. This would mean that the Scottish criminal courts would have had the final say on Convention rights as they applied in Scottish criminal cases. The final say would—of course—be subject to a right of individuals to complain to Strasbourg where it is alleged that the standards set by the domestic courts fell short of Convention standards. Although this would truly be bringing rights home, nevertheless it could lead to inconsistency in the treatment of human rights issues in the United Kingdom. This is because, apart from the absence of an appeal to the House of Lords, in criminal proceedings there is no appeal to the Privy Council except where a devolution issue is raised. However, such inconsistency will only be a problem if it is thought necessary or desirable that Convention rights should have the same application throughout the country. As it is a bitter disagreement has broken out between the Scots and English judges of the Privy Council on the application of Convention rights in a matter where Scots and English law diverge. We return to this in Ch.5. In the meantime, it is to be noted that it is thus a curious feature of devolution that Scottish criminal cases and Scottish criminal procedure is now subject to supervision by the old Imperial court.

VI. THE HUMAN RIGHTS ACT 1998

In addition to the Scotland Act and the obligations of the Scottish Parliament and the Scottish Executive, the legal status of the ECHR is enhanced also by the Human Rights Act 1998. This applies throughout the United Kingdom and has a number of potential implications for Scotland. These include legislation of the Westminster Parliament passed before and after devolution. In the case of pre-devolution legislation, the Act has implications for legislation applying specifically to Scotland, as well as for United Kingdom-wide legislation in terms of its application to Scotland. In the case of post-devolution legislation, the implications of the Act for Scots law will be confined to legislation dealing with reserved matters (such as immigration, employment law and national security). The Human Rights Act applies to Convention rights which are defined in s.1 to mean arts 2 to 12 of the Convention, as well as arts 1 to 3 of the First Protocol and arts 1 and 2 of the Sixth Protocol. These are to be "read with articles 16 to 18 of the Convention", and they are to have effect subject to any derogation or reservation (s.1). Section 2 of the Act requires the courts and tribunals, "when determining a question which has arisen in connection with a Convention right", to "take into account" any decision of the European Court of Human Rights, as well as any opinion or decision of the European Commission of Human Rights and the Committee of Ministers. However, the domestic courts are not bound to follow these decisions or opinions and may choose to apply Convention rights differently in their domestic context. But if they stray too far from the jurisprudence of the Strasbourg bodies, there is a possibility that the Strasbourg Court would find the United Kingdom in breach of the Convention.

Human Rights Act 1998

"Legislation

Interpretation of legislation.
    3.—(1) So far as it is possible to do so, primary legislation and subordinate legislation must be read and given effect in a way which is compatible with the Convention rights.
      (2) This section—
        (a) applies to primary legislation and subordinate legislation whenever enacted;
        (b) does not affect the validity, continuing operation or enforcement of any incompatible primary legislation; and

(c) does not affect the validity, continuing operation or enforcement of any incompatible subordinate legislation if (disregarding any possibility of revocation) primary legislation prevents removal of the incompatibility.

Declaration of incompatibility.

4.—(1) Subsection (2) applies in any proceedings in which a court determines whether a provision of primary legislation is compatible with a Convention right.

(2) If the court is satisfied that the provision is incompatible with a Convention right, it may make a declaration of that incompatibility.

(3) Subsection (4) applies in any proceedings in which a court determines whether a provision of subordinate legislation, made in the exercise of a power conferred by primary legislation, is compatible with a Convention right.

(4) If the court is satisfied—

(a) that the provision is incompatible with a Convention right, and

(b) that (disregarding any possibility of revocation) the primary legislation concerned prevents removal of the incompatibility,

it may make a declaration of that incompatibility.

(5) In this section 'court' means—

(a) the House of Lords;

(b) the Judicial Committee of the Privy Council;

(c) the Courts-Martial Appeal Court;

(d) in Scotland, the High Court of Justiciary sitting otherwise than as a trial court or the Court of Session;

(e) in England and Wales or Northern Ireland, the High Court or the Court of Appeal.

(6) A declaration under this section ('a declaration of incompatibility')—

(a) does not affect the validity, continuing operation or enforcement of the provision in respect of which it is given; and

(b) is not binding on the parties to the proceedings in which it is made."

Unlike the Scotland Act which enables the courts to strike down primary legislation of the Scottish Parliament, the Human Rights Act thus permits them only to interpret legislation of the Westminster Parliament consistently with Convention rights where it is possible to do so. However, this is by no means an insignificant power which makes nonsense of the duty of the courts to interpret legislation to give effect to the wishes of Parliament. As a result it is a power which has drawn a great deal of criticism from sceptics of Bill of Rights who contend that this is not the benign compromise that some contend. This is a matter to which we return in the next section. The power of the courts to declare primary legislation of the Westminster Parliament to be incompatible with Convention rights is also a significant power, placing the government under pressure to bring forward amending legislation, for the purposes of which an expedited parliamentary procedure is provided for urgent cases (s.10). Where a court is considering whether to make a declaration of incompatibility, the Crown must be informed, even though it is not a party to the proceedings (s.5(1)). Where a Minister of the Westminster Government or a member of the Scottish Executive have been informed, they are entitled to be joined in the proceedings (s.5(2)). Steps have been taken to help to ensure that it will not be necessary for the courts to intervene in this way, at least in relation to legislation passed after the Human Rights Act came into force. Thus all Bills must carry a statement on their face declaring that they are or are not compatible with Convention rights (s.19), while a new Joint Human Rights Committee has been established to enhance parliamentary scrutiny of legislation. However, apart from legislation, the Human Rights Act requires public authorities to comply with Convention rights, which means that British or United Kingdom public bodies can be restrained in the Scottish courts (s.6). These include bodies such as the public utility regulators, the Electoral Commission and ACAS. Unlike the Scotland Act which provides that the Scottish Executive has "no power" to do any act which is incompatible with Convention rights, the Human Rights Act provides that it is "unlawful" for a public authority to violate Convention rights.

Human Rights Act 1998

"Public authorities

Acts of public authorities.

6—(1) It is unlawful for a public authority to act in a way which is incompatible with a Convention right.

(2) Subsection (1) does not apply to an act if—

(a) as the result of one or more provisions of primary legislation, the authority could not have acted differently; or

(b) in the case of one or more provisions of, or made under, primary legislation which cannot be read or given effect in a way which is compatible with the Convention rights, the authority was acting so as to give effect to or enforce those provisions.

(3) In this section 'public authority' includes—

(a) a court or tribunal, and

(b) any person certain of whose functions are functions of a public nature,

but does not include either House of Parliament or a person exercising functions in connection with proceedings in Parliament.

(4) In subsection (3) 'Parliament' does not include the House of Lords in its judicial capacity.

(5) In relation to a particular act, a person is not a public authority by virtue only of subsection (3)(b) if the nature of the act is private.

(6) 'An act' includes a failure to act but does not include a failure to—

(a) introduce in, or lay before, Parliament a proposal for legislation; or

(b) make any primary legislation or remedial order.

Proceedings.

7—(1) A person who claims that a public authority has acted (or proposes to act) in a way which is made unlawful by section 6(1) may—

(a) bring proceedings against the authority under this Act in the appropriate court or tribunal, or

(b) rely on the Convention right or rights concerned in any legal proceedings,

but only if he is (or would be) a victim of the unlawful act.

(2) In subsection (1)(a) 'appropriate court or tribunal' means such court or tribunal as may be determined in accordance with rules; and proceedings against an authority include a counterclaim or similar proceedings.

(3) If the proceedings are brought on an application for judicial review, the applicant is to be taken to have a sufficient interest in relation to the unlawful act only if he is, or would be, a victim of that act.

(4) If the proceedings are made by way of a petition for judicial review in Scotland, the applicant shall be taken to have title and interest to sue in relation to the unlawful act only if he is, or would be, a victim of that act.

(5) Proceedings under subsection (1)(a) must be brought before the end of—

(a) the period of one year beginning with the date on which the act complained of took place; or

(b) such longer period as the court or tribunal considers equitable having regard to all the circumstances,

but that is subject to any rule imposing a stricter time limit in relation to the procedure in question.

(6) In subsection (1)(b) 'legal proceedings' includes—

(a) proceedings brought by or at the instigation of a public authority; and

(b) an appeal against the decision of a court or tribunal.

(7) For the purposes of this section, a person is a victim of an unlawful act only if he would be a victim for the purposes of Article 34 of the Convention if proceedings were

brought in the European Court of Human Rights in respect of that act.

(8) Nothing in this Act creates a criminal offence.

(9) In this section 'rules' means—

    (a) in relation to proceedings before a court or tribunal outside Scotland, rules made by the Lord Chancellor or the Secretary of State for the purposes of this section or rules of court,

    (b) in relation to proceedings before a court or tribunal in Scotland, rules made by the Secretary of State for those purposes, ...

(10) In making rules, regard must be had to section 9.

(11) The Minister who has power to make rules in relation to a particular tribunal may, to the extent he considers it necessary to ensure that the tribunal can provide an appropriate remedy in relation to an act (or proposed act) of a public authority which is (or would be) unlawful as a result of section 6(1), by order add to—

    (a) the relief or remedies which the tribunal may grant; or

    (b) the grounds on which it may grant any of them.

(12) An order made under subsection (11) may contain such incidental, supplemental, consequential or transitional provision as the Minister making it considers appropriate. . . .

Judicial remedies

8.—(1) In relation to any act (or proposed act) of a public authority which the court finds is (or would be) unlawful, it may grant such relief or remedy, or make such order, within its powers as it considers just and appropriate.

(2) But damages may be awarded only by a court which has power to award damages, or to order the payment of compensation, in civil proceedings.

(3) No award of damages is to be made unless, taking account of all the circumstances of the case, including—

    (a) any other relief or remedy granted, or order made, in relation to the act in question (by that or any other court), and

    (b) the consequences of any decision (of that or any other court) in respect of that act, the court is satisfied that the award is necessary to afford just satisfaction to the person in whose favour it is made.

(4) In determining—

    (a) whether to award damages, or

    (b) the amount of an award,

the court must take into account the principles applied by the European Court of Human Rights in relation to the award of compensation under Article 41 of the Convention.

(5) A public authority against which damages are awarded is to be treated—

    (a) in Scotland, for the purposes of section 3 of the Law Reform (Miscellaneous Provisions) (Scotland) Act 1940 as if the award were made in an action of damages in which the authority has been found liable in respect of loss or damage to the person to whom the award is made;

    (b) for the purposes of the Civil Liability (Contribution) Act 1978 as liable in respect of damage suffered by the person to whom the award is made.

(6) In this section—

'court' includes a tribunal;

'damages' means damages for an unlawful act of a public authority; and

'unlawful' means unlawful under section 6(1).

Judicial acts.

9.—(1) Proceedings under section 7(1)(a) in respect of a judicial act may be brought only—

    (a) by exercising a right of appeal;

    (b) on an application (in Scotland a petition) for judicial review; or

    (c) in such other forum as may be prescribed by rules.

(2) That does not affect any rule of law which prevents a court from being the subject of judicial review.

(3) In proceedings under this Act in respect of a judicial act done in good faith, damages may not be awarded otherwise than to compensate a person to the extent required by Article 5(5) of the Convention.

(4) An award of damages permitted by subsection (3) is to be made against the Crown; but no award may be made unless the appropriate person, if not a party to the proceedings, is joined.

(5) In this section—

'appropriate person' means the Minister responsible for the court concerned, or a person or government department nominated by him;

'court' includes a tribunal;

'judge' includes a member of a tribunal, a justice of the peace and a clerk or other officer entitled to exercise the jurisdiction of a court;

'judicial act' means a judicial act of a court and includes an act done on the instructions, or on behalf, of a judge; and

'rules' has the same meaning as in section 7(9)."

The Human Rights Act and the Common Law

The application of the Human Rights Act to the common law was considered in Karl Construction Ltd v Palisade Properties Ltd, *2002 S.L.T. 312, where in an important decision Lord Drummond Young held that the practice in the law of diligence of inhibition on the dependence of an action violated Art.1 of the First Protocol. Addressing wider questions Lord Drummond Young said:*

"[75] The Human Rights Act is not particularly helpful in determining the relationship of the Convention to the common law. Section 6(3)(a) states that a court is a 'public authority' for the purposes of section 6, and section 6(1) states that it is unlawful for a public authority to act in a way which is incompatible with a Convention right. It is therefore clear that a court is bound by the Convention to some extent. It has been suggested by at least one writer, Professor Sir William Wade (in a contribution to 'Constitutional Reform in the United Kingdom: Practice and Principles', edited by Beatson, Forsyth and Hare (Oxford, 1998), and an article, 'Horizons of Horizontality', (2000) 116 L.Q.R. 217) that the result is that a court must follow the Convention in any case where that there is a conflict between the common law and a Convention right. In my opinion that view is too extreme. In particular, it seems fundamentally at odds with the structure of the Human Rights Act, which does not make the Convention directly effective except in relation to public authorities. That limitation on direct effectiveness would not have been necessary if the Convention were intended to prevail over the common law in all cases; indeed, a wholly different structure would be expected if that were the intention of Parliament.

[76] The question thus arises as to how far the courts are bound by the Convention in common law matters. In my opinion the applicability of the Convention must extend at least to what may be described as the 'internal' processes of the court, as against the rights that individuals and other private legal persons have against one another as a matter of substantive law. Those 'internal' processes include the procedures that the court follows and, crucially, the remedies that the court makes available. I reach this conclusion because those are matters that involve the court's own processes. The statement in section 6(3)(a) that a court is a public authority must have some content, and the minimum content that can be given is in my opinion the subjection of the court's procedures and remedies to the Convention....

[77] In my opinion inhibition on the dependence is properly categorised as a remedy granted by the court. It is essentially a form of judicial security pending the resolution of litigation, and judicial securities of that nature are almost universally regarded as a form of interim remedy. If that is so, the court cannot grant an inhibition on the dependence in a

manner that is incompatible with a defender's Convention rights. That means that a court cannot grant inhibition on the dependence automatically, whether on the signeting of a summons or by letters of inhibition. Instead, inhibition on the dependence can only be granted if a specific justification is put forward for the grant. In addition, for the reasons discussed previously, I am of opinion that the court must be satisfied that the pursuer has a prima facie case.

[78] ... I must conclude that, if the pursuers have a right to inhibition on the dependence without establishing special circumstances, the present inhibition is incompatible with the defenders' Convention rights, and that section 6(1) and (3)(a) of the Human Rights Act requires that the court should give effect to those rights...."

VII. THE HUMAN RIGHTS ACT AND LEGISLATION

The Human Rights Act thus mainly addresses legislative and executive action. As we will see in Ch.5 below it also has implications for the common law. Yet although "beautifully drafted" (*Wilson v Department of Trade and Industry* [2003] UKHL 40, *per* Lord Rodger of Earlsberry), the Act has presented the courts with a number of difficult questions. The courts have also drawn some criticism from rights enthusiasts who campaigned for the introduction of the Human Rights Act. Thus one prominent commentator concluded after reviewing the record of the courts in the Act's first year, that "those who lobbied for the Human Rights Act were a little naïve because despite [some] optimistic signs from the courts ... overall the judiciary have [not] followed the principles of the Convention as well as they should" (J. Wadham, "The Human Rights Act: One Year On" [2001] E.H.R.L.R. 620). There are two types of issues which the Act raises: one relates to matters of scope, and the second to matter of substance. The former deals with how far the Act penetrates and depends on how the courts are prepared to use their powers to interpret legislation, declare legislation incompatible and determine what is and what is not a public authority: the wider these powers are used, the greater will be the reach of the Act. The latter deals with how rights are construed: even if the courts take a wide view of the scope of the Act, its impact could be limited by a narrow approach to the construction of Convention rights. In this chapter we are concerned with the first of these matters: questions relating to the content of Convention rights are dealt with in the following chapters. An issue that has come up for early consideration is how the new rule of statutory interpretation is to be applied.

R. v A
[2002] 2 A.C. 45

This is an important case about the so-called rape shield defence for alleged victims of sexual offences. Under the Youth Justice and Criminal Evidence Act 1999 the court in a sexual offence case could not examine the sexual history of the victim, except in the limited circumstances where s.41(3) to (5) applied. The effect was to prevent the court—as in this case—from considering evidence of recent sexual activity between the victim and the accused which the accused wished to lead as evidence of consent. This was not permitted under the express terms of s.41(3) which only allowed evidence to be admitted of other activity which took place at or about the same time as the alleged offence. There were, however, concerns that this might lead to a breach of the accused's right to a fair trial as protected by Art.6 of the ECHR. The question for the House of Lords was whether the Human Rights Act, s.3 would allow the 1999 Act to be interpreted to allow such evidence to be admitted.

LORD STEYN: "[44] On the other hand, the interpretative obligation under s 3 of the 1998 Act is a strong one. It applies even if there is no ambiguity in the language in the sense of the language being capable of two different meanings. It is an emphatic adjuration by the legislature (see *R v DPP, ex p Kebeline*, [2000] 2 AC 326 at 366, 373 per my judgment and that of Lord Cooke of Thorndon respectively). The White Paper made clear that the obligation goes far beyond the rule which enabled the courts to take the convention into account in resolving any ambiguity in a legislative provision (see *Rights Brought Home: The Human Rights Bill* (Cm 3782, 1997, para 2.7). The draftsman of the 1998 Act had before him the slightly weaker model in s 6 of the New Zealand Bill of Rights Act 1990 but preferred stronger language. Parliament specifically rejected the legislative model of requiring a reasonable interpretation. Section 3 of the 1998 Act places a duty on the court to strive to find a possible interpretation compatible with convention rights. Under ordinary methods of interpretation a court may depart from the language of the statute to avoid absurd consequences: s 3 goes much further. Undoubtedly, a court must always look for a contextual and purposive interpretation: s 3 is more radical in its effect. It is a general principle of the interpretation of legal instruments that the text is the primary source of interpretation: other sources are subordinate to it; compare, for example, arts 31 to 33 of the Vienna Convention on the Law of Treaties (Vienna, 23 May 1969, TS 58 (1980); Cmnd 7964). Section 3 of the 1998 Act qualifies this general principle because it requires a court to find an interpretation compatible with convention rights if it is possible to do so. In the progress of the Bill through Parliament the Lord Chancellor observed that 'in 99 per cent of the cases that will arise, there will be no need for judicial declarations of incompatibility' (see 585 HL Official Report (5th series) col 840) and the Home Secretary said 'We expect that, in almost all cases, the courts will be able to interpret the legislation compatibly with the Convention' (see 306 HC Official Report (6th series) col 778). For reasons which I explained in a recent paper, this is at least relevant as an aid to the interpretation of s 3 of the 1998 Act *against* the executive ('Pepper v Hart; A Re-examination' (2001) 21 OJLS 59). In accordance with the will of Parliament as reflected in s 3 it will sometimes be necessary to adopt an interpretation which linguistically may appear strained. The techniques to be used will not only involve the reading down of express language in a statute but also the implication of provisions. A declaration of incompatibility is a measure of last resort. It must be avoided unless it is plainly impossible to do so. If a *clear* limitation on convention rights is stated *in terms*, such an impossibility will arise (*R v Secretary of State for the Home Dept, ex p Simms* [2000] 2 AC 115 at 132 per Lord Hoffmann). There is, however, no limitation of such a nature in the present case.

[45] In my view s 3 of the 1998 Act requires the court to subordinate the niceties of the language of s 41(3)(c) of the 1999 Act, and in particular the touchstone of coincidence, to broader considerations of relevance judged by logical and commonsense criteria of time and circumstances. After all, it is realistic to proceed on the basis that the legislature would not, if alerted to the problem, have wished to deny the right to an accused to put forward a full and complete defence by advancing truly probative material. It is therefore possible under s 3 of the 1998 Act to read s 41 of the 1999 Act, and in particular s 41(3)(c), as subject to the implied provision that evidence or questioning which is required to ensure a fair trial under art 6 of the convention should not be treated as inadmissible. The result of such a reading would be that sometimes logically relevant sexual experiences between a complainant and an accused may be admitted under s 41(3)(c). On the other hand, there will be cases where previous sexual experience between a complainant and an accused will be irrelevant, eg an isolated episode distant in time and circumstances. Where the line is to be drawn must be left to the judgment of trial judges. On this basis a declaration of incompatibility can be avoided. If this approach is adopted, s 41 will have achieved a major part of its objective but its excessive reach will have been attenuated in accordance with the will of Parliament as reflected in s 3 of the 1998 Act. That is the approach which I would adopt.

LORD HOPE OF CRAIGHEAD: "[58] I would take, as my starting point for examining s 41 of the 1999 Act, the proposition that there are areas of law which lie within the discretionary area of judgment which the court ought to accord to the legislature. As I said in *R v DPP, ex p Kebeline* [2000] 2 AC 326 at 380–381, it is appropriate in some circumstances for the judiciary to defer, on democratic grounds, to the considered opinion of the elected body as to where the balance is to be struck between the rights of the individual and the needs of society (see also *Brown v Stott*, 2001 S.L.T. 59 per Lord Bingham of Cornhill and Lord Steyn respectively). I would hold that prima facie the circumstances in which s 41 was enacted bring this case into that category. As I shall explain in more detail later, the right to lead evidence and the right to put questions with which that section deals are not among the rights which are set out in unqualified terms in art 6 of the convention. They are open to modification or restriction so long as this is not incompatible with the right to a fair trial. The essential question for your Lordships, as I see it, is whether Parliament acted within its discretionary area of judgment when it was choosing the point of balance that is indicated by the ordinary meaning of the words used in s 41. If it did not, questions will arise as to whether the incompatibility that results can be avoided by making use of the rule of interpretation in s 3 of the 1998 Act, failing which whether a declaration of incompatibility should be made. But I think that the question which I have described as the essential question must be addressed first. As Lord Woolf CJ said in *Poplar Housing and Regeneration Community Association Ltd v Donaghue* [2001] 3 W.L.R. 183, unless the legislation would otherwise be in breach of the convention s 3 of the 1998 Act can be ignored. So the courts should always ascertain first whether, absent s 3, there would be any breach of the convention. ...

[69] It may be noted in passing that a statement of compatibility was attached to the Bill before second reading that its provisions were compatible with the 1998 Act. Statements to that effect are now required by s 19 of the Act, which was brought into force on 24 November 1998. But Mr Pannick QC for the Secretary of State did not seek to rely on this statement in the course of his argument. I consider that he was right not to do so. These statements may serve a useful purpose in Parliament. They may also be seen as part of the parliamentary history, indicating that it was not Parliament's intention to cut across a convention right (see Lord Irvine of Lairg LC 'The Development of Human Rights in Britain under an Unincorporated Convention on Human Rights' [1998] PL 221 at 228). No doubt they are based on the best advice that is available. But they are no more than expressions of opinion by the minister. They are not binding on the court, nor do they have any persuasive authority. ...

[108] I should like to add, however, that I would find it very difficult to accept that it was permissible under s 3 of the 1998 Act to read into s 41(3)(c) of the 1999 Act a provision to the effect that evidence or questioning which was required to ensure a fair trial under art 6 of the convention should not be treated as inadmissible. The rule of construction which s 3 lays down is quite unlike any previous rule of statutory interpretation. There is no need to identify an ambiguity or absurdity. Compatibility with convention rights is the sole guiding principle. That is the paramount object which the rule seeks to achieve. But the rule is only a rule of interpretation. It does not entitle the judges to act as legislators. As Lord Woolf CJ said in *Poplar Housing and Regeneration Community Association Ltd v Donaghue* [2001] 3 W.L.R. 183, s 3 of the 1998 Act does not entitle the court to legislate; its task is still one of interpretation. The compatibility is to be achieved only so far as this is possible. Plainly this will not be possible if the legislation contains provisions which expressly contradict the meaning which the enactment would have to be given to make it compatible. It seems to me that the same result must follow if they do so by necessary implication, as this too is a means of identifying the plain intention of Parliament (see Lord Hoffmann's observations in *R v Secretary of State for the Home Dept, ex p Simms* [2000] 2 AC 115 at 131)."

Section 3 has been raised in a number of Scottish cases: *Taylor v Advocate-General for Scotland*, 2003 S.L.T. 1158; *MacDonald v Advocate-General for Scotland*, 2003 S.L.T. 1158. It has been argued that it would be improper for judges to use s.3 of the Human Rights Act to stretch legislation to the limits of possibility when they have the power to declare statutes incompatible (even though a statute carrying such a statement remains in force):

"In order to preserve the democratic right of the citizens of the UK to determine the basic principles on which their society is to be governed and to have an equal say in how these principles are to be embodied in binding rules, it will be necessary to hold onto a plain—meaning approach to the interpretation of statutes, and to openly acknowledge that interpreting the ECHR is a matter of moral reasoning in which courts have no special expertise and in connection with which their decisions have no political legitimacy. From this perspective, it would be best if declarations of incompatibility were to be seen as routine and unproblematic." (T. Campbell, "Incorporation through Interpretation", in T. Campbell, K. D. Ewing and A. Tomkins (eds), *Sceptical Essays on Human Rights* (2001), p.99.)

In this way it would be for people, Parliament and Government to decide how to respond to any such declaration, and to ignore it if appropriate, bearing in mind that frequent use of the instrument will serve to undermine it. Since the decision in *R. v A*, there are signs that the courts are ready to pull back from the adventurism that characterised the use of s.3 in that case. In *Re S (FC)* [2002] A.C. 291, Lord Nicholls said that s.3 of the Human Rights Act 1998 "is a powerful tool whose use is obligatory. It is not an optional canon of construction. Nor is its use dependent on the existence of ambiguity. Further, the section applies retrospectively. So far as it is possible to do so, primary legislation 'must be read and given effect' to in a way which is compatible with Convention rights. This is forthright, uncompromising language". He continued:

"38. But the reach of this tool is not unlimited. Section 3 is concerned with interpretation. This is apparent from the opening words of section 3(1): 'so far as it is possible to do so'. The side heading of the section is 'Interpretation of legislation'. Section 4 (power to make a declaration of incompatibility) and, indeed, section 3(2)(b) presuppose that not all provisions in primary legislation can be rendered Convention compliant by the application of section 3(1). The existence of this limit on the scope of section 3(1) has already been the subject of judicial confirmation, more than once: see, for instance, Lord Woolf CJ in *Poplar Housing and Regeneration Community Association Ltd v Donoghue* [2001] 3 WLR 183, 204, para 75 and Lord Hope of Craighead in *R v Lambert* [2001] 3 WLR 206, 233–235, paras 79–81.

39. In applying section 3 courts must be ever mindful of this outer limit. The Human Rights Act reserves the amendment of primary legislation to Parliament. By this means the Act seeks to preserve parliamentary sovereignty. The Act maintains the constitutional boundary. Interpretation of statutes is a matter for the courts; the enactment of statutes, and the amendment of statutes, are matters for Parliament.

40. Up to this point there is no difficulty. The area of real difficulty lies in identifying the limits of interpretation in a particular case. This is not a novel problem. If anything, the problem is more acute today than in past times. Nowadays courts are more 'liberal' in the interpretation of all manner of documents. The greater the latitude with which courts construe documents, the less readily defined is the boundary. What one person regards as sensible, if robust, interpretation, another regards as impermissibly creative. For present purposes it is sufficient to say that a meaning which departs substantially from a fundamental feature of an Act of Parliament is likely to have crossed the boundary between interpretation and amendment. This is especially so where the departure has important practical repercussions which the court is not equipped to evaluate. In such a case the overall contextual setting may leave no scope for rendering the statutory provision Convention compliant by legitimate use of the process of interpretation. The boundary line may be crossed even though a limitation on Convention rights is not stated in express terms. Lord Steyn's observations in *R v A (No 2)* [2002] 2 AC 45, para 44 are not to be read as meaning that a clear limitation on Convention rights in terms is the only circumstance in which an interpretation incompatible with Convention rights may arise.

41. I should add a further general observation in the light of what happened in the present case. Section 3 directs courts on how legislation shall, as far as possible, be inter-

preted. When a court, called upon to construe legislation, ascribes a meaning and effect to the legislation pursuant to its obligation under section 3, it is important the court should identify clearly the particular statutory provision or provisions whose interpretation leads to that result. Apart from all else, this should assist in ensuring the court does not inadvertently stray outside its interpretation jurisdiction."

This approach has been welcomed by C. A. Gearty, "Reconciling Parliamentary Democracy and Human Rights" (2002) 118 L.Q.R. 248. However, where it is not possible to construe an Act of Parliament consistently with Convention rights, the courts will be forced back on s.4, which empowers them to declare primary legislation incompatible with Convention rights. But although there are now a few cases in which such declarations have been made, the following case suggests that a number of judicial barriers are being erected to ensure that this is not a power that will be frequently used.

The Human Rights Act and Parliamentary Sovereignty

In order to preserve the traditional supremacy of Parliament in the constitution of the United Kingdom, legislation cannot be invalidated by the Act even if it is incompatible with the Convention. This involves a recognition that the United Kingdom can, by reason of legislation on the statute book, be in breach of the Convention if Parliament should so choose and its is the statute which must be upheld and applied by the Judiciary.
(Wilson v Department of Trade and Industry *[2004] 1A.C. 816, per Lord Hobhouse of Woodbridge, at para.127.*)

Wilson v First County Trust Ltd (No.2)
[2004] 1 A.C. 816

This is an extraordinary case. Lord Nicholls recalls the facts as follows: "In January 1999 Penelope Wilson borrowed £5,000 from a pawnbroker for a period of six months. The pawned property was her car, a BMW 318 Convertible. She did not repay the loan. The pawnbroker sought repayment, failing which the car would be sold. Mrs Wilson's response was to commence proceedings in the ... County Court. She claimed the agreement was unenforceable because it did not contain all the prescribed terms. She sought on order for the return of her car. Alternatively she sought to reopen the agreement as grossly exorbitant. At the trial Mrs Wilson appeared in person. The pawnbroker was a two-man company, First County Trust Ltd. The company was represented in court by its finance director". The remaining facts are reproduced in the following extract from Lord Nicholl's speech.

LORD NICHOLLS OF BIRKENHEAD: "2. From these modest beginnings the County Court proceedings burgeoned into a case with wide-ranging implications. Neither Mrs Wilson nor First County Trust appeared before the House. But the Attorney General appeared on behalf of the Secretary of State for Trade and Industry. The Speaker of the House of Commons and the Clerk of the Parliaments intervened. They were represented by leading and junior counsel. The Finance and Leasing Association also intervened, as did four insurance companies which are among the largest providers of motor insurance in this country. And leading and junior counsel also appeared as amicus curi.

3. When Mrs Wilson signed her agreement and pawn receipt she was charged a "document fee" of £250. This was added to the amount of her loan. In the agreement the amount of the loan was stated as £5,250. The amount payable on redemption was £7,327, made up of £5,250 and interest of £1,827. The annual percentage rate of interest was stated to be 94.78%.

4. The agreement was a regulated agreement for the purposes of section 8 of the Consumer Credit Act 1974. A regulated agreement is not properly executed unless the document signed contains all the prescribed terms: section 61(1)(a). One of the prescribed terms is the 'amount of the credit': see the Consumer Credit (Agreements) Regulations 1983 (SI 1983/1553), regulation 6 and Schedule 6, para 2. The consequence of failure to state all the prescribed terms of the agreement is that the court is precluded, by section 127(3), from enforcing the agreement. In the absence of enforcement by the court the agreement is altogether unenforceable: section 65(1).

5. On 24 September 1999 His Honour Judge Hull QC, in a carefully reasoned judgment, held that the fee of £250 was part of the amount of the credit. So the agreement was enforceable. He reopened the agreement as an extortionate credit bargain and reduced the amount of interest payable by one half. Mrs Wilson appealed to the Court of Appeal. Pending the hearing of her appeal she paid First County Trust £6,900 to redeem her car. That was in December 1999.

6. The appeal was heard in November 2000, shortly after the Human Rights Act 1998 came into force. The Court of Appeal, comprising Sir Andrew Morritt V-C, and Chadwick and Rix LJJ, allowed Mrs Wilson's appeal: see [2001] QB 407. Sir Andrew Morritt V-C recognised there was considerable force in First County Trust's submissions in support of the judge's view. But having analysed the statutory provisions, the court held that the £250 added to the loan to enable Mrs Wilson to pay the document fee was not 'credit' for the purposes of the Consumer Credit Act. So one of the prescribed terms was not correctly stated. In consequence the agreement was unenforceable. So also was the security. First County Trust was ordered to repay the amount of £6,900 Mrs Wilson had paid the company after Judge Hull's judgment together with interest amounting to £662. The overall result was that Mrs Wilson was entitled to keep the amount of her loan, pay no interest and recover her car.

7. Sir Andrew Morritt V-C expressed concern at this outcome. He considered it might be arguable that section 127(3) of the Consumer Credit Act infringes article 6(1) of the European Convention on Human Rights and article 1 of the First Protocol to the Convention. The court adjourned the further hearing of the appeal for notice to be given to the Crown, pursuant to section 5 of the Human Rights Act, that the court was considering whether to make a declaration of incompatibility. The Secretary of State for Trade and Industry was then added as a party to the proceedings.

8. On 2 May 2001 the court gave judgment at the adjourned hearing: see [2002] QB 74. The court held that the inflexible exclusion of a judicial remedy by section 127(3), preventing the court from doing what is just in the circumstances of the case, is disproportionate to the legitimate policy objective of ensuring that particular attention is paid to the inclusion of certain terms in the document signed by the borrower. It is not possible to read and give effect to section 113 or section 127(3) in a way compatible with First County Trust's Convention rights. The court made a declaration, pursuant to section 4 of the Human Rights Act, that section 127(3), in so far as it prevents the court from making an enforcement order under section 65 of the Consumer Credit Act unless a document containing all the prescribed terms of the agreement has been signed by the debtor, is incompatible with the rights guaranteed to the creditor by article 6(1) of the Convention and article 1 of the First Protocol to the Convention.

9. The Secretary of State appealed to your Lordships' House. First County Trust did not. The Secretary of State accepted that Mrs Wilson's agreement was not 'properly executed' within the meaning of section 61 of the Consumer Credit Act. She accepted that, in consequence, no enforcement order could be made under section 65 and that the security over the car was unenforceable. The Secretary of State also accepted it is not possible to 'read down' the relevant provisions of the Consumer Credit Act and thereby save them from any Convention rights incompatibility otherwise existing. But she challenged the decision of the Court of Appeal on several grounds. Her primary submission was that the court has no jurisdiction to make a declaration of incompatibility in relation to events occurring before

the Human Rights Act came fully into force on 2 October 2000. Here, the agreement was made in January 1999 for a period of six months. Additionally, the parties' rights were determined before the Human Rights Act came into force. The County Court decision was in September 1999.

10. As everyone knows, the purpose of the Human Rights Act 1998 was to make the human rights and fundamental freedoms set out in the European Convention on Human Rights directly enforceable in this country as part of its domestic law. The question raised by the Secretary of State's submission is how the Act was intended to operate regarding events occurring before the Act came into force, that is to say, events taking place at a time when these human rights were not as such part of the domestic law of this country...

17. On its face section 3 is of general application. So far as possible legislation must be read and given effect in a way compatible with the Convention rights. Section 3 is retrospective in the sense that, expressly, it applies to legislation whenever enacted. Thus section 3 may have the effect of changing the interpretation and effect of legislation already in force. An interpretation appropriate before the Act came into force may have to be reconsidered and revised in post-Act proceedings. This effect of section 3(1) is implicit in section 3(2)(a). So much is clear.

18. Considerable difficulties, however, might arise if the new interpretation of legislation, consequent on an application of section 3, were always to apply to pre-Act events. It would mean that parties' rights under existing legislation in respect of a transaction completed before the Act came into force could be changed overnight, to the benefit of one party and the prejudice of the other. This change, moreover, would operate capriciously, with the outcome depending on whether the parties' rights were determined by a court before or after 2 October 2000. The outcome in one case involving pre-Act happenings could differ from the outcome in another comparable case depending solely on when the cases were heard by a court. Parliament cannot have intended section 3(1) should operate in this unfair and arbitrary fashion.

20. ... I agree with Mummery LJ in *Wainwright v Home Office* [2002] QB 1334, 1352, para 61, that in general the principle of interpretation set out in section 3(1) does not apply to causes of action accruing before the section came into force. The principle does not apply because to apply it in such cases, and thereby change the interpretation and effect of existing legislation, might well produce an unfair result for one party or the other. The Human Rights Act was not intended to have this effect.

21. I emphasise that this conclusion does not mean that section 3 never applies to pre-Act events...

22. In the present case Parliament cannot have intended that application of section 3(1) should have the effect of altering parties' existing rights and obligations under the Consumer Credit Act. For the purpose of identifying the rights of Mrs Wilson and First County Trust under their January 1999 agreement the Consumer Credit Act is to be interpreted without reference to section 3(1).

23. It follows that, in this transitional type of case concerning the Consumer Credit Act, no question can arise of the court making a declaration of incompatibility. For the reasons already considered, it is only when a court is called upon to interpret legislation in accordance with section 3(1) that the court may proceed, where appropriate, to make a declaration of incompatibility. The court can make a declaration of incompatibility only where section 3 is available as an interpretative tool. That is not this case...

26. For these reasons the appeal by the Secretary of State must succeed. In this transitional type of case section 3(1) is inapplicable to the interpretation of the Consumer Credit Act. Consequently, the court has no jurisdiction to make a declaration of incompatibility. The declaration made by the Court of Appeal should be set aside.

27. This conclusion makes it strictly unnecessary for the House to consider the further issues arising out of the judgment of the Court of Appeal. But it would not be satisfactory to leave these other issues unresolved. They have been fully argued by experienced counsel, the House has the benefit of the views of the Court of Appeal, and the issues are of

importance to innumerable transactions being entered into every day. . . .

68. I turn now to consider whether section 127(3) of the Consumer Credit Act is compatible with the rights guaranteed by article 1 of the First Protocol. Inherent in article 1 is the need to hold a fair balance between the public interest and the protection of the fundamental rights of creditors such as First County Trust. It is common ground that section 127(3) pursues a legitimate aim. The fairness of a system of law governing the contractual or property rights of private persons is a matter of public concern. Legislative provisions intended to bring about such fairness are capable of being in the public interest, even if they involve the compulsory transfer of property from one person to another: see the leasehold enfranchisement case of *James v United Kingdom* (1986) 8 EHRR 123, 141, para 41. More specifically, persons wishing to borrow money are often vulnerable. There is a public interest in protecting such persons from exploitation.

69. There must also be a reasonable relationship of proportionality between the means employed and the aim sought to be achieved. The means chosen to cure the social mischief must be appropriate and not disproportionate in its adverse impact. Whether that relationship exists in the case of section 127(3) is the key issue.

70. In approaching this issue, as noted in *R v Johnstone* [2003] 1 W.L.R. 1736, courts should have in mind that theirs is a reviewing role. Parliament is charged with the primary responsibility for deciding whether the means chosen to deal with a social problem are both necessary and appropriate. Assessment of the advantages and disadvantages of the various legislative alternatives is primarily a matter for Parliament. The possible existence of alternative solutions does not in itself render the contested legislation unjustified: see the Rent Act case of *Mellacher v Austria* (1989) 12 EHRR 391, 411, para 53. The court will reach a different conclusion from the legislature only when it is apparent that the legislature has attached insufficient importance to a person's Convention right. The readiness of a court to depart from the views of the legislature depends upon the circumstances, one of which is the subject matter of the legislation. The more the legislation concerns matters of broad social policy, the less ready will be a court to intervene.

71. I turn to the statutory setting of section 127(3). The Consumer Credit Act contains many requirements about the form and contents of regulated agreements. Parliament has singled out some obligations as having such importance that non-compliance leads automatically and inflexibly to a ban on the making of an enforcement order whatever the circumstances. These obligations are specified in section 127(3) and (4). In these two subsections Parliament has chosen, deliberately, to exclude consideration of what is just and equitable in the particular case. The latter approach, enabling the court to consider the circumstances of the particular case, was adopted as the general rule in section 127(1). Section 127(3) and (4) are, expressly, exceptions to the general rule. In prescribing these two exceptions Parliament must be taken to have considered that the sanction generally attaching to non-compliance with the statutory requirements was not sufficient to achieve compliance with the duty to include all the prescribed terms in the agreement (section 61(1)(a)) or the duties to provide copies and notice of cancellation rights (sections 62 to 64). Something more drastic was needed in order to focus attention on the need for lenders to comply strictly with these particular obligations.

72. Undoubtedly, as illustrated by the facts of the present case, section 127(3) may be drastic, even harsh, in its adverse consequences for a lender. He loses all his rights under the agreement, including his rights to any security which has been lodged. Conversely, the borrower acquires what can only be described as a windfall. He keeps the money and recovers his security. These consequences apply just as much where the lender was acting in good faith throughout and the error was due to a mistaken reading of the complex statutory requirements as in cases of deliberate non-compliance. These consequences also apply where, as in the present case, the borrower suffered no prejudice as a result of the non-compliance as they do where the borrower was misled. Parliament was painting here with a broad brush.

73. The unattractive feature of this approach is that it will sometimes involve punishing

the blameless pour encourager les autres. On its face, *considered in the context of one particular case*, a sanction having this effect is difficult to justify. The Moneylenders Act 1927 adopted a similarly severe approach. Infringement of statutory requirements rendered the loan and any security unenforceable. So did the Hire Purchase Act 1965, although to a lesser extent. This approach was roundly condemned in the Crowther report (Report of the Committee on Consumer Credit, under the presidency of Lord Crowther, March 1971) (Cmnd 4596), vol 1, p 311, para 6.11.4:

> 'It offends every notion of justice or fairness that because of some technical slip which in no way prejudices him, a borrower, having received a substantial sum of money, should be entitled to retain or spend it without any obligation to repay a single penny.'

74. Despite this criticism I have no difficulty in accepting that in suitable instances it is open to Parliament, when Parliament considers the public interest so requires, to decide that compliance with certain formalities is an essential prerequisite to enforcement of certain types of agreements. This course is open to Parliament even though this will sometimes yield a seemingly unreasonable result in a particular case. Considered overall, this course may well be a proportionate response in practice to a perceived social problem. Parliament may consider the response should be a uniform solution across the board. A tailor-made response, fitting the facts of each case as decided in an application to the court, may not be appropriate. This may be considered an insufficient incentive and insufficient deterrent. And it may fail to protect consumers adequately. Persons most in need of protection are perhaps the least likely to participate in court proceedings. They may well let proceedings go by default: see, in relation to money lending agreements, the Crowther report, p 236, para 6.1.19.

75. Nor do I have any difficulty in accepting that money lending transactions as a class give rise to significant social problems. Bargaining power lies with the lender, and the social evils flowing from this are notorious. The activities of some lenders have long given the business of money lending a bad reputation. Nor, becoming more specific, do I have any difficulty in accepting, in principle, that Parliament may properly make compliance with the formalities required by the Consumer Credit Act regarding 'prescribed terms' an essential prerequisite to enforcement. In principle that course must be open to Parliament. It must be open to Parliament to decide that, severe though this sanction may be, it is an appropriate way of protecting consumers as a matter of social policy. In making its decision in the present case Parliament had the benefit of experience gained over many years in the working of the Moneylenders Act 1927 and the hire purchase legislation, and also the views of the Crowther committee. Further, it must be open to Parliament so to decide even though the lender's inability to enforce an agreement will not assist a borrower who consents to the enforcement of the agreement in ignorance of the true legal position.

76. The one point which has caused me difficulty is whether the requirement to state the amount of 'credit' is sufficiently clear and certain. The more severe the sanction, the more important it is that the law should be unambiguous. In the present case the confusion over the treatment of the document fee of £250 as 'credit' may have been due to a widespread misunderstanding within the trade. Certainly it was shared by an experienced trial judge. Mr Hibbert on behalf of the Finance and Leasing Association submitted it is sometimes far from easy to apply the complex provisions of the Consumer Credit Act and the ancillary regulations. He gave examples of types of cases where, he said, identifying the amount of 'credit' is fraught with difficulty.

77. That there was genuine confusion in the present case is admitted. But I am not persuaded the degree of uncertainty involved in identifying the amount of 'credit' is unacceptably high. The consumer credit legislation has to cope with a wide range of types of transactions. It is not surprising that now and again problems of definition will arise. With the assistance of court decisions points of uncertainty, when they occur, can be clarified. The mere fact that a legal provision is capable of more than one interpretation

does not mean that it fails to meet the requirement implied in the Convention concept of 'prescribed by law': *Vogt v Germany* (1995) 21 EHRR 205, para 48. Moreover, I have in mind that the statutory provisions apply only to loans up to a prescribed financial limit, currently £25,000. So the exposure of a creditor in any one case is confined. The burden imposed on him is not excessive.

78. Accordingly, in my view section 127(3) is compatible with article 1 of the First Protocol.

VIII. THE HUMAN RIGHTS ACT AND PUBLIC AUTHORITIES

Moving from the relationship between the Human Rights Act and the legislative to the relationship between the Act and the Executive, here the crucial question is what is meant by "public authority" in s.6. Here it is recognised that there are three different kinds of bodies: "core" public authorities (such as government departments, local authorities and the police) on the one hand, and purely private bodies on the other (companies, trade unions and clubs). However, in between there are private bodies that exercise public functions (such as the utility companies, mixed medical practices, privately run prisons, housing associations, charities and so on). Apart from determining what is a core public authority, there are difficult questions about whether a body is a "functional" public authority. As the Joint Committee on Human Rights pointed out, this is an important issue particularly in the light of the privatisation and contracting out of private services. Both service providers and the beneficiaries of public services need to know whether the Human Rights Act applies to them. Some of the issues are explored in the following case.

Aston Cantlow and Wilmcote with Billesley Parochial Church Council v Wallbank
[2004] 1 A.C. 546

The defendants were lay rectors of land in Warwickshire. As such, they had a legal obligation to maintain the chancel of the parish church in good repair. The obligation of the defendants was enforced by the Parochial Church Council which was a body established by the Church of England. When the defendants refused to comply with a request to maintain the chancel of the parish church, legal proceedings were taken by the PCC to compel them to do so. The application succeeded and the defendants were ordered to pay £95,260.84. The defendants appealed, arguing that by their conduct in enforcing common law rights, the plaintiffs were violating the Convention rights of the defendants. The appeal succeeded. But the decision of the Court of Appeal was reversed by the House of Lords. One of the issues for the House of Lords was whether the church council was a public authority for the purpose of the Human Rights Act.

LORD NICHOLLS OF BIRKENHEAD: "7. ... the phrase 'a public authority' in section 6(1) is essentially a reference to a body whose nature is governmental in a broad sense of that expression. It is in respect of organisations of this nature that the government is answerable under the European Convention on Human Rights. Hence, under the Human Rights Act a body of this nature is required to act compatibly with Convention rights in everything it does. The most obvious examples are government departments, local authorities, the police and the armed forces. Behind the instinctive classification of these organisations as bodies whose nature is governmental lie factors such as the possession of special powers, democratic accountability, public funding in whole or in part, an obligation to act only in the public interest, and a statutory constitution: see the valuable article by Professor Dawn Oliver, 'The Frontiers of the State: Public Authorities and Public Functions under the Human Rights Act" [2000] PL 476.

8. A further, general point should be noted. One consequence of being a 'core' public authority, namely, an authority falling within section 6 without reference to section 6(3), is

that the body in question does not itself enjoy Convention rights. It is difficult to see how a core public authority could ever claim to be a victim of an infringement of a Convention rights. A core public authority seems inherently incapable of satisfying the Convention description of a victim: 'any person, *non-governmental organisation* or group of individuals' (article 34, with emphasis added). Only victims of an unlawful act may bring proceedings under section 7 of the Human Rights Act, and the Convention description of a victim has been incorporated into the Act, by section 7(7). This feature, that a core public authority is incapable of having Convention rights of its own, is a matter to be borne in mind when considering whether or not a particular body is a core public authority. In itself this feature throws some light on how the expression 'public authority' should be understood and applied. It must always be relevant to consider whether Parliament can have been intended that the body in question should have no Convention rights.

9. In a modern developed state governmental functions extend far beyond maintenance of law and order and defence of the realm. Further, the manner in which wide ranging governmental functions are discharged varies considerably. In the interests of efficiency and economy, and for other reasons, functions of a governmental nature are frequently discharged by non-govermental bodies. Sometimes this will be a consequence of privatisation, sometimes not. One obvious example is the running of prisons by commercial organisations. Another is the discharge of regulatory functions by organisations in the private sector, for instance, the Law Society. Section 6(3)(b) gathers this type of case into the embrace of section 6 by including within the phrase 'public authority' any person whose functions include 'functions of a public nature'. This extension of the expression 'public authority' does not apply to a person if the nature of the act in question is 'private'.

10. Again, the statute does not amplify what the expression 'public' and its counterpart 'private' mean in this context. But, here also, given the statutory context already mentioned and the repetition of the description 'public', essentially the contrast being drawn is between functions of a governmental nature and functions, or acts, which are not of that nature. I stress, however, that this is no more than a useful guide. The phrase used in the Act is public function, not governmental function.

11. Unlike a core public authority, a 'hybrid' public authority, exercising both public functions and non-public functions, is not absolutely disabled from having Convention rights. A hybrid public authority is not a public authority in respect of an act of a private nature. Here again, as with section 6(1), this feature throws some light on the approach to be adopted when interpreting section 6(3)(b). Giving a generously wide scope to the expression 'public function' in section 6(3)(b) will further the statutory aim of promoting the observance of human rights values without depriving the bodies in question of the ability themselves to rely on Convention rights when necessary.

12. What, then, is the touchstone to be used in deciding whether a function is public for this purpose? Clearly there is no single test of universal application. There cannot be, given the diverse nature of governmental functions and the variety of means by which these functions are discharged today. Factors to be taken into account include the extent to which in carrying out the relevant function the body is publicly funded, or is exercising statutory powers, or is taking the place of central government or local authorities, or is providing a public service.

13. Turning to the facts in the present case, I do not think parochial church councils are 'core' public authorities. Historically the Church of England has discharged an important and influential role in the life of this country. As the established church it still has special links with central government. But the Church of England remains essentially a religious organisation. This is so even though some of the emanations of the church discharge functions which may qualify as governmental. Church schools and the conduct of marriage services are two instances. The legislative powers of the General Synod of the Church of England are another. This should not be regarded as infecting the Church of England as a whole, or its emanations in general, with the character of a governmental organisation.

14. As to parochial church councils, their constitution and functions lend no support to

the view that they should be characterised as governmental organisations or, more precisely, in the language of the statute, public authorities. Parochial church councils are established as corporate bodies under a church measure, now the Parochial Church Councils (Powers) Measure 1956. For historical reasons this unique form of legislation, having the same force as a statute, is the way the Church of England governs its affairs. But the essential role of a parochial church council is to provide a formal means, prescribed by the Church of England, whereby ex officio and elected members of the local church promote the mission of the Church and discharge financial responsibilities in respect of their own parish church, including responsibilities regarding maintenance of the fabric of the building. This smacks of a church body engaged in self-governance and promotion of its affairs. This is far removed from the type of body whose acts engage the responsibility of the state under the European Convention.

15. The contrary conclusion, that the church authorities in general and parochial church councils in particular are 'core' public authorities, would mean these bodies are not capable of being victims within the meaning of the Human Rights Act. Accordingly they are not able to complain of infringements of Convention rights. That would be an extraordinary conclusion. The Human Rights Act goes out of its way, in section 13, to single out for express mention the exercise by religious organisations of the Convention right of freedom of thought, conscience and religion. One would expect that these and other Convention rights would be enjoyed by the Church of England as much as other religious bodies.

16. I turn next to consider whether a parochial church council is a hybrid public authority. For this purpose it is not necessary to analyse each of the functions of a parochial church council and see if any of them is a public function. What matters is whether the particular act done by the plaintiff council of which complaint is made is a private act as contrasted with the discharge of a public function. The impugned act is enforcement of Mr and Mrs Wallbank's liability, as lay rectors, for the repair of the chancel of the church of St John the Baptist at Aston Cantlow. As I see it, the only respect in which there is any 'public' involvement is that parishioners have certain rights to attend church services and in respect of marriage and burial services. To that extent the state of repair of the church building may be said to affect rights of the public. But I do not think this suffices to characterise actions taken by the parochial church council for the repair of the church as 'public'. If a parochial church council enters into a contract with a builder for the repair of the chancel arch, that could be hardly be described as a public act. Likewise when a parochial church council enforces, in accordance with the provisions of the Chancel Repairs Act 1932, a burdensome incident attached to the ownership of certain pieces of land: there is nothing particularly 'public' about this. This is no more a public act than is the enforcement of a restrictive covenant of which church land has the benefit.

17. For these reasons this appeal succeeds. A parochial church council is not a core public authority, nor does it become such by virtue of section 6(3)(b) when enforcing a lay rector's liability for chancel repairs. Accordingly the Human Rights Act affords lay rectors no relief from their liabilities. This conclusion should not be allowed to detract from the force of the recommendations, already mentioned, of the Law Commission. The need for reform has not lessened with the passage of time."

LORD HOPE OF CRAIGHEAD: "35. It is clear from these provisions that, for the purposes of this Act, public authorities fall into two distinct types or categories. Courts and tribunals, which are expressly included in the definition, can perhaps be said to constitute a third category but they can be left on one side for present purposes. The first category comprises those persons or bodies which are obviously public or 'standard' public authorities: Clayton and Tomlinson, *The Law of Human Rights* (2000), para 5.08. They were referred to in the course of the argument as 'core' public authorities. It appears to have been thought that no further description was needed as they obviously have the character of public authorities. In the Notes on Clauses which are quoted in Clayton and Tomlinson, para 5.06, it was explained that the legislation proceeds on the basis that some authorities are so obviously public authorities that it is not necessary to define them expressly. In other words, they are public authorities through and through. So section 6(5) does not apply to them. The second category comprises persons or bodies some of whose functions are of a public nature. They are described in Clayton and Tomlinson as 'functional' public authorities and were referred to in the argument as 'hybrid' public authorities. Section 6(5) applies to them, so in their case a distinction must be drawn between their public functions and the acts which they perform which are of a private nature.

36. Skilfully drawn though these provisions are, they leave a great deal of open ground. There is room for doubt and for argument. It has been left to the courts to resolve these issues when they arise. . . .

40. The Court of Appeal, in reaching the conclusion that the PCC is a 'core' public authority, appears to have proceeded in this way: (1) the PCC is an authority because it possesses powers which private individuals do not possess to enforce the lay rector's liability; and (2) it is public because it is created and empowered by law, it forms part of the Church of England as the established church and its functions include the enforcement of the liability on persons who need not be members of the church. By a similar process of reasoning the Court of Appeal concluded that the PCC is in any event a person some of whose functions, including chancel repairs, are functions of a public nature. In their view the fact that the PCC has the power and duty to enforce the obligation on persons with whom it has no other relationship showed that it has the character of a public authority, or at least that it is performing a function of a public nature when it is enforcing this liability.

41. This approach has the obvious merit of concentrating on the words of the statute. The words 'public' and 'authority' in section 6(1), 'functions of a public nature' in section 6(3)(b) and 'private' in section 6(5) are, of course, important. The word 'public' suggests that there some persons which may be described as authorities that are nevertheless private and not public. The word 'authority' suggests that the person has regulatory or coercive powers given to it by statute or by the common law. The combination of these two words in the single unqualified phrase 'public authority' suggests that it is the nature of the person itself, not the functions which it may perform, that is determinative. Section 6(1) does not distinguish between public and private functions. It assumes that everything that a 'core' public authority does is a public function. It applies to everything that a person does in that capacity. This suggests that some care needs to be taken to limit this category to cases where it is clear that this over-arching treatment is appropriate. The phrase 'functions of a public nature' in section 6(3), on the other hand, does not make that assumption. It requires a distinction to be drawn between functions which are public and those which are private. It has a much wider reach, and it is sensitive to the facts of each case. It is the function that the person is performing that is determinative of the question whether it is, for the purposes of that case, a 'hybrid' public authority. The question whether section 6(5) applies to a particular act depends on the nature of the act which is in question in each case.

42. The absence of a more precise definition of the expression 'public authority' for the purposes of section 6(1) of the Human Rights Act 1998 may be contrasted with the way that expression is used in the devolution legislation for Scotland and Northern Ireland. Sections 88–90 of the Scotland Act 1998 deal with what that Act calls 'cross-border public authorities'. 'Scottish public authorities' are dealt with in Part III of Schedule 5. Definitions of these expressions are provided in section 88(5), which requires 'cross-border authorities' to be specified by Order in Council and in section 126(1) which states that 'Scottish public authority' means any public body, public office or holder of such an office whose functions are exercisable only in or as regards Scotland. A list of public bodies was appended to the White Paper *Scotland's Parliament* (Cm 3658, 1997): see also the note to section 88 of the 1998 Act in *Current Law Statutes*. It included three nationalised industries, a group of tribunals, three statutory water authorities, health bodies and a large number of miscellaneous executive and advisory bodies. Sections 75 and 76 of the Northern Ireland Act

1998 impose a duty on public authorities to promote equality of opportunity and prohibit discrimination in the carrying out of their functions. The expression 'public authority' for the purposes of each of these sections is defined in a way that appears to leave no room for doubt as to which departments, corporations or other bodies are included: see sections 75(3), 76(7). . . .

47. The test as to whether a person or body is or is not a 'core' public authority for the purposes of section 6(1) is not capable of being defined precisely. But it can at least be said that a distinction should be drawn between those persons who, in Convention terms, are governmental organisations on the one hand and those who are non-governmental organisations on the other. A person who would be regarded as a non-governmental organisation within the meaning of article 34 ought not to be regarded as a 'core' public authority for the purposes of section 6. That would deprive it of the rights enjoyed by the victims of acts which are incompatible with Convention rights that are made unlawful by section 6(1) . . .

49. The phrase 'public functions' in this context is thus clearly linked to the functions and powers, whether centralised or distributed, of government. This point was developed more fully in *Holy Monasteries v Greece* (1995) 20 EHRR 1. The Government of Greece argued that the applicant monasteries, which were challenging legislation which provided for the transfer of a large part of the monastic property to the Greek State, were not non-governmental organisations within the meaning of article 25 (now 34) of the Convention. It was pointed out that the monasteries were hierarchically integrated into the organic structure of the Greek Orthodox Church, that legal personality was attributed to the Church and its constituent parts in public law and that the Church and its institutions, which played a direct and active part in public administration, took administrative decisions whose lawfulness was subject to judicial review by the Supreme Administrative court like those of any other public authority. Rejecting this argument, the court said at p 41, para 49:

> 'Like the Commission in its admissibility decision, the Court notes at the outset that the applicant monasteries do not exercise governmental powers. Section 39(1) of the Charter of the Greek Church describes the monasteries as ascetic religious institutions. Their objectives—essentially ecclesiastical and spiritual ones, but also cultural and social ones in some cases—are not such as to enable them to be classed with governmental organisations established for public administration purposes. From the classification as public law entities it may be inferred only that the legislature—on account of the special links between the monasteries and the State—wished to afford them the same legal protection *vis-à-vis* third parties as was accorded to other public law entities. Furthermore, the monastery councils' only power consists in making rules concerning the organisation and furtherance of spiritual life and the internal administration of each monastery.'

50. The phrase 'governmental organisations established for public administration purposes' in the third sentence of the passage which I have quoted from the *Holy Monasteries* case is significant. It indicates that test of whether a person or body is a 'non-governmental organisation' within the meaning of article 34 of the Convention is whether it was established with a view to public administration as part of the process of government. That too was the approach which was taken by the Commission in *Hautanemi v Sweden* (1996) 22 EHRR CD 156. At the relevant time the Church of Sweden and its member parishes were to be regarded as corporations of public law in the domestic legal order. It was held nevertheless that the applicant parish was a victim within the meaning of what was then article 25, on the ground that the Church and its member parishes could not be considered to have been exercising governmental powers and the parish was a non-governmental organisation.

51. It can be seen from what was said in these cases that the Convention institutions have

developed their own jurisprudence as to the meaning which is to be given to the expression 'non-governmental organisation' in article 34. We must take that jurisprudence into account in determining any question which has arisen in connection with a Convention right: Human Rights Act 1998, section 2(1).

52. The Court of Appeal left this jurisprudence out of account. They looked instead for guidance to cases about the amenability of bodies to judicial review, although they recognised that they were not necessarily determinative. But, as Professor Oliver has pointed out in her commentary on the decision of the Court of Appeal in this case, 'Chancel repairs and the Human Rights Act' [2001] PL 651, the decided cases on the amenability of bodies to judicial review have been made for purposes which have nothing to do with the liability of the state in international law. They cannot be regarded as determinative of a body's membership of the class of 'core' public authorities: see also Grosz, Beatson, Duffy, *Human Rights: The 1998 Act and the European Convention* (2000), p 61, para 4–04. Nor can they be regarded as determinative of the question whether a body falls within the 'hybrid' class. That is not to say that the case law on judicial review may not provide some assistance as to what does, and what does not, constitute a 'function of a public nature' within the meaning of section 6(3)(b). It may well be helpful. But the domestic case law must be examined in the light of the jurisprudence of the Strasbourg Court as to those bodies which engage the responsibility of the State for the purposes of the Convention.

53. At first sight there is a close link between the question whether a person is a non-governmental organisation for the purposes of article 34 and the question whether a person is a public authority against which the doctrine of the direct effect of directives operates under Community law: see article 249 EC. Both concepts lie at the heart of the obligations of the State under international law. Individual applications for a violation of Convention rights may be received under article 34 from 'any person, non-governmental organisation or group of individuals'. Direct effect exists only against the member state concerned 'and other public authorities': *ECSC v Faillite Acciaierie e ferriere Busseni SpA* [1990] ECR I–495, para 23; Brent, *Directives: Rights and Remedies in English and Community Law* (2001), para 15.11.

54. The types of organisations and bodies against whom the provisions of a directive could be relied on were discussed in *Foster v British Gas plc* [1990] ECR I–3313. The court noted in para 18 that it had been held in a series of cases that provisions of a directive could be relied on against organisations and bodies which were subject to the authority or control of the State or had special powers beyond those which result from the normal rules applicable to relations between individuals. Reference was made to a number of its decisions to illustrate this point. Its conclusions were set out in para 20:

'It follows from the foregoing that a body, whatever its legal form, which has been made responsible, pursuant to a measure adopted by the State, for providing a public service under the control of the State and has for that purpose special powers beyond those which result from the normal rules applicable in relations between individuals is included in any event among the bodies against which the provisions of a directive capable of having direct effect may be relied upon.'

55. This is a broad definition of the concept by which such bodies have come to be referred to as 'emanations of the State': eg *Johnston v Chief Constable of the Royal Ulster Constabulary* [1986] ECR 1651, para 56. It has been described as a starting point: *Doughty v Rolls-Royce plc* [1992] CMLR 1045, 1058, per Mustill LJ. As Brent, para 15.11, note 101, points out, the phrase 'emanation of the State' is an English legal concept derived from *Gilbert v Corporation of Trinity House* [1886] 17 QBD 795 which was later criticised by the courts as inappropriate and undefined. Whatever its value may be in the context of Community law, however, it would be neither safe nor helpful to use this concept as a short-hand way of describing the test that must be applied to determine whether a person or body is a non-governmental organisation for the purposes of article 34 of the Convention.

There is no right of individual application to the European Court of Justice in EC law. The phrase 'non-governmental organisation' has an autonomous meaning in Convention law...."

In a major study of the meaning of public authority in s.6 of the Human Rights Act, the Joint Committee on Human Rights noted that this was the only case to discuss in detail what is meant by a pure public authority. The Committee disagreed with the view expressed in the *Aston Cantlow* case that a pure public authority could not itself rely on Convention rights, and noted that the House of Lords appeared to take a narrow approach to the meaning of a pure public authority. Nevertheless the Joint Committee approved what appeared to be a wide interpretation of a functional public authority adopted by the Lords, and in particular a dictum of Lord Hope in para.41 of his speech where he said that: the s.6(3)(b) category of "functional" public authority:

> "... has a much wider reach, and is sensitive to the facts of each case. It is the function that the person is performing that is determinative of the question whether it is, for the purposes of the case, a 'hybrid' public authority."

The obligation under Art.13 of the ECHR to secure Convention rights to everyone in the territory was, in Lord Hope's view, 'crucial' to the interpretation of the meaning of public authority under s.6. The Joint Committee was concerned, however, that "the broad, functional approach to public authority responsibility under the Human Rights Act has not so far found favour in the lower courts", noting that:

> "26. ... In the relatively few decided cases, the courts have, in their application of section 6, taken as their starting point the amenability to judicial review of a body discharging a function, and have looked to the identity of the body, and its links with the State, as well as to the nature of the function performed
> 27. This is particularly the case as regards application of the definition to private sector providers of public services. The fully privatised public utilities such as the water companies are established in the case law as 'functional' public authorities, performing public functions in their delivery of services. By contrast, the application of section 6(3)(b) to smaller private or charitable organisations, often providing services under contract from local authorities, has been less clear-cut. The case law has considered the public authority status of organisations including housing associations, care homes, mental health care facilities and organisations managing public markets."

The Joint Committee was particularly concerned about *Poplar Housing and Regeneration Community Association Ltd v Donoghue* [2001] 3 W.L.R. 183 and *Callin v Leonard Cheshire Foundation* [2002] EWCA Civ 595. This concern led the Committee to conclude that: "A serious gap has opened in the protection which the Human Rights Act was intended to offer, and a more vigorous approach to re-establishing the proper ambit of the Act needs to be pursued" (para.41). In considering how this matter should be resolved, the Joint Committee made the following recommendations.

Joint Committee on Human Rights
'The Meaning of Public Authority under the Human Rights Act'
Seventh Report: H.L. 39/H.C. 382 (2004)

"A solution: principles of interpretation
25. The difficulties in defining two key terms—'public' and 'function'—have led to confusion in the application of section 6 through reliance on criteria, including statutory basis and institutional proximity to the State, which are not warranted either by the lan-

guage of the Act or by the ECHR. A function is a public one when government has taken responsibility for it.

26. On the principles we have set out, for a body to discharge a public function, it does not need to do so under direct statutory authority. A State programme or policy, with a basis in statute or otherwise, may delegate its powers or duties through contractual arrangements without changing the public nature of those powers or duties. Under section 6 of the Human Rights Act, there should be no distinction between a body providing housing because it itself is required to do so by statute, and a body providing housing because it has contracted with a local authority which is required by statute to provide the service. The loss of a single step in proximity to the statutory duty does not change the nature of the function, nor the nature of its capacity to interfere with Convention rights. ....

28. The attribution of public authority responsibilities to private sector bodies is justified on the basis that the private body operating to discharge a government programme is likely to exercise a degree of power and control (which in the absence of delegation would be State power and control) over the realisation of the individual's Convention rights.

Conclusion

30. It would be unsatisfactory to leave this matter to the present state of the case law. In his oral evidence, the Secretary of State for Constitutional Affairs told us that he would keep the matter of the interpretation of the meaning of 'public authority' by the courts 'under close review' and would 'pay particular attention to the need to intervene in future cases on the meaning of section 6(3)(b)'. We urge the Government to intervene in the public interest as a third party in cases where it can press the case for a broad, functional interpretation of the meaning of public authority under the Human Rights Act. In the interests of the full protection of Convention human rights which the Human Rights Act was designed to achieve, what is needed is a careful application of the current section 6 test so as to prevent any diminution in human rights protection arising from the contracting out of public services.

31. As a matter of broad principle, a body is a functional public authority performing a public function under section 6(3)(b) of the Human Rights Act where it exercises a function that has its origin in governmental responsibilities, in such a way as to compel individuals to rely on that body for realisation of their Convention human rights."

Is this the first time that a parliamentary body has complained that judges are not making enough use of their powers? Some may reflect that matters have come to a sorry pass when a parliamentary body must give judicial bodies a lesson in human rights.

IX. EC Law, Scots Law and the ECHR

The focus so far has been with the impact of human rights on Scots law and British or United Kingdom law. A third level where human rights have a bearing on the legal position in Scotland is at the EU level. At the time of writing, there is no human rights dimension to the EU Treaty, and the European Court of Justice has held that the European Community lacks the necessary authority to ratify the ECHR (*Re the Accession of the Community to the European Human Rights Convention* [1996] 2 C.M.L.R. 265). Although neither is ratified, the preamble to the EU Treaty recognises the Council of Europe's Social Charter of 1961, while art.6 includes an undertaking to "respect fundamental rights, as guaranteed by the [ECHR] as they result from the constitutional provisions common to Member States". Nor does it follow that the ECJ has no regard to fundamental rights when determining

- the scope and content of Community legislation (*P v S* [1996] E.C.R. I–2143);
- the legality of the actions of Community institutions (*Connelly v Commission* [1999] E.C.R. IA–87, II–463); or

- the legality of the actions of Member States (Case 36/75, *Rutili* [1975] E.C.R. 1219).

Moreover, as part of Community law, these obligations are binding on the national courts of Member States when considering community law. This is demonstrated by the following case. The question for consideration by the Court of Session was whether a directive had been properly implemented in circumstances where property was taken without compensating the owner.

Booker Acquaculture Ltd v Secretary of State for Scotland
2000 S.C. 9

The respondents were the proprietors of a fish farm. Acting under the authority of the Disease of Fish (Control) Regulations 1994, reg.7, the Secretary of State served a notice ordering diseased fish to be destroyed. The Regulations were made to implement an EC Directive of 1993. No provision was made in the Directive or the regulations for compensation and the fish farmers sought judicial review of the regulations and of the Secretary of State's decision not to pay compensation. The action succeeded before the Lord Ordinary, and the issue before the First Division on the Secretary of State's appeal was whether the Regulations were in breach of EC law as failing to protect the property rights of the fish farmers. The court decided to seek a preliminary ruling from the ECJ about whether Community law "binds a member state in respect of any liability to pay compensation for deprivation of property resulting from the application of a domestic measure adopted in implementation of the member state's obligation to provide control measures for … diseases under the 1993 Directive" (at 26). This is not a question which the Court of Session could resolve with "complete confidence". In the course of its decision, the court considered the right to property in EC law.

> LORD PRESIDENT (RODGER): "Counsel for both parties were agreed that, in implementing the 1993 Directive the United Kingdom had been subject to the general rules of the Treaty and in particular to the general principles of Community law, including the fundamental rights enshrined in Community law. That approach is fully vouched by the observations of Advocate-General Jacobs in *Wachauf v Bundesamt für Ernährung und Forstwirtschaft* (Case 5/88) [1989] E.C.R. 2609 at p 2629 where he says that 'it appears to me self-evident that when acting in pursuance of powers granted under Community law, Member States must be subject to the same constraints, in any event in relation to the principle of respect for fundamental rights, as the Community legislator'. This approach was adopted by the Court of Justice in para 19 of their judgment in the same case where they stated that, since the requirements of the protection of fundamental rights in the Community legal order 'are also binding on the Member States when they implement Community rules, the Member States must, as far as possible, apply those rules in accordance with those requirements'.
>
> Although there was therefore no dispute between the parties that in principle the fundamental rights would apply when a member state implemented Community rules, there is, as will be seen below, an issue between the parties as to whether, in determining compensation arising out of the application of the national measures implementing Community rules, the member state is acting within the scope of Community law or within the area of its own competence.
>
> *The Right to Property*
> Counsel for the respondent did not seek to question the existence of the fundamental right to property with which these proceedings are concerned. A convenient statement of the general approach to fundamental rights in Community law is to be found in *Nold KG v Commission* (Case 4–73) [1974] E.C.R. 491 in para 13 of the judgment of the court: 'As the Court has already stated, fundamental rights form an integral part of the general principles of law, the observance of which it ensures. In safeguarding these rights, the Court is bound

tendency widely shared by the legal orders of the Member States' (at p 3761).

In the light of these authorities I am satisfied that the right to property is recognised as a fundamental right under Community law and that the availability of compensation is relevant to any consideration of whether the right has been respected. Moreover, the right pervades the Community legal order and (as was said in *Wachauf* and other cases) will fall to be taken into account by any member state when implementing the obligations placed on it by a directive.

Does Community Law apply to the Determination of Compensation in this Case?
Counsel for the petitioners submitted that, in introducing and applying reg 7, the Minister and the Secretary of State were in effect implementing the obligations of the United Kingdom under the 1993 Directive. For this reason, they argued, the question of the duty of the Secretary of State to provide for compensation for owners whose fish were killed and destroyed, or the sale of which was controlled, under reg 7 was one which fell to be answered by reference to Community law and in particular by reference to the fundamental right to property recognised by Community law. It does indeed seem clear that, if the matter of compensation in the present case is governed by Community law, then the approach identified in the authorities to which I have referred would fall to be applied. In particular, the taking of property in the public interest without payment of compensation would be regarded as justifiable only in exceptional circumstances (*Lithgow*). Indeed, in his speech on behalf of the respondent, senior counsel really accepted that this would be the effect of the application of Community law—though he argued that the circumstances were sufficiently exceptional to justify ordering the destruction of the fish without the payment of compensation. On the other hand, if the matter of compensation is not controlled by Community law but by domestic law, then it seems equally clear that different considerations would apply, though what exactly those considerations would be it is unnecessary to determine since the petitioners case is perilled on Community law.

The Court of Justice emphasised the importance of this dividing line between Community and national law in *ERT v DEP* (Case C–260/89) [1991] E.C.R. I–2925 at para 42 of its judgment: 'As the court has held (see the judgment in Joined Cases C-60 and C-61/84 *Cinéthèque v Fédération Nationale des Cinémas Français* [1985] ECR 2605, para 25, and the judgment in Case C-12/86 *Demirel v Stadt Schwäbisch Gmund* [1987] ECR 3719, para 28), it has no power to examine the compatibility with the European Convention of Human Rights of national rules which do not fall within the scope of Community law. On the other hand, where such rules do fall within the scope of Community law, and reference is made to the Court for a preliminary ruling, it must provide all the criteria of interpretation needed by the national court to determine whether those rules are compatible with the fundamental rights the observance of which the Court ensures and which derive in particular from the European Convention on Human Rights.'

The fundamental question in this case therefore appears to me to be whether the matter of compensation for fish which are killed and destroyed or whose use is controlled by virtue of reg 7 is governed by Community or national law."

The place of human rights in EC law has been greatly enhanced by the EU Charter of Fundamental Rights "solemnly proclaimed" by the European Council at Nice in December 2000. This is a hugely significant document the content of which was greatly influenced by the ECHR, the Council of Europe Social Charter of 1961 and the Revised Social Charter of 1996, as well as the national constitutions of the then 15 Member States. As such the EU Charter is perhaps the most comprehensive human rights document ever drafted, in the sense that both civil and political rights shelter under its cover along with both social and economic rights. Moreover, they all stand together as equals, each enjoying an equal status with the other. This is a remarkable achievement in these neo-liberal times when ideas of equality and solidarity (to use the language of the Charter) have given way to rights promoting individual liberty. It is true that the EU Charter is of uncertain legal status and that it is not directly enforceable in the courts as such, whether by or against a Community institution, a Member State or an individual or company. It has, however, been referred to on many occasions now in proceedings in the European Court of Justice, the European Court of Human Rights and the domestic courts of the United Kingdom. It also forms the text of the fundamental rights chapter of the new EU Constitution to which the Charter was itself seen as a "prelude" (K. Lenaerts and E. E. De Smijter, "A 'Bill of Rights' for the European Union" (2001) 38 C.M.L.R. 273, at 300). Particularly important, however is art.51 of the Charter which makes it clear that it is designed to apply only in the admittedly expanding context of EU law and to Member States "only when they are implementing Union law". For a review of the Charter, see K. D. Ewing, *The EU Charter of Fundamental Rights: Waste of Time or Wasted Opportunity?* (Institute of Employment Rights, 2002).

EU Charter of Fundamental Rights 2000

"SOLEMN PROCLAMATION

The European Parliament, the Council and the Commission solemnly proclaim the text below as the Charter of Fundamental Rights of the European Union
   Done at Nice on the seventh day of December in the year two thousand
   For the European Parliament
   For the Council of the European Union
   For the European Commission

PREAMBLE

The peoples of Europe, in creating an ever closer union among them, are resolved to share a peaceful future based on common values.

Conscious of its spiritual and moral heritage, the Union is founded on the indivisible, universal values of human dignity, freedom, equality and solidarity; it is based on the principles of democracy and the rule of law. It places the individual at the heart of its activities, by establishing the citizenship of the Union and by creating an area of freedom, security and justice.

The Union contributes to the preservation and to the development of these common values while respecting the diversity of the cultures and traditions of the peoples of Europe as well as the national identities of the Member States and the organisation of their public authorities at national, regional and local levels; it seeks to promote balanced and sustainable development and ensures free movement of persons, goods, services and capital, and the freedom of establishment.

To this end, it is necessary to strengthen the protection of fundamental rights in the light of changes in society, social progress and scientific and technological developments by making those rights more visible in a Charter.

This Charter reaffirms, with due regard for the powers and tasks of the Community and the Union and the principle of subsidiarity, the rights as they result, in particular, from the constitutional traditions and international obligations common to the Member States, the Treaty on European Union, the Community Treaties, the European Convention for the Protection of Human Rights and Fundamental Freedoms, the Social Charters adopted by the Community and by the Council of Europe and the case-law of the Court of Justice of the European Communities and of the European Court of Human Rights.

Enjoyment of these rights entails responsibilities and duties with regard to other persons, to the human community and to future generations.

The Union therefore recognises the rights, freedoms and principles set out hereafter.

CHAPTER I DIGNITY

Article 1 Human dignity
Human dignity is inviolable. It must be respected and protected.

Article 2 Right to life
  1. Everyone has the right to life.
  2. No one shall be condemned to the death penalty, or executed.

Article 3 Right to the integrity of the person
  1. Everyone has the right to respect for his or her physical and mental integrity.
  2. In the fields of medicine and biology, the following must be respected in particular:
  — the free and informed consent of the person concerned, according to the procedures laid down by law,
  — the prohibition of eugenic practices, in particular those aiming at the selection of persons,
  — the prohibition on making the human body and its parts as such a source of financial gain,
  — the prohibition of the reproductive cloning of human beings.

Article 4 Prohibition of torture and inhuman or degrading treatment or punishment
No one shall be subjected to torture or to inhuman or degrading treatment or punishment.

Article 5 Prohibition of slavery and forced labour
  1. No one shall be held in slavery or servitude.
  2. No one shall be required to perform forced or compulsory labour.
  3. Trafficking in human beings is prohibited.

CHAPTER II FREEDOMS

Article 6 Right to liberty and security
Everyone has the right to liberty and security of person.

Article 7 Respect for private and family life
Everyone has the right to respect for his or her private and family life, home and communications.

Article 8 Protection of personal data
  1. Everyone has the right to the protection of personal data concerning him or her.
  2. Such data must be processed fairly for specified purposes and on the basis of the consent of the person concerned or some other legitimate basis laid down by law. Everyone has the right of access to data which has been collected concerning him or her, and the right to have it rectified.
  3. Compliance with these rules shall be subject to control by an independent authority.

Article 9 Right to marry and right to found a family
The right to marry and the right to found a family shall be guaranteed in accordance with the national laws governing the exercise of these right.

Article 10 Freedom of thought, conscience and religion
  1. Everyone has the right to freedom of thought, conscience and religion. This right includes freedom to change religion or belief and freedom, either alone or in community with others and in public or in private, to manifest religion or belief, in worship, teaching, practice and observance.

2. The right to conscientious objection is recognised, in accordance with the national laws governing the exercise of this right.

Article 11 Freedom of expression and information
1. Everyone has the right to freedom of expression. This right shall include freedom to hold opinions and to receive and impart information and ideas without interference by public authority and regardless of frontiers.
2. The freedom and pluralism of the media shall be respected.

Article 12 Freedom of assembly and of association
1. Everyone has the right to freedom of peaceful assembly and to freedom of association at all levels, in particular in political, trade union and civic matters, which implies the right of everyone to form and to join trade unions for the protection of his or her interests.
2. Political parties at Union level contribute to expressing the political will of the citizens of the Union.

Article 13 Freedom of the arts and sciences
The arts and scientific research shall be free of constraint. Academic freedom shall be respected.

Article 14 Right to education
1. Everyone has the right to education and to have access to vocational and continuing training.
2. This right includes the possibility to receive free compulsory education.
3. The freedom to found educational establishments with due respect for democratic principles and the right of parents to ensure the education and teaching of their children in conformity with their religious, philosophical and pedagogical convictions shall be respected, in accordance with the national laws governing the exercise of such freedom and right.

Article 15 Freedom to choose an occupation and right to engage in work
1. Everyone has the right to engage in work and to pursue a freely chosen or accepted occupation.
2. Every citizen of the Union has the freedom to seek employment, to work, to exercise the right of establishment and to provide services in any Member State.
3. Nationals of third countries who are authorised to work in the territories of the Member States are entitled to working conditions equivalent to those of citizens of the Union.

Article 16 Freedom to conduct a business
The freedom to conduct a business in accordance with Community law and national laws and practices is recognised.

Article 17 Right to property
1. Everyone has the right to own, use, dispose of and bequeath his or her lawfully acquired possessions. No one may be deprived of his or her possessions, except in the public interest and in the cases and under the conditions provided for by law, subject to fair compensation being paid in good time for their loss. The use of property may be regulated by law in so far as is necessary for the general interest.
2. Intellectual property shall be protected.

Article 18 Right to asylum
The right to asylum shall be guaranteed with due respect for the rules of the Geneva Convention of 28 July 1951 and the Protocol of 31 January 1967 relating to the status of

refugees and in accordance with the Treaty establishing the European Community.

Article 19 Protection in the event of removal, expulsion or extradition
   1. Collective expulsions are prohibited.
   2. No one may be removed, expelled or extradited to a State where there is a serious risk that he or she would be subjected to the death penalty, torture or other inhuman or degrading treatment or punishment.

CHAPTER III EQUALITY

Article 20 Equality before the law
Everyone is equal before the law.

Article 21 Non-discrimination
   1. Any discrimination based on any ground such as sex, race, colour, ethnic or social origin, genetic features, language, religion or belief, political or any other opinion, membership of a national minority, property, birth, disability, age or sexual orientation shall be prohibited.
   2. Within the scope of application of the Treaty establishing the European Community and of the Treaty on European Union, and without prejudice to the special provisions of those Treaties, any discrimination on grounds of nationality shall be prohibited.

Article 22 Cultural, religious and linguistic diversity
The Union shall respect cultural, religious and linguistic diversity.

Article 23 Equality between men and women
Equality between men and women must be ensured in all areas, including employment, work and pay. The principle of equality shall not prevent the maintenance or adoption of measures providing for specific advantages in favour of the under-represented sex.

Article 24 The rights of the child
   1. Children shall have the right to such protection and care as is necessary for their wellbeing. They may express their views freely. Such views shall be taken into consideration on matters which concern them in accordance with their age and maturity.
   2. In all actions relating to children, whether taken by public authorities or private institutions, the child's best interests must be a primary consideration. Every child shall have the right to maintain on a regular basis a personal relationship and direct contact with both his or her parents, unless that is contrary to his or her interests.

Article 25 The rights of the elderly
The Union recognises and respects the rights of the elderly to lead a life of dignity and independence and to participate in social and cultural life.

Article 26 Integration of persons with disabilities
The Union recognises and respects the right of persons with disabilities to benefit from measures designed to ensure their independence, social and occupational integration and participation in the life of the community.

CHAPTER IV SOLIDARITY

Article 27 Workers' right to information and consultation within the undertaking
Workers or their representatives must, at the appropriate levels, be guaranteed information and consultation in good time in the cases and under the conditions provided for by Community law and national laws and practices.

Article 28 Right of collective bargaining and action
Workers and employers, or their respective organisations, have, in accordance with Community law and national laws and practices, the right to negotiate and conclude collective agreements at the appropriate levels and, in cases of conflicts of interest, to take collective action to defend their interests, including strike action.

Article 29 Right of access to placement services
Everyone has the right of access to a free placement service.

Article 30 Protection in the event of unjustified dismissal
Every worker has the right to protection against unjustified dismissal, in accordance with Community law and national laws and practices.

Article 31 Fair and just working conditions
  1. Every worker has the right to working conditions which respect his or her health, safety and dignity.
  2. Every worker has the right to limitation of maximum working hours, to daily and weekly rest periods and to an annual period of paid leave.

Article 32 Prohibition of child labour and protection of young people at work
The employment of children is prohibited. The minimum age of admission to employment may not be lower than the minimum school-leaving age, without prejudice to such rules as may be more favourable to young people and except for limited derogations. Young people admitted to work must have working conditions appropriate to their age and be protected against economic exploitation and any work likely to harm their safety, health or physical, mental, moral or social development or to interfere with their education.

Article 33 Family and professional life
  1. The family shall enjoy legal, economic and social protection.
  2. To reconcile family and professional life, everyone shall have the right to protection from dismissal for a reason connected with maternity and the right to paid maternity leave and to parental leave following the birth or adoption of a child.

Article 34 Social security and social assistance
  1. The Union recognises and respects the entitlement to social security benefits and social services providing protection in cases such as maternity, illness, industrial accidents, dependency or old age, and in the case of loss of employment, in accordance with the rules laid down by Community law and national laws and practices.
  2. Everyone residing and moving legally within the European Union is entitled to social security benefits and social advantages in accordance with Community law and national laws and practices.
  3. In order to combat social exclusion and poverty, the Union recognises and respects the right to social and housing assistance so as to ensure a decent existence for all those who lack sufficient resources, in accordance with the rules laid down by Community law and national laws and practices.

Article 35 Health care
Everyone has the right of access to preventive health care and the right to benefit from medical treatment under the conditions established by national laws and practices. A high level of human health protection shall be ensured in the definition and implementation of all Union policies and activities.

Article 36 Access to services of general economic interest
The Union recognises and respects access to services of general economic interest as pro-

vided for in national laws and practices, in accordance with the Treaty establishing the European Community, in order to promote the social and territorial cohesion of the Union.

Article 37 Environmental protection
A high level of environmental protection and the improvement of the quality of the environment must be integrated into the policies of the Union and ensured in accordance with the principle of sustainable development.

Article 38 Consumer protection
Union policies shall ensure a high level of consumer protection.

CHAPTER V CITIZENS' RIGHTS

Article 39 Right to vote and to stand as a candidate at elections to the European Parliament
   1. Every citizen of the Union has the right to vote and to stand as a candidate at elections to the European Parliament in the Member State in which he or she resides, under the same conditions as nationals of that State.
   2. Members of the European Parliament shall be elected by direct universal suffrage in a free and secret ballot.

Article 40 Right to vote and to stand as a candidate at municipal elections
Every citizen of the Union has the right to vote and to stand as a candidate at municipal elections in the Member State in which he or she resides under the same conditions as nationals of that State.

Article 41 Right to good administration
   1. Every person has the right to have his or her affairs handled impartially, fairly and within a reasonable time by the institutions and bodies of the Union.
   2. This right includes:
     — the right of every person to be heard, before any individual measure which would affect him or her adversely is taken;
     — the right or every person to have access to his or her file, while respecting the legitimate interests of confidentiality and of professional and business secrecy;
     — the obligation of the administration to give reasons for its decisions.
   3. Every person has the right to have the Community make good any damage caused by its institutions or by its servants in the performance of their duties, in accordance with the general principles common to the laws of the Member States.
   4. Every person may write to the institutions of the Union in one of the languages of the Treaties and must have an answer in the same language.

Article 42 Right of access to documents
Any citizen of the Union, and any natural or legal person residing or having its registered office in a Member State, has a right of access to European Parliament, Council and Commission documents.

Article 43 Ombudsman
Any citizen of the Union, and any natural or legal person residing or having its registered office in a Member State, has the right to refer to the Ombudsman of the Union cases of maladministration in the activities of the Community institutions or bodies, with the exception of the Court of Justice and the Court of First instance acting in their judicial role.

Article 44 Right to petition
Any citizen of the Union, and any natural or legal person residing or having its registered office in a Member State, has the right to petition the European Parliament.

Article 45 Freedom of movement and of residence
1. Every citizen of the Union has the right to move and reside freely within the territory of the Member States.
2. Freedom of movement and residence may be granted, in accordance with the Treaty establishing the European Community, to nationals of third countries legally resident in the territory of a Member State.

Article 46 Diplomatic and consular protection
Every citizen of the Union shall, in the territory of a third country in which the Member State of which he or she is a national is not represented, be entitled to protection by the diplomatic or consular authorities of any Member State, on the same conditions as the nationals of that Member State.

CHAPTER VI JUSTICE

Article 47 Right to an effective remedy and to a fair trial
Everyone whose rights and freedoms guaranteed by the law of the Union are violated has the right to an effective remedy before a tribunal in compliance with the conditions laid down in this Article. Everyone is entitled to a fair and public hearing within a reasonable time by an independent and impartial tribunal previously established by law. Everyone shall have the possibility of being advised, defended and represented. Legal aid shall be made available to those who lack sufficient resources in so far as such aid is necessary to ensure effective access to justice.

Article 48 Presumption of innocence and right of defence
1. Everyone who has been charged shall be presumed innocent until proved guilty according to law.
2. Respect for the rights of the defence of anyone who has been charged shall be guaranteed.

Article 49 Principles of legality and proportionality of criminal offences and penalties
1. No one shall be held guilty of any criminal offence on account of any act or omission which did not constitute a criminal offence under national law or international law at the time when it was committed. Nor shall a heavier penalty be imposed than that which was applicable at the time the criminal offence was committed. If, subsequent to the commission of a criminal offence, the law provides for a lighter penalty, that penalty shall be applicable.
2. This Article shall not prejudice the trial and punishment of any person for any act or omission which, at the time when it was committed, was criminal according to the general principles recognised by the community of nations.
3. The severity of penalties must not be disproportionate to the criminal offence.

Article 50 Right not to be tried or punished twice in criminal proceedings for the same criminal offence
No one shall be liable to be tried or punished again in criminal proceedings for an offence for which he or she has already been finally acquitted or convicted within the Union in accordance with the law.

CHAPTER VII GENERAL PROVISIONS

Article 51 Scope
1. The provisions of this Charter are addressed to the institutions and bodies of the Union with due regard for the principle of subsidiarity and to the Member States only when they are implementing Union law. They shall therefore respect the rights, observe the principles and promote the application thereof in accordance with their respective powers.

2. This Charter does not establish any new power or task for the Community or the Union, or modify powers and tasks defined by the Treaties.

Article 52 Scope of guaranteed rights
1. Any limitation on the exercise of the rights and freedoms recognised by this Charter must be provided for by law and respect the essence of those rights and freedoms. Subject to the principle of proportionality, limitations may be made only if they are necessary and genuinely meet objectives of general interest recognised by the Union or the need to protect the rights and freedoms of others.
2. Rights recognised by this Charter which are based on the Community Treaties or the Treaty on European Union shall be exercised under the conditions and within the limits defined by those Treaties.
3. In so far as this Charter contains rights which correspond to rights guaranteed by the Convention for the Protection of Human Rights and Fundamental Freedoms, the meaning and scope of those rights shall be the same as those laid down by the said Convention. This provision shall not prevent Union law providing more extensive protection.

Article 53 Level of protection
Nothing in this Charter shall be interpreted as restricting or adversely affecting human rights and fundamental freedoms as recognised, in their respective fields of application, by Union law and international law and by international agreements to which the Union, the Community or all the Member States are party, including the European Convention for the Protection of Human Rights and Fundamental Freedoms, and by the Member States' constitutions.

Article 54 Prohibition of abuse of rights
Nothing in this Charter shall be interpreted as implying any right to engage in any activity or to perform any act aimed at the destruction of any of the rights and freedoms recognised in this Charter or at their limitation to a greater extent than is provided for herein."

X. CONCLUSION

The ECHR thus penetrates every level of government in Scotland. It binds local government bodies (as public authorities), it binds the Scottish Parliament and the Scottish Executive, it binds the Westminster Parliament and the United Kingdom Government in their administration of Scotland, and it binds the operation of EC law in Scotland. It is binding in the sense that it can be raised, applied or enforced (in different ways in different circumstances) in the Scottish courts. However, in having this effect, there is a tension which must now be addressed, and which has been one focus of this chapter. This is the tension between the protection of human rights and democracy: the tension between government by the judges and government by the people. The restraint that has been shown so far on the part of the courts has no doubt helped to conceal such tension, as has the fact that we now live in an era where there is a much greater ideological congruence between the courts and politicians. But the tension is unlikely to go away, and is likely to be felt more keenly in Scotland than elsewhere in Great Britain given the power of the courts effectively to strike down primary legislation of the Scottish Parliament. Yet devolution has not only brought potential institutional tension, but also curious paradox and political contradiction. Paradox in the sense that before devolution the people of Scotland were governed by a party that had little popular support and only minority parliamentary representation, with no safeguards against the abuse of sovereign power. Contradiction in the sense that although the people of Scotland now have their own Parliament, they are constrained as to what it may do even within the boundaries of the devolved authority. Yet this is not the only fuel for the sceptic, with the following extract revealing not that human rights adjudication is a threat to democracy in general, but that it is a threat to the liberating potential of devolution in particular. It is as if the people of Scotland are not to be trusted and that they need the supervision of Her Majesty's Privy Council.

C. Himsworth, "Rights versus Devolution"
in T. Campbell, K. D. Ewing and A. Tomkins (eds)
Sceptical Essays on Human Rights (2001)

"Rights versus devolution: nonsense in a kilt?
Even if the problems of smallness are not as great as supposed or if they turn out to be transitory, there will remain the question of whether the contribution of the human rights element in the devolution package will tend to be supportive or destructive of that package as a whole. This chapter is premised on the assumption that devolution itself is an honourable objective and that the commitment to Scotland-based power and accountability must be sustained. It is also premised on the assumption that the rights of citizens must be respected and that there is nothing objectionable in principle about their source in a European treaty. The chapter is not at all to be associated with the blanket antipathy to both devolution and European human rights reflected in some of the Scottish political debate. It insists simply that the centralizing tendency of a rights regime is at least problematic when superimposed on a constitutional system committed to the decentralization of power through devolution. If there is a generally centralizing tendency of human rights regimes, how far is it likely to be realized in the specific conditions established for the operation of Scottish government under the Scotland Act 1998 and then for human rights protection by that Act and the Human Rights Act 1998? There are, I think, a couple of pointers—one based on indications in the cases decided so far and the other which derives from the formal status given to the Scottish Parliament. ...

Practically all the litigation so far initiated has focused on challenges based on executive rather than legislative activity, and this may continue to be the case. Where such challenges are successful, however, a legislative response may be required; and, as suggested earlier, it seems inevitable that, in jurisdictions which force rights issues up to the same (or similarly constituted) supreme courts, there will be a similarity of outcome and, almost as inevitably, a similarity of response by the different administrations and legislatures. The common characteristics of human rights cases may produce a centralizing tendency across swathes of Scottish administration and, perhaps even more significantly, of areas of Scots private law previously untouched by UK or English decision-making. Human rights issues have the potential to reach deep into the Scottish legal system, and English court decisions on human rights may come to have a significant new effect on Scots law. With legal professional practice increasingly merging in the commercial areas, human rights practice may follow with even greater energy. If these sorts of development do occur, it may be that ultimate outcomes will not depend greatly on the formal status of the Scottish Parliament and its legislation .... A centralizing conformity may be achieved, even though few Acts of the Scottish Parliament are directly challenged and even fewer struck down."

Chapter 4

THE RIGHT TO LIBERTY

I. INTRODUCTION

Any consideration of the right to liberty protected by art.5 of the ECHR will inevitably be concerned predominantly with the exercise by the police of their powers for the suppression and detection of crime, namely arrest and detention. The deprivation of a person's freedom is an extremely significant power, and one which requires to be surrounded by safeguards to prevent abuse. But police powers do not end with arrest, and we shall also consider powers to carry out personal search and to take samples of blood and fingerprints. It might have been expected that the incorporation of the European Convention on Human Rights would have had an impact on law and practice in relation to police powers. But, with the exception of minor changes in relation to the granting of bail, Scottish courts appear to be satisfied that the existing measures designed to protect the rights of the accused are adequate.

II. POLICE POWERS SHORT OF ARREST

In this section, we consider the powers of the police which fall short of actual arrest. So far as the common law is concerned, the police have no power to stop and search prior to arrest, as the following case makes clear.

Jackson v Stevenson
(1897) 2 Adam 255

Jackson was searched by water-bailiffs who suspected him of poaching salmon. It was unclear whether the search was carried out before or after Jackson was arrested. He was convicted and one of two grounds on which he appealed was that the search was illegal, having been carried out prior to his arrest.

> LORD JUSTICE-GENERAL (ROBERTSON): "Now, a constable is entitled to arrest, without a warrant, any person seen by him committing a breach of the peace, and he may arrest on the direct information of eye witnesses. Having arrested him, I make no doubt that the constable could search him. But it is a totally different matter to search a man in order to find evidence to determine whether you will apprehend him or not. If the search succeeds (such is the condition of the argument), you will apprehend him; but if the search does not succeed you will not apprehend him. Now, I have only to say that I know no authority for ascribing to constables the right to make such tentative searches, and they seem contrary to constitutional principle. If the constable requires to make such a search, it can only be because without it he is not justified in apprehending; and, without a warrant, to search a person not liable to apprehension seems palpably illegal. A constable or bailiff must make

up his mind on what he sees (or hears on credible information) whether to arrest or not; and, if he does arrest in good faith, the law will protect him, whether his opinion at the time of the guilt of the person arrested prove accurate or not."

Lords Adam and Kinnear delivered concurring opinions on both grounds of appeal.

Nor do the police have the power at common law to take a citizen to the police station to help the police with their inquiries, a point made clear by Lord Justice-General Cooper in *Chalmers v HM Advocate*, 1954 S.L.T. 177, where he said in a memorable passage:

> LORD JUSTICE-GENERAL (COOPER): "Putting aside the case of proper apprehension without a warrant of persons caught more or less red-handed, no person can be lawfully detained except after a charge has been made against him, and it is for this reason that I view with some uneasiness the situation disclosed in this case, and illustrated by the recent cases of *Rigg*, 1946 S.L.T. 49 and *Short* (unreported), in which a suspect is neither apprehended nor charged but is simply 'asked' to accompany two police officers to a police office to be there questioned. In former times such questioning, if undertaken, would be conducted by police officers visiting the home or place of business of the suspect and there precognoscing him, probably in the presence of a relation or friend. However convenient the modern practice may be, it must normally create a situation very unfavourable to the suspect. In the eyes of every ordinary citizen the venue is a sinister one. When he stands alone in such a place confronted by several police officers, usually some of high rank, the dice are loaded against him, especially as he knows that there is no one to corroborate him as to what exactly occurred during the interrogation, how it was conducted, and how long it lasted."

The common law rule has, however, been eroded by a number of statutory provisions. These include the Misuse of Drugs Act 1971.

Misuse of Drugs Act 1971

"Powers to search and obtain evidence.

23...

(2) If a constable has reasonable grounds to suspect that any person is in possession of a controlled drug in contravention of this Act or of any regulations made thereunder, the constable may—

    (a) search that person, and detain him for the purpose of searching him;

    (b) search any vehicle or vessel in which the constable suspects that the drug may be found, and for that purpose require the person in control of the vehicle or vessel to stop it;

    (c) seize and detain, for the purposes of proceedings under this Act, anything found in the course of the search which appears to the constable to be evidence of an offence under this Act.

... nothing in this subsection shall prejudice any power of search or any power to seize or detain property which is exercisable by a constable apart from this subsection.

(4) A person commits an offence if he—

    (a) intentionally obstructs a person in the exercise of his powers under this section;

    ...."

Section 23 of the 1971 Act provides for the detention of a person in order that they may be searched for controlled drugs suspected of being in their possession. The suspicion must be "reasonable", and there is no requirement for a warrant. In the following case, the reasonable suspicion derived from a tip-off which turned out to be false.

Wither v Reid
1979 S.L.T. 192

Reid and a friend were met by police at Elgin railway station, as they were suspected of carrying drugs brought from Aberdeen. The tip-off on which the police were acting turned out to be false, and no drugs were found. However, Reid violently resisted attempts to search her and was charged with assaulting a police officer in the execution of her duties. Reid's defence was that her arrest and subsequent search of her person were unlawful, under s.24 of the Misuse of Drugs Act 1971, which makes provision for arrest without warrant where there is fear that the suspect will abscond if they are not arrested. It was argued for the Crown that the search was lawful by virtue of s.23 of the 1971 Act. The sheriff found that the arrest and subsequent search were illegal, and Reid was acquitted. An appeal by the Crown was unsuccessful. The questions for the opinion of the court were first whether the arrest of the respondent was lawful, and secondly, whether the sheriff was entitled to find her not guilty.

LORD ROBERTSON: "An accused person was charged with assaulting a police officer in the execution of her duty, contrary to s. 41 (1) (a) of the Police (Scotland) Act 1967. The alleged offence occurred while the accused was at Elgin police office being searched against her will to see if she was in possession of a controlled drug in contravention of the Misuse of Drugs Act 1971. At the trial, there was evidence that the police had received information to suggest that the accused was in possession of drugs, that they had told her when she was taken to the office that she was being arrested and that she would be searched for drugs. The accused had resisted the search, which was carried out forcibly. No drugs were found. The sheriff acquitted the accused on the view that the search was illegal, since it followed on an arrest which was itself illegal. While s. 24 (1) of the Misuse of Drugs Act 1971 permitted arrest without warrant, the conditions under which such an arrest might be made were not present in the instant case. While s. 23 (2) (a) of the Act authorised detention and search, in this case the police had arrested the accused, told her so and then purported to search her under the said s. 23 (2) (a). In such circumstances, the accused was entitled to use all necessary force, short of cruel excess, to resist the removal of her clothing and the indignity and humiliation of a body search. The Crown appealed by stated case.

The issue between the parties at the appeal was concerned with the first question. Counsel for the appellant conceded that if his submission that the search of the respondent was lawful was not accepted, his appeal must fail. The basis of that submission was that the respondent had not been under arrest at any time and that the words used by the detective sergeant when he approached the respondent at Elgin railway station, did not signify that he was 'arresting' her, despite the fact that it was made clear by him to her, according to finding 5, that she was 'under arrest'. What he did at that time, on this submission, did not depend only on the use of the word 'arrest' but also on the other words used and on the actions which followed the words used. The other words used by the detective sergeant as narrated in finding 5, would appear to indicate that he was relying on s. 23 (2) (a) of the Misuse of Drugs Act 1971 to search her and detain her only for the purpose of searching her.

Whatever may have been in the mind of the detective sergeant, he did tell the respondent that she was under arrest. He purported to arrest her. I cannot see how the later explanation to the respondent, apparently based on s. 23 (2) (a), can alter what he specifically said he was doing. His apparent confusion about his powers cannot, in my opinion, mean that he was not putting her under 'arrest', as he himself clearly thought he was doing despite the explanation. The actions which followed the 'arrest' and the events which occurred at Elgin police station are as consistent with a purported arrest as they are with search and detention under said s. 23 (2) (a). If one looks at the actions which followed the events at the Elgin railway station, as counsel for the appellant suggested should be done in order to ascertain whether there was an 'arrest', these actions did not show that she was not 'under arrest'. What the detective sergeant did was to arrest the respondent unlawfully prior to the search despite an explanation by him which indicated a limited statutory detention. The search which followed was referable to the purported arrest and was, therefore, in my opinion, unlawful. It follows accordingly that the sheriff was correct in the view which he reached.

In my opinion question 1 should be answered in the negative. It follows that question 2 should be answered in the affirmative. In terms of the Misuse of Drugs Act 1971, s. 23 (2): 'If a constable has reasonable grounds to suspect that any person is in possession of a controlled drug in contravention of the Act or of any regulations made thereunder, the constable may (a) search that person, and detain him for the purpose of searching him. ...' there is no definition in the Act of what is meant by the word 'detain' in that section.

Section 24 of the Act under the heading 'Power of Arrest' enacts:

> '(1) A constable may arrest without warrant a person who has committed, or whom the constable, with reasonable cause, suspects to have committed, an offence under this Act, if—
>
>   (a) he, with reasonable cause, believes that that person will abscond unless arrested; or
>   (b) the name and address of that person are unknown to, and cannot be ascertained by him;
>   (c) he is not satisfied that a name and address furnished by that person as his name and address are true; ...'

In the present case, according to finding-in-fact 5, the respondent was approached by police officers at Elgin railway station, who told her that she was being apprehended under the Misuse of Drugs Act 1971 on suspicion of being in possession of a controlled drug or drugs. It was made clear to the respondent that she was under arrest and was to be taken to Elgin police office and searched for drugs. She was told that she would not be kept there any longer than necessary. She was further told that when the police had received information of a suspected drug offence they were bound to take suspects to a police station to be searched for drugs; they told her she would be released as soon as possible. According to the sheriff, the police officers gave clear and unequivocal evidence that the respondent was arrested at the railway station under the Misuse of Drugs Act 1971.

If this is so, then the arrest in my opinion was unlawful. It was not an arrest under s. 24, but was a purported action under s. 23 (2) (a). But that section does not give authority to arrest, only to 'detain' for a limited purpose. There is a vital distinction between 'arrest' and 'detention' (*Swankie v Milne*, 1973 S.L.T.(Notes), Lord Cameron at p. 29). It is true that under s. 23 (2) (a) of the 1971 Act the police are entitled to detain the person suspected for the purpose of searching him, and for this purpose may be entitled to take him to a place where the search may take place. This place might conveniently be the nearest police station. But a penal statute must be construed strictly. In my opinion, in deference to the rights of the citizen, it must be made perfectly clear to the person against whom action is being taken under s. 23 (2) (a) that that is what is being done and that he is not being arrested. If, as apparently happened in this case, the respondent was arrested and told that she was to be taken to the police station under arrest, then in my opinion that was an unlawful arrest. It will not do, in my opinion, to say that she was bound to know the law and so was bound to realise that, although the police officers used the word 'arrest', they really meant 'detain', and were proceeding under s. 23 (2) (a). The police also should know the law and if they were proceeding under s. 23 they should have done so explicitly.

I think the sheriff was right."

A number of other statutes also confer a power to detain individuals. A general power of detention was introduced by Criminal Justice (Scotland) Act 1980 following the recommendations of the Thomson Committee some five years earlier.

Second Report of the Committee on Scottish Criminal Procedure
(Chairman: Lord Thomson)
Cmnd. 6218 (1975)

"Detention before arrest and charge

3.13 The policeman's real difficulty arises in investigations where he wants to interview a suspect or prevent him from interfering with evidence such as stolen property. At present the police are powerless to act without the consent of the very person who is likely to have most interest in refusing to give that consent. Clearly the police should not be entitled to arrest anyone they want to interview but it seems plainly wrong, for example, that a suspected violent criminal with significant evidence on his clothing has to be left at large while the police seek other evidence of his guilt sufficient to entitle them to charge.

3.14 We *recommend* that the practice of inviting persons to the police station should be regularised. We are convinced that it will continue if the law remains unchanged and that it can be controlled only by being recognised and made subject to clearly defined limits. We accept that certain people do and will continue to attend at police stations truly voluntarily, such as those who prefer to see the police there rather than have the police be seen to visit them, or those who call to confess to crime, but these are exceptional cases. Our recommendations will also cover the situation where the police stop in the street people who are suspected of committing or having recently committed an offence. At present, except where they act under Police Acts, which relate for the most part to stolen property, or under any other special statute such as the Road Traffic Act 1972, the police have no power to detain and question anyone in the street unless they are in a position to arrest him.

3.15 We *recommend*, therefore, a form of limited, or temporary arrest—arrest on suspicion. Since the rules governing this 'arrest' will differ from those governing arrest at the moment, we give it a separate name—detention. Detention will include power to take to and keep in a police station, but its duration will be limited by the following general rules:

    a. it should not last longer than is necessary in the interests of justice;

    b. it should be succeeded as soon as is reasonable by either release or arrest; and

    c. it should not in any event exceed a fixed period of time at the end of which the detainee must be either released or arrested and charged."

Although these recommendations were extremely controversial at the time they were implemented, they have been retained and are now to be found in the Criminal Procedure (Scotland) Act 1995. The difference in practice between an arrest on the one hand and detention on the other is one that would test the most gifted sophist: either way the individual is being held by the police.

Criminal Procedure (Scotland) Act 1995

"Powers relating to suspects and potential witnesses

13—(1) Where a constable has reasonable grounds for suspecting that a person has committed or is committing an offence at any place, he may require—

    (a) that person, if the constable finds him at that place or at any place where the constable is entitled to be, to give his name and address and may ask him for an explanation of the circumstances which have given rise to the constable's suspicion;

    (b) any other person whom the constable finds at that place or at any place where the constable is entitled to be and who the constable believes has information relating to the offence, to give his name and address.

(2) The constable may require the person mentioned in paragraph (a) of subsection (1) above to remain with him while he (either or both)—

    (a) subject to subsection (3) below, verifies any name and address given by the person;

(b) notes any explanation proffered by the person.

(3) The constable shall exercise his power under paragraph (a) of subsection (2) above only where it appears to him that such verification can be obtained quickly.

(4) A constable may use reasonable force to ensure that the person mentioned in paragraph (a) of subsection (1) above remains with him.

(5) A constable shall inform a person, when making a requirement of that person under—

(a) paragraph (a) of subsection (1) above, of his suspicion and of the general nature of the offence which he suspects that the person has committed or is committing;

(b) paragraph (b) of subsection (1) above, of his suspicion, of the general nature of the offence which he suspects has been or is being committed and that the reason for the requirement is that he believes the person has information relating to the offence;

(c) subsection (2) above, why the person is being required to remain with him;

(d) either of the said subsections, that failure to comply with the requirement may constitute an offence.

(6) A person mentioned in—

(a) paragraph (a) of subsection (1) above who having been required—

    (i) under that subsection to give his name and address; or

    (ii) under subsection (2) above to remain with a constable,

fails, without reasonable excuse, to do so, shall be guilty of an offence and liable on summary conviction to a fine not exceeding level 3 on the standard scale;

(b) paragraph (b) of the said subsection (1) who having been required under that subsection to give his name and address fails, without reasonable excuse, to do so shall be guilty of an offence and liable on summary conviction to a fine not exceeding level 2 on the standard scale.

(7) A constable may arrest without warrant any person who he has reasonable grounds for suspecting has committed an offence under subsection (6) above.

Detention and questioning at police station

14—(1) Where a constable has reasonable grounds for suspecting that a person has committed or is committing an offence punishable by imprisonment, the constable may, for the purpose of facilitating the carrying out of investigations—

(a) into the offence; and

(b) as to whether criminal proceedings should be instigated against the person, detain that person and take him as quickly as is reasonably practicable to a police station or other premises and may thereafter for that purpose take him to any other place and, subject to the following provisions of this section, the detention may continue at the police station or, as the case may be, the other premises or place.

(2) Detention under subsection (1) above shall be terminated not more than six hours after it begins or (if earlier)—

(a) when the person is arrested;

(b) when he is detained in pursuance of any other enactment; or

(c) where there are no longer such grounds as are mentioned in the said subsection (1), and when a person has been detained under subsection (1) above, he shall be informed immediately upon the termination of his detention in accordance with this subsection that his detention has been terminated.

(3) Where a person has been released at the termination of a period of detention under subsection (1) above he shall not thereafter be detained, under that subsection, on the same grounds or on any grounds arising out of the same circumstances.

(4) Subject to subsection (5) below, where a person has previously been detained in pursuance of any other enactment, and is detained under subsection (1) above on the same grounds or on grounds arising from the same circumstances as those which led to his earlier detention, the period of six hours mentioned in subsection (2) above shall be reduced by the

length of that earlier detention.

(5) Subsection (4) above shall not apply in relation to detention under section 41(3) of the Prisons (Scotland) Act 1989 (detention in relation to introduction etc. into prison of prohibited article), but where a person was detained under section 41(3) immediately prior to his detention under subsection (1) above the period of six hours mentioned in subsection (2) above shall be reduced by the length of that earlier detention.

(6) At the time when a constable detains a person under subsection (1) above, he shall inform the person of his suspicion, of the general nature of the offence which he suspects has been or is being committed and of the reason for the detention; and there shall be recorded—

　(a)　the place where detention begins and the police station or other premises to which the person is taken;

　(b)　any other place to which the person is, during the detention, thereafter taken;

　(c)　the general nature of the suspected offence;

　(d)　the time when detention under subsection (1) above begins and the time of the person's arrival at the police station or other premises;

　(e)　the time when the person is informed of his rights in terms of subsection (9) below and of subsection (1)(b) of section 15 of this Act and the identity of the constable so informing him;

　(f)　where the person requests such intimation to be sent as is specified in section 15(1)(b) of this Act, the time when such request is—

　　(i)　made;

　　(ii)　complied with; and

　(g)　the time of the person's release from detention or, where instead of being released he is arrested in respect of the alleged offence, the time of such arrest.

(7) Where a person is detained under subsection (1) above, a constable may—

　(a)　without prejudice to any relevant rule of law as regards the admissibility in evidence of any answer given, put questions to him in relation to the suspected offence;

　(b)　exercise the same powers of search as are available following an arrest.

(8) A constable may use reasonable force in exercising any power conferred by subsection (1), or by paragraph (b) of subsection (7), above.

(9) A person detained under subsection (1) above shall be under no obligation to answer any question other than to give his name and address, and a constable shall so inform him both on so detaining him and on arrival at the police station or other premises."

[Section 15 is reproduced below.]

The power of detention under s.13 allows a police officer to stop a person suspected of committing an offence and to require that the person gives his or her name and address. The person may be required to stay with the police officer while the name and address are verified. Section 14 is a more significant form of detention. A person may be detained for up to six hours where a police officer has reasonable suspicion that the person has committed an offence punishable by imprisonment. The purpose of the detention is to facilitate investigations into the offence or to determine whether proceedings should be instigated. Detention beyond the six-hour period is unlawful, unless the suspect is arrested during that time. The question arises as to what constitutes reasonable grounds for suspicion sufficient to justify detention. This is a matter considered in the following case.

Wilson v Robertson
1986 S.C.C.R. 701

The appellants were charged with breaking into vending machines in a social club, the fire door of which had been tampered with so that it would give access from the outside. The appellants were the only non-regulars in the club, were the last to leave and were loitering in the car park as the club was locked up. They challenged the legality of their detention and the admissibility of the statements made while so detained. However, the circumstances detailed were held to be sufficient to justify the suspicion that they had committed the offence and could thus be lawfully detained.

LORD JUSTICE GENERAL (EMSLIE): "The appellants are Alan Wilson and Timothy John Nolan. They went to trial on a complaint which libelled in the first instance theft by opening lockfast places, in particular, theft by opening lockfast cigarette vending machines in the Fishcross Miners Welfare Club and stealing therefrom cigarettes and money to a declared value. The second charge was a charge that by means of an instrument they attempted to force open a lockfast cupboard in these premises with intent to steal. At the conclusion of their trial Nolan was found guilty of both charges and Wilson was found guilty of charge (1) only. This appeal is concerned with the conviction of both appellants, and as can be seen from the stated case their conviction depended to a very large extent upon admissions which were allegedly made by the appellants to the police while they were detained in the Alloa Police Station. At the trial, after sundry evidence had been led, the procurator fiscal adduced police officers to speak to the alleged admissions and it became clear that at the time the alleged admissions were made the appellants had been detained under the purported authority of section 2(1) of the Criminal Justice (Scotland) Act 1980 [now section 14 of the 1995 Act]. When the evidence of the police constables was just about to be presented to the court, objection was taken to the leading of the evidence of any alleged confessions or admissions upon the ground that at the time when the alleged admissions were made the appellants had been illegally detained under and in terms of the subsection of the Act to which we have referred. What the sheriff did was to allow the trial to proceed under reservation of the question taken under objection. At the conclusion of the trial the objection was renewed in submissions on behalf of the appellants and the objection is recorded in the stated case in these words:

'For the appellant, Mr Brookens submitted that on the facts numbers 1 to 7 narrated aforesaid, a police officer could not have had reasonable grounds for suspecting the appellant of being the perpetrator of the theft libelled.'

Precisely the same submission is contained in each of the stated cases. The critical question in this appeal is question 1 and what question 1 says is this:

'On the facts found numbers 1 to 7, did the police have reasonable grounds for suspecting that the appellant had committed the crimes libelled in the complaint?'

The importance of that question lies in the language of section 2(1) of the Act of 1980. Reading short, what section 2(1) provides is as follows. Where a constable has reasonable grounds for suspecting that a person has committed an offence punishable by imprisonment, the constable may, for the purpose of facilitating the carrying out of investigations into the offence, detain that person and take him as quickly as is reasonably practicable to a police station. The submission for the appellants was a short one. On the facts found numbers 1 to 7 the sheriff was not entitled to hold that there were reasonable grounds for suspecting that the appellants had committed the offence libelled in the complaint. The facts narrated in these findings are, said Mr Moynihan, neutral, and they do not form any proper basis for a suspicion nor, indeed, do they form any proper basis for the existence of reasonable grounds for a suspicion, that the appellants were guilty of the offence. We have come to be of opinion, however, that short and simple though the submission for the appellants was, it should not receive effect. We are concerned here not with evidence as to guilt. We are concerned here simply to know whether there were reasonable grounds on which a police officer might entertain a suspicion that the appellants had committed the offence, and as the matter was put to us by the learned advocate-depute we have come to be of opinion that there were reasonable grounds upon which the police officers concerned were entitled to entertain the relevant suspicion.

The story really begins with finding 7 which is to the effect that the police formed the view that the fire door of the club concerned had been interfered with by somebody within the club before the theft took place. That is to say, the theft was an inside job in the sense that the thieves had made sure of their method of entry before they left the club that evening. Against that background there were a number of reasons, said the learned advocate-depute, and we think he was right in this, why the police might reasonably suspect the appellants as the people who used the means of entry which has been described. In the first place the appellants had, with others, been in the club that night. In the second place, however, they were not members of the club but were strangers and it is not unreasonable, at least in the first instance, as a matter of suspicion to look at the strangers before you look at the members. In any event the appellants were the only strangers present in the club that night according to the findings with which we are concerned, and what is more the appellants were the last to leave the club that night before it was locked up. As the learned advocate-depute pointed out, it is at least a matter for reasonable suspicion that persons who intend to leave the locking bar of fire doors open would want to make sure that the locking bar was still detached from its usual position when the premises were locked up and would accordingly be inclined to wait until the end to make sure that all was ready for a later intrusion. Again, as was pointed out to us from the findings, the appellants were in the vicinity of the club in the car park when the proper doors of the club were locked for the night. On that material we are of opinion that the sheriff was right to reject the objection which had been tendered on behalf of the appellants"...

Section 14 contains a number of safeguards for the individual suspect. Additional rights are to be found in s.15 of the 1995 Act. So far as s.14(9) is concerned, this is considered in the following case which deals with the equivalent provision in the Criminal Justice (Scotland) Act 1980. The following case also deals with the overlap between statutory and common law safeguards for the individual. The relevant common law provisions (the administration of a caution) are considered in Pt VIII below.

Tonge, Jack & Gray v H M Advocate
1982 S.L.T. 506

Tonge and Gray were detained by police on suspicion of rape. Tonge was not given a common law caution, but only a warning under s.2(7) of the Criminal Justice (Scotland) Act 1980. When Gray was detained he was given a common law caution, and later a similar warning under s.2(7). Subsequently, they each made incriminating statements. In each case, the police made an assertion of guilt when they went to speak to the suspects, whereupon they made their statements. Jack went voluntarily to the police station where he was given a warning (the precise nature of which was unclear) and he again made an incriminating statement in response to an assertion of his guilt. All were convicted, and appealed successfully on the basis that their statements were inadmissible as evidence.

LORD JUSTICE-GENERAL (EMSLIE): "... In the present case it is plain that on the relevant undisputed evidence no reasonable jury could have held that the alleged statements of Gray and Tonge had been voluntary and had not been extracted by unfair or improper means. It was, in the words of Lord Cameron, abundantly clear that the rules of fairness and fair dealing had been transgressed. A wholly new chapter began when Detective-Sergeant McMorran and Constable Jenkins approached these two appellants in detention. They had little or no evidence that the alleged crime had been committed or that either Gray or Tonge had been among its perpetrators. They hoped to get such evidence from Gray himself and it is an inescapable inference from the evidence that they hoped for the same response from Tonge. What they did was to accuse Gray and Tonge of participation in the alleged crime without first cautioning either. This was clearly calculated to provoke a response and the opening words of the response which the accusation elicited from each demonstrated that each was about to make a statement, possibly self-incriminating. Even then they did not caution either man and they did not caution either thereafter when it clearly began to appear that he was, in fact, about to incriminate himself. In these circumstances the unfairness of the police officers was manifest and it is clear from their own evidence that proper practice, prior to 1980, demanded the giving of a caution at least once to persons in the position of Gray and Tonge. Without their alleged statements there was no sufficient evidence to warrant their conviction and since the verdicts proceeded upon evidence which was inadmissible there has been a miscarriage of justice...

...I have come to be of the opinion that the alleged statements of Gray and Tonge were clearly inadmissible and should have been withheld from the jury. This was, in my opinion, one of those exceptional cases in which, upon the undisputed relevant evidence, it can be said that no reasonable jury could have held that the statements had been voluntary and had not been induced by unfair or improper means (vide *Balloch v H.M. Advocate*, 1977 S.L.T. (Notes) 29). In my judgment upon a close scrutiny of the notes of evidence it is abundantly clear that the rules of fairness and fair dealing were flagrantly transgressed (vide *H.M. Advocate v Whitelaw*, 1980 S.L.T. (Notes) 25). I do not say that in no circumstances will a statement by a detainee (a suspect within the meaning of s. 2(1)) be inadmissible merely because, when it was made, he had not received a full caution. What I do say is that the failure of the investigating officers to caution Gray and Tonge in the special circumstances of this case is fatal to the contention that the rules of fair dealing and fairness were properly observed.

In Gray's case the hope of the two officers was that when they saw him he would provide what was conspicuously lacking, namely, self-incriminating evidence. He was already impressed with the character of a suspect within the meaning of s. 2(1) and they undoubtedly approached him with the hope in their hearts, and with the intention of questioning him if necessary. It is of critical importance to notice what they did. They accused him of participation in the crime. Now, as is pointed out in Walkers' *Law of Evidence in Scotland*, p. 39, para. 45: 'It is proper practice that, when a person is charged with a crime, the caution should be given, since, without it, the reading of the charge may be interpreted by the accused as a question, or as an invitation to reply, in which case any statement then made is not spontaneous and voluntary.' I go further and say that the proper practice is now so long and so well entrenched that it may be taken that a full caution before a charge is made is a requirement of the law itself. The reading of a charge is calculated to provoke a response from the accused and it is quite essential that he should know, in advance, of his right to silence, and of the use which may be made of any response which he chooses to make. To charge an accused person without cautioning him is to put pressure upon him which may induce a response and I have no doubt that by accusing Gray, although not in the formal language of a charge, the accusation was clearly calculated, as a formal charge is calculated, to induce a response from the person accused. The accusation placed pressure upon Gray and I am persuaded that since no caution was administered before it was made, it is impossible to regard the statement made in response to it as spontaneous and voluntary. It was plainly induced by the accusation and in the circumstances was induced by unfair means. It cannot be left out of account either that no caution was administered when the first sentence uttered by Gray made it plain that he intended to make a statement, and that no caution was administered when it became obvious that he was about to incriminate himself. As the evidence of the police officers demonstrated it would have been proper practice to caution a suspect in Gray's position before he was allowed to proceed with a statement and, in my opinion, nothing in s. 2 of the Act of 1980 excuses compliance with that practice.

In Tonge's case I reach the same conclusion. Tonge, who had not received at any stage of the detention procedure a full caution in common law terms, was seen by the investigating officers with the single purpose of charging him. Had they carried out that purpose, they would have required to caution him. They did not do so. What they did, without cautioning him, was to accuse him of the crime, just as they had accused Gray of the crime. This, as Constable Jenkins agreed, was not a usual thing to do where the sole purpose of the encounter was to charge the suspect. Be that as it may the accusation was made without caution, no caution was administered when the first sentence of Tonge's response demonstrated that he was about to make a statement, and no caution was administered at any point while the alleged statement was being made. It is impossible to accept that the officers did not 'get a chance' to charge Tonge and the excuse for not cautioning him was the unfounded assumption that he had already received a full caution when he was detained under s. 2. For all the reasons which led me to hold that the alleged statement by Gray was inadmissible I also hold that the alleged statement by Tonge was inadmissible and should not have been left for consideration by the jury.

In light of what I have said, I would allow the appeals of Gray and Tonge and quash their conviction.

There remains for disposal the appeal of Jack ...

The submission on behalf of Jack in all these circumstances was that the trial judge on the quoted passage misdirected the jury on a matter of great material importance and that there was in Jack's case a miscarriage of justice. The alleged statements by Jack were of critical importance in the Crown case. The jury had to decide whether they could accept the evidence of the two police officers as reliable to the effect that statements were made, and that they were in the terms which they alleged. They also had to consider the whole context in which the alleged statements were made and in particular, whether before Jack said anything at all, he had received, as Constable Jenkins deponed, a full caution at common law. The reliability of the evidence of the two police officers who were already at odds with one another as to their purpose in approaching Jack, fell to be tested sharply upon this question. The trial judge's charge was so framed as to divert the jury's attention from these important issues. What he did, perhaps upon a misapprehension of the evidence, was to instruct the jury that on the one hand the police witnesses maintained that Jack had received a full caution, that Jack on the other hand denied this, and that since Jack had not been detained no question arose in relation to any warning in terms of the 1980 Act. These instructions were accordingly to the effect that they had only to decide one question, namely whether to believe the two police officers or to believe Jack, and the quoted passage from the charge read as a whole was likely to be under-stood by the jury to contain a direction in law that they must not consider at all the possibility that Jack only received a warning under s. 2 of the Act of 1980. What he ought to have done and omitted to do was focus clearly for the jury the vital question of the reliability of the police officers and to instruct them how they should examine that question. In particular he should have drawn the jury's close attention to the evidence of Detective-Sergeant McMorran upon the matter of the warning allegedly given to Jack by Constable Jenkins ...

For these reasons I am of opinion that in this difficult case ... the misdirections on a matter of real importance were such as to lead me to conclude that they were likely to have led to a miscarriage of justice. I reach this conclusion with the less hesitation since it is likely, if the alleged statements by Gray and Tonge had not gone before the jury, the trial would have taken a different course. I would accordingly allow the appeal by Jack and quash his conviction.

Before leaving this case, which has illustrated the problems and confusion created by the provisions of s. 2 of the Act of 1980, I would strongly urge police officers throughout Scotland who proceed to accuse a detainee or to question him or to take from him a voluntary statement, to rely not at all on the efficacy of the warning described in s. 2(7), and to appreciate that if any use is to be made in evidence of anything said by a detainee in these circumstances the ordinary rules of fairness and fair dealing which have been developed by the common law should be strictly observed. The wise course will be, inter alia, to administer to the detainee in the events which I have mentioned a full caution in common law terms. The omission to give such a caution will, by itself, at the very least place the admissibility of anything said by the detainee in peril and the appeals by Gray and Tonge demonstrate circumstances in which the omission of the interviewing officer to caution these men in such terms was fatal."

LORD CAMERON: ". . . In expressing my concurrence with your Lordship in the chair I would only venture to add certain observations of my own on the provisions and operation of s. 2 of the Act of 1980. It is not a happily drafted section, and in particular it is not easy to understand the reason which induced the legislature to enact subs. (7). . . . Now whatever else subs. (7) may mean, what it provides is neither an alternative to nor a substitute for the giving of a caution in the well-recognised and regular form in circumstances where the law and proper practice demands or requires. It is not indeed immediately apparent what useful purpose this innovative and possibly confusing provision is designed to serve, as the proviso to subs. (5) (a) states that: 'this paragraph [sic] shall be without prejudice to any existing rule of law as regards the admissibility in evidence of any answer given.' This, in my opinion means and can only mean that nothing in s. 2 alters the pre-existing rules of law or of safe and proper practice in the matters of cautioning persons who may be questioned in the course of police investigations of crimes or suspected crimes or at any time when a person is being charged with a crime or offence. It is of course well established that police officers are entitled to question a suspect as to his possible complicity in a crime which they are investigating, and that his replies will be admissible in evidence if they have not been extracted or compelled by unfair or improper means including threats, intimidations, offers of inducements, or cross-examination designed or intended to extract incriminating replies, but it is equally well recognised that in the case of one on whom suspicion of responsibility or complicity has centred, in order that his replies should be admissible in evidence, it is proper practice that any further questioning should be preceded by a caution in common form. The proviso to subs. 2(5) is of such wide generality that it leaves no doubt in my opinion that the warning specified in such limited terms which is required to be given in compliance with the provision of subs. (7), is not and cannot be in substitution for the cautions which the law and practice require to be given as a condition precedent to the admissibility of evidence obtained from questioning of a suspect or the replies to a charge made by an accused, but is of an entirely independent character which does not in any way determine the admissibility of evidence obtained by the questioning which the provisions of s. 2 permit.

It would appear to me to follow from this that in the case of a suspect of the kind figured in subs. (1) it would be wise and proper practice that he should receive a caution in recognised form before questions are put to him, in order that no conflict may arise as to the admissibility in evidence of any replies given by him, in the course of such questioning. This conclusion appears to me all the more necessary when it is kept in view that the whole basis on which the right to detain or to question rests on the very definite character of the police officer's suspicion as set out in subs. (1).

Apart however from the question as to what is required to make admissible in evidence any replies made by a suspect detained under the powers given by s. 2 to questions by a police officer in course of his authorised investigation, there are two other matters to which I would refer in relation to the actions of the police officers concerned in the investigations in this case. The first is as to the regular and well-known practice of police officers in taking a voluntary statement from one either suspected or actually charged with a crime, and the second is the rule of law which requires a caution to be given to an accused when a formal charge is made if his reply to the charge is to be admissible in evidence—either for or against him. The regular and proper practice when an accused or suspect indicates or intimates he wishes to make a voluntary statement is that the statement should be taken by officers unconnected with the particular investigation and authenticated by the signatures of the officers concerned and the maker of the statement himself. In the case of the appellants, although the detailed and incriminating statements ascribed to them are recorded in police notebooks, no attempt was made to have them given to or taken by independent officers, or even to have what is recorded in the officers' notebooks signed by the appellants themselves. The investigating officers in this case were fully aware of this proper practice and of the reasons for it, so that it cannot be argued that what is recorded in their notebooks and testified to in evidence were at the time regarded as 'voluntary statements' of the kind I have referred to.

As to the second, in my opinion it is a requirement, which goes beyond one of proper practice and is now a requirement of law, that when preferring a charge against an accused, police officers should caution him as to the possible use to be made of any reply made to that charge. Now the circumstances and manner in which the investigating officers proceeded in the case of all the appellants have already been fully set out by your Lordship, and I have no doubt that not only had the officers determined to prefer charges of rape even before they proceeded to interview the appellants, but also that their immediate intimation of their purpose and intention was in a form which, while lacking the precise formality of a charge, was no more and no less than the levelling, in words which were indistinguishable from those of the formal charge which immediately followed the 'voluntary statement,' a detailed accusation of rape—but one which in the case of the detainees Gray and Tonge was admittedly not preceded by a caution. At that stage of the inquiry there were at least serious grounds for doubt as to whether the police had sufficient evidence on which to justify making a charge, and it was thus a matter of the highest importance that the appellants should be induced to make some statements of an incriminatory character. In offering the explanation for their presence and the subject and purpose of their investigations the police officers concerned did so in a manner which was accusatorial in form and substance and, whether by design or inadvertence it matters not, would be likely to evoke from the person addressed some form of immediate response, explanatory or exculpatory or incriminating. That being so I am clearly of opinion that in the case of Gray and Tonge their statements, in the absence of a precedent caution, were inadmissible in evidence."

Lord Dunpark concurred.

III. POLICE POWERS OF ARREST

Arrest is self-evidently a significant invasion of a person's right to liberty, and accordingly may only take place where there is power to do so. The protections in place in relation to arrest have thus far proved sufficiently effective that art.5(1)(c) of the ECHR has yet to be fully examined in a domestic Scottish court. An arrest may be made by a police officer in the following circumstances:

- with a warrant;
- without a warrant under the common law; or
- without a warrant under the authority of a particular statute.

Each of these powers will be considered in turn, followed in the next section by a discussion of the citizen's power of arrest. It was said by Lord Hope of Craighead in *R. v Manchester Stipendiary Magistrate ex p. Granada Ltd* [2001] 1 A.C. 300:

" ... the entire system for the investigation and prosecution of crime in Scotland is in the hands of the public prosecutor. Overall responsibility for the investigation and prosecution of crime rests with the Lord Advocate. He presides over a system which is operated on his behalf in the sheriff and district courts by the procurator fiscal. The functions and powers of the procurator fiscal long pre-dated the inception of police forces in Scotland. So, while there is a close working relationship between the prosecutor and the police, the police remain subject to the control of the procurator fiscal: *Stair Memorial Encyclopaedia*, vol.

17, Procedure, para. 615. Moreover the organisation and administration of the police forces in Scotland is entirely separate from that in England and Wales. The principal enactment for Scotland is the Police (Scotland) Act 1967.

In practice the police carry out most of the preliminary inquiries themselves without reference to the procurator fiscal. But they have no authority to initiate prosecutions in their own name. Section 17(1)(*b*) of the 1967 Act provides that it shall be the duty of the constables of a police force, where an offence has been committed, to take all such lawful measures and make such reports to the public prosecutor as may be necessary for the purpose of bringing the offender with all due speed to justice. If the police consider that a crime has been committed or if they wish to obtain a warrant to enable them to conduct further investigations into an alleged crime, they must submit a report to the procurator fiscal. The application for a search warrant is made to the court by the procurator fiscal: Stoddart, *Criminal Warrants* (1991), para. 1.03. Once the procurator fiscal has taken charge of the case the police are bound by statute to obey his instructions: Police (Scotland) Act 1967, section 17(3) proviso."

(1) Arrest with Warrant

In order to obtain a warrant, a procurator fiscal will petition the appropriate court, which is usually the sheriff court, where it has been decided that there is sufficient evidence to charge the accused. The petition will specify the charge and crave warrant not only for the power to arrest, but also to search the person named and the premises in which he or she is found. Although for many years it was considered that a warrant would be granted as a matter of course, and would be presumed to be well-founded if presented by a responsible person, it is now the case that the person granting the warrant must be satisfied that there is reasonable cause for suspicion that a crime has been committed. It is sufficient for these purposes to proceed on the evidence of the police officer seeking the grant of the warrant.

Brown v Selfridge
2000 S.L.T. 437

The complainer was the procurator fiscal at Hamilton. The respondents were Alan Selfridge and Angela Helen Bain, both of whom appeared in the sheriff court at Hamilton in respect of a petition dated May 26, 1999 at the instance of the complainer. The petition contained a charge of being concerned in the supply of drugs. It began with a reference to "information received by the petitioner", but after setting out the charges added a narrative that the information received indicated that diamorphine of a quantity indicative of onward supply was found in S and B's house. The narrative reflected a change of practice by the Crown, after the Lord Advocate became a member of the Scottish Executive, in order to ensure compliance with the European Convention on Human Rights. The sheriff considered that the narrative was superfluous and prejudicial to the respondents as it might influence the sheriff's decision as to whether to grant bail. The Crown appealed against the sheriff's decision to refuse a warrant under the petition. The respondents argued that the Crown could use the additional narrative in the petition to argue against the grant of bail and the defence would be powerless to counter such arguments; and that it might be prejudicial if the petition was ever placed before a jury.

LORD JUSTICE GENERAL RODGER: "The date of the petition is of some significance since it was raised less than a week after 20 May 1999, the date on which the Lord Advocate was appointed by Her Majesty the Queen under s 48 (1) of the Scotland Act 1998. By virtue of that appointment he became a member of the Scottish Executive as defined by s 44 (1) and so has no power to do any act so far as it is incompatible with any of the rights under the provisions of the European Convention on Human Rights listed in s 1 (1) of the Human Rights Act 1998 (see ss 57 (2), 126 (1) and 129 (2) of the Scotland Act). As the advocate depute acknowledged, in the light of this legislation, the Crown changed its practice in drafting petitions of this kind. Although the advocate depute did not seek to specify precisely which articles of the Convention might apply, he could see that the provisions of arts 5 (1) (c), 5 (2), 5 (3), 5 (4) and 6 (3) (a) might all conceivably have a bearing on the position. The previous practice of simply referring to 'information received' was based on the acceptance by the courts that the officials of the Lord Advocate would not bring such petitions unless the information which they had received justified them in doing so. With the provisions of the Convention in mind, the Crown decided to include in such petitions a brief indication of the information which the procurator fiscal had received and upon which arrest and detention were sought. In this case the detail of the information received by the procurator fiscal is mentioned in a sentence on the face of the petition. In its original form the sentence said: 'The evidence against the accused Allan Selfridge and Angela Helen Bain is that diamorphine was found by police officers on the above date within the house occupied by them.' We were told that the agent for Mr Selfridge had suggested to the procurator fiscal depute that such evidence did not, on its face, support the charges of being concerned in supplying and of possession with intent to supply. In the light of that criticism the sentence was amended to read: 'The said information received by the petitioner indicates that diamorphine (of a quantity which in the opinion of a drug squad expert is indicative of onward supply) was found by police officers on the above date within the house occupied by the accused.'

From the averments in the bill and from her report, it appears probable that the sheriff did not accept this argument, which is in any event in our view misconceived. The inclusion in a petition of an indication of the information upon which the Crown seek the arrest and detention of an individual is plainly to the advantage of the individual concerned since it allows the court, and indeed the individual concerned, to see whether there is a proper basis for granting the warrant. We express no view, of course, as to what would constitute a proper basis for the grant of a warrant but, if no such proper basis were disclosed, the sheriff could refuse to grant the warrant sought. The change introduced by the Crown therefore tends to strengthen the role of the sheriff and in this way provides an additional safeguard for individuals against arbitrary arrest and detention. The amendment made to the petition in the light of the agent's criticism illustrates the point that the inclusion of the information can be of assistance to accused persons and their advisers.

For these reasons we are satisfied that the petition was competent and that the sheriff erred in upholding the submission for the respondents and dismissing it. We shall accordingly pass the bill and remit to the sheriff to proceed as accords.''

Form of complaint under section 138(1) of the Criminal Procedure (Scotland) Act 1995

IN THE SHERIFF [*or* DISTRICT] COURT
AT (*place*)
THE COMPLAINT OF THE PROCURATOR FISCAL AGAINST
(*name and address sufficient to distinguish person*)
[*or* at present in custody]
Date of birth:
The charge against you is that on (*date*) in [*or* at] you did (*set forth charge as nearly as may be in the form set out in Schedule 5 to the Criminal Procedure (Scotland) Act 1995*).
(*Signed*)

Procurator Fiscal

[*or* Complainer or Solicitor for Complainer]

Form of warrant to apprehend an accused person referred to in section 135 of the Criminal Procedure (Scotland) Act 1995

(*Place and date*). The court grants warrant to apprehend the said accused.
(*Signed*)

Sheriff

Form of warrant to search referred to in section 135 of the Criminal Procedure (Scotland) Act 1995

(*Place and date*). The court grants warrants to search the person, dwelling-house, and repositories of the accused, and any place where he may be found, and to take possession of the property mentioned or referred to in the complaint, and all articles and documents likely to afford evidence of his guilt or of guilty participation.
(*Signed*)

Sheriff

(2) Arrest Without Warrant at Common Law

While there has been no modern authority as to the common law power of arrest, the recognised principles that apply are fairly well settled. An arrest may be made where the police officer has reasonable grounds for suspecting that the person has committed a crime and that it is necessary in the interests of justice for the arrest to be carried out (*Peggie v Clark*, 1868 7 M. 89). The qualification that the arrest is necessary in the interests of justice is satisfied where there is the likelihood that the arrested person may attempt to flee, commit further crimes or dispose of stolen property. The more serious the crime that is committed, the greater the possibility of flight, and so the easier it is to meet the requirement of "necessary in the interests of justice". Hume identified the felonies of murder, house-breaking and robbery as cases where arrest without warrant might be necessary in the interests of justice (Hume ii, 80) but these categories have been reduced to a sliding scale such that "the arrest is more easily justified the more serious the offence" (*Renton & Brown's Criminal Procedure* (6th ed.), 1996, para.7–01). The leading case on arrest at common law relates to an action for damages brought against a police superintendent for wrongful search and arrest.

Peggie v Clark
1868 7 M. 89

Peggie was a carrier commissioned to carry a load of meat from Milnathort to Burntisland, and to deliver the price to the supplier immediately on return. However, rather than returning straightaway, Peggie spent the weekend at a wedding in Bridge of Earn, and the supplier reported the matter to the police. Peggie was arrested and held in custody for a period of about two hours, on suspicion of absconding with the proceeds of the load of meat. After his release, Peggie sued in the sheriff court claiming that the arrest was unlawful. He was successful, and the police constable appealed.

LORD PRESIDENT (INGLIS): "It appears to me that, if the superintendent had reasonable grounds for believing that the pursuer intended to appropriate the money, and for that purpose had absconded, it was right that he should take prompt measures for his apprehension; and the question therefore comes to be, whether he had reasonable grounds? Now, the event certainly goes far to justify him; for when the pursuer was apprehended on his return home, it appeared that he had spent a part of the money on his own account. Looking to all the circumstances, though it is a narrow case, I am inclined to agree with the Sheriff, that the defender had good ground for believing that the pursuer had committed a criminal breach of trust, and had thereupon absconded ...

The ground on which the Sheriff puts his judgment is somewhat delicate and hazardous. He rests almost entirely on the 12th section of the County Police Act ... I am not satisfied that that enactment introduced any new law, or extended the powers of police-officers to apprehend without warrant. But I am of the opinion that, under special circumstances, a police-officer is entitled to apprehend without warrant, and it will always be a question whether the circumstances justify the apprehension. There are some cases about which there can be no doubt,—thus, where a man is accused of murder, it would be a gross breach of duty on the part of a police-officer if, having an opportunity, he failed to apprehend the accused at once, and without a warrant. This is a different case, but, looking to the circumstances, I think they did justify the defender in proceeding without a warrant. But I rest my opinion on the common law, and not on the provision of the County Police Act. The Act, no doubt, fortifies a constable in the discharge of his duty, and defines it, but it gives him, in my opinion, no power beyond what he has at common law.''

LORD DEAS: "There are many exceptional cases in which police-officers or constables are entitled to apprehend without a written warrant, and for such cases no statute was required. If a policeman or constable sees a crime committed, it is his duty to apprehend the criminal at once; or if the criminal is pointed out to him running off from the spot, the same rule would apply. If again, the criminal is hiding, or the officer is credibly informed, or has good reason to believe, that he is about to abscond, the officer may *de plano* apprehend him, to prevent justice from being defeated. The same thing would hold if the crime believed to have been committed was murder or the like, the very nature of the punishment of which would render absconding the probable and natural result of the crime itself. Still further, if a suspected individual belongs to a class of persons reputed to live by crime, or who have no fixed-residence or known means of honest livelihood, in all such cases a police-officer or constable has large powers of apprehending without a warrant. But I agree with your Lordship that the officer is not entitled to overstep the necessity or reasonable requirements of the particular case; and there ought, moreover, in no case, to be undue delay in following out such summary apprehension, by obtaining the appropriate formal warrant for the offender's detention. If an individual, even although expressly charged with crime by an aggrieved party, be a well-known householder,—a person of respectability—what, in our justiciary practice, we call a 'law abiding party,' and where there are no reasonable grounds for supposing that he means to abscond or flee from justice, I find nothing ... to justify a police-officer or constable in apprehending him without a warrant.''

Lord Kinloch delivered a concurring opinion and Lord Ardmillan was absent.

It is usually not difficult for the police to establish that an arrest was justified on the basis of reasonable suspicion. An honest belief that grounds existed which justified arrest will normally be sufficient, unless there is a complete lack of reasonable grounds to support it. There are, however, surprising decisions reported from time to time, surprising in the sense that they provide a robust reminder of the importance of the right to liberty which underpins this area of the law. In *Twycross v Farrell*, 1973 S.L.T. (Notes) 85, the police were called to a school after receiving a complaint that the appellant was selling what may have been pornographic magazines to pupils. When the officer arrived he saw the appellant holding a magazine and talking to girls from the school. The officer asked the appellant what he was doing, the appellant refused to answer, swore at the officer and began to run away. The appellant was then seized by the officer, a struggle ensued and the appellant was convicted of resisting, obstructing, molesting and hindering the constable in the execution of his duty. In reversing the conviction the appeal court indicated that "since there were no findings in the case to support the existence of a reasonable belief by the constable that the appellant had committed an offence, the constable had no right to attempt to stop the appellant from moving smartly away from the spot and that the appellant having been so stopped was entitled to struggle as he did".

McLean v Jessop
1989 S.C.C.R. 13

In this rather unfortunate case, a policeman was charged with assault. He had been called to the scene of a housebreaking, where he saw two men running away. He pursued and caught one of the two, and struck him with his baton. It transpired that the injured party was a neighbour who was chasing after the thief. The sheriff convicted McLean, but he appealed.

LORD JUSTICE CLERK (ROSS): "We agree with Mr MacLean that the question which the sheriff ought to have asked was whether the appellant had reasonable grounds to suspect that a crime had been committed and that the complainer was implicated in it. On the findings we are quite satisfied that the appellant had reasonable grounds to suspect that a crime had been committed. The findings reveal that a radio message was broadcast to police officers in the area to the effect that persons suspected of housebreaking were at the rear of the complainer's home. There is a specific finding that houses in this area were often the target for housebreakers and that this fact was known to the appellant. The appellant, who was on duty in uniform, heard this message and proceeded to the address along with another police officer. Finding 4 states that shortly thereafter another message was broadcast saying that two persons were running from the rear gardens. Although it is not stated in terms that that message was heard by the appellant, the clear inference of the remainder of the finding is that it was. Accordingly, the situation is that the appellant, on duty in uniform, heard a report that persons suspected of housebreaking were at the rear at the complainer's home, that he proceeded there and that he then saw two persons running from the rear gardens of these houses. One of the two persons running was the complainer. That being so, we are satisfied that the appellant had reasonable grounds also to conclude that the complainer was implicated in the suspected housebreaking. In finding 5 it is stated that the complainer turned round and saw the appellant running at him; the appellant caught hold of the complainer who struggled with him and tried to explain that the was a neighbour who had called the police; it was at this stage that the appellant struck the complainer on the head with his police-issue baton. In finding 8 the sheriff states: 'The appellant had no reason to believe the complainer would attempt to run away from him or would succeed in doing so if he did not use his baton.' We regard that finding as being difficult to reconcile with the earlier finding 5 which recorded that after the appellant had caught hold of the complainer, the complainer struggled with him. In finding 11 reference is made to the standing orders of the Chief Constable of Strathclyde Police laying down the circumstances in which a uniformed officer is permitted to use his baton. One of these, namely paragraph (c), is in these terms: 'To secure an arrest, or prevent escape, of a person committing or charged with a serious crime'. In finding 8, as we have observed, it is stated that the appellant had no reason to believe the complainer would attempt to run away from him, but we agree with Mr MacLean that at the stage when the baton was used the clear inference from the findings is that the appellant was endeavouring to secure the arrest of the complainer.

The whole findings suggest to us that what occurred here was a most unfortunate but none the less genuine mistake on the part of the appellant, who had proceeded to the locus for the purpose of apprehending, if he could, the person suspected of housebreaking. He wrongly, but understandably, thought that the two persons whom he saw running were implicated and he took steps to apprehend one of them, namely the complainer. Although he was mistaken in concluding that the complainer was involved at all, it is quite intelligible that he should have made that mistake and once the complainer quite understandably struggled with him, it is, in our view, not unreasonable or improper that he should have made use of his baton in order to secure the arrest of that individual. The whole findings lead us to the conclusion that in the circumstances the appellant was justified in drawing his baton and in seeking to secure the arrest of the complainer, who was struggling with him. We cannot but feel sympathy for the wholly innocent complainer, who was struck by the baton, but in the circumstances we are not satisfied that he was the victim of an assault on the part of the appellant. We are quite satisfied that the Crown did not establish beyond reasonable doubt the necessary mens rea on the part of the appellant. We shall accordingly answer the question in the case in the negative and quash the conviction."

There are in addition to the foregoing, extensive powers to arrest without a warrant for breach of the peace. These are considered in Ch.9 below.

(3) Arrest Without Warrant under Statute

Many statutes confer power on the police to carry out an arrest without a warrant. We have already encountered one such example—the Misuse of Drugs Act 1971, s.24—in the previous section when dealing with *Wither v Reid*, 1979 S.L.T. 192. The breadth of this power of arrest without warrant under statute may vary from one statute to another, but will generally require reasonable suspicion on the part of the police officer that an offence under the statute is being committed. This requirement has been interpreted as necessitating little more than a subjective "honest belief" on the part of the police officer involved. The following cases illustrate the judicial interpretation of s.59 of the Civic Government (Scotland) Act 1982 as requiring reasonable suspicion that a crime was being committed before an arrest could lawfully be made. The Act covers such crimes as being on premises without authority with the intention of committing theft (s.57), and carrying tools for the purposes of housebreaking (s.58).

Civic Government (Scotland) Act 1982

"Powers of arrest and apprehension

59—(1) Subject to subsection (2) below, a constable may, where it is necessary in the interests of justice to do so, arrest without warrant a person whom he finds committing an offence to which this section applies or a person who is delivered into his custody in pursuance of subsection (3) below.

(2) A constable who is not in uniform shall produce his identification if required to do so by any person whom he is arresting under subsection (1) above.

(3) The owner, tenant or occupier of any property in, upon, or in respect of, which an offence to which this section applies is being committed or any person authorised by him may apprehend any person whom the owner or, as the case may be, the tenant, occupier or authorised person finds committing that offence and detain the apprehended person until he can be delivered into the custody of a constable.

In this subsection 'property' means heritable or moveable property.

(4) This section applies to offences under sections 50, 57 and 58 of this Act.

(5) This section shall not prejudice any power of arrest conferred by law apart from this section."

Sections 50, 57 and 58 deal with drunkeness and theft. What does this mean? In *Nicol v Lowe*, 1990 S.L.T. 543 the accused were arrested while coming out of the driveway of a house at 12.20 am with another youth. The police officer was suspicious about the youths' presence in the driveway at that time of night. The police arrested the youths, searched them and discovered in their possession certain articles of an incriminating nature. The youths were then charged under s.57, but objection was taken to the admissibility of the evidence relating to the search on the ground that the arrest and search were unlawful. The sheriff repelled the objection and convicted the accused who successfully appealed to the High Court. According to the Lord Justice Clerk (Ross):

"We appreciate, as the advocate-depute contended, that when police officers who are on patrol see persons emerging from private property it is really impossible for them to know whether they have lawful authority to be there and plainly they require to make further inquiries before they can determine that. In our opinion, however, in the state of knowledge of the two constables as described in finding 2 they cannot be said to have had reasonable grounds for believing that an offence had been committed or was being committed by these two youths. In cases brought under s. 57 (1) of the Act of 1982 it is not unusual to find other material being before the arresting officers. Thus it may be that they have observed individuals who have been acting in a suspicious manner, perhaps trying the door of lockfast premises or perhaps they have seen individuals who have attempted to hide when they heard the police approaching or, again this is very common, they have seen individuals who have taken one look at the police and have begun to run away. Where there is evidence of that kind one can well appreciate that police officers would have reasonable grounds for believing that an offence had been committed and therefore would be justified in arresting without a warrant. The present case however is not such a case. The advocate-depute reminded us that police officers are in a difficult position when they are on patrol and see something such as these officers saw at this late hour of the night when they are patrolling in their vehicle. In our opinion, however, in the state of knowledge which they are found to have had in this case they were not entitled to arrest the two youths there and then. As counsel for the appellant submitted they no doubt could have stopped the youths and asked them to wait while inquiries were made at the house to see if the householder could throw any light upon the question of whether the youths had any lawful authority to be there. Plainly if the youths had declined to wait or had run away then the police officers would no doubt have reasonable grounds for believing that an offence had been committed and thus would be entitled to detain or arrest the youths."

In this case, it was said that the police had "acted too fast in arresting the youths when they did", and consequently "exceeded the powers which were conferred upon them by s.59 (1) of the Act of 1982". Since the arrest was not lawful it followed that the subsequent search was unlawful and that the evidence should not have been admitted. The conviction was quashed. This was, however, a fairly rare instance of a judgment where reasonable grounds for suspicion were not established.

Keegan v Friel
1999 S.L.T. 1111

The three appellants had been recorded on closed circuit television acting suspiciously at the door to a night-club. The CCTV-operator contacted the police who intercepted and arrested the three, who were seen to discard implements which might have been used to break in to a locked building. The appellants challenged the lawfulness of their arrest given that the police had not come on them at the scene of the incident, but rather were going on the information of the CCTV-operator.

LORD CAPLAN: "When the solicitors acting for the appellants had each submitted to the sheriff at the end of the Crown case that there was no case to answer, they had done so on the basis that there had been no lawful arrest. If there had been no lawful arrest the appellants were entitled to object to the purported arrest and to resist it. The point had been made, and this was maintained at the appeal, that the arresting constables had no reasonable grounds for suspecting that the appellants had been committing an offence under s 57 (1) of the 1982 Act.

In our view the arrest of the three appellants was perfectly lawful. In the first place we should say that the comments by the Lord Justice Clerk in *Nicol v Lowe*, 1990 S.L.T. 543, to the effect that the test is whether there is reasonable ground for suspicion that the crime has been committed or is being committed does not rest unsupported. In the earlier case of *Breen v Pirie*, 1976 S.L.T. 136, the court was dealing with an arrest which purportedly was effected under s 5 (5) of the Road Traffic Act 1972. That provides that 'a constable may arrest without warrant a person committing an offence under this section'. We see, therefore, that once again the statutory power appears to be directed to a person who is in the course of committing an offence. At 1976 SLT, p 137 the Lord Justice General observes: 'The tests to which we have referred show that at the very least the arresting constable must, from his own observation and from facts within his own knowledge, have been in the position to form a conclusion that an offence was then being committed, or had shortly before that been committed, by the motorist concerned.'

It has to be observed that in *Breen* the arresting officers did not hear of an incident until some time after it had occurred. At p 137 of the report the Lord Justice General in criticising the arrest observes: 'they had no means of knowing, and there were no facts within their own knowledge to suggest, that that man was probably driving the vehicle'. We think it follows that the Lord Justice General was not objecting to the arrest on the basis that the police constables had not seen the offence being committed with their own eyes but was prepared to recognise that sufficient material to amount to 'means of knowing' the offence had been committed would satisfy the requirements of the Act.

The present case is a much stronger case for the justification of a statutory arrest than *Breen*. In our view the commission of an offence that justifies an arrest under s 59 (1) extends not only to the actions taken to commit the offence but extends to the immediate steps taken by the delinquents to get away from the scene of the crime. The arresting constables had been provided by the closed circuit television operator with a contemporaneous account of what was happening. The interception of the appellants was part of a combined operation in which, as would be necessary in such an arrangement, information is being shared. Moreover the police officers had an opportunity themselves to confirm the likelihood that what they had been told was accurate. When they arrived where they had been directed to proceed, they found three youths as had been described to them. Moreover the youths immediately on the arrival of the police acted suspiciously in that they dropped implements, which as the sheriff has held, were well suited to an attempt to effect illegal entry to premises. Thus for the purposes of the police operation the arresting constables had every reason to know that the three appellants were on the point of departure from the scene of the crime. Unlike the constables in *Breen* the constables in this case had a sound basis for concluding that a crime had very recently been committed. In the circumstances they were entitled to elect to exercise their statutory power of arrest rather than to adopt some alternative procedure such as taking the appellants into detention."

Another commonly used statute with powers of arrest without a warrant on reasonable suspicion has been the Road Traffic Act 1988. This provides by s.6(5):

"A constable may arrest a person without warrant if—
    (a) as a result of a breath test he has reasonable cause to suspect that the proportion of alcohol in that person's breath or blood exceeds the prescribed limit, or
    (b) that person has failed to provide a specimen of breath for a breath test when required to do so in pursuance of this section and the constable has reasonable cause to suspect that he has alcohol in his body,
but a person shall not be arrested by virtue of this subsection when he is at a hospital as a patient."

In *McLeod v Shaw*, 1981 S.C.C.R. 54, the court considered the forerunner to s.6(5), which was contained in the Road Traffic Act 1972. The accused was approached by a police officer as his car was stationary, four feet from the pavement. The police officer observed that his eyes were glazed and that his speech was very precise, but slightly slurred. The sheriff found that there was insufficient evidence to justify the police officer's belief that the accused was guilty of driving with excess alcohol, and thus his arrest was unlawful. The decision was appealed. According to Lord Justice General Emslie:

"It was not and could not be in dispute that under s. 5 (5) [of the 1972 Act] a constable may arrest a person 'apparently' committing an offence under s. 5 and upon that understanding of the subsection the sheriff proceeded to consider the legality of the arrest of the respondent. After examining the authorities to which he refers in his note he decided that the question he must ask himself was this:

> 'whether on their own observations the police officers were justified in concluding that the respondent was probably guilty of s. 5 (2)—being in charge of a motor vehicle when unfit to drive through drink and in arresting him without warrant.'

He then proceeded to look not only at the evidence of the police sergeant, the arresting officer, but at the evidence of the special constable as well. Having done so he decided that it had not been proved that unsteadiness on the part of the respondent had been a factor in the decision to arrest him and that the only factors had been that there was 'some slurring in the respondent's speech which was precise and some glazing in his eyes.' He then reached his own conclusion that these two factors did not justify the belief that the respondent was probably unfit to drive through drink and the result was the respondent's acquittal.

We have no doubt that in reaching his decision to acquit the respondent the learned sheriff misdirected himself. He asked himself the wrong question and having done so made the mistake of attempting to reconcile the evidence of the two police officers present with the result that he excluded from his consideration one of the facts as they appeared to be to the arresting officer, the police sergeant—one of the several grounds upon which she formed the honest belief that the respondent was apparently committing the s. 5 (2) offence. The question which the sheriff should have asked himself can in this case, be put in this way: 'Am I satisfied that the experienced arresting officer, the police sergeant, had no reasonable grounds for her admittedly honest belief that the respondent was apparently committing the s. 5 (2) offence which she had in mind?' That this was the proper question emerges from a consideration of the cases of *Wiltshire v Barrett* [1966] 1 Q.B. 312; *Woodage v Jones (No. 2)* [1975] R.T.R. 119; *Seaton v Allan*, 1974 S.L.T. 234; and *Breen v Pirie*, 1976 S.L.T. 136. It was the state of mind and knowledge of the arresting officer and of no other which is here in issue.

It is not surprising, therefore, that counsel for the respondent agreed that this was so. What the sheriff should have done, accordingly, was to ask himself that question with reference only to the facts as they appeared to the arresting officer, the police sergeant—the facts upon which her admittedly honest belief was founded. Had he done so he could not have held that she had no reasonable grounds for that honest belief. We are certainly not prepared so to hold."

It is clear that not only is the test for a reasonable belief not set unduly high, but also that it is to be viewed subjectively: the state of mind of the police officer is what is crucial, and the arrest will be lawful unless there is absolutely no basis for the belief that an offence has been committed. Difficult questions arise under the Road Traffic Act where the arrested person is arrested in England on suspicion of having committed an offence in Scotland. The matter is considered in the following case.

Binnie v Donnelly
1981 S.L.T. 294

SHERIFF PATERSON: "[The] appellant was driving his car in Scotland when he was involved in an accident. After that accident, he drove on for a matter of yards and in doing so crossed from Scotland into England. A matter of yards into England the appellant was involved in another accident. Police arrived at the locus of the second accident; those police officers were serving members of the Lothian and Borders Police Force. Those officers required the appellant at the locus of the second accident to give a specimen of breath. He did so. The reading was positive. The appellant was arrested, taken to Kelso Police Station where a specimen for analysis was obtained. That analysis brought out a blood-alcohol level above that permitted by law. In addition to the admission of the facts, the respondent and counsel for the appellant were at one that if there had been a departure from the procedure laid down in the Road Traffic Act for obtaining a specimen for analysis such a departure would vitiate the analysis and the prosecution would fail. Parties were also at one on the problem which arises in this prosecution namely whether or not Scottish police officers acted within their powers in requiring a specimen of breath from a motorist who at the time the requirement was made was in England. If that requirement was within their powers then the appellant fell to be convicted. If, on the other hand, the police officers in making that requirement had acted ultra vires the appellant must be acquitted."

The sheriff convicted and Binnie appealed.

Refusing the appeal, Lord Cameron (with whom Lords Emslie and Stott agreed) said:

"In my opinion the solution to the problem of jurisdiction presented by this case is to be found in an examination of the language of the relevant statutory provisions which define and govern the powers and jurisdiction of police constables in Scotland and by reference to the precise wording of s. 8(2) of the Road Traffic Act 1972. The governing statute is the Police (Scotland) Act 1967, and in s. 17 it defines the general functions and jurisdiction of constables. By s. 51(1) of that Act 'functions' are defined to include 'powers and duties'. By s. 17(4) the geographical boundaries of a constable's jurisdiction are defined in these words: 'Any constable of a police force shall have all the powers and privileges of a constable throughout Scotland.' Subsection (8) provides: 'this section shall be without prejudice to section 18 of this Act, and to any other enactment conferring powers on a constable for particular purposes.' 'Enactment' also and necessarily includes Acts of Parliament, as is made clear by s. 82 of and Sched. 4 to the Act. Section 18, which repeats a provision of the earlier Act of 1857, provides a limited extension of the jurisdiction of constables of border counties of England or Scotland as respects the execution of warrants in such border counties. The language of s. 8(2) of the Road Traffic Act 1972 repeats precisely that of s. 2 of the Road Safety Act 1967 and provides: 'If an accident occurs owing to the presence of a motor vehicle on a road or other public place, a constable in uniform may require any person whom he has reasonable cause to believe was driving ... the vehicle at the time of the accident to provide a specimen of breath for a breath test' and goes on in subss. (4) and (5) to give the constable power to arrest without warrant if the result of the test is positive or there is a failure to provide the requisite specimen of breath. Now the provisions of the statute are applicable to the whole United Kingdom and there is no limitative definition of a 'constable'. All that the statute prescribes in order to clothe the constable with the requisite power to require a breath test or without warrant to arrest is that he be in uniform. The police officers in the present case were constables and were in uniform and they had reasonable cause to believe that the appellant was the driver of the vehicle concerned in an accident on a road; and on a road in Scotland. The statute makes no reference to the border between England and Scotland or distinction between a Scottish or an English constable, though it is to be assumed that Parliament was fully aware of this fact in enacting legislation to be effectual throughout the United Kingdom. Now the powers conferred on a constable in uniform are powers conferred on him for a particular purpose, to operate the scheme of control over drivers of motor vehicles contained in the provisions of the Road Traffic Act 1972. It is also the case that s. 8 of the Act of 1972 repeats precisely the language of s. 2 of the Road Safety Act 1967, which received the Royal Assent prior to the passage of the Police (Scotland) Act of that year, so that the enactment of this particular extension of jurisdiction was on the statute book at the time the police legislation was before Parliament. Clearly therefore it was such an enactment as is covered by the language of s. 17(8) of the Police Act. The concept of trans-border jurisdiction was familiar to the legislature, as the provisions of s. 18 of the 1967 Act were a re-enactment of a provision which had been on the statute book since 1857. In my opinion the natural meaning to be given to the language of s. 8(2) is that no distinction is made between a constable according to whether he belongs to a police force raised and administered on one side of the border or the other, and that this conclusion is reinforced by consideration of the express wording of s. 17(8) of the 1967 Police Act where it clearly refers to an enactment which may for a particular purpose or particular purposes extend the jurisdiction and powers of a police officer beyond those normally possessed and exercisable by him. In my opinion the jurisdiction and power claimed in this case by the police officer are just such as the statute contemplates and the Road Traffic Act confers. For these reasons the learned sheriff in my view reached the right conclusion and his decision should be affirmed and the question in the case answered in the affirmative."

Other powers of arrest without a warrant are considered elsewhere in this book. For example, powers under the Terrorism Act 2000 are considered in Ch.10, below.

IV. THE CITIZEN'S RIGHT OF ARREST

The power of a private citizen to effect an arrest has historically been limited to situations where the person making the arrest is:

- the victim of the crime
- a witness to a serious crime being committed, or
- given information equivalent to personal observation.

(*Renton and Brown's Criminal Procedure* (6th ed.) para.7–03.)
    Any purported arrest which falls outwith these narrow confines may lead to a charge of assault, as the first of the following two cases reveals. *Codona v Cardle*, 1989 S.C.C.R. 287 also reveals that in making an arrest, the citizen must be aware of the need to use only reasonable force to make the arrest. The second of the following two cases (*Wightman v Lees*, 2000 S.L.T. 111) suggests a more generous approach to the courts to the public-spirited citizen. It suggests that the circumstances in which an arrest may be made extend to cover the situation where the citizen carrying out the arrest has a "moral certainty" that the arrested person has just committed a crime. The decision should perhaps be treated with a degree of caution given that it occurred in the context of an appeal against a conviction for theft on the ground that the citizen's arrest of the accused was unlawful.

Codona v Cardle
1989 S.C.C.R. 287

An accused person who was in partnership with his father in an amusement arcade, was charged with assault. The accused had approached the complainer whom he suspected of having broken a window in the arcade, and informed him and that he was going to effect a "citizen's arrest" and take him to the police station. The complainer was not prepared to go with the accused and the accused grabbed the complainer by the arm and twisted it up behind his back to the extent that the complainer protested loudly. The accused was convicted on the basis that he had used unreasonable force. The accused appealed against conviction contending that he had been entitled to use force in attempting to effect a citizen's arrest.

LORD JUSTICE CLERK (ROSS): "The justice explained to us that the defence in this case was that any assault upon the complainer was justified in that a citizen effecting an arrest had the same powers as a police officer and was permitted to use reasonable force. In presenting the appeal today counsel has referred to Renton and Brown, *Criminal Procedure* (5th ed.), para. 5–19, where the following statement appears: 'A private citizen is entitled to arrest without warrant for a serious crime he has witnessed, or perhaps where, being the victim of the crime, he has information equivalent to personal observation, as where the fleeing criminal is pointed out to him by an eyewitness.' Counsel for the appellant founded upon that passage, but having regard to the terms of the finding in this case, we are not satisfied that the appellant has brought himself within any of the categories described in that passage. He had not witnessed the breaking of the window. Since he was in partnership with his father in the arcade he was in a sense the victim of the crime, but on the basis of the findings it cannot be affirmed that he had any information equivalent to personal observation. Counsel had to concede that at best the appellant had a suspicion that the complainer was the perpetrator of the offence. In these circumstances we are not satisfied that the appellant was entitled to pursue the complainer as he did.

More importantly however we are not satisfied that he was entitled to exert the force which he did upon the complainer. In Gordon's *Criminal Law* (2nd ed.), para. 29–35, to which the justice was referred, it is stated: 'A man is, however, entitled to use reasonable force to seize and detain someone who is committing a crime, in the exercise of the citizen's right of arrest, and prosecution is unlikely in such cases unless excessive force is used.' Again we stress that this was not a case where the appellant was engaged upon attempting to arrest someone who was actually committing a crime. It is plain however that the issue must be whether reasonable force was used or whether the force which was used in the circumstances was excessive. In the present case even if one took the view that the appellant had reasonable grounds for concluding that the complainer had committed the offence of breaking the window, we are quite satisfied, on the findings, that the force which the appellant used after he grabbed hold of the complainer was excessive and was not reasonable. That being so we are of opinion that the justice was fully entitled to reach the conclusion that the appellant had used unreasonable force in the circumstances and that accordingly the justice was fully justified in finding the appellant guilty of the charge under the deletion to which we have referred. We shall accordingly answer the question in the case in the affirmative and the appeal is refused."

Wightman v Lees
2000 S.L.T. 111

The appellant had been arrested by a building contractor who had been checking flats which were being renovated. The appellant had been descending the stairs carrying a holdall, and when challenged he indicated he had come up the wrong close. The contractor was suspicious, and apprehended the appellant with the assistance of one of his employees. A drill belonging to the builders was discovered in the appellant's holdall. The lawfulness of this arrest and the subsequent discovery of the drill was challenged.

OPINION OF THE COURT: "During the course of the Crown case, objection was taken by the appellant's solicitor to the admissibility of any evidence from Barratt after he had apprehended the appellant. This was on the view that this was a citizen's arrest which was unlawful. The sheriff allowed the evidence to proceed subject to competency and relevancy but eventually rejected the submission. This was the principal issue which was raised in this appeal.

The advocate depute submitted that the rules stated in Renton and Brown were not absolutely rigid. While two examples were given of a situation where a citizen's arrest would be lawful, it is not said in terms that these are the only two situations. The observation in *Bryans v Guild*, 1990 S.L.T. 426 that the limits of the rule should not be departed from lightly again did not mean that the rules were absolutely rigid but did mean that in certain circumstances there could be an extension of them. Thus he submitted, in the two examples we have given, the citizen would be entitled to make an arrest and the law would be absurd if he was not so entitled. In the present case the information available to Barratt was that no person other than his employees had any right to be in the tenement. It was obvious that the building was unoccupied and therefore nobody could go up the stair by mistake on the excuse that they were looking for someone else. The appellant was carrying a holdall and tools had been stolen before. When he was followed downstairs, instead of going up another tenement stair in order to look for the person he said he was looking for, he ran away. In these circumstances Barratt had every reason to believe that a crime of theft had been committed and accordingly was entitled to make a citizen's arrest.

In our opinion the statement contained in Renton and Brown cannot be regarded with the same rigidity as was suggested by counsel. We are of opinion that a degree of common sense must be allowed to enter the equation. Accordingly while the rule is clear that a citizen is entitled to arrest in respect of a crime he has actually witnessed, this must be capable of extension to a situation where he is aware of circumstances which are strongly indicative of a crime having been committed, such as in the two examples we quoted above. To rule otherwise would, in our view, make a mockery of the law. Having said that, however, we agree with what was said in *Bryans* that the limits of the rule should not be departed from lightly, and that a citizen's arrest should not be made lawful just because the citizen has a suspicion that a crime may have been committed or a suspicion that the person arrested was the perpetrator of a crime. If, however, the citizen has a moral certainty that a crime has been committed and that a particular person has committed that crime, we consider that it cannot be said that the limits of the rule have been extended unduly if he makes a citizen's arrest of that person. It is, therefore, a question of degree in each case. The question in the present case therefore becomes whether the information available to Barratt was such that he was justified in coming to the conclusion that a crime had been committed rather than merely having a suspicion that a crime had been committed. Having regard to the facts that the appellant had no right whatever to be in the tenement, that he gave an explanation that was palpably false, that he was carrying a holdall, and that he ran away when he reached the street rather than simply walking off, we are satisfied that the circumstances pointed so strongly to the conclusion that a crime of theft had been committed that Barratt was justified in making a citizen's arrest."

V. THE MANNER OF ARREST

In addition to the requirement that the police officer has the **power** to carry out the arrest, there is also the matter of whether the correct **procedure** is used. Where the proper procedure is not applied, the arrest may be unlawful and the arrested person may be entitled to resist. Here two issues arise: the first is the need to bring to the attention of the arrested person the fact that he or she is under arrest; and secondly the need to explain the reasons for the arrest. A third issue is whether a police officer not in uniform must identify himself or herself as a police officer at the time of the arrest. This would be particularly important in the case of statutory offences which confer a power of arrest only on the police. As we have seen there is a duty in the Civic Government (Scotland) Act 1982, s.59(2), for a police officer not in uniform to identify himself or herself on request. The crucial issue in *Swankie v Milne*, 1973 S.L.T. (Notes) 128, arose due to the fact that the Road Traffic Act requires that a breath test is administered by a police officer in uniform. There is also the question of the force which may be used in making an arrest. This is considered in *Codona v Cardle*, 1989 S.C.C.R. 287, above.

Muir v Magistrates of Hamilton
1910 1 S.L.T. 164

Muir was standing on a street corner with some friends one Sunday when, as he averred:

"Sergeant Smith of the Hamilton Burgh Constabulary, accompanied by a constable, both in uniform, approached the pursuer in an ostentatious and aggressive manner, and charged him with an offence against the licensing laws, in that he had gained access to the County Hotel, Hamilton, on the morning of that day, by falsely representing himself to be a *bona fide* traveller; that he had written his name in the book specially kept for *bona fide* travellers; and that he had thereafter ordered and been supplied with exciseable liquor. The pursuer strenuously denied the accusation, but Sergeant Smith insisted on the charge, and stated that the pursuer must go with him there and then to the said hotel to be identified. At first the pursuer thought that Sergeant Smith was merely joking, but when he realised that the sergeant had really apprehended him and intended to take him through the streets in custody, the pursuer became alarmed and offered to meet the police at the said hotel at half-past eight in the evening, when the pursuer was in the habit of passing the hotel on his way to work ... Sergeant Smith refused to acquiesce in this proposal, and the pursuer was thereupon marched off through the crowded streets."

At the hotel the barmaid said definitely that Muir, whom she knew, had been nowhere near the hotel all day. Muir sued for wrongous arrest.

LORD ORDINARY (SALVESEN): "There is no suggestion that any force was used, or that anything happened but that the pursuer went in the company of the police to the hotel. It is not said that the sergeant acted maliciously; and, on the pursuer's own statement, he appears to have had probable cause. The only possible ground of action is that Sergeant Smith had no warrant for the alleged apprehension. In my opinion these facts do not disclose a case of apprehension at all. Had the pursuer refused to comply with Sergeant Smith's request, and had then been handcuffed and forcibly taken to the hotel for purposes of identification, the pursuer's case would have been stronger. All that happened, however, was that the sergeant asked the pursuer to accompany him to the County Hotel, and that the pursuer—fearing that if he did not comply with the request worse might happen—agreed to go. The pursuer being, in fact, innocent, I should have thought it in his interests to get himself cleared of suspicion by at once going down to the hotel."

In a not dissimilar case, *Swankie v Milne*, 1973 S.L.T. (Notes) 128, a man was suspected of driving under the influence of alcohol by police officers in plain clothes, who were accordingly unable lawfully to carry out a breath test. The officers contacted their uniformed colleagues, and confiscated the accused's car keys while they waited. In due course, uniformed officers arrived to carry out the test. The accused argued that he had been arrested by the plain-clothes officers, and thus the statutory procedure for the breath test was vitiated. On this occasion the uncertainty of the procedure again worked to the disadvantage of the accused. While the decision in *Swankie* recognised a state of police custody short of arrest, detention was placed on a formal footing by the Criminal Justice (Scotland) Act 1980. According to Lord Cameron:

"If there was no arrest then the first contention of counsel for the appellant necessarily falls to the ground. Had the plain-clothes officers in fact arrested or purported to arrest the appellant, then I can appreciate that a very difficult situation might arise with very difficult legal arrangements. In such a situation it could be argued with force that once arrested a person is in the custody of the police and it would or might be difficult to maintain that he could at the same time be in the category of a person 'driving or attempting to drive a motor vehicle'. An arrest is something which in law differs from a detention by the police at their invitation or suggestion. In the latter case a person detained or invited to accompany police officers is, at that stage, under no legal compulsion to accept the detention or invitation. It may well be that in a particular case refusal to comply could lead to formal arrest, but until that stage is reached there is theoretical freedom to exercise a right to refuse to accept detention at the hands of police officers who are not armed with a warrant. I think it is important always to keep clear the distinction between arrest, which is a legal act taken by officers of the law duly authorised to do so and while acting in the course of their duty, carrying with it certain important legal consequences, and the mere detention of a person by a police officer such as is referred to in findings 3 and 4. Once arrested not only is the freedom of action of the person arrested circumscribed, but he is also placed in the protection of the law in respect, e.g., of questioning by a police officer. None of these consequences flows from a mere 'detention' for inquiry or to enable the officers or their colleagues to pursue investigation or put forward (as in this case) certain statutory requests. And a person is either arrested or he is not; there is no half-way house. In my opinion it is plain that there was no arrest of the appellant by the plainclothes officers who stopped his van. No charge was preferred by them against the appellant nor is there any finding to establish or even suggest that at the stage when the officers stopped the van they had any intention of preferring the charge ultimately made or a charge under any other statute concerned with the driving of vehicles. If there was no arrest of the appellant by these constables then counsel's first contention necessarily fails."

Forbes v H M Advocate
1990 S.C.C.R. 69

Forbes was apprehended in terms of the Prevention of Terrorism (Temporary Provisions) Act 1984. The arresting officer told Forbes that he was being detained, rather than arrested, and Forbes challenged the validity of his arrest on the basis of the words used.

LORD HOPE: " ... in our opinion it does not follow that the police officer who effects the arrest must in every case use the word 'arrest' when he explains to the person what is happening when he is being taken into custody. It is desirable that he should do so, because it is necessary that it should be made clear to the person concerned that he is under legal compulsion and that his freedom of action is being curtailed. The clearer and more simple the words used in this regard the better, and the word 'arrest' satisfies this test since it is a word with a clear meaning which is widely known and well understood. On the other hand any form of words will suffice to inform the person that he is being arrested if they bring to his notice the fact that he is under compulsion and the person thereafter submits to that compulsion: *Alderson v Booth* [1969] 2 Q.B. 216 per Lord Parker C.J. at p.22I. And the nature of what the police officer is doing may be conveyed by actions as well as words.

In the present case, although the appellant was told that he was being detained, he was taken from his house at an early hour to the police office in handcuffs. On his arrival there he was invited to sign the custody record which stated inter alia that he had been made aware of the reason for his arrest. Leaving aside for the moment the question whether that reason had been made known to him, the use of the word 'arrest' on this form together with the manner which he was taken into custody would, in our opinion, have left no reasonable doubt in his mind that he was under legal compulsion and that he was being detained in consequence of an arrest. We were referred to *Wither v Reid*, 1979 S.L.T. 192 in which it was held that the accused had been arrested unlawfully because the police were proceeding under section 23(2)(a) of the Misuse of Drugs Act 1971 which gave them authority only to detain the person for the purpose of searching him. The police officers told the accused that she was being apprehended under the Act and that she was under arrest, prior to the search being carried out. If they had told her that she was being detained for the purpose of searching her, their actions would have been perfectly lawful, but Lord Kissen and Lord Robertson rejected the argument that the words used did not signify that she was being arrested but that she was being detained only for the purposes of the search. We do not doubt the soundness of that decision or of Lord Robertson's point at p. 15 that in deference to the rights of the citizen it must be made perfectly clear to the person against whom action is being taken under section 23(2)(a) of the 1971 Act that that is what is being done and that he is not being arrested. But the present case does not present the same difficulty. The police officers' conduct together with the words used point clearly to this being in fact an arrest, and there has been no suggestion in this case that this was not what the police officers at that stage were empowered to do.

The other issue as to the lawfulness of the arrest relates to what the appellant was told about the reason for his arrest. In approaching this matter it is important to bear in mind the nature and circumstances of the power of arrest which is being exercised. Where the arrest is one which proceeds upon a warrant of arrest the police officer who executes it should state the substance of the warrant: Macdonald on the Criminal Law of Scotland (5th edn), p. 199. As Hume on Crimes, vol ii, p. 79 puts it, 'the officer, when proceeding to arrest, should briefly acquaint the party with the substance of his warrant'. Where, as in this case, the arrest is without warrant the requirements of the law are in effect the same. The person must be told immediately upon his arrest of the reason why he is being arrested. Where the power of arrest is being exercised in consequence of a statutory power of arrest because the police officer has reasonable grounds for suspecting that the person has been guilty of a specific offence such as that referred to in section 12(1)(a) of the 1984 Act, the person arrested must be told of the general nature of the offence of which he is suspected. Special considerations will apply where the arrest proceeds upon a provision such as that which is to be found in section 12(1)(b) of the 1984 Act which empowers a police officer to arrest without warrant a person whom he has reasonable grounds for suspecting to be a person who is or has been concerned in the commission, preparation or instigation of acts of terrorism to which Part IV of that Act applies-that is to say, acts of terrorism connected with the affairs of Northern Ireland and acts of terrorism of any other description except acts connected solely with the affairs of the United Kingdom other than Northern Ireland: see section 12(3). In such a case the suspicion is related to something which has not yet reached the stage of being capable of being described in terms of a specific offence, and it will not be possible to go further than state the general nature of the suspicion. The distinction between section 12(1)(a) and (b) for these purposes was explained in *Ex parte Lynch* [1980] N.I. 126 by Lord Lowry L.C.J. at pp. 130–131. He began his examination of the matter by referring to *Christie v Leachinsky* [1947] A.C. 573 in which Viscount Simon at p. 587 and Lord Simmonds at p. 593 both made the point that the policeman is not entitled to keep the reason for the arrest to himself since the principle is the arrested man is entitled to know on what charge or on suspicion of what crime he is being arrested. He went on to say this, under reference to section 12(1) of the Prevention of Terrorism (Temporary Provisions) Act 1976 which was in substantially the same terms as those to be found in section 12 of the 1984 Act [at pp. 130F-131C]:

'These observations seem to us to lay down that what must be communicated to the suspected person at the time of his arrest is the true ground of arrest, which, in the context in which the observations were made, means informing the suspect of the felony or arrestable offence of which he is suspected. Such crimes can be described and communicated to the suspect in reasonably precise terms, if a police officer is making an arrest either under section 2 of the Criminal Law Act 1967 in respect of the alleged commission of an arrestable offence (usually an offence or an attempted offence carrying a penalty of imprisonment of 5 years or more) or under the former position at common law before the 1967 Act when the commission of felony was suspected. The power of arrest under section 12(1) of the 1976 Act exists when there is a reasonable suspicion of the suspect's guilt of specific offences, as in section 12(1)(a) or where a person is suspected of being subject to an exclusion order, as in section 12(1)(c). But the power conferred by section 12(1)(b) is wider and more general, being derived from a suspicion of the suspect's being concerned in the commission, preparation or instigation of acts of "terrorism". This word is defined in wide terms in section *14(1)* as meaning "the use of violence for political ends", and includes "any use of violence for the purpose of putting the public or any section of the public in fear". The scope of this language is such that no specific crime need be suspected in order to ground a proper arrest under section 12(1)(b). And it is further to be noted that an arrest under section 12(1) leads under section 12(2) to a permitted period of detention without preferring a charge. No charge may follow at all: thus an arrest is not necessarily (to use Scott L.J.'s phrase in the Court of Appeal in *Christie v Leachinsky* [1946] K.B. 124, 130) "the first step in a criminal proceeding against a suspected person on a charge which was intended to be judicially investigated". Rather it is usually the first step in the investigation of the suspected person's involvement in terrorism.'

The learned advocate-depute submitted that this passage provided a complete answer to the point which had been raised by the appellant. We note, however, that in that case the arrest was made expressly with reference to the provisions of section 12(1)(b) which is the wider and more general power of arrest which is derived from a suspicion of being concerned in the commission, preparation or instigation of acts of terrorism. The constable who effected the arrest in that case told the appellant that he was being arrested as he was suspected of being involved in terrorist activities. That was not what was done in the present case. The appellant was told that he was being detained under section 12 of the 1984 Act and he was shown a search warrant which narrated that there were reasonable grounds to believe that he had committed an offence contrary to section 10 of the 1984 Act. The position in this case therefore is that the arrest was made under section 12(1)(a), because the appellant was suspected of being a person guilty of an offence under section 10. That suspicion had already been taken to the point of formulating an offence with sufficient precision for the search warrant to be obtained. So this case must, in our opinion, be approached on the basis that the appellant was suspected was suspected of being guilty of an offence which was, as Lord Lowry puts it, capable of being described and communicated in reasonably precise terms. Had the only information which was given to the appellant been that he was being detained under section 12 of the Act we should have had little difficulty in holding that insufficient information was given to him to make this a valid arrest. But that is not all that he was told, because he was shown and given to read for himself the search warrant which narrated in the petition the grounds on which it had been sought and granted and made express reference to section 10 of the Act. In our opinion the information which was afforded to him by this means was sufficient, when taken together with the words used by the police officers, to provide the appellant with the information which he was entitled to have as to the general nature and true ground of his arrest."

The matter is now governed by statute in England and Wales: Police and Criminal Evidence Act 1984, s.28, which requires the arresting officer to explain the fact of and the reasons for the arrest. In light of the requirements of Art.5(2) of the ECHR, it is difficult to believe that there is not a similar obligation in Scotland. It is to be noted that on a slightly different point, where the Crown intends to have a person remanded in custody, it has served a so-called "custody statement" on the accused in which is given an outline of the Crown case so as to inform the accused of the reasons for his or her arrest. This has been done following the incorporation of Convention rights, though it is done some time after the arrest and is not contemporaneous with the arrest. The custody statement has been challenged (*Vannet v Hamilton*, 1999 S.C.C.R. 809), as has a similar practice where the Crown is seeking a warrant, of including an indication of the information on the basis of which arrest was sought (*Brown v Selfridge*, above). Neither challenge succeeded.

VI. Police Powers Incidental to Arrest

The arrest of an individual may involve not only the loss of liberty: it may also lead to interference with other human rights, most notably the right to privacy. Thus:

- an arrested person may be searched by the police;
- fingerprints may be taken, and
- other samples may be taken, perhaps for the purpose of DNA analysis.

Questions may also arise about the search of the arrested person's property including his or her home. These latter questions are discussed in Ch.6, below. Although all these matters raise acute human rights issues, it will be readily apparent that arrested persons had the protection of common law from long before the entry into force of the human rights legislation, albeit that the courts have oscillated as to what constitutes "fairness" to the accused.

(1) Personal Search

As we have seen it is unlawful to carry out a personal search in order to discover whether there is evidence justifying a subsequent arrest: *Jackson v Stevenson* (1897) 2 Adam 255. However, the police may search an arrested individual for evidence to prevent it from being lost. There is no need for a warrant in such circumstances. Indeed, the following case suggests that there may be a power of personal search even without an arrest having been made.

McHugh v H M Advocate
1978 J.C. 12

McHugh, along with another man, was suspected of assault and the theft of banknotes. Some of the banknotes had known numbers. The police, who did not have a warrant, went to the home of McHugh's co-accused, where they cautioned, charged and arrested McHugh. McHugh challenged the lawfulness of the subsequent search of his person, which yielded some of the numbered banknotes. The evidence was admitted and McHugh was convicted. He appealed.

> Lord Justice-General (Emslie) delivering the opinion of the court: "As we understood the argument, counsel began by saying that this was a cause in which the search was conducted without warrant. Although police who have lawfully arrested a person may quite properly search the arrested man without a warrant, it was not certain that an arrest had taken place in this case, or that if it had taken place, it had taken place legally. The only other circumstance in which a search of a citizen may be justified is where, although there is no warrant and no lawful arrest, the need to search is demanded as a matter of urgency to prevent the possible loss or destruction of important evidence. In this case, said Mr Taylor [for the appellant], it was by no means clear that the police were telling the truth when they said they arrested McHugh before they searched him. In any event, said Mr Taylor, it is by no means clear either that they had reasonable grounds for arresting McHugh, or that there were any considerations of urgency which could have justified the search which revealed the stolen property ... The evidence bearing upon the circumstances of the search was all one way and remained unshaken in cross-examination. It was to the effect that the officers had set out with the primary purpose of arresting McHugh, for that was their allotted task. They carried out that task and the search was a sequel to the arrest. They did not arrest without reasonable cause, and in particular merely to provide an excuse for a search. In any event it is perfectly clear that the search of McHugh, a prime suspect, was according to the evidence, essential as a matter of urgency, to avoid any risk that any of the numbered notes which he might have in his possession would be lost, hidden or destroyed. In this state of matters and particularly having regard to the sufficient evidence of the urgent need to search, the criticism of the direction given by the trial Judge is without real substance."

It may also be possible in the interests of urgency to search the home of an individual for evidence relating to an offence for which he or she was arrested. This is despite the fact that the suspect may not have been arrested there. In these circumstances the search may take place without a warrant: *HM Advocate v McGuigan*, 1936 S.L.T. 16. See Ch.6, below. The power of personal search may also include a power of intimate or strip search in certain circumstances, as the following case shows:

Gellatly v Heywood
1998 S.L.T. 287

The accused was charged under s.41(1) of the Police (Scotland) Act 1967 of resisting a search. He was arrested and detained in a police cell after having been strip-searched. Several hours later, he rang the cell alarm bell, and was seen with two "reefer" cigarettes and a tin box. It was decided to carry out a second strip-search, but the accused became agitated and resisted violently. He was convicted, and appealed on the basis that there were no reasonable grounds for the second search and that he was entitled to resist as a result.

LORD MCCLUSKEY: "We consider that both counsel have correctly identified the approach which the court is required to take. There must exist reasonable grounds for the decision to search before the search can be said to be one carried out in the execution of the officer's duty, within the meaning of s 41 (1) (a). We also consider, however, that the decision as to whether or not reasonable grounds existed is one primarily for the trial judge to make as a matter of fact. In this case the sheriff made such a finding by recording in finding in fact 8 that in the circumstances narrated there and elsewhere in the case, including Sergeant Fraser's decision, as custody officer, that he had reason to fear for the appellant's safety, the carrying out of a strip search was in the execution of that officer's duty. This court has not been persuaded of any good reason for going behind that conclusion. It is essentially a conclusion of fact which the sheriff was entitled to reach in the circumstances held by him to have been established. It will be seen from his note that the sheriff preferred the explanation as to the events given by the police officers to the explanation advanced by the appellant in giving evidence. The sheriff was also entitled to have regard to the fact that as Sergeant Fraser was the custody officer it was not irrelevant that he could have been severely criticised had he failed to search the appellant and thus left him in possession of concealed and dangerous material which might have caused the appellant himself to suffer harm. We also consider that the position taken by the Crown in relation to the duty to explain, which in substance corresponds with that advanced by counsel for the appellant, is the correct one. There cannot be an absolute duty to give an explanation, whatever the circumstances. The question as to whether or not a departure from the general practice of giving an explanation as to why the search is being carried out is permissible, is itself a judgment on the basis of the facts in the case. If the person whom the police decide should be searched is in such a condition that the explanation could not be received and understood—and there could be many reasons why an arrested person could not receive or understand an explanation—then the normal duty to give an explanation for the search would not need to be performed. Given the express finding that the appellant in the present case was at the material time in no way able to receive and accept rationally an explanation for the search, we consider that the sheriff was entitled to hold that the sergeant did not begin to act outwith his duty by failing to tender an explanation to the appellant.
Although we consider this to be a somewhat narrow case, given that it involved an intimate search in a police cell some hours after such a search had legitimately been carried out and had yielded no result, we consider that it is not for this court to reach a different conclusion on the two essential matters of fact that lie at the heart of the case, given the whole circumstances narrated by the sheriff."

Although a search may not normally take place before an arrest, it is to be noted that there may be circumstances where a search conducted with the authority of a warrant may authorise the search of anyone on the premises being searched. In the following case, the admission by the accused that he was at premises to buy drugs was held to be sufficient to justify a reasonable suspicion that he was in possession of drugs. He was searched and found to be in possession of a knife.

Gavin v Normand
1995 S.L.T. 741

An accused person was tried on summary complaint with a contravention of s.1(1) of the Prevention of Crime Act 1953. The accused called at a house which was being searched for controlled drugs by police officers under a warrant obtained in terms of s.23 (3) of the Misuse of Drugs Act 1971. When asked why he was there the accused stated that he wanted to buy some cannabis resin. The accused was then searched and a knife was found in his possession. Objection was taken to the admissibility of the evidence of the finding of the knife on the ground that the search was unlawful as the police officers had no reasonable grounds for suspecting that the accused was in possession of controlled drugs. The sheriff repelled the objection and convicted the accused who appealed, contending that his reply to the police indicated that he was not in possession of controlled drugs.

LORD JUSTICE GENERAL (HOPE): "The whole point therefore turns upon the circumstances of the search and whether that evidence was admissible. From the findings in fact it appears that on the date in question police officers were engaged in a search of the flat at 68 MacDuff Street, Glasgow, under the sanction of a search warrant which they had obtained in terms of the Misuse of Drugs Act 1971, s 23. It must be assumed that that warrant had been granted under subs (3) of that section which relates to the search of premises. At about 7 pm, while the search was still in progress, the appellant knocked at the door of the flat. A plain clothes police officer responded to the knock and invited the appellant to say why he was there. The appellant's reply was 'I'm here to buy some blaw'. The word which he used is a slang term for cannabis resin. He was then invited to enter the house, and he was then detained there for the purposes of a search in terms of s 23 of the Act. In this instance, since this was a search being conducted of a person who had not been found in the house, it would appear that the search was under subs (2) of the section. The finding is that the police officers involved had reasonable grounds to suspect that the appellant was in possession of a controlled drug. It was that last finding which counsel for the appellant challenged in the course of his submissions to us today.

As we understood his submissions, the argument was that the evidence did not justify the conclusion which is drawn in that finding. Counsel drew our attention to *Guthrie v Hamilton*, 1988 S.L.T. 823 in which it was said that, as the caller at the premises had no obvious innocent explanation for being there, the police were entitled to suspect that he was in possession of controlled drugs. The submission was that that was not the correct approach, having regard to the terms of the statute. Counsel emphasised that what the statute required was reasonable grounds to suspect that the person was in possession of controlled drugs. He said that, in the light of the reply which the appellant had given in response to the question put to him by the police officer, it was clear that the reason why the appellant had come to the house was to obtain drugs. It could not be inferred from what he said that he was already in possession of them, and unless there was a reasonable ground for suspicion that he was already in possession of a controlled drug, there was no basis upon which the search could properly have been carried out.

In his reply the learned advocate depute submitted that it was open to the police to conclude that any person who called at the house was there for the purpose of dealing in drugs, and that this was reinforced when one examined what the appellant said in reply to the question put to him by the police officer. What the appellant had said was that he was there to buy drugs. But, far from absolving the appellant, this enhanced the suspicion that he was in some way connected with dealing in drugs, and that was enough to justify the suspicion which the police officers formed about him. He drew our attention to *Stuart v Crowe*, 1993 SLT at p 440F where the Lord Justice Clerk said this: 'It appears to us to be a matter of common sense that if, as here, police officers are searching premises because they suspect that there are controlled drugs on these premises and someone arrives at the premises, the police are entitled to suspect that that person is also involved with controlled drugs and therefore to search his person'.

It was in reliance on that passage, and on the general submissions which he also made, that the learned advocate depute invited us to refuse this appeal.

The sheriff tells us in his note that the police officers said in their evidence that they had been informed that the flat was one where drugs were bought and sold. They anticipated that on occasion drugs would be delivered there, and they formed the view that any callers at the door should be considered suspect and should be searched. The police officers said that they were influenced in their decision to search the appellant by the comment which he made at the door, but that that was not the sole reason.

It is clear from that description of their evidence that the police officers, in conducting the search of these premises in the light of the information which they had been given, were entitled to be suspicious of any person who came to the door of those particular premises. We are not concerned therefore with the question as to whether the police are entitled to search any person who comes to any premises. This was a case where a search was already being conducted under warrant of premises which were thought to be associated with drug dealing. The significance of the remark made by the appellant in response to the question put to him by the police officer was that it confirmed that he was in some way associated with dealing in drugs. But the officers were not bound to accept every word that he said. It was enough for them that he had admitted that he was in some way connected with dealing in drugs. They were entitled to conclude that he might have some drugs in his possession as a result of this, and that was a sufficient basis for them to form the reasonable suspicion which would entitle them to search him.

For these reasons we are satisfied that the sheriff was right to repel the objection and to find that there was a sufficient basis in the evidence for a conviction."

(2) Prints and Samples

Adair v McGarry
1933 S.L.T. 482

McGarry was charged with theft by housebreaking. The only evidence against him was the correspondence between his finger-prints and the finger-prints found on one of certain stolen articles. The finger-prints of the accused were taken by the police while he was in detention at a police office after having been arrested and charged with theft by housebreaking. No magistrate's warrant was sought or procured for the purpose of taking the accused's finger-prints, nor was his consent asked. In these circumstances the sheriff-substitute held that the accused's finger-prints had not been taken according to law, and that the court was not entitled to take into consideration the evidence obtained from them. At the request of the procurator-fiscal the sheriff-substitute stated a case for the opinion of the High Court of Justiciary.

THE LORD JUSTICE-CLERK (ALNESS): "The question for decision in this case is whether the police are entitled to take finger-prints of persons who are detained by them as suspects though these persons have not yet been committed to prison. To that question the Crown answers—yea; the respondent replies—nay. As regards persons who have been committed to prison, no difficulty arises, inasmuch as the procedure to be followed in such cases is statutory in its character.

Manifestly the question before us is of importance, not only to the individual, but also to the public. On the one hand, the individual must be protected against any undue invasion of his rights; on the other hand, it is evident that the affirmation of the right claimed by the Crown may facilitate the investigation and detection of crime, and that the denial of that right may impede, if not frustrate, that process.

At the outset it is essential to bear in mind the distinction between the position of a person detained on suspicion of having committed a crime and the position of a person who has been committed to prison on a charge of crime. The rights of the police are wider in the former case than they are in the latter case. The police may arrest a suspect and may interrogate him; but that person may only be committed if a *prima facie* case against him is made out, and no interrogation is, after committal, permitted. Accordingly, the suggestion that finger-prints may be taken, once committal takes place, is far from meeting the demands of the situation.

I propose, first, to survey the problem apart from authority, and then to enquire whether the conclusion at which I arrive, on that survey, is rendered inadmissible by the state of the authorities.

Viewed apart from authority, then, the problem presents itself to my mind thus—the police must be armed with all adequate and reasonable powers for the investigation and detection of crime. Is finger-printing a reasonable incident in that process, not forbidden by the common law, and not unduly invading the rights of the accused?

I say 'not forbidden by the common law' because I think that phrase more correctly expounds the situation than the phrase 'authorised by the common law.' Let me explain what I mean by this. The system of detection of crime by means of finger-prints is a modern scientific discovery, later in date than any of the statutes to which reference was made in the course of the debate, and it would not therefore be reasonable to look for or to expect to find institutional or common law authority for its practice.

As regards undue invasion of the personal rights of the accused, one must have a sense of proportion. Certain it is that in practice, hitherto unchallenged, a person who is suspected of crime may be brought—with reasonable violence in the event of his resistance—to the police station, that he may be paraded for purposes of identification, that he may be stripped, and that he may be searched for any incriminating natural or artificial mark upon his person. That mark may include a birth mark or natural deformity, a tattoo mark, or bloodstains, or the like. All these things are done with a view to establishing the identity of the suspect. And yet it is argued that the comparatively innocuous process of taking a mould of the suspect's thumb is excluded from the rights of the police. I enquire—Why? To that question I have heard no adequate answer. The analogy of straining at a gnat and swallowing a camel suggests itself as apposite to the argument in question.

The suggestion seems to be that the existence of a warrant, such as is referred to in the Rules of 1904, to which I shall subsequently advert, removes all objection to finger-printing. If I could see that any substantial protection is afforded to the accused by the existence of such a warrant I could understand that view. But nothing is more certain than that such a warrant is a pure formality, is granted for the asking, is, so I am informed, never refused, and, moreover, is granted by a person who may know less about the matter than the police know. The suggested protection by way of warrant is quite illusory.

If the accused is innocent, no harm is done by finger-printing. He has not been subjected to so great 'humiliation'—to use counsel's words—as he may admittedly be subjected to in accordance with time-honoured and unchallengeable practice. If, on the other hand, he is guilty, the process renders it more likely that his guilt may be established. That is, I apprehend, desirable.

Bearing all these considerations in mind, I should have no difficulty in reaching the conclusion, authority apart, that the Crown possess the right which is claimed by them."

At common law, palm prints of an arrested person could also be taken without a warrant, where required by the urgency of the situation. In *Bell v Hogg*, 1967 S.L.T. 290 the taking of palm prints was justified as being necessary to prevent evidence from being lost. The current law relating to the taking of fingerprints, palmprints and other samples is found in the Criminal Procedure (Scotland) Act 1995.

Criminal Procedure (Scotland) Act 1995

"Prints and samples

18.—(1) This section applies where a person has been arrested and is in custody or is detained under section 14(1) of this Act.

(2) A constable may take from the person fingerprints, palm prints and such other prints and impressions of an external part of the body as the constable may, having regard to the circumstances of the suspected offence in respect of which the person has been arrested or detained, reasonably consider it appropriate to take.

(3) Subject to subsection (4) below, all record of any prints or impressions taken under subsection (2) above, all samples taken under subsection (6) below and all information derived from such samples shall be destroyed as soon as possible following a decision not to institute criminal proceedings against the person or on the conclusion of such proceedings otherwise than with a conviction or an order under section 246(3) of this Act.

(4) The duty under subsection (3) above to destroy samples taken under subsection (6) below and information derived from such samples shall not apply—

    (a) where the destruction of the sample or the information could have the effect of destroying any sample, or any information derived therefrom, lawfully held in relation to a person other than the person from whom the sample was taken; or

    (b) where the record, sample or information in question is of the same kind as a record, a sample or, as the case may be, information lawfully held by or on behalf of any police force in relation to the person.

(5) No sample, or information derived from a sample, retained by virtue of subsection (4) above shall be used—

    (a) in evidence against the person from whom the sample was taken; or

    (b) for the purposes of the investigation of any offence.

(6) A constable may, with the authority of an officer of a rank no lower than inspector, take from the person—

    (a) from the hair of an external part of the body other than pubic hair, by means of cutting, combing or plucking, a sample of hair or other material;

    (b) from a fingernail or toenail or from under any such nail, a sample of nail or other material;

    (c) from an external part of the body, by means of swabbing or rubbing, a sample of blood or other body fluid, of body tissue or of other material;

    (d) from the inside of the mouth, by means of swabbing, a sample of saliva or other material.

(7) A constable may use reasonable force in exercising any power conferred by subsection (2) or (6) above.

(8) Nothing in this section shall prejudice—

    (a) any power of search;

    (b) any power to take possession of evidence where there is imminent danger of its being lost or destroyed; or

    (c) any power to take prints, impressions or samples under the authority of a warrant."

The taking of other prints or samples (such as blood samples and dental impressions) may be authorised by a warrant at common law. Where a warrant is obtained, even fairly significant intrusions into the personal integrity of the suspect will be regarded as lawful. In *Hay v HM Advocate*, 1968 S.L.T. 334, a murder victim was found to have tooth marks on her breast. Her body was discovered near to an approved school and dental impressions were taken of 29 staff and pupils at the school. All but Hay were eliminated, and a warrant was sought to take him to a dental hospital for more detailed examination. The evidence secured his conviction, and he appealed unsuccessfully as to the lawfulness of the warrant. See Ch.6, below. Where there is suspicion that the suspect will attempt to thwart the terms of a warrant to take bodily samples, such a warrant may be granted without the requirement for intimation to the accused.

Mellors v Normand (No. 2)
1996 S.L.T. 1146

An accused person was charged on petition with rape and was remanded in custody. Prior to his committal for rape he had been fully committed on a charge of attempted murder and warrants had been granted for samples of blood and saliva and dental impressions to be taken, but he had refused to comply with these warrants. The accused was subsequently charged on petition with *inter alia* attempting to defeat the ends of justice by refusing to comply with the warrants and was remanded in custody in respect of that petition but liberated on the rape charge. Thereafter the Crown applied for a warrant in terms of s.18(6) of the Criminal Procedure (Scotland) Act 1995 to take a sample of the accused's hair for comparison purposes in respect of the rape charge. The sheriff granted the warrant without intimation of the petition being given to the accused, on the basis of information on oath that there was a real danger that the accused would frustrate the purposes of the warrant. The accused, after the warrant had been executed, sought suspension of it and an order for the destruction of the samples which had been obtained under the warrant, on the grounds that he had not been able to make representations to the sheriff who, in any event, had been misled as to the power which she was exercising.

> LORD JUSTICE GENERAL (HOPE): "The solicitor advocate put the matter in three ways in his submissions to us today. The first point which he raised, but then conceded, was whether there was a requirement in law for warrants of this kind to be intimated, whatever the circumstances, to the person who is under investigation. He accepted that while the normal and proper practice was that such warrants should be intimated, there may be circumstances where such intimation is not required where to do so would defeat the purpose for which the warrant was granted. He referred to *Harris, Complainer* at 1994 SLT, p 907I-J, where the Lord Justice Clerk narrated the averment by the complainer of her belief that there was a material risk that the person named in the petition would have an opportunity to retrieve the documents before any search for them took place and thus frustrate the inquiry into the commission of the alleged offences. In these circumstances the court accepted that it was not appropriate for intimation of the petition to be made to him and indeed that to do so would be undesirable. In the light of that case, very properly, the solicitor advocate accepted that there was no point in making further submissions in support of that argument here.
>
> The second point was that the sheriff did not have before her information to justify the exceptional step which she took. It was pointed out that it was said on oath before her that there was a real danger that the complainer would frustrate the purpose of the warrant. But it was said that the sheriff had not applied her mind to the simple administrative steps which could have been taken to prevent that happening, given that the complainer was already in custody. On this matter we note from the sheriff's report that a detective inspector informed her that he was aware of the history and circumstances of this case. He told her that he was in no doubt that the complainer would attempt to frustrate the purpose of the warrant were he to be made aware of the application or the fact that the sheriff had granted it. Various details were set out before her in answer to her concern on this point, to support the allegation which was being made. In the light of the information which she

received, in response to her understandable concern that this might be a case where inti-mation should nevertheless be made to the complainer, she was in the end satisfied that it was not appropriate for that step to be taken. She considered that it was in the interests of justice not to do this, and she has explained that it was for that reason and that reason only that she took this exceptional step.

We are satisfied that the sheriff did apply her mind carefully to the question to which the solicitor advocate addressed his argument. She had before her information which she was entitled to accept and, given the nature of the information with which she was provided, she was, in our opinion, entitled to proceed upon it. No doubt some administrative steps might have been taken to anticipate and prevent the complainer's attempts. But an element of risk was attached to that as they might not have been successful, and the sheriff was entitled to decide in the public interest that this was not a case where that risk should be undertaken.

The third point which was raised was in relation to a paragraph in the petition to the sheriff which made reference to s 18 of the Criminal Procedure (Scotland) Act 1995. The point which the solicitor advocate made about this was a short one. He submitted that the section was irrelevant to the complainer's case, as he was not a person to whom that provision applied. He accepted that the provision enables a constable in the situation to which it applies to take a sample of hair, other than pubic hair, from the external part of the body of a person who has been arrested. But he said that that was of no relevance to this case, partly because the section was not in force when the complainer was first taken into custody and partly because, in any event, he was not in the situation to which that section refers. All we need say about this argument is that the warrant in this case was sought at common law. This is not a situation where the sheriff was misled by the reference to the statute into thinking that she was exercising a statutory power which was not available to her. Indeed the reference to the statute may be taken as indicating that there were cir-cumstances where a warrant would be unnecessary if a statutory power was available, but that in this case, since that power was not available, a warrant was needed in accordance with the common law rules.

For these reasons we do not think that the sheriff misdirected herself when she granted the warrant complained against, and we note that nothing in her reports suggests that she did. We are quite satisfied that the decision which she took was soundly based on the information which was before her."

Questions arise about whether the taking of samples is consistent with art.6(2) of the ECHR which deals with the right not to incriminate oneself. The following case is concerned with the breath testing of suspected drink drivers under the Road Traffic Act 1988, s.7 which provides that:

"**7.**—(1) In the course of an investigation into whether a person has committed an offence under section ... 5 of this Act a constable may, subject to the following provisions of this section and section 9 of this Act, require him:—

   (a) to provide two specimens of breath for analysis by means of a device of a type approved by the Secretary of State, or

   (b) to provide a specimen of blood or urine for a laboratory test."

Brown v Gallacher
2002 S.L.T. 1135

The accused was charge with driving with excess alcohol. He challenged the leading of evidence obtained from an "Intoximeter" on the basis that it infringed his right not to incriminate himself.

LORD CAMERON: "As the sheriff records, the purpose of the minute is to seek to exclude the evidence of the printout from the Intoximeter device which was used to analyse breath samples provided by the appellant following upon his arrest. That is to say, it is directed at the evidence contained in printouts from the device upon which proof of the proportion of alcohol in the appellant's breath at the relevant time and hence establishment of the libel of the charge depends. For that reason, when opening his submissions for the appellant before us, counsel indicated that he was inviting the court to allow the appeal and to pronounce declarator that the procurator fiscal had no power to lead and rely upon evidence relating to the measured results produced by the Intoximeter device from samples of breath provided by the appellant. Such a declarator was consistent with the course adopted by this court in analogous circumstances in *Brown v Stott*, 2001 S.L.T. 59. The declarator is sought upon the basis that if such evidence were to be led at any subsequent trial of the appellant, the proceedings would not be fair and thus there would be a violation of the appellant's entitlement to a fair hearing under art 6 (1) of the European Human Rights Convention.

In his report the sheriff refers to the statutory scheme set out in the 1988 Act. The procedures leading up to an analysis by an Intoximeter device of specimens of breath provided by a person such as the appellant, begin with a roadside breath test administered by a constable in uniform in terms of s 6 of the Act. Where that roadside test shows an indication of alcohol in the breath, s 6 (5) empowers a constable to arrest that person without warrant. Consequent upon arrest and following conveyance of that person to a police station, s 7 empowers a constable to require him to provide two specimens of breath for analysis. For completeness, we set out the full terms of s 7 (1) so far as relevant: [his Lordship quoted its terms set out above and continued:] These specimens are not offered voluntarily. Section 7 (6) provides that it is an offence to refuse, without reasonable cause, to provide these specimens and imposes punishment upon conviction, the penalties extending to six months' imprisonment or a fine or both. Section 7 (7) requires that a constable must warn the suspect that failure to provide the samples may render him liable to prosecution. It is to be noted that the penalties for a contravention of s 7 (6) are the same as for a contravention of s 5 (1) (a) of the 1988 Act.

In our opinion, there is no support in either European jurisprudence or in domestic jurisprudence for the submissions for the appellant. We begin by bearing in mind that, as was said by Lord Hope of Craighead in *Brown v Stott* at 2001 SLT, p 79I-J, the right to silence and the right not to incriminate oneself have been recognised by the European Court as rights which, although not specifically mentioned in art 6 of the Convention, ought to be read in to that article to secure the right to a fair trial and that the fullest description of those rights is to be found in *Saunders v United Kingdom (1997) 23 E.H.R.R. 313* at paras 68–69.

In *Saunders* at paras 68 and 69 the court said:

> '68. The Court recalls that, although not specifically mentioned in Article 6 of the Convention, the right to silence and the right not to incriminate oneself, are generally recognised international standards which lie at the heart of the notion of a fair procedure under Article 6. Their rationale lies, *inter alia*, in the protection of the accused against improper compulsion by the authorities thereby contributing to the avoidance of miscarriages of justice and to the fulfilment of the aims of Article 6. The right not to incriminate oneself, in particular, presupposes that the prosecution in a criminal case seek to prove their case against the accused without resort to evidence obtained through methods of coercion or oppression in defiance of the will of the accused. In this sense the right is closely linked to the presumption of innocence contained in Article 6(2) of the Convention.
>
> 69. The right not to incriminate oneself is primarily concerned, however, with respecting the will of an accused person to remain silent. As commonly understood in the legal systems of the Contracting Parties to the Convention and elsewhere, it does not extend to the use in criminal proceedings of material which may be obtained from the accused through the use of compulsory powers but which has an existence independent of the will of the suspect such as, *inter alia*, documents acquired pursuant to a

warrant, breath, blood and urine samples and bodily tissue for the purpose of DNA testing.'

In *Cartledge v United Kingdom*, Application No. 30551/96, the Commission considered a complaint that the obtaining of a blood sample under compulsion involved a violation of the right of the suspect not to incriminate himself where the applicant was suspected of driving a motor vehicle with excess alcohol in his blood contrary to the Road Traffic Act 1972. The applicant had been stopped by the police and arrested for drinking and driving. At the police station, under alleged threat of prosecution for failure to provide a specimen, he allowed a police doctor to take a blood sample. The applicant had subsequently pleaded guilty but that gave rise to a separate issue before the Commission as to effective remedy if there had been a breach of art 6. The Commission noted that in appeal proceedings in England there was no suggestion that the crucial evidence of the analysis of the blood sample on which guilt or innocence depended was in any way open to doubt. Nor had there been any objection before the original court that the specimen of blood had been obtained contrary to the correct procedure. After recapitulating the terms of paras 68 and 69 in *Saunders*, the Commission said: 'As a result, in the light of the above considerations [i e those set out in para 69 in *Saunders*], the Commission does not find that the fact that the sample of blood was compulsorily obtained and admitted as evidence against the applicant could lead to the conclusion that the applicant was deprived of a fair trial within the meaning of Article 6 of the Convention.'

In *Brown v Stott* at 2001 SLT, p 71C-F Lord Bingham said:

'While the High Court was entitled to distinguish (as it did at pp 344–345) between the giving of an answer under sec 172 and the provision of physical samples, and had the authority of the European Court in *Saunders* (at para 69) for doing so, this distinction should not in my opinion be pushed too far. It is true that the respondent's answer, whether given orally or in writing, would create new evidence which did not exist until she spoke or wrote. In contrast, it may be acknowledged, the percentage of alcohol in her breath was a fact, existing before she blew into the breathalyser machine. But the whole purpose of requiring her to blow into the machine (on pain of a criminal penalty if she refused) was to obtain evidence not available until she did so and the reading so obtained could, in all save exceptional circumstances, be enough to convict a driver of an offence. If one applies the language of Wigmore on Evidence, vol 8, p 318, quoted by the High Court that an individual should "not be conscripted by his opponent to defeat himself" it is not easy to see why a requirement to answer is objectionable and a requirement to undergo a breath test is not. Yet no criticism is made of the requirement that the respondent undergo a breath test.'

In this passage Lord Bingham was countering the conclusion of the High Court, arising from the distinction referred to in *Saunders*, that since the appellant was subject to compulsion to make an incriminating reply under threat of being found guilty of an offence and punished with a fine and since the Crown proposed to make use of that reply as a significant part of the prosecution case, that use would offend her right not to incriminate herself, which is a constituent element of the basic principles of fair procedure inherent in art 6 (1) of the Convention. See also Lord Hope at p 76C-D (p 80D). But the passage quoted provides no foundation for the submission that a requirement to take a breath test under compulsion is an interference with the implied right on which the appellant relies in this appeal. Indeed in *Brown v Stott* it appears that following upon the answer given by Miss Brown, the police then required her to give a specimen of breath. This she did. The breath test was positive. Thereafter she was charged inter alia with driving her car after consuming an excess of alcohol in contravention of s 5 (1) (a) of the 1988 Act. Thus the decision cannot support the submission that the board in *Brown v Stott* were critical of the distinction made in *Saunders* between self incriminating statements and the provision of breath samples obtained under compulsion and thus that there was no real distinction between the two for the purpose of determining whether an individual's right not to incriminate himself had been interfered with. Rather, the issue to which the board addressed itself was whether evidence of an admission which Miss Brown was compelled to make under s 172 (2) (a) could be led at her trial for the offence charged under s 3, compatibly with her rights under art 6 of the Convention, against the background that the implied rights were not absolute. The board held that the rights not being absolute rights, were open to modification or restriction, that the statutory provisions for the detection and prosecution of road traffic offences serve a legitimate aim which would be at risk of being defeated if no means were available to enable the police to trace the driver of a vehicle after he had departed from the place of the offence before he could be identified and that the means employed were proportionate to that aim and were compatible with the right of the accused to a fair trial. The board reviewed the decision of this court because, as Lord Bingham said at p 61H-I (p 71J-K), the High Court interpreted the decision in *Saunders* as laying down more absolute a standard than the European Court intended, and that nowhere in the High Court judgments was there to be found any recognition of the need to balance the general interests of the community against the interests of the individual or to ask whether s 172 represented a proportionate response to what is undoubtedly a serious social problem.

The averments made in the minute do not raise any questions as to the propriety of the procedure which was followed by the police officers who made the requirement of the appellant. The procedure followed is not said to have been otherwise than in accordance with the relevant statutory provisions. Nor is there any suggestion that the evidence of measurement is tainted. That is to say, the evidence to which the minute is directed is not said to be otherwise objectionable than on the basis of an assertion that it was obtained in contravention of the implied right against self-incrimination. If there was no contravention of that right, it is not suggested that the admission of such evidence would prejudice a fair trial. We have emphasised this aspect of the averments, because when consideration is given to what is said by the court in *Saunders*, the assumption underlying the distinction made relative to material in the form of breath, blood or urine samples to be used in criminal proceedings, must have been that such material had been obtained lawfully and in accordance with the prescribed procedures laid down for a requirement to provide such material and could not be challenged on such grounds. Thus, for example, the court makes specific reference to documents 'acquired pursuant to a warrant'. Of course if such material was not obtained in accordance with the prescribed procedures, that is to say, according to law, then evidence relating to that material could be challenged at any subsequent trial as inadmissible. Furthermore, unlike the position in *Saunders* where the evidence used at his trial was derived from answers compulsorily obtained in a non-judicial investigation, the evidence in the present case was obtained in the course of a criminal investigation, as s 7 (1) of the 1988 Act makes clear.

The position in the present case is an exact parallel to the position in *Cartledge*. The obligation to provide the blood sample in that case can be equiparated in terms of the relevant road traffic legislation to the obligation to provide a breath sample in the present case. Each proceeded upon a requirement to be made with notice that if the suspect failed to provide the sample, he might be prosecuted for that failure. Indeed as appears from the provisions of s 7 (3) of the 1988 Act, so far as it is concerned with investigation of an offence under s 5 of the Act, the requirement for a specimen of blood or urine is only to made where the constable has reasonable cause to believe that for medical reasons a specimen of breath cannot be provided or should not be required or where either no or no reliable device is available or the device used has not produced a reliable indication of the proportion of alcohol in the breath. The decision of the Commission in *Cartledge* was determined by reference to what was said by the court in *Saunders* at paras 68 and 69. In later decisions the court has consistently referred to and supported the statements made there. In particular, in *JB v Switzerland* [2001] Crim. L.R. 748 the court clearly recognised that an obligation in criminal law to provide material by way of a breath sample fell into the same category as an obligation to provide a sample of blood or urine, namely, as material which had an existence independent of the person concerned and was not, therefore, obtained by means of coercion and in defiance of the will of that person. As the sheriff noted in his report, the provision of a sample of breath is to be regarded as no different in principle from other samples such as blood, urine or DNA, and its provision as much as the provision of blood, urine or DNA is of the kind of physical sample to which Lord Bingham referred in *Brown v Stott* at p 71C. Indeed, it is because of its physical nature that a specimen of breath is capable of being measured for the proportion of alcohol in it by means of the approved device, just as a specimen of blood or urine can be measured through a laboratory test. In our opinion, the requirement made of the appellant in this case to provide breath specimens, being made of him in accordance with the prescribed statutory procedures, was not an interference with the appellant's implied right not to incriminate himself, even though it was accompanied by notice that failure to provide it might make the suspect liable to prosecution. Accordingly, the making of such a requirement does not prejudice his right to a fair trial."

VII. RIGHTS OF SUSPECTS

Scots law recognises that those in police custody have a number of rights. These include:

- The right not to be held incommunicado.
- The right of access to a solicitor.
- The right to silence and not to incriminate oneself.

The nature of these rights may depend to some extent on whether the individual has been arrested or detained under the Criminal Procedure (Scotland) Act 1995, s.14. While a person arrested has the right of access to a solicitor, no such right exists for someone detained. Such a person is entitled only to have a solicitor informed of the fact of this detention.

(1) The Right Not to be Held Incommunicado

The first right of the suspect is to let someone know that he or she is in police custody. This was first introduced in 1980, and is now to be found in s.15 of the 1995 Act as follows. It will be noted that the right applies both where the individual has been arrested and where the individual has been detained for questioning.

Criminal Procedure (Scotland) Act 1995

"Rights of person arrested or detained
   15.—(1) Without prejudice to section 17 of this Act, a person who, not being a person in respect of whose custody or detention subsection (4) below applies—
   (a) has been arrested and is in custody in a police station or other premises, shall be entitled to have intimation of his custody and of the place where he is being held sent to a person reasonably named by him;
   (b) is being detained under section 14 of this Act and has been taken to a police station or other premises or place, shall be entitled to have intimation of his detention and of the police station or other premises or place sent to a solicitor and to one other person reasonably named by him,
   without delay or, where some delay is necessary in the interest of the investigation or the prevention of crime or the apprehension of offenders, with no more delay than is so necessary.
   (2) A person shall be informed of his entitlement under subsection (1) above—

    (a) on arrival at the police station or other premises; or
    (b) where he is not arrested, or as the case may be detained, until after such arrival, on
        such arrest or detention.
  (3) Where the person mentioned in paragraph (a) of subsection (1) above requests such
intimation to be sent as is specified in that paragraph there shall be recorded the time when
such request is—
    (a) made;
    (b) complied with.
  (4) Without prejudice to the said section 17, a constable shall, where a person who has
been arrested and is in such custody as is mentioned in paragraph (a) of subsection (1)
above or who is being detained as is mentioned in paragraph (b) of that subsection appears
to him to be a child, send without delay such intimation as is mentioned in the said
paragraph (a), or as the case may be paragraph (b), to that person's parent if known; and
the parent—
    (a) in a case where there is reasonable cause to suspect that he has been involved in the
        alleged offence in respect of which the person has been arrested or detained, may;
        and
    (b) in any other case shall,
be permitted access to the person.
  (5) The nature and extent of any access permitted under subsection (4) above shall be
subject to any restriction essential for the furtherance of the investigation or the well-being
of the person.
  (6) In subsection (4) above—
    (a) 'child' means a person under 16 years of age; and
    (b) 'parent' includes guardian and any person who has the actual custody of a child."

Thus it is not in fact the case that the detainee has a "right to a phone-call". Section 15(1)(a)
applies to arrest and allows only that a reasonably nominated person is informed of the fact of
an arrested person's whereabouts. The right of an arrested person to have access to a solicitor is
considered below. Section 15(1)(b) provides a right to have a reasonably nominated person
informed of the fact of a detainee's whereabouts, and also a right to have a solicitor informed of
a detained person's whereabouts. In the following case, it was held that the right contained in
s.15 does not amount to a right of access to a solicitor prior to interview. This rather begs the
question as to what benefit it is to the suspect to have a solicitor informed, where the solicitor is
not then present at the interview.

Paton v Ritchie
2000 S.L.T. 239

An accused was charged on a summary complaint with attempting to break into premises with
intent to steal or alternatively being found at the premises without lawful authority to be there
so that it might be inferred that he intended to commit theft. Before the accused was called on to
plead, his solicitor sought to raise as a devolution issue the procurator fiscal's intention to lead
evidence of a statement by the accused while detained by the police under the Criminal Procedure (Scotland) Act 1995, s.14. It was argued that as the police had failed to inform the
accused that he was entitled to have a solicitor present, this breached his right to a fair trial and
to defend himself through legal assistance of his own choosing, in terms of Art.6 (1) and (3) of
the European Convention on Human Rights.

LORD JUSTICE CLERK (CULLEN): "The circumstances out of which this appeal arises are set
  out in the minute and were elaborated to some extent by counsel who appeared on behalf of
  the appellant. The account on which we proceed is as follows. On 19 June the police
  received a 999 call about an alarm sounding at the premises. When police officers went to

the car park at the premises they saw the appellant walking from one side of the building. Although it was a warm evening, he was wearing a thick yellow jacket, a blue woollen tammy and black gloves. At the sight of the police vehicle he began to run. He was chased by police officers to a back garden. When they caught up with him he was still wearing the same clothes, but had put on a baseball cap in place of the tammy. At about 9.40 pm he was detained under s 14 (1) of the Criminal Procedure (Scotland) Act 1995. When he was searched a metal socket was found in a rear pocket of his jeans. He was taken to a police station. While he was there he indicated that he wanted to have a solicitor informed. At about 10.05 pm the police left a message on an answering machine at the home of his solicitor in which he was informed that the appellant had been detained and was at the police station. At about 11.50 pm the appellant was interviewed after being cautioned and without his solicitor being present. When he was asked to explain what he was doing near the premises he said that he had been trying to break in. He added that he had been wanting something to sell in order to get drugs. When he was asked what had stopped him getting in, he said that it was his hearing the police coming round the corner. He said that he had not used the socket. At about 1.27 am on the following morning he was arrested. Thereafter his solicitor was informed personally by a telephone message from the police. The appellant was not charged until 7.40 am. At that stage he said in response that he had been merely passing by when he was chased by the police. He had been going to 'tap' someone for a fiver.

The main question which we have to consider at this stage is whether the appellant has shown that he cannot receive a fair trial. Prior to the advent of devolution, the courts in Scotland required to consider such a question when it was maintained on behalf of an accused that by reason of some factor, such as delay or pre-trial publicity, he could not receive a fair trial and hence it was oppressive for the proceedings to continue. With the coming into operation of s 57 (2) of the Scotland Act 1998, the court now has to take into account the various rights which are comprehended in art 6 of the Convention in deciding that question.

From the decisions of the European Court of Human Rights and of the European Commission of Human Rights, to which we were referred, we can derive the following propositions. (1) The right set out in art 6 (3) (c) is one element among others of the concept of a fair trial in criminal proceedings to which art 6 (1) relates (*Imbrioscia v Switzerland* (1994) 17 E.H.R.R. 441, para 37). (2) Article 6, including para (3) (c), applies throughout, including at the stage of preliminary investigation (*Imbrioscia v Switzerland*, para 36; *Murray v United Kingdom* (1996) 22 E.H.R.R. 29, para 62). (3) Article 6 (3) (c) does not specify the manner by which the right to 'defend himself in person or through legal assistance of his own choosing' is to be exercised. It is left to the contracting state to choose the means of ensuring that it is secured. In considering whether the methods chosen are consistent with the requirements of a fair trial it has to be remembered, as we have already noted, that the Convention is designed to guarantee not rights that are theoretical or illusory but rights that are practical and effective. The European Court in *Imbrioscia* at para 38 also said: 'In addition, the court points out that the manner in which Article 6 (1) and (3) (c) is to be applied during the preliminary investigation depends on the special features of the proceedings involved and on the circumstances of the case; in order to determine whether the aim of Article 6—a fair trial—has been achieved, regard must be had to the entirety of the domestic proceedings conducted in the case'. (4) Article 6 (3) (c) does not state expressly, but it implies, the right of an accused to communicate with his lawyer as a fundamental part of the preparation of his defence (*Windsor v United Kingdom*, Application No. 13081/87). (5) However, that right cannot be said to be unsusceptible of restriction. If the accused has been questioned without his solicitor being present, the question is whether this is in conformity with the general principle of fairness laid down in art 6 (1) (*Windsor v United Kingdom; Robson v United Kingdom*, Application No. 25648/94).

It is clear from the above, as counsel accepted, that art 6 (3) (c) does not create a universal right in an accused to have access to his solicitor before or during questioning by the police. That there are cases in which this may be essential in order that the concept of fairness can be satisfied is demonstrated by the decision of the European Court in *Murray v United Kingdom*. Its circumstances were unusual in respect that the trial judge decided, as he was entitled to do under legislation relating to the prevention of terrorism, that an adverse inference should be drawn from the fact that the accused had elected to remain silent while he was questioned by the police. The accused had also been denied legal advice for 48 hours during which he had not answered their questions. At para 66 the court observed: 'To deny access to a lawyer for the first 48 hours of police questioning, in a situation where the rights of the defence may well be irretrievably prejudiced, is—whatever the justification for such denial—incompatible with the rights of the accused under Article 6'.

That case is far removed from the present. In Scotland no adverse inference can be drawn from the fact that an accused person was silent when he was questioned by the police (*Robertson v Maxwell*, 1951 S.L.T. 46). Further, as was pointed out by the advocate depute, the absence of a caution is likely to imperil the admissibility of anything said in response to a police officer who is exercising his power under s 14 (7) of the 1995 Act to question the person detained in relation to the suspected offence (see *Tonge v HM Advocate*, 1982 S.L.T. 506). The limited provision which was made by s 15 (1) (b) for the informing of a solicitor derived from the recommendations of the Second Report by the Thomson Committee on Criminal Procedure (paras 5.08 and 7.16). The committee recommended that it should be a matter of police discretion whether to allow a detainee an interview with his solicitor. The advocate depute also pointed out that, in accordance with well established practice, a person who wanted to make a voluntary statement would be informed that he was entitled to consult with a solicitor, and his statement would be taken by police officers who were unconnected with the investigation. Safeguards against the admission at the trial of evidence which had been unfairly obtained were provided. In the circumstances, he submitted, it was not possible to reach a conclusion that the appellant could not receive a fair trial.

In regard to the question whether the appellant can receive a fair trial, what was the practical effect of the fact that the solicitor was absent at the time when the appellant was being questioned by the police? We note that the appellant did not request that his solicitor should be present when he was questioned. Neither Scots law nor the Convention require that in all cases the person who is detained should be afforded the opportunity to have his solicitor present. We are not persuaded that the absence of the solicitor had a decisive effect upon the preparation of the appellant's defence. We do not accept the assertion that the appellant was prejudiced in regard to what was called his "statutory defence". It is clear from cases such as *Moran v Jessop*, 1989 S.C.C.R. 205, that there is an onus on the Crown to lead evidence which is such as to support the prima facie inference that the appellant had no lawful authority to be where he was found. In any event there is no question of the appellant being unable to avail himself of the services of a solicitor after he had been arrested. If so advised, he could have made a voluntary statement in order to explain the circumstances in which he came to be where he was found. The question whether a fair trial can be achieved depends not simply upon what happened during the preliminary investigation but on the whole proceedings. As we have already observed there are a number of safeguards both during that investigation and during the trial of the appellant. We are unable to affirm the view that, despite them, no fair trial could take place in the circumstances of the present case."

(2) Right of Access to a Solicitor

Criminal Procedure (Scotland) Act 1995

"Right of accused to have access to a solicitor

17.—(1) Where an accused has been arrested on any criminal charge, he shall be entitled immediately upon such arrest—

    (a) to have intimation sent to a solicitor that his professional assistance is required by
        the accused, and informing the solicitor—
            (i) of the place where the person is being detained;
            (ii) whether the person is to be liberated; and
            (iii) if the person is not to be liberated, the court to which he is to be taken and the
                 date when he is to be so taken; and
    (b) to be told what rights there are under—
            (i) paragraph (a) above;
            (ii) subsection (2) below; and
            (iii) section 35(1) and (2) of this Act.
    (2) The accused and the solicitor shall be entitled to have a private interview before the
examination or, as the case may be, first appearance."

The rights referred to under s.35 are to have judicial examination delayed for a period of up to
48 hours in order to allow attendance of a solicitor for the accused. The wording of the section is
that the arrested person is entitled to have immediate intimation sent to a solicitor, but there is
no sanction stipulated should intimation be delayed by the police, nor indeed if there is any
other breach of the rights of the accused under s.17. It might be that careful scrutiny would be
given to the admissibility of any confession evidence gathered before the solicitor arrived, but it
is certainly the case that it is no bar to subsequent proceedings where a private interview has
been refused.

Cheyne v McGregor
1941 J.C. 17

McGregor and another were charged with theft. He objected to the competency of the complaint on the basis that his right to a private interview in terms of s.15 of the Summary
Jurisdiction (Scotland) Act, 1908 had been denied. The sheriff sustained the objection and
dismissed the complaint against McGregor. An appeal by the Crown was unsuccessful, despite a
strongly worded dissent by Lord Mackay.

    LORD JUSTICE CLERK (AITCHISON): "I think this case has gone completely off the rails. The
respondents were arrested in Stirling on a charge of theft. On the evening of their arrest a
law agent called at the police office where they were detained and sought an interview with
one of the arrested men. He did so at the request of a brother of that man, and I shall take it
therefore that the man with whom he sought an interview desired to have an interview. The
inspector who was on duty at the time expressed his willingness to allow an interview, but
said to the law agent, 'But you won't see him alone, I will have to be there.' He also added
that it never was his practice to grant a private interview and he had never heard of the
practice being altered.
    Now I do not think that any of us can doubt for a moment that to refuse a private
interview to the law agent with his client was altogether wrong. It was contrary to the
express direction of section 15 of the Summary Jurisdiction (Scotland) Act, 1908. That
section runs: 'In any proceedings under this Act the accused if apprehended shall immediately on apprehension be entitled if he so desires, to have intimation sent to any law agent
and to have a private interview with such law agent prior to being brought before the
Court.' That of course is a very important and a very valuable right, and no officer of
police, whatever his rank and whatever the practice may be in any police station, has any
right to refuse a private interview to an arrested person.
    When the case was called in the Burgh Court on the following morning the respondents,
or at any rate the respondent who had been denied a private interview, was represented by
the law agent. No objection was taken that an interview had been refused, and the matter
indeed was not mentioned at all. At that diet the respondents were not called upon to plead,

so that, nothing took place beyond a formal appearance in Court and a formal remand of the accused until a later date. On the same day both respondents were liberated on bail, so that then, and from that time onward, they were at complete liberty to consult a law agent, and they have remained at liberty ever since. The proceedings in the Burgh Court did not go farther, the diet being deserted *pro loco et tempore*. A few days later another complaint was served in the Sheriff Court. On the diet being called certain objections of a preliminary kind to the competency of the complaint were tabled, including an objection that the accused, the respondent Robert M'Gregor, had been deprived of his legal rights under section 15 of the Act of 1908 in that he had been denied a private interview with his law agent upon his apprehension. When that objection was taken I think the obvious course was for the Sheriff-Substitute there and then to ascertain what the fact was, and I think that might have been done without holding a proof, which was the course adopted by the Sheriff. At any rate a proof was taken, and the Sheriff found it proved that an interview had been refused. He also found it proved that that had resulted in no prejudice to the accused. Thereupon, instead of appointing the case to proceed on the merits, he sustained the objection which had been tabled, which was an objection to the competency of the complaint, and he dismissed the complaint against both respondents.

Certain questions are put in the stated case, the material question being question 3, which is in these terms: 'Was I entitled to regard the refusal to grant an interview, when the respondents were charged on a Burgh Police Court complaint, as a bar to further proceedings on the Sheriff Court complaint?' Now there is no doubt that the view of the Sheriff-Substitute was that not only was the refusal to grant an interview a bar to the case proceeding immediately, but it was a bar to the case proceeding for all time. There is not the slightest doubt on the ground of his judgment that if a new complaint were brought he would be bound to sustain the same plea, and the result would be that the respondents could never be brought to trial at all upon a very serious charge. I should be very sorry to say anything to suggest that the right of an accused person to a private interview with his law agent immediately on apprehension was not a very important and valuable right—I should myself not object to it being described as a constitutional right—but I am not prepared to assent to the view that in every case where a mistake is made, and the accused person is wrongly refused an interview, the effect of that must be to bring the whole proceedings both at the time and for ever to an end. I do not find anything in the statute which compels me to take that view. I think the proper course to follow, and the course which I think in the circumstances of this case should have been followed, is to grant an adjournment—that is to adjourn the diet to a later date—to permit of an interview taking place, always under this caution, that if it should turn out in the course of the proceedings that there was any element of prejudice at all to the accused person, that fact would be decisive in his favour, and it might be that the proceedings could be stopped without following out the proceedings to an end."

Some indication that compliance with the statutory protections for the suspect will be significant in relation to the admissibility of confession evidence can be gleaned from the following case, where one of several co-accused of murder objected to the admissibility of incriminating statements he had made when initially interviewed as a witness rather than a suspect.

H M Advocate v Barrie
2002 S.L.T. 1053

Norwood was one of five co-accused who were charged with murder and assault. He was convicted on all three charges against him, and appealed on the basis that incriminating statements he made should not have been admitted as he had gone to the police initially as a witness, he was only 17 years old and that he had specifically asked for his lawyer to be present.

LORD COULSFIELD:

"At some time on 14 September 1999 either Norwood or a member of his family made contact with the police indicating that Norwood could give information about the murder which was being investigated at the time. After police officers had attended at Norwood's house, Norwood went voluntarily to the police station where there was some conversation with the officers, in the course of which Norwood gave certain information. In view of the nature of that information, the officers who had spoken to Norwood consulted senior officers and thereafter detained Norwood in terms of s 14 of the Criminal Procedure (Scotland) Act 1995 and cautioned him. The interview about which the question of admissibility arises took place thereafter, at about 8.30 pm. At the commencement of the interview, the interviewing officers went over what had happened in the course of the day, referred to the earlier detention and duly cautioned Norwood. Thereafter, the following exchange took place:

'*Suspect*: Am I allowed to talk with my lawyer here the now?
DC (1): Mm, did you ask for a lawyer to be advised?
Suspect: Aye.
DC (1): When you were at the bar there? Right, your lawyer will be informed and if indeed your lawyer decides to come and make representation—
Suspect: Mm hm.
DC (1): Advice will be taken as to whether or not your lawyer will be allowed access to you.
Suspect: Right.
DC (1): If your lawyer appears I don't see any reason why he wouldn't be allowed access.
Suspect: Right.
DC (1): All right, but it's important that we get this sorted out just now, particularly in the light of what you've been telling us earlier on.'

The interview then proceeded. In the course of it Norwood made statements which were capable of being incriminating. We were informed that the evidence of the interviewing officer was to the effect that in the earlier conversation Norwood had begun to talk about the supply of weapons and that this had led to him becoming a suspect. However, there was no attempt at the trial to have the question of admissibility determined at a trial within a trial.

In these circumstances, the submission for the appellant was that it was unfair to allow the incriminating answers to be admitted in evidence in view of the whole circumstances, including, in particular, the age of the accused, the fact that he had been interviewed originally as a witness before his status changed to that of suspect and the fact that he had specifically asked whether he could have access to his lawyer. It was pointed out that in the case of two other of the accused a lawyer had been present at the stage of initial interview. The advocate depute, on the other hand, submitted that the questions which had been put to Norwood had been spontaneously answered and that indeed he had, when initially asked to give an account of his involvement, given a full account without prompting. The procedure of detention and intimation to a solicitor and another person had been properly carried out and the judge had properly directed the jury to consider the question of the fairness of the procedure and to ignore the evidence if they thought that there had been unfairness.

We have considered the procedure followed and the terms of the interview as well as those of the judge's charge. It is sufficient, in our view, to say that we are satisfied that no sufficient ground has been stated for holding that the terms of the interview should not have been admitted in evidence. In these circumstances, this ground of appeal fails."

VIII. Questioning of Suspects

One of the purposes of detention of a person is to enable him or her to be questioned about possible involvement with the offence which is being investigated. In order to protect the rights of suspects to remain silent and not to incriminate themselves, the police will issue a caution, the normal form of which informs the accused that he or she is not obliged to say anything, but anything they do say may be recorded and used in evidence. Interviews will be tape-recorded as an added protection against unfair conduct by the police. The administration of a caution will be an important factor in assessing whether or not it is fair to admit particular evidence, but it is not necessarily fatal that a caution has not been given. As will be seen in this section, there has been a swing away from a fairly rigid test as to the admissibility of confession evidence to a more flexible approach, which depends largely on whether it is "fair" that the evidence is admitted. "Fairness" takes into account not only fairness to the accused, but also to the general public in ensuring the proper administration of justice. Although the test of fairness has altered over the course of years, *Chalmers v HM Advocate*, 1954 S.L.T. 177 decided in the aftermath of the Second World War and shortly after the United Kingdom had signed up to ECHR, marks a highpoint in judicial protection of a suspect under questioning.

Chalmers v HM Advocate
1954 S.L.T. 177

The appellant, who was under suspicion of having committed a murder, had after interrogation by the police at a police station burst into tears and made a confession. He had then led the police to a field and pointed out where the murdered man's purse was. Two hours later, after his father arrived, he was charged, and was said to have stated "I did it. He struck me". The trial judge held that the statement would have been inadmissible in evidence, but allowed evidence of the appellant's act in taking the police to the field. He was convicted and appealed. The High Court of Justiciary, quashing his conviction, held that the visit to the field was all part and parcel of the interrogation and that evidence of it was not admissible. The court made certain observations concerning the admissibility of statements made to the police by persons under suspicion.

> The Lord Justice-General (Cooper): "In the course of their investigations the police made many inquiries, and, on 26th July and again on 7th August, questioned the appellant. The statements then given by him were not incriminating. The police later obtained certain information from the witnesses, Mrs Oliver and her small son, which tended to cast some doubt upon the truth of the statements made by the appellant, and the police decided to see the appellant again. Their attitude at this point is frankly explained by the detective-inspector in charge of the investigations, who says that, from the information received from Mrs Oliver, he was 'inclined to suspect' that the appellant might have some connection with the crime, and that the appellant 'was under suspicion'. In that situation a police car with two officers was sent from Falkirk on 15th August to fetch the appellant from Clack-mannan, where he was still in bed; and he was brought to the police station at Falkirk at 11.10 a.m. and there interviewed by a detective-inspector in the presence of another officer of the same rank. The appellant (who was never at liberty again) was told that he was to be further questioned, and was cautioned in the usual terms. The inspector then proceeded to interrogate the appellant, telling him the information which had come into the possession of the police and reopening the statement made by him on 7th August. The inspector admits that he was 'cross-examining' the appellant, and making suggestions to him which were contradictory of his previous statement, saying, *inter alia,* that the police had reason to believe that he 'might have been' at the locus at the time when the crimes were committed. The interrogation lasted for about five minutes until the appellant was reduced to tears. He was then cautioned a second time, and asked whether he wanted his father or a

solicitor to be present 'when he did a certain thing'. The appellant declined. The second inspector was then asked to take a note of the appellant's statement, but before doing so he gave a third (or fourth) caution to the appellant and repeated the offer that his father or a solicitor should be present. A statement was then taken which we can only assume was highly incriminating; but this statement was not tendered in evidence by the Crown.

Matters did not end there. Immediately after the statement had been taken the first inspector questioned the appellant about certain matters contained in his statement, and in consequence of answers thus obtained, the appellant was taken about 11.45 a.m. in a police van by the inspector and two other police officers to a cornfield near the locus, where the purse of the deceased was found at a spot pointed out by the appellant under the surveillance of the police. The appellant was then taken back to the police station about 12.10 p.m. An interval of about two hours then ensued while the appellant's father was being fetched by the police, and at this stage, though there had been neither charge nor arrest, the appellant is described by the police as being 'detained in connection with the murder', whatever that may mean. The father arrived about 2.15 p.m. and the appellant again broke down. At 2.25 p.m. he was cautioned and formally charged in presence of his father, whereupon the appellant is said to have replied:

'I did it. He struck me.'

I have sympathy with the police in the difficult position in which they are often placed. We have no power to give instructions to the police, but we have the power and the duty to exclude from the cognisance of a jury evidence which, according to our practice and decisions, is inadmissible; and the police have an interest to know why such decisions are taken. Were it possible to do so I should like to be able to lay down comprehensive rules for the guidance of the police in all the situations which may arise in practice, but I am satisfied that this is impossible because in the border-line case so much turns upon the exact circumstances.

It is not the function of the police when investigating a crime to direct their endeavours to obtaining a confession from a suspect to be used as evidence against him at the trial. In some legal systems the inquisitorial method of investigation is allowed in different degrees and subject to various safeguards; but by our law self-incriminating statements when tendered in evidence at a criminal trial, are always jealously examined from the standpoint of being assured as to their spontaneity; and if, on a review of all the proved circumstances, that test is not satisfied, evidence of such statements will usually be excluded altogether. The theory of our law is that at the stage of initial investigation the police may question anyone with a view to acquiring information which may lead to the detection of the criminal; but that, when the stage has been reached at which suspicion, or more than suspicion, has in their view centred upon some person as the likely perpetrator of the crime, further interrogation of that person becomes very dangerous, and if carried too far, e.g. to the point of extracting a confession by what amounts to cross-examination, the evidence of that confession will almost certainly be excluded ... If under such circumstances cross-examination is pursued with the result, though perhaps not with the deliberate object, of causing him to break down and to condemn himself out of his own mouth, the impropriety of the proceedings cannot be cured by the giving of any number of formal cautions or by the introduction of some officer other than the questioner to record the ultimate statement. In the ordinary case, as many decisions now demonstrate, that statement if tendered in evidence at the trial will not be treated as possessing that quality of spontaneity on which our law insists, and its rejection, when tendered in evidence may, and sometimes does, wreck the prosecution. The practice exemplified by this and other recent cases in substance puts the suspect in much the same position as if he had been arrested, while depriving him of the privileges and safeguards which are extended by the statute and the decisions to an accused person who has been apprehended. The police have, of course, the right and the duty to produce all the incriminating evidence they can lay their hands on, from whatever source they may legitimately derive the clue which leads to its discovery, so long as any admission or confession by the accused is not elicited before the jury as an element in proof of guilt. The matter may be put in another way. The accused cannot be compelled to give evidence at his trial and to submit to cross-examination. If it were competent for the police at their own hand to subject the accused to interrogation and cross-examination and to adduce evidence of what he said, the prosecution would in effect be making the accused a compellable witness, and laying before the jury at second- hand evidence which could not be adduced at first hand, even subject to all the precautions which are available for the protection of the accused at a criminal trial."

THE LORD JUSTICE-CLERK (THOMSON): "I have hesitated whether to add anything but I venture to make some observations on the two general topics which were so fully discussed. These are (1) the circumstances under which statements made by an accused person to the police become inadmissible as evidence.

On the first of these topics the difficulty arises from the necessity of reconciling two principles: (1) that no accused person is bound to incriminate himself and need not submit himself as a witness, and (2) that what an accused person says—apart from what properly falls within the doctrine of *res gestae*—provided he says it freely and voluntarily, is admissible evidence against him. It is when the police in the course of their duty as investigators of crime interview someone in relation to some specific crime that the problem arises for decision whether something which has been said by an accused is admissible as evidence against him. Extreme cases are easy. At the one extreme once the investigation has gone to the extent that somebody is specifically cautioned and charged, thereafter nothing short of a voluntary statement is admissible against him. At the other extreme is the ordinary routine investigation of the police into the circumstances of the crime. In the course of such an investigation the man ultimately accused may be interviewed. It would unduly hamper the investigation of crime if the threat of inadmissibility were to tie hands of the police in asking questions. It would help to defeat the ends of justice if what the person so questioned said in answer to ordinary and legitimate questions were not admissible in evidence against him. I am assuming throughout that the questioning is not tainted by bullying, pressure, third degree methods and so forth. Evidence obtained by such methods can never be admissible in our Courts whatever stage the investigation has reached. But there comes a point of time in ordinary police investigation when the law intervenes to render inadmissible as evidence answers even to questions which are not tainted by such methods. After the point is reached, further interrogation is incompatible with the answers being regarded as a voluntary statement, and the law intervenes to safeguard the party questioned from possible self-incrimination. Just when that point of time is reached is in any particular case extremely difficult to define or even for an experienced police official to realise its arrival. There does come a time, however, when a police officer carrying out his duty honestly and conscientiously ought to be in a position to appreciate that the man whom he is in process of questioning is under serious consideration as the perpetrator of the crime. Once that stage of suspicion is reached, the suspect is in the position that thereafter the only evidence admissible against him is his own voluntary statement. A voluntary statement is one which is given freely not in response to pressure and inducement and not elicited by cross-examination. This does not mean that if a person elects to give a statement, it becomes inadmissible because he is asked some questions to clear his account of the matter up but such questions as he is asked must not go beyond elucidation. It is important to keep in mind also that the point of time at which the axe falls is not necessarily related to the person's being in custody or detention of some sort. The fact that he is detained may point to his being under suspicion but he may come under suspicion without having been detained."

The Lord Justice General identified three stages of police investigation:

- Initial stage: anyone may be questioned.
- Second stage: suspicion has fallen on one person. Further questioning is dangerous and if taken too far, will lead to evidence being inadmissible.
- Third stage: person apprehended and charged. Any statement must be voluntary and be made in non-prejudicial circumstances.

This mechanical approach was in due course moved away from in favour of a more flexible test of fairness, evident in the following case.

Miln v Cullen
1967 S.L.T. 35

About 20 minutes after a collision one of the drivers involved gave the police information about the respondent driver of the other car, which lead them to suspect the respondent of being drunk and responsible for the collision. The constables approached the respondent, formed the opinion that he was under the influence of drink, and one of them asked him if he was the driver of the car. The respondent admitted that he was, gave his name and address and produced his driving licence. He was then cautioned and charged under the Road Traffic Act 1960, s.6(1). Objection was taken to his replies to the questioning being given in evidence, because at the time of the questioning he was then under suspicion and not cautioned.

LORD JUSTICE-CLERK (GRANT): "While, according to our common law, no man is bound to incriminate himself, there is, in general, nothing to prevent a man making a voluntary and incriminating statement to the police if he chooses, and evidence being led of that statement at his subsequent trial on the charge to which his statement relates. It is said, however, that in the present case there are three factors which, when taken cumulatively, amount to unfairness—Constable Blair's 'suspicion', the absence of a caution and the fact that the respondent's admission was in reply to a question. One must, however, look at the realities of the situation. The two constables and Sievwright had apparently all formed the opinion that the respondent was unfit to drive through drink: but Constable Blair had only the uncorroborated statement of Sievwright that the respondent was the driver of the car. In that situation it seems to me that Constable Blair, in asking the simple question which he did, was not merely acting reasonably, properly and fairly, but was acting in accordance with the duties incumbent upon him.

In saying this I have fully in mind the well-known passage in Lord Justice- General Cooper's opinion in *Chalmers v H.M. Advocate*, 1954 S.L.T. 177 where he points out that 'the theory of our law is that at the stage of initial investigation the police may question anyone with a view to acquiring information which may lead to the detection of the criminal; but that, when the stage has been reached at which suspicion, or more than suspicion, has in their view centred upon some person as the likely perpetrator of the crime, further interrogation of that person becomes very dangerous, and, if carried too far, e.g., to the point of extracting a confession by what amounts to cross-examination the evidence of that confession will almost certainly be excluded'.

Where exactly the danger line is to be drawn will vary according to the particular circumstances . . . . But I am satisfied that we are well short of it in the present case. I would be prepared to hold that this case had never got beyond the investigation stage. In any event, however, there was no interrogation in the proper sense of that word, no extraction of a confession by cross-examination, no taint of undue pressure, cajoling or trapping, no bullying and nothing in the nature of third degree and it is not suggested that the respondent, by reason of low intelligence, immaturity or drink, was incapable of appreciating what was going on. Had Constable Blair gone on to interrogate the respondent about how the accident had happened, where he had been and what he had had to drink, a different situation might have been created. As it was, he merely asked what was, in my opinion, a fair and proper question and received a reply which can fairly and properly be admitted in evidence. It is well to keep in mind that, in applying the test of fairness, one must not look solely and in isolation at the situation of the suspect or accused: one must also have regard to the public interest in the ascertainment of the truth and in the detection and suppression of crime."

Lord Wheatley: "The legal principles in this field of evidence were exhaustively canvassed in *Chalmers v H.M. Advocate* (supra), and it would appear from the arguments addressed to us by counsel for the respondent and other expressions of opinion voiced elsewhere that certain misconceptions have arisen from the decision and opinions in that case. If that be so, then the sooner these misconceptions are cleared the better it is for all concerned. For instance, counsel for the respondent submitted that once a person came under suspicion no questions by a police officer and a fortiori no answers by the suspect were admissible in evidence. In *Chalmers*, the Lord Justice-General, supported by a full bench, reviewed the legal position at three different and progressive stages, namely (1) where routine investigations are being carried out and the person ultimately accused has not fallen under suspicion (2) where that person has fallen under suspicion but has not been cautioned and charged and (3) where that person has been cautioned and charged. I need not rehearse all that was said by Lord Cooper in that context, but I deem it important to stress that in the variety of circumstances which might attend cases in each of these categories the basic and ultimate test is fairness. While the law of Scotland has always very properly regarded fairness to an accused person as being an integral part of the administration of justice, fairness is not a unilateral consideration. Fairness to the public is also a legitimate consideration, and insofar as police officers in the exercise of their duties are prosecuting and protecting the public interest, it is the function of the Court to seek to provide a proper balance to secure that the rights of individuals are properly preserved while not hamstringing the police in their investigation of crime with a series of academic vetoes which ignore the realities and practicalities of the situation and discount completely the public interest. Even at the stage of routine investigations where much greater latitude is allowed, fairness is still the test, and that is always a question of circumstances. It is conceivable that even at that stage a question might be asked or some action might be perpetrated which produced an admission of guilt from the person being interviewed, and yet the evidence might be disallowed because the circumstances disclosed an unfairness to that person. At the other end of the scale, it is wrong to assume that after a person has been cautioned and charged questioning of that person is no longer admissible. All that was said in *Chalmers* and in the subsequent cases of *Manuel v H.M. Advocate*, 1958 S.L.T. (Notes) 44 and *Brown v H.M. Advocate*, 1966 S.L.T. 105 was that at that stage questions or indeed actions which induced by some means or another self-incriminating statements by an accused which were not voluntary or spontaneous were liable to be ruled out as inadmissible. But once again the test is one of fairness. A question asked merely to clear up an ambiguity and not calculated to produce an incriminating answer might result in a self-induced incriminating answer by an accused person. Whether such evidence should be admitted or not will always be a question for the Court, having regard to all the circumstances and the basic touchstone of fairness."

This more flexible approach was justified by Lord Wheatley as "fairness to the public" in that it allowed police to exercise their powers in order to prosecute and protect the public interest. Perhaps the highpoint of the test of fairness was reached in *Hartley v HM Advocate*, 1979 S.L.T. 26, where Lord Avonside held:

"*Brown v H.M. Advocate*, 1996 S.L.T. 105 was also quoted. I should have thought that case unhelpful to counsel for the accused. I refer to what was said by Lord Justice-General Clyde at p.107. He speaks of questioning and interrogation and concludes his remarks by saying:

'But the test in all of them is the simple and intelligible test which has worked well in practice—has what has taken place been fair or not?'

I pause to interject that that, in my understanding, is today in law the basic test and only test. There has been a steady move towards liberalisation so that justice must, of course, be done to the criminal, but equally justice must be done to the interest of the public and law and order."

Modern endorsement of this approach is found in the following case.

Pennycuick v Lees
1992 S.L.T. 763

The accused was followed by DSS inspectors as he was suspected of benefit fraud by claiming sickness benefit while he was still working. On the third occasion of being followed, he was interviewed without caution and admitted working more than 24 hours in that week. Four months later, the accused was seen again by the inspectors, who showed him four forms which he agreed he had signed. He was then cautioned and charged. He objected to the evidence as inadmissible due to not having been cautioned at the time of the questioning.

LORD JUSTICE-GENERAL (HOPE): "... in all these cases where inquiries are being conducted into activities which may be criminal the question is whether, looking at all the circumstances of the case, there has been unfairness to the accused in what took place. This was the test which was applied in *Miln v Cullen*, 1967 S.L.T. 35, in which it was conceded by the Crown that, when the accused was asked by the police officers whether he was the driver of the car, he was a suspected person. As Lord Strachan put it at 1967 S.L.T., p. 38: 'The whole circumstances must be taken into account, and the test in every case is whether in the particular circumstances there has been unfairness on the part of the police.'

In *Irving v Jessop*, 1988 S.L.T. 53, evidence was given by Post Office inquiry officers that when they visited the appellant and asked her if she had a television licence she admitted she had not. It was submitted that her reply to these officers was inadmissible because it had been unfairly obtained. The argument was that since she was a suspect she should have been warned that she might be prosecuted and that any reply which she made might be used in evidence. This argument was rejected on the ground that there was no unfairness on the part of the inquiry officers in their asking, in the course of their inquiries, whether someone with a television set had a television licence. Here again one can see the same test being applied. There is, therefore, no rule of law which requires that a suspect must always be cautioned before any question can be put to him by the police or by anyone else by whom the inquiries are being conducted. The question in each case is whether what was done was unfair to the accused.

The sheriff was satisfied that at the time of the interview on 28 April 1989 the officers of the department were investigating the possibility of an offence. But they still had to discover whether the person to whom they were speaking was the same James Pennycuick as the man whom they understood to be claiming benefit. The purpose of the interview was to find out whether the appellant was that man and whether or not he was entitled to the benefit which he was claiming from the social security office. The answer to the latter question depended on whether he was working and if so whether his earnings were in excess of the statutory earnings limit. It was only when they had all this information that they were able to determine whether the appellant had committed an offence. There is no suggestion in the findings that the officials were trying to trap the appellant into an admission or to provoke an incriminating reply from him which would provide them with evidence which they could not otherwise obtain. Their questions were designed merely to obtain information from him on matters relevant to their inquiries, at a stage when they were still unable to say whether or not he had committed an offence. This line of questioning was fair and proper in the circumstances, and we are in no doubt that the sheriff was entitled to hold that evidence as to what was said was admissible. The appellant was then asked to sign a written record of the interview and he agreed to do so. But here again there was no unfairness in what was done. He had already answered the questions which had been put to him, and the purpose was to enable him to say whether or not the written record was correct.

The sheriff tells us in his note that it was only after this interview had been completed that the officials were aware that a crime had been committed. This provides the background to the second interview, because it is clear that by that stage they knew that the man whom they proposed to interview was the James Pennycuick who had been claiming benefit and, in the light of information which they had already obtained, that he had committed an offence because he was not entitled to the benefits which he had received. On this occasion they advised the appellant at the outset of the purpose of their visit, which the sheriff said was sufficient to put him on his guard.

Nevertheless no caution was administered to him until after he had been shown and admitted signing the four forms claiming benefit, which became essential Crown productions in the case because they established that the appellant had been obtaining benefit from the social security office libelled in the charge. The officers said that the purpose of asking him whether he had signed these forms was to confirm his identity. That would have been a legitimate purpose and would have involved no unfairness if it was necessary for them to do this before the interview could proceed. But these officers, who were the same two officers as those who had conducted the previous interview, were already aware of the appellant's identity and they were also aware he had committed an offence. In these circumstances for them to show him the form merely to confirm his identity might seem to have been unnecessary, and the effect of the admissions was to provide them with evidence that the forms which were in their possession had been signed by the appellant.

Counsel submitted that it was not sufficient for the appellant in these circumstances merely to have been told the purpose of their visit before he was asked whether he had signed the forms. His argument was that in all the circumstances a caution was required, and that in its absence the evidence of the admissions should have been held to be inadmissible. At first sight there is some force in this submission, because the stage was no longer that of initial investigation. The officers were already in possession of the information which they needed to say whether or not the appellant had committed an offence. The question remains however whether, even at this stage, it was unfair for him to be asked whether he had signed the forms. This question has to be answered by taking into account the whole circumstances, and it is important to note that there is no suggestion in the case that any undue pressure, deception or other device was used to obtain the admissions. Nor can it be said that the appellant did not appreciate what was going on, because he was told at the outset by the officials what the purpose was of their visit. He was told that he was being interviewed in relation to an overpayment of supplementary benefit and income support. Taking all these factors into account, we consider that the sheriff was entitled to conclude that on this occasion also there was no unfairness to the appellant in what was done and to hold that the evidence of what he said was admissible."

Pennycuick was followed in 1999 by *Williams v Friel*, 1999 S.L.T. 366, where the accused was charged with presenting a false passport. He challenged evidence of his admission to a customs officer that he was Nigerian, which he made in response to the officer informing him of his suspicions. The evidence was held admissible as it disclosed no unfairness. According to Lord Bonomy:

"The question to be determined is whether, in all the circumstances of the case, there was unfairness to the appellant on the part of Gillespie [an immigration officer] which led to the acknowledgment by the appellant of his true identity. The appropriate test in such a situation is set out in *Pennycuick v Lees* at 1992 SLT, p 765E-F. That case deals with interviews conducted by officers of the DSS. The opinion of the court is expressed in the following terms:

> 'But in all these cases where inquiries are being conducted into activities which may be criminal the question is whether, looking at all the circumstances of the case, there has been unfairness to the accused in what took place. This was the test which was applied in *Miln v Cullen*, 1967 S.L.T. 35, in which it was conceded by the Crown that, when the accused was asked by the police officers whether he was the driver of the car, he was a suspected person.'

Counsel's contention was that the acknowledgment by the appellant of his true identity was unfairly elicited because at the time when the immigration officer spoke to the appellant en route to the office he suspected the appellant had committed an offence and made an accusation which was likely to evoke a response against interest without administering a caution. She did not suggest that the statement made in finding in fact 8 was made with a view to getting a response, but submitted that it was a statement which was likely to produce a response from a suspect.

In reply the advocate depute submitted that the circumstances of the present appeal were on all fours with those of *Pennycuick v Lees* and that the circumstances were not indicative of any unfairness to the appellant.

In his note the sheriff explains that the position of the immigration officer was that he suspected that the passport was not genuine in the absence of a UK entry stamp. That being the case, a question arose as to the identity and nationality of the appellant. It was for that purpose, and that purpose only, that the appellant had been invited to be interviewed at the immigration office. He had made the statement to the appellant en route to the office to let him know what he was thinking. The sheriff also made a finding that at that time the immigration officer did not have the information from the Canadian High Commission, which he obtained later, as to the genuineness or falsity of the passport or as to whether the appellant was entitled to be the holder of the passport.

In our opinion it cannot be said that there is any basis in the material before the sheriff for concluding that the acknowledgment of identity made by the appellant resulted from any unfair conduct on the part of the immigration officer. As finding in fact 8 shows, the immigration officer did not accuse the appellant of committing an offence but simply explained to him why he had invited him to be interviewed. The appellant chose to say what he did following on that explanation. In these circumstances the acknowledgment of identity was admissible and there was accordingly sufficient evidence to establish that the passport was false. That is sufficient for determination of the appeal and it will be refused."

The test of fairness has been described as 'simple and intelligible' by Lord Justice General Emslie (*Lord Advocate's Reference (No. 1 of 1983)*, 1984 S.L.T. 337). This may very well be the case, but the test does allow scope for individual interpretation in each case, with the attendant possibility of inconsistency.

IX. RIGHT TO A SPEEDY TRIAL

Here is a situation where the existing protections in Scots law have to a large extent precluded claims under the European Convention. Article 5(3) provides that a person detained within the scope of Art.5(1)(c):

- should appear "promptly" before a judge;
- should be tried within a "reasonable time"; or
- should be released pending trial.

The provisions of domestic law which currently apply are contained in the Criminal Procedure (Scotland) Act 1995. In terms of s.35(2), the sheriff may delay judicial examination for a period not exceeding 48 hours from and after the time of the accused's arrest, in order to allow time for the attendance of the accused's solicitor. In relation to summary procedure, s.135 provides that:

"(3) A person apprehended under a warrant or by virtue of power under any enactment or rule of law shall wherever practicable be brought before a court competent to deal with the case not later than in the course of the first day after he is taken into custody.

(4) The reference in subsection (3) above to the first day after he is taken into custody shall not include a Saturday, a Sunday or a court holiday prescribed for that court under section 8 of this Act; but nothing in this subsection shall prevent a person being brought before the court on a Saturday, a Sunday or such a court holiday where the court is, in pursuance of the said section 8, sitting on such day for the disposal of criminal business."

The second protection under art.5(3) is that a person detained should be tried within a reasonable time or released pending the trial taking place. Again, the Criminal Procedure (Scotland) Act 1995 makes provision for this:

Criminal Procedure (Scotland) Act 1995
[amended by Criminal Procedure (Amendment) (Scotland) Act 2004]

"Prevention of delay in trials

65.—(1) Subject to subsections (2) and (3) below, an accused shall not be tried on indictment for any offence unless—
> (a) where an indictment has been served on the accused in respect of the High Court, a preliminary hearing is commenced within the period of 11 months; and
> (b) in any case, the trial is commenced within the period of 12 months,
of the first appearance of the accused on petition in respect of the offence.

(1A) If the preliminary hearing (where subsection (1)(a) above applies) or the trial is not so commenced, the accused shall be discharged forthwith and thereafter he shall be for ever free from all question or process for that offence.

(2) Nothing in subsection (1) or (1A) above shall bar the trial of an accused for whose arrest a warrant has been granted for failure to appear at a diet in the case.

(3) On an application made for the purpose—
> (a) where an indictment has been served on the accused in respect of the High Court, a single judge of that court may, on cause shown, extend either or both of the periods of 11 and 12 months specified in subsection (1) above; or
> (b) in any other case, the sheriff may, on cause shown, extend the period of 12 months specified in that subsection.

(4) Subject to subsections (5) to (9) below, an accused who is committed for any offence until liberated in due course of law shall not be detained by virtue of that committal for a total period of more than—
> (a) 80 days, unless within that period the indictment is served on him, which failing he shall be entitled to be admitted to bail; or
> (aa) where an indictment has been served on the accused in respect of the High Court—
>> (i) 110 days, unless a preliminary hearing in respect of the case is commenced within that period, which failing he shall be entitled to be admitted to bail; or
>> (ii) 140 days, unless the trial of the case is commenced within that period, which failing he shall be entitled to be admitted to bail;
> (b) where an indictment has been served on the accused in respect of the sheriff court,

110 days, unless the trial of the case is commenced within that period, which failing he shall be entitled to be admitted to bail and thereafter he shall be for ever free from all question or process for that offence.

(4A) Where an indictment has been served on the accused in respect of the High Court, subsections (1)(a) and (4)(aa)(i) above shall not apply if the preliminary hearing has been dispensed with under section 72B(1) of this Act.

(5) On an application made for the purpose—

(a) in a case where, at the time the application is made, an indictment has not been served on the accused, a single judge of the High Court; or

(b) in any other case, the court specified in the notice served under section 66(6) of this Act,

may, on cause shown, extend any period mentioned in subsection (4) above.

(5A) Before determining an application under subsection (3) or (5) above, the judge or, as the case may be, the court shall give the parties an opportunity to be heard.

(5B) However, where all the parties join in the application, the judge or, as the case may be, the court may determine the application without hearing the parties and, accordingly, may dispense with any hearing previously appointed for the purpose of considering the application.

. . . . .

147.—(1) Subject to subsections (2) and (3) below, a person charged with an offence in summary proceedings shall not be detained in that respect for a total of more than 40 days after the bringing of the complaint in court unless his trial is commenced within that period, failing which he shall be liberated forthwith and thereafter he shall be for ever free from all question or process for that offence.

(2) The sheriff may, on application made to him for the purpose, extend the period mentioned in subsection (1) above and order the accused to be detained awaiting trial for such period as he thinks fit where he is satisfied that delay in the commencement of the trial is due to—

(a) the illness of the accused or of a judge;

(b) the absence or illness of any necessary witness; or

(c) any other sufficient cause which is not attributable to any fault on the part of the prosecutor.

(3) The grant or refusal of any application to extend the period mentioned in subsection (1) above may be appealed against by note of appeal presented to the High Court; and that Court may affirm, reverse or amend the determination made on such application.

(4) For the purposes of this section, a trial shall be taken to commence when the first witness is sworn."

As is evident, there is a discretion to extend the prescribed maximum periods in prison. The case below occurred well before the incorporation of the Convention, and it is unclear whether the same decision would be arrived at today.

Gildea v HM Advocate
1983 S.L.T. 458

An accused person was indicted for trial in the High Court. Shortly before the 110-day maximum period of pre-trial custody permitted by law was due to expire, the Crown successfully obtained from the trial judge an extension of 30 days, on the grounds that time-tabling, administrative difficulties and pressures had rendered it impossible for the Crown to proceed timeously. In particular, the preceding trial (for rape) overran by about three days. The accused appealed to the High Court against the order extending the 110 days.

OPINION OF THE COURT: "In this case the Crown sought to justify the grant of their application for extension in the following submission. It cannot be contended that in serving the indictment upon the appellant on 4 February 1983 there was any failure of due diligence, for it was then within reasonable contemplation that having regard to the business set down for disposal in Glasgow on the March circuit, the trial of the appellant would commence before 18 March 1983. The probabilities fall to be tested by consideration of the business set down for disposal in the South Court, for it was known that the first trial for disposal on that circuit in the North Court was quite unlikely to end before 18 March 1983. The first case for trial in the South Court involved charges of assault to severe injury and the danger of life, murder and a contravention of s. 3 (1) (b) of the Bail (Scotland) Act 1980. The accused was in custody and the 110-day period in his case was due to elapse on 20 March 1983. The wholly reasonable expectation that this trial would be concluded within two days was borne out in the result because it ended on 9 March 1983. The second trial for South Court disposal also involved an accused in custody and in his case the 110-day period was due to expire on 18 March 1983. This trial was reasonably estimated to require no more than two days to complete. In the event no trial took place because when the diet was called the accused pled guilty. The third trial was of a single accused charged with rape and there were only 23 witnesses on the Crown list. The entirely reasonable expectation was that this trial would be completed within two days and at worst on the third day. The fourth trial, that of the appellant, was accordingly expected to begin not later than 15 March and since it could not reasonably be expected to last more than two days it was confidently expected that the fifth trial of five accused, in the case of three of whom the 110-day period was due to expire on 18 March 1983, was likely to begin before that date. What in fact happened was unforeseen and was not reasonably foreseeable. The third trial on the South Court list, contrary to all reasonable expectation, and for reasons difficult to understand, consumed not two days nor three days but five days of the time of the court. It was not suggested that this expenditure of time was due to any cause for which the Crown was or could be held responsible. In this situation the Crown had a difficult decision to make. The decision was to proceed at once with the fifth case on the list involving the five accused and to apply in the case of the appellant for the extension of time granted by the judge on 15 March 1983.

For the appellant the submission was that this explanation by the Crown did not satisfy the test which was prescribed by s. 101 (4) (c) [now 1995 Act, s.65(7)(c)]. By delaying service of the indictment until 4 February 1983 the Crown failed to exercise due diligence and it was evident upon the explanation given by the advocate-depute that from that moment on they were at grave risk. Even if it be accepted that the forecasts of the time likely to be consumed by the first three South Court trials were those mentioned by the advocate-depute the Crown was allowing to itself a safety margin of only two days, at the most, if it were to be able to commence both the trial of the appellant and the fifth trial in the list before 18 March 1983. It is, it was said, notoriously difficult to predict the length of a trial on a charge of rape and it cannot be said that because the third trial in the list took five days to complete instead of two or three days this was not reasonably to be foreseen. The risk courted by the Crown was quite unacceptable, and by neglecting to requisition a special sitting for the disposal of the indictment against the appellant, or to release him from custody, the Crown cannot be held to have demonstrated that there was sufficient cause for which the Crown was not responsible, for their failure to be in a position to commence the trial of the appellant before 18 March 1983.

We do not pretend that the problem presented by this appeal is easy to resolve. With some hesitation, however, we have decided that the appeal should be refused. The Crown undoubtedly took a calculated risk in relation to the commencement of 110-day cases for disposal on the March circuit in the South Court. The question is whether the decision to take that risk was unreasonable and whether the judge who heard the application and was himself the presiding judge in the South Court was entitled to decide it was not. In our opinion he was so entitled and his decision was correct. The critical factor was the expected duration of the single-accused rape trial, number three in the list. In our judgment it was wholly reasonable to predict, for that trial, a disposal time of one-and-a-half days to two days, and at the very worst three days. That it should take five days to complete is, we think, almost impossible to understand, and it was not, from what we know of the case, reasonably to be anticipated. In the foregoing circumstances we are persuaded that the Crown was suddenly faced with such a difficulty as might happen without want of due diligence on the Crown's part, and that the judge who granted the extension sought, who incidentally was the trial judge in the disposal of the single-accused rape case which grossly overran its reasonably anticipated span, was well entitled to be satisfied that the Crown had established what required to be established in support of their application in terms of s. 101 (4) (c) of the Act of 1975."

The delay in *Gildea* can be attributed to a calculated risk taken by the prosecutor, rather than to circumstances which were beyond his control. Strasbourg jurisprudence would suggest that such delays attributable to the prosecuting authority are not looked on sympathetically: see *Assenov v Bulgaria* (1999) 25 E.H.R.R. 652.

Article 5(3) has had a significant effect on the law in Scotland relating to bail. The Bail, Judicial Appointments etc. (Scotland) Act 2000 amended the CPSA 1995 to make provision for a decision on bail to be taken on the first occasion that the accused appeared in court. This ensures compliance with the Art.5(3) requirement for an immediate judicial review of detention.

"Consideration of bail on first appearance

22A.—(1) On the first occasion on which—
  (a) a person accused on petition is brought before the sheriff prior to committal until liberated in due course of law; or
  (b) a person charged on complaint with an offence is brought before a judge having jurisdiction to try the offence,
the sheriff or, as the case may be, the judge shall, after giving that person and the prosecutor an opportunity to be heard and within the period specified in subsection (2) below, either admit or refuse to admit that person to bail.

(2) That period is the period of 24 hours beginning with the time when the person accused or charged is brought before the sheriff or judge.

(3) If, by the end of that period, the sheriff or judge has not admitted or refused to admit the person accused or charged to bail, then that person shall be forthwith liberated.

(4) This section applies whether or not the person accused or charged is in custody when that person is brought before the sheriff or judge."

Additionally, the Act allowed sheriffs to consider bail in relation to murder or treason.

Prior to the coming into force of the 2000 Act, but after Scotland Act 1998 had brought the provisions of ECHR into Scots law, the High Court considered whether the requirements of Art.5(3) in relation to bail were met in the case of *Burn Petitioner*, 2000 S.L.T. 538. The petitioner's application for bail had been opposed by the Crown on the basis of unspecified further inquiries which had to be carried out, and which would be compromised were the petitioner to be released. The sheriff refused bail, following the approach laid down in the earlier case of *Boyle v HM Advocate*, 1995 S.L.T. 162, wherein it was held that if the Crown asserted that it was necessary to keep the accused in custody, it was not for the sheriff to seek to look behind the assertion. According to Lord McCluskey:

"At the stage when accused persons are first brought before the sheriff on the procurator fiscal's petition, and the procurator fiscal makes a motion to commit the accused for further examination and states that the Crown are continuing to make inquiries and that it is necessary for the proper pursuit of these inquiries in the public interest that the accused should remain in custody at that stage, the court should not seek to go behind that statement. At that stage the procurator fiscal, as the petitioner, is asserting in the petition that he has information on the basis of which the charges are to be brought; the sheriff does not go behind that assertion. It appears to me that the assertion that it is necessary that the accused persons be kept in custody at that stage so that the inquiries will not be impeded by their release is an assertion of the same character. In my view, the sheriff should not seek to go behind that assertion but should accept that the procurator fiscal is acting for the public interest and in his role as a minister of justice. His judgment on the matter of the necessity of keeping the accused persons in custody at that stage should be respected."

The incompatibility of this decision with the accused's rights under art.5 were fully considered:

Burn, Petitioner
2000 S.L.T. 538

B petitioned the *nobile officium* after his application for bail was rejected by a sheriff who, following *Boyle v HM Advocate*, 1995 S.L.T. 162, had refused the application on the motion of the procurator fiscal without making any further inquiries as to the necessity of keeping B in custody. Both the accused and the Crown were content that the court should issue an opinion indicating the approach which should be adopted in applications for bail before full committal. B argued, *inter alia*, that by successfully opposing bail without supplying the sheriff with information as to the nature of any further inquiries, or as to why they necessitated keeping him in custody, the procurator fiscal, the Lord Advocate's representative, had in effect deprived the sheriff of any power to reach an independent view on B's application and had acted in a way incompatible with the European Convention on Human Rights 1950, art.5.

LORD JUSTICE GENERAL (RODGER): "We understand that, before the decision in *Boyle* there was no uniform practice as to the handling of such applications but that it was by no means unusual for sheriffs to ask the procurator fiscal why the Crown wished the particular accused to be kept in custody and, if the procurator fiscal was not able to give an explanation, many sheriffs would refuse the Crown motion and release the accused on bail. That situation changed with the decision in *Boyle* ... [His Lordship quoted the passage above, p.210.]

    ... we are satisfied that the law as laid down by Lord McCluskey in *Boyle* does not meet the requirements of art 5 (3) since the sheriff is directed not to seek to go behind any statement by the procurator fiscal that the Crown are continuing to make inquiries and that it is necessary for the proper pursuit of these inquiries in the public interest that the accused should remain in custody at that stage. In effect the law as there stated enjoins the sheriff not to consider the merits of the accused's continued detention for himself but to defer to the statement by the procurator fiscal. Now that the Convention has entered our law, we are satisfied that the approach laid down in *Boyle* can no longer be regarded as sound and that the decision must therefore be overruled.

    In future the Crown must provide sufficient general information relating to the particular case to allow the sheriff to consider the merits of their motion that the accused should be committed to prison and detained there for further examination. What will be required will depend on the facts of the particular case and for that reason we cannot lay down any hard and fast rule. We are satisfied, however, that it will not be necessary for the Crown to disclose operational details. On the other hand, where, for example, the Crown oppose bail on the ground of the risk that the accused would interfere with witnesses, the procurator fiscal depute should be in a position to explain the basis for that fear. The same would apply where opposition is based on a fear that the accused would interfere with a possible search of premises which the police wished to carry out. It follows also, as the advocate depute pointed out, that where opposition to bail is based on some such ground and the relevant inquiry is completed before the date for further examination, the Crown will wish to bring the matter back before the sheriff so that he can, if so advised, order the accused's release from custody."

X. CONCLUSION

There have yet to be many successful human rights claims in relation to police arrest and detention, which may indicate that the existing protections under statute and at common law are effective. On the other hand, what it may demonstrate is a certain complacency on the part of the courts that there is general compatibility with ECHR. "Fairness" can be seen as a judge's flexible friend, as in *Paton v Ritchie*, 2000 S.L.T. 239, where not only was it fair to admit as evidence a statement made by the accused before his solicitor arrived, but also this fairness extended to compliance with the right to a fair trial in terms of art.6 of the ECHR! Furthermore, the test of a police officer's "reasonable belief" justifying arrest or detention is so weighted in favour of the officer that it is arguably susceptible to challenge under art.5(1), in that it does not constitute a "lawful" arrest, where there is only a subjective view as to the suspicion falling on the arrestee.

There is one matter on which the ECHR can be seen to have a positive impact on the rights of suspects, and that is in relation to bail, both in terms of the statute, and also the requirement in *Burn* that there should be some explanation by the Crown as to why it is necessary that the accused remains in custody. But as has been identified earlier in this chapter, it is often unclear as to what remedy, if any, is available to a person whose rights are violated. There are occasional hints that account will be taken of the circumstances in which confession evidence was obtained in assessing its admissibility (*HM Advocate v Barrie*, 2002 S.L.T. 1053), but the absence of specific sanctions leaves the suspect in a vulnerable position. Conceivably, a claim for damages under s.8 of the Human Rights Act 1998 might be made where such rights are violated without redress in the initial proceedings. What is clear is the relatively limited impact that incorporation has had in relation to police powers. It will require determination and imagination on the part of those who are representing suspects to shake the judiciary free of the attitude that protections in place for many decades are not only adequate in their own terms, but also compatible with the new human rights based constitutional framework.

Chapter 5

THE RIGHT TO A FAIR TRIAL

I. INTRODUCTION

The right to a fair trial in Art.6 of the ECHR has given rise to more litigation in the Scottish courts than any other provision of the Convention. Of these cases a large number have been concerned with the question of delay in the conduct of criminal proceedings. Article 6 is also the provision that has been most frequently dealt with by the Privy Council in devolution references. These cases deal with a range of issues, but they have also exposed an important division between the English and Scottish judges about how to deal with the problem of delay. The Scottish judges have taken a much more robust protection of Convention rights than their English counterparts. In this chapter we deal with some of the more significant landmark cases under Art.6 which is reproduced in the above chapter.

II. "CIVIL RIGHTS AND OBLIGATIONS"

R. (Alconbury Properties) v Secretary of State for Environment, Transport and the Regions
[2003] 2 A.C. 295

This was a series of appeals dealing with different areas of planning law, highway improvement and compulsory purchase. The applicants were land owners who had either been refused permission to develop their land, or who had been given notice that their land was to be compulsorily acquired. The following account of the relevant legislation is drawn from the speech of Lord Clyde:

> "• The Town and Country Planning Act 1990 provides by section 77 that the Secretary of State for the Environment, Transport and the Regions may give directions requiring applications for planning permission to be referred to him instead of being dealt with by local planning authorities. Section 78 provides for the making of appeals to the Secretary of State against planning decisions or the failure to take such decisions and section 79 provides for the opportunity of a hearing before a person appointed by the Secretary of State for that purpose. By paragraph 3 of Schedule 6 to the Act the Secretary of State may direct that a planning appeal which would otherwise be determined by a person appointed by him shall instead be determined by the Secretary of State. By paragraph 4 he may revoke such a direction.
> • Provision is made in sections 14, 16, 18 and 125 of the Highways Act 1980 for the making of orders by the Secretary of State with regard to certain roadways and by paragraphs 1, 7 and 8 of Part I of Schedule I to that Act provision is made for the

hearing of objections at a local inquiry and the subsequent making or confirmation of the order by the Secretary of State. Section 2(3) of the Acquisition of Land
Act 1981 and paragraph 4 of Schedule 1 to that Act provide in relation to the
making of a compulsory purchase order by a minister for the hearing of objections
at a public local inquiry and the subsequent making of the order by the minister.
Under sections 1 and 3 of the Transport and Works Act 1992 the Secretary of
State may make orders in relation to among other things railways and waterways
and section 23(4) disentitles an inspector hearing objections into such orders from
authorising compulsory acquisitions or the compulsory creation or extinguish-
ment of rights over land."

The Divisional Court has held that these provisions were incompatible with Art.6(1) of the
ECHR, and it was against these decisions that leave had been given to appeal directly to the
House of Lords. As Lord Hoffmann pointed out in his speech:

"The issue in these three appeals is whether it is compatible with the Human Rights Act
1998 for Parliament to confer upon the Secretary of State the power to make decisions
which affect people's rights to the ownership, use or enjoyment of land".

LORD HOFFMANN: "66. Although the principle must be of general application, the contexts
in which the question has arisen in these appeals are planning, highway improvement and
compulsory purchase. In the first appeal ('the *Alconbury* case'), a company has applied for
planning permission to construct a distribution centre of national significance on a disused
American air base near Huntingdon. It could generate 7,000 new jobs but would obviously
affect the lives of many people living in the neighbourhood. In the second appeal ('the
Holding & Barnes case'), the respondents have applied for planning permission to use land
at Canvey Island for the storage and sale of wrecked cars. Again, the activity will generate
employment but the site is close to some gas storage installations and the Health and Safety
Executive thinks that this would create a danger to people living in the area. In the third
appeal ('the *Legal and General* case'), the respondent owns land near the interchange
between the M4 motorway and the A34 trunk road at Newbury. The Highways Agency, a
branch of the department of the Environment, Transport and the Regions, has promoted a
road improvement scheme which would involve taking the respondent's land.
67. In each of these cases the statutory decision maker is the Secretary of State. In the
first two, this is by virtue of his exercise of a statutory discretion. In the *Alconbury* case, the
application for planning permission has been refused by the Huntingdonshire District
Council and the developer has appealed to the Secretary of State. The appeal could have
been determined under Schedule 6 to the Town and Country Planning Act 1990 by an
inspector appointed to conduct a public inquiry, but the Secretary of State has exercised his
discretion under paragraph 3 of the Schedule to 'recover' the appeal and decide it himself.
In the *Holding & Barnes* case, the local planning authority was minded to grant permission
but the Secretary of State has exercised his power under section 77 of the 1990 Act to 'call
in' the application and decide it himself. In the *Legal and General* case, the Secretary of
State is the only statutory decision maker.
68. All three cases involve general social and economic issues. They concern the rights of
individuals to use, enjoy and own their land. But the number of persons potentially
interested is very large and the decisions involve the consideration of questions of general
welfare, such as the national or local economy, the preservation of the environment, the
public safety, the convenience of the road network, all of which transcend the interests of
any particular individual.

Democracy and the rule of law
69. In a democratic country, decisions as to what the general interest requires are made
by democratically elected bodies or persons accountable to them. Sometimes the subject-

matter is such that Parliament can itself lay down general rules for enforcement by the courts. Taxation is a good example; Parliament decides on grounds of general interest what taxation is required and the rules according to which it should be levied. The application of those rules, to determine the liability of a particular person, is then a matter for independent and impartial tribunals such as the General or Special Commissioners or the courts. On the other hand, sometimes one cannot formulate general rules and the question of what the general interest requires has to be determined on a case by case basis. Town and country planning or road construction, in which every decision is in some respects different, are archetypal examples. In such cases Parliament may delegate the decision-making power to local democratically elected bodies or to ministers of the Crown responsible to Parliament. In that way the democratic principle is preserved.

70. There is no conflict between human rights and the democratic principle. Respect for human rights requires that certain basic rights of individuals should not be capable in any circumstances of being overridden by the majority, even if they think that the public interest so requires. Other rights should be capable of being overridden only in very restricted circumstances. These are rights which belong to individuals simply by virtue of their humanity, independently of any utilitarian calculation. The protection of these basic rights from majority decision requires that independent and impartial tribunals should have the power to decide whether legislation infringes them and either (as in the United States) to declare such legislation invalid or (as in the United Kingdom) to declare that it is incompatible with the governing human rights instrument. But outside these basic rights, there are many decisions which have to be made every day (for example, about the allocation of resources) in which the only fair method of decision is by some person or body accountable to the electorate.

71. All democratic societies recognise that while there are certain basic rights which attach to the ownership of property, they are heavily qualified by considerations of the public interest. This is reflected in the terms of article 1 of Protocol 1 to the Convention: [Lord Hoffmann read article 1 and continued.]

72. Thus, under the first paragraph, property may be taken by the state, on payment of compensation, if the public interest so requires. And, under the second paragraph, the use of property may be restricted without compensation on similar grounds. Importantly, the question of what the public interest requires for the purpose of article 1 of Protocol 1 can, and in my opinion should, be determined according to the democratic principle—by elected local or central bodies or by ministers accountable to them. There is no principle of human rights which requires such decisions to be made by independent and impartial tribunals.

73. There is however another relevant principle which must exist in a democratic society. That is the rule of law. When ministers or officials make decisions affecting the rights of individuals, they must do so in accordance with the law. The legality of what they do must be subject to review by independent and impartial tribunals. This is reflected in the requirement in article 1 of Protocol 1 that a taking of property must be 'subject to the conditions provided for by law'. The principles of judicial review give effect to the rule of law. They ensure that administrative decisions will be taken rationally, in accordance with a fair procedure and within the powers conferred by Parliament. But this is not the occasion upon which to discuss the limits of judicial review. The only issue in this case is whether the Secretary of State is disqualified as a decision-maker because he will give effect to policies with which, ex hypothesi, the courts will not interfere."

Lord Clyde: "138. At the heart of the challenge is the objection that the Secretary of State cannot compatibly with article 6(1) himself determine the various issues to which these statutory provisions can give rise. No complaint is made where the decision is made by an inspector appointed by him. The objection is levelled against his taking upon himself the direct function of being the decision-maker.

The planning context

139. The general context in which this challenge is raised is that of planning and development. The functions of the Secretary of State in the context of planning may conveniently be referred to as 'administrative', in the sense that they are dealing with policy and expediency rather than with the regulation of rights. We are concerned with an administrative process and an administrative decision. Planning is a matter of the formation and application of policy. The policy is not matter for the courts but for the Executive. Where decisions are required in the planning process they are not made by judges, but by members of the administration. Members of the administration may be required in some of their functions to act in a judicial manner in that they may have to observe procedural rules and the overarching principles of fairness. But while they may on some occasions be required to act like judges, they are not judges and their determinations on matters affecting civil rights and obligations are not to be seen as judicial decisions. Even although there may be stages in the procedure leading up to the decision where what used to be described as a quasi-judicial character is superadded to the administrative task, the eventual decision is an administrative one. As was long ago observed by Lord Greene MR in (*B Johnson & Co (Builders) Ltd v Minister of Health* [1947] 2 All ER 395, 399:

'That decision must be an administrative decision, because it is not to be based purely on the view that he forms of the objections, vis-a-vis the desires of the local authority, but is to be guided by his view as to the policy which in the circumstances he ought to pursue.'

Moreover the decision requires to take into account not just the facts of the case but very much wider issues of public interest, national priorities. Thus the function of the Secretary of State as a decision-maker in planning matters is not in a proper sense a judicial function, although certain qualities of a judicial kind are required of him.

140. Planning and the development of land are matters which concern the community as a whole, not only the locality where the particular case arises. They involve wider social and economic interests, considerations which are properly to be subject to a central supervision. By means of a central authority some degree of coherence and consistency in the development of land can be secured. National planning guidance can be prepared and promulgated and that guidance will influence the local development plans and policies which the planning authorities will use in resolving their own local problems. As is explained in paragraph I of the Government's publication Planning Policy Guidance Notes, the need to take account of economic, environmental, social and other factors requires a framework which provides consistent, predictable and prompt decision-making. At the heart of that system are development plans. The guidance sets out the objectives and policies comprised in the framework within which the local authorities are required to draw up their development plans and in accordance with which their planning decisions should be made. One element which lies behind the framework is the policy of securing what is termed sustainable development, an objective which is essentially a matter of governmental strategy.

141. Once it is recognised that there should be a national planning policy under a central supervision, it is consistent with democratic principle that the responsibility for that work should lie on the shoulders of a minister answerable to Parliament. The whole scheme of the planning legislation involves an allocation of various functions respectively between local authorities and the Secretary of State. In placing some functions upon the Secretary of State it is of course recognised that he will not personally attend to every case himself. The responsibility is given to his department and the power rests in the department with the Secretary of State as its head and responsible for the carrying out of its work. Within his department a minister may well take advice on law and policy (*Bushell v Secretary of State for the Environment* [1981] AC 75) and the Secretary of State is entitled to seek elucidation on matters raised by the case which he has to decide, provided always that he observes the basic rules of fairness. In particular he should in fairness give the parties an opportunity to

comment if after a public inquiry some significant factual material of which the parties might not be aware comes to his notice through departmental inquiry.

142. There may be various agencies which will advise him on particular aspects of planning, as for example an agency skilled in the conservation of historic buildings. But it is a false analysis to claim that there is a lis between a developer and such an agency which will be heard and determined by the minister. As Lord Greene MR observed in *Johnson*, at p 399, in relation to objections to a compulsory purchase order proposed by a local authority:

> 'it is not a lis inter partes, and for the simple reason that the local authority and the objectors are not parties to anything that resembles litigation ... on the substantive matter, viz whether the order should be confirmed or not, there is a third party who is not present, viz, the public, and it is the function of the minister to consider the rights and interests of the public.'

The minister is not bound to follow the view of any agency, nor is he bound to follow the desires or interests of any other Government department. He is not bound to apply a particular policy if the circumstances seem to him inappropriate for its application. He is not independent. Indeed it is not suggested that he is. But that is not to say that in making the decisions on the matters in issue in the present appeals he is both judge and party. It does not seem to me correct to say of the Secretary of State that he is judex in sua causa, at least in any strict sense of that expression. He is, as I have already sought to explain, not strictly a judge. Moreover the cause is not in any precise sense his own. No one is suggesting that he, or the officials in his department, have any personal financial or proprietary interest in these cases. The concern of the Secretary of State and his department is to manage planning and development in accordance with the broad lines of policy which have been prepared in the national interest.

143. One criticism which is levelled at the system is that the minister has the functions both of making planning policy and of applying the policies which he has made. But that combination of functions does not necessarily give rise to unfairness. The formulation of policies is a perfectly proper course for the provision of guidance in the exercise of an administrative discretion. Indeed policies are an essential element in securing the coherent and consistent performance of administrative functions. There are advantages both to the public and the administrators in having such policies. Of course there are limits to be observed in the way policies are applied. Blanket decisions which leave no room for particular circumstances may be unreasonable. What is crucial is that the policy must not fetter the exercise of the discretion. The particular circumstances always require to be considered. Provided that the policy is not regarded as binding and the authority still retains a free exercise of discretion the policy may serve the useful purpose of giving a reasonable guidance both to applicants and decision-makers. Nor is this a point which can be made solely in relation to the Secretary of State. In a variety of administrative functions, in addition to planning, local authorities may devise and implement policies of their own.

144. It is now argued that the planning process is flawed in so far as the decision-maker is the Secretary of State. It is said that where he is making the decision the case falls foul of article 6 of the Convention. One possible solution which is proposed is that in the cases where at present the Secretary of State is himself the decision- maker, cases for the most part which are likely to give rise to issues of widespread or even national concern, which may well have a wide impact on the lives of many and involve major issues of policy, the decision should be removed from the minister, who is answerable to Parliament, to an independent body, answerable to no one. That would be a somewhat startling proposition and it would be surprising if the Convention which is rooted in the ideas of democracy and the rule of law should lead to such a result.

Applicability of the Convention

145. The first question is whether article 6 applies at all to decisions by planning authorities or by the Secretary of State. An attractive argument was presented on behalf of the Lord Advocate to the effect that article 6 was as regards civil matters concerned with the securing of justice in the resolution of a legal claim or dispute and not with the acts of an administrative body exercising a discretionary power. Article 6 would only come to affect matters of administrative discretionary decisions at the stage when a dispute arose on the grounds that the decision-maker had acted unlawfully, exceeding the parameters of his lawful discretion and erring in law. This argument looks to the whole terms of article 6(1) which can readily be seen as designed to cover judicial proceedings. Counsel pointed to the French text of the article and the use of the word 'contestations' which could be understood as relating to a dispute on civil rights and obligations and to litigation before a court of law. In support of this approach reference was made to a decision of the Commission in *Kaplan v United Kingdom* (1980) 4 EHRR 64, para 154 where, after referring to claims and disputes concerning legal rights and obligations of a civil character, the Commission stated:

'A distinction must be drawn between the acts of a body which is engaged in the resolution of such a claim or dispute and the acts of an administrative or other body purporting merely to exercise or apply a legal power vested in it and not to resolve a legal claim or dispute. Article 6(1) would not, in the Commission's opinion, apply to the acts of the latter even if they do affect "civil rights". It could not be considered as being engaged in a process of "determination" of civil rights and obligations. Its function would not be to decide ("décidera") on a claim, dispute or "contestation". Its acts may, on the other hand, give rise to a claim, dispute or "contestation" and article 6 may come into play in that way.'

146. This approach provides a clean and simple solution to the present problem. But I do not consider that it is sound. The observations in *Kaplan* on which the argument was supported have not been taken up by the court and reflect an earlier stage in the development of the jurisprudence on the scope and application of article 6(1). In the developing jurisprudence of the European Court of Human Rights it became recognised that a narrow view of the scope of article 6(1) was inappropriate. In *X v United Kingdom* (1998) 28 D. & R. 177, 186 the Commission held that a compulsory purchase order affected the applicant's private rights of ownership, that these were 'civil rights', and that in challenging the making of the order she was entitled to the protection of article 6(1). Counsel recognised the difficulty which that decision presented for his argument and was constrained to contend that the decision was wrong. His proposition involves a narrow understanding of the scope of the article.

147. In considering the scope of article 6(1) it is proper to take a broad approach to the language used and seek to give effect to the purpose of the provision. In *Ringeisen v Austria (No.1)* (1971) 1 EHRR 455, para 94 the phrase was taken to cover 'all proceedings the result of which is decisive for private rights and obligations.' This included cases where the proceedings concerned a dispute between a private individual and a public authority. In *Golder v United Kingdom* (1975) 1 EHRR 524, para 32 the court considered the French and English text of the article and concluded that the article covered a right of access to a court or 'tribunal' without there being already proceedings pending. The court held in paragraph 36 that 'article 6(1) secures to everyone the right to have any claim relating to his civil rights and obligations brought before a court or tribunal.' These two cases pre-date the decision in *Kaplan*. In *Le Compte, Van Leuven and De Meyere v Belgium* (1981) 4 EHRR 1, para 45 the court observed of the word 'contestation':

'Conformity with the spirit of the Convention requires that this word should not be construed too technically and that it should be given a substantive rather than a formal meaning besides, it has no counterpart in the English text of article 6(1).'

The court held that even if the use of the French word implied the existence of a disagreement, the evidence showed that there was one in that case where there were allegations of professional misconduct which were denied. The reference to a determination reflects the necessity for there to be a dispute. But it does not require to be a dispute in any formal sense. In *Moreira de Azevedo v Portugal* (1990) 13 EHRR 721, the court followed the approach taken in *Le Compte* and held that article 6(1) applied where the applicant had joined as an *assistente* in criminal proceedings with a view to securing financial reparation for injuries which he claimed he had suffered at the hands of the accused but had not filed any claim in civil proceedings. The distinction noticed by the Commission in *X v United Kingdom* (1998) 25 EHRR CD 88, 96 is not to be overlooked, that is the distinction between:

> 'the acts of a body which is engaged in the resolution of a dispute ("contestation") and the acts of an administrative or other body purporting merely to exercise or apply a legal power vested in it and not to resolve a legal claim or dispute.'

But at least from the time when a power has been exercised and objection is taken to that exercise the existence of a dispute for the purpose of article 6(1) can be identified.

148. The scope of article 6 accordingly extends to administrative determinations as well as judicial determinations. But, putting aside criminal proceedings with which we are not here concerned, the article also requires that the determination should be of a person's civil rights and obligations. The concept of civil rights in article 6(1) is an autonomous one (*König v Federal Republic of Germany* (1978) 2 EHRR 170). In *H v France* (1989) 12 EHRR 74, para 47 the court stated:

> 'It is clear from the court's established case law that the concept of "civil rights and obligations" is not to be interpreted solely by reference to the respondent state's domestic law and that article 6(1) applies irrespective of the parties' status, be it public or private, and of the nature of the legislation which governs the manner in which the dispute is to be determined; it is sufficient that the outcome of the proceedings should be "decisive for private rights and obligations".'

It relates to rights and obligations 'which can be said, at least on arguable grounds, to be recognised under domestic law' (*James v United Kingdom* (1986) 8 EHRR 123, para 81). The rights with which the present appeals are concerned are the rights of property which are affected by development or acquisition. Those clearly fall within the scope of 'civil rights'. But there is no issue about the existence of these rights and no determination of the rights in any strict sense is raised.

149. The opening words of article 6(1) are 'In the determination of his civil rights and obligations or of any criminal charge against him. . . .' Here again a broad interpretation is called for. The decision need not formally be a decision on the rights. Article 6 will still apply if the effect of the decision is directly to affect civil rights and obligations. In *Le Compte, Van Leuven & De Meyere*, para 46 the court observed:

> 'it must be shown that the "contestation" (dispute) related to "civil rights and obligations", in other words that the "result of the proceedings" was "decisive" for such a right.'

The dispute may relate to the existence of a right, and the scope or manner in which it may be exercised (*Le Compte*, at paragraph 49, also *Balmer-Schafroth v Switzerland* (1997) 25 EHRR 598). But it must have a direct effect of deciding rights or obligations. The court continued, at paragraph 47:

> 'As regards the question whether the dispute related to the above-mentioned right, the

court considers that a tenuous connection or remote consequences do not suffice for article 6 (1) in either of its official versions ("contestation sur"; "determination of"): civil rights and obligations must be the object—or one of the objects—of the "contestation" (dispute): the result of the proceedings must be directly decisive for such a right.'

That case was followed in *Sporrong and Lönnroth v Sweden* (1982) 5 EHRR 35, where at paragraph 80 the court noted that article 6(1) extended to a dispute concerning 'an administrative measure taken by the competent body in the exercise of public authority.' It is also said that the dispute must be 'genuine and of a serious nature': *Benthem v The Netherlands* (1985) 8 EHRR 1, para 32. In that case a genuine and serious dispute was held to have arisen 'at least' from the date when the licence which the applicant had earlier obtained from the local municipality was cancelled by the Crown.

150. It is thus clear that article 6(1) is engaged where the decision which is to be given is of an administrative character, that is to say one given in an exercise of a discretionary power, as well as a dispute in a court of law regarding the private rights of the citizen, provided that it directly affects civil rights and obligations and is of a genuine and serious nature. It applies then to the various exercises of discretion which are raised in the present appeals. But while the scope of the article extends to cover such discretionary decisions, the particular character of such decisions cannot be disregarded. And that particular factor has important consequences for the application of the article in such cases.

Compatibility with the Convention

151. If one was to take a narrow and literal view of the article, it would be easy to conclude that the respondents are correct and that the actions of the Secretary of State are incompatible with the article. It is accepted that he does not constitute an impartial and independent tribunal. In the context of a judicial proceeding that may well be fatal.

152. The first point to be noticed here, however, is that the opening phrase in article 6(1), 'in the determination', refers not only to the particular process of the making of the decision but extends more widely to the whole process which leads up to the final resolution. In *Zumtobal v Austria* (1993) 17 EHRR 116, para 64 the Commission under reference to *Ettl v Austria* (1987) 10 EHRR 255 paras 77 et seq, recalled that:

'article 6(1) of the Convention does not require that the procedure which determines civil rights and obligations is conducted at each of its stages before tribunals meeting the requirements of this provision. An administrative procedure may thus precede the determination of civil rights by the tribunal envisaged in article 6(1) of the Convention.'

It is possible that in some circumstances a breach in one respect can be overcome by the existence of a sufficient opportunity for appeal or review. While the failure to give reasons for a decision may in the context of some cases constitute a breach of the article, the existence of a right of appeal may provide a remedy in enabling a reasoned decision eventually to be given and so result in an overall compliance with the article. In the context of criminal cases article 6 will bite when a charge has been made, which could be long in advance of the trial or any subsequent appeal at which the actual resolution of the issue of guilt or innocence is made. In the civil context the whole process must be considered to see if the article has been breached. Not every stage need comply. If a global view is adopted one may then take into account not only the eventual opportunity for appeal or review to a court of law, but also the earlier processes and in particular the process of public inquiry at which essentially the facts can be explored in a quasi-judicial procedure and a determination on factual matters achieved.

153. Next, account has to be taken of the context and circumstances of the decision. Here an important distinction has been made by the European Court of Human Rights. The

distinction was explained in the context of medical disciplinary proceedings in *Albert and Le Compte v Belgium* (1983) 18 EHRR 533. In paragraph 29 of the judgment the court observed:

> 'In many member states of the Council of Europe, the duty of adjudicating on disciplinary offences is conferred on jurisdictional organs of professional associations. Even in instances where article 6(1) is applicable, conferring powers in this manner does not in itself infringe the Convention. Nonetheless, in such circumstances the Convention calls at least for one of the two following systems: either the jurisdictional organs themselves comply with the requirements of article 6(1), or they do not so comply but are subject to subsequent control by a judicial body that has full jurisdiction and does provide the guarantees of article 6(1).'

The court has recognised that planning decisions fall into a 'specialised area' (*Chapman v United Kingdom*, Application No 27238/95 (unreported) 2001) and have applied this distinction in relation to such decisions.

154. As regards the first of the two systems referred to in *Albert and Le Compte*, where the 'jurisdictional organ' is the Secretary of State it cannot be said that the requirements of Article 6(1) are met. So it is the second system which falls to be considered in the present context. In the first place consideration has to be given to the expression 'full jurisdiction.' At first sight the expression might seem to require in every case an exhaustive and comprehensive review of the decision including a thorough review of the facts as well as the law. If that were so a remedy by way of a statutory appeal or an application to the supervisory jurisdiction of the courts in judicial review would be inadequate. But it is evident that this is not a correct understanding of the expression. Full jurisdiction means a full jurisdiction in the context of the case. As Mr N Bratza stated in his concurring opinion in the decision of the Commission in *Bryan v United Kingdom* (1995) 21 EHRR 342, p 354:

> 'It appears to me that the requirement that a court or tribunal should have "full jurisdiction" cannot be mechanically applied with the result that, in all circumstances and whatever the subject matter of the dispute, the court or tribunal must have full power to substitute its own findings of fact, and its own inferences from those facts, for that of the administrative authority concerned.'

The nature and circumstances of the case have accordingly to be considered before one can determine what may comprise a 'full jurisdiction.' In the very different context of disciplinary proceedings a more exhaustive remedy may be required in order to satisfy article 6(1). In *Le Compte, Van Leuven & De Meyers* in the context of medical disciplinary proceedings the court stated, at paragraph 51:

> 'For civil cases, just as for criminal charges, article 6(1) draws no distinction between questions of fact and questions of law. Both categories of question are equally crucial for the outcome of proceedings relating to "civil rights and obligations". Hence, the "right to a court" and the right to a judicial determination of the dispute cover questions of fact just as much as questions of law.'

In that case the article was held not to be satisfied since the Court of Cassation had no jurisdiction to rectify factual errors or to examine whether the sanction was proportionate to the fault.

155. I turn then next to consider whether in the circumstances of the present cases as they presently stand the opportunities for appeal and review are such as to constitute a full jurisdiction. Guidance here may be found in *Bryan v United Kingdom*, above, where the court, echoing a passages from the opinion of Mr N Bratza in the Commission (see p 354) stated, at paragraph 45, that in assessing the sufficiency of the review available:

'it is necessary to have regard to matters such as the subject matter of the decision appealed against, the manner in which that decision was arrived at, and the content of the dispute, including the desired and actual grounds of appeal.'

These three matters may be considered separately.

156. First, the subject matter of the decisions are in each case matters of planning determination in relation to proposed developments which are of some considerable public importance. As planning decisions, even if they were not of some size and importance, they fall within what the court has recognised as a specialised class of case (*Chapman v United Kingdom*, above). The rights affected are principally rights to use land, which may be the subject of development or of compulsory acquisition. Moreover the right to use land is not an absolute right. It is under the domestic law subject to the controls of the planning regime, whereby permission may be required for the carrying out of a development or for the making of some change of use. Planning permission is not in general a matter of right.

157. So far as the manner in which the decisions will be taken is concerned it is to be noticed that in each case there will be a public inquiry before an inspector. That will be an occasion for the exploration of the facts, including the need and desirability of the development. The inquiry will be regulated by rules whose broad intention is to secure fairness in the procedure. The eventual decision in the present cases is to be taken by the Secretary of State. A remedy by way of appeal or judicial review is available, and there may be opportunities for judicial review at earlier stages as indeed is demonstrated in the present appeals.

158. So far as the content of the dispute is concerned, the present point is that the Secretary of State should not be the decision-maker. The challenge is advanced substantially as one of principle, although in relation to the Huntingdonshire case a variety of particular points were raised regarding the interest or involvement in the Alconbury proposals on the part of various persons connected with the department or the Government. But I find it unnecessary to explore these in detail. The Secretary of State is admittedly not independent for the purposes of article 6(1). I do not consider that it can be decided at this stage whether the interest or involvement of these other persons is going to provide grounds for challenging the legality of the eventual decision. Grounds for challenge which are at present unpredictable may possibly arise in due course. As matters presently stand the issue is whether article 6(1) is necessarily breached because the decision is to be taken by the Secretary of State with the assistance of his department. The challenge is directed not against the individual but against the office which he holds. The question which arises is whether the Secretary of State or some person altogether unconnected with the Secretary of State should make the decision.

159. As I indicated at the outset, Parliament, democratically elected, has entrusted the making of planning decisions to local authorities and to the Secretary of State with a general power of supervision and control in the latter. Thereby it is intended that some overall coherence and uniformity in national planning can be achieved in the public interest and that major decisions can be taken by a minister answerable to Parliament. Planning matters are essentially matters of policy and expediency, not of law. They are primarily matters for the executive and not for the courts to determine. Moreover as matter of generality the right of access to a court is not absolute. Limitations may be imposed so long as they do not so restrict or reduce the access that the very essence of the right is impaired (*Tinnelly & Sons Ltd v United Kingdom* (1998) 27 EHRR 249, para 72). Moreover the limitation must pursue a legitimate aim and the relationship between the means employed and the aim sought to be achieved must be reasonably proportionate (*Ashingdane v United Kingdom* (1985) 7 EHRR 528). In the context of the present cases the aim of reserving to a minister answerable to Parliament the determination of cases which will often be of very considerable public interest and importance is plainly a legitimate one. In light of the considerations which I have already canvassed it seems to me that there exists a reasonable balance between the scope of matters left to his decision and the scope of the control

possessed by the courts over the exercise of his discretionary power.

160. Accordingly as matters presently stand I find no evident incompatibility with article 6(1)."

This was an extremely important decision. As Lord Hoffmann pointed out, a decision the other way would mean "radical amendment to the system by which such decisions have been made for many years". It would indeed have been extraordinary if one of the earliest beneficiaries of the incorporation of Convention rights were property developers. The implications of the decision were immediately felt in Scotland. In *County Properties Ltd v Scottish Ministers*, 2002 S.L.T. 1125, the Inner House reversed a decision of Lord McFadyen that aspects of Scottish planning law violated Art.6. In this case the owners of a listed building in Glasgow applied to Glasgow City Council for planning permission and listed building consent to demolish it, and build a modern building in its place. Although granted by the council, the Scottish Ministers gave notice to say that the matter was of such importance that they would determine whether consent would be given or not. The developers challenged this decision as well as a decision by the Scottish Ministers appointing a Reporter to hear a public inquiry in relation to that application, and certain decisions said to have been made by the Reporter at a procedure meeting held in relation to the public inquiry. The decisions to hold a public inquiry and report were held by Lord McFadyen to be *ultra vires* the respondents by virtue of s.57(2) of the Scotland Act 1998 on the ground that they violated Art.6. He granted decree of reduction in respect of the decision to call in the application and the appointment of the Reporter. In reversing the Lord Ordinary in the light of *Alconbury*, the Inner House said:

"[18] We are satisfied that what was said in the *Alconbury* appeals did not relate merely to the specific facts and procedures which were under scrutiny in those cases. The crucial questions are issues of principle. We are satisfied that even upon the basis that there is contestation at the administrative stage, the nature of administrative and ministerial responsibilities and functions lies at the heart of any assessment of what is required in terms of Article 6(1). The distinctions drawn between the present case and what was in issue in the *Alconbury* appeals do not, in our opinion, make this case distinguishable in principle. We are satisfied that, in accordance with the principles identified in those appeals, it cannot be said that there is any inevitable incompatibility with Article 6(1) in the Scottish Ministers' decision to determine the petitioners' application for listed building consent, or in the appointment of a Reporter. The powers of the court to deal with genuinely justiciable issues arising in the administrative procedures are sufficient to ensure compatibility.

[19] We would add that, while the Reporter may not be, on his own, an 'independent and impartial tribunal' for the purposes of Article 6(1), it is important to bear in mind that he is bound to conduct the inquiry in accordance with statutory rules designed to give all parties to the inquiry fair notice of matters upon which they may wish to be heard, and a full opportunity to present to the Reporter any relevant evidence or submissions. Moreover, the written report to be prepared by the Reporter will require to contain findings in fact, a summary of the evidence upon which such findings in fact are based, details of the Reporter's assessment of those findings in fact and of the planning issues involved and reasons for the Reporter's recommendation to the Scottish Ministers. The Reporter's compliance with those safeguards is subject to the control of the court. They are as binding on a part-time Reporter as they are on a full-time Reporter. No submission was made as to the existence of any evidence of actual bias on the part of the Reporter, or as to the existence of any matter peculiar to this case, that might tend to dissuade or prevent the Reporter from following the correct procedures and practices. In the whole circumstances, accordingly, we are quite satisfied that the petitioners' Convention rights under Article 6 will not necessarily be breached if the Inquiry proceeds, the Reporter makes his report to the Scottish Ministers and they determine the application for listed building consent."

A similar emphasis on the need to look at procedures as a whole is to be found in the Outer

House decision in *Tehrani v United Kingdom Central Council for Nursing, Midwifery & Health Visiting*, 2001 S.L.T. 879. In that case the question arose whether disciplinary proceedings against a nurse by the Professional Conduct Committee of the UKCC (a statutory body constituted under the Nurses, Midwives and Health Visitors Act 1997) for misconduct was a violation of her civil rights. Addressing this matter, Lord MacKay said:

"[35] In considering this particular issue, I am required to take account of Strasbourg jurisprudence, which is relevant (section 2(1) of the 1998 Act). To assist me in doing so, I was referred to a number of cases decided by the European Court of Human Rights ('the EctHR'), relating to disciplinary proceedings against members of different professions. I am grateful to counsel for their considerable researches in this field. In *Le Compte, Van Leuven and De Meyere v Belgium* (1981) 4 E.H.R.R.1 the applicants were suspended from practising medicine by a disciplinary tribunal of the Belgian Ordre des Médecins. The applicants alleged that they had not received the benefit of the procedural guarantees required by Article 6(1). In its Judgment the ECtHR recognised that disciplinary proceedings do not normally involve a dispute over civil rights and obligations. It indicated, however, that depending upon the circumstances of a particular case, such a dispute might arise (para. 42). Having considered the factual circumstances that applied to the applicants, the ECtHR held that a dispute did exist and that the dispute directly and decisively affected the civil rights and obligations of the applicants, in that their private rights to practise their profession as doctors had been interfered with (paras. 45–48). That Judgment was followed in *Albert and Le Compte v Belgium* (1983) 5 E.H.R.R. 533, in which Dr. Le Compte was joined by another applicant, who was also a Belgian medical practitioner. Both applicants had been suspended from practise for two years by Provincial Councils of the Ordre des Médecins. Those decisions were unsuccessfully appealed to the Appeals Council of the Ordre of Médecins and from that tribunal to the Court of Cassation, on a point of law. In Dr. Le Compte's case, the Appeals Council changed the sanction of two years suspension to one of striking Dr. Le Compte's name from the register of the Ordre. As in the previous case involving Dr. Le Compte, the issues which arose for decision by the ECtHR included whether the applicants were involved in disputes, which fell within the ambit of Article 6(1). The ECtHR held that they were (paras 27–29). The ECtHR stressed that the effect of the disciplinary sanctions imposed was to divest the applicants, temporarily in the case of Dr. Albert and permanently in the case of Dr. Le Compte, of the right to continue to exercise the medical profession, which right they had duly acquired and which right allowed them to pursue what the ECtHR described as the 'goals of their professional life'. In reaching that decision, the ECtHR had regard to the fact that in Belgium it was by means of private arrangements, with clients and patients, that doctors in private practice availed themselves of the right to continue to practise. Such arrangements were usually contractual. In these circumstances, the ECtHR held that the right to continue to practise medicine constituted in the case of the applicants a private right and thus a civil right, within the meaning of Article 6(1), notwithstanding the fact that the medical profession is a profession exercised in the public interest.

[36] *Le Compte, van Leuven and De Meyere v Belgium* and *Albert and Le Compte v Belgium* were followed by the ECtHR in *Gautrin v France* (1999) 28 E.H.R.R. 221, which was another case involving members of the medical profession. The applicants in *Gautrin* were doctors, who were members of 'SOS Médecins', an association whose object is to provide emergency medical services on call to patients. A number of complaints against the applicants were lodged with their professional disciplinary body, the Regional Council of the Ordre des Médecins. It was alleged that the applicants, by using blue flashing lights on their vehicles and displaying the name of their association, 'SOS Médecins', on vehicles and other advertising materials, had contravened Article 23 of the Code of Conduct, which prohibits advertising. The complaints were upheld by the Regional Council. In respect of some of the applicants, short periods of suspension from practice were imposed. Other applicants were reprimanded. Appeals were taken to the National Council of the Ordre des

Médecins, which upheld the findings of breach of the Code of Professional Conduct, but reduced the periods of suspension in certain instances, substituted reprimands for periods of suspension in other cases and in yet further cases substituted warnings for reprimands. In *Gautrin*, it was not disputed that Article 6(1) applied to the case. Nevertheless in its Opinion, the ECtHR referred to the existence of settled case-law that disciplinary proceedings can give rise to disputes as to civil rights within the meaning of Article 6(1), if what is at stake is the right of the individual being disciplined to continue to practise medicine as a private practitioner, (para.33).

[37] Turning to cases involving members of the legal profession, I should record that counsel for the petitioner referred me to *H v Belgium* (1987) 10 E.H.R.R. 339 and *W R v Austria*, 21 December 1999, European Court of Human Rights, Unreported. In both cases, the ECtHR relied upon its previous judgments in the cases involving Dr. Le Compte. And in both cases the ECtHR held that the applicant's right to practise as a lawyer was a civil right within the meaning of Article 6(1). In particular in *WR v Austria*, the ECtHR recalled the case-law to the effect that disciplinary proceedings give rise to disputes over civil rights within the meaning of Article 6(1), if what is at stake is the right to continue to exercise a profession. For that reason, the ECtHR held that the provisions of Article 6(1) were applicable to the disciplinary proceedings against the applicant.

[38] I turn now to consider the possible consequences for the petitioner of the disciplinary proceedings initiated against her. If the petitioner is found guilty of misconduct, her name may be removed from the part of the Register that relates to qualified nurses. Were that to happen, the petitioner would cease to be a 'registered nurse', within the meaning of section 10(7) of the Nurses, Midwives and Health Visitors Act 1997. Whilst she would be able to seek employment as an auxiliary nurse or health care assistant, the petitioner would no longer be able to undertake nursing duties reserved to registered nurses. She would no longer be able to undertake duties involving the prescription, supply and administration of medicines. The provisions of section 58(1) of the Medicines Act 1968 ... authorise certain registered nurses to prescribe, supply and administer specified medicines to patients. I understood it to be accepted on behalf of the respondents and the Secretary of State for Health that were the petitioner's registration to be removed, she would be excluded from such activities.

[39] Counsel for the respondents and the Secretary of State for Health also conceded that there are other areas of employment from which the petitioner would be excluded as a matter of law, were her name to be removed from the Register. Such areas are those in which particular nursing duties are restricted by statute to 'registered nurses', within the meaning of section 7(7) of the 1997 Act. Miscellaneous examples drawn to my attention by counsel included the carrying out of 'intimate searches', in terms of section 164 (as amended) of the Customs and Excise Management Act 1979 and section 55 of the Police and Criminal Evidence Act 1984, and the discharge of certain powers in relation to children, by virtue of the provisions of sections 45 and 102 of the Children Act 1989. The petitioner would also be excluded by law from serving on various statutory bodies such a community health councils, the National Boards for Nursing, Midwifery and Health Visiting for England and Wales and as a member of the respondents themselves.

[40] The petitioner would also be unable to seek employment with employers, who specify registration in terms of section 7 of the 1997 Act, as being a necessary qualification, even although there is no legal necessity for their doing so. Various NHS trusts, hospitals, nursing homes and others adopt such a policy, by resolving that the 'nursing duties' they require should be only be carried out by registered nurses. Some employers adopt such a policy, even where the 'nursing duties' in question could be undertaken by nursing auxiliaries or health care assistants.

[41] Removal of the petitioner's name from the Register would also exclude the petitioner from employment in nursing homes, which is currently open to her, whether in a self-employed capacity or as an employed person. That would arise by reason of the provisions of regulation 10(2) of The Nursing Homes Registration (Scotland) Regulations 1990 (SI

1990/1310), to the effect that the 'person in charge' of a nursing home, registered under the Nursing Homes (Scotland) Act 1938, must be a medical practitioner or qualified nurse, whose name in entered in the Register. I understand that the petitioner held such employment in 1997 and 1998, during the period covered by the charge of misconduct she faces. Moreover, even if the petitioner was to find employment in a nursing home as a health care assistant, the financial consequences for the petitioner of having her name removed from the Register could be considerable.

[42] In these circumstances, I am satisfied that were the petitioner to have her name removed from the Register, following upon a finding of misconduct against her, such a determination would exclude her from certain nursing posts as a matter of law. It would exclude her from other posts, on account of criteria imposed by prospective employers. It would render it difficult, if not impossible, for the petitioner to find any employment in the nursing field, involving the same duties and attracting similar earnings, to those associated with the range of employment, which is currently open to her as a registered nurse."

But taken as a whole the disciplinary proceedings did not fall short of what Art.6 required. Although there were doubts about the independence of the PCC, it was nevertheless held that "the petitioner's right of appeal to the Court of Session, in terms of section 12 of the [Nurses, Midwives and Health Visitors Act 1997], ensures that any decision to remove her name from the Register would be one in which the determination involved had made in accordance with procedures which meet the requirements of Article 6(1)". Section 12 provides simply that "a person aggrieved by a decision to remove him from the register or to direct that his registration in the register be suspended or to remove or alter any entry in respect of him ... may, within three months after the date on which notice of the decision is given to him by the Council, appeal to the [Court of Session]". On appeal "(a) the court may give such directions in the matter as it thinks proper, including directions as to the costs of the appeal; and (b) the order of the court shall be final".

III. "A FAIR AND PUBLIC HEARING"

Brown v Stott
2001 S.L.T. 59

In the early hours of June 3, 1999 the police were called to a 24-hour superstore in Dunfermline where the respondent, Miss Brown, was suspected of having stolen a bottle of gin. The officers who attended judged her to be the worse for drink. Asked how she had come to the store, Brown said she had travelled by car. It seems that she made some reference to a kitten which was in the car. She was charged with theft and taken to the police station, but before leaving the store she pointed to a car in the store car park which she said was hers. At the police station the police found the keys of the car in her handbag. Exercising what they took to be their powers under s.172(2)(a) of the Road Traffic Act 1988, the police required her to say who had been driving her car at about 2.30 am when she would have travelled in it to the store car park. She replied "It was me". A breath test was then administered to her, which proved positive. So far as relevant s.172 of the Road Traffic Act 1988 provided that:

"(2) Where the driver of a vehicle is alleged to be guilty of an offence to which this section applies—
    (a) the person keeping the vehicle shall give such information as to the identity of the driver as he may be required to give by or on behalf of a chief officer of police, and
    (b) any other person shall if required as stated above give any information which it is in his power to give and may lead to identification of the driver.
  (3) Subject to the following provisions, a person who fails to comply with a requirement under subsection (2) above shall be guilty of an offence."

The respondent was prosecuted for two offences: theft; and driving a car after consuming excessive alcohol, contrary to s.5(1)(a) of the Road Traffic Act 1988. She indicated her intention to plead not guilty to both charges. On July 1, 1999 the respondent gave written notice of her intention to raise a devolution issue under s.98 of and Sch.6 to the Scotland Act 1998. The issue was whether, compatibly with the respondent's rights under Art.6 of the European Convention on Human Rights, the Procurator Fiscal at Dunfermline, as prosecutor, could rely at trial on the respondent's admission compulsorily obtained under s.172(2)(a) of the 1988 Act. The point was dismissed by the sheriff, but accepted on appeal by the High Court of Justiciary which declared that the Procurator Fiscal had no power to lead and rely on evidence of the admission which she had been compelled to make under s.172(2)(a) of the 1988 Act. The High Court took the view that the admission made under s.172 violated the right against self incrimination which the High Court thought to be part and parcel of the right to silence. The Privy Council reversed the decision of the High Court.

LORD BINGHAM OF CORNHILL: "What a fair trial requires cannot, however, be the subject of a single, unvarying rule or collection of rules. It is proper to take account of the facts and circumstances of particular cases, as the European Court has consistently done.
. . .
The European Convention is an international treaty by which the contracting states mutually undertake to secure to all within their respective jurisdictions certain rights and freedoms. The fundamental nature of these rights and freedoms is clear, not only from the full title and the content of the Convention but from its preamble in which the signatory governments declared

'their profound belief in those fundamental freedoms which are the foundation of justice and peace in the world and are best maintained on the one hand by an effective political democracy and on the other by a common understanding and observance of the human rights upon which they depend.'

Judicial recognition and assertion of the human rights defined in the Convention is not a substitute for the processes of democratic government but a complement to them. While a national court does not accord the margin of appreciation recognised by the European Court as a supra-national court, it will give weight to the decisions of a representative legislature and a democratic government within the discretionary area of judgment accorded to those bodies: see Lester and Pannick, *Human Rights Law and Practice*, (1999) at pp. 73–6. The Convention is concerned with rights and freedoms which are of real importance in a modern democracy governed by the rule of law. It does not, as is sometimes mistakenly thought, offer relief from 'The heart-ache and the thousand natural shocks That flesh is heir to'.
In interpreting the Convention, as any other treaty, it is generally to be assumed that the parties have included the terms which they wished to include and on which they were able to agree, omitting other terms which they did not wish to include or on which they were not able to agree. Thus particular regard must be had and reliance placed on the express terms of the Convention, which define the rights and freedoms which the contracting parties have undertaken to secure. This does not mean that nothing can be implied into the Convention. The language of the Convention is for the most part so general that some implication of terms is necessary, and the case law of the European Court shows that the Court has been willing to imply terms into the Convention when it was judged necessary or plainly right to do so. But the process of implication is one to be carried out with caution, if the risk is to be averted that the contracting parties may, by judicial interpretation, become bound by obligations which they did not expressly accept and might not have been willing to accept. As an important constitutional instrument the Convention is to be seen as a 'living tree capable of growth and expansion within its natural limits' (*Edwards v Attorney-General for Canada* [1930] A.C. 124 at 136 *per* Lord Sankey LC), but those limits will often call for very careful consideration.

Effect has been given to the right not to incriminate oneself in a variety of different ways. The Fifth Amendment to the Constitution of the United States provides that no person shall be compelled in any criminal case to be a witness against himself. The Indian Constitution (article 20(3)) provides that no person accused of any offence shall be compelled to be a witness against himself. The International Covenant on Civil and Political Rights 1966 provides in article 14(3)(g) that in determination of any criminal charge everyone shall be entitled to certain minimum guarantees, including a right not to be compelled to testify against himself or to confess guilt. The Canadian Charter of Rights and Freedoms confers on a person charged with an offence the right not to be compelled to be a witness in proceedings against himself in respect of that offence (section 11(c)). The New Zealand Bill of Rights Act 1990, in section 25(d), grants to everyone who is charged with an offence, in relation to the determination of the charge, certain minimum rights which include the right not to be compelled to be a witness or to confess guilt. The recently adopted constitution of South Africa grants rights to a suspect on arrest to remain silent and not to be compelled to make any confession or admission that could be used in evidence against him (section 35(1)(a) and (c)) and also a right to a fair trial, which includes rights to remain silent and not to testify during the proceedings and not to be compelled to give self-incriminating evidence (section 35(3)(h) and (j)). In contrast, the Universal Declaration of Human Rights 1948, in articles 10 and 11(1), grants a right to a fair trial in terms similar to the European Convention, but, like the Convention, contains no express guarantee of a privilege against self incrimination. Thus the right we have to consider in this case is an implied right. While it cannot be doubted that such a right must be implied, there is no treaty provision which expressly governs the effect or extent of what is to be implied.

The jurisprudence of the European Court very clearly establishes that while the overall fairness of a criminal trial cannot be compromised, the constituent rights comprised, whether expressly or implicitly, within article 6 are not themselves absolute. Limited qualification of these rights is acceptable if reasonably directed by national authorities towards a clear and proper public objective and if representing no greater qualification than the situation calls for. The general language of the Convention could have led to the formulation of hard-edged and inflexible statements of principle from which no departure could be sanctioned whatever the background or the circumstances. But this approach has been consistently eschewed by the Court throughout its history. The case law shows that the Court has paid very close attention to the facts of particular cases coming before it, giving effect to factual differences and recognising differences of degree. *Ex facto oritur jus.* The Court has also recognised the need for a fair balance between the general interest of the community and the personal rights of the individual, the search for which balance has been described as inherent in the whole of the Convention: see *Sporrong and Lönnroth v Sweden* (1982) 5 EHRR 35, at paragraph 69 of the judgment; *Sheffield and Horsham v United Kingdom* (1998) 27 EHRR, 163, at paragraph 52 of the judgment.

The high incidence of death and injury on the roads caused by the misuse of motor vehicles is a very serious problem common to almost all developed societies. The need to address it in an effective way, for the benefit of the public, cannot be doubted. Among other ways in which democratic governments have sought to address it is by subjecting the use of motor vehicles to a regime of regulation and making provision for enforcement by identifying, prosecuting and punishing offending drivers. Materials laid before the Board, incomplete though they are, reveal different responses to the problem of enforcement. Under some legal systems (Spain, Belgium and France are examples) the registered owner of a vehicle is assumed to be the driver guilty of minor traffic infractions unless he shows that some other person was driving at the relevant time or establishes some other ground of exoneration. There being a clear public interest in enforcement of road traffic legislation the crucial question in the present case is whether section 172 represents a disproportionate response, or one that undermines a defendant's right to a fair trial, if an admission of being the driver is relied on at trial.

I do not for my part consider that section 172, properly applied, does represent a disproportionate response to this serious social problem, nor do I think that reliance on the respondent's admission, in the present case, would undermine her right to a fair trial. I reach that conclusion for a number of reasons.

(1) Section 172 provides for the putting of a single, simple question. The answer cannot of itself incriminate the suspect, since it is not without more an offence to drive a car. An admission of driving may, of course, as here, provide proof of a fact necessary to convict, but the section does not sanction prolonged questioning about the facts alleged to give rise to criminal offences ... and the penalty for declining to answer under the section is moderate and non-custodial. There is in the present case no suggestion of improper coercion or oppression such as might give rise to unreliable admissions and so contribute to a miscarriage of justice, and if there were evidence of such conduct the trial judge would have ample power to exclude evidence of the admission.

(2) While the High Court was entitled to distinguish (as it did at pp. 390–391) between the giving of an answer under section 172 and the provision of physical samples, and had the authority of the European Court in *Saunders v United Kingdom* (1996) 23 E.H.R.R. 313 (at paragraph 69 of the judgment) for doing so, this distinction should not in my opinion be pushed too far. It is true that the respondent's answer, whether given orally or in writing, would create new evidence which did not exist until she spoke or wrote. In contrast, it may be acknowledged, the percentage of alcohol in her breath was a fact, existing before she blew into the breathalyser machine. But the whole purpose of requiring her to blow into the machine (on pain of a criminal penalty if she refused) was to obtain evidence not available until she did so and the reading so obtained could, in all save exceptional circumstances, be enough to convict a driver of an offence. If one applies the language of *Wigmore on Evidence*, volume 8, page 318, quoted by the High Court that an individual should 'not be conscripted by his opponent to defeat himself' it is not easy to see why a requirement to answer a question is objectionable and a requirement to undergo a breath test is not. Yet no criticism is made of the requirement that the respondent undergo a breath test.

(3) All who own or drive motor cars know that by doing so they subject themselves to a regulatory regime which does not apply to members of the public who do neither. Section 172 forms part of that regulatory regime. This regime is imposed not because owning or driving cars is a privilege or indulgence granted by the state but because the possession and use of cars (like, for example, shotguns, the possession of which is very closely regulated) are recognised to have the potential to cause grave injury. It is true that section 172(2)(b) permits a question to be asked of 'any other person' who, if not the owner or driver, might not be said to have impliedly accepted the regulatory regime, but someone who was not the owner or the driver would not incriminate himself whatever answer he gave. If, viewing this situation in the round, one asks whether section 172 represents a disproportionate legislative response to the problem of maintaining road safety, whether the balance between the interests of the community at large and the interests of the individual is struck in a manner unduly prejudicial to the individual, whether (in short) the leading of this evidence would infringe a basic human right of the respondent, I would feel bound to give negative answers. If the present argument is a good one it has been available to British citizens since 1966, but no one in this country has to my knowledge, criticised the legislation as unfair at any time up to now.

With much of the High Court judgment I am in respectful agreement. The United States Supreme Court decisions in *Hoffman v United States* 341 US 479 (1951) and *California v Byers* 402 US 424 (1971) and the decisions of the Supreme Court of Canada in *R. v Jones* [1994] 2 SCR 229 and *R. v White* [1999] 2 SCR 417 undoubtedly support the conclusion reached. Those courts were, however, considering different constitutional provisions. In the present case the High Court came very close to treating the right not to incriminate oneself as absolute, describing it as a 'central right' (at p. 391L) which permitted no gradations of fairness depending on the seriousness of the charge or the circumstances of the case. The High Court interpreted the decision in *Saunders* as laying down more absolute a standard than I think the European Court intended, and nowhere in the High Court judgments does one find any recognition of the need to balance the general interests of the community against the interests of the individual or to ask whether section 172 represents a proportionate response to what is undoubtedly a serious social problem.

In my opinion the Procurator Fiscal is entitled at the respondent's forthcoming trial to lead evidence of her answer given under section 172. I would allow the appeal and quash the declaration made by the High Court."

LORD HOPE OF CRAIGHEAD: "As the Lord Justice General (Rodger) observed (2000 S.L.T. 379, 385J), the right of silence and the right against self incrimination are not lately minted. They have been recognised as general principles of the law of Scotland at least since the beginning of the 19th century. In neither case was the right regarded as absolute, but the judges saw it as their function to see that they were jealously safeguarded. It was appreciated from an early stage that the accused's right to silence at trial would be worthless if his right of silence and his right against self incrimination were not available to him from the outset of the criminal investigation. So rules were developed by the judges to ensure that these rights were respected by the court and the police.

In *Chalmers v H.M. Advocate*, 1954 S.L.T. 177 Lord Justice General Cooper said that the principles which regulate the duties of the police when questioning suspects had been stated and restated in over a score of decisions in the past eighty or ninety years. As the jurisprudence on this subject developed the ultimate test was said to have been founded upon the principle of fairness. In *Brown v H.M. Advocate*, 1966 S.L.T. 105, 107 Lord Justice General Clyde observed that the test applied in all such cases was a simple and intelligible test which had worked well in practice—has what has taken place been fair or not? Other dicta to the same effect were referred to in *Codona v H.M. Advocate*, 1996 S.L.T. 1100, 1105A–E, where it was emphasised that that simple test must never be permitted to become a formality. The statutory rules relating to the questioning of persons detained at a police station and to judicial examination as a part of petition procedure, which are now to be found in sections 13–15 and 35–38 of the Criminal Procedure (Scotland) Act 1995, have been framed in such a way as to provide appropriate checks and balances in the interests of fairness to the accused.

As these provisions show, and as the judges have repeatedly emphasised in the common law context, the common law principle of fairness has always to be reconciled with the interests of society in the detection and punishment of crime: *Lawrie v Muir*, 1950 S.L.T. 137 per Lord Justice General Cooper; *H. M. Advocate v Hepper*, 1958 J.C. 39, 40 per Lord Guthrie. The rule of law requires that every person be protected from invasion by the authorities of his rights and liberties. But the preservation of law and order, on which the rule of law also depends, requires that those protections should not be framed in such a way as to make it impractical to bring those who are accused of crime to justice. The benefits of the rule of law must be extended to the public at large and to victims of crime also.

Now that the common law rights of the accused have been reinforced by the right under article 6(1) of the Convention to a fair trial it is necessary to re-examine and revise these principles. The scheme of the article involves the application of different tests at each stage of the inquiry from those applied by the common law. It requires that a more structured approach be taken when the overriding test of fairness is applied to the facts. But it is important to recognise nevertheless that the rule of law lies at the heart of the Convention.

The final indent of the preamble to the Convention refers to the common heritage of the European countries whose governments were signatory thereto of 'political traditions, ideals, freedom and the rule of law'. In *Salabiaku v France* (1988) 13 E.H.R.R. 379, para. 28 the European Court of Human Rights said that article 6, by protecting the right to a fair trial, was intended to enshrine 'the fundamental principle of the rule of law'. In *Golder v United Kingdom* (1975) 1 E.H.R.R. 524, para. 35 the Court said that in civil matters one could scarcely conceive of the rule of law without there being a possibility of access to the courts. These statements assert the right of the individual to the protection of the rule of law against the State. But the other side of the balance, which respects the public interest in the rule of law and the general interest of the community, was also recognised by the Court in *Salabiaku*. It said in para. 28 of its judgment in that case that the Convention did not prohibit presumptions of fact or of law in principle, and that they were not incompatible with article 6(2) so long as they were confined within reasonable limits which take account of what is at stake and maintain the rights of the defence. In *Pullar v United Kingdom* (1996) 22 E.H.R.R 391, para. 32, the Court said that the principle that a tribunal is to be presumed to be free of personal prejudice or partiality unless there is evidence to the contrary reflects 'an important element of the rule of law', which is that verdicts of a tribunal should be final and binding unless set aside by a superior court on the basis of irregularity or unfairness. A similar approach to the function of the rule of law can be seen in the fact that the Court has consistently recognised that, while the right to a fair trial is absolute in its terms and the public interest can never be invoked to deny that right to anybody under any circumstances, the rights which it has read into article 6 are neither absolute nor inflexible.

It is important therefore to distinguish between those Convention rights which are to be regarded as absolute and those which are not. The scheme of article 6, as Keir Starmer in *European Human Rights Law* (Legal Action Group 1999), pp. 118–119, para. 3.88, has explained, is that the rights listed in articles 6(2) and 6(3) which are supplementary to article 6(1) are not intended to be an exhaustive list of the requirements of fairness in criminal proceedings. Those which are listed in article 6(3) are described as minimum rights. Once the meaning of those rights has been determined, there is no room in their case for any implied modifications or restrictions. But the European Court and the European Commission have interpreted the article broadly by reading into it a variety of other rights to which the accused person is entitled in the criminal context. Their purpose is to give effect, in a practical way, to the fundamental and absolute right to a fair trial. They include the right to silence and the right against self incrimination with which this case is concerned. As these other rights are not set out in absolute terms in the article they are open, in principle, to modification or restriction so long as this is not incompatible with the absolute right to a fair trial. As Keir Starmer, p. 182, para. 4.75 has observed, where express restrictions are provided for by the Convention there is no room for implied restrictions. But where the European Court has read implied rights into the Convention, it has also read in implied restrictions on those rights.

The test of compatibility with article 6(1) which is to be applied where it is contended that those rights which are not absolute should be restricted or modified will not be satisfied if the modification or limitation 'does not pursue a legitimate aim and if there is not a reasonable relationship of proportionality between the means employed and the aim sought to be achieved': *Ashingdane v United Kingdom* (1985) 7 E.H.R.R. 528, para. 57. In *Sporrong and Lönnroth v Sweden* (1982) 5 E.H.R.R. 35, para. 69 the Court referred to the striking of a fair balance 'between the demands of the general interest of the community and the requirements of the protection of the individual's fundamental rights'. As that case and *Salabiaku v France* (1988) 13 E.H.R.R. 379 both demonstrate, that approach has been used to support the view that, although the presumption of innocence in article 6(2) is stated in absolute terms, it is not to be regarded as prohibiting the use of reverse onus clauses so long as they are confined within reasonable limits which strike a fair balance between these competing demands and requirements. The relevant principles described in *Ashingdane* were restated by the Court in *Lithgow v United Kingdom* (1986) 8 E.H.R.R. 329, para. 194 and again in *Fayed v United Kingdom* (1994) 18 E.H.R.R. 393, para. 65.

I would hold therefore that the jurisprudence of the European Court tells us that the questions that should be addressed when issues are raised about an alleged incompatibility with a right under article 6 of the Convention are the following: (1) is the right which is in question an absolute right, or is it a right which is open to modification or restriction because it is not absolute? (2) if it is not absolute, does the modification or restriction which is contended for have a legitimate aim in the public interest? (3) if so, is there a reasonable relationship of proportionality between the means employed and the aim sought to be realised? The answer to the question whether the right is or is not absolute is to be found by examining the terms of the article in the light of the judgments of the Court. The question whether a legitimate aim is being pursued enables account to be taken of the public interest in the rule of law. The principle of proportionality directs attention to the question whether a fair balance has been struck between the general interest of the community in the realisation of that aim and the protection of the fundamental rights of the individual."

[Lord Hope held that the legislation pursued a legitimate aim in a proportionate manner.]

A number of other cases have tested the general boundaries of Art.6, though there are few in which the courts have upheld complaints based simply on the ground that a trial was unfair. These cases include the following:

- *Brown v Gallacher*, 2002 S.L.T. 1135: the requirement that drivers submit to breath testing under the Road Traffic Act was not a breach of Art.6(1) as requiring the driver to incriminate himself or herself.
- *Irvine v Arco Atholl Ltd*, 2002 S.L.T. 931: the admission of hearsay evidence was not a breach of Art.6 despite the fact that there was no opportunity to cross-examine the party who produced the evidence.
- *H M Advocate v Beggs (No 3)*, 2002 S.L.T. 153: the admissibility of a witness statement from someone who died before the trial was not a breach of Art.6(1) or (3) in view of the need for corroboration.
- *Heasman v J M Taylor and Partners*, 2002 S.L.T. 451: assessment of damages by a jury in a civil action is not a breach of Art.6. (See also *McLeod v British Rail Board*, 2002 S.L.T. 238.)

Moving beyond Art.6(1), some of the provisions of Art.6 (2) and (3) also have a bearing on the fairness of a trial. However here too the courts have been careful to tread lightly. For example, the presumption of innocence in Art.6(2) does not apply to the making of a confiscation order under the Proceeds of Crime (Scotland) Act 1995 after a conviction has been secured. This is because in these proceedings the respondent is not charged with a criminal offence as Art.6(2) requires: *McIntosh Petitioner*, 2001 S.L.T. 305. Similarly the right to legal assistance in Art.6(3) does not appear to add greatly to the pre-existing rights of litigants or accused persons. It has been held by the Privy Council that the fixed payment system for the remuneration of solicitors in legal aid cases is consistent with Art.6, though concern was expressed about the potential for injustice to which the scheme gave rise: *Buchanan v McLean*, 2002 S.L.T. 780. However, according to Lord Hope:

"I am not persuaded that it has been shown that the fixed fee regime will give rise to any actual or inevitable prejudice at the appellants' trial. As I have already said, it would be wrong to assume that the solicitors who have been instructed in this case will reduce their standards of preparation simply because they consider that they will not receive adequate remuneration for their work when they are paid the fixed fee. The assumption must be, in the absence of any contrary evidence, that they will conduct the defence according to the standards which are expected of their profession as they are required to do by the codes. The fact that the solicitors have not indicated that they propose to withdraw from the case is also an important indication that, on the information which is available as this stage, the appellants are not being deprived of their right to a fair trial by the [scheme]. I am not persuaded that it has been shown that the fixed fee regime will give rise to any actual or inevitable prejudice at the appellants' trial."

It was subsequently held in *Vickers v Buchanan*, 2002 S.L.T. 686 that an accused person has no right to insist on a particular individual as his or her choice of solicitor. The accused had chosen a solicitor from Glasgow to represent her at her trial in Fort William. The solicitor in question had been unable to act because the fixed payment system did not provide adequate remuneration. On the other hand, however, the absence of legal assistance in children's panels was held to be a breach of Art.6(3)(c), leading to a declaration of incompatibility being issued: *S v Millar*, 2002 S.L.T. 531, and *S v Millar (No 2)*, 2002 S.L.T. 1304.

IV. "WITHIN A REASONABLE TIME"

The requirement that a trial must be held within a reasonable time has given rise to a great deal of litigation and to a great deal of difficulty. The issue was raised for the first time in *Dyer v Watson*, 2002 S.L.T. 229 which was a consolidated appeal dealing with two cases. In one it was held that a delay of 20 months was not too long in the case of perjury by police officers. In the other it was held that a delay of 28 months was too long in the case of alleged sexual offences alleged to have been committed when the accused was only 13. In the latter case the indictment was discharged, this being held by the Privy Council as being the only suitable way to dispose of the matter. However, the Privy Council left open the question of whether discharge should be the only remedy available when the Convention right of the accused had been violated. This matter was subsequently considered by the Privy Council in the following case, where an interesting split emerged between the Scottish and English members of the Committee. Before turning to that case, it is to be emphasised that the right to a fair trial "within a reasonable time" has two dimensions: the first is the need to bring a matter in a timely fashion, and the second is the need to process the trial in a timely manner when it has commenced.

R. v H M Advocate
2003 S.L.T. 4

The appellant had been charged with indecent behaviour towards two young girls. He claimed that because of the delay in bringing the matters to trial, there had been a violation of his right to have the charges determined within a reasonable time. He also claimed that the Lord Advocate had no power to prosecute him on these charges, having regard to the provisions of s.57(2) of the Scotland Act. The latter provides that "A member of the Scottish Executive has no power to make any subordinate legislation, or to do any other act, so far as the legislation or act is incompatible with any of the Convention rights or with Community law". The appellant sought the dismissal of the charges against him, but this was rejected by Lord Reed and by the Criminal Appeal Court. His appeal to the Privy Council was successful.

> LORD HOPE OF CRAIGHEAD: "31. The circumstances of this case are unusual. For the purposes of article 6(1) time begins to run from the date on which the person is first made subject to a 'criminal charge'. It ends when there is a 'determination' of the charge, and it includes the time taken by any appeal. The appellant was first charged with these offences on 13 August 1995 when he was cautioned and charged after the initial interview. The procurator fiscal then decided to take no proceedings. From the moment that this information was passed on to the appellant in 1996 he believed that the charges were not being proceeded with. ... He remained in that state of mind until he was indicted for trial at the High Court at Inverness on 16 July 2001 on an indictment which contained all six charges.
>
> ...
>
> 75. In my opinion the proper starting point for an analysis of all the article 6(1) rights is to be found in the wording of that article. It is important to put the words 'a fair and public hearing within a reasonable time' into their right context. That context is to be found in the opening words of the article. It begins by identifying the proceedings in which everyone is to be entitled to the protection of these rights. They are proceedings for 'the determination of his civil rights and obligations and of any criminal charge against him.' It has been held that the reasonable time guarantee begins to run as soon as a person is 'charged' within the meaning of the Convention: *Eckle v Federal Republic of Germany* (1983) 5 EHRR 1. The

wording of the article indicates that it continues until the charge has been determined. It includes the whole of the proceedings which are designed to achieve that purpose, including proceedings on appeal. It has been held that the purpose of the guarantee is to prevent an accused person from remaining too long in a state of uncertainty about his fate: *Stögmüller v Austria* (1969) 1 EHRR 155, 191, para 5. That decision indicates, as do the opening words of the article, that the guarantee relates to the proceedings as a whole. It is the time taken by the proceedings overall that matters. The guarantee does not concern itself with parts of the proceedings in isolation from other parts. What it is designed to do is to ensure that the *determination of the charge* takes place within a reasonable time.

76. It is clear that the concept of reasonableness implies that a relatively high threshold must be crossed before it can be said in any particular case that a period of delay is unreasonable: *Dyer v Watson*, 2002 S.L.T. 229, paras 51–52 per Lord Bingham of Cornhill. As Lord Bingham put it, the threshold is a high one, not easily crossed. Among the factors to be taken into account in deciding where that threshold lies is the public interest: see also *Martin v Tauranga District Court* [1995] 2 NZLR 419, 424–425, per Cooke P. A fair balance must be struck between the demands of the general interest of the community and the requirements of the protection of the individual's fundamental rights. But once that threshold has been crossed and it has been held that there has been a delay which is unreasonable within the meaning of the article, the position is irretrievable. It is simply not possible to say that what has happened so far has resulted in a delay in the determination of the criminal charge which is unreasonable, but that the delay in its determination can be removed by looking to what happens in the future. Once it has been established that there has been such a delay, any further proceedings will inevitably result in yet further delay in the determination of the charge. They cannot remove the effect of what has happened so far from the proceedings, which taken overall are bound to result in breach of the Convention right.

77. In *Dyer v Watson*, 2002 S.L.T. 229, para 128 Lord Millett said:

'The right to a hearing within a reasonable time clearly differs from the other rights in some respects. Once there has been unreasonable delay, it is no longer possible to bring the case to trial within a reasonable time from its inception. The most that can be achieved is to bring it to trial without further delay. On the other hand, a right not to be tried once there has been unreasonable delay prevents the case being heard at all. In this case alone the correlative right is destructive of the primary right, of fundamental importance in a society governed by the rule of law, that civil and criminal disputes should be determined by judicial process.'

78. The suggestion is—and it is right to mention that Lord Millett makes these points as no more than a suggestion—that there is no such thing as a Convention right not to be tried at all after unreasonable delay. But I do not think that there is any escape from the conclusion that, once it has been established that the right to a determination within a reasonable time has been breached, it will not be possible to avoid that breach simply by bringing the matter to trial without further delay. I also think that it is unhelpful, when one is attempting to analyse the Convention rights in article 6(1), to talk in terms of primary rights and correlative rights. The only correlative right under the Convention is the right under article 13 to an effective remedy.

79. On this analysis, and on the agreed facts, a finding that the Lord Advocate's act in continuing to prosecute the appellant on charges 1 and 3 is incompatible with the right to a determination of those charges within a reasonable time seems to me to be inevitable.

80. The conclusion which I would draw from an examination of the Convention right in the context of what Parliament has laid down in section 57(2) of the Scotland Act—and it has been said that, in law, context is everything—is that the stage at which the concerns of the individual, of society and of the system of criminal justice as a whole must be taken into account is the stage when one is considering whether the right to a determination of the

criminal charge within a reasonable time has been breached. That there has been such a breach has been conceded in this case. I make no criticism of that decision. But, as I indicated in *Mills v H M Advocate (No 2)*, 2002 SLT 939, 946, paras 29 and 30, concessions on this point ought not to be made in the future without taking full account of the observations which are set out in the Board's judgment in *Dyer v Watson*, 2002 S.L.T. 229. It should be remembered also that we are dealing in this case with what may be called 'pure' delay. There has been no suggestion of prejudice, nor—to put the matter in Convention terms—has it been suggested that in consequence of the delay the appellant will not receive a fair trial. The statutory protections for an accused are such that complaints of delay before trial unaccompanied by allegations of prejudice are seldom likely to arise in Scotland .... But I suggest that, if the issue is raised, the question whether the threshold has been crossed should be examined in the way that the judgment in *Dyer v Watson* has indicated with caution and with full regard to the consequences as to remedy which, in the case of proposed or continuing acts, section 57(2) of the Scotland Act 1998 makes inevitable.

81. I recognise that there is a genuine concern on the part of my noble and friends Lord Steyn and Lord Walker of Gestingthorpe about the implications of the decision in this case for the criminal justice system in England and Wales. Lord Steyn says that the interpretation of section 57(2) of the Scotland Act which I favour is contrary to the public interest and that it is detrimental to a fair and balanced criminal justice system. He refers also to the risk to the moral authority of human rights in the eyes of the public if they are allowed to run riot in our justice systems. These are powerful observations. I would be willing to accept that they may be justified if it were to be suggested that the decision had to be applied without question in England and Wales also, although this is a point on which I should like to hear further argument.

82. But I do not regard these observations as providing fair comment about the effect which this decision will have on the criminal justice system in Scotland. The Scottish system has accepted the imposition of statutory time limits on the prosecution of offences which are far more onerous than anything that the English system has been able to accept, and its common law jurisprudence proceeds along similar lines. As a result cases of pure delay are, as Lord Rodger has explained, indeed quite rare and they are likely to remain so. The bare fact that 39% of devolution minutes have raised issues of delay tells us nothing about the basis for these applications or the prospects of their being upheld when they are subjected to the appropriate threshold. My judgment is that the result of this case will be beneficial in Scotland, as it will tend to reinforce the philosophy which has always informed Scottish criminal justice that delays are contrary to the public interest and must be kept under strict control.

83. I think that it should also be recorded that the parties were informed at outset of the hearing before the Board that the decision of the Court of Appeal in *Attorney General's Reference (No 2 of 2001)* [2001] 1 WLR 1869 was not to be dealt with in the course of the argument as it was under appeal to the House of Lords. It is for this reason that I have not thought it appropriate to draw attention to defects in the reasoning in that case which will require to be examined in the appeal. All that needs to be said, with great emphasis as this is a case which has been brought under the Scotland Act and not the Human Rights Act, is that the decision in that case proceeds upon the assumption that under the Human Rights Act there is a choice of remedies. It does not address the particular issue which arises under section 57(2) of the Scotland Act, which provides that the Lord Advocate has no power to act incompatibly with any of the Convention rights.

84. For these reasons, and for those given by Lord Rodger with whose carefully reasoned judgment I am in full agreement, I would allow this appeal. I would hold that it would be incompatible with the appellant's right to a determination of a criminal charge against him within a reasonable time for the Lord Advocate to continue to prosecute him on charges 1 and 3 of the indictment and, as the Lord Advocate has no power to do an act which is incompatible with the Convention right, that the plea in bar should be sustained and these charges dismissed from the indictment.''

The decision in *R* has proved to be very controversial and to be the source of the major fissure that has opened up between the Scottish and English Law Lords on the interpretation of Convention rights. A majority of the members of the Judicial Committee in *R* were Scottish judges (Lords Hope, Clyde and Rodger). The two English Law Lords were Lords Steyn and Walker, both of whom dissented in strong terms. Lord Steyn cited Hardie Boys J. in *Martin v Tauranga District Court* [1995] 2 N.Z.L.R. 419, where he said that: "The right is to trial without undue delay: it is not a right not to be tried after undue delay" (at 432). After a review of English (*Attorney-General's Reference (No. 2 of 2001)* [2001] 1 W.L.R. 1869) and South African cases, Lord Steyn continued:

> "To hold otherwise would in my view be contrary to the public interest and detrimental to a fair and balanced criminal justice system. For my part the interpretation advocated by the appellant would result in severe disruption of the effective and just functioning of the criminal justice system. It is significant that since the commencement of the Scotland Act out of 1727 devolution minutes 675 raised issues of delay, ie 39%. If such a view were to be adopted in England, contrary to the decision in *Attorney-General's Reference (No. 2 of 2001)* [2001] 1 WLR 1869, the result would be a huge increase in stay applications in criminal courts at every level, with detrimental effect on the administration of justice."

Lord Steyn also expressed concern that "[t]he moral authority of human rights in the eyes of the public must not be undermined by allowing them to run riot in our justice systems. In working out solutions under the Scotland Act 1998 and the Human Rights Act 1998 courts in Scotland and England should at all times seek to adopt proportionate remedies". For his part, Lord Walker thought the result of the majority "surprising and inconvenient". He expressed concern about one consequence, namely: "the law of Scotland would appear to differ (on a very important human rights issue) from the law of England (as well as differing from other Commonwealth jurisdictions)".

The issue of delay was revisited by the House of Lords in *Attorney-General's Reference (No. 2 of 2001)* [2003] UKHL 68, an appeal in an English case where the majority of the court were English Law Lords. The majority took the opportunity to hold that *R* was wrongly decided, but they could not overrule it, as the House of Lords has no authority to reverse a decision of the Privy Council. Lord Hope said:

> "103. It would, of course, be open to the Judicial Committee, appropriately constituted, to overrule its own decision. But there are reasons for thinking that it ought to be cautious before doing so. Lord Bonomy has drawn attention to this problem in his Report: see *The 2002 Review of the Practices and Procedures of the High Court of Justiciary*, pp 107–109, paras 17.3–17.9. In paragraph 17.9 he states:

>> 'It is ironic that pre-devolution the High Court was the final arbiter in all matters of criminal procedure and evidence, and was entrusted with the responsibility of ensuring that our criminal practice was in keeping with our obligations in international law, but in post-devolution Scotland the High Court has had to cede that role to the Judicial Committee of the Privy Council when, but only when, an act of the Lord Advocate is involved. Should a similar point arise in relation to the conduct of the court itself or any other public authority, the final say reverts to the High Court.'

> 104. The fact that finality in all matters other than acts or failures to act of the prosecutor rests with the High Court of Justiciary indicates that, where the conduct of the court itself is in issue, it is in a position to make up its own mind as to how the reasonable time guarantee should be interpreted and given effect in the criminal courts in Scotland. It will be for the judges of that court to decide whether they can accept the decision of the majority in this case or whether they would prefer to follow the views of the majority in *R. v H M Advocate* 2003 S.L.T. 4, as amplified by the views which I and my noble and learned friend Lord

Rodger of Earlsferry have expressed in this case. They are, of course, bound by decisions of the Judicial Committee as to how devolution issues are to be disposed of. But the definition of the expression 'devolution issue' in paragraph 1 of Schedule 6 to the Scotland Act 1998 does not extend to acts of the court itself or those of other public authorities other than members of the Scottish Executive.

105. A declaration by your Lordships that *R v H M Advocate* should not be followed in this jurisdiction may be thought to be inevitable in view of the conclusion reached by the majority. But a declaration that that case was wrongly decided, as Lord Nicholls would have it, is undesirable. Section 103 of the Scotland Act 1998 provides that any decision of the Judicial Committee shall be binding in all legal proceedings (other than proceedings before the Committee). And there is no appeal to this House from decisions of the High Court of Justiciary in cases decided by that court under the Human Rights Act 1998. So it is open to the Scottish courts to go their own way on this issue.

106. The rule that the jurisdiction of the Scottish courts is separate from that in England and Wales has always been regarded in Scotland as an important part of the constitution of the United Kingdom. The provisions of the Scotland Act 1998 were designed to protect this rule. The Judicial Committee of the Privy Council forms part of the Scottish legal system when it is exercising its jurisdiction in a Scottish case under Schedule 6 to the Scotland Act: *Montgomery v H M Advocate*, 2002 S.L.T. 37. The jurisdiction which it was exercising in *R*'s case was as much part of the Scottish system as it would have been had the case been a Scottish appeal brought to this House under section 40 of the Court of Session Act 1988. In *Glasgow Corpn v Central Land Board*, 1956 SC (HL) 1, which was heard before the *Practice Statement (Judicial Precedent)* [1966] 1 WLR 1234 made it possible for it to depart from its previous decisions, the House was faced with the question whether it was obliged to follow its own decision in *Duncan v Cammell, Laird & Co Ltd* [1942] AC 624 when it was considering the question whether the Scottish courts had power to override a public interest objection by the Secretary of State where documents in the possession of a government department were sought to be recovered by a litigant. Viscount Simonds said at pp 9–10:

> 'At once it must be said that that decision was given upon an English appeal, in which the law of Scotland was not directly under review, that the common law of Scotland differs from that of England in regard to the liability of the Crown to be sued and has developed independently in regard to the right of discovery or recovery of documents in possession of the Crown, and that, desirable though it may be that in matters of constitutional importance the law of the two countries should not differ, yet it would be clearly improper for this House to treat the law of Scotland as finally determined by a decision upon an English appeal unless the case arose upon the interpretation of a statute common to both countries.'

107. The law of Scotland is not directly under review in this case. Moreover, questions arose in *R v H M Advocate* about the interpretation of the Scotland Act and aspects of Scottish criminal practice which are not common to the two countries. I would have much preferred it if your Lordships had felt able to arrive at a decision in this English appeal which could be reconciled with that of the Judicial Committee in *R*'s case. But it does not follow from the fact that this has not been possible that *R* should not be followed in Scotland.

108. A divergence of view between the two jurisdictions about the meaning of the reasonable time guarantee, as there is at present, is unfortunate but it may have to be accepted as inevitable. The last word as to its meaning must, of course, lie with Strasbourg. The doors of that court remain open to those who believe that, as a result of the decision in this case, they have not been provided in this jurisdiction with an effective domestic remedy."

Although the Scottish judges of the Privy Council have thus taken a robust view of cases involving delay in bringing cases to trial, it does not follow that even lengthy delays will be unreasonable. In *Morrison v H M Advocate*, 2002 S.L.T. 795, it was held that a three-year delay was not unreasonable where this was caused in part by the unwillingness of the accused's wife to give evidence against him. Moreover, in *O'Brien v H M Advocate*, 2002 S.L.T. 1101, a 23-month delay was held not to be unreasonable where this was due to limited resources in the forensic laboratory services. It is also the case that while the Scottish judges of the Privy Council have taken a robust view of cases involving delay in bringing cases to trial, they have taken a less absolute position when dealing with delays involving cases which are already in the system. This is a matter that was also considered by the Privy Council in *Dyer v Watson*, 2002 S.L.T. 229 where Lord Rodger said that:

"... the right of an accused person who is in custody to 'trial within a reasonable time or to release pending trial' under art 5 (3) ... has not featured significantly in cases coming before the courts in Scotland, presumably because Scots law imposes strict time limits in cases where the accused is remanded in custody. Any trial on indictment must begin within 110 days of the accused being committed to prison for trial (s 65 (4) (b) of the Criminal Procedure (Scotland) Act 1995 ("the 1995 Act")). Similarly, where the accused is in custody, any summary trial must begin within 40 days after the bringing of the complaint in court (s 147 (1)), unless the period is extended for a sufficient cause which is not attributable to any fault on the part of the prosecutor. These time limits mean that an infringement of art 5 (3) is very unlikely to occur or even to be alleged."

Yet these rules notwithstanding, delays may still occur, as the following case makes clear. Here the Privy Council was concerned with delay in processing an appeal and the remedy that would be appropriate where such a complaint is well founded.

Mills v H M Advocate (No.2)
2002 S.L.T. 939

On October 17, 1996 the appellant was convicted of the theft of a motor car and of assaulting a police officer by driving a car at him. He was on bail at the time of the offence of assaulting the police officer. On November 7, 1996 the appellant was sentenced to detention in a young offenders' institution for eight years and six months, six months of that period being attributable to the fact that he committed the offence while on bail. On May 8, 1997 he sought to appeal against his conviction on the ground of fresh evidence. A hearing to take this evidence was later fixed for May 6, 1999, but following a postponement at the request of the Crown the matter was not heard until May 9, 2001. On May 10, 2001 the High Court refused the appeal on the ground that the fresh evidence was not capable of being regarded by a reasonable jury as credible. On the same date the appellant was allowed to lodge a further ground of appeal in which he alleged that there had been a breach of his rights under Art.6(1) because of the delay in the hearing of the appeal. The court heard his appeal on this further ground on July 31, 2001. On August 1, 2001 it held that the appellant had established that there had been a breach of his Art.6(1) right by the Lord Advocate which fell within s.57(2) of the Scotland Act 1998. His appeal was allowed, and his original sentence of detention was reduced by a period of nine months. The appeal to the Privy Council was based on the claim by the appellant that the delay meant that his conviction should have been quashed.

LORD HOPE OF CRAIGHEAD: "... the Lord Advocate has not appealed against the decision by the High Court of Justiciary that there was an unexplained delay in the hearing of the appeal which could not be said to have been reasonable. Nor has he appealed against its decision that the appellant had established a breach of his article 6(1) right by the Lord Advocate which fell with section 57(2) of the Scotland Act.

...

Before I deal with the question as to the appropriate remedy in this case, I must say a little more about the facts. No complaint has been made in this case about pre-trial delay. Nor is there any complaint about delay in the appeal process up to the date of the diet of 6 May 1999 which had been originally fixed for the hearing of the fresh evidence. It is the delay which occurred during the period after that date that has been criticised.

The interlocutor of 6 May 1999 states that the court continued the appeal to a date to be afterwards fixed pending further preparations by the Crown. These preparations were to include the precognition of the appellant's witnesses, the recovery of certain productions used during the trial and an application to the Deputy Principal Clerk of Justiciary for the extension of the whole of the evidence in the trial including the speeches to the jury by both the Advocate Depute and counsel for the accused. Transcripts of the evidence at the trial were obtained and received in the Justiciary Office on 13 August 1999. On 19 August 1999 the Deputy Principal Clerk of Justiciary wrote to the Crown Office saying that, due to a misunderstanding, only the evidence and not the speeches had been extended. He said that some delay might be anticipated in obtaining a transcript of the speeches as the shorthand writer responsible for taking notes of part of the trial had left the employment of the firm of shorthand writers. He had already written to the firm of shorthand writers asking for the speeches to be transcribed as a matter of urgency. The precise date when a transcript of the speeches reached the Justiciary Office has not been identified, but it appears that they became available in December 1999. That date marks the beginning of the period which is under scrutiny on the ground that there was a delay which was unreasonable. It ends on 9 May 2001 when the court began hearing the fresh evidence.

The appellant accepts that it would not have been possible for the court to hear the fresh evidence as soon as the transcript of the speeches became available. The Crown was entitled to a little more time to complete its preparations for the appeal. A fresh diet then required to be fixed by the court, in accordance with the direction to this effect in the interlocutor of 6 May 1999. But, as Lord Coulsfield has explained, it would ordinarily have been expected that the hearing on the fresh evidence would take place within two or three months of the date of the request for a fresh diet. So the case has been argued on the basis that there was a delay of about twelve months prior to the hearing of the appeal for which the Crown was unable to give any explanation. The court held that a breach of article 6 by the Lord Advocate had been established because there had been a failure by the Crown to intimate when its preparations were complete.

. . .

The approach which I would take to the question which has been raised in this appeal is first to identify the remedy which would ordinarily be thought to be appropriate in domestic law for a breach of the kind which has taken place, and then to consider whether the remedy which has thus been identified would achieve just satisfaction for the breach as indicated by the jurisprudence of the European Court. I think that it is important to start with the position in domestic law because, as was emphasised in *Eckle v Federal Republic of Germany* (1982) 5 EHRR 1, 24, para 66, the Convention leaves to each contracting state, in the first place, the task of securing the enjoyment of the rights and freedoms which it enshrines. The machinery of protection established by the Convention, of which article 50 forms part, is of a subsidiary character.

In a case of pre-trial delay, for example, one of the remedies which is available in domestic law is to uphold the accused's plea in bar of trial. This was familiar ground long before the coming into effect of the Scotland Act 1998. It is available under the common law where there is such a grave risk of prejudice at the trial due to undue delay that no direction by the trial judge can be expected to remove it; see *McFadyen v Annan*, 1992 S.L.T.163; *Normand v Rooney*, 1992 S.L.T.275. It is available also where the point is taken as a devolution issue under the Scotland Act, for which purpose it is not necessary for the person charged to show that he has suffered, or will suffer, any actual prejudice: *Dyer v Watson, K v HM Advocate* 2002 SLT 229, 245I-J, para 79. In *K v HM Advocate*, where a breach of the article 6 guarantee was established, the Board held that to dismiss the indictment was the only appropriate course in the circumstances. As Lord Rodger of

Earlsferry said, at p 262K, para 182, it was, in the circumstances of that case, the only effective remedy. But different considerations apply where the delay has occurred between the date of a conviction and an appeal. There is no precedent in domestic law for the setting aside of a conviction which has been upheld on appeal as a sound conviction on the ground that there was an unreasonable delay between the date of the conviction and the hearing of the appeal.

The circumstances of the present case provide a clear example of a situation where the setting aside of the conviction would be regarded in domestic law as both unjustified and unnecessary. It would be regarded as unjustified because the appellant's appeal against his conviction was, as the High Court of Justiciary said in this case, wholly without merit. No grounds exist for regarding the conviction itself as unsound, nor is there any question of its having been affected in any way by the delay. And the setting aside of the conviction would be regarded as unnecessary, because the effects of the delay can be recognised perfectly well by a reduction in the appellant's sentence. Here again we are on familiar ground, as delay in bringing the accused to justice is widely recognised as a mitigating factor that can be taken into account when he is being sentenced.

The way in which effect can be given to this mitigating factor is plain in the present case. The purpose of the reasonable time guarantee is to avoid a person charged remaining too long in a state of uncertainty about his fate: *Stögmüller v Austria* (1969) 1 EHRR 155, 191, para 5. It has been held that article 6 does not require the person charged to co-operate with the judicial authorities: *Eckle v Federal Republic of Germany* (1982) 5 EHRR 1, 30, para 82. The appellant was under no obligation to take steps to obtain an earlier hearing of his appeal, and it cannot be held against him that if he was concerned about the delay he should have made an application to the court. So the only matter that needs to be examined is the extent to which the appellant has been prejudiced by the delay. As Lord Coulsfield observed, it might perhaps be said that the delay involved two elements of prejudice to him: 2000 SLT 1359, 1363L–1364A, para 15. One was the anxiety resulting from prolongation of the proceedings. The other was that his life had changed during the period of the delay. This could lead to additional problems and possibly hardships for himself and his family if he had to return to prison. Taking account of all these factors the court held that a reduction in sentence of nine months, leaving him with about six months of the original sentence to serve before he became eligible for parole, would produce an equitable result.

The question then is whether there is anything in the jurisprudence of the European Court which suggests that the reduction in sentence which was held to be appropriate in domestic law would be regarded as providing the appellant with less than just satisfaction for the purposes of article 41 of the Convention. The jurisprudence of the European Court indicates very clearly that the fact that an appeal against conviction on a criminal charge has been held not to have been decided within a reasonable time does not mean that the execution of the sentence has become unlawful: *Bunkate v The Netherlands* (1993) 19 EHRR 477, 484, para 25. On the other hand, it has been held that a person may be deprived of his status as a victim within the meaning of article 34 of the Convention if the national authorities have acknowledged in a sufficiently clear way the failure to observe the reasonable time requirement and have afforded redress by reducing the sentence in an express and reasonable manner: *Eckle v Federal Republic of Germany* (1982) 5 EHRR 1, 24, para 66; *Beck v Norway*, Application No 26390/95, para 27. It seems to me that these two requirements have been fully satisfied in this case.

I would hold therefore that the decision of the High Court of Justiciary to reduce the appellant's sentence by nine months in order to compensate him for the effects of the delay was an appropriate and sufficient remedy. It meets with the requirements indicated by the jurisprudence of the European Court. I would dismiss the appeal."

V. "BY AN INDEPENDENT AND IMPARTIAL TRIBUNAL"

Starrs v Ruxton
2000 S.L.T. 42

On May 5, 1999 Hugh Starrs and James Chalmers (the accused), appeared for trial before Temporary Sheriff Crowe in Linlithgow Sheriff Court on a summary complaint. The simple issue addressed at length in this case was whether a temporary sheriff was an "independent and impartial tribunal" in the sense of Art.6(1) of the Convention.

> LORD JUSTICE CLERK (CULLEN): "7. The first appearance of the temporary sheriff on the legislative scene was with the enactment of section 11 of the Sheriff Courts (Scotland) Act 1971...
>
> 9. Section 11 of the 1971 Act, as amended and in force during the period with which this case is concerned, makes provision by subsections (1), (1A) and (1B) for the appointment of a temporary sheriff principal where there is a vacancy or the sheriff principal is unable to perform, or rules that he is precluded from performing, all or some part of his duties. Section 11 provides thereafter:
>
>> '(2) Where as regards any sheriffdom—
>>> (a) a sheriff is by reason of illness or otherwise unable to perform his duties as sheriff, or
>>> (b) a vacancy occurs in the office of sheriff, or
>>> (c) for any other reason, it appears to the Secretary of State expedient so to do in order to avoid delay in the administration of justice in that sheriffdom,
>> the Secretary of State may appoint a person (to be known as a temporary sheriff) to act as a sheriff for the sheriffdom.
>>
>> (3) A person shall not be appointed to be a temporary sheriff principal or a temporary sheriff unless he is legally qualified and has been so qualified—
>>> (a) in the case of an appointment as a temporary sheriff principal, for at least ten years;
>>> (b) in the case of an appointment as a temporary sheriff, for at least five years.
>>   . . .
>> (4) The appointment of a temporary sheriff principal or of a temporary sheriff shall subsist until recalled by the Secretary of State.
>>
>> (4A) No appointment under this section of a person to be a temporary sheriff principal or temporary sheriff shall extend beyond the day on which the person reaches the age of 70.
>>   . . .
>
> 11. For the assistance of the court the Solicitor General provided a useful description of the manner in which temporary sheriffs are appointed and used. That description related almost entirely to the period since May 1997 when the present Lord Advocate assumed office. Its content is not a matter of general public knowledge. The Solicitor General explained that the Scottish Executive had announced its intention to consider proposals for changing the system of appointment. No final decision had been made as to how that function should be exercised. The Scottish Executive intended to consult on that subject as a number of interests were involved. It would then be for the Scottish Parliament to determine what method of appointment should be adopted.
>
> 12. The description given by the Solicitor General of the existing method of appointment was as follows. Although the power of appointment was vested in the Secretary of State, in practice a crucial role was played by the Lord Advocate. The decision that there was a requirement for temporary sheriffs was taken by the Lord Advocate, acting on advice from

Scottish Courts Administration (now the Scottish Executive Justice Department). If a requirement for temporary sheriffs was identified, this was advertised in the Scots Law Times. Intimation was also given in writing to those who had previously expressed an interest. A file on each candidate was kept by the Scottish Courts Administration. While there might be a requirement for a particular number of temporary sheriffs, this was treated as a flexible figure. Application forms, which were introduced by the present Lord Advocate, were issued to those who had expressed an interest. They requested information about the applicant's professional qualifications, experience and other details. The applicant was also asked whether he or she had ever been convicted or engaged as a party in any proceedings. The latter question was intended, for example, to find out whether the applicant had been sequestrated or disqualified as a director. The applicant had to supply the names of two referees, one of whom was a member of the judiciary with experience of his or her work in court. The referee required to state whether in his or her opinion the applicant was a fit person to be appointed to be a temporary sheriff. The references were confidential. Some applicants were eliminated at this stage.

13. A list of applicants was then drawn up by the Lord Advocate with a view to their being interviewed. In doing so he took account of a number of factors, such as geographical spread, gender, expertise, breadth of experience, age and professional qualifications. The aim was to achieve an appropriate balance and, if possible, to divide the appointments equally between men and women and between advocates and solicitors. The present Lord Advocate had a policy of not normally appointing someone to be a temporary sheriff when he was over the age of 65. It was also relevant whether the applicant might be an appropriate person to receive a permanent appointment and should be given some experience on the bench prior to that. The Solicitor General pointed out that, in making recommendations for the appointment of permanent sheriffs, sheriffs principal set store by the fact that a person had previous experience in sitting as a temporary sheriff. In general, appointment to the shrieval bench was made nowadays from those who had gained that experience. Service as a temporary sheriff could be regarded as providing proof of suitability for a permanent appointment. A sheriff principal, normally sitting with a sheriff, interviewed the applicants. The same sheriff principal and sheriff did not interview all of them. A report of the interview was prepared and sent to Scottish Courts Administration, and in turn to the Lord Advocate with any additional comments which were thought appropriate. The applicants were assessed as appointable or non-appointable, and the appointable were graded according to whether they were regarded as exceptional, 'good plus' or good. Some candidates were not required to be interviewed. These were persons who had a particular standing or expertise, such as Queen's Counsel, Advocate deputes, solicitors who had held high office and academic lawyers. This was the practice which had been followed in the case of recent holders of the office of Lord Advocate. The rationale of this was to persuade persons who might otherwise not apply, and to have the benefit of their knowledge and experience, so enhancing the standard of temporary sheriffs. In the case of Advocate deputes who had finished their period in Crown Office, it might assist them in re-establishing their practice, as well as taking advantage of the experience which they had gained. In addition a number of retired sheriffs had been put forward in this way.

14. With the benefit of the reports from the sheriffs principal and comments by officials, the Lord Advocate drew up a list of provisional candidates for appointment. He consulted with the Solicitor General and, more importantly, with the Lord President, on whose advice he placed considerable reliance. The Lord Advocate would then forward the finalised list to Scottish Courts Administration for the appointments to be made.

15. The Solicitor General observed that as the number of temporary sheriffs had increased over the years, the method by which their appointment was arrived at had undergone some change. It had become more formal to some extent. Application forms and interviews had been introduced.

16. Since the present Lord Advocate had taken office there had been two rounds of applications and appointments. In 1997 there had been 180 applications. 49 candidates had

been interviewed. 24 appointments were made, and 8 further persons were appointed without being interviewed. In 1998 there were 77 applications. 26 candidates were interviewed. 23 appointments were made, and in addition 3 persons were appointed without being interviewed. In each case appointments were made in December for one year only, being the following calendar year. Accordingly the appointments made as the result of the round in 1998, including those of [the temporary sheriiffs involved in this case], will expire on 31 December 1999. A number of isolated appointments had also been made outwith these rounds. The court was provided with a copy of the terms in which the appointment or 'commission' of a temporary sheriff is expressed. It stated:

> 'In exercise of the powers conferred by section 11 of the Sheriff Courts (Scotland) Act 1971, the Secretary of State hereby appoints . . . being a person qualified to fill the office of temporary sheriff, to act as a temporary sheriff for the undernoted sheriffdoms and at such courts within the said sheriffdoms from time to time as the Secretary of State may direct. The appointment shall subsist until the Thirty First Day of December . . . unless previously recalled by the Secretary of State.'

Undernoted were the names of all the sheriffdoms in Scotland. The document was signed by the Deputy Director, Scottish Courts Administration, on behalf of the Secretary of State for Scotland.

17. The Solicitor General provided the court with some information which illustrated the growth in the use of temporary sheriffs. In 1985 there were 88 permanent sheriffs and 61 temporary sheriffs. At the present time the corresponding numbers were respectively 110 and 129 respectively. In the light of the above, of the 129 temporary sheriffs, about 26 appointments had been appointed for the first time in 1998, and the remainder were persons whose commissions had been renewed. In 1989/90 the proportion of work, in terms of court days, carried out by temporary sheriffs was a little over 18%. In 1998/9 it was just under 25%.

18. Before embarking on his duties the temporary sheriff took two oaths, namely the oath of allegiance and the judicial oath, before the Lord President. He also required to undertake five days of judicial training, including training in respect of judicial standards. In addition he had two days training during the course of his first year of appointment. Each month the temporary sheriff required to provide Scottish Courts Administration with a list of the days on which he would be available. When there was a requirement for a temporary sheriff in a particular sheriff court, the sheriff clerk at that court would phone a booking clerk in Scottish Courts Administration. This could arise at short notice. The booking clerk had a list of the temporary sheriffs who were available. There was no restriction on the work which a temporary sheriff could undertake, but the majority of cases on which they sat were summary criminal cases. However, they could and did undertake jury trials and fatal accident inquiries. The booking of a temporary sheriff for a particular day was not on the basis that he was particularly well qualified for the case or cases which were to be heard by him that day. The booking clerk was instructed to make work available as fairly as possible depending, of course, on who was available to sit. A temporary sheriff who was a solicitor was not allowed to sit in the sheriff court of the area in which he practised, and the booking clerk required to observe that rule. There was no similar rule in the case of advocates. The Solicitor General said that there was a variation in the amount of work which was done by the individual temporary sheriff, ranging from a minimum of twenty days *per annum* to those few who were sitting almost full-time. The organisation of the sheriff courts within the sheriffdom was a matter for the sheriff principal, who was given primacy in regard to both permanent and temporary sheriffs. Reference was made to sections 15–17 of the 1971 Act. The Solicitor General emphasised that neither the Lord Advocate nor the procurator fiscal had any control over whether a given case was taken by a permanent sheriff or a temporary sheriff. Neither had any say as to whether a temporary sheriff was allocated to a particular sheriffdom or sheriff court.

19. The Solicitor General went on to explain that the practice was for the Lord Advocate to consider the re-appointment of each temporary sheriff. In doing so, he offered to consult with the sheriffs principal, the sheriff clerks, the President of the Law Society and the Dean of the Faculty of Advocates. This offer was not always taken up. Thereafter he consulted the Lord President. While a temporary sheriff would normally be expected to be re-appointed, there were a number of grounds on which he would not be re-appointed. Each temporary sheriff was expected to serve for a minimum of twenty days *per annum*. This requirement might be waived if there was good reason, such as illness. The commission would not be renewed if the temporary sheriff did not want this to happen, or if he reached the age of 65, although it was open to him to make representations for the renewal of his commission, which could be successful. The age limit was introduced by the present Lord Advocate in 1998 when the commissions of the temporary sheriff who had reached that age were not renewed. Since May 1997 no commission had been recalled during its currency. The Solicitor General emphasised that the renewal of a commission was 'virtually automatic' provided that the temporary sheriff served at least 20 days during the year and remained under the age of 65 and there were no adverse circumstances relating to the fitness for office. If there was a serious issue as to the behaviour or private life of the temporary sheriff, he was informed that the commission would not be renewed and was given an explanation. The Solicitor General gave a number of examples of cases in which this course of action had been taken by the Lord Advocate. In one case the temporary sheriff made a statement to a police officer which gave rise to an allegation of criminal conduct on his part. Crown counsel decided that he should not be prosecuted. Some months before the expiry of his commission he was sent a letter informing him that in view of his admitted conduct it was not appropriate that he should be re-appointed. He contested this and a meeting was held at which representations were made on his behalf by counsel, but having taken advice the Lord Advocate confirmed his decision, and Scottish Courts Administration were informed that the temporary sheriff was not to be used during the remainder of the year. On another occasion two temporary sheriffs were removed as they were the subject of proceedings in regard to disqualification from holding office as company directors. In the case of one of them there was a failure to inform the Lord Advocate and officials of certain matters where there was a clear obligation to do so. In the case of the other, certain personal difficulties had reflected on the temporary sheriff's fitness to hold office. In a further case the commission was suspended due to the health and private life the temporary sheriff, but no decision was taken as to his removal. There was also a case during the time of a previous Lord Advocate in which a commission was not renewed where the temporary sheriff had been unable to deal with civil work. The Solicitor General accepted that while the Lord Advocate was concerned with the question whether a temporary sheriff was fit to carry out the duties of his office, he did not apply a particular test in arriving at his decision. He was not able to say that in every case a temporary sheriff who was not re-appointed received an explanation. His understanding was that over the years the practice in dealing with such cases had evolved. What had been done some years ago would not be followed today.

20. The Solicitor General was unable to explain why a period of one year had been chosen. He accepted that, in practice, the system was not one of 'temporary' appointments (other than in the sense that the appointments were formally for a period of one year, and lacked security of tenure), but was one of part-time appointments which were intended to be long-term.

21. The Solicitor General accepted that it was also possible for a temporary sheriff to be 'sidelined' without any formal recall or non-renewal of his appointment. In other words, a temporary sheriff could simply not be 'used', as a matter of administrative practice. There was a suggestion made on behalf of the appellants, on the basis of anecdotal material, that this had happened to individuals as a result of the attitude of officials towards them (see e.g. H.L. Deb, 6 March 1997, col. 2063; cf. col. 2083).

22. The Solicitor General explained that temporary sheriffs were paid *per diem* and did

not qualify for a pension, unlike permanent sheriffs, who received a salary and a pension. He accepted that some temporary sheriffs, but by no means all, were dependent on their earnings from that source. He also accepted that some temporary sheriffs were seeking preferment to permanent appointments as sheriffs. Most persons now appointed as permanent sheriffs had previously served as temporary sheriffs. Temporary sheriffs formed in effect a pool from which permanent appointments might be made, although not all permanent appointments came from that pool. If a person were to apply for a permanent appointment without having previously served as a temporary sheriff, then he might be encouraged to seek a temporary appointment first, effectively as a form of probationary service.

23. ... [Lord Cullen referred to article 6 and continued.] The discussion in this court was directed to both independence and impartiality. The court was referred to a number of decisions of the European Court of Human Rights and of the European Commission. In *Findlay* v *United Kingdom* (1997) 24 E.H.R.R. 221, at para. 73 the court stated that:

> 'In order to establish whether a tribunal can be considered as "independent", regard must be had *inter alia* to the manner of appointment of its members and their term of office, the existence of guarantees against outside pressures and the question whether the body presents an appearance of independence.
>
> As to the question of "impartiality", there are two aspects to this requirement. First, the tribunal must be subjectively free of personal prejudice or bias. Secondly, it must also be impartial from an objective viewpoint, that is, it must offer sufficient guarantees to exclude any legitimate doubt in this respect.'

Similar statements may be found in the earlier cases of *Bryan* v *United Kingdom* (1995) 21 E.H.R.R. 342, at para.37 and *Pullar* v *United Kingdom* (1996) S.C.C.R. 755, at para.30.

24. As can be seen from this quotation and the decided cases the question whether a tribunal is independent and impartial embraces the question whether it presents the appearance of independence from an objective standpoint. For example in *De Cubber* v *Belgium* (1984) 7 E.H.R.R. 326 the fact that one of the judges of the court which had given judgment on the charges against the applicant had previously acted as investigating judge gave rise to the misgivings as to the court's impartiality. In that case the court observed, at para.30, that:

> 'a restrictive interpretation of article 6(1)—notably in regard to the observance of the fundamental principle of the impartiality of the courts—would not be consonant with the object and purpose of the provision, bearing in mind the prominent place which the right to a fair trial holds in a democratic society within the meaning of the Convention'.

In a number of cases the court has found that lack of independence and lack of impartiality are inter-linked. Thus in *Bryan* v *United Kingdom* the court recognised that the fact that the appointment of an inspector, who had the power to determine a planning appeal in which the policies of the appointing minister might be in issue, could be revoked by the minister at any time gave rise to a question as to his independence and impartiality. In the circumstances, it did not fall foul of article 6(1) by reason of the scope of review which was available to the High Court in England. In *Findlay* v *United Kingdom* the court was satisfied that there was objective justification for doubts as to the independence and impartiality of the members of a court martial where they were subordinate to the convening officer who acted as the prosecutor. In that case the process of review did not provide an adequate guarantee. In *Çiraklar* v *Turkey*, 28 October 1998 the court observed that it was difficult to disassociate impartiality from independence where the members of a national security court included a military judge. While there were certain constitutional safeguards, the members of the court were still servicemen and remained subject to military discipline and assessment. Their term of office was only four years. In these circumstances the court held (at para. 40) that there was a legitimate fear of their being influenced by considerations which had nothing to do with the nature of the case. There was objective justification for fear of lack of independence and impartiality. [Lord Cullen considered the arguments for both parties and continued]:

43. I turn to consider the terms of appointment of the temporary sheriff, and in particular the implication of the fact that the appointment was limited to one year at a time...

44. It is clear that in other parts of the world time-limited appointments of judges have given cause for concern. In the present case it might have been a reassurance if the reasons for this period were at least consistent with concepts of independence and impartiality. However, as I have already noted, the Solicitor-General was not able to give any reason why that period had been selected. He suggested that it might have been due to the possibility of a drop in the number of temporary sheriffs who were needed. That suggestion lacks plausibility in view of the manifest expansion in the use of temporary sheriffs as the demands on the system as a whole have increased over the years. Rather than a control over numbers, the use of the one year term suggests a reservation of control over the tenure of office by the individual, enabling it to be brought to an end within a comparatively short period. This reinforces the impression that the tenure of office by the individual temporary sheriff is at the discretion of the Lord Advocate. It does not, at least *prima facie*, square with the appearance of independence.

45. Then there are what I have referred to as the restrictions applied by the Lord Advocate in determining whether a temporary sheriff qualifies for re-appointment. I refer to the minimum period of work which the temporary sheriff is expected to perform and the age limit of 65 years. For present purposes it does not matter that these do not form part of the terms of his appointment. What matters is that they clearly form part of the basis on which the temporary sheriff's prospective tenure of office rests. Neither is sanctioned by statute. They are matters of ministerial policy. They may change as one Lord Advocate succeeds another. As the Solicitor-General made clear, his description of the policy applied by the present Lord Advocate cannot be regarded as binding a successor. How such restrictions are applied is evidently a matter for his discretion, as the practice of the present Lord Advocate in regard to the age limit demonstrates. The tendency of these restrictions is significant. The first tends, if anything, to eliminate the temporary sheriff who would prefer to sit only occasionally, and to encourage the participation of those who are interested in promotion to the office of permanent sheriff, or at least in their re-appointment as a temporary sheriff. The second may also have a similar effect.

46. There was, in my view, some force in the submission ... that the limits imposed by section 11(4) and the terms of appointment might tend to encourage the perception that temporary sheriffs who were interested in their advancement might be influenced in their decision-making to avoid unpopularity with the Lord Advocate. These restrictions tend to support the same argument.

47. As against these factors it is, of course, necessary to pay full regard to what were presented by the Solicitor-General as the guarantees of independence and impartiality of the temporary sheriff. The fact that the judicial oath is taken by the temporary sheriff and that he undergoes the training to which he referred are matters of importance. So too is the high standard of professional behaviour which is expected of and shown by those who practice law in Scotland. The practice followed by the present Lord Advocate in the appointment of temporary sheriffs, his lack of any connection with the way in which temporary sheriffs are used and the criteria used by him in determining whether a temporary sheriff has ceased to be fit for office are also important considerations. There is no question whatever as to the integrity and fair mindedness with which the Lord Advocate has acted. However, what I have to consider is whether the basis on which the temporary sheriff holds office is truly independent, that is independent of the executive, whether it presents an appearance of such independence, and whether and to what extent the lack of the former gives rise to the appearance of lack of impartiality. I do not have difficulty with

the fact that temporary sheriffs are appointed by the executive, following upon their selection by the Lord Advocate. ... However, appointment by the executive is consistent with independence only if it is supported by adequate guarantees that the appointed judge enjoys security of tenure. It is clear that temporary sheriffs are appointed in the expectation that they will hold office indefinitely, but the control which is exercised by means of the one year limit and the discretion exercised by the Lord Advocate detract from independence.

48. Part of the judgment in *Valente v The Queen* (1985) 34 D.L.R. (4th) 161 is of some interest in this connection. At p.180 Le Dain J. referred to the fact that the provision for the re-appointment of a judge after his retirement had been challenged on the ground that, unlike his original appointment, it was during the pleasure of the executive and that complete pension entitlement depended on such re-appointment. He pointed out that the Ontario Court of Appeal had relied on the fact that during his seven years in office the Attorney General had always acted with respect to such re-appointments on the recommendation of the Chief Judge of the provincial court in question. That practice was referred to as 'tradition'. At p.182 he accepted that tradition, reinforced by public opinion, operating as an effective restraint upon the executive or legislative action, was undoubtedly a very important objective condition tending to ensure the independence in fact of a tribunal. At p.183, however, he went on to say:

'It is a question of the relative importance that one is going to attach to tradition in a particular context as ensuring respect for judicial independence despite an apparent or potential power to interfere with it. Moreover, while tradition reinforced by public opinion may operate as a restraint on the exercise of power in a manner that interferes with judicial independence, it cannot supply essential conditions of independence for which specific provision of law is necessary.

With the greatest respect for the contrary view, where, as in the case of Provincial Court judges at the time Judge Sharpe declined jurisdiction, the legislature has expressly provided for two kinds of tenure—one under which a judge may be removed from office only for cause and the other under which a judge of the same court holds office during pleasure—I am of the opinion that the second class of tenure cannot reasonably be perceived as meeting the essential requirement of security of tenure for purposes of section 11(d) of the [Canadian] Charter. The reasonable perception is that the legislature has deliberately, in the case of one category of judges, reserved to the executive the right to terminate the holding of office without the necessity of any particular justification and without any inhibition or restraint arising from perceived tradition. I am thus of the view that a judge of the Provincial Court (Criminal Division) who held office during pleasure could not be an independent tribunal within the meaning of section 11(d) of the Charter.'

49. This line of reasoning seems to me to be persuasive and to support the view that even when full allowance is made for the matters relied upon by the Solicitor-General, the power of recall under section 11(4) is incompatible with the independence and appearance of independence of the temporary sheriff. For the reasons which I have already indicated, I regard the one year limit to the appointment as being a further critical factor arriving at the same result. As regards the difference in the basis of payment as between a temporary and a permanent sheriff, I would not be disposed to regard this in itself as critical. Rather it illustrates the difference in status to which I have already referred. I also accept that in this case there is a link between perceptions of independence and perceptions of impartiality, of the kind which has been categorised in Canada as institutional impartiality. I consider that there is a real risk that a well-informed observer would think that a temporary sheriff might be influenced by his hopes and fears as to his perspective advancement. I have reached the view that a temporary sheriff ... was not an 'independent and impartial tribunal' within the meaning of article 6(1) of the Convention.

51. As I have already stated I hold that the terms of section 11(4) of the 1971 Act are incompatible with article 6(1) of the Convention."

LORD PROSSER: "7. Quite apart from the shortness of the period of appointment, and the fact that in any event it can be recalled at any time, the dependence of a temporary Sheriff on the Executive is in my opinion all the more apparent when one considers other features of these appointments. The appointments are described as 'part-time'. But they are not part-time in the ordinary sense, according to which an employee works, say, 20 hours per week. The temporary Sheriff is not only liable to be 'suspended', no longer being used at all during the currency of his appointment. The extent to which he is used, and thus the extent to which he is remunerated, appears to be entirely at the discretion of the Executive. In such circumstances, while at one level he can be said to have been appointed to the office and to retain it, at another and more practical level he can be regarded as effectively 'appointed' each time that he is in fact used. For the purposes of the present cases, it is not necessary or appropriate to embark upon an assessment of the merits or demerits of such a system. But it appeared that those who were most available were likely to be most used, and that appointment to the permanent office of Sheriff could depend substantially upon whether and how an individual had served as a temporary Sheriff. While these were put forward as reasonable and indeed advantageous aspects of the system, they provide another vivid illustration of a temporary Sheriff's dependence on the Executive.

8. Given that a permanent appointment to the Shrieval bench is dependent on long years of experience in legal practice, it is by no means clear to me that one should be required to have a trial period, on the bench, prior to such appointment. But the fact that temporary Sheriffs will apparently often be hoping for a permanent appointment, and that they hold office during this period with no assurance that they will be used or reappointed, far less given a permanent position, constitutes, to my mind, a quite extreme form of dependence. One must not be Utopian, and a hope of promotion, for example, is no doubt present in the minds of many judges in many systems. I would stop short of saying that this is a general basis for alleging 'dependence' on those who can promote. But the possibility of obtaining a better post makes it more, not less, important that there should be security of tenure at any particular level.

9. If a person is appointed to judicial office *ad hoc*, for a particular purpose, the length of his tenure may be of no significance: he will go, and go only, when he is *functus*. Equally, length of tenure may be of little importance when the office is not a step in a career, but is something done out of a sense of duty, or at the end of a career. But in the case of temporary Sheriffs, where the appointment is frequently a 'career move', the combination of a one-year appointment with liability to either recall or suspension or limited use is in my opinion wholly inconsistent with the requirement of independence.

10. However long and secure the tenure of a judicial office may normally be, irremovability cannot be absolute. In the classic terminology, the appointment will be *ad vitam aut culpam*. (If not for life, appointment should be for a period which can be identified without discretionary intervention). It is not necessary here to consider what types of conduct might, in any given system, be regarded as '*culpa*' for this purpose. But if a judge's independence is to be preserved, notwithstanding the fact that he can thus be removed, two things seem to me to be important. First, the question of what will be regarded as '*culpa*' cannot be left to the discretion of any person upon whom the judge should not in principle be dependent. And secondly even if the scope of *culpa* is known and determined, the question of whether *culpa* on the part of the judge has been established cannot be left to the discretion of such a person. Even if, in practice, temporary Sheriffs were only removed by procedures identical with those which govern the removal of permanent Sheriffs, the temporary Sheriff could not in my opinion be regarded as independent in the requisite sense: as in other respects, a practice is no substitute for a right.

11. I would add one final point. Like your Lordships, I am not suggesting in any way that there has ever been any impropriety, either on the part of temporary Sheriffs or on the part of any holder of any ministerial office, or of their officials. But I would add that if a judge is not independent, then however great his integrity, it may be very difficult for him to know whether his want of independence affects the way in which he carries out his judicial duties.

And however determined a Minister or public servant may be to carry out his functions in relation to the judiciary only on the basis of wholly appropriate considerations, it will be important for him to remember that his own confidence in his own integrity is not, and cannot be regarded as, a guarantee."

LORD REED: "32. In my opinion, the most important of the ... factors relied upon by the appellants is the absence of security of tenure. It was common ground before us that, as a matter of law, a temporary sheriff can be removed from office at any time for any reason. It was also common ground that a temporary sheriff can be appointed on an annual basis and that his allocation to courts, and the renewal of his appointment, are thereafter within the unfettered discretion of the Executive....

33. There can be no doubt as to the importance of security of tenure to judicial independence: it can reasonably be said to be one of the cornerstones of judicial independence. The critical importance of judicial security of tenure has been recognised in Scots law since at least the declaration in Article 13 of the Claim of Right 1689 (cap. 28, APS IX 38) that 'the changing the nature of the judges' gifts *ad vitam aut culpam* into commissions *durante beneplacito*' is 'contrary to law'. As Lord Blackburn said in *Mackay and Esslement v Lord Advocate*, 1937 S.L.T. 577:

'... if the office (being salaried) is judicial, then it is inconsistent with the common law nature of the office that its tenure should be precarious.'

Security of tenure is similarly treated as fundamental in numerous international instruments. ... So far as the European Convention is concerned, the importance of security of tenure is equally well recognised. In *Zand v Austria* (1978) 15 D.R. 70, for example, the Commission stated (at para. 80):

'... according to the principles of the rule of law in democratic states which is the common heritage of the European countries, the irremovability of judges during their term of office, whether it be for a limited period of time or for lifetime, is a necessary corollary of their independence from the Administration and thus included in the guarantees of article 6(1) of the Convention.' ...

39. The Solicitor General emphasised that it is inconceivable that the Lord Advocate would interfere with the performance of judicial functions. I readily accept that; but that is not the point. Judicial independence can be threatened not only by interference by the Executive, but also by a judge's being influenced, consciously or unconsciously, by his hopes and fears as to his possible treatment by the Executive. It is for that reason that a judge must not be dependent on the Executive, however well the Executive may behave: 'independence' connotes the absence of dependence. It also has to be borne in mind that judicial independence exists to protect the integrity of the judiciary and confidence in the administration of justice, and thus society as a whole, in bad times as well as good. The adequacy of judicial independence cannot appropriately be tested on the assumption that the Executive will always behave with appropriate restraint: as the European Court of Human Rights has emphasised in its interpretation of article 6, it is important that there be 'guarantees' against outside pressures. In short, for the judiciary to be dependent on the Executive flies in the face of the principle of the separation of powers which is central to the requirement of judicial independence in article 6. ...

42. ... Conceptions of constitutional principles such as the independence of the judiciary, and of how those principles should be given effect in practice, change over time. Although the principle of judicial independence has found expression in similar language in Scotland and England since at least the late seventeenth century, conceptions of what it requires in substance—of what is necessary, or desirable, or feasible—have changed greatly since that time. What was regarded as acceptable even as recently as 1971 may no longer be regarded

as acceptable. The effect given to the European Convention by the Scotland Act and the Human Rights Act in particular represents, to my mind, a very important shift in thinking about the constitution. It is fundamental to that shift that human rights are no longer dependent solely on conventions, by which I mean values, customs and practices of the constitution which are not legally enforceable. Although the Convention protects rights which reflect democratic values and underpin democratic institutions, the Convention guarantees the protection of those rights through legal processes, rather than political processes. It is for that reason that article 6 guarantees access to independent courts. It would be inconsistent with the whole approach of the Convention if the independence of those courts itself rested upon convention rather than law.

43. The Solicitor General's reliance upon the role of the Lord Advocate also appears to me to rest upon a number of assumptions which may or may not prove to be justified. The independent role of the Lord Advocate as public prosecutor is well understood. It has been specifically protected by the Scotland Act (in particular, by sections 27(3), 29(2)(e) and 48(5)), since it cannot be assumed that the conventions and practice observed in Whitehall or Westminster, or the existing law, will necessarily be preserved in the new Scottish context. The Lord Advocate's role in the appointment and removal of members of the judiciary is not mentioned in the Scotland Act (e.g. in section 95) and continues to rest on convention. As the Solicitor General acknowledged, it has not yet been decided how these matters will be dealt with in the new context...

46. My conclusion is fortified by the requirement under article 6 that the tribunal must present an appearance of independence. I understand this requirement to mean that the test of independence must include the question whether the tribunal should reasonably be perceived as independent. The importance of that question is that the tribunal must be one which commands public confidence: otherwise, to adopt the words of Le Dain J. in *Valente* (at 172), 'the system will not command the respect and acceptance that are essential to its effective operation'. Even if I were mistaken in my conclusion that the necessary objective guarantees of independence were lacking, it seems to me that the need for the temporary sheriff's appointment to be renewed annually at the discretion of the Executive, and his lack of security of tenure, are in any event factors which could give rise to a reasonable perception of dependence upon the Executive. The necessary appearance of independence is therefore in my opinion absent...

61. Before concluding this part of my Opinion, I wish to make it plain that I am not suggesting that any temporary sheriff has ever allowed his judicial conduct to be influenced by any consideration of how he might best advance his prospects of obtaining the renewal of his appointment, or his promotion to a permanent appointment. Nor am I suggesting that any official or Minister has ever sought to interfere with the judicial conduct of a temporary sheriff or would ever be likely to do so. There is however no objective guarantee that something of that kind could never happen; and that is why these appeals must succeed."

As discussed in Ch.2 above, amending legislation provides for the creation of a new category of part-time sheriffs: ss.11A to 11D of the Sheriff Courts (Scotland) Act 1971, inserted by the Bail, Judicial Appointments, etc (Scotland) Act 2000, s.7. The appointment and removal from office of part-time sheriffs are the subject of new provisions which have been designed to be compatible with the Convention rights. Part-time sheriffs are appointed for five years and can only be removed for "inability, neglect of duty or misbehaviour", but, as Lord Hope pointed out in *Millar v Dickson*, 2001 S.L.T. 988:

"the Scottish legal system now faces the not inconsiderable problem of dealing with objections which have been taken under the devolution legislation since *Starrs v Ruxton* to the disposal by temporary sheriffs of criminal cases under both solemn and summary procedure between 20 May 1999, when section 57(2) of the 1998 Act came into force, and 11 November 1999, when their use was terminated by the Scottish Executive."

One of these issues was considered in the *Millar* case itself which was concerned with the question whether an individual could waive his right to be tried by an independent and impartial tribunal. The matter arose here when the appellants challenged their convictions following a trial before a temporary sheriff. Could it be argued that they had waived their right to a fair trial by failing to raise an objection to being tried by a temporary sheriff at the beginning of the proceedings? The Privy Council thought not.

According to Lord Hope in the *Millar* case, the jurisprudence of the European Court of Human Rights "shows that this element of the right to a fair trial, like the right to a public hearing, is not so fundamental that it is incapable of being waived if all the circumstances which give rise to the objection are known to the applicant and the waiver is unequivocal". In this case, however, these requirements of a valid waiver were not made out, for the following reasons:

"The Strasbourg jurisprudence shows that, unless the person is in full possession of all the facts, an alleged waiver of the right to an independent and impartial tribunal must be rejected as not being unequivocal. It was not suggested that in any of the four cases which are before us the appellants' agents were not aware that the sheriff before whom the case had called was a temporary sheriff or of the statutory provisions under which they had been appointed. But no evidence has been produced by the prosecutor, on whom the onus lies, to show that they were aware of the system which had been developed by the executive for making and not renewing these appointments. A full description of this system was given to the court in *Starrs v Ruxton*, 2000 S.L.T. 42. But, as the Lord Justice-Clerk (Cullen) said, the content of that description was not a matter of general public knowledge."

Lord Hope concluded in these terms:

"The decision in *Starrs v Ruxton* leads therefore to this result. Temporary sheriffs, viewed objectively, lacked the quality of independence and impartiality to which all accused persons are entitled under article 6(1) of the Convention. This lack of independence and impartiality, however slight, was sufficient to disqualify temporary sheriffs from taking any part in the determination of criminal charges at the instance of prosecutors acting under the authority of the Lord Advocate. It also made it unlawful for prosecutors to conduct proceedings in the sheriff court under the authority of the Lord Advocate with a view to the determination of criminal charges by temporary sheriffs in that court. The Lord Advocate had no power to conduct those proceedings before them in that court, as this was incompatible with the accused's Convention right: section 57(2) of the 1998 Act. The proceedings were thus vitiated from the moment when they were brought before the temporary sheriffs for their determination. The Convention right and the statutory fetter which the 1998 Act has imposed on the powers of the Lord Advocate thus march hand in hand. Under the devolved system the disqualification of a tribunal whose objective independence or impartiality is vitiated gives rise, at once and at the same time, to a lack of competence on the part of the Lord Advocate."

The right to be tried before an independent and impartial tribunal does not have implications only for temporary sheriffs. Questions have also been asked about juries, lay magistrates and children's panels as the following cases show.

Montgomery v H M Advocate
2001 S.L.T. 37

This case arose from the notorious killing of Surjit Chhokar. A man called Ronnie Coulter was convicted of assaulting Mr Chhokar, and at the end of the trial, Lord McCluskey (the trial judge) criticised the failure to prosecute two other men in connection with the death. The two other men were David Montgomery and Andrew Coulter. Lord McCluskey's remarks were widely reported in the press, as was a response from the Lord Advocate. Montgomery and

Coulter were subsequently charged with murder, whereupon they moved to challenge the prosecution for violating their right to a fair trial under art.6 of the Convention. The basis of the challenge was that the pre-trial publicity was of such a nature that there was an objectively justified fear that the jury would not be impartial.

LORD HOPE OF CRAIGHEAD: "Their Lordships were provided with volumes containing photocopies of the various reports and articles which have appeared in the press since 10 March 1999 when publicity was first given to the remarks which Lord McCluskey made at the end of the trial of Ronnie Coulter and they were shown a video recording of the reports which have appeared on television news broadcasts by BBC Scotland and Scottish Television. The bulk of this material relates to the period between that date and 26th August 1999 when further publicity was prohibited by the order made under section 4 of the Contempt of Court Act 1981. The articles which had appeared by the time the case was heard by the Appeal Court were said to have numbered in all about 181. A number of articles appeared in the press subsequently during the period from 28 November 1999 to 18 February 2000 regarding the activities of the Chhokar Family Justice Campaign. On 10 January 2000 a public demonstration was held outside Parliament House within sight of those entering the court building, including potential jurors, which also attracted publicity in the press and on television.

The Lord Justice General (Rodger) set out in his opinion at pp. 63–66 some of the more significant passages from the articles which appeared in the press in order to give a flavour of what they contained. I do not need to repeat this exercise. It is sufficient to say that the volume of the material is very considerable, and the tabloid and broadsheet newspapers and television broadcasts in which it appeared have a wide circulation throughout Scotland. When account is taken of the types of the print media involved and the times of day when the television news items were broadcast, it can be assumed that the coverage which has been given to this case was observed and absorbed at one time or another by most of the adult population in Scotland during the relevant period. Various themes were developed as one story followed upon another. One of these was the public dispute between Lord McCluskey and the Lord Advocate. Another was the similarity which was believed to exist with the Stephen Lawrence case. The suggestion was made that the murder was the product of a racist attack and that the issue of race hung over the fact that the killers of Surjit Singh Chhokar had not been brought to trial and convicted. After the appellants were indicted on 2 July 1999 articles appeared which linked their indictment to the campaign for justice by the deceased's family. A report was published containing a comment by the deceased's father that two of his son's murderers had been let off and that the third had been found guilty only of assault.
...

The test
The common law test, which is applied where pre-trial publicity is relied upon in support of a plea of oppression, is whether the risk of prejudice is so grave that no direction by a trial judge, however careful, could reasonably be expected to remove it. The question was first expressed in these terms by Lord Justice General Emslie in *Stewart v H.M. Advocate* 1980 S.L.T. 245. In that case the question was whether there was a substantial risk of prejudice to the accused where an attempt had been made to interfere with a juror during the trial and the other jurors knew of the attempt. He adopted the same wording when he was describing in *Stuurman v H.M. Advocate*, 1980 S.L.T. 182 the special circumstances in which the High Court of Justiciary has power under the common law to intervene to prevent the Lord Advocate from proceeding upon an indictment:

'The special circumstances must indeed be such as to satisfy the Court that, having regard to the principles of substantial justice and of fair trial, to require an accused to face trial would be oppressive. Each case will depend on its own merits, and where the alleged oppression is said to arise from events alleged to be prejudicial to the prospects of fair trial the question for the Court is whether the risk of prejudice is so grave that no direction of the trial Judge, however careful, could reasonably be expected to remove it.'

That was a case where the basis for the plea of oppression was pre-trial publicity. The same test was applied in *X. v Sweeney*, 1983 S.L.T. 48, where the Lord Advocate's decision not to prosecute three youths for rape had received wide publicity and it was contended on their behalf that it would be oppressive for authority to be given for them to be prosecuted privately by the alleged victim. In *McFadyen v Annan*, 1992 S.L.T. 163 the same test was applied by a court of five judges in a case where a complaint was objected to on the ground of undue delay; see also *Normand v Rooney*, 1992 S.L.T. 275, which was another case in which undue delay was alleged.

In the present case the issue which has been raised is not that of oppression under the common law but of incompatibility with the appellants' right to a fair trial under article 6 of the Convention. Two question then arise. The first is what guidance is to be found as to the relevant test in the jurisprudence of the Strasbourg Court. The second is whether the test which was laid down in *Stewart* and in *Stuurman* for use in cases of alleged oppression can also be applied in cases of alleged incompatibility with the Convention right.

The Strasbourg jurisprudence

...

The jurisprudence of the Strasbourg court indicates that a distinction is to be drawn between a subjective and an objective approach to the question of impartiality: *De Cubber v Belgium* (1984) 7 E.H.R.R. 236, 243, para. 24; *Hauschildt v Denmark* (1990) 12 E.H.R.R. 266, 279, para. 46. It is not suggested that the issue in this case is capable of being solved by the application of the subjective test, which involves ascertaining the personal conviction of a given judge in a given case. It is not the practice in Scotland for members of the jury to be questioned about their personal convictions or any knowledge which they may have gleaned from reports in the media before being sworn to try the case: *Spink v H.M. Advocate*, 1989 S.C.C.R. 413, per Lord Justice General Emslie at p. 416; *Pullar v H.M. Advocate*, 1993 J.C. 126. The question is one which has to be resolved by means of the objective approach. As the Court put it in para. 24 of its judgment, this involves determining whether sufficient guarantees have been offered to exclude any legitimate doubt as to the judge's impartiality. In *Remli v France* (1996) 22 E.H.R.R. 253, 271, para. 46 the court said that what was decisive was whether the fear that a particular judge lacks impartiality can be objectively justified. In *Gregory v United Kingdom* (1997) 25 E.H.R.R. 577, 593, para. 45 the court again said that an objective test must be applied, and added that it must be ascertained whether sufficient guarantees exist to exclude any legitimate doubt in this respect.

Of particular significance in this case are the observations which the Court made in *Pullar v United Kingdom* (1996) 22 E.H.R.R. 391, as that was a case in which it examined the issue of impartiality with regard to a criminal case which had been tried by a Scottish jury (for a report of the Scottish proceedings, see *Pullar v H.M. Advocate*, 1993 J.C. 126). At p. 402, para. 30 the Court said:

'It is well established in the case law of the court that there are two aspects to the requirement of impartiality in article 6(1). First, the tribunal must be subjectively impartial, that is, no member of the tribunal should hold any personal prejudice or bias. Personal impartiality is to be presumed unless there is evidence to the contrary. Secondly, the tribunal must also be impartial from an objective viewpoint, that is, it must offer sufficient guarantees to exclude any legitimate doubt in this respect.'

Commenting further on the principle that a tribunal shall be presumed to be free of personal prejudice or partiality at p. 403, para. 32, the court said:

'It reflects an important element of the rule of law, namely that the verdicts of a tribunal should be final and binding unless set aside by a superior court on the basis of irregularity or unfairness. This principle must apply equally to all forms of tribunal, including juries.

Although in some cases, not least the present, it may be difficult to procure evidence with which to rebut the presumption, it must be remembered that the requirement of objective impartiality provides a further important guarantee.'

At pp. 404–405, paras. 37–41 of its judgment in *Pullar* the court applied these principles to the facts of the case. The argument was directed to the fact that the jury which convicted the appellant included an employee of a key prosecution witness. That the question is one of fact and degree, taking account of the available safeguards, emerges clearly from what the court said in paragraphs 37–38 and 40–41:-

'37. It is recalled that P's misgivings as to the impartiality of the tribunal were based on the fact that one member of the jury, F, was employed by the firm in which the prosecution witness, M, was a partner. Understandably, this type of connection might give rise to some anxiety on the part of an accused. However, the view taken by the accused with regard to the impartiality of the tribunal cannot be regarded as conclusive. What is decisive is whether his doubts can be held to be objectively justified.
38. The principle of impartiality is an important element in support of the confidence which the courts must inspire in a democratic society. However, it does not necessarily follow from the fact that a member of a tribunal has some personal knowledge of one of the witnesses in a case that he will be prejudiced in favour of that person's testimony. In each individual case it must be decided whether the familiarity in question is of such a nature and degree as to indicate a lack of impartiality on the part of the tribunal. . .
40. In addition, regard must be had to the fact that the tribunal offered a number of important safeguards. It is significant that F was only one of 15 jurors, all of whom were selected at random from amongst the local population. It must also be recalled that the sheriff gave the jury directions to the effect that they should dispassionately assess the credibility of all the witnesses before them, and that all of the jurors took an oath to a similar effect.
41. Against this background, P's misgivings about the impartiality of the tribunal which tried him cannot be regarded as being objectively justified.'

These passages indicate that the decisive question is whether the doubts which the appellants have raised about the impartiality of the tribunal can be held to be objectively justified, and that in a case which is to be tried under the solemn procedure the 'tribunal' includes not only the jury but also the trial judge. Thus the question is not confined to the residual effect of the publicity on the minds of each of the jurors. Account must also be taken of the part which the judge will play in order to ensure, so far as possible, that the appellants will receive a fair trial. An examination of the measures which he can take under the system which has been laid down for the conduct of criminal jury trials forms an important part of the whole exercise.

. . .

Reference was also made to *Baragiola v Switzerland* (1993) 75 D.R. 76. In that case the Commission observed, at p. 120, that, while particular importance should be attached to the freedom of the press because of the public's right to information, a fair balance must nevertheless be struck between that freedom and the right to a fair trial guaranteed by article 6 of the Convention and that a restrictive interpretation of article 6(1) would not correspond to the aim and purpose of that provision. As I understand these observations, however, they were intended to emphasise the point that primacy must be given to the right to a fair trial. Article 6, unlike articles 8 to 11 of the Convention, is not subject to any words of limitation. It does not require, nor indeed does it permit, a balance to be struck between the rights which it sets out and other considerations such as the public interest. In so far as the *Baragiola* case may be taken as suggesting that in the application of article 6(1) a balance must be struck between the right of the individual to a fair trial and the freedom of the press or the public's right to information, I would be inclined not to follow it on the ground that this suggestion is inconsistent with the wording of the Convention. The suggestion is not, so far as I am aware, supported by any other authority.

The 'Stuurman' test

Although the Strasbourg jurisprudence indicates clearly that it is appropriate to have regard to the available safeguards, it does not lay down in any precise way the test which is to be applied in order to determine whether these safeguards can be relied upon to fulfil the requirement that the impartiality of the tribunal can be objectively justified. In the Court of Appeal the Lord Justice General (Rodger) said that, taking a cross-bearing by applying the *Stuurman* test, he would have reached substantially the same result if the appellants had chosen to advance their argument under the cover of a plea of oppression. Lord Coulsfield however expressed some doubts on this point.

There appear to be two reasons for doubting the utility of the *Stuurman* test, in the circumstances of the present case, as a means of solving the question which has been raised about the tribunal's impartiality. The first relates to the wording of the test itself, as it relates only to the effect of directions to be given by the trial judge. The second relates to the question raised by Lord Coulsfield as to whether a test which was designed to deal with cases of oppression is appropriate for use in the article 6 context, in view of dicta which indicate that the concept of oppression involves a balancing exercise which is not appropriate in the context of the article 6 right to a fair trial.

As regards the first reason, it will be recalled that the test was originally formulated in *Stewart v H.M. Advocate*, 1980 S.L.T. 245. That was a case where, close to the end of a long trial, one of the jurors was approached by a person claiming to be the brother of one of the accused, who offered her a bribe. She attempted to raise the matter with the trial judge the next day. The trial judge, due to a misunderstanding of the nature of her concern, told her to discuss the matter with the other jurors and to tell him if she still thought that it was important. She was seen later by both the clerk of court and the trial judge, when the true nature of her concern was revealed to them. She told them that she had discussed the matter with the other jurors. The only way in which a possible miscarriage of justice could be averted was by means of a direction by the trial judge. He directed the remaining members of the jury to put any information which they may have been given out of their minds when considering the evidence and what their verdicts were to be on that evidence. In that context the test was directed to the only issue in the case, which was whether the direction was a sufficient safeguard.

In *Stuurman v H.M. Advocate*, 1980 S.L.T. 182 the test was applied to a case of pre-trial publicity. The directions which the trial judge gave to deal with this matter were not said to have been defective in any way. The argument was that no direction by the trial judge, however careful, could reasonably be expected to remove the risk of prejudice to the fair trial. The reasons which the Lord Justice General (Emslie) gave for rejecting this argument were these:

'The publications occurred almost four months before the trial diet was called. In considering the effect of these publications at the date of the trial the Court was well entitled to bear in mind that the public memory of newspaper articles and news broadcasts and of their detailed contents is notoriously short and, that being so, that the residual risk of prejudice to the prospects of fair trial for the applicants could reasonably be expected to be removed by careful directions such as those which were in the event given by the trial Judge.'

This passage indicates that, when the test is being applied in practice, all the circumstances of the case require to be taken into account. It is only by having regard to all the circumstances that it can be determined whether the directions by the trial judge can reasonably be expected to remove the prejudice. This point is illustrated also by its application in *McFadyen v Annan*, 1992 S.L.T. 163. The three matters to which Schiemann L.J. referred in paragraph (10) in *Attorney General v MGN Ltd* [1997] 1 All E.R. 456, 461B—the length of time since publication, the focusing effect of listening to evidence over a prolonged period and the likely effect of the directions by the trial judge—are all taken into account in practice in the application of the *Stuurman* test in cases of alleged oppression due to pre-trial publicity. Applied in this way the test is, in my opinion, well suited for use in the context of a complaint which is made under article 6(1) of the Convention. It fits in well with the approach which the Strasbourg court took to this matter in *Pullar v United Kingdom* (1996) 22 E.H.R.R. 391.

The other reason for doubting its utility is based largely on passages from *X. v Sweeney*, 1983 S.L.T. 48 which, as Lord Coulsfield pointed out, suggest that when the test is applied a balancing exercise has to be performed between the risk of oppression and the public interest that justice should be done and should be seen to be done. In the common law context a balancing exercise of this kind has been applied in practice for many years. Its origin can be traced back at least as far as a series of cases dealing with the admissibility of evidence irregularly obtained. In the seven judge case of *Lawrie v Muir*, 1950 S.L.T. 37 Lord Justice General Cooper said:

'From the standpoint of principle it seems to me that the law must strive to reconcile two highly important interests which are liable to come into conflict—(a) the interest of the citizen to be protected from illegal or irregular invasions of his liberties by the authorities, and (b) the interest of the State to secure that evidence bearing upon the commission of crime and necessary to enable justice to be done shall not be withheld from Courts of law on any merely formal or technical ground.'

In *H.M. Advocate v Hepper*, 1958 S.L.T. 160 Lord Guthrie observed that the Lord Justice-Clerk, Lord Thomson, had repeatedly pointed out in recent years that the problem is always to reconcile the interest of society in the detection of crime with the requirement of fairness to an accused person.

In *X. v Sweeney* the issue was whether the massive publicity that had been given to criticisms of the Lord Advocate for not prosecuting the respondents in a case of alleged rape made it impossible for them to receive a fair trial if they were to be prosecuted by the alleged victim privately. The Lord Justice General (Emslie) said that, while he had not forgotten the public interest in securing a fair trial of accused persons, the public interest in the administration of justice and the detection and trial of alleged perpetrators of crime was matter to which great weight had to be given as the crimes alleged were of a particularly serious and horrible nature. Lord Avonside said, in regard to the public interest that justice should be done and be seen to be done and the interest of the respondents, the interest of justice must be paramount. Lord Cameron, while concurring in the result, appears to have taken a different view as to where the balance lay. He said that, while there was a public interest of paramount and permanent importance in the detection and suppression of crime, it was of equal importance that those charged with crime should receive a fair and impartial trial. Nevertheless it is clear that in that case the public interest that justice should be done—which is what much of the publicity in the present case also has been about—played a significant part in the decision.

In my opinion this feature of the case of *X. v Sweeney* does not deprive the *Stuurman* test of its utility in the article 6(1) context. It is sufficient, in order to preserve its integrity for this purpose, that it should be recognised that in the application of article 6(1) to the facts of the case there is no such balancing exercise. The right of the accused to a fair trial by an independent and impartial tribunal is unqualified. It is not to be subordinated to the public interest in the detection and suppression of crime. In this respect it may be said that the Convention right is superior to the common law right.

It needs to be emphasised, as was pointed out in *Pullar v United Kingdom* (1996) 22 E.H.R.R. 391, that the rule of law lies at the heart of the Convention. It is not the purpose of article 6 to make it impracticable to bring those who are accused of crime to justice. The approach which the Strasbourg court has taken to the question whether there are sufficient safeguards recognises this fact. It does not require the issue of objective impartiality to be resolved with mathematical accuracy. It calls instead for 'sufficient' guarantees or safe-guards and for the exclusion of any 'legitimate doubt': *Pullar v United Kingdom*, pp. 402–403, 405 paras. 30, 40. Account is taken of the fact that certainty in these matters is not achievable. That said, however, the only question to be addressed in terms of article 6(1) of the Convention is the right of the accused to a fair trial. An assessment of the weight to be given to the public interest does not come into the exercise. Provided this point of principle is recognised, I see no reason why the *Stuurman* test should not continue to be used in this context. The logical justification for doing so is that it directs attention to the effectiveness of the principal measures—short of deserting the diet *pro loco et tempore*—which the tribunal itself can provide. The likely effect of any warnings or directions given to the jury by the trial judge, in the light of the other circumstances of the trial, will in most cases be the critical issue.

The result in the present case

I am not persuaded that the judges in the court below were in error in their assessment of the effect of the publicity that has been given to this case and of the question whether, despite that publicity, the jury can be expected to act impartially. Recent research con-ducted for the New Zealand Law Commission suggests that the impact of pre-trial publicity and of prejudicial media coverage during the trial, even in high profile cases, is minimal: Warren Young, Neil Cameron and Yvette Tinsley, *Juries in Criminal Trials; Part Two*, Chapter 9, para. 287 (New Zealand Law Commission preliminary paper no. 37, November 1999). The lapse of time since the last exposure may increasingly be regarded, with each month that passes, in itself as some kind of a safeguard. Nevertheless the risk that the widespread, prolonged and prejudicial publicity that occurred in this case will have a residual effect on the minds of at least some members of the jury cannot be regarded as negligible. The principal safeguards of the objective impartiality of the tribunal lie in the trial process itself and the conduct of the trial by the trial judge. On the one hand there is the discipline to which the jury will be subjected of listening to and thinking about the evidence. The actions of seeing and hearing the witnesses may be expected to have a far greater impact on their minds than such residual recollections as may exist about reports about the case in the media. This impact can be expected to be reinforced on the other hand by such warnings and directions as the trial judge may think it appropriate to give them as the trial proceeds, in particular when he delivers his charge before they retire to consider their verdict.

The judges in the court below relied on their own experience, both as counsel and as judges, of the way in which juries behave and of the way in which criminal trials are conducted. Mr. O'Grady [for Coulter] submitted that there was no basis upon which one could assess the likely effect of any directions by the trial judge. He said that this was something that was incapable of being proved. But the entire system of trial by jury is based upon the assumption that the jury will follow the instructions which they receive from the trial judge and that they will return a true verdict in accordance with the evidence.

The Scottish judges are not alone in proceeding upon this assumption. In the Supreme Court of Canada, in *R. v Corbett* [1988] 1 S.C.R. 670, 692, Dickson C.J. said that jury directions are often long and difficult but that the experience of trial judges is that juries do perform their duty according to law. In *R. v Vermette* (1988) 50 D.L.R. (4th) 385, 392 La Forest J., under reference to the *Corbett* case, said that dicta in that case underlined the confidence that may be had in the ability of a jury to disabuse itself of information that it is not entitled to consider. In the High Court of Australia, in *The Queen v Glennon* (1992) 173 C.L.R. 592, 603 Mason C.J. and Toohey J. said that the law proceeds on the footing that the jury, acting in accordance with the instructions given to them by the trial judge, will render a true verdict in accordance with the evidence and that to conclude otherwise would be to underrate the integrity of the system of trial by jury and the effect on the jury of the instructions given by the trial judge. In the Irish High Court, in *Z v Director of Public Prosecutions* [1994] 2 I.R. 476, 496 Hamilton P., drawing upon his experience as counsel and as a judge, said that he shared in the confidence that his legal system has in juries to act with responsibility in accordance with the terms of their oath, to follow the directions given by the trial judge and a true verdict give in accordance with the evidence. I consider that the judges in the court below were entitled to draw upon their experience, and I see no reason in the light of my own experience to disagree with their assessment.

For these reasons the answer which I would give to the devolution issue is that the acts of the Lord Advocate which are complained of in this case are not incompatible with the appellants rights under article 6(1) of the Convention, as the careful directions which the judge may be expected to give to the jury in the course of the trial will be sufficient to remove any legitimate doubt that may exist at this stage about the objective impartiality of the tribunal. I would dismiss the appeal."

So far as lay magistrates are concerned, the issue arose in *Clark v Kelly*, 2003 S.L.T. 308 where objection was taken to the fact that the lay magistrates in the district courts are advised by legally qualified clerks appointed by the local authorities. Guidance on the role of the clerk provides as follows:

"2. The clerk is not a member of the court, and does not share the courts responsibility for its decisions. He is an official who is appointed and employed, on a full-time or part-time basis, by the local authority. He must be an advocate or solicitor. The post may be held by the same person who undertakes the duties of clerk of the peace.

[Note: the functions of the clerk of the peace, who acts as clerk to the justices of the area as a body, are set out in s.18(4) of the District Courts (Scotland) Act 1975.]

3. It is the clerk's duty, by statute, to advise the justices, either at their request or on his own initiative, on matters of law, practice and procedure, and so he is able to guard them against making mistakes, especially in respect of some of the technicalities of procedure and evidence. He does not offer judgement. Normally, he does not question witnesses although he may suggest questions to the justice. Unless there is good reason for not doing so, justices should accept the clerk's advice on procedural and legal matters. While some cases involve no special difficulties and can be decided without reference to the clerk for advice, there are occasions when there are legal arguments or difficulties in interpreting an Act of Parliament. At these times it is best that the justice retires for consultation with the clerk. However, the clerk takes no part in deliberations on conviction and sentence. On sentencing he is usually only concerned to advise on the powers of the court, though on occasions justices may be informed as to the level of penalty generally imposed by the court."

Three concerns were raised about the role of the clerk by counsel for the accused: "First, he submits that the clerk of court is in law part of the tribunal for the purposes of article 6(1) and that, as he lacks the security of tenure which is necessary to ensure his independence, the district court cannot be said to be an independent tribunal within the meaning of the article. Secondly, he submits that the practice by which advice on matters of law, practice and procedure is communicated privately by the clerk of court to the justices infringes the accused's right to a fair and public hearing. Thirdly, he submits that, if the clerk of court is not part of the tribunal, the district court surrenders its independence in accepting advice from someone who is not part of that court". As was pointed out, if these arguments were sound, no district court in Scotland could meet the requirements of art.6(1) except one which is presided over by a stipendiary magistrate. The Privy Council was clearly reluctant to face this prospect and it was held that the role of the clerk did not breach the Convention rights of the accused. However, Lord Hope did suggest that practice in the district court should be amended:

> "I suggest that the practice which should be followed by the clerks and justices in the district court in this matter should be as follows. Any advice which the clerk gives to the justice in private on matters of law, practice or procedure should be regarded by them as provisional until the substance of that advice has been repeated in open court and an opportunity has been given to the parties to comment on it. The clerk should then state in open court whether that advice is confirmed or is varied, and if it is varied in what respect, before the justice decides to act upon it. It would be helpful if guidance on this matter could be incorporated in the handbook and brought to the attention of justices and clerks by issuing an appropriate circular. It will, of course, be open to the parties to bring such guidance to the attention of the court if there is reason to think that it is not being observed by either the justice or the clerk at the trial. I would hold that, if these steps are taken in this case when it comes to trial, the giving of advice by the clerk to the justice will be compatible with the accused's Convention rights."

In other cases it has been held that the composition of children's panels does not violate art.6 (1), though it has also been held that the procedure before the panels violates art.6(3). See respectively *S v Millar*, 2002 S.L.T. 531, and *S v Millar (No. 2)*, 2002 S.L.T. 1304. These cases tend to confirm a degree of restraint on the part of the courts post *Starrs v Ruxton*, 2000 S.L.T. 42. The same restraint is to be found in the decision to reject a challenge to the planning system which allows major decisions affecting private property to be made by Ministers.

VI. CONCLUSION

The right to a fair trial in art.6 of the ECHR has thus given rise to extensive litigation at the highest level and to a significant body of case law, some of which has had important constitutional consequences. There are three major points which may be made by way of conclusion. The first is that in the earliest decisions the courts expressed a strong commitment to judicial independence, forcing a major rewriting of the arrangements for the appointment of part-time sheriffs. However, the robustness of the language used in that case in support of the principle of judicial independence has not been reflected in other cases where attempts have been made to challenge the independence of juries, district courts or children's panels. The difficulties which that case created in the early burst of enthusiasm may have led the courts to be more cautious about any future forays of this magnitude. Nevertheless it is difficult not to be impressed by the reluctance of the Privy Council to reclaim some ground in *Millar v Dickson* by rejecting what would have been an important limitation of the practical implications of the decision in *Starrs v Ruxton* without undermining its prospective impact.

The second point to emerge is the importance of legal formalism in the protection of Convention rights generally and the right to a fair trial in particular. This has been brought out most clearly in the debates about the right to be tried within a reasonable time. Here we find that proceedings under the Scotland Act 1998 have driven some members of the Privy Council to give a more effective protection to the right than might otherwise be the case in proceedings brought under the Human Rights Act 1998. The different route for bringing cases to court has thus had a real practical impact on the quality of the right of the accused. This last point is perhaps most visible in Lord Hope of Craighead's approach in the decision of the House of Lords in *Attorney-General's Reference (No. 2 of 2001)* [2003] UKHL 68, where he emphasised the importance of the different wording of the Scotland Act 1998, s.57 which says that Ministers have no power to act in breach of Convention rights. This contrasted with the Human Rights Act 1998, s.6 which says that it is unlawful for a public authority to breach Convention rights.

The third point is that apart from these two very important questions, art.6 has not otherwise been used radically to re-write either criminal or civil procedure. Although art.6 has been raised in a large number of cases to deal with a wide range of issues, the courts have generally found procedure to be consistent with its obligations. This is an important perspective to bear in mind when reflecting on the headline grabbing decisions in cases like *Starrs v Ruxton*, or the tensions revealed in *R. v H M Advocate*. Although Convention rights have generated matters of great constitutional significance in these cases, and although art.6 is by some way the most frequently used of all the Convention rights, it is nevertheless the case that art.6 claims are more likely to fail than to succeed in the cases where they are raised. This applies to matters as varied as self-incrimination, the nature of the evidence led against an accused and the conduct of juries. Scottish judges have not been readily willing to say that the common law rules over which they preside are an insufficient guarantee of a fair trial. Given the importance of fairness as a principle of the common law, this is not surprising.

Chapter 6

THE RIGHT TO PRIVACY

I. INTRODUCTION

Our concern in this chapter is with the right to privacy. An immediate problem, however, is that privacy is extremely difficult to define, and a comprehensive definition evaded the Younger Committee which had been established to examine the issue in the 1970s (Report of the Committee on Privacy, Cmnd 5102, 1972, paras 57 to 59). The principal reason for the problem is that privacy is a genus which offers shelter for many different species of interests. This can be demonstrated by the case law of the European Court of Human Rights on Art.8 of the ECHR which protects the right to private life, home and correspondence. The case law deals with a diverse range from sexuality, to the misuse of personal information, to telephone tapping, to the use of bugging devices, to the search of private property, to the activities of the security service. There are also issues relating to adoption and family life generally. The issue is complicated further by the fact that invasions of privacy are perpetrated not only by the state and its agents, but also by newspapers which are powerful commercial interests trading in current affairs as a commodity in pursuit of profit.

The task then is to present a chapter on privacy which is not only comprehensive but also coherent. Here we have chosen to focus on the private life of the individual and a series of different restraints on privacy which might be said to be progressively more invasive. We begin with surveillance, moving to the regulation of investigatory powers and from there to the interception of communications. From there we move to eavesdropping on individuals by means which require the covert entry onto property, and from there to the overt entry, search and seizure of property. In the final section we conclude with the question of unwanted publicity about an individual. The first of these questions of privacy is likely to arise as a result of the activities of both public authorities and private parties (such as employers, newspapers or insurance companies) while the second to the fifth of these categories are likely to arise mainly as a result of the activities of public authorities, such as the police or the security services. However, we should not be complacent in thinking that private bodies (such as insurance companies, newspapers and employers) do not indulge or have not indulged in surveillance or telephone tapping where their interests so dictate. In recent years the question of unwanted publicity is one that has been raised mainly as a result of the conduct of the press, though there are cases where the police have published photographs of suspects or otherwise disclosed information about individuals (*e.g.* that they have been convicted of sexual offences relating to children: *R. v Chief Constable of North Wales Police ex p. Thorpe* [1999] Q.B. 396).

II. SURVEILLANCE

One way by which the privacy of the individual may be violated is by way of surveillance, whether by public authorities or by private parties. Public authorities in the form of the security service or the police may engage in surveillance techniques for a number of reasons, notably the prevention and detection of crime. Private parties may engage in surveillance for a number of reasons, but perhaps to discover evidence of marital infidelity or evidence against a party in legal proceedings. The forms of surveillance vary, and include (1) the interception of telephone calls and mail; (2) the use of bugging or eavesdropping devices, (3) following an individual or watching his or her property, (4) photographing an individual or his or her property, and (5) the use of informers. By no means all of these practices will be unlawful at common law, for not all will involve the violation of any personal or property rights of the individual.

Robertson v Keith
1936 S.L.T. 9

Mrs Margaret Robertson, a chemist in Rutherglen, brought this action against the Chief Constable of Lanarkshire. The Chief Constable had arranged, for a period of five days, a continuous watch to be placed on the pursuer's house in order to establish the whereabouts of a member of his force, Detective Inspector Anderson. He had taken leave of absence and had given a false address as to where he might be found during his absence. This was regarded as a serious breach of discipline.

The pursuer claimed damages "for loss suffered through the wrongful and illegal actings of the defender." She also claimed damages for defamation, averring that the presence of the police near her house gave rise to alarming rumours, and that her neighbours, acquaintances and customers were led to believe that she had committed serious criminal offences. As a result of these rumours, she claimed that she "suffered in her feelings" and that her "business was very seriously injured." The Lord Ordinary (Moncrieff) assoilzied the defender, and his decision was upheld by a unanimous bench of seven judges.

THE LORD PRESIDENT (NORMAND): "The pursuer maintained that the defender was liable in damages because the watch which he set for the purpose of discovering the whereabouts of Detective Inspector Anderson was an unwarranted and unlawful invasion of the pursuer's rights, and her counsel sought to equiparate the alleged wrong with a wrongful arrest by the police. It is not doubtful that any unwarranted and unlawful proceeding by a public officer resulting in injury to anyone will subject him to liability, and that in such a case proof of malice and want of probable cause is not required of the pursuer. The first question, therefore, is whether the action of the defender in ordering the watch to be set falls into this category. It was admitted and it is, I think, the law that if the watch had been set in the course of investigating a crime, and if it had led to some injury to the pursuer, she would have had no case unless she could prove malice and want of probable cause. The protection which is thus given to the police and other public officials acting in the exercise of their duty is a privilege founded on the public interest (*Beaton v Ivory*, 1887 14 R. 1057), for it is of the highest importance that public officials should not be hindered in their duty by fears of incurring liability for damages if their conduct is subsequently impugned as indiscreet or imprudent or going beyond what the immediate necessities required. It was said, however, by pursuer's counsel that this privilege does not extend to the Chief Constable when he is acting under the powers vested in him for the maintenance of the discipline of the force. It would be strange if this distinction were valid, for the public interest is as deeply involved in the maintenance of the discipline of the police as it is in the investigation of any particular crime, though members of the public are not concerned in the actual maintenance of discipline in the way in which they may be concerned in the prevention or detection of crime. The Chief Constable is clearly acting in his public capacity whether he is exercising his disciplinary powers or his powers for the preservation of order and the prevention and detection of crime. In my opinion his privilege is the same in either case, and I think that the authorities are consistent with this principle (*McMurchy v Campbell*, 1887 14 R. 725; *Innes v Adamson*, 1889, 17 R. 11). If, therefore, it was lawful for the defender to set a watch for Anderson at or about a place where he thought he might be found, he is entitled to the protection implied in requiring the pursuer to prove malice and want of probable cause. Nor does it seem doubtful that the setting of a watch was within the defender's legal powers and an exercise of his powers and duties of discipline in relation to Anderson. There are averments that the police officers engaged on the watch committed trespass, and we were told that the watch amounted to an invasion of the pursuer's personal freedom and that it was an infringement of the law of neighbourhood, by which I understood counsel to mean that it amounted to a nuisance. But there is no proof that the watch instructed by the defender involved any wrongous act of any kind, nor that any trespass, invasion of the pursuer's personal liberty, or nuisance was committed. I accept the Lord Ordinary's findings of fact on the nature and incidents of the watch which was kept, and I agree with him that nothing was done beyond what was necessary if the watch was to be effective. I accordingly hold that the defender is entitled to the protection that the pursuer must prove malice and want of probable cause.

An argument was presented that malice should be inferred from the circumstances under which the watch was set. It was said that there was no urgent necessity to find Anderson, and that the Chief Constable might, have remained inactive till he returned to duty, as he did a few days later. It was further said that it was unreasonable to continue the watch from the Wednesday till the Monday morning when Anderson reported for duty, and that it could have been anticipated that a watch so long continued would cause annoyance to the pursuer and might give rise to public rumour hurtful to her reputation. The action of the defender was characterised as extravagant and unreasonable, and it was said that an inference of malice fell to be drawn from the circumstances to which I have referred. The reply made to this in law was that if what the defender did was an exercise of his disciplinary power and was unaccompanied by any unlawful act, the incidents of this lawful course of action could not be used to build up against him evidence of malice, and that if malice is to be established, extrinsic facts must be averred and proved.

In my view the question of malice is essentially a question of good faith. It has to be remembered that in order to succeed the pursuer has to prove both malice and want of probable cause. If there were proof of want of probable cause for any of the acts complained of, even though these acts were all of them singly within the lawful competence of the Chief Constable, it would be reasonable and possible to infer bad faith or malice either from extrinsic facts or from the manner in which the proceedings were carried out if, for example, they were accompanied by harshness, discourtesy, or inconsiderateness. But if there were probable cause, the presence or absence of malice matters not.

In the present case I hold that the watch and its incidents were in themselves lawful, and that there is no extrinsic evidence of malice. I may add that the evidence is that the police officers carried out their duty without discourtesy, and I consider that some of the comments made on the defender's conduct were exaggerated. I am also of opinion that the defender had probable cause for the action which he took."

The Lord Justice-Clerk (Aitchison): "Without entering upon further detailed examination of authority, the law, as I understand it, may be summarised in these propositions:

1. An act is *prima facie* within the competence of the public official doing or authorising it when it is the kind of act that is within his ordinary duty to discharge.
2. When a public official does an act that is *prima facie* within his ordinary duty, there is a presumption that he has acted within his authority.
3. This presumption is not absolute, but may be rebutted by shewing that the act was unrelated to any duty arising on the particular occasion, in which case the act ceases to be within the authority or competence of the public official and becomes unlawful.
4. Where an act is within the competence, no civil liability arises from the doing of the act unless it can be shewn that the act was done maliciously and without probable cause.

5. Want of probable cause and malice are not necessarily unrelated and independent. The absence of just cause may go to prove malice, and similarly the presence of oblique or dishonest motive may go to shew the absence of probable cause.
6. Malice may be inferred from recklessness, and the facts and circumstances from which it may be inferred need not be extrinsic to the circumstances in which the act is done or to the manner of doing it.
7. Circumstances may shew that an act was done with malice, or without probable cause, or that it was an act outwith the competence of the person doing or authorising it. In some cases, according to the angle from which the question is approached, the same facts may be habile to infer each of these conclusions.
8. The *onus probandi* is on the pursuer to shew that the act complained of is outwith the competence of the person doing or authorising it, or if, within the competence, that it was done maliciously and without probable cause.

There remains to consider the application of the law to the facts of this case. The questions are three: (1) Was what was done within the competence of the defender? (2) If so, was it done without probable cause? (3) Was it done maliciously? I will take these questions in the inverse order.

Where in this case is there evidence of malice or dishonest motive? There is no proved circumstance pointing to ill-will against the pursuer, or hostility, or even disagreement. It was said that the duration and severity of the watch disclosed an intention in the mind of the defender, reckless of consequences, to break Inspector Anderson at all costs, and that this, inferring a reckless disregard of the pursuer's interests, was proof of malice. It is, I think, a sufficient answer that when Anderson did report on the Monday he was allowed to tender his resignation. The defender might have chosen to arraign him on a grave charge of indiscipline, conviction upon which might have entailed a forfeiture of his pension rights. There is no evidence of antecedent ill-will against either Anderson or the pursuer.

Was there probable cause for the defender's action? Probable cause, as Sir John Salmond has pointed out (*Torts*, 7th ed. p. 619), really means provable cause—that is, excusable or just cause. Can it be said in this case that the defender acted without just occasion or lawful excuse? Anderson had gone on leave without leaving his communications intact, which was in itself a breach of police regulations, although, if done inadvertently, not of much moment; but what was a much graver matter, there was reason to think that Anderson was defying an order for his recall and that he was secreting himself in the pursuer's house. That being the position, I am unable to affirm that the Chief Constable was not entitled to take effective steps with a view to ascertaining the fact.

Was the setting and maintaining of the watch within the competence of the defender? This appears ultimately to be the real question in the case. I do not doubt that to set and maintain a police watch upon the house of a citizen, in circumstances that attract public attention and give rise to suspicion in the public mind, may, if done without just cause, amount to an invasion of the liberty of the citizen as truly and effectively as if the citizen were subjected to physical restraint. But whether in any case it is an unlawful invasion of liberty must depend upon the circumstances of the particular case. There are, and must be, many acts done by the police in the proper exercise of their functions that may affect injuriously innocent people and yet are acts done without legal wrong. It was conceded by counsel for the pursuer that if crime had been suspected as taking place in the pursuer's house it would have been a lawful exercise of police authority to watch the house. But it was argued that here there was no crime nor suspected crime, and that the indiscipline of Anderson was in truth a domestic matter that did not justify the steps that were taken. This argument is, in my view, unsound. Police discipline is primarily a domestic matter, a matter between the Chief Constable and his subordinates, but it is also a matter of vital public interest. No Chief Constable who had a proper sense of his responsibility could view with unconcern the deliberate defection of a superior officer committed within his jurisdiction in circumstances that pointed to wilful defiance. If the Chief Constable had reasonable ground for his suspicion (and this does not appear to be open to controversy) the conclusion is inevitable that he was entitled to set and maintain a watch so that he might have evidence of a grave dereliction of duty on the part of Anderson. The Lord Ordinary has held in fact that the actual watch was not made more onerous to the pursuer than was necessarily incidental to such a watch being maintained. This finding in fact has not been displaced.

A Chief Constable who is vested with high powers for the carrying out of his public office ought always to discharge his functions with a single eye to the public interest, and wherever possible in such a way as not to bring suspicion upon members of the community who have committed no breach of the law. In the present case I am not satisfied that the defender, as Chief Constable, acted imprudently or injudiciously, having regard to the difficult situation confronting him, although it may now appear, in the light of what has happened, that an alternative course might have been followed with advantage that would have been more in accord with caution and good sense."

Different surveillance practices may, however, constitute a breach of the Convention rights of the individual under surveillance, though this will not necessarily be true in every case. The question of police surveillance arose in *Connor v H M Advocate*, 2002 S.L.T. 671 where "police officers had subjected the [appellant] and his home at 3 Inverurie Street, Glasgow to systematic surveillance in pursuit of evidence in support of the charge that is libelled in the indictment. In consequence of said systematic surveillance and information obtained thereby police officers sought and were granted a warrant to enter and search the home of the (appellant) in pursuit of further evidence in the case." The appellant was subsequently charged under the Misuse of Drugs Act 1971, and it was argued that the surveillance outside his house violated his Convention rights. However, it was held that there was no breach of either Art.8 or Art.6. The Crown's case—which was accepted by the court—was that:

"Where surveillance was likely to breach article 8(1) rights, these matters were now regulated by the provisions of the Regulation of Investigatory Powers (Scotland) Act 2000. But in the present case all that could be said of the surveillance operation was that it involved observation of the public street outside the building in which appellant's flat was one of a number of flats and of the exterior of the door to the common close. That did not involve any interference with the appellant's rights under Article 8(1). There was no information directly gleaned from the appellant either by way of interference with his telephone or otherwise. There was no suggestion of police officers, either directly or indirectly by use of instruments or other equipment, looking into his flat, piercing, as it were, the integrity of his private space and observing what went on inside it. Nor could observation of persons entering and leaving the door to the common close be said to be an invasion of privacy so far as the appellant himself was concerned. The officer had undertaken observation as he did to determine whether the information on which he acted could be confirmed or enhanced so as to justify an application for a search warrant. He had come to the conclusion that he could make such an application by reference to his observation of the frequency of visitors to the building and what appeared to be visitors of a particular type. Thus the use of the information obtained was originally directed to the obtaining of the search warrant. No criticism was directed to the validity of the warrant. The fact that individuals were stopped by other police officers acting under appropriate statutory powers and that these individuals thereafter gave information relating to the appellant's activities, did not constitute an invasion of the appellant's rights since such information did not emanate from any area of the appellant's private life."

The following case also indicates the limited protection that Convention rights may provide for the individual who is under surveillance, in this case from an insurance company.

Martin v McGuiness
2003 S.L.T. 1424

The pursuer sought damages for injuries sustained in a road accident together with declarator that the conduct of private investigators employed by the defender was unlawful and a breach of Art.8 of the Convention, and also damages for the breach. At procedure roll the pursuer sought to have the investigators' evidence excluded from any proof arguing that to allow it would be in breach of s.6(1) of the Human Rights Act 1998. The pursuer averred that the investigators' inquiries targeted his family life, being designed to obtain private information about him from the most intimate family member, namely his wife, by deception, and that the surveillance intruded on his private life and property and was carried out covertly. He argued that although damages under the Human Rights Act 1998 could only be awarded against a public authority and although there was no existing common law remedy in Scotland apt to provide redress of the sort demanded by Art.8 for breach of a freestanding right of privacy, the court was bound to provide a remedy for any breach of a Convention right, which could be based either on *Robertson v Keith*, 1936 S.L.T. 9, or on the *actio iniuriarum*. The attempt to invoke art.8 failed, with Lord Bonomy allowing proof, but excluding the pursuer's averments relating to art.8.

LORD BONOMY: "[17] The declarator sought is that the attempt by the private investigator to elicit information about the pursuer from his wife and the subsequent surveillance of him and his family and visitors were unlawful acts. The conclusion for damages is for payment to him by the defender. Since he alone makes the claim for damages, only unlawful acts against him are relevant. While the lawfulness of the means employed to obtain evidence and the admissibility of that evidence may be two quite distinct issues and evidence may be admissible although it was gathered unlawfully, that is not the position in the present case. My decision on the admissibility of the evidence is based on my view that the conduct involved in gathering the evidence did not infringe the pursuer's Article 8 Convention right. Mr Summers [for the pursuer] explained that the declarator depended upon an infringement of Article 8 and the claim for damages depended on the declarator. It follows that the pursuer's case for declarator and damages is irrelevant on that ground alone. However, how a claim for damages for an infringement of Article 8 by one private individual against another private individual fits into the scheme of the Human Rights Act was debated at some length, and it is only right that I should reflect the submissions of counsel in this opinion.

[18] Mr Summers initially sought to suggest that the defender's conduct was unlawful because it was not undertaken in accordance with the provisions of the Regulation of Investigatory Power (Scotland) Act 2000. That Act regulates the activities of law enforcement and other public authorities and does not apply to the conduct of private individuals. Mr Summers did not elaborate upon the point.

[19] At one point in his submission Mr Summers suggested that, if the investigator's conduct was unlawful because it was incompatible with Article 8, then damages should be awarded against the defender 'under the Human Rights Act'. He later recognised that damages under that Act can only be awarded against a public authority. In Section 8(6) 'damages' are defined as 'damages for an unlawful act for public authority'. 'Unlawful' is defined as 'unlawful under Section 6(1)'. It follows that, if the admission by the Court of the evidence of the investigator is incompatible with Article 8, then admitting the evidence would be an unlawful act. That would be established by reclaiming any decision of this Court—Section 9(1)(a) of the Human Rights Act. However, if the evidence was admitted in good faith, it is not competent for an award of damages to be made against the Court as a public authority—Section 9(3).

[20] In the alternative, counsel submitted that the pursuer was entitled to damages 'at common law'. At page 12B it is averred that '... the said surveillance and enquiries made about the pursuer were in breach of his right to privacy at common law.' Later at 12E it is averred: 'the pursuer is entitled to reparation for the invasion of his right to privacy at

common law and for the distress caused to him thereby.' However, having made some general propositions to the effect that any breach of Article 8 which was unjustified was 'a delictual wrong', counsel then conceded that there was no existing remedy in Scotland apt to provide redress of the sort apparently demanded by Article 8 for breach of a free-standing right of privacy.

[21] He went on to make a number of submissions about the Court's duty to provide a remedy for a pursuer who was damaged by a breach of Article 8 by a private individual rather than a public authority. He submitted that it was the duty of the Court to develop existing remedies to take account of modern conditions including the introduction of Convention rights into Scots law. While the specific obligation to interpret the law in a way which is compatible with the Convention rights was confined in Section 3 of the Act to the interpretation of 'primary legislation and subordinate legislation', it followed, from the definition of the Court as a 'public authority' and the prohibition upon public authorities acting in a way which was incompatible with a Convention right, that the Court was bound to provide a remedy for any breach of a Convention right. If the Court were to hold the evidence obtained to be inadmissible because to admit it would be incompatible with Article 8, then the very gathering of the evidence itself was an unlawful act in contravention of Article 8. It followed that the right of the pursuer had been infringed; for every infringement of a right there must be a remedy. Mr McNeil for the defenders was broadly in agreement with that submission. While acknowledging that the emphasis of Section 5, 6 and 7 of the Act was on public authorities and that Section 8 restricted the liability to pay compensation under the Act to public authorities, he found it difficult to see why protection should exist for private individuals against actings by state and public authorities that were incompatible with a Convention right but not in respect of the actions of private individuals which were equally incompatible.

[22] As a result of this consensus, much of the debate centred on considering the remedies which currently exist in respect of unlawful conduct which might be said to involve an intrusion upon privacy, with a view to identifying one which might be extended or developed to provide a remedy for a private individual whose right to respect for his private and family life is infringed. Two possible sources of a potential remedy for infringement of privacy were advanced by Mr Summers.

[23] The first was in the opinions of the Lord President and the Lord Justice Clerk in the seven judge case of *Robertson v Keith*, 1936 S.L.T. 9. It is tempting to confine the ratio of this case to the conduct of public officials. A chief constable set up an intensive surveillance operation to observe the home of the pursuer because he suspected that one of his officers was concealing himself there and refusing to return to duty. Whether the officer was concealed in the pursuer's house was never established and was immaterial to the decision. The Court proceeded on the basis that the intensive surveillance operation had caused the pursuer's neighbours, acquaintances and customers to believe that she had committed serious criminal offences with the consequence that her business had failed and she had sustained financial loss. Mr Summers founded principally upon the opinion of the Lord Justice Clerk (Aitchison) to this effect:

> 'Was the setting and maintaining of the watch within the competence of the defender? This appears ultimately to be the real question in the case. I do not doubt that to set and maintain a police watch upon the house of a citizen, in circumstances that attract public attention and give rise to suspicion in the public mind, may, if done without just cause, amount to an invasion of the liberty of the citizen as truly and effectively as if the citizen were subjected to physical restraint. But whether in any case it is an unlawful invasion of liberty must depend upon the circumstances of the particular case.'

Mr Summers relied also on the opinion of the Lord President (Normand) as follows:

'It is not doubtful that any unwarranted and unlawful proceeding by a public officer resulting in injury to anyone will subject him to liability, and that in such a case proof of malice and want of probable cause is not required of the pursuer. The first question, therefore, is whether the action of the defender in ordering the watch to be set falls into this category. It was admitted, and it is, I think, the law, that, if the watch had been set in the course of investigating a crime, and if it had led to some injury to the pursuer, she would have had no case unless she could prove malice and want of probable cause. The protection which is thus given to the police and other public officials acting in the exercise of their duty is a privilege founded on the public interest—*Beaton* v *Ivory*, 1887 14 R.1057—for it is of the highest importance that public officials should not be hindered in their duty by fears of incurring liability for damages if their conduct is subsequently impugned as indiscreet or imprudent or going beyond what the immediate necessities required.'

Under reference to a brief discussion of this case by Lord Kilbrandon, then Law Commissioner, in the 1971 *Cambrian Law Review* at pages 42–43, Mr Summers submitted that the true ratio of *Robertson* v *Keith* was, not that special rules apply to public officials, but that an infringement of the liberty of the individual or of his peaceful enjoyment of his property or the peaceful enjoyment of his own private life by deliberate conduct causing him distress and annoyance was excused only if it was lawful. In the case of the chief constable the conduct was lawful since it fell within the scope of his duties and responsibilities. That being so, he could be held liable only if he had acted maliciously and without probable cause.

[24] It is difficult, submitted Mr Summers, to see why, as a matter of principle, there should be any distinction between conduct of an official and conduct of a private individual that has these effects. The Court could, therefore, provide redress for such conduct. However, redress will not be available where, as here, the conduct was lawful.

[25] Mr Summers recognised that the other potential source which he proposed involved a degree of judicial legislation. That appeared to be how the similar problem was being addressed in England and Wales. He found support for this approach in *Hansard*, H.L. November 3, 1997, col. 1230 where the Lord Chancellor expressed the expectation that, regardless of incorporation of the Convention, 'the judges are very likely to develop a common law right of privacy themselves.' He relied also on a similar view expressed by Lord Bingham in his article, 'Opinion: Should There be a Law to Protect Rights of Personal Privacy?' [1996] E.H.R.L.R. 450 at 461–462.

[26] He pointed to what he submitted were signs that the English courts were already following that course by extending the circumstances in which an action might lie for what is described in England as 'breach of confidence', defined by Lord Goff of Chieveley in *Attorney General* v *Guardian Newspapers Ltd* (*No. 2*) [1990] 1 A.C. 109 at 281 in the following terms:

'A duty of confidence will arise whenever the party subject to the duty is in a situation where he either knows or ought to know that the other person can reasonably expect his privacy to be protected.'

In delivering the opinion of the Court in *A* v *B plc* [2002] 3 WLR 542 Woolf C.J. adopted that definition and said this at page 550:

'It is most unlikely that any purpose will be served by a judge seeking to decide whether there exists a new cause of action in tort which protects privacy. In the great majority of situations, if not all situations, where the protection of privacy is justified, relating to events after the Human Rights Act 1998 came into force, an action for breach of confidence now will, where this is appropriate, provide the necessary protection.'

Examples of this development can be seen in *Naomi Campbell* v *MGN Ltd* [2002] EWCA Civ 1373; *Theakston* v *MGN* [2002] EWHC 137; *Douglas* v *Hello! Ltd* [2001] QB 967, [2001] 2 All ER 289 and *Venables* v *News Group Newspapers Ltd* [2001] Fam 430. These are all cases involving Article 10 of the Convention and its relationship with Article 8.

[27] Against that background Mr Summers made a rather cautious submission that the *actio iniuriarum* is sufficiently wide to cover any deliberate conduct causing affront or offence to the dignity, security or privacy of the individual. He unfortunately did not elaborate upon this, or attempt to establish by reference to authority the nature of and the basis for that remedy, nor indeed whether modern Scots law recognises it as a remedy. Mr McNeil on the other hand did consider in some detail whether resort to the *actio iniuriarum* would be one possible way of protecting rights of privacy. In doing so he considered its role in Roman law.

[28] That analysis was part of Mr McNeil's submission that Scots law has never recognised a specific right to privacy or to respect for private and family life and has tended to regard privacy as something indefinable—see *Stair Memorial Encyclopaedia*, Vol. 11 para. 1094. It was possible to identify specific legal wrongs against a person for which there was protection but, in general, the wrong arose because what was done or said came to the public notice. Mr McNeil pointed out by reference to *Walker on Delict*, 2nd ed., chapter 21, pages 704–708 that all the situations in which Scots law had recognised infringements of rights as the result of unjustifiable intrusion into private and personal affairs involved invoking recognised principles such as those relating to copyright or breach of contract or defamation. Of course it does not follow that, because a specific right to privacy has not so far been recognised, such a right does not fall within existing principles of the law. Significantly my attention was not drawn to any case in which it was said in terms that there is no right to privacy.

[29] By reference to Zimmerman, *The Law of Obligations*, at pages 1053–1059 and the *Digest of Justinian,* ed. Mommsen, at para. 21.7 and 21.18, Mr McNeil submitted that the *actio inuriarum* provides redress only where deliberate conduct involves an attack on personality for an unlawful purpose. Examples were insulting and abusive behaviour, harassment or stalking, which was seen as an attack on the honour of another, beating another man's slave, which was an insult to the honour of the owner, and intruding into another's home for an unlawful purpose. It may, however, be only a short step from an assault on personality of the nature of an insult to the dignity, honour or reputation of a person, causing hurt to his feelings, to deliberate conduct involving unwarranted intrusion into the personal or family life of which the natural consequence is distress.

[30] I have done no more than reflect the submissions made. Whether on infringement of Article 8 by one private individual causing loss to another, which has not in the past given rise to a successful claim, should now have that result, and the basis on which such a claim may be made remain to be determined in a case where these questions arise as live issues."

The foregoing decision makes it clear that there is no right to privacy yet recognised in Scots Law. It also makes it clear that the courts are not yet ready to bite the bait of the *actio iniuriarum* which is dangled before them as an inducement to create such a right. Indeed this bait has been around for some time, without so much as a nibble:

"72. Both Professor T. B. Smith (a Scottish Law Commissioner) and Professor David M. Walker have suggested that under existing law the Scottish Court might entertain an action for invasion of privacy at least where *animus injuriandi* could be established. Professor Walker states: 'It is submitted that the principle of the *actio injuriarum* would justify a Scottish Court in giving a remedy for invasion of privacy; the kinds of conduct which amount to such infringement are certainly affronts to personality likely to cause hurt feelings, and if the person is aggrieved a remedy should be given.' This is no doubt true in theory, but it is much in doubt if the Court would give a remedy except perhaps in an extreme case. In 1957 a Sheriff Substitute who had himself been convicted a year before for the offence of careless driving wrote a letter to a newspaper advocating heavier fines for some motoring offences. Another newspaper then published an ironical comment on the situation. The Sheriff Substitute then sued the latter newspaper for damages for invasion of privacy. The Inner House of the Court of Session (the Appeal Court) agreed with the judge of first instance that the action was irrelevant, *i.e.* had no sound basis in law. In the course of his opinion, Lord Justice-Clerk Thomson said: 'The basis of this argument is that an unwarranted invasion of privacy by a newspaper is actionable. This Court is a Court of law. It is not a court of manners, taste or journalistic propriety and so far as newspaper articles are concerned its function is to administer the law of defamation. Defamation consists in the making of a false statement derogatory of the character or reputation of the person spoken of. If such a statement is made, then unless the statement is privileged the pursuer has his remedy. But I know of no authority to the effect that mere invasion of privacy however hurtful and whatever its purpose and however repugnant to good taste is itself actionable. Whether such an invasion might amount to an ingredient in malice in circumstances where it is incumbent on the pursuer to establish that the defender acted maliciously it is unnecessary to consider.' This decision may be regarded as a weighty authority against the proposition that the Scottish courts would entertain an action for damages for invasion of privacy. On the other hand, in Scotland it has been said that the remedy depends upon the right rather than the right upon the remedy as in England, and, the Scottish court might grant a remedy in an extreme case even though the remedy had never been granted before."

(Report of the Committee on Privacy, Cmnd. 5102, 1972, para.306.)

III. REGULATION OF INVESTIGATORY POWERS

Despite the decisions in the foregoing cases, there appears to have been some concern that police surveillance practices may have breached the ECHR. However, this concern arose mainly on procedural grounds, and mainly by reason of the fact that the practice operated in a twilight zone without any legal authority or regulation. The position is now governed by the Regulation of Investigatory Powers (Scotland) Act 2000 (RIP(S)A). This is similar in terms to the Regulation of Investigatory Powers Act 2000 (RIPA), Pt II of which applies only to England and Wales. The rest of that Act (such as Pt I which applies to the interception of communications) extends to Scotland. The background to the RIP(S)A was explained in the Policy Memorandum which accompanied the Regulation of Investigatory Powers (Scotland) Bill:

"Covert investigation techniques, in particular the use of surveillance and human sources such as undercover officers and informants, often provide vital intelligence in preventing and detecting serious criminal activity. But criminals involved in such activity are often practised in the use of counter-measures. To combat this type of criminal the police must be able to use the most effective techniques available. These techniques need to be safeguarded, while at the same time ensuring that they are properly controlled and those employing them are accountable. It is important, too, that other public authorities in Scotland who use these techniques are also properly regulated and comply with controls and procedures."

The purpose of the Bill was "to ensure that certain covert investigation techniques are used in accordance with human rights", particularly Arts 6 and 8. According to the Policy Memorandum published with the Bill:

"To be acceptable in ECHR terms:
    (a) a framework of controls must have a basis in law;
    (b) the law must define the scope and manner of the exercise of a public authority's

functions with sufficient clarity to protect the individual from arbitrary interference and to ensure that it is the subject of effective control;
(c) the law must be sufficiently accessible and precise;
(d) the exceptions which allow interference should be constructed narrowly and interference with those rights should be necessary and proportionate to any offence."

The policy memorandum also addresses the policy objectives of the Bill in the following terms:

"POLICY OBJECTIVES
18. There are two important policy objectives:
— The first is to seek to achieve a balance between safeguarding the rights of individuals to their privacy without hindering the effective use of covert investigation techniques by law enforcement agencies as a valuable tool in tackling serious and dangerous crime.
— The second policy objective is to ensure that the regimes put in place to regulate the use of these techniques are similar north and south of the border. This is important from the point of view of law enforcement agencies who operate on both sides of the border and who have to deal with highly mobile and sophisticated criminals. It would clearly be undesirable if criminals were able to exploit differences in the regulatory regimes to their advantage. Both Scottish and UK Bills have been produced in close co-ordination between the Scottish Executive, the Home Office and law enforcement agencies.

ALTERNATIVE APPROACHES
19. Given the policy objectives set out in the paragraphs above, the only serious alternative approach would have been to have sought the consent of Parliament to the RIP Bill in Westminster covering the use of these techniques by the Scottish police. This would have had the advantage of ensuring consistency of approach so as to minimise cross-border policing problems. Further, it would have maintained the UK regulatory framework which has developed with Interception of Communications Act and Part III of the Police Act 1997. However, such an approach would have deprived the Scottish Parliament of the opportunity to scrutinise legislation that protects the rights of individuals and is important in the fight against crime in Scotland."

This desire to ensure that the legislation mirrored its English equivalent meant that there was no consultation on the Bill. The policy objectives of producing a regime that is compatible with the ECHR in order to protect the rights of the individual, while safeguarding the use of these techniques by law enforcement; and ensuring that there are similar regimes north and south of the border mean that there is very little room for manoeuvre. Not only has the Scottish Parliament followed the English legislation on this issue, but it has also made use of the same supervisory arrangements, that is to say the Chief Surveillance Commissioner and the Investigatory Powers Tribunal, both of which are based in London. Nevertheless the adoption of the English legislation as a fairly precise template for the Scottish legislation gives rise to the intriguing possibility that the RIP(S)A (or parts thereof) could be struck down by the Scottish courts as violating Convention rights, in circumstances where the English courts would have no such power.

Regulation of Investigatory Powers (Scotland) Act 2000

"1 Conduct to which this Act applies
(1) This Act applies to the following conduct—

    (a) directed surveillance;

    (b) intrusive surveillance; and

    (c) the conduct and use of covert human intelligence sources.

(2) For the purposes of this Act surveillance is directed if it is covert but not intrusive and is undertaken—

    (a) for the purposes of a specific investigation or a specific operation;

    (b) in such a manner as is likely to result in the obtaining of private information about a person (whether or not one specifically identified for the purposes of the investigation or operation); and

    (c) otherwise than by way of an immediate response to events or circumstances the nature of which is such that it would not be reasonably practicable for an authorisation under this Act to be sought for the carrying out of the surveillance.

(3) Subject to subsections (4) and (5) below, surveillance is intrusive for the purposes of this Act if, and only if, it is covert surveillance that—

    (a) is carried out in relation to anything taking place on any residential premises or in any private vehicle; and

    (b) involves the presence of an individual on the premises or in the vehicle or is carried out by means of a surveillance device.

(4) For the purposes of this Act surveillance is not intrusive to the extent that it is carried out by means only of a surveillance device designed or adapted principally for the purpose of providing information about the location of a vehicle.

(5) For the purposes of this Act surveillance which-

    (a) is carried out by means of a surveillance device in relation to anything taking place on any residential premises or in any private vehicle; but

    (b) is carried out without that device being present on the premises or in the vehicle,

is not intrusive unless the device is such that it consistently provides information of the same quality and detail as might be expected to be obtained from a device actually present on the premises or in the vehicle.

(6) In this Act—

    (a) references to the conduct of a covert human intelligence source are references to conduct of such a source which falls within any of paragraphs (a) to (c) of subsection (7) below, or is incidental to anything falling within any of those paragraphs; and

    (b) references to the use of a covert human intelligence source are references to inducing, asking or assisting a person to engage in the conduct of such a source, or to obtain information by means of the conduct of such a source.

(7) For the purposes of this Act a person is a covert human intelligence source if the person—

    (a) establishes or maintains a personal or other relationship with another person for the covert purpose of facilitating the doing of anything falling within paragraph (b) or (c) below;

    (b) covertly uses such a relationship to obtain information or to provide access to any information to another person; or

    (c) covertly discloses information obtained by the use of such a relationship or as a consequence of the existence of such a relationship.

(8) For the purposes of this section—

    (a) surveillance is covert if, and only if, it is carried out in a manner that is calculated to ensure that persons who are subject to the surveillance are unaware that it is or may be taking place;

    (b) a purpose is covert, in relation to the establishment or maintenance of a personal or other relationship, if and only if the relationship is conducted in a manner that is calculated to ensure that one of the parties to the relationship is unaware of the purpose; and

    (c) a relationship is used covertly, and information obtained as mentioned in subsection (7)(c) above is disclosed covertly, if and only if it is used or, as the case may be, disclosed in a manner that is calculated to ensure that one of the parties to the relationship is unaware of the use or disclosure in question.

(9) In this section 'private information', in relation to a person, includes any information relating to the person's private or family life.

(10) References in this section, in relation to a vehicle, to the presence of a surveillance device in the vehicle include references to its being located on or under the vehicle and also include references to its being attached to it."

A clearer picture of what the Act is designed to deal with is provided in the Policy Memorandum which gives some indication of what the different terms used in the Act will mean in practice:

- "● Surveillance is covert where it is undertaken in a manner calculated to ensure that the person or persons subject to the surveillance are unaware of it.
- ● 'Directed surveillance' is surveillance which is covert and which is undertaken in relation to a specific investigation in order to obtain information about, or identify, a particular person or to determine who is involved in a matter under investigation.
- ● 'Intrusive surveillance' is surveillance which is covert and carried out in relation to anything taking place on residential premises or in any private vehicle. This type of surveillance may take place by means either of a person or device located inside a residential premises or a private vehicle, or by means of a device placed outside which consistently provides a product of equivalent quality and detail as a product which would be obtained from a device located inside.
- ● The use of 'covert human intelligence sources' covers the use of informants, agents and undercover officers."

It is also made clear that "Less intrusive forms of surveillance where there is a general awareness on the part of the public that surveillance is taking place, such as CCTV for crime prevention, public order or traffic management purposes are excluded from the authorisation process".

Under s.2 of the 2000 Act, the Scottish Ministers are required to appoint, for the purposes of the Act, a Chief Surveillance Commissioner and such number of other Surveillance Commissioners as the Scottish Ministers think fit. The persons so appointed must hold or have held high judicial office within the meaning of the Appellate Jurisdiction Act 1876. Appointments are for a term of three years but are renewable. With some exceptions, a Surveillance Commissioner may be removed before the expiry of his or her appointment only after a resolution approving the removal has been passed by the Scottish Parliament. Decisions of the Commissioners (including decisions as to jurisdiction) are not to be subject to appeal or liable to be questioned in any court. Provision is also made in s.3 for the appointment of assistant surveillance commissioners. In this case, however, it is a condition of appointment that the individual is a sheriff, a Crown Court or circuit judge in England and Wales, or a county court judge in Northern Ireland. It was made clear at the time the Bill was introduced that the Commissioners for this purpose would be the Commissioners already appointed under the Police Act 1997, Pt III of which introduced other surveillance powers (relating to interference with property). These powers remain and complement the provisions of RIP(S)A 2000, and are considered below.

Regulation of Investigatory Powers (Scotland) Act 2000

"5 Lawful surveillance etc.
(1) Conduct to which this Act applies shall be lawful for all purposes if-
    (a) an authorisation under this Act confers an entitlement to engage in that conduct on the person whose conduct it is; and
    (b) that person's conduct is in accordance with the authorisation.

(2) A person shall not be subject to any civil liability in respect of any conduct of that person which—

    (a) is incidental to any conduct that is lawful by virtue of subsection (1) above; and

    (b) is not itself conduct an authorisation or warrant for which is capable of being granted under a relevant enactment and might reasonably have been expected to have been sought in the case in question.

(3) In this section 'relevant enactment' means—

    (a) an enactment contained in this Act; or

    (b) an enactment contained in Part III of the Police Act 1997 (authorisation of interference with property and wireless telegraphy) insofar as relating to a police force.

6 Authorisation of directed surveillance

(1) Subject to the following provisions of this Act, the persons designated for the purposes of this section shall each have power to grant authorisations for the carrying out of directed surveillance.

(2) A person shall not grant an authorisation for the carrying out of directed surveillance unless that person is satisfied-

    (a) that the authorisation is necessary on grounds falling within subsection (3) below; and

    (b) that the authorised surveillance is proportionate to what is sought to be achieved by carrying it out.

(3) An authorisation is necessary on grounds falling within this subsection if it is necessary—

    (a) for the purpose of preventing or detecting crime or of preventing disorder;

    (b) in the interests of public safety; or

    (c) for the purpose of protecting public health.

(4) The conduct that is authorised by an authorisation for the carrying out of directed surveillance is any conduct that—

    (a) consists in the carrying out of directed surveillance of any such description as is specified in the authorisation; and

    (b) is carried out in the circumstances described in the authorisation and for the purposes of the investigation or operation specified or described in the authorisation.

7 Authorisation of covert human intelligence sources

(1) Subject to the following provisions of this Act, the persons designated for the purposes of this section shall each have power to grant authorisations for the conduct or the use of a covert human intelligence source.

(2) A person shall not grant an authorisation for the conduct or the use of a covert human intelligence source unless that person is satisfied-

    (a) that the authorisation is necessary on grounds falling within subsection (3) below;

    (b) that the authorised conduct or use is proportionate to what is sought to be achieved by that conduct or use; and

    (c) that arrangements exist for the source's case that satisfy the requirements of subsection (6) below and such other requirements as may be imposed by order made by the Scottish Ministers.

(3) An authorisation is necessary on grounds falling within this subsection if it is necessary—

    (a) for the purpose of preventing or detecting crime or of preventing disorder;

    (b) in the interests of public safety; or

    (c) for the purpose of protecting public health.

(4) The Scottish Ministers may by order—

    (a) prohibit the authorisation under this section of any such conduct or uses of covert human intelligence sources as may be described in the order; and

(b) impose requirements, in addition to those provided for by subsection (2) above, that must be satisfied before an authorisation is granted under this section for any such conduct or uses of covert human intelligence sources as may be described.

(5) The conduct that is authorised by an authorisation for the conduct or the use of a covert human intelligence source is any conduct that—

(a) is comprised in any such activities involving conduct of a covert human source, or the use of a covert human intelligence source, as are specified or described in the authorisation;

(b) consists in conduct by or in relation to the person who is so specified or described as the person to whose actions as a covert human intelligence source the authorisation relates; and

(c) is carried out for the purposes of, or in connection with, the investigation or operation so specified or described.

(6) For the purposes of this Act there are arrangements for the source's case that satisfy the requirements of this subsection if such arrangements are in force as are necessary for ensuring—

(a) that there will at all times be a person holding an office, rank or position with the relevant investigating authority who will have day-to-day responsibility for dealing with the source on behalf of that authority, and for the source's security and welfare;

(b) that there will at all times be another person holding an office, rank or position with the relevant investigating authority who will have general oversight of the use made of the source;

(c) that there will at all times be a person holding an office, rank or position with the relevant investigating authority who will have responsibility for maintaining a record of the use made of the source;

(d) that the records relating to the source that are maintained by the relevant investigating authority will always contain particulars of all such matters (if any) as may be specified for the purposes of this paragraph in regulations made by the Scottish Ministers; and

(e) that records maintained by the relevant investigating authority that disclose the identity of the source will not be available to persons except to the extent that there is a need for access to them to be made available to those persons.

(7) In this section 'relevant investigating authority', in relation to an authorisation for the conduct or the use of an individual as a covert human intelligence source, means (subject to subsection (8) below) the public authority for whose benefit the activities of that individual as such a source are to take place.

(8) In the case of any authorisation for the conduct or the use of a covert human intelligence source whose activities are to be for the benefit of more than one public authority, the references in subsection (6) above to the relevant investigating authority are references to one of them (whether or not the same one in the case of each reference).

8 Persons entitled to grant authorisations under sections 6 and 7

(1) Subject to subsection (2) below, the persons designated for the purposes of sections 6 and 7 above are the individuals holding such offices, ranks or positions with relevant public authorities as are prescribed for the purposes of this subsection by order made by the Scottish Ministers.

(2) The Scottish Ministers may by order impose restrictions—

(a) on the authorisations under sections 6 and 7 above that may be granted by any individual holding an office, rank or position with a specified public authority; and

(b) on the circumstances in which, or the purposes for which, such authorisations may be granted by any such individual.

(3) A public authority is a relevant public authority for the purposes of this section in relation to sections 6 and 7 above if it is—

(a) a police force;
(b) the Scottish Administration;
(c) a council constituted under section 2 of the Local Government etc. (Scotland) Act 1994;
(d) the Common Services Agency for the Health Service;
(e) a health board;
(f) a special health board;
(g) a National Health Service trust established under section 12A of the National Health Service (Scotland) Act 1978;
(h) the Scottish Environment Protection Agency.
(4) The Scottish Ministers may by order amend subsection (3) above by—
(a) adding a public authority to those enumerated in that subsection;
(b) removing a public authority therefrom;
(c) making any change consequential on any change in the name of a public authority enumerated therein
(5) No order shall be made under subsection (4)(a) above unless it has been laid in draft before and approved by resolution of the Scottish Parliament."
[Regulations prescribe who may give authorisation in accordance with ss.6 and 7: SSI 2000/343. Special provision is made in s.9 for the Scottish Crime Squad.] ...

10 Authorisation of intrusive surveillance
(1) Subject to the following provisions of this Act, the chief constable of every police force shall have power to grant authorisations for the carrying out of intrusive surveillance.
(2) No such authorisation shall be granted unless the chief constable granting it is satisfied—
(a) that the authorisation is necessary for the purpose of preventing or detecting crime; and
(b) that the authorised surveillance is proportionate to what is sought to be achieved by carrying it out
(3) The matters to be taken into account in considering whether the requirements of subsection (2) above are satisfied in the case of any authorisation shall include whether the information which it is thought necessary to obtain by the authorised conduct could reasonably be obtained by other means.
(4) The conduct that is authorised by an authorisation for the carrying out of intrusive surveillance is any conduct that—
(a) consists in the carrying out of intrusive surveillance of any such description as is specified in the authorisation;
(b) is carried out in relation to the residential premises specified or described in the authorisation or in relation to the private vehicle so specified or described; and
(c) is carried out for the purposes of, or in connection with, the investigation or operation so specified or described."

By virtue of s.11, the police may only grant authorisations under ss.6, 7 and 10 if made from within the same police force. An application under the foregoing provisions may be combined with an application under the Police Act 1997 (on which see below). Provision is made to enable authorisations to be given under s.10 in cases of urgency where the chief constable or his or her designated deputy are unavailable: in these cases the authorisation may be given by an assistant chief constable (s.12). Any authorisation for instrusive surveillance under s.10 must be notified to an ordinary Surveillance Commissioner (s.13), who will normally be required to approve it except in cases of urgency (s.14). The Surveillance Commissioner may approve an authorisation "if, and only if, satisfied that there are reasonable grounds for being satisfied that the requirements of section 10(2)(a) and (b) above are satisfied in the case of the authorisation" (s.14(3)(a)). Surveillance Commissioners have the power to quash or cancel authorisations (s.15), and where the authorisation is cancelled, the Commissioner may also "order the destruction of any records relating, wholly or partly, to information obtained at such time by the authorised conduct" (s.15(5)). However no order may be made for the destruction of any records required for pending criminal or civil proceedings (s.15(6)). Under s.16, a chief constable of a police force may appeal to the Chief Surveillance Commissioner against a decision of the ordinary Commissioner.

The foregoing provisions of the RIP(S)A bear striking similarities not only to the RIPA 2000, but also to the Police Act 1997, Pt III. Not only are there similarities, but the institutional structure adopted by RIP(S)A 2000 for supervision of the powers is essentially the stucture put in place by the 1997 Act. The Commissioners under the RIP(S)A 2000 are the same as those appointed under the 1997 Act, and the same as those appointed under RIPA 2000 for England and Wales. The Chief Surveillance Commissioner is under a duty "to keep under review the exercise and performance, by the persons on whom they are conferred or imposed, of the powers and duties conferred or imposed by or under this Act" (s.21). It is also the duty of the Chief Surveillance Commissioner to report any breaches of the Act to the Scottish Ministers as and when they arise; and to report annually to the Scottish Ministers in respect of his or her functions under the Act: this report is to be laid before the Scottish Parliament, though some material may be withheld from publication in the public interest (s.22). The published reports of the Chief Commissioner contain little by way of illumination, though they do give some insight into the number of authorisations under the various powers. Finally an individual aggrieved by an authorisation under the RIP(S) or the Police Act 1997 may complain to the Investigatory Powers Tribunal established by the RIPA 2000.

Annual Report of the Chief Surveillance Commissioner to the Prime Minister and to Scottish Ministers for 2002–2003
Chief Commissioner: Sir Andrew leggatt
H.C. 1062: 2003

"6.7 There were 475 intrusive surveillance authorisations [throughout Great Britain] during 2002–2003, which represents a slight fall compared with 493 in the previous year. There were 80 renewals compared with 102 in the previous year.

6.8 There were 28 cases where urgency provisions were used. No authorisations were signed in the absence of the Chief Officer. In the previous year the figures were 35 and three.

6.9 One authorisation was quashed where the Commissioner was not satisfied that the serious crime criteria had been met.

. . .

7.1 In the course of the year I advised the Prison Service for England and Wales that their practice of obtaining intrusive surveillance authorisations through the Secretary of State was not necessary in hostage situations. The person holding someone hostage is engaged in crime and has no right to privacy. The person being held captive would be unlikely to raise concerns about invasion of privacy. The Home Secretary announced to Parliament on 12 December 2002 that he accepted this advice and that Prison Services procedures would be altered accordingly.

7.2 In response to an approach from the Association of Chief Police Officers, I expressed the view, subsequently reported in the press, that the police should not hesitate, where necessary, to use their powers under RIPA when investigating cases of unlawful sex with girls under the age of 13. But it is difficult to imagine circumstances in which a child could be left in peril while surveillance took place.

7.3 One of the Commissioners, Lord Bonomy, supported by the Chief Surveillance Inspector and the Secretary, chaired a seminar organised by Scottish police forces to review Police Act and RIP(S)A matters.

7.4 Following this event, the Scottish police forces and the Scottish Drugs Enforcement Agency have agreed on a general awareness training package to be distributed to all forces for delivery to officers from constable to Chief Inspector by all force training departments, and a similar, partly interactive, approach to improve awareness for non-specialist Superintendents. They have also agreed a further, more focused, input for newly promoted Superintendents attending the Scottish Police College (SPC), and more in-depth training for authorising officers under the legislation, especially those concerned with the management of CHIS.

...

8.1 The National Criminal Intelligence Service (NCIS), National Crime Squad (NCS), Scottish Drugs Enforcement Agency (SDEA), Her Majesty's Customs and Excise (HMCE) and UK police forces have provided statistics of their use of directed surveillance and CHIS. There were some 26,400 directed surveillance authorisations in 2002–2003, of which about 4,300 were current at the end of the year. This compares with about 28,000 (a corrected figure) and 4,800 respectively in the previous year ...

8.3 About 5900 CHIS were recruited during the same period; 5400 ceased to be used; and about 5000 were active at the end of the year. The figures for the previous year were 5400, 4900 and 5400 respectively.

...

9.1 There have been 276 inspections this year. This compares very favourably with 158 in the previous year ending 31 March (though that year's programme began in May). The aim is always to ensure proper recognition and acceptance, at senior management level, of the responsibilities which the legislation imposes, aided by the setting up of internal review processes and supported by focused training.

9.2 Law enforcement agencies
9.2.1 Law enforcement agencies may be defined as those bodies which are authorised to use intrusive surveillance. There were 62 inspections in the course of the year: 46 of police forces in England and Wales, including NCS and NCIS; nine of Scottish forces, plus the Police Service of Northern Ireland (PSNI), HM forces in Northern Ireland, HMCE, the British Transport Police and the Ministry of Defence Police.

9.2.2 While not itself able, because of its constitution, to authorise intrusive surveillance, the Scottish Drugs Enforcement Agency can be grouped with these bodies since it is closely involved in such operations.

9.2.3 Inspections of law enforcement agencies are usually conducted by individual inspectors. They normally take six days to complete, though longer is allowed for the larger forces. Five inspectors were deployed for the inspection of the Metropolitan Police, three each for NCS and HMCE, and two for PSNI.

9.2.4 Inspectors continue to focus on policies, procedures, training and the use of directed surveillance and CHIS. They also look at property interference and intrusive surveillance applications, though Commissioners scrutinise them directly at the time they are given.

9.2.5 There has been significant improvement as experience of the legislation has grown and as these bodies have learned from inspections. They have also been helped by the long-awaited publication of the Codes of Practice by the Home Office in August 2002 and by the Scottish Executive in March 2003.

9.2.6 My Office updates from time to time the examples of bad and good practice which we disseminate to all law enforcement agencies, so that they may continue to learn from each other. Bad practices that the Inspectors find include inadequate or non-existent policy documents, failure to review or cancel authorisations, inadequate applications and authorisations, authorisations that extend beyond their statutory limit, poor accountability for technical equipment, inadequate training, poor knowledge of the legislation, and no central record of authorisations.

9.2.7 Good practices are mostly the other side of the penny from the bad. They include excellent, detailed force guidance, first-rate central authorities bureaux which provide both oversight and quality control, exemplary reviews of force practice, frequent internal checking and dip-sampling, adoption of the ACPO best practice model for the management of CHIS, detailed risk assessments, and well-directed and imaginative training. Although good practices are now far commoner than bad, a checklist of bad practices is still useful. In future reports I intend to name forces that are notable for their good practices; and it may also be necessary to name any that remain notable for their bad practices.

9.2.8 Although it is my job to recommend to chief officers what should be done to achieve necessary improvement, it is for them to decide how it should be done. They face many pressures, not least in the allocation of time and resources to training and to IT systems. Nevertheless they are almost always responsive and ready to act. For that I am grateful.

9.2.9 On their visits to law enforcement agencies following inspections Commissioners have found that several topics often recur: training, the management of CHIS, the classification of confidential contacts, internal oversight by a central bureau, the quality and adequacy of applications and authorisations for directed surveillance, and crime hotspots (and the associated topic of private information) to which I have already referred. Matters of general discussion were the lack of co-ordination of training programmes in England and Wales, the limited use of covert activities in Scotland.

. . .

9.5 Local authorities in Scotland
9.5.1 Because a majority of Scottish authorities were inspected last year, only five were inspected this year, making 84% in all. Several had been slow to take account of RIP(S)A requirements, and policies had yet to be developed. Use of both directed surveillance and CHIS was extremely low."

IV. Interception of Communications

Telephone tapping gives rise to a dilemma in a democratic society. On the one hand the interception of communications taking place between private citizens is a major invasion of privacy, but on the other hand, it is an important weapon available to the police and security services whose business it is to maintain law and order and protect national security. Before 1985 the practice was not regulated by law but on the basis of administrative guidelines operated by the Home Office and the Scottish Office. According to official information, interceptions were made only on the authority of a warrant issued by the Home Secretary, the Secretary of State for Scotland or the Secretary of State for Northern Ireland. A warrant would be issued for the detection of serious crime or for gathering intelligence about subversive terrorist and espionage activities which were capable of constituting a threat to the peace or safety of the realm. In 1985 it was revealed that the Foreign Secretary also issued warrants for the gathering of intelligence to support the Government's foreign and defence policies. In the years 1980–85 the Home Secretary issued 1920 warrants, the Foreign Secretary 553 and the Scottish Secretary 302.

The legality of these arrangements was challenged in *Malone v Metropolitan Police Commissioner* [1979] Ch.344. During Malone's trial for handling stolen goods, the prosecution had said that the accused telephone had been tapped with the authority of a warrant. Malone then unsuccessfully sought a declaration that the tapping was unlawful as a violation of his right to privacy, his right to property, and his right to confidentiality in conversation on the telephone. In the absence of any unlawful conduct on any of these grounds, the court was unable to grant a remedy, for although there was no express authorisation of the practice, nor was there any express prohibition, and in the view of Sir Robert Megarry England is not a country where everything is forbidden unless it is expressly permitted. So, if the tapping of telephones could be carried out without breaking the law it did not require any statutory or common law powers to justify it. At this point Malone made an application to Strasbourg (Sir Robert Megarry having held that the ECHR could not form the basis of an action in the domestic courts). The essence of the complaint was that the practice of telephone tapping in Britain violated the right to privacy safeguarded by Art.8 of the Convention.

The main question for the Strasbourg court was whether the practice could be justified under

Art.8(2), on the ground that the practice was in accordance with law, and that it was necessary in a democratic society in the interests of national security, etc. In upholding the complaint, the court held that the practice was not in accordance with law (despite Sir Robert Megarry's decision that it was not unlawful). In the view of the court, the phrase "in accordance with law" means that the law "must be sufficiently clear in its terms to give citizens an adequate indication as to the circumstances in which and the conditions on which public authorities are empowered to resort to this secret and potentially dangerous interference with the right to respect for private life and correspondence." The British Government lost simply because domestic law did not regulate the circumstances in which the power to intercept could be exercised with sufficient clarity. Having so decided the court felt it unnecessary to decide whether the practice was unlawful on the additional ground that it exceeded what was necessary in a democratic society for the protection of national security. As a result, the Government was compelled to legislate, though no guidance was given by the court as to what should be the content of the legislation.

Legislation to give effect to the *Malone* judgment was introduced by the Interception of Communications Act 1985. The main features of the Act were the requirement that interception could take place only with the authority of a warrant issued by the Secretary of State. The warrant could be issued only for the limited purposes which included preventing and detecting serious crime and the interests of national security. Oversight of the arrangements was provided by a newly established tribunal and by an Interception Commissioner who was a senior judge. The similarities with the scheme operating before 1985 were thus very striking. These provisions were, however, found not to be fully compatible with the ECHR when another challenge was mounted in *Halford v United Kingdom* (1997) 24 E.H.R.R. 523. In this case a senior police officer complained that her employer had intercepted her telephone calls during the period when she was conducting litigation against them. The complaint was upheld, and it has been necessary to change the legislation. The amended legislation:

- extends the prohibition on unauthorised interceptions to include private tele-communications systems (such as those operated by employers);
- determines the circumstances in which a private telecommunications system may lawfully be intercepted;
- provides for civil as well as criminal liability for the unauthorised interception of private telecommunications systems.

Regulation of Investigatory Powers Act 2000

"Unlawful interception
1.—(1) It shall be an offence for a person intentionally and without lawful authority to intercept, at any place in the United Kingdom, any communication in the course of its transmission by means of—
    (a) a public postal service; or
    (b) a public telecommunication system.
  (2) It shall be an offence for a person—
    (a) intentionally and without lawful authority, and
    (b) otherwise than in circumstances in which his conduct is excluded by subsection (6) from criminal liability under this subsection,
to intercept, at any place in the United Kingdom, any communication in the course of its transmission by means of a private telecommunication system.
  (3) Any interception of a communication which is carried out at any place in the United Kingdom by, or with the express or implied consent of, a person having the right to control the operation or the use of a private telecommunication system shall be actionable at the suit or instance of the sender or recipient, or intended recipient, of the communication if it is without lawful authority and is either—
    (a) an interception of that communication in the course of its transmission by means

of that private system; or
    (b) an interception of that communication in the course of its transmission, by means of a public telecommunication system, to or from apparatus comprised in that private telecommunication system.
(4) Where the United Kingdom is a party to an international agreement which—
    (a) relates to the provision of mutual assistance in connection with, or in the form of, the interception of communications,
    (b) requires the issue of a warrant, order or equivalent instrument in cases in which assistance is given, and
    (c) is designated for the purposes of this subsection by an order made by the Secretary of State,
it shall be the duty of the Secretary of State to secure that no request for assistance in accordance with the agreement is made on behalf of a person in the United Kingdom to the competent authorities of a country or territory outside the United Kingdom except with lawful authority.
(5) Conduct has lawful authority for the purposes of this section if, and only if—
    (a) it is authorised by or under section 3 or 4;
    (b) it takes place in accordance with a warrant under section 5 ('an interception warrant'); or
    (c) it is in exercise, in relation to any stored communication, of any statutory power that is exercised (apart from this section) for the purpose of obtaining information or of taking possession of any document or other property;
and conduct (whether or not prohibited by this section) which has lawful authority for the purposes of this section by virtue of paragraph (a) or (b) shall also be taken to be lawful for all other purposes.
(6) The circumstances in which a person makes an interception of a communication in the course of its transmission by means of a private telecommunication system are such that his conduct is excluded from criminal liability under subsection (2) if—
    (a) he is a person with a right to control the operation or the use of the system; or
    (b) he has the express or implied consent of such a person to make the interception.
(7) A person who is guilty of an offence under subsection (1) or (2) shall be liable—
    (a) on conviction on indictment, to imprisonment for a term not exceeding two years or to a fine, or to both;
    (b) on summary conviction, to a fine not exceeding the statutory maximum…"

Section 1(5)(a) above provides that an interception may be lawful if authorised by ss.3 and 4. Otherwise a warrant is required unless s.1(6) applies. Section 3 authorises an interception where the person making the interception has reasonable grounds to believe that both the sender and the recipient have consented to the interception. It also authorises interception on a number of other grounds, including interception by the service provider for a purpose connected with the provision or operation of the service. Section 4 in turn authorises interception on a wide range of other grounds, including the interception of telephone calls or correspondence under the prison rules or in accordance with any direction given to the State Hospitals Board for Scotland under s.2(5) of the National Health Service (Scotland) Act 1978. So far as the issuing of warrants is concerned, s.5 provides that:

"(2) The Secretary of State shall not issue an interception warrant unless he believes—
    (a) that the warrant is necessary on grounds falling within subsection (3); and
    (b) that the conduct authorised by the warrant is proportionate to what is sought to be achieved by that conduct.
(3) Subject to the following provisions of this section, a warrant is necessary on grounds falling within this subsection if it is necessary—
    (a) in the interests of national security;
    (b) for the purpose of preventing or detecting serious crime;

> (c) for the purpose of safeguarding the economic well-being of the United Kingdom;
> or
> (d) for the purpose, in circumstances appearing to the Secretary of State to be
> equivalent to those in which he would issue a warrant by virtue of paragraph (b),
> of giving effect to the provisions of any international mutual assistance agreement.
> (4) The matters to be taken into account in considering whether the requirements of
> subsection (2) are satisfied in the case of any warrant shall include whether the information
> which it is thought necessary to obtain under the warrant could reasonably be obtained by
> other means.
> (5) A warrant shall not be considered necessary on the ground falling within subsection
> (3)(c) unless the information which it is thought necessary to obtain is information relating
> to the acts or intentions of persons outside the British Islands."

The Regulation of Investigatory Powers Act 2000 also defines who may apply for a warrant.
The category of applicants has been extended and s.6 now includes the following: the Director-
General of the Security Service; the Chief of the Secret Intelligence Service; the Director of
GCHQ; the chief constable of any police force in Scotland; and the Chief of Defence Intelli-
gence. By virtue of s.7 an interception warrant is to be issued only by a Secretary of State—or in
Scotland, the First Minister. In urgent cases the Secretary of State may authorise a warrant to
be signed by a senior official. Under s.8(1) the warrant must name or describe either—
> (a) one person as the interception subject; or
> (b) a single set of premises as the premises in relation to which the interception to which
> the warrant relates is to take place.
A warrant will be valid for three months, unless renewed. Once renewed a warrant will be valid
for another three months except those issued under s.5(1) (a) and (c) above: these are valid for
six months. There is no limit to the number of times a warrant can be renewed. A warrant
should be cancelled where the person requesting it "is no longer necessary on grounds falling
within section 5(3)" (s.9(3)).
An increasingly controversial feature of the 2000 Act (inherited from its predecessor) is s.17.
This provides for the exclusion of evidence about the interception of communications from legal
proceedings. Specifically, s.17(1) provides that:

> "no evidence shall be adduced, question asked, assertion or disclosure made or other thing
> done in, for the purposes of or in connection with any legal proceedings which (in any
> manner)—
> > (a) discloses, in circumstances from which its origin in anything falling within sub-
> > section (2) may be inferred, any of the contents of an intercepted communication
> > or any related communications data; or
> > (b) tends (apart from any such disclosure) to suggest that anything falling within
> > subsection (2) has or may have occurred or be going to occur.
> Subsection (2) provides that 'the following fall within this subsection—
> > (a) conduct by a person falling within subsection (3) that was or would be an offence
> > under section 1(1) or (2) of this Act or under section 1 of the Interception of
> > Communications Act 1985;
> > (b) a breach by the Secretary of State of his duty under section 1(4) of this Act;
> > (c) the issue of an interception warrant or of a warrant under the Interception of
> > Communications Act 1985;
> > (d) the making of an application by any person for an interception warrant, or for a
> > warrant under that Act;
> > (e) the imposition of any requirement on any person to provide assistance with giving
> > effect to an interception warrant."

Subsection (3) then lists a number of persons for the purposes of s.17(2)(a). These include the
persons to whom a warrant may be addressed, any person holding office under the Crown;

police officers and people employed by postal services or public telecommunication services. There are a number of exceptions in s.18 which relate mainly to proceedings for breach of the RIPA 2000 itself.

Not only may questions not be asked about interception, but the accused is not entitled to be told whether an interception has taken place, far less to be supplied with a copy of the transcripts. In *R. v Preston* [1994] 2 A.C. 130 an unsuccessful attempt was made to have a conviction quashed on the ground that the contents of an interception transcript were not available to the defence. The appeal failed with the House of Lords holding that there was no duty to disclose such evidence. According to Lord Jauncey of Tullichettle:

> "The defendants argued strenuously that failure to disclose intercepted material could result in prejudice to defendants. In my view, any prejudice which might result to the defence must be far outweighed by the inability of the prosecution to make use of incriminating material gleaned from an intercept. It is likely that in the great majority of cases in which a prosecution follows telephone-tapping the material of the intercept will incriminate rather than exculpate one or other of the parties to the intercepted conversation and would be of assistance to the prosecution if it were available in evidence."

Whether or not this is so, it may be a matter of concern in this case that during the trial arguments about the telephone tapping "had taken place in the judge's room in the absence of the defendants. Counsel were forbidden to tell their clients about the arguments exchanged and the information confided in the course of [these discussions]".

Section 18 of the Regulation of Investigatory Powers Act 2000 now provides that:

> "(7) Nothing in section 17(1) shall prohibit any such disclosure of any information that continues to be available for disclosure as is confined to—
>
> (a) a disclosure to a person conducting a criminal prosecution for the purpose only of enabling that person to determine what is required of him by his duty to secure the fairness of the prosecution; or
>
> (b) a disclosure to a relevant judge in a case in which that judge has ordered the disclosure to be made to him alone.
>
> (8) A relevant judge shall not order a disclosure under subsection (7)(b) except where he is satisfied that the exceptional circumstances of the case make the disclosure essential in the interests of justice.
>
> (9) Subject to subsection (10), where in any criminal proceedings—
>
> (a) a relevant judge does order a disclosure under subsection (7)(b), and
>
> (b) in consequence of that disclosure he is of the opinion that there are exceptional circumstances requiring him to do so,
>
> he may direct the person conducting the prosecution to make for the purposes of the proceedings any such admission of fact as that judge thinks essential in the interests of justice.
>
> (10) Nothing in any direction under subsection (9) shall authorise or require anything to be done in contravention of section 17(1).
>
> (11) In this section 'a relevant judge' means—
>
> (a) any judge of the High Court or of the Crown Court or any Circuit judge;
>
> (b) any judge of the High Court of Justiciary or any sheriff."

Proposals have been made from time to time to change the law to allow phone tapping evidence to be admitted, but these have always been rejected by the government. It is unclear whether this reflects a lack of confidence in the surveillance practices adopted or in the adequacy of the procedures against abuse. The following is an example of a recommendation for changing the law. The relevant law at the time was to be found in the Interception of Communications Act 1985, s.9.

Lord Lloyd of Berwick
Inquiry into Legislation against Terrorism
Cm. 3420, (1996)

"7.8 I come now to the arguments in favour of relaxing the strict embargo imposed by section 9 in terrorist cases. I have already explained that this would not require any amendment to [other provisions of the Act]. Nor would it require the repeal of section 9. It would require only that section 9 be amended to allow (not compel) the prosecution to adduce intercept material where so advised; so if, for example, the intercept material included a telephone conversation implicating the leader of a terrorist organisation in the commission of a terrorist offence, the intercept could be used, together with any other evidence in the case, to help secure his conviction. Obviously in such a case the whole of the intercept material relating to that defendant would have to be disclosed to the defence. But if the prosecution chose not to use the material, on the ground that it did not materially assist the prosecution, or on any other ground, then section 9 would continue to prevent the defence from asking any question tending to suggest that the interception had taken place, and, a *fortiori*, from calling for disclosure. The material would be fully protected.

7.9 What then are the arguments in favour of the proposed amendment?

7.10 The first and most obvious argument is that evidence of intercepted material is admissible to prove guilt in each of the countries which I have visited, and in every other country of which I have knowledge. The United Kingdom stands alone in excluding such material. Thus in the United States the use of intercept material in evidence is regarded as essential. In many instances, including high-profile cases involving the New York Mafia, convictions otherwise unobtainable have been secured by the use of intercept material. I put to officers of the FBI the suggestion that they were having second thoughts about the use of intercept material. I could find no support for this suggestion. In France I was told that intercept material has proved very valuable in terrorist cases. Thus, some 80% of the evidence against those suspected of involvement in the 1995 bombings is derived from intercept. Similarly, in Australia interception is regarded as an 'extremely valuable aid to the criminal prosecution'. The statistics with which I have been provided by the Security Division of the Attorney-General's Department show that in 1993–1994 668 warrants were issued under Part VI of the Telecommunications (Interception) Act 1979. 664 prosecutions for offences ranging from murder to serious fraud were based on intercepted material, nearly 500 of those prosecutions being for drug offences. Convictions were obtained in 87% of the cases. Often, when presented with the evidence of an intercept, the defendant pleads guilty.

7.11 If the use of intercept material is regarded as an essential tool in the prosecution hands in these and other countries, it does at least suggest that it would be of assistance to the prosecution authorities in the United Kingdom, if only in a small number of cases. It is always difficult to look backwards and point to specific cases in which interception material would have enabled a person to be charged or a conviction obtained. But I have been shown a list of some twenty cases, including four recent cases in which the intercept material would have been of assistance to the prosecution; and I was told of at least one terrorist investigation in which the interception evidence would have supplied 'the missing pieces in the jigsaw' and thus enabled a prosecution to be brought. One cannot also help wondering whether the admission of intercept evidence might not resolve some of the difficulties that arise in cases before the European Court of Human Rights.

7.12 The second argument in favour of some relaxation of section 9 is the curious disparity which now exists between IOCA on the one hand and the Security Service Act 1989 and the Intelligence Services Act 1994 on the other. Under the Security Service Act, for example, the Secretary of State may authorise the Security Service to enter on another's property in order to carry out eavesdropping operations. There is nothing in the Security Service Act which corresponds to section 9 of IOCA. On the contrary, section 2(2)(a) of the

Security Service Act as now amended, contemplates that the product of an eavesdropping operation will be admissible in evidence in criminal proceedings. Similarly the product of an eavesdropping operation carried out by the police in accordance with Home Office Guidelines is also admissible in evidence, as was decided by the House of Lords in the very recent case of *R v Khan* [1997] A.C. 558. No doubt when legislation is introduced to put the use of surveillance devices by the police on a statutory footing, as now at last proposed, eavesdropping by the police will continue to be admissible, subject to the discretion of the judge to exclude the evidence under PACE, section 78.

7.13 The position can be illustrated by an example: let us suppose that a telephone conversation takes place between two members of a terrorist organisation in which they discuss a forthcoming terrorist attack. Let us suppose that the Secretary of State has authorised a telephone intercept on the telephone line in question, and has also authorised the Security Service to place an eavesdropping device in the room where one end of the conversation takes place. An enterprising police officer, having obtained (mistakenly) the necessary authority from the assistant chief constable, places a second device in the same room. Tape recordings recovered from both devices of what was said by the man in the room would be admissible in evidence against him. But the intercept of the telephone conversation itself, and what was said by the man at the other end, would not be admissible; unless, of course there happened to be another enterprising police officer at the other end of the telephone conversation. This example, not all that far-fetched, would seem to produce a result so obviously absurd that something must have gone wrong.

7.14 There is another anomaly. In drugs cases, and other cases involving an alleged conspiracy, the prosecution often rely on the frequency of telephone conversations between two or more subscribers to prove the conspiracy. *R v Preston* [1994] 2 A.C. 130 was just such a case. The police can obtain this information without difficulty from the telephone operating company, since the company needs the information for the purpose of billing its customers. Hence the term 'metering'. There is nothing in IOCA to prevent the prosecution from adducing metering evidence, and inviting the jury to infer from the pattern and frequency of telephone calls that the defendants are parties to a conspiracy. It would surely seem odd to a member of the jury that he was being invited to infer guilt from the happening of one or more telephone conversations without being told what was actually said. Is it sensible that the prosecution should be obliged to get round the prohibition contained in section 9 of the Act by this indirect means?

7.15 I come now to the arguments on the other side. There are two main arguments. The first is that if interception material is used as evidence in court, the interception capability will become more widely known among terrorists, drug dealers and the criminal classes generally; as a result criminals would use more guarded language, or avoid the use of the telephone altogether.

7.16 I accept, of course, that the primary benefit of interception lies in detection, and, in the case of the Security Service, the Secret Intelligence Service and GCHQ, in the gathering of intelligence. If I thought that the intelligence effort would be materially affected by any relaxation of section 9, then I would have great hesitation in proposing any change.

7.17 But there is no evidence that the intelligence effort in other countries—eg the United States or Australia—has been affected in any way by the use of intercept material in court. Nor can I see any reason why it should be so affected. It is not as though the interception capability is still a well-kept secret, as it may have been when IOCA was introduced. Sophisticated criminals are all well aware that their telephones are, or may be, tapped. This is why they adopt coded language when discussing their plans, and often use telephones which they think may not be tapped. If intercept material were to be used in court in one or two terrorist cases a year, I cannot believe that drug dealers would learn anything that they do not already know. As for the fear that criminals would cease to use the telephone altogether, I regard this as fanciful. Drug dealers planning an importation, or terrorists planning to plant a bomb, must communicate with each other and with those who are directing the operation by some means. It cannot be done by pigeon post. There is no practicable alternative to the use of the telephone.

7.18 Similarly, I doubt whether the language used by criminals would become more opaque than it is at present. In any event those who have experience in listening to intercepted conversations are astute to pick up the meaning of new terms. I do not anticipate any difficulty on that score. All in all the risk that intelligence gathering, or the detection of drug dealers, will be jeopardized by the occasional use of intercept material in the conviction of terrorists can, I think, be discounted.

7.19 The second argument against any relaxation of section 9 is that it will result in pressure for increased disclosure by the prosecution. This would certainly be the consequence in any case in which the prosecution choose to rely on intercept evidence. Obviously in such a case the defence would be entitled to see the whole of the intercept evidence relating to that defendant. But where the prosecution chooses not to rely on intercept evidence, the position will be the same as it is today. The prosecution will not be obliged to disclose the existence of any intercept material, and the defence will not be permitted to ask whether such material exists.

7.20 Some fear was expressed that it would be open to the defence to argue along the lines 'my client must be innocent, since if he were guilty there would be incriminating material in existence on which the prosecution would have relied'. I suspect that section 9 already prohibits this line of argument by implication. If not, it would be easy enough to make it do so by amending section 9.

7.21 Another fear is that the use of intercept material in terrorist cases will add to the burden of the prosecution in preparing for trial, and to the expense of the agencies in storing intercept material pending a decision by prosecuting counsel on whether he intends to use the material or not. But I repeat: I am not proposing any change in the law or practice with regard to drugs cases, or other cases of serious crime under section 2(2)(b) of the [1985] Act. That would require an amendment to section 2(2)(b) as well as new arrangements under section 6. My proposal concerns only the relatively small number of cases affecting national security within section 2(2)(a). As I have already explained there is nothing in the Act which requires national security material to be destroyed before trial. Nor can I believe that the storage of such material would present insuperable problems. The material need not be transcribed until a decision has been taken by the prosecution whether to use it or not. Nor would my proposal add greatly, or indeed at all, to the burden on prosecution counsel, since, as I understand it, the prosecution must in any event be satisfied that there is nothing in the material which is inconsistent with the defendant's guilt.

7.22 This brings me to another problem. How can the court be satisfied that the undisclosed material does not assist the defence? I accept that there is a problem here. It was discussed by Lord Mustill in his speech in *R v Preston*. But it is not a problem which is made any worse by allowing the prosecution to use the material when it does not assist the defence. If there is undisclosed material which shows that the defendant is not guilty, then obviously the prosecution will be dropped, as it would be at present. If the material is neutral, counsel must ensure that the prosecution is not conducted in a manner which is inconsistent with that material. There may be difficult borderline cases. But there is no way of avoiding these.

7.23 Then is it in some way unfair that the prosecution should be allowed to use the material when it is helpful, but not disclose the material when it is not? This is a question on which different views might be held. But my own firmly held view is that in terrorist cases, where the terrorist has, in a sense, declared war on our society, and our democratic way of doing things, then society is surely entitled to defend itself. It should not be obliged to fight back with one arm tied behind its back. The arguments in favour of allowing a limited relaxation of section 9 in terrorist cases are, I think, overwhelming.

7.24 Finally I should say that I see no special difficulty in presenting the evidence in court for the consideration of the jury. Nor is there any great risk that interception techniques or methods would be compromised. Some aspects of the procedure, for example, to prove the integrity of the transcript, could, it necessary, be covered by a certificate signed by the relevant official. This is how it is done in Australia and other countries. It could be done here.

    7.25 I recommend that section 9 of IOCA be amended so as to allow the prosecution to adduce intercept material in cases affecting national security, that is to say, cases where the warrant authorising the interception has been issued under section 2(2)(a) of the Act, thus bringing IOCA into line with the Security Service Act 1989 and the Intelligence Servies Act 1994."

An important feature of the British regime for phone tapping is the lack of any judicial involvement in the process of granting warrants. This compares with the practice in most other countries, and it compares with the practice relating to the search of private property where a judicial rather than a ministerial warrant is required. However, although there is no judicial authorisation of warrants, there is judicial oversight of the procedure, though quite whether this is an adequate substitute for judicial authorisation is highly contestable. Section 57 of the RIPA 2000 makes provision for the appointment of an Interception of Communications Commissioner by the Prime Minister. He or she has general responsibilities to keep the operation of the legislation under review. Only people who have held high judicial office (within the meaning of the Appellate Jurisdiction Act 1876) are eligible for appointment. Appointments are presumably on terms agreed between the Commissioner and the Prime Minister. The first person appointed was Thomas L.J., a judge of the Court of Appeal in England and Wales who thus has jurisdiction over the First Minister in Scotland. His predecessors as Interception Commissioner (under the 1985 Act) included Lord Bingham and Lord Nolan.

    If in the course of his or her supervision the Commissioner uncovers any breach of the Act, he or she must report this to the Prime Minister. The Commissioner must in any event make an annual report to the Prime Minister, who may then decide to withhold some of the report before it is published. The reports of the Commissioner outline his working methods, which in recent years have included at least two visits to each of the agencies responsible for requesting warrants, as well as meetings with those who issue warrants:

"8.I have been very impressed by the quality, dedication and enthusiasm of the personnel carrying out this work on behalf of the government and the people of the United Kingdom. They show that they have a detailed understanding of the legislation and strive assiduously to comply with the statutory criteria and, in my view, there is very little, if any, danger that an application which is defective in substance will be placed before the Secretary of State. Where errors have occurred, which I refer to below (and in detail in the Confidential Annex) these have been errors of detail and not of substance. All errors are reported to me and if there is any product it is immediately destroyed. In conforming to the statutory duty placed on them, the agencies have made available to me everything that I have wished to see or hear. They welcome the oversight of the Commissioner, both from the point of view of seeking his advice, which they do quite frequently, and as a reassurance to the general public that their activities are overseen by an independent person who has held high judicial office. I am also left in no doubt as to the agencies' anxiety to comply with the law. In a case of doubt or difficulty, they do not hesitate to contact me.

    9. During the year I have also seen the Home Secretary, the Foreign Secretary, the Secretary of State for Northern Ireland, the Secretary of State for Defence and the First Minister for Scotland. I have been impressed with the care that they take to satisfy themselves that the warrants are necessary for the authorised purposes. If the Secretary of State has any doubts about the application and is minded to refuse it, further information or clarification would be sought so that reconsideration is given to issuing or renewing a warrant. Outright refusal of an application is comparatively rare because of the care with which applications are prepared by the agency concerned and scrutinised by the senior officials in the Secretary of State's department before they are submitted to him. However, I view the occurrence of occasional outright refusals, where for example, the strict require-

ments of necessity and proportionality are not met in the opinion of the Secretary of State, as a healthy sign. It shows that the Secretaries of State do not act as a 'rubber stamp'." (Report of the Interception of Communications Commissioner for 2002 (H.C. 1047, 2003), p.13.)

The Commissioner also visits the communications service providers (CSPs), that is to say the Post Office and major telephone companies. In recent reports the Commissioner has drawn attention to the fact that the system is working well with no evidence of abuse.

"10. Many members of the public are suspicious about the interception of communications, and some believe that their own conversations are subject to unlawful interception by the security, intelligence or law enforcement agencies. To an extent this may be understandable, because people do tend to be suspicious of what takes place in secret, and are worried by the 'big brother' concept. Interception for lawful purposes, of course, and inevitably, takes place in secret. In my oversight work I am conscious of these concerns. However, I am as satisfied as I can be that the concerns are, in fact, unfounded. Interception of an individual's communications can take place only after a Secretary of State has granted a warrant and the warrant can be granted on strictly limited grounds set out in section 5 of RIPA, essentially the interests of national security and the prevention or detection of serious crime. Of course, it would theoretically be possible to circumvent this procedure, but there are in place extensive safeguards to ensure that this cannot happen, and it is an important part of my work to ensure that these are in place, and that they are observed. Furthermore, any attempt to get round the procedures which provide for legal interception would, by reason of the safeguards, involve a major conspiracy within the agency concerned which I believe would, for practical purposes, be impossible. I am as satisfied as it is possible to be that deliberate unlawful interception of communications of the citizen does not take place. I say 'deliberate' because on rare occasions technical errors do occur which may render an interception unlawful in which case the product, if any has been received, from the interception is always destroyed.
11. As in the past, the Annex to this Report contains a summary of the numbers of warrants in force at the end of 2001 and those issued throughout the course of the year by the Home Secretary and the Scottish First Minister. The great majority of warrants issued in England and Wales and Scotland remain related to the prevention and detection of serious crime. The continuing incidence of serious and organised crime and an increased facility to counter it are the main cause of the larger numbers of warrants. The significantly high level of warrants sought each year, with a corresponding level of workload for the Secretaries of State and on the part of the relevant Agencies, clearly calls for the exercise of vigilant supervision. I can report that the level of scrutiny has been and continues to be generally well maintained."
(Report of the Interception of Communications Commissioner for 2001 (H.C. 1243, 2002), pp.2–3.)

Also in recent reports, the Commissioner has highlighted the importance of interception as an instrument for dealing with terrorism and serious crime (*ibid.*, p.7).
Concerns about the levels of interception in Scotland were addressed by the Commissioner in his report for 2001:

"12. There was some criticism of the level of the interception of communications in the year 2000 in Scotland in the Scottish Parliament and the Scottish media in February 2002. My inspections in Scotland show quite clearly that warrants for interception there have been granted by Ministers in Scotland only in cases which properly fall squarely within the definition of serious crime and within the upper echelons of that definition."
(Report of the Interception of Communications Commissioner for 2001 (H.C. 1243, 2002), p.3.)

The Commissioner's main concern has been with the number of errors that are made in executing warrants, which are said still be to "unacceptably high":

"39. One error was reported by the Scottish Executive although the fault for the error lies, not with them, but with a Scottish police force. The police force sought, and obtained, from the Scottish Executive a warrant, which was signed on 8 August 2002. By 13 August 2002 it became apparent that the intercept was not producing any intelligence. It transpired that the telephone number on the interception warrant was incorrect by one digit. Investigations revealed that the intelligence records in respect of the target showed the correct telephone number but that a mistake occurred within the police force when the number was transcribed into the warrant application form to the Scottish Executive."

   (Report of the Interception of Communications Commissioner for 2002 (H.C. 1047, 2003), p.13).

The volume of warrants issued is such that it would be physically impossible for the Commissioner to inspect all the warrants that are issued each year, far less inspect all the modifications to warrants that are made. As a result an examination is made of only a random sample:

"7. In accordance with these duties I have continued my practice of making twice yearly visits to the Security Service, the Secret Intelligence Service, GCHQ, the National Criminal Intelligence Service, the Special Branch of the Metropolitan Police, Strathclyde Police, the Police Service for Northern Ireland, HM Customs and Excise, the Foreign and Commonwealth Office, the Home Office, the Scottish Executive and the Ministry of Defence. Prior to each visit I obtain a complete list of warrants issued or renewed since my previous visit. I then select, largely at random although there have been occasions where I have indicated specific cases that I want to see, a sample of warrants for close inspection. In the course of my visit I satisfy myself that the warrants fully meet the requirements of RIPA, that proper procedures have been followed, that the relevant safeguards and codes of practice have been followed. During each visit I review each of the files and the supporting documents and discuss the cases directly with the operational officers concerned. I can view the product of interception. It is important to ensure that the facts justify the use of interception in each case and those concerned with interception fully understand the safeguards and the codes of practice."

   (Report of the Interception of Communications Commissioner for 2002 (H.C. 1047, 2003), p.2.)

   With the increase in the number of warrants granted, it remains to be seen whether this process of *ex post facto* judicial oversight will be a sufficient safeguard and a sufficient substitute for *ex ante* judicial authorisation. In the meantime it is to be noted that there is a right to apply to the Investigatory Powers Tribunal by anyone who claims that they have been the subject of interception under a warrant which has been improperly granted. The Investigatory Powers Tribunal replaces the Interception of Communications Tribunal which operated since 1985. The tribunal is chaired by a judge of the English Court of Appeal, and its other members include Sheriff Principal McInnes. This nevertheless seems a rather pointless jurisdiction, a judgment vindicated by the fact that despite several hundred applications having been made to these tribunals, none has ever succeeded in what is now some 20 years of their operation. Individuals are never informed that they are or have been the subject of interception, or of the reasons for it. Quite how they are expected to challenge the granting of a warrant is consequently difficult to fathom, however extensive the remedial powers of the tribunal may be on paper. It may also be noted that the tribunal is protected by a remarkable privative clause which purports to exclude judicial scrutiny of its activities. Section 67 of the 2000 Act provides:

"(8) Except to such extent as the Secretary of State may by order otherwise provide, determinations, awards, orders and other decisions of the Tribunal (including decisions as to whether they have jurisdiction) shall not be subject to appeal or be liable to be questioned in any court."

If the tribunal was a credible body, this would be a matter of some concern. As it is the Commissioner is generally satisfied that the powers in the RIPA are carried out within the law: (Report of the Interception of Communications Commissioner for 2001 (H.C 1243, 2002), p.7).

V. INTERFERENCE WITH PROPERTY

Moving beyond surveillance by interception to surveillance from within the premises of an individual, this requires taking another step in terms of violation of the privacy rights. Here the state is not simply watching the individual but is invading his or her property to do so, in this case by placing a bugging or eavesdropping device. This is a practice that may be resorted to by both the security service and the police, and which for a long time was unregulated by law. So far as the security service is concerned, the matter first came to judicial notice during the Spycatcher affair when it was famously claimed by a retired security service officer that MI5 had bugged and burgled its way across London. But rather than attract judicial condemnation, in *Attorney General v Guardian Newspapers Ltd (No. 2)* [1988] 3 All E.R. 545 Lord Donaldson expressed the view that:

"It would be a sad day for democracy and the rule of law if the service were ever to be considered to be above or exempt from the law of the land. And it is not. At any time any member of the service who breaks the law is liable to be prosecuted. But there is a need for some discretion and common sense. Let us suppose that the service has information which suggests that a spy may be operating from particular premises. It needs to have confirmation. It may well consider that, if he proves to be a spy, the interests of the nation are better served by letting him continue with his activities under surveillance and in ignorance that he has been detected rather than by arresting him. What is the service expected to do? A secret search of the premises is the obvious answer. Is this really 'wrongdoing'?

Let us test it in a mundane context known to us all. Prior to the passing of s 79 of the Road Traffic Regulation Act 1967, fire engines and ambulances, unlike police vehicles, had no exemption from the speed limits. Their drivers hurrying to an emergency broke the law. So far as I am aware that is still the position in relation to crossing traffic lights which are showing red and driving on the wrong side of the road to bypass a traffic jam. The responsible authorities in a very proper exercise of discretion simply do not prosecute them.

Even in the context of the work of the security service which, I must stress, is the defence of the realm, there must be stringent limits to what breaches of the law can be considered excusable. Thus I cannot conceive of physical violence ever coming within this category. Or physical restraint, other than in the powers of arrest enjoyed by every citizen or under the authority of a lawful warrant of arrest. But covert invasions of privacy, which I think is what Mr Wright means by 'burglary', may in some circumstances be a different matter.

It may be that the time has come when Parliament should regularise the position of the service. It is certainly a tenable view. The alternative view, which is equally tenable, is that the public interest is better served by leaving the members of the service liable to prosecution for any breach of the law at the instance of a private individual or of a public prosecuting authority, but they may expect that prosecuting authorities will exercise a wise discretion and that in an appropriate case the Attorney General would enter a nolle prosequi, justifying his action to Parliament if necessary."

This was clearly not an acceptable basis for the violation of human rights, and in the Security Service Act 1989 a procedure was introduced whereby the security service could apply to the Home Secretary for a warrant to authorise interference with property. The form of interference was unspecified, but it is clear that it was intended to deal with entry in order to place listening devices. A new Security Service Commissioner was appointed on the model of the Interception of Communications Commissioner to supervise the operation of the legislation. The matter is now governed by the Intelligence Services Act 1994.

Intelligence Services Act 1994

"**5.**—(1) No entry on or interference with property or with wireless telegraphy shall be unlawful if it is authorised by a warrant issued by the Secretary of State under this section.

(2) The Secretary of State may, on an application made by the Security Service, the Intelligence Service or GCHQ, issue a warrant under this section authorising the taking, subject to subsection (3) below, of such action as is specified in the warrant in respect of any property so specified or in respect of wireless telegraphy so specified if the Secretary of State—

    (a) thinks it necessary for the action to be taken for the purpose of assisting, as the case may be,—
      (i) the Security Service in carrying out any of its functions under the 1989 Act; or
      (ii) the Intelligence Service in carrying out any of its functions under section 1 above; or
      (iii) GCHQ in carrying out any function which falls within section 3(1)(a) above; and
    (b) is satisfied that the taking of the action is proportionate to what the action seeks to achieve; and
    (c) is satisfied that satisfactory arrangements are in force under section 2(2)(a) of the 1989 Act (duties of the Director-General of the Security Service), section 2(2)(a) above or section 4(2)(a) above with respect to the disclosure of information obtained by virtue of this section and that any information obtained under the warrant will be subject to those arrangements.

(2A) The matters to be taken into account in considering whether the requirements of subsection (2)(a) and (b) are satisfied in the case of any warrant shall include what it is thought necessary to achieve by the conduct authorised by the warrant could reasonably be achieved by other means.

(3) A warrant issued on the application of the Intelligence Service or GCHQ for the purposes of the exercise of their functions by virtue of section 1(2)(c) or 3(2)(c) above may not relate to property in the British Islands.

(3A) A warrant issued on the application of the Security Service for the purposes of the exercise of their function under section 1(4) of the Security Service Act 1989 may not relate to property in the British Islands unless it authorises the taking of action in relation to conduct within subsection (3B) below.

(3B) Conduct is within this subsection if it constitutes (or, if it took place in the United Kingdom, would constitute) one or more offences, and either

    (a) it involves the use of violence, results in substantial financial gain or is conduct by a large number of persons in pursuit of a common purpose; or
    (b) the offence or one of the offences is an offence for which a person who has attained the age of twenty-one [(eighteen in relation to England and Wales)] and has no previous convictions could reasonably be expected to be sentenced to imprisonment for a term of three years or more.

(4) Subject to subsection (S) below, the Security Service may make an application under subsection (2) above for a warrant to be issued authorising that Service (or a person acting on its behalf) to take such action as is specified in the warrant on behalf of the Intelligence Service or GCHQ and, where such a warrant is issued, the functions of the Security Service shall include the carrying out of the action so specified, whether or not it would otherwise be within its functions.

(5) The Security Service may not make an application for a warrant by virtue of sub-section (4) above except where the action proposed to be authorised by the warrant

    (a) is action in respect of which the Intelligence Service or, as the case may be, GCHQ could make such an application; and

    (b) is to be taken otherwise than in support of the prevention or detection of seriouscrime.

6 Warrants: procedure and duration, etc.

    (1) A warrant shall not be issued except—

    (a) under the hand of the Secretary of State or, in the case of a warrant by the Scottish Ministers (by virtue of provision made under section 63 of the Scotland Act 1998), a member of the Scottish Executive; or

    (b) in an urgent case where the Secretary of State has expressly authorised its issue and a statement of the fact is endorsed on it, under the hand of a senior official ... ; or

    (c) in an urgent case where, the Scottish Ministers have (by virtue of provision made under section 63 of the Scotland Act 1998) expressly authorised its issue and a statement of that fact is endorsed thereon, under the hand of a member of the staff of the Scottish Administration who is in the Senior Civil Service and is designated by the Scottish Ministers as a person under whose hand a warrant may be issued in such a case.

    (2) A warrant shall unless renewed under subsection (3) below, cease to have effect

    (a) if the warrant was under the hand of the Secretary of State or, in the case of a warrant issued by the Scottish Ministers (by virtue of provision made under section 63 of the Scotland Act 1998) a member of the Scottish Executive, at the end of the period of six months beginning with the day on which it was issued; and

    (b) in any other case, at the end of the period ending with the second working day following that day.

    (3) If at any time before the day on which a warrant would cease to have effect the Secretary of State considers it necessary for the warrant to continue to have effect for the purpose for which it was issued, he may by an instrument under his hand renew it for a period of six months beginning with that day.

    (4) The Secretary of State shall cancel a warrant if he is satisfied that the action authorised by it is no longer necessary.

The 1994 Act replaced the Security Service Commissioner with the Intelligence Services Commissioner with responsibilities to monitor the operation of all the security and intelligence services (and not just MI5 as under the 1989 Act). The Commissioner monitors the operation of the warrant procedure and reports annually to the Prime Minister. Although the non-confidential annex to the reports are published, they are not very illuminating and shed little light on the operation of this procedure.

Report of the Intelligence Services Commissioner for 2002
Commissioner: Rt. Hon. Lord Justice Simon Brown
H.C. 1048 (2003)

"27. As I have already explained, property (and/or intrusive surveillance) warrants for the Security Service are generally issued by the Home Secretary and the Secretary of State for Northern Ireland and those for the SIS and GCHQ by the Foreign Secretary. ... In carrying out my functions during 2002 I have, as usual, visited each of the security and intelligence agencies—the Security Service, SIS and GCHQ—as well as the warrant issuing government departments. In the course of these visits I have been concerned to satisfy myself that the respective agencies' object in obtaining the information being sought has been in the discharge of one of its statutory functions; that the action in question has appeared to be both necessary for obtaining information which could not reasonably be obtained by other less intrusive means and also proportionate to what is sought to be achieved; and that such information is likely to be of substantial value.

28. I have read the files relating to many of the warrants and authorisations issued during the course of the year and some of those where the warrants previously issued have been renewed. In so doing, I have also had the opportunity to review the material obtained from the operation. In a number of cases I have questioned those involved in the preparation of the warrant application, those who administer the warrant system and those who have implemented the warrant once it has been issued and acted on the information obtained under it. In the course of the year under review I have had meetings with the Home Secretary, the Foreign Secretary and the Secretary of State for Defence to discuss the warrantry/authorisation procedures.

29. In issuing warrants the Secretary of State is dependent on the accuracy of the information contained in the application and the candour of those applying for it. This is essentially a question of the integrity and quality of the personnel involved in the warrantry process both in the agencies and the government departments concerned. I regard it as one of my functions to check these matters so far as I can and as a result I am as satisfied as I believe I possibly can be that the applications made during the year in question properly reflected the position at the time of submission, and that the Secretaries of State have properly exercised their powers under the Acts. It is the duty of every member of each intelligence service, every official of the department of each relevant Secretary of State and every member of Her Majesty's Forces to disclose or provide to me all such documents and information as I may require to enable me to carry out my oversight functions—see section 60(1) of RIPA. I enjoy, therefore, very wide powers to ensure that I obtain maximum assistance from those I see during my reviews. In exercising these powers I have continued to experience the fullest possible co-operation on the part of all those concerned. Indeed, I have consistently gained the impression that the members of the various agencies at all levels are without exception keen rather than in any way reluctant to confide in me all possibly relevant information and, where appropriate, to share with me their deepest concerns.

30. Consistently with the practice followed since annual reporting by the respective statutory Commissioners began, I do not propose to disclose publicly the numbers of warrants or authorisations issued to the agencies. It would, I believe, assist the operation of those hostile to the state if they were able to estimate even approximately the extent of the work of the Security Service, SIS and GCHQ in fulfilling their functions. The figures are, however, of interest and I have included them in the confidential annex to this report."

So far as the police are concerned, the use of eavesdropping devices was unregulated by legislation until 1997. Before then the matter was governed by guidelines issued in England and Wales by the Home Office and in Scotland by the Scottish Office. Under the guidelines the use of such devices in any particular case could be authorised by a chief constable who was required to be satisfied that a number of criteria were met: (1) the investigation had to concern serious crime; (2) normal methods of investigation must have been tried and failed, or must, from the nature of things, be unlikely to have succeeded if tried; (3) there must have been good reason to think that the use of the equipment would have been likely to lead to an arrest and a conviction or, where appropriate, to the prevention of acts of terrorism; and (4) the use of equipment must have been operationally feasible. The authorising officer should also have satisfied himself that the degree of intrusion into the privacy of those affected by the surveillance was commensurate with the seriousness of the offence. The guidelines were considered by the House of Lords in *R. v Khan* [1997] A.C. 558 where the appellant had been convicted and jailed for offences connected with the importation of heroin.

The only evidence against the appellant was based on a tape recorded conversation of a meeting between him and another man. The meeting took place in the home of the latter and the evidence was obtained by means of a listening device that had been placed on the outside wall of the house in which the meeting was held. This had been done without the consent of the owner of the property, and was clearly unlawful in the sense that it had involved a civil trespass and some damage to the property. The Home Office Guidelines clearly could not authorise this illegality and the issue for the courts was whether evidence obtained by such illegal means was admissible. According to Lord Nolan, "as a matter of English law, evidence which is obtained improperly or even unlawfully remains admissible", subject to a discretion to exclude it on the grounds of fairness. However, the fact that evidence was obtained in improperly or, as in this case, in breach of the ECHR was not in itself reason to exclude it. In this case the evidence was properly admitted. Lord Nolan did, however, conclude by saying that:

"The sole cause of this case coming to your Lordships' House is the lack of a statutory system regulating the use of surveillance devices by the police. The absence of such a system seems astonishing, the more so in view of the statutory framework which has governed the use of such devices by the security service since 1989, and the interception of communications by the police as well as by other agencies since 1985."

It was subsequently held by the European Court of Human Rights that the practice of using surveillance devices based on Home Office Guidelines was a breach of art.8 of the ECHR: *Khan v United Kingdom* (2001) 30 E.H.R.R. 1016. This was both obvious and predictable in the light of the earlier decisions of the court, most notably *Malone v United Kingdom* (1984) 7 E.H.R.R. 14. This is simply because the practice was not prescribed by law, however justifiable a limitation it may be under art.8(2). However, the court also held that "the use at the applicant's trial of the secretly taped material did not conflict with the requirements of fairness guaranteed by Art.6(1) of the Convention". The position is now governed by the Police Act 1997 which was very controversial at the time it was passed, not least because it continues with the recent practice of allowing individual rights to be interfered with without a judicial warrant. Under Pt III of the Police Act 1997 (which applies to England and Wales as well as Scotland) provision is made for the creation of yet more Commissioners appointed by the Prime Minister. The Commissioners must be persons who hold or have held high judicial office within the meaning of the Appellate Jurisdiction Act 1876, and they hold office for fixed terms of three years. Appointments are made after consulting the First Minister, amongst others. The decisions of the Chief Commissioner or, subject to ss.104 and 106 (on which see below), any other Commissioner (including decisions as to his jurisdiction) shall not be subject to appeal or liable to be questioned in any court.

Police Act 1997

"Effect of authorisation under Part III

92. No entry on or interference with property or with wireless telegraphy shall be unlawful if it is authorised by an authorisation having effect under this Part.

93 Authorisations to interfere with property etc.

(1) Where subsection (2) applies, an authorising officer may authorise
    (a) the taking of such action, in respect of such property in the relevant area, as he may specify,
    (ab) the taking of such action falling within subsection (1A) in respect of property outside the relevant area, as he may specify, or
    (b) the taking of such action in the relevant aria as he may specify, in respect of wireless telegraphy.

(1A) The action falling within this subsection is action for maintaining or retrieving any equipment, apparatus or device the placing or use of which in the relevant area has been authorised under this Part or Part II of the Regulation of Investigatory Powers Act 2000 or under any enactment contained in or made under an Act of the Scottish Parliament which makes provision equivalent to that made by Part II of that Act of 2000.

(lB) Subsection (1) applies where the authorising officer is a customs officer [or an officer of the Office of Fair Trading] with the omission of—

    (a) the words "in the relevant area" in each place where they occur; and

    (b) paragraph (ab).

(2) This subsection applies where the authorising officer believes

    (a) that it is necessary for the action specified to be taken for the purpose of preventing or detecting serious crime, and

    (b) that the taking of the action is proportionate to what the action seeks to achieve.

(2AA) Where the authorising officer is the chairman of the Office of Fair Trading, the only purpose falling within subsection (2)(a) is the purpose of preventing or detecting an offence under section 188 of the Enterprise Act 2002.

(2B) The matters to be taken into account in considering whether the requirements of subsection (2) are satisfied in the case of any authorisation shall include whether what it is thought necessary to achieve by the authorised action could reasonably be achieved by other means.

(3) An authorising officer shall not give an authorisation under this section except on an application made—

    (a) if the authorising officer is within subsection (5)(a) to [(ea) or (ee)], by a member of his police force,

    (aa)if the authorising officer is within subsection (5)(eb) to (ed), by a member, as the case may be, of the Royal Navy Regulating Branch, the Royal Military Police or the Royal Air Force police,

    (b) if the authorising officer is within subsection (5)(f), by a member of the National Criminal Intelligence Service,

    (c) if the authorising officer is within subsection (5)(g), by a member of the National Crime Squad, or

    (d) if the authorising officer is within subsection (5)(h), by a customs officer, or.

    (e) if the authorising officer is within subsection (5)(i), by an officer of the Office of Fair Trading.

(4) For the purposes of subsection (2), conduct which constitutes one or more offences shall be regarded as serious crime if, and only if,—

    (a) it involves the use of violence, results in substantial financial gain or is conduct by a large number of persons in pursuit of a common purpose, or

    (b) the offence or one of the offences is an offence for which a person who has attained the age of twenty-one and has no previous convictions could reasonably be expected to be sentenced to imprisonment for a term of three years or more, and, where the authorising officer is within subsection (5)(h), it relates to an assigned matter within the meaning of section 1(1) of the Customs and Excise Management Act 1979.

(5) In this section "authorising officer" means—...

    (d) the chief constable of a police force maintained under or by virtue of section 1 of the Police (Scotland) Act 1967 (maintenance of police forces for areas in Scotland);...

    (ea) the Chief Constable of the Ministry of Defence Police;

    (eb) the Provost Marshal of the Royal Navy Regulating Branch;

    (ec) the Provost Marshal of the Royal Military Police;

    (ed) the Provost Marshal of the Royal Air Force Police;

    (ee) the Chief Constable of the British Transport Police;

    (f) the Director General of the National Criminal Intelligence Service;

    (g) the Director General of the National Crime Squad or any person holding the rank of assistant chief constable in that squad who is designated for the purposes of this paragraph by that Director General; or

(h) any customs officer designated by the Commissioners of Customs and Excise for the purposes of this paragraph ; or

(i) the chairman of the Office of Fair Trading....

(7) The powers conferred by, or by virtue of, this section are additional to any other powers which a person has as a constable either at common law or under or by virtue of any other enactment and are not to be taken to affect any of those other powers."

Section 94 makes provision for the giving of authorisation in the absence of the authorising officer. In that situation an assistant chief constable may give authorisation in cases of urgency. Under s.95, an authorisation shall be in writing, except that in an urgent case an authorisation (other than one given by virtue of s.94) may be given orally. Authorisations are valid for three months, except those issued under s.94 or those given orally: these exceptional authorisations are valid for 72 hours. All authorisations may be renewed for periods of three months, and all authorisations should be cancelled if no longer necessary. Under s.96, notice must be given to the Chief Surveillance Commissioner where an authorisation is given, cancelled or renewed, who must "scrutinise the notice", as soon as reasonably practicable after it is given (s.96(4)). In some cases there is a need for authorisations to be approved by a Commissioner. By virtue of s.97, prior approval is required where the property specified in the authorisation: (1) is used wholly or mainly as a dwelling or as a bedroom in a hotel, or (2) constitutes office premises. Prior approval is also required where the action authorised by it is likely to result in any person acquiring knowledge of (a) matters subject to legal privilege, (b) confidential personal information, or (c) confidential journalistic material. These last three terms are defined in ss.98, 99 and 100, with s.101 authorising a code of practice to be issued about the use of the powers which the 1997 Act introduced.

Scottish Executive
Covert Surveillance Code of Practice
2004

"7.1 Part III of the 1997 Act provides lawful authority for entry on or interference with property or wireless telegraphy by the police.

7.2 In many cases a covert surveillance operation may involve both intrusive surveillance and entry on or interference with property or with wireless telegraphy. This can be done as a combined authorisation, although the criteria for authorisation of each activity must be considered separately.

7.3 Responsibility for such authorisations rests with the authorising officer as defined in section 93(5) of the 1997 Act, that is the Chief Constable or equivalent. Authorisations require the personal authority of the authorising officer (or their designated deputy) except in urgent situations, where it is not reasonably practicable for the application to be considered by such a person. The person entitled to act in such cases is set out in section 94 of the 1997 Act.

7.4 Authorisations under the 1997 Act may not be necessary where the police are acting with the consent of a person able to give permission in respect of relevant property. However consideration should still be given to the need to obtain an authorisation under the RIP(S) Act.

7.5 Authorisations may only be given by an authorising officer on application by a member of his or her own force for entry on or interference with property or with wireless telegraphy within the authorising officer's own area of operation. However, an authorising officer may authorise the taking of action outside the relevant area solely for the purpose of maintaining or retrieving any device, apparatus or equipment.

7.6 Any person giving an authorisation for entry on or interference with property or with wireless telegraphy under section 93(2) of the 1997 Act must be satisfied that:

● it is necessary for the action specified to be taken for the purpose of preventing or detecting serious crime; and

- that the taking of the action is proportionate to what the action seeks to achieve.

7.7 The authorising officer must take into account whether what it is thought necessary to achieve by the authorised conduct could reasonably be achieved by other means.

7.8 Any person granting or applying for an authorisation to enter on or interfere with property or with wireless telegraphy will also need to be aware of particular sensitivities in the local community where entry or interference is taking place and of similar activities being undertaken by other public authorities which could impact on the deployment. In this regard, it is recommended that the authorising officers should consult a senior officer within the police force in which the investigation or operation takes place, where the authorising officer considers that conflicts might arise.

Authorisation procedures

7.9 Authorisations will generally be given in writing by the authorising officer. However, in urgent cases, they may be given orally by the authorising officer. In such cases, a statement that the authorising officer has expressly authorised the action should be recorded in writing by the applicant as soon as is reasonably practicable. This should be done by the person with whom the authorising officer spoke.

7.10 If the authorising officer is absent then as provided for in section 5(4) of the Police (Scotland) Act 1967, an authorisation can be given in writing or, in urgent cases, orally by the designated deputy.

7.11 Where, however, in an urgent case, it is not reasonably practicable for the designated deputy to consider an application, then written authorisation may be given by an Assistant Chief Constable (other than a designated deputy).

7.12 Applications to the authorising officer for authorisation must be made in writing by a police officer (within the terms of section 93(3) of the 1997 Act) and should specify:

- the identity or identities of those to be targeted (where known);
- the property which the entry or interference with will affect;
- the identity of individuals and/or categories of people, where known, who are likely to be affected by collateral intrusion;
- details of the offence planned or committed;
- details of the intrusive surveillance involved;
- how the authorisation criteria (as set out in paragraphs 7.6 and 7.7) have been met;
- any action which may be necessary to retrieve any equipment used in the surveillance;
- in case of a renewal, the results obtained so far, or a full explanation of the failure to obtain any results; and
- whether an authorisation was given or refused, by whom and the time and date.

7.13 Additionally, in urgent cases, the authorisation should record (as the case may be):

- the reasons why the authorising officer or designated deputy considered the case so urgent that an oral instead of a written authorisation was given; and
- the reasons why (if relevant) the person granting the authorisation did not consider it reasonably practicable for the application to be considered by the senior authorising officer or the designated deputy.

7.14 Where the application is oral, the information referred to above should be recorded in writing by the applicant as soon as reasonably practicable.

Notifications to Surveillance Commissioners

7.15 Where a person gives, renews or cancels an authorisation, they must, as soon as is reasonably practicable, give notice of it in writing to a Surveillance Commissioner, in accordance with arrangements made by the Chief Surveillance Commissioner. In urgent cases which would otherwise have required the approval of a Surveillance Commissioner, the notification must specify the grounds on which the case is believed to be one of urgency.

7.16 There may be cases which become urgent after approval has been sought but before a response has been received from a Surveillance Commissioner. In such a case, the authorising officer should notify the Surveillance Commissioner that the case is urgent (pointing out that it has become urgent since the previous notification). In these cases, the authorisation will take effect immediately.

7.17 Notifications to Surveillance Commissioners in relation to the authorisation, renewal and cancellation of authorisations in respect of entry on or interference with property should be in accordance with the requirements of The Police Act 1997 (Notifications of Authorisations etc) Order 1998; SI No. 3241.

Duration of authorisations

7.18 Written authorisations given by authorising officers will cease to have effect at the end of a period of three months beginning with the day on which they took effect. In cases requiring prior approval by a Surveillance Commissioner this means from the time the Surveillance Commissioner has approved the authorisation and the person who gave the authorisation has been notified. This means that the approval will not take effect until the notice has been received in the office of the person who granted the authorisation within the relevant police force. In cases not requiring prior approval, this means from the time the authorisation was given.

7.19 Oral authorisations given in urgent cases by:
- authorising officers; or
- designated deputies

and written authorisations given by:
- Assistant Chief Constables (other than a designated deputy).

will cease at the end of the period of seventy-two hours beginning with the time when they took effect.

Renewals

7.20 If at any time before the day on which an authorisation expires the authorising officer or, in his absence, the designated deputy considers the authorisation should continue to have effect for the purpose for which it was issued, the authorisation may be renewed in writing for a period of three months beginning with the day on which the authorisation would otherwise have ceased to have effect. Authorisations may be renewed more than once, if necessary, and the renewal should be recorded on the authorisation record (see paragraph 7.27).

7.21 Commissioners must be notified of renewals of authorisations. The information to be included in the notification is set out in The Police Act 1997 (Notifications of Authorisations etc) Order 1998; SI No: 3241.

7.22 If, at the time of renewal, the criteria in paragraph 7.30 exist, then the approval of a Surveillance Commissioner must be sought before the renewal can take effect. The fact that the initial authorisation required the approval of a Commissioner before taking effect does not mean that its renewal will automatically require such approval. It will only do so if, at the time of the renewal, it falls into one of the categories requiring approval (and is not urgent).

Reviews

7.23 Authorising officers should regularly review authorisations to assess the need for the entry on or interference with property or with wireless telegraphy to continue. This should be recorded on the authorisation record (see paragraph 7.27). The authorising officer should determine how often a review should take place when giving an authorisation. This should be as frequently as is considered necessary and practicable and at no greater interval than one month. Particular attention is drawn to the need to review authorisations and renewals regularly and frequently where the entry on or interference with property or with wireless telegraphy provides access to confidential information or involves collateral intrusion.

Cancellations

7.24 The senior authorising officer who granted or last renewed the authorisation must cancel it must apply for its cancellation, if that officer is satisfied that the authorisation no longer meets the criteria upon which it was authorised. Where the senior authorising officer is no longer available, this duty will fall on the person who has taken over the role of senior authorising officer or the person who is acting as the senior authorising officer (see The Regulation of Investigatory Powers (Cancellation of Authorisations) (Scotland) Regulations 2000; SSI No. 207).

7.25 The Surveillance Commissioners must be notified of cancellations of authorisations. The information to be included in the notification is set out in The Police Act 1997 (Notifications of Authorisations etc) Order 1998; SI No. 3421.

7.26 The Surveillance Commissioners have the power to cancel an authorisation if they are satisfied that, at any time after an authorisation was given or renewed, there were no reasonable grounds for believing the matters set out in paragraphs 7.6 and 7.7 above. In such circumstances, a Surveillance Commissioner may order the destruction of records, in whole or in part, other than any that are required for pending criminal or civil proceedings.

Authorisation record

7.27 An authorisation record should be created which records:
- the time and date when an authorisation is given;
- whether an authorisation is in written or oral form;
- the time and date when it was notified to a Surveillance Commissioner; and
- the time and date when the Surveillance Commissioner notified his approval (where appropriate).

The authorisation record should also record:
- every occasion when entry on or interference with property or with wireless telegraphy has occurred;
- the result of periodic reviews of the authorisation;
- the date of every renewal; and
- it should record the time and date when any instruction was given by the authorising officer to cease the interference with property or with wireless telegraphy.

Ceasing of entry on or interference with property or with wireless telegraphy

7.28 Once an authorisation or renewal expires or is cancelled or quashed, the authorising officer must immediately instruct those carrying out the surveillance to cease all the actions authorised for the entry on or interference with property or with wireless telegraphy. The time and date when such an instruction was given should be recorded on the authorisation record (see paragraph 7.27).

Retrieval of equipment

7.29 Where a Surveillance Commissioner quashes or cancels an authorisation or renewal, that Surveillance Commissioner will, if there are reasonable grounds for doing so, order that the authorisation remain effective for a specified period, to enable officers to retrieve anything left on the property by virtue of the authorisation. The Surveillance Commissioner can only do so if the authorisation or renewal makes provision for this. A decision by the Surveillance Commissioner not to give such an order can be the subject of an appeal to the Chief Surveillance Commissioner.

SPECIAL RULES

Cases requiring prior approval of a Surveillance Commissioner

7.30 In certain cases, an authorisation for entry on or interference with property will not take effect until a Surveillance Commissioner has approved it and the notice has been received in the office of the person who granted the authorisation within the relevant police

force. These are cases where the person giving the authorisation is satisfied that:
- any of the property specified in the authorisation:
- is used wholly or mainly as a dwelling or as a bedroom in a hotel; or
- constitutes office premises; or
- the action authorised is likely to result in any person acquiring knowledge of:
- matters subject to legal privilege;
- confidential personal information; or
- confidential journalistic material.

7.31 Office premises are defined as any building or part of a building whose sole or principal use is as an office or for office purposes (which means purposes of administration, clerical work, handling money and telephone or telegraph operation)."

Provision is also made in the Act for the powers of the Commissioners. As we have seen, in some—but not all—circumstances their prior approval is needed for an authorisation to have effect. In addition to these powers, complaints may also be made to a commissioner who must "investigate the complaint if and so far as it alleges that anything has been done in relation to any property of the complainant in pursuance of an authorisation under section 93(1)(a) or (b)" (s.102). The procedure is set out in Sch.7. There are also powers vested in the commissioners to quash an authorisation if satisfied that "at the time an authorisation was given or renewed, there were no reasonable grounds for believing the matters specified in section 93(2)" (s. 103). An authorisation may additionally be quashed where it was not issued with prior approval under s.97 and there are reasonable grounds for believing that any of the matters specified in s.97(2) apply. Where a commissioner quashes an authorisation, he or she "may order the destruction of any records relating to information obtained by virtue of the authorisation". However, the power to order the destruction of material does not apply to "records required for pending criminal or civil proceedings". An authorising officer has the right to appeal to the Chief Commissioner against a decision of the commissioner to refuse an authorisation under s.97, or to quash an authorisation under s.103. There is also a right of appeal by an authorising officer against a decision of the commissioner to order a destruction of records.

Annual Report of the Chief Surveillance Commissioner to the Prime Minister and to Scottish Ministers for 2002–2003.
Chief Commissioner: Sir Andrew Leggatt
H.C. 1062 (2003)

"Property interference and intrusive surveillance
6.1 The powers and duties of the Commissioners in scrutinising, and deciding whether to approve, authorisations under the 1997 Act and under RIPA or RIP(S)A, are explained in my Annual Report for 2000–2001. Again they are available from the OSC website.

Statistics
6.2 Statistics for property interference and intrusive surveillance authorisations for the past and previous years are set out in the tables at Annexes A and B. As before, I have not identified separately the number of authorisations given by each agency since this could give a misleading impression of their operating practices. Drugs offences continue to be the major target of authorisations.

Property Interference
6.3 Excluding renewals, there were 2511 property interference authorisations in 2002–2003, reflecting very little change on the previous year (2519).
6.4 I do not normally specify renewals of authorisations since they relate to ongoing operations and could confuse the figures. It is worth reporting, however, as an indicator of increased work undertaken by the OSC, that there were 543 in 2002–2003 compared with

437 in the previous year.

6.5 There were 244 cases where urgency provisions allowed for in the legislation were used. There were also two cases where authorisations were given in the absence of the Chief Officer. In the previous year these figures were 280 and 14. These reductions are mainly due to improved knowledge and efficiency as well as to an increasing familiarity with the requirements of authorisation.

6.6 Three authorisations were quashed. One related to the authorisation of interference outside the police force area which the Act does not permit. Another failed to meet the test of necessity and the third gave insufficient detail to persuade the Commissioner that it complied with the legislation."

VI. SEARCH AND SEIZURE OF PROPERTY

We move from the covert entry onto property to the overt entry onto property. This will normally arise in the context of criminal investigation by the police. We have already considered in Ch.4 the powers of the police to enter and search private property while looking for a suspect and as powers incidental to an arrest. In this chapter we are concerned more with entry, search and seizure at an earlier stage of an investigation (when the police are looking for evidence before anyone has been arrested) or when no crime has been committed and the police enter for preventive reasons to prevent a breach of the peace. The starting point is to acknowledge that the entry to and search of private property would be unlawful and could give rise to an action for damages. There may be other legal consequences, not the least of which is that any evidence obtained as a result of an illegal search may be ruled inadmissible by a court in criminal proceedings.

Although there is little doubt that a lawful entry and search would normally be a permissible restraint on the Art.8 right to respect for private life, one's home and one's correspondence, the requirements of Art.8(2) would of course have to be met. This means that any entry and search would have to be in accordance with law and necessary in a democratic society on one of the grounds listed there. It should not be presumed that the entry by the police onto private property (with or without a warrant) in the discharge of their duties will always be justified, as the following case reveals:

McLeod v United Kingdom
(1998) 27 E.H.R.R. 493

The applicant and her husband had divorced, following which there had been acrimonious litigation about the distribution of the assets. The applicant had been ordered by a court to deliver some furniture and other property to her husband by October 6, 1989. On October 3, 1989 the husband arranged with his brothers to attend the home of his former wife (which she shared with her elderly mother) to collect the items. This was done without the knowledge or agreement of the applicant who was not present when her former husband arrived. Fearing a breach of the peace because of the applicant's failure in the past to comply with court orders on this matter, the former husband's solicitor arranged for two police officers to be present while this was taking place. According to the report:

"When the police officers arrived, they were informed that Mr McLeod was there to collect his property pursuant to an agreement concluded between him and the applicant, and were given a copy of the list but not of the court order. According to one of the police officers, the solicitor's clerk offered to return to his office to get a copy of the order, but the police officer did not require that this be done.

One of the police officers knocked at the door of the house. It was answered by the applicant's mother who told him that her daughter was not at home, and that she was unaware of any arrangement concluded between the latter and Mr McLeod. In an affidavit sworn on 21 November 1990, the applicant's mother claimed that the police officer had told her to open the door because they were from the court and had a court order to execute. The applicant's mother opened the door and stepped aside, allowing Mr McLeod and his party access to the property."

The two police officers briefly entered the property at the beginning of the proceedings to remove the property but thereafter waited outside, mainly in the driveway. The applicant brought legal proceedings against the police for trespass. However, the application failed, the English courts taking the view that the police were entitled to enter the property to prevent a breach of the peace under exceptional common law powers, the continuing existence of which had been recognised by Parliament in the Police and Criminal Evidence Act 1984, s.17(6). The European Court of Human Rights held that the police had breached the Convention rights of the applicant.

"AS TO THE LAW:

I. ALLEGED VIOLATION OF ARTICLE 8 of the Convention

34. The applicant submitted that the police officers' entry into her home and their failure to prevent her ex-husband's entry violated Article 8 of the Convention [the Court then read article 8]

35. The Government contested these allegations, maintaining that the entry of the police into the applicant's home was 'in accordance with the law' within the meaning of Article 8(2) of the Convention, and was proportionate to the aim of preventing disorder and crime. The Commission agreed with the Government.

A. Alleged interference with the applicant's right to respect for her private life and home

1. Existence of an interference

36. It was not disputed that the entry of the police into the applicant's home on 3 October 1989 constituted an interference with her right to respect for her private life and home. The Court sees no reason to hold otherwise.

2. Justification for the interference

37. Such interference breaches article 8 unless it is 'in accordance with the law', pursues one or more of the legitimate aims set out in Article 8(2) and is, in addition, 'necessary in a democratic society' to achieve the aim or aims in question.

(a) 'In accordance with the law'

38. The applicant submitted that the common-law power of the police to enter private premises on the grounds of an anticipated breach of the peace was not 'in accordance with the law' within the meaning of Article 8(2). In this regard she argued, first, that the meaning of the concept 'breach of the peace' was insufficiently clear and precise and that, in particular, there was inconsistent jurisprudence as to the meaning of 'breach of the peace'...

41. The Court recalls that the expression 'in accordance with the law', within the meaning of Article 8(2), requires firstly that the impugned measures should have a basis in domestic law. It also refers to the quality of the law in question, requiring that it be accessible to the persons concerned and formulated with sufficient precision to enable them—if need be, with appropriate advice—to foresee, to a degree that is reasonable in the circumstances, the consequences which a given action may entail ... However, those consequences need not be foreseeable with absolute certainty, since such certainty might give rise to excessive rigidity, and the law must be able to keep pace with changing circumstances....

42. In this connection, the Court observes that the concept of breach of the peace has been clarified by the English courts over the last two decades, to the extent that it is now

sufficiently established that a breach of the peace is committed only when an individual causes harm, or appears likely to cause harm, to persons or property, or acts in a manner the natural consequence of which would be to provoke violence in others...

43. Furthermore, the English courts have recognised that the police have a duty to prevent a breach of the peace that they reasonably apprehend will occur and to stop a breach of the peace that is occurring. In the execution of this duty, the police have the power to enter into and remain on private property without the consent of the owner or occupier ... Despite the general abolition of common-law powers of entry without warrant, this power was preserved by section 17(6) of the 1984 Act...

44. When considering whether the national law was complied with, the Court recalls that it is primarily for the national authorities, notably the courts, to interpret and apply domestic law ... In this regard, the Court notes that in its decision the Court of Appeal took into account the criticisms of the common-law power of the police to enter private premises to prevent a breach of the peace cited by the applicant in her memorial to the Court, and found that the common-law power was applicable in situations involving domestic disturbance...

45. In conclusion, the Court finds that the power of the police to enter private premises without a warrant to deal with or prevent a breach of the peace was defined with sufficient precision for the foreseeability criterion to be satisfied. The interference was, therefore, 'in accordance with the law'.

(b) Legitimate aim

46. The applicant contended that, while the prevention of crime or disorder might be the objective behind the existence of the power, it was not the aim of the interference that took place in the present case. She submitted that the term 'prevention' should be interpreted narrowly and should not encompass a situation where police officers by their own actions caused a risk of disorder and then assumed powers of entry to prevent it.

47. The Government maintained that the purpose of the police officers' entry into the applicant's property was to prevent disorder or crime. In this regard, they drew attention to the fact that domestic strife was often the cause of considerable disorder and occasionally led to serious violence against persons or property....

48. The Court is of the view that the aim of the power enabling police officers to enter private premises to prevent a breach of the peace is clearly a legitimate one for the purposes of Article 8, namely the prevention of disorder or crime, and there is nothing to suggest that it was applied in the present case for any other purpose.

(c) "Necessary in a democratic society"

49. The applicant ... argued that, if the police chose to exercise their power of entry when there was no risk of physical injury or damage to property—which entailed a major infringement of the rights guaranteed under Article 8 of the Convention—the justification for the interference should be significant and indisputable. Furthermore, justification for the entry had to be made by reference to the degree of risk that existed at the time the police entered the property. In the present case, since there was no history of violence between the applicant and her ex-husband and the only person present at the house at the time of entry was her 74-year-old mother, the risk of harm was minimal or non-existent. Weighing this against the seriousness of the interference, the actions of the police could not be regarded as proportionate. In addition, they demonstrated such a lack of impartiality as to render the exercise of the powers disproportionate to the aim pursued.

50. The Government claimed that, because there was a clear pressing social need to prevent disorder or crime, the power of the police to enter private premises without permission to prevent a breach of the peace was 'necessary in a democratic society'. With regard to the present case, they submitted that the interference was proportionate to the legitimate aim pursued, as demonstrated by the fact that the visit to the applicant's home by her former husband to collect his possessions was made in the genuine, albeit mistaken,

belief that she had agreed to the arrangement; the ex-husband's solicitors feared that a breach of the peace might occur because of the history of the court proceedings between their client and the applicant; the police officers attended the applicant's home not to assist in the removal of the property but to maintain the peace; they acted in a discreet and reasonable manner; and the applicant's conduct on her return did call for their intervention. . . .

52. The Court recalls that, according to its established case-law, the notion of necessity implies that the interference corresponds to a pressing social need and, in particular, that it is proportionate to the legitimate aim pursued . . . .

53. The Court's task accordingly consists in ascertaining whether, in the circumstances of the present case, the entry of the police into the applicant's home struck a fair balance between the relevant interests, namely the applicant's right to respect for her private life and home, on the one hand, and the prevention of disorder and crime, on the other.

54. The Court notes that on the morning of 3 October 1989, Mr McLeod's solicitors, knowing the long and acrimonious history of the divorce proceedings, contacted the police requesting their attendance in order to avoid a breach of the peace occurring while their client's property was being removed from the applicant's home. Two police officers were instructed to attend. Upon arriving at the applicant's home, the police officers were shown a copy of the list of property that was to be removed, but not the order accompanying it.

One of the police officers knocked at the door of the house and was told by the applicant's mother that the applicant was not at home. Mr McLeod and his party entered the house and began removing the property. The police officers also entered the house, but did not participate in the removal of the property. One of them, however, checked that only items mentioned on the list were removed. When the applicant returned home, she became angry and demanded that the property that had been loaded into the van be put back into the house. One of the police officers intervened, insisting that the van be driven away and that any dispute should be left to the parties' solicitors.

55. The Court considers that, since Mr McLeod's solicitors genuinely believed that a breach of the peace might occur when their client removed his property from the former matrimonial home, the police could not be faulted for responding to their request for assistance. In this regard, it notes that the domestic courts accepted that a situation that might begin as a domestic quarrel could develop into a breach of the peace.

56. However, the Court observes that, notwithstanding the facts that the police were contacted in advance by Mr McLeod's solicitors and that the solicitor's clerk offered to return to his office and collect the court order . . ., the police did not take any steps to verify whether Mr McLeod was entitled to enter her home on 3 October 1989 and remove his property. Sight of the court order would have indicated that it was for the applicant to deliver the property, and not for her former husband to collect it, and moreover that she had three more days in which to do so. Admittedly, the court order would not have enabled the police officers to ascertain the correctness of Mr McLeod's genuinely held belief that an agreement had been made between himself and his ex-wife allowing him to remove his property from the former matrimonial home on 3 October 1989—a belief that was communicated to the police officers upon their arrival. Nonetheless, given the circumstances of the interference, and the fact that the applicant was not present and that her mother lacked any knowledge of the agreement, the police should not have taken it for granted that an agreement had been reached superseding the relevant parts of the court order.

57. The Court considers further that, upon being informed that the applicant was not present, the police officers should not have entered her house, as it should have been clear to them that there was little or no risk of disorder or crime occurring. It notes in this regard that the police officers remained outside the property for some of the time, suggesting a belief on their part that a breach of the peace was not likely to occur in the absence of the applicant. The fact that an altercation did occur upon her return is, in its opinion, immaterial in ascertaining whether the police officers were justified in entering the property initially.

58. For the above reasons, the Court finds that the means employed by the police officers were disproportionate to the legitimate aim pursued. Accordingly, there has been a violation of Article 8 of the Convention."

In examining the powers of entry, search and seizure in Scots law (other than those discussed in Ch.4), there are three questions for consideration:

- By what legal authority may the police enter and search private property?
- What formalities must be satisfied as a precondition for the exercise of legal powers to enter and search private property?
- What is the extent of the powers of the police while lawfully conducting a search of private property?

So far as the first of these questions is concerned, entry and search may take place with the consent of the occupier of the property, but as both *Hepper* (below) and *Leckie* (below) make clear, the search may take place only to the extent authorised or permitted by the occupier. In exceptional circumstances, entry and search may take place without either consent or a warrant. In the following case we give an account of the nature and extent of police powers to enter and search (a) with consent, (b) with a warrant and (c) with neither. The first case shows also that the consent must be genuine and not induced by misunderstanding about the authority of the police officers.

Lawrie v Muir
1950 S.L.T. 37

A shopkeeper was convicted of using milk bottles which did not belong to her, contrary to the Milk (Control and Maximum Prices) Order 1947. The crucial evidence was given by two inspectors of a milk-bottle collecting organisation who were authorised by contract with distributors to inspect the premises of any contracting distributor upon production of warrant cards. The accused was not a contracting distributor, but submitted to a search when the warrant cards were produced by the inspectors. As a result of this search the milk bottles were found. She appealed against conviction, *inter alia*, on the ground that the evidence, having been obtained by illegal search, was inadmissible. It was held that the evidence ought not to have been admitted and the conviction was quashed.

THE LORD JUSTICE GENERAL (COOPER): "The conviction obtained in this prosecution depends upon evidence given by two inspectors who in good faith conducted a search of the appellant's premises but who had no right to make that search. The Sheriff-Substitute repelled an objection to the admissibility of the evidence thus illegally obtained, and the main question is whether he was right in so doing. The matter has been remitted to a larger Court because of the importance and difficulty of the widest submission offered by the appellant, *viz.* that evidence obtained as a result of illegal entry, illegal search, illegal seizure or other like unlawful or irregular act, cannot be admitted in a criminal prosecution.

On this major issue there is little direct authority . . .

From the standpoint of principle it seems to me that the law must strive to reconcile two highly important interests which are liable to come into conflict—(a) the interest of the citizen to be protected from illegal or irregular invasions of his liberties by the authorities, and (b) the interest of the State to secure that evidence bearing upon the commission of crime and necessary to enable justice to be done shall not be withheld from courts of law on any merely formal or technical ground. Neither of these objects can be insisted upon to the uttermost. The protection of the citizen is primarily protection for the innocent citizen against unwarranted, wrongful and perhaps high-handed interference, and the common sanction is an action of damages. The protection is not intended as a protection for the guilty citizen against the efforts of the public prosecutor to vindicate the law. On the other hand the interest of the State cannot be magnified to the point of causing all the safeguards for the protection of the citizen to vanish, and of offering a positive inducement to the authorities to proceed by irregular methods. It is obvious that excessively rigid rules as to the exclusion of evidence bearing upon the commission of a crime might conceivably operate to the detriment and not the advantage of the accused, and might even lead to the conviction of the innocent; and extreme cases can easily be figured in which the exclusion of a vital piece of evidence from the knowledge of a jury because of some technical flaw in the conduct of the police would be an outrage upon common sense and a defiance of elementary justice. For these reasons, and in view of the expressions of judicial opinion to which I have referred, I find it quite impossible to affirm the appellant's extreme proposition. On the contrary I adopt as a first approximation to the true rule the statement of Lord Justice Clerk Aitchison in that 'an irregularity in the obtaining of evidence does not *necessarily* make that evidence inadmissible.'

It remains to consider the implications of the word 'necessarily' which I have italicised. By using this word and by proceeding to the sentence which follows, Lord Aitchison seems to me to have indicated that there was in his view no absolute rule and that the question was one of circumstances. I respectfully agree. It would greatly facilitate the task of judges were it possible to imprison the principle within the framework of a simple and unqualified maxim, but I do not think that it is feasible to do so. I attach weight to the fact that the word used by Lord Chancellor Chelmsford and by Horridge J., when referring to the disregarding of an irregularity in the obtaining of evidence, was 'excuse.' Irregularities require to be excused, and infringements of the formalities of the law in relation to these matters are not lightly to be condoned. Whether any given irregularity ought to be excused depends upon the nature of the irregularity and the circumstances under which it was committed. In particular, the case may bring into play the discretionary principle of fairness to the accused which has been developed so fully in our law in relation to the admission in evidence of confessions or admissions by a person suspected or charged with crime. That principle would obviously require consideration in any case in which the departure from the strict procedure had been adopted deliberately with a view to securing the admission of evidence obtained by an unfair trick. Again, there are many statutory offences in relation to which Parliament has prescribed in detail in the interests of fairness a special procedure to be followed in obtaining evidence; and in such cases (of which the Sale of Food and Drugs Acts provide one example) it is very easy to see why a departure from the strict rules has often been held to be fatal to the prosecution's case. On the other hand, to take an extreme instance figured in argument, it would usually be wrong to exclude some highly incriminating production in a murder trial merely because it was found by a police officer in the course of a search authorised for a different purpose or before a proper warrant had been obtained."

In the absence of consent to enter and search private property, the police will normally require a warrant. The common law vests a general power in magistrates to issue search warrants following an application by the police, while a number of statutes (such as the Misuse of Drugs Act 1971 and the Terrorism Act 2000) also confer specific powers on magistrates to grant search warrants for offences under the statutes in question. In addition courts of summary jurisdiction have the power by statute to grant search warrants "to grant warrant to search the person, dwelling-house and repositories of the accused and any place where he may be found for any documents, articles, or property likely to afford evidence of his guilt of, or guilty participation in, any offence charged in the complaint, and to take possession of such documents, articles or property": Criminal Procedure (Scotland) Act 1995, s.139(3). But the common law continues to provide the source of general authority to issue search warrants. Indeed the inherent common law power will not easily be displaced, as the following case makes clear, while also providing a helpful account of the nature of the power to issue search warrants.

MacNeill
1983 S.C.C.R. 450

The Procurator Fiscal in Aberdeen applied to the sheriff for a search warrant in connection with a suspected violation of the Civic Government (Scotland) Act 1982, s.51(2). This makes it an offence to publish, sell or distribute obscene material. The application was refused because the Act made no provision for search warrants. The fiscal appealed to the High Court.

LORD CAMERON: "The fact that there may or may not be in certain statutes specific provisions relative to the obtaining of warrants to search does not affect or diminish the common law powers of the procurator fiscal. The advocate-depute referred to the case of *Watson* v *Muir*, 1938 J.C. 181, especially Lord Justice-General Normand and Lord Fleming at p. 185, a case in which all the procedure under consideration took place before the service of a complaint, in support of his submission. In the Civic Government Act itself, the sections dealing with powers of arrest and search were directed towards the powers of a constable in relation to certain specified offences. These provisions could not be interpreted to limit or extinguish pro tanto the common law powers of the procurator fiscal. These powers could not be affected unless made the subject of specific statutory provisions. There was none such here. ... Where, as here, there was no mention of the procurator fiscal's common law powers, these remained entire; they could only be limited or extinguished by specific reference and express wording. The learned sheriff had misdirected himself and his decision should be recalled and the case remitted to him to grant the crave of the petition.

In my opinion the submission for the Crown is correct and in accordance with the principles of our criminal law. In the case of *McMillan* v *Grant; Rippie* v *Grant*, 1924 J.C. 13, Lord Sands in considering whether a procurator fiscal has power at common law to prosecute a statutory offence, said:

'The Sheriff Court is the King's Court in the Sheriffdom, and the King's Court has jurisdiction in common law to take cognisance of any offence against the King's peace within the Sheriffdom, unless its jurisdiction to do so is expressly excluded by statute. An offence against a statutory enactment is an offence against the King's peace, and accordingly the Sheriff Court has, at common law, jurisdiction to take cognisance of it. This consideration, as it appears to me, involves that the procurator-fiscal, as the representative of the Crown in the Sheriff Court, may prosecute any offence cognisable by that Court, unless his title to do so has, either expressly or by necessary implication, been withdrawn by statute' (at 22–23).

To enable him properly to discharge his functions the procurator fiscal has at common law certain powers which include the power to search under warrant, and as Lord Justice-General Normand put it in *Watson* v *Muir*, 1938 J.C. 181 at 184:

'[I]t must be remembered that, from ancient times, the procurator-fiscal as the public prosecutor in Scotland has had powers of search in the course of his duties when he is investigating crime. It is doubtless true that that power of search depends upon obtaining a legal warrant for search. But it has never been doubted that it is unnecessary for the procurator-fiscal to obtain a legal warrant to search if the party in possession of, or having the custody of, any article of which the procurator-fiscal desires to obtain possession is willing to yield possession.'

This common law power to search extends to a power to search premises under warrant in a case where no person has as yet been arrested or charged (c.f., *Stewart* v *Roach*, 1950 S.L.T. 245), the form of the requisite warrant being prescribed in section 310 of the Criminal Procedure (Scotland) Act 1975.

If then the procurator fiscal in virtue of his common law powers as representing the

Crown in the sheriff court has jurisdiction to prosecute all offences cognisable there, whether statutory or common law, it must necessarily follow that, unless his common law power of search is expressly and specifically abridged or excluded by the provisions of the statute or regulation creating the offence, his common law powers remain intact. It is significant that in none of the statutes referred to by the sheriff in his note, citing examples quoted in Renton and Brown, 4th edn, para. 5–29, with the single exception of the Public Order Act 1936, is the common law power of search exercisable by the procurator fiscal specifically and directly referred to. Thus the powers of arrest and search referred to in the Salmon and Freshwater Fisheries (Protection) Scotland Act 1951, and set out in section 11(1), relate specifically to water bailiffs, constables and persons authorised by the Secretary of State to exercise the powers of a water bailiff. No mention of or reference to the procurator fiscal or his powers is contained in the Act. In the Firearms Act 1968, which is a United Kingdom statute, there is no mention of the powers of a procurator fiscal, and section 58(4) of the Act provides inter alia: 'The powers of arrest and entry conferred by Part III of this Act shall be without prejudice to any power of arrest or entry which may exist apart from this Act ...', and Part III of the Act, headed 'Law Enforcement and Punishment of Offences', provides for the exercise by a constable of a power of search on a warrant obtained 'by information on oath'—but contains no reference to the common law power of the procurator fiscal. Clearly, where no specific reference is made to the power of the procurator fiscal eo nomine, no foundation can exist for the proposition that his common law jurisdiction or ancillary powers are limited or extinguished. In the Public Order Act 1936 the necessity for supporting an application for a search warrant by evidence on oath is specifically enacted by section 2(5) and this provision is made applicable in Scotland by section 8(3) which enacts that 'any application for a search warrant under the said subsection shall be made by the procurator fiscal instead of such officer as is therein mentioned'. This is a restrictive provision, restrictive in respect of the nature of the material upon which an application for a search warrant may be made but not of the power.

Parliament has given no reason for this restriction, though one may speculate that the politically sensitive subject-matter with which the statute deals could have led to such restriction on the manner of the exercise of the undoubted power of the procurator fiscal. Having regard to the position of the procurator fiscal in our Scottish scheme of criminal administration as representative of the Crown in the sheriff court charged with the duty of prosecuting offences cognisable in that court and with a consequent and necessary power of search in respect of all such offences be they common law or statutory, I am clearly of opinion that the power can only be taken away by express statutory provision or by necessary and inevitable implication. There is no such provision in the Civic Government (Scotland) Act 1982; it is of course true that in sections 59 and 60 of this Act specific powers to arrest and search persons and certain specified premises are given to be exercised without warrant, but as already noted these provisions and powers relate to constables: nowhere are the powers of the procurator fiscal in any way affected (except insofar as the provisions of section 8(3) of the Public Order Act 1936 are imported into the operation of the fasciculus of provisions in sections 62–65, a matter which does not arise in this case).

In my opinion therefore the learned sheriff misdirected himself in thinking that where a statute creating an offence did not specifically provide for a right and power to search on suspicion and for the manner in which that power was to be exercised in Scotland, whether the statute was of United Kingdom generality or applicable to Scotland alone, the common law power of the procurator fiscal was thereby extinguished in respect of such offence. In my opinion, having regard to the basic principles of this matter, the common law jurisdiction and powers of the procurator fiscal remain entire unless abridged or extinguished by specific and clear enactment. There being no such provision in the statute here the sheriff should have entertained the application for warrant to search. I would therefore pass the bill and remit to the sheriff to proceed as accords."

The scope of the common law authority to issue search warrants appears to be very wide and its boundaries are uncertain. In English law the position is now very different. The general power is vested in magistrates by statute, with the Police and Criminal Evidence Act 1984 authorising the issue of search warrants on application by the police where there is a serious arrestable offence. This is a term which is defined in the Act (s.116). In addition to this general power, there are a large number of individual statutes (such as the Misuse of Drugs Act 1971) which—as in Scotland—confer a power to grant a search warrant for the purpose of an investigation relating to an offence which the Act creates. An important feature of the 1984 Act, however, is that in addition to the power to issue warrants being confined to serious arrestable offences, there are special rules applicable to certain kinds of material even where it is sought in connection with an investigation for such an offence. These special rules apply to material which is subject to legal privilege, and to confidential personal records, human tissue or tissue fluid taken for the purposes of medical treatment and held in confidence, journalistic material (including photographs), and confidential business records. In the case of items subject to legal privilege no search warrant may be granted. In the case of other material, the application for a warrant must be made to a circuit judge, normally only after an order for production of the material in question granted in *inter partes* proceedings has not been complied with.

Stewart v Roach
1950 S.L.T. 245

The pursuer was the subject of police investigations following an anonymous tip off that he had stolen some goods from his workplace. He was questioned and a search warrant was issued to authorise the search of his house for the allegedly stolen items. In an action for damages a court of seven judges were asked to consider "whether it is illegal to grant and execute a warrant to search for stolen goods the premises of a person who has not been apprehended nor charged with an offence". The court answered in the negative.

> LORD PRESIDENT (COOPER): "The sole point taken is that the searches were wrongous because the pursuers were neither charged nor apprehended before the warrants were applied for and obtained. Prior charge or apprehension is said to be an essential pre-requisite. Otherwise, the warrants are admitted to be sufficiently specific and the procedure regular.
>
> It is difficult to see on principle why the lesser invasion of the pursuers' rights involved in a search of their houses for stolen goods should be objectionable simply because the more extreme step of charging or apprehending them had not been taken. However that may be, it was argued to us that the matter was concluded by authority, and particularly by a decision of the High Court of Justiciary—*M'Lauchlan v Renton*, 1911 S.C. (J.) 12. The situation in that case was set out by Lord Salvesen as follows: 'On 28th July 1910 a petition was presented in the Sheriff Court, at the instance of the procurator-fiscal of Midlothian, setting forth that Edward Jefferies, an inspector in the Leith police force, was prepared to make oath, as authorised by the 11th section of the Betting Act, 1853, that there was reason to suspect that the house known as Seafield Lodge, Leith occupied by the complainer, was kept or used as a betting-house or office, and that the petitioner was desirous of obtaining a special warrant, in terms of the said section of the Act. The petition concluded with a crave that the oath of Jefferies might be taken to the effect foresaid, and thereafter a special warrant granted authorising him to enter the house known as Seafield Lodge, and, if necessary, to use force for making such entry, "and to seize all letters, lists, cards, and other documents relating to racing or betting found in such house or premises". On the same day Jefferies deponed, upon oath, to the statements contained in the petition, and the Sheriff-Substitute granted warrant as craved.' Certain unopened letters were found in the house and the Court reached the view that unopened letters were not covered by the words of the Betting Act incorporated in the warrant. This view was overturned by a Full Bench in 1925,

Strathern v Benson, 1925 J.C. 40 , but the subsequent reversal does not deal with the general observations made by Lord Salvesen and concurred in by the Lord Justice-Clerk and Lord Ardwall on which the pursuers found. These observations are: 'There can be no doubt, at common law, it is illegal to grant a warrant to search the premises of any citizen who has not been charged with an offence, however much the Crown authorities may have reason for suspicion against him'. Lord Salvesen gives no authority for this pronouncement, but it is clear from the argument presented that the supposed basis of the doctrine is *Bell v Black and Morrison* (1865) 5 Irv. 57. In that case a procurator-fiscal presented to the Sheriff a petition which set forth that in the course of taking a precognition against A, he had recovered evidence showing that B and four other persons were implicated in the crimes with which A was charged; and prayed for 'warrant to officers of Court, and their assistants, to search the dwelling—house, repositories, and premises occupied by B,' etc., 'for written documents, and all other articles tending to establish guilt or participation in said crimes, and to take possession thereof'. Warrant was granted and, a suspension being brought, the Court, consisting of Lord Justice-Clerk Inglis, Lord Ardmillan and Lord Neaves, suspended the warrant as illegal. The opinion of the Court was delivered by the Lord Justice-Clerk. Three grounds for the decision are stated, 5 Irv. 57, at pp. 63, 64:

'In the first place, the warrant is granted against five different persons, none of whom is under a charge for any crime. It is stated in the petition that the persons against whom the warrant is asked are shown, by documents recovered in the course of the pre-cognition against Pringle, to have been engaged in the same conspiracy, and in writing and sending threatening letters. But as no charge has yet been made against any of these five persons, this amounts to no more than a statement of the suspicion or belief of the procurators-fiscal that they are implicated in the same crimes as Pringle. In the second place, the leading object of the warrant is to obtain possession of the papers of the parties against whom it is directed, without any limitation as to the kind of papers, for by the term "written documents" nothing else can be meant than all writings of every description. The only limitation is to be found in the words which follow— "tending to establish guilt or participation in said crimes,' and in the words in the body of the petition—"referring to and in connection with said conspiracy and threatening letters". But these words, while they may be supposed in one sense to have a limiting effect, are in another view capable of a very elastic interpretation: for it is not proposed to limit the seizure of papers in each person's house to those which inculpate himself; but, on the contrary, the words of the warrant would justify the seizure of papers tending to inculpate anybody in the crimes charged against Pringle, or at least, and in the most favourable sense would justify the seizure of all papers in the possession of the complainer Bell which would tend to inculpate any of the other four parties against whom the warrant is directed, in addition, of course, to Pringle, and so in regard to the papers of each of the four other persons against whom the warrant is issued. In the third place, the execution of the warrant is entrusted absolutely and without control to ordinary sheriff officers and their assistants, who are thereby commanded, whether in the presence or absence of the parties, who are under no criminal charge, and who have no notice of the application for or granting of the warrant, to seize their whole papers *per aversionem*, and themselves to read and examine all these papers for the purpose of finding traces or proofs of guilt either against the owners and possessors of the papers, or against some other person or persons.'

It will be observed that the first of these grounds is relevant to the present topic and indeed, as it turns out, is the only basis on which the argument for the pursuers rests. Had the Court regarded a charge as an essential prerequisite, we think that the opinion would have said so in terms and indeed that would have been decisive without further elaboration. It seems to us clear not only from the way in which the first ground is worded but also from the incidental reference to the absence of a criminal charge in the course of the formulation of the third ground, that they regarded the absence of charge as only one element for consideration in conjunction with the other circumstances of the case. The substance of the opinion is that in the whole circumstances disclosed, what was sought was far too wide and not fenced with sufficient safeguards, especially having in view that no charge had been preferred. That this is the true emphasis of the opinion appears from this later passage, 5 Irv. 57, at p. 64:

> 'The seizure of papers, as distinguished from their recovery as articles of evidence, and also as distinguished from the seizure of other articles which are invested with no character of confidentiality or secrecy, is, under all circumstances, a matter of extreme delicacy. But the seizure of papers made in the circumstances with which we have to deal, is a proceeding quite unknown to the law of Scotland.'

That this is the true view of this case is borne out by what was said by the Judges who took part in two subsequent cases in the Court of Session arising out of the same matter. The first of these was *Bell v Black and Morrison*, 1865, 3 Macph. 1026, where the successful complainer in the suspension brought an action for reparation which came before the Second Division consisting of Lord Justice-Clerk Inglis, Lord Cowan, Lord Benholme and Lord Neaves. The main topic of discussion was whether malice and want of probable cause should be inserted in the issue, but certain references were made to the question of the illegality of the warrant. The Lord Justice-Clerk expressed himself in strong terms but we do not consider that he added anything to what he had already said in the High Court of Justiciary as to his grounds for holding the warrant illegal. Lord Cowan said: 'It is sufficient for the case to say that there was here an illegal and altogether unprecedented application for a warrant of a very oppressive kind' (*ibid.* at p. 1029). Lord Benholme regarded the warrant as *ultra vires* of the Judge who granted it but did not say on what grounds he thought so. Lord Neaves said: 'An attempt has been here made to defend or excuse the warrant that was here granted. It seems to me to be one of the most illegal warrants I ever heard of. Some of us can remember a time when, if such a warrant had been obtained in connection with a political offence, the dissatisfaction that would have been excited would not have been appeased by a mere claim of damages against a procurator-fiscal. That a man's whole documents should be the subject of examination by inferior officers of the law, who are to read them all, and see if they tend to establish some crime with which he does not even stand charged, is a most unjustifiable violation of private rights' (*ibid.* at p. 1031). It seems to us that neither Lord Cowan nor Lord Neaves (the latter of whom was a member of the Court in the suspension) gives any support to the contention that charge or apprehension is an essential prerequisite to the grant of a special warrant to search.

A further civil action arising out of the same matter—*Nelson v Black and Morrison*, 1866, 4 Macph. 328—came before the First Division, consisting of Lord President M'Neill, Lord Curriehill, Lord Deas and Lord Ardmillan, who had been one of the Judges in the suspension proceedings. Nelson had been one of the parties against whom the search warrant was directed but a minute of withdrawal as against him was endorsed on the warrant a few days after its date. His action was for slander in respect of the statements in the petition. Again, the main question which arose was whether malice and want of probable cause should be inserted in the issues. The Lord President observed (*ibid.* at pp. 330, 331):

> 'But it is said that in this case it is not necessary for the pursuer to take this burden of proof upon him, because the warrant which the defenders asked for and obtained was in itself an illegal warrant, and, being of that character, was not a thing which they as procurators-fiscal were entitled to ask; and so it is argued that they had no privilege in making the statements upon which they did ask it.
> 'That may lead to a question of great nicety, viz., how far a procurator-fiscal puts himself outwith that protection which he would otherwise have, by asking something which he is not entitled to have; and that again may depend upon the nature of the

illegality involved in the demand. If it is out of all law and reason that a man's repositories should be searched, that is one form of illegality. If, on the other hand, the objection is merely that the premises ought not to have been searched in this particular form, that is another matter. The one relates to the substance of the proceedings; the other to the want of formality, or the want of caution in carrying them out. In regard to illegality of the first kind, I think the pursuer would be entitled to have an issue without malice and want of probable cause. In regard to the other, I am of a different opinion.

It appears to me that this case falls under the latter class. I think it was competent for the Sheriff, under this application, to grant a perfectly legal warrant. For example, if he had limited the search to particular documents, or appointed it to be carried out at the sight of the Sheriff himself, I cannot say that there would have been any illegality in such a warrant. That has not been done. But it does not follow that the defenders' application was out and out, and in substance, contrary to law.'

Lord Curriehill concurred with the Lord President. Lord Deas said (*ibid*. at pp. 331,332):

'I agree with your Lordship that this was an application under which a perfectly legal warrant might have been granted; and I think that if the qualification suggested by your Lordship had been introduced into the warrant, viz., that it was to be executed at the sight of the Sheriff or Sheriff-Substitute, it would have been difficult to say that any objection to it remained—particularly keeping in view that the charge, as to which evidence was sought, was a charge of conspiracy against a number of individuals, some of whom were known, and some were not known; and, although the pursuer was not then actually apprehended and under charge for this conspiracy, it is stated in the body of the petition that documentary evidence had already been recovered which showed that he was one of the parties engaged in the conspiracy. I think that in a case of that kind a perfectly legal warrant might have been granted under this petition; and I see nothing in the judgment of the Court of Justiciary inconsistent with this view, or with what has now been expressed by your Lordship.'

Lord Ardmillan said (*ibid*. at p. 332):

'I would add nothing to what your Lordship and Lord Deas have so clearly stated, if I had not been one of the Judges who in the Court of Justiciary suspended this warrant as executed against the party Bell therein named. I was then, and still am, of opinion that the warrant as taken and executed in the case of Bell was illegal. It was a wide and indefinite warrant to search for written documents tending to establish guilt, or participation in guilt, of a serious crime. The crime charged was a conspiracy and the writing of threatening letters, and an attempt to take the life of the Rev. Mr Edgar, and Mr Ballingall, farmer in Dunbog; and in the investigation of that offence, involving the very serious element of conspiracy, the public prosecutor is entitled to support. But, at the same time, a general warrant for a sweeping and indefinite search in the dwelling-house of a person not put under charge, for written documents, in regard to which there is this peculiarity that they must be read before it can be seen what they instruct, is a very strong and startling procedure; and if granted at all, such a warrant should have been accompanied by some security against oppression, and against the violation of private confidence. The most secret and sacred writings were, or might be, exposed to the perusal of a sheriff officer and his concurrents; and the personal attendance of the Sheriff, or some person of discretion and authority, to superintend the search, and to inspect and select the documents, was, in my opinion, necessary to secure the fair execution of the warrant and to prevent its having oppressive consequences. The illegality of the warrant lay in the absence of such securities.

I am not prepared to say that a general search warrant for articles of evidence, and, among other articles, for written documents tending to instruct an occult conspiracy, could not, in any case, be granted to the public prosecutor against parties named in the petition, if accompanied by proper securities against oppressive execution. I agree with your Lordship that such a warrant might have been legally granted. No such case was presented to the Court of Justiciary, or is now here. This warrant is without restriction, limitation, or security against prying curiosity, or reckless violation of confidence, and as taken and executed against Bell it was illegal.'

It is apparent that the First Division with both the previous cases before them give no countenance to the view that charge or apprehension is a prerequisite. Indeed the opinion of Lord Deas goes far to negative it, while the opinion of Lord Ardmillan shows that he did not understand the opinion of the Court in the suspension as turning on that point.

In these circumstances we come without hesitation to the conclusion that charge or apprehension is not an essential prerequisite to the granting of a search warrant and that the proposition in *M'Lauchlan v Renton*, 1911 S.C. (J.) 12 is too broadly stated. Special circumstances productive of exceptional hardship may make the granting of a search warrant illegal and in such cases the absence of charge or apprehension may be a relevant consideration but will not *per se* render the warrant illegal. That is a very different thing from stating as a proposition of general application that 'it is illegal to grant a warrant to search the premises of any citizen who has not been charged with an offence, however much the Crown authorities may have reason for suspicion against him' , 6 Adam, 378, Lord Salvesen at p. 383.

Accordingly in our view the question on which we have been consulted falls to be answered in the negative."

The above case reveals that the power to apply for a warrant is a wide one. Indeed it raises questions—to which there appear to be no answers—about the boundaries of that power. These questions are raised again by *Hay v H M Advocate*, 1968 J.C. 40 which reveals that the power to issue a warrant before arrest is not confined to a search of premises but could include a requirement that the individual subjects himself or herself to some form of medical examination. In that case a murder victim was found to have tooth marks on her breast. Her body was discovered near to an approved school, and dental impressions were taken of 29 staff and pupils at the school. All but Hay were eliminated, and a warrant was sought to take him to a dental hospital for more detailed examination. The evidence secured his conviction, and he appealed unsuccessfully as to the lawfulness of the warrant. In the view of the High Court (of five judges reflecting the importance of the matter):

"...two conflicting considerations arise. On the one hand, there is the need from the point of view of public interest for promptitude and facility in the identification of accused persons and the discovery on their persons or on their premises of indicia either of guilt or innocence. On the other hand, the liberty of the subject must be protected against any undue or unnecessary invasion of it.

In an endeavour as fairly as possible to hold the balance between these two considerations three general principles have been recognised and established by the Court. In the first place, once an accused has been apprehended, and therefore deprived of his liberty, the police have the right to search and examine him. In the second place, before the police have reached a stage in their investigations when they feel warranted in apprehending him they have in general no right by the common law of Scotland to search or examine him or his premises without his consent. There may be circumstances, such as urgency or risk of evidence being lost, which would justify an immediate search or examination, but in the general case they cannot take this step at their own hand. But in the third place, even before the apprehension of the accused they may he entitled to carry out a search of his premises or an examination of his person without his consent if they apply to a magistrate for a warrant for this purpose. Although the accused is not present nor legally represented at the hearing where the magistrate grants the warrant to examine or to search, the interposition of an independent judicial officer holds the basis for a fair reconciliation of the interests of the public in the suppression of crime and of the individual who is entitled not to have the liberty of his person or his premises unduly jeopardised. A warrant of this limited kind will only, however, be granted in special circumstances. The hearing before the magistrate is by no means a formality, and he must be satisfied that the circumstances justify the taking of this unusual course, and that the warrant asked for is not too wide or oppressive. For he is the safeguard against the grant of too general a warrant...

In the circumstances of the present case the obtaining of the warrant prior to the examination in question in our opinion rendered the examination quite legal, and the evidence which resulted from it was therefore competent."

But although there are wide powers to grant warrants to search, this does not mean that the warrant can authorise an unlimited power of search, as the following case establishes.

Bell v Black and Morrison
(1865) 5 Irv. 57

In 1863 a campaign of opposition to the person named as minister to the parish of Dunbog in Fife went so far as the sending to him of threatening letters and an explosion outside his house. In executing one search warrant (itself the subject of litigation) the prosecutors came across evidence suggesting the complicity of five other persons. They petitioned for and received a search warrant in very wide terms, which was then sought to be suspended in the present case.

The petition in terms of which warrant was granted read as follows:

"That the petitioners are informed, and have reason to believe, that written documents and other articles referring to, and connected with, said conspiracy and threatening letters are in the possession of the said John Bell, & C ... and as it is necessary, for the purpose of said precognition, to recover and take possession of the same, the present application for warrant to search becomes necessary. [The prayer was] to grant warrant to officers of Court, and their assistants, to search the dwelling-house, repositories, and premises, at Glenduckie, occupied by the said John Bell, & C ... for the said written documents, and all other articles tending to establish guilt, or participation in said crimes, and to take possession thereof, to be produced before your Lordship, or otherwise to do in the premises as to your Lordship shall seem proper."

The Lord Justice-Clerk (Inglis) delivered the opinion of the court (Lords Ardmillan and Neaves).

"There are some marked and important peculiarities in this petition and warrant ... In the first place, the warrant is granted against five different persons, none of whom is under a charge for any crime. It is stated in the petition that the persons against whom the warrant is asked are shown, by documents recovered in the course of the precognition against Pringle, to have been engaged in the same conspiracy, and in writing and sending threatening letters. But as no charge has yet been made against any of these five person, this amounts to no more than a statement of the suspicion or belief of the procurator-fiscal that they are implicated in the same crimes as Pringle. In the second place, the leading object of the warrant is to obtain possession of the papers of the parties against whom it is directed, without any limitation as to the kind of papers, for by the term "written documents" nothing else can be meant than all writings of every description. The only limitation is to be found in the words which follow—"tending to establish guilt or participation in said crimes," and in the words in the body of the petition—"referring to and connected with said conspiracy and threatening letters." But these words, while they may be supposed in one sense to have a limiting effect, are in another view capable of a very elastic interpretation: for it is not proposed to limit the seizure of papers in each person's house to those which inculpate himself; but, on the contrary, the words of the warrant would justify the seizure of papers tending to inculpate anybody in the crimes charged against Pringle, or at least, and in the most favourable sense, would justify the seizure of any papers in the possession of the complainer Bell which would tend to inculpate any of the other four parties against whom the warrant is directed, in addition, of course, to Pringle, and so in regard to the papers of each of the four other persons against whom the warrant is issued. In the third place, the execution of the warrant is entrusted absolutely and without control to ordinary sheriff-officers and their assistants, who are thereby commanded, whether in the presence or absence of the parties, who are under no criminal charge, and who have no notice of the application for or granting of the warrant, to seize their whole papers *per aversionem*, and themselves to read and examine all these papers for the purpose of finding traces or proofs of guilt either against the owners and possessors of the papers, or against some other person or persons.

The question which is thus raised for our decision has been represented to us by the learned counsel as one of great importance, and no one can doubt that it is so. It involves considerations of such high constitutional principle, that if we had felt any hesitation as to the judgment we should pronounce, we should have asked the assistance and advice of other Judges of this Court. But entertaining no doubt at all, we consider it our duty at once to pronounce this warrant to be illegal. The seizure of papers, as distinguished from their recovery as articles of evidence, and also as distinguished from the seizure of other articles which are invested with no character of confidentiality or secrecy, is, under all circumstance, a matter of extreme delicacy. But the seizure of papers made in the circumstances with which we have to deal, is a proceeding quite unknown to the law of Scotland. Something was said of practice, though no example of such seizure as this was mentioned. We think it right to say that no mere official practice would, in our eyes, justify such a warrant. Nothing short of an Act of Parliament, or a rule of the common law founded on a usage known to and recognised by the Court, would at all affect our judgment on this question. If any such practice really exists, which we do not believe, the sooner it is put an end to the better. The Court are therefore of opinion that the warrant must be suspended."

The foregoing case makes clear that the warrant must indicate with reasonable certainty what it is the police are entitled to look for: it should not be an open invitation to conduct a general search of the premises. In *Hammond v Howdle*, 1996 S.L.T. 1174, however, a warrant authorising the power to search everyone in a hotel where controlled drugs were suspected to be present. The warrant was granted under s.23 of the Misuse of Drugs Act 1971 which authorises a justice of the peace, a magistrate or a sheriff to grant a warrant authorising any constable acting for the police area in which the premises are situated at any time or times within one month from the date of the warrant to enter, if need be by force, the premises named in the warrant and to search the premises and any persons found therein. This can be done where the justice of the peace, magistrate or sheriff is satisfied by information on oath that there is reasonable ground for suspecting that any controlled drugs are, in contravention of the Act or any regulations made thereunder, in the possession of a person on any premises. It was complained that "the police were not in possession of any information which would enable them to suspect that any particular person was in possession of controlled drugs on these premises", and that "the intention of the police was to search patrons of the public house for drugs". However, in rejecting an argument that the police had no proper basis for applying for a warrant, the court held:

"that argument is based upon a misunderstanding of the basis upon which a warrant may be sought under this paragraph. What is required is that there should be reasonable grounds for suspecting that 'a person' on the premises concerned is in possession of controlled drugs. It is not necessary that a view should be formed as to precisely who that person may be. The name of the person is not important, and indeed counsel did not suggest that it was. Nor is it important that in any other way the individual or individuals should be identified. The crucial point is the connection between controlled drugs and the premises, and the existence of a reasonable ground for suspecting that a person on the premises, whoever he or she may be, is in possession of the controlled drugs."

Other safeguards in the execution of warrants are considered in the following case which discusses the nature of the evidence required by a justice of the peace before granting a warrant. It also indicates the possibility that the existing common law rules may have to be re-examined (though not necessarily changed) in the light of the incorporation of Convention rights and Art.8 in particular.

Birse v HM Advocate
2000 S.L.T. 869

Birse had been charged with the possession of cannabis. Part of the case against him was based on evidence obtained by a police search of the premises which he shared with his girlfriend who was the tenant of the property in question. He complained that the warrant was unlawful and a breach of his Convention rights.

LORD JUSTICE GENERAL (RODGER): "[2] We record at the outset that certain matters in relation to art 8 were not in controversy. First, the search of the premises was indeed an interference with the complainer's right to respect for his home. Secondly, if the warrant was granted in accordance with s 23 (3), then the search conducted under the warrant was in accordance with the law. It was also accepted that the purpose of the search was for the prevention of crime and that a warrant to search could be necessary in a democratic society for the purpose of preventing drugs offences. The focus of the attack on the warrant made on behalf of the complainer was, as we understood counsel's submissions, that the procedure adopted by the justice when granting the warrant had not afforded an adequate and effective safeguard against abuse of the police powers of search.

[3] The terms of the warrant indicate that it was granted under s 23 (3) of the Misuse of Drugs Act 1971. So far as relevant for present purposes, that subsection provides:

[His Lordship quoted its terms as set out supra and continued:]

The warrant, which is partly pre-printed and partly in writing, refers back to the application set out just above it and reads: 'At Galashiels (place) the Third day of June 1999 I Andrew Lyall Tulley Justice of the Peace for the Commission area of Scottish Borders, having examined the Informant on Oath and having considered the foregoing Application and being satisfied that there is reasonable ground for suspicion, GRANT WARRANT as craved. Andrew L Tulley Justice of the Peace 3/6/99 2015 hrs.'

[4] It is apparent that the warrant is ex facie valid and in accordance with the terms of s 23 (3) of the 1971 Act. Counsel for the appellant did not suggest otherwise. His contention was, however, that despite its appearance it was nonetheless invalid and that its grant had contravened art 8, by reason of what had—or perhaps more accurately what had not—occurred at the time when the warrant was granted. In advancing the submission in relation to our domestic law counsel referred to the opinion of Lord McCluskey in *HM Advocate v Rae* at 1992 SCCR, p 4 where his Lordship read an abbreviated version of s 23 (3) and commented: 'It is in my opinion clear that the information itself which has to be placed before the justice of the peace is not necessarily information about the circumstances which had given rise to the reasonable grounds for suspecting the presence of drugs or documents envisaged by the section. If an officer of the police appears before a justice of the peace and, on oath, says that he has such information, then in my opinion the justice of the peace is entitled, without further inquiry, to grant the warrant. The court has plainly proceeded upon that view in a number of cases to which I was not referred and I should briefly mention two of them.'

Lord McCluskey then went on to refer to the terms of the warrants in *Bell v HM*

Advocate, 1988 S.L.T. 820 and *Baird v HM Advocate*, 1989 S.C.C.R. 55 neither of which did more than indicate that the constable making the application had sworn that he had reasonable grounds for suspicion.

[5] As is well known, the applications for warrants of this kind—and indeed the warrants themselves—almost invariably take the form which they have in this case, where a pre-printed document was used. Since the terms of those documents are standard, they do not give any indication of the particular circumstances of the individual case. But in the present case at least—and we suspect that the same may well have applied in *Bell* and *Baird*—the formal words do not reveal the full picture. In any event, in this case it is clear that the justice did not simply proceed on the basis of a bare deposition by Constable Nisbet that he had reasonable ground for suspecting that controlled drugs were in the possession of a person on the premises concerned.

[6] As the Crown set out in their answers to the bill, Constable Nisbet confirmed that he had the authority of his inspector to seek the warrant and, in response to a question from the justice, explained the nature of the confidential information received by a fellow officer from a local resident. This indicated a concern both as to the irregular hours kept by the residents of the premises and as to the unusual and strange smells which had emanated in smoke from the windows. This occurred every weekend, especially on Friday and Saturday evenings.

In his report the justice says:

> 'With the passage of time I am unable to state precisely the questions put by to by [sic] DC Steven Nisbet on the date in question. However as a justice of the peace of 22 years' standing I can categorically state that it is invariably my practice when approached by police officers seeking search warrants to first check the identity of the officer, thereafter put him or her on oath, ascertain if they have the authority of their inspector to seek the warrant and then interrogate them as to the reasons for applying for the warrant.
>
> I always read the warrant and ask the officer to amplify the information contained therein.
>
> I am well aware that where an application is made for a warrant under the Misuse of Drugs Act 1971 I require to be satisfied that there are reasonable grounds for suspecting that controlled drugs are in the possession of any person on the premises specified and I never grant a warrant unless I am so satisfied.
>
> In addition to such other questions as might be proper, if the source of the police information is not named I ask the police to confirm that the information comes from a reliable source but do not require them to name that source.
>
> If I am satisfied that there are reasonable grounds for suspecting that controlled drugs are in the possession of any person on the premises specified, I then sign the warrant, adding the date and time of my signature and witness the police officer(s) signature(s) on the warrant...
>
> Given all the circumstances put to me in the application for the warrant and by the police officer present I was fully satisfied that reasonable grounds for suspicion existed and accordingly granted the warrant.'

[7] Counsel readily conceded that he had no basis for doubting or challenging these accounts of what had happened when the justice granted the warrant in question.

[8] At one point in his argument counsel suggested that the information placed before the justice would not in itself have been a proper basis for suspecting that someone was in possession of controlled drugs on the premises. That submission was in our view wholly unrealistic. For many years it has been common knowledge, even among judges, that the smoking of cannabis can produce an unusual and distinctive smell. Therefore, an unusual smell coming in smoke from the windows of premises, especially when this recurred on Friday and Saturday evenings, could well form a perfectly reasonable ground for sus-

pecting that someone was using, and was in possession of, cannabis on the premises.

[9] If that argument were once set on one side, counsel acknowledged that, if the justice had indeed been given the information which we have described, then he would have been entitled to be satisfied himself that there was reasonable ground for suspecting that someone was in possession of a controlled drug on the premises in question. In other words, the justice would have been in a position to grant a warrant in terms of s 23 (3) of the 1971 Act. Subject to the point which we deal with below, counsel did not demur to Lord Gill's observation in the course of argument that, if the justice had acted properly in terms of s 23 (3), the grant of the warrant would not have breached art 8, while if he had not acted properly in terms of the Act, the grant of the warrant would, arguably at least, have been in breach of art 8. The Convention argument was little more than a fifth wheel on the complainer's coach.

[10] In that situation, the observations of Lord McCluskey in *Rae* do not have any direct bearing on this case. We think it right, however, to indicate that, in our view, the whole point of the procedure for the grant of a warrant in terms of s 23 (3) is indeed to interpose an independent judicial figure who actually considers the circumstances and decides whether to grant the warrant.

... In particular, the justice or sheriff must himself be satisfied that there is reasonable ground for suspecting that controlled drugs are in the possession of a person on the premises. In some cases the information as originally presented by the officer will be enough for this, while in other cases the justice or sheriff may require to clarify the position.

[11] Counsel's final stance was that the procedure adopted by the justice, although it met the requirements of s 23 (3) as they are to be read on the face of the statute book, nonetheless contravened the requirements of art 8 of the Convention because no record had been kept of the proceedings. So, as the justice himself admitted, he could not actually recall the particular application, except for the address of the premises, or how he actually handled it, although he could say what his invariable practice was. The argument appeared to be that in this situation there had been an infringement of art 8 of the Convention because the complainer was effectively deprived of a proper basis for ensuring that the application had been considered properly. This appeared to us to come perilously close at least to being an argument based on art 13 of the Convention enshrining the right to an effective remedy before a national authority—the article which enjoys the singular honour of not being destined for incorporation into our law by the Human Rights Act 1998.

[12] Be that as it may, we are satisfied that the complainer's argument is without substance in this case. Here, admittedly, the justice could not recall the circumstances of this particular application. We pause to observe that, in part at least, this may be due to the complainer's delay in challenging the warrant. But the justice could and did explain what his invariable practice was in dealing with such applications and, as counsel accepted, that practice, if followed, would indeed mean that he acted as an independent judicial check that the circumstances justified the grant of the warrant. That information about the justice's invariable practice was backed up by information supplied by the Crown as to what had actually happened in this particular case and as to the details supplied to the justice before he granted the warrant. All that information is before this court and, in disposing of the bill of suspension, we can take account of that information. In another case we should equally take account of any information put before us which indicated that matters had not been handled properly and that the justice or sheriff had not been justified in granting the warrant. In such a case we should, of course, grant the appropriate remedy. The difficulty for the complainer is not, therefore, that the court lacks the power to grant the remedy which he seeks but simply that, on the facts of the case which we have outlined, the justice acted as an effective safeguard against any possible abuse by the police of their power of search. That being so, the complainer has not set out circumstances disclosing a breach of art 8 and is not therefore entitled to the remedy which he seeks."

The foregoing case makes clear that in addition to the substantive limits on the content of a warrant, there are certain procedural formalities to be observed. But the case is important also for indicating that the courts will not readily allow the police to be tripped up by claims about the irregularity in the granting of warrants: see also *Knaup v Hutchinson*, 2003 S.L.T. 1268. Otherwise *Birse* highlights the potentially limited significance of Convention rights in this area. Quite whether it is enough that Convention rights should be reduced so easily by evidence of the "invariable practice" of a witness without more is bound to raise eyebrows. In *H M Advocate v Bell*, 1985 S.L.T. 349 the warrant had been signed by the justice of the peace but not at the end as was the standard practice. It was held by the sheriff that the warrant (issued under the Misuse of Drugs Act 1971) was invalid because although signed by the justice of the peace, it had not been signed after the words "grant warrant as craved". According to the sheriff (whose decision was upheld by the High Court):

"From time immemorial, the law of Scotland has required that all deeds and writings of importance be authenticated to have any force or effect by subscription of the granter—the only recognised exceptions being those granted by the Sovereign who superscribes".

The corresponding procedure in England and Wales is set out in statute (Police and Criminal Evidence Act 1984, s.15) as follows:

"Search warrants—safeguards.
15.—(1) This section and section 16 below have effect in relation to the issue to constables under any enactment, including an enactment contained in an Act passed after this Act, of warrants to enter and search premises; and an entry on or search of premises under a warrant is unlawful unless it complies with this section and section 16 below.
(2) Where a constable applies for any such warrant, it shall be his duty—
    (a) to state—
        (i) the ground on which he makes the application; and
        (ii) the enactment under which the warrant would be issued;
    (b) to specify the premises which it is desired to enter and search; and
    (c) to identify, so far as is practicable, the articles or persons to be sought.
(3) An application for such a warrant shall be made ex parte and supported by an information in writing.
(4) The constable shall answer on oath any question that the justice of the peace or judge hearing the application asks him.
(5) A warrant shall authorise an entry on one occasion only.
(6) A warrant—
    (a) shall specify—
        (i) the name of the person who applies for it;
        (ii) the date on which it is issued;
        (iii) the enactment under which it is issued; and
        (iv) the premises to be searched; and
    (b) shall identify, so far as is practicable, the articles or persons to be sought.
(7) Two copies shall be made of a warrant.
(8) The copies shall be clearly certified as copies"

Leckie v Miln
1982 S.L.T. 177

An accused person was charged on summary complaint with four charges of theft, but was convicted of two charges only. The evidence disclosed that a search of the accused's home had been carried out and that certain items allegedly stolen were found therein. The defence had objected to the admission of evidence of what was found during the search on the ground that the articles were not referred to in the original petition for a warrant authorising the search, nor had consent to an unlimited search been given by the householder at the material time. The sheriff repelled the objection and convicted the accused, who appealed by stated case. The principal question for the High Court was whether the police were entitled to carry out the search.

OPINION OF THE COURT: "Both these charges tell the story of sneak thefts and in particular charge 1 libelled the theft of a wallet from certain office premises and proceeds to narrate that the wallet contained a number of articles including money and some business cards which turned out to be in the name of a Mr Eisner. So far as charge 2 is concerned that charge libelled the theft of a wallet, containing various items including a library card and a receipt, from a room in Harris Academy Annex in Dundee. Let it be said at once that the Crown case in support of conviction on these charges depended essentially upon evidence given by two police officers of finding, during a search of the appellant's dwelling-house which he occupied with a lady, of certain articles stolen during the thefts described in charges 1 and 2. The articles were in the first place certain business cards in the name of Mr Eisner and in the second place a library card in the name of the owner of the wallet taken from Harris Academy together with the receipt which had been in that wallet. The findings-in-fact which describe the search are findings 8, 9 and 10. According to finding 8 two police officers learned from their inspector that the appellant had been arrested on petition at Perth on a charge of sneak theft. That was all they were told. They were then instructed by the inspector to go to the appellant's house and search it. This they proceeded to do. But finding 8 tells us that the officers in question never saw the petition upon which the appellant had been arrested; that they were completely unaware of the nature of any charge in that petition except to the extent that it was a charge of theft of the sneak theft variety; that they did not know at all what articles had been stolen during that theft and did not, of course, in the circumstances, have the petition in their possession, containing the warrant to search, when they went to the appellant's house. On arrival at the house they met a lady called Miss Dailly (known as Mrs Leckie) and they informed her that they were police officers and that the appellant had been arrested by the police at Perth on a petition warrant. Having said that they informed Miss Dailly that they wished to search the house. No objection to the proposed search was made. Finding 10 then describes the search which took place and the discovery, in the course of that search, of the business cards to which we have referred in the top drawer of a chest of drawers in the only bedroom of the house, a top drawer which contained the clothing of Miss Dailly, and the discovery of the library ticket and the receipt which we have already mentioned inside a jacket hanging in the wardrobe of that bedroom. For the appellant the submission was that the search which was carried out in all the circumstances disclosed in findings 8, 9 and 10 was quite unlawful in respect that it was neither authorised by the warrant to search in the petition on which the appellant had been arrested in Perth nor was it authorised by any implied consent given by Miss Dailly. If that submission is sound, as counsel for the appellant urged us to accept, then it followed, according to counsel, that the evidence given by the police officers about their findings was inadmissible. This was not a case in which officers carrying out an active search within the scope of a lawful warrant came across articles unrelated to the particular crime with which they were concerned. In such a case the finding of other articles indicating guilt of other crimes may be perfectly admissible in evidence. The fundamental proposition here was that neither upon the warrant nor upon any implied consent was the active unlimited search carried out by the officers justified in law. The Crown position was simply this. There existed, no doubt, authority for a search of the appellant's premises and that authority was the warrant granted upon the petition on which the appellant had appeared in Perth. It is the case that the officers admittedly did not carry out an active search within the limitations of that warrant to search for they were wholly ignorant of the contents of the petition and the scope of the warrant to search granted upon its presentation. But given the authority for a lawful search of the premises, the search which was carried out was carried out by the officers in the manner in which they carried it out with the full consent given by Miss Dailly by plain implication. The question in the case therefore comes to be whether Miss Dailly did give consent for the unlimited search carried out by the officers, all as described in findings 8, 9 and 10. We are of opinion that by no stretch of the imagination can it be said that the consent given by Miss Dailly was consent for an active unlimited search regardless of the limitations in the warrant which admittedly existed. Finding 9 tells us that before Miss Dailly was informed that the officers wished to search the premises they told Miss Dailly that they were police officers and that the appellant had been arrested by the police at Perth on a petition warrant. It follows from that that any consent given by Miss Dailly must be assumed to have been given upon the footing that the officers intended to carry out a search within the authority contained in the warrant to which they referred, and that authority was, it is perfectly plain, an authority of a limited character. The search was nothing of the kind for, as we have already pointed out, the officers had no knowledge of the contents of the petition and what they did was to carry out a random search of the appellant's house in the hope of finding something which might conceivably have been the proceeds of a sneak theft anywhere. In these circumstances we are satisfied that the evidence of the finding of labels 2 and 4 should not have been admitted and if that is right then it follows that the conviction cannot stand for the evidence aliunde was insufficient to warrant the conviction of the appellant. The relevant questions in the case are three. The first question in the case we answer of consent in the affirmative in respect that no submission was made upon it. Question 2 goes to the entitlement of the officers to carry out the search which they did and to that question, which is perhaps not perfectly expressed to focus the argument, we give a negative answer. Having given a negative answer to question 2 it is inevitable that the answer to question 3 must also be in the negative. The conviction will accordingly be quashed."

The foregoing case makes clear that the warrant only authorises an entry and search for the purpose for which it was issued: it does not authorise entry and search for other purposes. The police must also notify their identity and the purposes of their visit, even when they have a warrant: Renton and Brown's *Criminal Procedure*, (6th ed, 1996), para.5.15. Nevertheless there are no statutory safeguards for the householder in Scotland that we find in England and Wales. The Police and Criminal Evidence Act 1984 (which applies only in England and Wales) provides by s.16 that:

Execution of warrants

    16.—(1) A warrant to enter and search premises may be executed by any constable.

    (2) Such a warrant may authorise persons to accompany any constable who is executing it.

    (3) Entry and search under a warrant must be within one month from the date of its issue.

    (4) Entry and search under a warrant must be at a reasonable hour unless it appears to the constable executing it that the purpose of a search may be frustrated on an entry at a reasonable hour.

    (5) Where the occupier of premises which are to be entered and searched is present at the time when a constable seeks to execute a warrant to enter and search them, the constable—

        (a) shall identify himself to the occupier and, if not in uniform, shall produce to him documentary evidence that he is a constable;

        (b) shall produce the warrant to him; and

        (c) shall supply him with a copy of it.

    (6) Where—

        (a) the occupier of such premises is not present at the time when a constable seeks to execute such a warrant; but

        (b) some other person who appears to the constable to be in charge of the premises is present,

subsection (5) above shall have effect as if any reference to the occupier were a reference to that other person.

(7) If there is no person present who appears to the constable to be in charge of the premises, he shall leave a copy of the warrant in a prominent place on the premises.

(8) A search under a warrant may only be a search to the extent required for the purpose for which the warrant was issued.

(9) A constable executing a warrant shall make an endorsement on it stating—

(a) whether the articles or persons sought were found; and

(b) whether any articles were seized, other than articles which were sought.

(10) A warrant which—

(a) has been executed; or

(b) has not been executed within the time authorised for its execution,

shall be returned—

(i) if it was issued by a justice of the peace, to the clerk to the justices for the petty sessions area for which he acts; and

(ii) if it was issued by a judge, to the appropriate officer of the court from which he issued it.

(11) A warrant which is returned under subsection (10) above shall be retained for 12 months from its return—

(a) by the clerk to the justices, if it was returned under paragraph (i) of that sub-section; and

(b) by the appropriate officer, if it was returned under paragraph (ii).

(12) If during the period for which a warrant is to be retained the occupier of the premises to which it relates asks to inspect it, he shall be allowed to do so."

There is also a Code of Practice which seeks to guide the police in their use of search powers. The Code of Practice is approved by Parliament and admissible in legal proceedings. There is nothing like this in Scotland.

H M Advocate v Hepper
1958 S.L.T. 160

An accused person was charged *inter alia* with, theft by housebreaking of 36 bottles of whisky and an attaché case. In the course of the trial a police witness deponed that he had visited the house of the accused on a matter unconnected with the crime for which the accused was being tried, and had been given permission by the accused to search his house. The advocate-depute proposed to ask what had been found with the object of eliciting that the attaché case, theft of which was libelled in the indictment, had been found. Counsel for the panel objected to the line of evidence on the ground that inasmuch as the search of his premises to which the accused consented had nothing to do with the crime for which he was on trial, the evidence of articles found during the said search was not admissible.

LORD GUTHRIE: "On 19th November 1957, police officers called at the residence of the accused on business not connected with the present charge. The accused was at home and consented to the police searching his house. In the course of his examination in the witness box, the detective superintendent who called at the accused's house was asked whether he had taken possession of anything, and objection was taken to the line of evidence. Counsel for the panel stated that the consent to a search was restricted to the business upon which the police had called at the accused's residence, and that, if the police in the course of that search discovered and removed an article which it was proposed to prove in evidence as relating to the present charge, such evidence should be excluded on the ground that it had been improperly obtained. Reference was made to *Turnbull*, 1951 S.L.T. 409, and *Jackson v Stevenson*, 1897, 2 Adam 255. In such cases, as the Lord Justice-Clerk, Lord Thomson, has repeatedly pointed out in recent years, the problem is always to reconcile the interest of society in the detection of crime with the requirement of fairness to an accused person. In the present case I am of opinion that the evidence is admissible. The police, in the course of their duty, when searching the accused's house with his consent in connection with another matter, came upon the article which they removed. In *Turnbull*, I distinguished that case, in which I excluded evidence as to documents taken possession of by police officers searching the accused's premises under a search warrant which clearly did not cover these documents, from a case in which police officers accidentally stumbled upon evidence of a plainly incriminating character in the course of a search for a different purpose. That distinction was based upon earlier authorities to which I was referred in *Turnbull's* case. It may be that the article which the police officers stumbled upon in their search of the accused's house was not an article of a plainly incriminating character, but it was at least an article of a very suspicious character, since it was an attaché case which contained within it the name and address of another person. In the circumstances, I do not think that the police officers acted in any way improperly in taking away that article in order to make further inquiries about it. If they had not done so, it might have disappeared. It appears to me that in the circumstances it was their duty, being officers charged with the protection of the public, to have acted as they did. But even if it cannot be put so highly, and if it be thought that their action was irregular, I am still of opinion that the evidence, even if irregularly obtained, is admissible in view of the interest of society in the detection of crime. I do not think this is a case in which the evidence ought to be excluded because of a breach of the principle of fairness to the accused. I therefore hold that the evidence is admissible."

The decision in *Hepper* was approved by *Burke v Wilson*, 1988 S.L.T. 749. Although the police may only use the warrant to gain entry for limited purposes, they may thus seize and remove anything they may stumble across in the course of the search which may be evidence of another offence. It will be noted in the *Hepper* case that the police officers entered and searched the premises without a warrant but with the consent of the occupier. They were lawfully on the premises and conducting a search for limited purposes authorised by the occupier. The same rule will apply where police officers are lawfully on the premises with a search warrant conducting a lawful search for the limited purpose authorised by the warrant. The warrant will not authorise a search for material unrelated to the offence which they are investigating (*Leckie v Miln*, 1982 S.L.T. 177) but it will allow them to remove material relating to another offence if they should stumble across it (*H M Advocate v Hepper*, 1958 S.L.T. 160). *Hepper* is to be distinguished from the earlier case of *H M Advocate v Turnbull*, 1951 S.L.T. 409 where the police entered premises with a search warrant to investigate tax fraud involving an accountant and his client. In the course of the search they removed a bundle of papers relating to other clients which were examined and subsequently formed the basis of criminal charges. The evidence from these latter files was ruled inadmissible, and the irregularity could not be remedied by a warrant granted six months later with retrospective effect. According to Lord Guthrie:

"To reach the opposite conclusion would largely destroy the protection which the law affords the citizen against the invasion of his liberties by its requirements of the specific warrant of a magistrate for interference with these liberties."

It has been held that in executing a warrant police officers may take with them specialists to help with securing access to and dealing with material being removed: *Lord Advocate's Reference (No. 1 of 2002)*, 2002 S.L.T. 1017.

Campbell v Vannet
1997 S.C.C.R. 787

The police in this case noticed activity at the door of the appellant which led them to believe that drugs were being bought and sold. Police officers (McKeown and Lapping) approached the house and rattled the letterbox, shouting to the occupant that they were the police with instructions to open. The police officers could see through the letter box that the occupant had rushed to the toilet where it was believed she was disposing of the drugs believed to be on the premises. When no one opened the door, the police officers forced their way in: they had no search warrant and no permission from the occupants. Did they act lawfully?

> LORD JUSTICE GENERAL (RODGER): "Mr McSherry [for the appellant] argued that it had been unlawful for the police officers to enter the premises in the way in which they did. He argued that any urgency in the situation had been created by Constable Lapping attempting to gain entry to the flat by rattling the letterbox. What the police should have done, Mr McSherry submitted, was to have waited and to have radioed for other officers to obtain a search warrant and then, armed with that search warrant, the constables should have entered the premises under the authority of that warrant. What had been done in this case amounted, in effect, to a circumnavigation of the procedures for obtaining a search warrant. Insofar as the sheriff had held that the urgent nature of the situation justified the action of the police, Mr McSherry submitted that the sheriff had relied on speculation, since certain at least of the factors which he had mentioned in disposing of that matter were not the subject of findings in fact.
>
> It will be apparent that Mr McSherry's approach rests on the fact that Constable Lapping and his colleague were entering premises to carry out a search. In our view, however, it is clear from the findings in fact that the police officers had just seen a serious crime of supplying or, to confine the matter to the terms of charge (3), offering to supply diamorphine being committed from within the premises. In that situation the police officers were entitled, in our view, to force entry to the premises with a view to detaining and apprehending the person who was suspected of having committed this serious crime. We note that Constable Lapping had first sought permission to enter and that this had not been given.
>
> For the proposition that in these circumstances the police officers were entitled to force entry we refer to the general statement of principle which is to be found at paragraph 7.05 of Renton and Brown under reference to the authorities of Hume, Alison and Macdonald. For these reasons we are satisfied that the entry to the premises by the police officers on this occasion was lawful. Since the legality of the entry was the only question which was argued before us, ... we shall dismiss the appeal against conviction."

The general rule is that entry and search of private property will normally be permitted only with the consent of the occupier or with the authority of a warrant: *Campbell v Vannet*, above, reveals that there are exceptions. As was pointed out in *Cairns v Keane*, 1983 S.C.C.R. 277 by Sheriff Macmillan:

> "In Scotland it has been said that the 'effect of all [the] authorities seemed to ... show that the 'rule of law in Scotland concerning the right of a constable to enter any premises for any purpose' was that, except when investigating serious crime, police officers are no more entitled than any other member of the public to enter upon private property without a warrant and without the consent of the owner; and that if they do they must be prepared to justify their conduct by reason of special circumstances before any evidence so obtained can be rendered admissible."(at 281.)

In *Cairns* it was held that the police were entitled to enter the home of the accused who was suspected by officers to have been driving while under the influence of alcohol. In these circumstances the police officers were entitled to follow the suspect into his house in order to breathalyse him. In addition:

- The police may enter private premises without a warrant and without consent to investigate a disturbance: *Moffat v McFadyen*, 1999 G.W.D. 22–1038.
- Parliament may confer on the police the power of entry without a warrant and without

consent: Civic Government (Scotland) Act 1982, Sch.2A (inserted by Crime and Disorder Act 1998). See also *Whitelaw v Haining*, 1992 S.L.T. 956.

- The police may on grounds of urgency enter and search private property without a warrant and without the owner's consent after an arrest: *McGuigan v H M Advocate*, 1936 S.L.T. 161. See Ch.4, above.

In England and Wales, the Police and Criminal Evidence Act 1984, s.17 gives a general statutory power to enter private premises without a warrant and without consent in specific and defined circumstances: *D'Souza v DPP* [1992] 4 All E.R. 545 (a decision of the House of Lords requiring an amendment to s.17).

VII. PRESS INTRUSION AND UNWANTED PUBLICITY

The issues discussed so far have been concerned mainly with invasion of privacy by the state. Here we consider the invasion of privacy not by the state but by the press, and it is here that difficult questions arise about conflicting rights. Parliament has intervened in the past to prevent the press from publishing salacious details disclosed in matrimonial litigation: Judicial Proceedings (Regulation of Reports) Act 1926, a provision still in force and occasionally the basis of prosecution. In recent years the issue has arisen in the context of unwanted publicity for actors and models who normally court publicity. On occasion, however, they may not want their wedding photographs printed in the newspapers before being touched up, or they may not want the public to know that they have been attending a clinic for drug abuse after telling the public that they do not take drugs. How is the matter to be resolved? Should the information be published or not? The exercise of the right to freedom of expression may be at the expense of the privacy of the individual, while any protection of the right to privacy may be at the expense of freedom of expression. One possible solution to these difficulties was alluded to by Lord Bonomy in *Martin v McGuiness*, 2003 S.L.T. 1424, is that the law of confidence could develop as the basis for protecting privacy. Although the law of confidence has been developed as an equitable doctrine in English law, it was received in Scotland in *Lord Advocate v Scotsman Publications Ltd*, 1989 S.L.T. 705. In that case an unsuccessful attempt was made to restrain the publication of information obtained by a former security service official which was said to been obtained in confidence.

In a number of cases the English Court of Appeal has also indicated that the law of confidentiality is an appropriate basis for protecting individuals from unwanted press publicity. This is a view now shared by the House of Lords in *Campbell v MGN Ltd* [2004] UKHL 22, where the leading speech for the majority in a 3:2 decision was given by Lord Hope of Craighead. In that major decision the House of Lords appeared to set the law on a different path from the Court of Appeal which had been generally unwilling readily to restrain press freedom in the interests of personal privacy. This is an approach which appears to have been developed independently of but in a manner which is consistent with the requirements of the Human Rights Act 1998, s.12. This provides as follows:

"(1) This section applies if a court is considering whether to grant any relief which, if granted, might affect the exercise of the Convention right to freedom of expression.
. . .
(3) No such relief is to be granted so as to restrain publication before trial unless the court is satisfied that the applicant is likely to establish that publication should not be allowed.

(4) The court must have particular regard to the importance of the Convention right to freedom of expression and, where the proceedings relate to material which the respondent claims, or which appears to the court, to be journalistic, literary or artistic material (or to conduct connected with such material), to—
(a) the extent to which—

(i) the material has, or is about to, become available to the public; or

(ii) it is, or would be, in the public interest for the material to be published;

(b) any relevant privacy code."

If a defendant can show that he or she has complied with a relevant privacy code, it is unlikely in these circumstances to have its claim to an entitlement to freedom of expression trumped by considerations of privacy: *Douglas v Hello!* [2001] Q.B. 967. Section 12 is designed in part to deal with the House of Lords decision in *American Cyanamid Co v Ethicon Ltd* [1975] A.C. 396, where it was held that in order to obtain an interim injunction the plaintiff need only show a serious issue to be tried and that the balance of convenience lay in favour of granting the restraining order. It was not the business of the courts at that stage to have regard to the legal merits of the case.

So what is a relevant privacy code? The best known such code is the Press Complaints Commission's Code of Practice. The Press Complaints Commission is a self-regulatory body established by the newspaper publishers in 1991. It deals with complaints by the public about breaches of the code of practice which the Commission itself has drawn up. If a complaint is well founded a newspaper may be required to give coverage to the complaint, but this will rarely be in a prominent place. The Commission has no power to award damages or otherwise compensate an individual aggrieved by a breach of the code. The independence of the Commission is hardly enhanced by the fact that its membership includes representatives of the very newspaper industry which the Commission purports to monitor. The Court of Appeal in *A v B plc* rightly indicated that it did not wish to have PCC rulings cited in proceedings before it as if they were legal decisions.

Press Complaints Commission
Code of Practice

"All members of the press have a duty to maintain the highest professional standards. This Code sets the benchmark for those ethical standards, protecting both the rights of the individual and the public's right to know. It is the cornerstone of the system of self-regulation to which the industry has made a binding commitment.

It is essential that an agreed code be honoured not only to the letter but in the full spirit. It should not be interpreted so narrowly as to compromise its commitment to respect the rights of the individual, nor so broadly that it constitutes an unnecessary interference with freedom of expression or prevents publication in the public interest.

It is the responsibility of editors and publishers to implement the Code and they should take care to ensure it is observed rigorously by all editorial staff and external contributors, including non-journalists, in printed and online versions of publications.

Editors should co-operate swiftly with the PCC in the resolution of complaints. Any publication judged to have breached the Code must print the adjudication in full and with due prominence, including headline reference to the PCC.

1   Accuracy

i) The Press must take care not to publish inaccurate, misleading or distorted information, including pictures.

ii) A significant inaccuracy, mis-leading statement or distortion once recognised must be corrected, promptly and with due prominence, and–where appropriate–an apology published.

iii) The Press, whilst free to be partisan, must distinguish clearly between comment, conjecture and fact.

iv) A publication must report fairly and accurately the outcome of an action for defamation to which it has been a party, unless an agreed settlement states otherwise, or an agreed statement is published.

2   Opportunity to reply

A fair opportunity for reply to inaccuracies must be given when reasonably called for.

3   *Privacy

   i) Everyone is entitled to respect for his or her private and family life, home, health and correspondence, including digital communications. Editors will be expected to justify intrusions into any individual's private life without consent.

   ii) It is unacceptable to photograph individuals in private places without their consent.

Note—Private places are public or private property where there is a reasonable expectation of privacy.

4   *Harassment

   i) Journalists must not engage in intimidation, harassment or persistent pursuit.

   ii) They must not persist in questioning, telephoning, pursuing or photographing individuals once asked to desist; nor remain on their property when asked to leave and must not follow them.

   iii) Editors must ensure these principles are observed by those working for them and take care not to use non-compliant material from other sources.

5   Intrusion into grief or shock

In cases involving personal grief or shock, enquiries and approaches must be made with sympathy and discretion and publication handled sensitively. This should not restrict the right to report legal proceedings, such as inquests.

6   *Children

   i) Young people should be free to complete their time at school without unnecessary intrusion.

   ii) A child under 16 must not be interviewed or photographed on issues involving their own or another child's welfare unless a custodial parent or similarly responsible adult consents.

   iii) Pupils must not be approached or photographed at school without the permission of the school authorities.

   iv) Minors must not be paid for material involving children's welfare, nor parents or guardians for material about their children or wards, unless it is clearly in the child's interest.

   v) Editors must not use the fame, notoriety or position of a parent or guardian as sole justification for publishing details of a child's private life.

7   *Children in sex cases

   1. The press must not, even if legally free to do so, identify children under 16 who are victims or witnesses in cases involving sex offences.

   2. In any press report of a case involving a sexual offence against a child–

   i) The child must not be identified.

   ii) The adult may be identified.

   iii) The word "incest" must not be used where a child victim might be identified.

   iv) Care must be taken that nothing in the report implies the relationship between the accused and the child.

8   *Hospitals

   i) Journalists must identify them-selves and obtain permission from a responsible executive before entering non-public areas of hospitals or similar institutions to pursue enquiries.

   ii) The restrictions on intruding into privacy are particularly relevant to enquiries about individuals in hospitals or similar institutions.

9 *Reporting of Crime
(i) Relatives or friends of persons convicted or accused of crime should not generally
     be identified without their consent, unless they are genuinely relevant to the story.
(ii)
     Particular regard should be paid to the potentially vulnerable position of children
     who witness, or are victims of, crime. This should not restrict the right to report
     legal proceedings.

10 *Clandestine devices and subterfuge
i) The press must not seek to obtain or publish material acquired by using hidden
    cameras or clandestine listening devices; or by intercepting private or mobile tele-
    phone calls, messages or emails; or by the unauthorised removal of documents or
    photographs.
ii) Engaging in misrepresentation or subterfuge, can generally be justified only in the
    public interest and then only when the material cannot be obtained by other means.

11 Victims of sexual assault
The press must not identify victims of sexual assault or publish material likely to contribute
to such identification unless there is adequate justification and they are legally free to do so.
...

The public interest
   There may be exceptions to the clauses marked * where they can be demonstrated to be
in the public interest.
   1. The public interest includes, but is not confined to:
   i) Detecting or exposing crime or serious impropriety.
   ii) Protecting public health and safety.
   iii) Preventing the public from being misled by an action or statement of an individual
        or organisation.
   2. There is a public interest in freedom of expression itself.
   3. Whenever the public interest is invoked, the PCC will require editors to demon-
      strate fully how the public interest was served.
   4. The PCC will consider the extent to which material is already in the public domain,
      or will become so.
   5. In cases involving children under 16, editors must demonstrate an exceptional
      public interest to over-ride the normally paramount interest of the child."

   The relationship between the Human Rights Act 1998, s.12 and the Press Complaints
Commission Code of Practice was considered in *Douglas v Hello!* [2001] Q.B. 967, where the
defendants had published unauthorised photographs of the plaintiffs' wedding. The plaintiffs
had signed an agreement with a rival magazine (*OK!*) giving them exclusive rights to publish the
photographs. Their application for an injunction to stop publication failed, with the Court of
Appeal taking into account a number of factors:

- "The plaintiffs' privacy claim was not strong: they did not choose to have a private
  wedding, attended by a few members of their family and a few friends, in the normal
  sense of the words 'private wedding'. Rather they invited 250 guests. Although they
  undertook to use their best efforts to ensure that their guests 'shall not publish and/or
  broadcast ... or write any article about, or give any extended comment, report or
  interview to any media concerning the Wedding', there was no evidence before the court
  which shows that they took any steps to enforce that undertaking, so far as their guests
  were concerned.
- So far as *Hello!'s* case is concerned, there was 'a substantial risk that if an injunction
  'killing' this weekly edition of *Hello!* were to turn out to have been wrongly granted,

Hello! would suffer damages which it would be extremely difficult to quantify in money terms. So far as *OK!* is concerned, if it won at the trial, it would be able 'to have recourse to the very powerful weapon, fashioned by equity, of requiring *Hello!* to account to it for all the profits it has made from the publication of Issue 639' [the issue which carried the disputed photographs]. The balance of convenience, as between *OK!* and *Hello!*, therefore favoured *Hello!*."

In so holding, Brooke L.J. concluded by noting that this was "essentially a commercial dispute between two magazine enterprises which are not averse to exercising spoiling tactics against each other". In the same case, Keene L.J. said that s.12(3):

"does not seek to give a priority to one Convention right over another. It is simply dealing with the interlocutory stage of proceedings and with how the court is to approach matters at that stage in advance of any ultimate balance being struck between rights which may be in potential conflict. It requires the court to look at the merits of the case and not merely to apply the American Cyanamid test. Thus the court has to look ahead to the ultimate stage and to be satisfied that the scales are likely to come down in the applicant's favour."

He did concede, however, that s.12(3) makes "prior restraint (*i.e.* before the trial) more difficult in cases where the right to freedom of expression is engaged than where it is not". But that was "not a novel concept in English law".

A v B plc
[2003] Q.B. 195

A was a footballer with a premier division football club. B was a national newspaper. C was one of two women with whom A, a married man, had affairs. An injunction was granted by Jack J. to restrain B from publishing the stories which C and the other woman, D, had sold to B recounting their affairs with A. The newspaper successfully appealed.

LORD WOOLF C.J.: "3. Since the coming into force of the Human Rights Act 1998 ('the 1998 Act') there has been an increase in the number of actions in which injunctions are being sought to protect the claimants from the publication of articles in newspapers on the grounds that the articles contain confidential information concerning the claimants, the publication of which, it is alleged, would infringe their privacy. Such actions can be against any part of the media.

4. The applications for interim injunctions have now to be considered in the context of articles 8 and 10 of the European Convention of Human Rights ('ECHR'). These articles have provided new parameters within which the court will decide, in an action for breach of confidence, whether a person is entitled to have his privacy protected by the court or whether the restriction of freedom of expression which such protection involves cannot be justified. The court's approach to the issues which the applications raise has been modified because under section 6 of the 1998 Act, the court, as a public authority, is required not to act 'in a way which is incompatible with a Convention right'. The court is able to achieve this by absorbing the rights which articles 8 and 10 protect into the long-established action for breach of confidence. This involves giving a new strength and breadth to the action so that it accommodates the requirements of those articles.

5. The court is assisted in achieving this because the equitable origins of the action for breach of confidence mean that historically the remedy for breach of confidence will only be granted when it is equitable for this to happen. As the headnote makes clear, in *Argyll v Argyll* [1967] Ch. 302 Ungoed-Thomas J decided that 'a contract or obligation of confidence need not be express, but could be implied, and a breach of contract or trust or faith could arise independently of any right to property or contract (other than any contract

which the imparting of the confidence might itself create); and that the court in the exercise of its equitable jurisdiction would restrain a breach of confidence independently of any right at law'. In *Stephens v Avery* [1988] 1 Ch 449, Sir Nicholas Browne-Wilkinson V-C made it clear that this approach could be extended to other relationships apart from that between husband and wife, though it would not necessarily apply in the same way.

6. The manner in which the two articles operate is entirely different. Article 8 operates so as to extend the areas in which an action for breach of confidence can provide protection for privacy. It requires a generous approach to the situations in which privacy is to be protected. Article 10 operates in the opposite direction. This is because it protects freedom of expression and to achieve this it is necessary to restrict the area in which remedies are available for breaches of confidence. There is a tension between the two articles which requires the court to hold the balance between the conflicting interests they are designed to protect. This is not an easy task but it can be achieved by the courts if, when holding the balance, they attach proper weight to the important rights both articles are designed to protect. Each article is qualified expressly in a way which allows the interests under the other article to be taken into account.

7. Actions for breach of confidence are usually brought at short notice and are followed by an immediate application for an interim injunction (as happened here) which has to be heard urgently without adequate time either for preparation or for the hearing of the application. If an interim injunction is to be granted it is essential that it is granted promptly because otherwise the newspaper will be published and then, from the claimant's point of view, the damage will have been done. Notwithstanding these constraints of time, the applications for injunctions in this class of action are frequently marked by the citation of very large numbers of authorities which the unfortunate judge has to do his best to digest prior to announcing his decision as to where the balance falls in the particular case.

8. In the present appeals the parties have placed before us three lever arch files of authorities. In addition, during the course of the hearing we were handed a number of other domestic and Strasbourg decisions. Finally we have another file which contains what was described as 'Press Complaints Commission Material', which includes 17 decisions of the Press Complaints Commission, as well as the Code of Practice of the Commission and a further judgment. It is understandable that, in what is a developing area of the law, citation of authority is necessary, but we would hope that the law has now, at least at the level below the House of Lords, become sufficiently clear to make the citation of authority on this scale unnecessary. This comment is not to be understood as a criticism of the counsel appearing before us on these appeals. They were seeking guidance as to the proper approach to the granting of injunctions in this sort of action. We do, however, hope that as a result of our decision the citation of authorities on this scale will be regarded as unnecessary and not accepted by judges of first instance who have to hear these applications. This action on the part of judges is necessary and part of their responsibilities because of the overriding objective to deal with cases justly .... The need for control of the excessive citation of authority should be borne in mind in deciding questions of costs since it leads to disproportionate expense which can in turn make litigation beyond the means of the ordinary person.

9. The authorities largely fall into two categories. The first category consists of the decisions of the Strasbourg Court on articles 8 and 10. These decisions are valuable sources of the principles which the articles embrace. The decisions do however tend to repeat the same principles in successive cases in order to apply them to different situations. The citation of a single case may therefore be all that is required. The application of the principles to the facts of a particular situation is largely unhelpful because that is primarily the task of the domestic court. The other category of cases are decisions given in this jurisdiction. If they are authorities which relate to the action for breach of confidence prior to the coming into force of the 1998 Act then they are largely of historic interest only.

10. The citation of authorities on the present scale adds hugely to the costs of litigation which is already inevitably high. It also creates huge problems for the judges hearing the

applications, particularly in view of the urgency with which they have to be dealt. In order to assist the parties we now set out guidelines which are intended to assist the judiciary and the parties to deal with the majority of these applications in a more proportionate manner.

THE GUIDELINES

11. We suggest that if judges direct themselves in accordance with the following paragraphs in many cases they will not need to be burdened by copious reference to other authorities:

i) The consideration of this type of application should generally begin with recognition that what is being considered is an interim application for an injunction. This means that whether any injunction is granted at all is a matter of discretion for the judge, to be exercised in accordance with what are now well-established principles which include the need to establish, as we will explain later, that after a trial it is likely that an injunction would be granted after a substantive hearing, while recognising that the grant or refusal of an interim injunction could well determine the outcome of the entire proceedings.

ii) The fact that the injunction is being sought to protect the privacy of the claimant, and if the injunction is not granted, the claimant may be deprived of the only remedy which is of any value is a relevant consideration. However, this consideration has to be weighed against the defendant's rights of freedom of expression. Even before the 1998 Act this would have been an important consideration. Its importance has been enhanced by section 12 of the 1998 Act. [Woolf L.J. then read the relevant provisions of section 12.]

iii) As to the word 'likely' in section 12(3) useful guidance is provided by Sir Andrew Morritt VC in *Imutran Ltd v Uncaged Campaigns Ltd* [2002] FSR 20. He said of section 12:

'17. Counsel for the defendants submitted that the requirement of likelihood imposed a higher standard than that formulated in *American Cyanamid*. I did not understand this to be disputed by counsel for Imutran. He submitted that whatever the standard was his case satisfied it. Theoretically and as a matter of language likelihood is slightly higher in the scale of probability than a real prospect of success. But the difference between the two is so small that I cannot believe that there will be many (if any) cases which would have succeeded under the *American Cyanamid* test but will now fail because of the terms of s.12(3). Accordingly I propose to apply the test of likelihood without any further consideration of how much more probable that now has to be.'

There is no conflict between section 12 (3) and the Convention. (See *Douglas v Hello! Ltd* [2001] QB 967; Keene LJ paragraph 150.)

iv) The fact that if the injunction is granted it will interfere with the freedom of expression of others and in particular the freedom of the press is a matter of particular importance. This well-established common law principle is underlined by section 12 (4). Any interference with the press has to be justified because it inevitably has some effect on the ability of the press to perform its role in society. This is the position irrespective of whether a particular publication is desirable in the public interest. The existence of a free press is in itself desirable and so any interference with it has to be justified. Here we would endorse the approach of Hoffmann LJ in *R v Central Independent Television plc* [1994] Fam 192, at p.201–204, where he said:

'publication may cause needless pain, distress and damage to individuals or harm to other aspects of the public interest. But a freedom which is restricted to what judges think to be responsible or in the public interest is no freedom.

Freedom means the right to publish things which Government and judges, however well motivated, think should not be published. It means the right to say things which "right thinking people" regard as dangerous or irresponsible. This freedom is subject only to clearly defined exceptions laid down by common law or statute ... the principle that the press is free from both Government and judicial control is more important than the particular case.'

v) The fact that under section 12 (4) the court is required to have particular regard to whether it would be in the public interest for the material to be published does not mean that the court is justified in interfering with the freedom of the press where there is no identifiable special public interest in any particular material being published. Such an approach would turn section 12 (4) upside down. Regardless of the quality of the material which it is intended to publish prima facie the court should not interfere with its publication. Any interference with publication must be justified.

vi) It is most unlikely that any purpose will be served by a judge seeking to decide whether there exists a new cause of action in tort which protects privacy. In the great majority of situations, if not all situations, where the protection of privacy is justified, relating to events after the Human Rights Act came into force, an action for breach of confidence now will, where this is appropriate, provide the necessary protection. This means that at first instance it can be readily accepted that it is not necessary to tackle the vexed question of whether there is a separate cause of action based upon a new tort involving the infringement of privacy.

vii) Furthermore in the majority of cases the question of whether there is an interest capable of being the subject of a claim for privacy should not be allowed to be the subject of detailed argument. There must be some interest of a private nature which the claimant wishes to protect, but usually the answer to the question whether there exists a private interest worthy of protection will be obvious. In those cases in which the answer is not obvious, an answer will often be unnecessary. This is because the weaker the claim for privacy the more likely that the claim for privacy will be outweighed by the claim based on freedom of expression. The advantage of not having to distinguish between acts which are public and those which are private in a difficult case is made clear by what Gleeson CJ had to say on the subject in *Australian Broadcasting Corporation v Lenah Game Meats Pty Ltd* [2001] HCA 63. He explained the difficulty of distinguishing between public and private information when he said at para. 42:

'[42] There is no bright line which can be drawn between what is private and what is not. Use of the term "public" is often a convenient method of contrast, but there is a large area in between what is necessarily public and what is necessarily private. An activity is not private simply because it is not done in public. It does not suffice to make an act private that, because it occurs on private property, it has such measure of protection from the public gaze as the characteristics of the property, the nature of the activity, the locality, and the disposition of the property owner combine to afford. Certain kinds of information about a person, such as information relating to health, personal relationships, or finances, may be easy to identify as private; as may certain kinds of activity, which a reasonable person, applying contemporary standards of morals and behaviour, would understand to be meant to be unobserved. The requirement that disclosure or observation of information or conduct would be highly offensive to a reasonable person of ordinary sensibilities is in many circumstances a useful practical test of what is private.'

viii) The same is true in cases in which the public interest in publication is relied on to oppose the grant of an injunction. We have already made clear that even where there is no public interest in a particular publication interference with freedom of expression has to be justified. However, the existence of a public interest in publication strengthens the case for not granting an injunction. Again in the majority of situations whether the public interest is involved or not will be obvious. In the grey area cases the public interest, if it exists, is unlikely to be decisive. Judges should therefore be reluctant in the difficult borderline cases to become involved in detailed argument as to whether the public interest is involved. In a borderline case the application will usually be capable of being resolved without deciding whether there is a public interest in publication. In any event, the citation of authority is unlikely to be helpful. The circumstances in any particular case under consideration can vary so much that a judgment in one case is unlikely to be decisive in another case, though it may be illustrative of an approach.

ix) The need for the existence of a confidential relationship should not give rise to problems as to the law. The difficulty will be as to the relevant facts. A duty of confidence will arise whenever the party subject to the duty is in a situation where he either knows or ought to know that the other person can reasonably expect his privacy to be protected. (See Lord Goff of Chieveley, in *Attorney General v Guardian Newspapers Ltd (No. 2)* [1990] 1 A C 109, at 281.) The range of situations in which protection can be provided is therefore extensive. Obviously, the necessary relationship can be expressly created. More often its existence will have to be inferred from the facts. Whether a duty of confidence does exist which courts can protect, if it is right to do so, will depend on all the circumstances of the relationship between the parties at the time of the threatened or actual breach of the alleged duty of confidence.

x) If there is an intrusion in a situation where a person can reasonably expect his privacy to be respected then that intrusion will be capable of giving rise to liability in an action for breach of confidence unless the intrusion can be justified. (See the approach of Dame Elizabeth Butler-Sloss P. in *Venables v Newsgroup Newspapers Ltd* [2001] 2 W.L.R. 1038 at para. 81) The bugging of someone's home or the use of other surveillance techniques are obvious examples of such an intrusion. But the fact that the information is obtained as a result of unlawful activities does not mean that its publication should necessarily be restrained by injunction on the grounds of breach of confidence (see the *Lenah Game* decision). Dependent on the nature of the unlawful activity there may be other remedies. On the other hand, the fact that unlawful means have been used to obtain the information could well be a compelling factor when it comes to exercising discretion.

xi) More difficult is the situation where the alleged intrusion into privacy is as a result of the reporting of the information to a third party by a party to the relationship which creates the privacy. This is a material factor in situations where two people have shared a sexual relationship outside marriage. If one wishes to exercise his or her article 10 rights that must impact on the other's right to maintain confidentiality. For example the information may relate, as in this case, to a situation where there is a sexual relationship between two parties and one of the parties informs the media about the relationship without the consent of the other party. Here the conflict between one party's right to privacy and the other party's right of freedom of expression is especially acute. In situations where the parties are not married (when they are, special considerations may arise) the fact that the confidence was a shared confidence which only one of the parties wishes to preserve does not extinguish the other party's right to have the confidence respected, but it does undermine that right. While recognising the special status of a lawful marriage under our law, the courts, for present purposes, have to recognise and give appropriate weight to the extensive range of relationships which now exist.

Obviously, the more stable the relationship the greater will be the significance which is attached to it.

xii) Where an individual is a public figure he is entitled to have his privacy respected in the appropriate circumstances. A public figure is entitled to a private life. The individual, however, should recognise that because of his public position he must expect and accept that his actions will be more closely scrutinised by the media. Even trivial facts relating to a public figure can be of great interest to readers and other observers of the media. Conduct which in the case of a private individual would not be the appropriate subject of comment can be the proper subject of comment in the case of a public figure. The public figure may hold a position where higher standards of conduct can be rightly expected by the public. The public figure may be a role model whose conduct could well be emulated by others. He may set the fashion. The higher the profile of the individual concerned the more likely that this will be the position. Whether you have courted publicity or not you may be a legitimate subject of public attention. If you have courted public attention then you have less ground to object to the intrusion which follows. In many of these situations it would be overstating the position to say that there is a public interest in the information being published. It would be more accurate to say that the public have an understandable and so a legitimate interest in being told the information. If this is the situation then it can be appropriately taken into account by a court when deciding on which side of the line a case falls. The courts must not ignore the fact that if newspapers do not publish information which the public are interested in, there will be fewer newspapers published, which will not be in the public interest. The same is true in relation to other parts of the media. ...

xiii) In drawing up a balance sheet between the respective interests of the parties courts should not act as censors or arbiters of taste. This is the task of others. If there is not a sufficient case for restraining publication the fact that a more lurid approach will be adopted by the publication than the court would regard as acceptable is not relevant. If the contents of the publication are untrue the law of defamation provides prohibition. Whether the publication will be attractive or unattractive should not affect the result of an application if the information is otherwise not the proper subject of restraint.

xiv) Section 12 (4) requires the court to take into account 'any relevant privacy code' but it is only one of a number of factors to be taken into account. The Press Complaints Commission Code of Practice provides that:

> 'It is essential to the workings of an agreed code that it be honoured not only to the letter but in the full spirit. The code should not be interpreted so narrowly as to compromise its commitment to respect the rights of the individual, nor so broadly that it prevents publication in the public interest.'

[He then read from the Privacy, Harassment and Public Interest sections of the Code.]
    Courts may well find this statement of practice of assistance. While recognising that section 12 (4) was primarily concerned with preserving the freedom of the press regard should be had to the guidance given by Brooke L.J. in *Douglas v Hello! Ltd*. ...

xv) However, the court should discourage advocates seeking to rely on individual decisions of the Press Commission which at best are no more than illustrative of how the Press Commission performs its different responsibilities.

12. In the above paragraphs we have attempted to assist courts as to how they should go about the task of holding the balance between the conflicting rights when hearing these applications. We are suggesting that frequently what is required is not a technical approach

to the law but a balancing of the facts. The weight which should be attached to each relevant consideration will vary depending on the precise circumstances. In many situations the balance may not point clearly in either direction. If this is the position, interim relief should be refused."

The Court of Appeal upheld the appeals and set aside the contested injunction on the ground that "the degree of confidentiality to which A was entitled, notwithstanding that C and D did not wish their relationships with A to be confidential, was very modest". In the view of the court: "Relationships of the sort which A had with C and D are not the categories of relationships which the court should be astute to protect when the other parties to the relationships do not want them to remain confidential. Any injunction granted after a trial would have to be permanent. It is most unlikely such an injunction would ever be granted". Lord Woolf concluded by saying that: "Once it is accepted that the freedom of the press should prevail, then the form of reporting in the press is not a matter for the courts but for the Press Commission and the customers of the newspaper concerned". A more robust defence of the right to privacy is to be found in the following landmark case, where a majority struck a balance for the competing interests in this area in a way that some may see as a blow to freedom of expression. It remains unclear at this stage just what is the status of the guidelines which were issued in *A v B plc*: although the House of Lords referred apparently approvingly to aspects of Lord Woolf's judgment, they were neither formally approved nor disapproved. It is also clear that this is an area of law in a process of some transition. It remains to be seen whether it will be possible for breach of confidence to continue to bear the load which this area of the law now demands. In his dissenting speech Lord Nicholls of Birkenhead referred to the need to acknowledge that the essence of the tort was the misuse in the following case of private information. It is important, however, not to exaggerate the implications of the following decision: the House of Lords is not saying that all personal information is protected, or that where it is that the right to privacy will always trump freedom of expression. It is interesting to reflect, for example, on how the House of Lords would have decided the *A v B plc* case: it cannot be assumed that the result would have been different.

Campbell v MGN Ltd
[2004] UKHL 22

The *Daily Mirror* carried articles about a model called Naomi Campbell, claiming that she was a drug addict who had attended a Narcotics Anonymous event. Campbell brought an action against the newspaper claiming damages for "breach of confidence and/or invasion of privacy". She also claimed that the newspaper was in breach of duty under the Data Protection Act 1998 and that she was entitled to compensation under s.13 of that Act. She succeeded on both counts before Morland J. whose decision was reversed by the Court of Appeal. By a majority of 3 (Lord Hope of Craighead, Baroness Hale of Richmond and Lord Carswell): 2 (Lord Nicholls of Birkenhead and Hoffmann), the House of Lords upheld her appeal on the first claim. The second claim was not pursued.

LORD HOPE OF CRAIGHEAD: "83. Miss Campbell's case is that information about the details of the treatment which she was receiving for the addiction falls to be treated differently. This is because it was not the subject of any falsehood that was in need of correction and because it was information which any reasonable person who came into possession of it would realise was obtained in confidence. The argument was put succinctly in the particulars of her claim, where it was stated:

'Information about whether a person is receiving medical or similar treatment for addiction, and in particular details relating to such treatment or the person's reaction to it, is obviously confidential. The confidentiality is the stronger where, as here, disclosure would tend to disrupt the treatment and/or its benefits for the person concerned and others sharing in, or giving, or wishing to take or participate in, the treatment. The very name "Narcotics Anonymous" underlines the importance of privacy in the context of treatment as do the defendants' own words—"To the rest of the group she is simply Naomi, the addict".'

84. The respondents' answer is based on the proposition that the information that was published about her treatment was peripheral and not sufficiently significant to amount to a breach of the duty of confidence that was owed to her. They also maintain that the right balance was struck between Miss Campbell's right to respect for her private life under article 8(1) of the European Convention for the Protection of Human Rights and Fundamental Freedoms and the right to freedom of expression that is enshrined in article 10(1) of the Convention.

85. The questions that I have just described seem to me to be essentially questions of fact and degree and not to raise any new issues of principle. As Lord Woolf CJ said in *A v B plc* [2003] QB 195, 207, paras 11(ix) and (x), the need for the existence of a confidential relationship should not give rise to problems as to the law because a duty of confidence will arise whenever the party subject to the duty is in a situation where he knows or ought to know that the other person can reasonably expect his privacy to be protected. The difficulty will be as to the relevant facts, bearing in mind that, if there is an intrusion in a situation where a person can reasonably expect his privacy to be respected, that intrusion will be capable of giving rise to liability unless the intrusion can be justified: see also the exposition in *Attorney-General v Guardian Newspapers Ltd (No 2)* [1990] 1 AC 109, 282 by Lord Goff of Chieveley, where he set out the three limiting principles to the broad general principle that a duty of confidence arises when confidential information comes to the knowledge of a person where he has notice that the information is confidential. The third limiting principle is particularly relevant in this case. This is the principle which may require a court to carry out a balancing operation, weighing the public interest in maintaining confidence against a countervailing public interest favouring disclosure.

86. The language has changed following the coming into operation of the Human Rights Act 1998 and the incorporation into domestic law of article 8 and article 10 of the Convention. We now talk about the right to respect for private life and the countervailing right to freedom of expression. The jurisprudence of the European Court offers important guidance as to how these competing rights ought to be approached and analysed. I doubt whether the result is that the centre of gravity, as my noble and learned friend Lord Hoffmann says, has shifted. It seems to me that the balancing exercise to which that guidance is directed is essentially the same exercise, although it is plainly now more carefully focussed and more penetrating. As Lord Woolf CJ said in *A v B plc* [2003] QB 195, 202, para 4, new breadth and strength is given to the action for breach of confidence by these articles.

87. Where a case has gone to trial it would normally be right to attach a great deal of weight to the views which the judge has formed about the facts and where he thought the balance should be struck after reading and hearing the evidence. The fact that the Court of Appeal felt able to differ from the conclusions which Morland J reached on these issues brings me to the first point on which I wish to comment.

Was the information confidential?

88. The information contained in the article consisted of the following five elements: (1) the fact that Miss Campbell was a drug addict; (2) the fact that she was receiving treatment for her addiction; (3) the fact that the treatment which she was receiving was provided by Narcotics Anonymous; (4) details of the treatment—for how long, how frequently and at what times of day she had been receiving it, the nature of it and extent of her commitment to the process; and (5) a visual portrayal by means of photographs of her when she was leaving the place where treatment had been taking place.

89. The trial judge drew the line between the first two and the last three elements. Mr Caldecott QC for Miss Campbell said that he was content with this distinction. So the fact that she was a drug addict was open to public comment in view of her denials, although he maintained that this would normally be treated as a medical condition that was entitled to protection. He accepted that the fact that she was receiving treatment for the condition was not in itself intrusive in this context. Moreover disclosure of this fact in itself could not harm her therapy. But he said that the line was crossed as soon as details of the nature and frequency of the treatment were given, especially when these details were accompanied by a covertly taken photograph which showed her leaving one of the places where she had been undertaking it. This was an area of privacy where she was entitled to be protected by an obligation of confidence. . . .

95. I think that the judge was right to regard the details of Miss Campbell's attendance at Narcotics Anonymous as private information which imported a duty of confidence. He said that information relating to Miss Campbells' therapy for drug addiction giving details that it was by regular attendance at Narcotics Anonymous meetings was easily identifiable as private. With reference to the guidance that the Court of Appeal gave in *A v B plc* [2003] QB 195, 206, para 11 (vii), he said that it was obvious that there existed a private interest in this fact that was worthy of protection. The Court of Appeal, on the other hand, seem to have regarded the receipt of therapy from Narcotics Anonymous as less worthy of protection in comparison with treatment for the condition administered by medical practitioners. I would not make that distinction. Views may differ as to what is the best treatment for an addiction. But it is well known that persons who are addicted to the taking of illegal drugs or to alcohol can benefit from meetings at which they discuss and face up to their addiction. The private nature of these meetings encourages addicts to attend them in the belief that they can do so anonymously. The assurance of privacy is an essential part of the exercise. The therapy is at risk of being damaged if the duty of confidence which the participants owe to each other is breached by making details of the therapy, such as where, when and how often it is being undertaken, public. I would hold that these details are obviously private.

96. If the information is obviously private, the situation will be one where the person to whom it relates can reasonably expect his privacy to be respected. So there is normally no need to go on and ask whether it would be highly offensive for it to be published. The trial judge nevertheless asked himself, as a check, whether the information that was disclosed about Miss Campbell's attendance at these meetings satisfied Gleeson CJ's test of confidentiality. His conclusion, echoing the words of Gleeson CJ, was that disclosure that her therapy for drug addiction was by regular attendance at meetings of Narcotics Anonymous would be highly offensive to a reasonable person of ordinary sensibilities. The Court of Appeal disagreed with this assessment. In para 53 they said that, given that it was legitimate for the respondents to publish the fact that Miss Campbell was a drug addict and that she was receiving treatment, it was not particularly significant to add the fact that the treatment consisted of attendance at meetings of Narcotics Anonymous. In para 54 they said that they did not consider that a reasonable person of ordinary sensibilities, on reading that Miss Campbell was a drug addict, would have found it highly offensive, or even offensive. They acknowledged that the reader might have found it offensive that what were obviously covert photographs had been taken of her, but that this of itself was not relied upon as a ground for legal complaint. Having drawn these conclusions they held in para 58 that the publication of the information of which Miss Campbell complains was not, in its context, sufficiently significant to amount to a breach of duty of confidence owed to her.

97. This part of the Court of Appeal's examination of the issue appears to have been influenced by the fact that they did not regard disclosure of the fact that Miss Campbell was receiving therapy from Narcotics Anonymous capable of being equated with treatment of a clinical nature. If one starts from the position that a course of therapy which takes this form is of a lower order, it is relatively easy to conclude that a reasonable person of ordinary sensibilities would not regard the publication of the further details of her therapy

as particularly significant. But I think that it is unrealistic to look through the eyes of a reasonable person of ordinary sensibilities at the degree of confidentiality that is to be attached to a therapy for drug addiction without relating this objective test to the particular circumstances.

98. Where the person is suffering from a condition that is in need of treatment one has to try, in order to assess whether the disclosure would be objectionable, to put oneself into the shoes of a reasonable person who is in need of that treatment. Otherwise the exercise is divorced from its context. The fact that no objection could be taken to disclosure of the first two elements in the article does not mean that they must be left out of account in a consideration as to whether disclosure of the other elements was objectionable. The article must be read as whole along with the photographs to give a proper perspective to each element. The context was that of a drug addict who was receiving treatment. It is her sensibilities that needed to be taken into account. Critical to this exercise was an assessment of whether disclosure of the details would be liable to disrupt her treatment. It does not require much imagination to appreciate the sense of unease that disclosure of these details would be liable to engender, especially when they were accompanied by a covertly taken photograph. The message that it conveyed was that somebody, somewhere, was following her, was well aware of what was going on and was prepared to disclose the facts to the media. I would expect a drug addict who was trying to benefit from meetings to discuss her problem anonymously with other addicts to find this distressing and highly offensive.

99. The approach which the Court of Appeal took to this issue seems to me, with great respect, to be quite unreal. I do not think that they had a sound basis for differing from the conclusion reached by the trial judge as to whether the information was private. They were also in error, in my opinion, when they were asking themselves whether the disclosure would have offended the reasonable man of ordinary susceptibilities. The mind that they examined was the mind of the reader: para 54. This is wrong. It greatly reduces the level of protection that is afforded to the right of privacy. The mind that has to be examined is that, not of the reader in general, but of the person who is affected by the publicity. The question is what a reasonable person of ordinary sensibilities would feel if she was placed in the same position as the claimant and faced with the same publicity.

. . .

101. These errors have an important bearing on the question whether the Court of Appeal were right to differ from the decision of the trial judge on the question where the balance lay between the private interest of Miss Campbell and the public interest in the publication of these details.

. . .

The competing rights of free speech and privacy

103. Morland J did not give any detailed reasons in para 70 of his judgment for his conclusion that, striking the balance between articles 8 and 10 and having full regard to section 12(4) of the Human Rights Act 1998, Miss Campbell was entitled to the remedy of damages. But he did recognise in para 98 that neither article 10 nor article 8 had pre-eminence, the one over the other. Court of Appeal's approach to the respondents' entitlement to publish what they described as the peripheral details was based on their view that the provision of these details as background to support the story that Miss Campbell was a drug addict was a legitimate part of the journalistic package which was designed to demonstrate that she had been deceiving the public when she said that she did not take drugs: [2003] QB 633, 662, para 62. In para 64 they said that its publication was justified in order to give a factual account that had the detail necessary to carry credibility. But they do not appear to have attempted to balance the competing Convention rights against each other. No doubt this was because they had already concluded that these details were peripheral and that their publication was not, in its context, sufficiently significant to amount to a breach of duty of confidence: para 58.

104. In my opinion the Court of Appeal's approach is open to the criticism that, because

they wrongly held that these details were not entitled to protection under the law of confidence, they failed to carry out the required balancing exercise.

105. The context for this exercise is provided by articles 8 and 10 of the Convention. The rights guaranteed by these articles are qualified rights. Article 8(1) protects the right to respect for private life, but recognition is given in article 8(2) to the protection of the rights and freedoms of others. Article 10(1) protects the right to freedom of expression, but article 10(2) recognises the need to protect the rights and freedoms of others. The effect of these provisions is that the right to privacy which lies at the heart of an action for breach of confidence has to be balanced against the right of the media to impart information to the public. And the right of the media to impart information to the public has to be balanced in its turn against the respect that must be given to private life.

106. There is nothing new about this, as the need for this kind of balancing exercise was already part of English law: *Attorney-General v Guardian Newspapers (No 2)* [1990] 1 AC 109, per Lord Goff of Chieveley. But account must now be taken of the guidance which has been given by the European Court on the application of these articles. As Sedley LJ pointed out in *Douglas v Hello! Ltd* [2001] 1 QB 967, 1004, para 135:

> 'The European Court of Human Rights has always recognised the high importance of free media of communication in a democracy, but its jurisprudence does not—and could not consistently with the Convention itself—give article 10(1) the presumptive priority which is given, for example, to the First Amendment in the jurisprudence of the United States' courts. Everything will ultimately depend on the proper balance between privacy and publicity in the situation facing the court.'

107. I accept, of course, that the importance which the Court of Appeal attached to the journalistic package finds support in the authorities. In *Jersild v Denmark* (1994) 19 EHRR 1, para 31 the European Court, repeating what was said in *Observer and Guardian v United Kingdom* (1992) 14 EHRR 153, para 59, declared that freedom of expression constitutes one of the essential foundations of a democratic society and that the safeguards to be afforded to the press are of particular importance. It then added these comments in para 31:

> 'Whilst the press must not overstep the bounds set, *inter alia*, in the interest of "the protection of the reputation and rights of others", it is nevertheless incumbent on it to impart information and ideas of public interest. Not only does the press have the task of imparting such information and ideas: the public also has a right to receive them. Were it otherwise, the press would be unable to play its vital role of "public watchdog".'

108. The freedom of the press to exercise its own judgment in the presentation of journalistic material was emphasised in a further passage in *Jersild's* case where the court said, at p 26, para 31:

> 'At the same time, the methods of objective and balanced reporting may vary considerably, depending among other things on the media in question. It is not for this court, nor for the national courts for that matter, to substitute their own views for those of the press as to what technique of reporting should be adopted by journalists. In this context the court recalls that article 10 protects not only the substance of the ideas and information expressed, but also the form in which they are conveyed.'

In *Fressoz v France* (2001) 31 EHRR 28, 60, para 54 the court said that in essence article 10 leaves it for journalists to decide whether or not it is necessary to reproduce material to ensure credibility, adding:

> 'It protects journalists' rights to divulge information on issues of general interest provided that they are acting in good faith and on an accurate factual basis and provide "reliable and precise" information in accordance with the ethics of journalism.'

109. There was no need for the court in *Jersild's* case to examine the question how the article 10 right which was relied on was to be balanced against a competing right under article 8 of the Convention. The applicants maintained that their right to freedom of expression under article 10 was infringed when they were charged and convicted of committing offences which resulted from their choice of the material that had been published. The objectionable remarks which were contained in the television broadcast of a news programme were of a racist nature. The focus of the case was on the right to impart information and ideas of public interest and the right of the public to receive such ideas. The *Fressoz* case on the other hand was about the disclosure of information which was confidential as it was contained in the taxpayer's tax file. It was lawful to disclose information about the taxpayer's income. The question was whether publication of the documents in which that information was contained could be justified under article 10. So the court addressed itself to the question whether the objective of preserving fiscal confidentiality, which in itself was legitimate, constituted a relevant and sufficient justification for the interference with the article 10 right. There was a balance to be struck by weighing the interference with freedom to disclose against the need for confidentiality.

110. The need for a balancing exercise to be carried out is also inherent in the provisions of article 10 itself, as the court explained in *Bladet Tromso and Stensaas v Norway* (2000) 29 EHRR 125. In that case a newspaper and its editor complained that their right to freedom of expression had been breached when they were found liable in defamation proceedings for statements in articles which they had published about the methods used by seal hunters in the hunting of harp seals. At p 167, para 59 the court said:

'Although the press must not overstep certain bounds, in particular in respect of the reputation and rights of others and the need to prevent the disclosure of confidential information, its duty is nevertheless to impart—in a manner consistent with its obligations and responsibilities—information and ideas on all matters of public interest.'

The court dealt with the question of balance at p 169, para 65:

'Article 10 of the Convention does not, however, guarantee a wholly freedom of expression even with respect to press coverage of matters of serious public concern. Under the terms of paragraph 2 of the Article the exercise of this freedom carries with it "duties and responsibilities" which also apply to the press. These "duties and responsibilities" are liable to assume significance when, as in the present case, there is question of attacking the reputation of private individuals and examining the "rights of others". As pointed out by the government, the seal hunters' right to protection of their honour and reputation is itself internationally recognised under Article 17 of the International Covenant on Civil and Political Rights. Also of relevance for the balancing of competing interests which the Court must carry out is the fact that under article 6(2) of the Convention the seal hunters had a right to be presumed innocent of any criminal offence until proved guilty. By reason of the duties and responsibilities' inherent in the exercise of the freedom of expression, the safeguard afforded by article 10 to journalists in relation to reporting on issues of general interest is subject to the proviso that they are acting in good faith to provide accurate and reliable information in accordance with the ethics of journalism.'

111. Section 12(4) of the Human Rights Act 1998 provides [Lord Hope read s 12(4) and continued] But, as Sedley LJ said in *Douglas v Hello! Ltd* [2001] QB 967, 1003, para 133, you cannot have particular regard to article 10 without having equally particular regard at the very least to article 8: see also *In re S (A Child) (Identifications: Restrictions on Publication)* [2003] 3 WLR 1425, 1450, para 52 where Hale LJ said that section 12(4) does not give either article pre-eminence over the other. These observations seem to me to be entirely consistent with the jurisprudence of the European Court, as is the following pas-

sage in Sedley LJ's opinion in *Douglas* at p 1005, para 137:

'The case being one which affects the Convention right of freedom of expression, section 12 of the Human Rights Act 1998 requires the court to have regard to article 10 (as, in its absence, would section 6). This, however, cannot, consistently with section 3 and article 17, give the article 10(1) right of free expression a presumptive priority over other rights. What it does is require the court to consider article 10(2) along with article 10(1), and by doing so to bring into the frame the conflicting right to respect for privacy. This right, contained in article 8 and reflected in English law, is in turn qualified in both contexts by the right of others to free expression. The outcome, which self-evidently has to be the same under both articles, is determined principally by considerations of proportionality.'

It is to be noted too that clause 3(i) of the Code of Practice of the Press Complaints Committee acknowledges this limitation. It states that a person may have a reasonable expectation of privacy in a public place.

Striking the balance

112. There is no doubt that the presentation of the material that it was legitimate to convey to the public in this case without breaching the duty of confidence was a matter for the journalists. The choice of language used to convey information and ideas, and decisions as to whether or not to accompany the printed word by the use of photographs, are pre-eminently editorial matters with which the court will not interfere. The respondents are also entitled to claim that they should be accorded a reasonable margin of appreciation in taking decisions as to what details needed to be included in the article to give it credibility. This is an essential part of the journalistic exercise.

113. But decisions about the publication of material that is private to the individual raise issues that are not simply about presentation and editing. Any interference with the public interest in disclosure has to be balanced against the interference with the right of the individual to respect for their private life. The decisions that are then taken are open to review by the court. The tests which the court must apply are the familiar ones. They are whether publication of the material pursues a legitimate aim and whether the benefits that will be achieved by its publication are proportionate to the harm that may be done by the interference with the right to privacy. The jurisprudence of the European Court of Human Rights explains how these principles are to be understood and applied in the context of the facts of each case. Any restriction of the right to freedom of expression must be subjected to very close scrutiny. But so too must any restriction of the right to respect for private life. Neither article 8 nor article 10 has any pre-eminence over the other in the conduct of this exercise. As Resolution 1165 of the Parliamentary Assembly of the Council of Europe (1998), para 11, pointed out, they are neither absolute not in any hierarchical order, since they are of equal value in a democratic society.

The article 10 right

114. In the present case it is convenient to begin by looking at the matter from the standpoint of the respondents' assertion of the article 10 right and the court's duty as a public authority under section 6(1) of the Human Rights Act 1998, which section 12(4) reinforces, not to act in a way which is incompatible with that Convention right.

115. The first question is whether the objective of the restriction on the article 10 right—the protection of Miss Campbell's right under article 8 to respect for her private life—is sufficiently important to justify limiting the fundamental right to freedom of expression which the press assert on behalf of the public. It follows from my conclusion that the details of Miss Campbell's treatment were private that I would answer this question in the affirmative. The second question is whether the means chosen to limit the article 10 right are rational, fair and not arbitrary and impair the right as minimally as is reasonably possible.

It is not enough to assert that it would be reasonable to exclude these details from the article. A close examination of the factual justification for the restriction on the freedom of expression is needed if the fundamental right enshrined in article 10 is to remain practical and effective. The restrictions which the court imposes on the article 10 right must be rational, fair and not arbitrary, and they must impair the right no more than is necessary.

116. In my opinion the factors that need to be weighed are, on the one hand, the duty that was recognised in *Jersild v Denmark* (1994) 19 EHRR 1, para 31 to impart information and ideas of public interest which the public has a right to receive, and the need that was recognised in *Fressoz v France* (2001) 31 EHRR 28, para 54 for the court to leave it to journalists to decide what material needs to be reproduced to ensure credibility; and, on the other hand, the degree of privacy to which Miss Campbell was entitled under the law of confidence as to the details of her therapy. Account should therefore be taken of the respondents' wish to put forward a story that was credible and to present Miss Campbell in a way that commended her for her efforts to overcome her addiction.

117. But it should also be recognised that the right of the public to receive information about the details of her treatment was of a much lower order than the undoubted right to know that she was misleading the public when she said that she did not take drugs. In *Dudgeon v United Kingdom* (1981) 4 EHRR 149, para 52 the European Court said that the more intimate the aspects of private life which are being interfered with, the more serious must be the reasons for doing so before the interference can be legitimate. Clayton and Tomlinson, The Law of Human Rights (2000), para 15.162, point out that the court has distinguished three kinds of expression: political expression, artistic expression and commercial expression, and that it consistently attaches great importance to political expression and applies rather less rigorous principles to expression which is artistic and commercial. According to the court's well-established case law, freedom of expression constitutes one of the essential foundations of a democratic society and one of the basic conditions for its progress and the self-fulfilment of each individual: *Tammer v Estonia* (2001) 37 EHRR 857, para 59. But there were no political or democratic values at stake here, nor has any pressing social need been identified: contrast *Goodwin v United Kingdom* (1996) 22 EHRR 123, para 40. . . . .

The article 8 right

119. Looking at the matter from Miss Campbell's point of view and the protection of her article 8 Convention right, publication of details of the treatment which she was undertaking to cure her addiction—that she was attending Narcotics Anonymous, for how long, how frequently and at what times of day she had been attending this therapy, the nature of it and extent of her commitment to the process and the publication of the covertly taken photographs (the third, fourth and fifth of the five elements contained in the article)—had the potential to cause harm to her, for the reasons which I have already given. So I would attach a good deal of weight to this factor.

120. As for the other side of the balance, a person's right to privacy may be limited by the public's interest in knowing about certain traits of her personality and certain aspects of her private life . . . But it is not enough to deprive Miss Campbell of her right to privacy that she is a celebrity and that her private life is newsworthy. A margin of appreciation must, of course, be given to the journalist. Weight must be given to this. But to treat these details merely as background was to undervalue the importance that was to be attached to the need, if Miss Campbell was to be protected, to keep these details private. And it is hard to see that there was any compelling need for the public to know the name of the organisation that she was attending for the therapy, or for the other details of it to be set out. The presentation of the article indicates that this was not fully appreciated when the decision was taken to publish these details. The decision to publish the photographs suggests that greater weight was being given to the wish to publish a story that would attract interest rather than to the wish to maintain its credibility.

121. Had it not been for the publication of the photographs, and looking to the text only,

I would have been inclined to regard the balance between these rights as about even. Such is the effect of the margin of appreciation that must, in a doubtful case, be given to the journalist. In that situation the proper conclusion to draw would have been that it had not been shown that the restriction on the article 10 right for which Miss Campbell argues was justified on grounds of proportionality. But the text cannot be separated from the photographs. The words 'Therapy: Naomi outside meeting' underneath the photograph on the front page and the words 'Hugs: Naomi, dressed in jeans and baseball hat, arrives for a lunchtime group meeting this week' underneath the photograph on page 13 were designed to link that what might otherwise have been anonymous and uninformative pictures with the main text. The reader would undoubtedly make that link, and so too would the reasonable person of ordinary sensibilities. The reasonable person of ordinary sensibilities would also regard publication of the covertly taken photographs, and the fact that they were linked with the text in this way, as adding greatly overall to the intrusion which the article as a whole made into her private life.

122. The photographs were taken of Miss Campbell while she was in a public place, as she was in the street outside the premises where she had been receiving therapy. The taking of photographs in a public street must, as Randerson J said in *Hosking v Runting* [2003] 3 NZLR 385, 415, para 138, be taken to be one of the ordinary incidents of living in a free community. The real issue is whether publicising the content of the photographs would be offensive: Gault and Blanchard JJ in the Court of Appeal (25 March 2004), para 165. A person who just happens to be in the street when the photograph was taken and appears in it only incidentally cannot as a general rule object to the publication of the photograph, for the reasons given by L'Heureux-Dubé and Bastarache JJ in *Aubry v Editions Vice-Versa Inc* [1998] 1 SCR 591, para 59. But the situation is different if the public nature of the place where a photograph is taken was simply used as background for one or more persons who constitute the true subject of the photograph. The question then arises, balancing the rights at issue, where the public's right to information can justify dissemination of a photograph taken without authorisation: *Aubry*, para 61. The European Court has recognised that a person who walks down a public street will inevitably be visible to any member of the public who is also present and, in the same way, to a security guard viewing the scene through closed circuit television: *PGJH v United Kingdom*, App No. 44787/98, para 57. But, as the court pointed out in the same paragraph, private life considerations may arise once any systematic or permanent record comes into existence of such material from the public domain. In *Peck v United Kingdom* (2003) 36 EHRR 719, para 62 the court held that the release and publication of CCTV forage which showed the applicant in the process of attempting to commit suicide resulted in the moment being viewed to an extent that far exceeded any exposure to a passer-by or to security observation that he could have foreseen when he was in that street.

123. The same process of reasoning that led to the findings in *Peck* that the article 8 right had been violated and by the majority in *Aubry* that there had been an infringement of the claimant's right to respect for her private life can be applied here. Miss Campbell could not have complained if the photographs had been taken to show the scene in the street by a passer-by and later published simply as street scenes. But these were not just pictures of a street scene where she happened to be when the photographs were taken. They were taken deliberately, in secret and with a view to their publication in conjunction with the article. The zoom lens was directed at the doorway of the place where the meeting had been taking place. The faces of others in the doorway were pixilated so as not to reveal their identity. Hers was not, the photographs were published and her privacy was invaded. The argument that the publication of the photograph added credibility to the story has little weight. The photograph was not self-explanatory. Neither the place nor the person were instantly recognisable. The reader only had the editor's word as to the truth of these details.

124. Any person in Miss Campbell's position, assuming her to be of ordinary sensibilities but assuming also that she had been photographed surreptitiously outside the place where she been receiving therapy for drug addiction, would have known what they were and

would have been distressed on seeing the photographs. She would have seen their publication, in conjunction with the article which revealed what she had been doing when she was photographed and other details about her engagement in the therapy, as a gross interference with her right to respect for her private life. In my opinion this additional element in the publication is more than enough to outweigh the right to freedom of expression which the defendants are asserting in this case.

Conclusion

125. Despite the weight that must be given to the right to freedom of expression that the press needs if it is to play its role effectively, I would hold that there was here an infringement of Miss Campbell's right to privacy that cannot be justified. In my opinion publication of the third, fourth and fifth elements in the article (see para 88) was an invasion of that right for which she is entitled to damages. I would allow the appeal and restore the orders that were made by the trial judge."

BARONESS HALE OF RICHMOND: "126. This case raises some big questions. How is the balance to be struck between everyone's right to respect for their private and family life under Article 8 of the European Convention on Human Rights and everyone's right to freedom of expression, including the freedom to receive and impart information and ideas under Article 10? How do those rights come into play in a dispute between two private persons? But the parties are largely agreed about the answers to these. They disagree about where that balance is to be struck in the individual case. In particular, how far is a newspaper able to go in publishing what would otherwise be confidential information about a celebrity in order to set the record straight? And does it matter that the article was illustrated by a covertly taken photograph?...

148. What was the nature of the freedom of expression which was being asserted on the other side? There are undoubtedly different types of speech, just as there are different types of private information, some of which are more deserving of protection in a democratic society than others. Top of the list is political speech. The free exchange of information and ideas on matters relevant to the organisation of the economic, social and political life of the country is crucial to any democracy. Without this, it can scarcely be called a democracy at all. This includes revealing information about public figures, especially those in elective office, which would otherwise be private but is relevant to their participation in public life. Intellectual and educational speech and expression are also important in a democracy, not least because they enable the development of individuals' potential to play a full part in society and in our democratic life. Artistic speech and expression is important for similar reasons, in fostering both individual originality and creativity and the free-thinking and dynamic society we so much value. No doubt there are other kinds of speech and expression for which similar claims can be made.

149. But it is difficult to make such claims on behalf of the publication with which we are concerned here. The political and social life of the community, and the intellectual, artistic or personal development of individuals, are not obviously assisted by pouring over the intimate details of a fashion model's private life. However, there is one way in which the article could be said to be educational. The editor had considered running a highly critical piece, adding the new information to the not inconsiderable list of Miss Campbell's faults and follies detailed in the article, emphasising the lies and hypocrisy it revealed. Instead he chose to run a sympathetic piece, still listing her faults and follies, but setting them in the context of her now-revealed addiction and her even more important efforts to overcome it. Newspaper and magazines often carry such pieces and they may well have a beneficial educational effect.

150. The crucial difference here is that such pieces are normally run with the co-operation of those involved. Private people are not identified without their consent. It is taken for granted that this is otherwise confidential information. The editor did offer Miss Campbell the opportunity of being involved with the story but this was refused. Her evidence suggests that she was concerned for the other people in the group. What entitled him to reveal this

private information about her without her consent?...

159. The judge was also obliged by section 12(4)(b) of the 1998 Act, not only to have particular regard to the importance of the Convention right to freedom of expression, but also to any relevant privacy code. The Press Complaints Commission Code of Practice supports rather than undermines the conclusion he reached [Baroness Hale read paragraph 3 of the code].

160. I would therefore allow this appeal and restore the order of the judge."

VIII. CONCLUSION

The right to privacy covers a large canvas. Apart from the areas discussed here, important developments have taken place in the area of sexual freedom (private life) and family life. However, in *MacDonald v Advocate-General for Scotland*, 2003 S.L.T. 1158 it was held that although discrimination by the military against service personnel on the ground of their homosexuality was a breach of Art.8. But it was also held that the Sex Discrimination Act 1975 could not be construed so as to apply to homosexual as well as gender discrimination. The matter is now governed by legislation. Similarly in *Saini v Home Secretary*, 1999 S.L.T. 1249 the forced deportation of an asylum seeker was found in the circumstances not to breach Art.8 even though he had married a British citizen with whom he had a child. Although the decision "bears hardly on the petitioner and his wife and child" that was said by Lord Nimmo Smith to be "inevitable where there is scope for the exercise of a discretion, the existence of which recognises that the weight to be attached to a particular marriage as a compassionate factor may not be sufficient to outweigh other considerations" (pp.1254 to 1255). All of which is to raise questions about just what the incorporation of Convention rights has achieved in the area of privacy, and questions about just how the law has changed as a result of the incorporation of these rights. It is true that the incorporation of Convention rights has required greater transparency in terms of police surveillance practices. However, the case law would suggest that the police still have more to fear from the Strasbourg Court than from the domestic courts. The case law would also tend to suggest that—with the limited exception of reporting aspects of the private lives of celebrities—the incorporation of Convention rights is not likely to be the catalyst for radical reform of Scots law and practice in any of the areas under discussion in this chapter.

Scots law on the power of the police to enter, search and seize private property in particular is extremely opaque, and an area where, as a result, Convention rights might have had a decisive impact. There is uncertainty about when a warrant may be issued and when a warrant is necessary. There is a lack of clarity about the procedures which must be followed before a warrant is issued and there is a lack of formal protection for the individual in the execution of warrants that we find in English law. This no doubt is convenient for the police in the sense that it provides a flexible framework for dealing with crime and suspected criminals. Nevertheless, it is not clear that the common law does enough to protect the individual from what is a grave invasion of privacy. At the very least it may be thought appropriate that there should be statutory rules which specify clearly

- when a search warrant may be granted;
- the circumstances when entry and search may take place without a warrant;
- the procedure to be followed before granting a search warrant;
- the rights of the person whose property is to be searched;
- the manner of execution of the warrant; and
- the circumstances in which property found in the course of a search may be seized.

If the Queen's subjects in England and Wales are entitled to expect some degree of certainty about police powers of entry, search and seizure, by what reason should her lieges in Scotland not be entitled to the same? In the absence of legislation, it remains to be seen how—if at all—Art.8 of the ECHR will lead to changes to Scots law on these points. But the decision in *Birse* is not a promising start.

Chapter 7

FREEDOM OF RELIGION

I. INTRODUCTION

IN this chapter we examine the nature and the limits of religious freedom in Scots law. We begin by briefly sketching the special legal status of the Church of Scotland and the Protestant religion. We then consider how these matters have been affected by the Human Rights Act 1998, before proceeding to examine how the courts and Parliament have taken steps to reinforce religious values and religious observance. Historically, the full panoply of the criminal law was used for this purpose, with blasphemy laws protecting the Christian religion from vilification, and the Sunday observance laws ensuring that there was nothing to distract the lieges from their holy duties. These provisions have given way in more recent times to a number of important facilities and privileges which have been extended to promote the spread of religious ideology and to assist the churches. Our third purpose in this chapter is to examine how far the state tolerates the practice of minority religions, given its commitment to the Church. We pursue this inquiry by looking at how religious beliefs and practices may present difficulties in a number of fields and by examining how, if at all, the law responds to any problems or conflicts which arise. A valuable account written from the perspective of English law is to be found in S. Poulter, *Ethnicity, Law and Human Rights* (1998).

II. THE CHURCH OF SCOTLAND

The status of the Church of Scotland as the national church was confirmed and preserved by the Treaty of Union. The Treaty states that as it is "reasonable and necessary that the True Protestant Religion, as presently professed within this Kingdom ... should be effectually and unalterably secured; Therefore Her Majesty with advice and consent of the ... Estates of Parliament Doth hereby Establish and Confirm the said True Protestant Religion ... to continue without any alteration ... in all succeeding generations." The Treaty further provides that presbyterian government shall be the only mode of government of the Church of Scotland. But although the Treaty established the supremacy of the presbyterian church in Scotland, the relationship between church and state was not always a happy one. In fact it was not until 1921 that it was satisfactorily settled. The Church of Scotland Act 1921 establishes the independence of the church from state control and, in so doing, permits a remarkable degree of internal freedom to the church in matters of doctrine, worship and discipline.

The Church of Scotland Act 1921

"Effect of Declaratory Articles

1. The Declaratory Articles are lawful articles, and the constitution of the Church of Scotland in matters spiritual is as therein set forth, and no limitation of the liberty, rights, and powers in matters spiritual therein set forth shall be derived from any statute or law affecting the Church of Scotland in matters spiritual at present in force, it being hereby declared that in all questions of construction the Declaratory Articles shall prevail, and that all such statutes and laws shall be construed in conformity therewith and in subordination thereto, and all such statutes and laws in so far as they are inconsistent with the Declaratory Articles are hereby repealed and declared to be of no effect.

Other Churches not to be prejudice

2. Nothing contained in this Act or in any other Act affecting the Church of Scotland shall prejudice the recognition of any other Church in Scotland as a Christian Church protected by law in the exercise of its spiritual functions.

Jurisdiction of Civil Courts

3. Subject to the recognition of the matters dealt with in the Declaratory Articles as matters spiritual, nothing in this Act contained shall affect or prejudice the jurisdiction of the civil courts in relation to any matter of a civil nature.

SCHEDULE

ARTICLES DECLARATORY OF THE CONSTITUTION OF THE CHURCH OF SCOTLAND IN MATTERS SPIRITUAL

II. The principal subordinate standard of the Church of Scotland is the Westminster Confession of Faith approved by the General Assembly of 1647, containing the sum and substance of the Faith of the Reformed Church. Its government is Presbyterian, and is exercised through Kirk Sessions, Presbyteries, Provincial Synods, and General Assemblies.

III. This Church is in historical continuity with the Church of Scotland which was reformed in 1560, whose liberties were ratified in 1592, and for whose security provision was made in the Treaty of Union of 1707. The continuity and identity of the Church of Scotland are not prejudiced by the adoption of these Articles. As a national Church representative of the Christian Faith of the Scottish people it acknowledges its distinctive call and duty to bring the ordinances of religion to the people in every parish of Scotland through a territorial ministry.

IV. This Church, as part of the Universal Church wherein the Lord Jesus Christ has appointed a government in the hands of Church office-bearers, receives from Him, its Divine King and Head, and from Him alone, the right and power subject to no civil authority to legislate, and to adjudicate finally, in all matters of doctrine, worship, government, and discipline in the Church, including the right to determine all questions concerning membership and office in the Church, the constitution and membership of its Courts, and the mode of election of its office-bearers, and to define the boundaries of the spheres of labour of its ministers and other office-bearers...

V. This Church has the inherent right, free from interference by civil authority, but under the safeguards for deliberate action and legislation provided by the Church itself, to frame or adopt its subordinate standards, to declare the sense in which it understands its Confession of Faith, to modify the forms of expression therein, or to formulate other doctrinal statements, and to define the relation thereto of its office-bearers and members, but always in agreement with the Word of God and the fundamental doctrines of the Christian Faith contained in the said Confession, of which agreement the Church shall be sole judge, and with due regard to liberty of opinion in points which do not enter into the substance of the Faith.

VI. This church acknowledges the divine appointment and authority of the civil magistrate within his own sphere.

VII. The Church has the right to interpret these Articles, and, subject to the safeguards for deliberate action and legislation provided by the Church itself, to modify or add to them."

An important feature of the 1921 Act is the fact that the civil courts cannot review matters properly within the jurisdiction of the judicatories of the church. The assemblies of other churches have no exclusive jurisdiction and are subject to judicial supervision. In the eyes of the law, these other churches are voluntary associations whose members are bound together by contract. But although a relationship based on contract could give the courts considerable scope for involvement in the domestic affairs of the churches, they have wisely refrained from such involvement. In *McDonald v Burns*, 1940 S.L.T. 325, Lord Justice-Clerk Aitchison said that the courts would only exceptionally interfere with the proceedings of a church, as in a case of *ultra vires*, or a breach of natural justice. This approach was confirmed in *Brentnall v Free Presbyterian Church of Scotland*, 1986 S.L.T. 471. For a full and interesting analysis of the development of the Church of Scotland, see F. Lyall, *Of Presbyters and Kings* (1980).

III. THE CHURCH OF SCOTLAND AND THE HUMAN RIGHTS ACT 1998

As we saw in Ch.1, the ECHR protects the right to freedom of religion. Yet paradoxically the Human Rights Act gave rise to great concern on the part of the Church of Scotland which feared that the Act would undermine its freedom to regulate its own internal affairs without intervention by the courts. That right had been expressed in strong terms in *Ballantyne v Presbytery of Wigtown*, 1936 S.L.T. 436, where the Lord Justice Clerk referred to "the right of the Church to self-government in all that concerned its own life and activity" (at p. 654). This right had been affirmed by the decision in *Logan v Presbytery of Dumbarton*, 1995 S.L.T. 1228 ((1996) J.R. 71) and again in *Percy v Board of National Mission of the Church of Scotland*, 2000 S.L.T. 475. *Logan* concerned judicial review proceedings by the minister of a parish church complaining about disciplinary decisions of the presbytery which were said to be in breach of natural justice. The decision was welcomed by Professor Lyall (1996) J.R. 71 "as a modern statement of the legal standing of the courts of the Church of Scotland and of the independent jurisdiction of the Kirk". However, as Professor Lyall also points out "it would be wrong ... to see *Logan* as wholly immunising the Church of Scotland from scrutiny by the civil courts. Were the Church to act outwith its jurisdiction, or so outrageously as to make it impossible to hold it as acting *intra vires*, no doubt the Court of Session would intervene if a patrimonial question were involved".

Logan v Presbytery of Dumbarton
1995 S.L.T. 1228

This was an application for reduction and interdict relating to disciplinary proceedings against the minister of Abbotsford Parish Church in Clydebank. The minister had been refused permission to be involved in a business, and it was alleged that he had continued his involvement despite the refusal of permission. Although the proceedings had not been completed, the minister complained that there had been a breach of natural justice in one of the preliminary stages of the case against him. An interim interdict was granted on March 17, 1995 on the ground that the petitioner had revealed a *prima facie* case. However, the interdict was recalled on April 26, 1995. In thus dismissing the application for an interdict Lord Osborne issued a lengthy and learned opinion about the constitutional position of the Church of Scotland. The following extract is only from the concluding passages of that opinion.

LORD OSBORNE: "Article IV of the Articles Declaratory of the Constitution of the Church of Scotland in Matters Spiritual provides as follows: [his Lordship quoted the terms of the Article and continued:]

In the course of the argument before me, it was accepted by counsel for the petitioner that the matter with which this petition is concerned was a 'matter of ... discipline'; furthermore, that it involved 'questions concerning ... office in the Church'; also that it involved 'the boundaries of the spheres of labour of its ministers'. In my opinion, it follows from these concessions that the subject matter of this petition falls within the exclusive jurisdiction of the courts of the Church of Scotland, in terms of Declaratory Article IV. That subject matter, in my opinion, plainly falls within the scope of the 'matters spiritual' referred to in the Declaratory Articles. Following the approach taken in *Ballantyne v Presbytery of Wigtown*, in particular that set forth by the Lord Justice Clerk at 1936 SLT 436, p 447, if that is so, 'the matter is at an end, and neither the statute nor the common law nor previous judicial decision, whether upon statute or upon the common law, can avail to bring the matter within the jurisdiction of the civil authority'.

As I understood the argument for the petitioner, it proceeded upon the basis that, since the powers of the Church had been the subject of parliamentary enactment, it followed that the decisions of the Church, albeit in relation to spiritual matters, fell within the scope of the supervisory jurisdiction of the Court of Session. It appears to me that such a proposition involves a non sequitur. In the first place, it overlooks the fact that, to quote the words of Lord Justice-Clerk Aitchison in *Ballantyne v Presbytery of Wigtown*, the Act of 1921 'is not an Act of Parliament conferring rights upon the Church, but it is a recognition by Parliament of Articles framed by the General Assembly of the Church as its Supreme Court in the exercise of what it claimed to be its own inherent powers'.

Furthermore, 'The Act came into operation by an Order of His Majesty in Council on 28th June 1926, and then only after the Declaratory Articles had been adopted by an Act of the General Assembly of the Church of Scotland with the consent of a majority of the Presbyteries of the Church. This adoption of the Articles by the free will of the Church after the Act was on the statute book, and as a condition of the Act becoming operative, was an assertion by the Church of its autonomy in matters affecting its own life and polity.'

In the light of these observations, it appears to me that the situation of the courts of the Church of Scotland cannot be equiparated with any tribunal created or upon which a power has been conferred by Parliament.

Reliance was placed by the petitioner upon the elucidation of the supervisory jurisdiction of the Court of Session to be found in *West v Secretary of State for Scotland*, 1992 S.L.T. 636 and, in particular, in the numbered paragraphs on p 650. Numbered para (1) is in the following terms: 'The Court of Session has power, in the exercise of its supervisory jurisdiction, to regulate the process by which decisions are taken by any person or body to whom a jurisdiction, power or authority has been delegated or entrusted by statute, agreement or any other instrument.'

In my opinion, it is quite plain that the courts of the Church of Scotland do not fall within the terms of this paragraph, since, in the light of what was said in *Ballantyne v Presbytery of Wigtown*, which I have just quoted, it cannot be said that those courts are bodies 'to whom a jurisdiction, power or authority has been delegated or entrusted by statute'. It appears to me that what was achieved in the Act of 1921 was a recognition by Parliament of certain pre-existing inherent powers in the Church of Scotland, rather than the conferring of powers upon it. Accordingly my conclusion is that the passage relied upon in *West v Secretary of State for Scotland*, when properly understood, does not assist the petitioner.

Quite apart from the foregoing considerations, in my opinion, the petitioner's arguments come into direct conflict with the provisions of Declaratory Article IV, given legal effect by s 1 of the Act of 1921. In particular, I have in mind the language used in the last sentence of the article, which I have already quoted. In effect, in that particular passage, Parliament has recognised that, within the sphere of the Church's spiritual government and jurisdiction, the civil authority has been denied any right of interference.

I would not wish to be understood as saying that this court possesses no power to determine the meaning and effect of the Act of 1921 and the appended Declaratory Articles."

The specific concern of the Church was that by virtue of s.6 of the Human Rights Act, the church courts would be regarded as public authorities and therefore subject to control by the civil courts. The points were considered by the Lord Advocate when these matters were raised at a late stage in the passing of the Bill. According to Lord Hardie:

"Courts of the Church of Scotland do not, as a matter of either their constitution or practice, carry out any judicial functions on behalf of the State. Nor do they adjudicate upon a citizen's legal rights or obligations, whether common law or statutory. They operate in relation to matters which are essentially of a private nature." (H.L. Debs, February 5, 1998, cols 794.)

Lord Hardie also emphasised that although the Church of Scotland was the national church, the effect of the 1921 Act was that it ceased being an established church: it was now a "non-public or private institution in the sense that its affairs were of no concern to the state" (*ibid*). The government nevertheless responded to these concerns—as well as concerns of other religious communities—by introducing what is now the Human Rights Act 1998, s.13. This provides that:

"(1) If a court's determination of any question arising under this Act might affect the exercise by a religious organisation (itself or its members collectively) of the Convention right to freedom of thought, conscience or religion, it must have particular regard to the importance of that right."

For this purpose a court includes a tribunal (s.13(2)). For an analysis of the wider implications of s.13, see P. Cumper, "The Protection of Religious Rights Under Section 13 of the Human Rights Act 1998" [2000] P.L. 254.

The introduction of this measure did not, however, satisfy the Church of Scotland, with Jim Wallace raising the matter when the House of Commons were considering Lords amendments to the Human Rights Bill. According to Mr Wallace:

"There has been much discussion between the Secretary of State and the former Moderator, and between the Prime Minister and the former moderator when he visited London at St. Andrewstide last year. The Church appreciates the time and consideration that the Government have given these matters. However, the package that has been presented to the Committee tonight has been considered by the Church of Scotland, and it is still not satisfied.

In a letter to the Secretary of State, the principal clerk of the Church of Scotland, Dr. McDonald, says:

'We appreciate any movement at all on the Government's part in this matter. However, we feel that this amendment will fall far short of anything that would meet our concerns. In the first place it would mean that the Church itself was relying on its rights under the convention, whereas the present position is that we rely on the 1921 Act. Moreover the amendment requires only that a court "must have particular regard to the importance of that right". It then remains open, presumably, to the court once it has had that "particular regard" to determine the issue. There is no automatic provision, as under the 1921 Act, that a determination that a matter is a spiritual one means that the court has no further jurisdiction.'

Furthermore, the General Assembly of the Church of Scotland, meeting in Edinburgh this week, passed a deliverance on Saturday morning deeply regretting that 'Her Majesty's

Government has, despite the representations of the Board, failed to agree to an amendment of the Human Rights Bill which would state explicitly that the position of the Church of Scotland in terms of the Church of Scotland Act, 1921, is not affected by the Bill.'

It goes on:

> 'Accordingly, we urge Her Majesty's Government either to give an assurance that the Human Rights Bill is entirely consistent with the provision of the 1921 Act or to amend the Bill to ensure that it will be so consistent.'

[Mr Wallace then refers to a letter to the former Moderator from the Secretary of State.]

In a further passage in his letter to the former Moderator, the Secretary of State for Scotland said:

> 'The civil courts have demonstrated their reluctance to involve themselves in the spiritual matters concerning doctrine, worship, government and discipline within the church, as defined in the Declaratory Articles recognised by the Church of Scotland Act 1921.'

It is not so much reluctance, but whether the courts have jurisdiction. When the case of *Logan*, to which I referred, first came before the Court of Session for an interdict, the counsel who moved for the interdict did not draw to the attention of the presiding judge the provisions of the Church of Scotland Act 1921, and the interdict was granted. Within a matter of days, the case came back to court and the provisions of the 1921 Act were drawn to Lord Osborne's attention. He immediately withdrew the interdict and said that the provisions of the 1921 Act prevailed. There was no further consideration of the merits of the case before the court.

My right hon. Friend the Member for Caithness, Sutherland and Easter Ross said that he found compelling the argument put by the Lord Advocate in another place, that because the courts of the Church of Scotland do not amount to public authorities, they would not fall within the scope of the Bill. However, it is fair to point out that although the Lord Advocate said that he found it extremely difficult to conjure up circumstances in which the courts of the Church of Scotland could be public authorities, he said on 5 February in the other place that it was possible, in some circumstances, that those courts of the Church could be public authorities. The Church of Scotland wants that possibility to be addressed.

The Secretary of State for Scotland suggested that there had been no case in 30 years in which any such issue arose, and he may make the fair point that the Bill brings human rights legislation home and makes our domestic courts, rather than Strasbourg, the appropriate forum. That, too, has been the case with the Church of Scotland. The Bill's purpose is to achieve a more convenient forum in which litigants can take action. There may have been no such case because people thought that going to Strasbourg was outwith their financial reach. It cannot clearly be shown that that is a game, set and match argument, but the Secretary of State fairly asked what was the difference in principle.

That case is more difficult to answer, but, if nothing in principle has changed and given that successive Governments have in no way departed from—indeed, have acknowledged and supported—the settlement between Church and state arrived at in 1921, there should be no difficulty in the Secretary of State giving the assurance that the exclusive jurisdiction of the Church of Scotland in matters spiritual, under the 1921 Act, will be unaffected by the Bill. If it has been unaffected in the past 30 years, the point that he made must also mean that it will be unaffected by the Bill. I would welcome such an assurance.

The Church of Scotland is anxious not to be thought to be in any way ignoring human rights or the United Kingdom's obligations under the convention. Paradoxically, the Church of Scotland, perhaps before some other Churches, accepted that it would be subject to human rights legislation in its secular affairs. The Church of Scotland would be subject to the convention's provisions in relation to human rights issues arising from its provision of eventide homes and clinics for drug addicts.

Furthermore, the committee on Church and nation has today been debating a resolution—I am not sure whether it has been passed—marking the 50th anniversary of the universal declaration of human rights and welcoming the incorporation of the European convention on human rights in to United Kingdom law. The General Assembly also had before it a motion stating:

> 'Instruct the Board of Practice and Procedure, in consultation with the Committee on Church and Nation, to consider whether, and if so how, the Church's commitment to the European Convention on Human Rights might be appropriately contained in an Act of Assembly, especially but not exclusively in relation to disciplinary and judicial procedures, and to report to the next General Assembly.'

The Church of Scotland is saying that it has exclusive jurisdiction in matters spiritual and that it would not be for the House to direct it to amend its legislation if, for the sake of argument and in extreme circumstances, the European Court of Human Rights had found that there had been a breach in a procedure and practice of a court of the Church. The Church of Scotland claims exclusive jurisdiction, but it is willing to consider, where appropriate, how it might incorporate the provisions into its practices."
(H.C. Debs, May 20, 1998, cols 1054–1055).

For its part the Government was unwilling to move any further. Mr Donald Dewar recognised that the Church's fears were "genuine" but believed that they were "unfounded" (*ibid.*, col.1064). The Government had "tried genuinely hard to think of such a circumstance [in which a problem could arise] and [could not] come up with anything that justifies the fear that has been raised" (*ibid.*, col.1065). Although the Government had made "considerable efforts to find a way forward", they had been unable to "find a form of amendment that meets in full the concerns of the Church of Scotland while preserving the integrity of ... the policy [of incorporating the ECHR]" (*ibid.*, col.1067).

It appears, however, that this may have been a storm in a font, with subsequent developments tending to confirm that the Church of Scotland is not a public authority, and so not directly affected by the Human Rights Act. In *Aston Cantlow and Wilmcote with Billesley Parochial Church Council v Wallbank* [2004] A.C. 546, Lord Rodger of Earlsferry said:

> LORD RODGER OF EARLSFERRY: "163. In the present case the question therefore comes to be whether a PCC is a public authority in the sense that it carries out, either generally or on the relevant occasion, the kind of public function of government which would engage the responsibility of the United Kingdom before the Strasbourg organs. It so happens that there are two cases from Strasbourg dealing with the position of churches in this regard. They suggest that, in general, church authorities should not be treated as public authorities in this sense.
>
> 164. The first case is *Holy Monasteries v Greece* (1995) 20 EHRR 1. On the basis of various provisions of the Convention, including article 1 of the First Protocol, the applicant monasteries challenged a Greek statute which changed the rules of administration of their patrimony and provided for the transfer of a large part of their estate to the Greek state. The links between the Greek Orthodox Church and the Greek state were particularly close. In Greek law the Holy Monasteries were public law entities that could be founded, merged or dissolved by means of a decree of the President of Greece. Another public law entity, under the supervision of the ministry of education and religious affairs, was responsible for managing the property belonging to the monasteries. In these circumstances the Greek government stated, as a preliminary objection to the Holy Monasteries' application, that they were not a non-governmental organisation which could make an application as a victim in terms of article 25(1) (now article 34) of the Convention. Repelling that objection, the European Court of Human Rights held, at p 41, para 49:

'Like the Commission in its admissibility decision, the court notes at the outset that the applicant monasteries do not exercise governmental powers. Section 39(1) of the Charter of the Greek Church describes the monasteries as ascetic religious institutions. Their objectives—essentially ecclesiastical and spiritual ones, but also cultural and social ones in some cases—are not such as to enable them to be classed with governmental organisations established for public administration purposes. From the classification as public law entities it may be inferred only that the legislature—on account of the special links between the monasteries and the state—wished to afford them the same legal protection vis à vis third parties as was accorded to other public law entities. Furthermore, the monastery councils' only power consists in making rules concerning the organisation and furtherance of spiritual life and the internal administration and furtherance of spiritual life and the internal administration of each monastery.

The monasteries come under the spiritual supervision of the local archbishop, not under the supervision of the state, and they are accordingly entities distinct from the state, of which they are completely independent.

The applicant monasteries are therefore to be regarded as non-governmental organisations within the meaning of article 25 of the Convention.'

While the positions of the Holy Monasteries and of a PCC are scarcely comparable, the judgment of the European Court is important for its reasoning that the nature of the objectives of the monasteries was not such that they could be classed with 'governmental organisations established for public administration purposes'. The court also attached importance to the fact that the monasteries came under the spiritual supervision of the local archbishop rather than under the supervision of the state, as an indication that they were entities distinct from the state.

165. In *Hautanemi v Sweden* (1996) 22 EHRR CD 155 the applicants were members of a parish of the Church of Sweden who complained of a violation of article 9 of the Convention because the Assembly of the Church of Sweden had prohibited the use of the liturgy of the Finnish Evangelical-Lutheran Church in their parish. Under reference to the judgment in the *Holy Monasteries* case, the Commission recalled article 25(1) (now article 34) of the Convention and observed, at p 155, that

'at the relevant time the Church of Sweden and its member parishes were to be regarded as corporations of public law. Since these religious bodies cannot be considered to have been exercising governmental powers, the Church of Sweden and notably the applicant parish can nevertheless be regarded as "non-governmental organisations" within the meaning of article 25(1).'

Having held that, as members of the parish, the applicants could be regarded as victims in terms of article 25(1), the Commission added, at p 156:

'The Commission has just found that, for the purposes of article 25 of the Convention, the Church of Sweden and its member parishes are to be regarded as "non-governmental organisations". It follows that the respondent state cannot be held responsible for the alleged violation of the applicants' freedom of religion resulting from the decision of the Church Assembly. ... There has thus been no State interference with that freedom.'

166. In the light of these decisions what matters is that the PCC's general function is to carry out the religious mission of the Church in the parish, rather than to exercise any governmental power. Moreover, the PCC is not in any sense under the supervision of the state: under section 9 of the 1956 Measure it is the bishop who has certain powers in relation to the PCC's activities. In these circumstances the fact that the PCC is constituted

as a body corporate under the 1956 Measure is irrelevant. For these reasons, in respectful disagreement with the Court of Appeal, I consider that the PCC is not a core public authority for purposes of section 6 of the Act.

167. This conclusion finds further support in the treatment of certain churches in relation to article 19(4) of the German Constitution or Grundgesetz. That article provides that, if any person's rights are infringed by "public power" ("öffentliche Gewalt"), recourse to the courts is open to him. The history of relations between Church and State in Germany is, of course, very different from the history of that relationship in any part of the United Kingdom. In Germany it has culminated in a declaration that there is to be no State Church (article 137(1) of the Weimar Constitution incorporated by article 140 of the Constitution). This important difference must not be overlooked. Nevertheless, as permitted by article 137, certain churches are constituted as public law corporations. In general, domestic public law entities are regarded as exercising public power in terms of article 19(4), whereas natural persons and private law associations are not. Despite this, because of their particular (religious) mission which does not derive from the state, the churches that are public law corporations are treated differently from other public law corporations that are organically integrated into the state. "Church power is indeed public, but not state power" ("ist kirchliche Gewalt zwar öffentliche, aber nicht staatliche Gewalt"): BVerfGE 18, 385, 386–387; BVerfGE 25, 226, 228–229. So, in relation to these churches, the Constitutional Court interprets the phrase "public power" in article 19(4) as being equivalent to "state power". Since within their own sphere the churches do not exercise state power, even if they exercise public power, the article 19(4) guarantee does not apply. This interpretation of "public power" tends to confirm the interpretation of "public authority" in section 6 which I prefer. Moreover, due allowance having been made for the particular position of the Church of England, the reasoning of the Constitutional Court also tends to confirm that the mere fact that section 3 of the 1956 Measure makes every PCC a body corporate does not carry with it any necessary implication that the PCC should, on that account alone, be regarded as a public authority for the purposes of section 6.

168. Of course, if the churches in Germany go outside their own unique sphere and undertake state functions, for example, in running schools, the constitutional guarantee in article 19(4) applies to them: BVerfGE 18, 385, 387–388; BVerfGE 25, 226, 229. In much the same way, for example, a Church of England body which was entrusted, as part of its responsibilities, with running a school or other educational establishment might find that it had stepped over into the sphere of governmental functions and was, in that respect, to be regarded as a public authority for purposes of section 6(1)."

IV. State Support for Religion and Public Worship

(1) Blasphemy

Bowman v Secular Society Ltd
[1917] A.C. 406

This case concerned the validity of a bequest to the Secular Society, a body which sought to promote the principle that human conduct should be based upon natural knowledge and not upon supernatural belief. The action was by a relative of the testator who challenged the bequest partly on the ground that any attack on Christian religion was illegal, however decent and temperate the form of attack. The House of Lords held the bequest valid.

Lord Finlay, L.C.: "In my opinion the appellants have failed to establish that all attacks upon religion are at common law punishable as blasphemous. There are no doubt to be found in the cases many expressions to the effect that Christianity is part of the law of England, but no decision has been brought to our notice in which a conviction took place for the advocacy of principles at variance with Christianity, apart from circumstances of scurrility or intemperance of language…

We have been referred by Lord Dunedin to the law of Scotland on this subjects as stated in Hume's Criminal Law (vol. 1, p. 5(68)), and it appears to be the case that in Scotland scurrility or indecency is an essential element of the crime of blasphemy at common law. Certain Scotch statutes which made it a crime to contravene certain doctrines have been repealed. The consequences of the view put forward on behalf of the appellants would be somewhat startling, and in the absence of any actual decision to the contrary I think we must hold that the law of England on this point is the same as that of Scotland, and that the crime of blasphemy is not constituted by a temperate attack on religion in which the decencies of controversy are maintained."

(Lord Finlay dissented on another ground.)

The last reported prosecution for blasphemy in Scotland is *Robinson* (1843) 1 Broun 643, where it was held that anything which vilified the Holy Scriptures and Christian religion was an offence. It was also said (by Lord Justice-Clerk Hope) that a mere denial of the truth and authority of the scriptures and the Christian religion was blasphemous. The passages in the *Bowman* case suggest that this no longer reflects the modern law, and indeed it has been argued that blasphemy is no longer a crime in Scotland (G.H. Gordon, *The Criminal Law of Scotland* (3rd ed., 2001), Vol.II, p.671). But whatever the legal status of blasphemy, it is unlikely that a prosecution would now be brought, it being more probable that the Crown would proceed on some other ground, such as breach of the peace if the circumstances justified such a charge. Although it is true that a conviction for blasphemy was more recently upheld by the House of Lords in *R. v Lemon* [1979] A.C. 617, that was initiated as a private prosecution, and it is only in exceptional circumstances that such a prosecution will be permitted in Scotland (see *H v Sweeney*, 1983 S.L.T. 48, and *McDonald v Lord Advocate*, 1988 S.L.T. 713). For an interesting review of blasphemy in Scotland, see G. Maher, "Blasphemy', 1977 S.L.T. (News) 257.

Yet although there may be a reluctance to prosecute, blasphemy may be used in order to restrain publications, as *Wingrove v United Kingdom* (1997) 24 EHRR 1 reveals. In that case the British Board of Film Classification was designated by the Video Recordings Act 1984 to issue classification certificates to video films. On this occasion it refused to issue a certificate for *The Visions of Ecstasy* which included an "intense erotic moment" between St Teresa and Jesus Christ. The reason for the decision was that the film was blasphemous and bound to give rise to outrage at the unacceptable treatment of a sacred subject. As a result of the decision, the film could not be sold, hired or otherwise supplied to the public. The decision was challenged as violating the right to freedom of expression in Art.10 of the Convention. The application failed. The court found that although there had been an undisputed interference with freedom of expression, it had been prescribed by law, pursued a legitimate aim, and was necessary in a democratic society. On the last point it was accepted by the court that only two prosecutions for blasphemy had been brought in the United Kingdom in the preceding 70 years and that strong arguments had been advanced in favour of abolishing blasphemy laws. Nevertheless "there is not yet sufficient common ground in the legal and social orders of the Member States of the Council of Europe to conclude that a system whereby a State can impose restrictions on the propagation of material on the basis that it is blasphemous is, in itself, unnecessary in a democratic society and thus incompatible with the Convention" (p.30).

In principle, the crime of blasphemy seems difficult to justify. In a multi-cultural and increasingly secular society, there is no reason why Christian values should enjoy any special status in the eyes of the criminal law. During the Second Reading debate of an unsuccessful Blasphemy Laws (Amendment) Bill in January 1930, the following point was forcefully made:

"If language is used by anyone which is genuinely indecent, or which so hurts the feelings of people that it tends to cause public disturbance, these offences can be adequately dealt with under the existing law. The offenders can be prosecuted either for indecent language or for language calculated to cause a breach of the peace. There will still be ample resources for the preservation of decency and public order." (234 H.C. Debs. 500.)

Attempts in England to extend the crime of blasphemy to include other religions have been unsuccessful: see *Ex p. Choudhury* [1991] 1 Q.B. 429.

(2) Sunday observance

The Sunday Act 1661

"Act for the due observation of the Sabbath day
Our Soverane Lord with advice and consent of his Estates of Parliament ... Inhibites and discharges ... keeping of mercats or using any sorts of Merchandise on the [sabbath day] under the pains and penalties following, viz. ten pounds."

Between 1503 and 1706 the Scots Parliament passed at least 13 statutes dealing with Sunday observance. The 1661 Act and the Sunday Trading Act 1579, which also prohibits the keeping of markets or fairs on Sundays, are almost all that survive (if, indeed, they are not in desuetude: *Middleton v Tough*, 1908 S.C. (J) 32). In practice, the courts have shown a marked reluctance to enforce these measures, and in any event the penalty of £10 Scots is unlikely to be an effective deterrent. It is difficult to see what useful purpose these provisions serve, and little would be lost if they were repealed by the next Statute Law (Repeals) Act. Unlike in England and Wales (Shops, Act 1950, Pt. IV), there was in Scotland no general prohibition against the opening of shops on Sundays, though it was possible for a local authority to require shops in its area to close early on Sundays (Shops Act 1950, s. 8).

English law was liberalised by the Sunday Trading Act 1994, though it is still more restrictive than the position in Scotland. While shops may now open on Sundays, many still cannot do so on the same terms as they may open on other days of the week. The Sunday Working (Scotland) Act 2003 extends to shop-workers and betting workers the right to opt out of Sunday working. These rights—contained in the Employment Rights Act 1996—had earlier applied to England and Wales only. Changing social values would make it extremely difficult to justify any serious control over what may now be lawfully done on Sundays. It is important to note that these changing values have informed the policies of both licensing authorities and legislators. Thus many licensing authorities permit theatres and cinemas to open on Sundays, and since 1976 it has been possible, and it is now standard practice, for public houses to obtain licenses for Sunday opening.

Report of the Departmental Committee on Scottish Licensing Laws
(Chairman: Dr Christopher Clayson) Cmnd. 5354 (1973)

"9.58 To take first the principle of Sunday observance we, like the Guest Committee before us, fully recognise that some people sincerely hold the view that only works of necessity and mercy should be carried out on Sundays. As our predecessors pointed out, however, for many years there has been an increasing tendency towards a less strict attitude towards Sunday observance and this is a fact which it would be wrong to ignore. There is no doubt that this trend has continued in the last ten years or so, and perhaps more quickly in that period than previously. Like the Guest Committee, therefore, we feel we would not be justified in recommending against Sunday opening of public houses on Sabbatarian grounds alone. Similarly, the change which our predecessors noted in the traditional Scottish attitude to Sunday has continued in the last decade, although the tradition clings more strongly in some parts of the country than in others. The Guest Committee formed the view in their day that Sunday opening would not necessarily be repugnant to Scottish sentiment. We share that view. On the question of the need for a rest day for publicans and those employed in public houses, we fully accept this point. We do not see, however, that if public houses were allowed to open on Sundays this would mean a seven-day working week for the publican and his staff. We would expect that those involved would ensure that if they worked on a Sunday they would have an equivalent rest day on some other day during the week. So far as the social benefits of the traditional day of rest for the population at large are concerned, it could be argued that the fact that public houses are closed on Sundays does in fact detract from these benefits. (In this connection the proposals which we make in a later chapter to facilitate access by families are relevant.) As to the point of an increase in crime, drunken driving and rowdyism on Sundays, we think it is significant that the Association of Chief Police Officers (Scotland) was among the organisations in favour of Sunday opening."

Sunday opening was permitted under the Licensing (Scotland) Act 1976, and the law was liberalised still further in 1990. The 1976 Act (as amended) now makes provision for permitted hours on Sunday of 12.30 pm to 2.30 pm, and 6.30 pm to 11.00 pm. Applications for a public house or refreshment licence must state whether the licensee proposes to open on Sundays: it is not necessary to make a separate application for Sunday opening. However, Sunday permitted hours may be refused, if there is evidence that "the opening and use on a Sunday of the premises" would cause "undue disturbance or public nuisance in the locality" (Licensing (Scotland) Act 1976, s.17(2A)). The Act also permits the licensing authorities to impose a Sunday restriction order where "the use of licensed premises is the cause of undue disturbance or public nuisance having regard to the way of life in the locality on a Sunday" (1976 Act, s.65(1)(b)). The effect of such a restriction is that there are no permitted hours on a Sunday. The reference in s.65 to "the way of life in the locality" is said to be a recognition that "the Sunday opening of licensed premises is, historically, a sensitive issue" (J.C. Cummins, *Licensing Law in Scotland* (2nd ed., 2000), p.238). However the permitted hours may also be extended, and it has been pointed out that:

"After its introduction by the Licensing (Scotland) Act 1976 Sunday opening was a contentious issue for a relatively short time. It is now seldom the source of opposition. Indeed, by May 1991, shortly after Sunday regular extensions first became available for public houses, approximately two-thirds of public houses in the country had obtained Sunday afternoon extensions." (*ibid.*, p.182.)

Yet further liberalisation was proposed by the Nicholson Committee's *Review of Liquor Licensing Law in Scotland* (2003). The Committee recommended that the "present system of statutory permitted licensing laws should be abolished and should be replaced by a system under which there will be no statutory prohibited hours; and actual opening hours will be those authorised, upon application, by a licensing board" (Recommendation 20). The Committee did, however, propose extended rights of objection for religious bodies. The list of those who may at present object to an application which has been made to a licensing board is to be found in the Licensing Act 1976, s.16 (1). This applies to:

"(a) any person owning or occupying property situated in the neighbourhood of the premises to which the application relates or any organisation which in the opinion of the board represents such persons;

(b) a community council ... for the area in which the premises are situated;

(c) any organised church which, in the opinion of the licensing board, represents a significant body of opinion among persons residing in the neighbourhood of the premises;

(d) the chief constable;

(e) the fire authority for the area in which the premises are situated;

(f) a local authority for the area in which the premises are situated."

The Nicholson Committee identified a number of shortcomings with this list. So far as relevant for immediate purposes:

"**6.23 ...** So far as churches are concerned we consider that it is unnecessary and inappropriate that they should be recognised as objectors only when, in the opinion of the board, they represent a significant body of opinion among persons residing in the neighbourhood of the premises. A church may, after all, wish to object to an application on its own account because of the proximity of proposed licensed premises to a church building or an adjacent graveyard. We should say, however, that it is not immediately clear to us what is intended by the statutory reference to any 'organised' church, though we suspect that this is intended to signify that 'church' should be read as meaning the summation of a whole religious denomination such as the Church of Scotland, or the Roman Catholic Church, rather than a particular church building in a particular locality. There is, however, a further matter which occurs to us in this context. The present provision relating to an 'organised church' was introduced into the 1976 Act as a result of a recommendation by the Clayson committee, but it appears that the committee made that recommendation solely on the basis of representations made by the Church of Scotland. Consequently, there does not appear to have been any explicit consideration given to religious faiths other than Christian. In our view it may be doubtful whether the word 'church' could be construed as including the Jewish faith, and all the more so it may be doubtful whether it would embrace other religions such as those of Islam. We consider that, in an increasingly multi-cultural society, any body representing an established religion should be entitled to object to an application if that body owns or occupies property in or near the neighbourhood of the premises to which the application relates. We therefore recommend:
      32. The following should be statutorily entitled to object to the grant of an application for a premises licence—(a) any persons who own, are tenants of, or reside in property situated in or near the neighbourhood of the premises to which an application relates, together with any body or organisation which represents, or bears to represent, people of the foregoing category; (b) a community council for the area in which the premises are situated; and (c) any body representing an established religion where that body owns or occupies property in or near the neighbourhood of the premises to which the application relates."

(3) Education

The Education (Scotland) Act 1980

"Religious instruction
      8.—(1) Whereas it has been the custom in the public schools of Scotland for religious observance to be practised and for instruction in religion to be given to pupils whose parents did not object to such observance of instruction, but with liberty to parents, without forfeiting any of the other advantages of the schools, to elect that their children should not take part in such observance or receive such instruction, be it enacted that education authorities shall be at liberty to continue the said custom, subject to the provisions of section 9 of this Act.
      (2) It shall not be lawful for an education authority to discontinue religious observance or the provision of instruction in religion in terms of subsection (1) above, unless and until a resolution in favour of such discontinuance duly passed by the authority has been submitted to a poll of the local government electors for the education area taken for the purpose, and has been approved by a majority of electors voting thereat.

Conscience clause
      9. Every public school and every grant-aided school shall be open to pupils of all denominations, and any pupil may be withdrawn by his parents from any instruction in religious subjects and from any religious observance in any such school; and no pupil shall

in any such school be placed at any disadvantage with respect to the secular instruction given therein by reason of the denomination to which such pupil or his parents belong, or by reason of his being withdrawn from any instruction in religious subjects."

In 1968 the Secretary of State appointed a committee under the chairmanship of Professor W.M. Millar to review the practice regarding moral and religious education in non-denominational schools. The committee, which reported in 1972, with a number of suggestions for improving the quality of religious education, found no evidence of any move in any local educational authority's area to have a poll taken to discontinue religious education in terms of what is now s.8(2). Very few parents exercise the right available to them in s.9 of the 1980 Act. The Millar Committee found that in 96 per cent of primary schools no parents, or less than 1 per cent of parents, exercised this right. In the remaining 4 per cent of primary schools, between 1 per cent and 10 per cent of parents elected to withdraw their children. In 93 per cent of secondary schools, no parents or less than 1 per cent exercised their right, and of the remaining 7 per cent, again between 1 per cent and 10 per cent of the parents sought the exemption of their children. The continuing relevance and future of the conscience clause was considered by the Millar Committee.

Report of a Committee on Moral and Religious Education in Scottish Schools
Scottish Office (1972)

"(a) Primary School
We have recommended ... that in the primary school religious education should largely avoid the kind of formal instruction in religion for which the 'conscience clause' was designed, and should be part of the children's exploration of their world and their relations with each other which the various activities in the classroom are designed to further. In this context it is particularly difficult—and indeed futile—to try to draw a line between what is religious and what is not, and the more a teacher has succeeded in removing the barriers between 'subjects' in the primary school the more difficult it will be for her to tell at which points a child who is to be withdrawn from religious education should be asked to do something else. The development of the integrated day and the use of project methods is likely to make withdrawal from 'instruction in religious subjects' less and less meaningful and may well create problems in the few cases where the parents insist on having their children withdrawn. It would be possible to simplify the problems by dealing with religious education in a fairly isolated way, but this would be to damage the real value of religious education, and we think it would be quite wrong to do this simply in order to make it easier to organise withdrawal of a child when it is requested. We recommend that when parents send a request to a primary school for withdrawal of their child or children the headteacher and the class teacher should discuss this with the parents to ensure that the parents understand the nature of the religious education being given in the school, the dislocation of the child's education that may be caused, and the problems that can result from a child being obviously isolated from his own group in certain circumstances. There should, of course, be no attempt to persuade the parents against their wishes to give up their right to have their children withdrawn, and if they insist the teacher should try to see that this is carried out with the minimum of disturbance both to the child concerned and the rest of the class. But we hope that if our general recommendations are followed parents will see religious education as an essential part of their children's education as a whole.

(b) Secondary School
From the section we have written on the secondary school in the previous chapter it will be clear that we regard religious education as an important element in every child's education at the secondary stage, and that we want it to move away completely from any attempt at indoctrination or conversion. So we expect that few parents will wish to have

their children withdrawn from the kind of religious education in the secondary school that we have proposed. There will not be the same difficulties in identifying 'religious education' as there is likely to be in the primary school, since even in a situation where a team of teachers is dealing with the group of related subjects ... it should generally be possible to mark out that time that could be described as religious education. But again we think the headteacher or an appropriate senior teacher should discuss with parents any request for withdrawal of children to make sure that the request is not based on a misconception of what religious education means in the school.

The right of withdrawal guaranteed by law belongs to the parent, but problems arise in the later years of secondary school when pupils themselves ask to be excused religious education, and particularly services of worship. Our view is that for pupils below the statutory school leaving age the question of withdrawal should be entirely a matter between the parent and the school. But the young people who remain at school for a fifth and a sixth year are beginning to be faced much more clearly with a range of situations where personal and moral choice is called for and are frequently exhorted to be responsible in using their freedom of choice; and they tend to feel—to some extent rightly—that the fact that they are at school through choice and not by compulsion should have implications for their freedom to be involved in or stay away from particular activities of the school. Requests from pupils in the fifth and sixth years of secondary school to withdraw from religious education should be treated seriously by the head teacher, and he or an appropriate deputy should discuss such a request with the pupil. If he is fairly certain that the pupil objects on grounds of genuine personal belief to being involved in religious education (even of the kind we propose) or services of worship, and if the parents raise no objection, we think such requests should be granted."

The position relating to the provision of religious instruction has been governed by the following guidance issued by the Scottish Office in 1991, which was influenced by the Millar Committee, as well as by others.

Scottish Office Circular 6/91
Provision of Religious Education and Religious Observance in Primary and Secondary Schools

1. This Circular describes and explains the Secretary of State's policy on the teaching of religious education and the provision of religious observance in primary and secondary schools; and sets out action which the Secretary of State invites education authorities to take in planning the provision of religious education and religious observance. The Circular is applicable to all primary and secondary schools, including special schools, although the Secretary of State recognises that a number of schools, and particularly denominational schools, by their nature already match its terms in their provision of religious education and religious observance.

2. In formulating this guidance the Secretary of State has taken into account the requirements of current legislation as contained in the Education (Scotland) Act 1980 and the advice contained in the following reports: the Millar Report, 'Moral and Religious Education in Scottish Schools' (1971); HM Inspectorate interim reports, 'Learning and Teaching in Religious Education' (1986) and 'Religious Observance in Primary and Secondary Schools' (1989); and Bulletins 1 and 2 of the former Consultative Committee on the Curriculum, 'A Curricular Approach to Religious Education' (1978) and 'Curriculum Guidelines for Religious Education' (1981). He has also sought and had regard to the views of representatives of churches and other interested bodies.

3. In this Circular 'religious education' refers to courses of religious education provided throughout primary, secondary and special schools (denominational or non-denominational); 'religious studies' refers to courses leading to certification in terms of the Scottish

Certificate of Education (SCE) or the National Certificate (NC); and 'religious observance' refers to occasions set aside for different forms of worship.

General

4. The Secretary of State is of the view that religious education and religious observance are valid and important educational experiences at all stages in primary and secondary schools. Religious education should receive the attention and facilities merited by its fundamental place in the curriculum. Syllabuses of religious education should in all schools be based on Christianity as the main religious tradition of Scotland but should also take account of the teaching and practices of other principal religions. Religious education should promote understanding of and respect for those who adhere to different faiths. This principle should inform religious education in all schools, but in schools where there are significant numbers of children of religious traditions other than Christianity it will have particular point. The aim should be as far as possible to adopt an approach to all faiths which is sensitive to the views of members of those faiths.

5. For those parents who are unable to give their acceptance there is a statutory right to withdraw their children from religious education and a parallel right to withdraw their children from religious observance. These rights should always be made known to parents and their wishes respected.

6. The Secretary of State considers that religious observance complements religious education and is an important contribution to pupils' spiritual development. It can also have a subsidiary role in promoting the ethos of a school by bringing pupils together and creating a feeling of corporate identity. In non-denominational schools religious observance should be of a broadly Christian character. But where appropriate schools may wish to organise special acts of observance for particular religions. Recommendations are given below about the frequency of religious observance. Regularity is necessary to ensure an impact on pupils' experience. It is, however, the quality of such occasions which is of paramount importance.

7. Most education authorities, and many schools, have policy guidelines governing the provision and content of religious education and religious observance. Education authorities are invited to review them in the light of this Circular. Education authorities and schools which do not have such policy statements are invited to develop them in the light of this Circular. It is important that such guidelines are widely known and observed. School Boards will have a particular interest in religious education and religious observance and policies should be formulated in discussion with them.

The Primary Stages

8. Religious education should be provided for all pupils in accordance with the guidance offered in the SED Working Paper No 1 on The Balance of the Primary Curriculum; this recommends a minimum of 10% of time for the curricular area of religious and moral education. Aspects of moral education will occur from time to time in other curricular areas which have their own recommended minimum time allocations. This should not detract from the time allocated to the religious and moral education curricular area. Advice on the content of religious and moral education will be offered within the 5–14 Development Programme.

9. All pupils should take part in religious observance not less than once a week. The precise form of observance will be determined by school policy which will take into account factors such as the roll of the school and the availability of accommodation but opportunities should be provided throughout each session for observance to take place in individual classes, or by stage or as a whole school; there should also be opportunities for the involvement of pupils and others including school chaplains in planning and presentation.

The Secondary stages

10. Religious education should be provided for all pupils in accordance with the recommendations of the SCCC's Curriculum Design for the Secondary Stages. This recommends for the Religious and Moral Education Mode a notional minimum of 5% of curriculum time in S1/S2, a minimum of 80 hours over 2 years in S3 and S4 and a continuing element within the context of personal and social development which should feature in the curriculum of all pupils in S5 and S6. Again, aspects of moral education will occur from time to time in other areas of the curriculum with their own time allocations but this should not detract from the time allocated to the Religious and Moral Education Mode. It is desirable that opportunities should be given to pupils to choose certificated courses in Religious Studies (See para 3). Where there is a shortage of staff or resources, however, priority should be given to the provision of religious and moral education for all pupils. Guidance on the content of religious education syllabuses is already available and will be supplemented for S1 and S2 within the 5–14 Development Programme.

11. All pupils should take part in religious observance at least once a month and preferably with greater frequency. The views of School Boards should be taken fully into account in determining frequency of observance. Again the precise form will be determined by schools policy but there should be opportunities for year, stage or whole school observance as well as involvement by pupils and others including school chaplains in planning and presentation. ...

Summary

14. The Secretary of State asks education authorities to review their policies on religious education and observance and to determine a times cale within which they can implement the advice given in this Circular. It should be possible to make good progress in the provision of religious observance. The Secretary of State accepts that the recommendation for religious education will have to be implemented as staff become available. He will monitor progress."

Scottish Executive
CONSULTATION PAPER:
REVIEW OF RELIGIOUS OBSERVANCE IN SCOTTISH SCHOOLS

"Preamble

Religious observance is a statutory requirement in schools under the Education (Scotland) Act 1980, which repeats the legislation of previous Acts in giving education authorities 'liberty to continue the said custom' and prohibits them from discontinuing it without a poll of local electors. Parents have the legal right to withdraw their children if they wish.

The HMIE report *Standards and Quality in Secondary Schools: Religious and Moral Education 1995–2000* stated that many secondary schools did not follow the advice contained in SOED Circular 6/91, where the Secretary of State advised that secondary schools should provide at least a monthly opportunity for religious observance. As a result of this report the Education Minister within the Scottish Executive set up a Review Group to advise on how schools could meet this requirement. Despite the focus on secondary schools in the report it was decided to expand the advice to include primary schools.

In the standards and quality report HMI stated that they did not believe that many secondary schools were deliberately negligent but that headteachers found it difficult to take account of the Circular in ways which were meaningful in the social, cultural and educational contexts of the present day. Schools have difficulty because they are not sure what is meant by religious observance in a predominantly secular and increasingly multi-faith society.

The Group believes that each individual within a school community has an entitlement to develop himself/herself as a spiritual being or 'whole person'. This entitlement includes being helped to recognise, reflect upon and develop a deeper understanding of the value and worth of each individual which comes from one's dignity as a person. Defined in this way, religious observance is educationally justifiable and contributes to the 'whole-person' development of all members of the school community.

Religious observance as defined above can be distinguished from an organised act of worship. Worship is a free response of an individual and a community to 'what is considered worthy of worship'. This response involves three elements: belief in the reality of the focus of worship, desire to offer worship to the focus of worship and commitment to life stances related to the focus of worship.

Where the school community, whether denominational or non-denominational, is continuous with a faith community, that community's faith in 'the focus of worship', may be assumed and worship may be considered to be appropriate as part of the formal activity of the school. Where, as in most non-denominational schools, there is a diversity of beliefs and practices, the Review Group believes that the appropriate context for an organised act of worship is within the informal curriculum as part of the range of activities offered for example by religions, groups, chaplains and other religious leaders.

In many schools there is a well-established tradition of using assemblies as a vehicle for religious observance, whether whole-school, year groups, stages or particular school groups such as houses. In any of these gatherings of the school community, the time set aside needs to be well planned to:

- provide opportunities for the community to reflect, with help, upon values, beliefs. commitments and hopes which are implicit in being human;
- provide opportunities for the school community to express and celebrate its shared values;
- give the school community time to reflect upon a range of stimuli from religious traditions and other sources such as literature, art and music;
- provide opportunities for the community to have space, stillness and time to respond to this reflection. In non-denominational, as well as denominational schools, the response of some members of the community may at times be in the form of worship, but for others it will be a period of meditation and reflection on what it is to be human or on the significant values of the school and wider community.

In the best practice, themes are carefully chosen to suit the school community's experience and understanding. The Review Group will develop exemplars that may help schools to review their present arrangements and provide genuine opportunities for the school community to reflect on educational and spiritual activities which enhance each member of the school community."

V. RELIGIOUS TOLERANCE

(1) Marriage

The Marriage (Scotland) Act 1977

"Persons who may solemnise marriage

8.—(1) A marriage may be solemnised by and only by—

    (a) a person who is—

        (i) a minister of the Church of Scotland; or

        (ii) a minister, clergyman, pastor, or priest of a religious body prescribed by regulations made by the Secretary of State, or who, not being one of the foregoing, is recognised by a religious body so prescribed as entitled to solemnise marriage on its behalf; or

        (iii) registered under section 9 of this Act; or

        (iv) temporarily authorised under section 12 of this Act; or

    (b) a person who is a district registrar or assistant registrar appointed under section 17 of this Act.

(2) In this Act—

    (a) any such person as is mentioned in subsection (1)(a) above is referred to as an 'approved celebrant,' and a marriage solemnised by an approved celebrant is referred to as a 'religious marriage';

    (b) any such person as is mentioned in subsection (1)(b) above is referred to as an 'authorised registrar,' and a marriage solemnised by an authorised registrar is referred to as a 'civil marriage.'

Registration of nominated persons as celebrants

9.—(1) A religious body, not being—

    (a) the Church of Scotland; or

    (b) prescribed by virtue of section 8(1)(a)(ii) of this Act,

may nominate to the Registrar General any of its members who it desires should be registered under this section as empowered to solemnise marriages:

Provided that any such nominee must, at the date of his nomination, be 21 years of age or over.

(2) The Registrar General shall reject a nomination made under subsection (1) above if in his opinion—

    (a) the nominating body is not a religious body; or

    (b) the marriage ceremony used by that body is not of an appropriate form; or

    (c) the nominee is not a fit and proper person to solemnise a marriage; or

    (d) there are already registered under this section sufficient members of the same religious body as the nominee to meet the needs of that body."

A religious body is defined in s.26 to mean "an organised group of people meeting regularly for common religious worship".

Section 10 of the 1977 Act makes provision for the removal of a celebrant's name from the authorised list by the Registrar General, generally on grounds relating to unfitness for office. Section 11 enables the religious body to change its celebrant or to cancel the registration of any such celebrant. Section 12 enables the Registrar General to grant a temporary authorisation to solemnise marriages. A marriage solemnised by an approved celebrant must be one in which both parties to the marriage are present and at which two witnesses purporting to be over 16 are present (s.13). Regulations made under s.8(1)(ii) have prescribed the following religious bodies: the Baptist Union of Scotland; the Congregational Church of Scotland; the Episcopal Church in

Scotland and other churches of the Anglican Communion; the Free Church of Scotland; the Free Presbyterian Church of Scotland; the Hebrew Congregation; the Methodist Church in Scotland; the Religious Society of Friends; the Roman Catholic Church; the Salvation Army; the Scottish Unitarian Association; and the United Free Church of Scotland: (Marriage (Prescription of Religious Bodies) (Scotland) Regulations SI 1977/1670).

The Matrimonial Proceedings (Polygamous Marriages) Act 1972

"Matrimonial relief and declarations as to validity in respect of polygamous marriages: Scotland
    2.—(1) A court in Scotland shall not be precluded from entertaining proceedings for, or granting, any such decree as is mentioned in subsection (2) below by reason only that the marriage to which the proceedings relate was entered into under a law which permits polygamy.
    (2) The decrees referred to in subsection (1) above are—
        (a) a decree of divorce;
        (b) a decree of nullity of marriage; ...
        ...
        (d) a decree of judicial separation;
        (e) a decree of separation and aliment, adherence and aliment, or interim aliment;
        (f) a decree of declarator that a marriage is valid or invalid;
        (g) any other decree involving a determination as to the validity of a marriage; and the reference in subsection (1) above to granting such a decree as aforesaid includes a reference to making any ancillary order which the court has power to make in proceedings for such a decree.
    (3) This section has effect whether or not either party to the marriage in question has for the time being any spouse additional to the other party; and provision may be made by rules of court—
        (a) for requiring notice of proceedings brought by virtue of this section to be served on any such other spouse; and
        (b) for conferring on any such other spouse the right to be heard in any such proceedings;
    in such cases as may be specified in the rules."

At common law the courts, in both England and Scotland, refused to recognise a marriage which was merely potentially polygamous. The marriage law of this country is based on Christian values, and so marriages must be monogamous. A spouse in a polygamous marriage was thus unable to obtain a matrimonial remedy where, say, his partner was guilty of adultery (*Muhammad v Suna*, 1956 S.C. 366). The 1972 Act was passed following criticism of the common law position by the Law Commission in 1971. Polygamous marriages are also recognised for social security purposes and for limited purposes at common law (see E.M. Clive, *Husband and Wife* (4th ed., 1997), pp.109–111). It should be emphasised, however, that the recognition of polygamous marriages is a limited one. In particular, it may be noted that a marriage contracted in this country while an earlier marriage survived would almost certainly be bigamous and therefore a crime, regardless of any claims that the parties' religion permitted such marriage: *cf. R. v Sarwan Singh* [1962] 3 All E.R. 612 and R.D. Leslie, "Polygamous Marriages and Bigamy" (1972) J.R.113. More recent legislation has addressed the validity of potentially polygamous marriages. The Private International Law (Miscellaneous Provisions) Act 1995 provides by s.7 that:

"Validity and effect in Scots law of potentially polygamous marriages

    7.—(1) A person domiciled in Scotland does not lack capacity to enter into a marriage by reason only that the marriage is entered into under a law which permits polygamy.
    (2) For the avoidance of doubt, a marriage valid by the law of Scotland and entered into—

(a) under a law which permits polygamy; and

(b) at a time when neither party to the marriage is already married,

has, so long as neither party marries a second spouse during the subsistence of the marriage, the same effects for all purposes of the law of Scotland as a marriage entered into under a law which does not permit polygamy."

(2) Education

The Education (Scotland) Act 1980

"Transference of denominational schools to education authorities

16.—(1) It shall be lawful for the person or persons vested with the titles of any school established after 21st November 1918, to which section 18 of the Act of 1918 would have applied had the school been in existence at that date, with the consent of the trustees of any trust upon which the school is held and of the Secretary of State, to transfer the school together with the site thereof and any land or buildings and furniture held and used in connection therewith, by sale, lease or otherwise, to the education authority, who shall be bound to accept such transfer, upon such terms as to price, rent, or other consideration as may be agreed, or as may be determined, failing agreement, by an arbiter appointed by the Secretary of State upon the application of either party.

Provision, maintenance and equipment of schools and other buildings

17.— ...

(2) In any case where an education authority are satisfied, whether upon representations made to them by any church or denominational body acting on behalf of the parents of children belonging to such church or body or otherwise, that a new school is required for the accommodation of children whose parents are resident within the area of the authority, regard being had to the religious belief of such parents, it shall be lawful for the education authority to provide a new school ...

Management of denominational schools

21.—(1) Any school transferred to an educational authority under section 16(1) of this Act shall be held, maintained and managed by the educational authority as a public school.

(2) Subject to subsections (2A) and (2B) below, in any such school the education authority shall have the sole power of regulating the curriculum and of appointing teachers:

(2A) A teacher appointed to any post on the staff of any such school by the education authority shall satisfy the Secretary of State as to qualification, and shall require to be approved as regards his religious belief and character by representatives of the church or denominational body in whose interest the school has been conducted;

(2B) Where the said representatives of a church or denominational body refuse to give the approval mentioned in subsection (2A) above they shall state their reasons for such refusal in writing.

(2C) Subject to the provisions of section 9 of this Act, the time set apart for religious instruction or observance in any such school shall not be less than that so set apart according to the use and wont of the former management of the school.

(3) For each school the education authority shall appoint as supervisor of religious instruction, without remuneration, a person approved as regards religious belief and character as aforesaid, and the supervisor so appointed shall report to the education authority as to the efficiency of the religious instruction given in such school, and shall be entitled to enter the school at all times set apart for religious instruction or observance.

(4) In every such school the education authority shall give facilities for the holding of religious examinations.

(5) Subsections (1) to (4) above, so far as applicable, shall have effect in relation to any school provided by an education authority under section 17(2) of this Act as they have

effect in relation to schools transferred to an education authority as mentioned in sub-section (1) above, subject to the modification that the time set apart for religious instruction in any school so provided shall be not less than that so set apart in schools in the same education area which have been transferred as mentioned in subsection (1) above.

(6) Any question which may arise as to the due fulfilment or observance of any provision or requirement of the foregoing provisions of this section shall be determined by the Secretary of State."

Compulsory education was introduced in 1872, but, in the belief that public education meant presbyterian education, the Roman Catholic community maintained its own voluntary schools independent of the state system. However, the financial burden of this system was a heavy one, and Roman Catholic schools were characterised by their inferior buildings and equipment and by their poorly-paid teachers. Partly in the belief that the inadequate education provided by these schools was contrary to the "national interest," the Education (Scotland) Act 1918 was passed to enable the schools to be brought within the state system and to be maintained at public expense, while retaining their distinctive religious flavour. Sections 16, 17 and 21 of the 1980 Act contain provisions almost identical in terms to those to be found in s.18 of the 1918 Act.

The transfer of schools under the 1918 Act appears to have taken place smoothly, and few difficulties were encountered. In January 2003, almost all denominational schools in Scotland were Roman Catholic, though there were also three Episcopalian, and one Jewish. Together they represented about 15 per cent of all publicly-funded schools. In addition to the state-funded faith schools, there were two privately funded Muslim schools. Although faith-based schools continue to be controversial, more than 90 per cent of Catholic parents make use of Catholic schools. On the other hand, a System Three opinion poll for the *Herald* newspaper in 2003 found that 48 per cent of those polled were in favour of abolishing faith based schools. But there is no political appetite for such a move, despite contentious and angrily denied claims that school segregation is divisive and contributes to sectariansim. In December 2002 the First Minister proposed the sharing of campus facilities (like sports grounds) by schools of different religious traditions, but there was concern on the part of the Catholic Church that this could affect the "ethos and identity" of their schools.

As pupil numbers have fallen dramatically in recent years and school closures have been necessitated in the interests of economy, extra pressure has been felt upon the denominational schools and litigation has ensued: *Deane v Lothian Regional Council*, 1986 S.L.T. 22; *Scottish Hierarchy of the Roman Catholic Church v Highland Regional Council*, 1987 S.L.T. 708. The latter case is a decision of the House of Lords about the closure of Roman Catholic schools at Arisaig and Mingarry by Highland Regional Council. Detailed procedures were introduced by the Education (Scotland) Act 1981, s.6, which inserted new ss.22A–22D of the Education (Scotland) Act 1980. The main purpose of these procedures—which according to Lord Mackay of Clashfern in the instant case—are not expressed with "conspicuous clarity"—was to require the closure of the schools to take place only after consultation and in some cases only with the consent of the Secretary of State for Scotland. In this case the application for judicial review failed because it could not be shown that the Secretary of State had failed to have regard to all the relevant circumstances and consequences of the proposals. In terms of the nature of the religious instruction that would apply after closure, it is reported by Lord Mackay that:

"In reaching his decision the Secretary of State noted particularly the concern of the Scottish Hierarchy of the Roman Catholic Church about the loss of separate denomina-tional schooling in the area. He also noted the undertaking given by the regional council in their consultative document of 26 October 1984 to maintain at least one member of (teaching) staff acceptable to Roman Catholic interests and at least one member of (teaching) staff acceptable to non-Roman Catholic interests, an undertaking reported to the meeting of the council on 3 July 1985. He further noted the council's intention that Roman Catholic pupils would continue to receive religious instruction in accordance with the specific arrangements they enjoy at present. The Secretary of State was also satisfied that closure would not place pupils at any educational disadvantage.

In reaching his decision on closure of Mingarry R.C. Primary School, the Secretary of State determined in terms of s. 22C (4) of the Education (Scotland) Act 1980, as amended, to impose the following conditions with regard to the religious instruction of pupils who, but for closure would have received their primary education at that school: (1) that Roman Catholic pupils should receive religious instruction separately from pupils of other denominations; (2) that such education should be provided by a person acceptable to the Scottish Hierarchy of the Roman Catholic Church; (3) that, in accordance with current arrangements, religious instruction be provided on four separate days per school week, with each period of instruction being of approximately one half hour's duration; (4) that if desired by the Scottish Hierarchy, a formal weekly service of approximately one hour's duration of religious observance for Roman Catholic pupils should be conducted separately from the service for pupils of other denominations." (pp. 711–712).

(3) Employment

Ahmad v Inner London Education Authority
[1976] I.C.R. 461; [1977] I.C.R. 490

Mr Ahmad was employed as a schoolteacher. He was a practising Muslim and insisted on taking time off work every Friday to attend a nearby mosque for prayers. The lunch break at school was between 12.30 and 1.30 pm, whereas the prayers were held between 1.00 and 2.00 pm, and Mr Ahmad did not return to the school until 2.15 or 2.20 pm. Following some protest from fellow employees, the ILEA eventually sought to deal with the issue by offering Mr Ahmad a new contract as a part-time teacher engaged for four and one-half days per week. His original contract was a full-time one. On receiving this offer, Mr Ahmad resigned, claiming that he had been unfairly dismissed. An industrial tribunal dismissed his claim and his appeals to both the Employment Appeal Tribunal and the Court of Appeal (by a majority) were unsuccessful.

PHILLIPS J. (E.A.T.): "The cause of the trouble lies in the employee's religious convictions: he is a devout Moslem ... The employee wished to attend the mosque on Fridays. This is, unless there is good reason to be excused, a matter of obligation for practising Moslems. It is said in the reasons given by the industrial tribunal that: 'The only acceptable excuses are to be a woman, a child, a traveller, a slave or to be sick.' At his previous schools, where there was no mosque within easy reach, it had sufficed for him to say his prayers in a room set aside for that purpose. When he was in the school where these matters came to a head there was a mosque nearer at hand.

The conflict arose from the fact that his absence to go to the mosque meant that he would not be available to take classes which otherwise it would have been his duty to take. So, on the one hand, the education authority required him to be present because he was a full-time primary teacher, and, on the other hand, he desired leave of absence so as to carry out his religious obligations. Those two requirements—his, to go to the mosque; the educational authority's, to have him present to teach—were irreconcilable. There was a long process of negotiation and discussion, but eventually the employee was informed that he could not be granted permission to be absent every Friday and, if he insisted, he must accept appointment as a four-and-half day temporary teacher ... He found that unacceptable and so he parted company with the employers...

There is no doubt at all that, as the industrial tribunal found, under his contract with the employers, the employee was duty bound to be in the school on Friday afternoons. It is equally clear that he was required to work full-time. Further, it found that under that contract, freely entered into, he had worked satisfactorily for something like five years, and that no mention had been made before he was employed of his requirement to attend a mosque. The industrial tribunal found, rightly, in our judgment, that there was no question of there having been any variation of the terms of his employment, though at various times, when employed in different schools, *ad hoc* arrangements had been made with individual headmasters, sometimes to pray in a room set aside for that purpose, on one or two occasions actually to attend a mosque. Accordingly, had the employee done what he wanted to do, that is, to absent himself for part of Friday afternoons, contrary to the wishes of his employers, he would have been acting in breach of his contract.

Reliance was placed by him on clause 9 of the staff code. That clause is set out in the tribunal's reasons and makes provision for absence of a full day's duration for religious observance on particular days. The tribunal found, in our judgment, correctly, that that did not extend to cover a case such as this, where a teacher desired to be absent every week, as here, on part of Friday. It is quite clear from the concluding words of that clause that the leave is to be 'restricted to days which are generally recognised in their religion as days when no work may be done.' No doubt what was in mind there was a day such as Good Friday, the Day of Atonement or something of that kind. Clearly it does not apply to a day every week during some part of which the member of that religion is required to attend his place of worship; so we are satisfied that the clause affords the employee no assistance.

The industrial tribunal concluded by looking at the matter quite generally and coming to the conclusion that in all the circumstances the employers had behaved quite reasonably in the course which they took in this difficult situation. They pointed out (and with this we would agree) that matters of this kind are better resolved by agreement at national level. The difficulties are obvious. We have now in this country persons of many different religions, and to accommodate them all in a workable time-table cannot be easy. Matters of this sort are far better dealt with by general agreement."

Greater protection against religious discrimination in employment is now provided by the Employment Equality (Religion or Belief) Regulations 2003 (SI 2003/1660). These Regulations are part of a radical overhaul of British discrimination law which has taken place as a result of the demands of EU law. The Regulations are modelled on the Sex Discrimination Act 1975 and the Race Relations Act 1976, though there is no new agency established to perform a role similar to that of the Equal Opportunity Commission or the Commission for Racial Equality. Similarly both sets of Regulations apply only in the employment field and do not apply to the provision of goods, services and facilities. On the other hand, however, the Regulations apply to a wide range of employment related matters and not just dismissal. Under the Religion or Belief Regulations, religion or belief means "any religion, religious belief, or similar philosophical belief" (reg.2). Discrimination is defined by reg.3 in the following terms:

"**3.**—(1) For the purposes of these Regulations, a person ('A') discriminates against another person ('B') if—

    (a) on grounds of religion or belief, A treats B less favourably than he treats or would treat other persons; or

    (b) A applies to B a provision, criterion or practice which he applies or would apply equally to persons not of the same religion or belief as B, but—

        (i) which puts or would put persons of the same religion or belief as B at a particular disadvantage when compared with other persons,

        (ii) which puts B at that disadvantage, and

        (iii) which A cannot show to be a proportionate means of achieving a legitimate aim.

    (2) The reference in paragraph (1)(a) to religion or belief does not include A's religion or belief.

    (3) A comparison of B's case with that of another person under paragraph (1) must be such that the relevant circumstances in the one case are the same, or not materially different, in the other."

Regulation 4 extends the definition of discrimination to include victimisation, and reg.5 to include harassment on the grounds of religion or belief. The most interesting of these provisions is reg.3(1)(b) which requires the employer to justify any practice which has the effect of discriminating against members of a particular religion. This will have implications for employers faced with employees who want time off or flexible working arrangements for reasons of religious worship or observance.

In terms of the conduct to which the Regulations apply, the key provision is reg.6 which applies to "applicants and employees" as follows:

"**6.**—(1) It is unlawful for an employer, in relation to employment by him at an establishment in Great Britain, to discriminate against a person—
   (a) in the arrangements he makes for the purpose of determining to whom he should offer employment;
   (b) in the terms on which he offers that person employment; or
   (c) by refusing to offer, or deliberately not offering, him employment.
(2) It is unlawful for an employer, in relation to a person whom he employs at an establishment in Great Britain, to discriminate against that person—
   (a) in the terms of employment which he affords him;
   (b) in the opportunities which he affords him for promotion, a transfer, training, or receiving any other benefit;
   (c) by refusing to afford him, or deliberately not affording him, any such opportunity; or
   (d) by dismissing him, or subjecting him to any other detriment.
(3) It is unlawful for an employer, in relation to employment by him at an establishment in Great Britain, to subject to harassment a person whom he employs or who has applied to him for employment.
(4) Paragraph (2) does not apply to benefits of any description if the employer is concerned with the provision (for payment or not) of benefits of that description to the public, or to a section of the public which includes the employee in question, unless—
   (a) that provision differs in a material respect from the provision of the benefits by the employer to his employees; or
   (b) the provision of the benefits to the employee in question is regulated by his contract of employment; or
   (c) the benefits relate to training.
(5) In paragraph (2)(d) reference to the dismissal of a person from employment includes reference—
   (a) to the termination of that person's employment by the expiration of any period (including a period expiring by reference to an event or circumstance), not being a termination immediately after which the employment is renewed on the same terms; and
   (b) to the termination of that person's employment by any act of his (including the giving of notice) in circumstances such that he is entitled to terminate it without notice by reason of the conduct of the employer."

There are, however, exceptions in reg.7 where "being of a particular religion or belief is a genuine and determining occupational requirement", or in other cases where "being of a particular religion or belief is a genuine occupational requirement for the job". The former applies "having regard to the nature of the job", and the latter where the employer has "an ethos based on religion and belief". Special provision is made for the application of the Regulations to a wide range of circumstances, such as contract workers, office-holders, the police, advocates, partnerships, and qualifications and training bodies (regs 8–21). There are also exceptions to protect national security, as well some forms of positive action (regs 24–25). Specific provision is made for Sikhs on construction sites (reg.26). Enforcement is principally by way of a complaint to an employment tribunal, though there are some matters over which the sheriff courts have jurisdiction (regs 27–34). For comment, see L.Vickers (2003) 32 I.L.J. 23 and 188.

VI. THE LIMITS OF TOLERANCE

In those and in other ways the state has by legislation taken steps to accommodate the non-Presbyterian minorities. There are, however, limits to the willingness of the state to accommodate. These arise particularly in the field of the criminal law.

R. v Senior
[1899] 1 Q.B. 283

The Prevention of Cruelty to Children Act 1894 provided by section 1 that if any person with custody, charge, or care of any child wilfully neglected the child in a manner likely to cause injury to the child's health, that person was guilty of a misdemeanour. In this case the prisoner was convicted of the manslaughter of his infant child for deliberately refusing to call in medical aid which would probably have saved the child's life. The prisoner was a member of a sect called the Peculiar People, who objected on religious grounds to medical treatment.

> LORD RUSSELL C.J.: "Neglect is the want of reasonable care—that is, the omission of such steps as a reasonable parent would take, such as are usually taken in the ordinary experience of mankind—that is, in such a case as the present, provided the parent had such means as would enable him to take the necessary steps. I agree with the statement in the summing-up, that the standard of neglect varied as time went on, and that many things might be legitimately looked upon as evidence of neglect in one generation, which would not have been thought so in a preceding generation, and that regard must be had to the habits and thoughts of the time. At the present day, when medical aid is within the reach of the humblest and poorest members of the community, it cannot reasonably be suggested that the omission to provide medical aid for a dying child does not amount to neglect. Mr Sutton contended that because the prisoner was proved to be an affectionate parent, and was willing to do all things for the benefit of his child, except the one thing which was necessary in the present case, he ought not to be found guilty of the offence of manslaughter, on the ground that he abstained from providing medical aid for his child in consequence of his peculiar views in the matter; but we cannot shut our eyes to the danger which might arise if we were to accede to that argument, for where is the line to be drawn? In the present case the prisoner is shewn to have had an objection to the use of medicine; but other cases might arise, such, for instance, as the case of a child with a broken thigh, where a surgical operation was necessary, which had to be performed with the aid of an anaesthetic; could the father refuse to allow the anaesthetic to be administered? Or take the case of a child that was in danger of suffocation, so that the operation of tracheotomy was necessary in order to save its life, and an anaesthetic was required to be administered. ...
>   I am of opinion that ... the conviction ought to be affirmed."
>
> GRANTHAM J.: "Taking the last of the two words, 'wilfully neglects,' first, was the omission of what was left undone by the prisoner neglect? The jury say it was. Then was what was left undone wilfully left undone—that is, was the neglect to provide medical aid the wilful act of the prisoner? Mr Sutton can only rely upon the fact that the prisoner was one of the sect called the 'Peculiar People'; but that fact of itself goes to shew that what he omitted he left undone with intent—that is, wilfully. Can it be said that this is not wilful neglect? I am clearly of the opinion that the prisoner's conduct amounted to wilful neglect, and that the summing-up of the learned judge was right."

The Scottish provisions corresponding to s.1 of the 1894 Act are to be found in the Children and Young Persons (Scotland) Act 1937, s.12. *Senior* was cited with apparent approval in *Clark v HM Advocate*, 1968 J.C. 53. The case is particularly relevant to the modern practice of Jehovah's Witnesses to refuse blood transfusions for themselves and their children. Following

Senior, the refusal to consent would almost certainly be an offence. But this will be of no assistance to the child who may die if denied treatment. Where the child's illness is known to the local authority, it may be possible for the local authority to intervene under the Children (Scotland) Act 1995. This empowers a child protection order to be made on application by the local authority to the sheriff where a child is suffering significant harm (s.57). Where an order is made, the local authority must do what is necessary to safeguard and promote the welfare of the child (s.15). Where, however, the doctor proceeds with treatment contrary to the wishes of the parent in an emergency, it seems highly unlikely that he or she would be prosecuted for assault or that an action for damages against him or her would succeed. Although it may be true that parental consent is normally necessary for an operation on a child (see *Whitehall v Whitehall*, 1958 S.C. 252), it would be difficult to resist the conclusion in a civil action that the doctor's assault was justified.

R. v John
[1974] 1 W.L.R. 624

The appellant refused to provide a specimen of blood when required to do so under the Road Safety Act 1967, s.3(3), because as a Mesmerist he considered this to be contrary to his religion. Section 3 provided that it was an offence to fail to provide a specimen without reasonable excuse. Did the appellant's religious beliefs provide him with a reasonable excuse for failing to provide the specimen?

ROSKILL L.J.: "It is right to say of course that any state of affairs which involve persons committing criminal offences because of beliefs sincerely held by them, is, to put it at its lowest, highly distasteful for any court. Ever since the early or middle part of the 18th century, the courts of this country have prided themselves on the liberality of their approach to matters of conscience. That attitude has continued for the last 200 years at least. Accordingly, any argument such as that to which this court has listened on behalf of the appellant is entitled to and must receive respect. For a man to be punished for an offence which is committed by reason only of his adherence to his own religion or belief can only be justified if the court is satisfied that the clear intention of the statute creating the offence was in the interests of the community as a whole to override the privileges otherwise attaching to freedom of conscience and belief, which it must always be the duty of the courts to protect and defend. There are examples mentioned in argument where this has happened. One is the National Service legislation before, during and after the war. Persons holding sincere objection to military service were nonetheless compelled to serve in one or other of various spheres of activity subject to due safeguards. Another is the recent case in the Divisional Court, *Hunter v Mann* [1974] 2 W.L.R. 742, where a doctor whose professional etiquette precluded him from giving certain information which the statute required him to give was prosecuted and fined. Other examples can be found in the law of evidence. There is no privilege attaching to the confessional. There is no privilege attaching to communications between doctor and patient. In these matters Parliament and the courts have found it necessary, in the interests of the community as a whole, to override the personal right of the individual to maintain his own belief. The position is by no means uncommon.

It is against that background that one turns to consider the position under the road traffic legislation. Anyone recollecting the introduction of these provisions in 1967 will recall that they were bitterly opposed, on the ground that they restricted individual liberty. They rendered persons liable to arrest on the road if a breath test proved to be positive. That was an infringement of personal liberty, albeit only for a limited period, by enabling the alleged offender to be taken to a police station. Nonetheless Parliament found it necessary, because of the difficulty of enforcing the former law in relation to driving when ability to drive was allegedly impaired through drink or drugs, to introduce the code which first found its place on the statute book in 1967. It was in many respects a drastic code which infringed the personal liberty of individuals. But Parliament found it necessary to introduce that code in the interests of the public as a whole, to prevent the public as a whole being victimised by those who were persistently driving after consuming an excessive quantity of alcohol but who all too often were not brought to justice because of the difficulty of bringing home a charge in the courts. The very introduction of the limit of 80 milligrammes of alcohol in 100 millilitres of blood was itself an infringement of individual rights.

It is therefore against the background of a statute which by its very terms does restrict individual rights that one has to construe the crucial words that are now in section 9 of the Act of 1972 'without reasonable excuse.' It is suggested that any excuse will do, if based upon belief sincerely held. But that, with great respect to the skill with which the argument has been advanced, involves making the person seeking to set up that excuse as reasonable being the judge in his own cause. He becomes entitled to say 'Because I believe a certain thing, that belief of my own, personal to myself, affords me a reasonable excuse for not complying with what other people would have to comply with.' In other words the person concerned is really seeking to say not 'I cannot,' but 'I ought not.'

In the view of this court, that is not well founded. As I said a few moments ago, the Road Traffic Act 1972 provides rules for the safety of the public. It provides rules in order to protect the public from certain classes of users of the road. The securing of that protection involves restriction on the liberty of individuals.

It is against that background that one returns to consider the language used in *R. v Lennard* [1973] 1 W.L.R. 483 It may be—and we say this with the utmost respect to Lawton and Scarman L.JJ.—that the language used, if construed too strictly, might involve an over-rigid approach to the language of the section. Certainly, in the view of this court and in the light of what was said by Scarman L.J. in *R. v Reid (Philip)* [1973] 1 W.L.R. 1283, 1289, the court did not intend to lay down something rigid and exhaustive. In truth what the court was saying was that for an excuse to be capable of being a reasonable excuse, it must be an excuse which is related to the capacity of the person concerned to supply a sample, be it of urine or be it of blood. It is not related to his belief whether or not he ought, because of his personal faith or belief, to be required to supply a sample of urine or blood. There is, in the view of this court, this very marked difference between the two positions. One depends on whether or not, for example, he is in a mental or physical condition which enables him physically to give the sample. It may be in some cases that he will not be in that condition. Such facts, if proved, may at least be capable of affording a reasonable excuse for not giving the sample. But it is not enough for someone to come along and say 'True others are obliged to comply with the law, but my personal faith or belief frees me from the obligations which rest upon others.'

That, with all respect to the appellant and to the sincerity of his beliefs, is what he is seeking to say in this court. This court must reject that argument. This conclusion does involve to some extent a restriction on the liberty of the individual, but it is a consequence that flows from what Parliament found necessary when these provisions were first introduced in 1967 for the benefit of the public as a whole."

Both *Senior* and *John* show clearly that religious belief will not normally be a good defence to a criminal charge. It is, of course open to Parliament to provide otherwise. One example of this is the Road Traffic Act 1988, s.12, which provides that the duty to wear a helmet does not apply to followers of the Sikh religion. However, that exception applies to an offence of little substance (albeit that the duty is controversial) which is designed mainly for the protection of the motor cyclist rather than his or her victim. If it were otherwise any such exemption would be extremely difficult to justify. And it is to be noted that just as the accused may not plead his or her own religious belief as a defence, nor may he or she plead the religious belief of his or her victim which may have led to more serious injury of the victim than might otherwise have been sustained. This is illustrated by *R. v Blaue* [1975] 1 W.L.R. 1411, where the accused was convicted of the manslaughter of a girl whom he had attacked with a knife and who had died after refusing a blood transfusion. She was a Jehovah's Witness. Blaue unsuccessfully appealed against his conviction arguing that unreasonable behaviour by the victim broke the chain of causation. In dismissing the appeal, Lawton L.J. said:

"The physical cause of death in this case was the bleeding into the pleural cavity arising from the penetration of the lung. This had not been brought about by any decision made by the deceased but by the stab wound.

Mr Comyn [for the defendant] tried to overcome this line of reasoning by submitting that the jury should have been directed that if they thought the deceased's decision not to have a blood transfusion was an unreasonable one, then the chain of causation would have been broken. At once the question arises—reasonable by whose standards? Those of Jehovah's Witnesses? Humanists? Roman Catholics? Protestants of Anglo-Saxon descent? The man on the Clapham omnibus? But he might well be an admirer of Eleazar who suffered death rather than eat the flesh of swine (2 Maccabees, ch.6, vv. 18–31) or of Sir Thomas More who, unlike nearly all his contemporaries, was unwilling to accept Henry VIII as Head of the Church of England. Those brought up in the Hebraic and Christian traditions would probably be reluctant to accept that these martyrs caused their own deaths.

As was pointed out to Mr Comyn in the course of argument, two cases, each raising the same issue of reasonableness because of religious beliefs, could produce different verdicts depending on where the cases were tried. It has long been the policy of the law that those who use violence on other people must take their victims as they find them. This in our judgment means the whole man, not just the physical man. It does not lie in the mouth of the assailant to say that his victim's religious beliefs which inhibited him from accepting certain kinds of treatment were unreasonable."

VII. CONCLUSION

The position relating to religious freedom has changed a great deal in recent years. The main points to emerge is that the Church of Scotland retains a privileged legal status, particularly in terms of the judicial supervision of its affairs. In practice this may be of greater symbolic than practical significance. But in the context of religion in particular, symbols are important. Secondly, we see the retreat of the coercive power of the state in the sense of imposing duties on individuals to participate in religious observance. Nevertheless, the residue of earlier times is still to be found, as the *Wingrove* case reminds us, while the duty to provide religious education in schools seems an unwarranted intrusion by the state into an area of personal choice rather than public obligation. Thirdly, there is growing concern to respect religious difference, with the energies of the state being devoted less to making people observe religion than to compel people to respect the religious freedom of others. Although the point is not to be exaggerated, the role of the state is thus changing. The Employment Equality (Religion or Belief) Regulations 2003 are a good example of this. So too is the following provision of the Criminal Justice (Scotland) Act 2003.

Criminal Justice (Scotland) Act 2003

"Offences aggravated by religious prejudice
    74.—(1) This section applies where it is—
      (a) libelled in an indictment; or
      (b) specified in a complaint,
    and, in either case, proved that an offence has been aggravated by religious prejudice.
    (2) For the purposes of this section, an offence is aggravated by religious prejudice if—
      (a) at the time of committing the offence or immediately before or after doing so, the

offender evinces towards the victim (if any) of the offence malice and ill-will based on the victim's membership (or presumed membership) of a religious group, or of a social or cultural group with a perceived religious affiliation; or

    (b) the offence is motivated (wholly or partly) by malice and ill-will towards members of a religious group, or of a social or cultural group with a perceived religious affiliation, based on their membership of that group.

(3) Where this section applies, the court must take the aggravation into account in determining the appropriate sentence.

(4) Where the sentence in respect of the offence is different from that which the court would have imposed had the offence not been aggravated by religious prejudice, the court must state the extent of and the reasons for that difference.

(5) For the purposes of this section, evidence from a single source is sufficient to prove that an offence is aggravated by religious prejudice.

(6) In subsection (2)(a)—

    'membership' in relation to a group includes association with members of that group; and

    'presumed' means presumed by the offender.

(7) In this section, 'religious group' means a group of persons defined by reference to their—

    (a) religious belief or lack of religious belief;

    (b) membership of or adherence to a church or religious organisation;

    (c) support for the culture and traditions of a church or religious organisation; or

    (d) participation in activities associated with such a culture or such traditions.''

These provisions came into force on June 27, 2003. By February 29, 2004, the police had reported 262 incidents of religious hatred to the Crown Office: *Scotland on Sunday*, April 4, 2004. It is not, however, yet an offence to incite religious hatred, and proposals to introduce such an offence in England and Wales in 2001 were never implemented. Quite whether such a law could be enforced in Scotland is open to question. The bigoted conduct of thousands of spectators at some football matches every week in Scotland is enough to indicate the scale of the challenge that would be presented to the police were such an offence to be introduced. It is also a depressing reminder of the need for such legislation.

Chapter 8

FREEDOM OF EXPRESSION

I. INTRODUCTION

The recognition of freedom of expression is fundamental to any society which lays claim to being democratic. As J. S. Mill observed: "The time ... is gone by, when any defence would be necessary of the 'liberty of the press' as one of the securities against corrupt or tyrannical government" (*On Liberty*, Ch. 2). In a similar vein, the United States Supreme Court remarked in *Stromberg v California*, 283 U.S. 359 (1931):

"The maintenance of the opportunity for free political discussion to the end that government may be responsive to the will of the people and that changes may be obtained by lawful means, an opportunity essential to the security of the Republic, is a fundamental principle of our constitutional system." (at 369).

These remarks apply with equal force to our own constitutional system, notwithstanding the substantial differences between it and the American constitution. Indeed in *R. v Home Secretary Ex p. Simms* [1999] 3 All E.R. 400, Lord Slynn said that: "freedom of speech is the lifeblood of democracy. The free flow of information and ideas informs political debate. It is a safety valve: people are more ready to accept decisions that go against them if they can in principle seek to influence them. It acts as a brake on the abuse of power by public officials. It facilitates the exposure of errors in the governance and administration of justice of the country." More recently, Lord Steyn has said that the ECHR "involved the idea that peaceful political debate about constitutional and governmental structures should be encouraged. Political free speech, criticising our existing form of government, was regarded as central to the development of European liberal democracies": *R. (Rusbridger) v Attorney General* [2004] 1 A.C. 309.

Yet, while freedom of expression is thus essential for the circulation of political ideas and the effective accountability of government, this is not the only function it serves. As was also pointed out by Lord Steyn in the *Simms* case, freedom of expression is "intrinsically important: it is valued for its own sake', as well as being 'instrumentally important". So far as the latter is concerned, it was said that, in addition to its contribution to democracy, freedom of expression promotes the "self fulfilment of individuals in society". Moreover, "in the famous words of Mr. Justice Holmes (echoing John Stuart Mill), 'the best test of truth is the power of the thought to get itself accepted in the competition of the market.': *Abrams v United States*, 250 U.S. 616, at 630 (1919), per Holmes J". Some of these wider considerations are addressed in the following extract.

Report of the Committee on Obscenity and Film Censorship
(Chairman: Bernard Williams) Cmnd. 7772 (1979)

"5.15. The freedom of expression is not for [J.S. Mill] just one more example of freedom from coercion but is a very special and fundamental form of freedom. It is clear that many of our witnesses share this view, some of them for Mill's own reasons, and we think it important to give those reasons some attention. Some of Mill's reasons we believe to be still very relevant today. Some of his arguments, however, were always flimsy and are yet more so in modern conditions. His basic thought was that human beings have no infallible source of knowledge about human nature or how human affairs may develop, and do not know in advance what arrangements or forms of life may make people happy or enable them to be, as Mill impassionately wanted them to be, original, tolerant and uncowed individuals. Since we do not know in advance, we do not know what new proposals, ideas or forms of expression may contribute to the development of man and society.

5.16. From this Mill drew the conclusion that we have no basis for suppressing or censoring any of them. He did so, in particular, because he thought (and many others have shared this view) that the only way the truth could emerge was by a form of natural selection in a 'free market' of ideas: if all ideas were allowed expression, good ideas would multiply, bad ideas would die out. This conception, if sound, would have very powerful consequences. It is important, for instance, that it would tell almost as much against restricting a publication as against suppressing it, since any constraint on a work's availability will reduce the chance of its message being heard. However, we do not find Mill's conception entirely convincing...

5.19. Even in the area of ideas, the notion of a 'free market' has to be regarded with some scepticism, and the faith in *laissez-faire* shown by the nineteenth century and earlier does not altogether meet modern conditions. If everyone talks at once, truth will not prevail, since no one can be heard and nothing will prevail: and falsehood indeed may prevail, if powerful agencies can gain an undue hold on the market. Even in natural science, which Mill regarded as the paradigm, he neglected the importance of scientific institutions and the filter against cranks which is operated, and necessarily operated, by expert opinion, excluding from serious consideration what it sees as incompetence. Against the principle that truth is strong and (given the chance) will prevail, must be set Gresham's Law, that bad money drives out good, which has some application in matters of culture and which predicts that it will not necessarily be the most interesting ideas or the most valuable works of art that survive in competition—above all, in commercial competition.

5.20. Thus we cannot entirely agree that 'the Truth certainly would do well enough if she were left to fend for herself'; she may need more of a chance than that. This point can surely justify intervention. Intervention, however, need not be and should not be negative intervention: it can take the form of such things as state subventions for the arts, or policies of refusing to design television programmes solely on the basis of ratings, or subsidising institutions of critical enquiry. This is not just a point about the rights of minorities; it involves Mill's own basic idea (though differently applied) that progress involves a belief or a value being first a minority belief or value, which must be preserved if it is ever to reach further.

5.21. The fact that the market-place model is an inadequate basis for the value of free expression does not mean that one replaces the market with monopoly, and institutes a censorship by the State or by worthy citizens. There is certainly no reason to think that that would do better in the detection of error or the advance of enlightenment. The more basic idea, to which Mill attached the market-place model, remains a correct and profound idea: that we do not know in advance what social, moral or intellectual developments will turn out to be possible, necessary or desirable for human beings and for their future, and free expression, intellectual and artistic—something which may need to be fostered and protected as well as merely permitted—is essential to human development, as a process which does not merely happen (in some form or another, it will happen anyway), but so far as possible is rationally understood. It is essential to it, moreover, not just as a means to it, but as part of it. Since human beings are not just subject to their history but aspire to be conscious of it, the development of human individuals, of society and of humanity in general, is a process itself properly constituted in part by free expression and the exchange of human communication.

5.22. We realise that some may disagree with this basic idea because they think that fundamental human moral truths have been laid down unchangeably for all time, for instance in religious terms. Mill, certainly, thought that there was no such revealed truth, and his arguments for freedom of expression and those of people who think like him are to that extent an expression of religious scepticism. We would suggest, however, that even those who believe that there are revealed truths of morality and religion should attend very anxiously to the argument for freedom of expression. First, the barest facts of cultural history show that any set of supposed revealed truths which have survived have received constantly new applications and interpretations, to which new moral perceptions have contributed. Second, every believer in some set of moral certainties has to share the world with other believers in some different set of moral certainties. If they share the same society, at least, and even if they could come to do so, they have some common interest in not accepting principles which would allow someone else's certainty to persecute their own. Third, many religious believers in moral certainties also believe that human beings have been created not just to obey or mirror those certainties, but freely to live by them, and that institutions of free expression can be in fact a more developed representation of the religious consciousness itself than authoritarian institutions. We have thus not been surprised, though we have been impressed, by the constructive concern for freedom of expression which has been shown by many of the submissions we have received from religious bodies, disturbed though most of them have been by the present situation.

5.23. Because we believe that the value of the freedom of expression is connected with the open future of human development, we do find a difficulty with certain proposals for obscenity law we have received, which both admit the fact of changing standards, and also invoke present standards to justify the actual suppression of certain publications. The Nationwide Festival of Light and others, following a formulation of Lord Longford's Committee, have recommended the suppression of what grossly affronts 'contemporary standards of decency or humanity accepted by the public at large.' But while some such provision might ground, as we shall ourselves suggest, a *restriction* of some material, to prevent its offending the public at large, the position of trying to justify suppression—which, if successful, is permanent—on the basis of what are acknowledged to be contemporary standards, seems to us to make, more than is justified, present views the determinant of the future."

But although the freedom of expression is recognised and cherished in most civilised societies, this will almost invariably be subject to exceptions. In the first place, it is normal to justify restrictions to protect individuals from harm. A question of some importance is, for whose benefit should the the freedom be restricted: other people who will be affected, or the citizen who may be harmed by his or her own exercise of the freedom? According to the Williams Committee:

"5.26. The presumption in favour of freedom of expression is strong, but it is a presumption, and it can be overruled by considerations of harms which the speech or publication in question may cause. The first question that arises is, harms to whom? ... In particular, in the case of publications, there is the question whether supposed harm to consumers—i.e. those who voluntarily choose to read the material—is, just in itself, to count. Mill and many others who advance what we have called the 'harm condition' for coercing behaviour would say that it did not. They say this because they accept the principle that, if one is dealing with adult persons, it is best to assume that each person is the best judge of whether he or she is being harmed. This additional principle makes an important difference. The harm condition by itself would not necessarily produce very liberal results. One might agree that laws should only suppress what does harm but think that disgusting books should be suppressed by law because their readers (though those readers would not themselves agree) are in fact harmed by them. With this other principle added, however, such paternalist laws would be ruled out."

The harm conditions would justify a number of controls, and there are in fact a number of restraints on freedom of expression in Scots Law on which—with one possible exception—the incorporation of Convention rights has had curiously little impact. Indeed it is not to be overlooked that although art.10(1) of the ECHR provides protection for the right to freedom of expression, it does so with a wide range of permitted restraints in art.10(2). In this chapter we look at three broad categories of control. The first is what is referred to as censorship in the sense that particular forms of expression may be restrained or restricted. This was a problem with the theatre in the past but is now one that arises in the context of the cinema and broadcasting. But we should not underestimate the extent to which commercial ownership of the press creates other forms of censorship which are outside the scope of the ECHR. The second category of control that we consider in this chapter is what is referred to as prohibited speech. This is rather self explanatory and reflects the fact that certain speech is forbidden in order to protect what is perceived to be a greater public interest. The examples discussed to illustrate this are pornographic speech (obscene publications), speech calculated to undermine the integrity of the judicial system and the right to a fair trial (contempt of court), and speech which involves the publication of confidential information relating to national security (official secrets). These are longstanding restraints on freedom of expression, with only the application of the law relating to contempt of court proving pervious to the demands of art.10. The third category of control examined here is what we refer to as restricted speech. This category does not focus so much on what is being said as on who says it, when it is said and under what conditions it is said. Although a number of examples could be given to illustrate these points, the focus is mainly on various forms of control that apply to political speech. We conclude with a brief account of private law remedies and the role of the interim interdict on freedom of expression following pioneering work by Professor Munro.

II. Censorship

(1) The Theatre

The Theatres Act 1846 provided that every new play or any new part of a play to be acted in any theatre in Great Britain was to be sent to the Lord Chamberlain who had power to disallow the presentation of the play or any part thereof (s.12). The Lord Chamberlain could forbid the presentation of a play or part thereof if he was of the "opinion that it is fitting for the Pre-servation of good Manners, Decorum, or of the public Peace so to do." There is evidence that the Lord Chamberlain sometimes used this power to exercise a political censorship, disallowing, for example, plays critical of the leadership of the USA. As was pointed out in *R. (BBC) v Pro-Life Alliance* [2004] 1 A.C. 185, however, it "now needs an effort of memory or imagination to call to mind the strict statutory censorship of theatres which continued until its final abolition by the Theatres Act 1968" (Lord Walker of Gestingthorpe).

In 1967 a Joint Committee on Censorship of the Theatre (H.C. 503, 1967) recommended that censorship of plays should cease and that there should be freedom of speech in the theatre, subject to overriding requirements of the criminal law. The Joint Committee seemed especially concerned that political censorship should be ended, on the ground that the existence of such powers was inappropriate in a modern democratic society. The position is now governed by the Theatres Act 1968, s.1 of which repeals the Theatres Act 1846. In abolishing pre-censorship, the 1968 Act did not, however, give *carte-blanche* to directors to do as they please. A number of statutory offences were introduced in order to prevent the presentation of obscene performances (s.2); to prevent the incitement of racial hatred by means of a public performance (s.5, now repealed and substituted by s.20, Public Order Act 1986); and to prevent the provocation of a breach of the peace by means of a public performance (s.6). A number of exceptions to these restraints are contained in s.7. Those responsible for theatrical production may also be subjected to criminal liability on several grounds discussed in the following sections of this chapter. These include the offence of public indecency as expressed in *Webster v Dominick*, 2003 S.L.T. 975. Dunoon.

(2) The Cinema

The Cinemas Act 1985

"Licence required for exhibitions
1.—(1) Subject to sections 5 to 8 below, no premises shall be used for a film exhibition unless they are licensed for the purpose under this section.
(2) A licensing authority may grant a licence under this section to such a person as they think fit to use any premises specified in the licence for the purpose of film exhibitions on such terms and conditions and subject to such restrictions as, subject to regulations under section 4 below, they may determine.
(3) Without prejudice to the generality of subsection (2) above, it shall be the duty of a licensing authority, in granting a licence under this section as respects any premises,—
  (a) to impose conditions or restrictions prohibiting the admission of children to film exhibitions involving the showing of works designated, by the authority or by such other body as may be specified in the licence, as works unsuitable for children; and
  (b) to consider what (if any) conditions or restrictions should be imposed as to the admission of children to other film exhibitions involving the showing of works designated, by the authority or by such other body as may be specified in the licence, as works of such other description as may be so specified.

Regulations by Secretary of State
4.—(1) Subject to sections 5 and 6 below, no film exhibition shall be given unless regulations made by the Secretary of State under this section are complied with.
(2) The matters for which provision may be made by regulations under this section are—
  (a) safety in connection with the giving of film exhibitions (including the keeping and handling, in premises where other entertainments are being given or meetings held, of cinematograph film used or to be used for the purposes of film exhibitions or other articles or equipment so used or to be used);
  (b) the health and welfare of children in relation to attendance at film exhibitions.
(3) Regulations under this section shall be made by statutory instrument which shall be subject to annulment in pursuance of a resolution of either House of Parliament.

Appeals against decisions of licensing authority
16.—(1) Any person aggrieved—
  (a) by the refusal or revocation of a licence,
  (b) by any terms, conditions or restrictions on or subject to which a licence is granted, or
  (c) by the refusal of a renewal or transfer of a licence,
may appeal to the Crown court or, in Scotland, to the sheriff."

The Cinemas Act 1985 is merely a consolidating measure. The law on film censorship has its origins in the Cinematograph Act 1909. The crucial provisions were ss.1 and 2 which corresponded with ss.1 (1) and 1 (2) of the 1985 Act. Sections 1 (3), 4 and 16 have their origins in the Cinematograph Act 1952. In commenting on these provisions, the Williams Committee said: "Parliament has never legislated for the censorship of films: it is purely a matter of accident that the film censorship system was able to find some statutory support when it first struggled into existence just before the First World War" (Williams, above, para.3.1)). Thus, as the historical account in App.2 of the Williams Report demonstrates, the exclusive purpose of the 1909 Act was to protect the public from the risk of fire and there is no evidence that the government anticipated that it might be used for censorship. However, it was soon realised that s.2 contained wide terms which enabled authorities to impose conditions other than those relating to public safety. In *LCC v Bermondsey Bioscope Co Ltd* [1911] 1 K.B. 445 a prohibition on Sunday opening of cinemas was upheld, with Alverstone L.C.J. adding the crucially important point that s.2 "is intended to confer on the [local authority] a discretion as to the conditions which they will impose, so long as these conditions are not unreasonable." It was feared that this dictum would permit local authorities to censor films. So, faced with the prospect of different local authorities adopting different approaches to the showing of films, which would thereby frustrate any system of national film distribution, the film industry established the British Board of Film Censors. The purpose of the board was to approve films before they were released, in the hope that the certificates issued by the board would be accepted by the licensing authorities throughout the country. In practice this is what happened, though it is important to note that licensing authorities retain the right not to show a film which has a BBFC certificate; or to show a film which has been denied such a certificate; or to vary the age restriction attached by the board to a film. The following case traces the development of the BBFC and reviews the practice relating to the issuing of certificates by it. The case is also important for highlighting the scope for judicial supervision of licensing authority decisions.

Classic Cinema Ltd v Motherwell DC
1977 S.L.T. (Sh. Ct.) 69

The licensing authority granted a licence under s.2 of the 1909 Act on the condition that no 'X' films would be shown on Sundays. The licensee successfully contested this condition, though another condition imposed by the authority was upheld.

THE SHERIFF PRINCIPAL (R. REID, Q.C.): "Section 6 (1)(b) and (5) of the Cinematograph Act 1952 provides that: 'Any person aggrieved . . . by any terms, conditions and restrictions on or subject to which such a license or consent is granted, may appeal to the sheriff.' It will be seen that the statute gives no indication of the approach to be adopted or the test to be applied by the sheriff in disposing of the appeal . . . I do not think that licensing decisions should have the privileged status accorded to bye-laws, but should be treated in much the same way as decisions relating to licences granted under the Gaming Act 1968. This approach requires that weight should be given to the decisions of the local authority, particularly in matters in which it represents local opinion, so that a judge should only differ on appeal when, having regard to the whole of the material before him, he is satisfied that the local authority's decision cannot be supported . . .

There was evidence in the appeal to the effect that the wide discretion granted to local authorities by section 2(1) of the 1909 Act had originally resulted in differences of opinion between local authorities as to films which might be exhibited in their areas. These differences caused serious difficulty to exhibitors and a typical British compromise came into being to avoid the worse results of the wide discretion Parliament had conferred. The film industry set up the British Board of Film Censors with the function of classifying films for the purpose of assisting local authorities to carry out their duties under the Act. Local authorities were not, of course, entitled to delegate their powers to the British Board of Film Censors or bind themselves to follow blindly the rulings of the Board, but classification by the Board became accepted and enabled a substantial measure of uniformity to be introduced into the licensing of films for public exhibition. Films were originally classified as suitable for universal exhibition ('U') or suitable for exhibition to adults only ('A'). In England, local authorities commonly imposed a condition that children could not attend an

'A' film unless accompanied by an adult. According to the evidence, in Scotland the general practice was to publicise the 'A' classification and to leave it to their parents to decide whether or not their children should see the film. As scenes of sex and violence became more common in films, it was felt that the classification was inadequate, and an 'AA' classification was introduced to designate films unsuitable for viewing by children under 14, and an 'X' classification to designate films unsuitable for viewing by persons under 18. When the new classifications were introduced the question arose between exhibitors and local authorities whether the latter should treat the 'AA' classification as advisory only and permit children under the age of 14, if accompanied by a responsible adult, to view such films, or whether children under 14 should be excluded from films so classified. In an attempt to resolve differences of approach the Cinematograph Exhibitors' Association attempted to agree a model licence with local authorities. The licence could not bind local authorities, but was a further attempt to introduce a measure of uniformity into film licensing. In the first draft of the model licence there were alternative clauses embodying both interpreations of the condition appropriate to the 'AA' classification. Finally, the association and local authorities agreed a condition which permitted children to see such films if accompanied by a responsible adult. The local authority in the present case have taken the other view. This refusal to follow the terms of the model licence, and the fact that the 'A' classification has been treated in Scotland as an advisory classification, provide the slender grounds on which the decision of a local authority embodied in condition 5 has been challenged.

The witness for the local authority explained that its licensing committee thought that 'AA' films were unsuitable viewing for children under 14 and that to permit children to see such films if accompanied by their parents, was misleading to parents in that it raised expectations that these films were suitable for viewing by children and put parents in a difficult position when scenes unsuitable for children were depicted. In these circumstances, the local authority preferred clear-cut prohibition. It appears to me that this is just the kind of decisions which a local authority is entitled to take. It is in no way unreasonable and I do not think I am entitled to interfere with it.

I turn to condition 11. This condition provides 'No "X" certificate films shall be shown on Sundays.' The local authority's witness explained that the condition had been imposed for moral reasons because members of the licensing committee considered that too many "X" films were being shown, because it was distasteful to many members of the community that such films should be shown on Sundays. There was also a fear that, owing to the lack of other entertainment on Sundays, there would be an unusually strong temptation for persons under 18 to seek admission to the cinema on Sunday evenings and there was, at the same time, a desire to provide wholesome entertainment for young persons on Sunday evenings. If matters had rested there, I would have felt it as difficult to interfere as in the case of condition 5, but there was abundant and unchallenged evidence of matters which did not appear to have been taken into consideration by the local authority which put a very different complexion on the matter. In the first place, there was evidence that young people rarely attended cinemas on Sunday even when 'U' or 'A' films were exhibited. A typical Sunday evening audience, according to the evidence, consisted of young adults and older single people, particularly those who lived alone and felt a need to seek entertainment on Sunday evenings. This audience will not come to see 'U' and 'A' films unless they are new showings of good quality. Second, and more important, the evidence showed that it was, in practice, impossible to obtain a sufficient number of 'U' and 'A' films with reasonable power to draw audiences for viewing on Sunday evenings. It appears that the number of 'X' films made each year exceeds the total of films in all other classifications. Moreover, such non-'X' films as are made are not freely available. Some of the cinema chains have preferential rights to the showing of films produced by particular film companies, and this inevitably restricts exhibitors in their choice of new films. There are other factors which restrict choice in the system adopted for distribution of films. All films are distributed through film distributors under contracts providing for payment to the distributor of a proportion of the takings at the box office. Because the distributor has an interest in the size of an audience he is concerned to see that films are shown which will attract the largest audiences. Copies of films are fairly expensive—they were said to cost about £600 each—and the distributor is also naturally anxious to maximise his return on the capital invested in the copy of a film. For these reasons, the choice of films offered by distributors to exhibitors is restricted. Moreover, because the distributor bears part of the cost of transporting films between distribution centres and cinemas, it is generally difficult to book a film for a one-day showing. Distributors much prefer bookings for three to seven days. The exhibitor's booking manager is not entirely without influence. There is some expertise in choosing films which will prove attractive in particular cinemas, but his choice is restricted by these various factors. Further, commercial considerations may restrict drastically the showing of 'U' and 'A' films which are offered by the distributor. Any 'U' and 'A' films more than five years old will probably have been shown on television and have no ability to attract an audience if screened in a cinema ... On this evidence I have come to accept the conclusion of a number of witnesses who gave evidence for the appellants that the consequence of allowing condition 11 to remain in force would be that the cinema would require to close on many Sundays, either because no non-'X' film was available or because such non-'X' films as were available were quite unprofitable to show ... The members of the licensing committee ... could not reasonably have imposed this condition. It is, in my view, so onerous that it comes near to endangering the continuance of the licensed activity. For this reason, I have decided that it should be deleted from the license."

The most detailed review of film censorship in modern times is to be found in the Williams Report, above. Some of those who submitted evidence to the Williams Committee argued that pre-censorship of films should be abolished. Some of these witnesses placed great emphasis on artistic freedom; others argued that the cinema should be treated in the same way as the theatre; and still others simply stressed the right of adults to freedom of choice and the unacceptability of the notion that certain people were qualified to judge what was right and wrong for everyone else to see (para.12.4). In rejecting these arguments, the Committee said:

"12.8 ... We are taken further towards accepting [pre-censorship of films] by the facts that the major part of our evidence supported the continuation of film censorship, that the present system has in the main worked effectively and well and that most other countries appear to regard film censorship as acceptable and desirable. What clinched the argument for some of us at least was the sight of some of the films with which the censorship presently interferes. We feel it necessary to say to many people who express liberal sentiments about the principle of adult freedom to choose that we were totally unprepared for the sadistic material that some film makers are prepared to produce. We are not here referring to the explicit portrayal of sexual activity or to anything which simply attracts charges of offensiveness. Films that exploit a taste for torture and sadistic violence do raise further, and disturbing, questions ...

　12.11 Some people told us that if there is material which we were satisfied should not be made available to the public, the proper way to suppress it is by way of making it the subject of determination by the courts, rather than by prior restraint. Prior restraint, it is commonly recognised, is a more effective means for suppressing material than is offered by the subsequent punishment approach. Its advantages are that it provides certainty, consistency and speed of decision and the possibility of continuous review by the same group of people; it avoids the delays of criminal trials and decisions by courts who know nothing of films and are not representative of the film-going public; it provides a more refined control, capable of identifying which elements of a film are objectionable and therefore allowing the distributor the opportunity of reacting; and it prevents objectionable material from becoming available at all rather than trying to retrieve it after publication and thereby giving it more publicity. We freely admit, and have already made clear, that we are in part encouraged to favour pre-censorship by the fact that it is what already exists. What we have to consider is, realistically, not whether we would institute a system of censorship if it were a novelty but whether we should abandon a functioning system; or rather, to put it more exactly, whether we should continue to use the system for the protection of young audiences (as almost all our witnesses considered necessary), but at the same time refuse to use the system to control films for adult viewing. We were very much impressed, moreover, by a different kind of argument. The impact of a film can depend on very subtle factors, which will not at all be caught by simple statements of what is being shown on the screen, and because of this the law is too inflexible an instrument through which to impose a control. An *ad hoc* judgment, grounded on certain guidelines, is a more efficient and sensitive way of controlling this medium. All these considerations together led us to the conclusion that films, even those shown to adults only, should continue to be censored."

But having accepted the case for some continued censorship, Williams also recommended reform of the arrangements then in force. First, it was proposed that local licensing, which featured so prominently in the *Classic Cinema* case, should be abolished: the committee concluded that the existence of such power could not "be justified by any local variation in taste and opinion" (para.12.19). Secondly, the committee recommended the creation of a new statutory body, the Film Examining Board, to replace the British Board of Film Censors. The FEB would establish policy and principles for the censorship of films and would appoint film examiners who would perform this task, with a right of appeal to the FEB against a decision of an examiner. Although the committee levelled no criticism at the BBFC, it was felt that it should be replaced. This was because the public esteem of the BBFC suffered from its close connections with the film industry and because it had no legal authority, and no power to ensure that its decisions were implemented. The third major change recommended by Williams was for new categories of certificate. New classifications have in fact been introduced and will be considered below.

The system of film censorship or classification in place today has undergone some changes since the Williams Committee reported, though these changes have not followed the path proposed by the Committee. The main change was the introduction of a classification scheme for videos by the Video Recordings Act 1984 (as amended by the Criminal Justice and Public Order Act 1994). The BBFC was designated by the government as the body responsible for this function, and an appeal lies from the decision of the BBFC to another non statutory body which is called the Video Appeals Committee, a Committee which we encountered in Ch.7 as part of the background to the decision in *Wingrove v United Kingdom* (1997) 24 E.H.R.R. 1. In 1985 the name of the BBFC was changed to the British Board of Film Classification, though it remains in essence the same body which was first established by the film industry in 1912. In its own words it is an independent non-governmental body. The BBFC has developed a number of classification principles by which it operates. These are as follows:

- adults should be free to choose what they see, providing that it remains within the law and is not potentially harmful to society;
- works should be allowed to reach the widest audience that is appropriate for their theme and treatment;
- the context in which something (*e.g.* sex or violence) is presented is central to the question of its acceptability;
- the BBFC's Guidelines will be reviewed periodically in the light of changes in public taste, attitudes and concerns.

There are now seven classification categories: U, Uc and PG which are advisory only; 12/12A, 15 and 18 which restrict viewing by age; and R18 which is only available to adults in licensed sex shops. The different classifications are explained as follows:

- U: Universal.
- Uc: Videos classified Uc are particularly suitable for pre-school children.
- "PG" Parental Guidance: Unaccompanied children of any age may watch. A "PG" film

should not disturb a child aged around eight or older. However, parents are advised to consider whether the content may upset younger or more sensitive children.

- 12A/12: No-one younger than 12 may see a "12A" film in a cinema unless accompanied by an adult. No-one younger than 12 may rent or buy a "12" rated video.
- 15: No-one younger than 15 may see a "15" film in a cinema. No-one younger than 15 may rent or buy a "15" rated video.
- 18: No-one younger than 18 may see an "18" film in a cinema. No-one younger than 18 may rent or buy an "18" rated video.
- R18: To be supplied only in licensed sex shops to adults of not less than 18 years.

The "R18" category is a special and legally restricted classification primarily for explicit videos of consenting sex between adults. Such videos may be supplied to adults only in licensed sex shops, of which there are currently about 90 in the UK. "R18" videos may not be supplied by mail order.

The BBFC is at pains to point out that statutory powers remain with the local councils, "which may overrule any of [the Board's] decisions, passing the films [the Board] rejects, banning films [it has] passed, and even waiving cuts, instituting new ones, or altering categories for films exhibited under their own licensing jurisdiction". Although "by the mid 1920's it had become general practice for local authorities to accept the decisions of the Board", there are still occasions when local authorities depart from them, even if this "does not happen very often". But, according to the Board:

"Examples where it has happened include the film MRS DOUBTFIRE, when pressure from parents led some local authorities to award a local 'PG' instead of the '12' originally awarded by the BBFC. Westminster Council banned CRASH, Bournemouth Council banned ROMANCE, and Camden Council gave '18' certificates to THE TEXAS CHAIN SAW MASSACRE and THE STORY OF O before the films came into the Board for classification. Both were subsequently classified '18' uncut by the Board. THE LAST HOUSE ON THE LEFT has also received local approval for individual screenings, most recently from Leicester Council."

(3) Broadcasting

The third area where powers exist to prevent speech relates to broadcasting. The BBC was created by Royal Charter in 1926 and operates under the terms of a Licence and Agreement which is renewed periodically by the government. Commercial television and radio companies operate under licences issued by the Independent Television Authority, a statutory body created by the Broadcasting Act 1990; a power now passed to OFCOM under the Communications Act 2003. Both the Licence and Agreement (in relation to the BBC) and the Broadcasting Act 1990 (in relation to the commercial sector) enable the government to prohibit particular broadcasts. These powers are discussed in the following extract.

T. Gibbons
Regulating the Media

"However, the idea of independence has a much more precarious status in broadcasting, for the state has never relinquished the potential for control that is entailed in the allocation of broadcasting frequencies and, in the case of public service broadcasting, the use of public finance and the guarantee of protection from competition in the market place. Independence has had a more negative aspect, being concerned with preventing direct interference from government rather than promoting the more critical tradition which the Press had claimed for itself and which broadcasting has attempted only relatively recently. Indeed, the scope for broadcasters to assert a 'Fourth Estate' role has always been ambiguous, especially for the BBC whose constitution has never clearly defined the nature of its association with government. Its independence has been secured in exchange for an understanding about what is acceptable political reporting and comment. The result has been what Burns has described as the BBC's 'politics of accommodation': serving the national interest, as Parliament sees it, on the one hand and the public good on the other.

More generally, and remarkably, both the BBC's Licence and Agreement and the legislation which governs commercial broadcasting have always contained provision for direct interference by government. Under clause 8.2 of the present Agreement, the Secretary of State 'may from time to time by notice in writing require the Corporation to refrain at any specified time or at all times from broadcasting or transmitting any matter or matter of any class specified in such notice, and the Secretary of State may at any time or times vary or revoke any such notice.' However, the Corporation 'may at its discretion announce or refrain from announcing that such a notice has been given or has been varied or revoked,' a provision which is intended to provide a safeguard by enabling the BBC to resist through public protest any attempt to exert pressure upon it. Almost identical provisions are contained in sections 10(3) and (4) and 94(3) and (4) of the 1990 Act. The power has never been used in relation to specific programmes and, although its use was threatened against the BBC in connection with a documentary about Northern Ireland in 1972, it was not implemented when the Chairman of the Governors indicated that he would reveal the Government's action.

As a general veto on broad classes of programme, however, the power has been used all too often. In 1927, the co-operation which Reith had afforded the Government during the General Strike was formalised into a prohibition on the broadcasting of matters of political, industrial or religious controversy. The restriction was lifted in 1928, but only when the Government accepted the recommendations of the Crawford Committee, made three years earlier, that controversial matter could be broadcast if it was of high quality, not too lengthy or insistent and distributed with 'scrupulous fairness', and the BBC had undertaken to deal with such matters on an impartial basis. Another matter which was also the subject of a veto, imposed in 1927 and never actually lifted, was a prohibition on the broadcasting of editorial opinion on current affairs or matters of public policy. The subjects of these vetoes were incorporated into undertakings which became attached to the Licence and they are now reflected in the duty of impartiality imposed by the current Agreement. They correspond with the similar duties which are placed on the ITC … Interestingly, the BBC has regarded its obligation as the mainstay of its position and defended it thus at the time of the Peacock inquiry:

> 'Without genuine independence, it is difficult, if not impossible, for broadcasters to maintain the highest standard of truthfulness and impartiality. Conversely, without having established a reputation for just those qualities it is difficult for any broadcasting organisation to be recognised as being truly independent and worthy of trust.'

This is a defensible rationalisation of the values of the Corporation, or indeed of public service broadcasting, but the genesis of such independence shows that a high price has been paid in the removal of any threat that the perceived power of the new medium would be used against politicians, whether in government or opposition.

The legal and regulator basis for the independence of the broadcasting media is, therefore, dependent on the goodwill of the government of the day. Where that goodwill is strained, the veto power is all too readily available. Its most significant use in recent times was the 'broadcasting ban' which occurred when the Secretary of State issued directives, in 1988, prohibiting the broadcasting of direct statements not only by members of terrorist organisations, but also by nationalist and loyalist political parties connected with Northern Ireland. The vagueness of the ban played on the broadcasters' reluctance to be branded as IRA sympathisers and, initially, they adopted a very restrictive interpretation of its effect. It was also difficult to tell whether material was being excluded from programmes; not every exclusion would necessarily carry a warning that it was being forced by government restrictions. Eventually, the broadcasters became less timid and they developed increasingly sophisticated means of dubbing actors' voices over film of the speakers. Yet it is clear that, despite the broadcasters' ability to publicise the fact that they were constrained by government restrictions, their editorial choices about matters concerning Northern Ireland were compromised. Some journalists did challenge the legality of the veto although, interestingly, the broadcasters themselves did not. Regrettably, the House of Lords was not prepared to hold that the Secretary of State had exercised his power unreasonably in his wish to combat terrorism and they refused to test the issue by reference to the proportionality test adopted by the European Court of Human Rights for applying Article 10 of the Convention."

The case referred to by Gibbons in the previous extract is *R. v Home Secretary ex p. Brind* [1991] 1 A.C. 696 which was concerned with directives issued by the Home Secretary to the broadcasters requiring them:

"1 ... to refrain from broadcasting any matter which consists of or includes—any words spoken, whether in the course of an interview or discussion or otherwise, by a person who appears or is heard on the programme in which the matter is broadcast where—(*a*) the person speaking the words represents or purports to represent an organization specified in paragraph 2 below, or (*b*) the words support or solicit or invite support for such an organisation, other than any matter specified in paragraph 3 below.
2. The organizations referred to in paragraph 1 above are—(*a*) any organization which is for the time being a proscribed organisation for the purposes of the Prevention of Terrorism (Temporary Provisions) Act 1984 or the Northern Ireland (Emergency Provisions) Act 1978; and (*b*) Sinn Fein, Republican Sinn Fein and the Ulster Defence Association.
3. The matter excluded from paragraph 1 above is any words spoken—(*a*) in the course of proceedings in Parliament, or (*b*) by or in support of a candidate at a parliamentary, European parliamentary or local election pending that election."

It was subsequently clarified that "the directives, as further defined and explained, do not restrict the reporting of statements made by terrorists or their supporters. What is restricted is the direct appearance on television of those who use or support violence, themselves making their statements ('actually reporting'). Thus the activities of terrorist organisations and statements of their apologists may still be reported, as they are in the press; but such persons are prevented from making the statement themselves on the television and radio. Publicity for their statements can be achieved, inter alia, by the dubbing of what they have said, using actors to impersonate their voices" (*R. v Home Secretary ex p. Brind*, above. (Lord Ackner)). Nevertheless, the ban was extremely wide, not least because it applied to organisations which were not proscribed (on which see Ch.10) and not least also because these organisations included lawful political parties. The question was whether the ban could be challenged in judicial review proceedings.

R. v Home Secretary Ex p. Brind
[1991] 1 A.C. 696

An application to challenge the ban was brought by a number of journalists who were members or employees of the National Union of Journalists. The action was brought before the Human Rights Act 1998, though it was argued that the Minister was bound to exercise his discretion in accordance with the terms of the Convention. This argument was rejected, as was the other argument for the applicants that the Minister had acted unreasonably in using his discretion to impose the ban.

LORD BRIDGE OF HARWICH: "My Lords, this appeal has been argued primarily on the basis that the power of the Secretary of State, under s 29(3) of the Broadcasting Act 1981 and under cl 13(4) of the licence and agreement which governs the operations of the British Broadcasting Corporation (the BBC) (Cmnd. 8233), to impose restrictions on the matters which the Independent Broadcasting Authority (the IBA) and the BBC respectively may broadcast may only be lawfully exercised in accordance with art.10 of the European Convention on Human Rights . . . . Any exercise by the Secretary of State of the power in question necessarily imposes some restriction on freedom of expression. The obligations of the United Kingdom, as a party to the convention, are to secure to every one within its jurisdiction the rights which the convention defines, including both the right to freedom of expression under art.10 and the right under art.13 to 'an effective remedy before a national authority' for any violation of the other rights secured by the convention. It is accepted, of course, by the appellants that, like any other treaty obligations which have not been embodied in the law by statute, the convention is not part of the domestic law, that the courts accordingly have no power to enforce convention rights directly and that, if domestic legislation conflicts with the convention, the courts must nevertheless enforce it. But it is already well settled that, in construing any provision in domestic legislation which is ambiguous in the sense that it is capable of a meaning which either conforms to or conflicts with the convention, the courts will presume that Parliament intended to legislate in conformity with the convention, not in conflict with it. Hence, it is submitted, when a statute confers upon an administrative authority a discretion capable of being exercised in a way which infringes any basic human right protected by the convention, it may similarly be presumed that the legislative intention was that the discretion should be exercised within the limitations which the convention imposes. I confess that I found considerable persuasive force in this submission. But in the end I have been convinced that the logic of it is flawed. When confronted with a simple choice between two possible interpretations of some specific statutory provision, the presumption whereby the courts prefer that which avoids conflict between our domestic legislation and our international treaty obligations is a mere canon of construction which involves no importation of international law into the domestic field. But where Parliament has conferred on the executive an administrative discretion without indicating the precise limits within which it must be exercised, to presume that it must be exercised within convention limits would be to go far beyond the resolution of an ambiguity. It would be to impute to Parliament an intention not only that the executive should exercise the discretion in conformity with the convention, but also that the domestic courts should enforce that conformity by the importation into domestic administrative law of the text of the convention and the jurisprudence of the European Court of Human Rights in the interpretation and application of it. If such a presumption is to apply to the statutory discretion exercised by the Secretary of State under s 29(3) of the 1981 Act in the instant case, it must also apply to any other statutory discretion exercised by the executive which is capable of involving an infringement of convention rights. When Parliament has been content for so long to leave those who complain that their convention rights have been infringed to seek their remedy in Strasbourg, it would be surprising suddenly to find that the judiciary had, without Parliament's aid, the means to incorporate the convention into such an important area of domestic law and I cannot escape the conclusion that this would be a judicial usurpation of the legislative function.

But I do not accept that this conclusion means that the courts are powerless to prevent the exercise by the executive of administrative discretions, even when conferred, as in the instant case, in terms which are on their face unlimited, in a way which infringes fundamental human rights. Most of the rights spelled out in terms in the convention, including the right to freedom of expression, are less than absolute and must in some cases yield to the claims of competing public interests. Thus, art 10(2) of the convention spells out and categorises the competing public interests by reference to which the right to freedom of expression may have to be curtailed. In exercising the power of judicial review we have neither the advantages nor the disadvantages of any comparable code to which we may refer or by which we are bound. But again, this surely does not mean that in deciding whether the Secretary of State, in the exercise of his discretion, could reasonably impose the restriction he has imposed on the broadcasting organisations, we are not perfectly entitled to start from the premise that any restriction of the right to freedom of expression requires to be justified and that nothing less than an important competing public interest will be sufficient to justify it. The primary judgment as to whether the particular competing public interest justifies the particular restriction imposed falls to be made by the Secretary of State to whom Parliament has entrusted the discretion. But we are entitled to exercise a secondary judgment by asking whether a reasonable Secretary of State, on the material before him, could reasonably make that primary judgment.

Applying these principles to the circumstances of the case ... I find it impossible to say that the Secretary of State exceeded the limits of his discretion. In any civilised and law-abiding society the defeat of the terrorist is a public interest of the first importance. That some restriction on the freedom of the terrorist and his supporters to propagate his cause may well be justified in support of that public interest is a proposition which I apprehend the appellants hardly dispute. Their real case is that they, in the exercise of their editorial judgment, may and must be trusted to ensure that the broadcasting media are not used in such a way as will afford any encouragement or support to terrorism and that any interference with that editorial judgment is necessarily an unjustifiable restriction on the right to freedom of expression. Accepting, as I do, their complete good faith, I nevertheless cannot accept this proposition. The Secretary of State, for the reasons he made so clear in Parliament, decided that it was necessary to deny to the terrorist and his supporters the opportunity to speak directly to the public through the most influential of all the media of communication and that this justified some interference with editorial freedom. I do not see how this judgment can be categorised as unreasonable. What is perhaps surprising is that the restriction imposed is of such limited scope. There is no restriction at all on the matter which may be broadcast, only on the manner of its presentation. The viewer may see the terrorist's face and hear his words provided only that they are not spoken in his own voice. I well understand the broadcast journalist's complaint that to put him to the trouble of dubbing the voice of the speaker he has interviwed before the television camera is an irritant which the difference in effect between the speaker's voice and the actor's voice hardly justifies. I well understand the political complaint that the restriction may be counter-productive in the sense that the adverse criticism it provokes outweighs any benefit it achieves. But these complaints fall very far short of demonstrating that a reasonable Secretary of State could not reasonably conclude that the restriction was justified by the important public interest of combating terrorism. I should add that I do not see how reliance on the doctrine of 'proportionality' can here advance the appellants' case. ...

I would dismiss the appeal."

Lords Ackner, Roskill, Templeman and Lord Lowry delivered concurring speeches.

If this case was decided today, the position would of course be very different because of the Human Rights Act. The applicants would now be able to argue directly that the Minister had breached Convention rights (assuming that they could be said to be victims of the Minister's action). It does not follow, however, that a direct challenge under the Human Rights Act would lead to a different outcome: the European Commission of Human Rights subsequently found that there had been no breach of Art.10: *Brind v United Kingdom* (1994) 18 E.H.R.R. C.D. 76. It is true—of course—that the British judges would not be bound by any such decision of the Strasbourg bodies, but it is a reminder that in this area the courts may take a tolerant view of state censorship. Yet the problem of censorship is not confined to the government. The broadcasters themselves may also indulge in the censorship of messages which cause them concern. This could arise, *e.g.* in the case of advertising or in the case of party political broadcasts. It is perhaps extraordinary to contemplate the possibility of television or radio companies in the United Kingdom seeking to veto a party political broadcast during a general election because of its political content. It is perhaps even more extraordinary to contemplate such a veto surviving judicial review under the Human Rights Act with its guarantee of freedom of expression. Yet this is precisely what happened in the following case.

R. (BBC) v Pro-Life Alliance
[2004] 1 A.C. 185

The Pro-Life Alliance is a registered political party which is opposed to abortion. At the general election in 2001, the Alliance contested enough seats in Wales to qualify for a party election broadcast there. It submitted a tape to the broadcasting authorities. The Court of Appeal ([2002] 3 W.L.R. 1080) said that it consisted mainly of "prolonged and deeply disturbing images" of aborted foetuses: "tiny limbs, bloodied and dismembered, a separated head, their human shape and form plainly recognisable" (Simon Brown L.J. at 1103, Laws L.J. at 1086). Laws L.J. went on to describe what was shown in the programme as "... certainly disturbing to any person of ordinary sensibilities". The broadcasting authorities unanimously refused to screen the broadcast on the ground that it contained material which would be offensive to public feeling. Under the Broadcasting Act 1990, the Independent Television Commission was required to take steps to ensure that "nothing is included in its programmes which offends against good taste or decency or is likely to encourage or incite to crime or to lead to disorder or to be offensive to public feeling." For its part the BBC is under a similar duty in its Licence under which it must ensure that its programmes "do not include anything which offends against good taste or decency or is likely to encourage or incite to crime or lead to disorder or to be offensive to public feeling." In the present case the BBC successfully appealed to the House of Lords from a decision of the Court of Appeal that it had acted unlawfully in refusing to broadcast the film submitted by the Alliance.

LORD HOFFMANN: "37. In requiring the application of standards of taste and decency, section 6(1)(a) of the 1990 Act makes no distinction between PEBs and other programmes. It applies to all programmes broadcast by a licensed service and section 202 defines 'programme', in relation to any service, as including 'any item included in that service'. The agreement between the BBC and the Secretary of State similarly makes no distinction.
...

52. The Alliance has never argued that section 6(1)(a) of the 1990 Act, in its application to PEBs, is inconsistent with its rights under article 10 of the Convention. But this is lip-service, because the thrust of its submissions, which found favour in the Court of Appeal, is that the statute should be disregarded or not taken seriously ...

54. I am fully conscious of the importance of free political speech. But I think that the Court of Appeal failed to make some important distinctions.

(a) The nature of the right under article 10

55. First, the primary right protected by article 10 is the right of every citizen not to be prevented from expressing his opinions. He has the right to "receive and impart information and ideas without interference by public authority".

56. In the present case, that primary right was not engaged. There was nothing that the Alliance was prevented from doing. It enjoyed the same free speech as every other citizen. By virtue of its entitlement to a PEB it had more access to the homes of its fellow citizens than other single-issue groups which could not afford to register as a political party and put up six deposits.

57. There is no human right to use a television channel. Parliament has required the broadcasters to allow political parties to broadcast but has done so subject to conditions, both as to qualification for a PEB and as to its contents. No one disputes the necessity for qualifying conditions. It would obviously not be possible to give every grouping which registers as a political party a PPB or PEB. The issue in this case is about the condition as to

contents, namely that it should not offend against standards of truth and decency.

58. The fact that no one has a right to broadcast on television does not mean that article 10 has no application to such broadcasts. But the nature of the right in such cases is different. Instead of being a right not to be prevented from expressing one's opinions, it becomes a right to fair consideration for being afforded the opportunity to do so; a right not to have one's access to public media denied on discriminatory, arbitrary or unreasonable grounds.

59. A recent example of the application of this principle is the decision of the Privy Council in *Benjamin v Minister of Information and Broadcasting* [2001] 1 WLR 1040. Mr Benjamin was host of a phone-in programme on government-controlled Anguilla Radio. The government suspended his programme because he had aired a politically controversial question (whether Anguilla should have a lottery) on which the government wished to stop discussion. Lord Slynn of Hadley (at p. 1048, paras 26, 27) accepted that Mr Benjamin had no primary right to broadcast. But he did have a right not to have his access to the medium denied on politically discriminatory grounds. Lord Slynn (at p 1052) described the government's action as "arbitrary or capricious". This is something which very much engages the freedom of political speech protected by article 10.

60. The same approach can be found in the jurisprudence of the European Court of Human Rights. In *Haider v Austria* (1995) 83 DR 66 the Commission rejected the complaint of Mr Haider, the Austrian politician, that (among other things) his opinions had not been given enough time on television, as manifestly unfounded. It said (at p. 74):

> "The Commission recalls that article 10 of the Convention cannot be taken to include a general and unfettered right for any private citizen or organisation to have access to broadcasting time on radio or television in order to forward his opinion, save under exceptional circumstances, for instance if one political party is excluded from broadcasting facilities at election time while other parties are given broadcasting time."

61. The emphasis, therefore, is on the right not to be denied access on discriminatory grounds. In *Huggett v United Kingdom* (1995) 82A DR 98 the Commission considered a complaint about the criteria for allocating PEBs in the 1994 European Parliament elections. Mr Huggett was an independent candidate who did not qualify. The Commission also rejected the complaint as manifestly unfounded because there was no "arbitrariness or discrimination" in the application of the criteria.

62. In my opinion, therefore, the Court of Appeal asked itself the wrong question. It treated the case as if it concerned the primary right not to be prevented from expressing one's political views and concluded that questions of taste and decency were not an adequate ground for censorship. The real issue in the case is whether the requirements of taste and decency are a discriminatory, arbitrary or unreasonable condition for allowing a political party free access at election time to a particular public medium, namely television.

(b) Contents conditions

63. The problem about conditions relating to the content of the broadcast, as opposed to conditions depending on such matters as the number of candidates fielded or votes obtained in the last election, is that they run a much greater risk of being considered discriminatory. After all, the government in *Benjamin's* case may be said in effect to have imposed a condition for access to the radio which related to the contents of the broadcast: the broadcaster should not discuss matters to which the government objected. But this was discriminatory on objectionable grounds. So conditions which concern the contents of the programmes which will be accepted for broadcasting must be carefully examined to make sure that they are truly neutral between different points of view, or that any lack of neutrality can be objectively justified.

64. That was the question in the recent controversial ECHR case of *VgT Verein Gegen Tierfabriken v Switzerland* (2002) 34 EHRR 159, which concerned the prohibition of

political advertising by section 18(5) of the Swiss Federal Radio and Television Act. An animal rights' association complained that the television authority had rejected as "political" its advertisement depicting commercial pig rearing as cruel and urging people to eat less meat, when it had accepted commercials from the meat industry extolling the pleasures of pork and bacon. As a matter of common sense, the association's complaint was not without merit. The Swiss government argued that no one had a right to television time and that the primary right under article 10 was not engaged. But the court took the view that for practical purposes it was. Prima facie, anyone was entitled to whatever television time for commercials he could afford to buy. Therefore a refusal to allow anyone a commercial on the grounds of the content of his broadcast was a discrimination which had to be justified. The court decided that there was no sufficient justification for discriminating against political advertising "in the particular circumstances of the applicant association's case": para. 75 at p. 177. This is a guarded, if somewhat opaque, decision. The court expressly said that such a prohibition might be compatible with article 10 "in certain situations." But the Secretary of State cautiously regarded the decision as a reason for being unable to certify that the proposed continuation of the UK ban on political advertising in clause 309 of the Communications Bill is compatible with the Convention.

(c) Are conditions as to taste and decency discriminatory?

65. A condition concerning standards of taste and decency is neutral in the sense that it applies across the board to all political parties wishing to broadcast PPBs. Until the Alliance produced its proposed PEB in the 1997 election, it does not appear to have caused difficulty to any political party. But the Alliance says that it is discriminatory against a party which feels the need to breach the standards in order to get its message across. That is true.

66. The question then is whether it can be objectively justified. In deciding this question, it must first be borne in mind that the quality of the article 10 right is different from that which was in issue in the *VgT* case. This is not a case in which the Alliance was exercising a right to buy television time which was prima facie open to everyone in order to express its views on whatever subject it thought fit. The BBC and Parliament have decided that in the public interest free television time should be made available to political parties for PEBs because they consider that this would advance the democratic interest in encouraging an informed choice at the ballot box.

67. In deciding whether a condition as to the content of a PEB is unreasonable or discriminatory, it is therefore in my opinion relevant to consider whether it has any impact upon the particular democratic interest which offering the PEB was intended to advance. For example, if political parties are given PEBs in connection with a referendum on whether we should join the Euro, it would be unreasonable to attach much weight to an objection by the Alliance that standards of taste and decency prevented them from using their PEB to best effect in advocating the case against abortion. The subject is unrelated to the democratic interest in providing a PEB.

68. Although it may be said that all questions of social and economic policy are open to discussion in a general election, the Alliance PEB was quite unrelated to the specific policy of encouraging an informed choice at the ballot box. Their views were of electoral concern, at any rate theoretically, to the voters in only six of the Welsh constituencies. And the results, which were not wholly unpredictable, showed that they were of concern to very few of those voters. In any case, abortion is not in this country a party political issue. It has for many years been the practice to allow members of Parliament a free vote on such issues. So, despite the reference by the Court of Appeal (at p. 1097) to the "cockpit of a general election", the Alliance broadcast had virtually nothing to do with the fact that a general election was taking place. The election merely gave it an opportunity to publicise its views in a way which would have been no more or less effective at any other time.

69. My Lords, I think that it is necessary to bring some degree of practicality and common sense to this question. The Electoral Commission, in its 2003 report (at p. 36),

expressed its concern about this aspect of the Court of Appeal's decision:

> "While we too would attach considerable weight to freedom of expression for political parties, especially during election campaigns, we are not convinced that this calls for PEBs to be exempted from the normal standards applied to all other broadcast material. It is not, in our view, realistic to conclude that the electorate necessarily stands to benefit from PPBs being outside the normal controls. In addition, we would be concerned if incentive was provided for organisations to register as political parties and field sufficient candidates in order to qualify for PPBs which would not only provide access to the media that would not otherwise be available but would enable material to be broadcast that would not otherwise be allowed."

70. Even assuming that the Alliance broadcast had been an ordinary PEB, relevant to the general election, I do not think it would have been unreasonable to require it to comply with standards of taste and decency. They are not particularly exacting and, as I have said, take into account the political context and the importance to the political party in getting its message across. But the rationale for having such standards applies to political as well as to any other broadcasts; the standards are part of the country's cultural life and have created expectations on the part of the viewers as to what they will and will not be shown on the screens in their homes.

71. Is there anything in European law which suggests that a taste and decency requirement would be regarded as unreasonable or discriminatory? In the *VgT* case the court made it clear that it was not considering a case in which the objection to an advertisement was that its content was offensive: see paragraph 76 at p. 177. And at this point it is also relevant to consider the response of the ECtHR to the complaint of the Alliance about the rejection of its PEB in the 1997 election. On 26 June 2000 the Registrar of the ECtHR wrote to the Alliance saying that "in accordance with the general instructions received from the Court" he drew their attention to "certain shortcomings" in the application. The indication given by the Registrar was that the court might consider that the taste and decency requirements were not an "arbitrary or unreasonable" interference with their access to television. Subsequently the court, after noting that the Alliance had been informed of "possible obstacles" to the admissibility of the application, rejected it as not disclosing "any appearance of a violation of the rights and freedoms set out in the Convention...."

72. The Court of Appeal treated this decision as an aberration to which no attention should be paid. But, like Scott Baker J., I think that it is very significant. The test applied in the letter from the Registrar, namely, whether the restriction on the content of the PEB was "arbitrary or unreasonable", seems to me precisely the test which ought to be applied. It is more in accordance with the jurisprudence of the ECtHR and a proper analysis of the nature of the right in question than the fundamentalist approach of the Court of Appeal.

73. In my opinion therefore, there is no public interest in exempting PEBs from the taste and decency requirements on the ground that their message requires them to broadcast offensive material. The Alliance had no human right to be invited to the party and it is not unreasonable for Parliament to provide that those invited should behave themselves."

Lords Nicholls of Birkenhead, Millett, and Walker of Gestingthorpe delivered concurring speeches. Lord Scott of Foscote dissented.

This is an important case which has attracted some criticism. But for the nature of the message that was banned and the unpopularity of the anti-abortion movement in liberal circles, it may have been even more heavily criticised by the human rights movement. The decision invites two questions to be asked. First: did the House of Lords give enough attention to the nature of the speech that was involved in this case? It was a case about the content of political speech, where the level of protection might be expected to be at its highest and where the courts may be expected to be most vigilant. Indeed as Lord Walker of Gestingthorpe pointed out: "The

European Court of Human Rights has recognised the special importance of freedom of expression at the time of an election (*Bowman v United Kingdom* (1998) 26 EHRR 1, para 42)". This is a dimension of the case raised very effectively by Lord Scott of Foscote in his dissenting speech where he said:

> "95...The restrictions on the broadcasting of material offending against good taste and decency and of material offensive to public feeling were drafted so as to be capable of application to all programmes, whether light entertainment, serious drama, historical or other documentaries, news reports, party political programmes, or whatever. But material that might be required to be rejected in one type of programme might be unexceptionable in another. The judgment of the decision maker would need to take into account the type of programme of which the material formed part as well as the audience at which the programme was directed. This was a party election broadcast directed at the electorate. He, or she, would need to apply the prescribed standard having regard to these factors and to the need that the application be compatible with the guarantees of freedom of expression contained in Article 10.
>
> 96. The conclusion to which the broadcasters came could not, in my opinion, have been reached without a significant and fatal undervaluing of two connected features of the case: first, that the programme was to constitute a party election broadcast; second, that the only relevant criterion for a justifiable rejection on offensiveness grounds was that the rejection be necessary for the protection of the right of homeowners not to be subjected to offensive material in their own homes.
>
> 97. The importance of the general election context of the Alliance's proposed programme cannot be overstated. We are fortunate enough to live in what is often described as, and I believe to be, a mature democracy. In a mature democracy political parties are entitled, and expected, to place their policies before the public so that the public can express its opinion on them at the polls. The constitutional importance of this entitlement and expectation is enhanced at election time.
>
> 98. If, as here, a political party's desired election broadcast is factually accurate, not sensationalised, and is relevant to a lawful policy on which its candidates are standing for election, I find it difficult to understand on what possible basis it could properly be rejected as being "offensive to public feeling". Voters in a mature democracy may strongly disagree with a policy being promoted by a televised party political broadcast but ought not to be offended by the fact that the policy is being promoted nor, if the promotion is factually accurate and not sensationalised, by the content of the programme. Indeed, in my opinion, the public in a mature democracy are not entitled to be offended by the broadcasting of such a programme. A refusal to transmit such a programme based upon the belief that the programme would be "offensive to very large numbers of viewers" (the letter of 17 May 2001) would not, in my opinion, be capable of being described as "necessary in a democratic society ... for the protection of ... rights of others". Such a refusal would, on the contrary, be positively inimical to the values of a democratic society, to which values it must be assumed that the public adhere."

The second question conversely is whether too much weight was given to other considerations. One of these was the nature of the Pro-Life Alliance which Lord Hoffman appeared to think did not merit equal respect for its position as other political parties. This is partly because of the nature of the party (a single issue party) and the nature of its message (confined to a single issue). But as was pointed out by Lord Scott, the Alliance was campaigning on "a lawful issue and one of public importance". The other issue which may have been overplayed is what Lord Walker of Gestingthorpe referred to as the citizen's "right not to be shocked or affronted by inappropriate material transmitted into the privacy of his home". In the same way Lord Nicholls chided the Court of Appeal which had "in effect carried out its own balancing exercise between the requirements of freedom of political speech and the protection of the public from being unduly distressed in their own homes. That was not a legitimate exercise for the courts in this case. Parliament has decided where the balance shall be held. The latter interest prevails over the former to the extent that the offensive material ban applies without distinction to all television programmes, including party broadcasts". However, as Lord Scott of Foscote pointed out

> "One of the disturbing features of our present democracy is so-called voter-apathy. The percentage of registered voters who vote at general elections is regrettably low. A broadcasters' mind-set that rejects a party election television programme, dealing with an issue of undeniable public importance such as abortion, on the ground that large numbers of the voting public would find the programme 'offensive' denigrates the voting public, treats them like children who need to be protected from the unpleasant realities of life, seriously undervalues their political maturity and can only promote the voter-apathy to which I have referred."

He might have added that television sets normally have an off button for those of sensitive disposition.

But for all that, the decision of the House of Lords has been a soft target for some critics wedded to freedom without adequate reflection about its consequences. So far as party election broadcasts are concerned, there is a great deal to reflect on in the views of the Electoral Commission quoted in para.69 of Lord Hoffmann's speech. The fact is that it is very easy for pressure groups to register as political parties under the Political Parties, Elections and Referendums Act 2000. There are no restrictions and few formalities, there now being an estimated 200 registered parties. Once registered as a political party, a pressure group can put up candidates in order to secure access to broadcasts that would otherwise be prohibited at other times because of their political content and the ban on political advertising. (The latter may also offend liberal opinion but it exists in order to ensure fair elections and to stop the wealthy from dominating the airwaves any more than they do at present.) In order to secure party election broadcasts, there is no need for the candidates put up by the party for the purpose to be serious and there is no restriction on organisations using this strategy as an opportunity to obtain publicity unrelated to the election. There is thus a legitimate concern about the eccentric messages of all manner of groups able to use the election for opportunistic reasons. The fact that the speech is uttered at election time does not make it electoral speech or even political speech. But even if it is, it does not follow that it should be unrestrained. If the broadcasters are not permitted to control the offensive (visual) material of the Pro-Life Alliance, what about the perceived racist propaganda of the British National Party which at least has the virtue of being a serious political party? We await with interest the fancy pirouettes of those critics who are simultaneously offended by the censorship of the Pro-Life Alliance's images (they were still allowed to broadcast) as well as the prospect of racist propaganda by parties such as the BNP. We are again about to enter the territory of the sophist and the pedant, manufacturing distinctions which will create hours of endless fun in the human rights class. But while we encounter liberal indignation at the decision in *Pro-Life*, we may also reflect on whether broadcasts of the kind proposed by the Alliance would ever be shown on mainstream television in the United States where the right to free speech is sometimes carried to its most absurd lengths: *Buckley v Valeo*, 424 U.S. 1 (1976).

The right of the government to censor the commercial broadcast media is now contained in the Communications Act 2003, which replaces the provisions of the Broadcasting Act 1990 which were referred to in the *Pro-Life Alliance* case. This 2003 Act establishes a new regulatory authority for broadcasting and communications. OFCOM has a number of responsibilities under the Act and will be the body responsible for issuing licences to television companies when the existing ones expire. For our purposes, however, the Act provides as follows:

Communications Act 2003

"Government requirements for licensed services

336—(1) If it appears to the Secretary of State or any other Minister of the Crown to be appropriate to do so in connection with any of his functions, the Secretary of State or that Minister may at any time by notice require OFCOM to give a direction under subsection (2).

(2) A direction under this subsection is a direction to the holders of the Broadcasting Act licences specified in the notice under subsection (1) to include an announcement so specified in their licensed services.

(3) The direction may specify the times at which the announcement is to be broadcast or otherwise transmitted.

(4) Where the holder of a Broadcasting Act licence includes an announcement in his licensed service in pursuance of a direction under this section, he may announce that he is doing so in pursuance of such a direction.

(5) The Secretary of State may, at any time, by notice require OFCOM to direct the holders of the Broadcasting Act licences specified in the notice to refrain from including in their licensed services any matter, or description of matter, specified in the notice.

(6) Where—

    (a) OFCOM have given the holder of a Broadcasting Act licence a direction in accordance with a notice under subsection (5),

    (b) in consequence of the revocation by the Secretary of State of such a notice, OFCOM have revoked such a direction, or

    (c) such a notice has expired,

the holder of the licence in question may include in the licensed service an announcement of the giving or revocation of the direction or of the expiration of the notice, as the case may be.

(7) OFCOM must comply with every requirement contained in a notice under this section.

(8) The powers conferred by this section are in addition to any powers specifically conferred on the Secretary of State by or under this Act or any other enactment.

(9) In this section 'Minister of the Crown' includes the Treasury."

In the case of the BBC the power of the Minister to intervene will be based on the power contained under the Licence and Agreement. The Communications Act 2003 also includes a number of other restraints on the broadcasters, some of which are new and some of which have been inherited from the earlier statutory regime.

III. PROHIBITED SPEECH

In this section we move from a consideration of censorship or preventing the freedom of expression to a category of speech which is prohibited or forbidden. Unlike censorship, this category of speech will not normally be prevented by a censor in the way that films or broadcasts may be prevented. Rather, this category of speech may attract civil liability or a criminal penalty after the event, though it is true that attempts may be made to restrain any such speech by way of interdict. As we will see in Pt V, however, the opportunities for restraint by court order should be greatly diminished by the Human Rights Act. The categories of prohibited speech are in fact wide ranging. We have already encountered blasphemy in Ch.7 (freedom of religion). In Ch.9 (freedom of assembly and association) we encounter sedition and incitement to racial hatred, while in Ch.10 (the war on terror) we encounter restraints on support for proscribed organisations). In this chapter we concentrate on three other examples of prohibited speech: obscene publications, publications which constitute a contempt of court, and publications which contain official secrets. In all cases, the European Court of Human Rights has accepted that it may be possible to impose restraints on freedom of expression. However, all these foregoing examples of speech by no means exhausts the circumstances in which speech may be prohibited. Also important are the law of defamation and the law of confidentiality.

(1) Obscenity

(a) The Background

The modern law on obscenity is to be found in the Civic Government (Scotland) Act 1982, s.51. Before the coming into force of this measure, the position was governed by a range of statutory provisions (notably the Burgh Police (Scotland) Act 1892), and more recently by the common law. The relevant provisions of the 1892 Act provided as follows:

> "380. Every person who is guilty of any of the following acts or omissions within the burgh shall, in respect thereof, be liable to a penalty not exceeding the respective amounts, or to imprisonment for a period not exceeding the respective periods herein after mentioned; videlicet,—
>
> To a penalty of twenty-five pounds, or alternatively without penalty, to imprisonment for sixty days, every person who . . .
>
> (3) Publishes, prints, or offers for sale or distribution, or sells, distributes, or exhibits to view, or causes to be published, printed, exhibited to view, or distributed, any indecent, or obscene book, paper, print, photograph, drawing, painting, representation, model or figure, or publicly exhibits any disgusting or indecent object, or writes or draws any indecent or obscene word, figure, or representation in or on any place where it can be seen by the public, or sings or recites in public any obscene song or ballad."

Local statutes in Dundee and Aberdeen made substantially similar provision. The Glasgow Corporation Consolidation (General Powers) Order Confirmation Act 1960 was slightly different. By s.162 a magistrate could, on a complaint by the procurator fiscal, grant a warrant to a police officer, not under the rank of inspector, to enter and search a shop or other place in which the magistrate had reasonable grounds for believing that any profane, indecent or obscene article, book, paper, print, photograph, drawing, painting, or representation was kept for sale, or lending, or hire, or for publication for purposes of gain. The police might seize and remove any relevant material found in the shop and the occupier who kept such material would if convicted be liable to a fine or to 60 days' imprisonment.

Galletly v Laird
1953 S.L.T. 67

William Galletly was charged in the police court at Paisley on a complaint that within his premises as a bookseller's shop he did "exhibit to view" books which were indecent or obscene, contrary to s.380(3) of the 1892 Act. He was convicted and the magistrate ordered the materials to be destroyed. Galletly appealed to the High Court.

Lord Justice-General (Cooper): "To justify a conviction in a case of this type the Court ought to be satisfied of two elements, viz.: (1) That the book or picture is of such a nature as to be calculated to produce a pernicious effect in depraving and corrupting those who are open to such influence; and (2) that such book or picture is being indiscriminately exhibited or circulated or offered for sale in such circumstances as to justify the inference that it is likely to fall (and perhaps intended to fall) into the hands of persons liable to be so corrupted.

The second of these elements seems to me the more important, for this reason that a book or picture, however indecent or obscene, will create no social evil of the type sought to be suppressed so long as it is kept in proper custody and under responsible control. The mischief resides not so much in the book or picture *per se* as in the use to which it is put, usually deliberately and for gain by the trafficker in pornography, who makes a business of inspiring and catering for depraved and perverted tastes. Such cases are usually not difficult to recognise, and it is easy to understand why Parliament should have confided to local officers of police and magistrates the recognition and detection of what is in a real sense a local public nuisance. These penal provisions are not aimed at setting up in each locality a *censor morum* with the duty of compiling on the principles of Mrs Grundy an *index expurgatorius* of the literary and artistic productions of all the ages, and with the power of imprisoning reputable dealers who justifiably stock literary, scientific, artistic and philosophic works which, however unsuitable for indiscriminate distribution to the curious adolescents, are perfectly appropriate for study by the serious scholar. I am quite unmoved by the suggestion that these prosecutions reveal a grave threat to the liberty of respectable booksellers, librarians and others, who were said to be afraid lest there might be discovered in their possession some work – perhaps a celebrated classic—which might offend the susceptibilities of the type of magistrate whom Lord Sands described as 'the morose Puritan'. It is impossible to read these provisions and the immediate context in which they occur without being convinced that their purpose is quite different, and that their use for the object suggested would be unjustifiable. I note, for example, that the other branches of the fasciculus in the Burgh Police Act are concerned *inter alia*, with penalising indecent exposure, the harbouring of prostitutes, and the allowance by the occupier of any building of 'riotous or disorderly conduct within the same'. Equally I am not dismayed by the idea that the opinion of the magistrate before whom the case is brought is virtually determinative of the question whether the books or pictures libelled are or are not indecent or obscene. Once it is understood that the emphais falls to be laid upon the second of the elements defined above, it seems to me to be not only intelligible but inevitable that the character of the offending books or pictures should be ascertained by the only method by which such a fact can be ascertained, *viz.*: by reading the books or looking at the pictures. The book or picture itself provides the best evidence of its own indecency or obscenity or of the absence of such qualities; and if in any case the magistrate's decision is challenged, the only method by which an appellate tribunal could determine whether the magistrate was entitled to reach the conclusion which he did would be by examing the book or picture, not with a view to re-trying the case but solely with a view to discovering whether they revealed evidence on which a reasonable magistrate would be entitled to condemn them as incident or obscene...

The magistrate [in this case] disallowed cross-examination by the complainer's solicitor and positive evidence tendered for the defence designed to show that books other than those referred to in the complaint circulated freely in Paisley and were available in the local public library, the suggestion apparently being that these other books were not materially different in character from those complained of. I consider that the magistrate's ruling was right. The character of other books is a collateral issue, the exploration of which would be endless and futile. If the books produced by the prosecution are indecent or obscene, their quality in that respect cannot be made any better by examining other books, or listening to the opinions of other people with regard to these other books...

The statute used the expression 'indecent or obscene', the complaint echoes the statutes, and the magistrate found the accused guilty as libelled as regards certain of the books. It was maintained that this was to return a general conviction on an alternative charge, and reference was made to the opinion of Lord Sands in *McGowan v Langmuir*, 1931 S.L.T. 94 where his Lordship engaged in a philological analysis of the vocabulary of indecency. I am willing to accept in that in general parlance 'obscene' is a stronger epithet than 'indecent', and even to adopt Lord Sands' suggestion that the former is the superlative and the latter is the comparative of the positive 'immodest'. But I do not believe, and I do not read the judgment in *McGowan* (*supra*) as deciding, that these subtleties played any part when this section was drafted in 1892. As applied in a penal provision to books or representations of the type in question the adjectives 'indecent or obscene' are, in my view, employed tautologically to convey a single idea and perfectly clear idea at that, and it would be palpably absurd to ask courts to wade through such a collection as has been produced in these cases for the purpose of uselessly classifying the condemned material into different grades of indecency.

In the result I consider that the attacks upon this conviction fail and that the bill should be refused."

Lords Carmont and Russell concurred.

There is an obvious difference in the approach adopted by Lord Cooper in *Galletly v Laird* and that adopted by Lord Sands in the earlier case, *McGowan v Langmuir*, 1931 S.L.T. 94. In *McGowan*, Lord Sands said at p.96:

"I do not think that the two words 'indecent' and 'obscene' are synonymous. The one may shade into the other, but there is a difference of meaning. It is easier to illustrate than define, and I illustrate thus. For a male bather to enter the water nude in the presence of ladies would be indecent, but it would not necessarily be obscene. But if he directed the attention of a lady to a certain member of his body his conduct would certainly be obscene. The matter might be roughly expressed thus in the ascending scale: Positive—Immodest; Comparative—Indecent; Superlative—Obscene. These, however, are not rigid categories. The same conduct which in certain circumstances may merit only the milder description, may in other circumstances deserve a harder one. 'Indecent' is a milder term than 'obscene', and as it satisfied the purposes of this case if the prints in question are indecent, I shall apply that test."

It appears, however, that Lord Cooper's approach is the one which was subsequently applied in practice.

(b) Entry and Retreat of the Common Law

Watt v Annan
1978 S.L.T. 198

Watt was charged and convicted on a summary complaint as follows:

"you did on 2nd October 1976 at the premises known as the Grapes Hotel, East Calder, conduct yourself in a shamelessly indecent manner and did exhibit or cause to be exhibited to a number of persons a film of an obscene or indecent nature, which depicted *inter alia* sexual intercourse, involving a number of male and female persons, acts of masturbation, oral sex and unnatural acts and practices, including the drinking of urine and inserting a candle into the private parts of female persons appearing in said film, and said film was liable to create depraved, inordinate and lustful desires in those watching said film and to corrupt the morals of the lieges."

The film was shown behind locked doors in the lounge bar of the hotel. Watt was the supplier and owner of the film and a member of a social club of which all others present were also members.

LORD CAMERON: "The statement that 'all shamelessly indecent conduct is criminal' makes its first appearance in the first edition of MacDonald's *Criminal Law* and is repeated in all subsequent editions without comment or criticism in any decided case. It was approved by Lord Clyde in *McLaughlan v Boyd*, 1933 S.L.T. 629 at p. 631 when he declared it to be sound and correctly expressing the law of Scotland. It is true that this observation was obiter but it was concurred in by the other members of the court and has not been since subjected to criticism or doubt. It is clear however that, as the Crown maintained, it is not the indencency of the conduct itself which makes it criminal but it is the quality of 'shameless-ness', and the question is what is the content of this qualification? It was accepted, and rightly so, in the submission for the Crown that for the conduct to be criminal, in such circum-stances as the facts in the present case disclose, it must be directed towards some person or persons with an intention or knowledge that it should corrupt or be calculated or liable to corrupt or deprave those towards whom the indecent or obscene conduct was directed. Whether or not conduct which is admittedly indecent or obscene is to be held criminal will depend on the proof of the necessary mens rea and upon the facts and circumstances of the particular case. It would be impracticable as well as undesirable to attempt to define precisely the limits and ambit of this particular offence, far less to decide that the nature of the premises or place in which the conduct charged has occurred should alone be decisive in transforming conduct which would otherwise be the proper subject of prosecution into conduct which may do no more than offend the canons of personal propriety or standards of contemporary morals. If it were considered desirable or necessary that this was a chapter of the criminal law in which precise boundaries or limits were to be set then it might be thought that the task is one which is more appropriate for the hand of the legislator.

In the present case there is no dispute that the film displayed amply deserved the description of indecent or obscene or that its display was calculated or liable to corrupt or deprave the morals of those who viewed it, whether they were consenters or otherwise. The question is then narrowed to this, whether the circumstances of the display as found by the sheriff in this case were such as to render the conduct of the appellant shamelessly indecent ... Neither the publicity nor the privacy of the locus of the conduct charged necessarily affects far less determines the criminal quality of indecent conduct libelled as shameless. That this is so can be readily inferred from the context in which this statement of the law appears, particularly in MacDonald's first edition and in those subsequent editions which were revised by the Lord Justice-Clerk himself. In my opinion therefore it is not essential to the relevancy of a charge of shamelessly indecent conduct that it must be libelled that the conduct in question occurred in a public place or was a matter of public exhibition...

The criminal character of the act of indecency must therefore depend on proof of the necessary criminal intent as well as proof of the nature of the conduct itself and of the circumstances in which it takes place. Conduct that may be legitimate and innocent in the laboratory of the anthropologist may well be shamelessly indecent if carried on or exhibited in other places or circumstances, and whether these can be characterised as private or public may be no matter. In any event, it may well be asked what should be the criterion of 'publicity' as opposed to 'privacy' which is to determine the critical issue of deciding that conduct which might otherwise be regarded only as in conflict with accepted morals becomes in breach of the criminal law. To this question the submissions for the appellant provide no answer and the obscene publication cases are no guide. In these circumstances and for these reasons I am of opinion that the appellant's attack on the relevancy of this complaint fails..."

The Lord Justice-General (Emslie) and Lord Johnston agreed.

Before *Watt v Annan*, the last reported prosecution at common law was *Robinson* (1843) 1 Broun 590, where the accused was charged with exposing for sale obscene work "intended to vitiate and corrupt the morals of the lieges ... and to raise and create in their minds inordinate and lustful desires." Although Lord Justice-General Clyde alluded to the existence of common law liability in *McGowan v Langmuir*, the common law lay dormant, perhaps appropriate only in those areas where the statutory offences did not apply. Yet to the prosecutor the re-intro-duction of some form of common law liability must have appeared desirable on several counts, not the least of these being that the statutes controlled only a limited range of activity and did not extend, *e.g.* to the conduct which led to the prosecution in *Watt v Annan*. A second and perhaps more important advantage of the common law to the prosecutor is that the penalties which could be exacted were substantially greater than the £25 fine (or 60 days' imprisonment) then permitted by the statutes. It seems that for this reason the Crown resorted to the common law as a basis for prosecution even in those areas where the statutes applied. In *Robertson v Smith*, 1979 S.L.T. (Notes) 51, the accused was convicted at Dundee sheriff court on a complaint which libelled *inter alia* that he conducted himself "in a shamelessly indecent manner, that he did sell, expose for sale and have for sale 1,060 indecent and obscene books and magazines ... five indecent and obscene films ... and a pack of indecent and obscene playing cards, which books, magazines, films and playing cards were likely to deprave and corrupt the morals of the lieges and to create in their minds inordinate and lustful desires." The evidence was broadly that following a search of the accused's shop premises the police found the offending articles, some on display in the front shop and some in the back room. The shop was constructed so that it was impossible to see inside the shop from outside, but there was a sign outside indicating that it was a bookseller's shop and that no one under 18 would be admitted. The accused appealed by stated case. The appeal was dismissed. In delivering the opinion of the court, Lord Cameron said:

"I would, as at present advised, be disposed to regard the offence of exposure of obscene material for sale as one which may competently be comprehended within the general category of shameless and indecent conduct according to the common law of Scotland. If indecent exposure of the person falls within the generic of 'shameless indecent conduct' at common law, exposure for sale of obscene publications or reproductions would not appear to me to differ in quality but only in species ...

Counsel for the appellant's second principal argument was founded upon the assertion that the sheriff did not apply his mind to the issue of mens rea or to the facts and circumstances of the particular case, in respect that he made no finding that the appellant's conduct as occupier of the premises was indecent or shameless. There was, in particular, no finding as to the mode of display of the publications libelled within the front shop. There was thus no finding indicative of mens rea, more especially that there was no specific finding that the appellant owned or ran the business. In the absence of any such necessary findings the material for conviction was insufficient. In my opinion there is no substance in this argument. The appellant is found to be occupier of the premises, the stock of material in the back shop is found to be *his* 'reserve' stock, the premises advertise a bookselling business with access denied to persons under 18. There is no window display, but on the contrary the contents of the shop are screened effectively from outside view and it is impossible to see into the shop from outside. All this appears to me more than ample to demonstrate that the appellant was fully aware of the type of custom he was seeking to cultivate and of the nature of the wares that he was offering to the adult public for sale. The care taken to conceal the wares from outward view was both an invitation and an indication of the character and quality of the goods inside."

Having thus established that the exposure of obscene material for sale was an offence at common law, three questions arose as to the scope of the offence. The first related to the essence of the offence, a matter considered in *Ingram v Macari*, 1982 S.L.T. 92 where remarkable similiarities with the statutory offences were revealed. The respondent had been charged in the following terms: "that ... in the shop premises occupied by you at 90 East High Street, Forfar ... you did conduct yourself in a shamelessly indecent manner, and sell one magazine of an indecent and obscene nature, namely 'Rustler, Vol. 5, No. 8', and did further expose for sale and have for sale 262 indecent and obscene books and magazines." The sheriff held that the charge was irrelevant and he dismissed the complaint on the ground that the charge did not aver that the indecent and obscene material was liable or likely to deprave and corrupt the morals of the lieges and to create in their minds inordinate and lustful desires. The Crown appealed successfully against the dismissal, with the High Court writing:

"In our opinion the submission for the Crown is sound and must receive effect. As the Crown concedes, the substance of offences of the kind with which this complaint is concerned is sale or exposure for sale of indecent and obscene material (*Robertson v Smith*, 1979 S.L.T. (Notes) 51 at p. 52). The question is whether for the purposes of pure relevancy of a charge at common law that charge must libel expressly that the allegedly indecent and obscene articles are liable to corrupt and deprave those likely to be exposed to their influence. There can be no doubt that the answer to that question is no. It is to be found in the opinion of the court delivered by the Lord Justice-General (Cooper) in *Galletly*. That case establishes that under the statutory provisions such as those with which the case was concerned, which make it an offence to sell or expose for sale 'indecent or obscene' articles of publications, the words 'indecent or obscene' imply the liability of the articles or publications concerned to corrupt and deprave. As the Lord Justice-General said in his opinion (1953 S.L.T. at p. 71): 'different as these and other like provisions are in detail, there seems to me to run through all the provisions on the subject, and also through the rules of our own common law as exemplified by such cases as *Robinson* (1843) 1 Broun 590, 643, a common policy aimed at providing a remedy for an undoubted social evil; and in view of the argument to which we listened it will be simplest to begin with certain general observations, derived from a survey of the statutes and of a series of decisions both in Scotland and in England. To justify a conviction in a case of this type the Court ought to be satisfied of two elements, viz. (1) that the book or picture is of such a nature as to be calculated to produce a pernicious effect in depraving and corrupting those who are open to such influences; and (2) that such book or picture is being indiscriminately exhibited or circulated or offered for sale in such circumstances as to justify the inference that it is likely to fall (and perhaps intended to fall) into the hands of persons liable to be so corrupted.'

If, therefore, for the purposes of statutory offences the words 'indecent or obscene' convey a single idea involving the liability of articles so described to corrupt and deprave, there is no reason whatever for supposing that at common law the words 'indecent and obscene' do not carry the same implication. In the result the liability of the allegedly indecent and obscene publications to corrupt and deprave is of the essence of the common law offence just as it is of the statutory offences and must be established. This liability, however, is implied in the words 'indecent or obscene' in their statutory context or 'indecent and obscene' in the context of a common law charge. They do not therefore require to be expressly libelled for the purposes of relevancy."

The second question raised by the offence admitted in *Robertson v Smith*, was to establish what was meant by "exposure for sale." This was subsequently considered in *Scott v Smith*, 1981 S.L.T. (Notes) 22, where the accused did not openly display the articles in question but produced a selection of materials from a drawer when asked by a customer whether he had any adult magazines for sale. In his opinion, Lord Cameron said:

"What in fact he did was, at the request of a customer, to lay before the customer a number of magazines which have been found to be obscene publications, and that finding is not challenged. In respect of these articles they were certainly displayed for one purpose alone—to attract the customer and for sale. They were taken from a drawer in the shop which contained other obscene magazines ... Other similar magazines were found, not in a drawer but (1) on a shelf behind the counter, and (2) on the shop floor behind the counter. Even though they were 'not visible to the casual visitor' equally they were not concealed. All were of the same character according to the sheriff's findings, and these are not challenged.

It is not open to dispute that all the magazines found were held by the appellant for sale to members of the public and formed part of his stock held in immediate readiness to meet the desires or requests of any member of the public who came to the shop as a prospective customer for 'adult books' as indicative of the type and character of the literary works desired. The appellant at once recognised the nature and purpose of his customer's request and consequently offered and displayed a selection of his wares in this particular line of literature.

There must be many bookshops—both new and second-hand—where significant parts of the books on sale are not visible to the casual visitor, but because of this fact it could scarcely be argued that the books in question were not being exposed for sale. It seems to me that decision of the issue of what is 'exposure for sale' in any given case is largely one of fact and circumstance. I do not think it would be practicable or profitable to attempt to define within rigid limits or boundaries what is comprised within the words 'exposed for sale'.

In the present case the sheriff had before him facts which made it clear that a substantial stock of obscene magazines was kept in immediate readiness for sale in drawers and on shelves and even on the floor adjacent to the counter over which sales took place. Further, there was undoubted display of a selection of the stock when the general request was made 'whether he [the appellant] had any adult books'. This was not the case of a sale of a particularly requested item, but a display of a representative selection of stock in response to a general question as to whether a particular type of periodical or book was kept in stock by the shopkeeper. It was in reference to this general request that there was what may fairly enough be described as an 'exposure' of stock—for the purpose of securing a sale. I think that on the facts found by the sheriff in this case he was entitled to hold established that the appellant had 'exposed for sale' the magazines and periodicals specified in the schedules annexed to the complaint."

The third issue raised by the cases after *Robertson v Smith* is whether there were any limitations on the scope of the offence. In *Tudhope v Sommerville*, 1981 S.L.T. 117 the High Court held that the crime did not extend to wholesalers of indecent material. In delivering the opinion of the court, Lord Cameron said:

"No doubt it is a crime at common law to expose for sale in premises to which the public are invited to resort or to which they are given access for the purpose of being invited to purchase or be supplied with obscene or indecent literature, but that is a very different matter from warehousing literature of that type. It has not as yet been suggested that to do so constitutes a common law offence according to the law of Scotland. While disclaiming a intention to describe what is charged here as falling within the category of shameless and indecent conduct, the advocate-depute sought to formulate the offence as falling within the category of 'trafficking in obscene material' by analogy with 'trafficking' by actual exposure for sale. In effect, the argument for the Crown was that what is libelled in this complaint was an 'aspect' of what had already and for long been held to be criminal conduct. In my opinion this will not do: the criminal element in charges of exposure for sale of obscene or indecent material lies in the exposure to the public. The mere possession of such material is not by that fact alone rendered criminal at common law; here there is no affront to public decency or morals nor any action which of itself is designed or calculated to corrupt the morals of the lieges. The lieges are in no sense brought in actual contact or potential contact with the (assumedly) corrupting influence so long as it remains passively in the accused's warehouse. On the other hand, possession in retail shop premises in circumstances indicative that such material is part of that retailer's stock in trade and is kept in such manner and in such place as to yield the conclusion that that stock is being offered for sale, may well however provide the necessary basis for conviction of the offence of shameless and indecent conduct. ... The Crown in the present appeal seek to push the boundaries of criminal responsibility further than has been recognised in the past, by contending that it is the purpose for which the possession exists which constitutes its criminal character, as it is an 'aspect' of what has already been held criminal, namely the exposure for sale. But at what point is the line to be drawn? At the wholesaler? But if he is to be held liable at common law and the offence is not 'shameless and indecent conduct,' on what ground should the publisher or printer escape? The argument for the Crown—and in a case in which neither conspiracy nor concert is alleged (and I reserve my opinion on the relevancy of such a charge affecting the retailer, wholesaler or publisher or printer)—went beyond the bounds of conduct which directly affected or might affect members of the public."

The other limitation had emerged earlier in *Dean v John Menzies (Holdings) Ltd*, 1981 S.L.T. 50 where it was held that the offence cannot be committed by a limited liability company on the ground that shamelessness is an attribute of which human beings alone are capable and is not something which can be imputed to a company. The case is also important for the indications of dissent by Lords Stott and Maxwell about developments of shameless indecency generally. In his opinion, Lord Stott said this was "an area of law in which (as is perhaps indicated by the archaic and faintly ludicrous wording of the complaint) commonsense is not noticeably at a premium" (at 60). But notwithstanding this decision, the Crown seemed undaunted and continued to fish for small fry, with prosecutions being brought against the proprietors of small businesses, and remarkably, against junior employees (including shop assistants) of the corporate bodies which could not be prosecuted. Sensibly, however, sheriffs appeared reluctant to convict the latter such people, who after all will bear no responsibility for the policy of their employer: see *Tudhope v Barlow*, 1981 S.L.T. (Sh. Ct) 94. This was a clear abuse of power by the Crown Office which ought to have been firmly dealt with by the courts. Even if it is conceded that the Executive needed more powers than those contained in the Burgh Police (Scotland) Act 1892, it is a constitutional impropriety to take an initiative which by-passes Parliament by seeking the endorsement of a compliant court. Certainly reports of shameless indecency cases have declined, and in one which *has* recently been reported (*Lockhart v Stephen*, 1987 S.C.C.R. 642) the sheriff (Stewart) emphasised that the standard, as said in *Tudhope v Barlow*, is the current standards of ordinary decent people, that those standards have changed enormously since the offence of shameless indecency was revived, and that a live performace in a pub which, though perhaps vulgar, disgusting and offensive, gave no encouragement to violent sadistic practices, but only encouraged normal sexual activity among adults according to the general standards of today is not likely to deprave and corrupt and so is not shamelessly indecent. The interested reader should compare the facts alleged in the complaint, as compared with that in *Watt v Annan*, to appreciate just how much the current standards of ordinary decent people have changed!

The offence of shameless indecency was strongly criticised in the academic literature and reported prosecutions in connection with indecent or obscene publications began to decline in the 1980s. As a result, shameless indecency began to play a marginal role in the control of such publications. Many would argue that it should have had no such role in the first place. Nevertheless shameless indecency grew and developed in new directions. In one line of cases it was used against men who had improper sexual relationships with young people in their care, while in another it was used against men who showed indecent videos to young people. In *Webster v Dominick*, 2003 S.L.T. 975, however, the High Court (consisting of five judges) re-examined the foundations of the crime in the light of claims that it was too vague to meet the requirements of Art.7 of the ECHR. The High Court reached a major decision in which the offence was disapproved and a new common law offence of public indecency created in its place. The new offence of public indecency bears some similarities to the English common law offence of outraging public decency, which by no means had a painless labour. Indeed in *Knuller v DPP* [1973] A.C. 435, Lord Reid said that: "To recognise this new crime would go contrary to the whole trend of public policy followed by Parliament in recent times". Some of the objections to a judge-made offence of shameless indecency apply with equal force to a judge-made offence of public indecency. For our immediate purposes, however, it is important to note that Lord Cullen (L.J.–C.) expressly stated that this new offence would not apply to obscene publications which would now be governed only by statute (the Civic Government (Scotland) Act 1982, on which see below). The Lord Justice Clerk delivered the only opinion, with which the other members of the court concurred.

(c) The Modern Statutory Regime

Report of the Committee on Obscenity and Film Censorship
(Chairman: Bernard Williams) Cmnd. 7772 (1979)

"SUMMARY OF PROPOSALS

General

1. The existing variety of laws in this field should be scrapped and a comprehensive new statute should start afresh (see paragraph 2.29).

2. Terms such as 'obscene', 'indecent' and 'deprave and corrupt' should be abandoned as having outlived their usefulness (paragraph 9.21).

3. The law should rest partly on the basis of harms caused by or involved in the existence of the material: these alone can justify prohibitions; and partly on the basis of the public's legitimate interests in not being offended by the display and availability of the material: this can justify no more than the imposition of restrictions designed to protect the ordinary citizen from unreasonable offence (paragraphs 9.7 and 10.2).

4. The principle object of the law should be to prevent certain kinds of material causing offence to reasonable people or being made available to young people (paragraph 9.7).

5. Only a small class of material should be forbidden to those who want it, because an objective assessment of likely harm does not support a wider prohibition (paragraph 10.8)

6. The printed word should be neither restricted nor prohibited since its nature makes it neither immediately offensive nor capable of involving the harms we identify, and because of its importance in conveying ideas (paragraph 7.22).

Restriction

7. Restrictions should apply to matter (other than the printed word) and to a performance whose unrestricted availability is offensive to reasonable people by reason of the manner in which it portrays, deals with or relates to violence, cruelty or horror, or sexual, faecal or urinary functions or genital organs (paragraph 9.36 and 11.8).

8. Restriction is to consist in a ban
   (i) on the display, sale, hire etc. of restricted material other than by way of postal or other delivery and
   (ii) on the presentation of any restricted performance other than in premises (or part of premises having a separate access from the street)
      (a) to which persons under the age of eighteen are not admitted, and
      (b) to which access is possible only by passing a prominent warning notice in specified terms, and
      (c) which make no display to persons not passing beyond the warning notice, other than the name of the business and an indication of its nature (paragraphs 9.15 and 11.8)...

13. It should not be an offence for a person under the age of eighteen to seek to gain entry to premises in which restricted material is being displayed, sold or hired or in which a restricted performance is being presented, or to order restricted material to be sent to him or her (paragraph 9.44)...

Prohibition

19. Prohibited material should consist of photographs and films whose production appears to the court to have involved the exploitation for sexual purposes of any person where either
      (a) that person appears from the evidence as a whole to have been at the relevant time under the age of sixteen, or
      (b) the material gives reason to believe that actual physical harm was inflicted on that

person (paragraph 10.6).

20. It should be an offence to take any prohibited photograph or film, to distribute or show it, to have it with a view to its being distributed or shown, or to advertise it as being available for distribution or showing (paragraph 10.13)...

24. A live performance should be prohibited if

    (a) it involves actual sexual activity of a kind which, in the circumstances in which it was given, would be offensive to reasonable people (sexual activity including the act of masturbation and forms of genital, anal or oral connection between humans and animals as well as between humans), or

    (b) it involves the sexual exploitation of any person under the age of sixteen (paragraph 11.15)."

No action was taken to implement the proposals of the Williams Committee. There have, however, been two major statutory initiatives since Williams. The first was the enactment of the Indecent Displays (Control) Act 1981, sponsored by a backbencher, Mr Tim Sainsbury. The Act (which repealed the provisions of s.380(3) of the Burgh Police (Scotland) Act 1892 which made it an offence to exhibit to view indecent or obscene materials) gives substantial effect to the recommendations in para. 8 above. However, the major departure is that the Act applies to "indecent" material whereas Williams had recommended the abolition of the old legal standards and their replacement with a provision based on offence to reasonable people. The Act provides that it is an offence to display indecent material in a public place. A public place is defined as a place to which the public have or are permitted to have access (whether on payment or otherwise) while the matter is displayed. The Act does not apply where:

    (1) the place is one to which the public are permitted to have access only on payment which is or includes payment for the display; or

    (2) the place is a shop or any part of a shop to which the public can only gain access by passing beyond an adequate warning notice. The notice must state that persons passing beyond it will find material on display which they may consider indecent. Persons under 18 must not be permitted entry and this must be stated on the notice.

The Act specifically adopts a number of exclusions which deal with the theatre, television, the cinema, art galleries and museums. Prosecution under the Act may lead to imprisonment or a fine, or both.

The Civic Government (Scotland) Act 1982

"Obscene material

51.—(1) Subject to subsection (4) below, any person who displays any obscene material in any public place or in any other place where it can be seen by the public shall be guilty of an offence under this section.

(2) Subject to subsection (4) below, any person who publishes, sells or distributes or, with a view to its eventual sale or distribution, makes, prints, has or keeps any obscene material shall be guilty of an offence under this section.

(4) A person shall not be convicted of an offence under this section if he proves that he had used all due diligence to avoid committing the offence.

A major feature of s.51 (which does not apply to television programmes or plays) is that it applies only to obscene material, whereas the 1892 Act applied to both indecent and obscene material. The reason was explained in the House of Lords in the following terms:

"The one major difference between Clause 51 and the existing law on obscenity in the 1892 Act, is that, unlike the provision in the 1892 Act, which covers indecent and obscene material,. Clause 51 is restricted to obscene material. This has been done primarily in order to remove an inconsistency which now arises under Scottish law as a result of the passing of the Indecent Displays (Control) Act 1981. The 1981 Act implicitly permits the display of indecent material in certain clearly defined circumstances—for instance, behind a warning notice. Under the present law on obscenity in Scotland, however, a shopkeeper who complies with the 1981 Act and withdraws behind such a notice material which could be regarded as indecent could still find himself falling foul of the criminal law on the grounds that he is offering indecent material for sale. This difficulty does not arise in England and Wales because the prohibition on offering for sale under the Obscene Publications Act 1959 applies only to obscene material. The restriction of Clause 51 to obscene material only thus not only removes this inconsistency but secures a greater measure of uniformity in relation to the law on obscenity throughout Great Britain. The clause does not attempt a definition of 'obscene' but leaves it, as at present, to the courts to interpret that term in light of the prevailing moral consensus." (425 H.L. Debs, November 24, 1981, col. 673).

One consequence of this change is that the courts will have to embark upon the inquiry disapproved by Lord Cooper in *Galletly v Laird*, 1953 S.L.T. 67; that is to say, "it will now be the task of the Scottish courts to draw [a] distinction between 'indecent' and 'obscene'" (Solicitor-General for Scotland, First Scottish Standing Committee, June 22, 1982, 16th sitting, col. 552). Thus, it will not be unlawful to sell indecent material, provided that a warning notice is put up. But even if a warning notice is put up, it will be unlawful to sell obscene material.

A second major feature of s. 51 is that it does not define "obscene". This is a point which was raised in Standing Committee where the Solicitor-General for Scotland asserted that: "Obscenity is a relative concept which may vary according to the circumstances and locality, and it would be difficult if not impossible to produce a workable and generally acceptable definition" (*ibid.*, col. 551). It was therefore thought that the term "should be left to the interpretation of the courts in the light of the prevailing moral consensus" (*ibid.*), albeit that "the courts are unlikely to welcome this burden" (*ibid.*, col. 552). It was anticipated, however (on the basis of a dictum in *Ingram v Macari*, 1982 S.L.T. 92), that "the words 'deprave and corrupt' [will be] read into the legislation automatically as a definition of obscenity. The courts already apply the test [under the previous statutes and the common law]." The Solicitor-General continued by expressing the view that this would be a reasonable qualification to attach to the statute (*ibid.*, col. 552). The continuing application of this test would thus appear to expose Scots law to the range of difficulties which the similar test in English law has presented to the courts.

One question which has arisen is whether the offence is limited to sexual matters. The English courts have been prepared to hold that the glorification of drug-taking is obscene because of the tendency to deprave and corrupt (*John Calder (Publications) Ltd v Powell* [1965] 1 Q.B. 509). A second question is whether it is unlawful to offer for sale material which has an adverse effect in the sense that it is likely to repel people rather than cause them to behave in a depraved or corrupted fashion. In *R. v Anderson* [1972] 1 Q.B. 304, it was held that failure by a trial judge to deal with this in his direction to the jury amounted to "a substantial and serious misdirection". A third question is whether it is unlawful to offer for sale material to a likely audience which is already corrupted. In *DPP v Whyte* [1972] A.C. 849 the House of Lords divided three to two in replying in the affirmative. In the course of his speech, Lord Wilberforce said at 862–863:

"Let us see what they have done. Having confined the class of likely readers to males of middle age and upwards they have held that they were not satisfied that the books would have a tendency to deprave and corrupt a significant proportion of them. They reached this result by a process of inference: none of the readers was called to the witness box. The process was:

'(i) the significant proportion of future recipients of the ... articles were going to be the 'hard core'—note the conclusory words—'of regular customers of the ... said shop'; (ii) the regular customers they saw as 'inadequate, pathetic, dirty minded men, seeking cheap thrills—addicts to this type of material, whose morals were already in a state of depravity and corruption'; (iii) there was grave doubt 'whether such minds could be said to be open to any immoral influences which the ... articles were capable of exerting.'

My Lords, I appreciate genuinely the efforts which the justices made to administer this legislation; it is obvious that they gave the case a great deal of attention and thought. It is no reflection on their ability that in this very difficult task they fell into error. But, in my opinion, the process I have just stated was erroneous in itself and the facts to which it was applied lead clearly to the conclusion that the respondents should have been convicted. Putting aside the considerable deficiencies in the factual basis of the process (is it really to be supposed that every, or with minor exceptions, every male of forty and upwards who has visited or may visit this shop is of the character described—what is meant by 'significant proportion'?), to state as a proposition that all these men are incapable of being depraved and corrupted because they are addicts is not a finding of fact, but an assumption contrary to the whole basis of the Act. The Act's purpose is to prevent the depraving and corrupting of men's minds by certain types of writing: it could never have been intended to except from the legislative protection a large body of citizens merely because, in different degrees, they had previously been exposed, or exposed themselves, to the 'obscene' material. The Act is not merely concerned with the once and for all corruption of the wholly innocent; it equally protects the less innocent from further corruption, the addict from feeding or increasing his addiction. To say this is not to negate the principle of relative 'obscenity': certainly the tendency to deprave and corrupt is not to be estimated in relation to some assumed standard of purity of some reasonable man. It is the likely reader. And to apply different tests to teenagers, members of men's clubs or men in various occupations or localities would be a matter of common sense. But the argument here is not: 'Well, nobody reads this until he is over forty and by then he won't come to any harm': it is quite different. It assumes the possibility of corruption by the articles in question, indeed the fact of it is found, and argues from that to an absence of corrupting tendency. The passage contains its own refutation. These very men, it states, are depraved and corrupted by these very articles. In itself it proves the case: it should have led to conviction."

English statutes contain two important defences to a charge of obscenity. The first is the defence of public good whereby a conviction will not lie if it is proved that the publication of the article in question was justified in the interests of science, literature, art or learning, or of other subjects of general concern. The existence of this defence in Scotland appears to have been conceded by Lord Cooper in *Galletly* and was certainly anticipated by Lord Sands in *McGowan v Langmuir*. As was made clear in the parliamentary debates these cases will continue to be authoritative under the new statutory régime. The second defence recognised by English law is that of innocent publication whereby a conviction will not lie if the accused proves that he had not examined the article in question and had no reasonable cause to suspect that by having it he risked prosecution. Although this defence is perhaps limited in scope, it would not be difficult to establish its existence from Lord Cooper's remarks that what the law is aiming to control is the deliberate trafficking in pornography by those who make a business of catering for depraved and perverted tastes. It may be noted that this defence was explicitly recognised by the Edinburgh Corporation Order Confirmation Act 1967 (s.453(2)), but by none of the other of the local statutes in force before 1982. And it may well be, of course, that the activity covered by this defence will also be covered by the only explicit defence in s.51, that is to say, the provision in subs. (4). It was pointed out in Standing Committee that s.51(4) would operate to protect employees from being prosecuted. In view of the fact that corporations may now be convicted (thus dealing with the *John Menzies* problem), it is hoped that the Crown would in any event move against employees.

Before leaving this subject, it is to be noted that many will regret that the Scottish Office did not act more adventurously. The "deprave and corrupt" test has been widely criticised, and it is a pity perhaps that the opportunity was not taken to meet these criticisms. Thus, in *Whyte's* case Lord Wilberforce said (at p. 862):

"It can only have been the pressure of Parliamentary compromise which can have produced a test so difficult for the courts. No definition of 'deprave and corrupt' is offered—no guideline as to what kind of influence is meant. Is it criminal conduct, general or sexual, that is feared (and we may note that the articles here treated of sadistic and violent behaviour), or departure from some mode of morality, sexual or otherwise, and if so whose code, or from accepted or other beliefs, or the arousing of erotic desires 'normal' or 'abnormal,' or, as the justices have said, 'private fantasies.' Some, perhaps most, of these alternatives involve deep questions of psychology and ethics: how are the courts to deal with them? Well might they have said that such words provide a formula which cannot in practice be applied. What they have said is, first, that no definition of deprave and corrupt can be provided (*R. v Calder & Boyars Ltd.* [1969] 1 Q.B. 151), though the words are meant to be strong and emphatic (see *R. v Knuller (Publishing, Printing and Promotions) Ltd.* [1972] 3 W.L.R. 143, 148, 180, *per* Lord Reid and Lord Simon of Glaisdale); secondly, that judges or juries must decide for or against a tendency to deprave and corrupt as a question of fact and must do so without expert, that is psychological or sociological or medical, advice (*R. v Anderson*). I simply state this attitude as a fact; it is not appropriate to endorse or to disapprove it on this present occasion. I have serious doubts whether the Act will continue to be workable in this way, or whether it will produce tolerable results. The present is, or in any rational system ought to be, a simple case, yet the illogical and unscientific character of the Act has forced the justices into untenable positions."

(2) Contempt of court

Contempt of court covers a multitude of sins. In *Johnson v Grant*, 1923 S.C. 789, the Lord Justice-General (Clyde) expressed the following view:

"The phrase 'contempt of Court' does not in the least describe the true nature of the class of offence with which we are here concerned, and which is prosecuted in the civil Court by petition and complaint with the concurrence of the Lord Advocate. The offence consists in interfering with the administration of the law; in impeding and perverting the course of justice. The malversation of an officer of Court is an example of it. Another, and often venial, example is the publication in the press of references to a pending litigation calculated to prejudice one of the parties or to bias the jury. A third, and a much more serious, instance is where people take upon themselves to break the law and then to defy its administration—in short directly to impede and to pervert the course of justice. The currency of the phrase is particularly regrettable, inasmuch as it seems to have encouraged the idea that all that has to be done by a person who has, however deliberately, committed this class of offence, and then wishes to avoid the consequences of his conduct, is to present an apology, as for an offence against the dignity of the Court. It is not the dignity of the Court which is offended—a petty and misleading view of the issues involved—it is the fundamental supremacy of the law which is challenged. That is why conduct of this kind is properly treated as deserving of criminal punishment; it is intolerable in any civilised and well-ordered society. Further, not only has no one the power to purge himself of a deliberate offence by saying he is sorry, but the mere circumstance that he presents a belated expression of contrition has, with regard to the public aspect of the matter, almost no importance at all."

For our purposes, we are concerned only with how the law of contempt restricts free expression in the press and elsewhere. We look first at how the law protects judges from criticism and secondly at how it is used to ensure that accused persons are given a fair trial.

(a) The Strict Liability Rule

An important second function of the law of contempt is to regulate a conflict between two fundamental civil liberties: freedom of expression on the one hand, and the right to a fair trial on the other. Unlimited press freedom may lead to excessive pre-trial publicity (with accusations of guilt against the accused) which may make it impossible to guarantee a fair trial before a jury which has not already prejudged the issues. It is a function of the law of contempt to strike a balance between these competing claims. In Scotland, the balance has been struck clearly in favour of the right of the accused, and the law seeks to prohibit expression to the extent that it conflicts with this basic right. In *Stirling v Associated Newspapers Ltd,* 1960 S.L.T. 5, the Lord Justice-General (Clyde) said:

> "... the Press in this country is free, free in particular fairly to report anything that occurs in open Court, when a trial takes place, free to publicise anything that is said or done by a Judge, or a counsel, or a witness, or by the jury at that trial. For, in doing so, the Press is performing a genuine public service in enabling the public to see for themselves whether justice is being done. The high standard of discrimination and fairness with which this work has been done by responsible Scottish newspapers has made it unnecessary for our Courts to lay down rules in this matter. We have been content to rely on their honour, their good sense and their discrimination. But freedom does not mean license, and the freedom which the Press rightly enjoys carries its own responsibilities. If that freedom is abused, and if the content of a newspaper is such as to be likely to endanger the prospects of a fair and impartial trial in Scotland, then, it is the duty of this Court, and it has always been recognised to be the duty of this Court, to take cognisance of it, and to punish the wrong that such conduct involves.
>
> We are not concerned with the motive for which the wrong is done, whether it is to pander to sensationalism, to increase the circulation of the newspaper, or whatever else it may be. Our duty is always to prevent any violation of those principles of fair play which it is the pride of this country to extend even to the worst of criminals."

The legal position is now governed by the Contempt of Court Act 1981, which was passed for two reasons. The first was to implement the major recommendations of the Phillimore Committee on Contempt of Court. The second was to bring English law into line with the European Convention on Human Rights following the decision in *Sunday Times v United Kingdom* (1979) 2 E.H.R.R. 245.

The Contempt of Court Act 1981

"The strict liability rule"

1. In this Act 'the strict liability rule' means the rule of law whereby conduct may be treated as a contempt of court as tending to interfere with the course of justice in particular legal proceedings regardless of intent to do so.

Limitation of scope of strict liability

2.—(1) The strict liability rule applies only in relation to publications, and for this purpose 'publication' includes any speech, writing, broadcast or other communication in whatever form, which is addressed to the public at large or any section of the public.

(2) The strict liability rule applies only to a publication which creates a substantial risk that the course of justice in the proceedings in question will be seriously impeded or prejudiced.

(3) The strict liability rule applies to a publication only if the proceedings in question are active within the meaning of this section at the time of the publication.

(4) Schedule 1 applies for determining the times at which proceedings are to be treated as active within the meaning of this section.

SCHEDULE 1

Times when Proceedings are Active for Purposes of Section 2

Preliminary

1. In this Schedule 'criminal proceedings' means proceedings against a person in respect of an offence, not being appellate proceedings ... and 'appellate proceedings' means proceedings on appeal from or for the review of the decision of a court in any proceedings.

2. Criminal, appellate and other proceedings are active within the meaning of section 2 at times respectively prescribed by the following paragraphs of this Schedule; and in relation to proceedings in which more than one of the steps described in any of those paragraphs is taken, the reference in that paragraph is a reference to the first of those steps.

Criminal proceedings

3. Subject to the following provisions of this Schedule, criminal proceedings are active from the relevant initial step specified in paragraph 4 until concluded as described in paragraph 5.

4. The initial steps of criminal proceedings are:—

    (a) arrest without warrant;

    (b) ... the grant of a warrant for arrest;

    (c) the issue of a summons to appear, or in Scotland the grant of a warrant to cite;

    (d) the service of an indictment or other document specifying the charge; ...

5. Criminal proceedings are concluded—

    (a) by acquittal or, as the case may be, by sentence;

    (b) by any other verdict, finding, order or decision which puts an end to the proceedings;

    (c) by discontinuance or by operation of law.

6. The reference in paragraph 5(a) to sentence includes any order or decision consequent on conviction or finding of guilt which disposes of the case, either absolutely or subject to future events...

7. Proceedings are discontinued within the meaning of paragraph 5(c) ... in Scotland, if the proceedings are expressly abandoned by the prosecutor or are deserted *simpliciter*...

11. Criminal proceedings against a person which become active on the issue or the grant of a warrant for his arrest cease to be active at the end of the period of twelve months beginning with the date of the warrant unless he has been arrested within that period, but become active again if he is subsequently arrested.

Other proceedings at first instance

12. Proceedings other than criminal proceedings and appellate proceedings are active from the time when arrangements for the hearing are made or, if no such arrangements are previously made, from the time the hearing begins, until the proceedings are disposed of or discontinued or withdrawn...

14. In Scotland arrangements for the hearing of proceedings to which paragraph 12 applies are made within the meaning of that paragraph—

    (a) in the case of an ordinary action in the Court of Session or in the sheriff court, when the Record is closed;

    (b) in the case of a motion or application, when it is enrolled or made;

    (c) in any other case, when the date for a hearing is fixed or a hearing is allowed.

Appellate proceedings

15. Appellate proceedings are active from the time when they are commenced—
   (a) by application for leave to appeal or apply for review, or by notice of such an application;
   (b) by notice of appeal or of application for review;
   (c) by other originating process,
until disposed of or abandoned, discontinued or withdrawn.

16. Where, in appellate proceedings relating to criminal proceedings, the court—
   (a) remits the case to the court below; or
   (b) orders a new trial or a *venire de novo*, or in Scotland grants authority to bring a new prosecution,
any further or new proceedings which result shall be treated as active from the conclusion of the appellate proceedings."

The period since the enactment of the Contempt of Court Act 1981 has seen a gradual liberalisation of Scots law which was traditionally very tough on the press. As initially applied in the first wave of post 1981 Act cases, the test applied by the courts under the legislation appeared to be little different in practice from the test operating under the pre–1981 common law. So far as the latter is concerned, the leading case is *Atkins v London Weekend Television Ltd*, 1978 S.L.T. 76, where it was said that the test was whether "the contents of a [television] programme complained of were such as to give rise to a real risk of prejudice to the fair and impartial trial of the petitioner on the charges on which she stood indicted" (at 78). The test adopted in *H M Advocate v News Group Newspapers Ltd*, 1989 S.C.C.R. 156 was not much different: "there can be no contempt unless there is some risk, greater than a minimal one, that the course of justice in the proceedings in question will be seriously impeded or prejudiced. The adverb 'previously' does not require translation. It must be given its familiar and ordinary meaning" (at 161). Similarly in *H M Advocate v Caledonian Newspapers Ltd*, 1995 S.L.T. 926, where the High Court was moved to disagree "with counsel that the strict liability rule imposes a very high test in regard to a publication of the kind referred to in s 2 while the proceedings in question are active". In the *Caledonian Newspapers* case, it was explained that "the public policy that underlines the strict liability rule is that of deterrence. The court must do what it can to minimise the risk of prejudice, because it is in the public interest that proceedings for the detection and punishment of crime should not be interrupted by the effect on the course of justice by publicity" (at 1193).

There was no recognition in these cases of the importance of freedom of expression. But, this was to change in *Cox, Petitioner*, 1998 S.L.T. 1172 where the Lord Justice General said that:

"It is important, however, to recall that the due course of justice is only one of the values with which the Contempt of Court Act 1981 was concerned. The other value was freedom of expression. Parliament passed the 1981 Act in order to change the law of the United Kingdom and so to bring it into conformity with the interpretation of art 10 of the European Convention on Human Rights which the European Court of Human Rights had established in *Sunday Times v United Kingdom*. ... As its origins demonstrate, the Act was designed to regulate the boundary, which had always, of course, existed, between freedom of expression and the requirements of the due course of justice. That boundary may have been displaced from the familiar place where once it ran; Parliament may have redrawn the boundary at a point which would not have been chosen by people looking at the matter primarily from the standpoint of the administration of justice. But these factors simply make it all the more important that the courts faithfully observe the boundary which Parliament has settled in order to meet the international obligations of the United Kingdom." (at 1176)

In the same case Lord Prosser said in similar terms that:

"Whatever defining words are chosen to express the risk and degree of prejudice which will constitute contempt, and define its boundary, I think it worth emphasising that quite apart from the 1981 Act, and quite apart from the European Convention on Human Rights, there was ... never any excuse for the courts extending the boundary, and diminishing freedom of speech, on the basis that some wider boundary is more convenient, or simpler, or provides a useful cordon sanitaire." (at 1177)

It does not follow, however, that the law of contempt is free from danger for the press, as the following case indicates.

H M Advocate v The Scotsman Publications
1999 S.L.T. 466

This was a petition and complaint relating to the trial of Mohammed Sarwar who had been accused of electoral offences. On February 2, 1998 an article appeared on the front page of *The Scotsman* with the following headline: "Sarwar charge witnesses ask for protection". A smaller headline proclaimed: "Exclusive: Police told of pressure over evidence". So far as relevant the article read as follows:

"TWO key witnesses in the Glasgow Govan fraud inquiry have asked for police protection because they fear intimidation and attempts to persuade them to change their evidence.

The Scotsman understands that one witness has contacted police after facing pressure from friends and family in Glasgow and abroad. . . .

Strathclyde Police refused to comment on any of the allegations of intimidation while the Crown prepares its case against Mohammad Sarwar, the Govan MP who is charged with election fraud, attempting to pervert the course of justice and breaking the law on election expenses. . . .

The procurator-fiscal in Glasgow is now precognising witnesses for the Crown and is expected to report to the Crown office within two to three months".

A petition was presented by the Lord Advocate to have the publisher, the editor and the journalist punished for contempt of court.

LORD MARNOCH: "During the hearing reference was made to four authorities which, in chronological order, were *Kemp and Others, Petitioners*, 1982 S.L.T. 357; *H.M. Advocate v Newsgroup Newspapers Limited*, 1989 S.C.C.R. 156, particularly at p. 161F; *H.M. Advocate v Caledonian Newspapers Limited* 1995 S.L.T. 926 at p. 929B, and *Attorney General v M.G.N. Limited* [1997] 1 All E.R. 456 at pp. 460–461. The last reference provides a particularly useful index of the various matters which should be borne in mind in a case of this sort. In the end, however, I did not understand there to be any serious doubt as to the law which was applicable. In that connection the advocate depute made it clear that the petitioner relied exclusively on section 2(2) of the Contempt of Court Act 1981 and it was not, I think, disputed that the test which accordingly fell to be applied was whether, at the time it was made, the publication in question created a 'substantial' or 'material' or, to use the words of Lord Emslie in *H.M. Advocate v Newsgroup Newspapers Limited.*, 'greater than minimal' risk that the course of justice in the proceedings commenced against Mr. Sarwar would be, to use the words of the Act, 'seriously impeded or prejudiced'. There was also, I think, no dispute but that the effect of the publication had to be judged according to its likely impact on the ordinary reader at the time of publication;—*Attorney General v M.G.N. Limited* at p. 460.

As to the likely impact of the publication on the ordinary reader at the time I am not in any doubt that he would be left with the impression that two 'key' witnesses had asked for police protection because they feared intimidation from Mr. Sarwar or associates of Mr.

Sarwar for whose actings Mr. Sarwar was directly or indirectly responsible. That, it seems to me, is the natural inference which would be drawn from the first paragraph of the article in question;—and that, I think, was by and large the submission of the advocate depute. In particular, I did not understand him to make any separate or independent submission regarding the first sentence of article 7 of the petition. As regards what I have just said, it is, of course, true that there are other possible candidates for the role of intimidator, namely persons not acting under the control of Mr. Sarwar but for one reason or another well disposed or sympathetic to his cause. That, according to Mr. Mitchell for the respondents, was 'the furthest the article could go'. In my opinion, however, where, in the context of a criminal prosecution, particularly one involving charges of election fraud and attempting to pervert the course of justice, there is reference to feared intimidation,—without further particulars,—the ordinary reader is likely to assume that the accused is ultimately the person whose intimidation is feared. He, after all, is the person with the most obvious interest in the outcome of the trial.

If I am right so far then I have to say that in my opinion there could hardly be a more prejudicial suggestion in advance of trial than the one in question. The fact that an accused should stoop to intimidating witnesses is one which many readers, including the ordinary reader, would regard as almost tantamount to guilt. Moreover, once the ordinary reader has formed that impression I do not consider that he is likely to forget it, particularly when applied to someone as well-known as Mr. Sarwar. It is, in short, an impression which, in my opinion, is likely to 'stick'. For these reasons I am not, myself, much moved by the submission that the effect of the article would have been spent or forgotten by the time, some months later, the hypothetical juror took his place in the jury box. Nor do I think that its effect would necessarily be removed by the ordinary directions of a trial judge to have regard only to the evidence in the case. Whatever directions along these lines may be given jurors will, I think, always form some impression of the sort of person they are dealing with and, if they had read the article in question, I cannot but think that that impression might well be coloured in a manner prejudicial to the accused. I emphasise, here, that what I have in mind are what I have described as the 'ordinary directions' of a trial judge since these are the only ones which can be assumed as at the date of publication. Particular directions, sensitively given, to ignore entirely any suggestion of intimidation from any quarter might be in a different category but in my opinion that sort of direction cannot be prayed in aid by the present respondents.

It remains only to consider a submission which was made, I think, rather hesitantly on behalf of the respondents to the effect that the *Scotsman's* principal readership, as one might expect, was in the Lothians and that its circulation in the region of Strathclyde was no more than around 12,000 copies. Again, for myself, I do not find this a very compelling consideration. As I understand it the *Scotsman* does see itself as a national newspaper and in my view there would be a material risk of serious prejudice if even one juror had read the article and was affected by it in the way which I have envisaged. In any event, it cannot nowadays be assumed that High Court trials will always take place where the crime or crimes are said to have been committed.

In the result, and for all the foregoing reasons, I am of opinion that the petitioner has made out his case and that the respondents are guilty of contempt under the provisions of section 2 of the Contempt of Court Act 1981."

In other cases the courts have pointed out that it would be improper to reveal that the accused has previous convictions (*Cox, Petitioner, op cit.*, at 1178). Also likely to give rise to contempt proceedings would be the publication of a photograph where the identity of the offender is an issue (*Caledonian Newspapers Ltd, op cit.*). Similarly with any explicit inference that the accused was guilty of the offence for which he was to be tried (*Al Megrahi v Times Newspapers Ltd*, 1999 S.C.C.R. 824). In the last case, however, a finding of contempt against the *Sunday Times* was avoided where the trial of the accused (charged with the Lockerbie bombing) was to be by three Scottish judges sitting in the Netherlands rather than by a jury in Scotland. This is a conclusion which follows the House of Lords in *Re Lonrho* [1990] 2 A.C. 154 where Lord Bridge said:

> "The possibility that a professional judge will be influenced by anything he has read about the issues in a case which he has to try is very much more remote. He will not consciously allow himself to take account of anything other than the evidence and argument presented to him in court."

However, in the new liberal era of contempt of court the judges have been more willing to trust the ability of the jury to "stick to the evidence which they have heard, and exclude other considerations from their mind" (*Cox, Petitioner, op cit.*, at p. 1177 (Lord Prosser)). Indeed Lord Prosser was to point out that: "Juries are healthy bodies. They do not need a germ free atmosphere. Even when articles in the press do contain germs of prejudice, it will rarely be appropriate ... to bring these to the attention of the court, far less for specific directions to have to be given, far less for the issue to be treated as even potentially one of contempt" (*ibid.*, at p. 1178).

(b) Defences to Strict Liability

The Contempt of Court Act 1981

"Defence of innocent publication or distribution

3.—(1) A person is not guilty of contempt of court under the strict liability rule as the publisher of any matter to which that rule applies if at the time of the publication (having taken all reasonable care) he does not know and has no reason to suspect that relevant proceedings are active.

(2) A person is not guilty of contempt of court under the strict liability rule as the distributor of a publication containing any such matter if at the time of distribution (having taken all reasonable care) he does not know that it contains such matter and has no reason to suspect that it is likely to do so.

(3) The burden of proof of any fact tending to establish a defence afforded by this section to any person lies upon that person ...

Contemporary reports of proceedings

4.—(1) Subject to this section a person is not guilty of contempt of court under the strict liability rule in respect of a fair and accurate report of legal proceedings held in public, published contemporaneously and in good faith.

(2) In any such proceedings the court may, where it appears to be necessary for avoiding a substantial risk of prejudice to the administration of justice in those proceedings, or in any other proceedings pending or imminent, order that the publication of any report of the proceedings, or any part of the proceedings, be postponed for such a period as the court thinks necessary for that purpose ...

Discussion of public affairs

5. A publication made as or as part of a discussion in good faith of public affairs or other matters of general public interest is not to be treated as a contempt of court under the strict liability rule if the risk of impediment or prejudice to particular legal proceedings is merely incidental to the discussion.

Savings

6. Nothing in the foregoing provisions of this Act—

(a) prejudices any defence available at common law to a charge of contempt of court under the strict liability rule;

(b) implies that any publication is punishable as contempt of court under that rule which would not be so punishable apart from those provisions;

(c) restricts liability for contempt of court in respect of conduct intended to impede or prejudice the administration of justice."

These provisions allow for three circumstances in which the strict liability rule will not apply. The first is the defence of innocent publication, a defence which has existed in England and Wales since 1960, following the enactment of the Administration of Justice Act 1960, s.11, a measure which did not extend to Scotland. Although a Scots equivalent now exists, its limits should be appreciated. It is to be borne in mind that the offence is one of strict liability and that it will be no defence that the publisher honestly believed that the content of the publication did not constitute a contempt. In particular, the courts have held on several occasions that a conviction will lie even though the information was supplied by the police. See *MacAlister v Associated Newspapers Ltd*, 1954 S.L.T. 14, and *Hall v Associated Newspapers Ltd*, 1978 S.L.T. 241 above. More recently, in *HM Advocate v George Outram and Co Ltd*, 1980 S.L.T. (Notes) 13, the High Court struck the following warning:

"We have had occasion before to question the wisdom of the provision of such information by the police to the press at least at any time after a person to whom it relates has been arrested on criminal charges. However that may be there can surely be no lingering doubt that if information, even from police sources, about a person who has been charged with criminal offences and arrested, is such that if published it would constitute the offence labelled contempt of court, the source of the offending material cannot be relied upon in mitigation of the offence."

This applies with equal force to the new statutory régime. Section 3 only protects a publisher who does not know the proceedings are active: it offers no protection based on the content of the publication.

The second ground on which liability may be excluded is with regard to the contemporary reporting of judicial proceedings. Before the enactment of the 1981 Act, this defence was not recognised by statute. There was, however, authority for the view that it existed at common law. In *Stirling v Associated Newspapers Ltd*, 1960 S.L.T. 5, Lord Justice-General Clyde said that: "when a trial takes place, [the press is] free to publicise anything that is said or done by a Judge or a counsel, or a witness, or by the jury at that trial." The common law, and now the statute, would of course be subject to any statutory exceptions, one of which is the Judicial Proceedings (Regulation of Reports) Act 1926 which seeks to prohibit the salacious reporting of details revealed in matrimonial litigation. It is to be noted that the right to report legal proceedings is otherwise not unlimited, with s.4(2) permitting the courts to order that any reporting should be postponed. The nature and purpose of s.4(2) were considered in *Galbraith v H M Advocate*, 2001 S.L.T. 465 where it was said that:

"In terms of Section 2(2) a person commits an offence if he publishes something which creates a substantial risk that the course of justice in particular proceedings will be seriously impeded or prejudiced. Section 4(1) then creates an exception to Section 2(2): even though a publication creates a substantial risk that the course of justice will be seriously impeded or prejudiced, nonetheless the person publishing it does not commit an offence if the publication is simply a fair and accurate report of legal proceedings held in public, published contemporaneously and in good faith. This exception does not apply, however, where the court has made an order requiring that publication of the report should be postponed and the report is published during the period of postponement.

[9] When Parliament created the presumption in favour of allowing contemporaneous publication of a fair and accurate report of legal proceedings, even though it might have potentially detrimental effects on the proceedings or on certain other proceedings, it was recognising that such reports act as a safeguard 'against judicial arbitrariness or idiosyncrasy' and help to maintain public confidence in the administration of justice: *Attorney-General v Leveller Magazine Ltd.* [1979] A.C. 440 at p. 449 per Lord Diplock. But this

particular benefit to the public and to the administration of justice flows only from reports of the proceedings in court and, moreover, only from reports which are fair and accurate. It is therefore only to such reports that the presumption applies and it is only in the case of such reports that the court needs—and is given by section 4(2)—a power to require that in an appropriate case publication be postponed in the interests of justice."

In that case it was held that a s.4(2) order could only be issued to postpone the reporting of the proceedings to safeguard the administration of justice. It does not enable the court to impose an order to prevent the publication of comment which is adverse to the accused. In that case the strict liability rule will apply if the comment is prejudicial: "That is the mechanism which Parliament has provided for protecting the course of justice from the effects of publications of that kind. The court's power in s.4(2) is not intended to be used to deal with such publications but to deal, rather, with reports of its proceedings which are fair and accurate but should nonetheless be postponed": *Galbraith, ibid.* The following case suggests that the power under s.4(2) to issue such orders should be exercised with restraint, though it may be noted that 37 such orders were posted on the Scottish Courts website between 2000 and 2003.

British Broadcasting Corporation, Petitioners
2002 S.L.T. 2

This was an appeal by the BBC against an order under s.4(2) which had been made by Lord Osborne in the trial of Graeme Donaldson for the murder of Gurmit Singh Basra. The order required that any reporting which tended to show the participation of another person (Ward) suspected by the police in the events leading to the death of the deceased should be postponed until 24 hours after the conclusion of Donaldson's trial.

OPINION OF THE COURT: "[12] In Britain the general rule is that trials take place in public. This promotes not only the interests of the individual accused by ensuring that others can see whether he is being tried fairly but also the interests of the wider public who can see and, if appropriate, 'endorse, criticise, applaud or castigate the conduct of their courts': *The State v Mamabolo*, 11 April 2001, unreported, at paragraph 29 per Kriegler J. writing for the majority of the Constitutional Court of South Africa. The reporting of court proceedings in the media serves these two important but separate purposes. Not surprisingly, therefore, the need for the public to have access in this way to court proceedings is reflected in the terms of article 6(1) of the European Convention on Human Rights and Fundamental Freedoms which provides that the press and public may be excluded from a trial only 'to the extent strictly necessary in the opinion of the court in special circumstances where publicity would prejudice the interests of justice'. Similarly, article 10, on freedom of expression, provides in paragraph (2) that the exercise of the right to freedom of expression may be 'subject to such formalities, conditions, restrictions or penalties as are prescribed by law and are necessary in a democratic society ... for maintaining the authority and impartiality of the judiciary.'

[13] As this court has recalled on a number of occasions, the 1981 Act was enacted to bring our law into line with the requirements of the European Convention and, in interpreting and applying its provisions, we must bear in mind not only the terms of the Convention but also the jurisprudence of the European Court of Human Rights. A convenient summary of that Court's application of article 10(2) is to be found in their judgment in *Observer and Guardian v United Kingdom* (1991) 14 E.H.R.R. 153 at paragraph 59:

'The Court's judgments relating to Article 10 ... enounce the following major principles.

   (a) Freedom of expression constitutes one of the essential foundations of a democratic society; subject to paragraph 2 of Article 10, it is applicable not only to "information" or "ideas" that are favourably received or regarded as inoffensive or as a matter of indifference, but also to those that offend, shock or disturb. Freedom of expression, as enshrined in Article 10, is subject to a number of exceptions which, however, must be narrowly interpreted and the necessity for any restrictions must be convincingly established.

(b) These principles are of particular importance as far as the press is concerned. Whilst it must not overstep the bounds set, *inter alia,* in the "interests of national security" or for "maintaining the authority of the judiciary", it is nevertheless incumbent on it to impart information and ideas on matters of public interest. Not only does the press have the task of imparting such information and ideas: the public also has a right to receive them. Were it otherwise, the press would be unable to play its vital role of "public watchdog".

(c) The adjective "necessary", within the meaning of Article 10(2), implies the existence of a "pressing social need". The Contracting States have a certain margin of appreciation in assessing whether such a need exists, but it goes hand in hand with a European supervision, embracing both the law and the decisions applying it, even those given by independent courts. The Court is therefore empowered to give the final ruling on whether a "restriction" is reconcilable with freedom of expression as protected by article 10.'

[14] In enacting the provisions of the 1981 Act ... , Parliament recognised the need for the press and media to be able to impart to the public information about proceedings in our courts. In particular, to allow this to be done, section 4(1) contains an exception to the strict liability rule. The effect is that, even where the contemporaneous publication of a fair and accurate report of court proceedings creates a substantial risk that the course of justice will be seriously impeded or prejudiced, the publisher is not to be guilty of contempt of court under the strict liability rule. This exception in favour of the freedom of the media to report proceedings is not unlimited, however. For one thing, it applies only to the contemporaneous publication of reports of proceedings and only to reports which are fair and accurate. It does not apply, for instance, to delayed reports or to comments about the proceedings—where appropriate, they are covered by the strict liability rule. Parliament also recognised that, in certain circumstances, the interests of justice would require the balance to be struck in favour of restricting publication, even of a fair and accurate report of public court proceedings. So, in section 4(2), the courts are given the power to make an order requiring that publication of the report of proceedings, or of a particular part of the proceedings, should be postponed. Where such an order has been pronounced, publication during the period of postponement constitutes contempt of court in terms of section 1. See paragraphs 8 and 9 of the opinion of this court delivered by the Lord Justice General in *Galbraith*, 2001 S.L.T. at p. 468 A–E. Of course, a court which is called upon to make an order under section 4(2) must bear in mind that restrictions on the publication of the proceedings of our courts are exceptions to the general rule in favour of publication. As we have explained, in part at least, that public interest is distinct from the interest of the parties in having the proceedings conducted under the eyes of the public. A court must be careful to bear that wider public interest in mind, especially in those cases where—for whatever reason—the parties themselves would wish the court to make an order postponing publication, or where, as here, one of the parties adopts a neutral stance. Even in these situations, the court must consider not only whether such an order is 'necessary' but also what the appropriate scope of any order might be.

[15] In the present case the Advocate Depute asked for the order to avert what she saw as a risk of prejudice to any proceedings that the Crown might take against Ward. She apparently contended that those proceedings were 'pending' even though, as we have explained, the sheriff had refused to extend the twelve-month period for bringing Ward to trial on indictment and that period had run out. The trial judge rejected that argument. In our view he was correct to do so. The Advocate Depute's alternative contention was that the proceedings against Ward were 'imminent' since, if they took place at all, they would be likely to take place as soon as convenient after the accused's trial. The mere fact that the Lord Advocate might decide not to proceed did not mean that such possible proceedings

were not 'imminent' for the purposes of section 4(2). The trial judge acceded to that argument, holding that 'imminent'.

> 'is used to suggest something which is impending, or threatening, or hanging over a person's head, ready to overtake a person, or coming on shortly. I do not understand the word to mean that the threatened evil, or danger, or event is something which will necessarily occur or materialise. It may be a sword of Damocles which will not necessarily fall.'

This approach would seem to be in line with the view of Shaw L.J. that the words 'pending or imminent' would include 'the possible (not necessarily the inevitable) outcome of legal process': *R. v Horsham Justices, ex p. Farquharson* [1982] Q.B. 762 at p. 797 E. As in *Galbraith* (2001 S.L.T. 468 J–K), we prefer to reserve our opinion on this point, since we are able to decide the appeal on the basis of the other arguments advanced by counsel.

[16] As Lord Taylor L.C.J. observed in *Ex p. Telegraph plc* [1993] 1 W.L.R. 980, section 4(2) contains two requirements for the making of an order. The first is that publication would create 'a substantial risk of prejudice to the administration of justice' and the second is that postponement of publication 'appears to be necessary for avoiding' that risk. He continued ([1993] 1 W.L.R. at p. 984 D–G):

> 'It has been said that there is a third requirement, derived from the word "may" at the beginning of the subsection, namely, that a court, in the exercise of its discretion, having regard to the competing public interests of ensuring a fair trial and of open justice, considers it appropriate to make an order. ... It seems to us the discretion indicated by the use of the word "may" in the provision is catered for by the second requirement that the court may only make an order where it appears to it to be "necessary for avoiding" the substantial risk of prejudice to the administration of justice that it perceives. In forming a view whether it is necessary to make an order for avoiding such a risk a court will inevitably have regard to the competing public considerations of ensuring a fair trial and of open justice. It is noteworthy that whether the element of discretion is to be regarded as part of the "necessity" test or as a third requirement, the courts as a matter of practice have tended to merge the requirement of necessity and the exercise of discretion.' (citations omitted)

We respectfully incline to share the view of the Court of Appeal, Criminal Division, as to the appropriate analysis of the subsection but, in any event, as they point out, in considering whether it is 'necessary' to make an order a court will inevitably have regard to the competing public considerations of ensuring a fair trial and of open justice. It is by considering these rival considerations that the court determines, in terms of the Convention jurisprudence, whether there is a 'pressing social need' to make the order.

[17] Even where publication of a report of proceedings would give rise to a substantial risk of prejudice to proceedings which are pending or imminent, there may be other means of eliminating or reducing the risk. In former times moving any trial in the other proceedings to a different part of the country might usually have been an effective way of ensuring that potential jurors were drawn from an area where a local newspaper did not circulate and where the matter would, accordingly, have gone unreported or would have been reported to only a lesser extent. In an era of radio and television broadcasts covering the whole of Scotland, however, that remedy by itself may often not be effective. And Mr. Keen specifically acknowledged that it would not have been effective in the present case. Mr. Keen also accepted that the Crown could not be expected to delay any trial in this case, where the events in question were already almost eighteen months old. On the other hand, it will be relevant for a court to consider whether the usual directions to a jury to proceed simply on the evidence led before them would be sufficient to deal with any prejudice arising out of a report of the proceedings. Even if they would not, the court would have to ask itself

whether the risk of prejudice could be avoided by giving the jury special directions tailored to deal with the particular circumstances. It would only be if the court concluded that these or similar measures would not be adequate to deal with the risk of prejudice that the court could conclude that a section 4(2) order might be necessary. In pondering these issues, the court can draw upon the experience of judges in our own system and in other systems in which juries play a similar role. That experience suggests that jurors understand and apply the directions which are given to them and that they can successfully concentrate on the evidence led in court, while excluding extraneous material from consideration. We refer to the discussion in paragraph 13 of the opinion in *Galbraith* and to the authorities cited there (2001 S.L.T. at p. 469 C–E), as well as to the subsequent decision of the Privy Council in *Montgomery v H. M. Advocate*, 2001 S.L.T. 37.

[18] The trial judge explained why he had concluded that he should make an order in this case:

'I was influenced firstly by the consideration that the nature of the alleged crime and the fact that the victim had been a member of a minority ethnic community, in the present climate of opinion and on the basis of past experience, would inevitably mean that reporting of the present proceedings would be very extensive and most intense. Secondly, it had been stated on behalf of the accused in the present proceedings that a feature of his defence would be the "prosecution" of William Ward, which indicated to me that the conduct of the defence would involve the vigorous support of the allegation contained in the special defence in evidence. That would be likely to entail frequent references to William Ward of a nature highly prejudicial to him. Thirdly, it had also been indicated by the Advocate-depute that there would be likely to be in evidence frequent references to the possible involvement of William Ward in the offence. Having regard to these various factors, it appeared to me that much publicity of a high-profile nature would be likely to be given to the allegations to be made against and the evidence concerning William Ward, in the event of no order being made. While there have indeed been recent expressions of confidence in the jury system and, in particular, in the ability of juries to follow directions given to them ... , it appeared to me that, having regard to the factors mentioned, there remained a substantial risk of prejudice, in the absence of an order. Indeed, I consider that it would be difficult to envisage a stronger case for the exercise of the power conferred by Parliament in section 4(2) of the Act 1981 than the present one.'

We accept that, for the reasons which the trial judge gives, the reporting of the accused's trial was likely to be more extensive and more intense than in the average case. We were not given any detailed account of the evidence about Ward's role which it was anticipated would be heard in the accused's trial, nor yet of the evidence which had actually been led. We are prepared to accept, however, that the conduct of both the Crown and the defence cases was likely to result in the leading of a considerable amount of evidence suggesting that Ward had been involved in the offence. We are further prepared to assume that at least some potential jurors at any possible trial of Ward might notice the reports of that evidence and might recall it at the time of that trial.

[19] For our part—unlike the trial judge—we have no real difficulty in envisaging stronger cases for the exercise of the section 4(2) power. But that is really beside the point. More importantly, we simply find ourselves unable to agree with his conclusion that an order should be made in the circumstances of this case. We have to consider both the interests of justice in any proceedings against Ward and the public interest in having fair and accurate reports of the proceedings in the accused's trial. Both these interests are substantial. But, having regard to the circumstances of this case, we are not satisfied that an order was 'necessary' to deal with the risk of prejudice to the course of justice in any trial of Ward. In saying this, we have in mind, in particular, the experience of the judges in Scotland and elsewhere who have found that, when evidence is led at a trial, jurors con-

centrate on that evidence, on the submissions of counsel and on the directions of the judge in the trial. When they come to consider their verdict, they do so on that basis, rather than on the basis of what they may have read, heard or seen in the media some weeks or months before. Were it not so, jury trials would long ago have ceased to command the confidence of the public and of the legal profession. Applying that experience to the present case, we see no reason to think that anything said in evidence in the accused's trial about the role of Ward would have made it impossible for a jury to reach a proper verdict in any subsequent trial of Ward. In considering possible prejudice to Ward from the leading of this evidence, it should not be forgotten that, in so far as it tended to incriminate Ward, some at least of the evidence at the accused's trial might well be replicated or indeed supplemented at Ward's trial. The jury would therefore be likely to base their decision on the version of the evidence led at that trial, which would be fresh in their minds, rather than on their recollection of a report of what had been said in the accused's trial. In these circumstances we are satisfied that this is a case where directions by the judge at any trial of Ward could deal perfectly adequately with any risk of prejudice to Ward from the reporting of the proceedings in the accused's trial. Should that assessment turn out to be incorrect, and the judge presiding at Ward's trial considered that the jury could not return a fair and impartial verdict, then the court could deal with that eventuality by deserting the diet.

[20] For these reasons we allowed the appeal and, in terms of the crave, recalled the order under section 4(2) of the Contempt of Court Act 1981 which the trial judge had pronounced on 19 April 2001."

The third situation in which the strict liability rule does not apply is with regard to the good faith discussion of public affairs. This provision (which like the previous two had been recommended by the Phillimore Committee) had also been anticipated by the common law in *Atkins v London Weekend Television Ltd* (above). In that case, however, the exclusion of strict liability for this reason did not succeed, partly because there was still a serious risk of prejudice to the chances of a fair trial. The source of the defence at common law is acknowledged to be *Ex parte Bread Manufacturers* (1937) S.R. (N.S.W.) 242 where Jordan C.J. said (at 249):

"... if in the course of ventilation of a question of public concern matter is published which may prejudice a party on the conduct of a lawsuit it does not follow that a contempt has been committed. The case may be one in which as between competing matters of public interest the possibility of prejudice to a litigant may be required to yield to other and superior considerations. The discussion of public affairs and the denunciation of public abuses, actual or supposed, cannot be required to be suspended merely because the discussion or denunciation may, as an incidental but not intended by-product, cause a risk of prejudice to a person who happens to be a litigant at the time."

It is to be noted, however, that the defence has an older pedigree in Scotland. See *Cowie v George Outram & Co Ltd*, 1912 S.C.(J.) 14. The leading case on s.5 follows.

Attorney-General v English
[1983] A.C. 116

Dr Arthur, a well-known paediatrician, was charged with murdering a three-day old Down's Syndrome boy by giving him a drug which caused him to die of starvation. During the trial a by-election was held in North West Croydon, one of the candidates being Mrs Marilyn Carr who had been born without arms and who was standing as an independent pro-life candidate taking as a main plank in her campaign the stopping of the practice of killing newborn handicapped babies. During the campaign, and during the trial of Dr Arthur, the *Daily Mail* published an article by Mr Malcolm Muggeridge, who supported Mrs Carr. In his speech, Lord Diplock referred to the article in the following terms:

"The article complained of was directed exclusively to Mr Muggeridge's support of Mrs Carr's candidature in the by-election because of her support of the pro-life cause and in particular her opposition to deliberate failure to keep alive newly-born babies suffering from what are presently regarded as incurable physical or mental disabilities so severe as to deprive them of all possibility of their enjoying what a normal person would regard as a life that was worth living. For any human being to arrogate to himself the right to decide whether a human being was fit to be born or to go on living was regarded by Mr Muggeridge as contrary to Christian morality which regarded all human life as sacred. There was no mention in the article of Dr Arthur's trial.

The first part of the article described Mrs Carr herself and how she had succeeded in overcoming the terrible physical handicap with which she had been born and in carving out a useful career for herself. '*Today,*' he wrote, in a passage principally relied upon by the Attorney-General as amounting to contempt of court, '*the chances of such a baby surviving would be very small indeed. Someone would surely recommend letting her die of starvation, or otherwise disposing of her.*' The article then continued with a skilful piece of polemical journalism which concluded with the following passages derisive of those whose views he was condemning:

'Are human beings to be culled like livestock? No more sick or misshapen bodies, no more disturbed or twisted minds, no more hereditary idiots or mongoloid children. Babies not up to scratch to be destroyed, before or after birth, as would also the old beyond repair. *With the developing skills of modern medicine, the human race could be pruned and carefully tended until only the perfect blooms—the beauty queens, the Mensa I.Q.s, the athletes—remained.*'

The article then went on to contrast this with what the writer claimed to be the Christian view of the equal sanctity of all human life, whatever might be the individual human being's physical or mental qualities or deficiencies. As an example of a devotion to this view of Christian morality, he cited Mother Teresa of Calcutta."

The Divisional Court held that this was a contempt. The editor appealed.

LORD DIPLOCK: "There is, of course, no question that the article in the *Daily Mail* of which complaint is made by the Attorney-General was a 'publication' within the meaning of section 2(1). That being so, it appears to have been accepted in the Divisional Court by both parties that the onus of proving that the article satisfied the conditions stated in section 2(2) lay upon the Attorney-General and that, if he satisfied that onus, the onus lay upon the appellants to prove that it satisfied the conditions stated in section 5. For my part, I am unable to accept that this represents the effect of the relationship of section 5 to section 2(2). Section 5 does not take the form of a proviso or an exception to section 2(2). It stands on an equal footing with it. It does not set out exculpatory matter. Like section 2(2) it states what publications shall *not* amount to contempt of court despite their tendency to interfere with the course of justice in particular legal proceedings.

For the publication to constitute a contempt of court under the strict liability rule, it must be shown that the publication satisfies the criterion for which section 2(2) provides, *viz.* that it 'creates a substantial risk that the course of justice in the proceedings in question will be seriously impeded or prejudiced.' It is only if it falls within section 5 that anything more need be shown. So logically the first question always is: has the publication satisfied the criterion laid down by section 2(2).

My Lords, the first thing to be observed about this criterion is that the risk that has to be assessed is that which was created by the publication of the allegedly offending matter at the time when it was published. The public policy that underlies the strict liability rule in contempt of court is deterrence. Trial by newspaper or, as it should be more compendiously expressed today, trial by the media, is not to be permitted in this country. That the risk that was created by the publication when it was actually published does not ultimately affect the outcome of the proceedings is, as Lord Goddard C.J. said in *R. v Evening Standard Co. Ltd.*

[1954] 1 Q.B. 578, 582 'neither here nor there.' If there was a reasonable possibility that it might have done so if in the period subsequent to the publication the proceedings had not taken the course that in fact they did and Dr Arthur was acquitted, the offence was complete. The true course of justice must not at any stage be put at risk.

Next for consideration is the concatenation in the subsection of the adjective 'substantial' and the adverb 'seriously,' the former to describe the degree of risk, the latter to describe the degree of impediment or prejudice to the course of justice. 'Substantial' is hardly the most apt word to apply to 'risk' which is a noumenon. In combination I take the two words to be intended to exclude a risk that is only remote. With regard to the adverb 'seriously' a perusal of the cases cited in *Attorney-General v Times Newspapers Ltd.* [1974] A.C. 273 discloses that the adjective 'serious' has from time to time been used as an alternative to 'real' to describe the degree of risk of interfering with the course of justice, but not the degree of interference itself. It is, however, an ordinary English word that is not intrinsically inapt when used to describe the extent of an impediment or prejudice to the cause of justice in particular legal proceedings, and I do not think that for the purposes of the instant appeal any attempt to paraphrase it is necessary or would be helpful. The subsection applies to all kinds of legal proceedings, not only criminal prosecutions before a jury. If, as in the instant case and probably in most other criminal trials upon indictment, it is the outcome of the trial or the need to discharge the jury without proceeding to a verdict that is put at risk, there can be no question that that which in the course of justice is put at risk is as serious as anything could be.

My Lords, that Mr Malcolm Muggeridge's article was capable of prejudicing the jury against Dr Arthur at the early stage of his trial when it was published, seems to me to be clear. It suggested that it was a common practice among paediatricians to do that which Dr Arthur was charged with having done, because they thought that it was justifiable in the interest of humanity even though it was against the law. At this stage of the trial the jury did not know what Dr Arthur's defence was going to be; and whether at that time the risk of the jury's being influenced by their recollection of the article when they came eventually to consider their verdict appeared to be more than a remote one, and was a matter which the judge before whom the trial was being conducted was in the best position to evaluate, even though his evaluation, although it should carry weight, would not be binding on the Divisional Court or on your Lordships. The judge thought at that stage of the trial that the risk was substantial, not remote. So, too, looking at the matter in retrospect, did the Divisional Court despite the fact that the risk had not turned into an actuality since Dr Arthur had by then been acquitted. For my part I am not prepared to dissent from this evaluation. I consider that the publication of the article on the third day of what was to prove a lengthy trial satisfied the criterion for which section 2(2) of the Act provides.

The article, however, fell also within the category dealt with in section 5. It was made, in undisputed good faith, as a discussion in itself of public affairs, *viz.* Mrs Carr's candidature as an independent pro-life candidate in the North West Croydon by-election for which the polling day was in one week's time. It was also part of a wider discussion on a matter of general public interest that had been proceeding intermittently over the last three months, upon the moral justification of mercy killing and in particular of allowing newly-born hopelessly handicapped babies to die. So it was for the Attorney-General to show that the risk of prejudice to the fair trial of Dr Arthur, which I agree was created by the publication of the article at the stage the trial had reached when it was published, was not 'merely incidental' to the discussion of the matter with which the article dealt.

My Lords, any article published at the time when Dr Arthur was being tried which asserted that it was a common practice among paediatricians to let severely physically or mentally handicapped newborn babies die of starvation or otherwise dispose of them would (as, in common with the trial judge and the Divisional Court, I have already accepted) involve a substantial risk of prejudicing his fair trial. But an article supporting Mrs Carr's candidature in the by-election as a pro-life candidate that contained no such assertion would depict her as tilting at imaginary windmills. One of the main planks of the policy for which she sought the suffrage of the electors was that these things did happen and ought to be stopped.

I have drawn attention to the passages principally relied upon by the Divisional Court as causing a risk of prejudice that was not 'merely incidental to the discussion.' The court described them as 'unnecessary' to the discussion and as 'accusations.' The test, however, is not whether an article could have been written as effectively without these passages or whether some other phraseology might have been substituted for them that could have reduced the risk of prejudicing Dr Arthur's fair trial; it is whether the risk created by the words actually chosen by the author was 'merely incidental to the discussion,' which I take to mean: no more than an incidental consequence of expounding its main theme. The Divisional Court also apparently regarded the passages complained of as disqualified from the immunity conferred by section 5 because they consisted of 'accusations' whereas the court considered, *ante*, p. 128 E-F, that 'discussion' was confined to 'the airing of views and the propounding and debating of principles and arguments.' I cannot accept this limited meaning of 'discussion' in the section. As already pointed out, in the absence of any accusation, believed to be true by Mrs Carr and Mr Muggeridge, that it was a common practice among some doctors to do what they are accused of doing in the passages complained of, the article would lose all its point whether as support for Mrs Carr's parliamentary candidature or as a contribution to the wider controversy as to the justifiability of mercy killing. The article would be emasculated into a mere contribution to a purely hypothetical problem appropriate, it may be, for debate between academic successors of the mediaeval schoolmen, but remote from all public affairs and devoid of any general public interest to readers of the *Daily Mail*.

My Lords, the article that is the subject of the instant case appears to me to be in nearly all respects the antithesis of the article which this House (*pace* a majority of the judges of the European Court of Human Rights) held to be a contempt of court in *Attorney-General v Times Newspapers Ltd.* [1974] A.C. 273. There the whole subject of the article was the pending civil actions against Distillers Co. (Biochemicals) Ltd. arising out of their having placed upon the market the new drug thalidomide, and the whole purpose of it was to put pressure upon that company in the lawful conduct of their defence in those actions. In the instant case, in contrast, there is in the article no mention at all of Dr Arthur's trial. It may well be that many readers of the *Daily Mail* who saw the article and had read also the previous day's report of Dr Arthur's trial, and certainly if they were members of the jury at that trial, would think, 'that is the sort of thing that Dr Arthur is being tried for; it appears to be something that quite a lot of doctors do.' But the risk of their thinking that and allowing it to prejudice their minds in favour of finding him guilty on evidence that did not justify such a finding seems to me to be properly described in ordinary English language as 'merely incidental' to any meaningful discussion of Mrs Carr's election policy as a pro-life candidate in the by-election due to be held before Dr Arthur's trial was likely to be concluded, or to any meaningful discussion of the wider matters of general public interest involved in the current controversy as to the justification of mercy killing. To hold otherwise would have prevented Mrs Carr from putting forward and obtaining publicity for what was a main plank in her election programme and would have stifled all discussion in the press upon the wider controversy about mercy killing from the time that Dr Arthur was charged in the magistrates' court in February 1981 until the date of his acquittal at the beginning of November of that year; for those are the dates between which, under section 2(3) and Schedule 1, the legal proceedings against Dr Arthur would be 'active' and so attract the strict liability rule.

Such gagging of *bona fide* public discussion in the press of controversial matters of general public interest, merely because there are in existence contemporaneous legal proceedings in which some particular instance of those controversial matters may be in issue, is what section 5 of the Contempt of Court Act 1981 was in my view intended to prevent. I would allow this appeal."

Lords Elwyn-Jones, Keith of Kinkel, Scarman and Brandon of Oakbrook agreed.

(c) Residual Common Law Liability

Questions arise about whether there is liability for contempt of court which is separate from and additional to the 1981 Act. That is to say, there are questions about whether there is a residual liability for contempt at common law which may fill in any gaps which the Act has missed, and which may be wider than the Act provides. Section 6 of the 1981 Act clearly anticipates liability for conduct "intended to impede or prejudice the administration of justice". The following case, however, questions whether there is a wider category of contempt at common law. In expressing unease about a residual liability of indeterminate scope, the High Court also takes the opportunity to comment on *Muir v BBC*, 1997 S.L.T. 425 where the existence of such liability had most recently been suggested.

Al Megrahi v Times Newspapers Ltd
1999 S.C.C.R. 824

In this case the *Sunday Times* published an article in which it suggested that the accused were guilty of the murder of the 270 people killed as a result of a bomb exploding on a Pan American World Airways aircraft on flight 103 over Lockerbie. The article was published before the trial, which, however, was to take place in The Netherlands before three High Court judges, under the terms of an agreement between the US and British Governments which was implemented by the High Court of Justiciary (Proceedings in the Netherlands)(United Nations) Order 1998. There was no jury. Nevertheless the petitioners moved against the respondents for contempt of court. They also sought an order prohibiting the respondents, pending the completion of the trial, from publishing any article, feature or comment relating to the proceedings against the petitioners which was liable to prejudice the administration of justice in general and the case against the petitioners in particular.

> LORD JUSTICE CLERK (CULLEN): "Counsel for the petitioners maintained that the article and editorial contained a series of assertions of fact in regard to allegations which the Crown would require to prove at the trial. A fair and dispassionate reader would be left with the impression that the guilt of the petitioners could be taken for granted, and that if there were to be an acquittal, it would not be because the petitioners were innocent, but because the evidence had been adversely affected by the passage of time. The effect of what was written was all the greater as it was partly contained in an editorial in a quality newspaper.
>
> Mr. Taylor and Mr. Keen [for the petitioners] both invoked the strict liability rule as it is expressed in sections 1 and 2 of the Contempt of Court Act 1981. They pointed out that, by reason of the terms of paras. 4 and 11 of Schedule 1 to that Act, the criminal proceedings against the petitioners had become 'active' again for the purposes of the Act with their arrest after they reached the Netherlands on or about 5 April. [After referring to s 2 of the 1981 Act his Lordship continued] ... Counsel referred to a number of authorities for the propositions—which were not in dispute—that (i) the 'risk' must be more than minimal or remote; (ii) 'seriously' required a real impediment or prejudice to the course of justice; and (iii) the test fell to be applied at the stage of publication, without regard to what might have happened or might happen thereafter. (*Att. Gen. v English* [1983] 1 A.C. 116, per Lord Diplock at page 141; *H.M. Advocate v Caledonian Newspapers Limited*, 1995 S.L.T. 926 at pages 929–930; and *H.M. Advocate v Scotsman Publications Limited*, 1999 S.C.C.R. 163 at page 167).
>
> Mr. Taylor also sought to rely on the pre-existing common law of contempt of court. However, he made it clear that he was not relying on section 6 of the 1981 Act ... That provision plainly ensures that the Act is not to affect liability in respect of conduct which is specifically intended to impede or prejudice the administration of justice, either in relation

to particular proceedings or more generally (*Att.-Gen. v Newspaper Publishing plc* [1988] Ch. 333, per Sir John Donaldson M.R. at page 374). There is no suggestion to that effect in the present case. However, Mr. Taylor relied on *Smith v Ritchie*, 1892 3 White 408, in which an accused who had been committed for trial on a charge of uttering as genuine certain forged manuscripts or other documents sought to have the editors and publishers of a newspaper prohibited from publishing or circulating any statement relating to the alleged forgeries or anything prejudicial to him until the proceedings had been brought to a conclusion. At page 411 the Lord Justice Clerk (Macdonald) said:

> 'When any person has been committed for trial, that person is necessarily under the protection of the court, and is accordingly entitled to apply to the court to prevent anything being done which may in any way prejudice him in his trial.'

I have no doubt that it is as true today as it was then that a person who has been committed for trial is under the protection of the court. However, it is also clear that liability for contempt of court in regard to the effect of a publication on proceedings which are 'active', that is to say liability regardless of any intent to interfere with the course of justice, is regulated by sections 1 and 2 of the 1981 Act. As was pointed out by the Lord Justice General in the recent case of *Cox and Griffiths, Petitioners*, 1998 J.C. 267 at page 273, the Act was passed in order to change the law of the United Kingdom and so to bring it into conformity with the interpretation of Article 10 of the European Convention on Human Rights by the European Court on Human Rights in *Sunday Times v United Kingdom* (1979) 2 E.H.R.R. 245. The Act represented a distinct shift in favour of freedom of expression (*Att. Gen v Newspaper Publishing plc*, per Lloyd L.J. at page 382). On any view it could hardly be supposed that, in regard to the possible effect of a publication on the course of justice in particular proceedings which are 'active', a publisher is exposed to liability according to one test under the statute and another test according to the common law.

The court was also referred to a passage in the Opinion of the Court in *Muir v B.B.C.*, 1997 S.L.T. 425, which was concerned with the prohibition of the broadcasting of a television programme. In that case the court indicated (at page 427) that it had the power in the exercise of its nobile officium to make an order even if there was not a contempt of court under the Act. However, when those remarks are read in context, it is plain that the court was distinguishing what fell within section 2(2) of the Act from what would properly constitute contempt of court after consideration of the defence under section 5. In these circumstances I am satisfied that any liability for contempt of court in regard to the effect of the publication on the course of justice in the current proceedings is regulated by the relevant provisions of the 1981 Act.

If the petitioners were in custody in Scotland and were to stand trial on indictment before a jury in Scotland, I would have had little difficulty in accepting that the statements contained in the article and editorial raised a serious question as to their effect on the minds of potential jurors. ... It is obvious that the arrangements in accordance with the Agreement and the Order were made in order to meet objections to the petitioners standing trial before a jury in Scotland. As at the date of publication of the article and the editorial there was nothing to indicate that the petitioners might wish instead to be tried in Scotland and the same applies at the present time. Thus, while the possibility of that happening could be absolutely ruled out, it was extremely remote. Accordingly I consider that, as matters stood at the date of publication, it is unrealistic to consider the effect of the article and editorial on potential jurors in Scotland.

Counsel for the petitioners then went on to submit that, even on the footing that their clients were to stand trial in the Netherlands before judges in accordance with the Order, the article and editorial represented a contempt of court.

Counsel did not maintain that there was any risk of a judge being influenced by the publication complained of. Further, counsel did not submit that there was any risk of the evidence or conduct of particular witnesses being affected. However, Mr.Taylor submitted that in two respects the publication complained of gave cause for concern. Firstly, the court should take action to prevent public confidence in the course of justice in the current proceedings from being undermined. Secondly, the petitioners were entitled to be assured that they would be tried by an impartial tribunal. Mr.Taylor stated that his client was concerned lest, if the press was not subject to regulation, there might be a trial by the media and not by a court of law. There was every indication that matters were going to get worse. Instead the court should exercise its nobile officium to prevent unfairness to his client between the present time and the conclusion of the trial. The media should not be allowed to think that the 1981 Act did not apply. Mr.Keen accepted that the position of the petitioners should be looked at from an objective standpoint. Pre-judgment of matters by the media usurped the function of a court by suggesting to the public that the court might be influenced by what was published. Each publication created a further risk. The petitioners had been assured, before they surrendered themselves to the United Kingdom authorities, that they would receive a fair and objective trial. His client had no detailed knowledge of the Scottish legal system. His reactions to the publication were understandable. . . .

Where a court is concerned with the question whether a publication has attracted strict liability for the purposes of sections 1 and 2 of the Act, it has to consider the prospective effect of the publication as at the date when it was made. In *In re Lonrho plc* [1990] 2 A.C. 154 Lord Bridge of Harwich said at page 209:

> 'The question whether a particular publication, in relation to particular legal proceedings which are active, creates a substantial risk that the course of justice in those proceedings will be seriously impeded or prejudiced is ultimately one of fact. Whether the course of justice in particular proceedings will be impeded or prejudiced by a publication must depend primarily on whether the publication will bring influence to bear which is likely to divert the proceedings in some way from the course which they would otherwise have followed. The influence may affect the conduct of witnesses, the parties or the court.'

The submissions made by counsel for the petitioners in this branch of the argument, which assumes a trial before judges in the Netherlands, plainly did not suggest that the article and editorial complained of might affect the conduct of anyone in such a way as to influence or divert the proceedings. Instead they concentrated on the way in which the administration of justice in these proceedings might be perceived from the point of view of the public on the one hand and the petitioners on the other.

In support of their submissions counsel for the petitioners referred to a decision of the Court of Appeal in *Att.-Gen. v Channel 4 Television*, 16 December 1987, unreported. That case was later the subject of a decision of the European Commission on Human Rights on 13 April 1989 (Application No. 14132/88).

In its decision the Court of Appeal refused to discharge an injunction which it had granted on the application of the Attorney-General to prohibit the broadcasting of a television programme which reconstructed a prominent criminal appeal which was currently being heard. In giving the decision of the Court, the Lord Chief Justice, Lord Lane, said (at pages 8–9 of the transcript):

> 'The portrayal by actors of a witness, albeit using words or some of the words which the witness has used, is pretending to be the real thing and is subtly inviting the viewer, as Mr. Laws put it, to sit in the judgment seat, and subtly inviting the viewer to make what he thinks is his own comment or judgment, but in truth that comment and judgment will be conditioned, and predictably conditioned, by the way in which the actor, as he has been directed, has played the part of the witness. The actor has it in his power to make a truthful witness appear to be a liar and vice versa.
>
> Such a representation would not, in normal circumstances, directly affect the

judgment of the court. It would, or it certainly might, affect the public's view of the judgment of the court. As to that it might be said that a broadcast of this nature after judgment is delivered would have the same effect, but we doubt if that is true. Even if it is true, there is a further reason for at least postponing such a programme until after all the proceedings are over. That is this. Whatever may be the nature of the present programme, which we have not seen despite invitations to us to do so, the defendant in any case, or the appellants in the present case, in circumstances such as these, are entitled to be assured that so far as possible the court has not been influenced by external matters.

The broadcast of this sort of programme before the case is finally over may leave the defendant, or the appellants in this case, without such assurance. He will know that the court in all probability has seen the programme before judgment has been delivered. He may harbour doubts, however unjustified those doubts may be, about the effect which the programme may have had upon the judgment of the court.'

The Commission was satisfied that the injunction constituted an interference with the television company's freedom of expression within the meaning of Article 10(1) of the European Convention on Human Rights. However, it held that, for the purposes of Article 10(2), the restriction was 'prescribed by law', pursued the legitimate aims of protecting the rights of others and of maintaining the authority and impartiality of the judiciary, and was justified by a 'pressing social need'. Accordingly the Commission found that the case failed to disclose an arguable claim of a violation of Article 10. It was not, of course, for the Commission to determine whether the Court of Appeal had correctly interpreted or applied the law of contempt. It was concerned with whether the decision of the Court of Appeal was or was not compatible with Article 10. Accordingly I propose to concentrate on the basis of that decision.

It is reasonably plain that in arriving at its decision the Court of Appeal did not treat the injunction as justified by section 4(2) of the Contempt of Court Act 1981 which empowers the court to order the postponement of the publication of any report of proceedings or any part of proceedings 'where it appears to be necessary for avoiding a substantial risk of prejudice to the administration of justice in those proceedings, or in any other proceedings pending or imminent'. The court did not examine whether the test of necessity was satisfied. It did not proceed on the basis that the judgment of the court in the criminal appeal might be affected. It plainly distinguished the programme from the reporting of, or comment on, the proceedings in the appeal. It appears therefore that the injunction was sought to be justified on broader considerations relating to the administration of justice where contempt of court was in question.

In considering the value which should be attached to this decision, which was the sole decision founded upon by counsel for the petitioners in support of the submissions which they made in this branch of the case, it is of some importance to consider the legal basis on which it rested. At page 6 of the transcript the Lord Chief Justice referred to the following passage from the speech of Lord Diplock in *Att. Gen. v Times Newspapers Limited* [1974] A.C. 273 at page 309:

'The due administration of justice requires first that all citizens should have unhindered access to the constitutionally established courts of criminal or civil jurisdiction for the determination of disputes as to their legal rights and liabilities; secondly, that they should be able to rely upon obtaining in the courts the arbitrament of a tribunal which is free from bias against any party and whose decision will be based upon those facts only that have been proved in evidence adduced before it in accordance with the procedure adopted in courts of law; and thirdly that, once the dispute has been submitted to a court of law, they should be able to rely upon there being no usurpation by any other person of the function of that court to decide it according to law. Conduct which is calculated to prejudice any of these three requirements or to undermine the public confidence that they will be observed is contempt of court.'

The Lord Chief Justice rejected the argument that this dictum was not applicable to the case with which the court was concerned, stating that it was one of general application and that if conduct fell within the words used by Lord Diplock properly construed, that was the basis on which the court could exercise jurisdiction to grant an injunction. It appears that the third of the three requirements of the administration of justice which he stated was treated as being of most relevance.

From the speech of Lord Diplock and other speeches in the House of Lords in *Att. Gen. v Times Newspapers Limited* it is plain that the members of the House sought to establish a general rule in the law of contempt that it was offensive to that law for the press to pre-judge issues in pending cases and hence 'usurp the function of the court'. Thus, for example, Lord Reid at page 300 said:

> 'I do not think that the freedom of the press would suffer, and I think the law would be clearer and easier to apply in practice if it is made the general rule that it is not permissible to pre-judge issues in pending cases.'

It can be seen that, underlying the adoption of such a rule in that case there were a number of considerations. These included that pre-judgment by the press might lead the public to an opinion on the subject matter of the litigation (a claim of damages for the effects of the marketing of the drug thalidomide) before the issue had been adjudicated on by the court; and, of particular relevance to that case, that pre-judgment was liable to lead to replies by the parties in what Lord Morris of Borthy-y-Gest described at page 304 as 'flurries of pre-trial publicity'.

The same approach to pre-judgment may be found in a passage from the judgment of Shaw L.J. in *Schering Chemicals Limited v Falkman Limited* [1982] Q.B. 1 at page 30, which the Lord Chief Justice quoted at page 7 of the transcript:

> 'There is the larger question of the undesirability of presenting simulated trials of the subject matter of pending or prospective litigation on so influential a medium of publicity as television. This must be a matter of degree. When the presentation appears to encroach upon the function and authority of the judicature, the limits of tolerance are clearly exceeded.'

The difficulty about the pre-judgment test as such, i.e. irrespective of the circumstances of the particular case, is that it cannot stand with the enactment of sections 1 and 2 of the Contempt of Court Act, in which Parliament adopted a different test, following on the recommendations of the Report of the Committee on Contempt of Court (the Phillimore Report) in December 1974 (Cmnd. 5794). As Lord Bridge of Harwich observed in *In re Lonrho* at page 208, the pre-judgment test propounded in the speeches in *Att. Gen. v Times Newspapers Limited* was criticised in the Phillimore Report, paras. 106–111. The decision of the House of Lords was held by the European Court of Human Rights (in *The Sunday Times v United Kingdom*) to constitute an infringement of the right to freedom of expression under Article 10 in respect that, while the interference with the freedom of expression was for the legitimate aim of maintaining the 'authority . . . of the judiciary' under Article 10(2), it was not justified by a 'pressing social need' and could not therefore be regarded as 'necessary' within the meaning of Article 10(2). As I have pointed out earlier in this opinion it is recognised that the 1981 Act represented a distinct shift in favour of freedom of expression, in conformity with Article 10 of the European Convention. Accordingly I do not consider that the judicial statements which were relied on by the Court of Appeal in *Att. Gen v Channel 4 Television* could still be regarded as authoritative as at the time of its decision.

Quite apart from that, the ratio of the decision of the Court of Appeal does not appear to me to square with the 1981 Act. Where a court is asked to prohibit a publication in a case where proceedings are active its task is to determine the effect of the publication on the course of those proceedings. There is nothing in the Act which enjoins the court to apply as the test the perception of others as to whether the course of justice may be affected. The administration of justice has to be robust enough to withstand criticism and mis-understanding. It would, of course, be an entirely different matter if the court were faced with conduct intended to impede or prejudice the administration of justice, either in the context of particular proceedings or more generally. The court would be well justified in making an order to prevent a deliberate affront to the administration of justice, for example, where a publication was regarded as impugning the integrity of the court or attacking its authority....

In the present case it is sufficient for me to say that I am not satisfied that the article and editorial, whether taken together or individually, fell foul of the strict liability rule under section 2(2) of the 1981 Act. In any event, even if it had been correct to use as a test the question whether they might undermine public confidence in the administration of justice, I would have held that such a test was not met. Neither contained any direct reference to those who were to act as judges at the trial or to the functions which they were to discharge. They contained certain allegations of fact in regard to matters which, as Mr. Davidson [for the respondents] demonstrated, have been the subject of considerable press coverage for some time. The main thrust of what was published was directed to the complaint that, despite information as to the alleged involvement of Colonel Gadaffi, the United Kingdom Government was taking steps with a view to restoring certain relations with Libya. The references to the case and to the first petitioner in particular, appeared to be incidental. Further, in considering any suggestion that this publication might tend to undermine public confidence in the administration of justice, one has to bear in mind that that question should be considered in a wider context. In this country the public and those who are the subject of criminal proceedings enjoy the benefit of an independent judiciary, the members of which are well used to concentrating on the evidence, and only the evidence, which is put before them in the proceedings, and to arriving at decisions in an impartial manner. Accordingly I do not consider that the article and editorial complained of constituted a contempt of court. In the circumstances I do not find it necessary to deal with the respondents' defence under section 5 of the 1981 Act. The question of pronouncing an order against the respondents in regard to their future conduct does not arise."

Lords Coulsfield and Caplan delivered concurring judgments.

(3) National Security and Official Secrets

A third area where speech is prohibited relates to national security where a number of restraints operate. The issue has arisen in modern times as a result of a spate of "spy and tell" books and articles which have been produced by a number of former security service officers: these include Peter Wright, Anthony Cavendish, George Blake, Richard Tomlinson, and David Shayler. The first obstacle to be faced lies in the civil law and, in particular, breach of confidence whereby an interdict or an injunction can be obtained to prevent the publication of confidential material. It was on this basis that temporary injunctions (pending the trial of the matter) were granted in *Attorney General v Guardian Newspapers Ltd* [1987] 3 All E.R. 316 to prevent the publication by the *Guardian* and *Observer* newspapers of extracts from the memoirs of Peter Wright, a retired member of the security service. In order to obtain an injunction, it has to be shown not only that the material in question was obtained in breach of confidence but also that it would be in the public interest to restrain the publication. In this case (the *Spycatcher* case after the title of Mr Wright's book), it was held that the public interest lay in favour of granting the interim injunctions sought by the Attorney General.

Shortly after the temporary injunctions were granted, the book was published in the US, and copies began to appear in the United Kingdom. Indeed the book became available to anyone who wanted it. As a result, the two newspapers moved to have the temporary injunctions discharged. With the contents of the book now being public knowledge, there could hardly be any public interest in maintaining the injunctions against the newspapers. However, the application failed and the injunctions were maintained. The Government's application for permanent injunctions was heard in 1989 and at this stage it was accepted that there was no case to maintain the ban in view of the fact that the allegations made by Peter Wright were already in the public domain. The House of Lords also accepted that publication by the newspapers was unlikely to cause any harm to the national interest: *Attorney General v Guardian Newspapers Ltd (No. 2)* [1990] 1 AC 109. It was subsequently held by the European Court of Human Rights that the granting of the temporary injunctions in 1986 did not violate Art.10 of the ECHR, but that the failure to discharge them in the following year did amount to a breach. This is because the interests of national security could no longer be served by the injunctions in light of the widespread circulation of the book (which had become a bestseller in the US).

Lord Advocate v Scotsman Publications Ltd
1989 S.L.T. 705

Anthony Cavendish—a former member of the security services—had privately circulated copies of a book *Inside Intelligence* to a number of friends. Copies of the book had fallen into the hands of the *Scotsman*, Scottish Television and the *Glasgow Herald*. On January 5, 1988 the *Scotsman* had published an article containing some of the material in the book. The Lord Advocate sought an interim interdict to restrain the *Scotsman* and anyone having notice of the interdict from publishing any information contained in the book. The petition was refused by the Lord Ordinary and his decision was upheld by both the Inner House and the House of Lords.

LORD KEITH OF KINKEL: "In the course of the argument for the appellant before the Second Division it became clear, as apparently it had not been before the Lord Ordinary, that the Crown did not maintain that *Inside Intelligence* contained any information disclosure of which was capable of damaging national security. From that point of view the whole contents of the book were entirely innocuous. So the grounds upon which the Second Division refused interim interdict were different from those relied on by the Lord Ordinary, which in the circumstances need not be examined. The judges of the Second Division, having considered such authorities upon the law of confidentiality as existed in the Scottish corpus juris, came to the conclusion that Scots law in this field was the same as that of England, in particular as respects the circumstances under which a person coming into possession of confidential information knowing it to be such, but not having received it directly from the original confider, himself comes under an obligation of confidence. That conclusion was, in my opinion, undoubtedly correct. While the juridical basis may differ to some extent in the two jurisdictions, the substance of the law in both of them is the same. If it had not been for the acceptance by counsel for the appellant that further publication of the information contained in the book would not be prejudicial to national security, the Second Division would have been disposed to grant interim interdict. They would not, at the interlocutory stage, have been prepared to hold that such limited publication as had already taken place had placed the contents of the book in the public domain to such an extent that a restriction on further publication would serve no useful purpose. But in the face of the concession about absence of prejudice to national security the Second Division were unable to find that a prima facie case for permanent interdict had been pleaded. ...

    At the time of the decision by the Second Division the *Spycatcher* case had passed through the stages of trial before Scott J. and appeal to the Court of Appeal: *Att. Gen. v Guardian Newspapers Ltd. (No. 2)* [1990] 1 AC. 109. The decision on appeal to your Lordships' House, which affirmed the Court of Appeal, was given on 13 October 1988. That decision authoritatively established that a member or former member of the British security or intelligence service owes a lifelong duty of confidentiality to the Crown which renders him liable to be restrained by injunction or interdict from revealing information which came into his possession in the course of his work. Disclosure of such information is by its nature damaging to national security and there is no room for close examination of the precise manner in which revelation of any particular information would cause damage. A publisher or other person acting on behalf of the member or former member of the service was held to be subject to similar restraint. It was the prospect of damage to the public interest which necessitated the fetter on freedom of speech, and the House accepted the principle that in general the Crown was not in a position to insist on confidentiality as regards governmental matters unless it could demonstrate the likelihood of such damage being caused by disclosure. I said at [1988] 3 W.L.R., pp. 782–783: 'In so far as the Crown acts to prevent such disclosure or to seek redress for it on confidentiality grounds, it must necessarily, in my opinion, be in a position to show that the disclosure is likely to damage or has damaged the public interest. How far the Crown has to go in order to show this must depend on the circumstances of each case. In a question with a Crown servant himself, or others acting as his agents, the general public interest in the preservation of confidentiality, and in encouraging other Crown servants to preserve it, may suffice. But where the publication is proposed to be made by third parties unconnected with the particular confidant, the position may be different. The Crown's argument in the present case would go the length that in all circumstances where the original disclosure has been made by a Crown servant in breach of his obligation of confidence any person to whose knowledge the information comes and who is aware of the breach comes under an equitable duty binding his conscience not to communicate the information to anyone else irrespective of the circumstances under which he acquired the knowledge. In my opinion that general proposition is untenable and impracticable, in addition to being unsupported by any authority. The general rule is that anyone is entitled to communicate anything he pleases to anyone else, by speech or in writing or in any other way. That rule is limited by the law of defamation and other restrictions similar to these mentioned in article 10 of the Convention for the Protection of Human Rights and Fundamental Freedoms (1953) (Cmd. 8969). All those restrictions are imposed in the light of considerations of public interest such as to countervail the public interest in freedom of expression. A communication about some aspect of government activity which does no harm to the interests of the nation cannot, even where the original disclosure has been made in breach of confidence, be restrained on the ground of a nebulous equitable duty of conscience serving no useful practical purpose.'

This passage recognises that there may be some circumstances under which a third party may come into possession of information, originally confidential, which has been revealed by a Crown servant in breach of his own duty of confidence, and yet may not be liable to be restrained from passing it on to others. In *Spycatcher* itself the circumstances which resulted in the defendant newspapers not being restrained from publishing and commenting on material contained in the book were that it had been disseminated worldwide to the extent of over 1,000,000 copies and that it was freely available in this country. In that situation it was impossible for the Crown to demonstrate that further publication by the defendants would add to any extent to the damage to the public interest which had already been brought about.

One particular circumstance of the present case, which gives it a peculiar and perhaps unique character, is the abandonment by the appellant of any contention that the contents of *Inside Intelligence* include any material damaging to national security. The other most relevant circumstance is that the book has been distributed by Mr Cavendish to 279 recipients. These two circumstances in combination must lead inevitably to the conclusion that the appellant has not pleaded a good arguable prima facie case that further publication by the respondents would do any material damage to the public interest. ...

It was argued for the appellant that dismissal of this appeal would have the effect that any newspaper which received an unsolicited book of memoirs by a present or former member of the security or intelligence service would be free to publish it. That is not so. If there had been no previous publication at all and no concession that the contents of the book were innocuous the newspaper would undoubtedly itself come under an obligation of confidence and be subject to restraint. If there had been a minor degree of prior publication, and no such concession, it would be a matter for investigation whether further publication would be prejudicial to the public interest, and interim interdict would normally be appropriate.

My Lords, I can find no material misdirection in law in the opinions of the judges of the Second Division, nor anything unreasonable in the manner of exercise of their discretion. I would accordingly dismiss the appeal and find it unnecessary to deal with the argument of the third and fourth respondents regarding the form of the interim interdict asked for."

Lords Templeman and Jauncey of Tullichettle delivered concurring speeches. Lords Griffiths and Goff of Chieveley concurred with Lord Keith. For comment and criticism of the "myopic tendencies" of the judges revealed by this case, see N. Walker, "Spycatcher's Scottish Sequel" [1990] P.L. 354.

The other source of liability for disclosures and publications of the kind that featured in *Lord Advocate v Scotsman Publications Ltd*, 1989 S.L.T. 705 is criminal liability under the Official Secrets Act 1989. The 1989 Act repealed and replaced the highly controversial Official Secrets Act 1911, s.2 which provided in wide terms that it was an offence for a civil servant to disclose any official information without authorisation. As a departmental committee (the so-called Franks Committee after its chair) pointed out in 1972:

"The leading characteristic of this offence is its catch-all quality. It catches all official documents and information. It makes no distinctions of kind, and no distinctions of degree. All information which a Crown servant learns in the course of his duty is 'official' for the purposes of section 2, whatever its nature, whatever its importance, whatever its original source. A blanket is thrown over everything; nothing escapes. The section catches all Crown servants as well as official information. Again, it makes no distinctions according to the nature or importance of a Crown servant's duties. All are covered. Every Minister of the Crown, every civil servant, every member of the Armed Forces, every police officer, performs his duties subject to section 2."

The committee continued:

"Nevertheless governments regularly reveal a great deal of official information. These disclosures do not contravene section 2. A Crown servant who discloses official information commits an offence under the section only if the information is disclosed to someone 'other than a person to whom he is authorised to communicate it, or a person to whom it is in the interest of the State his duty to communicate it.' The Act does not explain the meaning of the quoted words. We found that they were commonly supposed, by persons outside the Government, to imply a fairly formal process of express authorisation. Actual practice within the Government rests heavily on a doctrine of implied authorisation, flowing from the nature of each Crown servant's job. In the words of the Home Office, 'the communication of official information is proper if such communication can be fairly regarded as part of the job of the officer concerned.' Ministers are, in effect, self-authorising. They decide for themselves what to reveal. Senior civil servants exercise a considerable degree of personal judgment in deciding what disclosures of official information they may properly make, and to whom. More junior civil servants, and those whose duties do not involve contact with members of the public, may have a very limited discretion, or none at all."

(Report of a Departmental Committee on: Section 2 of the Official Secrets Act 1911, Cmnd. 5104 (1972)).

Section 2 was important because it restricted the circulation of information, by making it an offence to disclose and receive unauthorised information. The Franks Committee pointed out, however, that:

"Prosecutions have been few. Recently they have averaged about one a year. From 1945 to 1971 twenty-three prosecutions were brought, involving thirty-four defendants, of whom twenty-seven were convicted and six acquitted; in one case the charge was withdrawn. Nearly two-thirds of the defendants were Crown servants or former Crown servants, including a number of police and prison officers. Only two case since the war have involved professional journalists. Well over one-third of the twenty-three cases involved information relating to matters of defence, national security or intelligence. One-third concerned police or prison information. In three cases the information related to international affairs."

The effect of the section was not, however, to be judged by the number of unauthorised disclosures actually resulting in prosecution. A number of Government witnesses told the Franks Committee that "section 2 had a widespread deterrent effect in preventing improper disclosures by Crown servants." For their part, the news media said that "the section frequently deterred or prevented Crown servants from disclosing information of public interest which, in their view, should have been disclosed." The committee concluded that section 2 "is rarely activated in the courtroom, but is seen by many as having a pervasive influence on the work and the behaviour of hundreds of thousands of people." Although there were many prosecutions under s.2, very few of the cases were reported, despite the obscure drafting and difficulties in interpretation which the section raised.

Official Secrets Act 1989

"Security and intelligence.
    1.—(1) A person who is or has been—
        (a) a member of the security and intelligence services; or
        (b) a person notified that he is subject to the provisions of this subsection, is guilty of
            an offence if without lawful authority he discloses any information, document or
            other article relating to security or intelligence which is or has been in his pos-
            session by virtue of his position as a member of any of those services or in the
            course of his work while the notification is or was in force.
    (2) The reference in subsection (1) above to disclosing information relating to security or intelligence includes a reference to making any statement which purports to be a disclosure of such information or is intended to be taken by those to whom it is addressed as being such a disclosure.
    (3) A person who is or has been a Crown servant or government contractor is guilty of an offence if without lawful authority he makes a damaging disclosure of any information, document or other article relating to security or intelligence which is or has been in his possession by virtue of his position as such but otherwise than as mentioned in subsection (1) above.
    (4) For the purposes of subsection (3) above a disclosure is damaging if—
        (a) it causes damage to the work of, or of any part of, the security and intelligence
            services; or
        (b) it is of information or a document or other article which is such that its unau-
            thorised disclosure would be likely to cause such damage or which falls within a
            class or description of information, documents or articles the unauthorised dis-
            closure of which would be likely to have that effect.
    (5) It is a defence for a person charged with an offence under this section to prove that at the time of the alleged offence he did not know, and had no reasonable cause to believe, that the information, document or article in question related to security or intelligence or,

in the case of an offence under subsection (3), that the disclosure would be damaging within the meaning of that subsection.

(6) Notification that a person is subject to subsection (1) above shall be effected by a notice in writing served on him by a Minister of the Crown; and such a notice may be served if, in the Minister's opinion, the work undertaken by the person in question is or includes work connected with the security and intelligence services and its nature is such that the interests of national security require that he should be subject to the provisions of that subsection.

(7) Subject to subsection (8) below, a notification for the purposes of subsection (1) above shall be in force for the period of five years beginning with the day on which it is served but may be renewed by further notices under subsection (6) above for periods of five years at a time.

(8) A notification for the purposes of subsection (1) above may at any time be revoked by a further notice in writing served by the Minister on the person concerned; and the Minister shall serve such a further notice as soon as, in his opinion, the work undertaken by that person ceases to be such as is mentioned in subsection (6) above.

(9) In this section 'security or intelligence' means the work of, or in support of, the security and intelligence services or any part of them, and references to information relating to security or intelligence include references to information held or transmitted by those services or by persons in support of, or of any part of, them.

Defence.

2.—(1) A person who is or has been a Crown servant or government contractor is guilty of an offence if without lawful authority he makes a damaging disclosure of any information, document or other article relating to defence which is or has been in his possession by virtue of his position as such.

(2) For the purposes of subsection (1) above a disclosure is damaging if—
  (a) it damages the capability of, or of any part of, the armed forces of the Crown to carry out their tasks or leads to loss of life or injury to members of those forces or serious damage to the equipment or installations of those forces; or
  (b) otherwise than as mentioned in paragraph (a) above, it endangers the interests of the United Kingdom abroad, seriously obstructs the promotion or protection by the United Kingdom of those interests or endangers the safety of British citizens abroad; or
  (c) it is of information or of a document or article which is such that its unauthorised disclosure would be likely to have any of those effects.

(3) It is a defence for a person charged with an offence under this section to prove that at the time of the alleged offence he did not know, and had no reasonable cause to believe, that the information, document or article in question related to defence or that its disclosure would be damaging within the meaning of subsection (1) above.

(4) In this section 'defence' means—
  (a) the size, shape, organisation, logistics, order of battle, deployment, operations, state of readiness and training of the armed forces of the Crown;
  (b) the weapons, stores or other equipment of those forces and the invention, development, production and operation of such equipment and research relating to it;
  (c) defence policy and strategy and military planning and intelligence;
  (d) plans and measures for the maintenance of essential supplies and services that are or would be needed in time of war.

International relations.

3.—(1) A person who is or has been a Crown servant or government contractor is guilty of an offence if without lawful authority he makes a damaging disclosure of—
  (a) any information, document or other article relating to international relations; or
  (b) any confidential information, document or other article which was obtained from

a State other than the United Kingdom or an international organisation,
being information or a document or article which is or has been in his possession by
virtue of his position as a Crown servant or government contractor.

(2) For the purposes of subsection (1) above a disclosure is damaging if—

(a) it endangers the interests of the United Kingdom abroad, seriously obstructs the
promotion or protection by the United Kingdom of those interests or endangers
the safety of British citizens abroad; or

(b) it is of information or of a document or article which is such that its unauthorised
disclosure would be likely to have any of those effects.

(3) In the case of information or a document or article within subsection (1)(b) above—

(a) the fact that it is confidential, or

(b) its nature or contents,

may be sufficient to establish for the purposes of subsection (2)(b) above that the information, document or article is such that its unauthorised disclosure would be likely to have
any of the effects there mentioned.

(4) It is a defence for a person charged with an offence under this section to prove that at
the time of the alleged offence he did not know, and had no reasonable cause to believe,
that the information, document or article in question was such as is mentioned in subsection (1) above or that its disclosure would be damaging within the meaning of that
subsection.

(5) In this section 'international relations' means the relations between States, between
international organisations or between one or more States and one or more such organisations and includes any matter relating to a State other than the United Kingdom or
to an international organisation which is capable of affecting the relations of the United
Kingdom with another State or with an international organisation.

(6) For the purposes of this section any information, document or article obtained from a
State or organisation is confidential at any time while the terms on which it was obtained
require it to be held in confidence or while the circumstances in which it was obtained make
it reasonable for the State or organisation to expect that it would be so held.

Crime and special investigation powers.

4.—(1) A person who is or has been a Crown servant or government contractor is guilty
of an offence if without lawful authority he discloses any information, document or other
article to which this section applies and which is or has been in his possession by virtue of
his position as such.

(2) This section applies to any information, document or other article—

(a) the disclosure of which—

(i) results in the commission of an offence; or

(ii) facilitates an escape from legal custody or the doing of any other act prejudicial to the safekeeping of persons in legal custody; or

(iii) impedes the prevention or detection of offences or the apprehension or prosecution of suspected offenders; or

(b) which is such that its unauthorised disclosure would be likely to have any of those
effects.

(3) This section also applies to—

(a) any information obtained by reason of the interception of any communication in
obedience to a warrant issued under section 2 of the Interception of Communications Act 1985 [or under the authority of an interception warrant under
section 5 of the Regulation of Investigatory Powers Act 2000], any information
relating to the obtaining of information by reason of any such interception and
any document or other article which is or has been used or held for use in, or has
been obtained by reason of, any such interception; and

(b) any information obtained by reason of action authorised by a warrant issued
under section 3 of the Security Service Act 1989 [or under section 5 of the Intel-

ligence Services Act 1994 or by an authorisation given under section 7 of that Act], any information relating to the obtaining of information by reason of any such action and any document or other article which is or has been used or held for use in, or has been obtained by reason of, any such action.

(4) It is a defence for a person charged with an offence under this section in respect of a disclosure falling within subsection (2)(a) above to prove that at the time of the alleged offence he did not know, and had no reasonable cause to believe, that the disclosure would have any of the effects there mentioned.

(5) It is a defence for a person charged with an offence under this section in respect of any other disclosure to prove that at the time of the alleged offence he did not know, and had no reasonable cause to believe, that the information, document or article in question was information or a document or article to which this section applies.

(6) In this section 'legal custody' includes detention in pursuance of any enactment or any instrument made under an enactment."

The foregoing provisions of the 1989 Act are addressed to security and intelligence officers, civil servants and government contractors. They are addressed to the people who disclose the information. As such they are wide ranging and far reaching but still narrower than the corresponding provisions of s.2 of the 1911 Act which they replace. Section 5, however, addresses a wider audience and deals with the receipt of information. For this purpose the recipient could be a newspaper reporter or editor who acquires the information which he or she then publishes. Section 5 provides as follows:

"(1) Subsection (2) below applies where—
   (a) any information, document or other article protected against disclosure by the foregoing provisions of this Act has come into a person's possession as a result of having been—
      (i) disclosed (whether to him or another) by a Crown servant or government contractor without lawful authority; or
      (ii) entrusted to him by a Crown servant or government contractor on terms requiring it to be held in confidence or in circumstances in which the Crown servant or government contractor could reasonably expect that it would be so held; or
      (iii) disclosed (whether to him or another) without lawful authority by a person to whom it was entrusted as mentioned in sub-paragraph (ii) above; and
   (b) the disclosure without lawful authority of the information, document or article by the person into whose possession it has come is not an offence under any of those provisions.

(2) Subject to subsections (3) and (4) below, the person into whose possession the information, document or article has come is guilty of an offence if he discloses it without lawful authority knowing, or having reasonable cause to believe, that it is protected against disclosure by the foregoing provisions of this Act and that it has come into his possession as mentioned in subsection (1) above.

(3) In the case of information or a document or article protected against disclosure by sections 1 to 3 above, a person does not commit an offence under subsection (2) above unless—
   (a) the disclosure by him is damaging; and
   (b) he makes it knowing, or having reasonable cause to believe, that it would be damaging;
   and the question whether a disclosure is damaging shall be determined for the purposes of this subsection as it would be in relation to a disclosure of that information, document or article by a Crown servant in contravention of section 1(3), 2(1) or 3(1) above."

Although in principle s.5 could be used against the press, there is no case so far of this having been done.

An issue which is central to ss.1 to 5 is the question whether a disclosure is authorised. On this s.7 provides that a disclosure is authorised only if it is made by a crown servant or government contractor in accordance with his or her official duty or in accordance with an official authorisation. Section 7 also provides that it is a defence for a person charged with an offence under the Act "to prove that at the time of the alleged offence he believed that he had lawful authority to make the disclosure in question and had no reasonable cause to believe otherwise". Other provisions of the Act make it an offence to retain or return documents covered by the Act (s.8). By virtue of s.10, conviction under the Act for an offence (other than those in s.8), could lead to imprisonment of up to two years, or a fine or both. Trials may take place *in camera* on the grounds of national safety (except again for those relating to s.8) (s.11). For the purposes of the Act a crown servant is widely defined to include a Minister of the Crown; a member of the Scottish Executive or a junior Scottish Minister; a civil servant; a member of the naval, military or air forces of the Crown; a police constable; and other prescribed persons (s.12). A "government contractor" in turn means, subject to subs.(3), any person who is not a Crown servant but who provides, "or is employed in the provision of", goods or services to the government (s.12). It was perhaps inevitable that these provisions would be challenged under the Human Rights Act 1998 as violating the right to freedom of expression, particularly in light of the fact that, unlike the action for breach of confidence, there is no public interest defence in a prosecution under the Act. It is perhaps just as inevitable that any challenge would fail.

R. v Shayler
[2003] 1 A.C. 247

The appellant was a member of the security service who was charged under ss.1 and 4 of the Official Secrets Act 1989. He had disclosed at least 29 documents relating to security and intelligence to *The Mail on Sunday*, and these formed the basis of articles in that newspaper. Mr Shayler also wrote an article. Some of the information was classified as "Top Secret", and some of the documents were said to have included material obtained by or relating to the interception of communications in obedience to warrants issued under s.2 of the Interception of Communications Act 1985. At a preliminary hearing held under the Criminal Procedure and Investigations Act 1996 an issue arose about whether the appellant had been entitled to disclose the information in the public interest in order to expose "illegal, unlawful and inefficient workings of the security and intelligence services". However the contention was rejected by the trial judge (Moses J.) who held that there was no public interest defence to a prosecution under ss.1 or 4 of the 1989 Act and that none was required by the ECHR, Art.10. The Act was not incompatible with the Human Rights Act, and there was no need to read it consistently with the Human Rights Act or to entertain a declaration of incompatibility. This decision was upheld by the Court of Appeal and ultimately by the House of Lords.

LORD BINGHAM OF CORNHILL: "12. As enacted the OSA 1989 makes important distinctions leading to differences of treatment:
  (1) The Act distinguishes between different classes of discloser. Thus, in section 1, members and former members of the intelligence and security services and persons notified that they are subject to the subsection are covered by subsection (1), whereas past and present Crown servants and government contractors are covered by sub-section (3).
  (2) The Act distinguishes between different kinds of information. Section 1 deals with security and intelligence information. Successive sections deal with information relating to defence, international relations and crime.
  (3) The Act provides specific defences on which reliance may be placed in different circumstances: thus, in addition to the defence expressly provided in section 1(5) ..., further defences are provided in sections 2(3), 3(4), 4(4) and (5), 5(3) and (4), 6(3), 7(4) and 8(2).

(4) The requirement to prove damage differs according to the nature of the disclosure and the information disclosed. Thus the provisions in section 1(3) and (4) are to be contrasted with the lack of any express requirement of damage in section 1(1), and are in line with similar provisions in sections 2(1) and (2), 3(1), (2) and (3), 4(2), 5(3) and 6(2).

Construction of section 1(2) and 4(1) of the OSA 1989

18. Section 1(1)(a) of the OSA 1989 imposes criminal liability on a member or former member of the security and intelligence services if, without lawful authority (as defined in section 7), he discloses any information or document relating to security or intelligence which is or has been in his possession by virtue of his position as a member of any of those services. The only defence expressly provided is, under subsection (5), that at the time of the disclosure he did not know and had no reasonable cause to believe that the information or documents in question related to security or intelligence. As already demonstrated, a member or former member of the security and intelligence services is treated differently under the Act from other persons, and information and documents relating to security and intelligence are treated differently from information and documents relating to other matters. Importantly, the section does not require the prosecution to prove that any disclosure made by a member or former member of the security and intelligence services was damaging to the interests of that service or the public service generally.

19. Section 4(1), read in conjunction with section 4(3)(a), imposes criminal liability on a serving or former crown servant if, without lawful authority (as defined in section 7), he discloses any information obtained by reason of the interception of any communication in obedience to a warrant issued under section 2 of the Interception of Communications Act 1985 which has been in his possession by virtue of his position as a serving or former crown servant. The only defence expressly provided is, under subsection (5), that at the time of the disclosure he did not know and had no reasonable cause to believe that any information or document disclosed was information or a document to which the section applied. In a prosecution under the subsections referred to the prosecution do not have to prove damage or the likelihood of damage (as required under section 4(2)) and a limited defence based on lack of knowledge that damage would be caused (as provided under section 4(4)) does not apply.

20. It is in my opinion plain, giving sections 1(1)(a) and 4(1) and (3)(a) their natural and ordinary meaning and reading them in the context of the OSA 1989 as a whole, that a defendant prosecuted under these sections is not entitled to be acquitted if he shows that it was or that he believed that it was in the public or national interest to make the disclosure in question or if the jury conclude that it may have been or that the defendant may have believed it to be in the public or national interest to make the disclosure in question. The sections impose no obligation on the prosecution to prove that the disclosure was not in the public interest and give the defendant no opportunity to show that the disclosure was in the public interest or that he thought it was. The sections leave no room for doubt, and if they did the 1988 white paper [which preceded the 1989 Act], which is a legitimate aid to construction, makes the intention of Parliament clear beyond argument.

The right to free expression

21. The fundamental right of free expression has been recognised at common law for very many years .... The reasons why the right to free expression is regarded as fundamental are familiar, but merit brief restatement in the present context. Modern democratic government means government of the people by the people for the people. But there can be no government by the people if they are ignorant of the issues to be resolved, the arguments for and against different solutions and the facts underlying those arguments. The business of government is not an activity about which only those professionally engaged are entitled to receive information and express opinions. It is, or should be, a participatory process. But there can be no assurance that government is carried out for the people unless the facts are

made known, the issues publicly ventilated. Sometimes, inevitably, those involved in the conduct of government, as in any other walk of life, are guilty of error, incompetence, misbehaviour, dereliction of duty, even dishonesty and malpractice. Those concerned may very strongly wish that the facts relating to such matters are not made public. Publicity may reflect discredit on them or their predecessors. It may embarrass the authorities. It may impede the process of administration. Experience however shows, in this country and elsewhere, that publicity is a powerful disinfectant. Where abuses are exposed, they can be remedied. Even where abuses have already been remedied, the public may be entitled to know that they occurred. The role of the press in exposing abuses and miscarriages of justice has been a potent and honourable one. But the press cannot expose that of which it is denied knowledge.

22. Despite the high value placed by the common law on freedom of expression, it was not until incorporation of the European Convention into our domestic law by the Human Rights Act 1998 that this fundamental right was underpinned by statute. Article 10(1) of the Convention, so far as relevant, provides: [He then read parts of article 10.] Section 12 of the 1998 Act reflects the central importance which attaches to the right to freedom of expression. ... Thus for purposes of the present proceedings the starting point must be that the appellant is entitled if he wishes to disclose information and documents in his possession unless the law imposes a valid restraint upon his doing so.

Article 10(2)

23. Despite the high importance attached to it, the right to free expression was never regarded in domestic law as absolute. Publication could render a party liable to civil or criminal penalties or restraints on a number of grounds which included, for instance, libel, breach of confidence, incitement to racial hatred, blasphemy, publication of pornography and, as noted above, disclosure of official secrets. The European Convention similarly recognises that the right is not absolute: article 10(2) qualifies the broad language of article 10(1) ... It is plain from the language of article 10(2), and the European Court has repeatedly held, that any national restriction on freedom of expression can be consistent with article 10(2) only if it is prescribed by law, is directed to one or more of the objectives specified in the article and is shown by the state concerned to be necessary in a democratic society. 'Necessary' has been strongly interpreted: it is not synonymous with 'indispensable', neither has it the flexibility of such expressions as 'admissible', 'ordinary', 'useful', 'reasonable' or 'desirable': *Handyside v United Kingdom* (1976) 1 EHRR 737, 754, para 48. One must consider whether the interference complained of corresponded to a pressing social need, whether it was proportionate to the legitimate aim pursued and whether the reasons given by the national authority to justify it are relevant and sufficient under article 10(2): *The Sunday Times v United Kingdom* (1979) 2 EHRR 245, 277–278, para 62.

24. In the present case there can be no doubt but that the sections under which the appellant has been prosecuted, construed as I have construed them, restricted his prima facie right to free expression. There can equally be no doubt but that the restriction was directed to objectives specified in article 10(2) .... It was suggested in argument that the restriction was not prescribed by law because the procedure for obtaining authorisation was not precisely specified in the OSA 1989, but I cannot accept this. The restriction on disclosure is prescribed with complete clarity. A member or former member of any of the security or intelligence services wishing to obtain authority to disclose could be in no doubt but that he should seek authorisation from his superior or former superior in the relevant service or the head of that service, either of whom might no doubt refer the request to higher authority. It was common ground below, in my view, rightly, that the relevant restriction was prescribed by law. It is on the question of necessity, pressing social need and proportionality that the real issue between the parties arises.

25. There is much domestic authority pointing to the need for a security or intelligence service to be secure. The commodity in which such a service deals is secret and confidential

information. If the service is not secure those working against the interests of the state, whether terrorists, other criminals or foreign agents, will be alerted, and able to take evasive action; its own agents may be unmasked; members of the service will feel unable to rely on each other; those upon whom the service relies as sources of information will feel unable to rely on their identity remaining secret; and foreign countries will decline to entrust their own secrets to an insecure recipient …

26. The need to preserve the secrecy of information relating to intelligence and military operations in order to counter terrorism, criminal activity, hostile activity and subversion has been recognised by the European Commission and the Court in relation to complaints made under article 10 and other articles under the convention … . The thrust of these decisions and judgments has not been to discount or disparage the need for strict and enforceable rules but to insist on adequate safeguards to ensure that the restriction does not exceed what is necessary to achieve the end in question. The acid test is whether, in all the circumstances, the interference with the individual's convention right prescribed by national law is greater than is required to meet the legitimate object which the state seeks to achieve. The OSA 1989, as it applies to the appellant, must be considered in that context.

27. The OSA 1989 imposes a ban on disclosure of information or documents relating to security or intelligence by a former member of the service. But it is not an absolute ban. It is a ban on disclosure without lawful authority. It is in effect a ban subject to two conditions. First of all, the former member may, under section 7(3)(a), make disclosure to a Crown servant for the purposes of his functions as such:

(1.) The former member may make disclosure to the staff counsellor, whose appointment was announced in the House of Commons in November 1987 (Hansard (HC Debates), 2 November 1987, written answers col 512), before enactment of the OSA 1989 and in obvious response to the grievances ventilated by Mr Peter Wright in *Spycatcher*. The staff counsellor, a high ranking former civil servant, is available to be consulted:

'by any member of the security and intelligence services who has anxieties relating to the work of his or her service which it has not been possible to allay through the ordinary processes of management-staff relations.'

In February 1989 the role of the staff counsellor was further explained: see the judgment of the Court of Appeal, [2001] 1 WLR 2206, para 39.

(2.) If the former member has concerns about the lawfulness of what the service has done or is doing, he may disclose his concerns to (among others) the Attorney General, the Director of Public Prosecutions or the Commissioner of Metropolitan Police. These officers are subject to a clear duty, in the public interest, to uphold the law, investigate alleged infractions and prosecute where offences appear to have been committed, irrespective of any party affiliation or service loyalty.

(3.) If a former member has concerns about misbehaviour, irregularity, maladministration, waste of resources or incompetence in the service he may disclose these to the Home Secretary, the Foreign Secretary, the Secretary of State for Northern Ireland or Scotland, the Prime Minister, the Secretary to the Cabinet or the Joint Intelligence Committee. He may also make disclosure to the secretariat, provided (as the House was told) by the Home Office, of the parliamentary Intelligence and Security Committee. He may further make disclosure, by virtue of article 3 of and Schedule 2 to the Official Secrets Act 1989 (Prescription) Order 1990 (SI 1990/200) to the staff of the Controller and Auditor General, the National Audit Office and the Parliamentary Commissioner for Administration.

28. Since one count of the indictment against the appellant is laid under section 4(1) and (3) of the OSA 1989, considerable attention was directed by the judge and the Court of Appeal to the role of the commissioners appointed under section 8(1) of the Interception of Communications Act 1985, section 4(1) of the Security Service Act 1989 and section 8(1) of the Intelligence Services Act 1994. The appellant submits, correctly, that none of these commissioners is a minister or a civil servant, that their functions defined by the three

statutes do not include general oversight of the three security services, and that the secretariat serving the commissioners is, or was, of modest size. But under each of the three Acts, the commissioner was given power to require documents and information to be supplied to him by any crown servant or member of the relevant services for the purposes of his functions (section 8(3) of the 1985 Act, section 4(4) of the 1989 Act, section 8(4) of the 1994 Act), and if it were intimated to the commissioner, in terms so general as to involve no disclosure, that serious abuse of the power to intercept communications or enter premises to obtain information was taking or had taken place, it seems unlikely that the commissioner would not exercise his power to obtain information or at least refer the warning to the Home Secretary or (as the case might be) the Foreign Secretary.

29. One would hope that, if disclosure were made to one or other of the persons listed above, effective action would be taken to ensure that abuses were remedied and offenders punished. But the possibility must exist that such action would not be taken when it should be taken or that, despite the taking of effective action to remedy past abuses and punish past delinquencies, there would remain facts which should in the public interest be revealed to a wider audience. This is where, under the OSA 1989 the second condition comes into play: the former member may seek official authorisation to make disclosure to a wider audience.

30. As already indicated, it is open to a former member of the service to seek authorisation from his former superior or the head of the service, who may no doubt seek authority from the secretary to the cabinet or a minister. Whoever is called upon to consider the grant of authorisation must consider with care the particular information or document which the former member seeks to disclose and weigh the merits of that request bearing in mind (and if necessary taking advice on) the object or objects which the statutory ban on disclosure seeks to achieve and the harm (if any) which would be done by the disclosure in question. If the information or document in question were liable to disclose the identity of agents or compromise the security of informers, one would not expect authorisation to be given. If, on the other hand, the document or information revealed matters which, however, scandalous or embarrassing, would not damage any security or intelligence interest or impede the effective discharge by the service of its very important public functions, another decision might be appropriate. Consideration of a request for authorisation should never be a routine or mechanical process: it should be undertaken bearing in mind the importance attached to the right of free expression and the need for any restriction to be necessary, responsive to a pressing social need and proportionate.

31. One would, again, hope that requests for authorisation to disclose would be granted where no adequate justification existed for denying it and that authorisation would be refused only where such justification existed. But the possibility would of course exist that authority might be refused where no adequate justification existed for refusal, or at any rate where the former member firmly believed that no adequate justification existed. In this situation the former member is entitled to seek judicial review of the decision to refuse, a course which the OSA 1989 does not seek to inhibit. In considering an application for judicial review of a decision to refuse authorisation to disclose, the court must apply (albeit from a judicial standpoint, and on the evidence before it) the same tests as are described in the last paragraph. It also will bear in mind the importance attached to the convention right of free expression. It also will bear in mind the need for any restriction to be necessary to achieve one or more of the ends specified in article 10(2), to be responsive to a pressing social need and to be no more restrictive than is necessary to achieve that end.

32. For the appellant it was argued that judicial review offered a person in his position no effective protection, since courts were reluctant to intervene in matters concerning national security and the threshold of showing a decision to be irrational was so high as to give the applicant little chance of crossing it. ....

33. There are in my opinion two answers to this submission. First the court's willingness to intervene will very much depend on the nature of the material which it is sought to disclose. If the issue concerns the disclosure of documents bearing a high security classi-

fication and there is apparently credible unchallenged evidence that disclosure is liable to lead to the identification of agents or the compromise of informers, the court may very well be unwilling to intervene. If, at the other end of the spectrum, it appears that while disclosure of the material may cause embarrassment or arouse criticism, it will not damage any security or intelligence interest, the court's reaction is likely to be very different. Usually, a proposed disclosure will fall between these two extremes and the court must exercise its judgment, informed by article 10 considerations. The second answer is that in any application for judicial review alleging an alleged violation of a convention right the court will now conduct a much more rigorous and intrusive review than was once thought to be permissible. The change was described by Lord Steyn in *R (Daly) v Secretary of State for the Home Department* [2001] 2 AC 532, 546 where after referring to the standards of review reflected in *Associated Provincial Picture Houses Ltd v Wednesbury Corporation* [1948] 1 KB 223 and *R v Ministry of Defence, Ex p. Smith* [1996] QB 517, he said:

'26. ... There is a material difference between the *Wednesbury* and *Smith* grounds of review and the approach of proportionality applicable in respect of review where Convention rights are at stake.

27. The contours of the principle of proportionality are familiar. In *de Freitas v Permanent Secretary of Ministry of Agriculture, Fisheries, Lands and Housing* [1999] 1 AC 69 the Privy Council adopted a three-stage test. Lord Clyde observed, at p 80, that in determining whether a limitation (by an act, rule or decision) is arbitrary or excessive the court should ask itself:

"whether: (i) the legislative objective is sufficiently important to justify limiting a fundamental right; (ii) the measures designed to meet the legislative objective are rationally connected to it; and (iii) the means used to impair the right or freedom are no more than is necessary to accomplish the objective."'

Clearly, these criteria are more precise and more sophisticated than the traditional grounds of review. ...

36. The special position of those employed in the security and intelligence services, and the special nature of the work they carry out, impose duties and responsibilities on them within the meaning of article 10 (2): *Engel v The Netherlands (No 1)* (1976) 1 EHRR 647, para 100; *Hadjianastassiou v Greece* (1992) 16 EHRR 219, para 46. These justify what Lord Griffiths called a bright line rule against disclosure of information of documents relating to security or intelligence obtained in the course of their duties by members or former members of those services. (While Lord Griffiths was willing to accept the theoretical possibility of a public interest defence, he made no allowance for judicial review: *Attorney General v Guardian Newspapers Ltd (No 2)* [1990] 1 AC 109, 269G). If, within this limited category of case, a defendant is prosecuted for making an unauthorised disclosure it is necessary to relieve the prosecutor of the need to prove damage (beyond the damage inherent in disclosure by a former member of these services) and to deny the defendant a defence based on the public interest; otherwise the detailed facts concerning the disclosure and the arguments for and against making it would be canvassed before the court and the cure would be even worse than the disease. But it is plain that a sweeping, blanket ban, permitting of no exceptions, would be inconsistent with the general right guaranteed by article 10(1) and would not survive the rigorous and particular scrutiny required to give effect to article 10(2). The crux of this case is whether the safeguards built into the OSA 1989 are sufficient to ensure that unlawfulness and irregularity can be reported to those with the power and duty to take effective action, that the power to withhold authorisation to publish is not abused and that proper disclosures are not stifled. In my opinion the procedures discussed above, properly applied, provide sufficient and effective safeguards. It is, however, necessary that a member or former member of a relevant service should avail himself of the procedures available to him under the Act. A former member of a relevant service, prosecuted for making an unauthorised disclosure, cannot defend himself by

contending that if he had made disclosure under section 7(3)(a) no notice or action would have been taken or that if he had sought authorisation under section 7(3)(b) it would have been refused. If a person who has given a binding undertaking of confidentiality seeks to be relieved, even in part, from that undertaking he must seek authorisation and, if so advised, challenge any refusal of authorisation. If that refusal is upheld by the courts, it must, however reluctantly, be accepted. I am satisfied that sections 1(1) and 4(1) and (3) of the OSA 1989 are compatible with article 10 of the convention; no question of reading those sections conformably with the convention or making a declaration of incompatibility therefore arises. On these crucial issues I am in agreement with both the judge and the Court of Appeal. They are issues on which the House can form its own opinion. But they are also issues on which Parliament has expressed a clear democratic judgment ...

38. I would dismiss the appeal."

Lords Hope of Craighead and Hutton delivered concurring speeches. Lords Hobhouse and Scott of Foscote concurred.

The *Shayler* case thus gives rise to the curious situation that conduct that cannot be restrained by interdict or injunction for breach of confidence could nevertheless form the basis of a prosecution under the Official Secrets Act 1989. There is also the possibility that an application for an interdict or injunction could be made by the government law officers to prevent a breach of the Official Secrets Act 1989, thereby circumventing potential difficulties created by the *Spycatcher* and *Inside Intelligence* cases. There is, however, one other issue that needs to be addressed. In the cases discussed so far the newspapers have published material from officials whose identity has been known to the government. However, what happens if an official secretly provides security sensitive information to a newspaper, as happened in 1984 when information about the arrival of US cruise missiles was provided to *The Guardian*. In such a case the government may want to know the identity of the person who supplied the information, for a number of reasons. In order to ensure that there are no further leaks, the government may want to dismiss the individual in question, may want to consider a criminal prosecution under the Official Secrets Act 1989.

The question which arises in these cases is whether the newspaper is under a duty to reveal its sources? The protection by journalists of their sources is an important principle which relates directly to the right to freedom of expression. The willingness of people to speak freely to journalists and the ability of journalists to conduct investigative reporting would be greatly impaired if the journalist was to be compelled to hand over names. The names handed over might then be subject to prosecution, civil action, or dismissal. The right of journalists to protect their sources is thus protected by the Contempt of Court Act 1981, s.10, which forms the basis of the newspaper's unsuccessful defence to an action for the return of documents in the following case. But the right is not an unlimited one, with s.10 carrying many significant exceptions which go a long way to swallow the basic rule against discloure. In *Secretary of State for Defense v Guardian Newspapers Ltd* [1985] 1 A.C. 359 it was held by the House of Lords that the right to protect sources had to yield in that case to the demands of national security. As a result, *The Guardian* was required to return documents to the government which enabled the government to identify the source of the leak of information about the arrival of US cruise missiles. The hapless Ms Tisdall was prosecuted under the Official Secrets Act 1911, s.2, convicted and imprisoned.

IV. RESTRICTED SPEECH

So far we have considered forms of speech which are either censored or prohibited. There is of course a fine line between the two in the sense that prohibition is itself a form of censorship. Not only is it likely to restrain what the individual may say, it may also form the basis of intervention by the courts by way of interdict if they are alerted in time to be able to prevent a publication or broadcast. Nevertheless, there remains a crucial difference between censorship and prohibition: in the case of the former the speech is prevented (as in the *Pro-Life Alliance* case); in the the case of the latter it is typically punished after the event (as in the *Shayler* case). In addition to these two categories of speech, there is a third category of speech. This category does not involve the censorship or prohibition of speech so much as its restriction. Here we are not concerned so much with the content of the speech, but with who is making the speech, or when they are making the speech, or the conditions under which they are making the speech. The category of restricted speech is thus defined by these three different forms of restriction.

(1) Restrictions on the Source of Speech

One form of restriction relates to the identity of the speaker. Here we are not offended by the message, but by the fact that the message is being conveyed by someone who is regarded as an inappropriate person to make it. Perhaps the best example of such a restriction applies in relation to civil servants and local government staff in order to ensure that we have a politically neutral public service. The restrictions on the speech of civil servants are to be found in the Civil Service Management Code. These restrictions have been revised over many years, generally to relax the political disabilities under which civil servants labour. The restrictions are directed not only at candidature in a general election but also a wide range of other political activities. Under the Civil Service Management Code, there are three groups of civil servants, so far as political activities are concerned. These are the politically free, the politically restricted, and an inter-mediate category who can take part in political activities with consent. It is clear from the Civil Service Management Code that the political restrictions on civil servants apply to speech and the expression of political opinions in public. In addition to the restrictions on civil servants, there are also similar restrictions on local government officers, though these are of much more recent vintage. Although the political restrictions on civil servants have a long pedigree, the corresponding local government restrictions were not introduced until 1990 following the report of the Widdicombe Committee of Inquiry into the Conduct of Local Authority Business (Cmnd. 9797, 1986).

The Local Government and Housing Act 1989 empowered the Secretary of State for the Environment to make regulations to restrict the political activities of certain categories of local government officers, and restrictions were introduced by the Local Government Officers (Political Restrictions) Regulations 1990 (SI 1990/851). The Regulations applied to all persons holding a politically restricted post as defined in s.2(1) of the Act. As pointed out by the European Court of Human Rights in *Ahmed v United Kingdom* (2000) 29 E.H.R.R. 1:

"This term covers three broad categories of local government officials: the most senior post-holders in local government (category one); officials remunerated in excess of a prescribed level and whose posts are listed for the purposes of the application of the Regulations (category two); and officials paid less than the prescribed level but who hold a listed post (category three)."

Each local authority was obliged to draw up a list of posts falling within the second and third categories (s.2(2)). A local government officer in the second and third categories could apply to an independent adjudicator to have his or her post removed from the list of posts to which the Regulations applied (s.3). Although the restrictions on civil servants have never been challenged as breaching Convention rights, an application was made to Strasbourg complaining that these restrictions on local government employees violated Arts 10 and 11 of the ECHR.

Ahmed v United Kingdom
(2000) 29 E.H.R.R. 1

The four applicants were employed by different local government authorities in England. Each was designated as politically restricted, with the result that the first had to give up being a Labour candidate at the forthcoming general election. The second had to give up his position as Vice-Chair of his Constituency Labour Party, and to refrain from supporting and assisting Labour candidates (including his wife) in local authority elections. The third had to resign as Chairman of his Constituency Labour Party and to stop giving radio interviews in his capacity as Chairman of the Plymouth Health Emergency, a body concerned with National Health policies. And the fourth could no longer act as parliamentary chairman of his political party in Harrow East and was prevented from speaking at public meetings on issues such as housing and the health service. The European Court of Human Rights nevertheless held that there had been no breach of the Convention.

JUDGMENT: "40. ... The Government did not dispute that the applicants could rely on the guarantees contained in Article 10; nor did they deny that the application of the Regulations interfered with the exercise of their rights under that Article. They contended however that the interferences which resulted from the application of the Regulations to the applicants were justified under the second paragraph of Article 10.

...

[The Court considered whether the restrictions satisfied a legitimate aim:]

50. The Government defended their view that the Regulations were essential to the proper functioning of the democratic system of local government in the United Kingdom. They stressed that, in line with the conclusions and recommendations of the Widdicombe Committee (see paragraphs 9 and 10 above), the restrictions contained in the Regulations were intended to strengthen the tradition of political neutrality on the part of specific categories of local government officers by prohibiting them from participating in forms of political activity which could compromise the duty of loyalty and impartiality which they owed to the democratically elected members of local authorities....

52. The Court does not accept the applicants' argument that the protection of effective democracy can only be invoked as a justification for limitations on the rights guaranteed under Article 10 in circumstances where there is a threat to the stability of the constitutional or political order. To limit this notion to that context would be to overlook both the interests served by democratic institutions such as local authorities and the need to make provision to secure their proper functioning where this is considered necessary to safeguard those interests. The Court recalls in this respect that democracy is a fundamental feature of the European public order. That is apparent from the Preamble to the Convention, which establishes a very clear connection between the Convention and democracy by stating that the maintenance and further realisation of human rights and fundamental freedoms are best ensured on the one hand by an effective political democracy and on the other by a common understanding and observance of human rights (see, mutatis mutandis, the *United Communist Party of Turkey and Others v Turkey* (1998) 26 E.H.R.R. 121). For the Court this notion of effective political democracy is just as applicable to the local level as it is to the national level bearing in mind the extent of decision-making entrusted to local authorities and the proximity of the local electorate to the policies which their local politicians adopt. It also notes in this respect that the Preamble to the Council of Europe's European Charter of Local Self-Government (European Treaty Series no. 122) proclaims that 'local authorities are one of the main foundations of any democratic regime'.

53. The Court observes that the local government system of the respondent State has long rested on a bond of trust between elected members and a permanent corps of local government officers who both advise them on policy and assume responsibility for the implementation of the policies adopted. That relationship of trust stems from the right of council members to expect that they are being assisted in their functions by officers who are politically neutral and whose loyalty is to the council as a whole. Members of the public also have a right to expect that the members whom they voted into office will discharge their mandate in accordance with the commitments they made during an electoral campaign and that the pursuit of that mandate will not founder on the political opposition of

their members' own advisers; it is also to be noted that members of the public are equally entitled to expect that in their own dealings with local government departments they will be advised by politically neutral officers who are detached from the political fray.

The aim pursued by the Regulations was to underpin that tradition and to ensure that the effectiveness of the system of local political democracy was not diminished through the corrosion of the political neutrality of certain categories of officers.

54. For the above reasons, the Court concludes that the interferences which resulted from the application of the Regulations to the applicants pursued a legitimate aim within the meaning of paragraph 2 of Article 10, namely to protect the rights of others, council members and the electorate alike, to effective political democracy at the local level.

[The Court then considered whether the restraints could be said to be 'necessary in a democratic society]

(a) General principles
55. The Court recalls that in [*Vogt v Germany* (1995) 21 E.H.R.R. 205] it articulated as follows the basic principles laid down in its judgments concerning Article 10:

    (i) Freedom of expression constitutes one of the essential foundations of a democratic society and one of the basic conditions for its progress and each individual's self-fulfilment. Subject to paragraph 2 of Article 10, it is applicable not only to 'information' or 'ideas' that are favourably received or regarded as inoffensive or as a matter of indifference, but also to those that offend, shock or disturb; such are the demands of that pluralism, tolerance and broadmindedness without which there is no 'democratic society'. Freedom of expression, as enshrined in Article 10, is subject to a number of exceptions which, however, must be narrowly interpreted and the necessity for any exceptions must be convincingly established.

    (ii) The adjective 'necessary', within the meaning of Article 10 § 2 implies the existence of a 'pressing social need'. The Contracting States have a certain margin of appreciation in assessing whether such a need exists, but it goes hand in hand with a European supervision, embracing both the law and the decisions applying it, even those given by independent courts. The Court is therefore empowered to give the final ruling on whether a 'restriction' is reconcilable with freedom of expression as protected by Article 10.

    (iii) The Court's task, in exercising its supervisory jurisdiction, is not to take the place of the competent national authorities but rather to review under Article 10 the decisions they delivered pursuant to their power of appreciation. This does not mean that the supervision is limited to ascertaining whether the respondent State exercised its discretion reasonably, carefully or in good faith; what the Court has to do is to look at the interference complained of in the light of the case as a whole and determine whether it is 'proportionate to the legitimate aim pursued' and whether the reasons adduced by the national authorities to justify it are 'relevant and sufficient'. In so doing, the Court has to satisfy itself that the national authorities applied standards which were in conformity with the principles embodied in Article 10 and, moreover, that they based their decisions on an acceptable assessment of the relevant facts.

56. In the same judgment the Court declared that these principles apply also to civil servants. Although it is legitimate for a State to impose on civil servants, on account of their status, a duty of discretion, civil servants are individuals and, as such, qualify for the protection of Article 10 of the Convention...

61. The Court's task is to ascertain in view of the above-mentioned principles (see paragraphs 55 and 56 above) whether the restrictions imposed on the applicants corresponded to a 'pressing social need' and whether they were 'proportionate' to the aim of protecting the rights of others to effective political democracy at the local level (see paragraph 54 above). In so doing it must also have regard to the fact that whenever the right to freedom of expression of public servants such as the applicants is in issue the 'duties and

responsibilities' referred to in Article 10(2) assume a special significance, which justifies leaving to the authorities of the respondent State a certain margin of appreciation in determining whether the impugned interference is proportionate to the aim as stated ....

62. It is to be observed at the outset that the Widdicombe Committee reported back to the government at the time that it had found specific instances of abuse of power by certain local government officers. The Committee was concerned both about the impact which the increase in confrontational politics in local government affairs would have on the main- tenance of the long-standing tradition of political neutrality of senior officers whose advice and guidance were relied on by the members elected to local councils as well as about the increased potential for more widespread abuse by senior officers of their key positions in a changed political context. Those concerns emerged from the Committee's detailed analysis of the state of local government at the time and its wide-ranging rounds of consultations with interested parties. There was a consensus among those consulted on the need for action to strengthen the tradition of political neutrality either through legislation or modification of the terms and conditions of officers' contracts of employment.

In the Court's view, the Widdicombe Committee had identified a pressing social need for action in this area. The adoption of the Regulations restricting the participation of certain categories of local government officers, distinguished by the sensitivity of their duties, in forms of political activity can be considered a valid response by the legislature to addressing that need and one which was within the respondent State's margin of appreciation. It is to be observed in this regard that the organisation of local democracy and the arrangements for securing the functioning, funding and accountability of local authorities are matters which can vary from State to State having regard to national traditions. Such is no doubt also the case with respect to the regulation of the political activities of local government officers where these are perceived to present a risk to the effective operation of local democracy, especially so where, as in the respondent State, the system is historically based on the role of a permanent corps of politically neutral advisers, managers and arbitrators above factional politics and loyal to the council as a whole.

The scope of the ban on local government officers arose for consideration in *Darroch v Strathclyde Regional Council*, 1993 S.L.T. 1111 where it was held that a depute assessor, depute electoral registration officer and depute community charge registration officer did not occupy a politically restricted post. The Outer House reached this decision expressing surprise in the process, given the objectives in ss.1–3 of the 1990 Act which was to "prohibit those holding certain posts in a local authority's employment from becoming or remaining members of a local authority or from standing for election to Parliament" (at 1116). According to Lord MacLean, "[o]ne might reasonably think an assessor in Scotland would be so prohibited given the nature of his post and his position as an officer of the local authority", and that it was "odd that he was not included amongst those defined as statutory chief officers in the Act". Lord MacLean had earlier quoted with approval a passage in the *Stair Memorial Encyclopaedia* about assessors. There Lord Clyde had written that: "The nature of the assessor's office and the duties which he has to carry out require him to possess a degree of independence of the local authority. Although he is employed by and is an officer of the valuation authority, it has always been recognised that in the carrying out of his responsibilities in the field of valuation he is free from any interference or interference from the authority". A notable feature of the *Darroch* case is that in granting the declarator sought by the petitioner, the court elided the rule that judicial review is not available in employment disputes. This was not a case "involving simply a con- tractual dispute between employee and employer. It is obvious that the decision made by the respondents, if not challenged, may have consequences for others in their employment, such as the assessor himself and other deputes. The restrictions placed on the activities of the petitioner ... raise a matter of public law since they affect his freedom of speech and association as well as that of others" (at 1993).

(2) Restrictions on the Manner and Timing of Speech

A second form of restriction on speech moves from questions about the identity of the speaker, to questions about the manner and form of the speech. Here we concentrate on manner and form restrictions that apply to speech particularly in the context of elections. The most obvious form of restraint is the prohibition on the use of television and radio for the purposes of political advertising. The new regulator (OFCOM) has a duty under the Communications Act 2003, s.319 to set programme standards which must meet a number of standards objectives also set out in s.319. These standards objectives include s.319(2)(g) which provides that that "advertising that contravenes the prohibition on political advertising set out in section 321(2) is not included in television or radio services". Section 321 (2) then provides that:

> "(2) For the purposes of section 319(2)(g) an advertisement contravenes the prohibition on political advertising if it is—
>
> (a) an advertisement which is inserted by or on behalf of a body whose objects are wholly or mainly of a political nature;
>
> (b) an advertisement which is directed towards a political end; or
>
> (c) an advertisement which has a connection with an industrial dispute.
>
> (3) For the purposes of this section objects of a political nature and political ends include each of the following—
>
> (a) influencing the outcome of elections or referendums, whether in the United Kingdom or elsewhere;
>
> (b) bringing about changes of the law in the whole or a part of the United Kingdom or elsewhere, or otherwise influencing the legislative process in any country or territory;
>
> (c) influencing the policies or decisions of local, regional or national governments, whether in the United Kingdom or elsewhere;
>
> (d) influencing the policies or decisions of persons on whom public functions are conferred by or under the law of the United Kingdom or of a country or territory outside the United Kingdom;
>
> (e) influencing the policies or decisions of persons on whom functions are conferred by or under international agreements;
>
> (f) influencing public opinion on a matter which, in the United Kingdom, is a matter of public controversy;
>
> (g) promoting the interests of a party or other group of persons organised, in the United Kingdom or elsewhere, for political ends."

The ban on political advertising was first introduced in the Television Act 1954 and has been retained ever since. The measure has enjoyed judicial support, in the form of the following dictum by Kennedy J. in *R. v Radio Authority ex parte Bull* [1995] 4 All E.R. 481: "in addition to freedom of communication there are other rights to be protected, such as freedom from being virtually forced to listen to unsolicited information of a contentious kind, and the danger of the wealthy distorting the democratic process" (at 495). But these views were expressed before the Human Rights Act 1998 was introduced, and there is some uncertainty about whether the ban is consistent with Art.10. Some of these uncertainties surfaced during the parliamentary history of the Communications Act 2003 during which the Government re-affirmed its commitment to the advertising ban. According to the Minister (Dr Kim Howells), "[t]he current ban safeguards public and democratic debate and protects broadcasters' impartiality by denying powerful interests the chance to skew political debate" (Official Report, Standing Committee E, January 28, 2003, cols 796–7). There is, however, some uncertainty about whether the ban is consistent with Art.10 of the ECHR. The uncertainty is caused by the decision in the following case.

Vgt Verein Gegen Tierfabriken v Switzerland
(2002) 34 E.H.R.R. 159

The applicants were an animal welfare organisation that wanted to broadcast a commercial in response to a number of commercials placed by the meat industry. The proposed commercial urged people to eat less meat to protect animals and the environment. The television company refused to broadcast the advertisement in view of its "clear political character", and an application to the courts was unsuccessful, with one of the courts holding that the prohibition of political advertising laid down in s.18(5) of the Swiss Federal Radio and Television Act served various purposes:

> "It should prevent financially powerful groups from obtaining a competitive political advantage. In the interest of the democratic process it is designed to protect the formation of public opinion from undue commercial influence and to bring about a certain equality of opportunity among the different forces of society. The prohibition contributes towards the independence of the radio and television broadcasters in editorial matters, which could be endangered by powerful political advertising sponsors. According to the Swiss law on communication the press remains the most important means for paid political advertising. Already, financially powerful groups are in a position to secure themselves more space; admitting political advertising on radio and television would reinforce this tendency and substantially influence the democratic process of opinion-forming—all the more so as it is established that with its dissemination and its immediacy television will have a stronger effect on the public than the other means of communication ... Reserving political advertising to the print media secures for them a certain part of the advertising market and thereby contributes to their financing; this in turn counteracts an undesirable concentration of the press and thus indirectly contributes to the pluralistic system of media required under Article 10 of the Convention."

The court also observed that the applicant association had other means of disseminating its political ideas, for instance in foreign programmes which were broadcast in Switzerland, or in the cinema and the press. The European Court of Human Rights held that there had been a breach of Art.10 of the ECHR. Although the television company was not a state authority, the court nevertheless held that the liability of the state was engaged because the advertisement had been banned as a result of legislation. The responsibility of the respondent state having been established, the refusal to broadcast the applicant association's commercial was held to be an "interference by public authority" in the exercise of the rights guaranteed by Art.10. The question then was whether the interference infringed the requirements of Art.10(2).

JUDGMENT OF THE COURT:

"D. Whether the interference pursued a legitimate aim
   59. The applicant association further maintained that there was no legitimate aim which justified the interference with its rights.
   60. The Government submitted that the refusal to broadcast the commercial at issue aimed at enabling the formation of public opinion protected from the pressures of powerful financial groups, while at the same time promoting equal opportunities for the different components of society. The refusal also secured for the press a segment of the advertising market, thus contributing towards its financial autonomy. In the Government's opinion, therefore, the measure was justified 'for the protection of the ... rights of others' within the meaning of Article 10(2) of the Convention.
   61. The Court notes the Federal Council's message to the Swiss Federal Parliament in which it was explained that the prohibition of political advertising in section 18(5) of the Swiss Radio and Television Act served to prevent financially powerful groups from obtaining a competitive political advantage. The Federal Court in its judgment of 20

August 1997 considered that the prohibition served, in addition, to ensure the independence of broadcasters, spare the political process from undue commercial influence, provide for a degree of equality of opportunity among the different forces of society and to support the press, which remained free to publish political advertisements.

62. The Court is, therefore, satisfied that the measure aimed at the 'protection of the ... rights of others' within the meaning of Article 10(2) of the Convention.

E. Whether the interference was 'necessary in a democratic society'

63. The applicant association submitted that the measure had not been proportionate, as it did not have other valid means at its disposal to broadcast the commercial at issue. The television programmes of the Swiss Radio and Television Company were the only ones to be broadcast and seen throughout Switzerland. The evening news programme and the subsequent national weather forecasts had the highest ratings, namely between 50% and 70% of all viewers. Even with the use of considerable financial resources it would not be possible to reach so many persons via the private regional channels or the foreign channels which could be received in Switzerland.

64. The Government considered that the measure was proportionate as being 'necessary in a democratic society' within the meaning of Article 10(2) of the Convention. It was not up to the Court to take the place of the national authorities; indeed, Contracting States remained free to choose the measures which they considered appropriate, and the Court could not be oblivious of the substantive or procedural features of their respective domestic laws ... . In the present case, the Federal Court in its judgment of 20 August 1997 was called upon to examine conflicting interests protected by the same basic right: namely the freedom of the applicant association to broadcast its ideas, and the freedom of the Commercial Television Company and the Swiss Radio and Television Company to communicate information. To admit the applicant association's point of view would be to grant a 'right to broadcast', which right would substantially interfere with the right of the Commercial Television Company and the Swiss Radio and Television Company to decide which information they chose to bring to the attention of the public. In fact, Article 10 would then oblige a third party to broadcast information which it did not wish to. Finally, the public had to be protected from untimely interruptions in television programmes by commercials.

65. In this respect the Government pointed out the various other possibilities open to the applicant association to broadcast the information at issue, namely by means of local radio and television stations, the print media and internet. Moreover, the Commercial Television Company had offered the applicant association the possibility of discussing the conditions for broadcasting its commercials, but this had been categorically refused by the latter.

66. The Court recalls that freedom of expression constitutes one of the essential foundations of a democratic society and one of the basic conditions for its progress and for each individual's self-fulfilment. Subject to paragraph 2 of Article 10, it is applicable not only to 'information' or 'ideas' that are favourably received or regarded as inoffensive or as a matter of indifference, but also to those that offend, shock or disturb. Such are the demands of pluralism, tolerance and broadmindedness without which there is no 'democratic society'. As set forth in Article 10, this freedom is subject to exceptions. Such exceptions must, however, be construed strictly, and the need for any restrictions must be established convincingly, particularly where the nature of the speech is political rather than commercial ... .

67. Under the Court's case-law, the adjective 'necessary', within the meaning of Article 10(2), implies the existence of a 'pressing social need'. The Contracting States have a certain margin of appreciation in assessing whether such a need exists, but it goes hand in hand with a European supervision, embracing both the legislation and the decisions applying it, even those given by an independent court. The Court is therefore empowered to give the final ruling on whether a 'restriction' is reconcilable with freedom of expression as protected by Article 10.

68. The Court's task, in exercising its supervisory jurisdiction, is not to take the place of the competent national authorities but rather to review under Article 10 the decisions they delivered pursuant to their power of appreciation. This does not mean that the supervision is limited to ascertaining whether the respondent State exercised its discretion reasonably, carefully and in good faith; what the Court has to do is to look at the interference complained of in the light of the case as a whole and determine whether it was 'proportionate to the legitimate aim pursued' and whether the reasons adduced by the national authorities to justify it are 'relevant and sufficient' .... In doing so, the Court has to satisfy itself that the national authorities applied standards which were in conformity with the principles embodied in Article 10 and, moreover, that they relied on an acceptable assessment of the relevant facts ....

69. It follows that the Swiss authorities had a certain margin of appreciation to decide whether there was a 'pressing social need' to refuse the broadcasting of the commercial. Such a margin of appreciation is particularly essential in commercial matters, especially in an area as complex and fluctuating as that of advertising ....

70. However, the Court has found above that the applicant association's film fell outside the regular commercial context inciting the public to purchase a particular product. Rather, it reflected controversial opinions pertaining to modern society in general .... The Swiss authorities themselves regarded the content of the applicant association's commercial as being 'political' within the meaning of section 18(5) of the Federal Radio and Television Act. Indeed, it cannot be denied that in many European societies there was, and is, an ongoing general debate on the protection of animals and the manner in which they are reared.

71. As a result, in the present case the extent of the margin of appreciation is reduced, since what is at stake is not a given individual's purely 'commercial' interests, but his participation in a debate affecting the general interest.

72. The Court will consequently examine carefully whether the measure in issue was proportionate to the aim pursued. In that regard, it must balance the applicant association's freedom of expression, on the one hand, with the reasons adduced by the Swiss authorities for the prohibition of political advertising, on the other, namely to protect public opinion from the pressures of powerful financial groups and from undue commercial influence; to provide for a certain equality of opportunity among the different forces of society; to ensure the independence of broadcasters in editorial matters from powerful sponsors; and to support the press.

73. It is true that powerful financial groups can obtain competitive advantages in the area of commercial advertising and may thereby exercise pressure on, and eventually curtail the freedom of, the radio and television stations broadcasting the commercials. Such situations undermine the fundamental role of freedom of expression in a democratic society as enshrined in Article 10 of the Convention, in particular where it serves to impart information and ideas of general interest, which the public is moreover entitled to receive. Such an undertaking cannot be successfully accomplished unless it is grounded in the principle of pluralism of which the State is the ultimate guarantor. This observation is especially valid in relation to audio-visual media, whose programmes are often broadcast very widely ....

74. In the present case, the contested measure, namely the prohibition of political advertising as provided in section 18(5) of the Federal Radio and Television Act, was applied only to radio and television broadcasts, and not to other media such as the press. The Federal Court explained in this respect in its judgment of 20 August 1997 that television had a stronger effect on the public on account of its dissemination and immediacy. In the Court's opinion, however, while the domestic authorities may have had valid reasons for this differential treatment, a prohibition of political advertising which applies only to certain media, and not to others, does not appear to be of a particularly pressing nature.

75. Moreover, it has not been argued that the applicant association itself constituted a powerful financial group which, with its proposed commercial, aimed at endangering the independence of the broadcaster; at unduly influencing public opinion or at endangering

equality of opportunity among the different forces of society. Indeed, rather than abusing a competitive advantage, all the applicant association intended to do with its commercial was to participate in an ongoing general debate on animal protection and the rearing of animals. The Court cannot exclude that a prohibition of 'political advertising' may be compatible with the requirements of Article 10 of the Convention in certain situations. Nevertheless, the reasons must be 'relevant' and ' ''sufficient' in respect of the particular interference with the rights under Article 10. In the present case, the Federal Court, in its judgment of 20 August 1997, discussed at length the general reasons which justified a prohibition of 'political advertising'. In the Court's opinion, however, the domestic authorities have not demonstrated in a 'relevant and sufficient' manner why the grounds generally advanced in support of the prohibition of political advertising also served to justify the interference in the particular circumstances of the applicant association's case.

76. The domestic authorities did not adduce the disturbing nature of any particular sequence, or of any particular words, of the commercial as a ground for refusing to broadcast it. It therefore mattered little that the pictures and words employed in the commercial at issue may have appeared provocative or even disagreeable.

77. In so far as the Government pointed out that there were various other possibilities to broadcast the information at issue, the Court observes that the applicant association, aiming at reaching the entire Swiss public, had no other means than the national television programmes of the Swiss Radio and Television Company at its disposal, since these programmes were the only ones broadcast throughout Switzerland. The Commercial Television Company was the sole instance responsible for the broadcasting of commercials within these national programmes. Private regional television channels and foreign television stations cannot be received throughout Switzerland. ...

79. In the light of the foregoing, the measure in issue cannot be considered as 'necessary in a democratic society'. Consequently, there has been a violation of Article 10 of the Convention.''

The ban on political advertising on British television and radio was examined by the Joint Committee on Human Rights which appeared to conclude that the provisions of the Communications Bill did not evince a disrespect for human rights on the part of the government. According to the Committee in a report issued on February 3, 2003:

"40. In our First Report, we set out six factors which we provisionally thought were relevant to an assessment by Parliament of the propriety of proceeding to legislate in a way that would give rise to an acknowledged risk of incompatibility with a Convention right. Taking those matters into account, and in the light of the correspondence mentioned above, we are satisfied that—

- in any litigation about the ban on political advertising and sponsorship in the broadcast media under clause 309 of the Bill, the Government would argue that the decision in *Vgt Verein Gegeng Tierfabriken v Switzerland* (2002) 34 E.H.R.R. 159 should not be followed, or alternatively that the decision does not necessarily entail the incompatibility of clause 309 with the right to freedom of expression under ECHR Article 10, and that such an argument would have a reasonable chance of success;
- the Government would feel obliged to amend the law if that particular provision were held by the European Court of Human Rights, after argument, to be incompatible with Article 10, and would consider its position if a court in the United Kingdom were to make a declaration of incompatibility under section 4 of the Human Rights Act 1998; and
- in the meantime, pending the opportunity to advance before the courts its arguments relating to the compatibility of a ban with Article 10, the Government has good reasons for believing that the policy reasons for maintaining the ban outweigh the reasons for restricting it, particularly as it would be difficult to produce a workable compromise solution.

41. We are satisfied that the course of action taken by the Government in introducing the Communications Bill with a statement under section 19(1)(b) of the Human Rights Act 1998, rather than a statement of compatibility under section 19(1)(a), does not evince a lack of respect for human rights, and is legitimate in the circumstances." (Joint Committee on Human Rights—Fourth Report (2002–2003))

The Government thus appears to take the view that the benefits of the broadcasting ban in terms of electoral fairness outweigh any potential breach of the ECHR. It is also the case that political parties are not prohibited from using television and radio at election time. As we have already seen earlier in this chapter, free time is made available to political parties for party election broadcasts, provided they meet the qualifying conditions. It is to be pointed out, however, that even if the qualifying conditions are met, this facility is not available to all parties on the same terms, with the larger national parties having greater access than the small parties. It is also the case that there are no free broadcasts for other organisations that may wish to influence the conduct of an election which nevertheless remain prohibited from using this particular medium of communication.

Apart from restraints on the medium that may be used for the purpose of expressing views and opinions, there are also restraints based on the timing of speech. These restraints do not prohibit speech altogether, but they tend to limit the amount or volume of the speech. The best example of this arises under electoral law, where the Representation of the People Act 1983, s.76 imposes a tight limit on the amount that may be spent by candidates at elections. This is a measure that was introduced in the Representation of the People Act 1918, and has been re-enacted in several statutes consolidating election law. As enacted in 1983, s.76 provided that:

"No expenses shall, with a view to promoting or procuring the election of a candidate at an election, be incurred by any person other than the candidate, his election agent and persons authorised in writing by the election agent on account—
(a) of holding public meetings or organising any public display; or
(b) of issuing advertisements, circulars or publications; or
(c) of otherwise presenting to the electors the candidate or his views or the extent or nature of his backing or disparaging another candidate,
but paragraph (c) of this subsection shall not—
(i) restrict the publication of any matter relating to the election in a newspaper or other periodical or in a broadcast made by the British Broadcasting Corporation ... [or the Independent Broadcasting Authority];
(ii) apply to any expenses *not exceeding in aggregate the sum of GBP 5.*"

These provisions were first introduced in the cause of electoral fairness. (The words in parenthesis were amended in 2000, a matter to which we return below.) Since 1883 there have been limits on the amount that candidates could spend in an election. It was thought to be unfair to candidates that individuals or organisations could come into a constituency and seek to influence the outcome by producing literature or holding meetings attacking one or more of the candidates. It was thought to be unfair because the candidates in question would have to use some of their limited expenditure to respond to these attacks. Nevertheless these provisions obviously impose a restraint on the freedom of expression of the individuals or organisations who may want to incur expenditure supporting or opposing a particular candidate at an election.

Bowman v United Kingdom
(1998) 26 E.H.R.R. 1

Mrs Bowman was the executive director of the Society for the Protection of the Unborn Child ("SPUC"), an organisation of approximately 50,000 members which is opposed to abortion and human embryo experimentation. SPUC sought to change the law to restrict both abortion and embryo experimentation. At the general election in 1992 Mrs Bowman arranged to have material distributed in a number of constituencies informing electors about the views of different parliamentary candidates on abortion and other matters. One of the constituencies was Halifax where 25,000 leaflets were distributed, setting out the views of the four candidates. The leaflets made it clear that SPUC was not telling people how to vote, but urged the reader to check candidates' "voting intentions on abortion and on the use of the human embryo as a guinea-pig". Mrs Bowman was prosecuted under s.75 of the 1983 Act for incurring unauthorised expenditure to convey information to electors with a view to promoting or procuring the election of a candidate. Mrs Bowman was, however, acquitted because the summons charging her with the offence had not been issued within one year of the alleged prohibited expenditure, in accordance with the time-limit stipulated in s.176 of the 1983 Act. Despite the acquittal, Mrs Bowman nevertheless complained that the British Government had violated her Convention rights. By a majority, the European Court of Human Rights agreed. After holding that the prohibition in s 75 of the 1983 Act amounted to a restriction on freedom of expression, which directly affected Mrs Bowman, the Court considered whether the restriction could be justified under article 10(2) of the Convention. It was not disputed that the restriction was 'prescribed by law', so the only matters for consideration were whether the restriction pursued a legitimate aim and was 'necessary in a democratic society'.

JUDGMENT OF THE COURT:
"C. Legitimate aim

36. The Government maintained that the spending limit in section 75 of the 1983 Act pursued the aim of protecting the rights of others in three ways. First, it promoted fairness between competing candidates for election by preventing wealthy third parties from campaigning for or against a particular candidate or issuing material which necessitated the devotion of part of a candidate's election budget, which was limited by law, to a response. Secondly, the restriction on third-party expenditure helped to ensure that candidates remained independent of the influence of powerful interest groups. Thirdly, it prevented the political debate at election times from being distorted by having the discussion shifted away from matters of general concern to centre on single issues.

37. In the applicant's view, section 75, far from pursuing a legitimate aim, only operated to curtail democratic freedom of expression. It was improbable in the extreme that single-issue groups, such as SPUC, could distract voters from the mainstream political platforms to such a degree as to hinder the electoral process. Furthermore, the restriction on expenditure could not properly be said to ensure equality between candidates, because they were already subject to inequalities depending on whether or not they received the support of one of the major political parties, which were free to spend unlimited amounts on campaigning at national level as long as they did not attempt to promote or prejudice any particular candidate .... .

38. The Court finds it clear that the purpose of section 75, particularly taken in the context of the other detailed provisions on election expenditure in the 1983 Act, is to contribute towards securing equality between candidates. It therefore concludes, as did the Commission, that the application of this law to Mrs Bowman pursued the legitimate aim of protecting the rights of others, namely the candidates for election and the electorate in Halifax and, to the extent that the prosecution was intended to have a deterrent effect, elsewhere in the United Kingdom.

It considers that the arguments advanced by the applicant on this point are of greater relevance to the issue whether the restriction was 'necessary in a democratic society', to which question it now turns.

D. 'Necessary in a democratic society'

39. The Government maintained that section 75 of the 1983 Act imposed only a partial restriction on expenditure ... , which was no more extensive than was necessary to achieve the legitimate aims pursued. They pointed out that there had been other means of communication open to Mrs Bowman, for example, she could have started her own newspaper, had letters or articles published in the press, given interviews on radio or television, stood for election herself or published leaflets with the purpose of informing the electorate without promoting or opposing any particular candidate.

40. The applicant, as did the Commission, considered that the restriction was disproportionate. She contended that there was no pressing social need to suppress the dissemination of factually accurate information about the position of candidates for public office on important moral issues; on the contrary, there was a pressing need to permit such matters to be put on the political agenda prior to elections. Despite the Government's submission that the restriction was necessary to ensure equality between candidates, there was no indication that Mrs Bowman's leaflets had operated to disadvantage any particular candidate, since it was possible that the information they contained attracted as many supporters as opponents of the different policies on abortion. Furthermore, she asserted that the restriction was illogical since no limit was placed on the powers of the mass media to publish material in support of or opposition to candidates or on the political parties and their supporters to pay for advertising at national or regional levels as long as they did not attempt to promote or prejudice the electoral prospects of any particular candidate.

41. The Court observes, in the first place, that the limitation on expenditure prescribed by section 75 of the 1983 Act is only one of the many detailed checks and balances which make up United Kingdom electoral law. In such a context, it is necessary to consider the right to freedom of expression under Article 10 in the light of the right to free elections protected by Article 3 of Protocol No. 1 to the Convention ...

42. Free elections and freedom of expression, particularly freedom of political debate, together form the bedrock of any democratic system .... The two rights are inter-related and operate to reinforce each other: for example, as the Court has observed in the past, freedom of expression is one of the 'conditions' necessary to 'ensure the free expression of the opinion of the people in the choice of the legislature' .... For this reason, it is particularly important in the period preceding an election that opinions and information of all kinds are permitted to circulate freely.

43. Nonetheless, in certain circumstances the two rights may come into conflict and it may be considered necessary, in the period preceding or during an election, to place certain restrictions, of a type which would not usually be acceptable, on freedom of expression, in order to secure the 'free expression of the opinion of the people in the choice of the legislature'. The Court recognises that, in striking the balance between these two rights, the Contracting States have a margin of appreciation, as they do generally with regard to the organisation of their electoral systems ....

44. Turning to the facts of the present case, the Court's task is to determine whether, in all the circumstances, the restriction on Mrs Bowman's freedom of expression was proportionate to the legitimate aim pursued and whether the reasons adduced by the national authorities in justification of it were relevant and sufficient ....

45. In this connection it finds it significant that the limitation on expenditure contained in section 75 of the 1983 Act was set as low as GBP 5. It recalls that this restriction applied only during the four to six weeks preceding the general election (see paragraphs 16 and 18–19 above). However, although it is true that Mrs Bowman could have campaigned freely at any other time, this would not, in the Court's view, have served her purpose in publishing the leaflets which was, at the very least, to inform the people of Halifax about the three candidates' voting records and attitudes on abortion, during the critical period when their minds were focused on their choice of representative ....

46. The Court notes the Government's submission that the applicant could have made use of alternative methods to convey the information to the electorate. However, it is not

satisfied that, in practice, she had access to any other effective channels of communication. For example, it has not been demonstrated that she had any way of ensuring that the material contained in the leaflets was published in a newspaper or broadcast on radio or television. Although she could herself have stood for election and thus become entitled to incur the statutory amount of expenses allowed to candidates, this would have required her to pay a deposit of GBP 500, which she would in all probability have forfeited .... Furthermore, it was not her desire to be elected to Parliament, but only to distribute leaflets to voters.

47. In summary, therefore, the Court finds that section 75 of the 1983 Act operated, for all practical purposes, as a total barrier to Mrs Bowman's publishing information with a view to influencing the voters of Halifax in favour of an anti-abortion candidate. It is not satisfied that it was necessary thus to limit her expenditure to GBP 5 in order to achieve the legitimate aim of securing equality between candidates, particularly in view of the fact that there were no restrictions placed upon the freedom of the press to support or oppose the election of any particular candidate or upon political parties and their supporters to advertise at national or regional level, provided that such advertisements were not intended to promote or prejudice the electoral prospects of any particular candidate in any particular constituency. It accordingly concludes that the restriction in question was disproportionate to the aim pursued.

It follows that there has been a violation of Article 10 of the Convention."

One of the six dissenting judges (Judge Valticos) was unable to accept that "the fact that the British electoral system restricts the expenditure which 'unauthorised' persons may incur in promoting or prejudicing the chances of a particular candidate in the period leading up to an election amounts to a breach of the Convention". In his view there was:

"something slightly ridiculous in seeking to give the British Government lessons in how to hold elections and run a democracy; above all, it is wrong to seek the repeal of a provision aimed at precluding a person, other than a member of political parties, from influencing the way people vote and—as Mr Martínez rightly noted in his dissenting opinion annexed to the Commission's report—at preventing candidates with substantial financial resources ultimately gaining an advantage over other less well-off candidates."

Nevertheless a breach is a breach, however misconceived it may be. Following the *Bowman* judgment, s.75 of the 1983 Act was amended. In place of the words in parenthesis in s.75 (reproduced above), there were substituted "incurred by any person which do not exceed in the aggregate the permitted sum (and are not incurred by that person as part of a concerted plan of action)". For this purpose the permitted sum means £500 in respect of a candidate at a parliamentary election, and £50 plus .5p for every elector in respect of a local government candidate. By raising the amount of permitted expenditure in this way, the Government will hope that it has avoided the risk that the restraints will remain in breach of Art.10 without doing too much violence to the policy which s.75 is designed to promote. However, additional restraints on electoral speech were introduced by the Political Parties, Elections and Referendums Act 2000. As the Court pointed out in the *Bowman* case, the 1983 Act applied to impose spending limits only on candidates and those who incurred expenditure to promote or oppose a particular candidate. It did not apply to the expenditure incurred in an election by the political parties or by those who incurred expenditure to support or oppose one or more political parties: *Walker v UNISON*, 1995 S.L.T. 1226. As part of the reform of the law relating to political funding, the Political Parties, Elections and Referendums Act 2000 introduced limits on the national spending of political parties. The limits vary according to the number of candidates the party in question puts up at the election. The 2000 Act also introduced limits on national third party spending in an election, that is to say spending incurred by individuals and organisations in order to promote or oppose a particular party in an election.

(3) Restrictions in the Form of Qualifications and Conditions

The third category of restriction on speech are those which permit speech but which do so only if prescribed qualifications or conditions are met. Restrictions of this kind may take several forms.

- There may be restrictions in terms of the dissemination of (and therefore access to) the material in question. An example of this is the Indecent Displays Act 1981 which is designed to protect and prevent children from having access to indecent material by making it available only in parts of a shop to which they may go.
- There may be restrictions in the sense that certain forms of expression will be permitted but only on the condition that others are also allowed to speak. This arises in the context of broadcasting where there is a concern that a powerful medium should not be dominated or controlled by a few voices at the expense of others.
- There may be restrictions in terms of the persons to whom the information may lawfully be made. A good example of this is the Public Interest Disclosure Act 1998 which authorises whistleblowing. However, the whistleblower must express any concerns in the first instance to his or her employer. It is only exceptionally that concerns may be communicated to the public at large.

Our concern in this chapter is with the second of these three different forms of restriction. As indicated a good example are the balance restrictions which apply to broadcasters in terms of political balance. Under the Communications Act 2003, s.320 it is provided that:

"(1) The requirements of this section are—
   (a) the exclusion, in the case of television and radio services (other than a restricted service within the meaning of section 245), from programmes included in any of those services of all expressions of the views or opinions of the person providing the service on any of the matters mentioned in subsection (2);
   (b) the preservation, in the case of every television programme service, teletext service, national radio service and national digital sound programme service, of due impartiality, on the part of the person providing the service, as respects all of those matters;
   (c) the prevention, in the case of every local radio service, local digital sound programme service or radio licensable content service, of the giving of undue prominence in the programmes included in the service to the views and opinions of particular persons or bodies on any of those matters.
(2) Those matters are—
   (a) matters of political or industrial controversy; and
   (b) matters relating to current public policy.
(3) Subsection (1)(a) does not require—
   (a) the exclusion from television programmes of views or opinions relating to the provision of programme services; or
   (b) the exclusion from radio programmes of views or opinions relating to the provision of programme services.
(4) For the purposes of this section—
   (a) the requirement specified in subsection (1)(b) is one that (subject to any rules under subsection (5)) may be satisfied by being satisfied in relation to a series of programmes taken as a whole;
   (b) the requirement specified in subsection (1)(c) is one that needs to be satisfied only in relation to all the programmes included in the service in question, taken as a whole.
(5) OFCOM's standards code shall contain provision setting out the rules to be observed in connection with the following matters—
   (a) the application of the requirement specified in subsection (1)(b);

   (b) the determination of what, in relation to that requirement, constitutes a series of
       programmes for the purposes of subsection (4)(a);
   (c) the application of the requirement in subsection (1)(c).
  (6) Any provision made for the purposes of subsection (5)(a) must, in particular, take
account of the need to ensure the preservation of impartiality in relation to the following
matters (taking each matter separately)—
   (a) matters of major political or industrial controversy, and
   (b) major matters relating to current public policy,
as well as of the need to ensure that the requirement specified in subsection (1)(b) is satisfied
generally in relation to a series of programmes taken as a whole."

The foregoing is an important provision which helps to ensure that commercial radio and
television are not used explicitly as platforms for the political views of proprietors or editors. A
similar duty applies to the BBC under the terms of its Licence and Agreement with the Government. The statutory provisions have formed the basis of a number of attempts to challenge
some forms of political broadcast in particular. The issue arose for consideration during the first
devolution referendum (in 1979) when time was made available to the political parties by the
broadcasting authorities in order to present their views on the Scotland Act 1978 to the voters.

Wilson v Independent Broadcasting Authority
1979 S.L.T. 279

This was a petition for an interim interdict to restrain the IBA from proceeding with broadcasts
on the Scottish devolution referendum in 1979. The petitioners claimed that the schedule proposed by the IBA was in breach of sections 2(2)(b) and 4(1)(f) of the Independent Broadcasting
Authority Act 1973 because more broadcasting time would be given to the side campaigning for
a "No" vote. Section 2(2)(b) of the 1973 Act imposed a duty on the IBA to ensure that the
programmes broadcast by it maintained a proper balance and wide range in their subject-
matter, while s.4(1)(f) imposed an obligation of due impartiality in respect of matters of political
or industrial controversy or relating to current public policy.

> LORD ROSS: "The petitioners' complaint is that the arrangements for party political
> broadcasts which the respondents have made, if implemented, would constitute a breach by
> the respondents of a statutory duty to ensure that programmes broadcast by them main-
> tained a proper balance.

> Counsel for the respondents argued with great persuasiveness that s.2(2)(b) was not con-
> cerned with ensuring a balanced viewpoint, but related only to the subject-matter in its
> quantitative and qualitative sense. If that were so, and if the petitioners were correct,
> counsel submitted that there would be no need for s.4(1)(f) which would have no content.
>   Although I feel that there is considerable force in respondent's counsel's submission I
> have come to be of opinion that the construction which he seeks to place on s.2(2)(b) is
> unduly restrictive. It may well be that the duty in question would require the respondents to
> maintain a proper balance between programmes containing different subject-matters. For
> example, a balance would require to be maintained between religious programmes, sport,
> current affairs and so on. But I do not consider that that is the only balance that s.2(2)(b)
> requires the respondents to ensure is maintained. The statute does not state that pro-
> grammes should maintain a proper balance between different subject-matters but that the
> programmes should maintain a proper balance in their subject-matter. In my opinion the
> subsection would also require inter alia a proper balance to be maintained in relation to
> programmes on any particular subject-matter. The Scottish referendum is in itself a subject-
> matter and in my opinion, s.2(2)(b) places on the respondents a duty to ensure that pro-
> grammes broadcast by them on the subject of the referendum maintain a proper balance.

I accept that when arranging party political broadcasts in connection with a general election, all possible political viewpoints cannot be covered, and, for example, some participants in a general election and some minor parties may be excluded (see *Grieve v Douglas-Home*, 1965 S.L.T. at p. 193 per Lord Kilbrandon). But the situation is different with a referendum where the electorate is being invited to answer a question 'Yes' or 'No'. Where the subject matter of programmes being broadcast is the referendum, I am of the opinion that a proper balance must be maintained between programmes favouring 'Yes' and programmes favouring 'No'. It is plain from both the petition and the answers that the party political broadcasts with which the petitioners are concerned are not normal party political broadcasts but are to be devoted specifically to the issue to be put to the electorate in the referendum. This puts them in a special category and they cannot be treated as if they were ordinary political broadcasts...

Being satisfied that a prima facie case of breach has been averred, the question then arises as to whether the court has power to pronounce interdict in such a situation.

Where such a breach has been averred, I am of the opinion that the court is entitled to grant the remedy sought. It is important that the Act does not provide any specific method of enforcing the duty. It creates no offence and imposes no sanctions. It provides no remedy for the breach. In that situation I am of the opinion that the court does have power to interdict the continuance of the breach of duty. Indeed, if the court does not have power, how is the duty imposed on the respondents to be enforced?"

There were no referendum broadcasts in 1997. The position is now governed by the Political Parties, Elections and Referendums Act 2000. This provides in the event of a national referendum (such as a referendum on the voting system or a referendum on entry to the single European currency), the Electoral Commission must designate two organisations (the yes side and the no side). These designated organisations may apply for public funding for their campaigns, and they are subject to a spending limit. However the limit which applies to the designated bodies is higher than the spending limit that applies to other organisations (with the exception of the main national political parties which are permitted to spend the same). It is also the case that the designated organisations are now entitled to referendum campaign broadcasts during the period of a referendum campaign. The length and frequency of the referendum campaign broadcasts are to be determined by OFCOM which is obliged to consult the Electoral Commission about any rules relating to such broadcasts (Political Parties, Elections, and Referendums Act 2000, Sch.12). In the absence of a referendum to which these provisions apply, they appear rather quixotic at the time of writing. A more serious concern relates to party election broadcasts.

Wilson v Independent Broadcasting Authority
1988 S.L.T. 276

This was a petition for judicial review by the SNP challenging the allocation of time to the political parties for party election broadcasts during the 1987 general election. The Conservatives, Labour and the SDP/Liberal Alliance were each allocated five broadcast slots of 10 minutes, while the SNP was allocated only two (for broadcast in Scotland only) and Plaid Cymru only one (for broadcast in Wales only). The SNP claimed that by this allocation, the Independent Broadcasting Authority (then the regulatory body) had breached its statutory duties under what was then the Broadcasting Act 1981, s.2(2)(b) and s.4(1)(f). The former imposed a duty on the Authority to ensure that the programmes broadcast by the Authority in each area maintained a "proper balance" in their subject area. The latter imposed another duty on the Authority, this time to ensure that "due impartiality is preserved on the part of persons providing the programmes as respects matters of political or industrial controversy or relating to current public policy". The petition was refused.

LORD PROSSER: "I turn to the issue between the parties...

Taking questions of statutory construction first I consider an argument advanced by counsel for the respondents to the effect that s.2(2)(b) imposed no requirement relevant to the present circumstances. What had to be ensured was a proper balance in the subject matter of programmes. This, it was contended, meant a proper balance between various categories of subject matter, such as sport on the one hand or politics on the other. There was no requirement of balance within any one such category: if coverage of sport were wholly devoted to football or indeed to the exploits of a single football club, then that would constitute no imbalance with which this subsection at least was concerned. So, too, any imbalance between the treatment of one political party and another would be untouched by this section. Politics was one 'subject matter' and the proper balance required by the subsection was not a balance within that subject matter but between it and other subject matters.

Reference was made to the opinion of Lord Robertson in *Wolfe v I.B.A.* [unreported] which it was submitted I should prefer on this point to the opinion of Lord Ross in *Wilson v I.B.A.*, 1979 S.L.T. 279. The words of the subsection and its predecessors are not perhaps very happily drafted; and I am not at all sure how a 'proper' balance between such broad topics as sport and politics would be judged. I am not however persuaded that a statute which provides for that imponderable question to be put in the balance would be likely to ignore the need for balance within what might be called one particular subject matter. The words of the subsection appear to me to be equally referable to such internal balance or to the balance between subjects. In particular they appear to me to be referable to a balance between various programmes in a field such as politics, even if there is a problem in relation to the balancing of viewpoints within a single programme. I concur with Lord Ross's opinion in *Wilson*, and consider that in the rather different area now in issue, s.2(2)(b) requires the respondents to ensure a proper balance in the presentation of party politics through election broadcasts. ...

What then of s.2(2)(b)? On behalf of the petitioners it was contended that television is now a major element in any election as a means of communication with the electorate. To allow the United Kingdom parties five broadcasts against the petitioners' two was to give a significant advantage to each of these parties' candidates, and to put the petitioners' candidate in any constituency in Scotland at a serious disadvantage.

It was contended for the petitioners that the 'Scottish dimension' was something distinct from the United Kingdom dimension. This was recognised in many aspects of the constitution: the Union itself, the law, the Scottish Office, and other examples were cited. The reference of the Scotland Act 1978 to a referendum in Scotland alone was stressed. In the particular field of broadcasting, the structure of the broadcasting authorities in general and their practice of having 'Scottish' election broadcasts in particular were identified as illustrating the existence of a Scottish dimension, separate from and requiring consideration separately from, the ordinary United Kingdom dimension. That United Kingdom dimension justified an initial allocation of election broadcasts; but in final allocation, one could not ignore the Scottish dimension and give the petitioners a share which would merely reflect their share of United Kingdom votes or seats or candidates. One must consider the petitioners, in Scotland, on the basis of a comparison with United Kingdom parties in Scotland. In that context, which it was maintained the respondents had failed properly to consider, the petitioners were to be regarded as of equivalent significance with the other parties, and should receive an equivalent share of election broadcasts. ...

It is clear that the so called 'Scottish dimension' has been acknowledged (whether adequately or not) in the respondents' proposals. Allocations are not based simply on proportions of the total number of United Kingdom votes, or seats, or candidates. The petitioners' allocation of two election broadcasts flows from an acknowledgement of their position in Scotland, since in United Kingdom terms they would, under the respondents' general proposals, receive only one broadcast, and that of half the length.

The word 'dimension' is not perhaps an adequate one. A Scottish or United Kingdom dimension might take many forms. There are no doubt certain topics of 'purely' Scottish concern in the election, and many of predominantly Scottish concern. There will be other topics of concern throughout the United Kingdom, but which in Scotland take a different form, requiring special policies or special treatment. There will be other topics which are not thus special to Scotland, but which in their general form may nonetheless be seen from a peculiarly Scottish viewpoint. There are no doubt many other ways of seeing and describing this Scottish element or dimension in the matters which the political parties may wish to raise in their broadcasts. The need to raise them is acknowledged not merely in the allocation of four times as much broadcasting time to the petitioners as they would otherwise receive, but also in the division of the United Kingdom parties' time into three 'United Kingdom' broadcasts and two which can be devoted to such Scottish treatment without being transmitted to an audience outside Scotland. The broadcasts which can be expected to deal with the Scottish dimension in this sense are thus indeed on a basis of parity, at two each for all four contenders.

The Scottish dimension is, however, to be observed also in the parties' own functions and aims. The petitioners do not, as the other political parties do, aspire to United Kingdom office. Correspondingly, the petitioners do not in general, as I understand matters, seek to present policies which meet specifically non-Scottish problems, or non-Scottish aspects of general problems, or non-Scottish view points on matters which are otherwise common to all United Kingdom voters. Correspondingly, the petitioners do not seek to present candidates outside Scotland, or to persuade non-Scottish voters to support them. Counsel for the respondents submitted that it was not they who were ignoring the Scottish dimension, but the petitioners who were under estimating this United Kingdom dimension. It was necessary to give the United Kingdom parties broadcasting time, not only through the two non-Scottish transmissions (which could be used for material which at least need not be presented to Scottish voters) but through additional broadcasts—the three United Kingdom broadcasts allocated to each—which would allow them to present to all the electorate, including the electorate in Scotland, the party policies upon which they sought election to Parliament and indeed government, as a United Kingdom party.

It is contended for the petitioners that by having these three 'extra' broadcasts, which are denied to the petitioners, the other parties have an advantage in 'persuasion time' over the petitioners. It would however surprise many Scots, I think—and not least the petitioners— if any of the other parties were to use their United Kingdom platform on these occasions to concentrate on Scottish concerns or to respond to specifically Scottish viewpoints. If they were to do so, no doubt they might have an advantage over the petitioners in that respect. But having regard to the United Kingdom dimension of their aims and interests, I can see no improper balance in an allocation of time to the United Kingdom parties to deal with that dimension and broadcast on that plane. Whether the allocation is the best, or is right, is not for me to judge. But there would be at least a problem, if parity were granted to the petitioners, in the availability to them of five programmes devoted to Scottish policies and viewpoints, while the other parties would be forced to cover much else in the same time, or to split their transmissions so that Scottish voters would see only Scottish angled material. The rejection of such an approach, and the adoption of an allocation which gives extra time to the United Kingdom parties for United Kingdom transmissions, must in my opinion be regarded as a tenable decision, reflecting United Kingdom dimensions as well as a Scottish dimension, and consistent with the respondents' duty to ensure a proper balance.

In these circumstances I do not consider that on the pleadings or the factual material before me the petitioners have shown that they are entitled to the remedy they seek. That being so, I refuse the declarators sought."

The *Wilson* case was one of a number of attempts made to challenge broadcast allocation, which has been controversial from time to time. All other attempts to challenge the broadcasters have also failed, with different grounds being used in a series of ingenious attempts to mount legal challenges. The position is now governed by the Communications Act 2003 which provides by s.333 that:

"**Party political broadcasts**

(1) The regulatory regime for every licensed public service channel, and the regulatory regime for every national radio service, includes—

    (a) conditions requiring the inclusion in that channel or service of party political broadcasts and of referendum campaign broadcasts; and

    (b) conditions requiring that licence holder to observe such rules with respect to party political broadcasts and referendum campaign broadcasts as may be made by OFCOM.

(2) The rules made by OFCOM for the purposes of this section may, in particular, include provision for determining—

    (a) the political parties on whose behalf party political broadcasts may be made;

    (b) in relation to each political party on whose behalf such broadcasts may be made, the length and frequency of the broadcasts; and

    (c) in relation to each designated organisation on whose behalf referendum campaign broadcasts are required to be broadcast, the length and frequency of such broadcasts.

(3) Those rules are to have effect subject to sections 37 and 127 of the Political Parties, Elections and Referendums Act 2000 (only registered parties and designated organisations to be entitled to party political broadcasts or referendum campaign broadcasts).

(4) Rules made by OFCOM for the purposes of this section may make different provision for different cases.

(5) Before making any rules for the purposes of this section, OFCOM must have regard to any views expressed by the Electoral Commission."

These various provisions of the Communications Act 2003 are designed so far as possible to ensure that the free time is allocated fairly to the political parties. In this way the broadcaster is required by law to carry the broadcasts, but is free to do so provided that the conditions and qualifications of the 2003 Act are met. In other words, it cannot carry the broadcasts of one eligible party and refuse to carry the broadcasts of another.

V. CONCLUSION

We have thus identified three broad categories of speech: speech which is censored, speech which is prohibited, and speech which is restricted. Although these are helpful categories for the purposes of presentation, they are not watertight. For the individual whose speech falls within the category of restricted speech, the speech is in effect prohibited, and if it is prohibited it is liable to be restrained by interdict if an interested party can move quickly enough to deal with it. Restraint by interdict in fact brings us back to where we started in the sense that an interdict is a form of prior restraint if not strictly a form of censorship. The material presented so far reveals that an interdict may be sought to prevent the publication of prohibited or restricted speech in three different types of case. The first is where the speaker is in breach of a statutory or other obligation enforceable in public law. The second is where the speaker is in breach of an obligation under criminal law which causes particular damage to the petitioner. The third is where the speaker has violated the private law rights of the petitioner, or otherwise violated an enforceable duty recognised by private law, such as the duty of confidentiality.

  In a valuable article Munro has shown just how serious a danger to freedom of expression the granting of interdicts has been in the past: C.R. Munro, "Prior Restraint of the Media and Human Rights Law" (2002) J.R. 1:

"Just a couple of years ago, a Scottish judge presented with a petition for interim interdict against the media would typically have been quickly apprised of the facts, have heard brief arguments on the merits and law, and would have come summarily to a decision (p 33)."

The interim interdict may be granted *ex parte*, and it will be sought at short notice with little time available to either party to prepare full arguments. In order to succeed the petitioner does not have to convince the court that his or her legal rights have been infringed. Rather, the petitioner must satisfy the lower standard that there is a serious question and that the balance of convenience is in favour of restraining the publication until the matter is resolved at the trial of the action. The ease with which interim relief could be obtained in such cases led Munro to doubt whether Scottish judges "have regarded prior restraint as a 'drastic interference', to be ordered only exceptionally" (*ibid.*, p 34). The effect of the interim interdict is thus to maintain the *status quo* until the trial which may not take place for several years. At best this means that a publication may be postponed pending the trial, but at worst it may mean that the publication never takes place if the author feels that its purpose would be lost at a later date. It is thus possible that the interim order could have the effect of stopping a publication altogether if the respondent elects to give up. Some of the problems are compounded by the fact that these cases are not only heard at short notice without full examination of the issues but by the fact also that the appeal process may by necessity be perfunctory or in some cases non-existent, as the following case highlights.

Houston v BBC
1995 S.L.T. 1305

The BBC proposed to broadcast an interview with the Prime Minister on April 3, 1995 three days before local government elections in Scotland on April 6, 1995. On April 3,1995, two candidates applied for an interim interdict to prevent the broadcast being made until after the elections were held, contending that the BBC would breach its duty of impartiality, as contained in its Licence and Agreement with the Government. The interdict was granted by the Lord Ordinary on the afternoon of April 3, and the appeal was heard later that day, shortly before the broadcast was due to be made. The appeal was dismissed, thereby preventing the broadcast being made on April 3. On the following day the BBC sought leave to appeal to the House of Lords, presumably to give them an opportunity to carry the broadcast before April 6 if they so wished.

OPINION OF THE COURT: "When this case came before the Lord Ordinary yesterday afternoon he was asked to consider two issues. The first was whether the pursuers had made out a prima facie case that, if the corporation were to broadcast in Scotland an extended interview with the Prime Minister on the *Panorama* programme that evening, they would be in breach of their duty, under the conditions of their licence, to treat controversial subjects with due impartiality. The second was whether, if such a prima facie case had been made out, the balance of convenience favoured the granting of interim interdict to prevent the programme being broadcast until after 9 pm on Thursday 6 April, following the close of the poll in the local government elections which are to take place in Scotland on that day. The Lord Ordinary reached a decision in favour of the pursuers in both of these issues and granted interim interdict in the terms sought by them.

The Lord Ordinary's decision was then brought before this court on a reclaiming motion for review. The solicitor advocate for the defenders made it clear at the outset of his argument that he was not seeking to challenge the decision of the Lord Ordinary on either of the two issues which had been debated before him. What he sought to do was to present a further argument, to the effect that the pursuers had not made out a prima facie case that they had a title and interest to bring these proceedings before this court. He accepted that there was a duty on the corporation to act with due impartiality in terms of the licence. The issue was whether the pursuers, who are candidates at the local government election, had the locus standi which was required to bring proceedings against the corporation based on an apprehended breach of conditions of the licence to which they were not a party.

The matter came before us half an hour before the programme was due to be broadcast. For obvious reasons it was not possible for the important issue which was raised by the solicitor advocate for the defenders to be debated in detail under reference to a full citation of authority. We were however persuaded, under reference in particular to *Wilson v Independent Broadcasting Authority*, 1979 S.L.T. 279, to which we were referred by the Dean of Faculty, that on this new issue a prima facie case had been made out which was sufficient to justify the granting of interim interdict on the balance of convenience. We were not asked to decide, and did not decide, any issue about the content of the programme. Nor were we asked to reach, or were we in a position to reach, a final decision on the issue of principle. The only issue for us was whether a prima facie case existed on a point which was not frivolous or vexatious but was open to argument. The issue of balance of convenience was not in dispute before us.

The corporation have now enrolled for leave to appeal to the House of Lords against our interlocutor. That leave to appeal is required is not in question, as it was not disputed that both in form and substance our interlocutor was an interlocutory judgment. Section 40 (1) (b) of the Court of Session Act 1988 requires leave of the Inner House before an interlocutory judgment of this court can be appealed to the House of Lords. On that matter our decision is final and not subject to review by the House of Lords: see *Ross v Ross*, per Viscount Dunedin at 1927 SLT, p 2. The question is whether we would be justified in granting leave, having regard to the nature of the issue which was before us in the reclaiming motion and various practical considerations to which we shall refer.

The issue which was before us in the reclaiming motion was described by the solicitor advocate for the defenders as a matter of considerable public importance, not only in Scotland but throughout the United Kingdom. For our part we do not doubt for a moment that an important point of law has been raised in this case. It is one on which there is, so far as we are aware, no clear previous authority. The Dean of Faculty did not seek to challenge the defenders' submission as to the importance of the issue. It is equally clear however that it is not a matter which can be the subject of a final or definitive decision at this stage. It is well established, both in England and in Scotland, that it is no part of the court's function at the interlocutory stage in a litigation to try to resolve difficult questions of law which call for detailed argument and mature consideration: *American Cyanamid Co v Ethicon Ltd*, per Lord Diplock at [1975] AC, p 407; *Group 4 Total Security Ltd v Ferrier* at 1985 SLT, p 290. It was not possible for us in the time available to attempt to resolve that issue, nor was it possible for either side to present us with a carefully researched and fully developed argument. Nor indeed would it be possible for the House of Lords to resolve the issue in the event that we were to grant leave to appeal. The House of Lords would be in no better position than we were to determine the important issue of principle. It is also clear that the question for the House of Lords in the exercise of their appellate function, in a matter of this kind which depends so much on the exercise of a discretion by this court, would not be whether they would have decided the issue differently but whether we have gone so far wrong that they must set aside our decision to adhere to the decision of the Lord Ordinary to grant the interim interdict: *Hadmor Productions Ltd v Hamilton*, per Lord Diplock at [1983] 1 AC, p 220B-E. For these reasons, any idea which the corporation may have that this court has decided the issue of principle by coming to a definitive view upon it is misconceived. So also is any idea that the House of Lords in an appeal against our interlocutor affirming the decision of the Lord Ordinary would be able to come to such a view.

The importance of the issue and its novelty points clearly, in our opinion, to the conclusion that it is one which should be carefully and thoroughly debated in a proper manner without the pressure of urgency which has inevitably arisen in this case at the interlocutory stage. As the Dean of Faculty put it, the importance of the issue makes it all the more important that it should be addressed after full argument. It was not disputed on either side that, whatever the result of today's proceedings, that issue was capable of being properly litigated before the court at the appropriate stage.

The solicitor advocate for the defenders then said that there were considerations pointing to the balance of convenience which justified our granting leave to appeal. He said that the corporation were anxious to broadcast the programme as early as possible. It dealt with topical matters, and it was at least possible that they would lose their topicality if the broadcasting of the programme was to be further delayed. We were not impressed by this argument. In the first place the Lord Ordinary's decision on the balance of convenience was not challenged in the reclaiming motion before us. In the second place it is far from clear— and the solicitor advocate was unable to elaborate on this point – that the issues which were discussed in the programme were of such a nature that it is a matter of urgency that they be broadcast. Further, the closer the broadcasting comes to the election day the stronger the pursuers' case becomes that the risk of prejudice would arise which has led them to bring the matter before this court.

Then there are the practical considerations. Whatever the situation may be in England, the position in the case of an appeal to the House of Lords from the Court of Session in Scotland in terms of the statute requires various stages to be gone through. The first is the seeking of leave from this court, where this is required. If leave is granted, the papers must then be made up for the use of the Appellate Committee in London. Among these there will require to be a written opinion from this court giving the reasons for the decision so that there may be a basis for discussion in the appeal. The Appellate Committee must then decide whether the matter is of such urgency that it is willing to sit to deal with the appeal at very short notice. Its decision must then be reported to the House on a motion which may be open to debate before the judgment can be pronounced. Even then matters are not over, because a judgment of the House of Lords has no effect in Scotland until this court has pronounced a further interlocutor under rule 56.1 of the Rules of the Court of Session to apply the judgment. Before a motion to that effect can be enrolled, copies of the judgment must be lodged in process in this court.

It seems to us to be clear that, unless this could be regarded as a case of extreme urgency and importance—which it is not, in our opinion—there is no reasonable prospect of all these steps being completed today. At best for the corporation, therefore, the process would be completed tomorrow in time for the programme to be shown on Wednesday evening, but that is the evening before the local elections are due to be held. In our opinion these considerations far outweigh any advantage that the corporation are likely to achieve by showing the programme 24 hours earlier than they could lawfully do so in terms of the Lord Ordinary's interlocutor.

For these reasons we shall refuse the motion for leave to appeal to the House of Lords."

The problem of improper restraints on freedom of expression by way of interim interdict is addressed now by the Human Rights Act 1998, s.12 which we encountered already in Ch.6.

The provisions of s.12 bear a striking resemblance to corresponding provisions in the Trade Union and Labour Relations (Consolidation) Act 1992, s.221 which is designed to protect trade unions from interim relief sought by employers when organising lawful industrial action. (These provisions of the 1992 Act curiously do not apply to Scotland, perhaps because of a mis-understanding that the position in Scots law is in practice no different from the position in English law. Lord Fraser of Tullybelton claimed that the Scottish courts took into account the relative merits of the parties when considering the balance of convenience (*NWL Ltd v Woods* [1979] I.C.R. 867 at 884). But there is no evidence that employers found it harder to obtain interim relief in Scotland than they did in England.) Reflecting the terms of the 1992 Act and extending it all to Scotland, the Human Rights Act addresses the problem of *ex parte* interdicts (s.12(2)) and the problem of interim relief being granted on the basis of a *prima facie* case only (s.12(3)). The Human Rights Act also addresses the problem of freedom of expression being constrained by claims that a publication violates the petitioner's right to privacy. The effect of s.12(4) is that no interdict should normally be granted in such circumstances where the respondent has complied with a relevant privacy code, such as that issued by the Press Complaints Commission.

It has been suggested that "prior restraints affecting the media should be harder to obtain", and that "in practice, interim relief will depend on the higher hurdle for applicants that they must establish that they would be likely to succeed at trial in having publication disallowed" (Munro, above, at 33). It has also been suggested that in Scotland "the difference may be most noticeable in defamation cases, but there is some room for reduction of availability in confidence cases and contempt as well" (*ibid.*, at 33–34). It thus ought no longer to be enough for the petitioner simply to turn up to collect his or her order from the duty judge. However, for all that, the experience of TULRCA 1992, s.221 suggests that we should not overstate the importance of s.12 which is only as good as the HRA itself. As we have seen the main restraints on freedom of expression in place at the time the HRA was introduced remain largely in place, and have survived judicial scrutiny. We also still have a system of censorship of films and television, while the categories of prohibited and restricted speech also remain in place. More importantly, as we saw in Ch.6 when discussing *Douglas v Hello!* [2001] Q.B. 967 the Court of Appeal in England has warned against using s.12 to elevate freedom of expression to a higher plane than is warranted. Indeed it might be argued that the Court of Appeal has rendered s.12 largely redundant. Sedley L.J. reminded us of the need to read Art.10(1) along with Art.10(2), with all its permitted qualifications, in the interests of striking a "proper balance". Keene L.J. appeared to go further by suggesting that whatever the outcome of a deliberation under s.12 "there remains a discretion in the court". Admittedly it is unclear whether this discretion would not only enable the court to refuse an injunction (or interdict) where the applicant had made out a case, as well as enable the court to issue an injunction (or interdict) where the applicant had not made out a case. More recently, however, the same court has held that "likely" in s.12(3) means "a real prospect of success" rather than "more probable than not": *Cream Holdings Ltd v Banerjee* [2003] 3 W.L.R. 999. It is on such fine distinctions that human rights depend.

Chapter 9

FREEDOM OF ASSEMBLY AND ASSOCIATION

I. INTRODUCTION

In this chapter we move from a consideration of the right to freedom of expression to consider the right to freedom of assembly. The two are of course closely related in the sense that an assembly is one means by which people may collectively express themselves. It is a particularly important form of expression, as conveying the strength of community support or opposition to government action. Good examples of this are the demonstrations against the war in Iraq which took place in Edinburgh early in 2003. Freedom of assembly is also important to draw public attention to the activities of companies by protesting outside shops and workplaces. A good example of this is the picketing of fur shops by animal rights activists or the picketing of workplaces by striking trade unionists. However, although it facilitates protest against public and private power, the right to freedom of assembly is important for giving a voice to those who have no access to other means of communication. Most citizens are neither newspaper proprietors nor columnists and very few are invited to take part in radio or television programmes to impress their views on others. Nevertheless they will still have opinions on matters of current concern, and these opinions may be deeply felt. Public protest in association with others who feel the same way about an issue provides an opportunity for views to be expressed. We should not underestimate the extent to which popular protest can help shape the political agenda. The demonstrations against the "poll tax" are thought by some not only to lead to a reversal of government policy, but also to pave the way for the removal of Margaret Thatcher as its chief architect.

II. FREEDOM OF ASSEMBLY AND SCOTS LAW

A remarkable feature of Scots law — which it shares with English law — is that there was no formal legal protection of the right to freedom of assembly. This is despite the claim by the Home Office that "the rights of peaceful protest and assembly are amongst our fundamental freedoms: they are numbered among the touchstones which distinguish a free society from a totalitarian one": Home Office, *Review of Public Order Law* (Cmnd. 9510, 1985), p.2. The position in Scots law was represented by Lord President Dunedin in *McAra v Magistrates of Edinburgh*, 1913 S.C. 1059 where he said:

"As regards the common law, I wish most distinctly to state it as my opinion that the primary and overruling object for which streets exist is passage. The streets are public, but they are public for passage, and there is no such thing as a right in the public to hold meetings as such in the streets ... What I mean is this: streets are for passage, and passage is paramount to everything else. That does not necessarily mean that anyone is doing an illegal act if he is not at the moment passing along. It is quite clear that citizens may meet in the streets and may stop and speak to each other. The whole thing is a question of degree and nothing else, and it is a question of degree which the Magistrates are the proper persons to consider in each case, and it is for them to take such measures as are necessary to preserve to the citizens in general that use which is paramount to all other uses of the streets. I say this because there is a good deal in the pursuer's pleadings about what he calls 'exercising his right to free speech in public places.' Now the right of free speech undoubtedly exists and the right of free speech is to promulgate your opinions by speech so long as you do not utter what is treasonable or libellous, or make yourself obnoxious to the statutes that deal with blasphemy and obscenity. But the right of free speech is a perfectly separate thing from the question of the place where that right is to be exercised. You may say what you like provided it is not obnoxious in the ways I have indicated, but that does not mean that you may say it anywhere."

So there was no right to freedom of assembly, whether conferred by statute or recognised by common law. At best there was a freedom to assemble, that is to say a freedom to assemble to the extent that it was not prohibited by law, or to the extent that those who assemble do nothing that is unlawful. The position relating to freedom of assembly has been changed following the incorporation of Convention rights by the Scotland Act 1998 and the Human Rights Act 1998, with the right to freedom of assembly expressly protected by art.11 of the E.C.H.R. It is not clear, however, whether this will fundamentally alter the way in which freedom of assembly is protected in Scots law or require much revision of the legal restraints in force at the time Convention rights were introduced. The following case is an important reconsideration of the right to freedom of assembly, decided in England shortly after the Human Rights Act was introduced, but shortly before it was brought into force. Although the case is an appeal in an English case, it includes some consideration of the position in Scotland. Indeed as Lord Hope pointed out the statute which was being considered in the case applies in Scotland as it does in England and Wales. However, the two participating Scottish Law Lords ended up on different sides, with Lord Clyde deciding with the majority and Lord Hope dissenting.

DPP v Jones
[1999] 2 A.C. 240

The appellant had been found guilty of taking part in a trespassory assembly on the A344, adjacent to the perimeter fence of the monument at Stonehenge. She was taking part in a peaceful assembly with 21 other people and refused to disperse when told to do so by the police. An hour before Dr Jones had been arrested, a group of protestors had scaled the perimeter fence of the monument and were escorted away by the police. The Public Order Act 1986, s.14A(5) provides that:

"An order prohibiting the holding of trespassory assemblies operates to prohibit any assembly which (a) is held on land to which the public has no right of access or only a limited right of access, and (b) takes place in prohibited circumstances, that is to say, without the permission of the occupier of the land or *so as to exceed* the limits of any permission of his or *the limits of the public's right of access.*" (Emphasis added.)

The question for the House of Lords was whether a peaceful non obstructive assembly of 20 or more people on the public highway exceeded the public's right of access to the highway so as to constitute a trespassory assembly within the terms of s.14A of the 1986 Act. In a ground-breaking decision a majority (the Lord Chancellor, Lord Hutton and Lord Clyde) held that the defendant had not exceeded her authority to use the highway. Lords Slynn of Hadley and Hope dissented.

LORD CLYDE: "There is no doubt but that the assembly in the present case took place on a highway and that a highway is land to which the public had a limited right of access. So one has next to consider the prohibited circumstances. Those circumstances are defined in section 14A(5)(b). The critical qualification here claimed is that the assembly so took place 'as to exceed ... the limits of the public's right of access.' So the question comes to be what is the extent of the public's right of access. That is a quite general question which will apply universally, whether an individual member of the public or a group of people is involved. It will also be applicable to any other kind of public road, subject to any particular limitations which may restrict the use of such a road, whenever or however imposed.

The Act gives a little further explanation. Section 14A(9) defines 'limited' in relation to a right of access by the public to land as meaning that 'their use of it is restricted to use for a particular purpose (as in the case of a highway or road) or is subject to other restrictions.' So one has to consider what was the particular purpose for which Parliament considered the use of a highway was restricted.

The fundamental purpose for which roads have always been accepted to be used is the purpose of travel, that is to say, passing and re-passing along it. But it has also been recognised that the use comprises more than the mere movement of persons or vehicles along the highway. The right to use a highway includes the doing of certain other things subsidiary to the user for passage. It is within the scope of the right that the traveller may stop for a while at some point along the way. If he wishes to refresh himself, or if there is some particular object which he wishes to view from that point, or if there is some particular association with the place which he wishes to keep alive, his presence on the road for that purpose is within the scope of the acceptable user of the road. The view was expressed by A. L. Smith L.J., in *Hickman v Maisey* [1900] 1 Q.B. 752, 756, that if a man took a sketch from the highway no reasonable person would treat that as an act of trespass. So as it seems to me the particular purpose for which a highway may be used within the scope of the public's right of access includes a variety of activities, whether or not involving movement, which are consistent with what people reasonably and customarily do on a highway. In *Harrison v Duke of Rutland* [1893] 1 Q.B. 142, 146 Lord Esher M.R. defined trespass in terms of a person being on the highway 'not for the purpose of using it in order to pass and repass, or for any reasonable or usual mode of using the highway as a highway.' But what is reasonable or usual may develop and change from one period of history to another. That was recognised by Collins L.J. where in *Hickman v Maisey* [1900] 1 Q.B. 752, 758 he said:

> 'The right of the public to pass and repass on a highway is subject to all those reasonable extensions which may from time to time be recognised as necessary to its exercise in accordance with the enlarged notions of people in a country becoming more populous and highly civilised, but they must be such as are not inconsistent with the maintenance of the paramount idea that the right of the public is that of passage.'

On the other hand the purpose for which the road is used must be for ordinary and lawful uses of a roadway and not for some ulterior purpose for which the road was not intended to be used. Thus in the case of *Hickman v Maisey* to which I have already referred, it was held to be a trespass for someone to use the road as a vantage point for observing the performance of racehorses undergoing trial. To use the language of Collins L.J. (at p. 758) that was a use of the highway 'in a manner which is altogether outside the purpose for which it was dedicated.' So also in the earlier case of *Harrison v Duke of Rutland* (1893) Q.B.D. 142 it was held to be a trespass for a person to use the road for the purpose of disrupting the adjoining landowner's enjoyment of his sporting rights.

But it must immediately be noticed that the public's right is fenced with limitations affecting both the extent and the nature of the user. So far as the extent is concerned the user may not extend beyond the physical limits of the highway. That may often include the verges. It may also include a lay-by. Moreover, the law does not recognise any jus spatiendi which would entitle a member of the public simply to wander about the road, far less beyond its limits, at will. Further, the public have no jus manendi on a highway, so that any stopping and standing must be reasonably limited in time. While the right may extend to a picnic on the verge, it would not extend to camping there.

So far as the manner of the exercise of the right is concerned, any use of the highway must not be so conducted as to interfere unreasonably with the lawful use by other members of the public for passage along it. The fundamental element in the right is the use of the highway for undisturbed travel. Certain forms of behaviour may of course constitute criminal actings in themselves, such as a breach of the peace. But the necessity also is that travel by the public should not be obstructed. The use of the highway for passage is reflected in all the limitations, whether on extent, purpose or manner. While the right to use the highway comprises activities within those limits, those activities are subsidiary to the use for passage, and they must be not only usual and reasonable but consistent with that use even if they are not strictly ancillary to it. As was pointed out in *McAra v Magistrates of Edinburgh* 1913 S.C. 1059 and in *Aldred v Miller* 1924 J.C. 117 the use of a public street for free unrestricted passage is the most important of all the public uses to which public streets are legally dedicated. No issue regarding the nature of the user arises in the present case. It appears that everyone was behaving with courtesy and civility and restraint. Moreover there was no obstruction at all to any traffic.

In the generality there is no doubt but that there is a public right of assembly. But there are restrictions on the exercise of that right in the public interest. There are limitations at common law and there are express limitations laid down in Article 11 of the Convention on Human Rights. I would not be prepared to affirm as a matter of generality that there is a right of assembly on any place on a highway at any time and in any event I am not persuaded that the present case has to be decided by reference to public rights of assembly. If a group of people stand in the street to sing hymns or Christmas carols they are in my view using the street within the legitimate scope of the public right of access to it, provided of course that they do so for a reasonable period and without any unreasonable obstruction to traffic. If there are shops in the street and people gather to stand and view a shop window, or form a queue to enter the shop, that is within the normal and reasonable use which is a matter of public right. A road may properly be used for the purposes of a procession. It would still be a perfectly proper use of the road if the procession was intended to serve some particular purpose, such as commemorating some particular event or achievement. And if an individual may properly stop at a point on the road for any lawful purpose, so too should a group of people be entitled to do so. All such activities seem to me to be subsidiary to the use for passage. So I have no difficulty in holding that in principle a gathering of people at the side of a highway within the limits of the restraints which I have noted may be within the scope of the public's right of access to the highway.

In my view the argument for the appellants, and indeed the reasoning of the Crown Court, went further than it needed to go in suggesting that any reasonable use of the highway, provided that it was peaceful and not obstructive, was lawful, and so a matter of public right. Such an approach opens a door of uncertain dimensions into an ill-defined area of uses which might erode the basic predominance of the essential use of a highway as a highway. I do not consider that by using the language which it used Parliament intended to include some distinct right in addition to the right to use the road for the purpose of passage.

I am not persuaded that in any case where there is a peaceful non-obstructive assembly it will necessarily exceed the public's right of access to the highway. The question then is, as in this kind of case it may often turn out to be, whether on the facts here the limit was passed and the exceeding of it established. The test then is not one which can be defined in general terms but has to depend upon the circumstances as a matter of degree. It requires a careful assessment of the nature and extent of the activity in question. If the purpose of the activity becomes the predominant purpose of the occupation of the highway, or if the occupation becomes more than reasonably transitional in terms of either time or space, then it may come to exceed the right to use the highway.

The only point which has caused me some hesitation in the circumstances of the present case is the evident determination by the two appellants to remain where they were. That does seem to look as if they were intending to go beyond their right and to stay longer than would constitute a reasonable period. But I find it far from clear that there was an assembly of twenty or more persons who were so determined and in light of the fluidity in the composition of the grouping and in the consistency of its component individuals I consider that the Crown Court reached the correct conclusion.

I do not find it possible to return any general answer to the certified question. The matter is essentially one to be judged in light of the particular facts of the case. But I am prepared to hold that a peaceful assembly which does not obstruct the highway does not necessarily constitute a trespassory assembly so as to constitute the circumstances for an offence where an order under section 14A(2) is in force. I would allow the appeal."

An important feature of the speeches of both Lords Clyde and Hope is their emphasis on the restrictions which may be imposed on the right to freedom of assembly under Art.11 of the ECHR. Particularly significant is the emphasis attached by Lord Hope to private property rights as a restraint on the right to freedom of assembly. The same emphasis is to be found in cases on freedom of assembly over a 100 years ago, giving rise to concerns that the enactment of the Human Rights Act may do little to alter the fundamental pre-occupation of the common law. It is of course the case that these speeches were delivered before the Human Rights Act was introduced and that matters will be transformed by its coming into force. That, however, would be a rather optimistic view. There is nothing in the case law since 1998 to suggest that any of the statutory or common law restraints on the right to freedom of assembly are in any way vulnerable. This is true despite attempts to use provisions other than Art.11 to challenge restraints on the right of public protest. In the *Pamela Smith* case below, an attempt was made unsuccessfully to argue that the arrest of a protestor for breach of the peace was a violation of Arts 7 and 10: but this challenge to the offence of breach of the peace was unsuccessful. What the cases do suggest, however, is that the discretion which the law confers on the police and others to restrain assemblies or other forms of public protest may have to be exercised with a greater degree of caution than might otherwise have been the case: *Redmond-Bate v DPP* (1999) 7 B.H.R.C. 375.

Convention rights have been super-imposed upon a large volume of statute and common law. For the purposes of analysing this body of law, it is important to distinguish between the regulation of processions and meetings on the one hand, and offences which may be committed by those who take part in such activities on the other. The main regulatory burden in relation to the former is carried by the Civic Government (Scotland) Act 1982 (CGSA) which introduced common rules throughout Scotland. Previously the position varied. Each of the four cities and Greenock were governed by local Acts of Parliament (such as the Edinburgh Corporation Order Confirmation Act 1967), while the other towns were governed by the Burgh Police Act 1892 (see W. Finnie, "The Burgh Police Act" (1981) 26 J.L.S.S. 447). However it is to be pointed out that the CGSA is not a comprehensive code, and that the Public Order Act 1986 and the Criminal Justice and Public Order Act 1994 apply in Scotland also to empower the police and local authorities to regulate public assemblies. So far as offences which might be committed by taking part in an assembly are concerned, these have grown over the years and some are not as important now as they were in earlier times. Parliament and the courts tend to respond to events with new laws, but are very slow in removing these laws when they appear no longer to be necessary: the pressure inexorably is for more. It is also the case that the substance of the law and the vigour with which it is enforced depend to a large extent to the political climate of the time. That said, those who take part in public assemblies are most likely to feel the policeman's hand on their shoulder because they are committing a breach of the peace. But criminal law is not the only source of potential restraint or liability: so too is the civil law where the interim interdict is a potential menace to the right to freedom of assembly.

III. Processions

(1) Duty to Notify in Advance

Before the enactment of the CGSA, there was no general statutory duty on the organisers of a march or procession to give notice in advance to the public authorities. There were, however, obligations imposed by two of the local statutes. The Edinburgh Corporation Order Confirmation Act 1967 provided by s.184 for example that 7 days notice of a procession had to be given to the town clerk.

Similar (though not identical) provision existed in Aberdeen. It was this measure which formed the basis of the new controls introduced by the CGSA: Scottish Office, *Report of the Working Party on Civic Government* (1976).

The Civic Government (Scotland) Act 1982

"Notification of processions

    62.—(1) A person proposing to hold a procession in public shall give written notice of that proposal in accordance with subsections (2) and (3) below—

      (a) to the local authority in whose area the procession is to be held, or if it is to be held in the areas of more than one such authority, to each such authority;

      (aa) if the procession is to be held to any extent in a National Park, to the National Park authority for the National Park; and

      (b) to the chief constable.

    (2) Notice shall be given for the purposes of subsection (1) above by—

      (a) its being posted to the main office of the local authority and (where subsection (1)(aa) above applies) of the National Park authority, and to the office of the chief constable so that in the normal course of post it might be expected to arrive not later than seven days before the date when the procession is to be held; or

      (b) its being delivered by hand to those offices not later than seven days before that date.

    (3) The notice to be given under subsection (1) above shall specify—

      (a) the date and time when the procession is to be held;

      (b) its route;

      (c) the number of persons likely to take part in it;

      (d) the arrangements for its control being made by the person proposing to hold it; and

      (e) the name and address of that person.

    (4) A local authority may, on application in accordance with subsection (5) below by a person proposing to hold a procession in public in their area—

      (a) made to them;

      (aa) if the procession is to be held to any extent in a National Park, intimated to the National Park authority for the National Park; and

      (b) intimated to the chief constable,

within the period of seven days before the date when the procession is to be held, make an order dispensing with the requirements of subsection (2) above in relation to the time limits for the giving of notice of that proposal.

(5) An application under subsection (4) above shall specify the matters mentioned in subsection (3) above and, where an order has been made under the said subsection (4), the application for it shall be treated as notice duly given for the purposes of subsection (1) above.

(6) A local authority may (whether upon application made to them or not) make an order exempting any person proposing to hold any procession in public being a procession specified in the order or one of a class of processions so specified from the requirement under this section to give notice to the authority of the proposal to hold that procession.

(7) This section does not apply in relation to processions commonly or customarily held; but a local authority may, as respects their area, order that it shall apply to any such procession so held or any such class or procession so held as is specified in the order.

(8) An order under subsection (6) or (7) above may—

    (a) provide that its application in any case or class of cases is subject to such conditions as may be specified in the order;

    (b) classify processions by reference to any factor or factors whatsoever;

    (c) be varied or revoked by subsequent order made in like manner.

(9) The local authority shall, before making an order under subsection (4) above or making, varying or revoking an order under subsection (6) or (7) above, consult the chief constable.

(10) The local authority shall as soon as a notice under subsections (1) to (3) above, or an application under subsection (4), is received send a copy of that notice or application to the chief constable.

(11) The local authority shall, as soon as possible after they make, vary or revoke an order under subsection (6) or (7) above, give public notice of that fact in a newspaper or newspapers circulating in their area.

(12) In this section and in sections 63 to 65 of this Act—

    'Procession in public' means a procession in a public place;

    'chief constable' means, in relation to a local authority, the chief constable of the police force for the area which comprises or includes the area of the authority; and

    'public place' has the same meaning as in Part II of the Public Order Act 1986."

The enactment of this measure attracted surprisingly little resistance in Parliament. The Opposition accepted the need for s.62, with Mr Donald Dewar conceding in Standing Committee that:

"controlling processions needs police manpower, if only to ensure that there are not traffic accidents, traffic jams, foul-ups, snarl-ups, or malicious people causing trouble on the fringes. Given the size of that problem and that the measure is an intimation to allow effective regulation, I think that it would be wrong for us in any way to stand against the clause becoming part of the Bill." (First Scottish Standing Committee, 18th sitting, June 24, 1982, col. 691).

This is not to deny that some aspects of the section gave rise to difficulty. In the House of Lords concern was expressed that the duty to notify was a duty to notify the regional council rather than the district council: "It does not make sense that everything in relation to a small town in South Ayrshire has got to go way up to Glasgow" (428 H.L. Debs., March 9, 1982, Col. 125 (Lord Ross of Marnock)). Indeed, it had been proposed by the Working Party on Civic Government in Scotland that the "regulating authority should be the district or islands council" (Scottish Office, above). The Government, however, was persuaded otherwise by the Committee on Local Government in Scotland that the matter should be dealt with by the regional councils: "this is consistent with regional councils' responsibilities for police and the highways".

A second difficulty related to the fact that the clause as originally published appeared without what is now subs. (7) on its face. The concern of some members of both Houses was that the Act would thereby impose a duty to notify in the case of all processions, including customary and ceremonial processions. In the House of Lords examples were given of activities far removed from the mischief behind the Act, but which would nevertheless be caught by its terms. Thus reference was made to the Salvation Army, the Boy Scouts, Girl Guides and Boys' Brigade. In the words of Viscount Thurso: "They are not holding a procession in the customary way in which we understand the word 'procession,' but they are indeed probably holding a procession in a technical sense if they march from their headquarters to a church, or if they march down the street with their band playing and their banners flying" (428 H.L. Debs., March 9, 1982, col. 125–126). Lord Ross of Marnock gave examples of "local gala days, the processions of the children and the floats, and, in the Borders, the Common Riding processions" (*ibid.*, col. 127). The Government's view was that local authorities could make an exemption order under subs. (6) exempting such activity. This, however, did not satisfy the Opposition: "Local authorities being what they are, you could get a patchwork of different attitudes over the whole country and different administrative conditions laid down in respect of processions that would never have caused any trouble and which delight the people of Scotland" (*ibid.*, col. 128).

Subsection (7) was in fact designed principally to preserve the freedom of religious expression, with the Salvation Army particularly in mind. As a result of the amendment, which was carried despite initial government resistance (expressed in strong terms in the Lords), all such processions are now presumed excluded from the duty to notify, though it is open to the authority to use its powers under the second limb of subs. (7) to impose a duty on the part of the organisation in question. The burden of apathy is thus now in favour of freedom to this limited extent. This is not to say that there was no substance in the Government's case. The Earl of Mansfield objected to the amendment on three grounds (though he later supported the amendment). First:

> "As one of the objects of advance notice, coupled with powers to impose conditions in a march, is to help minimise the disruption which processions cause to the community, it would seem right, on the whole, not to have any exceptions at all, or, failing that, to draw any exemptions narrowly." (*ibid.*, col. 132).

Second, he argued that it was now

> "uncertain in particular cases whether any notice was required to be given, because it may not be clear whether a particular procession is one which is 'commonly or customarily held.' This could result in the organiser of a procession committing an offence by failing to give notice of a procession in the belief, which may prove to be mistaken, that his procession fitted the description of 'commonly or customarily held.' So this is a weakness ... and it might adversely affect those whom it seeks to protect." (*ibid.*, cols. 132–133).

Thirdly, the Minister saw no threat to religious freedom in the clause as originally introduced, since if local councillors displayed any religious intolerance, they would pay the electoral penalty. More credible was the argument that "we are treading on very dangerous ground so far as religious tolerance is concerned, because ... the Orange Order could make some claim to be religious and that could cause problems too" (*ibid.*, col. 133). However, it would be open to a council to require the Orange Order to give notification of its Twelfth of July parades.

In its final form, then, s.62 creates five classes or potential classes of procession:
   (1) processions commonly or customarily held. Section 62(7) *prima facie* exempts them from the need to be notified;
   (2) processions commonly or customarily held in respect of which the local authority has disapplied the exemption (s.62(7));
   (3) processions with respect to which, because they are in response to currents events or for some similar reason there is not time to give seven days' notice. The authority *may* dispense with the notice of requirement in such cases (s.62(4)), but the other matters specified in s.62(3) must still be notified;
   (4) processions or classes of procession in relation to which generally, the local authority has given an exemption from the requirement to notify (s.62(6)); and
   (5) processions which do not fall into any of the preceding classes. In respect of these the full notification requirements apply.

West Lothian Council

"Street Processions And Parades Permit

Summary

Anyone organising a street procession or parade has to apply for approval from the Council.

Eligibility

Each application is judged on its own merits.

. . .

Service Standards

We will acknowledge receipt of your application within three working days of receipt. arrange for any road closures which might be necessary;

inform you of the date, time and place of the Community Safety Committee meeting which will have to consider your application in the event of any unresolved difficulties. invite comments on your application from the police and highways services, within one working day of receipt of receiving your completed application; (acting on the council's behalf, the police will contact parade organisers to establish the extent of road disruption and highlight any difficulties arising from their applications);

issue a permit, by letter, at least 28 days prior to the event taking place, provided it presents no problems;

Note: Events which require the closure of major roads or which involve adult sectarian organisations with more than 500 participants are automatically referred to Committee."

The Council also undertakes as follows: "Within one working day, Council officials will contact Police and Highways staff for comment on your application. Within three working days, the Council will also contact you to say it is dealing with your letter. Provided there are no problems, the council aims to issue you with a permit at least 28 days before your event is due to take place. However: if there are objections or worries about the parade; or if the parade involves the closure of major roads; or if the parade is a sectarian march involving 500 or more people ... the application must be referred to the Council's Community Safety Committee for a final decision". The Council points out that "there is no current legislation that allows objections to temporary or minor road closures, the closure will however be removed as quickly as possible after the event".

---

(2) Forbidding and Regulating Processions

Before 1982 the power to prohibit and regulate processions was governed by three different measures. First, the Public Order Act 1936 empowered the chief officer of police to give directions imposing on both the organisers and the participants "such conditions as appear to him necessary for the preservation of public order." This power was exercisable only where the chief of police had "reasonable grounds for apprehending that the procession may occasion serious public disorder." The power to impose conditions did not include the power to ban a march altogether. Secondly, the local Acts generally contained powers exercisable by the magistrates. In Aberdeen, for example, the Aberdeen Corporation (General Powers) Order Confirmation Act 1938 provided by s.182(3):

"The magistrates may, if the conducting of any procession would or would be likely to cause or result in disorderly behaviour or a breach of the peace or any nuisance or annoyance or any obstruction to traffic, prohibit the conducting of such procession or may make an order prescribing a different route for such procession."

So, unlike the power of the police under s.3 of the Public Order Act 1936, the magistrates had a power to ban marches. The power was used in Aberdeen in 1981 to ban an Orange march, on the ground that it would be "composed of bands of imported religious zealots," would "outrage" many citizens, and would introduce for the first time to the city the "taint of religious bigotry" (*The Scotsman*, September 8, 1981). Similar powers existed in Edinburgh, though not in Glasgow or Dundee. The third source of power which permitted the prohibition and regulation of processions was a group of measures intended to be exercised with traffic considerations uppermost. One such measure was the Burgh Police (Scotland) Act 1892, s.385, which enabled highway authorities to issue notices and orders

> "(2) Diverting temporarily out of any street or streets, traffic of every kind, or such particular kinds of traffic as may be specified in any such order or notice: and the islands or district council may from time to time make bye-laws and issue notices and orders prohibiting or regulating public processions. And every breach of any such bye-law, notice, or order shall be deemed an offence against this Act, and every person committing such an offence shall be liable to a penalty not exceeding twenty-five pounds."

In *Loyal Orange Lodge No. 493 Hawick First Purple v Roxburgh District Council*, 1981 S.L.T. 33, it was held by the Inner House that this measure could be invoked by a local authority to forbid a march on public order grounds. The position is now governed by the CGSA.

The Civic Government (Scotland) Act 1982

"63—(1) The local authority may, after consulting the chief constable and (where s.62(1)(aa) of this Act applies) the National Park authority in respect of a procession notice of which has been given or falls to be treated as having been given in accordance with section 62(1) of this Act, make an order—

(i) prohibiting the holding of the procession; or

(ii) imposing conditions on the holding of it.

(1A) Where notice of a proposal to hold a procession has been given or falls to be treated as having been given in accordance with section 62(1) of this Act—

(a) if a local authority have made an order under subsection (1) above they may at any time thereafter, after consulting the chief constable and (where s.62(1)(aa) of this Act applies) the National Park authority, vary or revoke the order and, where they revoke it, make any order which they were empowered to make under that subsection;

(b) If they have decided not to make an order they may at any time thereafter, after consulting the chief constable and (where section 62(1)(aa) of this Act applies) the National Park authority, make any order which they were empowered to make under that subsection.

(2) The conditions which may be imposed under subsection (1) or (1A) above on the holding of a procession may include conditions—

(a) as to the date, time and duration of the procession;

(b) as to the route to be taken by it;

(c) prohibiting its entry into any public place specified in the order.

(3) A local authority shall—

(a) where notice of a proposal to hold a procession has been given or falls to be treated as having been given in accordance with section 62(1) of this Act, deliver at least 2 days before the date when, in terms of the notice, the procession is to be held, to the person who gave the notice—

(i) where they have made an order under subsection (1) or (1A) above, a copy of it and a written statement of the reason for it; or

(ii) where they decide not to make an order under subsection (1) above or to revoke an order already made under subsection (1) or (1A) above notification of that fact; and

      (iii) where they have, under subsection (1A) above, varied such an order a copy of
           the order as varied and a written statement of the reasons for the variation,
           and
    (b) where they have made an order under subsection (1) or (1A) above in relation to a
       proposal to hold a procession, make such arrangements as will ensure that persons
       who might take or are taking part in that procession are made aware of the fact
       the order has been made and, if the order has been varied under subsection (1A)
       above, that it has been so varied and of its effect; and
    (c) where they have revoked an order made under subsection (1) or (1A) above in
       relation to a proposal to hold a procession, make such arrangements as will ensure
       that persons who might take or are taking part in that procession are made aware
       of the fact that the order has been revoked.
  (4) The local authority shall comply with subsection (3) above."

Section 63 confers important powers on local authorities. They may ban a procession, or they may impose conditions on the holding of it. The power to ban contrasts with the powers of local authorities in England and Wales under the Public Order Act 1986, s.13. That measure, being based on s.3(2) of the Public Order Act 1936, does not permit the banning of individual marches or processions, but provides that a banning order shall apply to all such activity in the locality for a period of up to three months. A second important feature of the s.63 power is the remarkably wide discretion given to local authorities in the exercise of the power to ban or impose conditions. The banning power in England and Wales may be exercised only to prevent serious public disorder (POA 1986, s.13(1)). And although the power to impose conditions has been extended, it is still nevertheless constrained by s.12 of the Public Order Act 1986 which is reproduced below.

In Scotland, in contrast, the public authorities appear empowered to ban or impose conditions for any reason, though the exercise of this power would now have to be consistent with art.11 of the ECHR.

This point was raised in Standing Committee by Mr Donald Dewar for the Opposition, who pointed out that local authorities have been given a wide discretion, but that nowhere is a test specified, with the result that there is a danger of the authorities becoming censors or passing moral judgments on parades they did not like (First Scottish Standing Committee, 18th sitting, June 24, 1982, col. 691). In reply, the Solicitor General for Scotland pointed to three safeguards: first, the duty to intimate (s.63 (3)); secondly, the duty to give reasons (s.63 (3)); and thirdly, the right of appeal to the sheriff in s.64, which provides as follows:

"The sheriff may uphold an appeal under this section only if he considers that the local authority in arriving at their decision to make the order—
    (a) erred in law;
    (b) based their decision an any incorrect material fact;
    (c) exercised their discretion in an unreasonable manner; or
    (d) otherwise acted beyond their powers."

The introduction of this statutory right of appeal is an important innovation. There was no corresponding provision under the Public Order Act 1936, s.3, nor is there such a right in England and Wales under the Public Order Act 1986. The only means of redress under these measures was or is judicial review. The Government has pointed out that "the availability of judicial review as an effective remedy has been greatly extended, by the law and by the procedural reforms of recent years" (Home Office, *Review of Public Order Law* (Cmnd. 9510, 1985)). Nevertheless, a remedy by way of judicial review alone has been criticised because the courts have been reluctant to use their powers under this procedure (P. Thornton, *We Protest* (1985), p.52). It is the case that the English courts appear to tread very warily in cases which seek to challenge the exercise of discretionary powers relating to public order.

Yet although the introduction of this statutory right is important, it should not be exaggerated. It is an appeal from the exercise of an unlimited discretion on very limited grounds. The limited nature of the appeal was stressed by the government in the House of Lords when the Earl of Mansfield said that it "is not some sort of rehearsing before a lawyer on the part of somebody who is dissatisfied with the determination of the matter by the local authority" (428 H.L. Debs. March 9, 1982, 143). In fact s.63(4) adds very little. This decision of the local authority would have been subject to judicial review on precisely the grounds specified in the subsection anyway. All the subsection does is to give statutory force to the grounds of judicial review and to provide that they are actionable before the sheriff. This is confirmed by the Secretary of State, who said that s.63(4) (c) "would not put the sheriff in the position of being the substitute local authority looking *de novo* at the circumstances and saying 'I would allow the march.' He would have to consider, because of this discretion, whether the decision was such that no reasonable local authority could have reached that view" (First Scottish Standing Committee, 18th sitting, June 24, 1982, col. 700). This stung Mr Donald Dewar to suggest that sheriffs "will not be keen to upset the discretion that has been exercised by the local authority" and to question whether the right of appeal is "as impressive and reassuring as might appear at first sight" (*ibid.*, 19th sitting, June 24, 1982, col. 704). This is not to deny that there will be cases where judicial accountability could be important. It does at least offer a check against the arbitrary and capricious use of power. An example given in Committee of where the right of appeal would be useful is "if a local authority were to say, following its own internal party political diktats, that there were to be no processions of any military character within its area, there would be a good chance that the sheriff would consider that that was an unreasonable exercise of discretion" (*ibid.*, col. 693, the Solicitor General for Scotland).

Edinburgh City Council

"Minutes: Licensing Committee 20/02/98

Loyal Orange Institution of Scotland—East of Scotland Processions—Edinburgh— 27 June 1998

Notification had been received from the Loyal Orange Institution of Scotland of its intention to hold processions in Edinburgh on Saturday 27 June 1998.

The Chief Constable reported that he had no objections to the arrangements for two processions which had been discussed with the organiser, subject to certain conditions which were detailed in his report.

The first procession would commence at 10 am and proceed to the Martyrs Memorial in the Grassmarket via Academy Street, Duke Street, Leith Walk, Leith Street, Princes Street, North Bridge, High Street, George IV Bridge, Victoria Street and West Bow. Following a short service at the Memorial, the procession would continue to Waterloo Place via Cowgatehead, Cowgate, Holyrood Road, Horse Wynd, Abbeyhill, Abbeymount and Regent Road. The procession would then proceed to the front of the assembling body for the second procession.

The second procession was to commence at 12 noon and proceed westwards towards the Meadows via Waterloo Place, Princes Street, The Mound, North Bank Street, Bank Street, George IV Bridge, Bristo Place, Lothian Street, Potterrow, Chapel Street and Buccleuch Street. The procession would terminate in East Meadow Park, between Middle Meadow Walk and Boys' Brigade Walk, and a rally lasting approximately 11/2 hours would be held. Thereafter, participants would disperse by coach.

DECISION

(1) To make an Order imposing conditions stipulating the time and route recommended by the Chief Constable for two processions by the Loyal Orange Institution of Scotland in Edinburgh on 27 June 1998.

(2) To note that delegated authority would be used imposing a temporary ban or restriction on traffic, as detailed in the Chief Constable's report."

Angus Council

"Civic Licensing Committee

MINUTE of MEETING of the CIVIC LICENSING COMMITTEE held in the Town and County Hall, Forfar on Friday 31 March 2000 at 12.30 pm.

1. URGENT BUSINESS

The Committee noted that, in terms of Section 50B of the Local Government (Scotland) Act 1973, (as amended), the Vice-Convener was of the opinion that the following item of business be considered as a matter of urgency, because the Sheriff's Interlocutor had directed that a special meeting of the Committee be held no later than today to reconsider the proposed procession.

2. PUBLIC PROCESSION 'PROPOSED PARADE, FORFAR' SUNDAY 2 APRIL 2000

With reference to Article 1 of the minute of meeting of this Committee of 27 March 2000, there was submitted Report No 394/00 by the Director of Law and Administration advising that notification, in terms of Section 62 of the Civic Government (Scotland) Act 1982, had been received from the Wishart Arch Defenders Loyal Orange Lodge 444 of their intention to hold a short parade in Forfar on 2 April 2000. There was also tabled at the meeting, and circulated to all those present, a procedure note which was adopted by the Committee.

The Head of Legal Services updated the meeting on the events following the meeting held on 27 March 2000. An appeal had been held in the Sheriff Court, Forfar on Thursday 30 March 2000. The Sheriff had upheld the appeal and remitted the matter back to the Committee to reconvene a meeting excluding Councillors Bill Roberton, Bill Middleton and Glennis Middleton, because as local members, they had expressed objections prior to the Committee's consideration of the procession.

Mr James G McLean, County Grand Master of the Loyal Orange Lodge, and Ms Ann McKeown, Solicitor, addressed the Committee in support of the parade. Chief Inspector Robson, of Tayside Police Eastern Division, commented on the Chief Constable's response to the road safety and public order aspects and confirmed that he had no objection to the proposed procession.

After various questions had been asked and answered, and members had commented on the proposed procession, the organisers were invited to sum up.

Thereafter, the Committee unanimously agreed that an Order be made under Section 63(1) of the Civic Government (Scotland) Act 1982 prohibiting the proposed procession for the following reasons:—

    i. that the Committee apprehended that the procession, if it proceeded, would lead to disorder.

    ii. that the procession, if permitted, could lead to religious intolerance and division in the community.

    iii. that there was no history of such processions in Forfar or in the Angus area and, as such, there was no overriding reason why the procession should proceed.

    iv. that, in any event, prohibition of the procession was necessary in a democratic society for the prevention of disorder and for the protection of the rights and freedom of others."

The Public Order Act 1986

"Imposing conditions on public processions

12.—(1) If the senior police officer, having regard to the time or place at which and the circumstances in which any public procession is being held or is intended to be held and to its route or proposed route, reasonably believes that—

    (a) it may result in serious public disorder, serious damage to property or serious disruption to the life of the community, or

    (b) the purpose of the persons organising it is the intimidation of others with a view to compelling them not to do an act they have a right to do, or to do an act they have a right not to do.

He may give directions imposing on the persons organising or taking part in the procession or prohibiting it from entering any public place specified in the directions.

(2) In subsection (1) the 'senior police officer' means—

    (a) in relation to a procession being held, or to a procession intended to be held in a case where persons are assembling with a view to taking part in it, the most senior in rank of the police officers present at the scene, and

    (b) in relation to a procession intended to be held in a case where paragraph (a) does not apply, the chief officer of police.

(3) A direction given by a chief officer of police by virtue of subsection (2)(b) shall be given in writing.

(4) A person who organises a public procession and knowingly fails to comply with a condition imposed under this section is guilty of an offence, but it is a defence for him to prove that the failure arose from circumstances beyond his control.

(5) A person who takes part in a public procession and knowingly fails to comply with a condition imposed under this section is guilty of an offence, but it is a defence for him to prove that the failure arose from circumstances beyond his control.

(6) A person who incites another to commit an offence under subsection (5) is guilty of an offence.

(7) A constable may arrest without warrant anyone he reasonably suspects is committing an offence under subsection (4), (5) or (6). . . .

(11) In Scotland this section applies only in relation to a procession being held, and to a procession intended to be held in a case where persons are assembling with a view to taking part in it."

This measure supplements the power of the local authorities under the 1982 Act. Section 12(11) does, however, impose an important limit on the power of the police in Scotland. Generally, conditions in advance should be imposed by local authorities (albeit in consultation with the police). But the government was of the view that this was insufficient, pointing out in the White Paper that "it seems desirable that the police should have clear statutory authority to issue directions for the control of a procession should this be seen to be necessary either immediately before the procession starts or when it is in progress": Home Office, *Review of Public Order Law* (Cmnd. 9510, 1985). The power of the police is not as wide as that of the local authorities, though it is much wider than that which existed under the Public Order Act 1936, s.3(1). This enabled the police to issue directions only to prevent serious public disorder. The police power to impose conditions overrides any decision of a local authority not to impose conditions under the 1982 Act and the police conditions take priority over any which the local authority may have issued (CGSA, s.66). The function of the new extended police powers was explained by the government in the White Paper (Home Office, *ibid.*, pp.27–28)) in the following terms:

"4.21. In proposing an extension of the police's power to impose conditions the Government has no intention of altering the present arrangements whereby the police negotiate agreements with the march organisers. The Government anticipates that in the great majority of cases the police will continue to proceed on the basis of informal agreements. But the Government does intend to alter the legal framework within which agreements are negotiated, by widening the circumstances in which the police will be empowered to impose conditions in default of agreement, or where they suspect that an agreement will not be kept. This means widening the present test of serious public disorder in section 3(1) [of the POA 1936] by adding other criteria to it. The Green Paper suggested a reduction in the test for imposing conditions to one of public disorder. But there has been no evidence from the police that they have experienced difficulties in imposing conditions on marches where this was necessary *to prevent disorder*. The only change the Government would propose to the existing test is to make it clear that serious public disorder can include serious damage to property. But in addition the Government believes that greater flexibility can usefully be conferred by the introduction of two new tests.

4.22. The first test is one proposed by the Select Committee, who vividly described the degree of disruption which can be caused even by a procession of average size. Some degree of disruption must of course be accepted by the wider community; but it does not seem right that the police should have no power to re-route a procession in order to limit traffic congestion, or to prevent a bridge from being blocked, or to reduce the severe disruption sometimes suffered by pedestrians, business and commerce. The Committee therefore suggested an additional test which would enable the police to impose conditions on a procession in order to prevent serious disruption to the normal life of the community. The Government agrees that a new test of this kind is required, in order to prevent marches from causing unreasonable disruption to local residents, other users of the highway, and adjoining shops and businesses. An example of the circumstances in which the test might operate is provided by the policy of the Metropolitan Police in seeking to discourage demonstrators from using Oxford Street during business hours. A number of other police forces have given examples of marches being held through shopping centres on Saturdays or through city centres in the rush hour. At present the police have no legal powers should the organisers of a march be minded to defy police efforts to persuade them to change their plans. The proposed test would enable the police to re-route a march if they believed that it was likely to be seriously disruptive to the traffic, the shops or the shoppers.

4.23. Serious disruption can be caused by marches organised with the best of intentions. But the second new test proposed by the Government is directed at those who organise processions with more malicious intent. It would confer on the police a power to impose conditions in order to prevent the coercion of individuals. This is a libertarian safeguard designed to prevent demonstrations whose overt purpose is to persuade people, from being used as a cloak by those whose real purpose is to intimidate or coerce. Sometimes, however, their purpose is not even concealed: their literature proclaims their intention as being to 'stop' or 'smash' their opponents. (An example was provided last year in Manchester by the National Front, who when organising a counter-demonstration to a march by the Troops Out Movement described their purpose as being to 'stop this vermin ... don't let them march').

4.24. On some such occasions the police will often need to impose conditions in order to prevent serious public disorder. Sometimes there is no clear risk of disorder because the target of the demonstration is a single individual, or a peaceful group who are unlikely to respond with violence. When the National Front march through Asian districts the reaction of the local community may be to board up their shops and businesses and to stay at home. It is on these occasions that the law needs to give the police powers to ensure that individuals are free to go about their business without fear of intimidation. Another example of marches whose purpose is to coerce is provided by animal rights protesters, who on occasion have marched on furriers' shops or food factories with the intention of preventing the employees from working. On other occasions a march may be coercive simply by reason of the number of marchers compared with its objective (for example, 1,000 people marching on the home of a local councillor, or an inquiry inspector). On such occasions there may not be a risk of public disorder, but the police may need to impose conditions on the march in order to protect the individual or individuals who are its target. In maintaining the balance between the freedom to demonstrate and the rights of the wider community the law must ensure that people are not so harassed by demonstrators that they are no longer free to come and go without fear of coercion or intimidation."

In view of the fact that they are imposed on the spot, and unlike the conditions imposed by the local authority, there is effectively no means of challenging the conditions imposed by the police. In England and Wales (where police powers are not subject to s.12(11)) the police may issue the instructions well in advance of the procession. In such circumstances judicial review would be available in theory, though perhaps not in practice. But although great reforms have taken place in judicial review in recent years, there is no way in which an organiser could get judicial review of conditions imposed by the police officer on the spot. The only control then is after the event. It is a criminal offence to fail to comply with a police instruction. Presumably, it would be open to someone arrested and charged to offer the defence that the conditions were unlawful because the police had no reasonable grounds to believe that there would be serious disruption, serious damage, or whatever. It is not clear, however, whether the courts would be anxious to challenge the exercise of the police officers' discretion, save in palpably absurd cases such as a clear breach of Convention rights. Nor in a sense is this the point. The demonstration is killed by the conditions. Arrests may be made. Prosecutions may not be brought. Even if a prosecution is brought and fails, this hardly compensates the defence for the invasion of their liberties and the disruption of the march.

IV. MEETINGS AND ASSEMBLIES

We turn now from the question of prior restraints on marches and processions to the question of prior restraints on meetings and assemblies. The statutory position here contrasts sharply with that which applies to processions. In the first place, there is no general power to ban meetings or assemblies. The government considered but rejected the introduction of such a power:

"5.3. A new power to ban static demonstrations would be a substantial limitation on the right of assembly and the right to demonstrate. The Government has been very concerned not to extend statutory controls over static demonstrations any further than is strictly necessary. Meetings and assemblies are a more important means of exercising freedom of speech than are marches: a power to ban them, even as a last resort, would be potentially a major infringement of freedom of speech (especially at election time). It might also be difficult to enforce: and there was no strong request from the police for a power to ban. The Government has concluded that the new controls which it proposes over static demonstrations should not include a power to ban. The power to impose conditions should in most cases be sufficient to control those demonstrations which threaten to be disorderly, disruptive or intimidatory." (Home Office, *Review of Public Order Law* (Cmnd. 9510, 1985)).

There is, in addition, no general duty on the part of the organisers to notify the public authorities, whether it be the local council (as under the CGSA for processions), or the police (as under the CGSA as amended by the Public Order Act 1986, s.12 for processions). Again the Government considered but rejected any such duty:

"5.4 The Government has been greatly assisted by advice from the police as to what powers they consider would be useful and practicable in relation to static demonstrations. Discussion of an advance notice requirement has made it clear that it would produce much unnecessary work for the police to little purpose. There is no legal definition of a static demonstration: an assembly covers the whole range of public gatherings, from political rallies to religious services and pop festivals to football matches. The Government has considered possible definitions based on the nature of an assembly, or its likely size; but it has not proved possible to devise a definition which restricts the category to those events of interest to the police. An advance notice requirement would therefore inundate the police with notifications of perfectly peaceful meetings. The administrative burden would far outweigh the information gain." (*ibid.*)

It does not follow, however, that there is no power to impose prior restraints. First, restrictions may be imposed by local byelaws; and secondly the Public Order Act 1986, s.14 extends additional powers to the police.

(1) Bye-Laws and Prior Restraint

The power to make bye-laws is one which has important implications for the holding of meetings and public assemblies. Bye-laws are a kind of delegated legislation, with the power to make them being vested in local authorities. The general bye-law making power is contained in the Local Government (Scotland) Act 1973 which provides by s.201:

"(1) A local authority may make byelaws for the good rule and government of the whole of any part of the region, islands area or district, as the case may be, and for the prevention and suppression of nuisances therein.

(2) The confirming authority in relation to byelaws made under this section shall be the Scottish Ministers.

(3) Byelaws shall not be made under this section for any purpose as respects any area if provision for that purpose as respects that area is made by, or is or may be made under, any other enactment."

Section 201(2) provides that bye-laws must be "confirmed" by the Scottish Ministers. Before they are confirmed, however, they must be published and anyone aggrieved has a right to make representation to the confirming authority. Any objections must be considered by the Scottish Ministers, and if necessary a local inquiry must be held (s.202(8)). Any such inquiry must be held by the sheriff, unless the Scottish Ministers otherwise direct. In addition to this general power to make bye-laws, there may also be specific power conferred by statute. Although made by popularly elected bodies, the bye-law making power is not unlimited, and is constrained first by the *ultra vires* rule, and secondly by the requirement of reasonableness. As a result, bye-laws may be challenged at two points in the legal process. First, they may be questioned at the point of confirmation (see *Rothesay Town Council, Petitioners* (1898) 14 Sh. Ct. Rep. 189 and *Burgh of Dunblane, Petitioners*, 1947 S.L.T. (Sh.Ct.) 27). Secondly, they can be challenged collaterally as a defence in criminal proceedings for breach of the bye-law. In *McCallum v Procurator Fiscal, East Kilbride (Appeal No: 120/99)* the High Court of Justiciary pointed out that "in cases such as *Aldred v Miller*, 1925 JC 21 it has been held that there is a strong presumption in favour of the validity of a byelaw passed by a local authority, particularly if it has been confirmed, in accordance with the provisions of the statute authorising it, by some public official such as the Secretary of State for Scotland or the sheriff". It was also pointed out that the "the power conferred by section 201 is a wide and general one".

Aldred v Langmuir
1932 J.C. 22

"The following facts were admitted or proved:—'On Sunday, 5th July 1931, a large demonstration consisting of five to six thousand persons was observed by police officers approaching Glasgow Green, one of the public parks of the City of Glasgow. The officers followed the demonstrators, who entered the Green and proceeded as far as the Nelson Monument, where, from an improvised platform, the appellant, as well as the other accused, lectured to the crowd. The accused Andrew Reilly acted as chairman, and each speaker spoke from five to fifteen minutes, the subject being "Free Speech" and the

"Imprisonment of the Tramp Preachers." The meeting, which lasted from 3.15 p.m. until 5 p.m., was quite an orderly one, and during its progress a collection was taken by means of a hat. The name of each speaker was taken by the police officers, and all frankly admitted that they had not the written authority of the Corporation or the Director of Parks for the holding of said meeting as required by No. 20 of the bye-laws libelled. Neither the appellant nor any of the other accused, with the exception of the accused Daniel Lanaghan, had ever at any such time applied to the Corporation or the Director of Parks for such a written authority. An application by the accused Langhan to hold a meeting in the Green on 1st May last under the auspices of the Irish Labour League was refused by the Parks Committee of the Corporation. Lanaghan's object in going to the Green on 5th July 1931 was to protest against this refusal. Between the years 1916 and 1931 116 applications for permits to hold meetings in Glasgow Green have been made to the Corporation. Of that number, 94 were granted, and 22 refused. No permits have ever been issued by the Director of Parks personally. He has left that matter entirely in the hands of the Parks Committee of the Corporation. For some years prior to 1922 Bye-law No. 20 was not uniformly enforced, but since then it has been consistently applied."

The stipendiary magistrate found each of the accused guilty as libelled and imposed a fine on each of them. Aldred appealed to the High Court of Justiciary. One of the grounds of his appeal was that the bye-law under which he was convicted was *ultra vires*. The bye-law is reproduced in the opinion of the Lord Justice-General:

LORD JUSTICE-GENERAL (Clyde): "The power of the Corporation to regulate the public parks of the city is a power exercisable by bye-law, the power being conferred by section 37 of the Glasgow Public Parks Act 1878, which is in the following terms:—'The Lord Provost, Magistrates, and Council may from time to time *make such bye-laws* as they shall think fit *for the good government and regulation of the said public parks*, gardens, and open spaces, and of the museums, galleries, and collections of natural history, science, and art, and other buildings, *and persons frequenting the same*, and of the superintendents, curators, rangers, park-keepers, and other officers or servants appointed and employed by them, and may impose such penalties for breaches of the bye-laws so to be made, not exceeding five pounds for each offence, as may be considered by them expedient, and from time to time, as they shall think fit, may repeal, alter, or re-enact any such bye-laws: Provided that such bye-laws shall not be repugnant to the law of Scotland, and shall be reduced into writing, and have affixed thereto the signatures of at least two of the magistrates of the city.' The bye-law which the appellant is said to have contravened is No. 20 of a set of bye-laws for the management and regulation of the public parks enacted by the Corporation, in virtue of the powers of the section just quoted, on 13th April 1916, and approved by the Sheriff of Lanarkshire on 20th June of the same year. It is in the following terms:—'No person shall, in any of the parks, sing, preach, lecture, or take part in any service, discussion, meeting, or demonstration, or hold any exhibition or public show, for any purpose whatsoever, or play any musical instrument, except with the written authority of the Corporation or the Superintendent, and then only on such places as may from time to time be by the Corporation or the Superintendent set apart by notice for such purposes.' The superintendent referred to is an officer of the Corporation in the parks department. It is not in dispute that Glasgow Green is one of the public parks of the city.

The attack upon the validity of Bye-law No. 20 rests on the principle of the decision pronounced in *McGregor v Disselduff*, 1907 S.C. (J) 21. In that case the power of the magistrate to regulate the places and hours for bathing on or from the seashore of Dunoon was derived from a statute which authorised such regulation by bye-law. The bye-law enacted by the magistrates simply prohibited bathing on or from the seashore except at such places as might from time to time be appointed by the magistrates. It was held that a bye-law in these prohibitory terms was not one which regulated the places and hours of bathing, but merely reserved the power of regulation to the discretion of the magistrates as such discretion might be exercised from time to time. The power committed by the statute to the magistrates was a power exercisable by means of bye-laws, not a power of discretionary regulation. The bye-law was therefore held to be *ultra vires*.

If the power of regulation given to the Corporation by the Public Parks Act 1878, had been no more than a power to regulate the use of the parks of the city for the purpose of lectures, meetings, and demonstrations, it is probable that the principle of the decision above referred to would have applied, to the effect of invalidating Bye-law No. 20. But the power conferred on the Corporation is much wider than that; it is a general power to regulate the public parks of the city and the persons resorting thereto. Broadly speaking, public parks are provided in the interests of the health of a city population—as the city's 'lungs,' to use a common expression—and for recreation from the crowded labours of an urban population. It is therefore that the power of regulation should include the prohibition of the use of the parks for purposes which are, or may be, inconsistent with, or detrimental or alien to, these general interests, or which may be harmful to the parks themselves. The Corporation's bye-laws contain many examples of prohibitory regulation of this kind besides Bye-law No. 20—Bye-law No. 9, for instance, which prohibits any person from bringing a dog into a public park except on leash; and also many examples of prohibitory regulations which are subject to exception by way of special permission, Bye-law No. 18, for instance, which prohibits picnics in a public park without special permission. All these bye-laws are, I think, plainly *intra vires* of a corporation empowered to regulate, by bye-law, the public parks under its administration and the public resorting thereto."

Lords Sands and Blackburn delivered concurring opinions. The fine imposed was reduced to a sum of 10 shillings.

(2) Police Powers to Regulate Public Assemblies

The Public Order Act 1986

"Imposing conditions on public assemblies

14.—(1) If the senior police officer, having regard to the time or place at which and the circumstances in which any public assembly is being held or is intended to be held, reasonably believes that—

(a) it may result in serious public disorder, serious damage to property or serious disruption to the life of the community, or

(b) the purpose of the person organising it is the intimidation of others with a view to compelling them not to do an act they have a right to do, or to do an act they have a right not to do.

He may give directions imposing on the persons organising or taking part in the assembly any conditions which prescribe the place at which the assembly may be (or continue to be) held, its maximum duration, or the maximum number of persons who may constitute it, provided they are conditions which appear to the senior police officer necessary to prevent such disorder, damage, disruption or intimidation.

(2) In this section 'the senior police officer' means the chief officer of police (in relation to an assembly intended to be held) or the most senior in rank of police officers present at the scene (in relation to an assembly being held).

(3) A direction given by a chief officer of police by virtue of subsection (2)(b) shall be given in writing.

(4) A person who organises a public assembly and knowingly fails to comply with a condition imposed under this section is guilty of an offence, but it is a defence for him to prove that the failure arose from circumstances beyond his control.

(5) A person who takes part in a public assembly and knowingly fails to comply with a condition imposed under this section is guilty of an offence, but it is a defence for him to

prove that the failure arose from circumstances beyond his control.

(6) A person who incites another to commit an offence under subsection (5) is guilty of an offence.

(7) A constable may arrest without warrant anyone he reasonably suspects is committing an offence under subsection (4), (5) or (6). ...

16. In this Part—

... 'public assembly' means an assembly of 20 or more persons in a public place which is wholly or partly open to the air;

'public place' means—

(a) any highway, or in Scotland any road within the meaning of the Roads (Scotland) Act 1984, and

(b) any place to which at the material time the public or any section of the public has access, on payment or otherwise, as of right or by virtue of express or implied permission;

'public procession' means a procession in a public place."

The conditions which may be imposed under s.14 are identical to those which may be imposed by the police officer on the spot under s.12 with regard to processions. Although there is no duty of advance notification, if the police are aware of an assembly which is imminent, they may impose conditions well in advance of the proposed day. Alternatively, conditions may be imposed on the spot. The conditions which may be imposed relate to numbers, location and duration. The background to s.14 was explained by the Home Office (*Review of Public Order Law* (Cmnd. 9510, 1985)) in the following terms:

"5.7. It is right to give examples of how the Government anticipates that the new powers might operate in practice. The first test would enable the police to take preventative action to avoid serious public disorder. This might have proved useful on occasions in the past when marches have been banned and the organisers have announced their intention to hold a meeting instead. The National Front has on occasion staged a rally, after a march has been banned. The new power would not enable the police to ban the rally: but if they apprehended serious public disorder they would be able to insist that it was held in a less sensitive area. The power might also prove useful in relation to picketing which has resulted in outbreaks of serious public disorder: at Grunwick's or Warrington, for example, the police could have imposed conditions limiting the numbers of demonstrators, or moving the demonstration in support of the pickets further away from the factory. And the power could in suitable cases be used in relation to football matches: where the police apprehend serious public disorder in connection with a fixture they could where necessary impose conditions limiting the number of spectators.

5.8. As with marches, the test of serious public disorder will include serious damage to property. In most cases serious or widespread damage cannot be committed by demonstrators without engendering serious public disorder; but on occasion the clarification might prove useful in enabling the police to impose conditions on a demonstration where the main risk is damage to property (for example, animal rights protesters demonstrating outside an isolated laboratory or mink farm).

5.9. The second test is serious disruption to the life of the community. Static demonstrations may be thought in general to be less disruptive than marches, but on occasion they can deliberately or inadvertently result in serious disruption, and where this occurs it is right that the police should have power to take preventative action. An example of deliberate disruption is provided by the Stop The City demonstrations in 1983–84. These were intended to bring the City of London, and on one occasion Leeds, to a halt by a variety of disruptive activities. In the City of London the Commissioner had powers under the City of London Police Act 1839 to issue directions to his constables to keep order and to prevent any obstruction of the thoroughfares. No equivalent powers exist outside London. In such circumstances the police might on occasion find it helpful to be able to impose conditions limiting the numbers of demonstrators or indicating that certain areas would be out of bounds to them. In the diplomatic quarter of London residents have occasionally complained about the disruption caused by demonstrations outside neighbouring embassies: if the disruption was shown to be serious the police could limit the numbers or duration of a demonstration, or move it further away.

5.10. The third test is the coercion of individuals. The obvious example is picketing: where pickets deliberately try to obstruct the passage of those going to work, as they did at Grunwick's and during the miners' dispute, the police should be able to limit their numbers, or move them further away from the path of the workers. But examples can be given of other demonstrations which have attempted by force to obstruct the free movement of people or vehicles: in such cases it is right to give the police preventative powers to ensure that this does not happen. And examples of coercion go wider than deliberate obstruction: in the South Wales picketing case (*Thomas v National Union of Mineworkers (South Wales Area)* [1986] Ch.20) the judge held that mass picketing which was not obstructive could nevertheless be intimidatory, especially outside someone's home.

5.11. It is not envisaged that the police will need formally to impose conditions at all frequently. But as with marches, their ability to do so will affect the legal framework within which negotiations with demonstration organisers are conducted. The police and the demonstrators will know that, in default of obtaining agreement about the ground rules, the police will be able to impose conditions if they apprehend that the demonstration will result in disorder, disruption or coercion. The organisers will have an incentive to negotiate: and the police will have to be reasonable, because if they impose conditions unreasonably, their decision will be open to challenge in the courts by judicial review."

It is important to stress that this power under s.14 may be utilised in advance of or at the time of the assembly. Unlike the CGSA, but like the other provisions of the Public Order Act 1986, there is no right of appeal against the conditions which the police may impose. At best there may be the possibility of judicial review, but the prospect of this does seem rather remote. If the police are late in imposing their conditions, it will be difficult to move quickly enough to persuade the court to intervene, and again the point has to be made that where police discretion is concerned the judges seem reluctant to second-guess the exercise of this power. Realistically, we are again left with ineffective safeguards against abuse, a situation which has aroused some concern. That concern was expressed as follows:

"11.5. The proposed tests for imposing conditions on static demonstrations are the same as for marches and processions: the reasonable apprehension of *serious disruption to the local community* or of *the coercion of individuals*. As we have argued above ... these tests are unacceptably wide and vague. They involve the application of subjective judgment by the police, often in a political context. The exercise of police power in this way will provoke resentment and hostility. A test of disruption to the local community will become a test of convenience and a protest is never convenient to those against whom it is directed. A test of coercion of individuals is undoubtedly aimed at picketing. Every employer whose premises are picketed will call for the police to impose conditions by saying that the picket is disruptive and/or coercive to those seeking to enter the premises. The police will be obliged to act accordingly.

11.6. How will the police act? They will have no power to ban the static demonstration, but they will have the power to do the next best thing: to impose conditions on the static demonstration in relation to *location, numbers* and *duration*. In many circumstances the restrictions will be tantamount to a ban, a danger which the White Paper foresees, but fails to avoid. Parents protesting outside the Town Hall about inadequate child-care facilities could be removed to the local park, to what the White Paper calls a 'less sensitive area'. Pickets could be reduced to one in number. A proposed assembly at Greenham Common of 10,000 people could be restricted to 50 people for half an hour. The White Paper even suggests that the police should limit the numbers of spectators at football matches. These proposals undermine the necessary level of tolerance of the right of protest required in a free society. What price inconvenience? Will fireworks for a royal wedding, the carnival in Notting Hill, a 24-hour vigil outside South Africa House, a CND protest at Molesworth all fail the test?" (P. Thornton, *We Protest* (1985), pp.59–60)

Although there are no safeguards, there is nevertheless one crucial limitation. This is to be found in the definition of public place. The power to impose conditions applies only to public assemblies, which is defined to mean assemblies of 20 or more people in a public place which is wholly or partly open to the air. However, if the police anticipate that 20 or more people will assemble in a public place (such as a park), they can issue instructions to the organisers that no more than six may assemble. Or if no conditions have been imposed and an assembly of 20 or more gather, the police can then insist that all but six people disperse. The power to issue instructions applies if 20 or more are anticipated, or if 20 or more attend. If as a result of these numbers the section is activated, then the police may impose conditions as to numbers which they deem necessary to prevent disorder, damage, disruption or intimidation. But what if less than 20 people assemble? Can the police issue conditions as to numbers, duration or location? The answer is not under s.14, but that they may in appropriate cases use common law powers which are probably as extensive as those conferred by the Public Order Act. This is a matter to which we return. There are many other powers for dealing with demonstrations or protests on private land. They include the Conspiracy and Protection of Property Act 1875, on which see below; and byelaws made under the Military Lands Act 1892, on which see *Francis v Cardle*, 1988 S.L.T. 578. Additional powers for dealing with public assemblies were introduced by the Criminal Justice and Public Order Act 1994. Under s.61 this empowers the police in certain defined circumstances to remove trespassers from land. More importantly, s.70 amended the Public Order Act 1986 by inserting new sections 14A to 14C. These new provisions enable local authorities on the request of the police to ban certain assemblies, and to enable the police to prevent people from travelling to them. We have already encountered s.14A in the account of *DPP v Jones* [1999] 2 A.C. 240. Sections 14A to 14C provide as follows:

Public Order Act 1986

"Prohibiting trespassory assemblies
    14A.—(1) If at any time the chief officer of police reasonably believes that an assembly is intended to be held in any district at a place on land to which the public has no right of access or only a limited right of access and that the assembly—
        (a) is likely to be held without the permission of the occupier of the land or to conduct itself in such a way as to exceed the limits of any permission of his or the limits of the public's right of access, and
        (b) may result—
            (i) in serious disruption to the life of the community, or
            (ii) where the land, or a building or monument on it, is of historical, architectural, archaeological or scientific importance, in significant damage to the land, building or monument,
he may apply to the council of the district for an order prohibiting for a specified period the holding of all trespassory assemblies in the district or a part of it, as specified.
    (2) On receiving such an application, a council may—
        . . .
        (b) in Scotland, make an order in the terms of the application.
        . . .
    (5) An order prohibiting the holding of trespassory assemblies operates to prohibit any assembly which—

    (a) is held on land to which the public has no right of access or only a limited right of access, and

    (b) takes place in the prohibited circumstances, that is to say, without the permission of the occupier of the land or so as to exceed the limits of any permission of his or the limits of the public's right of access.

(6) No order under this section shall prohibit the holding of assemblies for a period exceeding 4 days or in an area exceeding an area represented by a circle with a radius of 5 miles from a specified centre.

(7) An order made under this section may be revoked or varied by a subsequent order made in the same way, that is, in accordance with subsection (1) and (2) or subsection (4), as the case may be.

(8) Any order under this section shall, if not made in writing, be recorded in writing as soon as practicable after being made.

(9) In this section and sections 14B and 14C—

    'assembly' means an assembly of 20 or more persons;

    'land' means land in the open air;

    'limited', in relation to a right of access by the public to land, means that their use of it is restricted to use for a particular purpose (as in the case of a highway or road) or is subject to other restrictions;

    'occupier' means—

        (a) ...; or

        (b) in Scotland, the person lawfully entitled to natural possession of the land, and in subsections (1) and (4) includes the person reasonably believed by the authority applying for or making the order to be the occupier;

    'public' includes a section of the public; and

    'specified' means specified in an order under this section.

. . .

Offences in connection with trespassory assemblies and arrest therefor

14B.—(1) A person who organises an assembly the holding of which he knows is prohibited by an order under section 14A is guilty of an offence.

(2) A person who takes part in an assembly which he knows is prohibited by an order under section 14A is guilty of an offence.

(3)...

(4) A constable in uniform may arrest without a warrant anyone he reasonably suspects to be committing an offence under this section.

. . .

Stopping persons from proceeding to trespassory assemblies

14C.—(1) If a constable in uniform reasonably believes that a person is on his way to an assembly within the area to which an order under section 14A applies which the constable reasonably believes is likely to be an assembly which is prohibited by that order, he may, subject to subsection (2) below—

    (a) stop that person, and

    (b) direct him not to proceed in the direction of the assembly.

(2) The power conferred by subsection (1) may only be exercised within the area to which the order applies.

(3) A person who fails to comply with a direction under subsection (1) which he knows has been given to him is guilty of an offence.

(4) A constable in uniform may arrest without a warrant anyone he reasonably suspects to be committing an offence under this section. . . .

There are important differences between s.14 of the 1986 Act and s.14A. Section 14 (a power to impose conditions) applies to all assemblies in public, whereas s.14A (a power to ban an assembly) applies to places where the public have no right of access or only a limited right of access. One overlap between the two provisions however relates to assemblies held on the highway. This would be a public place for the purposes of s.14, but it would also be a place to which the public have only a limited right of access under s.14A. As a result such an assembly could be the subject of conditions imposed by the police under s.14, or it could be banned under s.14A. However as we have seen, in *DPP v Jones* [1999] 2 A.C. 240, the House of Lords cut down the scope of the power to ban assemblies on the highway using the powers in s.14A. In that case it was held that a peaceful assembly on the highway was not a trespassory assembly. This was because the use of the highway for peaceful purposes was a lawful use of the highway. However, much will depend on the circumstances of each case, and the facts of another case may lead a court to conclude that the form of protest used goes beyond the limited right to use the highway for the purposes of peaceful protest. An example might be where the protest causes an obstruction of the highway.

V. STATUTORY OFFENCES

In addition to the offences which may be committed under the provisions so far discussed, there is a range of other offences which may be committed by those who take part in assemblies of one form or another. Statutory restraints effectively address three quite different though overlapping concerns, though it is not suggested that there is any coherence to the patchwork of statutory regulation. It has grown over a large number of years to deal with specific matters, some of which are only incidentally related to public protest. Nevertheless, the first concern reflected in the legislation relates to the message being projected by the assembly with restraints on assemblies designed to demonstrate support for fascist political parties (Public Order Act 1936, s.1) and to incite racial hatred (Public Order Act 1986, ss.18 and 19). This is the **what** question. The second concern relates to the location of the assembly, with a number of provisions prohibiting some forms of trespass (Trespass (Scotland) Act 1865, s.3, and the Criminal Justice and Public Order Act 1994, s.68). However public assemblies which obstruct pedestrians are also unlawful. This is the **where** question. The third form of restraint relates to the purpose of the assembly (Civic Government (Scotland) Act 1982, s.53). Here the concern is with activity which is designed by intimidation to prevent people from doing what they are lawfully entitled to do (Trade Union and Labour Relations (Consolidation) Act 1992, s.241). This is the **why** question. It is to be noted in addition that there are some statutory provisions which make it an offence to disrupt public meetings. These include the Public Meeting Act 1908 whereby it is an offence to act in a disorderly manner at a lawful public meeting. Otherwise it is an illegal practice to act in a disorderly manner at an election meeting: Representation of the People Act 1983, s.97

(1) The nature of the assembly

The Public Order Act 1936

"Prohibition of uniforms in connection with political objects
    1.—(1) Subject as hereinafter provided, any person who in any public place or at any public meeting wears uniform signifying his association with any political organisation or with the promotion of any political object shall be guilty of an offence:
    Provided that, if the chief officer of police is satisfied that the wearing of any such uniform aforesaid on any ceremonial, anniversary, or other special occasion will not be likely to involve risk of public disorder, he may, with the consent of a Secretary of State, by order permit the wearing of such uniform on that occasion either absolutely or subject to such conditions as may be specified in the order...

    9.—(1)...
'Meeting' means a meeting held for the purpose of the discussion of matters of public

interest or for the purpose of the expression of views on such matters...

'Public meeting' includes any meeting which the public or any section thereof are permitted to attend, whether on payment or otherwise;

'Public place' includes any highway, or in Scotland any road within the meaning of the Roads (Scotland) Act 1984, and any other premises or place to which at the material time the public have or are permitted to have access, whether on payment or otherwise."

This section was introduced in response to the adoption of uniforms by a number of groups, but principally the Fascists, in the 1930s, their aim being, of course, to give themselves a paramilitary air, a feeling of strength and a more fear-inspiring presence. What was desired was to suppress this intimidating use of uniform without preventing such uses of uniform as that by the Boy Scouts. As J.R. Clynes put it on Second Reading (317 H.C. Debs. 1369):

"We have no objection to the continued use of that innocent regalia associated with so many groups in this country, a ribbon, a sash, or some distinctive piece of pageantry has usually been used without complaint or even notice, and has been accepted as a gesture to some treasured memory or to some historical or worthy purpose. Shirts, jackets and jerseys are in themselves unimportant. The real point is what they signify and what they are intended to denote. A garb answering to a uniform and worn in what really is a military march and in a military manner and spirit brings into our political activities alien elements making for conflict and disorder."

The solution was the provision of a dispensing power to the chief constable and a deliberate avoidance of any definition of "uniform," leaving it as a matter of fact for local judges. A few prosecutions occurred in the 1930s establishing *inter alia* that a uniform need not be a complete livery and that a Fascist belt-buckle and armband were sufficient to constitute an offence (*R. v Charnley* (1937) 81 S.J. 108; for other examples see E.H.R. Ivamy "The Right of Public Meeting" (1949) 2 C.L.P. 183. The use of uniforms is not part of current street politics, though the Act briefly found a new use against the IRA.

O'Moran v DPP; Whelan v DPP
[1975] 1 All E.R. 473

In one of these cases the accused was one of the bearers at the funeral of an IRA prisoner. He was wearing a black roll-neck pullover, dark glasses and black beret. In the other case the accused was arrested for wearing a black beret, one of a number distributed at a Sinn Fein rally in London. They were charged with, and convicted of, an offence against s.1(1) of the Public Order Act 1936. On appeal:

LORD WIDGERY C.J.: "The question arises whether in those circumstances the magistrate acted within the law in finding that the charges were proved. I go back to the section itself which creates the offence...

The section, as will be remembered, refers to a person in a public place wearing a uniform. 'Wearing,' in my judgment, implies some article of wearing apparel. I agree with the submission made in argument that one would not describe a badge pinned to the lapel as being a uniform worn for present purposes. In the present instance, however, the various items relied on, such as the beret, dark glasses, the pullovers and the other dark clothing, were clearly worn and therefore satisfy the first requirement of the section.

The next requirement is that that which was worn was a uniform, so one has to consider the meaning of that word. It seems to me that in deciding whether a person is wearing a uniform different considerations may apply according to whether he is alone or in company with others. If a man is seen walking down Whitehall wearing the uniform of a policeman or a soldier, it is unnecessary to prove that that is uniform of any sort because it is so universally recognised or known as being clothing worn by a member of the Metropolitan Police or the Army, as the case may be, that it is described as uniform on that account, and judges can take judicial notice of the fact that it is uniform in that sense.

If a man was seen walking down Whitehall wearing a black beret, that certainly would not be regarded as uniform unless evidence were called to show that that black beret, in conjunction with any other items appropriate to associate it, had been used and was recognised as the uniform of some body...

In this case of course the eight men in question were together. They were not seen in isolation. Where an article such as a beret is used in order to indicate that a group of men are together and in association, it seems to me that that article can be regarded as uniform without any proof that it has been previously used as such...

In this case of course the articles did go beyond the beret. They extended to the pullover, the dark glasses and the dark clothing, and I have no doubt at all in my own mind that those men wearing those clothes on that occasion were wearing uniform within the meaning of the Act.

Evidence has been called in this case from a police sergeant to the effect that the black beret was commonly used, or had been frequently used, by the members of the I.R.A., and I recognise that it is possible to prove that an article constitutes uniform by that means as well. But what I stress, first of all, is that it is not necessary to prove previous use of the article as uniform if it is clear from the activities of the accused on the day in question that they were adopting a similar style of dress in order to show their mutual association one with the other.

The next point, and perhaps the most difficult problem of all, is the requirement of the section that the uniform so worn shall signify the wearer's association with any political organisation. This can be done in my judgment in two ways. The first I have already referred to. It is open to the prosecution, if they have the evidence and wish to call it, to show that the particular article relied on as uniform has been used in the past as the uniform of a recognised association, and they can by that means, if the evidence is strong enough, and the court accepts it, prove that the black beret, or whatever it may be, is associated with a particular organisation. In my judgement it is not necessary for them to specify the particular organisation because in many instances the name of the organisation will be unknown or may have been recently changed. But if they can prove that the article in question has been associated with a political organisation capable of identification in some manner, then that would suffice for the purposes of the section.

Alternatively, in my judgement the significance of the uniform and its power to show the association of the wearer with a political organisation can be judged from the events to be seen on the occasion when the alleged uniform was worn. In other words it can be judged and proved without necessarily referring to the past history at all because in my judgment if a group of persons assemble together and wear a piece of uniform such as a black beret to indicate their association one with the other, and furthermore by their conduct indicate that that beret associates them with other activity of a political character, that is enough for the purposes of the section...

Turning finally to the questions which are submitted for the opinion of this court, the first one is:

'Was the dress worn capable of being a uniform and was the common denominator, the black beret, a uniform within the meaning of section 1(1) of the Public Order Act of 1936?' I have already given sufficient reasons for my conclusion that it undoubtedly was.

The second question is:

'Is it necessary under this subsection for the prosecution to prove exactly which political organisation is concerned?' The answer is no..."

Melford Stevenson and Watkins JJ. concurred.

These provisions of the 1936 Act remain in force, but they have not been widely used, and they are in any event largely overshadowed by the Terrorism Act 2000. Section 13 of the 2000 Act provides that it is an offence for a person in a public place to wear an item of clothing, "in such a way or in such circumstances as to arouse reasonable suspicion that he is a member or supporter of a proscribed organisation". It is also an offence to wear, carry or display an article in such a way or in such circumstances as to arouse a similar suspicion. Where there is reasonable grounds to suspect someone of committing an offence under s.13, a constable may arrest without a warrant. Conviction could lead to imprisonment of up to six months, a fine not exceeding level 5 on the standard scale, or both. See *Rankin v Procurator Fiscal, Ayr*, Appeal No. XJ343/03.

The Public Order Act 1986

"Acts intended or likely to stir up racial hatred

Use of words or behaviour or display of written material

18.—(1) A person who uses threatening, abusive or insulting words or behaviour, or displays any written material which is threatening, abusive or insulting, is guilty of an offence if—

(a) he intends thereby to stir up racial hatred, or

(b) having regard to all the circumstances racial hatred is likely to be stirred up thereby.

(2) An offence under this section may be committed in a public or a private place, except that no offence is committed where the words or behaviour are used, or the written material is displayed, by a person inside a dwelling and are not heard or seen except by other persons in that or another dwelling.

(3) A constable may arrest without warrant anyone he reasonably suspects is committing an offence under this section.

(4) In proceedings for an offence under this section it is a defence for the accused to prove that he was inside a dwelling and had no reason to believe that the words or behaviour used, or the written material displayed, would be heard or seen by a person outside that or any other dwelling.

(5) A person who is not shown to have intended to stir up racial hatred is not guilty of an offence under this section if he did not intend his words or behaviour, or the written material, to be, and was not aware that it might be, threatening, abusive or insulting.

(6) This section does not apply to words or behaviour used, or written material displayed, solely for the purpose of being included in a programme service.

Publishing or distributing written material

19—(1) A person who publishes or distributes written material which is threatening, abusive or insulting is guilty of an offence if—

(a) he intends thereby to stir up racial hatred, or

(b) having regard to all the circumstances racial hatred is likely to be stirred up thereby.

(2) In proceedings for an offence under this section it is a defence for an accused who is not shown to have intended to stir up racial hatred to prove that he was not aware of the content of the material and did not suspect, and had no reason to suspect, that it was threatening, abusive or insulting.

(3) References in this Part to the publication or distribution of written material are to its publication or distribution to the public or a section of the public."

These measuress—also directed at racists and fascists—have their origins in s.6 of the Race

Relations Act 1965 which made it an offence, with intent to stir up hatred against any section of the public on grounds of colour, race, or ethnic or national origin, to use in a public place or at a public meeting threatening, abusive or insulting words which are likely to stir up such hatred. As originally enacted, s.6 was, however, widely criticised. Lord Scarman referred to it as "an embarrassment to the police. Hedged about with restrictions (proof of intent, requirement of the Attorney-General's consent) it is useless to a policeman on the street." (Scarman, *The Red Lion Square Disorders of 15 June 1974* (Cmnd. 5919, 1974)) The measure was repealed in 1976 and a new provision substituted in its place: this became s.5A of the POA 1936. This provided that it was an offence in a public place or at a public meeting to use words which are threatening, abusive or insulting where hatred is likely to be stirred up against any racial group. But this too was criticised as inadequate (Home Office, *Review of the Public Order Act 1936 and Related Legislation* (Cmnd. 7891, 1981)), with the Government expressing the view in the White Paper that s.5A "should be re-cast to penalise conduct which is either likely to stir up racial hatred or which is intended to do so": Home Office, *Review of Public Order Law* (Cmnd. 9510, 1985). This proposed change, which has been incorporated in s.19 of the 1986 Act, was welcomed by the NCCL (now Liberty):

"N.C.C.L. welcomes the moves to strengthen the law against stirring up racial hatred. It is right to penalise conduct which is *intended* to stir up racial hatred even though it may not be possible to prove that it is likely to do so. This arises where those confronted with the conduct either agree with it or are so implacably opposed to it that there is no chance of their being influenced by it. But for the present inadequacy of the law, two of the best known failed prosecutions would probably have been successful. The first case concerned the delivery of inflammatory material, a pamphlet entitled 'Blacks not wanted here', to Sidney Bidwell MP. The Court of Appeal decided that distribution of a pamphlet to the home of a Member of Parliament was not publication to the public at large. The other case was the prosecution of John Kingsley Read, leader of the British Movement, who addressed his supporters, after an Asian youth was killed in Southall, with the words 'One down, a million to go.'"

(P. Thornton, *We Protest* (1985), p. 41)

(2) The Location of the Assembly

The Trespass (Scotland) Act 1865

"Interpretation
2. In this Act the following words shall have the meanings hereby assigned to them:

'Premises' shall mean and include any house, barn, stable, shed, loft, granary, out-house, garden, stackyard, court, close, or inclosed space...

Parties lodging in premises or encamping on land, without permission or on turnpike or public road, guilty of an offence
3.—(1) Every person who lodges in any premises, or occupies or encamps on any land, being private property, without the consent and permission of the owner or legal occupier of such premises or land, and every person who encamps or lights a fire on or near any private road or enclosed or cultivated land, or in or near any plantation, without the consent and permission of the owner or legal occupier of such road, land, or plantation, or on or near any turnpike road, statute labour road, or other highway, shall be guilty of an offence punishable as herein-after provided.
[(2) Subsection (1) above does not extend to anything done by a person in the exercise of the access rights created by the Land Reform (Scotland) Act 2003.]"

This Act does not apply to processions, or at least to the overwhelming majority of them which take place on public streets; it is restricted to private land or buildings, though of course much land and many buildings owned by public authorities are "private" in this sense. As it applies to assemblies the major restriction is that it refers to "lodging" and "encamping," which imply some degree of duration. Clearly "protest camps" such as Greenham Common or Faslane in the 1980s would fall within the Act. "Sit-ins" or occupations may do so also (see *Galt v Philp* [1984] I.R.L.R. 156, discussed later in this chapter). Whether a two-hour rally would do so seems much less likely. Where the Act *would* require the owner's permission the owner may be as arbitrary or politically-biased as he or she wishes. This may be acceptable if the owner is a private body, but wholly objectionable if the owner is a public body. Conceivably, though the matter has never been tested, general administrative law principles would prevent such a body from acting unreasonably (*Wheeler v Leicester City Council* [1985] A.C. 1054), while public bodies in particular would have to have regard to Convention rights.

In more recent years a number of fresh statutory initiatives have been taken to deal with trespass, in response to new forms of public protest.

Criminal Justice and Public Order Act 1994

"Offence of aggravated trespass.

68.—(1) A person commits the offence of aggravated trespass if he trespasses on land in the open air and, in relation to any lawful activity which persons are engaging in or are about to engage in on that or adjoining land in the open air, does there anything which is intended by him to have the effect—

(a) of intimidating those persons or any of them so as to deter them or any of them from engaging in that activity,

(b) of obstructing that activity, or

(c) of disrupting that activity. ...

(2) Activity on any occasion on the part of a person or persons on land is 'lawful' for the purposes of this section if he or they may engage in the activity on the land on that occasion without committing an offence or trespassing on the land.

(4) A constable in uniform who reasonably suspects that a person is committing an offence under this section may arrest him without a warrant.

(5) In this section 'land' does not include—

(a) the highways and roads excluded from the application of section 61 by paragraph

(b) of the definition of 'land' in subsection (9) of that section

...

Powers to remove persons committing or participating in aggravated trespass.

69.—(1) If the senior police officer present at the scene reasonably believes—

(a) that a person is committing, has committed or intends to commit the offence of aggravated trespass on land in the open air; or

(b) that two or more persons are trespassing on land in the open air and are present there with the common purpose of intimidating persons so as to deter them from engaging in a lawful activity or of obstructing or disrupting a lawful activity,

he may direct that person or (as the case may be) those persons (or any of them) to leave the land.

(2) A direction under subsection (1) above, if not communicated to the persons referred to in subsection (1) by the police officer giving the direction, may be communicated to them by any constable at the scene.

(3) If a person knowing that a direction under subsection (1) above has been given which applies to him—

(a) fails to leave the land as soon as practicable, or

(b) having left again enters the land as a trespasser within the period of three months

> beginning with the day on which the direction was given,
> he commits an offence ...

(4) In proceedings for an offence under subsection (3) it is a defence for the accused to show—

(a) that he was not trespassing on the land, or

(b) that he had a reasonable excuse for failing to leave the land as soon as practicable or, as the case may be, for again entering the land as a trespasser.

(5) A constable in uniform who reasonably suspects that a person is committing an offence under this section may arrest him without a warrant.

(6) In this section 'lawful activity' and 'land' have the same meaning as in section 68."

These provisions were considered in Scotland in *Procurator Fiscal, Dingwall v McAdam*, March 6, 2003, where five accused were charged under s.68 of the 1994 Act for trespassing on to a farm (Tullich farm) to disrupt the sowing of genetically modified oil seed rape. Two issues arose for consideration by Sheriff MacFadyen: Were the accused trespassing on land? If so, was the activity which persons were engaged on, namely the sowing of genetically modified seed, a lawful activity? So far as the first of these issues is concerned, the sheriff had "no doubt that all of the accused were trespassing at the time of their engaging in obstructive and disruptive behaviour". He continued:

"The evidence of the owner of the land, Mr. Grant, which I accepted was to the effect that he had not given consent to the presence of protesters, including the accused, thereon. He did however agree to leave matters to the police to regulate the conduct of parties in the field. The police, in the person of Temporary Assistant Chief Constable, Ramsay McGhee, indicated to the protesters present that they could enter into and remain on the field. However that was subject to the caveat that if they interfered with the tractor or other machinery then they would be arrested for breach of the peace. Protesters, including all of these accused entered the land thereafter. It is not clear from the evidence if any of the accused were aware of that statement by Mr. McGhee. In my view, there is no difficulty in finding that any consent, if that is what it was, which in fact did not come from the landowner, was conditional on the good behaviour of the accused. Once a person forms the intention of behaving disruptively or obstructively then, provided the activity about to be or being disrupted or obstructed is lawful, then he or she is trespassing on the land. The accused were on another's land. They were behaving disruptively and obstructively. They had no permission to behave in that way from anyone. In my view, in determining whether trespass has occurred, there is an inextricable link between the nature of the conduct of the accused and his or her presence on the land. It would be quite possible for a person A to obstruct, or disrupt lawful activity without entering into private land and indeed to intimidate person B so as to deter him from engaging in an activity without person A entering into private land. If that were the situation, for example by protesters standing on a public road shouting intimidatory threats at persons about to embark on a lawful activity within private property, then no contravention of section 68 would occur. That would be because the persons carrying out the intimidation were not trespassing at the time. If however, such conduct took place within the private property without permission to be present in order to disrupt, obstruct or intimidate, then trespass would be committed. I therefore reject the submissions made by all accused to the effect that the Crown had failed to prove trespass, on the assumption above stated."

So far as the second issue is concerned, it will be recalled that before the court can convict under s.68 it must be satisfied that any activity which the accused intends to disrupt or obstruct is lawful activity. Under the Environmental Protection Act 1990, s.111, it is provided that no person shall release any genetically modified organisms (GMOs) except in pursuance of a consent granted by the Secretary of State and in accordance with any limitations and conditions to which the consent is subject. In this case it was accepted that the sowing of the seeds was being done with proper authority and under the conditions set down by the Scottish Ministers. The accused were found guilty as libelled, and appealed unsuccessfully to the High Court: *McAdan v Urquhart*, 2004 S.L.T. 790.

The Civic Government (Scotland) Act 1982

"Obstruction by pedestrians

53 Any person who, being on foot in any public place—

(a) obstructs, along with another or others, the lawful passage of any other person and fails to desist on being required to do so by a constable in uniform, or

(b) wilfully obstructs the lawful passage of any other person shall be guilty of an offence ... ."

This is a potentially important power in the policing of public assemblies. Although the penalty on conviction is not high, the police are nevertheless entitled to arrest without a warrant, and they may do so to disperse a crowd or to thin out a crowd. The crucial question is what amounts to obstruction? The answer supplied by the following case would appear to be "not very much". This is an area, however, where the operation of the law may be affected by Art.11 of the ECHR and also by the dicta in *DPP v Jones* [1999] 2 A.C. 240. At the very least the ECHR may invite a more reasonable accommodation of competing interests in the use of the highway than was evident in the following case.

Aldred v Miller
1924 J.C. 117

This was a charge under the Glasgow (Police) Act 1866, s.149(47) of which made liable to a penalty "Every person who occasions any kind of obstruction, nuisance, or annoyance in any road, street, court, or common stair, or obstructs or incommodes, hinders, or prevents the free passage along or through the same, or prejudices or annoys in any manner whatsoever any other person using the same." It was alleged that Aldred caused an obstruction by standing in Hamilton Drive near Great Western Road, Glasgow, and lecturing in a loud voice, thereby causing a crowd of persons to assemble, with the result that the streets were wholly or to a large extent blocked up so as to obstruct, incommode, hinder, or prevent free passage along or through the streets. The accused was convicted by the magistrates, whereupon he brought a bill of suspension in which it was stated:

"3. The *locus* libelled in the said complaint adjoins the Botanic Gardens, Glasgow, and is a favourite spot for the holding of open-air meetings for political and other purposes. The complainer had been, prior to the date libelled in said complaint, in the habit of addressing meetings at said *locus* on Sunday afternoons, and was doing so on Sunday, 10th February 1924, the date libelled. His said meetings were widely advertised, and were well known to the police. Said meetings were largely attended, and it was the duty of the police to regulate the crowd of people who attended the complainer's said meeting, and to see that the said people did not impede the passage of pedestrains or vehicular traffic at said *locus*.

4. Evidence was led on said 28th March 1924 in support of said complaint as follows:— Sergeant Thomas Ross, a police-sergeant, stated that he was on duty in Hamilton Drive on said date, and saw the complainer commence his lecture at 3.30 p.m. at said *locus*, and about 4 p.m. there would be nearly 300 persons present; that these persons blocked the east pavement, but the west pavement was not blocked at any time; that several motors came along and had to slow down, but were not held up, as the crowd made way for them to pass; that, after some time, a motor was brought to a standstill till a passage was made; that the driver of this motor complained to the witness, who spoke to the present complainer and asked the latter to stop lecturing; that the present complainer offered the witness his

name and address, but said he was not going to give up his right to address a public meeting; and that there appeared to be no one in connexion with the meeting regulating the crowd. In cross-examination this witness stated (1) that he expected the complainer to keep the street clear, and (2) that he was not aware that it had been laid down in Glasgow that the police had to regulate the traffic. This witness was in general corroborated by Constable John Lyall. Mrs Eliza Gray, who was with her husband in the motor car said to have been brought to a standstill, stated that the said car had not been long held up, as the crowd made way for it. Mr Graeme Hunter stated that he was not personally obstructed, but that he saw the meeting in progress, and saw the said delay to the motor car.

5. For the defence the following evidence was led:—Mr William Forbes stated that he was chairman at the said meeting; that he was going round about the crowd during the meeting; that people were standing at the side of the pavement; that neither pavement was blocked; that there was sufficient room for motors to pass; that the complainer at his meetings asked the crowd to keep a passage clear for traffic; that at the meeting in question he carried out his said custom, and made the said request of the crowd present. Mr Charles Dorran stated that he was selling literature at the said meeting; that he saw two or three motors slow down, but none stop. Mr William C. Stark stated that he was not a member of any political organisation; that he was present at the meeting in question; that the number of persons was smaller than the number attending meetings at the same place under the auspices of the Scottish Economic League and the Reconstruction Society; that he saw one or two cars slow down as they approached the meeting, but that motors usually slowed down near that point to take the corner.'...

The complainer pleaded, *inter alia*:—'(1) The complaint condescended on being irrelevant and not containing averments sufficient in law to constitute the offence libelled under the section of the Act therein described, the conviction and sentence complained of should be suspended, and the respondent ordered to repay the fine to the complainer, with expenses as craved. (2) The complainer having, at the time and place libelled in said complaint, conducted himself in an orderly manner in the exercise of his lawful right of addressing the lieges on his political views, the conviction and sentence complained of should be suspended, and the respondent ordered to repay the said fine to the complainer, with expense as craved.' The case was heard before the High Court on 20th June 1924, when the complainer appeared in person and argued;—The evidence led for the prosecution pointed to an ordinary public meeting, which did not necessarily constitute an obstruction. It was held in a place where meetings were often held, and in such circumstances it was the duty of the police to do their best to keep the roadway clear, and this they did not do. There was no evidence that the complainer refused to cooperate in abating the obstruction. If there was any obstruction, it was of the most trifling character, and there was no evidence that it continued after the warning by the police. Accordingly, the conviction was not supported by evidence."

LORD JUSTICE-GENERAL (Clyde): "The complainer objected, and objects, to the relevancy of the complaint, but I do not think the objection is sound. The reasons adduced in argument in support of the objection appear to me to be vitiated by a fallacy which arises from the failure to distinguish between a private right and a public right. When a man exercises a private right, he is using that which is his own; and, because the right is his own, it is exclusive of the rights of others. But when a man exercises a public right he uses that which is not his own, but belongs to the community of which he is only a constituent unit. His participation in the benefits of the public right is not exclusive of, but must be so restricted as to be consistent with, the equal participation of the other constituent members of the public community to whom the right belongs. In short, the exercise of a public right is circumscribed on every hand by the duty (which arises out of the very nature of public rights) to respect the equal rights of the others to participate in them. Apart from questions regarding the special rights of frontagers, the right to use a public street, for any of the public purposes to which it is dedicated as such, is a public right, not a private one.

Accordingly, if anybody does what the section on which the complaint was founded prohibits—if, that is to say, anybody causes an obstruction in a public street or hinders other members of the public in exercising the public right of free passage upon it—he selfishly engrosses the public right to himself, and his action is justly condemned.

The complaint is not against holding a public meeting; the complaint is that the accused caused an obstruction on a public street by holding a public meeting there. An obstruction to the exercise by members of the public of the public uses for which the streets exist—passage in particular—can certainly be created in that way: and an obstruction so caused is not any the less objectionable because the author of it is a person who advertises, or otherwise convenes, a public meeting in order that it may stand on the street and listen to his speeches. As I have already indicated, there is no such thing as a private right in any individual to make use of any public street for holding public meetings. If the thing is done at all, it must be done with due regard to the equal participation of all the members of the public in the various uses for which public streets are kept open.

I do not attempt to define the uses to which a public street, as such, is legally devoted. I have assumed in what I have said that the use for public meeting is not wholly excluded from the catalogue of legal public uses. But, assuming that it is such a use (like the use of part of the surface of a street as a stance for vehicles plying for hire), it must be conducted under the many and serious restrictions which are imposed by the necessity of avoiding interferences with other public uses. If those restrictions are not observed—and it is not always easy to observe them—the Magistrates have the duty of enforcing them. The section under which the present complaint was brought provides one of the means of enforcement. It must be remembered, as Lord Dunedin pointed out in *McAra v Magistrates of Edinburgh*, 1913 S.C. 1059, that of all the public uses to which public streets are legally dedicated, that of free unrestricted passage is the most important.

It is impossible to say that there was no evidence in the case to support the conviction. There was clear evidence of obstruction. A large part of the street was blocked, and wheeled vehicles had to slow down in order to make a way through, or even to stop. It is no answer whatever, in the complainer's mouth, to say that the police ought to have come to his aid. The duty of the police is to vindicate public right, and not to facilitate abuse of the street by any individual for purposes of his own.

It seems to me that there is no ground of challenge of this conviction, and I propose that we should refuse the bill of suspension."

LORD SANDS: "I agree, I do not think that any question of the right to use a street as a place of public meeting arises in this case. There is no doubt that when meetings in such places are customary they are not interfered with. On the other hand, there is also no doubt that, if they cause an obstruction, they are an offence. The question whether an obstruction has been caused is one of fact; it is left to the local judge who tries the case. It may happen that he may take a view which another judge might not have taken. But we cannot interfere with his decision on a question of fact, whether or not we should have come to the same conclusion. But, on the facts stated in this particular case, I do not think there is any reason to doubt that the Judge was properly satisfied that there had been an obstruction. It may not have been a very grave or serious obstruction; but there was an obstruction, and he was entitled to convict."

Lord Cullen agreed.

(3) The Purpose of the Assembly

Trade Union and Labour Relations (Consolidation) Act 1992

Intimidation or annoyance by violence or otherwise

241. A person commits an offense who, with a view to compel any other person to abstain from doing or to do any act which such other person has a legal right to do or abstain from doing, wrongfully and without legal authority—

(a) Uses violence to or intimidates such other person or his wife or children, or injures his property; or,

(b) Persistently follows such other person about from place to place; or

(c) Hides any tools, clothes, or other property owned or used by such other person, or deprives him of or hinders him in the use thereof; or,

(d) Watches or besets the house or other place where such other person resides, or works, or carries on business, or happens to be, or the approach to such house or place; or,

(e) Follows such other person with two or more other persons in a disorderly manner in or through any street or road ...

(3) A constable may arrest without warrant anyone he reasonably suspects is committing an offence under this section."

This provision was first introduced as the Conspiracy and Protection of Property Act 1875, s.7 and thus has a long history, being resurrected from time to time. It has been applied mainly in the context of labour picketing, though there is no reason in principle why it could not be used to deal with consumer or other picketing if the ingredients of the offence are met. These are three in number: first, that the action is done with a view to compel; secondly, that it is so done wrongfully and without legal authority; and thirdly, that the conduct takes one of the forms listed in s.241(1). The main source of controversy caused by this section relates to s.241(1)(d) that is to say watching and besetting. This means that picketing *per se* will be criminal if it is done wrongfully and without legal authority. So far as labour picketing is concerned, lawful authority has in fact been provided since 1875. The present authority is now to be found in the Trade Union and Labour Relations (Consolidation) Act 1992, s.220. This provides:

"(1) It is lawful for a person in contemplation or furtherance of a trade dispute to attend—

(a) at or near his own place of work, or

(b) if he is an official of a trade union, at or near the place of work of a member of that union whom he is accompanying and whom he represents,

for the purpose only of peacefully obtaining or communicating information, or peacefully persuading any person to work or abstain from working.

(2) If a person works or normally works—

(a) otherwise than at any one place, or

(b) at a place the location of which is such that attendance there for a purpose mentioned in subsection (1) above is impracticable,

his place of work for the purposes of that subsection shall be any premises of his employer from which he works or from which his work is administered.

(3) In the case of a worker who is not in employment where—

(a) his last employment was terminated in connection with a trade dispute, or

(b) the termination of his employment was one of the circumstances giving rise to a trade dispute,

in relation to that dispute his former place of work shall be treated for the purposes of subsection (1) as being his place of work.

(4) A person who is an official of a trade union by virtue only of having been elected or

appointed to be a representative of some of the members of the union shall be regarded for the purposes of subsection (1) above as representing only those members; but otherwise an official of a trade union shall be regarded for those purposes as representing all its members."

But the question which arises is simply this: what is the status of picketing which is not labour picketing within the meaning of s.220 or is labour picketing outside the scope of the area of legality? Is the simple act of picketing (watching and besetting) wrongful? The issue is a controversial one, which has been considered on several occasions by the English courts. In *J. Lyons & Sons v Wilkins* [1896] 1 Ch. 811 and [1899] 1 Ch. 255 there was a strike by the Society of Fancy Leather Workers at the premises of J. Lyons & Sons. A picket of two men was mounted to persuade workers not to work for the employer until the dispute was resolved. No violence, threats or intimidation were used. In an action for an injunction by the employer—based on what was then s.7 of the 1875 Act—it was argued for the union that the picketing must be independently actionable at common law, civilly or criminally; otherwise s.7 could not apply. This argument was rejected, however, with the court holding first that the use of the word "wrongful" in s.7 was superfluous, being only an indication of the phraseology to be used by the pleader. In other words the items in what is now s.241(1)(a)–(e) were criminal; and secondly, it was argued that in any event watching and besetting is wrongful in the sense that it is an actionable tort (*i.e.* civil wrong), being a nuisance.

Some 10 years later, however, the matter was reconsidered by a differently-constituted Court of Appeal. In *Ward, Lock & Co v OPAS* (1906) 22 T.L.R. 327, a picket was set up with two aims. One was to induce men employed in printing works to join the union; and the second was to induce new members to join the strike which was being conducted. The aim of the strike was to force the employer to hire union-only labour. Again, there was no evidence of violence, threats or intimidation. This time, however, the court adopted a different construction. It was held that in order to constitute an offence, the acts listed in s.241(1) must at least give rise to liability in reparation, thereby rejecting the view that the word "wrongfully" is superfluous. So to secure a conviction, the prosecution must show that the picketing was at least civilly actionable. The court then went on to hold, again in contrast to the *Lyons* case, that picketing is not *per se* a nuisance and that the tortious quality of the picketing would depend on the facts. In the case in question it was held that the peaceful picketing was not wrongful in this sense. So there is a direct conflict in these two decisions of the Court of Appeal. Later cases tend to favour *Ward, Lock*, which was endorsed in *Fowler v Kibble* [1922] 1 Ch. 487 and, by Lord Denning, in *Hubbard v Pitt* [1975] I.C.R. 308. It was also followed by Scott J. in the following case, though it has to be said that the learned judge also breathed new fire into the section by increasing the range of potential plaintiffs or pursuers, if his decision is followed in Scotland.

Thomas v National Union of Mineworkers (South Wales Area)
[1986] Ch. 20

The plaintiffs included miners who were known to have returned to work during the strike of 1984–85. In doing so, they were met by large gatherings of pickets and demonstrators, sometimes as many as 200–300. The crowds were kept back from the roads in to the collieries to allow the working miners to pass. Abuse was hurled at the men including "you scabby bastards", "you'll get your heads kicked in", and similar phrases which counsel for the defendants reassuringly claimed were merely "a little rough language", not likely to upset "a tough, self-reliant, down-to-earth miner". The plaintiffs nevertheless sought injunctions to restrain this picketing of their own places of work, and also of other sites which included collieries, power stations and steelworks.

SCOTT J.: "The working miners are entitled to use the highway for the purpose of entering and leaving their respective places of work. In the exercise of that right they are at present having to suffer the presence and behaviour of the pickets and demonstrators. The law has long recognised that unreasonable interference with the rights of others is actionable in tort. The law of nuisance is a classic example and was classically described by Lindley M.R. in *J Lyons & Sons v Wilkins* [1899] Ch. 255 at p. 267. I have already cited the passage. It is, however, not every act of interference with the enjoyment by an individual of his property rights that will be actionable in nuisance. The law must strike a balance between conflicting rights and interests. The point is made in *Clark and Lindsell*, para. 23/01: 'A variety of different things may amount to a nuisance *in fact* but whether they are *actionable* as the *tort* of nuisance will depend upon a variety of considerations and a balance of conflicting interests.'

Nuisance is strictly concerned with, and may be regarded as confined to, activity which unduly interferes with the use or enjoyment of land or of easements. But there is no reason why the law should not protect on a similar basis the enjoyment of other rights. All citizens have the right to use the public highway. Suppose an individual were persistently to follow another in a public highway, making rude gestures or remarks in order to annoy or vex. If continuance of such conduct were threatened no one can doubt but that a civil court would, at the suit of the victim, restrain by an injunction the continuance of the conduct. The tort might be described as a species of private nuisance, namely unreasonable interference with the victim's rights to use the highway. But the label for the tort does not, in my view, matter.

In the present case, the working miners have the right to use the highway for the purpose of going to work. They are, in my judgment, entitled under the general law to exercise that right without unreasonable harassment by others. Unreasonable harassment of them in their exercise of that right would, in my judgment, be tortious.

A decision whether in this, or in any other similar case, the presence or conduct of pickets represents a tortious interference with the right of those who wish to go to work to do so without harassment must depend on the particular circumstances of the particular case. The balance to which I have earlier referred must be struck between the rights of those going to work and the rights of the pickets.

It was made clear in *Ward Lock & Co. Ltd. v Operative Printers' Assistants' Society* (1906) 22 T.L.R. 327 that picketing was not, *per se*, a common law nuisance. The Court of Appeal was in that case considering the question from the point of view of the owner of the premises being picketed. The picketing was peaceful and *per* Vaughan Williams L.J. (at 329), 'there was no evidence that the comfort of the plaintiffs or the ordinary enjoyment of the Botolph Printing Works was seriously interfered with by the watching and besetting.' He held in effect, that there was no common law nuisance being committed.

Similarly, in the present case, the working miners cannot complain of picketing *per se* or of demonstrations *per se*. They can only complain of picketing or demonstrations which unreasonably harass them in their entry into and egress from their place of work.

From the comments I have already made earlier in this judgment it will be apparent that I think it plain from the evidence before me that the picketing at the colliery gates is of a nature and is carried out in a manner that represents an unreasonable harassment of the working miners. A daily congregation on average of 50 to 70 men hurling abuse and in circumstances that require a police presence and require the working miners to be conveyed in vehicles do not in my view leave any real room for argument. The working miners have the right to go to work. Neither they nor any other working man should be required, in order to exercise that right, to tolerate the situation I have described. Accordingly in my judgement the colliery gates picketing is tortious at the suit of the plaintiff or plaintiffs who work at the collieries in question...

The form of the injunctions is important and difficult. The injunctions must state the nature of the picketing which is to be restrained. The plaintiffs' rights are rights, in my view, not to be unreasonably harassed on their way to or from work. But an injunction cast in that form would be useless. It would beg practically every question raised by this application. The injunction must deal with the two aspects of the picketing that, in my view, have justified the plaintiffs' application for relief, namely the intimidatory quality of the picketing and the abuse and threats which accompany the picketing.

I have already expressed the view that given the temper of the local communities and the strong feelings that have plainly been raised by the return to work of some of the members of the union, sheer weight of sufficient numbers on the picket lines would be sufficient by itself to be intimidatory. It is, in my judgment, tortious for the South Wales branch by its lodges to organise or participate in picketing on an intimidatory scale. So the injunction must, in my view, restrain the union from organising or participating in picketing by more than some specified number of persons. What should that number be? Counsel for the first to seventh defendants pointed out that two or three might by their words and gestures intimidate, whereas a dozen might, by the calmness and reasonableness of their behaviour, not be intimidatory at all. I agree with that. Any number chosen is necessarily arbitrary. I am, however, given some statutory guidance.

Section 3 of the Employment Act 1980, provided, by subs. (1) for the Secretary of State to 'issue Codes of Practice containing such practical guidance as he thinks fit for the purpose of promoting the improvement of industrial relations.' The section provides for any such code to be preceded by consultation with ACAS, and, by subs. (4), to be approved by resolution of both Houses of Parliament. Subsection (8) provides:

'A failure on the part of any person to observe any provision of a Code of Practice issued under this section shall not of itself render him liable to any proceedings; but in any proceedings before a court or industrial tribunal or the Central Arbitration Committee—(a) any such Code shall be admissible in evidence, and (b) any provision of the Code which appears to the court, tribunal or committee to be relevant to any question arising in the proceedings shall be taken into account in determining that question.'

A code of practice has been issued by the Secretary of State under s.3, and has been approved by both Houses of Parliament. It came into force on 17 December 1980 under the Employment Code of Practice (Picketing) Order 1980. Section E of the code is headed 'Limiting numbers of Pickets.' Paragraph 29 is in these terms:

'The main cause of violence and disorder on the picket line is excessive numbers. Wherever large number of people with strong feelings are involved there is a danger that the situation will get out of control and that those concerned will run the risk of arrest and prosecution.'

I need not read para. 30, but para. 31 is important:

'Large numbers on a picket line are also likely to give rise to fear and resentment amongst those seeking to cross that picket line, even where no criminal offence is committed. They exacerbate disputes and sour relations not only between management and employees but between the pickets and their fellow employees. Accordingly pickets and their organisers should ensure that in general the number of pickets does not exceed six at any entrance to a workplace. Frequently a smaller number would be appropriate.'

Paragraph 31 does not make it a criminal offence or tortious to have more than six persons on a picket line. Nor is less than six any guarantee of lawfulness. The paragraph simply provides a guide as to a sensible number for a picket line in order that the weight of numbers should not intimidate those who wish to go to work. I am directed by subs. (8) of s.3 of the 1980 Act to take this guidance into account.

I do so and propose, therefore, to restrain the South Wales branch by its lodges, from organising picketing or demonstrations at colliery-gates by more than six persons. I should make it clear that there is, in my judgment, no legitimate distinction to be drawn between so-called pickets who are stationed close to the gates of the colliery and the rest, so-called demonstrators, who stand nearby.

I now come to the matter of verbal abuse and threats. The legitimate purpose of picketing is peaceful persuasion or the peaceful communication or obtaining of information. Threats of violence and intimidatory language are inconsistent with peaceful persuasion. Some use of insulting language may perhaps be consistent with peaceful persuasion, but nevertheless if carried to extremes and persisted in over a long period it would become, in my view, tortious. There is obviously a risk in a case such as this that pickets may use strong language. It is part of the defendant's case that on the South Wales picket lines strong language is almost bound to be used. But in order that picketing should remain peaceful picketing it is, in my judgment, the duty of those who organise the picketing to do their best to see that threats of violence are not offered by the pickets and that use of strong language does not get out of hand. If the number of pickets is kept down to six or thereabouts the problems about verbal abuse and threats may well become unimportant.

The evidence of the officers of the Abernant lodge, to which I have already referred, was that, as a matter of practice, they always advised pickets not to make threats to working miners. This is a practice which, it seems to me, ought to be adopted by all the lodges, and it should, in my view, be the responsibility of the South Wales branch to take such steps as are practicable to ensure that its lodges do so.

Accordingly I propose to grant an injunction in respect of each of the five collieries I have mentioned, restraining the union and its servants, agents and officers, including the officers of the lodge of the colliery in question, in these terms: from inciting, procuring, assisting, encouraging or organising members of the union or others, to congregate or assemble at or near the entrance to the colliery (a) otherwise than for the purpose of peacefully obtaining or communicating information or peacefully persuading any person to work or abstain from working, and (b) otherwise than in numbers not exceeding six."

It was once thought that what is now s.241 of the 1992 Act was largely redundant. The provision was, however, revived in the 1980s. The decision in *Thomas* will clearly help that revival by extending its potential use. Scott J. comes close to saying that in certain circumstances a large attendance of pickets will *per se* give rise to liability in tort (reparation), is therefore wrongful, and therefore a violation of what is now s.241 of the 1992 Act. Parliament has also helped the revival of what is now s.241 of the 1992 Act. The government claimed in 1985:

"5.16. The section has been criticised as archaic; but the circumstances of the miners' dispute have shown how important it is to have an offence penalising conduct of this kind. The provision was used mainly in dealing with intimidation away from the picket line, in particular the besetting of people's homes. It was also used for offences on the picket line; but its effectiveness is hampered by the fact that it is not an arrestable offence, and by the maximum penalty being three months' imprisonment or a fine of £100. To enable the police to deal more effectively with criminal intimidation, the Government proposes that section 7 of the 1875 Act should be made an arrestable offence; and that the maximum penalty should be increased to six months' imprisonment or a fine of £2000."

(Home Office, *Review of Public Order Law* (Cmnd. 9510, 1985)).

Parliament responded in the Public Order Act 1986, which amended the section to provide that suspects could be arrested without a warrant and by increasing the penalty. That amendment has been carried forward to the 1992 consolidation. As suggested, the revival was due mainly to the miners' strike, with 643 charges in England and Wales (P.Wallington, "Policing the Miners' Strike" (1985) 14 I.L.J. 145), though with much fewer arrests and prosecutions in Scotland (only four) (*ibid.*). Nevertheless, the revival of what is now s.241 of the 1992 Act was led by the Scottish prosecution authorities. It was used during a strike of tax inspectors in *Elsey v Smith* [1983] I.R.L.R. 292. Moreover, in 1984 a new use was found for the section in a very controversial incident which led to judicial criticism of the conduct of the police.

Galt v Philp
[1984] I.R.L.R. 156

A dispute existed between medical laboratory scientific officers and medical consultants employed by Fife Health Board which was responsible for running hospital services in Fife, including the Victoria Hospital in Kirkcaldy. In the course of the dispute one of the medical laboratory scientific officers was suspended. In response, a sit-in in the laboratory was organised. The MLSOs refused entry to other hospital staff. Police officers, including the chief constable, were called and negotiations continued for some hours. Eventually, the police made a forced entry and arrested those inside, charging them under the Trespass (Scotland) Act 1865. For reasons which are not clear from the report, these charges were not proceeded with. A new charge was, however, brought under s.7(4) of the 1875 Act (now s.241 (1)(d) of the 1992 Act). One of the questions on an appeal from the sheriff (who refused to convict) to the High Court of Justiciary (which reversed the sheriff) was whether the section applied to sit-ins of this kind. The court held that it did.

LORD CAMERON: "The evidence, so far as led, indicates that certain named persons were prevented from obtaining entry to the laboratory to which in performance of their contract of employment, they were entitled and required to have access at any time. Such action, if not warranted by legal authority, as this was not, would constitute a legal wrong and attract civil liability either by way of interdict or, if loss could be demonstrated, by action of damages. As to that I do not think there can be room for doubt: if that view of the circumstances disclosed be correct, as I think it is, then, should it amount to 'besetting' as is libelled in this complaint, the conduct of the respondents would be in contravention of s.7 of the 1875 Act. The evidence so well and carefully narrated by the sheriff, (and it was not said that his narrative was in any way inaccurate), appears to me to demonstrate that access to the hospital laboratories was effectively blocked by the action of the respondents and therefore this could most properly be characterised as 'besetting.' The words of the statute used to describe the offence are: 'Watches or besets the house or other place ... Where such other persons ... works or carries on business ... or the approach to such house or place.' The use of this language and of the alternative 'watches or besets' in my opinion is indicative that the offence is not limited to the maintenance of an external watch, nor does recourse to the *Oxford Dictionary* suggest that the word 'beset' is to receive so limited an interpretation. It would in any event be manifestly absurd, having regard to the evil which the statute seeks to suppress, so to construe the statute that the external watcher should be held guilty of an offence, but scatheless if he were to force his way in and occupy the house or place concerned, for precisely the same purpose and objective. In view of the fact that articles indicative of an occupation to be undertaken by a number of people and prolonged at least overnight, were recovered on the premises by the police, it appears to me that, in the absence of evidence pointing to the contrary, the sheriff would be entitled, if he accepted that evidence, to draw the inference of guilt in respect of all respondents remaining in the complaint."

VI. COMMON LAW OFFENCES

We turn now to consider the common law offences that may be deployed to deal with various forms of public protest. In view of the restraints already identified, it is perhaps difficult to contemplate the need for any more. However the common law operated before the statutory framework was established and to some extent was dealing with different concerns from those which exist today. As a result some of the common law provisions are largely redundant, although formally still in force. This may be true particularly of sedition, the redundancy of which is probably reinforced by Convention rights and by a desire generally not to use the law in an overtly partisan way to quash dissent and opposition. However, it is by no means true that all common law powers are redundant, and it remains the case that breach of peace is a potent force for dealing with forms of political protest (relating to form, purpose and location) which are thought by the political authorities to be unacceptable. In this section we address three common law offences: sedition, mobbing and rioting and breach of the peace. Although it is true that the material relating to the first of these (sedition) belongs to a bygone age, the reader may perhaps forgive the self-indulgence of the authors. We present the material of a famous political trial to show how law can be used to crush those who would question existing forms of political authority. It is for the reader to reflect on whether there are any contemporary parallels.

As we saw in the previous section, the statutory restraints on freedom of assembly fall into three categories. They address the message of the protestors (racism), the place of their protest (trespass and obstruction in a public place), and the purpose of their protest (intimidation). The common law rules also address three (related) concerns. First there is a concern with the message, with the law of sedition being addressed to forms of protest designed to challenge the authority of government. Secondly, there is concern about the method or purpose of the assembly, with the law on mobbing and rioting designed to deal with protest by intimidation, a form of law which may yet find a use against anti-globalisation protestors. Thirdly, there is a concern about the consequences of the action, with breach of the peace addressing concerns that people may be alarmed or provoked by the protestors. However, as we will see, the elasticity of breach of the peace is such that it effectively gives the police powers which can be used depending on the message, location and conduct of the demonstrators, all of which may be relevant in assessing consequences. As such it gives the police wide powers to disperse an assembly, impose conditions on the conduct of an assembly and prevent an assembly from gathering. Breach of the peace does not of course just apply to political protest, and has a wide range of other purposes, but it has been a useful tool for dealing with different generations of protestors concerned over the years with many different causes.

(1) Sedition

A number of Scottish radicals were prosecuted for sedition between 1793 and 1820, including Thomas Muir: see Berresford Ellis and Mac a' Ghobhainn, *The Scottish Insurrection of 1820* (1989). The punishments included capital punishment and transportation. Prosecutions for sedition occurred again during the Chartist campaigns in 1848. Indeed *H M Advocate v Cumming, Grant* (1848) J. Shaw 17 is the last reported prosecutions for sedition in Scotland. The nature of the offence was defined as follows by the Lord Justice Clerk (Hope):

"The crime of sedition consists in wilfully, unlawfully, mischievously, and in violation of the party's allegiance, and in breach of the peace, and to the public danger, uttering language calculated to produce popular disaffection, disloyalty, resistance to lawful authority, or, in more aggravated cases, violence and insurrection. The party must be made out not to be exercising his right of free discussion for legitimate objects, but to be purposely, mischievously, without regard to his allegiance, and to the public danger, scattering burning firebrands, calculated to stimulate and excite such effects as I have mentioned— reckless of all consequences. As Mr Clark said in Palmer's case, 'He, whose speeches or writings have that tendency, is seditious, unless, in either case, the speaker or writer has a legal object in view.'

Now, in this case, I apprehend that the law does not look for or require, beside this illegal spirit, this general dole or legal malice, the additional and special element of the intention, or *purpose*, with reference to the precise *effects* which the words are *calculated* to produce. If such purpose is also proved, the case will be one of more deliberate, more dangerous, and more aggravated sedition. But very often the precise *effects* which the words are calculated to produce, are not at all what the party *intends*, and still more, not what he has brought his own mind up to, just because they point to immediate violence. The party guilty of sedition in uttering such language is often only playing the part of a field orator, hallooed on by shouts from an excited and turbulent crowd—often of the worst characters: He has to sustain his part as a leader; has to outbid in exaggeration and violence the man who spoke before him; has got so familiarized to violent and dangerous language that he does not think how they may affect others; has to secure a liberty for bold language, and often to secure pay for such achievements: He is aiming, perhaps, at being chosen as a delegate; thinks, perhaps, that by *intimidation* he may concuss and frighten others into an exaggerated notion of the numbers and power of those who venture to utter such language: He is reckless as to what he says; thinks and cares little about it, if it answers the object at the time; but all the while he may not desire or intend the precise effects which his words are calculated to produce—it may be of instant violence. Yet of sedition he is clearly guilty, if these reckless words are calculated to produce such results."

There have been prosecutions for sedition in the twentieth century, most famously of John MacLean, the great Scottish socialist. However, these prosecutions were conducted under the Defence of the Realm Regulations during the First World War, so strictly they were prosecutions under statute rather than common law. Yet they were prosecutions for sedition nevertheless. Regulation 42 of the Defence of the Realm Regulations provided that it was an offence for any person to cause mutiny, sedition or disaffection among any of His Majesty's forces or among the civilian population. MacLean was prosecuted on at least seven occasions, on account of his anti-war speeches during the First World War. The first of the prosecutions was in 1915 as a result of a speech in Bath Street, Glasgow. On at least three of these occasions, he was prosecuted for sedition, and he was jailed at least five times. The story of the most famous trial is told in the following extract.

Nan Milton
John MacLean

"As he took his seat in the dock Maclean 'looked paler than usual', according to a newspaper report. And well might he be pale—not because in front of him loomed the dread prospect of prison, but because he knew that this was the greatest hour of his life. This was his great opportunity. Tomorrow millions of people all over the country would read a detailed report of the trial. Could he make the most of this great chance to transmit his message far and wide? Could he use the dock, revealed by history as the greatest propaganda platform of all time, to stir the people into consciousness that the real criminal was not the man in the dock but the hideous and bloody system represented by the man with the judge's wig?

Maclean had decided to conduct his own defence this time and, unhampered by legal caution, raise a threatening fist in the face of authority. His very first words showed quite clearly that he was not there to defend, but to attack.

'Are you guilty or not guilty?' asked the Lord Justice-General.

'I refuse to plead!'

This reply having been taken as a plea of not guilty, His Lordship went on to remind him that he had the right to object to any member of the jury. Maclean replied like lightening:

'I object to the whole of them!'

That sentence will stand as the most powerful protest of his time against contemporary 'justice'. He objected to all the trappings of a legal system which had for its primary purpose the protection of that very system of private property-ownership which was poisoning the roots of society and driving millions of men to violent death.

The indictment, which took fully ten minutes to read, accused Maclean of addressing meetings in Glasgow, Lanarkshire and Fife between the dates of 20 January and 4 April 1918, and there making statements likely to prejudice recruiting and cause mutiny and sedition among the people. There were eleven charges in all, but in essence his main crime was his call to the workers to follow the example of their Russian comrades, go forward, and strike the first blow for revolution on 1 May.

There were 28 witnesses for the prosecution, 15 policemen, 8 special constables, 2 shorthand writers employed by the police, one newspaper reporter, one mining inspector, and one slater.

Evidence regarding meetings held in Glasgow was given by three special constables. One asserted that he heard Maclean call himself a 'Socialist Democrat'. He advocated the downing of tools and said that the socialists should break through all laws and establish their own rules and regulations; he stated that the Clyde district had helped to win the Russian revolution, and that the revolutionary spirit on the Clyde was at present ten times as strong as it was two years ago. At another meeting Maclean said that the workers should take control of the City Chambers and retain hostages, take control of the Post Office and the banks, compel the farmers to produce food and if they did not, burn the farms; he stated that this movement would have the support of French-Canadians and the workers in New York and that when it became known what the Clyde was doing, other districts would follow suit; he stated that the present House of Commons should be superseded by a Soviet and that he did not care whether it met in the usual place or in Buckingham Palace; and he advised the workers in Beardmore's munition works to 'ca' canny' and restrict their output of munitions.

The other two witness corroborated.

Maclean cross-examined them at considerable length, and it transpired that one had not taken a verbatim report of the speeches, but only a 'good note'. Another had taken no notes at all of the first meeting and only a 'few notes' of the second, while the third 'might have taken a word or two on a slip of paper' but went home and wrote his notes from memory. Yet, as Maclean pointed out, all three gave exactly the same evidence!

Several policemen testified that during a meeting at Shettleston Football Park, Maclean had said that the workers in Russia had caused a revolution and he wished to impress them that the workers here should be prepared for the same.

In the course of evidence one witness pointed out that he did not consider it wise to take notes at the meeting because of the attitude of the crowd. He went instead to the Police Office and made notes there. The other witnesses also chose the better part of valour and took 'nothing but mental notes'.

Further evidence was led regarding meetings in Fife. Maclean was accused of saying that the men of Fife should come out against the Manpower Bill as the government was simply waiting to drag more young men away to be slaughtered. An interesting point was raised by Maclean during the cross-examination of the Police Superintendent of Fife. This witness had notes supplied to him by a press reporter who was present at Maclean's meetings in the interests of the police and the press. The Superintendent admitted that he had paid little attention to what Maclean had said. Maclean protested against small portions being taken out of his speeches here and there:

> 'The consequences of any man's speech are always based upon what goes before. The main parts of my speech, in which my themes are developed, are omitted. I want to expose the trickery of the British government and their police and their lawyers.'

One witness declared in the course of his evidence that Maclean had stated that he was quite prepared to run any risk if he thought he could bring about a social revolution in Glasgow.

> **Maclean** Do you think it is a correct report of what I said at Hartshill to say that I talked about bringing about a social revolution in Glasgow?
> **Witness** You did.
> **Maclean** It seems to me a very bad slip, because a social revolution cannot be brought about in a city. It is either a slip on your part or a slip on my part.
> **Witness** It is not a slip on my part. You spoke about seizing the Municipal Buildings in Glasgow, and it seems to me that you meant that the revolution would have its

beginning in Glasgow.

Maclean There is a difference between a social revolution in Glasgow, and *beginning* a social revolution in Glasgow.'

A mining inspector in the service of the Fife Coal Co gave evidence regarding a meeting at Crossgates in Fife. He considered the speech a dangerous one and made a report of it to his employers. He took no notes.

In the course of cross-examination, Maclean asked if he was not aware that in the past the land had been violently seized from the people, and did he not object to the present owners holding the land when they had got it violently?

'**Witness** I might object to that, but it is a question of how you take it from them. For instance, in answer to a question as to how these things should be got, the question being. "Could we get these things by peaceful action?" you said, "I am here to develop a revolution."

Maclean Do you infer that revolution means violence?

Witness You could not have put any other construction on your words after you said that revolution here was to be on the same lines as in Russia. I understand that the Russian Revolution was a violent revolution.

Maclean It is the most peaceful revolution the world has ever seen, and it is the biggest. Don't you know that this war is the most bloody that has ever taken place, and that revolution and bloodshed do not go together?

Witness No.

Maclean You said it was a dangerous speech. Dangerous to whom? To the Fife Coal Co?

Witness I was a servant of the Fife Coal Company, and I was an official, and it was my duty to report to them.'

A slater also gave evidence regarding this meeting. He took no notes, but remembered a few things said. The speech was a bit strong on revolution and was likely to unsettle the audience.

Cross-examined by Maclean, he said that the speech was likely to carry people away, especially the younger people, and was therefore unsettling.

'**Maclean** A canny place, Fife?

Witness Yes.

Maclean I should say the last place in which a revolution would take place would be in Fife?

Witness It will take some working up for you.

Maclean Don't you think the war also has unsettled the people, that it has had an unsettling influence?'

Evidence was given by a Glasgow Special Constable regarding a meeting which he attended in Glasgow on 13 March, and at which Maclean was alleged to have said that when peace was proclaimed the Army and Navy would rally to the Red Flag, and to have urged the audience to make the May Day demonstration a one-day strike for peace, to empty the workshops on that day, so that the first day of May might be the first blow for the revolution.

'**Maclean** You were instructed not to take notes openly?

Witness Yes.

Maclean Why?

Witness I don't know. No reason was given.

Maclean You were not afraid to take notes openly?

> **Witness** I was not afraid, but I did not think it was judicious.
> **Maclean** You thought you would go there as a spy, and not let people know you were there?'

Maclean called no witnesses, and in reply to the Lord Justice-General said he did not wish to go into the witness-box. He would reserve what he had to say until later.

The Lord Advocate addressed the jury. There was nothing in the law of the country as at present framed to prevent people getting up and talking about socialism, however inappropriate it might be, but there came a time when such discussion of social questions became seditious. They could not afford that—indeed the truth was that society could not afford that at any time. The prisoner had by a long and persistent series of violent, inflammatory, and revolutionary addresses done the best he could to create sedition and disaffection among the civilian population. He did not pretend to see into Maclean's heart, to understand the motives that had tempted him, but just because they could never know that, they must judge Maclean by what he did. It was their duty to protect themselves from men like Maclean unless they wanted to be overtaken by the same catastrophe as befell Russia.

In an impassioned speech lasting seventy-five minutes, Maclean addressed the jury. Fifty-five years of world turmoil and upheaval have passed since then and another even more bloody world war has confirmed his darkest forebodings, but the years have added to the depth of his words. Today the 'Holy War' of 1914–18 has been stripped of its glamour. Maclean's statements and prophecies, regarded by many in 1918 as the ravings of an unbalanced fanatic, have been revealed in their historical truth.

There is not a socialist today who can fail to be moved by his efforts to unmask the real meaning of the war. There is not a socialist worthy of the name who can fail to be stirred by the revolutionary passion with which he, not as the accused but as the accuser, poured out fierce denunciations of his 'judges' and the State they represented.

The Lord Advocate had said he could not fathom his motives, he began. If they were not clean and genuine, would he have made his statements in the presence of shorthand reporters? He had simply been proceeding along the lines upon which he had proceeded for many years. For the full period of his active life he had been a teacher of economics to the working classes, and his contention had always been that capitalism was rotten to its foundations and must give place to a new society. He was out for the benefit of society, not for any individual human being, but he realized that justice and freedom could only be obtained when placed on a sound economic basis. He knew that in the reconstruction of society the class interests of those who were on top would resist the change and that the only factor that could make for a clean sweep was the working class.

In his economics classes he had pointed out for years that because of the inability of the workers to purchase the wealth they created, it was necessary to create markets abroad, and in order to have these markets it was necessary to have empire. The capitalist development of Germany since the Franco-Prussian War had forced on her also the need for empire and a clash must come between the two countries.

In one lecture which he had delivered regularly before the war, he had taken as his theme "Thou shalt not steal! Thou shalt not kill!", and had pointed out that as a result of the robbery going on in all civilized countries they had to keep armies, but these armies must inevitably clash. In another called "Edward the Peacemaker" he had pointed out that Edward VII's alliance with France and Russia was for the purpose of encircling Germany in preparation for the coming struggle.

He considered capitalism the most infamous, bloody and evil system that mankind had ever witnessed. He wished no harm to any human being, but he, as one man, was going to exercise his freedom of speech. "No human being on the face of the earth", he challenged, "no government, is going to take from me my right to speak, my right to protest against wrong, my right to do everything that is for the benefit of mankind. I AM NOT HERE, THEN, AS THE ACCUSED: I AM HERE AS THE ACCUSER OF CAPITALISM

DRIPPING WITH BLOOD FROM HEAD TO FOOT."

He poured ridicule on the self-righteous indignation displayed by the warmongers when the Germans killed women and children in this country, when not a voice was raised to protest against the deaths of women and children through terrible housing and factory conditions. The government was responsible for these deaths, just as they were responsible for the deaths of the Russian women who had been left without adequate means of life. He took this opportunity to advertise the plight of these women, in the hope that public opinion would press the government to see that they got paid at least as well as the dependants of British soldiers.

The Edinburgh press had been preparing public opinion for this trial by slanders against the Bolsheviks. The truth was that since the Bolsheviks came into power there had been fewer deaths in Russia than for the same period under any Czar for 300 years. The White Guards had been responsible for more deaths than the Soviets. Under the Bolsheviks the co-operative movement had grown more rapidly than ever before, the universities, theatres, picture houses, music halls, schools, were open day and night for the purpose of training the workers to manage the affairs of the country and to organize production. The Bolsheviks wanted peace throughout the world and had entered into negotiations with the Germans at Brest Litovsk. A pause had been made in the negotiations to allow Great Britain and the Allies to have time to take part, but they had refused.

The Bolsheviks were accused of being in the pay of the Germans, but the truth was that while the peace meeting was being held Trotsky had been playing a very bold game. He had spread millions of leaflets amongst the German soldiers in the trenches urging them to stop fighting and to overthrow the Kaiser and the capitalist class of Germany.

Britain had been doing that same thing since the very beginning of the war. The learned gentleman for the prosecution had said that revolution inside Germany was good, but revolution inside Britain was bad. He could square it if he could. Maclean could not. The conditions of Germany, economically, were the same conditions as Britain; there was only a slight difference between the political super-structure of the two countries. And the workers were not concerned with the political super-structure, but with the economic foundation.

More serious strikes than in this country had been taking place in Germany. Soldiers and sailors had mutinied and been shot down by the German government. Revolution in Germany was near, but it would be a very bad thing for the workers of the world if a revolution were unsuccessful in Germany and no similar effort made here. The workers' enemy was the same in all countries, and if the German workers overthrew their autocratic government, it was our duty to see that they were not enslaved at the dictates of the capitalists of other parts of the world.

He was convinced that the problems of capitalism would not be solved by the war. With improved methods of speeding up, improved machinery and technique, the workers would be able to produce five times the amount of wealth that they did before the war and the problem of the disposal of surplus goods would be greater than ever. The new rush for empire had already begun. America had got hold of one or two islands in the West Indies, and had seized Dutch Guiana. She had prevented Japan getting control of North China and when Japan had been incited by the Allies to land at Vladivostok in order to crush the Bolsheviks, America began to back up the Bolsheviks because she was afraid that if Japan got half Siberian Russia it would give her strategic control of Siberia. Britain had taken the German colonies, and was taking control of Mesopotamia and Palestine. The secret treaties made public by the Bolsheviks had shown that all the nations had been making plans so that when Germany was crushed they would get this territory or that territory. "THEY WERE ALL OUT FOR EMPIRE."

"All the property destroyed during the war will be replaced. In the next five years there is going to be a great world trade depression and the respective Governments, to stave off trouble, must turn more and more into the markets of the world to get rid of their produce, and in fifteen years' time from the close of this war—I have pointed this out at all my meetings—we are into the next war if Capitalism lasts; we cannot escape it."

He had taken up constitutional action at this time because of the abnormal circumstances and because precedent had been given by the British government. If it was right for the government to throw aside law and order and adopt methods that mankind had never seen before, then it was equally right for members of the working class. They must take abnormal lines of action, and he urged them to follow the example of their comrades in Russia.

"The Lord Advocate pointed out here that I was probably a more dangerous enemy that you have got to face than the Germans. THE WORKING CLASS WHEN THEY RISE FOR THEIR OWN ARE MORE DANGEROUS TO CAPITALISTS THAN EVEN THE GERMAN ENEMIES AT YOUR GATES. I am glad that you have made this statement at this, the most historic trial that has ever been held in Scotland, when the working-class and the capitalist class meet face to face."

He had nothing to retract, nothing to be ashamed of. He had acted clean and square for his principles:

"I am a Socialist, and have been fighting and will fight for an absolute reconstruction of society for the benefit of all. I am proud of my conduct. I have squared my conscience with my intellect, and if everyone had done so this war would not have taken place...
      No matter what your accusations against me may be; no matter what reservations you keep at the back of your head, my appeal is to the working class. I appeal exclusively to them because they, and they only, can bring about the time when the whole world will be one brotherhood, on a sound economic foundation. That, and that alone, can be the means of bringing about a reorganization of society. That can only be obtained when the people of the world get the world and retain the world."

The jury felt no need to retire. They intimated through their foreman a verdict of guilty on all charges. The Lord Justice-General asked Maclean if he had anything more to say, but no, he thought he had said enough for one day.
      The Lord Justice-General pronounced sentence. He said the accused was obviously a highly-educated and intelligent man, who thoroughly realized the seriousness of the offences he had committed. The sentence of the court was that he be sent to penal servitude for a period of five years.
      Maclean appeared somewhat taken aback by the severity of the sentence, but on being led to the cells he turned to his comrades in the gallery and cried: 'Keep it going, boys: keep it going!' "

MacLean was released without serving his full sentence and the penalties imposed on him in the other cases were much less severe. However, he was subsequently re-arrested and jailed at least twice more before his death in 1923. The war time powers under which MacLean was prosecuted and convicted were revoked in 1921. For an account of the use of these powers see K.D. Ewing and C.A. Gearty, *The Struggle for Civil Liberties* (1999), Ch.2, and R.S. Shiels, "The Criminal Trials of John MacLean" (2001) J.R. 1. There appears not to have been a prosecution for sedition in Scotland since 1922 when Guy Aldred was given a 12-month prison sentence for the publication of a newspaper entitled the *Red Commune*. Three other people were also convicted in the same case, which gave rise to unusual proceedings subsequently when the Crown petitioned the High Court to retain the exhibits used at the trial. It was held that the convicted socialists were not entitled to their costs arising from these latter proceeedings, even though the petition was abandoned: *H M Advocate v Aldred*, 1922 J.C. 13. It has been said in the House of Lords: "Whatever may have been the position before the Human Rights Act 1998 came into operation, it is difficult to think of any rational argument justifying the criminalisation of conduct of citizens who wish to argue for a different form of government": *R. (Rusbridger) v Attorney General* [2004] 1 A.C. 309.

(2) Mobbing and Rioting

The second common law offence of relevance is mobbing and rioting. It is possible to distinguish between "mobbing" as the behaviour or a group viewed as such, and "rioting" which is the behaviour of an individual (Alison, *Principles and Practice of the Criminal Law of Scotland* (1833, vol.ii)), and one modern writer has suggested that there still lingers in Scots law a separate offence of "rioting" (I.M. Fleming, "Rioting Revived", 1984 S.L.T. (News) 36). However, this view finds no general acceptance and the word "mobbing" and the full phrase are generally used interchangeably. There is no single authoritative definition of the offence, but a mid-nineteenth century one, which was recently approved by the High Court in *Hancock v H.M. Advocate*, 1981 S.C.C.R. 32, is to be found in the following case.

John Robertson et al.
(1842) 1 Broun 152

The accused were charged with mobbing and rioting committed with intent to prevent a presbytery from performing its duty. The charge arose from the presentation of an unpopular person as minister of a parish and the intention of the appropriate presbytery to proceed to his induction. A crowd assembled and broke up the deliberations. The trial was very much concerned with conflicting evidence, but the Lord Justice-Clerk delivered an extensive charge to the jury on the law of mobbing and rioting.

> LORD JUSTICE-CLERK (Hope): "I have to state to you, in point of law, that an illegal mob is any assemblage of people, acting together for a common and illegal purpose, effecting, or attempting to effect their purpose, either by violence or by demonstration of force or numbers, or by any species of intimidation, impediment, or obstruction, calculated to effect their object, and to impede, obstruct, and defeat others employed in discharge of duty...
>
> It is not necessary that the purpose or object of the mob should have been previously concerted, or that they should be brought together and congregated with the view previously formed of effecting the object subsequently attempted. It is enough, that after they have been so assembled and brought together, finding their numbers, and ascertaining a common feeling, they then act in concert, and take up and resolve to effect a common purpose. There must, however, be a common purpose and object, for which they are combined and acting in concert, after they are congregated, and operating as such throughout the acts alleged to be acts of mobbing. That purpose or object must be unlawful. But then, such an unlawful purpose or object may consist in attempts to effect by violence and numbers, and not by legal measures, an object, the pursuit of which, in a lawful and peaceable manner, is lawful and laudable...
>
> A charge of Mobbing and Rioting against a few of a great crowd, implies that only certain acts, and a certain share of what was going on, can be proved as to any individuals. But, when a jury is once satisfied of the existence of a common object, that parties were combined to effect, and were acting in union in order to effect, that common object, these acts of a whole body, done in furtherance, and to effect that object, and naturally arising out of the exertions of a mob to effect that common object, become necessarily, in the eye of the law, the acts of all who take part in the proceedings of the mob, who act along with them in any degree, and who aid, countenance, and support, even by presence, that object for which the mob are acting in concert. Presence in a mob, if such presence is in order to countenance what is done, will be a fact sufficient to establish a party's guilt of all that is done by the mob...

The *continued* presence of a party in a mob after its character has shewn itself, without any aid to those against whom the mob is directing its acts, may (I only say *may*) in common cases become very speedily accession to the mob; for such continued presence, especially by a person looked up to by the mob, and known to take a deep and keen interest in the object and feelings of the mob, though he may not declare his approbation of the acts of violence, gives them boldness, additional confidence, and, perhaps, a mistaken notion that they are encouraged by him; but, at all events, does give them, sanction and encouragement...

Any person present ought either to aid in quelling the disturbance, or at least instantly withdraw. If he continues in the heart of the scene without opposing himself, and, much more, if before or after, he is found in friendly communication with the mob, or even simply remains among them, then his continued presence constitutes accession, though the degree of his guilt may be greatly less than that of others. And this is justly so held, for he truly adds by his presence to the numbers of the mob, and to the apparent concert and union among them...

On the same general grounds, the law holds a party, who is shewn to be one of a mob, answerable for all the acts of Mobbing and Rioting committed by that mob, in prosecution and furtherance of their common object...

You cannot separate all the acts of a mob into distinct crimes, so that no one shall be guilty of mobbing, except in respect of his own individual acts of accession. He may be the ringleader, and yet not an act of violence, after the mob begins, may be proved against him individually...

I have reserved for my last remark, in point of law, a point of the utmost importance in this case, and by the application of which, I presume, your verdict will be much influenced. You will observe, that the duty which the Presbytery had to discharge, was one in which all the parishioners had an interest,—at which all were entitled to be present, none more so than those opposed to the settlement. They were all entitled to be present at and watch the proceedings. All parishioners and communicants are invited, as well as entitled in law, to be present. Hence the fact of being present, of being one of the crowd, nay, of remaining in the crowd, in itself, in this case, implies *by itself* no accession at all, in point of law, to the common and illegal purpose of the mob ... if a person, entitled as a parishioner and communicant to be present throughout the whole scene, was perfectly quiet and peaceable during that scene,—never having been desired, even along with others, to leave the church,—his presence alone does not in this case make him responsible for the acts of the mob, or prove his secret concert with them. The fact that he was a ringleader or instigator, or otherwise a part of the mob, must be separately proved to your satisfaction, so as to shew that presence, apparently legal and peaceable, was yet in truth presence, in order to back, aid, countenance, support, and encourage the mob...

In the present case, the burden of giving this character to continued presence in the mob, is much more onerous than when a party has no legal interest or right in remaining to witness the whole proceedings which are going on."

The accused were acquitted.

From this it transpires that the effect of a finding of mobbing and rioting is that each individual is presumptively responsible for all the acts of the mob committed in furtherance of its common end. As to the elements of the offence, there are three: (1) a number of people, (2) intimidation, and (3) a common illegal purpose. The number of people required is not fixed. In *Sloan v Macmillan*, 1922 J.C. 1 the court did not have to consider counsel's submission that five would be too few, but observed that it depends on "what these people do, the violence they show, the threats they use." As to intimidation, normally violence accompanies mobbing but this need not be so, although the threat of it probably is. Thus in *Sloan* the compliance of strike-breakers during a strike was secured by a parade of strength, but no recourse to violence.

Most legal problems with mobbing are associated with the common illegal purpose. This illegal purpose is to be understood in the sense of immediate purpose. A crowd may lawfully assemble to urge a lawful end, but if its purpose is, or becomes, to effect that end by violence or intimidation then that is its immediate purpose and the crowd becomes a mob (*McDonald et al. v Mackay* (1842) 1 Broun 435). In modern times mobbing has been used mainly to deal with gang fights and street violence: *Hancock v H M Advocate*, 1981 S.C.C.R. 32. It was, however, deployed during the miners' strike in 1972, though its unsuccessful use in that case (combined with its unsuccessful use in *Sloan*, above) suggests that it is of rather limited relevance for dealing with protesting workers in the modern era. However it might be premature to write it off altogether as a restraint on protests.

P. Wallington
"The Case of the Longannet Miners and the Criminal Liability of Pickets"
(1972) 1 I.L.J. 219

"What happened at Longannet
Longannet Power Station, on the shores of the Forth, was not immediately affected by the critical shortage of coal that developed during the miners' strike, and was able to continue generating when other power stations had to close—allegedly using oil delivered in foreign ships. The N.U.M. arranged a mass picket of the power station to persuade staff to stay away from work. On February 14, some 2,000 pickets were present at Longannet, with 400 police on duty; in the course of the day, thirteen of the pickets were arrested and charged with mobbing and rioting. It is difficult to be certain what happened, but clearly there was some disorder, since three policemen suffered injuries; two newspapers reported that there were 'clashes' when pickets 'surged forward and tried to break through the police cordon'. At the subsequent trial at Dunfermline Sheriff Court, evidence was given by the police of pushing and shouting and provocative conduct, and individual cases of assaults; presumably the jury disbelieved this evidence, at least in respect of the accused, as they were all acquitted. It is perhaps sufficient to conclude that a large number of pickets confronted a large force of police; that the main object of the pickets was to induce workers at the power station not to work; and that some breaches of the peace and assaults occurred.

The remainder of the story may be summarised briefly: the thirteen pickets were detained in custody for three days, and then released on bail until their trial on June 6. One of the accused was discharged for lack of evidence at the conclusion of the prosecution's case, and the remainder were acquitted of all charges by the jury on June 16, the ninth day of the trial. Eleven of the acquittals were by majority verdict, but the jury's verdict was reached in twenty minutes....

Mobbing and rioting is not an offence that is unknown to the industrial scene in Scotland; the leading case in 1921 [*Sloan v Macmillan*, 1922 J.C. 1.] involved seventeen striking miners in Ayrshire who intimidated 'voluntary workers' into abandoning work at a pumphouse at Houldsworth Colliery (thus causing the workings to be flooded), by representing that they were supported by a gang of hundreds of desperate men. Nor did the offence fall into obsolescence after 1921; in a number of instances immediately prior to Longannet it had been charged in cases of gang fights and mob hooliganism. The essence of the offence can be seen from the colourful language of the indictment in the Longannet case, which libelled that the accused

> 'formed part of a riotous mob of evil disposed persons which, acting with a common purpose, did conduct itself in a violent, riotous and tumultuous manner to the great terror and alarm of the lieges, and in breach of the peace did curse, swear and utter threats of violence'...

In other words the offence is intimidation by force of numbers or threats of violence. Willing presence in such a mob is sufficient to establish guilt, and participation in specific acts of intimidation or violence need not be proved. The purposes of the mob may be lawful or even laudable, as in a case where a group of Highlanders gathered on the jetty at Stromeferry and forcibly prevented the unloading of ships on the Sabbath, a purpose which the court took to be sufficiently praiseworthy to justify lenience in sentencing, but not to affect guilt [*Alexander Gollan*, 1883 5 Coup. 31.] In the Longannet case, the jury presumably took the view that the picket as a whole was not a 'riotous mob' but this serious charge is available where a mass picket does attempt to intimidate or threaten those passing through its ranks, or becomes violent."

In one of the omitted footnotes, Wallington records that the sheriff, directing the jury, said that "it was not necessary that there should be any actual violence: mere presence of sufficient numbers of persons preventing access to the power station would be sufficient to constitute the offence".

(3) Breach of the Peace

One reason why mobbing and rioting is an unusual charge "is the availability of the catch-all offence of breach of the peace, which is sufficient to cover any minor disorder, and is the charge regularly used where pickets are prosecuted. Breach of the peace in Scots law is an offence of wide and ill-defined scope..." (Wallington, *ibid.*). In *Wilson v Brown*, 1982 S.C.C.R. 49, it was said by Lord Dunpark:

"It is well settled that a test which may be applied in charges of breach of the peace is whether the proved conduct may reasonably be expected to cause any person to be alarmed, upset or annoyed or to provoke a disturbance of the peace. Positive evidence of actual harm, upset, annoyance or disturbance created by reprisal is not a prerequisite of conviction."

It was said to be enough that the conduct of the accused "was likely to lead to a disturbance if allowed to continue" (p. 52). It is important to note, then, that conduct likely to cause (though not necessarily causing) alarm, upset or annoyance could constitute the offence. Indeed, in *Sinclair v Annan*, 1980 S.L.T. (Notes) 55, the High Court approved a conviction for conduct which caused embarrassment. And remarkably in 1986 when a Caithness newspaper published an article on fire risks in churches under the title "Hellish worry of church fires", the local procurator fiscal wrote to the editor stating that in his view such a title amounted to a breach of the peace and that similar conduct in the future would lead to prosecution. Whether or not such a prosecution would have succeeded is to some extent immaterial. The affair highlights the extent to which breach of the peace had ceased to be a justifiable restriction on public disorder, having become concerned with enforcing standards of good taste and decorum. As the result of the incorporation of Convention rights, however, the law of breach of the peace has been tightened up, or if the reader prefers, better explained.

(a) The nature of the offence

Smith v Donnelly
2001 S.L.T. 1007

The appellant was charged by the respondent on a complaint in the following terms:

"On 15 February 1999 on the A814, North Gate entrance to H.M. Naval Base, Clyde, District of Argyll and Bute, you Pamela Smith did conduct yourself in a disorderly manner, lie down on the roadway, disrupt the free flow of traffic, refuse to desist when requested to do so and commit a breach of the peace."

In proceedings before the magistrate, the appellant indicated that she wished to raise a devolution issue. After hearing parties, the magistrate decided that no devolution issue had been shown to exist but granted the appellant leave to appeal. The appellant argued that "the charge of breach of the peace is an all-encompassing charge which has been used to cover any type of behaviour deemed inappropriate in various circumstances and is therefore too vague to be aligned with the European Convention for the Protection of Human Rights". It was claimed in particular that the charge of breach of the peace violated art.7 of the Convention.

LORD COULSFIELD: "[6] Counsel for the appellant informed us that this was the first case in which the question whether the charge of breach of the peace was compatible with Article 7 of the Convention had been directly raised. He submitted that Article 7 was directed to the provision of effective safeguards against arbitrary prosecution and pointed out that no derogation from the Article was permissible under Article 15. A person must be able to know from the text of the law and the court's interpretation of it what acts are criminal. The way in which breach of the peace had come to be defined by the court in Scotland was so wide as to violate Article 7 in that a citizen could not know with reasonable certainty what actions would breach criminal law. ...

[11] Both counsel for the appellant and the advocate depute took the case of *Raffaelli v Heatly*, 1949 J.C. 101, as the starting point for consideration of the modern law of breach of the peace. There is, however, in our view, something to be gained by looking first at the earlier decision in *Ferguson v Carnochan*, 1889 16 R. (J.) 93 which was a prosecution of a man who had used loud language and oaths and imprecations in a street in a Burgh early on a Sunday morning. In the course of his opinion Lord Justice Clerk Macdonald said:

'Breach of the peace consists in such acts as will reasonably produce alarm in the minds of the lieges, not necessarily alarm in the sense of personal fear, but alarm lest if what is going on is allowed to continue it will lead to the breaking up of the social peace. The words 'to the alarm of the lieges' in a charge of breach of the peace mean that what is alleged was likely to alarm ordinary people and if continued might cause serious disturbance to the community.'

[12] Lord Maclaren said (at p. 94):

'The clearest case of breach of the peace consists in engaging in hostilities either in the street or in a private ground, for I agree that it makes no difference whether the offence be committed in a public or private place, provided the lieges be alarmed. But breach of the peace is not confined to acts of this description. Breach of the peace means breach of public order and decorum. All accompanied always by the qualification that it is to the alarm and annoyance of the public. Articulate noises and cries not calculated to be offensive to anyone have been held not to amount to breach of the peace. On the other hand, where the brawling is of such a kind as to be offensive and alarming, it is not necessary that those who hear it should be alarmed for themselves. It is enough that offensive language should be uttered in a noising and clamorous manner so as to cause reasonable apprehension in the minds of those who hear it that some mischief may result to the public peace.'

[13] In *Raffaelli v Heatly, supra* the accused was charged with conducting himself in a disorderly manner by peering in at a lighted window of a dwellinghouse at about 11.50 p.m. and putting residents in the street in a state of fear and alarm and committing a breach of the peace. It was established that the appellant had walked down the street and stared through a chink in curtains into a room in a dwellinghouse in which there was a light and he had done so on two occasions. On his behalf, it was submitted that that was all that had been proved, since there was no evidence that any person had been alarmed or upset or that anything took place that might reasonably be expected to alarm anyone. Having set out the argument for the appellant, Lord Justice Clerk Thomson said (at p. 104):

'It is usual to charge this offence as a breach of the peace, because it is a species of disorderly conduct; where something is done in breach of public order or decorum which might reasonably be expected to lead to the lieges being alarmed or upset or tempted to make reprisals at their own hand, the circumstances are such as to amount to breach of the peace.'

[14] The Lord Justice Clerk went on to comment on the evidence and on the evidence of one female witness in particular and to hold that that evidence, taken in conjunction with the whole circumstances, warranted the conclusion that there was a breach of the peace. Lord Mackay gave an opinion to the same effect, but employed the phrase 'to the alarm and annoyance of the public'.

[15] *Young v Heatly*, 1959 J.C. 66 was a case in which a teacher was charged with making improper remarks of a sexual nature to pupils in the school. The point considered was whether it was necessary that there should be any evidence of alarm either to the pupils or to anyone else. Lord Justice General Clyde, at p. 70, said that breach of the peace was an offence the limits of which had never been sharply defined because it was so largely a question of circumstances and degree in each case and went on to refer to various authorities including *Ferguson v Carnochan* and *Raffaelli v Heatly, supra*. Having done so, he said:

'It follows therefore that it is not essential for the constitution of this crime that witnesses should be produced who speak to being alarmed or annoyed. At the same time, however, I consider that a very special case requires to be made out by the prosecution if a conviction for breach of the peace is to follow in the absence of such evidence of alarm or annoyance. For then the nature of the conduct giving rise to the offence must be so flagrant as to entitle the court to draw the necessary inference from the conduct itself.'

[16] There have, of course, been a very large number of decisions of the High Court on appeals from courts of summary jurisdiction dealing with charges of breach of the peace in many different situations. Counsel appearing in this case, however, agreed that the essential nature of the charge as it is understood in Scotland is to be found in these authorities, if it is to be found anywhere. The first question for us, therefore, is whether these authorities can be seen as providing a definition of a crime which is of sufficient certainty to meet the requirements of the Convention. In our opinion, they do provide such a definition. The requirement which is found in English law, that there should be harm or a threat of harm to person or property, is not part of the law of Scotland. In the absence of that requirement, we agree that there must be sufficient clarity as to what it is that is required in Scots law to constitute the crime.

[17] The crime of breach of the peace can be committed in a wide variety of circumstances, and, in many cases, it is a relatively minor crime. It has therefore been said, more than once, that a comprehensive definition which would cover all possible circumstances is neither possible nor desirable. Equally, in our view, it is neither possible nor desirable to derive a comprehensive definition from a close analysis of the facts of individual cases in which it has been held that a breach of the peace had been committed. If, however, we take as our starting point what was said by L.J.C. Macdonald in *Ferguson v Carnochan, supra* it is, in our view, clear that what is required to constitute the crime is conduct severe enough to cause alarm to ordinary people and threaten serious disturbance to the community. The opinions in *Ferguson* are reported differently in 19 R. (J.) and in 2 White 278 but so far as the Lord Justice Clerk is concerned the differences not appear to us to be material for the present purpose. It is true that, as has been pointed out, Lord Maclaren referred to breach of public order and decorum and to annoyance to the public: and that these phrases were taken up in the opinions in *Raffaelli v Heatly*. On that basis it has been suggested that since a very wide range of types of conduct could be seen as an annoyance to someone or in some

circumstances, there is no sufficient certainty as to what the essential element is. We have come to the conclusion that that criticism is not made out. If words like annoyance or upset or breach of decorum are taken in isolation they might, it is true, be taken as applicable to something minor in the way of conduct which could be considered inappropriate or irritating. If, however, the opinions in the leading cases are read as a whole, we think it sufficiently clear that something substantially greater than mere irritation is involved. Lord Maclaren himself does not speak of 'annoyance' in isolation but of 'alarm and annoyance' and says that a reasonable apprehension of disturbance to the public peace is necessary to the proof of the crime. What is required, therefore, it seems to us, is conduct which does present as genuinely alarming and disturbing, in its context, to any reasonable person.

[18] That interpretation is supported by the fact that, as Lord Justice General Clyde pointed out, if there is no evidence of actual alarm, the conduct must be 'flagrant' if it is to justify a conviction. 'Flagrant' is a strong word and the use of that word points to a standard of conduct which would be alarming or seriously disturbing to any reasonable person in the particular circumstances. The point can be further reinforced by reference to some older authorities. In *Buist v Linton*, 1865 5 Irv. 210, a complaint that an accused did 'annoy and interrupt' two persons and 'did use opprobrious epithets towards them whereby they were annoyed and disturbed' was held irrelevant. In *Banks v McLennan* (1876) 3 Couper 359 a complaint of disorderly conduct 'by using insulting and abusive language of an individual' including calling the individual a thief was held irrelevant, the court observing that a conviction would be an interference with the liberty of the subject which it could not sanction. *Kinnaird v Higson*, 2001 G.W.D. 16–592 is a modern instance in which the court held that the mere fact that bad language has been used does not justify a conviction for breach of the peace. We therefore conclude that the definition of the crime found in the principal authorities does meet the requirements of the Convention.

[19] The appellant argued, however, that subsequent decisions have either widened the definition of the crime or shown that the definition is so meaningless as to be capable of infinite extension, or, indeed, both. In considering this argument, we are not in a position to review any earlier decisions of this court. At one stage, it was suggested that it might be appropriate to convene a larger court to review some of the decisions but we do not think that it is necessary to take that step. While there are cases in which a breach of the peace has been held established on grounds which might charitably be described as tenuous, none of the later decisions, as we read them, has attempted to redefine or modify in any way the central statements of the nature of the crime found in *Ferguson*, and the other cases cited. Given the nature of the charge, and the need to apply it in a wide variety of circumstances, it is inevitable that there will be cases which are at or near the borderline and decisions will have to be taken upon those cases as they arise. That is, however, not an uncommon situation in dealing with criminal law which is not statutory, and, provided that the central statements of the nature of the crime are kept in mind we do not see any need for a comprehensive re-examination of the authorities which have ensued since *Young v Heatly*. As we have said, we would not favour any attempt to derive a definition or redefinition of breach of the peace from close analysis of the facts of particular marginal decisions.

[20] Having said that, however, it may be of some assistance to comment on some recurrent themes. As we have observed, there are both old and recent authorities which support what might be called a robust approach to cases involving the use of bad language. Secondly, there have been repeated instances in which refusal to co-operate with police or other officials has led to a charge of breach of the peace: but such a refusal, even if forcefully or even truculently stated, is not likely to be sufficient in itself to justify a conviction. Thirdly, there have been cases in which actions done or words spoken in private have been held to amount to breach of the peace, or conduct likely to provoke such a breach, more because of some perceived unpleasant or disgusting character than because of any real risk of disturbance. In such cases, it is perhaps particularly necessary to bear in mind what the essential character of the crime is. Fourthly, there will be cases in which the court will require to bear in mind the importance of freedom of expression, an issue which

now involves reference to Article 10 of the Convention. However, no argument was addressed to us in regard to Article 10, and we think it better not to attempt to discuss it in this case. We would add that it seems to us that, notwithstanding the decision in *Butcher v Jessop*, 1989 S.L.T. 593, that a charge of breach of the peace in statutory form is sufficient to meet the requirements of notice it will normally be proper, now that regard must be had to the Convention, to specify the conduct said to form the breach of the peace in a charge, as indeed is common practice already.

[21] One further point may be worth making. In the argument before the magistrate, the appellant, as an experienced protester, made the point that she had sometimes been subject to police action and sometimes not in respect of very similar conduct. That may have been so, but police officers do have a certain discretion to act or not act in difficult circumstances and their action or inaction cannot be taken to reflect on the central question of the definition of breach of the peace.

[22] In the whole circumstances, we are satisfied the appellant's argument is not well-founded and we shall refuse this appeal."

Although the law has thus been tightened up, it nevertheless continues to confer a wide power on the police to restrict the exercise of the right to freedom of assembly. It should perhaps be noted that challenges to breach of the peace convictions by demonstrators alleging a breach of arts 10 and 11 have also failed: *Jones v Carnegie*, 2004 S.L.T. 609. For further analysis, see P. Ferguson, 'Breach of the Peace and the European Convention on Human Rights' (2001) 5 Edin. L.R. 145. In the following pages we consider how these wide powers enable the police to impose conditions on the conduct of a meeting or assembly; how they enable the police to disperse an assembly; and whether they enable the police to prevent an assembly from taking place at all. But before considering these matters, two preliminary points must be made. First, some of the authorities are drawn from English law and from Ireland. In most of the cases, the accused have been convicted under the Police Act 1996, s.89 (or its predecessors). This provides that it is an offence to obstruct a police officer in the execution of his duty the Scottish equivalent being s.41(1) of the Police (Scotland) Act 1967. For present purposes, failure to comply with an instruction from a police officer is not an offence under the English statute (and its predecessors) unless the instruction was given by a police officer who apprehended a breach of the peace. So an apprehended breach of the peace is necessary for a successful prosecution under s.89. The English cases which follow relate to the question whether the police officer had reasonable grounds to apprehend a breach of the peace. For that reason they are of interest in Scotland, though in English law a breach of the peace means an actual or apprehended threat to a person or property: *R. v Howell* [1981] 3 All E.R. 383.

The second point to be made relates to the scope of these powers and in particular whether the powers of the police apply to private as well as public meetings. It has been held by the English courts in a celebrated case that the police have the power to enter private property without a warrant to prevent a breach of the peace. This is so even though the breach of the peace is apprehended at a political meeting which the organisers have asked the police not to attend or to leave once in attendance: *Thomas v Sawkins* [1935] 2 K.B. 249. This common law power of entry is expressly acknowledged by statute: Police and Criminal Evidence Act 1984, s.17(6) but this applies in England and Wales only. It was claimed in the aftermath of the *Thomas* decision that the police in Scotland had a similar power to attend a political meeting:

"I am advised that under the existing [Scots] law the police are entitled to enter and remain in a hall during a meeting, if they are requested by the promoters to do so; also, if they have reason to believe that a breach of the law is being committed; or further, if they have reasonable grounds for apprehending that a breach of the law is about to be committed." (Sir G. Collins, Secretary of State for Scotland, 312 H.C. Debs. 1807.)

Some support for this view may be found in the judgment of Lord McLaren in *Ferguson v Carnochan*, 1889 16 R. (J.) 93 which is discussed in the *Pamela Smith* case, above. But, although this confirms that a breach of the peace may take place in private, it is not authority for the view that the police may enter private premises and remain there against the wishes of the organisers of the meeting. There is, however, recent authority for the view that the police may enter private premises to investigate a disturbance (*Moffat v McFadyen*, 1999 G.W.D. 22–1038), though it is unclear whether this would authorise entry only where a disturbance was apprehended, as in *Thomas v Sawkins*, above.

(b) The Power to Disperse

One consequence of the discretion conferred on the police by breach of the peace is the power to disperse an assembly in order to prevent a breach of the peace from taking place. Very often the power of dispersal presents a choice as to which assembly to disperse, for often one gathering may attract a hostile audience intent on preventing an assembly from being held. Clearly the police would be empowered to disperse the hecklers or the counter-demonstrators in order to maintain the peace. An important question, however, is whether they may also disperse those who are being heckled. Is there a heckler's veto in Scots law? The classic decision in *Beatty v Gillbanks* (1882) 9 Q.B.D. 308 suggests that there is no such veto in English law. Beatty was arrested after having assembled with more than 100 other people with a view to participating through Weston-super-Mare in a Salvation Army parade. In the past Salvation Army processions had attracted disorder from a rival organisation, the Skeleton Army. On this occasion, the magistrates had issued an order directing all persons to abstain from assembling to the disturbance of the public peace. The instruction was defied and Beatty was arrested. In the course of his judgment, Field J. said:

"Now, without doubt, as a general rule it must be taken that every person intends what are the natural and necessary consequences of his own acts, and if in the present case it had been their intention, or if it had been the natural and necessary consequence of their acts, to produce the disturbance of the peace which occurred, then the appellants would have been responsible for it, and the magistrates would have been right in binding them over to keep the peace. But the evidence as set forth in the case shows that, so far from that being the case, the acts and conduct of the appellants caused nothing of the kind, but, on the contrary, that the disturbance that did take place was caused entirely by the unlawful and unjustifiable interference of the Skeleton Army, a body of persons opposed to the religious views of the appellants and the Salvation Army, and that but for the opposition and molestation offered to the Salvationists by these other persons, no disturbance of any kind would have taken place. The appellants were guilty of no offence in their passing through the streets, and why should any other person interfere with or molest them? What right had they to do so? If they were doing anything unlawful it was for the magistrates and police, the appointed guardians of law and order, to interpose...

Here the only terror that existed was caused by the unlawful resistance wilfully and designedly offered to the proceedings of the Salvation Army by an unlawful organisation outside and distict from them, called the Skeleton Army. It was suggested by the respondent's counsel that, if these Salvation processions were allowed, similar opposition would be offered to them in future, and that similar disturbances would ensue. But I cannot believe that that will be so. I hope, and I cannot but think, that when the Skeleton Army, and all other persons who are opposed to the proceedings of the Salvation Army, come to learn, as they surely will learn, that they have no possible right to interfere with or in any way obstruct the Salvation Army in their lawful and peaceable processions, they will abstain from opposing or disturbing them. It is usual happily in this country for people to respect and obey the law when once declared and understood, and I have hope and have no doubt that it will be so in the present case. But, if it should not be so, there is no doubt that the magistrates and police, both at Weston-super-Mare and everywhere else, will understand their duty and not fail to do it efficiently, or hesitate, should the necessity arise, to deal with the Skeleton Army and other disturbers of the public peace as they did in the present instance with the appellants, for no one can doubt that the authorities are only anxious to do their duty and to prevent a disturbance of the public peace. The present decision of the justices, however, amounts to this, that a man may be punished for acting lawfully if he knows that his so doing may induce another man to act unlawfully—a proposition without any authority whatever to support it. Under these circumstances, the question put to us by the justices must be negatively answered, and the order appealed against be discharged."

A rather different conclusion was reached in the same year by a Scottish court faced with a similar problem also involving the Salvation Army.

Deakin v Milne
(1882) 10 R. (J.) 22

At the time of this case the Salvation Army was in rivalry with the Skeleton Army to such an extent that almost any procession organised by the Salvation Army was likely by its mere existence to promote opposition by the Skeleton Army and consequent disorder. This happened on several occasions in Arbroath, the magistrates of which were stung to make a proclamation prohibiting these processions.

LORD JUSTICE-CLERK (MONCREIFF): "In the opinion which I have formed in this case I do not desire to say anything that could for a moment be considered to reflect on the motives or objects of the persons whose conduct has here been brought in question ... The question relates to the preservation of the order and peace of the burgh.

It appears that this class of persons called the Salvation Army, and another band who have a designation of their own, have been in the habit of making processions on Sunday forenoons to the great disturbance of the inhabitants, and also, as the prosecutor says and the magistrates have found, to the endangering of the public peace. The magistrates made various attempts to stop these proceedings, but, finding that the evil by no means diminished, they issued a proclamation on the 17th of March to prevent these disturbances. It appears to me that this was an exceedingly proper and discreet proceeding on the part of the magistrates, and that it was entirely within their power, not if these persons neither endangered the public peace nor annoyed the inhabitants, but if they were satisfied on reasonable grounds that what these people did had a tendency to these things ... But notwithstanding this proclamation these persons did turn out, and there was a breach of the peace, and the result is that they are charged with a breach of the peace, or inciting to a breach of the peace, and, secondly, with a breach of the proclamation by the magistrates.

I am of the opinion that the proceedings of the magistrates were perfectly proper. There are many processions that may take place in the streets of a burgh which may attract a good deal of attention, but which the magistrates are quite entitled to permit. There are objects in which the inhabitants of the towns may take a legitimate interest, but the limit to that necessarily is that the assembling of persons, and the behaviour of persons when they so assemble, shall be within the law. But when it leads to breach of the peace, however good the intentions of the persons may be, the magistrates are entitled to interfere; and therefore I hold that the magistrates, having decided upon the facts, in the first place, that this procession and crowd had a tendency to cause, and did cause, a breach of the peace, came to a conclusion which they were entitled to reach. I am not here to say what the facts are. That is a matter for the magistrates alone. But I think it is impossible to say that they had not the means of reaching the conclusion they did on these facts. In the second place, I think that a breach of the proclamation which the magistrates were entitled to issue was a municipal offence. On the whole matter, therefore, I think that there is no ground whatever for the appeal."

Lords Young and Craighall delivered concurring opinions.

A similar position to that in *Deakin v Milne* was adopted in the following year in Ireland. In *O'Kelly v Harvey* (1883) 14 L.R. Ir. 105, justices of the peace for an area where a meeting pressing for reforms of land law was to be held apprehended that the meeting would lead to breach of the peace and, deciding that the dissolution of the meeting was the only means of preserving the peace, called upon those present to disperse. When they refused the defendant laid hands upon one participant, who thereupon sued for damages for assault. The judgment of the court was delivered by Law C., who said:

"The defence, however, positively states that the Defendant being a Justice of the Peace, and present, believed, and had reasonable grounds for believing, that the peace could not otherwise be preserved than by separating and dispersing the Plaintiff's land meeting; and justified his action on that ground. The question then seems to be reduced to this:— assuming the Plaintiff and others assembled with him to be doing nothing unlawful, but yet that there were reasonable grounds for the Defendant believing, as he did, that there would be a breach of the peace if they continued so assembled, and that there was no other way in which the breach of the peace could be avoided but by stopping and dispersing the Plaintiff's meeting—was the Defendant justified in taking the necessary steps to stop and disperse it? In my opinion he was so justified, under the peculiar circumstances stated in the defence, and which for the present must be taken as admitted to be there truly stated. Under such circumstances the Defendant was not to defer action until a breach of the peace had actually been committed. His paramount duty was to *preserve the peace unbroken*, and that, by whatever means were available for the purpose."

It is almost certainly also the case that the power of dispersal is not confined to Scotland and Ireland. Despite *Beatty v Gillbanks* it is likely that English law would also recognise a power of dispersal, where a police officer could show that this was necessary in order to prevent a breach of the peace. This follows inexorably from *Duncan v Jones* [1936] 1 K.B. 218, *Piddington v Bates* [1961] 1 W.L.R. 162 and *Moss v McLachlan* [1985] I.R.L.R. 76, which we discuss later in the chapter.

It is not to be assumed that because the police have the power to disperse an assembly to maintain the peace they will always do so. Sometimes they will disperse the counter demonstration, a step apparently encouraged by the dictum of O'Brien J. in *R. v Justices of Londonderry* (1891) Ir. L.R. 440, who said that if "danger arises from the exercise of lawful rights resulting in a breach of the peace, the remedy is the presence of sufficient force to prevent that result, not the legal condemnation of those who exercise those rights." But the fact remains that the police have a discretion as to how to respond, and this they may exercise to permit or suppress the freedom of assembly. Their power of suppression was illustrated by *Alexander v Smith* 1984, S.L.T. 176, where the accused was charged with breach of peace. He was convicted and appealed by stated case, the justice finding the following facts admitted or proved:

"1. That the witnesses, Police Constables T. Taylor and N. Ward were on duty at McLeod Street on 8 January 1982; that a large crowd was making its way to Tynecastle Football Ground to watch a football match. 2. That the presence of the appellant at the locus was brought to the attention of said constables by some members of said crowd. That said members of the crowd shouted to the police officers as they passed, appeared to take exception to the appellant, told said police officers to get rid of him from the area and informed the said police officers that, if they took no action with regard to the appellant, there would be trouble. That the appellant was at that time attempting to sell *Bulldog*, a newspaper of the National Front political party. That the appellant was jumping up and down advertising said newspaper and was shouting things such as 'Get your *Bulldog* here, *Bulldog* 10 pence.' That the said police officers were concerned lest a more serious incident develop and were concerned for the safety of the appellant. That said members of the crowd, having intimated their attitude to the appellant to the said police officers, continued on to said football match. (The said police officers did not note the names and addresses of any of the persons referred to above and none was called as a witness by the respondent.) One of the said police officers, P.C. Taylor, gave evidence to the effect that the appellant had shouted at some members of the crowd and had called them 'nigger lovers.' This evidence was not spoken to by P.C. Ward. 3. That the appellant was shouting at the crowd and had called members of the public 'nigger lovers.' 4. That members of the crowd near the appellant seemed incensed by his attempts to sell the newspapers. That the appellant's hat was knocked off by a member of the crowd. 5. That the said police officers approached the appellant, asked him what he was selling, whereupon the appellant said 'You can't take them from me, it's not illegal to sell them'. That said police officers told the appellant to move on from the locus. That the appellant continued to try to sell said newspapers saying that he was doing nothing wrong and that it was lawful for him so to do (the newspapers were produced and identified by said police officers). 6. That said police officers then took said newspapers from the appellant, took hold of his arms and removed him from the locus. That the appellant then shouted at said police officers. That the appellant was protesting that he had done nothing unlawful."

The principal question for the High Court was whether the justice was entitled to convict. The court answered in the affirmative and, without delivering a formal opinion, refused the appeal. It is important to stress, however, that the power to disperse is not a licence to censor those who are a nuisance. Here it is appropriate to refer to *Hutton v Main*, 1891 19 R. (J.) 5, where the accused were charged that they "did loudly read, sing, pray and preach, and did continue to do so for half-an-hour, by which a large crowd was collected, and the residents and others in the neighbourhood were annoyed and disturbed". In dismissing the complaint as irrelevant, the Lord Justice Clerk said:

"There is no doubt that people who have the best intentions, and whose sole desire is to do good, may commit a breach of the peace by forming a procession, or even, it may be, by standing upon the street doing nothing further than these appellants are said to have done. And plainly in the *Arbroath* case to which we were referred there was a relevant charge. The members of the Salvation Army, in defiance of a proclamation by the magistrates, who in their discretion considered that a continuance of the conduct in which the members of the army engaged was likely to cause a breach of the peace and ought to be stopped, persisted in that conduct and continued their processions. A conviction obtained against certain of them was most properly upheld.

On the other hand, it is equally plain that a prosecutor who libels a breach of the peace is not ordinarily bound to use the words 'breach of the peace,' if he states facts which amount to that crime.

Now, street-preaching is a familiar thing. Respectable persons gather, sing in order to attract the attention of those near, and thereafter preach to them. It is matter of common knowledge that such things are done without anyone having an idea of these persons committing a breach of the peace. Accordingly it is a delicate matter to charge persons who have so acted as to gather people together to hear the Gospel preached on the street, and such cases require careful libelling. It is just one of the cases in which a mere bald statement that the accused did sing, preach, and pray, whereby a crowd was collected and persons were disturbed is insufficient, indeed utterly inadequate to suggest a breach of the peace. There must be more specification, and it is easy to give more if the acts done were truly in breach of the peace. In this particular case I am not surprised that the prosecutor did not add to what he has said that a breach of the peace was committed. I am satisfied that if he had done so it would not have made the complaint relevant. The expression 'breach of the peace' would not have been more than a summing up of the act charged. It is necessary in such a case to set forth the acts said to be done, and these acts must amount to an offence. Now, the words here, 'did loudly read, sing, pray, and preach,' do not seem to import more than that these things were done aloud. Then we come to the words, 'did continue to do so for half-an-hour, whereby a large crowd was collected,' and persons were disturbed. There do not at all suggest the gathering of a riotous and disorderly crowd, such that it would have been the duty of the police to disperse it.

As has been remarked in previous cases, such matters require to be dealt with on a reasonable way. What on one day may be quite legitimate may at another time, and under other circumstances, be illegitimate even at the same place. As I read the complaint, it does not import that the assembly of the crowd was to the annoyance and disturbance of the lieges."

Where the power to disperse is lawfully exercised, the police may use considerable force for the purpose: *Ward v Strathclyde Chief Constable*, 1991 S.L.T. 392 (use of cantering horses to disperse groups of rival football fans).

(c) The power to impose conditions

Rather than order an assembly to disperse, the police officer on the spot may decide instead to intervene by imposing conditions on those taking part. The origin of the powers of the police to impose conditions on the conduct of a meeting or assembly is often traced back to the Irish case, *Humphries v Connor* (1864) 17 Ir. C.L.R. 1, where the defendant, a police officer, was sued for assault, having removed an orange lily from the clothing of the plaintiff. The defendant took this step on the ground that it was necessary to prevent a breach of the peace. The court (by a majority) agreed. In accepting that this was a good defence to the action, O'Brien J. said:

"The defence states, that the defendant was Constabulary Inspector in the district in which the transaction occurred; and I need not say that it was his duty, as such, to preserve the public peace and prevent a breach of it. The defence also states in substance, that plaintiff's wearing the orange lily at that time was calculated and tended to provoke animosity among different classes of her Majesty's subjects; that several persons, who were provoked by it, followed the plaintiff, made a great disturbance, and threatened plaintiff with personal violence; that the defendant, in order to preserve the public peace and prevent a breach of it ... and to restore order, &c., requested plaintiff to remove the lily; that plaintiff refused to do so, and on the contrary continued to wear it, and thereby to excite and provoke those persons to inflict personal violence on her, and to cause such disturbance and threats. It further states, that it was likely the public peace would be broken ... in consequence of her continuing to wear the lily; and that in order to preserve the public peace ... the defendant *gently and quietly, and necessarily and unavoidably*, removed the lily from plaintiff, doing her no injury whatever, and thereby ... preserved the public peace, which would otherwise have been broken. Such is the substance of the defence ... But assuming (as on the present demurrer we are bound to do) that the defence truly states and represents the facts, it appears from it that the act complained of—namely, the removal of the lily from plaintiff, gently and without doing her any injury whatever, was necessary for the purposes of restoring order and preserving the public peace ... that it had such an effect; and that but for it the public peace would have been broken."

It is to be noted, however, that in a powerful dissent Fitzgerald J. said:

"But the doubt which I have is, whether a constable is entitled to interfere with one who is not about to commit a breach of the peace, or to do, or join in any illegal act, but who is likely to be made an object of insult or injury by other persons who are about to break the Queen's peace. I would not have ventured to express my doubt except that very important consequences may result from the principle of the decision of my Brothers in this case.

I do not see where we are to draw the line. If a constable is at liberty to take a lily from one person, because the wearing of it is displeasing to others, who may make it an excuse for a breach of the peace, where are we to stop? It seems to me that we are making, not the law of the land, but the law of the mob supreme, and recognising in constables a power of interference with the rights of the Queen's subjects, which, if carried into effect to the full extent of the principle, might be accompanied by constitutional danger."

It is clear that in Scots Law this power to impose conditions is a power that is available to the police, as the following case makes clear.

McAvoy v Jessop
1989 S.C.C.R. 301

The appellant was the Master of the Provincial Black Chapter of Scotland which is an branch of the Orange Order. On August 8, 1987, he was leading a parade which passed in front of a Roman Catholic church. A police officer instructed him to request the band which accompanied the parade not to play while passing the church. According to the findings of fact by the stipendiary magistrate:

"4. The band was playing music as it approached said church. James Wilkie, Inspector of Strathclyde Police, approached the marchers and requested a member of the parade to have the band cease playing as the procession was approaching St Theresa's Church and a service was due to start at 6.30 p.m., i.e., within a very few minutes, and the music ceased. Inspector Wilkie did so because he believed a service was in progress. No service was in progress. A man identified as the appellant approached Inspector Wilkie and said, 'I'm in charge of the parade, and I'll tell the band when to stop.' The appellant was agitated. The inspector twice requested the appellant to instruct the band to cease playing until the procession passed the Roman Catholic church. It was obvious to those present, namely those marching in the procession, followers and passers-by, that Inspector Wilkie accompanied by two uniformed sergeants was involved in a heated discussion or confrontation with the appellant. The inspector subsequently ordered the appellant to have the band cease playing till it passed the Roman Catholic church. The appellent ordered the band to start playing, which it did and music was played as the band passed said church. When the band recommenced playing a loud cheer emanated from the supporters.

5. The area was busy and quite a number of people were entering the grounds of St Theresa's Church and other parishioners were being welcomed by a priest at the church door prior to entering the church. On hearing the loud cheer a number of persons in the church grounds turned round. There was no other reaction and no evidence that these persons were alarmed, annoyed or disturbed—there was no complaint made by them to the police.

6. To discourage any reaction from the public, Inspector James Wilkie moved to the head of the procession and accompanied it to its premises in nearby Sunnylaw Street, Glasgow, where the parade disbanded. The appellant then apologised to Inspector Wilkie for the confrontation with the police but was adamant that he was within his rights.

7. On 10th August 1987, the appellant was cautioned and charge, with failing to obey a police instruction and made no reply."

Master McAvoy was convicted of breach of the peace, and his conviction was upheld on appeal, with the Lord Justice Clerk delivering the opinion of the court.

LORD JUSTICE CLERK (ROSS): "Mr Findlay [for the defence] maintained that this was a lawful parade, that the playing of music is part of the procession was lawful, and that the procession was following a lawful route. No doubt that is so. The question, however, must be whether the magistrate was entitled to hold that ordering the band to play music in the circumstances was conduct likely to cause a breach of the peace. It does not matter that there was no evidence that persons were in fact alarmed, annoyed or disturbed by the band starting up again. The test is well recognised and the question is as was put in *Raffaelli* v *Heatly*, 1949 J.C. 101:

'[W]here something is done in breach of public order or decorum which might reasonably be expected to lead to the lieges being alarmed or upset or tempted to make reprisals at their own hand, the circumstances are such as to amount to breach of the peace.'

Mr Findlay maintained that the appellant was within his lawful rights; the police request that music should stop and not be recommenced, was based upon a misconception, in that the police officer apparently thought a service was in progress whereas in fact the service had not yet begun. In our opinion, however, whether or not the police inspector was mistaken in thinking that a service was in progress, the stipendiary magistrate was entitled to have regard to the fact that at the material time a police officer had reasonably taken the view that for the band to play at that time was something which was likely to cause a breach of the peace. Quite apart from any conditions which may or may not have been imposed upon the procession, the fact was that at the material time the parade which was an Orange parade was passing a Roman Catholic church outside of which there were parishioners being welcomed by their priest prior to entering the church. In such circumstances, we are of opinion that it was quite reasonable for the police inspector to make the request that the music should stop and it should not be recommenced. That request having been made to the appellant in the circumstances, we are of opinion that it was provocative for him to insist upon the band playing at that particular time. That it was indeed provocative is evidenced by the fact that the recommencement of the band playing was met by a loud cheer from the appellant's supporters. In the circumstances as we have described them and as they are described in the findings, we are satisfied that the stipendiary magistrate was entitled to take the view that the appellant's conduct in ordering the band to play music as it was passing this place of worship while persons were entering the church grounds was conduct likely to cause a breach of the peace. It follows that the stipendiary magistrate was entitled to convict the appellant and accordingly we shall answer the one question in the case in the affirmative."

The leading English authority on the right of the police to regulate public assemblies is *Duncan v Jones* [1936] 1 K.B. 218. In that case a disturbance had taken place following an address the appellant had previously given to a crowd outside an unemployed workers' centre. A later meeting at the same place was announced, but a police officer tried to prevent any disorder by asking Mrs Duncan to conduct her address some yards down the street. She refused and was charged and convicted of obstructing a police officer in the execution of his duty. In dismissing her appeal, Lord Hewart C.J. said:

"There have been moments during the argument in this case when it appeared to be suggested that the court had to do with a grave case involving what is called the right of public meeting. I say 'called,' because English law does not recognise any special right of public meeting for political or other purposes. The right of assembly, as Professor Dicey puts it, is nothing more than a view taken by the court of the individual liberty of the subject. If I thought that the present case raised a question which has been held in suspense by more than one writer on constitutional law—namely, whether an assembly can properly be held to be unlawful merely because the holding of it is expected to give rise to a breach of the peace on the part of the persons opposed to those who are holding a meeting—I should wish to hear more argument before I expressed an opinion. This case, however, does not even touch that important question."

In a similar vein, Humphrey J. said:

"I regard this as a plain case. It has nothing to do with the law of unlawful assembly. No charge of that sort was even suggested against the appellant. The sole question raised by the case is whether the respondent, who was admittedly obstructed, was so obstructed when in the execution of his duty.

It does not require authority to emphasise the statement that it is the duty of a police officer to prevent apprehended breaches of the peace. Here it is found as a fact that the respondent reasonably apprehended a breach of the peace. It then, as is rightly expressed in the case, became his duty to prevent anything which in his view would cause that breach of the peace. While he was taking steps so to do he was wilfully obstructed by the appellant. I can conceive no clearer case within the statutes than that."

In a later case the Divisional Court held that the police could not only give directions as to the location of an assembly, but also the numbers who may attend. In *Piddington v Bates* [1961] 1 W.L.R. 162, a police officer directed that only two pickets should be permitted outside the entrance to a workplace. The appellant was arrested for breach of the peace for refusing to comply with this instruction, and subsequently convicted with obstruction of a police officer in the execution of his duty. In dismissing the appeal, the Lord Chief Justice (Parker) said:

"The court has been referred to a great number of cases, both Irish and English, dealing with the position when a police constable can be said to contemplate a breach of the peace and to take action to preserve it because, of course, the question here is whether the constables in question were acting in the course of the execution of their duty when they were obstructed. I find it unnecessary to refer to those cases. It seems to me that the law is reasonably plain. First, the mere statement by a constable that he did anticipate that there might be a breach of the peace is clearly not enough. There must exist proved facts from which a constable could reasonably anticipate such a breach. Secondly, it is not enough that his contemplation is that there is a remote possibility; there must be a real possibility of a breach of the peace. Accordingly, in every case, it becomes a question of whether, on the particular facts, it can be said that there were reasonable grounds on which a constable charged with this duty reasonably anticipated that a breach of the peace might occur ...

The other point goes to an analysis of the evidence, from which it is said that no reasonable man could possibly anticipate a breach of the peace. It is pointed out that there was no obstruction in the street; that there was no actual intimidation; and that there were no threats or intimations of violence. It is said that there was really nothing save the fact that picketing was going on to suggest that a breach of the peace was a real possibility.

As I have said, every case must depend upon its exact facts, and the matter which influences me in this case is the matter of numbers. It is, I think, perfectly clear from the wording of the case, although it is not expressly so found, that the police knew in these small works there were only eight people working. They found two vehicles arriving, with 18 people milling about the street trying to form pickets at the doors. On that ground alone, coupled with the telephone calls which, I should have thought, intimated some sense of urgency and apprehension, the police were fully entitled to think as reasonable men that there was a real danger of something more than mere picketing to collect or impart information or peaceably to persuade. I think that in those circumstances the prosecutor had reasonable grounds for anticipating that a breach of the peace was a real possibility. It may be, and I think this is the real criticism, that it can be said: Well, to say that only two pickets should be allowed is purely arbitrary; why two? Why not three? Where do you draw the line? I think that a police officer charged with the duty of preserving the Queen's peace must be left to take such steps as on the evidence before him he thinks are proper. I am far from saying that there should be any rule that only two pickets should be allowed at any particular door. There, one gets into an arbitrary area, but so far as this case is concerned I cannot see that there was anything wrong in the action of the prosecutor.

Finally, I would like to say that all these matters are so much matters of degree that I would hesitate, except on the clearest evidence, to interfere with the findings of magistrates who have had the advantage of hearing the whole case and observing the witnesses. I am of opinion that the appeal of Piddington should be dismissed."

On similar facts, it is difficult to believe that a Scottish court would not reach a similar conclusion in either of these two cases, particularly in view of the fact that the definition of breach of the peace is wider in Scotland than in England. Independently of the Public Order Act 1986, s.14 it thus appears to be open to the police to impose conditions as to the numbers, conduct and location of an assembly. It is perhaps partly for this reason that there is little evidence of s.14 being widely used in Scotland. Breach of the peace continues to be a flexible tool of the police to deal with new forms of protest by new generations of political activists, as the following case makes clear.

Colhoun v Friel
1996 S.C.C.R. 497

This was a case which arose out of the construction of the M77. The construction work involved the felling of trees, to which the appellant objected. He was charged with conducting himself in a disorderly manner by sitting on a felled tree which was being cut up by workmen using power saws. This would enable the trees to be removed from the site. The accused refused to move when told to do so by a security officer and a police officer. His conviction for breach of the peace was upheld by the High Court.

> LORD JUSTICE GENERAL (HOPE): "In his note the sheriff has explained that he felt that the appellant's actions constituted a real danger because the workman was using a power-operated chain saw with his back to the accused, who was sitting with his back against the place to which the workman was proceeding. The sheriff also refers to the fact that the appellant was asked three times to move and that he refused to do so. The appellant told the security officer that he could not hear what he was saying, but the two requests by the police officer were heard by the appellant.
>
> Miss Scott for the appellant pointed out that there was no finding in the case of any alarm or annoyance having been caused to anybody. She submitted that the acts described in these findings were minimal and that they were insufficient to enable the inference to be drawn that this was conduct of a kind likely to cause fear, alarm or annoyance. She referred to the well-known passage in *Raffaelli* v *Heatly*, 1949 J.C. 101, where at p. 104 the Lord Justice-Clerk said:
>
>> "It is usual to charge this offence as a breach of the peace, because it is a species of disorderly conduct; where something is done in breach of public order or decorum which might reasonably be expected to lead to the lieges being alarmed or upset or tempted to make reprisals at their own hand, the circumstances are such as to amount to a breach of the peace."
>
> We were referred also to a passage in the opinion of Lord Mackay at p. 105, where he said that, if acts are repeated and are calculated to cause alarm and annoyance and are indecorous, that is enough. The nature of the crime of breach of the peace has been described in numerous authorities and we do not need to go over all the references which we were given by Miss Scott. It can at least be said that it is well settled that the test to be applied is whether the proved conduct may reasonably be expected to cause any person who observed it to be alarmed, upset or annoyed or to provoke a disturbance. In the present case the submission, as we have said, was that the nature and the quality of the acts proved in the evidence were not such as to entitle that inference to be drawn.
>
> In his reply the advocate-depute submitted that there was sufficient evidence to entitle the sheriff to reach the conclusion which he did. What had happened here was that the

appellant had deliberately sat down on the tree with his back to the workman as the work was in progress. He had been asked three times to move and he had refused to do so. His refusal had taken place in circumstances which put both the appellant himself and the workman into a position of risk, if the operation of sawing the tree had been continued in the face of the refusal to move. All that was necessary was sufficient evidence to entitle the sheriff to hold that the conduct might reasonably cause any person to be alarmed or annoyed and that test was clearly satisfied here.

We have reached the conclusion that the sheriff was entitled to reach the decision which he did in the light of the conduct which was established in this case. There were clearly several requests to the appellant to move, two of which at least he heard, with which he refused to comply. He had sat down on the tree deliberately while it was in the course of being cut up, and he placed himself and the workman in a position of danger by his refusal to move as the workman proceeded in the task of cutting the tree up with the power-operated saw. This was disorderly conduct which might reasonably have caused a person to be alarmed by virtue of what might ensue if the appellant was to remain in that position as the work proceeded."

(d) The Power to Prevent an Assembly?

It is evident from the foregoing that the police have a quite remarkable power to deal with meetings and demonstrations. They may insist on being present; they may issue instructions as to location and numbers; and ultimately they may disperse. The final question is whether there is a common-law power on the part of the police to ban particular meetings and processions. This indeed would be a logical extension of the powers discussed so far, and it is unsurprising that the police should eventually claim to have just such a power. Although there were several examples of such a power being claimed earlier, it was during the miners' strike of 1984/85 that it was formally recognised by the courts to authorise the use of road blocks by the police to prevent the movement of picketing miners.

The police road blocks had two purposes. The first was to prevent miners from leaving their own counties. This was true particularly of the road blocks set up at the Dartford Tunnel to prevent miners from leaving Kent on the way to picket lines in Nottinghamshire. The second purpose was to prevent miners from entering the vicinity of coalfields or other sites for picketing. This is true, for example, of the road blocks set up at the county boundary in Nottinghamshire and those set up to prevent miners from travelling to Hunterston where coal was being brought into the country from overseas. It is to be noted that the police operation led to thousands of people being turned away. Thus, the Chief Constable of Nottinghamshire estimated that 164,508 individuals, whom he described as presumed pickets, were prevented from entering the county in the first 27 weeks of the dispute.

An inquiry into the policing of the dispute reported:

"We have received evidence from many people not connected with the dispute, and from miners travelling for purposes unconnected with the dispute, of police officers at road blocks requiring proof of identity and refusing under threat of arrest to allow people to pass; some non-miners have been arrested for obstructing the police in refusing to comply with instructions to turn back. Miners travelling to picket have reported variously being warned that they would be liable to arrest if they proceeded to a pit to picket, or told to turn back on pain of arrest for obstruction. Some have been arrested in these circumstances."

Not surprisingly, the practice was condemned:

"In many cases individuals have been inconvenienced or even prevented from making important journeys because the police did not accept their explanations. This smacks of the Soviet internal passport system or South African pass laws. There have moreover been reports of police officers at roadblocks causing gratuitous damage to pickets' cars. The balance between the liberties of working miners to travel to work and of striking miners to picket has been struck almost entirely in favour of the former, creating among the strikers an understandable impression that they were all assumed to be engaged on an enterprise of violence."

What then is the authority for this quite remarkable power? In England and Wales there was no statutory authority for the practice, though it is almost arguable that the Police and Criminal Evidence Act 1984 conferred such a power, but only from the commencement date, January 1, 1985. Nevertheless, this would require a particularly generous construction of ss.4 and 116 of that Act. But even so there was and still is no statutory power authorising the practice in Scotland. So what about the common law? In the House of Commons the Attorney-General said:

"There is no doubt that if a constable reasonably comes to a conclusion that persons are travelling for the purpose of taking part in a picket in circumstances where there is likely to be a breach of the peace, he has the power at common law to call upon them not to continue their journey and to call upon drivers to take them no further. Any person who fails to comply with a police request in those circumstance will be committing the offence of obstructing a police officer in the course of his duty." (56, H.C. Debs 279–280, March 16, 1984.)

Similarly, according to the Solicitor-General for Scotland:

"the police in Scotland have the authority—where they apprehend that there is the prospect of an offence—to ensure that that offence is not committed, whether it is a breach of the peace, obstruction of the highway or anything else ... they have power to precent the commission of offences, not being restricted simply to acting when an offence has already occurred." (60, H.C. Debs 358–359, May 14, 1984.)

These views are endorsed by the following decision. Although it is true that it is a decision of the Divisional Court in England, under the Police Act 1964, s.51(3) (now Police Act 1996, s.89), it is difficult to believe that a similar result would not be reached in Scotland.

Moss v McLachlan
[1985] I.R.L.R. 76

SKINNER J. "The judgment I am about to deliver is the judgment of the Court. This is an appeal by way of case stated by four appellants against decisions of the Justices of the Petty Sessional Division of Mansfield in the county of Nottingham. Each appellant was convicted in June of this year of wilfully obstructing a police officer in the execution of his duty on 25 April last contrary to s.51(3) of the Police Act, 1964 as amended by the Criminal Law Act, 1977....

The facts were as follows. On the day in question, as a result of a trade dispute between the National Union of Mineworkers and the National Coal Board, a number of policemen were stationed at Junction 27 of the M1 at Annesley, in the county of Nottingham. The junction is between one-and-a-half and two miles from two collieries which are half a mile apart from one another and between four and five miles from two more collieries, also half a mile apart. The police had reason to believe that striking miners from outside the county were intending to demonstrate and form a mass picket at one or more of the four collieries near to the junction.

The object of the police was to stop cars carrying persons who appeared to be striking miners. Persons who satisfied them that they were not intent on a course of mass picketing were allowed to proceed. The object with the rest was to dissuade them, if possible, from taking part in any demonstration or mass picket and, if persuasion failed, to order them to turn back and prevent them from going further in the direction of the adjacent collieries.

Shortly after 10 a.m. some 25 or more cars arrived at the junction from the north carrying 60 to 80 men who, from their badges and the stickers on their cars, were clearly identifiable as striking miners. These cars were stopped and the occupants were addressed by Inspector Brammar, who was in charge of the police operation. He identified himself to the men and continued: 'I have reason to believe that you are all intent on going to the pits in this county to demonstrate. I have reason to fear a breach of the peace if you continue to the pits, and I am asking you all to turn back. I have a duty at common law to prevent a breach of the peace and the power at common law to act to prevent a breach of the peace. If you continue you will be obstructing an officer in the execution of his duty and therefore liable to arrest.'

The group of men discussed this advice among themselves and then returned to their vehicles and started to drive off. During the discussion the appellant Moss was heard to say: 'We're all agreed then lads. We won't follow the car round and we'll continue on to the pits.' The police had believed that they were going to accede to the request that had been made of them by going around the traffic island and returning north up the motorway. In the event the first car in the convoy driven by the appellant Moss drove right up to a contingent of Surrey officers who had just arrived at the scene and had formed themselves into three cordons, thereby blocking access to the A608 road. The other vehicles drew up close behind one another and eventually a second parallel line of vehicles drew up alongside the first. The exit from the motorway was eventually blocked. The occupants alighted.

They were advised by Inspector Brammar of the danger that the obstruction was causing and requested to remove their vehicles. There was however an impasse of some 35 or 40 minutes during which time the men seemed undecided as to what course of action to follow. During that period angry shouts from the men at passing National Coal Board vehicles and other comments by them made it plain that the police's suspicions that the men were intent on a mass demonstration or picket were justified. Further vehicles arrived during this interlude: the drivers of some were prevailed upon to return north, but others declined the advice.

Eventually the men advanced towards the Surrey officers who were blockading the road. Inspector Brammar shouted to them: 'I have every reason to fear a breach of the peace if you are allowed to continue. If you insist on going on then you are liable to arrest.' The miners' response made it clear that the majority were determined to continue, although one or two expressed reservations about the wisdom of doing so.

The first group to approach the cordon consisted of an estimated 15 men. Police Sergeant Crampton of the Surrey Constabulary gave a warning similar to Inspector Brammar's and added, 'Do you understand?' Several of the men replied 'Yes.' Police Sergeant Crampton continued: 'What do you intend to do—go on or go back?' Several indicated that they were going on, and endeavoured to push their way through the cordon. Those that did so were arrested.

In the upshot some 40 miners who insisted on going on towards the collieries and attempted to force their way through the cordon despite further warnings were arrested on the ground that if they proceeded the police feared a breach of the peace at one of the four collieries. The appellants were four of those arrested, charged, tried and convicted. They were each sentenced to be confined in the precincts of the court until the rising of the court and ordered to pay £30 towards the cost of the prosecution within 28 days of the end of the strike.

The appellants concede that they cannot challenge the magistrates' findings of wilful obstruction by them of the officers named in the charges. However they contend that the police orders to turn back and their subsequent refusal to allow them to pass were unlawful. In reality, they say, the police were restricting their right to freedom of movement. Though the police have a duty to ensure that the peace is kept, they had no power to take the steps they did in this case: their only power was to admonish. In these circumstances the police were not acting in the execution of their duty and the offence accordingly was not proved.

Subject to one submission by Mr Mansfield [for the appellants], to which I shall return later, the law on this subject is clear. If a constable apprehends, on reasonable grounds, that a breach of the peace may be committed, he is not only entitled but is under a duty to take reasonable steps to prevent that breach occurring.

The magistrates concluded that: 'The police honestly and on reasonable grounds feared that there would be a breach of the peace if there were a mass demonstration at whichever Nottinghamshire colliery the appellants and their colleagues chose to congregate.'

The appellants submit that there was no finding of fact by the magistrates to support that conclusion: there was no conduct from which any constable could reasonably have apprehended a breach of the peace. Mr Mansfield submits that the conduct in question must be conduct by the appellants themselves in the presence of the arresting officer, though he concedes that the latter is entitled to take into account the conduct of a group of which the appellants were members. He also contends that the fears must be specific. It is not enough, he says, to fear a breach of the peace at one or more of the collieries involved by some or all of the miners involved. The officer must be able to say which pit, which miners and when.

Mr Milmo replies that a police officer has to look at all the facts within his knowledge. He has the power to act if they raise in his mind a fear that the person or persons he is dealing with may cause a breach of the peace, even if he cannot precisely pinpoint when and where.

On this basis he relies on the magistrates' findings that: (a) there were four pits within five miles of the cordon; (b) over 25 cars carrying over 60 striking miners were involved in the attempt to break through the police cordon; (c) while waiting at the junction, angry shouts from the National Union of Mineworkers members at passing National Coal Board lorries and other comments by them made it plain that the police's suspicions that the men were intent on a mass demonstration or picket were justified; (d) the police suspicions that the gathering of a large picket would lead to a breach of the peace were based on their own experiences in the current and other trade disputes, on the knowledge gleaned from those experiences, from their colleagues and from the widespread public dissemination of the news that there had been severe disruptions of the peace, including many incidents of violence, at collieries within the Nottinghamshire coalfield area in the days and weeks of the dispute before 20.4.84. The officers however had no way of knowing which colliery it was the intention of the miners to picket.

The appellants say this is not enough. The police were not entitled to take into account the experiences of others of what they had heard or read on television or in the press. They could only prevent the men from proceeding if it was clear from the words and deeds of the man at the junction that a breach of the peace was intended.

In our judgment there was ample evidence before the magistrates to support their conclusion. That is enough to dispose of Mr Mansfield's argument that the magistrates here were dealing with action by the police to prevent the appellants from exercising their undoubted right to demonstrate peacefully in order to show support for and solidarity with fellow trade unionists.

On the magistrates' findings of fact anyone with knowledge of the current strike would realise that there was a substantial risk of an outbreak of violence. The mere presence of such a body of men at the junction in question in the context of the current situation in the Nottinghamshire coalfields would have been enough to justify the police in taking preventative action. In reaching their conclusion the police themselves are bound to take into account all they have heard and read and to exercise their judgment and common sense on that material as well as on the events which are taking place before their eyes.

The situation has to be assessed by the senior police officers present. Provided they honestly and reasonably form the opinion that there is a real risk of a breach of the peace in the sense that it is in close proximity both in place and time, then the conditions exist for reasonable preventive acting including, if necessary, the measures taken in this case.

The findings of fact by the magistrates therefore dispel any suggestions that (1) the belief of the officers present was other than honest or reasonable, or (2) that the steps taken were other than reasonable.

But, says Mr Mansfield, the police can only take preventive action if a breach of the peace is imminent and there was no such imminence here. In support of this proposition he relies on a passage in the judgment of Lord Justice Watkins in *R. v Howell* [1981] 3 All E.R. 383 at p. 388: '... there is a power of arrest for breach of the peace where ... (2) the arrestor reasonably believes that such a breach will be committed in the immediate future by the person arrested although he has not yet committed any breach...'

This passage must be read in the light of the judgment of Lord Parker, Chief Justice, in *Piddington v Bates* [1960] 3 All E.R. 660 at p. 663, in which he says the police must anticipate 'a real, not a remote, possibility' of a breach of the peace before they are justified in taking preventive action.

We do not think that there is any conflict between the two approaches. The possibility of a breach of the peace must be real to justify any preventive action. The imminence or immediacy of the threat to the peace determines what action is reasonable. If the police feared that a convoy of cars travelling toward a working coal field bearing banners and broadcasting, by sight or sound, hostility or threats towards working miners might cause a violent episode, they would be justified in halting the convoy to enquire into its destination and purpose. If, on stopping the vehicles, the police were satisfied that there was a real possibility of the occupants causing a breach of the peace one-and-a-half miles away, a journey of less than five minutes by car, then in our judgment it would be their duty to prevent the convoy from proceeding further and they have the power to do so.

If and in so far as there may be any difference between the two approaches (and we do not believe there is), we respectfully prefer that of Lord Parker, Chief Justice, in *Piddington v Bates*.

We also repeat the words of Lord Parker, Chief Justice, at p. 663 of that case: 'For my part, I think that a police officer charged with the duty of preserving the Queen's peace must be left to take such steps as, on the evidence before him, he thinks proper.'

For the reasons we have given, on the facts found by the magistrates, a breach of the peace was not only a real possibility but also, because of the proximity of the pits and the availability of cars, imminent, immediate and not remote. In our judgment the magistrates were correct in their reasoning and conclusions and we would dismiss these appeals."

A new use for this power was found in *R. (Laporte) v Chief Constable of Gloucestershire Constabulary* [2004] EWHC 253, relating to the demonstrations against the war in Iraq which took place in various parts of the country in 2003. On one occasion a coach carrying a group of demonstrators from London to RAF Fairford in Gloucestershire was stopped outside the town of Lechlade (some five kilometres from the base) by the police and prevented from travelling to its destination. The police officers were acting on instructions from a Chief Superintendent Lambert and were exercising powers under the Criminal Justice and Public Order Act 1994, s.60. The police apprehended a breach of the peace at the demonstration from a number of "hard line" protestors, which the High Court accepted that they had good cause to anticipate. According to May L.J.:

"37. Mr Freeland on behalf of the defendant submits that at common law police officers have the power to take all reasonable steps to prevent a breach of the peace. This includes, not only a power of arrest, but a power of detention using reasonable force short of arrest. He relies on *Albert v Lavin*, [1982] A.C. 546. In addition to the passage from the opinion of Lord Diplock which I have already referred to, Mr Freeland refers to the judgment of Hodgson J in the Divisional Court at page 553 where he said:

'It is however clear law that a police officer, reasonably believing that a breach of the peace is about to take place, is entitled to take such steps as are necessary to prevent it, including the reasonable use of force: ... If those steps include physical restraint of someone then that restraint is not an unlawful detention but a reasonable use of force. It is a question of fact and degree when a restraint has continued for so long that there must be either a release or an arrest, but on the facts found in this case it seems to me to be clear that that point had not been reached. Obviously where a constable is restraining someone to prevent a breach of the peace he must release (or arrest) him as soon as the restrained person no longer presents a danger to the peace.'

...

38. Mr Freeland submits that the circumstances in which a breach of the peace may be apprehended vary infinitely, and that whether the apprehended breach of the peace is 'imminent' or 'about to happen' (to use the words of Lord Diplock in *Albert v Lavin*) will depend on all the circumstances. I accept this submission so far as it goes, but there must be a limit beyond which the concept of imminence will not stretch. I also consider that it may be relevant to consider what actions on their part the police are seeking to justify, and what preventive steps are practical. Preventing a single person from committing a breach of the peace is a different thing from preventing a large number of people from doing so. Different preventive measures may be justified in each case and this in turn may lend colour to what is properly apprehended as imminent. Mr Freeland submits that, when a coach contains passengers who are expected to resort to violence on reaching their destination, that is a sufficient basis for preventing them reaching the destination by stopping them at a convenient place which in the context of motor travel by road is close to the destination and where the preventive measures can be taken in an orderly way. He draws attention to the similarities between the present case and *Moss*. On the facts of the present case, he submits that a breach of the peace was properly to be regarded as imminent.

39. In my view, there are difficulties with this submission. It is necessary to distinguish between arrest and preventive action short of arrest. On the facts of the present case, Mr Freeland struggles to submit persuasively that any apprehended breach of the peace justifying arrest was imminent at the time when the coaches were in the lay-by. Mr Lambert's own assessment at the time had been that it was not. He did not consider that anticipated circumstances in the lay-by would justify the arrest of the passengers in the coaches. In my view, he was correct in this. His view was that arrest would have been justified if they had reached RAF Fairford itself. If in law the circumstances which justify preventive measures short of arrest, which interfere with a person's freedom under articles 10 and 11 of the Convention, are the same as those which justify arrest, it is difficult to justify the preventive measures in the present case. On the other hand, *Moss* is an authority providing strong support for Mr Freeland's case that the preventive measures in the present case falling short of detention were legitimate. To comply with articles 10(2) and 11(2) of the Convention, restrictions of this kind have to be prescribed by law and necessary in the democratic society in the interests of public safety or for the prevention of disorder or crime. It is, in my judgment, a question of fact in each case whether preventive measures of this kind are necessary in this context and thus proportionate. For them to be prescribed by law, it is necessary that the law sufficiently defines the circumstances in which the police may lawfully take preventive measures of this kind. In my view, this requirement is in substance satisfied by the judgment of Skinner J in *Moss*. The essential features are that a senior police officer should honestly and reasonably form the opinion that there is a real risk of a breach of the peace in close proximity both in place and time; that the possibility of a breach must be real; that the preventive measures must be reasonable; and that the imminence or immediacy of the threat to the peace determines what action is reasonable. I would add that the police are entitled to have regard to what is practical and that the number of people from whom a breach of the peace is apprehended may be relevant. The question of imminence is thus relevant to the lawfulness of preventive measures of this kind, but the degree of imminence may not be as great as that which would justify arrest.

40. In the present case, Mr Lambert reasonably and honestly believed that, if the coaches

were allowed to proceed to Fairford, there would be breaches of the peace. He was in my judgment in these circumstances lawfully entitled to give instructions for preventive measures. It was his duty to do so. As in *Moss*, anyone seeking to override the preventive measures would be obstructing a police officer in the execution of his duty. But Mr Lambert himself acknowledged that the circumstances in the lay-by did not justify the arrest of the coach passengers generally.

41. The principle that the police are, in the circumstances which I have stated, entitled to take preventive measures does not entitle them to take those measures indiscriminately. But there may be circumstances in which individual discrimination among a large number of uncooperative people is impractical. In my judgment, Mr Lambert was entitled to regard the circumstances in the lay-by at Lechlade as such. For these reasons I do not consider that the police action in preventing the coaches from proceeding to Fairford was unlawful. I would reject this part of the claimant's claim."

It was also held, however, that the police did not have the power to order that the coaches be sent back to London under police escort without being allowed to stop on the way.

VII. RESTRAINT BY INTERDICT

An important but sometimes overlooked restraint on freedom of assembly comes not from the criminal law but from the civil law. This is likely to arise where the target of protest action is a private party rather than the state. It may be an employer in dispute with a trade union, a farmer in dispute with environmentalists, or political activists directing their ire at sheriff officers as part of their campaign against the poll tax. In these cases the employer, the farmer or the sheriff officer may of course seek the assistance of the police who may attend in numbers to keep the peace. But, they may also take legal steps of their own to have the action restrained because it violates their rights in private law. Typically this is action that might be taken by an employer to deal with picketing outside his or her place of business. We have already encountered the TULRCA 1992, s.241 which makes various forms of picketing and related activity a criminal offence. Although this provision (and its predecessor) has been used periodically as a basis of prosecution, many of the cases discussed above are cases which have been brought by employers in the English courts to restrain what they claim to be criminal conduct which prejudices their legal rights. There are, however, other grounds for the granting of interdicts to restrain picketing, as the following case makes clear.

Timex Electronics Corporation v Amalgamated Engineering and Electrical Union
1994 S.L.T. 438

This was an appeal against an interim interdict granted to the petitioners who carried on business in Dundee. They alleged that unlawful mass picketing was being organised by the respondents outside their premises during a strike by employees of the corporation. The first respondent was the union and the second to fifth respondents were officials of the union. It was alleged that the picketing was having an intimidatory effect on employees who attended for work, and as such amounted to "unlawful inducement to employees to break their contracts of employment, unlawful interference with the performance of the contracts of employment and unlawful inducement to persons to interfere with the performance of such contracts". The remaining facts are explained in the Opinion of the court as delivered by the Lord President.

LORD PRESIDENT HOPE: "The respondents' counsel accepted that the averments in the petition, if true, indicated that there was a case to try. His opposition to the motion for interim interdict was based partly on the balance of convenience and partly on the terms of the proposed interdict, which he maintained was wide enough to cover activities which were lawful. The Lord Ordinary was satisfied that there was a case to try in respect of the individual respondents, but not in respect of the AEEU itself. He was also satisfied that it was appropriate for interim interdict to be pronounced on the balance of convenience. He considered that there was merit in the criticisms of the prayer of the petition on the ground that it included actions which were not unlawful, and the petitioners' counsel sought and was granted leave to amend in order to meet these criticisms.

The Lord Ordinary then pronounced interim interdict against the second, third, fourth and fifth named respondents and each of them in which they were prohibited 'by themselves, their servants or agents or howsoever from inciting, procuring, assisting, encouraging or organising in any manner whatsoever, any person (i) to congregate or assemble at or near the entrance to the petitioners' factory premises at Harrison Road, Dundee for the purpose of obtaining or communicating information or persuading any person to work or abstain from working (a) otherwise than peacefully and (b) in numbers exceeding six for that purpose or (ii) to attend elsewhere for the purpose of persuading or inducing employees of the petitioners by whatever manner not to work'.

The second, third, fourth and fifth respondents have reclaimed against this interlocutor on the grounds that its terms are unclear, unspecific and wider than necessary to prevent any unlawful conduct, and that its effect is to prevent them by interdict from conduct which is lawful. Counsel for the fourth and fifth respondents submitted that the terms of the interim interdict failed to give sufficiently clear and precise notice of the conduct which was intended to be prohibited. She pointed out that it was confined largely to a repetition of words used in s 220 (1) of the Trade Union and Labour Relations (Consolidation) Act 1992 which deals with peaceful picketing. She said that it had failed to define the particular conduct which the petitioners in this case complained of as being unlawful. When she directed our attention to the particular passages in the interim interdict which she said were objectionable counsel for the petitioners informed us that he recognised the force of these criticisms. He sought leave to amend the prayer of the petition in order to deal with them, and we adjourned the hearing for a while in order that the respondents' counsel could consider his proposed amendments and decide whether they would be acceptable. When the hearing resumed we were informed by counsel for the third respondent that he was content with the proposed amendments, and that he would not oppose the granting of a fresh order for interim interdict if the prayer of the petition were to be amended as counsel proposed. Counsel for the fourth and fifth respondents was content to accept all of the amendments proposed by counsel for the petitioners but she submitted that one further amendment was necessary in order to deal fully with her argument.

The effect of the amendments proposed by counsel for the petitioners and agreed to by counsel for the third respondent would be to interdict the second, third, fourth and fifth respondents ad interim 'by themselves, their servants or agents or howsoever from inciting, procuring, assisting, encouraging or organising in any manner whatsoever, any person (i) to congregate or assemble at or near the main middle gates leading to the entrance to the petitioners' factory premises at Harrison Road, Dundee for the purpose of obtaining or communicating information from or to any person entering or leaving or seeking to enter or leave the petitioners' said premises or for the purpose of persuading any such person to abstain from working (a) otherwise than peacefully and (b) in numbers exceeding six for that purpose or (ii) to attend wherever employees of the petitioners are being picked up for work for the purpose of persuading or inducing such employees by whatever manner not to work'.

The only point which remained at issue between counsel for the petitioners and counsel for the fourth and fifth respondents related to the use of the phrase 'at or near' before the words 'the main middle gates leading to the entrance to the petitioners' factory premises'. We then heard further argument from both counsel directed to this point.

Counsel for the fourth and fifth respondents submitted that this phrase was too imprecise to be appropriate for inclusion in an order for interim interdict. She referred to the following observation by Lord President Emslie in *Murdoch v Murdoch*, 1973 SLT (Notes) at p 13: 'Interdict, as is well known, is an equitable remedy designed to afford protection against an anticipated violation of the legal rights of the pursuer. In all cases, however, where interdict is granted by the court the terms of the interdict must be no wider than are necessary to curb the illegal actings complained of, and so precise and clear that the person interdicted is left in no doubt what he is forbidden to do.'

She said that the use of the word 'near' was likely to create a problem for her clients in identifying the geographical extent of the prohibition which had been imposed on them. In *Rayware Ltd v Transport and General Workers' Union* [1989] 1 W.L.R. 675, Nourse LJ said that the word 'near' was not a restricting but an expanding word. In that case picketing on a private road seven tenths of a mile from the entrance to the estate where the plaintiff carried on business was held to be 'at or near' the employee's place of work within the meaning of s 15 of the Trade Union and Labour Relations Act 1974, as amended. This decision indicated the latitude which was inherent in the word, and it would be difficult for advisers to say where the clients could carry on their activities without infringing the interdict.

We do not consider that the words 'at or near' are too imprecise to be appropriate for an interdict against unlawful picketing. These words must be read in their context. In the present case this describes not only the place but also the purpose of congregating or assembling there. It is that purpose which is the essence of the illegal actings complained of, and we regard the words 'at or near' as being no wider than is necessary to give effect to the restraint. In view of the nature of these actings, and the numbers of people who might otherwise be expected to be encouraged or organised to congregate or assemble in order to take part in them, the word 'at' may well be too precise for the interdict to be effective. It would be unreasonable to limit the effect of the interdict in a way which would create that risk. It was accepted that it would be impracticable to deal with the matter by means of a precise measurement.

Furthermore, the words 'at or near' are commonly used to describe the place where picketing can or cannot be undertaken, Section 220 of the 1992 Act provides that it is lawful for a person in contemplation or furtherance of a trade dispute to attend 'at or near his own place of work' for the purpose only of peacefully obtaining or communicating information, or peacefully persuading any person to work or abstain from working. It was pointed out in *Rayware Ltd* that the words 'at or near' in this provision must be construed in a geographical sense with due regard for the intent and purpose of the legislation. In *Thomas v National Union of Mineworkers* [1986] Ch.20, Stuart-Smith J granted an injunction restraining the union and its servants, agents and officers from inciting, pro-curing, assisting, encouraging or organising members of the union or others to congregate or assemble 'at or near the entrance to the colliery' otherwise than for the purpose of peaceful picketing. In *News Group Newspapers Ltd v SOGAT '82* [1987] I.C.R. 81, the same judge granted an injunction against the unions and the relevant officials from carrying on unlawful picketing 'at or near the Wapping Plant'. These examples illustrate counsel for the petitioners' point that, when regard is had to the purpose of the interdict, the use of these words is both necessary and appropriate. We agree with him that any reasonable person, putting himself in the position of the respondents in this case, would understand what was meant by them, and that they require to be included in the interdict if the acts complained of are to be restrained effectively.

We shall therefore allow the prayer of the petition to be amended in the terms proposed by counsel for the petitioner at the bar."

For a full account of the *Timex* case, see K. Millar and C. Woolfson, 'Timex: Industrial Relations and the Use of the Law in the 1990s' (1994) 23 I.L.J. 209. It is to be noted that the decision in *Thomas v NUM (South Wales Area)* [1986] Ch. 20 to which Lord President Hope referred is a decision of Scott J. and not Stuart Smith J. (Indeed in *News Group Newspapers Ltd v SOGAT 82 (No 2)* [1987] I.C.R. 81, Stuart Smith J. cast doubt on the desire of Scott J. in the former case to extend the tort of private nuisance to cover the workers crossing the picket lines as well as the owner or occupier of the property being picketed. But this was not material to the use of either case by Lord Hope.)

The problem with interim interdicts is a procedural one in the sense that they can be granted *ex parte* (without the other party being present), as in *McIntyre v Sheridan*, 1993 S.L.T. 412. It is true that an *ex parte* order can be challenged, but as *McIntyre v Sheridan* reveals this depends on the interdict being served on the respondent in good time. The other problem with interim interdicts is that they can be granted on the ground that the respondent has not violated the rights of the petitioner. At the stage that the interim interdict is granted, the question of whether the petitioner's rights have been violated cannot be determined with certainty, and cannot be determined until the trial of the action which may not take place for several months or years. In the meantime the respondent will be restrained from taking what may be perfectly lawful action, and indeed the restraint may be permanent if the interim interdict has the effect of preventing a particular event or a particular series of events. All that the petitioner needs to establish is that the balance of convenience is in favour of granting the interim interdict. According to Lord Fraser of Tullybelton, the courts may have regard to the legal merits at the interim stage but only to determine where the balance of convenience lies (*NWL Ltd v Woods* [1979] I.C.R. 867). This is a particular problem in trade disputes, where Parliament has intervened in England and Wales to require the courts to have regard to the likelihood of the defendant succeeding at the trial of the action before granting an interim injunction where the defendant claims to have been acting in contemplation or furtherance of a trade dispute. This provision does not apply to Scotland. The granting of interim interdicts to deal with protestors is not confined to trade disputes, as the following case makes clear. The following case also highlights the procedural disadvantages for respondents while revealing the serious consequences of failing to comply with an interdict.

McIntyre v Sheridan
1993 S.L.T. 412

Mr Sheridan was the chairman of the Scottish Anti-Poll Tax Union. The union was opposed to the use of warrant sales by sheriff officers to recover unpaid poll tax from defaulters. An *ex parte* interim interdict had been granted on Friday, September 27, 1991 against Mr Sheridan to restrain him from attending a warrant sale in Glasgow on October 1, 1991. It also sought to restrain him from disrupting, impeding or otherwise interfering with the day-to-day business of the petitioner sheriff officers. The interim interdict was not served on the respondent until the afternoon of September 30, though according to the Lord Ordinary this was thought to be "perfectly understandable" in the circumstances. It was established that the respondent knew about the interdict at the time of the facts which were the subject of the complaint. Nevertheless Mr Sheridan was said to have been angered by the late delivery which did not give him adequate time to have it recalled. The relevant facts are told by Lord Caplan in the following terms:

"The effects of Mrs Brennan to be sold at the sale were five items of furniture with an appraised value of £360. At Turnbull Street there is an enclosed yard where the sale was to take place and the effects to be sold were in a van which had been left overnight in the yard. Robert McIntyre who was proposing to conduct the auction sale and Freda Reilly who was to assist him arrived at the yard early in the morning of 1 October. After checking the sale items they sat in the cabin of the van. About 9.50 am 30 or 40 people came into the yard. They battered the side of the van. They let down the tyres of the van. They began to shake the van to and fro from side to side and someone asked the crowd to stand clear of one side of the van, giving the occupants of the van the impression that the intention was to overturn the van. Mr McIntyre managed to avert that possibility by edging the van forward a short distance so that it stood between two pillars. £1,400 worth of damage was done to the van by these actions. During this phase of the incident Mr McIntyre and Mrs Reilly were terrified. Mr McIntyre pumped his horn frantically, hoping to attract police assistance. Meanwhile the crowd in the yard were increasing.

Inspector Cattell was in Turnbull Street outside the yard and he had a sizeable police contingent of about 60 officers at his disposal. When he saw the size of the crowd pouring into the yard, he instructed some of his policemen to follow them in. After a struggle the policemen who entered the yard were able to interpose themselves between the van and the assembled crowd. They were also able to restore order. The respondent, according to his own evidence, entered the yard towards the rear of the crowd. He stated that at the time there was some shouting, there was a clatter of metal against metal, the van was moving to and fro and its horn was sounding. Eventually there was a crowd of about 200–250 people in the yard.

After the police had surrounded the van the crowd became more pacific particularly as the sale was not due to take place for about an hour and no other action was imminent. Many of the assembled crowd carried placards protesting against the sale, some chanted 'No no warrant sale' and shouts of 'Scum' were directed at the two sheriff officers. There was some waving of fists and some isolated scuffling. During this stage of the incident the respondent stood on some kind of platform on a number of occasions and addressed the crowd. He was the only person present who thus addressed the crowd. On one occasion he said: 'We would appeal to the polis not to protect these people. These people are nothing but scum and they shouldnae allow the warrant sale to take place'. At another point of time in addressing the crowd the respondent held up a piece of paper and said: 'This interdict is to stop me and every single one of youse from being here today. As far as I'm concerned this is what they can do with their bloody interdict'. The respondent then tore the paper he was holding and threw the bits into the crowd. There was some division of view as to the precise expletive that Mr Sheridan used when he referred to the interdict but I hardly think this is important. At another point of time Mr Sheridan said to the crowd: 'The sale that they're going to try and carry out is due to take place at 11 o'clock. That's one hour and five minutes. As far as we're concerned there will be no sale'. The witnesses got the impression that the respondent was a person the crowd looked to for leadership. When he addressed the crowd he spoke with an obvious degree of aggression. The crowd listened attentively and responded to him enthusiastically. Moreover members of the crowd who appeared to be active in the demonstration conferred with him from time to time.

As the time for the sale approached some members of the crowd began again to concentrate their attention in the direction of the van and the mood of a section of the crowd became distinctly more menacing. Mr McIntyre heard a voice shout: 'If they try to take the furniture out of the van', although because of the noise from the crowd he could not hear the end of the sentence, Mr McIntyre consulted with Inspector Cattell, Inspector Cattell also adjudged the mood of the crowd to be menacing and he informed the sheriff officers that although he could ensure that they would not be murdered he could not guarantee that they might not suffer some injury if the sale were to proceed. It was therefore decided to cancel the sale and Mr Doherty announced this through a megaphone about 10.50 am. The crowd responded to the news with jubilation. Given the numbers of persons gathered at the yard and the threatening behaviour that some elements had shown themselves to be capable of, there was no practical possibility that the sale could have taken place.

Even after the sale was cancelled the crowd remained in the yard. The respondent again addressed the crowd and said: 'When this van goes out of the yard we're prepared to go out of the yard. What we are saying loud and clear is that this warrant sale is cancelled and so is every other one. Let's go back to all the housing estates and all the colleges and let's build the campaign. If any of these people turn up in the Polloks, Drumchapels, the Castlemilks we'll chase them to hell'. Thereafter Mr Sheridan approached Inspector Cattell and said that he could arrange to allow the van to leave the yard but the crowd would not leave before the van. Mr McIntyre signified he was prepared to drive the van away. Thereafter the respondent once more addressed the crowd and said: 'We've got a guarantee now folks. They're going to take the van away. If we let them get out of here the van's away. The warrant sale's off so we can get everybody this end.' After Mr Sheridan spoke the crowd cleared a path for the van and Mr McIntyre drove it away."

Two sheriff officers brought proceedings for breach of the interdict, which Lord Caplan found to have been established. Mr Sheridan was sentenced to six months' imprisonment. He appealed unsuccessfully, the opinion of the court being delivered by the Lord Justice Clerk (Ross).

LORD JUSTICE CLERK (ROSS): "On the basis of the facts which the Lord Ordinary found proved, we are satisfied that he was fully entitled to conclude that there had been breach of interdict. We are not persuaded that before the first respondent could be held to have interfered with the day to day business of the sheriff officers or their employees in the carrying out of their lawful duties, it was necessary to show that he had carried out some physical act. ...

We agree with counsel for the minuters that the words 'impede' and 'interfere' should be given their ordinary and natural meaning, and that there is no justification for placing some narrow interpretation upon them as counsel for the first respondent suggested. In particular we are satisfied that interference need not have a physical element. However, although that is so, we are inclined to the view that in the present case there was in any event a physical element to the interference by the first respondent. The Lord Ordinary makes it plain in his opinion that the first respondent himself accepted that he entered the yard towards the rear of the crowd at a time when there was shouting, a clatter of metal against metal, and the van was being moved to and fro with its horn sounding. This accordingly must have been towards the end of the stage when the crowd was behaving in a violent manner towards the sheriff officers in the van. Having arrived there it is plain from the Lord Ordinary's findings that the first respondent proceeded to associate himself with the crowd and indeed to take charge of the crowd. He addressed the crowd, and he was the only person to address the crowd. Witnesses got the impression that the first respondent was a person to whom the crowd looked for leadership. When he addressed the crowd before the decision to cancel the sale was made he spoke with an obvious degree of aggression and the crowd listened attentively to him and responded enthusiastically. In these circumstances we are of opinion that the Lord Ordinary would have been entitled to conclude that there had been a physical element in the first respondent's interference with the day to day business of the minuters and the carrying out of their lawful duties.

As it was in his opinion the Lord Ordinary expressed the view that an individual impeded or interfered with sheriff officers if he did anything calculated and likely to obstruct the conduct of their lawful activities. He pointed out that to a large extent a crowd or mob gathers its intimidatory character by force of numbers and that if a person deliberately attaches himself to a crowd bent upon impeding sheriff officers, then at the simplest level, adding weight to the mob or crowd can itself be an act of interference when this is done with a view to associating oneself with the activities of those assembled. We agree with that expression of opinion by the Lord Ordinary. Moreover, as the Lord Ordinary himself recognised, the activities of the first respondent went beyond mere attachment to the crowd. As we have already observed, the first respondent appears to have assumed leadership of the crowd, and to have been treated by the crowd as their leader. Indeed, when one has regard to the speeches made by the first respondent to the crowd, we are satisfied that there was ample material to justify the conclusion that the first respondent not only impeded or interfered with the sheriff officers in their day to day business and the carrying out of their lawful duties, but also encouraged others to do the same. ...

We agree with the Lord Ordinary that the manner in which the first respondent addressed the crowd could properly be described as inflammatory both in content and in manner of delivery. By declaring: 'The sale they're going to try to carry out is due to take place at 11 o'clock', and: 'As far as we're concerned there will be no sale', the first respondent was plainly inferring that difficulties would and should be placed in the way of the intention to carry out the sale. We also agree with the Lord Ordinary that the first respondent's action in tearing up what appeared to be the interim interdict could only be taken as a representation to the crowd that their purposes merited ignoring the rule of law. The Lord Ordinary mentions that at the end of his evidence, the first respondent declared that it was obvious from his statements and acts that he had no intention of being bound by the interdict.

In these circumstances we are quite satisfied that the Lord Ordinary was well founded in concluding that there had been what he described as 'a flagrant and calculated breach of interim interdict'. The findings made by the Lord Ordinary fully support the conclusion at which he arrived, and counsel for the first respondent failed to persuade us that any error could be detected in the Lord Ordinary's reasoning. As regards counsel's criticisms of the width of the interim interdict, it is unnecessary for us to express any view upon the question of whether the first respondent might have breached the interdict by making a speech against warrant sales in another part of Scotland. The speeches upon which the minuter founds were speeches which were made at the place where the warrant sale was to take place.

Counsel's second ground of appeal was that the period of imprisonment of six months was excessive. Under reference to the second ground of appeal, he contended that it was excessive having regard to the non-physical involvement of the first respondent, the non-interference by the crowd whilst he was present, and his right to express lawfully his opposition to the use of warrant sales. We are quite satisfied that there is no merit in this ground of appeal. As we have already observed there was a real physical element in the first respondent's involvement. In any event even if his involvement could properly be categorised as non-physical, what he did was to commit a flagrant and calculated breach of interim interdict. Although the main violence appears to have taken place just before the first respondent arrived, there can be no doubt that the crowd continued to behave in an intimidatory manner whilst he was present, and the speeches which he made would certainly have encouraged them to do so. We entirely accept that the first respondent, if so advised, is entitled to express lawfully his opposition to the use of warrant sales to enforce payments of arrears of the community charge, but that is, as the ground of appeal recognises, subject to the terms of the interim interdict.

In his supplementary opinion the Lord Ordinary explains that the first respondent's actions on the day in question had been deliberate and calculated, and that he had chosen publicly to challenge the authority of the courts. He flagrantly flouted the interim interdict pronounced by the court in front of a crowd which he knew contained violent and disorderly elements. Not only that but he actively participated in the crowd, and assumed leadership of the crowd.

Counsel for the first respondent himself recognised that if the Lord Ordinary was well founded in concluding that there had been a flagrant and calculated breach of interim interdict, then civil imprisonment was well nigh inevitable. He urged us however to substitute a lesser period for the period of six months selected by the Lord Ordinary.

We are satisfied that the Lord Ordinary was fully entitled to select a period of six months as the period of imprisonment in this case. We fully agree with the Lord Ordinary that if the evidence had shown that the first respondent had been directly involved in the serious violence directed against the sheriff officers at the beginning of the incident a heavier sentence would have been called for. Nothing which counsel for the first respondent said persuaded us that a period of six months in the circumstances could be regarded as excessive."

Additional powers to obtain a civil remedy to deal with protestors is to be found in the Protection from Harassment Act 1997 which deals specifically with harassment. The Act is much narrower in its application in Scotland than in England and Wales, but nevertheless provides that an interdict may be obtained to stop a course of conduct which amounts to harassment of another. For this purpose "conduct" includes speech; and "harassment" of a person includes causing the person alarm or distress. A course of conduct must involve conduct on at least two occasions. In practice conduct of this kind in the past has been dealt with as a breach of the peace: *Lees v Greer*, 1996 S.L.T. 1096; and *McKenzie v Normand*, 1992 S.L.T. 130 (without the need for the conduct to be repeated). Although the Protection from Harassment

Act 1997 has been used in England to deal with animal rights protestors, it is to be noted that it gives rise to criminal as well as civil liability in that jurisdiction. In Scotland its use appears to be confined in practice to matrimonial or personal disputes, though it clearly has wider implications. However, equally, there is no shortage of measures available to deal with the type of problems to which the Act might be directed.

VIII. CONCLUSION: THE LIMITED IMPACT OF CONVENTION RIGHTS

The right to freedom of assembly in Scotland is thus subject to a number of statutory and common law restraints. All of the restraints discussed in this chapter were introduced before—and in many cases long before—the enactment of the Scotland Act 1998 and the Human Rights Act 1998. The introduction of these measures raises questions about how far—if at all—the balance between liberty and restraint will have to be restruck in the light of the right to freedom of assembly which has now been introduced into Scots law. There is, however, no reason to believe that the incorporation of Convention rights will make much difference to the substance of the law. In particular it does not follow that any of the statutory or common law offences will themselves have to be reconsidered. Indeed it was already held by the European Commission of Human Rights that the power to ban marches on public order grounds under the Public Order Act 1936 did not violate Art.11: *Christians against Racism and Facism v United Kingdom* (1981) 21 D.R. 138. The decision in *Smith v Donnelly*, 2001 S.L.T. 1007 is a particularly important decision of the High Court of Justiciary in the Convention rights era. Rights enthusiasts will be disappointed that even the law of breach of the peace has survived a challenge brought on the ground that its wide and indeterminate scope violates Convention rights. It is perhaps revealing that the challenge was based on Art.7 rather than Art.10 & Art.11. It seems that the legitimacy of restraints on the latter is beyond contest, a view subsequently confirmed by *Jones v Carnegie*, 2004 S.L.T. 609.

But although the structure of the law is likely to be unaffected by the introduction of a right to freedom of assembly, we should not overlook the fact that public authorities and the police will be obliged to have regard to Convention rights when exercising discretionary powers. But we should not also overlook that this means having regard not only to the right to freedom assembly in Art.11(1) but also the permitted restrictions in Art.11(2). As we saw in the Angus Council example above, this may mean that while Art.11 is taken into account, it does not necessarily mean that an assembly will be allowed to proceed. Similarly, while the police may have to take into account an individual's right to freedom of assembly (as in *Redmond-Bate v D.P.P.* (1999) 7 B.H.R.C. 375) this may prove to be a rather insignificant matter where the individual is arrested for breach of the peace or obstruction of the highway. It ought, however, to provide some defence against the arbitrary and capricious exercise of the power of arrest. Apart from local authorities and the police, the courts too will be required to address Convention rights before convicting and before issuing interdicts. So far as the latter are concerned, the introduction of Convention rights ought to require a review of the circumstances in which interim interdicts are granted to restrain the exercise of Convention rights. It is hard to see how the issuing and serving of the interdicts in *McIntyre v Sheridan*, 1993 S.L.T. 412 can be said to be consistent with Art.6 of the Convention.

Chapter 10

"THE WAR ON TERROR" AND EMERGENCY POWERS

I. INTRODUCTION

In the materials presented so far we have considered how human rights are protected by Scots law in a wide range of circumstances. But it is not to be assumed that these rights will be protected in the same way in all circumstances regardless of context. Indeed many Convention rights permit qualifications in order to protect the rights or interests of others, and the nature of the qualification may vary according to the nature of the right or interest to be protected. One area which gives rise to major restrictions on human rights is the area of national security. Here we find that when public safety or national security are under threat great powers may be taken by the government in response, with the result that human rights may be sacrificed or subordinated for what some regard as a more urgent cause. Indeed under Art.15 it is possible to derogate from some (though not all) Convention rights. In this chapter we consider the restrictions on human rights which exist to deal with the issue of national and international terrorism.

The bomb explosion on Pam Am flight 103 over Lockerbie in 1988 was a devastating reminder that even small countries such as Scotland are not immune from the consequences of international conflict. In the same way, the legislation introduced since the incidents in New York and Washington DC in the US on September 11, 2001 are a reminder that conflict involving other countries can have a profound impact on the laws of a small country like Scotland. It should also be pointed out, however, that much of the modern Scots law dealing with terrorism has its origins in the United Kingdom Government's response to the conflict in Northern Ireland since 1969. The current law has grown gradually since the first Prevention of Terrorism (Temporary Provisions) Act was introduced in 1974. The law has developed since in response to decisions of the European Court of Human Rights, as well as the changing nature of the problem to which the legislation is addressed.

Before proceeding to discuss these matters, it may be pointed out that the present situation is simply part of a historical process of continuing legal restraints on civil liberties which has presented in a number of cycles. The process begins in modern times with the First World War, moving to the international war against communism in the 1920s and 1930s, the Second World War in 1939, the Cold War in the 1940s and 1950s, and the war against Irish republicanism in the 1970s. Now the war against international terrorism provides the occasion for greater powers. It is in effect the sixth cycle of restraint since 1914, and the sixth occasion for the introduction of emergency powers, many of which will be permanent and which will remain long after the emergency which produced them. What is different is that we have moved from a situation in war time in which we had temporary powers under the Defence of the Realm Acts to one in which we have permanent powers under legislation of various kinds.

II. 'TERRORISM' AND THE ECHR

It is often commented that the United Kingdom has been found on many occasions to be in breach of the ECHR by the European Court of Human Rights. Some of the most important—and shocking—of these decisions relate to measures taken to deal with terrorism in Northern Ireland. This is a battle that was fought by the British Government on a number of fronts: in Northern Ireland; on the British mainland; and overseas (including Gibraltar where a number of IRA suspects were shot dead in brutal circumstances by British security personnel). Special powers were taken to deal with the challenge to established authority, including emergency powers legislation in Northern Ireland and the Prevention of Terrorism Acts in the rest of Great Britain. As already mentioned, the first Prevention of Terrorism (Temporary Provisions) Act was passed in 1974, this being replaced in 1976 and then by the Prevention of Terrorism (Temporary Provisions) Act 1984, which was in turn replaced by the Prevention of Terrorism (Temporary Provisions) Act 1989. The last gave way to the Terrorism Act 2000, a measure which unlike the statutes it replaces does not expire after five years (unless renewed annually by Parliament). These different measures brought the United Kingdom into conflict with various provisions of the Convention, notably Arts 3, 5 and 6, but these were not the only measures to give rise to difficulty. The Gibraltar killings already referred to led to a finding that the United Kingdom had breached the right to life guarantees in Art.2 of the Convention: *McCann v United Kingdom* (1995) 21 E.H.R.R. 27.

Republic of Ireland v United Kingdom
(1978) 2 E.H.R.R. 25

This was an important complaint brought by the Republic of Ireland about the detention of a large number of nationalists, the powers being directed mainly at the IRA. The detentions took a number of forms and included detention for interrogation and what was referred to as preventive detention (internment). The detentions took place under special powers and then emergency powers. Those interned were detained indefinitely without the authority of a court or a judge. Some of the people detained were subjected to ill-treatment. The mistreatment included methods of sensory deprivation, sometimes termed "disorientation". The techniques consisted of:

- wall-standing: forcing the detainees to remain for periods of some hours in a "stress position", described by those who underwent it as being "spreadeagled against the wall, with their fingers put high above the head against the wall, the legs spread apart and the feet back, causing them to stand on their toes with the weight of the body mainly on the fingers";
- hooding: putting a black or navy coloured bag over the detainees' heads and, at least initially, keeping it there all the time except during interrogation;
- subjection to noise: pending their interrogations, holding the detainees in a room where there was a continuous loud and hissing noise;
- deprivation of sleep: pending their interrogations, depriving the detainees of sleep;
- deprivation of food and drink: subjecting the detainees to a reduced diet during their stay at the detention centre and pending interrogations.

The European Commission of Human Rights found that these practices amounted to torture. However, the European Court of Human Rights found that it amounted to inhuman and degrading treatment:

AS TO THE LAW: "97. From the start, it has been conceded by the respondent Government that the use of the five techniques was authorised at 'high level'. Although never committed to writing or authorised in any official document, the techniques had been orally taught to members of the RUC by the English Intelligence Centre at a seminar held in April 1971.

98. The two operations of interrogation in depth by means of the five techniques led to

the obtaining of a considerable quantity of intelligence information, including the identification of 700 members of both IRA factions and the discovery of individual responsibility for about 85 previously unexplained criminal incidents....

167. The five techniques were applied in combination, with premeditation and for hours at a stretch; they caused, if not actual bodily injury, at least intense physical and mental suffering to the persons subjected thereto and also led to acute psychiatric disturbances during interrogation. They accordingly fell into the category of inhuman treatment within the meaning of Article 3. The techniques were also degrading since they were such as to arouse in their victims feelings of fear, anguish and inferiority capable of humiliating and debasing them and possibly breaking their physical or moral resistance. On these two points, the Court is of the same view as the Commission.

In order to determine whether the five techniques should also be qualified as torture, the Court must have regard to the distinction embodied in Article 3, between this notion and that of inhuman or degrading treatment. In the Court's view, this distinction derives principally from a difference in the intensity of the suffering inflicted. The Court considers in fact that, whilst there exists on the one hand violence which is to be condemned both on moral grounds and also in most cases under the domestic law of the Contracting States but which does not fall within Article 3 of the Convention, it appears on the other hand that it was the intention that the Convention, with its distinction between 'torture' and 'inhuman or degrading treatment', should by the first of these terms attach a special stigma to deliberate inhuman treatment causing very serious and cruel suffering.

Moreover, this seems to be the thinking lying behind Article 1 in fine of Resolution 3452 (XXX) adopted by the General Assembly of the United Nations on 9 December 1975, which declares: 'Torture constitutes an aggravated and deliberate form of cruel, inhuman or degrading treatment or punishment'.

Although the five techniques, as applied in combination, undoubtedly amounted to inhuman and degrading treatment, although their object was the extraction of confessions, the naming of others and/or information and although they were used systematically, they did not occasion suffering of the particular intensity and cruelty implied by the word torture as so understood.

168. The Court concludes that recourse to the five techniques amounted to a practice of inhuman and degrading treatment, which practice was in breach of Article 3."

Another issue which arose in this case related to the detention of individuals which was held to be in breach of Art.5. The British government had, however, derogated from Art.5 under the provisions of Art.15. (It could not derogate from Art.3, as derogation from this particular article is not permitted.) The Court had to consider the claim for the Irish government that the derogation was not justified under Art.15. The court disagreed, but in doing so made clear that this is a matter that would not attract an especially rigorous standard of scrutiny on its part. In rejecting the challenge to the derogation, the court said:

"211. ... It falls in the first place to each Contracting State, with its responsibility for 'the life of [its] nation', to determine whether that life is threatened by a 'public emergency' and, if so, how far it is necessary to go in attempting to overcome the emergency. By reason of their direct and continuous contact with the pressing needs of the moment, the national authorities are in principle in a better position than the international judge to decide both on the presence of such an emergency and on the nature and scope of derogations necessary to avert it. In this matter Article 15(1) leaves those authorities a wide margin of appreciation. Nevertheless, the States do not enjoy an unlimited power in this respect. The Court, which, with the Commission, is responsible for ensuring the observance of the States' engagements (Article 19) (art. 19), is empowered to rule on whether the States have gone beyond the 'extent strictly required by the exigencies' of the crisis .... The domestic margin of appreciation is thus accompanied by a European supervision.

212. Unquestionably, the exercise of the special powers was mainly, and before 5 Feb-

ruary 1973 even exclusively, directed against the IRA as an underground military force. The intention was to combat an organisation which had played a considerable subversive rôle throughout the recent history of Ireland and which was creating, in August 1971 and thereafter, a particularly far-reaching and acute danger for the territorial integrity of the United Kingdom, the institutions of the six counties and the lives of the province's inhabitants .... Being confronted with a massive wave of violence and intimidation, the Northern Ireland Government and then, after the introduction of direct rule (30 March 1972), the British Government were reasonably entitled to consider that normal legislation offered insufficient resources for the campaign against terrorism and that recourse to measures outside the scope of the ordinary law, in the shape of extrajudicial deprivation of liberty, was called for. When the Irish Republic was faced with a serious crisis in 1957, it adopted the same approach and the Court did not conclude that the 'extent strictly required' had been exceeded ....

However, under one of the provisions complained of, namely Regulation 10, a person who was in no way suspected of a crime or offence or of activities prejudicial to peace and order could be arrested for the sole purpose of obtaining from him information about others—and this sometimes occurred .... This sort of arrest can be justifiable only in a very exceptional situation, but the circumstances prevailing in Northern Ireland did fall into such a category. Many witnesses could not give evidence freely without running the greatest risks ... ; the competent authorities were entitled to take the view, without exceeding their margin of appreciation, that it was indispensable to arrest such witnesses so that they could be questioned in conditions of relative security and not be exposed to reprisals. Moreover and above all, Regulation 10 authorised deprivation of liberty only for a maximum of forty-eight hours."

The Court thus held that the requirements of Art.15 were met, and that the derogations from Art.5 were not in breach of the Convention. The practice of internment—which was confined to Northern Ireland—was discontinued in 1975—though the power to re-introduce it was retained in legislation until 2000. The derogations which protected the British Government from challenge under Art.5 in the foregoing case were also withdrawn subsequently. However, fresh derogations were issued after the following decision.

Brogan v United Kingdom
(1988) 11 E.H.R.R. 117

Brogan was arrested at his home at 6.15 am. on September 17, 1984 by police officers under s.12 of the Prevention of Terrorism (Temporary Provisions) Act 1984. He was then taken to Gough Barracks, Armagh, where he was detained until his release at 5.20 pm on September 22, 1984, that is a period of detention of five days and 11 hours. Within a few hours of his arrest, he was questioned about his suspected involvement in an attack on a police mobile patrol which occurred on August 11, 1984 in County Tyrone and resulted in the death of a police sergeant and serious injuries to another police officer. He was also interrogated concerning his suspected membership of the Provisional Irish Republican Army ("IRA"), a proscribed organisation for the purposes of the 1984 Act. He maintained total silence and refused to answer any questions put to him. Other applicants (Dermot Coyle, William McFadden and Michael Tracey) were also detained under s.12 on the ground that there were reasonable grounds for suspecting them to have been involved in the commission, preparation or instigation of acts of terrorism connected with the affairs of Northern Ireland. On the day following his arrest, each applicant was informed by police officers that the Secretary of State for Northern Ireland had agreed to extend his detention by a further five days under s.12(4) of the 1984 Act. The latter provides that anyone arrested under s.12(1) could be detained for up to 48 hours and up to another five days on the authority of the Secretary of State. None of the applicants was brought before a judge or other officer authorised by law to exercise judicial power, nor were any of them charged after their release. The question for the European Court of Human Rights was whether the detention breached Art.5 of the ECHR.

As to the Law:

"III. ALLEGED BREACH OF ARTICLE 5 PARA. 1

49. ... There was no dispute that the applicants' arrest and detention were 'lawful' under Northern Ireland law and, in particular, 'in accordance with a procedure prescribed by law'. The applicants argued that the deprivation of liberty they suffered by virtue of section 12 of the 1984 Act failed to comply with Article 5 para. 1 (c), on the ground that they were not arrested on suspicion of an 'offence', nor was the purpose of their arrest to bring them before the competent legal authority.

50. Under the first head of argument, the applicants maintained that their arrest and detention were grounded on suspicion, not of having committed a specific offence, but rather of involvement in unspecified acts of terrorism, something which did not constitute a breach of the criminal law in Northern Ireland and could not be regarded as an 'offence' under Article 5 para. 1 (c).

The Government have not disputed that the 1984 Act did not require an arrest to be based on suspicion of a specific offence but argued that the definition of terrorism in the Act was compatible with the concept of an offence and satisfied the requirements of paragraph 1 (c) in this respect, as the Court's case-law confirmed. In this connection, the Government pointed out that the applicants were not in fact suspected of involvement in terrorism in general, but of membership of a proscribed organisation and involvement in specific acts of terrorism, each of which constituted an offence under the law of Northern Ireland and each of which was expressly put to the applicants during the course of their interviews following their arrests.

51. Section 14 of the 1984 Act defines terrorism as 'the use of violence for political ends', which includes 'the use of violence for the purpose of putting the public or any section of the public in fear'. The same definition of acts of terrorism—as contained in the Detention of Terrorists (Northern Ireland) Order 1972 and the Northern Ireland (Emergency Provisions) Act 1973—has already been found by the Court to be 'well in keeping with the idea of an offence' (see the *Ireland v United Kingdom* (1978) 2 E.H.R.R. 25, para. 196).

In addition, all of the applicants were questioned within a few hours of their arrest about their suspected involvement in specific offences and their suspected membership of proscribed organisations.

Accordingly, the arrest and subsequent detention of the applicants were based on a reasonable suspicion of commission of an offence within the meaning of Article 5 para. 1 (c).

52. Article 5 para. 1 (c) also requires that the purpose of the arrest or detention should be to bring the person concerned before the competent legal authority.

The Government and the Commission have argued that such an intention was present and that if sufficient and usable evidence had been obtained during the police investigation that followed the applicants' arrest, they would undoubtedly have been charged and brought to trial.

The applicants contested these arguments and referred to the fact that they were neither charged nor brought before a court during their detention. No charge had necessarily to follow an arrest under section 12 of the 1984 Act and the requirement under the ordinary law to bring the person before a court had been made inapplicable to detention under this Act. In the applicants' contention, this was therefore a power of administrative detention exercised for the purpose of gathering information, as the use in practice of the special powers corroborated.

53. The Court is not required to examine the impugned legislation in abstracto, but must confine itself to the circumstances of the case before it.

The fact that the applicants were neither charged nor brought before a court does not necessarily mean that the purpose of their detention was not in accordance with Article 5 para. 1 (c). As the Government and the Commission have stated, the existence of such a purpose must be considered independently of its achievement and sub-paragraph (c) of Article 5 para. 1 does not presuppose that the police should have obtained sufficient evidence to bring charges, either at the point of arrest or while the applicants were in custody.

Such evidence may have been unobtainable or, in view of the nature of the suspected offences, impossible to produce in court without endangering the lives of others. There is no reason to believe that the police investigation in this case was not in good faith or that the detention of the applicants was not intended to further that investigation by way of confirming or dispelling the concrete suspicions which, as the Court has found, grounded their arrest (see paragraph 51 above). Had it been possible, the police would, it can be assumed, have laid charges and the applicants would have been brought before the competent legal authority.

Their arrest and detention must therefore be taken to have been effected for the purpose specified in paragraph 1 (c).

54. In conclusion, there has been no violation of Article 5 para. 1.

IV. ALLEGED BREACH OF ARTICLE 5 PARA. 3

55. Under the 1984 Act, a person arrested under section 12 on reasonable suspicion of involvement in acts of terrorism may be detained by police for an initial period of forty-eight hours, and, on the authorisation of the Secretary of State for Northern Ireland, for a further period or periods of up to five days.

The applicants claimed, as a consequence of their arrest and detention under this legislation, to have been the victims of a violation of Article 5 para. 3, which provides [the Court read Art.5(3) and continued]. The applicants noted that a person arrested under the ordinary law of Northern Ireland must be brought before a Magistrates' Court within forty-eight hours ... ; and that under the ordinary law in England and Wales (Police and Criminal Evidence Act 1984) the maximum period of detention permitted without charge is four days, judicial approval being required at the thirty-six hour stage. In their submission, there was no plausible reason why a seven-day detention period was necessary, marking as it did such a radical departure from ordinary law and even from the three-day period permitted under the special powers of detention embodied in the Northern Ireland (Emergency Provisions) Act 1978. Nor was there any justification for not entrusting such decisions to the judiciary of Northern Ireland.

56. The Government have argued that in view of the nature and extent of the terrorist threat and the resulting problems in obtaining evidence sufficient to bring charges, the maximum statutory period of detention of seven days was an indispensable part of the effort to combat that threat, as successive parliamentary debates and reviews of the legislation had confirmed. In particular, they drew attention to the difficulty faced by the security forces in obtaining evidence which is both admissible and usable in consequence of training in anti-interrogation techniques adopted by those involved in terrorism. Time was also needed to undertake necessary scientific examinations, to correlate information from other detainees and to liaise with other security forces. The Government claimed that the need for a power of extension of the period of detention was borne out by statistics. For instance, in 1987 extensions were granted in Northern Ireland in respect of 365 persons. Some 83 were detained in excess of five days and of this number 39 were charged with serious terrorist offences during the extended period.

As regards the suggestion that extensions of detention beyond the initial forty-eight-hour period should be controlled or even authorised by a judge, the Government pointed out the difficulty, in view of the acute sensitivity of some of the information on which the suspicion was based, of producing it in court. Not only would the court have to sit in camera but neither the detained person nor his legal advisers could be present or told any of the details. This would require a fundamental and undesirable change in the law and procedure of the United Kingdom under which an individual who is deprived of his liberty is entitled to be represented by his legal advisers at any proceedings before a court relating to his detention. If entrusted with the power to grant extensions of detention, the judges would be seen to be exercising an executive rather than a judicial function. It would add nothing to the safe-guards against abuse which the present arrangements are designed to achieve and could lead to unanswerable criticism of the judiciary. In all the circumstances, the Secretary of State was better placed to take such decisions and to ensure a consistent approach. Moreover, the merits of each request to extend detention were personally scrutinised by the Secretary of State or, if he was unavailable, by another Minister.

...

58. The fact that a detained person is not charged or brought before a court does not in itself amount to a violation of the first part of Article 5 para. 3. No violation of Article 5 para. 3 can arise if the arrested person is released 'promptly' before any judicial control of his detention would have been feasible .... If the arrested person is not released promptly, he is entitled to a prompt appearance before a judge or judicial officer.

The assessment of 'promptness' has to be made in the light of the object and purpose of Article 5. The Court has regard to the importance of this Article in the Convention system: it enshrines a fundamental human right, namely the protection of the individual against arbitrary interferences by the State with his right to liberty .... Judicial control of inter-ferences by the executive with the individual's right to liberty is an essential feature of the guarantee embodied in Article 5 para. 3, which is intended to minimise the risk of arbi-trariness. Judicial control is implied by the rule of law, 'one of the fundamental principles of a democratic society ..., which is expressly referred to in the Preamble to the Convention' (see, mutatis mutandis, *Klass v Germany* (1978) 2 E.H.R.R. 214, para. 55) and 'from which the whole Convention draws its inspiration' (see, mutatis mutandis, *Engel v Netherlands* (1976) 1 E.H.R.R. 647, para. 69).

59. The obligation expressed in English by the word 'promptly' and in French by the word 'aussitôt' is clearly distinguishable from the less strict requirement in the second part of paragraph 3 ('reasonable time'/'délai raisonnable') and even from that in paragraph 4 of Article 5 ('speedily'/'à bref délai'). The term 'promptly' also occurs in the English text of paragraph 2, where the French text uses the words 'dans le plus court délai'. As indicated in the *Ireland v United Kingdom* (1978) 2 E.H.R.R. 25, 'promptly' in paragraph 3 may be understood as having a broader significance than 'aussitôt', which literally means imme-diately. Thus confronted with versions of a law-making treaty which are equally authentic but not exactly the same, the Court must interpret them in a way that reconciles them as far as possible and is most appropriate in order to realise the aim and achieve the object of the treaty ....

The use in the French text of the word 'aussitôt', with its constraining connotation of immediacy, confirms that the degree of flexibility attaching to the notion of 'promptness' is limited, even if the attendant circumstances can never be ignored for the purposes of the assessment under paragraph 3. Whereas promptness is to be assessed in each case according to its special features ... , the significance to be attached to those features can never be taken to the point of impairing the very essence of the right guaranteed by Article 5 para. 3, that is to the point of effectively negativing the State's obligation to ensure a prompt release or a prompt appearance before a judicial authority.

60. The instant case is exclusively concerned with the arrest and detention, by virtue of powers granted under special legislation, of persons suspected of involvement in terrorism in Northern Ireland. The requirements under the ordinary law in Northern Ireland as to bringing an accused before a court were expressly made inapplicable to such arrest and detention by section 12(6) of the 1984 Act. There is no call to determine in the present judgment whether in an ordinary criminal case any given period, such as four days, in police or administrative custody would as a general rule be capable of being compatible with the first part of Article 5 para. 3.

None of the applicants was in fact brought before a judge or judicial officer during his time in custody. The issue to be decided is therefore whether, having regard to the special features relied on by the Government, each applicant's release can be considered as 'prompt' for the purposes of Article 5 para. 3.

61. The investigation of terrorist offences undoubtedly presents the authorities with special problems, partial reference to which has already been made under Article 5 para. 1. The Court takes full judicial notice of the factors adverted to by the Government in this connection. It is also true that in Northern Ireland the referral of police requests for extended detention to the Secretary of State and the individual scrutiny of each police request by a Minister do provide a form of executive control. In addition, the need for the continuation of the special powers has been constantly monitored by Parliament and their operation regularly reviewed by independent personalities. The Court accepts that, subject to the existence of adequate safeguards, the context of terrorism in Northern Ireland has the effect of prolonging the period during which the authorities may, without violating Article 5 para. 3, keep a person suspected of serious terrorist offences in custody before bringing him before a judge or other judicial officer.

The difficulties, alluded to by the Government, of judicial control over decisions to arrest and detain suspected terrorists may affect the manner of implementation of Article 5 para. 3, for example in calling for appropriate procedural precautions in view of the nature of the suspected offences. However, they cannot justify, under Article 5 para. 3, dispensing altogether with 'prompt' judicial control.

62. As indicated above (paragraph 59), the scope for flexibility in interpreting and applying the notion of 'promptness' is very limited. In the Court's view, even the shortest of the four periods of detention, namely the four days and six hours spent in police custody by Mr McFadden, falls outside the strict constraints as to time permitted by the first part of Article 5 para. 3. To attach such importance to the special features of this case as to justify so lengthy a period of detention without appearance before a judge or other judicial officer would be an unacceptably wide interpretation of the plain meaning of the word 'promptly'. An interpretation to this effect would import into Article 5 para. 3 a serious weakening of a procedural guarantee to the detriment of the individual and would entail consequences impairing the very essence of the right protected by this provision. The Court thus has to conclude that none of the applicants was either brought 'promptly' before a judicial authority or released 'promptly' following his arrest. The undoubted fact that the arrest and detention of the applicants were inspired by the legitimate aim of protecting the community as a whole from terrorism is not on its own sufficient to ensure compliance with the specific requirements of Article 5 para. 3. There has thus been a breach of Article 5 para. 3 in respect of all four applicants.

V. ALLEGED BREACH OF ARTICLE 5 PARA. 4

63. The applicants argued that as Article 5 had not been incorporated into United Kingdom law, an effective review of the lawfulness of their detention, as required by paragraph 4 of Article 5, was precluded....

64. The remedy of habeas corpus was available to the applicants in the present case, though they chose not to avail themselves of it. Such proceedings would have led to a review of the lawfulness of their arrest and detention under the terms of the 1984 Act and the applicable principles developed by case-law.

The Commission found that the requirements of Article 5 para. 4 (art. 5-4) were satisfied since the review available in Northern Ireland would have encompassed the procedural and substantive basis, under the Convention, for their detention. The Government have adopted the same reasoning.

65. According to the Court's established case-law, the notion of 'lawfulness' under paragraph 4 has the same meaning as in paragraph 1; and whether an 'arrest' or 'detention' can be regarded as 'lawful' has to be determined in the light not only of domestic law, but also of the text of the Convention, the general principles embodied therein and the aim of the restrictions permitted by Article 5 para. 1 .... By virtue of paragraph 4 of Article 5 (art. 5-4), arrested or detained persons are entitled to a review bearing upon the procedural and

substantive conditions which are essential for the 'lawfulness', in the sense of the Convention, of their deprivation of liberty. This means that, in the instant case, the applicants should have had available to them a remedy allowing the competent court to examine not only compliance with the procedural requirements set out in section 12 of the 1984 Act but also the reasonableness of the suspicion grounding the arrest and the legitimacy of the purpose pursued by the arrest and the ensuing detention.

As is shown by the relevant case-law, ..., these conditions are met in the practice of the Northern Ireland courts in relation to the remedy of habeas corpus.

Accordingly, there has been no violation of Article 5 para. 4.

VI. ALLEGED BREACH OF ARTICLE 5 PARA. 5

66. The applicants further alleged breach of Article 5 para. 5. ... A claim for compensation for unlawful deprivation of liberty may be made in the United Kingdom in respect of a breach of domestic law. As Article 5 is not considered part of the domestic law of the United Kingdom, no claim for compensation lies for a breach of any provision of Article 5 which does not at the same time constitute a breach of United Kingdom law.

The Government argued, inter alia, that the aim of paragraph 5 is to ensure that the victim of an 'unlawful' arrest or detention should have an enforceable right to compensation. In this regard, they have also contended that 'lawful' for the purposes of the various paragraphs of Article 5 is to be construed as essentially referring back to domestic law and in addition as excluding any element of arbitrariness. They concluded that even in the event of a violation being found of any of the first four paragraphs, there has been no violation of paragraph 5 because the applicants' deprivation of liberty was lawful under Northern Ireland law and was not arbitrary.

67. The Court, like the Commission, considers that such a restrictive interpretation is incompatible with the terms of paragraph 5 which refers to arrest or detention 'in contravention of the provisions of this Article'. In the instant case, the applicants were arrested and detained lawfully under domestic law but in breach of paragraph 3 of Article 5. This violation could not give rise, either before or after the findings made by the European Court in the present judgment, to an enforceable claim for compensation by the victims before the domestic courts; this was not disputed by the Government.

Accordingly, there has also been a breach of paragraph 5 in this case in respect of all four applicants."

It might have been expected after the *Brogan* decision that the government would change the law relating to executive detention. But rather than do so, as already suggested, the Government chose instead to renew its derogation from Art.5(3). The derogation was in the following terms:

"Following [the *Brogan* judgment], the Secretary of State for the Home Department informed Parliament on 6 December 1988 that, against the background of the terrorist campaign, and the over-riding need to bring terrorists to justice, the Government did not believe that the maximum period of detention should be reduced. He informed Parliament that the Government were examining the matter with a view to responding to the judgment. On 22 December 1988, the Secretary of State further informed Parliament that it remained the Government's wish, if it could be achieved, to find a judicial process under which extended detention might be reviewed and where appropriate authorised by a judge or other judicial officer. But a further period of reflection and consultation was necessary before the Government could bring forward a firm and final view. Since the judgment of 29 November 1988 as well as previously, the Government have found it necessary to continue to exercise, in relation to terrorism connected with the affairs of Northern Ireland, the powers ... enabling further detention without charge, for periods of up to 5 days, on the authority of the Secretary of State, to the extent strictly required by the exigencies of the situation to enable necessary enquiries and investigations properly to be completed in order to decide whether criminal proceedings should be instituted. To the extent that the exercise of these powers may be inconsistent with the obligations imposed by the Convention the Government have availed themselves of the right of derogation conferred by Article 15(1) of the Convention and will continue to do so until further notice..."

This meant that the law did not have to be changed, but it also meant that those detained under these powers were unable to challenge the detention. In *Brannigan and McBride v United Kingdom* (1994) 17 E.H.R.R. 539, however, an attempt was made unsuccessfully to challenge the derogation on the ground that it could not be justified as being necessary under Art.15. In the view of the Court:

"43. ... it falls to each Contracting State, with its responsibility for 'the life of [its] nation', to determine whether that life is threatened by a 'public emergency' and, if so, how far it is necessary to go in attempting to overcome the emergency. By reason of their direct and continuous contact with the pressing needs of the moment, the national authorities are in principle in a better position than the international judge to decide both on the presence of such an emergency and on the nature and scope of derogations necessary to avert it. Accordingly, in this matter a wide margin of appreciation should be left to the national authorities (see *Ireland v United Kingdom* (1978) 2 E.H.R.R. 25, para. 207). Nevertheless, Contracting Parties do not enjoy an unlimited power of appreciation. It is for the Court to rule on whether inter alia the States have gone beyond the 'extent strictly required by the exigencies' of the crisis. The domestic margin of appreciation is thus accompanied by a European supervision (ibid.). At the same time, in exercising its supervision the Court must give appropriate weight to such relevant factors as the nature of the rights affected by the derogation, the circumstances leading to, and the duration of, the emergency situation."

It was held that the circumstances in Northern Ireland constituted a public emergency threatening the life of the nation and the question was whether the measures taken were strictly required by the exigencies of the situation. In the view of the court the derogation was a genuine response to an emergency. It was also held that the absence of judicial control of extended detention was justified. On the last point the court said:

"58. The Court notes the opinions expressed in the various reports reviewing the operation of the Prevention of Terrorism legislation that the difficulties of investigating and prosecuting terrorist crime give rise to the need for an extended period of detention which would not be subject to judicial control. Moreover, these special difficulties were recognised in its above-mentioned Brogan judgment, para. 61.

It further observes that it remains the view of the respondent Government that it is essential to prevent the disclosure to the detainee and his legal adviser of information on the basis of which decisions on the extension of detention are made and that, in the adversarial system of the common law, the independence of the judiciary would be compromised if judges or other judicial officers were to be involved in the granting or approval of extensions....

59. It is not the Court's role to substitute its view as to what measures were most appropriate or expedient at the relevant time in dealing with an emergency situation for that of the Government which have direct responsibility for establishing the balance between the taking of effective measures to combat terrorism on the one hand, and respecting individual rights on the other .... In the context of Northern Ireland, where the judiciary is small and vulnerable to terrorist attacks, public confidence in the independence of the judiciary is understandably a matter to which the Government attach great importance.

60. In the light of these considerations it cannot be said that the Government have exceeded their margin of appreciation in deciding, in the prevailing circumstances, against judicial control."

The court concluded that: "Having regard to the nature of the terrorist threat in Northern Ireland, the limited scope of the derogation and the reasons advanced in support of it, as well as the existence of basic safeguards against abuse, ... the Government have not exceeded their margin of appreciation in considering that the derogation was strictly required by the exigencies of the situation". This derogation was not withdrawn until the 1989 Act was repealed (though as we shall see, it was quickly followed by another). In the meantime, the derogation from Art.5 did not protect the government from challenge under Art.6, as the following case reveals.

Withdrawal of derogation contained in a Note Verbale from the Permanent Representative of the United Kingdom, dated 19 February 2001, handed to the Secretary General on 19 February 2001

The United Kingdom Permanent Representative to the Council of Europe presents his compliments to the Secretary General of the Council, and has the honour to refer to Article 15, paragraph 3, of the Convention for the Protection of Human Rights and Fundamental Freedoms, signed at Rome on 4 November 1950, as well as to the notification made by the then United Kingdom Permanent Representative to the then Secretary General under the Article 15, paragraph 3, and dated 23 December 1988 and 23 March 1989.

The provisions referred to in the March 1989 notification, namely section 14 and paragraph 6 of Schedule 5 to the Prevention of Terrorism Act 1989, have been replaced by section 41 and paragraph 6 of Schedule 7 to the Terrorism Act 2000. Under section 41 a person who has been arrested by a constable upon reasonable suspicion of being guilty of an offence under Sections, 11, 12, 15, to 18, 54 and 56 to 63 of the Act, or being concerned in the commission, preparation or instigation of acts of terrorism, can be detained by virtue of the arrest for up to 48 hours and thereafter, where a judicial authority extends the detention period, for up to a further five days. The judicial authority will extend detention only to the point strictly necessary for the completion of investigations and enquiries or to preserve relevant evidence in order to decide whether criminal proceedings should be instituted. Under paragraph 6 of Schedule 7 to the Act a person who is being examined at a port or in a border area by an examining officer for the purpose of determining whether he is a person who is or has been involved in the commission, preparation or instigation of acts of terrorism, or for the purpose of determining whether his presence in the border area is connected with his entering or leaving Northern Ireland, may be detained pending the conclusion of his examination. The period of his detention under this power shall not exceed nine hours. No extension of detention is possible.

In the light of these developments, the measures referred to in the notifications dated 23 December 1988 and 23 March 1989 will cease to operate as of Monday, 26 February 2001. Accordingly, the two notifications are withdrawn as from that date, and the Government of the United Kingdom confirms that the provisions of the Convention will again be executed as from then.

However, this withdrawal of the derogation only applies to the United Kingdom of Great Britain and Northern Ireland. It is not yet possible to withdraw the derogation in respect of the Crown Dependencies, that is the Bailiwick of Jersey, the Bailiwick of Guernsey and the Isle of Man. The Crown Dependencies are actively considering enacting or amending their current Prevention of Terrorism legislation to reflect the changes in the United Kingdom legislation made under the Terrorism Act 2000. (The letter from the Permanent Representative of 12 November 1998 to the previous Secretary General explains the position in relation to the legislation in the Crown Dependencies.)

Period covered: 26/2/2001—
The preceding statement concerns Article(s): 15

Murray v United Kingdom
(1996) 22 E.H.R.R. 29

The applicant was arrested by police officers at 5.40 pm on January 7, 1990 under s.14 of the Prevention of Terrorism (Temporary Provisions) Act 1989. He was cautioned under the terms of the Criminal Evidence (Northern Ireland) Order 1988 which allowed adverse inferences to be drawn from his refusal to say anything that he might subsequently rely on at his trial. He was taken to a police station where he was denied access to a solicitor for 48 hours under the Northern Ireland (Emergency Provisions) Act 1987. While in custody the applicant was cautioned pursuant to art.6 of the Criminal Evidence (Northern Ireland) Order 1988. He was asked to account for his presence at the house where he was arrested. He was warned that if he failed or refused to do so, a court, judge or jury might draw such inference from his failure or refusal as appeared proper. In reply to this caution the applicant stated: "Nothing to say". In May 1991 the applicant was tried for the offences of conspiracy to murder, the unlawful imprisonment, with seven other people, of a certain Mr L and of belonging to a proscribed organisation, the Provisional Irish Republican Army (IRA). The applicant was found guilty of the offence of aiding and abetting the unlawful imprisonment of Mr L and sentenced to eight years' imprisonment. He was acquitted on the remaining charges. In concluding that the applicant was guilty of the offence of aiding and abetting false imprisonment, the trial judge drew adverse inferences against the applicant. An appeal to the Court of Appeal was unsuccessful, and a complaint was then made to Strasbourg alleging a breach of art.6(1) and (2) that he had been deprived of the right to silence in the criminal proceedings against him. He further complained, under art.6 (3) of his lack of access to a solicitor during his detention.

AS TO THE LAW:

"I. ALLEGED VIOLATION OF ARTICLE 6 (art. 6) OF THE CONVENTION

45. Although not specifically mentioned in Article 6 of the Convention, there can be no doubt that the right to remain silent under police questioning and the privilege against self-incrimination are generally recognised international standards which lie at the heart of the notion of a fair procedure under Article 6 .... By providing the accused with protection against improper compulsion by the authorities these immunities contribute to avoiding miscarriages of justice and to securing the aims of Article 6 (art. 6).

46. The Court does not consider that it is called upon to give an abstract analysis of the scope of these immunities and, in particular, of what constitutes in this context 'improper compulsion'. What is at stake in the present case is whether these immunities are absolute in the sense that the exercise by an accused of the right to silence cannot under any circumstances be used against him at trial or, alternatively, whether informing him in advance that, under certain conditions, his silence may be so used, is always to be regarded as 'improper compulsion'.

47. On the one hand, it is self-evident that it is incompatible with the immunities under consideration to base a conviction solely or mainly on the accused's silence or on a refusal to answer questions or to give evidence himself. On the other hand, the Court deems it equally obvious that these immunities cannot and should not prevent that the accused's silence, in situations which clearly call for an explanation from him, be taken into account in assessing the persuasiveness of the evidence adduced by the prosecution.

Wherever the line between these two extremes is to be drawn, it follows from this understanding of 'the right to silence' that the question whether the right is absolute must be answered in the negative.

It cannot be said therefore that an accused's decision to remain silent throughout criminal proceedings should necessarily have no implications when the trial court seeks to evaluate the evidence against him. In particular, as the Government have pointed out, established international standards in this area, while providing for the right to silence and the privilege against self-incrimination, are silent on this point.

Whether the drawing of adverse inferences from an accused's silence infringes Article 6 is a matter to be determined in the light of all the circumstances of the case, having particular regard to the situations where inferences may be drawn, the weight attached to them by the national courts in their assessment of the evidence and the degree of compulsion inherent in the situation.

48. As regards the degree of compulsion involved in the present case, it is recalled that the applicant was in fact able to remain silent. Notwithstanding the repeated warnings as to the possibility that inferences might be drawn from his silence, he did not make any statements to the police and did not give evidence during his trial. Moreover under Article 4 (5) of the Order he remained a non-compellable witness. Thus his insistence in maintaining silence throughout the proceedings did not amount to a criminal offence or contempt of court. Furthermore, as has been stressed in national court decisions, silence, in itself, cannot be regarded as an indication of guilt.

49. The facts of the present case accordingly fall to be distinguished from those in *Funke v France* (1993) 16 E.H.R.R. 297 where criminal proceedings were brought against the applicant by the customs authorities in an attempt to compel him to provide evidence of offences he had allegedly committed. Such a degree of compulsion in that case was found by the Court to be incompatible with Article 6 since, in effect, it destroyed the very essence of the privilege against self-incrimination.

50. Admittedly a system which warns the accused—who is possibly without legal assistance (as in the applicant's case)—that adverse inferences may be drawn from a refusal to provide an explanation to the police for his presence at the scene of a crime or to testify during his trial, when taken in conjunction with the weight of the case against him, involves a certain level of indirect compulsion. However, since the applicant could not be compelled to speak or to testify, as indicated above, this factor on its own cannot be decisive. The Court must rather concentrate its attention on the role played by the inferences in the proceedings against the applicant and especially in his conviction.

51. In this context, it is recalled that these were proceedings without a jury, the trier of fact being an experienced judge. Furthermore, the drawing of inferences under the Order is subject to an important series of safeguards designed to respect the rights of the defence and to limit the extent to which reliance can be placed on inferences.

In the first place, before inferences can be drawn under Article 4 and 6 of the Order appropriate warnings must have been given to the accused as to the legal effects of maintaining silence. Moreover, as indicated by the judgment of the House of Lords in *R. v Murray* (1993) 97 Cr. App. R. 151 the prosecutor must first establish a prima facie case against the accused, i.e. a case consisting of direct evidence which, if believed and combined with legitimate inferences based upon it, could lead a properly directed jury to be satisfied beyond reasonable doubt that each of the essential elements of the offence is proved.

The question in each particular case is whether the evidence adduced by the prosecution is sufficiently strong to require an answer. The national court cannot conclude that the accused is guilty merely because he chooses to remain silent. It is only if the evidence against the accused 'calls' for an explanation which the accused ought to be in a position to give that a failure to give any explanation 'may as a matter of common sense allow the drawing of an inference that there is no explanation and that the accused is guilty'. Conversely if the case presented by the prosecution had so little evidential value that it called for no answer, a failure to provide one could not justify an inference of guilt (ibid.). In sum, it is only common-sense inferences which the judge considers proper, in the light of the evidence against the accused, that can be drawn under the Order.

In addition, the trial judge has a discretion whether, on the facts of the particular case, an inference should be drawn. As indicated by the Court of Appeal in the present case, if a judge accepted that an accused did not understand the warning given or if he had doubts about it, 'we are confident that he would not activate Article 6 against him'. Furthermore in Northern Ireland, where trial judges sit without a jury, the judge must explain the reasons for the decision to draw inferences and the weight attached to them. The exercise of discretion in this regard is subject to review by the appellate courts.

52. In the present case, the evidence presented against the applicant by the prosecution was considered by the Court of Appeal to constitute a 'formidable' case against him. It is recalled that when the police entered the house some appreciable time after they knocked on the door, they found the applicant coming down the flight of stairs in the house where Mr L. had been held captive by the IRA. Evidence had been given by Mr L—evidence which in the opinion of the trial judge had been corroborated—that he had been forced to make a taped confession and that after the arrival of the police at the house and the removal of his blindfold he saw the applicant at the top of the stairs. He had been told by him to go downstairs and watch television. The applicant was pulling a tape out of a cassette. The tangled tape and cassette recorder were later found on the premises. Evidence by the applicant's co-accused that he had recently arrived at the house was discounted as not being credible.

53. The trial judge drew strong inferences against the applicant under Article 6 of the Order by reason of his failure to give an account of his presence in the house when arrested and interrogated by the police. He also drew strong inferences under Article 4 of the Order by reason of the applicant's refusal to give evidence in his own defence when asked by the court to do so.

54. In the Court's view, having regard to the weight of the evidence against the applicant, as outlined above, the drawing of inferences from his refusal, at arrest, during police questioning and at trial, to provide an explanation for his presence in the house was a matter of common sense and cannot be regarded as unfair or unreasonable in the circumstances....

Nor can it be said, against this background, that the drawing of reasonable inferences from the applicant's behaviour had the effect of shifting the burden of proof from the prosecution to the defence so as to infringe the principle of the presumption of innocence....

57. Against the above background, and taking into account the role played by inferences under the Order during the trial and their impact on the rights of the defence, the Court does not consider that the criminal proceedings were unfair or that there had been an infringement of the presumption of innocence.

58. Accordingly, there has been no violation of Article 6 (1) and (2) of the Convention.

B. Access to lawyer

...

62. The Court observes that it has not been disputed by the Government that Article 6 applies even at the stage of the preliminary investigation into an offence by the police. In this respect it recalls its finding in the *Imbrioscia v Switzerland* (1993) 17 E.H.R.R. 441 that Article 6—especially paragraph 3—may be relevant before a case is sent for trial if and so far as the fairness of the trial is likely to be seriously prejudiced by an initial failure to comply with its provisions. As it pointed out in that judgment, the manner in which Article 6 para. 3 (c) is to be applied during the preliminary investigation depends on the special features of the proceedings involved and on the circumstances of the case (loc. cit., p. 14, para. 38).

63. National laws may attach consequences to the attitude of an accused at the initial stages of police interrogation which are decisive for the prospects of the defence in any subsequent criminal proceedings. In such circumstances Article 6 will normally require that the accused be allowed to benefit from the assistance of a lawyer already at the initial stages of police interrogation. However, this right, which is not explicitly set out in the Convention, may be subject to restrictions for good cause. The question, in each case, is whether the restriction, in the light of the entirety of the proceedings, has deprived the accused of a fair hearing.

64. In the present case, the applicant's right of access to a lawyer during the first 48 hours of police detention was restricted under section 15 of the Northern Ireland (Emergency

Provisions) Act 1987 on the basis that the police had reasonable grounds to believe that the exercise of the right of access would, inter alia, interfere with the gathering of information about the commission of acts of terrorism or make it more difficult to prevent such an act.

65. It is observed that the applicant did not seek to challenge the exercise of this power by instituting proceedings for judicial review although, before the Court, he now contests its lawfulness. The Court, however, has no reason to doubt that it amounted to a lawful exercise of the power to restrict access. Nevertheless, although it is an important element to be taken into account, even a lawfully exercised power of restriction is capable of depriving an accused, in certain circumstances, of a fair procedure.

66. The Court is of the opinion that the scheme contained in the Order is such that it is of paramount importance for the rights of the defence that an accused has access to a lawyer at the initial stages of police interrogation. It observes in this context that, under the Order, at the beginning of police interrogation, an accused is confronted with a fundamental dilemma relating to his defence. If he chooses to remain silent, adverse inferences may be drawn against him in accordance with the provisions of the Order. On the other hand, if the accused opts to break his silence during the course of interrogation, he runs the risk of prejudicing his defence without necessarily removing the possibility of inferences being drawn against him. Under such conditions the concept of fairness enshrined in Article 6 requires that the accused has the benefit of the assistance of a lawyer already at the initial stages of police interrogation. To deny access to a lawyer for the first 48 hours of police questioning, in a situation where the rights of the defence may well be irretrievably pre-judiced, is—whatever the justification for such denial—incompatible with the rights of the accused under Article 6.

67. The Government have argued that in order to complain under Article 6 of denial of access to a lawyer it must be clear that, had the applicant been able to consult with his solicitor earlier, he would have acted differently from the way he did. It is contended that the applicant has not shown this to be the case.

68. It is true, as pointed out by the Government, that when the applicant was able to consult with his solicitor he was advised to continue to remain silent and that during the trial the applicant chose not to give evidence or call witnesses on his behalf. However, it is not for the Court to speculate on what the applicant's reaction, or his lawyer's advice, would have been had access not been denied during this initial period. As matters stand, the applicant was undoubtedly directly affected by the denial of access and the ensuing inter-ference with the rights of the defence. The Court's conclusion as to the drawing of inferences does not alter that.

69. In his written submissions to the Court, the applicant appeared to make the further complaint under this head that his solicitor was unable to be present during police inter-views. However, whether or not this issue formed part of the complaints admitted by the Commission, in any event its examination of the case was limited to that of the question of his access to a lawyer. Moreover, the case as argued before the Court was, in the main, confined to this issue. In these circumstances, and having regard to the Court's finding that he ought to have had access to a lawyer, it is not necessary to examine this point.

70. There has therefore been a breach of Article 6 (1) in conjunction with paragraph 6 (3) of the Convention as regards the applicant's denial of access to a lawyer during the first 48 hours of his police detention."

Other important cases on Art.6 include *Magee v United Kingdom* (2001) 31 E.H.R.R. 822 and *Brennan v United Kingdom* (2002) 34 E.H.R.R. 507. In the latter case the complainant had been arrested on suspicion of being a member of the IRA. He was denied access to a solicitor for 24 hours, and was not allowed to have a solicitor present while being interviewed by the police. The court held that Art.6 had not been breached on either ground. It did, however, hold that there had been a breach in relation to the refusal to allow the complainant to consult his solicitor privately: when he was eventually allowed to see his solicitor, the complainant was permitted to do so only in the presence of a police officer. According to the court:

"58. The Court has noted above that Article 6(3) normally requires that an accused be allowed to benefit from the assistance of a lawyer at the initial stages of an interrogation. Furthermore, an accused's right to communicate with his advocate out of hearing of a third person is part of the basic requirements of a fair trial and follows from Article 6(3) (c). If a lawyer were unable to confer with his client and receive confidential instructions from him without surveillance, his assistance would lose much of its usefulness, whereas the Convention is intended to guarantee rights that are practical and effective ... However, the Court's case-law indicates that the right of access to a solicitor may be subject to restrictions for good cause and the question in each case is whether the restriction, in the light of the entirety of the proceedings, has deprived the accused of a fair hearing. While it is not necessary for the applicant to prove, assuming such were possible, that the restriction had a prejudicial effect on the course of the trial, the applicant must be able to be claim to have been directly affected by the restriction in the exercise of the rights of the defence.

59. In this case, the trial judge found that the restriction served the purpose identified under section 45 of the 1991 Act of preventing information being passed on to suspects still at large. There was, however, no allegation that the solicitor was in fact likely to collaborate in such an attempt, and it was unclear to what extent a police officer would be able to spot a coded message if one was in fact passed. At most, it appears that the presence of the police officer would have had some effect in inhibiting any improper communication of information, assuming there was any risk that such might take place. While the Court finds that there is no reason to doubt the good faith of the police in imposing and implementing this measure—there is no suggestion, as pointed out by the Government, that the police sought to use the opportunity to obtain evidence for their own purposes—, it nonetheless finds no compelling reason arising in this case for the imposition of the restriction.

60. As regards the proportionality of the restriction, the Court notes that the police officer was only present at one interview. Indeed, the measure could only apply during the first 48-hour period after the arrest, after which the applicant was able to consult out of hearing with his solicitor until his trial some months later. It was a restriction therefore of very limited duration, and may in that respect be distinguished from the breach found in *S. v Switzerland* (1992) 14 E.H.R.R. 670, where the restriction on consultations lasted for about eight months.

61. The consultation was, however, the first occasion since his arrest at which the applicant was able to seek advice from his lawyer. He had been cautioned under Article 3 of the 1988 Order and, as noted in *John Murray* (1996) 22 E.H.R.R. 29, his decision as to whether to answer particular questions or to risk inferences being drawn against him later was potentially of great importance to his defence at trial. The Government have argued that the solicitor would have been able to advise him concerning the application of Article 3, even in the presence of the police officer. It also appears that the trial judge, after hearing the solicitor and applicant give evidence concerning the interview, considered that the solicitor had not been inhibited in any way in giving advice to the applicant.

62. Nonetheless, the Court cannot but conclude that the presence of the police officer would have inevitably prevented the applicant from speaking frankly to his solicitor and given him reason to hesitate before broaching questions of potential significance to the case against him. Both the applicant and the solicitor had been warned that no names should be mentioned and that the interview would be stopped if anything was said which was perceived as hindering the investigation. It is immaterial that it is not shown that there were particular matters which the applicant and his solicitor were thereby stopped from discussing. The ability of an accused to communicate freely with his defence lawyer, recognised, *inter alia*, in Article 93 of the Standard Minimum Rules for the Treatment of Prisoners, was subject to express limitation. The applicant had already made admissions before the consultation, and made admissions afterwards. It is indisputable that he was in need of legal advice at that time, and that his responses in subsequent interviews, which were to be carried out in the absence of his solicitor, would continue to be of potential relevance to his trial and could irretrievably prejudice his defence."

III. THE TERRORISM ACT 2000

The Terrorism Act 2000 contains permanent powers and replaces the Prevention of Terrorism (Temporary Provisions) Act 1989. The 2000 Act was passed following the report of Lord Lloyd who conducted an *Inquiry into Legislation Against Terrorism* (Cm. 3420, 1996). In his report Lord Lloyd concluded that even after lasting peace was established in Northern Ireland, there would still be a need for permanent anti-terrorist legislation (para.5.15). He recommended that a new Act should apply throughout the United Kingdom and should cover domestic as well as international terrorism (para.5.21). He also recommended that the law dealing with terrorism should be based on the following principles.

Lord Lloyd of Berwick
Inquiry into Legislation Against Terrorism
Cm. 3420 (1996)

"(i) Legislation against terrorism should approximate as closely as possible to the ordinary criminal law and procedure;
(ii) Additional statutory offences and powers may be justified, but only if they are necessary to meet the anticipated threat. They must then strike the right balance between the needs of security and the rights and liberties of the individual;
(iii) The need for additional safeguards should be considered alongside any additional powers;
(iv) The law should comply with the UK's obligations in international law."

These principles were subsequently endorsed as a "useful framework" by a Joint Committee of Privy Councillors in 2003 which examined the operation of the Anti-terrorism, Crime and Security Act 2001. The Report of the Joint Committee is considered more fully below.

The starting point of the Terrorism Act 2000 is the definition of terrorism in s.1 of the Act. The term is widely and controversially defined and gave rise to considerable discussion in Parliament. As defined, terrorism includes not only international terrorism (including those such as the African National Congress (ANC) involved in national liberation struggles against oppressive regimes), but also to include those involved in potentially violent acts of political protest, such as animal rights protestors or anti-war protestors whose violence includes serious damage to property. The Government acknowledged the wide scope of the definition but argued that the operation of the Act would be constrained by the Human Rights Act, and that a common sense view would be adopted when it came to prosecution. Section 1 of the Act provides as follows:

Terrorism Act 2000

"Terrorism: interpretation
    1.—(1) In this Act "terrorism" means the use or threat of action where—
      (a) the action falls within subsection (2),
      (b) the use or threat is designed to influence the government or to intimidate the public or a section of the public, and
      (c) the use or threat is made for the purpose of advancing a political, religious or ideological cause.
    (2) Action falls within this subsection if it—
      (a) involves serious violence against a person,
      (b) involves serious damage to property,
      (c) endangers a person's life, other than that of the person committing the action,
      (d) creates a serious risk to the health or safety of the public or a section of the public,

or

(e) is designed seriously to interfere with or seriously to disrupt an electronic system.

(3) The use or threat of action falling within subsection (2) which involves the use of firearms or explosives is terrorism whether or not subsection (1)(b) is satisfied.

(4) In this section—

(a) 'action' includes action outside the United Kingdom,

(b) a reference to any person or to property is a reference to any person, or to property, wherever situated,

(c) a reference to the public includes a reference to the public of a country other than the United Kingdom, and

(d) 'the government' means the government of the United Kingdom, of a Part of the United Kingdom or of a country other than the United Kingdom.

(5) In this Act a reference to action taken for the purposes of terrorism includes a reference to action taken for the benefit of a proscribed organisation."

(1) Terrorist Organisations and Terrorist Fundraising

In terms of conduct prohibited by the Terrorism Act 2000, the starting point relates to membership and support of certain proscribed organisations. Section 3 of the Act provides as follows.

Terrorism Act 2000

"Proscription

3.—(1) For the purposes of this Act an organisation is proscribed if—

(a) it is listed in Schedule 2, or

(b) it operates under the same name as an organisation listed in that Schedule.

(2) Subsection (1)(b) shall not apply in relation to an organisation listed in Schedule 2 if its entry is the subject of a note in that Schedule.

(3) The Secretary of State may by order—

(a) add an organisation to Schedule 2;

(b) remove an organisation from that Schedule;

(c) amend that Schedule in some other way.

(4) The Secretary of State may exercise his power under subsection (3)(a) in respect of an organisation only if he believes that it is concerned in terrorism.

(5) For the purposes of subsection (4) an organisation is concerned in terrorism if it—

(a) commits or participates in acts of terrorism,

(b) prepares for terrorism,

(c) promotes or encourages terrorism, or

(d) is otherwise concerned in terrorism."

Fourteen organisations were proscribed at the time the Act was introduced. These are all related to the situation in Northern Ireland and include republican organisations such as the IRA and loyalist groups such as the UDA. Since the enactment of the Terrorism Act 2000 a number of other organisations have been added to the list by the Government. At the time of writing there were 39 proscribed organisations, of which only 14 were connected with Northern Ireland.

PROSCRIBED INTERNATIONAL ORGANISATIONS

Twenty-five international terrorist organisations are proscribed under the Terrorism Act 2000, which means they are outlawed in the UK.

- 17 November Revolutionary Organisation (N17): N17 is a terrorist organisation that aims to highlight and protest at what it deems to be imperialist and corrupt actions, using violence. Formed in 1974 to oppose the Greek military Junta, its stance was initially anti-Junta and anti-US, which it blamed for supporting the Junta.
- Abu Nidal Organisation (ANO): The principal aim of ANO is the destruction of the state of Israel. It is also hostile to "reactionary" Arab regimes and states supporting Israel.
- Abu Sayyaf Group (ASG): The precise aims of the ASG are unclear, but its objectives appear to include the establishment of an autonomous Islamic state in the Southern Philippine island of Mindanao.
- Al-Gama'at al-Islamiya (GI): The main aim of GI is through all means, including the use of violence, to overthrow the Egyptian Government and replace it with an Islamic state. Some members also want the removal of Western influence from the Arab world.
- Al Qaida: Inspired and led by Osama Bin Laden, its aims are the explusion of Western forces from Saudi Arabia, the destruction of Israel and the end of Western influence in the Muslim world.
- Armed Islamic Group (Groupe Islamique Armée) (GIA): The aim of the GIA is to create an Islamic state in Algeria using all necessary means, including violence.
- Asbat Al-Ansar ('League of Parisans' or 'Band of Helpers'): Sometimes going by the aliases of 'The Abu Muhjin' group/faction or the 'Jama'at Nour', this group aims to enforce its extremist interpretation of Islamic law within Lebanon, and increasingly further afield.
- Babbar Khalsa (BK): BK is a Sikh movement that aims to establish an independent Khalistan within the Punjab region of India.
- Basque Homeland and Liberty (Euskadi ta Askatasuna) (ETA): ETA seeks the creation of an independent state comprising the Basque regions of both Spain and France.
- Egyptian Islamic Jihad (EIJ): The main aim of the EIJ is to overthrow the Egyptian Government and replace it with an Islamic state. However, since September 1988, the leadership of the group has also allied itself to the 'global Jihad' ideology expounded by Osama Bin Laden and has threatened Western interests.
- Hamas Izz al-Din al-Qassem Brigades: Hamas aims to end Israeli occupation in Palestine and establish an Islamic state.
- Harakat Mujahideen (HM): HM, previously known as Harakat Ul Ansar (HuA), seeks independence for Indian-administered Kashmir. The HM leadership was also a signatory to Osama Bin Laden's 1998 fatwa, which called for worldwide attacks against US and Western interests.
- Hizballah External Security Organisation: Hizballah is committed to armed resistance to the state of Israel and aims to liberate all Palestinian territories and Jerusalem from Israeli occupation. It maintains a terrorist wing, the External Security Organisation (ESO), to help it achieve this.
- International Sikh Youth Federation (ISYF): ISYF is an organisation committed to the creation of an independent state of Khalistan for Sikhs within India.
- Islamic Army of Aden (IAA): The IAA's aims are the overthrow of the current

Yemeni government and the establishment of an Islamic State following Sharia Law.

- Islamic Movement of Uzbekistan (IMU): The primary aim of IMU is to establish an Islamic state in the model of the Taleban in Uzbekistan. However, the IMU is reported to also seek to establish a broader state over the entire Turkestan area.
- Jaish e Mohammed (JeM): JeM seeks the 'liberation' of Kashmir from Indian control as well as the 'destruction' of America and India. JeM has a stated objective of unifying the various Kashmiri militant groups.
- Jeemah Islamiyah (JI): JI's aim is the creation of a unified Islamic state in Singapore, Malaysia, Indonesia and the Southern Philippines.
- Kurdistan Workers' Party (Partiya Karkeren Kurdistan) PKK): The PKK is primarily a separatist movement that has sought an independent Kurdish state in southeast Turkey.
- Lashkar e Tayyaba (LT): LT seeks independence for Kashmir and the creation of an Islamic state using violent means.
- Liberation Tigers of Tamil Eelam (LTTE): The LTTE is a terrorist group fighting for a separate Tamil state in the North and East of Sri Lanka.
- Mujaheddin e Khalq (MeK): The MeK is an Iranian dissident organisation based in Iraq. It claims to be seeking the establishment of a democratic, socialist, Islamic republic in Iran.
- Palestinian Islamic Jihad—Shaqaqi (PIJ): PIJ is a Shi' group which aims to end the Israeli occupation of Palestine and create an Islamic state similar to that in Iran. It opposes the existence of the state of Israel, the Middle East Peace Process and the Palestinian Authority.
- Revolutionary Peoples' Liberation Party—Front (Devrimci Kurtulus Partisi—Cephesi) (DHKP-C): DHKP-C aims to establish a Marxist Leninist regime in Turkey by means of armed revolutionary struggle.
- Salafist Group for Call and Combat (Groupe Salafiste pour la Predication et le Combat) (GSPC): Its aim is to create an Islamic state in Algeria using all necessary means, including violence.

SOURCE: Home Office, 2004

PROSCRIBED 'IRISH GROUPS'

- Continuity Army Council
- Comann un mBan
- Fianna na hEireann
- Irish National Liberation Army
- Irish People's Liberation Organisation
- Irish Republican Army
- Loyalist Volunteer Force
- Orange Volunteers
- Red Hand Commando
- Red Hand Defenders
- Saor Eire
- Ulster Defence Association
- Ulster Freedom Fighters
- Ulster Volunteer Force

SOURCE: Home Office, 2004

It has been recognised judicially that proscription brings with it "very serious consequences ... for rights as important as those of free speech and free assembly" (*R (Kurdistan Workers' Party) v Home Secretary* [2002] EWHC (Admin) 644, Richards J.). Yet there is no right for any organisation to be consulted before it is proscribed. If, however, an organisation is proscribed, an application may be made for its deproscription. The application is made to the Secretary of State by the proscribed organisation itself or by anyone affected by the organisation's proscription (s.4). Where an application is rejected, an appeal may be made to the Proscribed Organisations Appeal Commission which must apply the principles of judicial review to determine whether the Secretary of State's decision was flawed (s.5). The three judicial members of the Commission are retired judges of the English courts: there are no Scottish members amongst them. A further appeal lies from the Commission to the Court of Session or the Court of Appeal in England and Wales (s.6).

R. (Kurdistan Workers' Party) v Home Secretary
[2002] EWHC (Admin) 644

Three organisations were proscribed by ministerial order. The organisations in question were the People's Mojahedin Organisation of Iran (the PMOI), the Kurdistan Workers' Party (the PKK) and Lashkare Tayyabah (the LeT). They each challenged the proscriptions in judicial review was not an appropriate remedy in view of the right to seek deproscription under the statutory procedure.

RICHARDS J: "70. The next, and to my mind the most important, question for consideration is whether it is appropriate for the various challenges to proceed by way of judicial review. For the Secretary of State, Mr Sales submits in essence that permission should be refused because POAC can and should determine the substantive issues raised and is the appropriate forum for that purpose. He has an alternative, fall-back position that judicial review should be allowed to proceed on individual procedural issues but not on issues that depend on an assessment of the underlying facts. Counsel for the claimants, on the other hand, submit that POAC cannot review the specific decisions under challenge, cannot consider the full grounds that the claimants wish to raise and cannot give the remedies they seek. By contrast, the Administrative Court can consider the entirety of the claims and can grant the full range of relief and is therefore the appropriate forum....

72. Mr Sales points to statements of principle to the effect that judicial review is a remedy of last resort and that judicial review will not normally be allowed where there is an alternative remedy by way of appeal (see e.g. *R v Panel on Take-overs and Mergers, ex p. Guinness plc* [1990] 1 QB 146 at 177E–178A and *R v Chief Constable of Merseyside Police, ex p. Calveley* [1986] QB 424). He also relies, by way of analogy, on statements in *R v DPP, ex p. Kebilene* [2000] 2 AC 326 and *R (Pretty) v DPP* [2002] 1 A.C. 800 to the broad effect that satellite litigation by way of judicial review is to be avoided in relation to issues arising in the context of criminal proceedings. The same principle, he submits, applies in relation to issues that have been or could be raised in proceedings before POAC.

73. The claimants' counsel, ... submits that the true principle is that an alternative procedure should be exhausted first if it is at least as extensive as judicial review ... , that one potential exception is where the ground of challenge is based on procedural fairness (*ex p. Guinness plc*, above, at 184G–185A) and that where the suggested alternative forum cannot consider the entirety of a complaint which can be raised by way of judicial review, the court should entertain a claim for judicial review (*R v Inland Revenue Commissioners, ex p. Mead* [1993] 1 All ER 772 at 781–2).

74. All such statements of principle and illustrations of their application provide helpful guidance, but an exercise of discretion in a matter of this kind depends very much upon the particular subject-matter and context of the claim.

75. It is plain that Parliament, although not seeking to exclude the possibility of judicial

review, intended POAC to be the forum of first resort for the determination of claims relating to the lawfulness of proscription under the 2000 Act. The procedure established for challenging proscription, whether by inclusion in Schedule 2 as originally enacted or by subsequent addition to the list by means of an order under s.3, is an application to the Secretary of State for removal from the list and an appeal to POAC if the application is refused, with a further avenue of appeal to the Court of Appeal on a question of law.

76. POAC is, as Mr Sales submits, a specialist tribunal with procedures designed specifically to deal with the determination of claims relating to proscription, a context heavily laden with issues of national security: cf. the observations of Lord Steyn in *Secretary of State for the Home Department v Rehman* [2003] 1 A.C. 153, para 30, in relation to the equivalent composition and procedures of the Special Immigration Appeals Commission under the Special Immigration Appeals Commission Act 1997 (though POAC and SIAC do not have an identical status). The special advocate procedure and the exist- ence of extensive powers in relation to the reception of evidence, including otherwise   non-disclosable evidence, place POAC at a clear advantage over the Administrative Court in such an area. In many respects the Administrative Court might be able to devise something equivalent: Lord Lester [for one of the claimants] referred to the observation of the Strasbourg Court at paragraph 78 of the judgment in *Tinnelly & Sons Ltd. v United Kingdom* (1998) 27 EHHR 249, that 'in other contexts it has been found possible to modify judicial procedures in such a way as to safeguard national security concerns about the nature and sources of intelligence information and yet accord the individual a substantial degree of procedural justice'. But it would be far less satisfactory to go down that route than to utilise the POAC procedure already carefully formulated for the purpose.

77. Moreover proceedings before POAC are expressly excluded from the prohibition on the disclosure of intercepted communications, potentially a very important area of evidence; and although it was submitted for the claimants that the same or a similar result could be achieved in the Administrative Court by a Convention-compliant construction of the Regulation of Investigatory Powers Act 2000, in particular the power under s.18(7)–(8) to order disclosure to a judge of the High Court, this is at best very uncertain and would again be a less satisfactory route than reliance on the clear and general exception under s.18(1)(f) in respect of any proceedings before POAC or any proceedings arising out of proceedings before POAC.

78. POAC has also been designated as the appropriate tribunal for the purposes of s.7 of the Human Rights Act in relation to proceedings against the Secretary of State in respect of a refusal to deproscribe.

79. All those considerations tell strongly in favour of POAC being the appropriate tribunal for consideration of issues falling within what I have previously termed category (2), namely whether proscription was necessary in a democratic society and whether it was non-discriminatory. Those are important parts of the PMOI and LeT claims. They depend heavily on a scrutiny of all the evidence, including any sensitive intelligence information, concerning the aims and activities of the organisations concerned and a comparison between them and other organisations proscribed or not proscribed. I recognise that POAC's appellate jurisdiction relates not to the original proscription but to a refusal to deproscribe, whereas by these proceedings the claimants challenge the original decision to proscribe. But in relation to these substantive issues, at least, I do not think that anything turns on that point. The issues are materially the same whether they are raised in the context of the original proscription or in the context of a refusal to deproscribe. In the case of the PMOI and the LeT, where there have been applications to deproscribe and appeals have been lodged with POAC in respect of the refusal to deproscribe, the issues are already before POAC in materially the same form as they are sought to be raised in this court, as is apparent from a comparison between the written cases in the two fora. If the claimants' arguments are well founded, they will succeed before POAC or on appeal from POAC and this will result in their deproscription. Indeed, it is asserted in the PMOI's amended claim form that '[h]ad the Secretary of State acceded to the claimants' application ... it would

have been unnecessary to bring legal proceedings of any kind' (para 90). If, therefore, the substantive issues stood alone, there would to my mind be no question but that POAC is the appropriate forum and permission to apply for judicial review should be refused.

80. The problems arise out of the fact that such issues do not stand alone. The PMOI and LeT claimants also raise issues falling within what I have previously termed category (1), i.e. a procedural challenge to the original decision to include the organisations in the draft Order and to the Order itself. Moreover the PKK claimants have not even raised issues within category (2) and have not themselves sought deproscription or appealed to POAC, but have focused their challenge, so far as the proscription of the PKK is concerned, on the broad submission that the original decision and Order are vitiated by a failure to observe the procedural guarantees required by the Convention.

81. In my view it would be possible for those procedural issues, taken by themselves, to be determined in the Administrative Court as effectively as in POAC. Moreover the natural targets of any challenge on those grounds are the original decision and Order, which lie within the jurisdiction of the Administrative Court but not of POAC. If there was a procedural defect as alleged, it occurred at that original stage and not at the stage of the subsequent refusal to deproscribe; and it would generally be considered artificial and inappropriate to challenge a subsequent decision on grounds relating to a defect in the original decision.

82. The present context strikes me, however, as exceptional. The legislative intention is in my view that challenges to an organisation's presence in the list of proscribed organisations should be brought by way of an application for deproscription and appeal to POAC. It is possible to give effect to that legislative intention even in relation to a challenge based on procedural defects vitiating the original decision to proscribe. That is because, as Mr Sales submits, the Secretary of State can be requested to deproscribe on the basis that the original proscription was unlawful on procedural as well as substantive grounds; and if the Secretary of State refuses to deproscribe, an appeal can be brought on the basis that he has erred in law and/or acted in breach of the claimants' Convention rights in so refusing. Mr Emmerson [for one of the claimants] expressed the concern that the Secretary of State might be able to avoid any appealable error by expressing no view one way or the other on the lawfulness of the original proscription. Whatever the theoretical merit of that argument, I cannot see this happening in practice, given the Secretary of State's stance that all matters are more appropriately dealt with on appeal to POAC rather than by way of judicial review. It would be extraordinary if the Secretary of State were to adopt a course that threw the claimants back onto judicial review as the only means of obtaining an effective remedy, the very thing that the Secretary of State seeks so strenuously to avoid.

83. If the various aspects of the procedural challenge to the original decision can be raised in this way before POAC on an appeal from a refusal to deproscribe, as I think they can, one comes back to whether that is the more appropriate course than to allow a direct challenge to the original decision by way of judicial review. In my judgment it is. That applies with particular force to the PMOI and LeT, since it is much better that their challenge to proscription on substantive grounds be determined by POAC and there is an obvious advantage in all issues being determined by the same tribunal (especially given the inevitable existence of a degree of overlap between what I have termed the substantive and the procedural issues). It is less obvious in the case of the PKK, where there are no proceedings before POAC and the procedural grounds advanced in relation to proscription could all be dealt with as satisfactorily by the Administrative Court. Since, however, POAC is intended to be the forum of first resort and is the appropriate forum for the PMOI and LeT claims, and since there is a heavy overlap between PKK's procedural grounds and the procedural grounds advanced by the PMOI and LeT, POAC is also in my view the appropriate forum for the PKK claim. It is better for all these matters to be determined by POAC, with an appeal if necessary to the Court of Appeal on questions of law, than to allow the claims to be spread between two jurisdictions or to allow the entirety of the claims to proceed in the Administrative Court. As already mentioned, it is still open to the PKK to

go down the POAC route even though it has not yet done so.

84. In considering the appropriateness of POAC as a forum for issues relating to pro-scription/deproscription, I have taken into account the fact that there is no material difference between POAC and the Administrative Court in terms of the legal principles to be applied: by s.5(3) of the 2000 Act, POAC is required to allow an appeal if it considers that the decision to refuse to deproscribe was flawed 'when considered in the light of the principles applicable on an application for judicial review'. I see no reason why POAC should be any less able than the Administrative Court to provide effective scrutiny of the matters under challenge.

85. I have also taken into account, however, that there is a difference as regards available remedies. The first material difference is that, unlike the Administrative Court, POAC has no power to quash the original decision or Order. By s.5(4)–(5), it may make an order to which the Secretary of State must give effect by means of a further Order removing the organisation from the list in Schedule 2. This means that the proscription remains valid as from the date when the original Order came into effect until the date of the further Order removing the organisation from the list. That might be relevant if any of the claimants were subject to sanctions dependent upon the validity of the proscription in the interim period (though account would have to be taken of the mitigating effect of s.7). I do not think, however, that this difference in the form of order available to POAC as compared with the Administrative Court would have any practical consequence for the claimants. In parti-cular, I do not think that it would affect the substance of their damages claims, to which I refer below.

86. The second difference as regards available relief is that POAC does not have the power to grant a declaration of incompatibility under s.4 of the Human Rights Act. Such a declaration is sought by the claimants in the alternative to their arguments that proscrip-tion is unlawful under the existing legislation when construed compatibly with the Convention. In my judgment, however, POAC's lack of such a power does not render the POAC procedure inappropriate, since there exists an avenue of appeal to the Court of Appeal on a point of law and the Court of Appeal does have such a power. The fact that a declaration of incompatibility cannot be made by an inferior tribunal, but only on appeal to the High Court or Court of Appeal, does not generally render proceedings before the inferior tribunal inappropriate or render an application for judicial review appropriate. The appropriate course is still generally to pursue the proceedings before the inferior tribunal and then on appeal to the High Court or Court of Appeal, rather than to apply for judicial review. An obvious example is that of criminal proceedings in the Crown Court, where a declaration of incompatibility is available only on appeal to the Court of Appeal but the general appropriateness of pursuing all issues in the criminal proceedings instead of applying for judicial review has been stressed in *Kebilene* and in *R (Pretty) v DPP*. Thus in the PMOI and LeT appeals to POAC the incompatibility arguments have properly been advanced with a view to seeking declarations from the Court of Appeal on a further appeal if that becomes necessary.

87. The third difference is that POAC does not have the power to award damages whereas in the present proceedings the claimants, by late amendments, have claimed damages pursuant to s.8 of the Human Rights Act. I do not regard this as telling sig-nificantly in favour of the grant of permission for the claims to proceed by way of judicial review. That would be to allow the tail to wag the dog. A claim for damages can properly be made as part of an otherwise appropriate claim for judicial review, but is not in itself a good reason for permitting judicial review. In practice, where there is a claim for damages as part of an otherwise appropriate claim for judicial review, the claim for damages would normally be left over to be dealt with as a discrete issue, if still relevant, after the main issues of public law had been determined. ... Thus there is no particular reason why the damages claim should proceed by way of judicial review and the claimants would be under no real disadvantage in relation to this part of their claim if they had to bring a separate claim for damages following a successful appeal to POAC for deproscription. Although

s.7(5) of the Human Rights Act lays down a basic time limit of one year for the bringing of such a claim, a longer period is permitted where considered equitable and there would be an overwhelming case for allowing a longer period if matters got that far. . . .

92. Accordingly I take the view that it would not be appropriate to allow any of the present claims for judicial review to proceed. Most of the issues can and should be canvassed before POAC on an appeal under s.5, and thereafter as necessary in the Court of Appeal on a further appeal on a question of law. To the extent that issues cannot be canvassed in that way, it is inappropriate to allow them to be canvassed now by way of judicial review. They should at least await a determination by POAC of those issues that POAC can deal with. In my view to require the claimants to proceed in this way is to meet the requirement to provide an effective remedy for breach of Convention rights."

As already indicated, proscription of an organisation has a number of consequences, both for the organisation and its members and supporters. There are not only issues of freedom of expression and freedom of assembly, but also freedom of association and freedom to the peaceful enjoyment of possessions. The starting point is the offences which may be committed by individuals who are associated with such organisations. The Terrorism Act 2000 provides as follows:

Terrorism Act 2000

"Membership
    11.—(1) A person commits an offence if he belongs or professes to belong to a proscribed organisation.
    (2) It is a defence for a person charged with an offence under subsection (1) to prove—
        (a) that the organisation was not proscribed on the last (or only) occasion on which he became a member or began to profess to be a member, and
        (b) that he has not taken part in the activities of the organisation at any time while it was proscribed.
    (3) A person guilty of an offence under this section shall be liable—
        (a) on conviction on indictment, to imprisonment for a term not exceeding ten years, to a fine or to both, or
        (b) on summary conviction, to imprisonment for a term not exceeding six months, to a fine not exceeding the statutory maximum or to both.

. . .

Support
    12.—(1) A person commits an offence if—
        (a) he invites support for a proscribed organisation, and
        (b) the support is not, or is not restricted to, the provision of money or other property (within the meaning of section 15).
    (2) A person commits an offence if he arranges, manages or assists in arranging or managing a meeting which he knows is—
        (a) to support a proscribed organisation,
        (b) to further the activities of a proscribed organisation, or
        (c) to be addressed by a person who belongs or professes to belong to a proscribed organisation.
    (3) A person commits an offence if he addresses a meeting and the purpose of his address is to encourage support for a proscribed organisation or to further its activities.
    (4) Where a person is charged with an offence under subsection (2)(c) in respect of a private meeting it is a defence for him to prove that he had no reasonable cause to believe that the address mentioned in subsection (2)(c) would support a proscribed organisation or

further its activities.
(5) In subsections (2) to (4)—
    (a) 'meeting' means a meeting of three or more persons, whether or not the public are
        admitted, and
    (b) a meeting is private if the public are not admitted.
(6) A person guilty of an offence under this section shall be liable—
    (a) on conviction on indictment, to imprisonment for a term not exceeding ten years,
        to a fine or to both, or
    (b) on summary conviction, to imprisonment for a term not exceeding six months, to
        a fine not exceeding the statutory maximum or to both.

Uniform
13.—(1) A person in a public place commits an offence if he—
    (a) wears an item of clothing, or
    (b) wears, carries or displays an article,
in such a way or in such circumstances as to arouse reasonable suspicion that he is a
member or supporter of a proscribed organisation.
(2) A constable in Scotland may arrest a person without a warrant if he has reasonable
grounds to suspect that the person is guilty of an offence under this section.
(3) A person guilty of an offence under this section shall be liable on summary conviction
to—
    (a) imprisonment for a term not exceeding six months,
    (b) a fine not exceeding level 5 on the standard scale, or
    (c) both."

Part III of the Act applies to terrorist property which is defined to mean, among other things,
money or property which is likely to be used for the purposes of terrorism (including the
resources of a proscribed organisation). Specifically, it is an offence to solicit, receive or provide
money for the purposes of terrorism (s.15). It is also an offence to use or possess money for the
purposes of terrorism (s.16), or take part in the laundering of terrorist property (s.18). Where
someone believes that any of the foregoing offences have been committed (those in ss.15–18) it is
an offence to fail to disclose the information to the police. This is aimed principally at banks and
others whose suspicion is based on information which comes to their attention "in the course of
a trade, profession, business or employment" (s.19). There is an exception for legal advisers who
are not required to disclose information obtained from a client. Anyone found guilty of an
offence under s 19 is liable to imprisonment of up to five years. There are also provisions
enabling people to disclose information to the police in other circumstances "notwithstanding
any restriction on the disclosure of information imposed by statute or otherwise" (s.20). Where
someone is convicted of an offence under ss.15–18, the court may make a forfeiture order.
This will apply to any terrorist property in the possession or under the control of the person
convicted (s.23).

(2) Investigating Terrorist Activity

Parts II and III of the 2000 Act thus deal with questions of membership and support for terrorist
organisations on the one hand, and financial support for terrorist activities on the other. As such
they deal heavy blows to the right to freedom of association as well as the right to peaceful
enjoyment of one's possessions. Parts IV and V of the Act move in different directions and deal
with police powers to investigate terrorist activities (Pt IV) and to deal with suspected terrorists
(Pt V). Here we encounter other far-reaching powers with implications for the right to liberty,
the right to respect for one's home and private life, and the right to freedom of assembly. So far
as Pt IV is concerned, terrorist investigations are defined as follows:

Terrorism Act 2000

"Terrorist investigation
    32. In this Act 'terrorist investigation' means an investigation of—
        (a) the commission, preparation or instigation of acts of terrorism,
        (b) an act which appears to have been done for the purposes of terrorism,
        (c) the resources of a proscribed organisation,
        (d) the possibility of making an order under section 3(3), or
        (e) the commission, preparation or instigation of an offence under this Act."

Although there are a number of powers for the purposes of terrorist investigations, the most important of these are to be found in Sch.5. This allows the police to obtain a warrant to require the provision of information for the purposes of terrorist investigations. So far as these provisions apply to Scotland, Sch.5 provides as follows.

Terrorism Act 2000
Schedule 5
Terrorist Investigations: Information

"Order for Production of Material
    22.—(1) The procurator fiscal may apply to the sheriff for an order under this paragraph for the purposes of a terrorist investigation.
    (2) An application for an order shall relate to particular material, or material of a particular description.
    (3) An order under this paragraph may require a specified person—
        (a) to produce to a constable within a specified period for seizure and retention any material which he has in his possession, custody or power and to which the application relates;
        (b) to give a constable access to any material of the kind mentioned in paragraph (a) within a specified period;
        (c) to state to the best of his knowledge and belief the location of material to which the application relates if it is not in, and it will not come into, his possession, custody or power within the period specified under paragraph (a) or (b).
    (4) For the purposes of this paragraph—
        (a) an order may specify a person only if he appears to the sheriff to have in his possession, custody or power any of the material to which the application relates, and
        (b) a period specified in an order shall be the period of seven days beginning with the date of the order unless it appears to the sheriff that a different period would be appropriate in the particular circumstances of the application.
    (5) Where the sheriff makes an order under sub-paragraph (3)(b) in relation to material on any premises, he may, on the application of the procurator fiscal, order any person who appears to the sheriff to be entitled to grant entry to the premises to allow any constable to enter the premises to obtain access to the material.
    23.—(1) The sheriff may grant an application under paragraph 22 if satisfied that the conditions in sub-paragraphs (2) and (3) are satisfied in respect of that material.
    (2) The first condition is that—
        (a) the order is sought for the purposes of a terrorist investigation, and
        (b) there are reasonable grounds for believing that the material is likely to be of substantial value, whether by itself or together with other material, to a terrorist investigation.
    (3) The second condition is that there are reasonable grounds for believing that it is in the public interest that the material should be produced or that access to it should be given

having regard—
- (a) to the benefit likely to accrue to a terrorist investigation if the material is obtained, and
- (b) to the circumstances under which the person concerned has any of the material in his possession, custody or power.

24.—(1) An order under paragraph 22 may be made in relation to a person who appears to the sheriff to be likely to have any of the material to which the application relates in his possession, custody or power within the period of 28 days beginning with the date of the order.

(2) Where an order is made under paragraph 22 by virtue of this paragraph, paragraph 22(3) shall apply with the following modifications—
- (a) the order shall require the specified person to notify a named constable as soon as is reasonably practicable after any material to which the application relates comes into his possession, custody or power,
- (b) the reference in paragraph 22(3)(a) to material which the specified person has in his possession, custody or power shall be taken as a reference to the material referred to in paragraph (a) above which comes into his possession, custody or power, and
- (c) the reference in paragraph 22(3)(c) to the specified period shall be taken as a reference to the period of 28 days beginning with the date of the order.

(3) Where an order is made under paragraph 22 by virtue of this paragraph, paragraph 22(4) shall not apply and the order—
- (a) may only specify a person falling within sub-paragraph (1), and
- (b) shall specify the period of seven days beginning with the date of notification required under sub-paragraph (2)(a) unless it appears to the sheriff that a different period would be appropriate in the particular circumstances of the application.

25.—(1) Subject to paragraph 33(1), an order under paragraph 22 shall have effect notwithstanding any obligation as to secrecy or other restriction on the disclosure of the information imposed by statute or otherwise.

(2) Where the material to which an application under paragraph 22 relates consists of information contained in a computer—
- (a) an order under paragraph 22(3)(a) shall have effect as an order to produce the material in a form in which it can be taken away and in which it is visible and legible, and
- (b) an order under paragraph 22(3)(b) shall have effect as an order to give access to the material in a form in which it is visible and legible.

26.—(1) An order under paragraph 22 may be made in relation to material in the possession, custody or power of a government department.

(2) Where an order is made by virtue of sub-paragraph (1)—
- (a) it shall be served as if the proceedings were civil proceedings against the department, and
- (b) it may require any officer of the department, whether named in the order or not, who may for the time being have in his possession, custody or power the material concerned, to comply with it.

(3) In this paragraph 'government department' means a public department within the meaning of the Crown Suits Scotland Act 1857 and any part of the Scottish Administration. ...

Searches

28.—(1) The procurator fiscal may apply to the sheriff to grant a warrant under this paragraph for the purposes of a terrorist investigation.

(2) A warrant under this paragraph shall authorise any constable—
- (a) to enter the premises specified in the warrant,
- (b) to search the premises and any person found there, and

(c) to seize and retain any relevant material which is found on a search under paragraph (b).

(3) For the purpose of sub-paragraph (2)(c) material is relevant if the constable has reasonable grounds for believing that it is likely to be of substantial value, whether by itself or together with other material, to a terrorist investigation.

(4) The sheriff may grant an application under this paragraph if satisfied—

(a) that the warrant is sought for the purposes of a terrorist investigation,

(b) that there are reasonable grounds for believing that there is material on premises specified in the application which is likely to be of substantial value to a terrorist investigation, and

(c) that one of the conditions in paragraph 29 is satisfied.

(5) Where a warrant is granted in relation to non-residential premises, the entry and search must be within the period of 24 hours beginning with the time when the warrant is granted.

(6) For the purpose of sub-paragraph (5) 'non-residential premises' means any premises other than those which the procurator fiscal has reasonable grounds for believing are used wholly or mainly as a dwelling.

(7) A warrant under this paragraph may authorise the persons named in the warrant to accompany the constable who is executing it.

29.—(1) The conditions referred to in paragraph 28(4)(c) are—

(a) that an order made under paragraph 28 in relation to material on the premises has not been complied with, or

(b) that for any of the reasons mentioned in sub-paragraph (2) it would not be appropriate to make such an order.

(2) The reasons are—

(a) it is not practicable to communicate with any person entitled to produce the material,

(b) it is not practicable to communicate with any person entitled to grant access to the material or entitled to grant entry to the premises on which the material is situated, or

(c) the investigation for the purposes of which the application is made may be seriously prejudiced unless a constable can secure immediate access to the material.

Explanations

30.—(1) The procurator fiscal may apply to the sheriff for an order under this paragraph requiring any person specified in the order to provide an explanation of any material—

(a) seized in pursuance of a warrant under paragraph 28, or

(b) produced or made available to a constable under paragraph 22.

(2) Without prejudice to paragraph 33(1), an order under this paragraph may require a lawyer to provide the name and address of his client.

(3) A statement by a person in response to a requirement imposed by an order under this paragraph may only be used in evidence against him—

(a) on a prosecution for an offence under section 2 of the False Oaths (Scotland) Act 1933, or

(b) on a prosecution for some other offence where in giving evidence he makes a statement inconsistent with it.

(4) Paragraphs 26 and 27 shall apply to orders under this paragraph as they apply to orders under paragraph 22.

Urgent cases

31.—(1) A police officer of at least the rank of superintendent may by a written order signed by him give to any constable the authority which may be given by a search warrant under paragraph 28.

(2) An order shall not be made under this paragraph unless the officer has reasonable grounds for believing—

    (a) that the case is one of great emergency, and

    (b) that immediate action is necessary.

(3) Where an order is made under this paragraph particulars of the case shall be notified as soon as is reasonably practicable to the Secretary of State.

32.—(1) If a police officer of at least the rank of superintendent has reasonable grounds for believing that the case is one of great emergency he may by a written notice signed by him require any person specified in the notice to provide an explanation of any material seized in pursuance of an order under paragraph 22.

(2) Sub-paragraphs (2) and (3) of paragraph 30 shall apply to a notice under this paragraph as they apply to an order under that paragraph.

(3) A person commits an offence if he fails to comply with a notice under this paragraph.

(4) It is a defence for a person charged with an offence under sub-paragraph (3) to show that he had a reasonable excuse for his failure.

(5) A person guilty of an offence under sub-paragraph (3) is liable on summary conviction to imprisonment for a term not exceeding six months, to a fine not exceeding level 5 on the standard scale or to both.

Supplementary

33.—(1) This Part of this Schedule is without prejudice to any rule of law whereby—

    (a) communications between a professional legal adviser and his client, or

    (b) communications made in connection with or in contemplation of legal proceedings and for the purposes of those proceedings,

are in legal proceedings protected from disclosure on the ground of confidentiality.

(2) For the purpose of exercising any powers conferred on him under this Part of this Schedule a constable may, if necessary, open lockfast places on premises specified in an order under paragraph 22, a warrant under paragraph 28 or a notice under paragraph 32.

(3) A search of a person under this Part of this Schedule may only be carried out by a person of the same sex."

In addition to these powers in Sch.5, Sch.6 provides that the procurator fiscal may seek an order from a sheriff requiring a financial institution to provide certain information about a customer's account to the police. The order may only be made by the sheriff if he or she is satisfied that the order is sought for the purpose of a terrorist investigation, the tracing of terrorist property is desirable for the purpose of the investigation, and the order will enhance the effectiveness of the investigation (Sch.6, para.5). It is a criminal offence for the financial institution to fail to provide the information.

(3) Counter-Terrorist Powers

Part V of the Act deals with police powers to arrest and search, as well as powers of stop and search. These powers apply to suspected terrorists, with a terrorist being defined for this purpose by s.40 to mean a person who:

    "(a) has committed an offence under any of sections 11, 12, 15 to 18, 54 and 56 to 63, or

    (b) is or has been concerned in the commission, preparation or instigation of acts of terrorism."

The powers of arrest and search are to be found in ss.41–43 of the Act, with s.41(1) providing that "a constable may arrest without a warrant a person whom he reasonably suspects to be a terrorist". By virtue of s.41(3), a person detained under this provision must be released within 48 hours, unless further detention has been authorised in Scotland by a judicial authority which in Scotland means a sheriff (Sch.8). It is important to note that arrest is a precondition of detention: *Forbes v H M Advocate*, 1990 S.C.C.R. 69 (see Ch.4 above). Under Sch.8, para.32 (1) a judicial authority may grant a warrant for further detention if satisfied that:

"(a) there are reasonable grounds for believing that the further detention of the person to whom the application relates is necessary to obtain relevant evidence whether by questioning him or otherwise or to preserve relevant evidence, and

(b) the investigation in connection with which the person is detained is being conducted diligently and expeditiously."

For this purpose "relevant evidence" is defined by para.32(2) to mean evidence which relates to his commission of an offence under any of the provisions mentioned in s.40(1)(a), or indicates that he is a person falling within s.40(1)(b). A person may be detained for up to 14 days in total from the time of arrest (Sch.8, para.36, as amended by the Criminal Justice Act 2003, s.306). Section 42 authorises a justice of the peace (including a sheriff) to issue a search warrant "if he is satisfied that there are reasonable grounds for suspecting that a person whom the constable reasonably suspects to be a person falling within section 40(1)(b) is to be found there".

In addition to these powers of arrest, there are also extensive powers of stop and search. The first of these applies in relation to suspected terrorists, with s.43 providing that:

"A constable may stop and search a person whom he reasonably suspects to be a terrorist to discover whether he has in his possession anything which may constitute evidence that he is a terrorist."

In addition to the power to stop and search a suspected terrorist, there are also powers of random stop and search which can be used not only against terrorist suspects:

Terrorism Act 2000

"Authorisations

44.—(1) An authorisation under this subsection authorises any constable in uniform to stop a vehicle in an area or at a place specified in the authorisation and to search—

    (a) the vehicle;

    (b) the driver of the vehicle;

    (c) a passenger in the vehicle;

    (d) anything in or on the vehicle or carried by the driver or a passenger.

(2) An authorisation under this subsection authorises any constable in uniform to stop a pedestrian in an area or at a place specified in the authorisation and to search—

    (a) the pedestrian;

    (b) anything carried by him.

(3) An authorisation under subsection (1) or (2) may be given only if the person giving it considers it expedient for the prevention of acts of terrorism.

(4) An authorisation may be given—

    (a) where the specified area or place is the whole or part of a police area outside Northern Ireland other than one mentioned in paragraph (b) or (c), by a police officer for the area who is of at least the rank of assistant chief constable;

    (b) where the specified area or place is the whole or part of the metropolitan police district, by a police officer for the district who is of at least the rank of commander of the metropolitan police;

    (c) where the specified area or place is the whole or part of the City of London, by a police officer for the City who is of at least the rank of commander in the City of London police force; . . .

(5) If an authorisation is given orally, the person giving it shall confirm it in writing as soon as is reasonably practicable.

Exercise of power

45.—(1) The power conferred by an authorisation under section 44(1) or (2)—

(a) may be exercised only for the purpose of searching for articles of a kind which could be used in connection with terrorism, and

(b) may be exercised whether or not the constable has grounds for suspecting the presence of articles of that kind.

(2) A constable may seize and retain an article which he discovers in the course of a search by virtue of section 44(1) or (2) and which he reasonably suspects is intended to be used in connection with terrorism.

(3) A constable exercising the power conferred by an authorisation may not require a person to remove any clothing in public except for headgear, footwear, an outer coat, a jacket or gloves.

(4) Where a constable proposes to search a person or vehicle by virtue of section 44(1) or (2) he may detain the person or vehicle for such time as is reasonably required to permit the search to be carried out at or near the place where the person or vehicle is stopped.

(5) Where—

(a) a vehicle or pedestrian is stopped by virtue of section 44(1) or (2), and

(b) the driver of the vehicle or the pedestrian applies for a written statement that the vehicle was stopped, or that he was stopped, by virtue of section 44(1) or (2), the written statement shall be provided.

(6) An application under subsection (5) must be made within the period of 12 months beginning with the date on which the vehicle or pedestrian was stopped."

By virtue of s.46, an authorisation under these powers expires after 28 days, though it may be renewed. The authorisation must be notified by the person making it to the Home Secretary who must then approve it. It is an offence to fail to stop a vehicle when required to do so by a constable exercising powers conferred by such an authorisation. It is also an offence for an individual to fail to stop when required to do so (s.47). Conviction could lead to imprisonment or a fine, or both. Significantly these powers to grant an authorisation require the approval of a Minister rather than a judge, but it has been commented judicially that the powers are of such a nature that most British people would have hoped they were completely unnecessary in this country, particularly in a time of peace. It was also said that the power of authorisation and random stop and search that it authorises is an extraordinary power not to be misused: *R. (Gillan and Quinton) v Metropolitan Police Commissioner* [2003] EWHC 2545 (Admin) (Brooke L.J.). The exercise of the power was subject to scrutiny in the courts in the following case.

R. (Gillan) v Metropolitan Police Commissioner
[2004] EWCA Civ 1067

In this case the two applicants had tried to join a demonstration against an arms fair held in Docklands, East London. The first applicant was stopped and his rucksack searched. It contained a sandwich, notebook and print outs from websites which the police confiscated after contacting central command. The other applicant was a journalist who was detained for half an hour, despite wearing a photographer's jacket and having a press pass. She too was stopped and searched, and was so shaken by the incident that she went home. These steps were all taken following an authorisation granted under the Terrorism Act 2000, s.44. Both were of good character, and nothing was found. Three issues arose for consideration by the High Court: the decision to grant the authorisation; the manner of its exercise in this particular case; and the Convention rights of the applicants. The High Court held that there had been no violation of the appellants' convention rights. On appeal to the Court of Appeal:

LORD CHIEF JUSTICE (LORD WOOLF): "27. To resolve the issues to which this appeal gives rise it is important to have clearly in mind the different levels at which the complaints need to be considered. These levels are as follows:

  i) that of the 2000 Act. What is suggested is that section 44, in view of its subject matter; should be construed restrictively. We will describe this as the 'Interpretation Question';

  ii) that of the Assistant Chief Constable (here Mr Veness) who in his discretion granted the authorisations. We will describe this as the 'Authorisation Question',

  iii) that of the Secretary of State, in exercising his discretion to confirm the authorisations. We will refer to this as the 'Confirmation Question';

  iv) that of the officer (here Commander Messinger) who was in charge of the police officers who were to exercise the power to stop and search. We will refer to this as the 'Command Question'; and

  v) that of the officers who respectively stopped and searched each of the appellants. We will refer to this as the 'Operational Question'.

28. Consideration of the issues at each level has in common the need to take into account the nature of the statutory power granted by the 2000 Act and the impact on such a power of both the common law and the Human Rights Act 1998. Random searching is a significant interference with the rights of the individual and, if challenged, requires those responsible to establish that it is legally justified. . . .

The Interpretation Question

30. The interpretation of the 2000 Act is a matter of law for the courts. There is no question of this Court showing deference or respect to the views of the respondents because of the subject matter of the legislation. On the contrary, as the statutory power enables the appropriate senior police officer to authorise interference with the freedom of the citizen, backed by a criminal sanction to support compliance, the power has to be restrictively construed. However, this does not assist the appellants, since even adopting a restrictive approach to the construction there is no justification for giving other than the ordinary meaning to the language of section 44 and section 45 of the 2000 Act. It is clear that Parliament, unusually, has permitted random stopping and searching, but, as we have already indicated when examining the language of the relevant sections, made the use of that power subject to safeguards. The power is only to be used for a single specified purpose for a period of an authorisation granted by a senior officer and confirmed by the Secretary of State. Furthermore, the authorisation only has a limited life unless renewed.

31. We do not find it surprising that the word 'expedient' should appear in section 44(3) in conjunction with the power to authorise. The statutory scheme is to leave how the power is to be used to the discretion of the senior officer. In agreement with the Divisional Court, we would give the word its ordinary meaning of advantageous. It is entirely consistent with the framework of the legislation that a power of this sort should be exercised when a senior police officer considers it is advantageous to exercise the power for the prevention of acts of terrorism.

32. Interpreted in this way, sections 44 and 45 could not conflict with the provisions of the Articles of the ECHR. If those Articles were to be infringed it would be because of the manner of the exercise of the power, not its existence. Any possible infringement of the ECHR would depend on the circumstances in which the power that the sections give is exercised.

The Supervision by the Court

33. This brings us to the general approach that the courts should adopt when reviewing the exercise of a power which is provided by Parliament for the prevention of terrorism. Possible terrorist activities create unusual difficulties for the authorities who have the responsibility for preventing them happening. Quite apart from the serious direct damage that they can cause, there is the continuing damage that can result from the fear of the

public of further incidents. In addition, the range and nature of the terrorist incidents that are possible increase the difficulty in taking preventive action. For this reason, the courts will not readily interfere with the judgement of the authorities as to the action that is necessary. They will therefore usually not interfere with the authorities' assessment of the risk and the action that should be taken to counter the risk.

34. This does not mean the courts do not have an important role in supervising the decisions and actions of the authorities. . . .Courts can ensure the authorities do not stray beyond the four corners of the power they have been given. They can ensure that the power is used only in furtherance of the purpose for which the power was provided and they can ensure its use is necessary and proportionate.

35. Avoiding the use of the word 'deference' because of its inaccurate connotations, the position is that, while the courts will respect the authorities' view as to matters of security, this does not mean that the court has no role as to proportionality. What action is or is not proportionate is still very much an issue for the judgment of the court. The court will usually place in the scales the authorities' evaluation of the action needed to avoid the terrorist incident as against the court's assessment of the effect on the member of the public. But the ultimate determination of what is or is not proportionate still rests with the court. This task has to be performed in accordance with the approach indicated by Lord Steyn in *R. (Daly) v. Home Secretary* [2001] 2 A.C. 532 at p. 547.

Articles 5, 8, 10 and 11

36. In addition, the Court can and will here have to determine whether there is any infringement of the Articles of the ECHR relied on by the appellants. On the facts of these appeals the question arises how far Articles 5, 10 and 11 can assist the appellants. Here, Article 5 creates a difficulty of a more general nature. When a stop and search takes place the individual is detained in the sense that, if he does not stop and permit the search, the individual will commit an offence but if the process is carried out with due expedition it should only last minutes. Does such a process constitute detention within the meaning of that term in Article 5? If it does many activities that are routine today will be within the reach of Article 5, including the search of bags on entering certain public premises and security checks at airports.

37. Whilst, under the ECHR, an arrest clearly triggers Article 5 protection, the exercise of police powers that fall short of arrest but nonetheless prevent an individual from doing what he or she likes, falls into a grey area. Article 5 is concerned with the deprivation of liberty and not with mere restrictions on freedom of movement. In line with its previous approach in *Engel v. Netherlands* (1976) I E.H.R.R. 647, para. 58, in *Guzzardi v. Italy*, (1980) 3 E.H.R.R. 333, at para. 92 of its judgment the European Court of Human Rights (the "EctHR") reminded itself that Article 5 contemplates the 'physical liberty of the person' and that its aim is to ensure that no one should be deprived of this liberty in an 'arbitrary' fashion. The Court recognised that mere restrictions on *liberty of movement* are governed by Article 2 of Protocol 4 which provides that:

'Everyone lawfully within the territory of a State shall, within that territory, have the right to liberty of movement and freedom to choose his residence.'

38. However, this distinction between 'deprivation of liberty' and 'deprivation of liberty of movement' can prove very difficult to make; as the court noted in *Guzzardi*, at para. 93 of its judgment:

'The difference between deprivation of and restriction upon liberty is nonetheless merely one of **degree or intensity**, and not one of nature or substance. Although the process of classification into one or other of these categories sometimes proves to be no easy task in that some borderline cases are a matter of pure opinion, the Court cannot avoid making the selection upon which the applicability or inapplicability of Article 5 depends.' [emphasis added]

39. In determining whether the level of restraint involved amounts to a detention within the meaning of Article 5, the Court stated that:

'The starting point must be [the] concrete situation and account must be taken of a whole range of criteria such as the type, duration, effects and manner of implementation of the measure in question.' [emphasis added]

40. Based on these criteria, cases will, depending on their specific facts, fall on one side or the other of the 'dividing line'. Lester and Pannick, *Human Rights Law and Practice* (2004), p. 163, provides a number of examples of what will constitute an infringement of Article 5. In *Guzzardi* itself, the EctHR held that a suspected mafia member was deprived of his liberty during one phase of his detention, when he was made the subject of a compulsory residence order requiring him to live on a small island subject to strict police supervision. In *Engel v Netherlands* the EctHR held that 'strict arrest' imposed on soldiers for disciplinary offences amounted to a deprivation of liberty despite the different standards that apply to army personnel. In the unreported case of *Hojemeister v Germany*, the Commission held that detention incidental to a lawful search was not sufficient to trigger Article 5 protection.

41. Pannick and Lester [2004:164] note that '[d]etention does, however, depend upon the intention of the authorities'. Accordingly, where the police intend merely to question a suspect without detaining him, Article 5 will not apply. In *X v. Germany* (1981) 24 DR 158 at 161, the Commission decided that the object of police action was not clearly to deprive those involved of their liberty; the police action was: '... simply to obtain information from them about how they obtained possession of the objects found on them and about thefts which had occurred in the school previously.' The Commission therefore held that a 10 year-old girl who was questioned at a police station for two hours without being arrested, locked into a cell or formally detained was not deprived of her liberty for the purposes of Article 5.

42. On the other hand, Professor Feldman, in *Civil Liberties and Human Rights in England and Wales* (2002), p.304, recognises that, at least *prima facie*, brief detainment of the type associated with stop and search powers could fall within the ambit of Article 5:

'Where a person is briefly detained on the street or at a customs post in order to check for stolen, prohibited, or dutiable goods, there is a deprivation of liberty, albeit only for a short period: the person is not free to move anywhere without the agreement of the officer until the procedure is complete.'

43. He does note, however, that the detainment would only, in the general course, last a very short time, and therefore makes the qualification that:

'Under ECHR Article 5(1) and the Human Rights Act 1998, a deprivation of liberty does not take place if someone is detained for a very limited time. Searches of the person falling short of arrest entail a detention for only a short period.'

44. In the current appeal it is not essential to decide whether the stopping and searching of the appellants, using the powers vested in the police under the authorisation pursuant to section 44 of the 2000 Act, fell within Article 5 because, as we will see, it was justifiable under Article 5(1)(b) as detention in order 'to secure the fulfilment of [any] objective prescribed by law'.

45. However, if this point had to be decided, we would conclude that the stop and search powers should not be considered to constitute an infringement of Article 5. We agree with Sir Gerald Fitzmaurice, who in a dissenting opinion in *Guzzardi* at para. 6, urges that, in the light of the existence of Article 2 of Protocol 4, the ambit of Article 5 should be construed strictly:

'The existence of [Article 2 of Protocol 4] shows either that those who originally framed the Convention on Human Rights did not contemplate that [Article 5] should go beyond preventing actual deprivation of liberty, or extend to mere restrictions on freedom of movement [...] The resulting picture is that [Article 5] of the Convention guaranteed the individual against illegitimate [...] imprisonment, or confinement so close as to amount to the same thing – in sum against deprivation of liberty stricto sensu but it afforded no guarantee against restrictions [...] falling short of that'.

46. Taking into account:

   i)   the likely limited nature of any infringement of Article 5 in any normal stop and search;

ii) the fact that the main aim of a stop and search will not be to deprive an individual of his liberty but rather to effect a verification of one form or another (for example, the rapid verification that the person stopped is not carrying articles of a kind that could be used in connection with terrorism); and

iii) Article 2 of Protocol 4 which, in dealing specifically with the right to liberty of movement, gives some indication of the intended scope of Article 5,

the better view is that a short detainment pursuant to a stop and search power will normally fall outside Article 5.

47. The application of the other Articles is more straightforward. The first respondent was prepared to accept that Article 8 applies to the stop and search process and we accept that this is the correct approach. However, we do not consider that Articles 10 and 11 could be invoked. This is because insofar as this complaint relates to the general powers created by the terms of the 2000 Act and of the authorisations given under it, (see para. 26(d) above) those powers are, by section 45(1)(a) of the 2000 Act, strictly limited to searching for articles of a kind which could be used in connection with terrorism. So exercised, and in particular in view of the very limited powers of detention that are created by section 45(4), there is nothing in them that threatens either the right of freedom of expression or the right of assembly. Furthermore, the power if properly exercised by the police would not have any chilling effect on the rights protected by Articles 10 and 11.

48. The case might be different if the powers, ostensibly granted for the limited purposes of the 2000 Act, were in fact used, wrongly, in order to control or deter attendance at demonstrations. The evidence of the two appellants, that we have recorded at para. 16-17 above, gives some cause for concern in those respects, particularly in view of the alleged seizure from the first appellant of papers relating to the demonstration, and the alleged prevention of the second appellant from filming. However, as we indicate in paras. 56-57 below, those issues were not tested in these proceedings, because the thrust of the appellants' case, and thus the response of the respondents, was directed primarily at the general conformity of the legislation with articles 10 and 11: on which issue, as we have said above, the legislation itself cannot be criticised.

49. The appellants suggest that the exceptions to Article 5, 8, 10 and 11 cannot be relied upon because either what took place was 'not in accordance with a procedure prescribed by law' or 'not in accordance with the law'. This is because the law was not published and was arbitrary. We do not accept that this is the position. 'The law' that is under criticism here is the statute, not the authorisation. That law is just as much a public record as is any other statute. And the provisions are not arbitrary in any relevant sense. Although the police officer does not have to have grounds for suspecting the presence of suspicious articles before stopping a citizen in any particular case (section 45(1)(b)), he can only be authorised to use those powers for limited purposes, and where a decision has been made that the exercise of the powers is expedient for the serious purpose of the prevention of acts of terrorism (section 44(3)). The system, so controlled, cannot be said to be arbitrary in any sense that deprives it of the status of 'law' in the autonomous meaning of that term as understood in Convention jurisprudence. In addition, while the authorisations and their confirmation are not published because not unreasonably it is considered publication could damage the effectiveness of the stop and search powers and as the individual who is stopped has the right to a written statement under section 45(5), in this context the lack of publication does not mean that what occurred was not a procedure prescribed by law.

The Authorisation and Confirmation Questions

50. We turn to the authorisations made by Mr Veness and their confirmation by the Secretary of State. The scale of terrorist incidents around the globe is so well known it hardly required evidence to establish that this country is faced with a real possibility of terrorist incidents. However, the evidence surveys the history of global and national incidents (connected with the problems in Northern Ireland) that have already occurred. In

such a situation the authorisation and confirmation of a random power of search, provided by Parliament subject to the safeguards we have identified, cannot, as a matter of general principle, be said to be an unacceptable intrusion, that is neither necessary nor proportionate (as those terms are used in an ECHR context) into the human rights of those who are searched in the absence of some identified specific threat. The disadvantage of the intrusion and restraint imposed on even a large number of individuals by being stopped and searched cannot possibly match the advantage that accrues from the possibility of a terrorist attack being foiled or deterred by the use of the power.

51. Does the fact that we now know what has been taking place is an extensive blanket or "rolling" programme alter the situation? We do not think so. The evidence justifying this way of using the power could be more satisfactory, but in view of the evidence provided by the Secretary of State as to the process of confirmation, we are satisfied that the rolling programme is justified in the present situation. It did no more than enable the commander in a particular area to have the powers available when this was operationally required without going back to the Secretary of State for confirmation of a particular use. At this level there is nothing to support the suggestion of the appellants that authorisation and confirmation were not being granted and obtained for the purpose identified by the 2000 Act but rather for day-to-day policing. It is clear that there is no ground on which it would be appropriate for a court to interfere with or even criticise the authorisation and confirmation programme.

The Command Question

52. This is confirmed by the evidence that is available relating to the use of the authorisation and confirmation in conjunction with the arms fair that led to these proceedings. Having regard to the nature of the fair, its location near an airport and a previous site of a terrorist incident (connected with the Northern Ireland problems) and the fact that a protest was taking place, Command Messenger was entitled to decide that section 44 powers should be exercised in connection with the arms fair.

53. The Commander's responsibilities in relation to section 44 did not end with his designating the fair as an appropriate event in connection with which stop and search powers should be used. Indeed, we do not believe for a moment that he would regard it as all that was required. We expect that he would agree with us that officers who were to exercise the powers should receive carefully designed instructions (or if this had been done previously, a reminder) on their use. The evidence as to what happened is lamentable. There is reference to the officers being told they could use their powers and a slide being shown. There is little else, and there is no evidence of an explanation being given to the officers who would be dealing with the public as to the limits on their powers and as to how the powers should be deployed.

54. The inadequate nature of the evidence (of which the Divisional Court also complained without any attempt to rectify the position being made for the appeal, possibly for technical reasons) is particularly surprising because this is clearly a test case. It is important that, if the police are given exceptional powers (such as those under consideration here) because of threats to the safety of the public, they are prepared to demonstrate that they are being used with appropriate circumspection. This is in addition to the general obligation on parties conducting judicial review proceedings to do so openly or, as it has been said by Lord Donaldson of Lymington MR, with the cards face up. We appreciate that in this area discretion as to disclosure needs to be exercised so that information that could be operationally prejudicial is not disclosed. However, this consideration would not apply to making clear that proper instructions were given to officers exercising the powers. While it was legitimate to use the power if those doing so were made properly aware of their responsibilities, it is quite a different matter if the basic requirements of good administration were being neglected.

The Operational Question

55. We received no satisfactory explanation from the first respondent as to the inadequacies of the evidence. However, it was clear to us that part of the explanation could be that while the nature of the appellants' case has changed as the proceedings progressed, it has been, as Mr Rabinder Singh [for the appellants] accepts, focused on the issues of principle and not on the circumstances of the individual appellants. It was no doubt also recognised that proceedings for judicial review are not the correct forum in which to investigate factual issues. Nonetheless, it is still regrettably the position that in answer to the respondents' statements of what happened to them, the only response is the notes made by the police officers. We are without any statements from the officers.

56. The onus is on the first respondents to show that the interference with the appellants of which complaint is made was lawful. It is not possible to say that the onus has been discharged on the evidence before us. On the appellants' evidence remarks were made that suggest that the powers could have been used in order "to police" the protest. This would not be a lawful use of the power. We have also pointed out in para. 49 above to the potential evidential difficulties under Articles 10 and 11 that are presented by some parts of the appellants' evidence. As we have said, the form of these proceedings does not permit the resolution of those matters; but we feel sure that the respondents will wish to review very carefully those aspects of this operation, and of the briefing that the officers on the ground received before performing their powers and duties under the Act. This is the sum of what can be said on the limited evidence available.

Remedies

58. Mr Rabinder Singh accepted that, in view of the history of these proceedings, the only appropriate remedy to which the appellants could be entitled would be a declaration. We are prepared to hear the parties on the question of relief. However, it may be of assistance if we indicate that our provisional view is that this judgment is best left to speak for itself and that no order should be made on the appeal either as to the merits or costs."

(4) Terrorist Offences

The Terrorism Act 2000 introduces a number of offences. It is an offence to be a member of or to support in various ways a proscribed organisation. There are a number of offences relating to terrorist property and to counter-terrorist activities (such as failing to stop to be searched). The Act is, however, concerned more to attack organisations and their funds on the one hand and designed to give the police sufficient powers of investigation on the other, than it is to create specific offences relating to terrorism. Indeed although there are powers to arrest someone because he or she is suspected of being a terrorist, it is not an offence to be a terrorist. However, someone who falls within the definition of a terrorist will do so because he or she has committed one of more of the foregoing offences or one or more crimes of violence. Many of the terrorist activities to which the Act is addressed would constitute offences under the criminal law as it is, without the need for additional offences to be created. The most notorious example of this is *Megrahi v H M Advocate*, 2002 S.L.T. 1433. There are, however, a number of specific terrorist offences which have been introduced which are aimed at terrorist activity to supplement the existing criminal law. These offences are directed not at the support for or funding of terrorist organisations but at their activities.

Terrorism Act 2000

"Weapons training

54.—(1) A person commits an offence if he provides instruction or training in the making or use of—

    (a) firearms,

    (b) explosives, or

    (c) chemical, biological or nuclear weapons.

(2) A person commits an offence if he receives instruction or training in the making or use of—

    (a) firearms,

    (b) explosives, or

    (c) chemical, biological or nuclear weapons.

(3) A person commits an offence if he invites another to receive instruction or training and the receipt—

    (a) would constitute an offence under subsection (2), or

    (b) would constitute an offence under subsection (2) but for the fact that it is to take place outside the United Kingdom.

(4) For the purpose of subsections (1) and (3)—

    (a) a reference to the provision of instruction includes a reference to making it available either generally or to one or more specific persons, and

    (b) an invitation to receive instruction or training may be either general or addressed to one or more specific persons.

(5) It is a defence for a person charged with an offence under this section in relation to instruction or training to prove that his action or involvement was wholly for a purpose other than assisting, preparing for or participating in terrorism.

(6) A person guilty of an offence under this section shall be liable—

    (a) on conviction on indictment, to imprisonment for a term not exceeding ten years, to a fine or to both, or

    (b) on summary conviction, to imprisonment for a term not exceeding six months, to a fine not exceeding the statutory maximum or to both.

(7) A court by or before which a person is convicted of an offence under this section may order the forfeiture of anything which the court considers to have been in the person's possession for purposes connected with the offence.

(8) Before making an order under subsection (7) a court must give an opportunity to be heard to any person, other than the convicted person, who claims to be the owner of or otherwise interested in anything which can be forfeited under that subsection.

(9) An order under subsection (7) shall not come into force until there is no further possibility of it being varied, or set aside, on appeal (disregarding any power of a court to grant leave to appeal out of time). ...

Directing terrorist organisation

56.—(1) A person commits an offence if he directs, at any level, the activities of an organisation which is concerned in the commission of acts of terrorism.

(2) A person guilty of an offence under this section is liable on conviction on indictment to imprisonment for life.

Possession for terrorist purposes

57.—(1) A person commits an offence if he possesses an article in circumstances which give rise to a reasonable suspicion that his possession is for a purpose connected with the commission, preparation or instigation of an act of terrorism.

(2) It is a defence for a person charged with an offence under this section to prove that his possession of the article was not for a purpose connected with the commission, preparation or instigation of an act of terrorism.

(3) In proceedings for an offence under this section, if it is proved that an article—

    (a) was on any premises at the same time as the accused, or

(b) was on premises of which the accused was the occupier or which he habitually used otherwise than as a member of the public,

the court may assume that the accused possessed the article, unless he proves that he did not know of its presence on the premises or that he had no control over it.

(4) A person guilty of an offence under this section shall be liable—

(a) on conviction on indictment, to imprisonment for a term not exceeding 10 years, to a fine or to both, or

(b) on summary conviction, to imprisonment for a term not exceeding six months, to a fine not exceeding the statutory maximum or to both.

Collection of information

58.—(1) A person commits an offence if—

(a) he collects or makes a record of information of a kind likely to be useful to a person committing or preparing an act of terrorism, or

(b) he possesses a document or record containing information of that kind.

(2) In this section 'record' includes a photographic or electronic record.

(3) It is a defence for a person charged with an offence under this section to prove that he had a reasonable excuse for his action or possession.

(4) A person guilty of an offence under this section shall be liable—

(a) on conviction on indictment, to imprisonment for a term not exceeding 10 years, to a fine or to both, or

(b) on summary conviction, to imprisonment for a term not exceeding six months, to a fine not exceeding the statutory maximum or to both.

(5) A court by or before which a person is convicted of an offence under this section may order the forfeiture of any document or record containing information of the kind mentioned in subsection (1)(a).

(6) Before making an order under subsection (5) a court must give an opportunity to be heard to any person, other than the convicted person, who claims to be the owner of or otherwise interested in anything which can be forfeited under that subsection.

(7) An order under subsection (5) shall not come into force until there is no further possibility of it being varied, or set aside, on appeal (disregarding any power of a court to grant leave to appeal out of time)."

In addition to the foregoing, s.61 provides that a person commits an offence if he or she incites another person to commit an act of terrorism wholly or partly outside the United Kingdom, and the act would, if committed in Scotland, constitute one of the offences listed in s.61(2). The offences to which s.61(2) applies are (1) murder, (2) assault to severe injury, and (3) reckless conduct which causes actual injury. It is both interesting and important to note that s.62(5) provides that: "Nothing in this section imposes criminal liability on any person acting on behalf of, or holding office under, the Crown". This would include members of the security and intelligence services as well members of the armed forces.

Terrorism Act 2000—Arrest and charge statistics Between September 11, 2001 and June 30, 2004:

Police records show that from September 11, 2001 until June 30, 2004, 609 people were arrested under the Terrorism Act 2000. 61 of these were charged under the Act and 38 under both the Terrorism Act and other legislation.

The remainder were either released without charge, bailed to return, cautioned, charged under other legislation (such as the legislation for murder, grievous bodily harm, use of firearms or explosives and so forth), or dealt with under immigration or mental health legislation. Of the 99 individuals charged under the Terrorism Act, there have been 15 convictions to date.

Source: Home Office (2004)

IV. THE ANTI-TERRORISM, CRIME AND SECURITY ACT 2001

Hot on the heels of the Terrorism Act 2000 came the Anti-terrorism, Crime and Security Act 2001. This was passed in the immediate aftermath of the incidents in New York and Washington on September 11, 2001. According to the Home Secretary (Mr David Blunkett) who introduced the measure in the House of Commons:

> "Circumstances and public opinion demanded urgent action and appropriate action after the 11 September attacks on the World Trade Centre and the Pentagon. Many parliamentarians understandably demanded caution, proportionality and a response that would last for the future. Over the five weeks following the attacks, in which thousands of men and women lost their lives, it was the Government's task to appraise the measures that would be necessary to close loopholes and set aside anomalies that had developed over many years in existing legislation." (H.C. Debs, November 19, 2001, col.22.)

According to Mr Blunkett, the measures proposed were "rational, reasonable and proportionate steps to deal with an internal threat and an external, organised terrorist group that could threaten at any time not just our population, but the populations of other friendly countries" (*ibid.*, col.25). Not everyone agrees with the "rational, reasonable and proportionate" part. Other countries have also introduced tough new laws in the wake of the events in New York and Washington, including the US itself where the so called Patriot Act has proved to be very controversial. The US has also attracted international opprobrium (including criticism from British judges) for its indefinite detention without trial in barbaric conditions of "enemy combatants" (including a number of British citizens) following the bombing, invasion and occupation of Afghanistan in 2002. The Anti-terrorism, Crime and Security Act 2001 has also attracted an intense level of criticism, notwithstanding Mr Blunkett's claims about it being "rational, reasonable and proportionate". One concession made by the Government to its critics is that the Act would have to be reviewed by a Committee of Privy Councillors: 2001 Act, s.122. The report was published on December 18, 2003, and various provisions are referred to below: Privy Councillor Review Committee, *Anti-terrorism, Crime and Security Act 2001 Review: Report*, H.C. 100 (2003) (Newton Review Committee). The Government also agreed to a review of Pt 4 of the Act. This has been conducted by Lord Carlile and was published on February 11, 2004. It is also considered below. Other reviews have been conducted by parliamentary committees, most notably by the Joint Committee on Human Rights.

(1) Cutting the Source of Funding

The Anti-terrorism, Crime and Security Act 2001 is best known for the provisions it introduces for the detention of people without trial, but in a long measure of 129 sections, it does much else besides. Part 1 deals with terrorist property and replaces provisions found earlier in the Terrorism Act 2000. The new provisions apply to the seizure and forfeiture of terrorist cash, which is defined to include coins and notes in any currency, postal orders, cheques, travellers' cheques and bankers' drafts.

The Anti-terrorism, Crime and Security Act 2001
Schedule 1

"Seizure of cash

2 (1) An authorised officer may seize any cash if he has reasonable grounds for suspecting that it is terrorist cash.

(2) An authorised officer may also seize cash part of which he has reasonable grounds for suspecting to be terrorist cash if it is not reasonably practicable to seize only that part.

Detention of seized cash

3 (1) While the authorised officer continues to have reasonable grounds for his suspicion, cash seized under this Schedule may be detained initially for a period of 48 hours.

(2) The period for which the cash or any part of it may be detained may be extended by an order made by a magistrates' court or (in Scotland) the sheriff; but the order may not authorise the detention of any of the cash—

    (a) beyond the end of the period of three months beginning with the date of the order, and

    (b) in the case of any further order under this paragraph, beyond the end of the period of two years beginning with the date of the first order.

...

(4) An order under sub-paragraph (2) must provide for notice to be given to persons affected by it.

(5) An application for an order under sub-paragraph (2)—

...

    (b) in relation to Scotland, may be made by a procurator fiscal, and the ... sheriff ... may make the order if satisfied, in relation to any cash to be further detained, that one of the following conditions is met.

(6) The first condition is that there are reasonable grounds for suspecting that the cash is intended to be used for the purposes of terrorism and that either—

    (a) its continued detention is justified while its intended use is further investigated or consideration is given to bringing (in the United Kingdom or elsewhere) proceedings against any person for an offence with which the cash is connected, or

    (b) proceedings against any person for an offence with which the cash is connected have been started and have not been concluded.

(7) The second condition is that there are reasonable grounds for suspecting that the cash consists of resources of an organisation which is a proscribed organisation and that either—

    (a) its continued detention is justified while investigation is made into whether or not it consists of such resources or consideration is given to bringing (in the United Kingdom or elsewhere) proceedings against any person for an offence with which the cash is connected, or

    (b) proceedings against any person for an offence with which the cash is connected have been started and have not been concluded.

(8) The third condition is that there are reasonable grounds for suspecting that the cash is property earmarked as terrorist property and that either—

    (a) its continued detention is justified while its derivation is further investigated or consideration is given to bringing (in the United Kingdom or elsewhere) proceedings against any person for an offence with which the cash is connected, or

    (b) proceedings against any person for an offence with which the cash is connected have been started and have not been concluded.

Payment of detained cash into an account

4 (1) If cash is detained under this Schedule for more than 48 hours, it is to be held in an interest-bearing account and the interest accruing on it is to be added to it on its forfeiture or release.

...

Release of detained cash

5 (1) This paragraph applies while any cash is detained under this Schedule.

(2) ... the sheriff may direct the release of the whole or any part of the cash if satisfied, on an application by the person from whom it was seized, that the conditions in paragraph 3 for the detention of cash are no longer met in relation to the cash to be released.

(3) A ... procurator fiscal may, after notifying the ... sheriff ... under whose order cash

is being detained, release the whole or any part of it if satisfied that the detention of the cash
to be released is no longer justified.

(4) But cash is not to be released—

(a) if an application for its forfeiture under paragraph 6, or for its release under
paragraph 9, is made, until any proceedings in pursuance of the application
(including any proceedings on appeal) are concluded,

(b) if (in the United Kingdom or elsewhere) proceedings are started against any
person for an offence with which the cash is connected, until the proceedings are
concluded."

Provision is made in paras 6–10 for the forfeiture of terrorist cash on an application by the
Scottish Ministers to the sheriff. An appeal lies to the Court of Session which may order a
release of the cash if the appeal is successful. Any cash forfeited as a result of a forfeiture order is
to be paid into the Scottish Consolidated Fund. If no forfeiture order is made in respect of any
cash which has been detained, the person to whom the cash belongs or from whom it was seized
may make an application to the sheriff for compensation. The Newton Review Committee (*op.
cit.*) thought these measures to be "proportionate and effective" (para.122), and reported that
the power to seize cash had been used 18 times, netting £270,000. It was recommended that the
powers should be extended to non-cash items, but the Committee did highlight a number of
difficulties associated with the targeting of terrorist finance:

"Terrorist finance presents particular challenges for law enforcement. The funds in question may not derive from illegal activities; the sums involved can be small; and the
individuals who use those funds may avoid conspicuously expensive lifestyles in seeking to
maintain effective cover for their operations."

The foregoing powers were said by Newton nevertheless to be a "useful point of intervention
in disrupting the planning of terrorist activities before they occur". These powers are not,
however, the only powers directed to the financing of terrorism, and they are complemented by
a number of other provisions of the 2001 Act. These include the remarkable provisions of Pt II
of the Act which appear to be addressed mainly at the possibility of international terrorism
being funded from the United Kingdom. In order to combat this, the Treasury is empowered
effectively to freeze bank accounts. What is unusual about the procedure, however, is that this is
to be done in individual cases not with the authority of the courts but with the approval of
Parliament.

The Anti-terrorism, Crime and Security Act 2001

"Power to make order

4 (1) The Treasury may make a freezing order if the following two conditions are
satisfied.

(2) The first condition is that the Treasury reasonably believe that—

(a) action to the detriment of the United Kingdom's economy (or part of it) has been
or is likely to be taken by a person or persons, or

(b) action constituting a threat to the life or property of one or more nationals of the
United Kingdom or residents of the United Kingdom has been or is likely to be
taken by a person or persons.

(3) If one person is believed to have taken or to be likely to take the action the second
condition is that the person is—

(a) the government of a country or territory outside the United Kingdom, or

(b) a resident of a country or territory outside the United Kingdom.

(4) If two or more persons are believed to have taken or to be likely to take the action the
second condition is that each of them falls within paragraph (a) or (b) of subsection (3); and

different persons may fall within different paragraphs.

Contents of order

5 (1) A freezing order is an order which prohibits persons from making funds available to or for the benefit of a person or persons specified in the order.

(2) The order must provide that these are the persons who are prohibited—

    (a) all persons in the United Kingdom, and

    (b) all persons elsewhere who are nationals of the United Kingdom or are bodies incorporated under the law of any part of the United Kingdom or are Scottish partnerships.

(3) The order may specify the following (and only the following) as the person or persons to whom or for whose benefit funds are not to be made available—

    (a) the person or persons reasonably believed by the Treasury to have taken or to be likely to take the action referred to in section 4;

    (b) any person the Treasury reasonably believe has provided or is likely to provide assistance (directly or indirectly) to that person or any of those persons.

(4) A person may be specified under subsection (3) by—

    (a) being named in the order, or

    (b) falling within a description of persons set out in the order.

(5) The description must be such that a reasonable person would know whether he fell within it.

(6) Funds are financial assets and economic benefits of any kind."

The Act further provides that the Treasury must keep a freezing order under review, and that an order ceases to have effect at the end of the period of two years starting with the day on which it is made. The power to make an order is exercisable by statutory instrument which must be approved by a resolution of each House of Parliament. At the time of writing these powers had never been used, but the Newton Review Committee pointed out that they are broad and that there is no appeal against the making of an order. The Committee also pointed out that these powers overlap with the provisions of the Terrorism (United Nations Measures) Order 2001, SI 2001/3365 which deal with the freezing of terrorist assets. The Order gives the Treasury power to freeze the funds of persons provided certain criteria set out in the Order are met. These include a requirement that there are reasonable grounds for suspecting that the person is or may be:

- within Article 4(1)(a): "a person who commits, attempts to commit, facilitates or participates in the commission of acts of terrorism";
- within Article 4(1)(b): "a person controlled or owned (*sic*) directly or indirectly by a person in (a)"; or
- within Article 4(1)(c): "a person acting on behalf, or at the direction, of a person in (a)".

According to the Newton Review Committee at para.148:

"From the counter-terrorist point of view, the Terrorism Order has a number of advantages which distinguish it from Part 2 [of the 2001 Act]:

    a. it gives a clear and narrowly limited definition of terrorism, drawn directly from the Terrorism Act 2000;

    b. it is not limited in application to foreign nationals (and thus for instance has been used against the assets of ... UK suicide bombers);

    c. it explictly permits an appeal by individuals and affected firms [to the Court of Session against a direction to freeze assets], unlike Part 2 [of the 2001 Act] where the only provision for scrutiny after an order is made is by a process of internal review of an unspecified character by the Treasury."

In the view of the Committee, the power to make freezing orders for use against terrorism should be reviewed, with the legislation based on "the well tested" provisions of the Terrorism (United Nations Measures) Order 2001, SI 2001/3365. In 2004 the Chancellor of the Exchequer instructed the Bank of England to add to its list of individuals and terrorist groups subject to an asset freeze the names "Kadek" and "Kongra-Gel" as aliases of the terrorist Kurdistan Worker's Party (PKK), which is already subject to such a freeze. He also directed financial institutions that any funds which they hold for or on behalf of five senior members of Hamas must be frozen. This action was taken because the Treasury had reasonable grounds for suspecting that four of the individuals were, or may have been, persons who facilitated or participated in the commission of acts of terrorism while the other was or may have been a person who committed, facilitated or participated in such acts. In March 2004 the Treasury reported that:

- Both before and after September 11, 2001 the UK froze a total of around £70 million of terrorist assets. The bulk of these assets have now been unfrozen, and made available to the 'legitimate government in Afghanistan'.
- 38 bank accounts were currently frozen in UK institutions under Treasury powers to implement UN measures against terrorist financing (presumably the Terrorism (United Nations Measures) Order 2001).

(2) Securing Information from Government Departments

In addition to these funding issues, another theme of the 2001 Act is to enable the police and security services to have access to information held by other government departments or public bodies. This information is usually protected by statute which often restricts the purposes for which the information may be used. Take a random example: the Race Relations Act 1976, s.52 provides that no information given to the Commission for Racial Equality by any person in connection with a formal investigation (by the Commission) shall be disclosed by the Commission except in certain prescribed circumstances. These circumstances do not include requests from the police or other agencies. Section 17 of the 2001 Act authorises the disclosure of information obtained by various public authorities for:

"(a) the purposes of any criminal investigation whatever which is being or may be carried out, whether in the United Kingdom or elsewhere;
(b) the purposes of any criminal proceedings whatever which have been or may be initiated, whether in the United Kingdom or elsewhere;
(c) the purposes of the initiation or bringing to an end of any such investigation or proceedings;
(d) the purpose of facilitating a determination of whether any such investigation or proceedings should be initiated or brought to an end."

These provisions apply to 66 provisions listed in Sch.4 of the Act, and it was said by Newton that they represent a "significant extension of the government's power to use information obtained for one purpose, in some cases under compulsory powers, for a completely different purpose". It will be noted that this power to disclose information in this way is not related directly or exclusively to terrorist investigations or terrorist-related offences. Indeed these measures were first introduced in the Criminal Justice and Police Bill 2001 and were dropped from the Bill following opposition in the House of Lords. It appears that the powers are being used for purposes other than terrorism. Thus, it was revealed by the Newton Review Committee that only 21 per cent of disclosures made by Customs and Excise under the 2001 Act relate to terrorism, and only 4 per cent of Inland Revenue disclosures were so related. Specific provision is made authorising the disclosure of information by the Inland Revenue.

The Anti-terrorism, Crime and Security Act 2001

"Disclosure of information held by revenue departments

19 (1) This section applies to information which is held by or on behalf of the Commissioners of Inland Revenue or by or on behalf of the Commissioners of Customs and Excise, including information obtained before the coming into force of this section.

(2) No obligation of secrecy imposed by statute or otherwise prevents the disclosure, in accordance with the following provisions of this section, of information to which this section applies if the disclosure is made—

(a) for the purpose of facilitating the carrying out by any of the intelligence services of any of that service's functions;

(b) for the purposes of any criminal investigation whatever which is being or may be carried out, whether in the United Kingdom or elsewhere;

(c) for the purposes of any criminal proceedings whatever which have been or may be initiated, whether in the United Kingdom or elsewhere;

(d) for the purposes of the initiation or bringing to an end of any such investigation or proceedings; or

(e) for the purpose of facilitating a determination of whether any such investigation or proceedings should be initiated or brought to an end.

(3) No disclosure of information to which this section applies shall be made by virtue of this section unless the person by whom the disclosure is made is satisfied that the making of the disclosure is proportionate to what is sought to be achieved by it.

(4) Information to which this section applies shall not be disclosed by virtue of this section except by the Commissioners by or on whose behalf it is held or with their authority.

(5) Information obtained by means of a disclosure authorised by subsection (2) shall not be further disclosed except—

(a) for a purpose mentioned in that subsection; and

(b) with the consent of the Commissioners by whom or with whose authority it was initially disclosed;

and information so obtained otherwise than by or on behalf of any of the intelligence services shall not be further disclosed (with or without such consent) to any of those services, or to any person acting on behalf of any of those services, except for a purpose mentioned in paragraphs (b) to (e) of that subsection.

(6) A consent for the purposes of subsection (5) may be given either in relation to a particular disclosure or in relation to disclosures made in such circumstances as may be specified or described in the consent.

(7) Nothing in this section authorises the making of any disclosure which is prohibited by any provision of the Data Protection Act 1998."

Strong concerns were expressed about the scope of these powers by the Newton Committee Review of the Act. The Committee said that it attached particular importance to Art.8 of the ECHR but thought that the protection of the Human Rights Act was illusory in this context. This is because "the burden will lie on the individual to complain about the disclosure of their confidential information in circumstances where, almost by definition, he or she will be unlikely to know that disclosure has occurred"(para.164). The Committee recommended that "the Government (sic) should legislate to provide independent external oversight of the whole disclosure regime (eg by the Information or one of the other statutory Commissioners) to provide a safeguard against abuse and to ensure that rigorous procedural standards governing disclosure are applied across the range of public bodies, prosecuting authorities and intelligence and security agencies" (para.166). The Committee was also of the view that while external oversight was a necessary safeguard, it was not sufficient. It was pointed out that in the past, when a statute conferred intrusive powers on the Executive:

"Parliament has normally made their exercise subject to the prior approval of a judge or other independent person (eg search warrants). Independent authorisation or scrutiny has been considered particularly important when an individual is unlikely to know that such powers are being exercised against him, as is the case here."

In the view of the Committee prior authorisation should be required before information is divulged, with the authorisation to be given either by a "senior person" or by a judicial officer, depending on the nature of the information on the one hand and the nature of the offence on the other.

(3) Excluding and Detaining Suspected International Terrorists

Part 4 of the Act is by far the most controversial, dealing with immigration and asylum. It is not hard to see why it should be so controversial: it permits the indefinite detention without trial of individuals who are suspected international terrorists under powers which have been introduced only after derogating from Convention rights. Under the pre-existing law, there were limited powers to remove people whose presence in this country was thought not to be conducive to the public good. These included people with only a limited right to remain here and people who had been convicted of an offence. Anyone to be deported in this way had a right of appeal to the Special Immigration Appeals Commission which was established by the Special Immigration Appeals Commission Act 1997. There is an appeal from the Commission to the Court of Session and then to the House of Lords. It has been said in the House of Lords that "issues of national security do not fall beyond the competence of the courts" (*Secretary of State v Rehman* [2003] 1 A.C. 153 (Lord Steyn)). Nevertheless, it has also been made clear that the courts will only reluctantly question ministerial judgments relating to national security. In what is likely to be a much quoted postscript to his decision in *Rehman, ibid.*, Lord Hoffmann said that:

"I wrote this speech some three months before the recent events in New York and Washington. They are a reminder that in matters of national security, the cost of failure can be high. This seems to me to underline the need for the judicial arm of government to respect the decisions of ministers of the Crown on the question of whether support for terrorist activities in a foreign country constitutes a threat to national security. It is not only that the executive has access to special information and expertise in these matters. It is also that such decisions, with serious potential results for the community, require a legitimacy which can be conferred only by entrusting them to persons responsible to the community through the democratic process. If the people are to accept the consequences of such decisions, they must be made by persons whom the people have elected and whom they can remove."

The Government sought wider powers to remove suspected international terrorists, without necessarily waiting for them to commit an offence or provide other grounds for removal. However, in taking such powers the Government encountered another obstacle in the form of Art.3 of the ECHR. It will be recalled that this provides that no one shall be subjected to torture or to inhuman or degrading treatment or punishment. In *Chahal v United Kingdom* (1996) 23 E.H.R.R. 413, it was held that it was a breach of this provision to return someone to a country where they may be subjected to torture or inhuman or degrading punishment or treatment. Article 3 is a non-derogable provision of the Convention. The next best option for the government then was to detain (that is to say imprison) the people who could not be removed or deported. This has been done in the past, most recently in the case of internment in Northern Ireland in the early stages of the "Troubles". But internment without trial (or executive detention) was found to be a breach of Art.5 of the ECHR which generally provides for detention only after conviction or only after arrest on suspicion of having committed a crime (*Ireland v United Kingdom* (1978) 2 E.H.R.R. 25). Unlike Art.3, however, it is possible to derogate from Art.5 where—in the words of Art.15—"there is a public emergency threatening the life of the nation", provided the measures taken are "strictly required by the exigencies of the situation". The British Government gave fresh notice of its intention to derogate from Art.5 on December 18, 2001 in order to permit the detention of suspected international terrorists it was unable to deport.

Declaration contained in a Note Verbale from the Permanent Representative of the United Kingdom, dated 18 December 2001, registered by the Secretariat General on 18 December 2001

The United Kingdom Permanent Representative to the Council of Europe presents his compliments to the Secretary General of the Council, and has the honour to convey the following information in order to ensure compliance with the obligations of Her Majesty's Government in the United Kingdom under Article 15(3) of the Convention for the Protection of Human Rights and Fundamental Freedoms signed at Rome on 5 November 1950.

Public emergency in the United Kingdom
The terrorist attacks in New York, Washington, D.C. and Pennsylvania on 11th September 2001 resulted in several thousand deaths, including many British victims and others from 70 different countries. In its resolutions 1368 (2001) and 1373 (2001), the United Nations Council recognised the attacks as a threat to international peace and security.

The threat from international terrorism is a continuing one. In its resolution 1373 (2001), the Security Council, acting under Chapter VII of the United Nations Charter, required all States to take measures to prevent the commission of terrorist attacks, including by denying safe haven to those who finance, plan, support or commit terrorist attacks.
There exists a terrorist threat to the United Kingdom from persons suspected of involvement in international terrorism. In particular, there are foreign nationals present in the United Kingdom who are suspected of being concerned in the commission, preparation or instigation of acts of international terrorism, of being members of organisations or groups which are so concerned or of having links with members of such organisations or groups, and who are a threat to the national security of the United Kingdom.
As a result, a public emergency, within the meaning of Article 15 (1) of the Convention, exists in the United Kingdom.

The Anti-terrorism, Crime and Security Act 2001
As a result of the public emergency, provision is made in the Anti-terrorism, Crime and Security Act 2001, *inter alia*, for an extended power to arrest and detain a foreign national which will apply where it is intended to remove or deport the person from the United Kingdom but where removal or deportation is not for the time being possible, with the consequence that the detention would be unlawful under existing domestic law powers. The extended power to arrest and detain will apply where the Secretary of State issues a certificate indicating his belief that the person's presence in the United Kingdom is a risk to national security and that he suspects the person of being an international terrorist. That certificate will be subject to an appeal to the Special Immigration Appeals Commission ("SIAC"), established under the Special Immigration Appeals Commission Act 1997, which will have power to cancel it if it considers that the certificate should not have been issued. There will be an appeal on a point of law from a ruling by SIAC. In addition, the certificate will be reviewed by SIAC at regular intervals. SIAC will also be able to grant bail, where appropriate, subject to conditions. It will be open to a detainee to end his detention at any time by agreeing to leave the United Kingdom.

The extended power of arrest and detention in the Anti-terrorism, Crime and Security Act 2001 is a measure which is strictly required by the exigencies of the situation. It is a temporary provision which comes into force for an initial period of 15 months and then expires unless renewed by Parliament. Thereafter, it is subject to annual renewal by Parliament. If, at any time, in the Government's assessment, the public emergency no longer exists or the extended power is no longer strictly required by the exigencies of the situation, then the Secretary of State will, by Order, repeal the provision.

Domestic law powers of detention (other than under the Anti-terrorism, Crime and Security Act 2001)

The Government has powers under the Immigration Act 1971 ("the 1971 Act") to remove or deport persons on the ground that their presence in the United Kingdom is not conducive to the public good on national security grounds. Persons can also be arrested and detained under Schedules 2 and 3 to the 1971 Act pending their removal or deportation. The courts in the United Kingdom have ruled that this power of detention can only be exercised during the period necessary, in all the circumstances of the particular case, to effect removal and that, if it becomes clear that removal is not going to be possible within a reasonable time, detention will be unlawful (*R. v Governor of Durham Prison, ex parte Singh* [1984] All ER 983).

Article 5(1)(f) of the Convention

It is well established that Article 5(1)(f) permits the detention of a person with a view to deportation only in circumstances where "action is being taken with a view to deportation" (*Chahal v United Kingdom* (1996) 23 EHRR 413 at paragraph 112). In that case the European Court of Human Rights indicated that detention will cease to be permissible under Article 5(1)(f) if deportation proceedings are not prosecuted with due diligence and that it was necessary in such cases to determine whether the duration of the deportation proceedings was excessive (paragraph 113).

In some cases, where the intention remains to remove or deport a person on national security grounds, continued detention may not be consistent with Article 5(1)(f) as interpreted by the Court in the *Chahal* case. This may be the case, for example, if the person has established that removal to their own country might result in treatment contrary to Article 3 of the Convention. In such circumstances, irrespective of the gravity of the threat to national security posed by the person concerned, it is well established that Article 3 prevents removal or deportation to a place where there is a real risk that the person will suffer treatment contrary to that article. If no alternative destination is immediately available then removal or deportation may not, for the time being, be possible even though the ultimate intention remains to remove or deport the person once satisfactory arrangements can be made. In addition, it may not be possible to prosecute the person for a criminal offence given the strict rules on the admissibility of evidence in the criminal justice system of the United Kingdom and the high standard of proof required.

Derogation under Article 15 of the Convention

The Government has considered whether the exercise of the extended power to detain contained in the Anti-terrorism, Crime and Security Act 2001 may be inconsistent with the obligations under Article 5(1) of the Convention. As indicated above, there may be cases where, notwithstanding a continuing intention to remove or deport a person who is being detained, it is not possible to say that "action is being taken with a view to deportation" within the meaning of Article 5(1)(f) as interpreted by the Court in the *Chahal* case. To the extent, therefore, that the exercise of the extended power may be inconsistent with the United Kingdom's obligations under Article 5(1), the Government has decided to avail itself of the right of derogation conferred by Article 15(1) of the Convention and will continue to do so until further notice.

Period covered: 18/12/2001—

The preceding statement concerns Article(s) : 15

The Anti-terrorism, Crime and Security Act 2001

"Suspected international terrorist: certification

21 (1) The Secretary of State may issue a certificate under this section in respect of a person if the Secretary of State reasonably—

    (a) believes that the person's presence in the United Kingdom is a risk to national security, and

    (b) suspects that the person is a terrorist.

(2) In subsection (1)(b) 'terrorist' means a person who—

    (a) is or has been concerned in the commission, preparation or instigation of acts of international terrorism,

    (b) is a member of or belongs to an international terrorist group, or

    (c) has links with an international terrorist group.

(3) A group is an international terrorist group for the purposes of subsection (2)(b) and (c) if—

    (a) it is subject to the control or influence of persons outside the United Kingdom, and

    (b) the Secretary of State suspects that it is concerned in the commission, preparation or instigation of acts of international terrorism.

(4) For the purposes of subsection (2)(c) a person has links with an international terrorist group only if he supports or assists it.

(5) In this Part—

'terrorism' has the meaning given by section 1 of the Terrorism Act 2000, and 'suspected international terrorist' means a person certified under subsection (1).

(6) Where the Secretary of State issues a certificate under subsection (1) he shall as soon as is reasonably practicable—

    (a) take reasonable steps to notify the person certified, and

    (b) send a copy of the certificate to the Special Immigration Appeals Commission.

(7) The Secretary of State may revoke a certificate issued under subsection (1).

(8) A decision of the Secretary of State in connection with certification under this section may be questioned in legal proceedings only under section 25 or 26.

(9) An action of the Secretary of State taken wholly or partly in reliance on a certificate under this section may be questioned in legal proceedings only by or in the course of proceedings under—

    (a) section 25 or 26, or

    (b) section 2 of the Special Immigration Appeals Commission Act 1997 (appeal).

Deportation, removal, &c.

22 (1) An action of a kind specified in subsection (2) may be taken in respect of a suspected international terrorist despite the fact that (whether temporarily or indefinitely) the action cannot result in his removal from the United Kingdom because of—

    (a) a point of law which wholly or partly relates to an international agreement, or

    (b) a practical consideration.

(2) The actions mentioned in subsection (1) are—

    (a) refusing leave to enter or remain in the United Kingdom in accordance with provision made by or by virtue of any of sections 3 to 3B of the Immigration Act 1971 (control of entry to United Kingdom),

    (b) varying a limited leave to enter or remain in the United Kingdom in accordance with provision made by or by virtue of any of those sections,

    (c) recommending deportation in accordance with section 3(6) of that Act (recommendation by court),

    (d) taking a decision to make a deportation order under section 5(1) of that Act (deportation by Secretary of State),

    (e) making a deportation order under section 5(1) of that Act,

   (f) refusing to revoke a deportation order,

   (g) cancelling leave to enter the United Kingdom in accordance with paragraph 2A of Schedule 2 to that Act (person arriving with continuous leave),

   (h) giving directions for a person's removal from the United Kingdom under any of paragraphs 8 to 10 or 12 to 14 of Schedule 2 to that Act (control of entry to United Kingdom),

   (i) giving directions for a person's removal from the United Kingdom under section 10 of the Immigration and Asylum Act 1999 (person unlawfully in United Kingdom), and

   (j) giving notice to a person in accordance with regulations under paragraph 1 of Schedule 4 to that Act of a decision to make a deportation order against him.

(3) Action of a kind specified in subsection (2) which has effect in respect of a suspected international terrorist at the time of his certification under section 21 shall be treated as taken again (in reliance on subsection (1) above) immediately after certification.

Detention

23 (1) A suspected international terrorist may be detained under a provision specified in subsection (2) despite the fact that his removal or departure from the United Kingdom is prevented (whether temporarily or indefinitely) by—

   (a) a point of law which wholly or partly relates to an international agreement, or

   (b) a practical consideration.

(2) The provisions mentioned in subsection (1) are—

   (a) paragraph 16 of Schedule 2 to the Immigration Act 1971 (detention of persons liable to examination or removal), and

   (b) paragraph 2 of Schedule 3 to that Act (detention pending deportation).

Bail

24 (1) A suspected international terrorist who is detained under a provision of the Immigration Act 1971 may be released on bail. . . .

Certification: appeal

25 (1) A suspected international terrorist may appeal to the Special Immigration Appeals Commission against his certification under section 21.

(2) On an appeal the Commission must cancel the certificate if—

   (a) it considers that there are no reasonable grounds for a belief or suspicion of the kind referred to in section 21(1)(a) or (b), or

   (b) it considers that for some other reason the certificate should not have been issued.

(3) If the Commission determines not to cancel a certificate it must dismiss the appeal.

(4) Where a certificate is cancelled under subsection (2) it shall be treated as never having been issued.

(5) An appeal against certification may be commenced only—

   (a) within the period of three months beginning with the date on which the certificate is issued, or

   (b) with the leave of the Commission, after the end of that period but before the commencement of the first review under section 26.

Certification: review

26 (1) The Special Immigration Appeals Commission must hold a first review of each certificate issued under section 21 as soon as is reasonably practicable after the expiry of the period of six months beginning with the date on which the certificate is issued.

(2) But—

   (a) in a case where before the first review would fall to be held in accordance with subsection (1) an appeal under section 25 is commenced (whether or not it is finally determined before that time) or leave to appeal is given under section 25(5)(b), the first review shall be held as soon as is reasonably practicable after the expiry of the period of six months beginning with the date on which the appeal is finally determined, and

(b) in a case where an application for leave under section 25(5)(b) has been commenced but not determined at the time when the first review would fall to be held in accordance with subsection (1), if leave is granted the first review shall be held as soon as is reasonably practicable after the expiry of the period of six months beginning with the date on which the appeal is finally determined.

(3) The Commission must review each certificate issued under section 21 as soon as is reasonably practicable after the expiry of the period of three months beginning with the date on which the first review or a review under this subsection is finally determined.

(4) The Commission may review a certificate during a period mentioned in subsection (1), (2) or (3) if—

(a) the person certified applies for a review, and

(b) the Commission considers that a review should be held because of a change in circumstance.

(5) On a review the Commission—

(a) must cancel the certificate if it considers that there are no reasonable grounds for a belief or suspicion of the kind referred to in section 21(1)(a) or (b), and

(b) otherwise, may not make any order (save as to leave to appeal).

(6) A certificate cancelled by order of the Commission under subsection (5) ceases to have effect at the end of the day on which the order is made.

(7) Where the Commission reviews a certificate under subsection (4), the period for determining the next review of the certificate under subsection (3) shall begin with the date of the final determination of the review under subsection (4).

. . .

Review of sections 21 to 23

28 (1) The Secretary of State shall appoint a person to review the operation of sections 21 to 23.

(2) The person appointed under subsection (1) shall review the operation of those sections not later than—

(a) the expiry of the period of 14 months beginning with the day on which this Act is passed;

(b) one month before the expiry of a period specified in accordance with section 29(2)(b) or (c).

(3) Where that person conducts a review under subsection (2) he shall send a report to the Secretary of State as soon as is reasonably practicable.

(4) Where the Secretary of State receives a report under subsection (3) he shall lay a copy of it before Parliament as soon as is reasonably practicable. . . .

Duration of sections 21 to 23

29 (1) Sections 21 to 23 shall, subject to the following provisions of this section, expire at the end of the period of 15 months beginning with the day on which this Act is passed.

(2) The Secretary of State may by order—

(a) repeal sections 21 to 23;

(b) revive those sections for a period not exceeding one year;

(c) provide that those sections shall not expire in accordance with subsection (1) or an order under paragraph (b) or this paragraph, but shall continue in force for a period not exceeding one year.

(3) An order under subsection (2)—

(a) must be made by statutory instrument, and

(b) may not be made unless a draft has been laid before and approved by resolution of each House of Parliament.

(4) An order may be made without compliance with subsection (3)(b) if it contains a

declaration by the Secretary of State that by reason of urgency it is necessary to make the order without laying a draft before Parliament; in which case the order—

    (a) must be laid before Parliament, and

    (b) shall cease to have effect at the end of the period specified in subsection (5) unless the order is approved during that period by resolution of each House of Parliament.

(5) The period referred to in subsection (4)(b) is the period of 40 days—

    (a) beginning with the day on which the order is made, and

    (b) ignoring any period during which Parliament is dissolved or prorogued or during which both Houses are adjourned for more than four days.

(6) The fact that an order ceases to have effect by virtue of subsection (4)—

    (a) shall not affect the lawfulness of anything done before the order ceases to have effect, and

    (b) shall not prevent the making of a new order.

(7) Sections 21 to 23 shall by virtue of this subsection cease to have effect at the end of 10th November 2006.

Legal proceedings: derogation

30 (1) In this section "derogation matter" means—

    (a) a derogation by the United Kingdom from Article 5(1) of the Convention on Human Rights which relates to the detention of a person where there is an intention to remove or deport him from the United Kingdom, or

    (b) the designation under section 14(1) of the Human Rights Act 1998 of a derogation within paragraph (a) above.

(2) A derogation matter may be questioned in legal proceedings only before the Special Immigration Appeals Commission; and the Commission—

    (a) is the appropriate tribunal for the purpose of section 7 of the Human Rights Act 1998 in relation to proceedings all or part of which call a derogation matter into question; and

    (b) may hear proceedings which could, but for this subsection, be brought in the High Court or the Court of Session.

(3) In relation to proceedings brought by virtue of subsection (2)—

    (a) section 6 of the Special Immigration Appeals Commission Act 1997 (person to represent appellant's interests) shall apply with the reference to the appellant being treated as a reference to any party to the proceedings,

    (b) rules under section 5 or 8 of that Act (general procedure; and leave to appeal) shall apply with any modification which the Commission considers necessary, and

    (c) in the case of proceedings brought by virtue of subsection (2)(b), the Commission may do anything which the High Court may do (in the case of proceedings which could have been brought in that court) or which the Court of Session may do (in the case of proceedings which could have been brought in that court).

(4) The Commission's power to award costs (or, in Scotland, expenses) by virtue of subsection (3)(c) may be exercised only in relation to such part of proceedings before it as calls a derogation matter into question.

(5) In relation to proceedings brought by virtue of subsection (2)(a) or (b)—

    (a) an appeal may be brought to the appropriate appeal court (within the meaning of section 7 of the Special Immigration Appeals Commission Act 1997) with the leave of the Commission or, if that leave is refused, with the leave of the appropriate appeal court, and

    (b) the appropriate appeal court may consider and do only those things which it could consider and do in an appeal brought from the High Court or the Court of Session in proceedings for judicial review.

(6) In relation to proceedings which are entertained by the Commission under subsection (2) but are not brought by virtue of subsection (2)(a) or (b), subsection (4) shall apply in so

far as the proceedings call a derogation matter into question...."

These provisions were extremely controversial, and drew strong criticism in Parliament. They were examined—and criticised—by a number of parliamentary committees, including the Joint Committee on Human Rights. They have also been strongly criticised by a number of NGO's, such as Amnesty International and Liberty, by the Committee of Privy Councillors (the Newton Review Committee) and by Lord Carlile's statutory review of Pt 4. The Newton and Carlile Reports are considered below in the JCHR report of February 24, 2004. The powers of detention have also been challenged in the courts in the following case.

A, X and Y v Home Secretary
[2004] Q.B. 335

This was an appeal from a decision of the Special Immigration Appeals Commission (SIAC) quashing the Human Rights Act 1998 (Designated Derogation) Order 2001 ("the Order") and granting a declaration under the Human Rights Act 1998, s.4 that the Anti-Terrorism, Crime and Security Act 2001, s.23 is incompatible with Arts 5 and 14 of the ECHR in so far as it permits detention of suspected international terrorists in a way that discriminates against them on the ground of nationality. The alleged discrimination was based on the fact that the 2001 Order and Act allow only suspected terrorists who are non-nationals to be detained when there are equally dangerous British nationals who are in exactly the same position but who cannot be detained.

LORD CHIEF JUSTICE (WOOLF):

"First Submission

40. Whether the Secretary of State was entitled to come to the conclusion that action was only necessary in relation to non-national suspected terrorists, who could not be deported, is an issue on which it is impossible for this court in this case to differ from the Secretary of State. Decisions as to what is required in the interest of national security are self-evidently within the category of decisions in relation to which the court is required to show considerable deference to the Secretary of State because he is better qualified to make an assessment as to what action is called for. If authority is required for this proposition, then it is provided by *Brown v Stott*, 2001 S.L.T. 59, *Home Secretary v Rehman* [2003] A.C. 153, *Ireland v UK* [1978] 2 EHRR 25 para 206 p 91, *R v Secretary of State ex p. Farrakhan* [2002] EWCA Civ 606, and *International Transport Roth GmbH v Secretary of State for the Home Department* [2002] EWCA Civ 158 at [77] and [80]–[87]; dealing with the parallel situation as to whether there was a 'public emergency' and *Chahal v United Kingdom* (1996) 23 E.H.R.R. 413, para 138). However, as the ECtHR pointed out, the court retains its supervisory role.

41. In addition, it is wrong to suggest, as this submission does, that it is on the choice of immigration control that the Secretary of State's case is based. His case is based on his decision that, in order to meet the present situation, he need only take action against suspected terrorists who have no right to remain in this country but cannot be deported.

Second Submission

42. I turn to the second core submission that Part 4 of the 2001 Act is both over-inclusive and under-inclusive. The over-inclusive contention arises because the terrorist activities, to which Part 4 of the 2001 Act applies, go beyond those required by the emergency in relation to which the derogation was made. ... I accept that on the language of Part 4 it is over-inclusive. But in practice this is not a point of substance. Lord Goldsmith gave SIAC on behalf of the government an undertaking that Part 4 would be only used for the emergency which was the subject of the derogation. I agree ... that the court should not allow an

undertaking on behalf of the government 'ameliorating the potential effect of the legislation to shift the concept of legal certainty and rights away from the solid bedrock to sandy foundations'. However, here the powers contained in Part 4 could only be used to the extent that they were covered by the Order, otherwise they would fall foul of Article 5. The Secretary of State is required to give reasons for his decision and those reasons can be inquired into by SIAC so there is no real risk of anyone being prejudiced by Lord Gold-smith's undertaking not being complied with. This was the view of SIAC, who also referred to section 3 HRA which could be used, if necessary, to restrict the use of Part 4. However, I do not consider this would be necessary because of the other reasons I have given.

43. As to under-inclusion, it is necessary to consider at least two candidates. First, there are the suspected terrorists who are nationals. Then there are the suspected terrorists who are not nationals, who once they leave the country will be free to engage in activities hostile to this country. Mr Whalley, who has made a statement on behalf of the Secretary of State covering this point, contends that irrespective of whether non-national suspect terrorists are detained or leave this country, the terrorist organisation in the UK will be disrupted. He also relies on the fact that the detention or deporting of non-national suspected terrorists will indicate that this country is not a safe haven for terrorists. Placing on one side the issue of discrimination, these are points which depend on the evidence before SIAC and do not call for resolution on this appeal.

Third to Fifth Submissions

44. The third, fourth and fifth core submissions cover very much the same ground and so are covered by what I have already stated. The exception is Mr Emmerson's submissions about *Secretary of State for Home Department v Rehman* [2003] A.C. 153. That case is important for the clear statements contained in the speeches of the House of Lords as to the deference which should be extended to the executive on matters of national security (see in particular the speeches of Lord Steyn and Lord Hoffmann). It is also important because it recognises that conduct which is directed at a foreign state can have direct implications for the national security of this country. The extent of the threat, required as a pre-condition to derogation, is more extensive than that required by the interests of national security. It is a public emergency threatening the life of the nation. It is the broader formulation of national security which was considered in *Rehman*. Despite this the same general approach is clearly appropriate. Where international terrorists are operating globally and committing acts designed to terrorise the population in one country, that can have implications which threaten the life of another. This is why a collective approach to international terrorism is important. As the Order recognises, we are concerned here with a threat identified by the United Nations Security Council as 'a threat to international peace and security', a threat which required all States to take measures 'to prevent the commission of terrorist attacks, including by denying safe haven to those who finance, plan, support or commit terrorist attacks'. While the courts must carefully scrutinise the explanations given by the executive for its actions, the courts must extend the appropriate degree of deference when it comes to judging those actions.

Submissions Six to Eight: Discrimination

45. The remaining core submissions, while in part also covering the same ground as the earlier submissions, go to what is the main issue, namely, discrimination. Was the UK government entitled to single out non-nationals who could not be deported in the fore-seeable future as the subject of the Order and the 2001 Act? Here I differ from SIAC, largely because of the tension between Article 15 and Article 14. Article 15 restricts the extent of the derogation to what is strictly necessary. That is what the Secretary of State has done on his evidence. Of course, he did so for national security reasons. No doubt, by taking action against nationals as well as non-nationals the action from a security point of view would have been more effective. Equally, if the non-nationals were detained notwithstanding the fact that they wanted to leave this country, the action would be more effective. However, on

his assessment of the situation, the Secretary of State was debarred from taking more effective action because it was not strictly necessary.

46. SIAC came to the conclusion at paragraph 94 that if an 'alien cannot be deported he must be allowed to remain'. That is correct, but as already stated that does not create a right to remain, only a right not to be removed. For example, if later the alien can be deported, he can be removed and pending removal detained. Because of this difference alone, aliens can be objectively distinguished from non-aliens.

47. SIAC go on to say that the threat is not confined to aliens (and that is agreed), but SIAC then wrongly conclude that this means there must be discrimination on the grounds of nationality as aliens are not nationals. This is an over-simplification. It was eloquently urged on behalf of the respondents, and particularly by Mr Pannick. It is an over-simplification because the position here is that the Secretary of State has come to the conclusion that he can achieve what is necessary by either detaining or deporting only the terrorists who are aliens. If the Secretary of State has come to that conclusion, then the critical question is, are there objective, justifiable and relevant grounds for selecting only the alien terrorists, or is the discrimination on the grounds of nationality? As to this critical question, I have come to the conclusion that there are objectively justifiable and relevant grounds which do not involve impermissible discrimination. The grounds are the fact that the aliens who cannot be deported have, unlike nationals, no more right to remain, only a right not to be removed, which means legally that they come into a different class from those who have a right of abode.

48. The class of aliens is in a different situation because when they can be deported to a country that will not torture them this can happen. It is only the need to protect them from torture that means that for the time being they cannot be removed.

49. In these circumstances it would be surprising indeed if Article 14, or any international requirement not to discriminate, prevented the Secretary of State taking the restricted action which he thought was necessary. As the respondents accept, the consequences of their approach is that because of the requirement not to discriminate, the Secretary of State would, presumably, have to decide on more extensive action, which applied both to nationals and non-nationals, than he would otherwise have thought necessary. Such a result would not promote human rights, it would achieve the opposite result. There would be an additional intrusion into the rights of the nationals so that their position would be the same as non-nationals.

50. The ECHR is essentially a pragmatic document. In its application it is intended to achieve practical benefits for those who are entitled to its protection. The Secretary of State is not entitled to adopt an irrational approach, either under the Convention or at common law. He is required to point to an objective justification for adopting the distinction which he is making. This he does here, in my judgment, on solid ground because of the distinction between aliens and nationals which is part of domestic and international law. As I have stressed, an alien's right to reside in this country is not unconditional. True it is that the respondents cannot be deported, but that does not mean that they are in the same position as nationals. They are still liable to be deported, subject to the decision of SIAC on their personal circumstances, when and if this is practical.

51. It is to be hoped that although there is no time limit which at present can be imposed upon their detention, the regular review of their positions, which the legislation requires, will result in their detention being of limited duration.

52. However, contrary to the view of SIAC, I consider the approach adopted by the Secretary of State, which involves detaining the respondents for no longer than is necessary before they can be deported, or until the emergency resolves, or they cease to be a threat to the safety of this country, is one which can be objectively justified. The individuals subject to the policy are an identifiable class. There is a rational connection between their detention and the purpose which the Secretary of State wishes to achieve. It is a purpose which cannot be applied to nationals, namely detention pending deportation, irrespective of when that deportation will take place.

53. The fact that deportation cannot take place immediately does not mean that it ceases to be part of the objective. This is confirmed by the fact that two of the respondents were able to leave this country. It is suggested that the action is not proportionate. However, I disagree. By limiting the number of those who are subject to the special measures, the Secretary of State is ensuring that his actions are proportionate to what is necessary. There is no alternative which the respondents can point to which is remotely practical. It is wrong to regard the *Chahal* case as establishing that those who cannot be removed have a legally enforceable right to remain. They have a right not to be removed so as to protect their right not to be subject to treatment in breach of Article 3, but that is not the same thing as having 'a legally enforceable (Convention) right to remain'...

The Joint Committee of Parliament on Human Rights

63. I have also considered the second and fifth reports of the Joint Committee of Parliament on Human Rights. The Committee examined the Bill which became the 2001 Act. Both reports expressed concerns about the Bill which the Committee had to examine at great speed. In the fifth report the Committee acknowledged that there had been improvements to the Bill as a result of the second report. However, the Committee still had a number of concerns. The first concern related to the power of detention. This should only be used where it is impossible or inappropriate to prosecute the detained person and the Secretary of State is searching diligently for a safe country. There is nothing to suggest at this stage that this concern is not being met. The second and third concern, which relates to the jurisdiction of SIAC and the ability of the Secretary of State to rectify, also do not apply to the respondents at the present time. The fourth and final concern relates to special advocates being available to this Court. At the beginning of the hearing such advocates were available but we released them, as they would not be required. The reports, while valuable, do not therefore affect these appeals.

64. What I have set out above means that I would allow this appeal. In those circumstances, the question does arise as to what added protection the HRA has provided for the respondents. I believe that additional protection is substantial. Before SIAC, two of whose members were senior judges, and before this court, the issues raised by the respondents were examined in a way which would not have been possible before the HRA came into force. Before both tribunals the standards that the ECHR requires were applied by SIAC and this court, but this court has concluded that applying those standards the action which has been taken by the appellant is lawful and complies with the ECHR. While the respondents are detained the same scrutiny can be repeated if the circumstances change sufficiently to justify this. This is a very considerable protection which would not have been available either to nationals or non-nationals prior to the HRA coming into force. The unfortunate fact is that the emergency which the government believes to exist justifies the taking of action which would not otherwise be acceptable. The ECHR recognises that there can be circumstances where action of this sort is fully justified. It is my conclusion here, as a matter of law, and that is what we are concerned with, that action is justified. The important point is that the courts are able to protect the rule of law."

Lord Justice Brooke: "72. As SIAC noted, the language of ECHR Article 15 has been considered on a number of occasions at Strasbourg. Earliest in time is *Lawless v Ireland (No 3)* (1961) 1 EHRR 15, where the applicant was complaining that the Irish Government had detained him without trial for five months under legislation directed against the IRA. The ECtHR directed itself (at para 28) that:

> '... the natural and customary meaning of the words "other public emergency which affects the life of the nation" is sufficiently clear; they refer to an exceptional situation of crisis or emergency which affects the whole population and constitutes a threat to the organised life of the community of which the State is composed.'

73. It went on to determine whether the facts and circumstances which led to the making of the relevant proclamation by the Irish Government came within this concept, and it found that the existence of such an emergency *was reasonably deduced* by the Irish Government from a combination of several factors:

(i) the existence in its territory of a secret army engaged in unconstitutional activities and using violence to attain its purposes;

(ii) the fact that this army was also operating outside the territory of the state, thus seriously jeopardising its relations with its neighbour; and

(iii) the steady and alarming increase in terrorist activities for nine months, culminating in a homicidal ambush in the territory of Northern Ireland near the border which brought to light the imminent danger to the nation caused by the continuance of unlawful activities in Northern Ireland by the IRA and various associated groups, operating from the territory of the Republic of Ireland.

74. I have referred to the facts of this case because we received submissions to the effect that the language of ECHR Article 15 should be narrowly construed. This case shows the Strasbourg court more than willing to consider the effect on the life of a nation of terrorists whose activities outside its territory were seriously jeopardising its relations with a neighbouring state.

75. In its report on the *Greek case* (1969) 12 Yearbook 170 para 153, the European Commission on Human Rights suggested that a public emergency should have the following characteristics if it was to qualify under ECHR Article 15:

'(1) It must be actual or imminent.

(2) Its effects must involve the whole nation.

(3) The continuance of the organised life of the community must be threatened.

(4) The crisis or danger must be exceptional, in that the normal measures or restrictions, permitted by the Convention for the maintenance of public safety, health and order, are plainly inadequate.'

76. The Commission derived the notion of an imminent danger from the French text of the Convention, and it went on to suggest that when the ECtHR in *Lawless* said that the Irish Government reasonably deduced that the requisite state of affairs existed it was using the language of a margin of appreciation. In *Greece v United Kingdom* (1958) 18 H.R.L.J. 348 the Commission at para 136 had spoken of 'discretion in appreciating the threat to the life of the nation'.

77. In *Brannigan and McBride v United Kingdom* (1993) 17 EHRR 539 the ECtHR returned to this topic at paragraph 43. From this important passage the following principles can be derived:

(1) Each Contracting State has a responsibility for the life of its nation, so that it falls to the state to determine both whether the relevant emergency exists and how far it is necessary to go in attempting to overcome it.

(2) The state is in a better position than an international judge to decide such questions, and a wide margin of appreciation must therefore be left to the national authorities in this matter.

(3) This domestic margin of appreciation must be accompanied by a European supervision, but in exercising its supervision the court must give appropriate weight to all relevant factors.

78. When it came to apply this approach and make *its own assessment* (at para 47), the ECtHR considered in the light of all the material before it that there could be no doubt that a relevant public emergency existed at the relevant time.

79. In its recent decision on admissibility in *Marshall v United Kingdom* (10th July 2001) the ECtHR revisited this topic and applied the same tests. The following matters emerge from this decision (at pp 11–13):

(i) The proper function of the European supervising court on the second main issue (see para 65(2) above) is to decide whether the derogation was a genuine response to an emergency situation and whether the absence of judicial control of extended detention was justified;

(ii) In making this assessment the supervising court should have regard to the authorities' margin of appreciation and the nature of the safeguards which existed to prevent abuse;

(iii) Nothing had happened in the nine years since *Brannigan and McBride* were detained such as to lead the court to controvert the authorities' assessment of the situation in Northern Ireland;

(iv) As to the measures the authorities took in the present case it was not the role of the supervising court to substitute its view as to what measures were most appropriate or expedient at the relevant time in dealing with an emergency situation for that of the Government, which had direct responsibility for establishing the balance between the taking of effective measures to combat terrorism on the one hand and respecting individual rights on the other.

Judicial supervision in human rights cases, and issues of deference

81. In all the cases concerned with Northern Ireland prior to October 2000, however, there was no mechanism for judicial supervision of the relevant decisions of the government or the legislature of this country at national level. A number of recent decisions of the courts, however, have pegged out the course a national court should adopt, particularly in a matter affecting national security. They are now well known, and like Lord Woolf CJ, I will content myself with giving the leading references: *R v DPP ex p Kebilene* [2000] 2 AC 326, 380–1; *Brown v Stott*. 2001 S.L.T. 59; *International Transport Roth GmbH v Secretary of State for the Home Department* [2002] EWCA Civ 158 at [77] and [80]–[87]; and *Home Secretary v Rehman* (see para 64 above). It is convenient only to set out certain principles which I derive from Lord Hoffmann's speech in *Rehman*, at paras 57–58 and 64:

(1) When there is an appeal to SIAC it is the Home Secretary, not SIAC, who is the principal decision-maker;

(2) It must be remembered that the Home Secretary has the advantage of a wide range of advice from people with day to day involvement in security matters which SIAC cannot match;

(3) Because what is at issue is an evaluation of risk, an appellate body traditionally allows a considerable margin to the original decision-maker. It should not ordinarily interfere with a case in which the Home Secretary's view is one which could reasonably be entertained;

(4) Even though a very different approach may be needed when determining whether an appellant's ECHR Article 3 rights are likely to be infringed, this deferential approach is certainly required in relation to the question whether a deportation is in the interests of national security;

(5) Although SIAC has the express power to reverse the exercise of a discretion, they should exercise restraint by reason of a common-sense recognition of the nature of the issue and of the differences in the decision-making processes and responsibilities of the Home Secretary and SIAC;

(6) The events of 11th September are a reminder that in matters of national security the cost of failure can be high. Decisions by ministers on such questions, with serious potential rights for the community, therefore require a legitimacy which can be conferred only by entrusting them to persons responsible to the community through the democratic process.

The meaning of 'public emergency' in ECHR Article 15

82. Any judicial assessment of the quality of the Home Secretary's decision-making process in the present case is inevitably made more complicated by the fact that he told a Parliamentary Committee in October 2001 that there was no immediate intelligence

pointing to a specific threat to this country. There is, however, as I understand it, no direct challenge to his good faith. It appears to me that the answer to the conundrum posed by the language he used must be found in identifying the proper meaning of the word 'imminent' as it appears in the French text of ECHR Article 15. This is a necessary part of the process of determining what the expression 'public emergency threatening the life of the nation' really means.

83. SIAC considered this issue in paragraph 24 of their determination. They made the following points:

(1) It is not the imminence of a threat which is required, but the actuality or imminence of an emergency. This distinction is by no means an unreal one;

(2) The measures which involve the need to derogate are required to try to prevent the outrages which would have a disastrous effect if they occurred. It would be absurd to require the authorities to wait until they were aware of an imminent attack before taking the necessary steps to avoid such an attack;

(3) What is required is a real risk that an attack will take place unless the necessary measures are taken to prevent it;

(4) An emergency can exist and can certainly be imminent if there is an intention and a capacity to carry out serious terrorist violence even if nothing has yet been done, and even if plans have not reached the stage when an attack is actually about to happen.

84. I have not found this issue of interpretation an easy one. The importance the ECHR attaches to personal liberty and the rule of law is underlined by the fact that it requires an actual or imminent emergency of the type described in Article 15 before a Contracting State may lawfully derogate from the protections afforded by Article 5(1). While considering the issues in this anxious case I have constantly reminded myself of the powerful dissenting opinion of Mr Justice Jackson, with whom Mr Justice Frankfurter joined, in *Shaughnessy v United States*, 345 US 205, 218–228 (1953). I quote just two passages:

'Fortunately it still is startling, in this country, to find a person held indefinitely in executive custody without accusation of crime or judicial trial. Executive imprisonment has been considered oppressive and lawless since John, at Runnymede, pledged that no free man should be imprisoned, dispossessed, outlawed or exiled save by the judgment of his peers or by the law of the land (p 218)...

Quite unconsciously, I am sure, the Government's theory of custody for "safekeeping" without disclosure to the victim of charges, evidence, informers or reasons, even in an administrative proceeding, has unmistakable overtones of the "protective custody" of the Nazis more than of any determining procedure known to the common law (p 226).'

85. After a good deal of hesitation I have concluded that it would be wrong to give an over-literal interpretation to the word 'imminent' in the present context. Absent such an interpretation, there was ample material on which the Home Secretary could conclude that an emergency of the requisite quality existed. And if it did, even Mr Justice Jackson accepted (at p 223) that 'due process of law will tolerate some impounding of an alien where it is deemed essential to the safety of the State'. Although the rights of the claimants to liberty and due process are potent considerations, so, too, as SIAC observed, are the rights of very many other people which the Home Secretary judged to be threatened if the claimants remain at large, including the right to life itself. I would therefore endorse SIAC's approach to this issue.

Reliance on intelligence material

86. Turning to another point, I have read with great care the witness statements of the respondents' solicitors and the other matters of factual detail which have been brought together conveniently in an appendix to Mr Gill's skeleton argument. The Security Service

has made a fairly brief reply to some of the points that have been made. Nobody who has read in any depth the history of miscarriages of justice in this country over the last 50 years, or who knows anything about the difficult problems that confront the intelligence community when they try to assess the quality and reliability of the information they receive, could approach the issues in this case with anything other than great anxiety. The difficulties which face the intelligence community, and those who have to decide how much reliance they can place on their advice, are compounded in a case like the present. Differences in language, differences in culture, and often very subtle differences in political or religious ideology abound. All these differences present formidable problems for the dispassionate assessor. Mistakes may well be made. That anxiety is heightened when one reads and re-reads the evidence of Gareth Peirce, a solicitor who has great experience in these matters, and of Natalia Garcia, the solicitors for X and Y.

87. But unless one is willing to adopt a purist approach, saying that it is better that this country should be destroyed, together with the ideals it stands for, than that a single suspected terrorist should be detained without due process, it seems to me inevitable that the judiciary must be willing, as SIAC was, to put an appropriate degree of trust in the willingness and capacity of ministers and Parliament, who are publicly accountable for their decisions, to satisfy themselves about the integrity and professionalism of the Security Service. If the security of the nation may be at risk from terrorist violence, and if the lives of informers may be at risk, or the flow of valuable information they represent may dry up if sources of intelligence have to be revealed, there comes a stage when judicial scrutiny can go no further.

88. In this context two passages in the Security Service evidence are of particular importance. The first is when its witness, whose credentials are impressive, speaks of the care the Service takes in determining whether it is safe to rely on intelligence information. The second is when he says that it is for practical reasons impossible to prosecute some of those the Service believes to be foreign terrorists because to attempt to do so would itself imperil national security.

89. On this appeal we are concerned not only with matters of personal liberty but with matters of life and death for possibly thousands of people. In these circumstances it appears to me that the arrangements that have been made for judicial supervision of the decision of Parliament, imperfect as they are, are the best that can be devised for a situation like this. ... Contrast, for example, section 4 of the Prevention of Terrorism (Temporary Provisions) Act 1974, whereby the Home Secretary received advice in private from an independent adviser in relation to challenges against an exclusion order and was not obliged to disclose the content of the advice, or to say whether he accepted it or not.

90. Like Lord Woolf CJ, I do not consider that SIAC misunderstood their function or misdirected themselves as to the nature of the job they were to do. ... For these reasons I am unable to hold that SIAC was wrong ... to refuse to controvert the Home Secretary's judgment on the question whether an emergency of the requisite seriousness existed. I would therefore dismiss the claimants' appeal on the first main issue."

(4) Reviews of the Act

The 2001 Act deals with a range of other matters beyond those already considered. These include provisions dealing with weapons of mass destruction (Pt 6); the security of pathogens and toxins (Pt 7); the security of the nuclear industry (Pt 8); aviation security (Pt 9); and police powers (Pt 10). There is also a remarkable provision in Pt 14 which deals with the review of the Act. As we have seen provision is made in s.28 for the review of Pt 4 of the Act. Section 122 also makes provision for the review of the Act as a whole by a committee of privy councillors, the review to be conducted within two years of the date the Act was passed. Remarkably, s.123 then provides that the privy councillors "may specify any provision of this Act as a provision to which this section applies". The effect is that subject "to subsection (3), any provision specified under subsection (1) ceases to have effect at the end of the period of 6 months beginning with the day on which the report is laid before Parliament under section 122(5)" (s 123(2)). This last provision does not apply "if before the end of that period a motion has been made in each House of Parliament considering the report" (s.123(3)). No doubt to the great embarrassment of the Government the Newton Review Committee specified the whole Act. As already indicated, the report by Lord Carlile on Pt 4 and the Privy Council report on the Act as a whole are considered in the following extract from yet another report on the Act. This is the report of the Joint Committee on Human Rights which was published on February 24, 2004: "a report on the reviews". The following extract deals with its findings on Pt 4 only. Other provisions are referred to in the summary in the box on p.578–579 below.

Joint Committee on Human Rights
Anti-terrorism, Crime and Security Act 2001: Statutory Review and Continuance of Part 4
Sixth Report: H.L. 38/H.C. 381 (2003–2004)

"1 Introduction

The various statutory reviews of the Anti-terrorism, Crime and Security Act 2001
   1. The Anti-terrorism, Crime and Security Act 2001 was passed at great speed by both Houses in the wake of the attacks on the World Trade Centre and other targets in the USA on 11 September 2001. The Act contained a number of provisions affecting human rights. One such set of provisions, sections 21 to 23 in Part 4 of the Act, provides for the indefinite detention without charge of people certified by the Secretary of State as being suspected of links to international terrorism, if they are not United Kingdom nationals and cannot be removed from the country for practical or legal reasons. The Government accepted that this is incompatible with the right to liberty of the person under ECHR Article 5, and that it necessitated a derogation from that right under Article 15 of the ECHR.
   2. At a late stage in its passage through Parliament, a number of safeguards were inserted in the Bill. One of these is the 'sunset' clause which became section 29(1) of the Act. It provides that Part 4 of the Act will cease to operate at the end of 10 November 2006. Before that date, Part 4 was to cease to operate fifteen months after the Act received the Royal Assent, unless renewed earlier for a period of no more than one year by a statutory instrument made by the Secretary of State under section 29(2) and (3) of the Act. Further orders can renew Part 4 for subsequent periods of no more than one year, up to 10 November 2006, are permitted. Before the Secretary of State may make an order, section 29(3)(b) requires that a draft order has to be laid before each House and approved by both Houses by an affirmative resolution (except in cases of urgent necessity, when an order may be made temporarily under section 29(4) without first being laid and approved in draft).
   3. Parliament thus has an annual opportunity to debate the continuance of the powers in Part 4 of the Act. As an additional safeguard, and in order to inform the debate, section 28 of the Act requires the Secretary of State to appoint a person to review the operation of the certification and detention provisions, who must report at least one month before the date when the provisions are due to expire if not renewed. This task is performed by Lord Carlile of Berriew QC. His report on the operation of sections 21 to 23 in 2003 was published on 11 February 2004.
   4. In addition, section 122 of the Act provided that the whole Act was to be subject to a single, comprehensive review by a committee of Privy Councillors appointed by the Secretary of State, which was to report to the Secretary of State not later than 13 December 2003, two years after the Act was passed. The committee's report was to be laid before Parliament. This task was undertaken by a committee under the chairmanship of Lord Newton of Braintree. After taking evidence and deliberating through much of 2003, it reported in December 2003. Its report was laid before Parliament on 18 December 2003.
   5. Section 123 of the Act allowed the committee of Privy Councillors to specify any

provision of the Act as one which is to cease to have effect six months from the day on which the committee's report was laid before Parliament, unless the Committee's Report had first been debated by each House. The Committee was so concerned about the speed with which the Act had been passed and the lack of fit between the Act and other legislation in related areas that it designated the whole Act for the purpose of section 123. The committee stressed that this was to enable Parliament to review the report and the Act as a whole, and made it clear that there were many parts of the Act which the committee considered to be unexceptionable.

6. As a result, the whole Act will automatically cease to have effect in June 2004 unless, before the relevant date, each House holds a debate on the committee's report. The House of Commons is expected to debate the report on 25 February 2004, and the House of Lords is expected to do so in the first week in March.

7. After our initial consideration of the committee's report, our Chair wrote to the Home Secretary on 21 January 2004 asking a number of questions about the Government's intentions in the light of it. The Home Secretary responded in a letter dated 6 February 2004.

The draft Anti-terrorism, Crime and Security Act 2001 (Continuance in Force of Sections 21 to 23) Order 2004

8. The Home Secretary has laid before each House the draft Anti-terrorism, Crime and Security Act 2001 (Continuance in Force of Sections 21 to 23) Order 2004, to continue sections 21 to 23 in force for a further twelve months from 14 March 2004. A standing committee of the House of Commons is expected to consider the draft Continuance Order on 26 February 2004, and the House of Lords is expected to debate the draft order in the first week in March.

Our report

9. We have considered the Newton Committee report, the report by Lord Carlile of Berriew QC, and the draft Continuance Order, and now report our conclusions on their human rights implications to each House in the hope that it will help to inform the debates on the Newton Committee report and the draft Continuance Order in the two Houses from a human rights perspective.

. . .

3 The Draft Continuance Order 2004

Background

17. Part 4 contains some of the most controversial aspects of the 2001 Act. It is also the one which raises the most intense problems of compatibility with human rights, and led to a derogation by the United Kingdom from the right to liberty of the person under ECHR Article 5. Part 4 contains the power in sections 21 to 23 of the Act to detain a person indefinitely without any criminal charge, let alone a trial, if:

   a) the Secretary of State has certified that he reasonably believes that the person is a terrorist (including in this category anyone who 'has links with an international terrorist group');
   b) the person is a foreign national; and
   c) for legal or practical reasons, the person cannot be removed from the United Kingdom.

18. In order to avoid a situation in which this detention would be held to amount to a violation of the right to liberty of the person under ECHR Article 5(1), the Secretary of State made a derogation order under section 14 of the Human Rights Act 1998 designating a derogation from Article 5 for the purpose of combating the threat of terrorism as one of the derogations to which the Convention rights are subject under section 1 of that Act. The Government subsequently gave notice to the Secretary General of the Council of Europe

that it considered that sections 21 to 23 of the 2001 Act were a justifiable derogation under Article 15 of the ECHR, on the ground that the terrorist attacks on the USA in September 2001 showed that there was a public emergency threatening the life of the nation and the measures derogated from the United Kingdom's obligations under Article 5 no further than was strictly required by the exigencies of the situation and consistently with the United Kingdom's other obligations under international law. An equivalent notice of derogation was given under the International Covenant on Civil and Political Rights, Article 4, in respect of the right to liberty of the person under Article 9. No other State party to the Convention or the International Covenant has made such a derogation in the wake of 11 September 2001.

OUR PREVIOUS REPORTS RELATING TO PART 4 OF THE ACT

19. When we considered the derogation and this Part of the Bill in 2001, we noted that we had not been shown any evidence of a public emergency threatening the life of the nation, although we accepted that there might be such evidence. We considered that the safeguards attached to the powers were insufficient to ensure that the measures in the Bill could be said to be strictly required by the exigencies of the situation. We also drew attention (a) to the risk that the provisions would unlawfully discriminate on the ground of nationality, since only foreign nationals would be liable to be detained, (b) to the need for stronger procedural protections for appellants before the Special Immigration Appeals Commission and the courts, and (c) to the need for more frequent reviews of detention. In addition, we drew attention to a number of other procedural problems.

20. The sections were to cease to have effect after fifteen months (in March 2003) unless continued by affirmative resolution of each House. In preparation for the debate, Lord Carlile of Berriew QC conducted a statutory review of the operation of sections 21 to 23. We then reported to each House on its view as to the propriety of continuing the operation of the sections. We adopted the following position:

a) we expressed doubts about the compatibility of the derogation with the Convention;

b) we took the view that the derogation was likely to have been valid and effective in municipal law under the Human Rights Act 1998, although we considered that it had not been proper to make the order in the abstract, before the detailed provisions to which it related had been endorsed by Parliament;

c) we recognised that it was for the courts to decide whether the detention of particular suspects was vitiated by unlawful discrimination;

d) we repeated its earlier recommendation, and endorsed that of Lord Carlile of Berriew, that the nature of the 'links' with international terrorism sufficient to form the basis of a certificate made by the Secretary of State should be clarified; and

e) we came to the conclusion that the two Houses could legitimately rely on the review by Lord Carlile of Berriew and decide that the measures were being operated fairly, although we drew attention to systemic weaknesses in the protection for human rights, which might properly be reasons for refusing to continue the measures in force, stemming from:

   i) the time it had taken the Special Immigration Appeals Commission to hold any substantive hearing into the merits of the detainees' appeals;

   ii) the shortage of properly qualified, high-quality legal advice available to detainees;

   iii) doubts as to whether evidence was being categorized as 'open' or 'closed', for the purpose of withholding it from appellants and their legal advisers, in a way that properly reflected the importance to procedural due process of withholding evidence from parties only when making it available would compromise the effort to protect the public against the national emergency which gave rise to the derogation under ECHR Article 15 and justified the detention;

iv) concern to ensure that the services of the special advocate, who could see and make submissions in the detainees' interests about 'closed' material, would be able to participate in proceedings in the Court of Appeal and House of Lords on appeal from the Special Immigration Appeals Commission; and

v) concern to ensure that the detainees' conditions of detention should reflect their status as people who have been neither charged with nor convicted of any offence.

21. In the event, the operation of the powers was extended for twelve months from March 2003, and the two Houses must now consider whether to renew them again for a further twelve months.

The views of the Newton Committee on Part 4 of the Act

22. The Newton Committee drew attention to a number of features of Part 4 of the Act which, in its view, make it an inappropriate basis for continuing to deal with the threat from international terrorists. Several of these features stem from the fact that the detention power is based on immigration law, rather than being a measure specifically designed for the needs of counter-terrorism. There are objections of principle, namely:

a)   the need for the United Kingdom, alone among Council of Europe member states, to derogate from Article 5 of the ECHR; and

b)   the indefinite period for which detention can continue; and the fact that selective use of a power such as this opens the door to arbitrary action.

23. The Newton Committee thought that there were also objections relating to efficacy, since the terrorist threat is not limited to foreign nationals.

24. Finally, the Newton Committee thought that there was evidence of a lack of proactive, focused, case-management in determining whether any particular detainee should continue to be detained.

25. The Newton Committee considered the shortcomings to be sufficiently serious to allow it to recommend strongly that the provisions of Part 4 should be replaced as a matter of urgency. The Committee recommended that new legislation should deal with all terrorism, whatever its origin or the nationality of its suspected perpetrators, and should not require a derogation from the ECHR.

The Home Secretary's views

26. These factors are relevant to the continuance in force of sections 21 to 23 of the Act after 13 March 2004. Our Chair therefore asked the Home Secretary for the Government's response. The Home Secretary replied, 'The need for these powers will continue to exist whilst the public emergency remains and whilst we are unable to take action to remove suspected international terrorists'. However, he continued, 'It is not possible to predict for how long the current state of public emergency will continue to subsist'. The Home Secretary told us he plans to launch a consultation exercise on possible measures to replace or complement the detention powers, looking towards a possible reform 'in the longer term' (answers to questions 2 and 4). It is clear that no developed proposal will be ready before the debates take place in the two Houses.

27. In a written statement made by the Home Secretary on 20 January 2004 when he laid the draft Continuance Order before each House, he said that the detention powers in Part 4 of the Act 'are a cornerstone of the UK's anti-terrorism measures. It is essential that we are able to take firm, swift action against those who threaten the safety of this country .... [W]e continue to believe that the Part 4 powers are a necessary and proportionate response to the current threat'. He disclosed that 16 people had been detained under the Part 4 powers. Two had subsequently left the country. The Special Immigration Appeals Commission (SIAC) had rejected appeals by ten detainees, and judgment is awaited in respect of two more.

28. In his letter to our Chair, the Home Secretary informed us that he did not accept the criticisms made by the Newton Committee about the management of individual cases. In his written statement of 20 January 2004 he had already stated, 'My decisions to certify and detain these individuals were made on the basis of detailed and compelling evidence'. In his letter, he further assured us that the cases had been fully considered again in preparation for the detainees' appeals to the SIAC, and that the individual cases were kept actively under review, a process which had led to one detainee being convicted on criminal charges and another currently being prosecuted. He pointed out that some delay had occurred in getting individual cases heard by SIAC as a result of the need to litigate the lawfulness of the derogation from rights under ECHR Article 5 as a preliminary issue, and mentioned that some difficulty was being experienced in returning detainees to their countries of origin because SIAC had imposed an order requiring the detainees' anonymity to be maintained.

Lord Carlile's Report on the operation of sections 21 to 23 in 2003

THE CONTEXT OF LORD CARLILE'S REPORT

29. Lord Carlile begins his report by pointing out that he is required to report on the operation of sections 21 to 23 of the Act on the premise that they are in effect, whereas the Newton Committee was required to advise as to whether they considered that those sections should remain in effect. He referred to comparisons with other countries which he had undertaken, and mentioned the risk of '*function creep*'—the tendency of the control authorities such as the police to want to use information provided for counter-terrorism purposes in a wider context.

30. Lord Carlile noted that we had not been persuaded in 2001 that the conditions for the derogation had been met, but that the SIAC and the Court of Appeal had concluded that they were met, although the matter is subject to an appeal to the House of Lords in which judgment is expected early in the Spring of 2004. He also commented on the fact that the detention provisions 'are wide in their scope and have a significant impact on a particular group of the resident community ... who do not hold British nationality'. He agreed with a view expressed by the SIAC that grounds for detention which may be reasonable for an arrest and a short period of detention 'may be insufficient for indefinite detention. Taking into account all the circumstances as one should, the passage of time may alter significantly the threat posed by an individual or even a group or former cell'.

31. Lord Carlile noted that the Government had rejected his suggestion, in his report last year, that the 'links' to international terrorism which would justify detention under section 21(2) and (4) of the Act should be clarified. He accepted the rejection, and drew attention to the judgment of the SIAC that it is possible, within the scope of the SIAC's powers under section 25, to allow a detainee 'to contend that even if what is said against him were true, recourse to so draconian a power was disproportionate in the light of other circumstances'. Lord Carlile considered that this set the notion of 'links' in 'an acceptable context'.

LORD CARLILE'S FINDINGS AND RECOMMENDATIONS

32. After a full and careful examination of the operation of the whole of the procedure for operating sections 21 to 23 of the Act, Lord Carlile concluded that:

a) 'there remain in the United Kingdom individuals and groups who pose a present and real threat to the safety of the public here and abroad';

b) in every individual case, the criteria for detention were met;

c) civil servants in the Home Office exert pressure to decrease rather than increase the level of detentions;

d) criminal charges are being brought whenever possible (although not necessarily for terrorism-related offences), in order to bring the detention into line with conventional ideas of lawfulness and due process: like the Newton Committee,

Lord Carlile considered (as we do) that normal criminal proceedings should be the preferred approach;

e) the Home Secretary considers each case in an active and inquiring way;

f) appropriate levels of political executive judgment are generally being applied to certification decisions;

g) there is, however, a tendency to over-estimate the risk that a person would be exposed to the risk of death, torture, or inhuman or degrading treatment or punishment, in violation of ECHR Article 2 or 3, if returned to his or her country of origin; the Foreign and Commonwealth Office is inclined to rely on a generic assessment of risk in a country, rather than to enter into bilateral discussions with the country as to the likely experience of the people being considered for removal to that country; and the Government should investigate the possibility that in some cases it might be possible to return a person to his or her country of origin, avoiding the need for indefinite detention in this country;

h) overall, the SIAC procedure is proceeding according to 'a determined and managed timetable' (albeit one which faces delays because of the preliminary litigation over the lawfulness of the derogation from ECHR Article 5 rights and a possible future application to the European Court of Human Rights); it 'operates effectively and proportionately to the risks of national security, especially in the light of the disclosure and hearing constraints applicable';

i) the statutory review periods, which we had considered to be insufficiently frequent, have not caused difficulties to the SIAC;

j) at present a detainee who leaves the country cannot continue his or her appeal from outside the country; the Act should be amended to allow such a person to protect his or her future position by continuing an appeal on the merits against certification from outside the country;

k) the Special Advocates (who represent the interests of appellants in relation to material which is too sensitive to be disclosed to the appellants or their legal advisers) have done a good job within the scope of their powers, and 'the special advocate procedure works reasonably well to achieve its purpose of assisting SIAC to reach decisions correct in fact and law';

l) however, as the shortage of Special Advocates has delayed hearings, there should be—

    i) organised training opportunities at which Special Advocates can share problems and develop common approaches to procedural and ethical issues, and receive training,

    ii) a security-cleared assistant in every case to help the Special Advocate, for example by categorising papers and acting as a conduit of information, and

    iii) a widening in the range of people who are appointed as Special Advocates beyond the ranks of those with specialist knowledge in administrative law, for example by including people with expertise in the practise of criminal law;

m) it should be made clear that the Special Advocate should continue to represent the interests of the appellant in closed proceedings before the SIAC even if the appellant instructs his or her representatives to withdraw from the open proceedings;

n) those in authority should consider whether Special Advocates should have greater access to the appellants in relation to the closed material, to assist the Special Advocates in the performance of their duties and the SIAC in its procedure;

o) as much relevant information as possible should be disclosed; but that

p) taken as a whole, the present system is 'workable and working reasonably well'.

Our conclusions in the light of the two reports

33. We consider that the reports of the Newton Committee and Lord Carlile in relation to Part 4 of the Act are valuable and complementary. In the light of them, and of our

previous scrutiny of the Act and its operation, we have come to the conclusion there are serious weaknesses in the protection for human rights under Part 4. We continue to doubt whether the very wide powers conferred by Part 4 are, in Convention terms, strictly required by the exigencies of the situation.

34. Like the Newton Committee, we have grave concerns about long-term detention without trial on the basis of suspicion of links with international terrorism, necessitating an indefinite derogation from the important right to liberty under ECHR Article 5. Insufficient evidence has been presented to Parliament to make it possible for us to accept that derogation under ECHR Article 15 is strictly required by the exigencies of the situation to deal with a public emergency threatening the life of the nation. Even if the derogation were found by the courts to be justified under Article 15 we would still consider it to be deeply undesirable.

35. We remain deeply concerned about the human rights implications of making the detention power an aspect of immigration law rather than anti-terrorism law. We agree with the Newton Committee that applying the power only to people who are not United Kingdom nationals reduces its efficacy as an anti-terrorism tool, and with Lord Carlile that it has a particular impact on one part of the resident community. We have previously expressed the view that this means that Part 4 is incompatible with the right to be free of discrimination in the enjoyment of Convention rights under ECHR Article 14. The SIAC took the same view, but the Court of Appeal considered that the difference of treatment was justifiable as having an objective and rational justification. Until the matter is finally and authoritatively settled (which may require an application to the European Court of Human Rights in Strasbourg) we remain of the view that there is a significant risk that Part 4 violates the right to be free of discrimination under ECHR Article 14.

36. As both the Newton Committee and Lord Carlile accept, we are convinced that there is a need for other measures to respond to the threat of terrorism. While we note that Lord Carlile has found that the certification and detention of those detained so far under Part 4 was fully in accordance with the statutory criteria, and that the SIAC is capable of applying those criteria in a proportionate and context-sensitive way, provided that it acts in accordance with the requirements of Article 6 of the Convention; and while we appreciate that at least some of those who are currently in detention may pose a threat which would make it undesirable to release them while a search is taking place for an alternative; we are nevertheless certain that a more satisfactory legal framework is urgently required which would be both effective and compatible with the United Kingdom's human rights obligations including full compliance with Article 5 of the ECHR.

37. We are not persuaded that it is appropriate to renew Part 4 when there is no end in sight of the 'emergency' by which these exceptional powers were considered to be justified. If the Government argue that it is necessary to continue Part 4 in force this should be limited to six months and should be subject to a firm undertaking that the Government will actively seek, as a matter of priority, a new legal basis for its anti-terrorism tactics to be put in place speedily and in accordance with the principles developed in the Newton Committee Report.

38. In the event that the Government persuades Parliament that these exceptional powers should be continued, we support the recommendation of the Newton Committee that the Government should publish up-to-date, anonymised information about each individual Part 4 certification and the number of detentions there have been under the Terrorism Acts (including the Terrorism Act 2000 as well as the 2001 Act) and their outcomes (for example prosecution, certification under Part 4, release, etc.). This would help Parliament to assess the continuing need for these, or other, measures, as well as providing a degree of openness for the process which could be a safeguard for the human rights of detainees.

39. We also support the recommendations of Lord Carlile for improving the way in which the current procedures operate while they continue to have effect, particularly those noted above in paragraph 32 (g), (j), (l), (m) (subject to the outcome of appropriate consultations with the Bar Council and the Law Society on the ethical implications of requiring

a Special Advocate to continue to act without the support of the appellant), (n) and (o).

   40. **Finally, we draw the attention of each House once more to the substantial concerns which we expressed in our earlier reports on this Part of the Act, summarised in paragraphs 19 and 20 above, not least to those in paragraph 20(e)(v) about which we believe there are real grounds for anxiety.''**

As indicated by the Joint Committee in para. 6 above, steps have been taken to ensure that all provisions of the Act still continue in force.

Joint Committee on Human Rights
Anti-terrorism, Crime and Security Act 2001: Statutory Review and Continuance of Part 4
Sixth Report: HL 38/HC 381 (2003–2004)

Summary

This Report considers the human rights implications of the Anti-terrorism, Crime and Security Act 2001 in the context of (a) the review of the whole Act by a Committee of Privy Councillors chaired by Lord Newton of Braintree, (b) the report by Lord Carlile of Berriew QC on the operation in 2003–04 of Part 4 of the Act, which allow suspected international terrorists who are not United Kingdom nationals and cannot be removed from the country to be detained indefinitely without charge, and (c) the draft Order laid before each House to continue in force for a further twelve months from 14 March 2004 those provisions.

   In relation to Part 4 of the Act, the Committee's conclusions are as follows:
   a) there are serious weaknesses in the protection for human rights under the detention provisions of Part 4 of the Act (paragraph 33);
   b) in the light of the evidence so far presented to Parliament, the Committee continues to doubt whether the powers under Part 4 are strictly required by the exigencies of the situation to deal with a public emergency threatening the life of the nation, and so continues to doubt whether the derogation from ECHR Article 5 is justified (paragraphs 33 to 34);
   c) even if the courts were ultimately to decide that the derogation from Article 5 is justified, the Committee would still consider an indefinite derogation from the important right to liberty under Article 5 to be deeply undesirable (paragraph 34);
   d) the Committee remains of the view that there is a significant risk that the powers under Part 4 violate the right to be free of discrimination under ECHR Article 14 because they have a particular impact on only one part of the resident community of the United Kingdom (namely those who are not nationals of the United Kingdom) on the ground of nationality (paragraph 35);
   e) a more satisfactory legal framework is urgently required which would be both effective and compatible with the United Kingdom's human rights obligations including full compliance with ECHR Article 5 (paragraph 36);
   f) the Committee is not persuaded that it is appropriate to renew Part 4 when there is no end in sight to the "emergency" by reference to which the exceptional powers were considered to be justified (paragraph 37);
   g) if the Government argues that it is necessary to continue Part 4 in force, it should be for a period of no more than six months, and the Government should give a firm undertaking that it will actively seek, as a matter of priority, a new legal basis for its anti-terrorism to be put in place speedily and in accordance with the principles developed in the Newton Committee Report (paragraph 37);
   h) if the Government persuades Parliament that the powers should be continued, it should publish anonymised information about each individual Part 4 certification and the number of detentions there have been under the Terrorism Acts and their outcomes (paragraph 38);

    i) the Committee supports the recommendations of Lord Carlile for improving the way in which the current procedures operate while they continue to have effect, subject to the outcome of appropriate consultations with the Bar Council and the Law Society on the ethical implications of requiring a Special Advocate to continue to act without the support of the appellant (paragraph 39);

    j) the Committee draws the attention of each House to the substantial concerns expressed in its earlier reports on this Part of the Act, ... not least the need to ensure that detainees' conditions of detention reflect their status as people who have been neither charged with nor convicted of any offence (paragraph 40).

In relation to the Newton Committee's recommendations on other parts of the Act:

    k) the Committee endorses the recommendations of the Newton Committee that freezing orders for specific use against terrorism should be addressed again in primary legislation and that such orders for other emergency situations, and the safeguards which should accompany them, should be reconsidered on their own merits in the context of more appropriate legislation for emergencies (paragraphs 41 to 43);

    l) the Committee welcomes the Newton Committee's analysis of provisions on disclosure of information, and endorses its recommendations for independent external oversight of the whole disclosure regime and for prior authorisation by a senior person in terrorism cases and by a judge in other cases (paragraphs 44 to 47);

    m) the Committee accepts the Newton Committee's conclusion that there was no reason to object to the provisions in Part 8 of the Act on security in the nuclear industry, in the light of assurances which the Government had given about the way in which the provisions would operate (paragraphs 48 to 49);

    n) the Committee endorses the views of the Newton Committee that police powers conferred or extended by Part 10 of the Act to identify people and to retain fingerprints indefinitely ought not to have been included in emergency legislation, and should be limited to cases where a person has been charged with an offence, or is authoritatively certified as being of ongoing importance in a terrorist investigation (paragraphs 50 to 52), and that the power to remove and confiscate disguises should be limited to situations where a senior police officer believes that the measure is necessary in response to a specific terrorist threat (paragraphs 53 to 55);

...

V. TAKING NEW LIBERTIES:

(1) The Civil Contingencies Bill 2004

Hot on the heels of the Anti-terrorism, Crime and Security Act 2001 is the Civil Contingencies Bill 2004. According to the Government, the purpose of the Bill is:

> "To deliver a single framework for civil protection in the United Kingdom. This is a key element of the Government's work to enhance our resilience to disruptive challenge. The current framework is disjointed in places, and the [Act] will deliver consistency of approach and outcome. And those parts of the current arrangements that are outdated will be modernised, to deliver a new framework to meet the challenges of the twenty first century." (Cabinet Office, *Draft Civil Contingencies Bill* (2003), p.5).

The need to "modernise" the existing law had been revealed by the flooding that occurred in much of England and Wales in 2000, and in the same year by the crisis caused by the protests by fuel tanker drivers. Reference was also made to the events in the US on September 11, 2001, which were said to have "changed the frame of reference for counter-terrorism" (*ibid.*, p.5). The emphasis in the Bill is thus said to be "resilience", and this takes two forms. Part 1 deals with contingency planning for and civil protection during periods of emergency, while Pt 2 authorises the making of emergency regulations to deal with an emergency. According to the Government, some "disruptive challenges are of such a nature or scale that they may require extraordinary measures to be taken to deal with their effects and aftermath which would not be appropriate in normal circumstances" (*ibid.*, p.27).

(2) Background

Although not designed to deal exclusively with terrorism, it is clearly anticipated that this would be one of the purposes for which the Bill might be used. Under the guise of "modernisation", Pt 2 of the Bill replaces the Emergency Powers Act 1920 with a new framework for dealing with emergencies. The Emergency Powers Act 1920—introduced to deal with industrial action though capable of being used for other purposes—permits a proclamation of emergency to be issued in very limited circumstances: in response to action "*of such a nature and on so extensive a scale as to be calculated, by interfering with the supply and distribution of food, water, fuel, or light, or with the means of locomotion, to deprive the community, or any substantial portion of the community, of the essentials of life*" (s.1(1)). The Civil Contingencies Bill 2004 will authorise emergency powers to be taken for many other reasons, and will enable the application of these powers to be confined to particular parts of the country. The background to this particular aspect of the Act is explained in the following passages from a Cabinet Office report.

Cabinet Office
Draft Civil Contingencies Bill
Consultation Document—June 2003
Chapter 5

"Modernisation of Emergency Powers legislation
    13. In the UK [emergency] legislation currently takes the form of the Emergency Powers Act 1920, which applies to Great Britain, and the Emergency Powers Act (Northern Ireland) 1926 as amended by the Emergency Powers Act 1964 and the Emergency Powers (Northern Ireland) Act 1964 respectively. This legislation is not as sophisticated and flexible as that which many other countries operate and adds very little to the resilience of the UK. The Civil Contingencies Bill offers an opportunity to develop a more effective and flexible framework.
    14. The Emergency Powers Act was introduced in the face of what was seen as the growing threat of nationally disruptive industrial action and the risk of civil unrest. It has been used twelve times in its eighty-year history, the last time being in 1974, and only ever in times of industrial unrest. In the years since 1920, individual government departments have introduced many of their own emergency legislative measures to deal with times of crisis affecting their individual policy sectors, in part out of a recognition that Emergency Powers legislation was inadequate if emergency situations were to arise in their areas. There is though still a need for a latent capacity to rapidly make new temporary statutory provision where this is the most effective way of enabling the resolution of an emergency. As currently constituted the Emergency Powers Acts only allow this in a relatively small number of scenarios which means they are not currently a tool that can be deployed to address all forms of disruptive challenge.
    15. The existing legislation does not reflect the realities of the early twenty-first century. It is based upon an assumption regarding the services needed by society in the 1920s that no longer holds in the much more integrated, technologically dependent, twenty-first century. This narrow and outdated focus coupled with the fact that the 1920 legislation allows only

for a Great Britain-wide response when emergencies tend to affect only part of the country at a time, and the fact that the legislation does not incorporate the devolution settlements, means it is in serious need of modernisation. As currently constituted the Act does not serve a useful function in the early twenty-first century. It cannot be used rapidly and effectively to provide temporary statutory powers in many situations where the lack of these can prevent effective measures being taken to deal with an emergency.

16. This is why the Bill includes modern and flexible provision for the use of special legislative measures in times of serious emergency. The overall policy aim is to enhance the Government's capability to respond to an emergency. The new powers will:

Provide a useable tool in the Government's crisis management tool-kit, a mechanism for enabling the most effective response to an emergency situation.

Be capable of being deployed in any situation where its deployment would be beneficial to attempts to respond to or recover from a severe disruptive challenge but limited by appropriate democratic and other safeguards against the possibility of misuse.

Be able to provide for a response proportionate to the emergency in question.

Address devolution issues.

...

Territorial extent

21. Under the existing legislation the territorial extent of a declaration must be GB or NI wide. Given that disruptive challenges more frequently appear at sub-national levels while other parts of the country remain unaffected, there is a strong argument for allowing special legislative measures to be used on a sub-national basis. The ability to declare a need for special legislative measures in a specific area is useful and common internationally but does not exist in the UK (except NI). The new framework will allow for this as a more flexible, targeted and proportional use of special legislative measures. It is proposed special legislative measures should operate on the following basis:

- UK—applying to the entire UK.
- Sub-UK—applying to one or more of the English Regions and/or the devolved countries.

22. The declaration of a sub-UK need for special legislative measures would allow for these to be used within a specified part of the UK without recourse to a full national declaration. This would demonstrate proportionality of response.

...

(3) Extending the Definition of Emergency

The new definition of emergency goes far beyond the Emergency Powers Act 1920, though it is not as extensive as the Government had first proposed in the Draft Bill. The Government yielded to political pressure and accepted that its original proposals went much too far. In what is now cl.17 it was proposed that an emergency would arise where the event or situation caused "serious harm" rather than "serious damage". More importantly, the three criteria in cl.18(1) were originally four, with the fourth being a serious threat to "the political, administrative or economic stability of the United Kingdom or a Part or region". This in turn was defined to mean an event or situation which causes or may cause disruption to the activities of the Government, the performance of public functions, or the activities of banks or other financial institutions. Public functions is a term which was then widely defined. In addition, it was proposed that education should be an essential service, and that a threat to welfare should include disruption of an essential commodity, or disruption of an essential service. Neither an essential commodity nor an essential service was defined, giving the Government potentially extremely wide powers as a result. The revised definition is as follows.

Civil Contingencies Bill 2004

"Meaning of 'emergency'

18.—(1) In this Part "emergency" means an event or situation which threatens serious damage to—

    (a) human welfare in the United Kingdom or in a Part or region,

    (b) the environment of the United Kingdom or of a Part or region, or

    (c) the security of the United Kingdom or a Part or region.

(2) For the purposes of subsection (1)(a) an event or situation threatens damage to human welfare only if it involves, causes or may cause—

    (a) loss of human life,

    (b) human illness or injury,

    (c) homelessness,

    (d) damage to property,

    (e) disruption of a supply of money, food, water, energy or fuel,

    (f) disruption of an electronic or other system of communication,

    (g) disruption of facilities for transport, or

    (h) disruption of services relating to health.

(3) For the purposes of subsection (1)(b) an event or situation threatens damage to the environment only if it involves, causes or may cause—

    (a) contamination of land, water or air with—

        (i) harmful biological, chemical or radio-active matter, or

        (ii) oil,

    (b) flooding, or

    (c) disruption or destruction of plant life or animal life.

(4) For the purposes of subsection (1)(c) the following threaten damage to security—

    (a) war or armed conflict, and

    (b) terrorism, within the meaning given by section 1 of the Terrorism Act 2000.

(5) The Secretary of State may by order—

    (a) provide that a specified event or situation, or class of event or situation, is to be treated as falling, or as not falling, within any of paragraphs (a) to (c) of subsection (1);

    (b) amend subsection (2) so as to provide that involving or causing disruption of a specified supply, system, facility or service—

        (i) is to be treated as threatening damage to human welfare, or

        (ii) is no longer to be treated as threatening damage to human welfare.

(6) An order under subsection (5)—

    (a) may make consequential amendment of this Part, and

    (b) may not be made unless a draft has been laid before, and approved by resolution of, each House of Parliament.

(7) The event or situation mentioned in subsection (1) may occur or be inside or outside the United Kingdom."

(4) Emergency Regulations

But it is not just that there is a wider definition of an emergency: there is also a greatly enhanced power to make regulations to deal with it. One preliminary point is that there is now no need for a royal proclamation to be made and no need for a state of emergency to be declared. Clause 19 simply allows an Order in Council to be made if the conditions in cl.20 are satisfied. This reduces the likelihood of parliamentary scrutiny of the decision to invoke the Act, though there must normally be parliamentary approval of the emergency regulations. It is perhaps curious that this formality has disappeared and that Parliament should surrender the power formally to review the invoking of emergency powers, content only to scrutinise the scope and content of the powers taken. The point was addressed by the Joint Committee on the Civil Contingencies Bill which reported that:

> "188. The Defence Committee has pointed out that the draft Bill gives Parliament no role in endorsing the declaration of emergency. It is easy to argue the case for not requiring any specific parliamentary approval: historically such actions have been taken by the Crown and Government without the need for formal parliamentary approval; the circumstances of the emergency may make it impossible for Parliament to meet; and, in reality, no Government would be able to sustain such a declaration of emergency if it did not command a majority in the House of Commons.
>
> 189. On the other hand, specific parliamentary endorsement for such a declaration would give democratic legitimacy to a whole range of measures which could not be examined in detail, would give confidence to those carrying them out that they were properly authorised and would assure the courts that Ministers were not acting beyond their political authority. It would also overcome the problem that, theoretically, it would be possible under the Bill for an emergency to be declared and successive sets of regulations to be made every seven days without any meeting of Parliament."

(Report of the Joint Committee on the Draft Civil Contingencies Bill H.L. 184/H.C. 1074 (2002/2003).)

The point was not fully pursued either by the Joint Committee or by the Government in its response. There are, however, a number of political safeguards built into the Bill, some of which have been carried over from the Emergency Powers Act 1920. The emergency regulations need parliamentary approval, otherwise they lapse after seven days (cl.26), and if approved by Parliament they expire after 30 days unless renewed (cl.25). Parliament has the power to amend the regulations (cl.25), and it is expressly provided that no regulations applying wholly or partly to Scotland may be made without the Scottish Ministers having first been consulted (cl.28).

Civil Contingencies Act 2004

"Power to make emergency regulations

19.—(1) Her Majesty may by Order in Council make emergency regulations if satisfied that the conditions in section 20 are satisfied.

(2) A senior Minister of the Crown may make emergency regulations if satisfied—

(a) that the conditions in section 20 are satisfied, and

(b) that it would not be possible, without serious delay, to arrange for an Order in Council under subsection (1).

(3) In this Part 'senior Minister of the Crown' means—

(a) the First Lord of the Treasury (the Prime Minister),

(b) any of Her Majesty's Principal Secretaries of State, and

(c) the Commissioners of Her Majesty's Treasury.

(4) In this Part 'serious delay' means a delay that might—

(a) cause serious damage, or

(b) seriously obstruct the prevention, control or mitigation of serious damage.

(5) Regulations under this section must be prefaced by a statement by the person making the regulations—

(a) specifying the nature of the emergency in respect of which the regulations are made, and

(b) declaring that the person making the regulations—

(i) is satisfied that the conditions in section 20 are met,

(ii) is satisfied that the regulations contain only provision which is for the purpose of preventing, controlling or mitigating an aspect or effect of the emergency in respect of which the regulations are made,

(iii) is satisfied that the effect of the regulations is in due proportion to that aspect

or effect of the emergency, and
(iv) in the case of regulations made under subsection (2), is satisfied as to the matter specified in subsection (2)(b).

Conditions for making emergency regulations
    20.—(1) This section specifies the conditions mentioned in section 19.
    (2) The first condition is that an emergency has occurred, is occurring or is about to occur.
    (3) The second condition is that it is necessary to make provision for the purpose of preventing, controlling or mitigating an aspect or effect of the emergency.
    (4) The third condition is that the need for provision referred to in subsection (3) is urgent.
    (5) For the purpose of subsection (3) provision which is the same as an enactment ('the existing legislation') is necessary if, in particular—
    (a) the existing legislation cannot be relied upon without the risk of serious delay,
    (b) it is not possible without the risk of serious delay to ascertain whether the existing legislation can be relied upon, or
    (c) the existing legislation might be insufficiently effective.
    (6) For the purpose of subsection (3) provision which could be made under an enactment other than section 19 ('the existing legislation') is necessary if, in particular—
    (a) the provision cannot be made under the existing legislation without the risk of serious delay,
    (b) it is not possible without the risk of serious delay to ascertain whether the provision can be made under the existing legislation, or
    (c) the provision might be insufficiently effective if made under the existing legislation.

Scope of emergency regulations
    21.—(1) Emergency regulations may make any provision which the person making the regulations thinks is for the purpose of preventing, controlling or mitigating an aspect or effect of the emergency in respect of which the regulations are made.
    (2) In particular, emergency regulations may make any provision which the person making the regulations thinks is for the purpose of—
    (a) protecting human life, health or safety,
    (b) treating human illness or injury,
    (c) protecting or restoring property,
    (d) protecting or restoring a supply of money, food, water, energy or fuel,
    (e) protecting or restoring an electronic or other system of communication,
    (f) protecting or restoring facilities for transport,
    (g) protecting or restoring the provision of services relating to health,
    (h) protecting or restoring the activities of banks or other financial institutions,
    (i) preventing, containing or reducing the contamination of land, water or air,
    (j) preventing, or mitigating the effects of, flooding,
    (k) preventing, reducing or mitigating the effects of disruption or destruction of plant life or animal life,
    (l) protecting or restoring activities of Her Majesty's Government,
    (m) protecting or restoring activities of Parliament, of the Scottish Parliament, of the Northern Ireland Assembly or of the National Assembly for Wales, or
    (n) protecting or restoring the performance of public functions.
    (3) Emergency regulations may make provision of any kind that could be made by Act of Parliament or by the exercise of the Royal Prerogative; in particular, regulations may—
    (a) confer a function on a Minister of the Crown, on the Scottish Ministers, on the National Assembly for Wales, on a Northern Ireland department, on a coordinator appointed under section 23 or on any other specified person (and a function conferred may, in particular, be—

        (i) a power, or duty, to exercise a discretion;

        (ii) a power to give directions or orders, whether written or oral);

(b) provide for or enable the requisition or confiscation of property (with or without compensation);

(c) provide for or enable the destruction of property, animal life or plant life (with or without compensation);

(d) prohibit, or enable the prohibition of, movement to or from a specified place;

(e) require, or enable the requirement of, movement to or from a specified place;

(f) prohibit, or enable the prohibition of, assemblies of specified kinds, at specified places or at specified times;

(g) prohibit, or enable the prohibition of, travel at specified times;

(h) prohibit, or enable the prohibition of, other specified activities;

(i) create an offence of—

        (i) failing to comply with a provision of the regulations;

        (ii) failing to comply with a direction or order given or made under the regulations;

        (iii) obstructing a person in the performance of a function under or by virtue of the regulations;

(j) disapply or modify an enactment (other than a provision of this Part) or a provision made under or by virtue of an enactment;

(k) require a person or body to act in performance of a function (whether the function is conferred by the regulations or otherwise and whether or not the regulations also make provision for remuneration or compensation);

(l) enable the Defence Council to authorise the deployment of Her Majesty's armed forces;

(m) make provision (which may include conferring powers in relation to property) for facilitating any deployment of Her Majesty's armed forces;

(n) confer jurisdiction on a court or tribunal (which may include a tribunal established by the regulations);

(o) make provision which has effect in relation to, or to anything done in—

        (i) an area of the territorial sea,

        (ii) an area within British fishery limits, or

        (iii) an area of the continental shelf;

(p) make provision which applies generally or only in specified circumstances or for a specified purpose;

(q) make different provision for different circumstances or purposes.

(4) In subsection (3) 'specified' means specified by, or to be specified in accordance with, the regulations.

Limitations of emergency regulations

22.—(1) Emergency regulations may make provision only if and in so far as the person making the regulations thinks—

(a) that the provision is for the purpose of preventing, controlling or mitigating an aspect or effect of the emergency in respect of which the regulations are made, and

(b) that the effect of the provision is in due proportion to that aspect or effect of the emergency.

(2) Emergency regulations must specify the Parts of the United Kingdom or regions in relation to which the regulations have effect.

(3) Emergency regulations may not—

(a) require a person, or enable a person to be required, to provide military service, or

(b) prohibit or enable the prohibition of participation in, or any activity in connection with, a strike or other industrial action.

(4) Emergency regulations may not—

(a) create an offence other than one of the kind described in section 21(3)(i),

    (b) create an offence other than one which is triable only before a magistrates' court or, in Scotland, before a sheriff under summary procedure,

    (c) create an offence which is punishable—

        (i) with imprisonment for a period exceeding three months, or

        (ii) with a fine exceeding level 5 on the standard scale, or

    (d) alter procedure in relation to criminal proceedings."

(5) The Civil Contingencies Bill 2004 and Human Rights

Clauses 20 and 21 confer wide powers, though there are some welcome restraints on ministerial power: these include the requirements of necessity (cl.20(3), urgency (cl.20(4), and proportionality (cl.22(1)(b)). Nevertheless there are still wide regulation-making powers, including the power to:

- confiscate or destroy property (with or without compensation),
- prohibit freedom of movement (with a power to "prohibit" and "require" movement "to or from a specified place",
- prohibit, or enable the prohibition of, assemblies,
- prohibit, or enable the prohibition of, travel at specified times.

A matter of particular concern in view of contemporary international developments (Guantanamo Bay) is the power to make regulations to "confer jurisdiction on a court or tribunal (which may include a tribunal established by the regulations)". So too is the rather enigmatic power to "prohibit, or enable the prohibition of, other specified activities". A particular issue of controversy with the new Act is the extent to which emergency regulations should be subject to judicial review. In particular, should emergency regulations be subject to scrutiny under the Human Rights Act? We have already seen how the Government contrived to exclude the Human Rights Act from Pt 4 of the Anti-terrorism, Crime and Security Act 2001 by derogating from Art.5 to allow legislation in breach of Convention rights to be introduced. The Government's evident weariness of the Human Rights Act was revealed in a different form when the Draft Civil Contingencies Bill was published. This proposed that any emergency regulations should be treated as if they were primary legislation, for reasons and with consequences explained in the following extract.

Cabinet Office
Draft Civil Contingencies Bill
Consultation Document—June 2003
Chapter 5

"30. The legislation will, as all legislation must, operate within the confines placed upon it by human rights legislation. The Bill is compatible with the European Convention on Human Rights.

    31. During serious emergencies, the balance between individual rights and the need for action to mitigate the emergency can be difficult to achieve. That is why a procedure already exists to allow the Government to derogate from the Convention, and to make immediate adjustments to the Human Rights Act to reflect the derogation, in the event of a serious emergency.

    32. As part of the work to modernise emergency powers, the Government has considered whether any additional flexibility is necessary.

    33. Primary legislation can be challenged in the Courts, but cannot be quashed or prevented by injunctions on human rights grounds. Secondary legislation is subject to injunction and can be quashed. In an emergency, where speed is of the essence, it is not desirable for any emergency regulations to be held up by injunctions, especially where delay may prevent effective resolution of an emergency which threatens the safety of the com-

munity. Claims that human rights are being infringed may in the end prove unfounded, but a Court might on an interim basis order that emergency regulations be suspended.

34. The counter point to this argument is that the regulations should be subject to the standard process for dealing with human rights challenges to secondary legislation, with the usual safeguards and derogations available. In particular there is a procedure under which many, but not all, of the rights protected by the Human Rights Act may be suspended when there is a public emergency which threatens the life of the nation. If that derogation is relied on, and assuming that Courts would not lightly intervene in the Government's efforts to respond to an emergency, the risk of successful legal challenge is not substantial.

35. The Government is considering whether regulations introduced as emergency measures should be considered as primary legislation made by Parliament for human rights purposes. That way, emergency regulations are not slowed up or prevented by injunctions, but there is still the redress to the law courts if individuals or organisations considered that their rights had been infringed. The reasons for considering emergency regulations as primary legislation are that they would only be introduced in extreme, and very rare, special circumstances; they operate in effect as temporary primary legislation; they have a limited life-span; and, they have to be approved by Parliament as soon as practicable once made. The proposal would prevent the suspension or quashing of emergency regulations themselves, but it would not prevent courts suspending or quashing the actions of persons under the regulations on human rights grounds unless any violation of human rights were specifically required by the regulations.

36. The Bill includes a clause to this effect, but the Government believes that the case for its inclusion in the final Bill is by no means certain. The Government will be seeking further evidence from the consultation and pre-legislative scrutiny processes before it forms a final view."

These proposals met with little approval and with a great deal of opposition. The effect of the Government's proposals was that emergency regulations would not be open to effective challenge by the courts under the Human Rights Act 1998. This is true no matter how far these instruments may have violated Convention rights. All that a court would have been able to do is issue a declaration of incompatibility. As we know, the Government would be free to ignore any such declaration. The critics included four parliamentary committees (the Commons Defence Committee, Lords Constitutional Committee, the Joint Committee on Human Rights, and the Joint Committee on the Draft Civil Contingencies Bill). The views of the last are to be found in the following extract. It should also be noted that the critics of the Government's proposals also included a number of NGO's, such as Liberty and Justice.

Report of the Joint Committee on the Draft Civil Contingencies Bill
H.L. 184/H.C. 1074 (2002/2003)

"138. The human rights concerns arise most acutely in relation to Part 2 of the draft Bill (Emergency Powers). In this respect, the draft Bill replaces the Emergency Powers Act 1920, which was passed three decades before the United Kingdom ratified the European Convention on Human Rights and nearly eight decades before the Human Rights Act 1998 incorporated the Convention rights into UK law and provided for remedies in the UK courts. As a result of these developments, there is heightened attention and perhaps precision to the issue of infringement of rights than was previously the case. In addition, since 1920, wartime legislation and laws against terrorism have provided experience of the relevance of rights, the powers and limitations of judicial and parliamentary protection, as well as the relevance of mechanisms such as notices of derogation.

139. Of the constitutional principles which must be observed in civil contingency planning and in times of extreme crisis, disaster and emergency, the first we consider is the values of individual rights. We deal below with other constitutional aspects of the draft Bill.

These concepts closely correlate with the requirements of the European Convention on Human Rights, as embodied in the Human Rights Act 1998. The Convention is evidently infused with the values of rights and, within that context, seeks to proffer principles such as:

- Legality—is there a clear and accessible legal basis for processes and powers on the part of public authorities, the basis of which can be tested?
- Necessity—was the invocation of the public authority's emergency power which infringed rights strictly required in response to the threat or crisis, or could "normal" powers have been utilised?
- Proportionality—even if new provisions are in principle necessary, were actions taken by public authorities proportionate to the threat or crisis which they are seeking to act against?

...

144. Of all the human rights issues, most witnesses regarded as the most serious the power in clause 25 to treat secondary legislation as if it is an Act of Parliament for the purposes of the Human Rights Act 1998. The problem it seeks to address is as follows. In theory, a court might rule that regulations made under Part 2 of the Civil Contingencies Bill were invalid, or might grant an injunction against action being taken pursuant to them before the legal issues had been fully argued in court. This might occur within the seven days between the regulations being made and their being approved by Parliament. The scenario envisaged is therefore of a Government unable to respond effectively to an emergency because the courts have ruled their measures actually or potentially illegal.

145. Both the Defence Committee and the Joint Committee on Human Rights have said:

'... this new provision should not be included in the Bill unless the Government can demonstrate a clear and compelling need for the additional powers which it provides.'

146. The Constitution Committee has told us:

'We are not satisfied that the Government has demonstrated a compelling need for this departure from the structure for the protection of Convention rights created by the 1998 Act, and we consider that this approach would run the risk of creating an undesirable precedent.'

147. The ability of Ministers to make draconian regulations which breach human rights would not be entirely unfettered even with clause 25 remaining part of the Bill. The regulations would be subject to approval by Parliament within seven days and might not receive that approval. It would still be open to a court to declare that a regulation was incompatible with the Convention under section 4 of the Human Rights Act, though, as with primary legislation, this would not invalidate the regulation. The prospect of subsequent litigation might also act a deterrent. And regulations would still be subject to normal judicial review ... . Nevertheless, the Government recognises that the restraint imposed on striking down on human rights grounds under clause 25 would be an important departure from normal practice and so 'believes that the case for its inclusion in the draft Bill is by no means certain'.

148. The effect of clause 25 is viewed with concern for three main reasons:

- One is on grounds of precedent—that the Human Rights Act is a finely balanced statute which governs the relationship between state and individuals—and should not be changed even in an emergency or, perhaps, especially in an emergency. Allied to the ground of principle is the fear of the slippery slope—that a precedent will be set which other legislation will follow, perhaps dealing with such serious issues as terrorism, serious frauds and drug trafficking.
- The second is that in practical terms the value of rights is being diminished. It

removes the possibility of the courts striking down the secondary legislation on grounds of incompatibility with Convention rights.

- The third reason for criticism of clause 25 is simply that the curtailment under clause 25 is not necessary.

149. Three reasons may be adduced for questioning the need for clause 25:

  i) There is little evidence that judges are overly 'activist' in dealing with challenges to emergency powers.

  ii) Judges are unlikely to prevent the Government taking action when the balance of convenience is against interfering with measures to protect public safety.

  iii) It is always possible for the Government to derogate from parts of the European Convention.

150. Though it is true that there has been some shift from the very deferential attitudes which tended to prevail in wartime, the vast majority of challenges to emergency powers (for example against terrorism) have been rejected by the courts. On this point we have been told by human rights experts:

'The courts have been traditionally deferential towards the Executive in times of public emergency, that is in general the approach that courts have taken. That is true not just of the UK but other comparable jurisdictions, the United States as well. You will find a general attitude in common law jurisdictions that courts in times of emergency will give proper deference to the role of the Executive in making [the] regulations.

... there is nothing in our constitutional or legal history to suggest that our courts are anything other than deferential to the Executive and indeed to Parliament in times of national emergency or fear of national emergency.

If the Government is coming to court for, say, emergency flood relief, the court will have regard to the balance of convenience and I question whether any UK court or High Court judge would ever strike down regulations that gave the Government power if needed to address a clear state of emergency.

There can be no suggestion in reality that it would be realistic that the courts would wish to or be able to strike down in any serious and enduring way these regulations before Parliament had a chance to give them primary legislative effect.'

151. Nor are the judges very ready to grant injunctions even when they decide that a challenge is sustainable, recognising that the balance of convenience is against interfering with executive action intended to protect public safety.

152. Finally, the possibility of derogation under article 15 of the European Convention must be considered quite feasible. This process takes little time—the Secretary General of the Council of Europe has to be notified after the derogation is made. To give effect to the derogation in UK law, the Secretary of State has to make an order under section 14 of the Human Rights Act 1998. The Government followed this path when bringing forward the Anti-Terrorism, Crime and Security Bill in 2001. Derogations have persisted as a common feature of emergency and anti-terrorism legislation to prevent terrorism in Northern Ireland since 1968. If the circumstances demand some temporary encroachment on human rights, it could be argued that a derogation from the European Convention would be the most Convention-compliant way of proceeding.

...

155. Assuming that there persists a remote risk of the courts frustrating the ability of the Government to cope with an emergency, we have considered what other legal devices might be available to avoid the consequent disruption which might arise.

- One possibility is that a court should not be able to implement any finding of invalidity until there had been an opportunity for the exhaustion of all appeal processes. Normally, this power to stay its decision pending an appeal would be at the discretion of the court, but legislation could delimit that discretion, and this interference with normal judicial discretion would still be preferable to the total abolition of Human Rights challenge.

- Another possibility would be to provide for a stay pending the opportunity for parliamentary scrutiny. On this scenario, rather than awaiting the exhaustion of appeal processes, the courts might fix a set time (say 40 days) for suspension of a judgment sufficient for Parliament to take action by way of amending regulations.
- An additional option to both of the foregoing would be to provide for some changes to judicial process. For example, it might be suggested that challenges to the legality of such regulations could only be made directly to a higher judicial body—the High Court at least, or perhaps even to the proposed Supreme Court. In addition, challenges could be fast-tracked.

156. We conclude that the Government has not demonstrated a clear and compelling need to treat regulations under the Civil Contingencies Bill as having the status of Acts of Parliament for the purposes of the Human Rights Act. At most, there may be a need for some procedural changes, such as a fast track process within a higher court, plus a compulsory stay on the enforcement of any court order until the appeal is exhausted. We welcome the Government's willingness to reconsider this matter."

The Government yielded to political pressure and the proposal that emergency regulations should be treated as if they were primary legislation has been dropped. Emergency regulations will thus be subject to review by the courts in the same way as other secondary legislation. It does not follow, however, that the regulations will be subject to intensive scrutiny or indeed that the Government's change of heart will mean a great deal in practice. In now accepting that "emergency powers should always be operated within the confines of the Human Rights Act", the Government pointed out that:

"It should be noted that many of the Convention rights are qualified rights. Such rights can be interfered with where this is in accordance with the law, necessary in a democratic society and the interference is proportionate to the end to be achieved. Thus the Convention rights will not necessarily impede the taking of appropriate action to respond to an emergency. As the [Joint] Committee has indicated, it is also possible to derogate from the Convention under Article 15 in certain cases. Once derogation has been designated for the purposes of the Human Rights Act, emergency regulations could be made in reliance on that derogation without contravening the Human Rights Act.

The Government has considered whether provision should be included in the Bill to give emergency regulations procedural protection from successful challenge in the courts. The courts have a number of tools available to them already to ensure that their determinations do not impede inappropriately action taken in an emergency. An interim injunction, for example, is a discretionary remedy. In determining whether to grant an injunction under the 'balance of convenience' test, the courts will consider the wider public interest in not granting an interim injunction. Should a challenge to emergency regulations be successful, the court will have discretion to strike the regulations down. And should the court consider that it is appropriate to do so, it may 'sever' the offending provision and allow the rest of the regulations to continue. In other words, the courts are unlikely ever to strike down emergency regulations in their entirety.

The Government has also considered the courts' attitude to the exercise of emergency powers. The Government largely agrees with the Committee's analysis of this point. In light of the range of tools available to the court to ensure that the response to an emergency is not impeded inappropriately by successful legal challenges, and the likely approach that the courts would take to emergency powers, the Government has concluded that no further provision is needed to protect procedurally emergency regulations from challenge in the courts." (Cabinet Office, *The Government's Response to the Report of the Joint Committee on the Draft Civil Contingencies Bill* (2004), p.15.)

VI. EMERGENCY POWERS, THE COURTS AND HUMAN RIGHTS

It is a curious irony that so much restrictive legislation should be introduced within such a short period since the enactment of the Human Rights Act 1998. The measures discussed in this chapter reveal a number of restrictions—of varying degrees of seriousness—to the human rights set out in the ECHR. These include:

- The right to liberty.
- The right to respect for one's private life.
- The right to freedom of expression.
- The right to freedom of association and assembly.
- The right to the peaceful enjoyment of one's possessions.

As we have seen the Government has had formally to derogate from its obligations under the Convention in order to introduce some of these measures. It was also prepared in the Draft Civil Contingencies Bill to exclude effective judicial scrutiny by proposing that emergency regulations should be treated as if they were primary legislation, thereby protecting them from being overruled by the courts. However, it is not only the inexorable rise of illiberal legislation in the Human Rights Act era that is a cause for concern. So too is the self-denying role of the courts in areas where greater scrutiny is most needed. As has been recognised by the American courts recently, "Even in times of national emergency—indeed, particularly in such times—it is the obligation of the Judicial Branch to ensure the preservation of our constitutional values and to prevent the Executive Branch from running roughshod over the citizens and aliens alike": David Cole, "The War on our Rights', *The Nation*, January 12/19, 2004, p.5. In the same vein, the President of the Supreme Court of Israel has written that:

> "Judicial review of the legality of the war on terrorism may make this war harder in the short term, but it also fortifies and strengthens the people in the long term. The rule of law is an essential element in national security."
> (A. Barak, 'Foreword: A Judge on Judging: The Role of a Supreme Court in a Democracy' [2002] 116 *Harvard Law Review* 19.)

We have seen, however, that in recent cases the courts in this country have shown little inclination to become involved in national security questions, save only to endorse the conduct of the Government. We are witnessing a contemporary example of a well established phenomenon, which is that the courts are extremely deferential to the Executive in times of crisis, real or imagined. The point was well made by Lord Bingham in a published lecture when he said:

> "In times of emergency, crises and serious disorder it [freedom from executive detention] is almost the first right to be curtailed. It is in that sense vulnerable. At such times public opinion is an unreliable source of protection for those detained. So too are representative institutions. So too are courts of law. Yet retrospective inquiry tends to show that the infringement of personal liberty thought to be justified at the time were significantly greater than the necessity of the circumstances required." (T. Bingham, "Personal Freedom and the Dilemma of Democracies" (2003) 52 I.C.L.Q. 841.)

During the First World War the government introduced executive detention without express statutory authority. In *R. v Halliday* [1917] A.C. 260 Lord Chancellor Finlay said that: "It appears to me to be a sufficient answer to this argument that it may be necessary in time of great public danger to entrust great powers to His Majesty in Council, and that Parliament may do so feeling certain such powers will be reasonably exercised" (at pp.268–269). Moving forward to the Second World War we come to *Liversidge v Anderson* [1942] A.C. 206. This too was concerned with executive detention. According to Lord Macmillan:

> "The liberty which we so justly extol is itself the gift of the law and as Magna Carta recognises may by law be forfeited or abridged. At a time when it is the undoubted law of the land that a citizen may by conscription or requisition be compelled to give up his life and all that he possesses for his country's cause it will be no matter for surprise that there should be confided to the Secretary of State a discretionary power of enforcing the relatively mild precaution of detention."(at 267)

The incorporation of Convention rights nevertheless adds a new dimension to the story. Courts are empowered to ensure that public authorities comply with these rights and may declare Acts of Parliament incompatible with them, thereby putting pressure on the Government to bring forward amending legislation. However, as we have seen, the incorporation of Convention rights has made little difference. It is true that incorporation allows fresh questions to be raised before the courts, but it also enables these fresh questions to be answered just as easily. None of this will surprise the alert comparative lawyer, not even the student of countries such as the US where we find a Bill of Rights to protect the individual from the State. In the US, the emergence of Communism brought a legislative response against promoting the socialist message which after the First World War the First Amendment was unable to prevent: *Schenck v US*, 249 U.S. 211 (1919); *Debs v US*, 249 U.S. 211 (1919); *Abrams v US*, 250 U.S. 616 (1919). During the Second World War Japanese Americans were detained without trial, again in circumstances upheld by the Supreme Court: *Korematsu v United States*, 323 U.S. 214 (1944). Moreover, during the Cold War a federal ban on the Communist Party was upheld by the Supreme Court despite constitutional guarantees of freedom of expression and association: *Dennis v US*, 341 U.S. 494 (1951). Now of course we have the situation in Guantanamo Bay which has drawn a response even from British Law Lords who claim that the treatment of detainees by the US government violates international law.

Second law lord criticises detentions at Guantanamo Bay

The Independent, 28 January 2004

A second law lord is to question US policy over the detention of 660 terror suspects at Guantanamo Bay.

Lord Hope of Craighead, one of the country's senior judges, will tell an audience of lawyers and academics tonight that the men are being held in a place beyond the rule of law without the protection of any court.

He will warn them not to let "the smiling charming faces of our American allies divert us from seeking to discover the reality of what is being done by their interrogators."

Last year, Lord Steyn, another of the 12 members of the judicial committee of the House of Lords, spoke out against the detention when he described Guantanamo Bay as a "monstrous failure of justice" and the military tribunals that will try suspects as kangaroo courts.

His intervention was quickly seized upon by the families of the nine British detainees because it broke with judicial protocol that prevents judges from making public comments on live political issues.

Lord Hope does not go as far as Lord Steyn but he does say "it is no understatement to say the detainees are at the victors' mercy". In a lecture on the history of torture, jointly organised by international law firm Clifford Chance and Essex University, Lord Hope asks: "How can we expect to eliminate torture elsewhere if there is no sure way of knowing whether or not it has been practised at Guantanamo Bay by the Americans?"

He adds: "We can assume that whatever has been done and is being done to the prisoners has and is being done with the cold and ruthless efficiency that characterises the actions of officials who are determined to obtain results and whose actions are not subjected to international inspection or to the control of any independent judicial authority."

He argues that people have every right to be suspicious about the conditions under which the detainees are being held because the outside world has no means of testing American assurances that "all appropriate measures" are used in their interrogation.

Nine Britons and three British residents are among the 660 people who have been held at the American naval base in Cuba for more than two years without charge or access to lawyers.

In recent weeks the Americans signalled they are ready to repatriate European suspects if given assurances that they will be properly managed by the police when they return to their communities.

But the Home Secretary, David Blunkett, has said that such restrictions would have to comply with British law, making such a condition impossible to enforce.

Lawyers argue that, since there is no offence with which they could be charged, because no admissible evidence was gathered at the time of their capture, they would be freed upon arrival in Britain.

Since this article the US Supreme Court has held that these detained at Guatonamo Bay have the right to challenge the legality of their detention, *Haudi v Rumsfeld*; *Rasul v Bush*, June 28, 2004. Some—though not all—of the British detainees were returned home and released from police custody.

So what are the implications of these developments? It appears that despite the incorporation of Convention rights, there is an extraordinary continuity in the approach of the domestic courts in times of crisis.

- Convention rights cannot stop the inexorable drive in the direction of more and more state powers, whether it be identity cards, police powers of stop and search, or greater

emergency powers.
- In times of crisis, the courts do not and will not protect the individual from the state whether the crisis be caused by external or internal threats, whether it be world war, cold war or the war against terror.

The law reports are studded by cases which make these points very clearly: *R. v Halliday* [1917] A.C. 260 and *Liversidge v Anderson* [1942] A.C. 206 may be the best known; but they have more modern parallels, of which *R. v Minister for Civil Service ex p. CCSU* [1985] A.C. 374 is prominent. In that case the House of Lords upheld a ban on trade union membership imposed by the Government on staff employed at Government Communications Headquarters. The courts—it seems—consider it their role to protect public safety and national security at all costs, with the principle expressed by Darling J. in 1916 still being as pertinent today as it was then: *salus populi suprema lex* (*Ronnfeldt v Philips* (1918) 34 T.L.R. 356). This is not to say that Convention rights are insignificant and unimportant, or to deny that important common law developments have taken place in their shadow. But it is to say that they are of marginal importance when the individual comes face to face with the might of the state in the most sensitive areas, though the record of the Strasbourg Court is more impressive than the domestic courts. The experience of the Convention rights in the domestic courts is likely to be one of abject disappointment and growing disillusionment. This is because the radicals who supported it failed to engage properly with the empirical evidence: since *Entick v Carrington* (1765) 19 St. Tr. 1930 there have been few cases where the courts have been prepared to stand up to government where liberty comes face to face with security. It will take more than the incorporation of Convention rights to change the judicial role, or indeed the judicial perception of their role.

Judges and National Security

In the first extract in chapter 1 we deal with *Agee v Lord Advocate* 1977 SLT (Notes) 54. Philip Agee was one of two Americans deported because their presence was deemed not conducive to the public good. The other was Mark Hosenball who challenged his deportation in the English courts. He too was unsuccessful. In the course of his judgment, Lord Denning said:

"There is a conflict here between the interests of national security on the one hand and the freedom of the individual on the other. The balance between these two is not for a court of law. It is for the Home Secretary. He is the person entrusted by Parliament with the task. In some parts of the world national security has on occasions been used as an excuse for all sorts of infringements of individual liberty. But not in England. Both during the wars and after them, successive ministers have discharged their duties to the complete satisfaction of the people at large. They have set up advisory committees to help them, usually with a chairman who has done everything he can to ensure that justice is done. They have never interfered with the liberty or the freedom of movement of any individual except where it is absolutely necessary for the safety of the state. In this case we are assured that the Home Secretary himself gave it his personal consideration, and I have no reason whatever to doubt the care with which he considered the whole matter. He is answerable to Parliament as to the way in which he did it and not to the courts here I would dismiss the appeal."

(*R. v Home Secretary, ex p. Hosenball* [1977] 1 W.L.R. 766.

However, this is not to deny that the judges now have a problem, which is one largely of their own making. Many judges campaigned actively and publicly for the incorporation of the European Convention on Human Rights. In doing so created an expectation that if given the new powers that they craved, they would make a difference and things would be different. "Give us the tools and we will do the job". Yet since the introduction of Convention rights the jurisprudence has generally been very cautious on a range of issues, with the exceptions and qualifications to Convention rights generally swallowing the rights themselves. Although this is true particularly of the national security cases, it is also true in a number of other areas discussed elsewhere in this book. The enactment of Convention rights has not made a significant contribution to freedom of expression or freedom of assembly, with a range of legal restrictions and practices surviving judicial scrutiny. In the difficult times in which we now live, it is incumbent on the courts to be more assertive in the protection of the vulnerable individual. There is no virtue in attacking the Americans for Guantanamo Bay while—as in *R. (Abbassi) v Foreign Secretary* [2002] EWCA 1598—simultaneously refusing to require the British Government to do more on behalf of British citizens being detained there. Nor is there any virtue in attacking the Americans for Guantanamo Bay while tolerating the indefinite imprisonment of foreign nationals without trial in HMP Belmarsh in south London. The incorporation of Convention rights has to mean something more than simply new lyrics for old songs. Otherwise the disappointment that turns to disillusionment will lead to a loss of confidence not only in the Convention rights (and the legislation by which they were incorporated), but in the judges themselves.

INDEX